Encyclopedia of
Educational
Research

Encyclopedia of Educational Research

FIFTH EDITION

Sponsored by the American Educational Research Association

Editor in Chief
Harold E. Mitzel

Associate Editors
John Hardin Best and William Rabinowitz

Volume 2

THE FREE PRESS, *A Division of Macmillan Publishing Co., Inc.*, NEW YORK
Collier Macmillan Publishers, LONDON

THE FREE PRESS
A Division of Macmillan Publishing Co., Inc.
866 Third Avenue, New York, NY 10022

Collier Macmillan Canada, Inc.

Library of Congress Catalog Card Number: 82–2332

Printed in the United States of America

printing number

1 2 3 4 5 6 7 8 9 10

Library of Congress Cataloging in Publication Data
Main entry under title:

Encyclopedia of educational research.

  Includes bibliographies and index.
  1. Educational research—United States—Directories.
2. Education—Bibliography. 3. Universities and colleges
—United States—Directories. 4. Education—Dictionaries.
I. Mitzel, Harold E. II. Best, John Hardin. III. Rabinowitz, William. IV. American Educational Research Association.
L901.E57   1982   370'.7'8073   82–2332
ISBN 0–02–900450–0 (set)   AACR2

Contributors' acknowledgments, some of which are relevant
to the copyright status of certain articles, appear in a
special section at the back of volume 4.

E

(CONTINUED)

ECONOMICS AND EDUCATION

Whereas economists have long recognized that schooling contributes to individual occupational position and wage differentiation (Adam Smith, e.g., discussed schooling in this context), analysis of the relationship between education and the economic system—the economics of education—is essentially an intellectual issue of the last quarter century.

In the mid-1950s, the interest in expenditures on education as a possible source of increasing material output grew out of the failure of traditional development models—in which inputs were defined as homogeneous labor and capital—to explain more than about one-half of the total economic growth in long-term growth periods. The early works on economics and education therefore concentrated on establishing education as an input into the growth process, a form of increasing the productive "quality" of labor. More recently, however, serious questions have been raised about what expenditures on schooling actually do to increase output, or, for that matter, whether more schooling raises output at all. Some economists began to ask whether economic growth is the only process of change concerning the political economy, and whether, indeed, the most important function of education is not its distribution role, within and between generations of workers.

The subject of economics and education, while relatively new, is therefore very broad. It addresses the fundamental connections between the acquisition of skills, economic change, and social structure. It directly involves, on the one hand, labor market income-distribution theory, and on the other, the theory of public finance, for public education is one of the public sector's largest social expenditures.

This article reviews the rich and varied theoretical and empirical literature on economics and education, a literature extensive enough to occasion the publication of a major bibliography (Blaug, 1978). It is clearly impossible to do more than touch the surface of this richness; and I have chosen to discuss those topics that seem to clarify where the subject has been and where it is going.

Education as an Input. Economists found in the 1950s that increases in labor and capital, as measured by man-hours of work and the value of capital, explained only a part of a country's growth rate. The "residual" of unexplained growth was at first ascribed to technology (Solow, 1957), but later, this general term was defined to include improvements in the quality of capital (Denison, 1962; Griliches & Jorgenson, 1964) and the investment in human beings (Schultz, 1959, 1961). In a series of pioneering studies, Schultz developed the idea that expenditures on education were not primarily consumption, but rather an investment in the increased capacity of labor to produce material goods. Hence, formal schooling was at least in part an investment in *human capital*, an investment with economic yield in terms of increased product per worker, holding physical capital constant.

Human capital theory. At the same time, Denison (1962) applied measurements of investment in human capital and others' estimates of the economic return to such investment in an effort to account for unexplained growth in the postwar U.S. economy. Denison found that expenditures on education seemed to explain about 23 percent of the 1909–1929 growth rate in employed income per person and 42 percent between 1929 and 1957, whereas increased capital per worker accounted for 29 percent and 9 percent, respectively, in the two periods. Denison concluded that additional education played a significant role in increasing U.S. material growth, particularly after the first period of rapid physical capital increase.

This concept may have rankled some educators who saw education primarily as a means for elevating culture and civilization, not for increasing production. As T. W. Schultz (1963) wrote, "Those who value schooling highly, which includes most of those who are part of the educational establishment, are likely to look upon an effort such

519

as this as an intrusion which can only debase the cultural purposes of education. In their view, education lies beyond the economic calculus, because they believe that education is much more than a matter of costs and returns" (p. viii). Nevertheless, human capital theory ultimately provided a rationale for a massive expansion of schooling in most countries: if expenditures on such schooling contributed to economic growth, governments could satisfy demands by their populations for schooling while simultaneously contributing to the overall material growth of the economy. Further rationale was provided by another type of study; for example, Harbison and Myers (1964) argued that per capita secondary and higher education is highly correlated with per capita income. Therefore, they reasoned, increasing the per capita level of intermediate and higher education would lead to higher levels of income per capita.

In the second wave of empirical work on education as human capital, the cost of (investment in) education was related to the increase in income (productivity) realized, on the average, by individuals in the labor force to show the worth of expenditures on education relative to other investments in the economy. Studies by Hansen (1963), Becker (1964), and Hanoch (1967) for the United States, Blaug (1967) for England, and Carnoy (1967a, 1967b) for Mexico and other Latin American countries indicated that the rate of return to education as an investment was high compared to investment in physical capital. On the other hand, Gounden's data for India (1967) suggested just the opposite: physical capital seemed to be a better investment in India than education. No matter what they showed, however, the implication of these studies, like Denison's work, was that income differences between groups of people with different amounts of schooling in the labor force could be used to estimate the expected value of education not only to the marginal individual taking more schooling, but to the aggregate economy in the form of increased output produced by those with more education. These economists were arguing that increasing the level of education increased the level of material output; for every additional dollar, peso, or rupee invested at the margin, gross national product (GNP) would increase approximately by the rate of return to education multiplied by labor's share in GNP.

Income differentiation and schooling.   One of the first questions to be asked by these same analysts, however, was whether the entire income difference between groups with different levels of schooling could be ascribed to schooling. Mincer (1962) noted that differences in individual earnings not only varied with differential schooling, but that the differences seemed to increase with age. He argued that this was owing to investment in on-the-job training and that those with more schooling had, as part of the return to their investment, greater access to on-the-job training opportunities than those with less schooling.

Denison (1962) had introduced the concept of correcting earnings differences for nonschooling, nontraining variables such as IQ by adjusting his estimates of such differentials by an "alpha coefficient" of 0.6; this assumed that 60 percent of income (productivity) differences was due to schooling alone. Morgan and David (1963) adjusted earnings differentials of white male heads of nonfarm households in the U.S. labor force in terms of measures of religion, personality, father's education, labor market conditions, mobility, and supervisory responsibilities. The adjustment was intended to separate the effect of schooling on earnings from motivation and ability. They found that, although the adjustment varied by level of schooling and age, for those less than 35 years old the 60 percent adjustment used by Denison seemed generally to hold.

Later studies, using different statistical techniques, by sociologists such as Blau and Duncan (1967) and by economists such as Griliches and Mason (1972) and Hause (1972) in the United States and Carnoy (1967a) in Mexico tended to confirm further that the part explained by schooling, of the explainable differences in earnings among individuals of the same race and sex, was the largest. Eckhaus (1973) and Chiswick and Mincer (1972) in the United States and Thias and Carnoy (1972) in Kenya showed that the employment factor was also crucial in understanding why individuals earned differentially. Correcting for differential unemployment rate among individuals with different levels of schooling, these studies indicated that the role of schooling in earnings was greatly reduced, particularly at certain levels of schooling. Their studies cast some doubt upon the previously high estimate of the "productive" value of schooling, since annual income is a function of the amount of time worked and wages paid per unit of time; it is the latter that supposedly reflect productivity differences (although it could be argued that more schooling makes people prefer to work more).

Schooling and Individual Income.   It was not universally agreed upon that the correlation of schooling with earnings reflected a causal relation between schooling as an investment good and the higher productivity of labor. First, some educators probably felt that the principal function of schooling was to prepare better, happier citizens, and not inputs into the production process. Similarly, some economists felt that the observed correlation could be explained by the conception of schooling as a consumption good: an individual with higher income tended to have a higher-income family that purchased more schooling for their children. In this consumption interpretation, of course, more schooling did not result in more income, but, rather, more income resulted in more schooling consumed. (A number of studies attempt to measure the income elasticity of schooling expenditures, for example, Shapiro (1962) and Hirsch (1959). Thus, schooling was not seen principally as a policy variable in increasing economic growth.

However, more sophisticated statistical analysis—Blau and Duncan (1967) and Duncan, Featherman, and Duncan (1972)—indicated that even when parents' education and occupation (highly correlated with family income) were accounted for, an individual's schooling was still a significant explainer of his occupational position and earnings. This implied that additional schooling is a factor in additional earnings even when the possible correlation between socioeconomic family position and schooling of children is accounted for. Although this did not prove that schooling was not primarily a consumption good, it strengthened the argument that a direct relation between schooling and earnings (more schooling leading to higher earnings) existed and had to be explained in some way. Bowles (1972) argued that such studies generally underestimate the effect of social class upon present earnings and occupational status relative to the effect of schooling on those variables for two reasons: (1) There is a bias in remembering parents' education and occupation relative to the amount of schooling taken by a person. People with high education tend to remember their parents as having less education and lower-status occupations than they actually had, and those with less schooling tend to remember their parents with higher education and status than they actually had, thus reducing the variance in social class relative to the variance in the education of the interviewee. (2) The use of parents' education and occupation is only a proxy for the parents' class position; parents' income and wealth are better predictors of the effect of social class and son's earnings than parents' education or occupation. Indeed, Sewell and Hauser's work (1974) on Wisconsin data bears out this second contention.

Earnings and productivity. Another discussion that questioned the contribution of schooling to growth revolved around the relation of earnings to productivity. Given that more schooling leads to higher earnings for the individual, does this mean that increasing schooling produces higher productivity? Do earnings equal productivity? Vaizey (1961) and others were willing to concede that the individual saw schooling as an investment; that is, that he correctly expected to earn more if he went further in school, but that this did not necessarily imply that schooling actually produced more aggregate output. Education could be an allocator of the share of output going to labor, assigning more earnings to those with more schooling, and less earnings to those with less, even though the marginal product of both groups could be approximately equal. In that model, higher investment by society in schooling would not necessarily produce more goods for distribution among the labor force, but the pattern of investment among individuals and groups would be important in determining who received the share of output going to labor. Neither would a higher average level of schooling lead to higher income per capita.

Support for this argument came indirectly from two sources. The first was Berg's work (1970), followed by Ful-

ler's study (1970), which showed that within carefully defined occupational categories, schooling and physical productivity of workers were not significantly correlated. The second was Thurow's study (1968) of the relation between labor's marginal productivity, as derived from aggregate production function estimates, and wages paid to labor. Thurow's comparison indicated that, in the United States, workers received, on average, earnings less than their marginal product (on the average 63 percent of productivity), whereas workers in those sectors (nonfarm, nonmanufacturing) that are less union-organized and require lower average education received, on average, less earnings relative to marginal product (60 percent) than workers in manufacturing (80 percent). Both studies, of course, only suggested that the correlation between schooling and productivity—if it could be measured properly—would be less than the correlation between schooling and income. If the suggested relation was borne out, the contribution of schooling to growth, by implication, was less than indicated by estimates based on earnings differences.

However, Berg's, Fuller's, and Thurow's work have methodological problems serious enough to cast doubt on their conclusions. Berg's and Fuller's correlations of productivity and schooling within an occupation yield good productivity comparisons in the sense that they can be measured in physically comparable units; but they necessarily exclude those workers at the lower end of the occupation's schooling spectrum who are in lower-paying and, supposedly, less productive occupations where the average level of schooling is also lower. At the same time, these correlations exclude those workers at the higher end of the occupation's education spectrum who are in higher-paying, more "productive" jobs where the average levels of schooling are also higher. Put another way, within a single occupation we will find usually workers with a fairly wide range of schooling, but a fairly low variance of income relative to the overall earnings variance in the labor force. We have to assume that the workers with much less or much more than the occupation's average schooling are extraordinary in some way that may be related to their productivity and earnings, but which is not measured by the schooling variable. Since, on average, those with different amounts of schooling are in different occupations producing different goods, it is virtually impossible to estimate the relation between physical productivity and schooling. On average, people with more schooling receive higher incomes than those with less schooling because they produce goods that are defined as "worth" more.

Thurow's methodology is also questionable: his results indicate that even in terms of the value of goods produced, more skilled and organized workers are doing better relative to their marginal product than less skilled and/or less organized workers (Thurow, 1968). But he faces the counterargument that estimates of aggregate production functions are not a meaningful reflection of what is happening in any real economic sense (Blaug, 1974). Thurow's estimates of marginal productivity may or may not measure the productivity of different groups, and consequently his comparisons with average wages may or may not be valid.

"Queue" or "screening" concepts. In later work, Thurow and Lucas (1972) contended that education and training are not important factors in determining potential productivity of workers because "productivity" is an attribute of *jobs,* not people. Jobs associated with a lot of modern capital equipment are high-productivity jobs, and workers queue up for them. Once a worker is hired, the cognitive skills necessary to raise his productivity up to the productivity of the job are learned through formal and informal training programs. The chief criterion that employers use in selecting workers for jobs is "trainability": those who possess background characteristics that employers feel reduce training costs go to the head of the queue and receive the best work.

The "queue" concept of education in the labor market sees the correlation between schooling and earnings as unrelated to any specific knowledge that schooling imparts to workers that makes them more productive; rather, schooling provides a convenient device for employers to identify those workers who can be trained more easily, based, it seems, primarily upon noncognitive values and norms acquired by students as they go further in school. Is this a contribution to worker productivity? Or is it a subsidy to employers that makes it easier for them to select workers for various jobs—a transfer of resources from the public sector to owners of capital?

Similarly, Arrow (1972) suggested that schooling may act as a mechansim to screen "desirable" from less desirable employees. The "screening" hypothesis and the "queue" concept both implied that education did not contribute directly to economic growth but served as a means to sort people for jobs, higher-productivity and lower-productivity jobs paying higher and lower wages. Although some economists retorted that screening did contribute to higher output because it made employers' labor search costs lower, Arrow showed that such a transfer to employers made the economy no better off. This left the discussion back at the level of determining whether there were persuasive reasons to believe that education did contribute directly to higher worker productivity or whether it was primarily a sorter of individuals for differentially paying jobs.

The argument for schooling contributing to growth lies in the productivity-raising skills that schooling allegedly provides to students as potential workers. Unlike the "queue" theory, in which more schooling made students more trainable as workers, the screening argument rests upon the certificates awarded to students as they progress in school. For the screen to function, some types of criteria have to be used, but these need not be cognitive, productivity-raising, or even "trainability" ones.

Labor market segmentation. Segmentation theory goes further: in its most technical version, it reinforces queue theory, arguing that wages are a function of the level of technology in particular industries, and that barriers exist to entry into the high-pay, high-technology jobs. This is the *dual labor market* theory (Doeringer & Piore, 1971). Labor markets in high-technology industries have different promotion rules, different payoffs to schooling, and different rules than in low-paying, low-technology industries. In the Marxian version of the theory, segmentation is the product of capitalist development and the class struggle between labor and capital; that is, segmentation of the labor force is a structure of the labor market that develops as part of capital's attempts to extract increased surplus through a more sophisticated division of labor (Reich, Gordon, & Edwards, 1973; Carter & Carnoy, 1974; Rosenberg, 1975; Rumberger & Carnoy, 1980. In both versions, wages are structured by the nature of jobs and job differentiation, according to the type of capital associated with each job, and not according to the human capital characteristics of workers in the jobs. Indeed, there is a subset of studies in segmentation analysis that estimates the low increase in employment probability and wages of those in "secondary" (menial, repetitive, low-wage) jobs as a result of education and training programs (Harrison, 1972; Rumberger & Carnoy, 1980; Levin, 1979). These studies suggest that the 1960s' War on Poverty programs were not successful because they incorrectly assumed that poverty could be reduced by marginal increases in the skills of the poor, when, in fact, the job market itself is much more crucial in explaining the wage structure.

Bowles (1975) and Gintis (1971) complemented this perspective: they suggested that young people were allocated to different occupations and earnings in large part on the basis of parents' social class (income, occupation, education), and that the principal function of schooling was to legitimize the reproduction of the class structure through a façade of meritocracy. Thus, the Bowles–Gintis view contends that schooling is more than a screening device for labor as an input to production (a benefit to employers as entrepreneurs); it is an institution that serves employers' class interest in perpetuating the capitalist social hierarchy. In this view, the growth function of schooling is not rejected: Bowles and Gintis argue that there is cognitive component to schooling, but that this cognitive component is overshadowed by the importance of class values and norms in school output and in assigning groups of individuals to various economic roles. But Carnoy (1974) pointed out that the function of schooling as an ideological arm of the state, reinforcing and reproducing the social structure, may have a negative effect on economic growth, since it gives priority to distribution of power (profit) and hierarchical rules rather than maximization of output.

Evaluation. Where does all this leave us? Does schooling contribute to increased output, or does it allocate people to jobs with higher training, productivity, and earnings possibilities? Is it a subsidy to employers? Does it legitimize an unequal social structure and hence contribute to higher output by helping to produce acceptance of unequal work roles and hence political stability (or to lower output through political stability)?

We can imagine how schooling could contribute to economic growth; the breaking of abstract codes in a systematic way (reading and arithmetic) allegedly helps develop deductive and inductive logic, which, in turn, helps people solve problems associated with production. More important, even though such logical capability may not contribute directly to increased production, it may make the physical capital with which people work more productive, since workers probably would be more aware of the nature of machinery and its required care. More schooling, especially centrally controlled, or common, schooling, also probably makes for better communication among workers and between workers and supervisors. If people have shared a common communicative experience with a common knowledge base (the school), workers from different family backgrounds, age groups, or cultures should be able to relate at least at that common experiential level. Welch (1970) suggests that the main contribution of education in production is yet something different: it makes producers better decision makers in the allocation of resources, including time. Welch's model implies that the greater the decision-making functions associated with a job, the greater would be the potential effect of education on productivity. All of these possible effects of schooling on productivity form the implicit bases for studies of correlation between education in the labor force and the level of gross national product (Bowman & Anderson, 1963; Harbison & Myers, 1964).

We can also understand the basis for the screening or "legitimization" argument: there is, after all, no way to prove that those with higher wages produce more than those with lower wages. It is a persuasive point that more schooling requires the expenditure of real resources, so that society would be wasteful and irrational to spend such resources if they did not result in some positive return. But the return might *not* be in the form of higher total output; if "society" is defined as a particular subset of the population, that subset may profit from a shift of product among groups, such as between those who are less and those who are more educated or between workers and capitalists. Schooling, in the screening argument, helps perform this shift, and the return to schooling may represent not a net contribution to total output but the transfer of labor's product from the less schooled to the more schooled, or the form of legitimizing that transfer. Thus, we could observe a positive return (as measured by wage differences) to expenditures on schooling as a result of people with lower wages being paid much less than their product, those with higher wages being paid their product, and capital increasing its return at the expense of the less schooled, although schooling does not contribute to a net increase in total product. Higher-schooled groups would have succeeded in such a case in using schooling to shift relative consumption power from the schooled to the more schooled through wage and income policies.

Finally, it is also possible that the principal function of schooling in economic growth lies in its legitimization of the existing or emerging social order. The acceptance by the masses of a particular social structure could have a positive effect on economic output. However, if the accepted economic organization—acceptable in part because schools have helped legitimize that organization—is not maximizing total output, but only the return to capital and the income of certain groups, schooling could have a negative effect on economic growth (Carnoy, 1974).

Bowles and Gintis's more recent, comprehensive work (1975), argues that the relation between the economy and education must be traced through schooling's effect on the consciousness, interpersonal behavior, and personality it fosters and reinforces in students. Any explanation of what schooling does depends on understanding the economy, and understanding the economy means—in the United States—understanding the essential elements of capitalism. For Bowles and Gintis, this means dealing with the social process of extracting surplus from workers and the inherently antagonistic and always potentially explosive process that requires.

Schooling probably does all of these things, but the main issue concerns which of these functions best characterizes schooling's role (Blaug, 1973). The question is not so much whether schooling contributes to growth, but how much and how it contributes. We conclude that the contribution is probably smaller than the early human capital theorists and development economists thought, and the process more complex. The correlation between earnings and schooling measures many other influences on earnings that are also correlated with schooling. There is also little evidence that earnings and productivity are equal; indeed, it is likely (on political grounds) that societies in which the higher educated are more powerful socially and politically reward those with higher education more relative to their productivity and those with less education less relative to their productivity, even if, in neoclassical terms, this prevents an "optimum" allocation of resources.

Education and Income Distribution. Social implications point up a different issue: should economic change be interpreted only as aggregate economic growth per capita? Economists in the last decade became increasingly interested in the distribution aspect of the economy. For example, a number of studies found that increased output per capita did not necessarily mean that all groups in the economy participated in that increase (Barkin, 1971; Fishlow, 1973). This raised serious questions about the meaning of economic change that may benefit only a minority of the labor force and population and a definition of development—aggregate economic growth per capita—that does not distinguish between those situations in which all groups participate in an income increase and those in which the income increase is highly concentrated in a small percentage of the population. Furthermore, the achievement of rapid growth of material output in societies that placed distribution considerations on a par with (or even above) growth considerations—such as the Soviet Union, Eastern Europe, China, and now Cuba—placed alternative models of economic and social change in direct competition with each other, a competition in which the distribution of output played a key role. See Adelman and Robinson (1978) and Adelman and Morris (1973) for a summary of the "efficiency" versus "equality" development models debate.

What function does schooling play in income distribution? The literature on screening, queue theory, and labor market segmentation indicates that schooling may designate who gets the high-paying and low-paying jobs in an economy. But, according to this theory, the variation of income among jobs would not be affected by the distribution of schooling in a society: income distribution is a function of the types of jobs available and the incomes attached to those jobs. Arguments for the legitimization and reproduction of class structure also imply a distribution role for schooling, primarily in maintaining groups of people in the same relative income position from generation to generation. In order to sort out these relationships and what we know about them, the discussion will focus upon two issues: the effect of education on intergenerational changes in relative income position (mobility), and its relation to intragenerational changes in income distribution.

Schooling and mobility. The first of these issues has been the object of many studies, particularly by sociologists (Floud, Halsey, & Martin, 1957; Havighurst & Gouveia, 1969; Jencks et al., 1972; Sewell & Hauser, 1974). In a review of these studies in the United States, Sewell and Hauser (1974) found that education and occupational status of parents are highly correlated with children's educational attainment, but that while the overall effect of parents' status and income is the single most important variable explaining son's current income, son's educational attainment is almost as important, and the overall explainability of earnings variation by parents' socioeconomic status and son's IQ and educational attainment is very low (less than 10 percent). This was Jencks's argument as well. On the other hand, a person's occupational status seems to be largely explained by educational attainment, not parents' social status. If these results are correct, schooling appears to increase mobility, even when parents' social class background is accounted for in explaining both the amount of schooling taken and the income equation.

In low-income countries, the effect of schooling on earnings appears to be greater than in the United States (Psacharopoulos, 1973; Carnoy et al., 1979); but very few of the low-income country studies carry out an analysis relating the effect of parents' social class background to both child's school attainment and child's income. In those cases where this is done, the results indicate that the effect of schooling on earnings is much greater than in the United States. And schooling and social class variables together explain a higher fraction of variance in low-income

countries. In the studies where the "social class of parents" variable does not enter, schooling alone as an explainer of earnings is more important than in U.S. estimates.

These results lead us to believe that much more than in high-income countries, schooling and socioeconomic background variables in developing economies are together highly related to earnings and occupational position. In other words, less of a "chance" factor appears to effect a person's attaining his or her economic position in the low-income situation. Although not very much information exists to indicate whether parents' social class in low-income countries is important in explaining the amount of schooling taken by children, recent work in Brazil indicates that parents' social class explains about 50 percent of the variance in individual educational attainment (Belloni & Vasquez, 1975). Other work in Kenya also shows a high correlation between father's income and the amount and kind of schooling taken (Mwaniki, 1973). As far as intergenerational mobility is concerned, then, schooling undoubtedly contributes in developing societies to such mobility, but parents' social class seems to be very influential in determining how much schooling a person gets. Schooling to an important degree appears to confirm a person's parents' social class, and legitimizes the passing of that social position from one generation to the next. The relation varies from country to country: we tend to believe that this role of schooling is more pronounced in Latin America, for example, than in Africa, where multiple social structures still exist (tribal versus colonial). But even in Africa, as Mwaniki's work indicates, new social structures based on European-type divisions between peasant, worker, and urban bourgeoisie are developing rapidly.

Intragenerational income variation. The issue of schooling's role in intragenerational variation in income is much more complex. As early as the mid-1950s Kuznets (1955) argued in his presidential address to the American Economic Association that the distribution of income became more equalized as an economy reached higher levels of income per capita (Mincer, 1958; Kuznets, 1959). One of the principal reasons for this equalization, in Kuznets's view, was the higher education of the labor force in higher-income economies. In other words, an increased level of schooling in the labor force contributes to a more equal distribution of earnings.

In part, Kuznets came to this conclusion because he felt that a more educated labor force is more likely to agitate politically for a more equal wage structure, but there are also good economic reasons in the neoclassical framework for believing that higher average schooling will contribute to a lower variance in earnings. If there is a direct connection between education and productivity, and between productivity and earnings, raising the average level of schooling could eventually reduce the variance of years of schooling in the labor force. There is probably an upper limit to how much schooling people would be willing to take, since there are fewer and fewer years in which to collect increased earnings from such additional schooling; and governments seem increasingly committed to providing a minimum level of schooling to their young population, with that minimum rising as the average level of schooling in the labor force rises. These two effects reduce the variance of schooling in the labor force over time and should, if the connection between education, productivity, and earnings holds, also reduce the variance in productivity and hence in earnings. Reduction in the variance of schooling in the labor force can be effected directly by concentrating investment in lower levels of schooling (Fishlow, 1973). In any case, varying the distribution of schooling in the labor force should have a direct effect upon the distribution of earnings if the causal connection between these two variables really exists.

In his study of the drastic decrease in income equality in Brazil between 1960 and 1970, Langoni (1973) explains the change in precisely this way: the distribution became more unequal in part because the distribution of schooling became more unequal, Brazilian university education expanding much more rapidly than primary school education. Indeed, Langoni (1973) agrees with Kuznets on another implicit assumption (made explicit in Langoni's work): not only was the change in distribution of schooling partly responsible for the change in earnings distribution, but the pattern of educational expansion was a "natural" phenomenon in the economic growth process. So, just as Kuznets uses "natural" forces in the economic growth process to predict an evolution to more equal income distribution, Langoni uses them to explain an increasingly unequal income distribution.

Jobs and income distribution. But if productivity is primarily a function of jobs, not characteristics of workers, as in the queue and segmentation theory, the effect on income distribution of changing the distribution of schooling in the labor force should be negligible. It would be the job or income structure itself that would have to be changed in order to influence income distribution. Education would serve to allocate people to jobs with various earnings attached to them; in the case where their distribution were highly unequal, the value of additional schooling would be high, and in the case where their distribution were more equal, the value of additional schooling would be correspondingly lower. Again in the Brazilian case, Malan and Wells (1973) present evidence that the increased inequality of Brazilian incomes did not occur during the rapid growth period of the late sixties, but rather in a two-year period, 1965–1966, when the Brazilian government intervened directly in the wage structure by holding wages fixed during an inflationary period, and allowing salaries of higher-paid workers to rise more rapidly than prices. Although no other country has had an empirical debate of this sort, data for Chile (Johnston, 1973; Frank, 1975) also indicate that changes in the distribution of schooling during the 1960s apparently had a negligible effect upon income distribution, whereas direct government wage policy during three successive regimes (1964–1975) significantly increased inequality (1966–1970), re-

duced inequality (1970–1973), and drastically increased inequality (1973–1975).

Unemployment. United States data, furthermore, point to unemployment as a key factor in income distribution, apparently more important than either the level of education or its distribution (Chiswick & Mincer, 1972). The fact that employment (number of days worked annually) is a function of policies that have little to do with schooling (business cycles, the direct intervention of the state in fiscal and monetary policy, or even direct controls over investment and employment) again suggests that the distribution of income, although possibly related to the distribution of education in the labor force, is more closely related to government macroeconomic strategy directly affecting incomes policies. If a government is dedicated to ensuring full employment and reducing the variance of earnings in the labor force as part of its development policy (Israel and Sweden, for example), the income distribution will be more equal than in economies where the government is primarily concerned with shifting income to professionals and administrators (Brazil and Mexico, for example). It is likely that, in both cases, educational investment will tend to be consistent with the overall incomes policy (although in Chile between 1964 and 1973 it was not); and it may be a moot point to separate the effect of education from the direct intervention of the state. Nevertheless, in the studies we have cited, education seems to play a rather limited role.

It is important to note that in most of the literature on both intergenerational and intragenerational relations between education and earnings, the dependent variable is wages salaries (earnings), not income. But wages and salaries represent only a fraction of the total product of the economy, about 65 percent to 75 percent in the United States (Kuznets, 1959; Machlup, 1963); 70 percent to 75 percent in Western Europe (Denison & Poullier, 1967); and perhaps as low as 50 percent or less in Latin America. Even if changing the distribution of wages and salaries through an educational policy could work, it would therefore affect less than three-fifths of the total income distribution in low-income countries unless other measures were taken to equalize wealth. Similarly, making the access to wages and salaries less dependent on father's education and earnings (through making access to education more equal for various groups, for example) would probably have little effect on the access to nonwage and nonsalary income derived from capital wealth (land and physical capital). Although there are large variations in wage and salary income in every nonsocialist country, these variations are considerably smaller than the distribution of all income (including income from physical wealth).

Education and Discrimination. In the United States, income distribution and mobility issues are closely tied to racial and sexual discrimination. The economics of education has considered discrimination an important area of study, particularly in assessing of changes in incomes of blacks relative to whites and women relative to men as well as the role that education plays in those changes; and for women, estimating the relationship between education and labor force participation.

The discussion of these issues has paralleled closely the discussion of the relationship between education and productivity (for a summary of the race discrimination discussion, see Marshall, 1974; Levin, 1979; and Reich, 1981; for a summary of the discussion on women's labor force participation and wage discrimination, see Standing, 1978; and Amsden, 1980). Those analysts who assume that productivity is a function of human capital characteristics have also stressed that race and sex discrimination can be explained largely by a combination of employer profit-maximizing behavior and human capital differences between black and white people and women and men (Becker, 1957; Freeman, 1973; Fuchs, 1974; Mincer & Polachek, 1974; Smith & Welch, 1977, 1978).

Racial discrimination. According to Becker, racism is fundamentally a problem of attitude toward race. Whites are defined to have a "taste for discrimination" if they are willing to forfeit income in order to be associated with other whites instead of blacks. Since white employees and employers prefer not to associate with blacks, they require a monetary compensation for the psychic cost of such an association. Becker tries to show that white employers lose financially from discrimination, although white workers gain. Smith and Welch (1977) make a different argument. They explain converging incomes of blacks and whites in the post–World War II period (particularly since 1964) by converging quantity and quality of the black educational experience. Thus, discrimination is not discrimination at all, but the logical result of differences in human capital. As human capital converges, productivity and hence earnings equalize. They disagree with Freeman's findings (1973) that the principal influence on increasing black-white earnings ratios since 1964 was reduced discrimination. Levin (1979) supports Freeman and questions the human capital interpretation on three grounds: (1) convergence in educational patterns between the races has taken place for at least the last fifty years, yet convergence in income is a relatively recent phenomenon; (2) returns to college education have risen for black people relative to white people in the post-1964 period, but the opposite has happened for returns to elementary and secondary education, seriously questioning the human capital hypothesis; (3) the black-white income ratios rose for older as well as younger workers, indicating that even those whose schooling experience did not change were affected by the general trend of the 1960s and early 1970s. Levin (1979) concludes, "Rather, the improvements in the black-white earnings ratio were pervasive and the shift appears to have been an abrupt one coinciding with the intense civil rights activity and passage of major civil rights legislation in the early and middle sixties" (p. 107).

If the issue is discrimination and not human capital, does this mean that Becker's "taste for discrimination" has been reduced? Reich (1981) contends, along with Levin, that it is not "taste" (an exogenous factor) that has changed, but that increased struggle by black people changed the political possibilities for exploiting black workers more than white workers. He sees racism (discrimination) as rooted in the economic system and not in "exogenously-determined attitudes." Reich shows, in his exhaustive study, that the economic consequences of racism are not only lower incomes for black workers, but also higher incomes for employers coupled with lower incomes for white workers—exactly the opposite of Becker's results.

Sexual discrimination. Wage discrimination against women is a subject of similar debate. Mincer and Polachek (1974) argue that much of the difference in wages between men and women can be explained by differences in work histories and by difference in job investment and depreciation. Thus, years of work experience differ significantly among men and women 30–44 years old in their sample (19.4 years for men, 15.6 for single women, and 9.6 for married women). They contend that equalizing work experience would eliminate about 45 percent of the male-female wage gap for married women and 7 percent of the much smaller gap for single women.

However, other analysts see the problem from the point of view of a segmented labor market, or occupational segregation (Bergmann, 1974; Chiplin & Sloane, 1974). In those analyses, women are limited in their occupational choice by employers (and male workers), and wages are "customarily" lower in "women's" occupations. Thus, it is not human capital differences, but labor market conditions that set wages lower. This position corresponds to the queue and segmentation view of education and labor markets.

Educational Finance. A major role of the educational economist has been to analyze and design the system of financing education. This concern arises out of the very central role that the field of government finance has played in economics. During the period 1960–1980, four major shifts occurred in the area of educational finance, and each had major consequences for the economics of education. These are (1) the rising federal role; (2) school finance equalization at the state level; (3) financial retrenchment; and (4) encroachment of the private sector.

Rising federal role. In 1960 the federal government accounted for only about 3 percent of federal elementary and secondary expenditures. With the thrust of the "War on Poverty," the federal contribution rose to over 7 percent in 1965 and has maintained that level ever since. Since education is a constitutional responsibility of the states, any federal intervention must be based upon a national interest in education. Although prior to 1960 such an interest was reflected in federal funds for vocational education and aid for schools in federally impacted areas, it was not until the national effort to improve equity in the 1960s that the federal role increased substantially. In essence the rising federal presence took the form of categorical grants for particular groups of students or services that would improve educational opportunities for students with special needs.

Foremost among these were Title I of the Elementary and Secondary Education Act of 1965, which was designed to provide compensatory educational services to children from low-income backgrounds. Of the approximately $7 billion in federal expenditures on elementary and secondary education in 1980, almost half was accounted for by Title I. Other important programs established during the 1960s and 1970s include services for students from non-English-speaking backgrounds, for the handicapped, and for school districts undergoing desegregation.

These programs have generated large numbers of studies in the economics of education addressing the most appropriate ways to design federal grant programs and the overall federal role in education. Examples of the types of studies generated and their conclusions can be found in Timpane (1978). The federal role in financing postsecondary education also increased over this period as a result of substantial loan and grant programs. Most important was the Higher Education Act of 1965 and its 1972 amendments. The latter legislation provided Basic Educational Opportunity Grants (BEOGs) for student tuition on the basis of family income. These programs have also stimulated substantial research on appropriate policies for financing postsecondary education (Hartman, 1971; Bowen, 1977; Hartman, 1978).

Equalization at state level. At the state level, the major changes over the 1960–1980 period have been the attempt to more nearly equalize educational funding for local school districts. Prior to 1970, the vast majority of states funded their educational systems through the use of a local property tax. Since property wealth is distributed rather unequally within states, this led to large differences in the amount of funding available for the education of each student among wealthy and poorer school districts. Although the states intervened by providing a nominal amount of equalization aid and funding for each child in average daily attendance, the overall spending patterns were highly unequal.

In the late 1960s and early 1970s, economic researchers and legal scholars began to challenge the state systems of educational finance on the basis of their constitutional validity and highly unequal results (Wise, 1968; Coons, Clune, & Sugarman, 1970). This led to legal challenges in many states, with the courts declaring many of the state systems unconstitutional, as in the *Serrano* case in California, because they make a child's educational expenditures a function of the wealth of his or her parents or neighbors rather than of the wealth of the state as a whole. In other cases, such as New Jersey, the older property tax-based approach was declared unconstitutional because it was not "thorough and efficient" as required by that state's constitution.

These cases resulted in major shifts in the financing of education at the state level, with a greater state share of funding and a strong trend toward equalizing educa-

tional expenditures among school districts (Odden, Berne, & Stiefel, 1979). A number of different approaches were taken to bring about these changes as reviewed in Benson et al. (1974). In addition, more recent approaches for equalization emphasize adjusting state aid to local educational agencies to account for differences in the cost of educational resources among such agencies (Chambers, 1979).

Financial retrenchment. In contrast to the growth in financial support for education in the 1960s and previously, the 1970s began a period of financial retrenchment. Although federal funds for categorical programs kept growing, there were increasing restraints on funding from other sources. Even though state and local support grew over this period, it grew at a slower pace than previously, when inflation is taken into account. Three factors that contributed to retrenchment were (1) annual rates of inflation that were often in the 10 percent or higher range; (2) declines in enrollment; and (3) attempts in the late 1970s to limit tax and expenditure levels.

In California, Proposition 13 was passed in 1978 to limit revenues from the local property tax (Catterall & Thresher, 1979). In 1979 a state expenditure measure was passed limiting increases in state expenditures. And in 1980 a measure was passed in Massachusetts that cut property tax revenues—the main source of school support—by about 40 percent. All of these revenue measures as well as milder tax and expenditure limitation movements in other states had important effects upon educational budgets. Indeed, they represent a prelude to the attempts by the Reagan administration to propse a 25 percent reduction in federal funding for education in 1981.

To a large degree, the field of economics of education is faced with the challenges of understanding the impacts of these cuts and suggesting ways to minimize their effects. Further, alternative ways of allocating resources in response to the cuts as well as searches for other sources of revenue have become an important research agenda.

Encroachment of the private sector. A final trend of the 1960–1980 period was the increasing consideration of ways to promote public support for private educational alternatives. The voucher proposal was popularized by the Office of Economic Opportunity to promote an experiment in which parents would be given tuition vouchers that could be used at any eligible school that wished to compete for them (Center for the Study of Public Policy, 1970). A limited version of the plan was attempted in San Jose, California with provocative results (Weiler, 1974). A more comprehensive approach, based upon the work of Coons and Sugarman (1978), was the basis for a constitutional initiative in California. Although that initiative failed to obtain enough votes, the voucher alternative is being considered by a number of states and is being discussed at the federal level. It has also been an object of scrutiny in the economics of education literature (Levin, 1980).

At the federal level, the principal form of subsidy discussed for nonpublic education has been the tuition tax credit. Legislation for federal tuition tax credits has been proposed throughout the late 1970s, providing credit on the federal income tax for a portion of tuition payments for each child in a private educational institution. The advocates of this proposal and the voucher approach argue that the exclusion of private school students from public support is unfair because it requires their families to pay twice for education, one through taxes and once through tutition. Further, they assert that by increasing the competition between public and private schools, the former will become more efficient. Detractors argue that parents of children in private schools always have the option of paying once by sending their children to public schools, and that what is taught in private schools is not in the public interest. Further, they suggest that either plan will not improve the public schools, but will further erode both political and financial support in a period of retrenchment (Catterall, 1981; Levin, 1980). Whatever the immediate outcome of the debate and political activity, this issue is not likely to disappear in the foreseeable future.

Research and Policy Implications. Analysis of the role of education in economic change has developed rapidly in the last twenty years. Although there are a number of conflicting hypotheses concerning the relationship between education and productivity, education and discrimination, and between education and the distribution of wages and salaries, we have learned quite a lot about the possible nature of these relationships. The principal confrontation now taking place concerns the interpretation of a large body of data and the emphasis upon some empirical results rather than others.

A major deficiency to date is that both theoretical and empirical studies of education's role in social change have tended to be ahistorical. The understanding and knowledge we have gleaned has been based almost entirely on cross-sectional studies at a single point in time. In part, this is true because the issue is so young and data have not been gathered over past time; but in part, the problem also lies in the ahistorical nature of social science in the United States. To delve deeper into the role of schooling requires more historical studies of education; this including longitudinal studies, using data collected on individuals or groups over time, and historiography, which studies the expansion of education in the past and the role it has played in social change.

Longitudinal studies. Longitudinal work has, of course, already been done, and its results have generally confirmed cross-sectional studies. Husén (1969) analyzed follow-up data on a group in Malmö, Sweden, who were first tested in 1938, when they were ten years old. His twenty-six-year follow-up, begun in 1964, showed that schooling was the single most important factor explaining economic success of individuals in this group, but that the amount of schooling taken is heavily influenced by the social class background of students. In later work with the same sample, Fägerlind (1975) found that the effect

upon earnings of education and its social class and IQ precedents increases as individuals get older.

Other longitudinal work is proceeding in the United States based on a sample taken by Parnes (1972) and his associates at Ohio State University as well as the Project Talent survey taken in the early 1960s (Hause, 1972). Although the United States analyses do not span the length of time covered by the Swedish data, they help reveal the effect of schooling upon individuals' early employment and income, and, in the case of the Parnes data, on schooling's role in determining what happens to people in mid-career.

Another type of "longitudinal" study that has already yielded some results but will be more important in the future is the analysis of cross-section results over time, using comparable samples. Freeman (1973), Fuchs (1974), Carnoy and Marenbach (1975), Levin (1979), Reich (1981), and Smith and Welch (1978) are just several examples in the United States of studies that utilized surveys to make such intertemporal comparisons of the economic payoff to various groups in the labor force (black people, women, and white males) and the possible role of schooling in affecting economic position. Chiswick and Mincer (1972) in the United States, and Langoni (1973), Malan and Wells (1973), and Velloso (1975) in Brazil have similarly analyzed the role of schooling in changing income distribution over time.

The important contribution that longitudinal studies make to our understanding of educational development is their analysis of change over time within a single country. When we make estimates from cross-sectional studies, inferences from such estimates require the assumption that different groups of individuals or countries will follow the same process through time as other groups that have higher education and higher earnings or more or less equal income distribution. Although the assumption may be a valid one, we have little knowledge of the process of getting from one point to another; the theory of economic change is, after all, primarily a theory of process.

Such empirical studies, however, do share one serious deficiency with cross-section analysis: both rely on correlations for understanding causality. They do not usually tell us, for example, whether the correlation between education and earnings is an education-productivity relation, and they do not reveal whether the relation between the distribution of earnings and education is the result of productivity effects of simultaneous income distribution and schooling distribution policies by the same government.

Historical studies. To study these issues, some economists are paying closer attention to the historical role of education in economic change. Histories of education have been written, of course (although not many outside of the United States and Western Europe), but these usually take a "cultural" point of view, namely, that education was spread as an end in itself to liberate people from ignorance or to bring them into a new, more civilized culture. Recently, sociologists, economists, and revisionist historians have questioned this approach by writing new interpretations of educational expansion within the context of economic and social change. Katz (1968, 1971), Karrier (1972), Spring (1972), Bowles and Gintis (1975), and Tyack (1974) for the United States; Foster (1965) for Ghana; Quick (1974) for England; and Carnoy (1974) for the Third World in general, all provide us with insight into the role of education in the process of economic and social change. They claim that education serves the needs of the economic and social system, particularly the dominant economic groups in that system and the bureaucracy of the educational system itself (Tyack, 1974). Foster stresses the impact of individual investor sovereignty when faced by a set of educational choices within a given social structure. Other studies (Carnoy, 1974; Bowles & Gintis, 1975) emphasize the correspondence between the constrained likelihood of individual educational decisions and the economic and social needs of a dominant class of capitalists or capitalist intermediaries.

The important point about these different views of educational expansion is not so much their difference, as the theoretical frameworks they develop for social scientific studies of education and economic change. Much of the controversy about the relation between schooling and change occurs (explicitly and implicitly) because of differences in theoretical interpretation of historical relationships.

Theoretical issues. There are two branches of theoretical work that are especially crucial to our understanding of the issue of the relation between education and economic change. The first group of studies has already been mentioned—the study of labor markets. The second group involves studies of the role of the State in economic and social development. Neoclassical economic theory has left us with deficiencies in both these areas: in understanding labor market institutions, because in neoclassical theory the labor market is a derivative of the market for goods and the number of people available for various kinds of jobs; in understanding the State, because neoclassical theory views the State as distorting, for obscure political reasons, the optimum allocation of resources by the free market.

The discussion of the theory of labor markets (including individual workers' formal education as a variable) is now extensive, including the neoclassical view (Cain, 1975); the dual view (Doeringer & Piore, 1971); and the segmented view (Reich, Gordon, & Edwards, 1973; Carter & Carnoy, 1974; Edwards, 1979; Rumberger & Carnoy, 1980; Carnoy and Levin, 1982). The president of the American Economic Association considered the debate important enough to feature it in a recent presidential address (Solow, 1980). The operation of labor markets is central to the discussion of whether education increases productivity, and hence contributes to growth, or whether schooling is primarily a means of subsidizing the return to capital (the screen) or primarily a means of reproducing the capitalist (or postcapitalist) organization of production, and

hence does not contribute much to growth, although it does maintain the hierarchy of power largely unchanged from generation to generation.

Whether or not the State should provide free education, a source of debate among neoclassical economists in the past (Blaug, 1970), the fact is that the State is and has been massively involved with trying to control formal schooling for a long time in most countries. The way the State provides education may have a lot to do with intergenerational mobility and changes in the distribution of income over time; thus, understanding the process of public investment in education is necessary to any theory of education and economic change.

As we have shown, part of this theoretical discussion has taken place in the historical literature, but, more recently economists (Bowles & Gintis, 1975; Carnoy, 1980; Carnoy and Levin, 1982), political sociologists (Offe, 1980; Lenhardt, 1980; Weiler, 1980), and even philosophers (Althusser, 1971) have made the State a primary focus of analyzing the relationship between education and the economy. In that discussion, the State in capitalist economies is seen in one form or another as mediating between the needs of employers to increase profits and the needs of workers for increased wages and employment in better jobs. In order for the democratic State to be "legitimate," it must give in to the demands of the mass of voting workers; but to maintain its revenue base and the basis of its social function, the State must also reproduce the dominance by the capital owners and managers of the investment and production process. In this context, education plays a variety of roles: it supplies skills for production and makes possible the allocation of skills to various kinds of jobs; it socializes youth to work in particular ways and to accept the work system; and it also inculcates a general ideology in the population that promotes the existing production system and political process as fair and rational. Yet, as Carnoy and Levin (1982), suggest, this mediating role can also be the source of contradiction within the economic and political process: for example, young people may become "overeducated" for existing jobs (Rumberger, 1981), or school idealizations of an equitable and just society may be taken seriously by youth and translated into demands on the work place and on politicians.

It is important to note that now the economics of education not only presents us with information about specific relations between education and economic change, but also attempts to integrate this knowledge into broader understandings of the social change process and the role of education in that process. Economists of education have graduated from narrow estimates of the productive value of formal schooling to explaining, by means of both statistical and historical methodologies, the complex relations between education, the State, and the labor market.

Martin Carnoy

See also Comparative Education; National Development and Education.

REFERENCES

Adelman, I., & Morris, C. T. *Economic Growth and Social Equity in Developing Countries.* Stanford, Calif.: Stanford University Press, 1973.

Adelman, I., & Robinson, S. *Income Distribution Policy in Developing Countries: A Case Study of Korea.* Stanford, Calif.: Stanford University Press, 1978.

Althusser, L. *Lenin and Philosophy and Other Essays.* New York: Monthly Review Press, 1971.

Amsden, A. H. *The Economics of Women and Work.* New York: St. Martin's Press, 1980.

Arrow, K. *Higher Education as a Filter* (Technical Report No. 71). Stanford, Calif.: Stanford University, Institute for Mathematical Studies in the Social Sciences, September 1972.

Barkin, D. Acceso a la educación superior y beneficios que reporta en Mexico. *Revista del Centro de Estudios Educativos,* 1971.

Becker, G. *The Economics of Discrimination.* Chicago: University of Chicago Press, 1957.

Becker, G. *Human Capital.* New York: Columbia University Press, 1964.

Belloni, I., & Vasquez de Miranda, G. *The Determinants of Educational Attainment in Minas Gerais, Brazil.* Paper presented at Estudios Conjuntos de Inegración Económica Latinoamericana (ECIEL) Conference, Lima, Peru, 1975.

Benson, C.; Goldfinger, P.; Hoachlander, E. G.; & Pers, J. *Planning for Educational Reform: Financial and Social Alternatives.* New York: Harper & Row, 1974.

Berg, I. *Education and Jobs: The Great Training Robbery.* New York: Praeger, 1970.

Bergmann, B. Occupational segregation, wages, and profits when employers discriminate by sex. *Eastern Economics Journal,* April–July 1974, *1*(2–3), 103–110.

Blau, P., & Duncan, O. D. *The American Occupational Structure.* New York: Wiley, 1967.

Blaug, M. The private and social returns on investment in education: Some results for Great Britain. *Journal of Human Resources,* Summer 1967, *2*(3), 330–346.

Blaug, M. *An Introduction to the Economics of Education.* London: Penguin Press, 1970.

Blaug, M. The correlation between education and income: What does it signify? *Higher Education,* Amsterdam; 1973.

Blaug, M. *Neo-Keynesian Theory of Value and Distribution: Revolution or Dead End?* London: University of London, Institute of Education, 1974. (Mimeo)

Blaug, M. *Economics of Education* (3rd ed.) Elmsford, N.Y.: Pergamon Press, 1978.

Bowen, H. *Investment in Learning.* San Francisco: Jossey-Bass, 1977.

Bowles, S. Schooling and inequality from generation to generation. *Journal of Political Economy* (Part 2), May–June 1972, *80*(3), S219–S251.

Bowles, S. Unequal education and the reproduction of the social division of labor. In M. Carnoy (Ed.), *Schooling in a Corporate Society* (2nd ed.). New York: McKay, 1975.

Bowles, S., & Gintis, H. *Schooling in Capitalist America.* New York: Basic Books, 1975.

Bowman, M. J., & Anderson, A. Concerning the role of education in development. In C. Gertz (Ed.), *Old Societies and New States.* New York: Free Press, 1963.

Cain, G. The challenge of dual and radical theories of the labor market to orthodox theory. *American Economic Review,* May 1975, *65*(2), 16–22.

Carnoy, M. Earnings and schooling in Mexico. *Economic Development and Cultural Change,* July 1967, pp. 408–419. (a)

Carnoy, M. Rates of return to schooling in Latin America. *Journal of Human Resources,* Summer 1967, *2*(3) 359–374. (b)

Carnoy, M. *Education as Cultural Imperialism.* New York: McKay, 1974.

Carnoy, M. *Marxian Approaches to Education* (Program Report No. 80-B13). Stanford, Calif.: Stanford University, Institute for Research on Educational Finance and Governance, July 1980. (ERIC Document Reproduction Service No. ED 193 799)

Carnoy, M., & Levin, H. M. *The Dialectics of Education and Work.* Stanford University Press, 1982.

Carnoy, M.; Lobo, J.; Toledo, A.; & Belloso, J. *Can Educational Policy Equalize Income Distribution in Latin America?* Geneva: International Labor Organization, 1979.

Carnoy, M., & Marenbach, D. The rate of return to education in the United States, 1939–1969. *Journal of Human Resources,* Summer 1975, *10*(3), 312–331.

Carter, M., & Carnoy, M. *Theories of Labor Markets and Worker Productivity.* Palo Alto, Calif.: Center for Economic Studies, 1974. (Mimeo)

Catterall, J. Tuition tax credits for schools. In *IFG Policy Perspectives.* Stanford, Calif.: Stanford University, Institute for Research on Educational Finance and Governance, 1981.

Catterall, J., & Thresher, T. *Proposition 13: The Campaign, the Vote, and the Immediate Aftereffects for California Schools* (Program Report No. 79-B5). Stanford, Calif.: Stanford University, Institute for Research on Educational Finance and Governance, March 1979. (ERIC Document Reproduction Service No. ED 172 381)

Center for the Study of Public Policy. *Education Vouchers.* Cambridge, Mass.: The Center, March 1970.

Chambers, J. *Educational Cost Differentials and Allocation of State Aid for Elementary/Secondary Education* (Report No. 79-B4). Stanford, Calif.: Stanford University, Institute for Research on Educational Finance and Governance, March 1979.

Chiplin, B., & Sloane, P. J. Sexual discrimination in the labour market. *British Journal of Industrial Relations,* November 1974, *12*(3), 371–402.

Chiswick, B., & Mincer, J. Time series change in personal income inequality in the United States from 1939, with projections to 1985. *Journal of Political Economy* (Part 2), May-June 1972, *80*(3), S34–S66.

Coons, J.; Clune, W.; & Sugarman, S. *Private Wealth and Public Education.* Cambridge, Mass.: Belknap Press, 1970.

Coons, J., & Sugarman, S. *Education by Choice.* Berkeley: University of California Press, 1978.

Denison, E. F. *The Sources of Economic Growth in the United States and the Alternatives before Us.* New York: Committee for Economic Development, 1962.

Denison, E., & Poullier, J. P. *Why Growth Rates Differ.* Washington, D.C.: Brookings Institution, 1967.

Doeringer, P., & Piore, M. *Internal Labor Markets and Manpower Training.* Lexington, Mass.: Heath, Lexington Books, 1971.

Duncan, O. D.; Featherman, D. L.; & Duncan, B. *Socioeconomic Background and Achievements.* New York: Seminar Press, 1972.

Eckhaus, R. *Estimating the Returns to Education: A Disaggregated Approach.* Berkeley, Calif.: Carnegie Corporation, 1973.

Edwards, R. *Contested Terrain.* New York: Basic Books, 1979.

Fägerlind, I. *Formal Education and Adult Earnings.* Stockholm: Almqvist & Wiksell, 1975.

Fishlow, A. *Brazilian Income Size Distribution: Another Look.* Berkeley: University of California, 1973. (Mimeo)

Floud, J. E.; Halsey, A. H.; & Martin, F. M. *Social Class and Educational Opportunity.* London: Heinemann, 1957.

Foster, P. *Education and Social Change in Ghana.* London: Routledge & Kegan Paul, 1965.

Frank, A. G. An open letter about Chile to Arnold Harberger and Milton Friedman. *Radical Review of Political Economics,* Fall 1975, pp. 61–76.

Freeman, R. Changes in the labor market for black Americans, 1948–1972. *Brookings Papers on Economic Activity.* (Washington, D.C.: The Brookings Institution, 1973), pp. 67–120.

Fuchs, V. Recent trends and long-run prospects for female earnings. *American Economic Review,* May 1974, *64*(2).

Fuller, W. *Education, Training, and Worker Productivity: Study of Skilled Workers in Two Firms in South India.* Unpublished doctoral dissertation, Stanford University, 1970.

Gintis, H. Education, technology, and worker productivity. *American Economic Association Proceedings,* May 1971, *61*(2), 266–271.

Gounden, N. Investment in education in India. *Journal of Human Resources,* Summer 1967, *2*(3), 347–358.

Griliches, Z., & Jorgenson, D. Sources of measured productivity change: Capital input. *American Economic Review,* May 1964, *61*, 50–61.

Griliches, Z., & Mason, W. Education, income, and ability. *Journal of Political Economy* (Part 2), May-June 1972, *80*(3), S74–S103.

Hanoch, G. An economic analysis of earnings and schooling. *Journal of Human Resources,* Summer 1967, *2*(3), 310–329.

Hansen, W. L. Total and private rates of return to investment in schooling. *Journal of Political Economy,* April 1963, *71*.

Harbison, F., & Myers, C. *Education, Manpower, and Economic Growth.* New York: McGraw-Hill, 1964.

Harrison, B. Education and underemployment in the urban ghetto. *American Economic Review,* December 1972, pp. 796–812.

Hartman, R. *Credit for College: Public Policy for Student Loans.* New York: McGraw-Hill, 1971.

Hartman, R. Federal options for student aid. In D. Breneman & C. Finn (Eds.), *Public Policy and Private Higher Education.* Washington, D.C.: Brookings Institution, 1978.

Hause, J. Earnings profile: Ability and schooling. *Journal of Political Economy* (Part 2), May-June 1972, *80*(3), S108–S138.

Havighurst, R., & Gouveia, A. *Brazilian Secondary Education and Socioeconomic Development.* New York: Praeger, 1969.

Hirsch, Z. *Analysis of the Rising Costs of Public Education* (Congressional Joint Economic Committee, 86th Congress, 1st Session). Washington, D.C.: U.S. Government Printing Office, 1959.

Husén, T. *Talent, Opportunity, and Career.* Stockholm: Almqvist & Wiksell, 1969.

Jencks, C., et al. *Inequality.* New York: Basic Books, 1972.

Johnston, C. *Educación y Distribución del Ingreso.* Thesis presented to the Faculty of Economics, University of Chile, December 1973.

Karrier, C. *Testing for Order and Control in the Corporate State.* Urbana: University of Illinois, 1972. (Mimeo)

Katz, M. *The Irony of Early School Reform.* Cambridge, Mass.: Harvard University Press, 1968.

Katz, M. *Class, Bureaucracy, and Schools.* New York: Praeger, 1971.

Kuznets, S. Economic growth and income inequality. *American Economic Review,* May 1955, *45*(1).

Kuznets, S. Quantitative aspects of economic growth of nations, Part 4. Distribution of national income by factor shares. *Economic Development and Cultural Change* (Part 2), April 1959.

Langoni, C. *A Distribucão da Renda e Desenvolvimento Econômica da Brasil.* Rio de Janeiro: Editora Expressão e Cultura, 1973.

Lenhardt, G. *On Legal Authority, Crisis of Legitimacy, and Schooling in the Writings of Max Weber.* (Program Report No. 80-B19). Stanford, Calif.: Stanford University, Institute for Research on Educational Finance and Governance, November 1980.

Levin, H. M. *Education and Earnings of Blacks and the Brown Decision* (Program Report No. 79-B13). Stanford, Calif.: Stanford University, Institute for Research on Educational Finance and Governance, October 1979. (ERIC Document Reproduction Service No. ED 176 374)

Levin, H. Educational vouchers and social policy. In R. Haskins & J. Gallagher (Eds.), *Care and Education of Young Children in America.* Norwood, N.J.: Ablex 1980.

Machlup, F. Micro- and macro-economics. In *Essays in Economic Semantics.* Englewood Cliffs, N.J.: Prentice-Hall, 1963.

Malan, P., & Wells, J. Distribucão da renda e desenvolvimento econômico do Brasil. *Pesquisa e Planejamento Econômico,* December 1973.

Marshall, R. The economics of racial discrimination: A survey. *Journal of Economic Literature,* September 1974, *12*, 849–871.

Mincer, J. Investment in human capital and personal distribution of income. *Journal of Political Economy,* August 1958, *66*, 281–301.

Mincer, J. On-the-job training: Costs, returns, and some implications. *Journal of Political Economy* (Supplement), October 1962, *70*. S50–S80.

Mincer, J., & Polachek, S. Family investment in human capital. *Journal of Political Economy* (Part 2), March–April 1974, *82*(2), S76–S108.

Morgan, J., & David, M. Education and income. *Quarterly Journal of Economics,* 1963, *77*, 423–437.

Mwaniki, D. *Education and Socio-economic Development in Kenya: A Study of the Distribution of Resources for Education.* Unpublished doctoral dissertation, Stanford University, 1973.

Odden, A.; Berne, R.; & Stiefel, L. *Equity in School Finance.* Denver, Colo.: Education Finance Center, October 1979. (ERIC Document Reproduction Service No. ED 182 821)

Offe, C. *Notes on the "Laws of Motion" of Reformist State Policies.* Bielefeld, Germany: Bielefeld University, 1980. (Mimeo)

Parnes, H. Longitudinal surveys: Prospects and problems. *Monthly Labor Review,* February 1972.

Psacharopoulos, G. *Returns to Education: An International Comparison.* New York: Elsevier, 1973.

Quick, P. M. *Education and Industrialization: Elementary Education in Nineteenth-century England and Wales.* Unpublished doctoral dissertation, Harvard University, 1974.

Reich, M. *Racial Inequality: A Political Economic Analysis.* Princeton, N.J.: Princeton University Press, 1981.

Reich, M.; Gordon, D.; & Edwards, R. A theory of labor-market segmentation. *American Economic Review,* May 1973, *63*, 359–365.

Rosenberg, S. *The Dual Labor Market: Its Existence and Consequences.* Unpublished doctoral dissertation, University of California at Berkeley, 1975.

Rumberger, R. *Overeducation in the U.S. Labor Market.* New York: Praeger Special Studies, 1981.

Rumberger, R., & Carnoy, M. Segmentation in the U.S. labor market: Its effects on the mobility and earnings of whites and blacks. *Cambridge Journal of Economics,* 1980, *4,* 117–132.

Schultz, T. W. Investment in man: An economist's view. *Social Service Review,* June 1959, *33,* 110–117.

Schultz, T. Investment in human capital. *American Economic Review,* March 1961, *51,* 1–17.

Schultz, T. *The Economic Value of Education.* New York: Columbia University Press, 1963.

Sewell, W., & Hauser, R. *Education, Occupation, and Earnings: Achievement in the Early Career.* University of Wisconsin, Department of Sociology, March 1974. (ERIC Document Reproduction Service No. ED 116 041)

Shapiro, S. *An Analysis of the Determinants of Current Public and Societal Expenditures per Pupil in Elementary and Secondary Schools, Decennially, 1920–1950.* Unpublished doctoral dissertation, University of Chicago, 1962.

Smith, J., & Welch, F. Black-white male wage ratios: 1960–1970. *American Economic Review,* June 1977, *67,* 323–338.

Smith, J., & Welch, F. *Race Difference in Earnings: A Survey and New Evidence.* Santa Monica, Calif.: Rand Corporation, 1978.

Solow, R. Technical change and the aggregate production function. *Review of Economics and Statistics,* August 1957, *39,* 312–320.

Solow, R. On theories of unemployment. *American Economic Review,* March 1980, pp. 1–11.

Spring, J. Education and the corporate state. *Socialist Revolution,* March-April 1972, *8.*

Standing, G. *Labour-Force Participation and Development.* Geneva: International Labor Organization, 1978.

Thias, H., & Carnoy, M. *Cost-Benefit Analysis in Education: A Case Study of Kenya.* Washington, D.C.: World Bank, 1972.

Thurow, L. Disequilibrium and the marginal productivity of capital and labor. *Review of Economics and Statistics,* February 1968.

Thurow, L., & Lucas, R. The American distribution of income: A structural problem. In *Hearings before the Joint Economic Committee.* Washington, D.C.: U.S. Government Printing Office. 1972.

Timpane, M. (Ed.). *The Federal Interest in Financing Schooling.* Cambridge, Mass.: Ballinger, 1978.

Tyack, D. *The One Best System.* Cambridge, Mass.: Harvard University Press, 1974.

Vaizey, J. *The Economics of Education.* London: Faber & Faber, 1961.

Velloso, J. *Human Capital and Market Segmentation. An Analysis of the Distribution of Earnings in Brazil, 1970.* Unpublished doctoral dissertation, Stanford University, 1975.

Weiler, D. *A Public School Voucher Demonstration: The First Year at Alum Rock.* Santa Monica, Calif.: Rand Corporation, 1974. (ERIC Document Reproduction Service No. ED 093 091)

Weiler, H. N. *Legalization, Expertise, and Participation: Strategies of Compensatory Legitimation in Educational Policy.* Paper prepared for delivery at the Conference of Europeanists, Council for European Studies, Washington, D.C., October 1980.

Welch, F. Education in production. *Journal of Political Economy,* January-February 1970, *78,* 35–59.

Wise, A. *Rich School, Poor School.* Chicago: University of Chicago Press, 1968.

EDUCATIONAL FOUNDATIONS

See Anthropology; Comparative Education; Economics and Education; History of Education; Philosophy of Education; Political Science; Psychology; Sociology of Education.

EDUCATIONAL PHILOSOPHY

See Philosophy of Education.

EDUCATIONAL PSYCHOLOGY

See Psychology.

EDUCATIONAL RESEARCH ASSOCIATIONS

Voluntary professional and scholarly associations (councils, societies) of individuals and organizations engaged in educational research exist in a variety of forms and sizes. They do, however, share a number of common characteristics: (1) association membership is voluntary, that is, membership is not required for professional entry or employment certification in the field of educational research; (2) members pay annual dues and receive specific benefits for participation; (3) all or part of the association's membership views the field of education, or some part of it, as a principal subject of inquiry; and (4) the members engage in such professional activities as basic research, development, dissemination, evaluation, statistics, policy study, and analysis in education.

Educational research associations, among their purposes and missions, have several common functions. They all provide for the exchange of knowledge and information derived from the research and related inquiry of their members. These associations promote the study of education as an important professional endeavor. They encourage, directly or indirectly, the improvement of education through a base of knowledge and information produced by educational inquiry. They also provide their members with information of common interest related to policies, issues, opportunities, and other matters affecting the conduct of research and membership in the association.

In addition to these generally shared functions, several educational research associations perform additional collective activities for their members. Individually or in collaboration with other groups, educational research associations provide forums for the development of performance and ethical standards covering one or more forms of educational inquiry (e.g., evaluation, testing, and so on).

A number of educational research associations represent their membership in governmental, professional, and public arenas. For example, some educational research associations, on their own and through coalitions, provide information and testimony to the legislative and executive branches of government. Such information relates to policies and programs affecting opportunities for and the conduct of educational research. These associations also promote the funding of government research programs. These liaison activities with governmental, educational, and scholarly groups are designed to inform others of the value, character, and purposes of educational research, and the consequences of policies and actions for the field of research.

Additionally, educational research associations engage in efforts to improve the quality of research methods and performance. A number of these associations have also initiated programs or specific efforts to increase the participation of minorities, women, and other underrepresented groups in the conduct of educational research. Finally, several educational research associations conduct occasional studies and data collection activities about their members, the field of educational research, and educational policies and issues affecting their members' professional activities.

These association functions are accomplished through a wide variety of activities. Knowledge and information are shared through journals, newsletters, monographs, reviews, annual meetings, topical conferences, and so on. Publications also inform the external public with regard to the results of research efforts. Meetings, in addition to the formal sharing of information through paper presentations and symposia, offer informal exchange and network opportunities for association members. Educational research associations sponsor training programs and colloquia for members to learn new techniques and findings in educational research. Much of the work of educational research associations is accomplished through standing committees or temporary groups of members, with the support of the association staff.

Types of Associations. The range of associations involving educational researchers and organizations engaged in educational inquiry attests to the diversity and complexity of both the field of education and the forms of educational study. Education is the largest single enterprise in the United States, involving over 64 million people (engaged in education as their primary activity), and a national investment of over $160 billion. Educational researchers conduct studies on teaching, learning, education policy, management, organization, and the societal forces affecting education at all levels. Most educational researchers are in academic institutions; however, they are also located in federal, state, and local education agencies, independent research and development organizations, the military, business, industry, and human-service institutions. Educational research organizations have been formed to accommodate the collective professional interests among researchers working in this heterogeneous field.

A number of national professional associations are composed of members whose primary professional activity is the conduct of educational research. The American Educational Research Association (AERA) serves as an umbrella association for these groups. These associations may focus on a particular area of education, a type of research methodology, an education curriculum, or they may represent a subset of institutions or individuals engaged in educational research. Similar associations exist at regional and state levels.

Educational research divisions are included in professional associations and science societies for such disciplines as psychology, sociology, political science, anthropology, economics, and statistics. In addition, a number of professional education associations, which focus primarily on teaching, administration, governance, and support services, include research divisions for researchers.

AERA has fourteen thousand individual members and over one hundred institutional affiliates. The association has ten divisions and over seventy-five special interest groups to provide its members with different forums for interaction and exchange. The divisions include (A) administration, (B) curriculum and objectives, (C) learning and instruction, (D) measurement and research methodology, (E) counseling and human development, (F) history and historiography, (G) the social context of education, (H) school evaluation and program development, (I) education in the professions, and (J) postsecondary education. AERA special interest groups range in size from thirty members to several hundred and cover a broad range of research subjects (e.g., politics of education, mathematics education, early childhood education, and education finance), methods and purposes of research (e.g., research use, organizational theory, psycholinguistics, and survey research), and the location or role of researchers (e.g., state education, agencies, professors of research). In addition to its periodical journals, meetings, and other publications, the association provides a research training program, a governmental and professional liaison service, and special committees for women, minorities, and students.

State and regional educational research associations (e.g., California, the Northeast, and Pennsylvania) are also broad-reaching in member interest, and they provide members with geographic proximity for meetings and other forms of exchange. Several of the AERA special interest groups have formed their own associations, such as the Politics of Education Association, and researchers in mathematics education. Examples of other national associations composed primarily of educational researchers include the National Council on Measurement in Education (primarily concerned with test and other data collection instruments on student ability and achievement), the Evaluation Research Society, the American Educational Finance Association, and the National Reading Conference.

Several institutional associations include educational research organizations among their members. The American Association of Colleges for Teacher Education has several subgroups of schools of education with major research missions (e.g., the Deans' Network, and the Association of Schools and Colleges of Education in State Universities and Land-Grant Colleges). The Council for Educational Development and Research serves as a forum for information exchange, and as an advocacy body for several university educational research and development centers, and regional education laboratories funded by the federal government. AERA's institutional affiliates have also formed an organization in conjunction with the association's Governmental and Professional Liaison program. The AERA Organization of Institutional Affiliates includes universities (R & D centers, schools of education), state and local education agencies, and independent research and development organizations.

The American Psychological Association (APA) is the discipline-based association with the largest number of educational researchers. APA has six divisions concerned with educational research interests, namely, educational psychology, school psychology, experimental psychology, evaluation and measurement, developmental psychology, and teaching of psychology. The American Sociological Association, American Political Science Association, American Statistical Association, and the American Anthropological Association (AAA) are examples of other academic societies with significant numbers of education researchers. AAA also administers the Council on Education and Anthropology, with members primarily engaged in educational studies.

The Society for Research on Child Development, American Personnel and Guidance Association, American Association for Higher Education, and the Association for Supervision and Curriculum Development are examples of professional associations that include educational researchers among their members. Research membership subdivisions are included in a number of the subject areas and curricular associations, for example, teachers of English, mathematics, social studies, reading, and science. The Council for Exceptional Children, an umbrella association for education of the handicapped, includes educational researchers working on problems of education for the handicapped.

Phi Delta Kappa, a general national association of professional educators, includes programs and publications for educational researchers, evaluators, and those engaged in the use of research for educational improvement. Other associations provide similar outlets for the products and outcomes of educational research, for example, the National Society for the Study of Education, and the University Council for Educational Administration. The American Association for the Advancement of Science, an umbrella association of individuals, organizations, and affiliated associations, also includes an educational research division.

A number of professional and institutional education associations, although not educational research associations, provide research services, publications of educational research findings, and other opportunities for educa-

tional researchers to share the fruits of their labor. These include the teacher unions, school administrator associations, higher education associations, and national associations of school boards, state school officials, and so on. The American Council on Education (the umbrella association of higher education institutions and associations), the National Education Association, the American Federation of Teachers, the American Association of School Administrators, and the Education Commission of the States (ECS) are some of the large national education associations that conduct their own research programs or serve as clearinghouses for policy and research studies of importance to their members. ECS, for example, administers the National Assessment of Educational Progress, a periodic study of student achievement in reading, mathematics, writing, science, and other subjects.

Contributions. Educational research associations play a significant gatekeeper role with regard to what is published in the various fields of educational study. Association publications provide a significant outlet for the work of their members. In addition, they provide the field of educational research with a variety of forums and opportunities for researchers to share their products and outcomes. As a general observation, however, the impact of these associations on the formation of general education policy or on the conduct of educational practice is limited by the perceived relevance of the educational research that they sponsor and publicize. That is, association members are responsible for production of knowledge and information with potential use in policy making and practice, but influence is not guaranteed by association membership or publication of members' work. Only recently have these associations taken an active role in federal policy that affects opportunities for and the conduct of educational research. Since many of the associations are based in Washington, opportunities to provide legislative and executive branch officials with information resources are increased. Research groups can also share information with educational practitioners through their association publications and meetings.

In summary, educational research associations, by number, type, and focus of member interest, reflect the diversity and complexity of education and research in general. They provide for the exchange of information and knowledge among their members, and an outlet for members' work among a larger pool of professional and public audiences. They promote and clarify the achievements and character of their members' work. In turn, they inform their members about policies, issues, and other concerns that affect the conduct of educational research. In the general field of education, they are not seen as "power brokers"; however, directly and indirectly, they shape the literature and knowledge base in this multifaceted arena.

David H. Florio

See also Professional Organizations; Research Laboratories and Centers.

EDUCATIONAL SOCIOLOGY

See Sociology of Education.

EDUCATIONAL TECHNOLOGY

See Computer-Based Education; Information Management and Computing; Media Use in Education; New Technologies in Education; Systems Design in Instruction.

EFFECTS OF COLLEGE EXPERIENCE

Several metaphors have been used to describe higher education. One of the most widely used, taken from the business or production model, refers to graduates as "products," and identifies the important questions as "How efficient is the industry?" and "How much do we get for our investment?" Higher education is sometimes thought of in computer terms, with variables conceptualized as "inputs," "manipulations," and "outputs." Here the questions are more likely to be "How much of the output of college experience can be accounted for by the input characteristics?" or "Given these input variables, what operations do we need to perform to obtain desired output characteristics?" Even more mechanistic is the physical metaphor of "impact." One is likely to think of the effects of a cue ball striking a rack of balls on a billiard table. The most common question consistent with this metaphor is "What is the impact of college on students?"

None of these metaphors is acceptable as a way of construing the college experience because in each of them the student is seen as passive and somewhat helpless. How the student *uses* college resources will make a substantial difference in personal development; in the ability to make contributions to friends, family, and the larger society; in personal welfare as reflected in quality of life and income; and in the general welfare of society. These are not small issues. Consequently, it is important to underscore that students choose and act on available resources, as well as to recognize that higher education is a powerful environment that encourages students to move in certain directions. As a result, we believe that "dialogue" is a much more descriptive metaphor of the mutually enhancing interchange that occurs among students, faculty, student service personnel, peers, and the surrounding community. In a dialogue, each participant is contributing to the other. Each modifies and is modified as the dialogue proceeds. Ideas are reconstructed and shared. Thus, we believe it is most accurate to speak of the "value added" (Whitla, 1977) of the college experience rather than "impact" or "output" because of what each member of the dialogue gains from the interaction with others.

Sanford (1958), drawing from his Vassar studies, illustrated the nature of that dialogue and the dilemma found by researchers in attempting to identify the causes of changes observed in college students. He recounted the case of a young woman from a conventional, middle-class background who changed markedly during her junior year in college. She credited the change to the influences of a young professor of political science and a rather intellectual and offbeat roommate. However, a study of her life history reflected a capacity for nonconformity, as evidenced by an unusual pattern of high school interests. Sanford asked: "How do we account for the development of independence and wide-ranging interests in college?" In this case, was the impetus to change really the professor, the roommate, or the student's earlier high school interests?

In addition to the questions raised by Sanford, we might ask "Would the trends established in childhood have continued to be nurtured by some other experience had the student chosen not to go to college?" "Would some other professor or an alternative set of collegiate experiences have had a similar effect?" or even "How many students made similar changes under the tutelage of this professor or as a result of the influence of roommates like the one involved in this case?" In asking such questions, we put into bold relief the underlying dilemma of research into the value-added question "Can we ignore the dynamics of the individual student and gain any meaningful understanding of what actually happens to students in college?"

In order to isolate the relative contributions of such factors, it is necessary to combine methods that focus on change in individual students (idiographic studies) and methods that focus on group changes (nomothetic studies). Madison (1969), White (1975), and R. Heath (1964) attempted to fuse the two approaches by first studying individuals in some depth and then formulating general theories about the development of students in general. Madison attempted to show a relationship between early childhood and personality development in college. White's *Lives in Progress* took a case history approach to the college experience and to changes that occur after college. Heath, on the other hand, has traced the progress of college students toward more mature functioning, toward being what he calls a "reasonable adventurer." Such theoretical descriptions, which move from the specific individual to the general case, provide us with more holistic perspectives on the development of students.

However, they are less helpful with answers to frequently asked quantitative questions such as "How much change can we expect students to make in attitudes, values, beliefs, and knowledge?" "Are there economic benefits for the student who attends college?" "Is there a social benefit to be derived from a society's support of higher education?" "If so, how much and what kind?" Such questions must be approached nomothetically.

Thus, there are two basic problems in studying the influence of college on students. The first is deciding what changes it is important to identify and assess. The second is separating the effects of the college experience from those of maturation and concurrent life experiences. In the following sections, we shall first discuss the criterion problem and then consider several research designs that have been used in the study of the college student. After a section illustrating how one particular criterion (intellectual development) has been studied, we shall present a brief summary of the present state of knowledge on the value-added question.

Intended Changes. The criterion problem can be expressed in a question such as "What value *should* one expect to obtain from higher education?" This question is particularly valid now that the burden of expense is placed largely on public funds (Garcia & Garcia, 1978). Even if that were not the case, however, the question would be valid because of the costly investment of private funds, time, and energy. This question can be answered at two levels and with two different criteria. First, the question can be addressed at the individual and societal level, and second, it can be considered in terms of economic as well as psychosocial benefits.

Education, in the minds of some people, has never had economic gain as a primary aim; instead, the psychosocial welfare of both individuals and society has been a principal concern. Indeed, the tension between career (economic) and liberal (psychosocial) outcomes of education has had a long history. We will give consideration to both.

Psychosocial models. A major stimulus of concern over the effects of college on the psychosocial development of students was the publication of *Changing Values in College* (Jacob, 1957). Prior to that time, there had been relatively little interest in the issue. Drawing on data from five principal sources covering thirty institutions, Jacob concluded that students were (1) "remarkably homogeneous" in their values (p. 1); (2) "gloriously contented" (p. 1); (3) "unabashedly self-centered" (p. 1); (4) conformists yet highly tolerant of diversity; (5) traditional in their respect for sincerity, honesty, loyalty, and religion; (6) "dutifully responsive towards government" (p. 2); and (7) committed to higher education. Further, he found little evidence for the effects of a liberal arts curriculum on student values, or for the effects of the instruction or particular teaching methods. He did find that certain colleges with a "high level of expectancy" and a distinctive mission seemed to have marked effect on student values. He further identified certain students as more impervious to the college experience than others.

Jacob's report was widely quoted and criticized (Reisman, 1958), and served as the impetus for many studies intending to confirm or discredit his generalizations. The decades of the 1960s and 1970s were marked by large numbers of such studies. For example, the Feldman and Newcomb (1969) review contains over 2,500 bibliographic entries.

Individual models. Early in the decade, Sanford (1962) laid the groundwork for combining personality theory and educational practice. Drawing heavily on his studies at Vassar College, he and his colleagues began to fashion

a developmental framework for understanding students and guiding their educational experiences. Some studies of the college experience sought to identify and track changes in students as they occur without consideration of the desirability of those changes. Astin (1978), for example, documented increases in student hedonism, including smoking and drinking. By contrast, Sanford (1966) placed emphasis on *development* as an outcome. Furthermore, he distinguished development from both growth and change. "Change," the more general term, refers to a different state of being. "Growth" refers to enlarging and getting bigger. "Development" is the more limited term and, for Sanford, refers to the process of increased differentiation and integration that leads to greater complexity.

Knefelkamp, Widick, and Parker (1978) review the work of a number of developmental theorists who consider the college influence in terms of increasing cognitive complexity and resulting ability to deal with life issues. Independent efforts by Sanford and others (see Webster, Freedman, & Heist, 1962) at Vassar, R. Heath (1964) at Princeton, D. Heath (1968, 1978) at Haverford, Perry (1970) at Harvard, Chickering (1969) at Goddard, and Kohlberg at Harvard (Boyd, 1976) were all successful in demonstrating that college students change in predictable directions and that these changes can be described by coherent theoretical terms and models.

The work of the Sanford group led eventually to a standardized research instrument named the Omnibus Personality Theory (OPI) (Heist & Yonge, 1962). The scales of the OPI identify the constructs of the theory and include both intellectual and psychosocial domains. Chickering (1969) used the OPI scales in his thirteen-college study and conceptualized a seven-vector theory of student development. The central vector, "establishing identity," is based on a concept borrowed from Erikson (1963).

D. Heath (1968), bolstered by the writings of twenty-five educational theorists, believes that growth toward maturity is encouraged by the college experience. In a longitudinal study of men at Haverford College in which he compared "mature" and "immature" men, Heath found that they could be differentiated by his model which includes four personality sectors and the five dimensions. He has continued to validate his model in two ways: (1) a cross-cultural study of university men in Turkey, northern Italy, and southern Italy (D. Heath, 1977), and (2) a follow-up study of graduates from Haverford College in their thirties (D. Heath, 1976). Both studies produced evidence that the model is descriptive of mature men and that it is predictive of later life adjustment.

Societal models. Bowen (1980), an economist, has explicated a model that predicts the effects of higher education on society as a whole. He suggests higher education can be expected to be responsible for six effects on society. The first is greater openness to change. A society of educated people should be more cognizant of the inadequacy of existing conditions and should encourage new and better ways of meeting human needs. Second, there should be wider participation by citizens in public affairs and greater accountability of government to the citizenry. Third, humane values and social responsibility should be in more evidence while prejudice and discrimination lessen. Fourth, knowledge and technology should be more widely diffused, to the greater benefit of all citizens. Fifth, there should be increased international understanding. Sixth, the life style that is common among educated people should become more pervasive. These effects should be manifested in a decreased crime rate, improved health, increased graciousness of living, and greater appreciation of cultural activities. Thus, if the effects of a liberal education are identifiable in individual students, they should likewise be identifiable in the society at large.

Economic models. Most economists present the value-added problem of higher education in different terms than those employed by psychologists and sociologists. Economists typically pose the question as a relative trade of costs for benefits (Solmon, 1973). Costs may be direct or indirect and may be assessed to the individual, the family, or society in general. Most obvious is the direct cost to either the individual or the family of tuition, books, board and room, and so forth. An equally obvious direct cost is the taxes levied to support higher education. Another direct cost was often overlooked in early research identifying pecuniary gains from higher education: this is "opportunity cost," or income that is *not* earned during the period of additional schooling.

The economic benefit that is most frequently of interest is the relative income of students with higher levels of schooling as compared to that of individuals who do not attend college. Indirect economic returns include consumer efficiency, better use of time, and increased enjoyment of leisure. Just as there are indirect costs to society as a whole, there may be indirect benefits to society as a whole (Raymond, 1975; Rich, 1976). The expected benefits cited by Bowen would be illustrative. The point to be made is that though the individual benefits may be very small, the cumulative effect in society may be very large indeed. For example, Clark (1973) suggests that the greatest social benefits may be felt not from student contributions but from the direct contribution of scholarly work by faculty to changing the knowledge base available for public decision making and technological advancement.

One important issue is raised by studies of the economic benefits of higher education. Some have argued that higher education does not contribute directly to the economic benefits enjoyed by graduates; rather, it serves a credentialing or screening function for society (Berg, 1970; Taubman & Wales, 1975). That is, employers require higher education credentials even though graduates are not superior to nongraduates in terms of relevant skills or knowledge. Thus, the benefits are the indirect results of having graduated. Those who hold to this view argue that it may be more economical for employers to rely on a diploma than to devise elaborate screening mechanisms of their own because either (1) those who choose to go to college, on the average, have more of the relevant knowledge and skill than those who do not go to college or (2) the personality characteristics of those who choose to attend and who persist through higher education are important correlates of success on the job; examples of such characteristics are persistence, risk-taking capacity, and congeniality.

Estimating Change. Most of the interest in the value-added question centers on changes in student characteristics that can be attributed to the college experience. However, if one is to *attribute* change, it must first be properly *identified* and then linked to one or more "causes."

The nature of change. Most early studies compared the mean scores of one group of students with those of another group to ascertain whether change had occurred. This entailed a comparison of freshmen with seniors or of college students with non-college students, or a comparison of the scores of the same group tested at two points in time. The results were often disappointing because the differences in the means were not large enough to be statistically significant. Feldman and Newcomb (1969) were able to demonstrate that such findings were misleading because of an inadequate understanding of group differences as reflected by mean scores. They noted that groups may differ in one or more of the following ways, only a few of which would be detected by a comparison of group means.

Assume that a freshman group is being compared with a senior group. With a given mean and standard deviation of the freshman group, there may be significant differences in the senior group that would not be detected using a simple comparison of the two means. More specifically, the seniors may be (1) more homogeneous: smaller standard deviation; (2) more heterogeneous: larger standard deviation; or (3) fractionalized, that is, divided into two or more clusters, with the total group being either more homogeneous or more heterogeneous. Any of these differences may or may not be accompanied by a difference in the means (Feldman, 1970).

A second problem in detecting change may occur when an individual undergoes considerable change in thinking, attitudes, values, or beliefs and yet has the same score when the attribute is measured a second time. In the group variation of this problem, a number of individuals may change from time 1 to time 2, but the changes may be in opposite directions. Thus, the indication of change in either the means or the standard deviations of the groups is masked when the two testings are compared.

Detecting sources of change. In addition to dealing with the problems just described, the research design must separate the effect of the college environment from (1) the effects of maturation and time, and (2) the effects of existing individual characteristics. Cross-sectional designs do not provide for (1) effects that may be due to some students dropping out or (2) cohort differences. Even longitudinal studies are not without complications. Repeated testing may contaminate results; dropouts must still be

FIGURE 1. *Conceptual model for research on informal student-faculty contact*

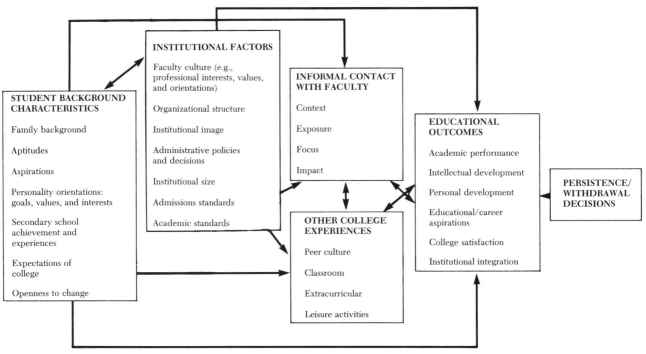

SOURCE: Pascarella, 1980.

accounted for in the analysis; and it is rarely possible to obtain adequate resources to follow students over long periods. A combination of cross-sectional and longitudinal strategies can help overcome some of the difficulties of single-design studies.

To separate the effects of the college experience from maturation, it is necessary to include noncollege samples. Unfortunately, such samples are rarely accessible to the researcher. Recruitment of research subjects is difficult, and characteristics related to attending college (IQ, socioeconomic status, maturation) are hard to match in the non–college-going population. Such factors cannot be overcome with existing methodologies and must be approached using logical or statistical analysis rather than experimental design.

Research designs and methodology. Several models for accomplishing statistical control are available. Thoma and Davison (1981) have suggested that results can be logically inferred through the process of patterning. Astin (1970a, 1970b) proposed a general model for studying the effects of the college experience. The three critical variables include (1) student characteristics at college entrance, (2) elements of the college experience, and (3) student characteristics at graduation or later. Though we are interested mostly in how (2) and (3) are related, the design must include adequate measures of all three variables. Furthermore, the analytic method must be able to separate the effects of (2) on (3) from those of (1) on (3).

In order to detect the effects of institutional environment versus student input characteristics, Astin concluded that linear regression with particular emphasis on the use of partial correlations was the most appropriate form of analysis, given his design model. He maintained that it is possible to have particular confidence in inferences drawn under the following conditions: (1) the environmental variable is uncorrelated with the input variables; (2) the correlation between environment and output is substantially higher than that between environment and input; and (3) there is a significant interaction effect between certain input characteristics, the environmental variable, and output characteristics.

A problem of some consequence in attempting to ferret out the value added by the college experience is the dynamic interaction among all variables of consequence. The most descriptive model of this interaction available is that of Pascarella (1980) (see Figure 1), which suggests the interrelations of important student and environmental variables. The picture presented is one of complex, mutually shaping influences. Students not only are "impacted" by the college, but, as would be true in a dialogue, are themselves a potent source of effects.

The schematic has the advantage of outlining clearly the complexity of interacting variables so that research can be better conceptualized. Unfortunately, if the question is "Does college have an impact on student development?" no designs exist that are capable of handling the total complexity. Indeed, the entire attempt to isolate "impact variables" may be misdirected. At best, the researcher will find incremental change attributable to single variables only *on the average*. Change in individuals, as suggested earlier, is highly dependent upon how students themselves choose to use the opportunities provided.

Thus far we have discussed the guiding theoretical models and methodological problems encountered when investigating the value-added or outcome question of higher education. In an article of this scope we cannot review in detail the thousands of studies that have attempted to determine the nature and extent of those outcomes. Fortunately, there have been several such reviews in the past decade (see Feldman & Newcomb, 1969; Pace, 1979; Bowen, 1980). Instead, we will illustrate the nature of the research strategies and outcomes with a more detailed review of the intellectual development research, and then provide a short summary of findings concerning college "outcome" that are generally accepted by most researchers and reviewers.

Intellectual Development. Although the academic achievement of college students is probably the most highly researched aspect of higher education (Astin, 1978), there is increased emphasis on understanding the process of intellectual development during the college years.

Apart from instilling specific subject matter knowledge, higher education is claimed to be influential in the development of rationality (Bowen, 1980). Rationality, or the ability to think and reason critically, has been shown to increase with the number of years of education (Brabeck, 1980). Typically, instruments such as the Watson-Glaser Critical Thinking Test (Watson & Glaser, 1964) or the Cornell Critical Thinking Test (Ennis & Millman, 1971) have been used to assess students' abilities to weigh evidence, separate facts from inferences, and synthesize a logical outcome from available data. While such instruments document general shifts in the ability to reason complexly, Perry (1970) has developed a scheme that outlines the specific transformations or stages of intellectual development.

Perry claims that cognitive development proceeds through nine "positions," or stages, each with its own discernible set of characteristics. The central quality that varies with each position is the student's understanding of the nature of knowledge. Classifying the nine positions into four general descriptive categories, Perry posits that student's understanding of knowledge moves from a black-white perception of absolutes (termed "dualism"), through an appreciation of a variety of equally legitimate alternative ways of knowing ("multiplicity"), to a recognition that these options must be viewed in their context ("relativism"), culminating in the realization that each person must make a personal commitment to particular ways of knowing and understanding ("commitment"). In sum, each of the nine positions can be viewed as a transformation that demonstrates increasing complexity of thought and incorporates the thinking patterns of previous levels.

In addition to Perry's original study (Perry, 1970), subsequent research (Meyer, 1975; Clinchy, Leif, & Young, 1977; Blake, 1976) has substantiated the progressive increase of intellectual development from the freshman year to the senior year. Significantly, the scheme has also proved to be a heuristic tool helping college personnel understand and devise programs to facilitate the development of college students in a variety of contexts (see Parker, 1978).

However, despite its usefulness in providing a more detailed description of the process of intellectual development, and its application in various counseling and educational settings, Perry's work is not without critics (King, 1977; Boyd, 1972). In general, the criticism has centered on a perceived shift in focus occurring at the point of relativism: epistemological issues appear to give way to moral and stylistic concerns. Perry (1981) and others (e.g., Kurfiss, 1977) have maintained that this mixture of intellectual and identity components preserves the richness and complexity of students' thinking. On the other hand, such a treatment may result in a less than comprehensive description of presumably different developmental domains (epistemological, moral, and identity issues) as well as promoting confusion about underlying structural features and constructs.

Recently King (1977) and Kitchener (1977) have devised a seven-stage scheme of intellectual development called "reflective judgment" (RJ) that largely avoids the criticism of Perry's work noted earlier and concentrates on the development of students' changing perception of the nature of knowledge. Influenced by the work of the philosophers Popper (1972), Kuhn (1975), and Dewey (1933) as well as that of the psychologists Boyd (1972), Riegel (1973), and Broughton (1975) and the seminal contribution of Perry (1970), King and Kitchener have argued persuasively that epistemological development continues beyond Perry's stage of relativism. Their highest level of development, "probabilism," essentially describes how a person makes judgments within a relativistic framework. In other words, if one cannot say for certain which theory, interpretation, or observation is correct, King and Kitchener suggest that the decision can be made on the basis of which is more probable.

Although a relatively recent conceptualization, the RJ scheme has been used in a number of studies. In their original work, King (1977) and Kitchener (1977) demonstrated significant and progressively increasing levels of reflective judgment for a sample consisting of high school students, college juniors, and students completing their third year of graduate school. Suggestive of the importance of education to cognitive development, this finding has been consistently replicated using cross-sectional designs (Welfel, 1979; Mines, 1980; Brabeck, 1980; Strange, 1978; Lawson, 1980; King & Parker, 1978), and in a recently completed longitudinal follow-up of their original sample Kitchener et al. (1981) find support for the sequential and hierarchical nature of their construct.

Since this has become a uniformly replicated result, attention has shifted to examining possible explanations for the differences between the groups studied. Two important studies (Strange, 1978; Lawson, 1980) sought to investigate whether maturation or increase in chronological age promotes cognitive development or whether level of education is the more salient variable. Strange compared freshmen, age 18, and seniors, age 22, with older, nontraditional freshmen and older seniors (ages 22 and 26, respectively). His results indicated that the scores of the two freshman groups (18 and 22 years old) and those of the two senior groups (22 and 26 years old) were more similar to each other than to those of fellow students of similar age. In other words, his findings suggest that educational level is a more potent variable than chronological age in accounting for intellectual development.

In a similarly designed study, Lawson (1980) added to these findings by employing a sample of older advanced graduate students and a comparison group of nonstudents. In order to properly assess the effect of educational level on RJ, Lawson compared currently enrolled students with a matched *nonstudent* group. In her study, graduate students were found to score higher than nonstudents of comparable age and undergraduate education. Older subjects scored higher than younger subjects. The findings only partially support Lawson's prediction of a significant education effect at the graduate level: changes among the graduate students were larger than for the nonstudent group, but the difference was not significant. She speculates that the difference between undergraduate and graduate students found in previous research (King, 1977; Kitchener, 1977) is in part due to a combined selection and maturation effect, rather than to the impact of education alone. However, it may well be that the effects of undergraduate education continue to increase after graduation even though one is not in graduate school.

The impact of curricular emphasis or major field has also been investigated using the RJ scheme. King and Parker (1978) and Welfel (1979) sought to investigate whether students in different majors would vary significantly in level of reflective judgment. Neither study reported evidence that college major or academic program had a significant effect on level of reflective judgment.

As noted earlier, although few could argue that college has no effect on the intellectual development of students, the nature and extent of its impact are often unclear. Theories such as Perry's and King and Kitchener's offer useful descriptions of the transformations that take place during the important college years. Although substantive knowledge or recognition of particular facts may fade with the passage of time, the ability to think with sophistication or to reason about alternatives on the basis of evidence instead of whim is of lifelong use to the college graduate.

Summary of Added Value. The preceding review of the research on intellectual development in college illustrates the use of various research designs to identify the nature and causes of change. Now we briefly summarize

what has been determined to be the added value of the college experience.

Academic gains. Pace (1979) has reviewed the evidence from five major studies of the achievement of college students. These studies were conducted over a period of nearly fifty years. The results from all of them are clear and convincing. The longer students are in school, the more they know. And, not surprisingly, what they know depends upon what they study; for example, students who major in the physical sciences know more about such sciences than those who do not. One interesting finding, however, is that there is less difference in achievement between majors and nonmajors in the social sciences than in other fields.

Further, the achievement differences continue after graduation. College graduates know more than nongraduates about the specific content taught in college, but more important, they keep learning and know more about current events, public affairs, important people, and recent discoveries.

Psychosocial gains. Two major reviews and one major longitudinal study summarize the available research in this area. The conclusions are highly consistent (Feldman & Newcomb, 1969; Bowen, 1980; Astin, 1978) and suggest that college students

develop a more positive self-image as reflected in greater interpersonal and intellectual competence, and they develop more liberal political views and attitudes toward social issues. At the same time, they show less religiousness and altruism and show reduced interest in athletics, business, music and status. [There is also an] increase in hedonistic behavior. Freshmen appear to be less studious and to interact less with instructors than they did in high school, but studiousness and interaction with faculty increase with time in college. (Astin, 1978, p. 212)

The effort to account for these changes has been fraught with the methodological difficulties that were the subject of the first part of this article. However, patterns emerge both from the accumulated research and from careful application of stringent analytical techniques. Among the most important general findings is that students with higher abilities tend to change more than those with lower abilities, thus accentuating initial differences (Mayes, 1977). This is no doubt due to the interaction of higher abilities with other significant change factors. A second important variable is involvement: this may be academic involvement, such as longer study time, honors programs, or classroom participation; peer involvement in residence halls, fraternities or sororities, student government, or clubs; athletic involvement, such as varsity or informal sports programs; or direct student-faculty interaction. A third important variable is the type of institution: private or public, selective or nonselective, large or small (Chickering, 1969, 1974).

As one might suppose, these factors tend to cluster in patterns so that students with high academic ability are inclined to attend select private colleges, become academically involved, and have greater faculty-student interaction. Students with high social interaction skills tend to become involved in peer group activities, spend less time with faculty, and attend less selective colleges. Those with high athletic ability tend to become involved in athletic programs and less involved in academic programs or student government. Thus, each of these involvement patterns sets other conditions, which in turn strengthen existing characteristics and heighten differences among students.

Students who do not get involved in any of the three general involvement patterns tend to take less from their college investment and consequently change less. Peers are among the most powerful contributors to change. If students become involved with other students who are academically inclined, they become more academically inclined; if they become involved with students who are more interested in social activities, they become more so. In either case, the peer group contributes more to psychosocial development than classroom activities or faculty (Lenning, 1978; Wallace, 1966; Walsh, 1973).

Economic gains. Whether one considers economic gains in terms of the individual or in terms of society, the aggregated results of many studies show consistent evidence that higher education contributes significant traits and necessary skills to the labor force (Bowen, 1980). While in college, students are helped to identify their vocational interests and begin making career choices (Kessler, 1979). Even when individual ability, family status and influence, and opportunity cost are controlled, there is evidence that graduates can anticipate earnings from 8 to 15 percent above those of nongraduates (Renshaw, 1972; Grasso, 1977). However, because of the increase in the educational level of the overall population, these differences are decreasing. The decrease in differences at the individual level tends to add to the evidence that the indirect effects on society as a whole are greater.

Thus, the evidence gathered through many studies, using many criteria, and applying ever more precise research models is that higher education adds considerably to the well-being of individuals and to the welfare of society. The differences at the individual level are, in many cases, small and significant only in a statistical sense. However, when these differences are accumulated over many individuals and over many years, the social benefits are clearly discernible and may be primarily responsible for the quality of life now enjoyed by millions of Americans.

Looking Forward. In spite of the massive amount of evidence accumulated since the early 1960s, important unsolved problems remain. We began this review by pointing to the predicament faced by the researcher working with group data when he or she is concerned with individual development. There is not, as yet, any satisfactory research model that will solve this dilemma. Lamiell (1981) has proposed an "idiothetic psychology of personality" as one possible answer, but we do not find his arguments persuasive. Given our current level of research sophistication, idiographic case studies may need to be used in conjunction with nomothetic comparative group research designs.

One of the most perplexing and resistant problems from a social perspective is continuing inequality. Bowen (1980) comments: "One of the most compelling beliefs underlying American society is that glaring differences among people in freedom, power, status, and income are wrong and should be ameliorated" (p. 325). Among the great liberal hopes of the 1950s and 1960s was that access to higher education for all would help reduce social inequality. However, from our current vantage point there is little evidence that such equality of access has brought about the desired changes. Existing data suggest that people with greater initial ability or achievement become more capable than those with less even when the proportion added is the same. Such results suggest a moderation of the expectation that higher education will end inequality.

A third problem is the lack of long-term follow-up studies of the psychosocial benefits of higher education. Among the few available are *Persistence and Change* (Newcomb et al., 1967), a twenty-five-year follow-up of Bennington College graduates; *Princeton Retrospectives* (R. Heath, 1979), a twenty-five-year follow-up; and D. Heath's follow-up of Haverford graduates (1976). Although the economic studies have required comparisons of gains many years after graduation, studies of psychosocial benefits have been limited to examining immediate outcomes.

Finally, efforts such as those of Astin (1978), Newcomb and Wilson (1966), and Chickering (1974) have been helpful in identifying what aspects of the college experience contribute significantly to the development of students. Yet there is little evidence that such information has been used by policy makers (see Astin, 1978). Questions of economic efficiency such as "How does an organization deliver the greatest number of credits to the greatest number of students at the least possible cost?" seem to have dominated the thinking of policy makers in the 1970s. We suggest instead that emphasis on education as dialogue will lead to consideration of how the college experience can be deliberately designed so that increased numbers of students will enjoy "value-added" benefits by gaining academic knowledge, developing their intellect, increasing their interpersonal competence, and achieving a sense of personal identity and integrity.

Clyde A. Parker
Janet A. Schmidt

See also Curriculum and Instruction in Higher Education; Higher Education; Undergraduate Instruction.

REFERENCES

Astin, A. The methodology of research on college impact (I). *Sociology of Education*, 1970, *43*, 223–254. (a)
Astin, A. The methodology of research on college impact (II). *Sociology of Education*, 1970, *43*, 437–450. (b)

Astin, A. *Four Critical Years: Effects of College on Beliefs, Attitudes, and Knowledge.* San Francisco: Jossey-Bass, 1978.

Berg, I. *Education and Jobs: The Great Training Robbery.* New York: Praeger, 1970.

Blake, L. *A Measure of Developmental Change: A Cross-sectional Study.* Paper presented at the annual meeting of the American Psychological Association, Washington, D.C., 1976.

Bowen, H. *Investment in Learning.* San Francisco: Jossey-Bass, 1980.

Boyd, D. *Some Thoughts on a Comparison of Perry and Kohlberg.* Unpublished manuscript, Harvard University, 1972.

Boyd, D. *Education toward Principled Moral Judgment: An Analysis of an Experimental Course in Undergraduate Moral Education Applying Lawrence Kohlberg's Theory of Moral Development.* Unpublished doctoral dissertation, Harvard University, 1976.

Brabeck, M. *The Relationship between Critical Thinking Skills and the Development of Reflective Judgment among Adolescent and Adult Women.* Unpublished doctoral dissertation, University of Minnesota, 1980.

Broughton, J. *The Cognitive Developmental Approach to Epistemology and Its Relation to Logical and Moral Stages.* Paper presented at the meeting of the Society for Research in Child Development, Denver, 1975. (ERIC Document Reproduction Service No. ED 122 923)

Chickering, A. *Education and Identity.* San Francisco: Jossey-Bass, 1969.

Chickering, A. *Commuting versus Resident Students.* San Francisco: Jossey-Bass, 1974.

Clark, K. A slightly different approach. In L. Solomon & P. Taubman (Eds.), *Does College Matter?* New York: Academic Press, 1973.

Clinchy, B.; Leif, J.; & Young, P. Epistemological and moral development in girls from a traditional and progressive high school. *Journal of Educational Psychology,* 1977, *69*(4), 337–343.

Dewey, J. *How We Think.* Lexington, Mass.: Heath, 1933.

Ennis, R., & Millman, J. *Cornell Critical Thinking Test Manual.* Champaign-Urbana: University of Illinois, Critical Thinking Project, 1971.

Erikson, E. H. *Childhood and Society.* New York: Norton, 1963.

Feldman, K. *Research Strategies in Studying College Impact.* Iowa City. American College Testing Program, 1970.

Feldman, K., & Newcomb, T. *The Impact of College on Students* (Vol. 1). San Francisco: Jossey-Bass, 1969.

Garcia, G., & Garcia, R. Higher education: What is the payoff? *Journal of the National Association of College Admission Counselors,* 1978, *22*(3), 24–26.

Grasso, J. *On the Declining Labor Market Value of Schooling.* Paper presented at the annual meeting of the American Educational Research Association, New York, April 1977. (ERIC Document Reproduction Service No. ED 137 580)

Heath, D. *Growing Up in College.* San Francisco: Jossey-Bass, 1968.

Heath, D. What the enduring effects of higher education tell us about a liberal education. *Journal of Higher Education,* 1976, *47,* 173–190.

Heath, D. *Maturity and Competence: A Transcultural View.* New York: Gardner Press, 1977.

Heath, R. *The Reasonable Adventurer: The Nature and Development of Students in Higher Education.* Pittsburgh, Pa.: University of Pittsburgh Press, 1964.

Heath, R. *Princeton Retrospectives.* Princeton, N.J.: Princeton University Press, 1979.

Heist, P., & Yonge, G. *Manual for the Omnibus Personality Inventory.* New York: Psychological Corporation, 1962.

Jacob, P. *Changing Values in College.* New Haven, Conn.: Edward Harper Foundation, 1957.

Kessler, J. Needed: Career-related data. In L. Soloman & N. Ochsner (Eds.), *Using Longitudinal Data in Career Counseling: New Directions for Education (Work and Careers Series).* San Francisco: Jossey-Bass, 1979.

King, P. *The Development of Reflective Judgment and Formal Operational Thinking in Adolescents and Young Adults.* Unpublished doctoral dissertation, University of Minnesota, 1977.

King, P., & Parker, C. *Assessing Intellectual Development in the College Years: A Report of the Instructional Improvement Project, 1976–1977.* Unpublished manuscript, University of Minnesota, 1978.

Kitchener, K. *Intellectual Development in Late Adolescents and Young Adults: Reflective Judgment and Verbal Reasoning.* Unpublished doctoral dissertation, University of Minnesota, 1977.

Kitchener, K.; King, P.; Davison, M.; & Parker, C. A longitudinal study of reflective judgment. In preparation, 1981.

Knefelkamp, L.; Widick, C.; & Parker, C. (Eds.). Applying new developmental findings. In *New Directions for Student Services Series* (No. 4). San Francisco: Jossey-Bass, 1978.

Kuhn, T. *The Structure of Scientific Revolutions.* Chicago: University of Chicago Press, 1975.

Kurfiss, J. Sequentiality and structure in a cognitive model of college student development. *Developmental Psychology,* 1977, *13*(6), 565–571.

Lamiell, J. Toward an idiothetic psychology of personality. *American Psychologist,* 1981, *36*(3), 276–289.

Lawson, J. *The Relationship between Graduate Education and the Development of Reflective Judgment: A Function of Age or Educational Experience.* Unpublished doctoral dissertation, University of Minnesota, 1980.

Lenning, O. Assessing student educational progress. *AAHE-ERIC/ Higher Education Research Currents,* April 1978. (ERIC Document Reproduction Service No. ED 166994)

Madison, P. *Personality Development during College.* Reading, Mass.: Addison-Wesley, 1969.

Mayes, S. The increasing stratification of higher education: Ideology and consequence. *Journal of Educational Thought,* 1977, *11*(1), 16–27.

Meyer, P. *Intellectual Development of College Students as Measured by Analysis of Religious Content.* Unpublished doctoral dissertation, University of Minnesota, 1975.

Mines, R. *Levels of Intellectual Development and Associated Critical Thinking Skills in Young Adults.* Unpublished doctoral dissertation, University of Iowa, 1980.

Newcomb, T.; Koenig, K.; Flacks, R.; & Warwick, D. *Persistence and Change.* New York: Wiley, 1967.

Newcomb, T., & Wilson, E. (Eds.) *College Peer Groups.* Hawthorne, N.Y.: Aldine, 1966.

Pace, C. *Measuring Outcomes of College.* San Francisco: Jossey-Bass, 1979.

Parker, C. A. (Ed.) *Encouraging Development in College Students.* Minneapolis: University of Minnesota Press, 1978.

Pascarella, E. Student-faculty informal contact and college outcomes. *Review of Educational Research,* 1980, *50*(4), 545–595.

Perry, W. *Forms of Intellectual and Ethical Development in the College Years.* New York: Holt, Rinehart & Winston, 1970.

Perry, W. Cognitive and ethical growth: The making of meaning. In A. W. Chickering (Ed.), *The Modern American College.* San Francisco: Jossey-Bass, 1981.

Popper, K. *Objective Knowledge.* New York: Oxford University Press, 1972.

Raymond, R. The returns to investments in higher education: Some new evidence. *Journal of Human Resources,* 1975, *10*(2), 139–154.

Reisman, D. The Jacob report. *American Sociological Review,* 1958, *23,* 732–738.

Renshaw, E. Are we overestimating the return from a college education? *School Review,* 1972, *80*(3), 459–475.

Rich, H. The effect of college on political awareness and knowledge. *Youth and Society,* 1976, *8*(1), 67–80.

Riegel, K. Dialectical operations: The final period of cognitive development. *Human Development,* 1973, *16,* 346–370.

Sanford, N. The professor looks at the student. In R. M. Cooper (Ed.), *The Two Ends of the Log.* Minneapolis: University of Minnesota Press, 1958.

Sanford, N. *The American College.* New York: Wiley, 1962.

Sanford, N. *Self and Society.* New York: Atherton Press, 1966.

Solmon, L. Schooling and subsequent success: Influence of ability, background, and formal education. In *ACT Research Report* (No. 57). American College Testing Program, Iowa City, Iowa, 1973. (ERIC Document Reproduction Service No. ED 078 774)

Strange, C. *Intellectual Development, Motive for Education, and Learning Styles during the College Years: A Comparison of Adult and Traditional-age College Students.* Unpublished doctoral dissertation, University of Iowa, 1978.

Taubman, P., & Wales, T. Education as an investment and a screening device. In F. T. Juster (Ed.), *Education, Income, and Human Behavior* (Carnegie Commission Higher Education Report). New York: McGraw-Hill, 1975.

Thoma, S., & Davison, M. *Graduate Education: Moral Judgment Development and Ego Development.* Unpublished manuscript, Project Report No. 7, Higher Education and Cognitive-Social Development Project, University of Minnesota, 1981.

Wallace, W. *Student Culture.* Chicago: Aldine, 1966.

Walsh, W. *Theories of Person-Environment: Implications for the College Student.* Iowa City: American College Testing Program, 1973.

Watson, G., & Glaser, E. *Watson-Glaser Critical Thinking Appraisal Manual.* New York: Harcourt, Brace, & World, 1964.

Webster, H.; Freedman, M.; & Heist, P. Personality changes in college students. In N. Sanford (Ed.), *The American College.* New York: Wiley, 1962.

Welfel, E. *Reflective Judgment and Its Relationship to Years in College, Major Field, Academic Performance and Satisfaction with Major among College Students.* Unpublished doctoral dissertation, University of Minnesota, 1979.

White, R. *Lives in Progress.* (3rd ed.). New York: Dryden Press, 1975.

Whitla, D. *Value Added: Measuring the Outcomes of Undergraduate Education* (Summary and Test Battery Report, Office of Instructional Research and Evaluation). Cambridge, Mass.: Harvard University, 1977.

ELEMENTARY EDUCATION

The meaning of the term "elementary education" has evolved over the years. At one time it referred to grade levels 1–8; and at other times kindergarten has been in-

TABLE 1. *Elementary school enrollment in the United States, 1870–1980*

Year	Enrollment
1870	6,722,000
1880	9,757,000
1890	12,181,000
1900	16,225,000
1910	18,457,000
1920	20,864,000
1930	23,588,000
1940	20,995,000
1950	19,405,000
1960	27,500,000
1970	33,249,000
1980	24,157,000

SOURCE OF DATA: Sheridan, 1980.

cluded with the elementary school. Practice in some school districts includes grades 7 and 8 with the junior high school or the middle school. In others, elementary school is restricted to kindergarten through grade 6. Middle schools have been known to include grades 5 and 6 as well. Where middle schools encompass upper elementary grades, the definition of an elementary school would include grades K–4. No standard definition for elementary education has been accepted that is appropriate for all school systems.

Table 1 indicates how elementary school enrollments have continually increased until the 1969/70 school year and now have begun to decline (Dolmatch, 1981; Sheridan, 1980). Clearly, elementary school education is an extensive activity. These figures include both public and nonpublic data.

Development. The elementary education school system to which we refer did not emerge rapidly; it has evolved through the last 330 years. The beginning was very meager, and it has had to struggle to evolve into the elementary schools that we know today.

Educational theorists. The early American school was greatly influenced by four major educational theorists. The earliest of these was Jean Jacques Rousseau (1712–1778). The second theorist who influenced education was Pestalozzi (1746–1827). He developed a theory and put it into actual use in several experimental schools. He emphasized the importance of understanding of the students' intellectual, moral, and personal needs. The use of instructional materials was proposed by Pestalozzi in his education doctrine "Anschauung," which has been translated to mean observation, sense experience, or perception. Essentially he was stating that education comes from actual experiences with real things rather than from a vicarious experience through a book.

Froebel (1782–1852) was the third writer who had a powerful effect on our educational system. His basic theory contends that knowledge cannot be passed from teacher to pupil but that knowledge is only acquired by self-activity of the learner. Learning is directly proportional to the doing. He believed that each child has certain urges or desires that are a part of the child's innate ability and that the teacher's influence either fosters or thwarts this intellectual development.

Fourth, Herbart (1776–1841) insisted upon the importance of the learner's interest in what is being studied. Instruction should be geared toward developing many-sided interests. Herbert's doctrine of apperception was central to his system of psychology of learning. "Apperception" was defined as a kind of process of mental ingestion in which new ideas were fused into old ideas.

Organization plans. In the United States beginning about 1850, the period of expansion and system building in elementary schooling began. Education was now established as an integral part of American society, with tax support, with state control, and with the extension of the educational system into the secondary and university levels. It was a period during which different types of school organizations were examined. Horace Mann became consultant to many states and school systems advocating more taxation for public education, which more than doubled the money available to public schools. In his *Reports* he advocated improved teaching methods with emphasis upon Pestalozzian reforms, new emphasis upon school hygiene, and the introduction of school libraries. Mann's famous *Seventh Annual Report* dealt mainly with the Prussian implementation of the Pestalozzian procedures in German schools. The Oswego plan (Dearborn, 1925), as initiated and advocated by Edward Sheldon, was the first real introduction of the Pestalozzian concepts into American schools, and the Oswego schools became a show place for the Pestalozzian method. Prominent educators reported favorably on the school system and as a result Sheldon explained his work before the National Teachers' Association. He helped change education from memorizing and recitation teaching to "oral instruction" and "object teaching." Oswego also had a center for training teachers in the new method of instruction.

Another school organization that gained momentum during the last quarter of the nineteenth century was the kindergarten. The Froebelian concept of the nature of the child was the directing theory (Reisner, 1930). Froebel emphasized that play and games are children's work. The first kindergarten in the United States was established in Watertown, Wisconsin, in 1855. This concept constantly has been expanded and has come to influence broadly the development of nursery school and day care centers. Outgrowths of the play concept were more physical activity for all children and new interest in development of the hand and muscles as well as of the mind.

The first elementary school organized on the graded plan was probably Quincy Grammar School in Massachusetts under the leadership of J. D. Philbrick in 1848. The majority of elementary schools in the United States are still organized on the graded plan. By 1860 nearly all cities in the United States had adopted the graded plan. The graded plan had great influence on the construction of elementary schools for many years. Elementary schools were composed of many rooms constructed to accommodate about thirty elementary school students at a given time. (See Cubberley, 1934.)

St. Louis schools, about 1872, under the leadership of Superintendent Harris, developed the quarterly promotion plan. The elementary school year's work was separated into four ten-week units, and promotion was made at the end of each ten-week period. Otto (1932) studied the quarterly promotion plan and found that only 5 out of 555 school systems used the quarterly promotion plan in 1932.

In time, protest developed against the "lock-step" method of organizing the elementary school into the grade plan. In 1889 Superintendent of Pueblo, Colorado, schools, Preston W. Search, urged complete individual progress for each pupil. By 1910 it was reported that 203 out of 965 cities had tried the Pueblo Plan. This effort at individualization was the groundwork for establishment of the Winnetka plan by Superintendent Carleton Washburne and also the Gary plan as inaugurated by Superintendent Will Wirt. The Winnetka curriculum was separated into two main parts; the traditional knowledge and skills, and group activity and self-expression. All children need common essentials and the time required to master these essentials varies with learning ability. The content remains constant for all students but the rate at which the student masters the knowledge or skill varies. The traditional part of the curriculum requires certain quality of work but the time in which it is mastered varies. In the second part of the curriculum no standards are fixed, students can vary according to individual ability.

Many different plans of organization for elementary school can be found in the literature, such as Cambridge Plan, Portland (Oregon) Plan, Batavia (New York) Plan, North Denver (Colorado) Plan, Santa Barbara (California) Concentric Plan, and others.

Education Laws. Laws enacted to formalize public control of education have resulted in highly uniform educational practices, especially at the elementary school level.

Compulsory education. The first laws of 1789 in the new state of Massachusetts provided for the establishment of schools but no provision was made for compulsory attendance. Massachusetts in fact did not pass a compulsory school attendance law until 1852. By 1892 only 28 of the 44 states had passed a compulsory school attendance law, and it was not until 1918 that every state had passed such a law. Even then the compulsory attendance laws were not strictly enforced (Ensign, 1969). Note that there is a difference between compulsory education and compulsory school attendance. Compulsory education only requires children to be educated; it does not require children to attend school. Children could be educated at home with-

TABLE 2. *Compulsory school attendance laws*

Entrance age	Exit age	Number of states	Percentage of states
6	16	9	17.6%
6	17	2	2.2%
6	18	3	5.9%
7	13	1	1.9%
7	15	3	5.9%
7	16	26	53.0%
7	17	2	2.2%
7	18	1	1.9%
8	15	1	1.9%
8	16	2	2.2%
8	17	1	1.9%
		Total 51[a]	

[a] Includes Washington, D.C.

SOURCE OF DATA: Sheridan, 1980.

out attending school. Early laws did not compel school attendance, but only required education. Today every state requires school attendance but there seem to be liberal exemptions such as attendance in private or parochial schools or tutoring at home.

All fifty states and Washington, D.C., have compulsory school laws. The present compulsory school entrance age varies from 6 to 8 and the exit age varies from 13 to age 18. The mode of compulsory attendance is 7–16 with 50 percent of the states using these limits. Table 2 summarizes the state compulsory attendance ages (Dolmatch, 1981; Sheridan, 1980).

Elementary and Secondary Act. The Elementary and Secondary Act of 1965 has had a significant impact upon elementary school education. This law, Public Law 89-10, was designed to deal with the many deficiencies apparent in the 16,056 school districts in the United States (Sheridan, 1980). The law had five different titles with each title designed to address a particular public school deficiency.

Title I of Public Law 89-10 was designed to provide assistance to schools for the education of children from families whose total yearly income was less than $2,000. A school district that could identify an area with a concentration of such families was entitled to receive benefits to improve education for all children in that area.

Title II of Public Law 89-10 allotted about $100 million to provide schools (both public and private) with certain resources such as audio materials, visual equipment, textbooks, school libraries, and other instructional materials.

Title III of Public Law 89-10 was designed to encourage schools to initiate innovative practices into their school systems. Application was made to the U.S. Secretary of Education for funds to support a wide variety of programs that would use community resources, cultural advantages, and talents of local leaders.

Title IV of Public Law 89-10 was designed to initiate and operate national and regional laboratories dedicated to research in education. A fund of $100 million to be used over a five-year period was set aside, which enabled the Educational Resources Information Center (ERIC), several regional laboratories, and other research and development centers to be developed.

Title V of Public Law 89-10 was designed to provide federal funds for state departments of education to fund specific projects within each state that would strengthen educational programs.

Curriculum. Cubberley (1934) discusses the evolution of the curriculum in American schools. He states that all schools from the first included reading and writing as the required subjects to be taught in all the colonies. Rhode Island was the first to include ciphering in the school curriculum and it spread to other colonies. The three subjects of reading, writing, and ciphering formed the basis of the 3 Rs in the American school.

Soon the curriculum evolved to include reading, spelling, word analysis, declamation, and ciphering as the fundamental subjects of all common schools. Some city schools included arithmetic, grammar, history of the United States, and civics. By 1830 the curriculum in the better city elementary schools for children was

- *Young children.* Letters and syllables, reading, writing, spelling, numbers, elementary languages, good behavior.
- *Older children.* Advanced reading, advanced spelling, word analysis, penmanship, arithmetic, geography, grammar, United States history, manners and morals.

Sewing and darning very often were required subjects for girls.

Boston began the graded school by having writing schools and reading schools. The curriculum of the writing school included writing and arithmetic. The curriculum of the reading school included spelling, accentuation, reading prose and verse, and English grammar and composition.

TABLE 3. *Mid–nineteenth-century curriculum in Providence, Rhode Island, schools*

Primary schools	Intermediate schools	Grammar school	High school
(Ages 5–7½)	(Ages 7½–10)		
Reading	Reading	Reading	Twenty different
Spelling	Spelling	Writing	high school subjects
Arithmetic	Writing	Arithmetic	were offered.
Music	Arithmetic	Geography	
	Music	Grammar	
	Geography	Composition	
		U.S. history	
		Declamation	
		General history	

By 1823 geography was added to the curriculum of the reading school and later United States history. School buildings were constructed of two large rooms (180–200 seats each), one room for the reading school and one room for the writing school. Three teachers were usually placed in each room for listening to recitations. The students attended part of each day in each of the two rooms with two different sets of teachers.

As the school curriculum continually evolved, it became more segmented. The curriculum of the primary school became separated into six steps. A primary teacher took all children through the six steps. Schools also became separated into primary schools, intermediate schools, grammar schools, and high schools.

The school curriculum for Providence, Rhode Island, in 1848 included ages 5–17, and the subjects are shown in Table 3.

Today, the elementary school curriculum is not nationally standardized. A National Education Association (NEA) survey (Bartholomew, 1980) found that reading was the only subject required in all elementary schools. Between 95 and 99 percent of the surveyed schools say they require American history, spelling, general science, and physical education. At the other extreme, only 5 percent require a foreign language.

Instructional Innovations. American education has repeatedly tried educational innovations in the classroom. During the late 1960s and 1970s one could find such efforts as team teaching, nongraded, vertical, or heterogeneous grouping of students.

Team teaching. Team teaching is defined by Olsen (1968) as "instructional situation where two or more teachers, possessing complementary teaching skills, cooperatively plan and implement the instruction for a single group of students, using flexible grouping to meet the particular needs of the students." By teaming it is felt that the knowledge, competence, and skills of each teacher may be used at a maximum. Each team will develop its own personality depending upon the personal style, value systems, and teaching styles of the team members.

Armstrong (1977) states that "a teaching team is a group of two or more persons assigned to the same students at the same time for instructional purposes in a particular subject or combination of subjects." Shaplin and Olds (cited by Shaplin, 1964) write that "team teaching ordinarily refers to a type of instructional organization in which two or more teachers jointly carry out instructional operations for the same group of students rather than each working alone with his own class."

Coleman and Budahl (1973) indicate that a necessary ingredient for good team teaching is a harmonious working together toward common objectives. Research by Seyforth and Canady (1973) and Traut (1971) indicates that team members must be able to share space and students, and at the same time give up traditional ideas of "rights" to a classroom and particular children.

Many researchers (Gaskell & Sheridan, 1968; Funaro, 1968; Brunetti, 1970; Pellegrin, 1970a, 1970b; Deibel, 1971; Traut, 1971) seem to indicate that successful teams of teachers depend upon the extent of task-oriented interactions, degree of independence among the teachers, decision making in collegial groups of teachers, with more decisions concerning school-wide matters. Successful teams work together to develop their own programs (Davis, 1966; Olsen, 1968; Funaro, 1968; Engman, 1973).

Olsen (1968) stressed that team teaching increased grouping and scheduling flexibility and that the quality of education improved. The literature, however, does not support Olsen (1968) that the quality of education will improve. Research studies designed to evaluate student achievement in team-teaching schools (Burchyett, 1972; Burningham, 1968; Cooper & Sterns, 1973; Jackson, 1964; Lambert, Goodwin & Wiersma, 1965; Rhodes, 1971; Stearns, Green & David, 1979) consistently find significant difference in achievement scores between team-taught and self-contained classrooms. Bair and Woodward (1964) reviewed the research on team teaching and concluded that there were no significant differences in academic achievement between children taught by team teaching and children taught in self-contained classrooms. They found, however, that team teachers willingly worked longer hours.

Charters and Jones (1974), after carefully studying the research in team teaching and academic achievement, discovered that there really were no substantive differences between the two teaching conditions. Most of the studies on academic achievement were conducted for short periods of time, one academic year. This did not provide ample time for team members to become acclimated to the new teaching strategy. Team teaching has not been intensively or systematically researched. Support for team teaching is based on affirmation rather than on empirical evidence.

Mastery learning. Mastery learning is based on the assumption that every student can learn most things to a specified level of competence in more or less the same amount of time (Bloom, 1976). Carroll (1963) was one of the first to formulate a model of school learning based upon this idea. "Learning for mastery" (LFM) has been the basis for many school models such as those in New York City in the 1960s (Hyman & Cohen, 1979), New Orleans in the 1970s (Geisert, 1979), and Philadelphia in the 1980s (Kopple & Conner, 1980).

In a mastery learning situation, students receive instruction focused upon predetermined and specific objectives. Whole class, group, or individual situations can be used to implement instruction. After a period of time, a criterion-referenced test (CRT) is given to test the specific objective(s) studied in the teaching situation. These CRT responses are evaluated to determine whether the test takers have reached a level of mastery that has been predetermined by the creators or implementors of the teaching unit. Often a 75, 80, or 85 percent level is required to indicate "mastery" of the objectives. In a group situation the students who do not reach this criterion level are retaught the material, ideally using alternative strategies, while other students do practice and enrichment work. In an individualized situation, a student would simply study the material until mastery is attained before continuing to the next objectives for study (Block, 1971, 1972; Kersch, 1972; Mayo, 1970).

Individually Guided Education. Individually Guided Education (IGE) is an approach that provides a framework for individualizing education. Its structure provides for individualizing through a team-teaching situation. A continuous cycle is developed for each student by assessment of the student's present knowledge, deciding what each student needs next (stated as objectives), adapting the material available to the student's learning style, and then reassessing the student to ascertain if the objectives were accomplished.

The organizational structure for an IGE school has been designated as the multiunit organization. Students, teachers, and aides are separated into units that include children of overlapping ages. Within each unit children are grouped and regrouped based upon student interests, needs, and objectives. Teachers work together within a unit plan, discuss, analyze, and make decisions about the educative process for a unique group of children.

Nongrading. Graded elementary schools place students together because they are similar in age and the children are expected to proceed through a set curriculum (often a textbook) at a set pace. All children are expected to do the same work in one academic year. Nongraded learning implies that children will proceed through the same elementary school curriculum but that the rate will vary depending upon the child. A specified amount of content will not be delineated for each grade level.

Research studies overwhelmingly conclude that nongraded schoolchildren's achievement scores are significantly higher than those of graded schoolchildren. (Bowman, 1971; Brody, 1970; Gumpper, Meyer & Kaufman, 1971; Killough, 1972; Remacle, 1971; Wilt, 1971). Martin and Pavan (1973) reviewed the research on nongraded classrooms from 1968 to 1973. They found that in twelve of sixteen studies nongraded schoolchildren were significantly higher achievers. The other four found no significant difference. It was also noted that fewer children were retained and that nongraded schools were particularly beneficial for blacks, boys, and underachievers. Yarborough and Johnson (1978) noted that average and below-average children developed better attitudes toward school in a nongraded environment.

Most research on nongraded school organization was conducted in the early 1970s with little research available since 1973. The research supports nongraded programs as enhancing students' academic achievement and reinforcing positive attitudes toward school for most children. One must constantly be reminded, as Wilt (1971) concludes, that "no single organizational change can hope to solve the needs of learners in a mass, heterogeneous society."

Grouping. Two commonly accepted methods for assigning children to classroom-structured schools have been heterogeneous or homogeneous grouping (Wilson & Schmits, 1978). Heterogeneous grouping places children into classrooms haphazardly and allows for different levels of ability for children with different needs to interact. Homogeneous grouping organizes children according to similarities or specific characteristics such as mental ability achievement, social maturity, learning style, or a combination of these and other variables. Shane (1960) has identified thirty-two different grouping strategies for homogeneous grouping. It seems apparent then that homogeneous grouping serves to restrict the range of individual differences with respect to certain criterion dimensions, whereas heterogeneous grouping tends to expand the range of individual differences on all dimensions.

In grouping children for instruction, Esposito (1973) states that a careful review of ability-grouping research indicates that few studies have considered the educational relevance of ethnic and socioeconomic status in the placement of children into ability groups or curricular tracks, and that few have examined the social, economic, and political consequences of grouping schemes with respect to ethnic and socioeconomic separation of children. Esposito (1973) goes on to state that emphasis in the placement of children resides mainly in academic achievement, intelligence, and reading achievement levels (alone or in combination), whereas the consequences of grouping schemes are examined with respect to academic achievement, attitude, and personality development.

Proponents of heterogeneous groups argue that undue stigma is placed upon the self-concept of the child with low ability and that high-ability students receive an inflated sense of their own self-worth. Adult life experiences occur in heterogeneous populations and we cannot prepare students for life when they learn to deal only with children who have like characteristics. Findlay and Bryan (1971) concluded that when considering all children, no clear-cut positive or negative effect upon achievement can be attributed to grouping.

Physical Environment. The standard learning environment of a self-contained classroom filled with rows of desks has been replaced with a number of different arrangements that are designed to be more compatible with the intellectual and physical characteristics of the students. The effects of these new arrangements on learning have recently received some research attention.

Open space schools. "Open space schools" describes a type of building designed to allow children and teachers to share space in some way. This type of structure permits young children the freedom of movement that is necessary for muscular development and it allows more interaction with peers and environment. A large, open space may be used by different groups in different ways for different purposes. Brunetti (1970) indicates that "the open space school is composed of instructional areas without interior walls, ranging in size from two to over thirty equivalent classrooms." Of schools built between 1967 and 1970, George (1975) reported that more than 50 percent of all schools were of open space design. However, there still is a wide variation in internal structure.

Research evidence available about open space schools does not support real differences in learning or teaching outcomes (Armstrong, 1975). Any type of innovative educational program can exist in either an open space school or in a traditional classroom. Changes in architectural design in and of themselves do not make a difference. Several studies conclude that no difference exists between open space schools and conventional schools (Holmquist, 1972; Jaworowicz, 1972; Leroy, 1973; Warner, 1970).

Teachers within an open space school have a more positive attitude toward education, teaching, and pupils than teachers in architecturally closed schools (Khan & Traub, 1980; Mills, 1972; Wren, 1972). There also is an increased feeling of professionalism among teachers. Most of the studies have been conducted in schools that have been operating as open schools for a short period of time. Because of the operating time the Hawthorne effect may have a bearing upon the results of these studies.

Brunetti (1970) concluded that there was a reduction in the physical and organizational structure for teachers in open space schools and that a high degree of colleague interaction and cooperative task performance were present. In contrast Warner (1970) did not find significant differences.

A self-concept study by Heimgartner (1972) in both open space and self-contained classrooms found children in open space schools had more identification with children in their school group than children in self-contained classrooms; children in open space schools had an increase in self-esteem, and children in open space schools were found not to identify with any one teacher more than another. Studies by Beckley (1973), and Purkey, Graves, and Zellner (1970) agreed with Heimgartner (1972) but studies by Lovin (1972) and Sackett (1971) found negative effects. Studies by Kling (1971), Reudi and West (1973), and Wright (1974) indicated no significant differences in self-concept between children in open space or traditional classrooms. Hendry and Matheson (1979) studied the social effects of open class on primary children and found a difference in their informal social interactions. LaForge (1972) found no significant difference in total personality that could be attributed to children's experiences in either self-contained or open space classrooms. However, he noted that children from open space schools were more tender-minded and were more sensitive to the needs of others. Hallinan (1976) studied 60 elementary classrooms from open space and traditional classrooms and concluded that children's friendship patterns are affected by the structure of the classroom. Anifant's (1972) data indicated that children from open space schools were significantly more risk-taking than children from self-contained classrooms.

Comparative research findings on the cognitive achievement of students in open space schools and in traditional schools is conflicting. Killough (1971) found that after pupils had remained in an open space school for at least two years their mean achievement gains were significantly better during the third year and for the total three-year period than the achievements of their counterparts in a traditional school. The open space school children also achieved significantly better as they moved into a traditional junior high program.

Olson (1973), Read (1973), and Warner (1970), in three different studies, found that there was no significant difference in achievement between students in open space schools and students in more conventional classrooms.

Achievement of two groups of first-grade children, one in open space schools and one in a traditional school, was studied by Bell, Switzer, and Zepursky (1974). They found children in the traditional school to be significantly ahead of the open space children on all reading tests. Number concept scores did not differ significantly.

Reiss and Dydhalo (1975) reached similar conclusions

as they studied thirty second-grade children in three open space and three traditional schools. Comparison of scores from standardized achievement tests indicated no significant difference between the two groups. However, they found that children from the open space schools were significantly more persistent than children from the traditional schools.

Spigel (1974) and Grapko (1972) found similar results as they compared children in open space schools and traditional schools. There was no difference in academic achievement between the two types of organization. However, Grapko (1972) found that children with a lower average IQ functioned more poorly in open space schools. He conjectured that low-ability students need more direct instruction, more guidance, and more direction than they received in an open space school. Spigel (1974) found similar results with no difference in achievement for high-ability and middle-ability students. Low-ability fourth-grade children in open space scored significantly higher on the reading subtest than their counterparts, and low-ability seventh-grade students in traditional schools scored significantly higher on the vocabulary subtest.

Studies of this type experience difficulty in control techniques. Random assignment of teachers and students to school is almost impossible. We risk attributing differences in achievement to physical environment when we really may be measuring differences in instructional program, teacher effectiveness, and a myriad of other variables that may be unrelated to the physical structure. Generalizability is missing in many of the studies as comparisons are made of only one open space school with one traditional school (Anifant, 1972; Heimgartner, 1972; Jeffreys, 1970; Killough, 1972; LaForge, 1972; Sackett, 1972; Townsend, 1972; Wren, 1972; Wright, 1974). Very little evidence is available to verify that an attempt was made to match the two different types of schools. Most open space schools and traditional schools will vary in more ways than in structural design. They will vary in educational philosophy, materials, teachers' attitudes, and instructional techniques. Conclusions drawn from such limited data and limited studies must be viewed very cautiously.

Seating arrangement. Considerable research has been conducted to assess the effects of seating arrangements and student-teacher interaction. At the elementary school level Adams (1969) and Adams and Biddle (1970) extensively studied the verbal interaction that took place in 32 mathematics and social studies classes involving two classes each of sixteen different teachers. The investigators found that verbal interaction within the classroom is clustered in the center front and in a line directly up the center of the classroom. The data were so convincing that they termed this area the "action zone." From this, Adams (1969) developed a principle that he called "location-communication participation principle." His principle states that the greater the distance a seat is located from the frontmost and centermost part of the room, the less likelihood that the occupants of that location will be involved

in overt verbal interaction. Koneya (1976) found evidence that substantiated the existence of an "action zone." Delefes and Jackson (1972) studied 53 students in a grade 5 language arts and a grade 8 social studies class (two teachers) and from this very limited sample they failed to find a well-defined "action zone." However, they found that teachers have a tendency to call upon students seated in the front more often than on the students seated toward the back of the room.

Schwebel and Cherlin (1972) studied the physical and social distancing in teacher-pupil relationships in 14 classrooms ranging from kindergarten through grade 5. They found that students who had been assigned seats in the front rows were more attentive and engaged in more on-task behavior than students situated in other parts of the room. During the experiment, teachers reassigned the students to new seats at random. Students who were moved forward showed the greatest mean increase in the amount of time engaged in work and the greatest mean decrease in the amount of time spent in inactivity and unassigned activity. It was also noted that teacher's ratings of student attentiveness and likability also changed. Students moved forward in the classroom received more favorable ratings and students moved toward the back of the room received less favorable ratings.

The evidence suggests that a seat in the front and center of a classroom facilitates achievement, participation, and a positive attitude. Teachers seem to attend more to students sitting in the front and center of the classroom. It can be hypothesized that because of the proximity to the teacher, students in the front and center have increased eye contact and more opportunity for nonverbal communication. It might be concluded that teachers should have alternate seating arrangements that allow for teaching from different sections of the classroom and that they should make a concerted effort to interact with students who are seated at a distance or in peripheral positions. Rivlin and Rothenberg (1976) collected data on the location and activities of students and teachers in eight open education classrooms. It was found that in seven of the classrooms the teacher's prime location was in the front of the room.

Furniture arrangement. Prescott, Jones, and Kritchevsky (1967) have conducted one of the most extensive anlyses of classroom space use. Although their study involved day care centers and is not directly related to the elementary school, the investigators examined the availability and placement of equipment and materials specifically, and their data suggest that as the quality of physical space decreased there was a corresponding increase in the amount of teacher restriction control. The number of lessons on arbitrary rules of social living increased, and conflict among the children increased with decreased quality of physical space.

Zifferblatt (1972) examined two third-grade classrooms in which the teacher's instructional styles, the curricula, and the activities were similar. The difference between the two classrooms was the arrangement of space within the classroom. In one classroom, the furniture was arranged so that only two or three children could work together. Desks were placed in less accessible areas of the room, providing a certain degree of privacy. Teacher's desk was placed in a corner, which required the teacher to move around the room more. The second classroom had as many as twelve student desks clustered together. The teacher's desk was centrally located and areas for different activities were not clearly designated and set apart by barriers. Areas for quiet study and areas for activities were contiguous. Zifferblatt (1971) concluded that the more satisfactory space arrangement was two or three children together. Attention span was longer, there was less non–task-oriented activity, and that there was less loud conversation.

The findings of Prescott, Jones and Kritchevsky (1967) and of Zifferblatt (1972) seem to support each other. Weinstein's (1977) study of second- and third-grade children demonstrated that changes in behavior of children are related to furniture arrangement and room design. The range of behaviors was broadened within certain room locations, and the frequency of specific behaviors was changed.

Winett, Battersby, and Edwards (1975) examined the effects of replacing one piece chair-desks in rows with clusters of eight movable desks and chairs along with individualized instruction and behavior-modification techniques on the academic and social behavior of sixth-grade students and concluded that the type of seating furniture was unrelated to behavior.

Santrock (1976) studied another aspect of the environment—the affective quality. He studied motor task performance of first-grade and second-grade school children and concluded that environmental manipulation had an impact on persistence—students worked longer at the task in the happy environment.

Windowless classrooms. Collins (1975) reviewed the research on windowless classrooms and concluded that the absence of windows does not appear to have much influence on students. Despite the differences of preferences, research evidence does not support the idea that freedom from excessive, heat, glare, and distraction will allow increased concentration, which will in turn lead to higher academic achievement. On the other hand, evidence does not support the conclusion that lack of visual access will lead to claustrophobia or psychological and physical harm.

Noise. Teachers have been known frequently to remind students that the classroom is too noisy. This seems to indicate that teachers feel that noise is detrimental to concentration and achievement. Slater (1968) experimented with seventh-grade students' performance on a standardized reading test under three different conditions: (1) in a quiet classroom (45–55 dB), (2) in an average classroom (55–70 dB),(3) in an extremely noisy classroom (75–90 dB). He concluded that the noise effect was neither detrimental nor facilitating on speed or accuracy of performance.

Weinstein and Weinstein (1979) conducted a study in an open space school on reading comprehension. Fourth-grade children in a quiet room (47 dB) and in normal classroom noise (60 dB) were compared and it was found that there was no significant difference in performance. Results of this study cannot be generalized to situations where noise levels are high.

Bronzaft and McCarthy (1975) studied children in New York City in a school located near the elevated subway. In reading scores it was found that children housed on the noisy side (89 dB) of the building performed at a significantly lower level than children housed on the opposite side (65 dB) of the building. Reasons for the difference in scores may be that the noise interfered with the communication, students may have been unable to hear the teacher and may have missed valuable information. Teachers may also stop instruction during the time the trains are passing the school (30 seconds out of every 4½ minutes). Eleven percent of classroom time was lost because of noise.

Cohen, Glass, and Singer (1973) examined the auditory discrimination and reading achievement scores of fifty-four second-, third-, fourth-, and fifth-grade children living in a thirty-two–story apartment building along a major highway. They found significant correlations between floor level and performance on an auditory discrimination test and between auditory discrimination and reading test scores. Nober (1973) demonstrated in a short-term study that tape-recorded classroom noise (65 dB) played in the background adversely affects performance.

The conflicting data indicate the obvious need for additional research to clarify the relationship between noise and school achievement. Internal classroom noise as compared with external classroom noise may be significant. Longitudinal studies need to be conducted to assess the effects of long-term and short-term noise exposure.

The evidence suggests that design factors can have a significant influence on general behavior and on attitudes toward the class and other students. However, there is no evidence to support the notion that classroom design has an impact on achievement.

Recent Trends. The 1980 National Education Association survey (Bartholomew, 1980) of school programs indicated that 61 percent of school systems feel pressure to enforce stricter discipline. Smaller school systems seem to feel less pressure than larger school systems. Seventy-three percent of the elementary schools feel growing pressure to increase the time spent on basic curriculum, and 74 percent to require higher student achievement standards. Fifty-nine percent of the schools require schoolchildren to pass a test prior to promotion or graduation, and 62 percent of the schools are now enforcing stricter attendance requirements than in the past, while 28 percent of the schools feel pressure to increase the amount of student homework.

TABLE 4. *Incidence of elementary schools that provide for instruction of the handicapped*

| | Percentage of elementary schools that | | | |
Handicap	Make no provision for instruction	Instruct in special classes	Mainstream for some instruction	Mainstream for all instruction
Speech impaired	0%	4%	34%	62%
Hearing impaired	5	15	62	18
Visually impaired	5	12	57	26
Mentally impaired	0	17	79	3
Emotionally impaired	3	36	57	4
Orthopedically impaired	2	16	59	22

SOURCE OF DATA: Sheridan, 1980.

Thirty-eight percent of the elementary schoolchildren who do not successfully complete the requirements for a given grade are retained in that grade until the goals are attained. Fifty-three percent are promoted to the next grade level while receiving specially designed remedial help and only 9 percent of the children are assigned to specially designed programs.

Discipline. The NEA survey of schools (Bartholomew, 1980) reported that 42 percent of the schools have moderate-to-major student discipline problems with 3 percent of the schools indicating that student discipline is a major problem. It is estimated that, on the average, 7 percent of the individual schools in the school systems have serious student discipline problems.

Elementary teachers, on the average, have about three students they consider chronic behavior problems. When elementary school teachers are asked to respond to inquiries about student discipline and violence and the extent to which they interfere with teaching, 23 percent said "to a great extent," 33 percent "to a moderate extent," 37 percent "to a small extent," and 8 percent did not reply at all.

Special services. Fifty-five percent of the school systems report that handicapped students attend school in their own attendance area, 20 percent of the schools bus handicapped children to selected schools, and 11 percent bus the children to specifically designed centers for handicapped students. From the data in Table 4 it seems apparent that a majority of the elementary schools are mainstreaming handicapped students for some instruction.

Some elementary schools provide specialists for certain curricular areas. Table 5, Column 1, indicates the percent of the schools that do not have a specialist in that particular area. Column 2 indicates the percent of schools that have specialists available but not housed in a particular school. They may be housed in some other building but are available upon request. Column 3 indicates the proportion of specialists who are housed in schools but are responsible

TABLE 5. *Extent of specialists in elementary schools*

Service	Not available	Available on request	Limited provision	Fully provided
School nurse	10	12	45	33
Librarian	4	3	29	65
Guidance counselor	30	9	34	28
Psychologist	6	33	29	32
Social worker	33	26	22	19
Psychiatrist	51	37	8	4
Speech therapist	1	11	31	57
Teacher aides	4	2	42	52
Unpaid volunteer aides	18	15	43	25
Special reading teacher	3	3	26	69
Special art teacher	26	5	28	41
Special music teacher	5	3	28	64
Special physical education teacher	14	2	24	60

SOURCE OF DATA: Sheridan, 1980.

TABLE 6. *Methods of reporting pupil progress to parents according to elementary teachers*

Method of reporting	Percentage of elementary teachers using the technique
Teacher-parent conference	84.2%
Classified scale of letters (A,B,C,D, etc.)	55.9
Formal letter or written paragraph to parents	26.0
Descriptive word grade	29.2
Percent grade	4.4
Pass/fail	7.3
Classified scale of numbers	6.4
Dual marking system	4.0
Other	7.4

for working in several schools, and Column 4 shows the percent of the elementary schools that have the specialists available in that particular school. Note that 69 percent of the schools have a reading teacher within the school.

The respondents to the NEA Nationwide Teacher Opinion Poll (Bartholomew, 1980) indicated that there is an average of twenty-seven teachers in the elementary schools and that the mean number of students in the respondent's elementary school is 554.

Reporting to parents. How do teachers report pupil school progress to parents? An NEA Research Bulletin (1971) shows that at least eight different methods are used to report pupil progress to parents with some schools having their own unique procedure. Most elementary schools used the parent conference as the major method. Table 6 indicates the percent of elementary school teachers that used the identified technique for reporting to parents.

Concluding Remarks. During the past decade, elementary education has received unprecedented scrutiny. Concern for educational effectiveness has prompted the development of new techniques and not only have traditional instructional practices been altered, and in some cases replaced by innovations that have produced some radical changes in the classroom, but increased attention is now being paid to the effects of these changes on instructional processes and learning outcomes. Comparison of old and new practices is becoming standard procedure.

Also apparent is a growing interest in gathering broad descriptive information about elementary education. Thus, management information systems on local, state, and national levels are becoming commonplace. The availability of this broad information base coupled with the interest in monitoring instructional effects increases the potential for improving local instruction policy decisions.

James W. Heddens

See also Home-School Relationships; Instruction Processes; Instructional Time and Learning; Middle Years Development.

REFERENCES

Adams, R. S. Location as a feature of instructional interaction. *Merrill Palmer Quaterly,* 1969, *15*(4), 309–322.

Adams, R. S., & Biddle, B. J. *Realities of Teaching: Explorations with Video Tapes.* New York: Holt, Rinehart & Winston, 1970.

Anifant, D. C. Risk-taking behavior in children experiencing open space and traditional school environments (Doctoral dissertation, University of Maryland, 1972). *Dissertation Abstracts International,* 1972, *33,* 2491A. (University Microfilms, No. 72–29, 596)

Armstrong, D. G. Open space vs. self-contained. *Educational Leadership,* 1975, *32*(4), 291–295.

Armstrong, D. G. Team teaching and academic achievement. *Review of Educational Research,* 1977, *47,* 65–86.

Bair, M., & Woodward, R. G. *Team Teaching in Action.* Boston: Houghton Mifflin, 1964.

Bartholomew, B. R. (Project Director). Nationwide teacher opinion poll, 1980. In *National Education Association Research Memo.* Washington, D.C.: National Education Association, 1980.

Beckley, L. L. Comparative study of elementary school student attitudes toward school and self in open concept and self-contained environments (Doctoral dissertation, Purdue University, 1972). *Dissertation Abstracts International,* 1973, *34,* 206A. (University Microfilms No. 73–15, 769)

Bell, A. E.; Switzer, F.; & Zipursky, M. A. Open area education: An advantage or disadvantage for beginners? *Perceptual and Motor Skills,* 1974, *39*(1), 407–416.

Block, J. H. *Student evaluation: Toward the setting of mastery performance standards.* Paper presented at the American Educational Research Association, Chicago, April 1972. (ERIC Document Reproduction Service No. ED 065 605)

Block, J. H. (Ed.). *Mastery Learning: Theory and Practice.* New York: Holt, Rinehart & Winston, 1971.

Bloom, B. S. *Human Characteristics and School Learning.* New York: McGraw-Hill, 1976.

Bowman, B. L. A comparison of pupil achievement and attitude in a graded school with pupil achievement and attitude in a nongraded school: 1968–69, 1969–70 school years (Doctoral dissertation, University of North Carolina, 1970). *Dissertation Abstracts International,* 1971, *32,* 660A. (University Microfilms No. 71–20, 958)

Brody, E. B. Achievement of first- and second-year pupils in graded and nongraded classrooms. *Elementary School Journal,* 1970, *71,* 391–394.

Bronzaft, A. L., & McCarthy, D. P. The effect of elevated train noise on reading ability. *Environment and Behavior,* 1975, *1*(4), 517–527.

Brunetti, F. A., Jr. The teacher in the authority structure of the elementary school: A study of open-space and self-contained classroom schools (Doctoral dissertation, Ohio State University, 1970). *Dissertation Abstracts International,* 1970, *31,* 4405A. (University Microfilms No. 71–2740)

Burchyett, J. A. A comparison of the effects of nongraded, multi-age, team teaching versus the modified self-contained classroom at the elementary school level. (Doctoral dissertation, Michigan State University, 1972). *Dissertation Abstracts International,* 1972, *33,* 5998A. (University Microfilms No. 73–22, 686)

Burningham, G. L. A study and evaluation of the team teaching of the fourth grade at Woodstock Elementary School. (Doctoral dissertation, University of Utah, 1968). *Dissertation Abstracts International,* 1968, *29*(3-A), 770. (University Microfilms No. 68–11, 905).

Carroll, J. A model of school learning. *Teachers College Record,* 1963, *64,* 723–733.

Charters, W. W., Jr.; & Jones, J. E. *On Neglect of the Independent Variable in Program Evaluation* (Project MITT Occasional Paper). Eugene: University of Oregon, Eugene Center for Educational Policy and Management, 1974.

Cohen, S.; Glass, D.; & Singer, J. Apartment noise, auditory discrimination, and reading ability in children. *Journal of Experimental Social Psychology,* 1973, *9,* 407–422.

Coleman, C. H., & Budahl, I. Necessary ingredients for good team teaching. *National Association of Secondary School Principals Bulletin,* January 1973, 41–46.

Collings, B. L. *Windows and People—A Literature Survey: Psychological Reaction to Environments with and without Windows* (National Bureau of Standards Building Science Series, No. 70). Washington, D.C.: Institute for Applied Technology, 1975.

Cooper, D. H., & Sterns, H. N. Team teaching, student adjustment, and achievement. *Journal of Educational Research,* 1973, *66,* 323–327.

Cubberley, E. P. *Public Education in the United States.* Boston: Houghton Mifflin, 1934.

Davis, R. J., Jr. Teacher assessment of team teaching. *Science Teacher,* 1966, *33,* 38–39.

Dearborn, N. H. *The Oswego Movement in American Education* (Contributions to Education, No. 183). New York: Columbia University, Teachers College, 1925.

Deibel, R. F. An investigation of factors in creating and utilizing open space elementary schools (Doctoral dissertation, Ohio State University, 1971). *Dissertation Abstracts International,* 1972, *32,* 6261A. (University Microfilms No. 72–15, 196)

Delefes, P., & Jackson, B. Teacher-pupil interaction as a function of location in the classroom. *Psychology in the Schools,* 1972, *9*(2), 119–123.

Dolmatch, T. B. (Ed.). *Information Please Almanac, 1981.* New York: Simon & Schuster, 1981.

Engman, L. *Team Teaching Will Work.* State College, Pa., 1973. (ERIC Document Reproduction Service No. Ed 085 374)

Ensign, F. C. *Compulsory School Attendance and Child Labor.* New York: Arno Press and the New York Times, 1969.

Esposito, D. Homogeneous and heterogeneous ability grouping: Principal findings and implications for evaluating and designing more effective educational environments. *Review of Educational Research,* 1973, *43*(2), 163–179.

Findlay, W. G., & Bryan, M. M. *Ability Grouping, 1970: Status, Impact,* and Alternatives. Athens: University of Georgia, Center for Educational Improvement, 1971.

Funaro, G. J. Team teaching: The danger and the promise. *Clearing House,* 1968, *43,* 401–410.

Gaskell, W., & Sheridan, J. Team teaching and the social studies in the elementary school. *Elementary School Journal,* 1968, *68,* 246–250.

Geisert, G. SCIP: A New Orleans solution to a national problem. *Educational Leadership,* 1979, *37,* 128–134.

George, P. S. *Ten Years of Open Space Schools: A Review of the Research.* Gainesville: Florida Educational Research and Development Council and University of Florida, 1975.

Glass, G. V., & Smith, M. L. *Meta-analysis of Research on the Relationship of Class Size and Achievement.* San Francisco: Far West Laboratory for Educational Research and Development, 1978.

Grapko, M. F. *A Comparison of Open Space and Traditional Classroom Structures according to Independence Measures in Children, Teachers' Awareness of Children's Personality Variables, and Children's Academic Progress: Final Report.* Toronto: Ontario Department of Education, 1972. (ERIC Document Reproduction Service No. ED 088 180)

Gumpper, D. C.; Meyer, J. H.: & Kaufman, J. J. *Nongraded Elementary Education: Individualized Learning—Teacher Leadership—Student Responsibility.* University Park: Pennsylvania State University, 1971. (ERIC Document Reproduction Service No. ED 057 440)

Hallinan, M. T. Friendship patterns in open and traditional classrooms. *Sociology of Education,* 1976, *49*(4), 254–265.

Hartwell, C. S. The grading and promotion of pupils. *N.E.A. Addresses and Proceedings,* 1910.

Heimgartner, N. L. *A Comparative Study of Self-concept: Open Space versus Self-contained* (Study No. 4). Greeley: University of Northern Colorado, 1972. (ERIC Document Reproduction Service No. ED 069 389)

Hendry, L. B., & Matheson, P. A. Teachers and pupils in open-plan and conventional classrooms. *Scottish Education Review,* 1979, *11*(2), 107–117.

Holmquist, A. L. A study of the organizational climate of twelve elementary schools in the Albuquerque Public School System; each having architecturally open and architecturally closed classrooms (Doctoral dissertation, University of New Mexico, 1972). *Dissertation Abstracts International,* 1972, *33,* 5472A. (University Microfilms No. 73–8394)

Hyman, J. S., & Cohen, S. A. Learning for mastery: Ten conclusions after fifteen years and three thousand schools. *Educational Leadership,* 1979, *37,* 104–110.

Jackson, J. Analysis of team teaching and a self-contained homeroom experiment in grades five and six. *Journal of Experimental Education,* 1964, *32,* 317–331.

Jaworowicz, E. H. Open space school design as a situational determinant of organizational climate and principal leader behavior (Doctoral dissertation, Wayne State University, 1972). *Dissertation Abstracts International,* 1972, *33,* 2028A. (University Microfilms No. 72–28, 448)

Jeffreys, J. S. An investigation of the effects of innovation educational practices on pupil-centeredness of observed behaviors and on learner outcome variables (Doctoral dissertation, University of Maryland, 1970). *Dissertation Abstracts International,* 1971, *31,* 5766A. (University Microfilms No. 71–13, 201)

Kersh, M. E. *A Study of Mastery Learning in Fifth-grade Arithmetic.* Unpublished doctoral dissertation, University of Chicago, 1972.

Khan, S. B., & Traub, R. E. Teachers' attitudes in open and traditional schools. *Canadian Journal of Education,* 1980, *5*(3), 5–14.

Killough, C. K. An analysis of the longitudinal effect that a nongraded elementary program, conducted in an open space school, had on the cognitive achievement of pupils (Doctoral dissertation, University of Houston, 1971). *Dissertation Abstracts International,* 1972, *32,* 3614A. (University Microfilms No. 72–2265)

Kling, G. W. The relationship between classroom space and self-concept of learners (Doctoral dissertation, University of Northern Colorado, 1971). *Dissertation Abstracts International,* 1972, *32,* 3616A–3617A. (University Microfilms No. 72–3276)

Koneya, M. Location and interaction in row and column seating arrangements. *Environment and Behavior,* 1976, *8*(2), 265.

Kopple, H., & Conner, K. *The Mastery Learning Manual.* Philadelphia: Philadelphia Public Schools, 1980.

Laforge, H. E. The effect of the open space design of an elementary school upon personality characteristics of students (Doctoral dissertation, University of Houston, 1972). *Dissertation Abstracts International,* 1973, *33,* 1365A. (University Microfilms No. 72–26, 322)

Lambert, P.; Goodwin, W. L.: & Wiersma, W. A. A comparison of pupil achievement in team and self-contained organizations. *Journal of Experimental Education,* 1965, *33,* 217–224.

Leroy, J. M. Classroom climate and student perceptions: An exploratory study of third-grade classrooms in selected open space and self-contained schools (Doctoral dissertation, University of Wisconsin, 1973). *Dissertation Abstracts International,* 1973, *34,* 568A. (University Microfilms No. 73–15, 977)

Lovin, J. C. The effect of the school's physical environment on the self-concepts of elementary school students (Doctoral dissertation, University of Georgia, 1972). *Dissertation Abstracts International,* 1973, *33,* 4744A–4745A. (University Microfilms No. 73–5730)

Martin, L. S., & Pavan, B. N. Current research on open space, nongrading, vertical grouping, and team teaching. *Phi Delta Kappan,* 1976, *57*(5), 310–315.

Mayo, S. T. *Measurement in Education: Mastery Learning and Mastery Teaching.* Paper presented at the National Council on Measurement in Education, East Lansing, Mich., March 1970. (ERIC Document Reproduction Service No. ED 051 299).

Mills, F. M. A comparison of teacher performance and attitudes of teachers performing independently in self-contained classrooms and teachers performing cooperatively in open instructional areas (Doctoral dissertation, Arizona State University, 1972). *Dissertation Abstracts International,* 1972, *33,* 2038A. (University Microfilms No. 72–30, 132)

National Education Association Research Bulletin. October 1971, *49*(3).

Nober, L. W. Auditory discrimination and classroom noise. *Reading Teacher,* 1973, *27*(3), 288–291.

Olsen, C. O. Team teaching in the elementary school. *Education,* 1968, *88,* 345–349.

Olson, C. A comparative study involving achievement and attitudes of senior high school students from an open-concept elementary school and a self-contained elementary school (Doctoral dissertation, University of Nebraska, Lincoln, 1973). *Dissertation Abstracts International,* 1973–1974, *34,* 3708A–3709A. (University Microfilms No. 74–650).

Otto, H. J. *Current Practices in the Organization of Elementary Schools* (Contributions to Education, No. 5). Evanston, Ill.: Northwestern University, 1932.

Packard, J. S.: Carlson, R. O.: Charters, W. W., Jr.; Moser, R. H.; & Schmuck, P. A. *Governance and Task Interdependence in Schools: First Report of a Longitudinal Study.* Eugene: Oregon University, 1976. (ERIC Document Reproduction Service No. ED 143 134)

Pavan, B. N. Good news: Research on the nongraded elementary school. *Elementary School Journal,* 1973, *73,* 333–342.

Pellegrin, R. J. *Professional Satisfaction and Decision Making in the Multiunit School* (Technical Report, No. 7). Eugene, Oreg.: Center for Advanced Study of Educational Administration, May 1970. (a)

Pellegrin, R. J. *Some Organizational Characteristics of Multiunit Schools* (Technical Report, No. 8). Eugene, Oreg.: Center for Advanced Study of Educational Administration, May 1970. (b)

Prescott, E.; Jones, E.; & Kritchevsky, S. *Group Day Care as a Child Rearing Environment: An Observational Study of Day Care Programs.* Pasadena, Calif.: Pacific Oaks College, 1967. (ERIC Document Reproduction Service No. ED 024 453)

Purkey, W. W.; Graves, W.; & Zellner, M. Self-perceptions of pupils in an experimental elementary school. *Elementary School Journal,* 1970, *71,* 166–171.

Pyecha, J. *A National Survey of Individualized Education Programs (IEPs) for Handicapped Children* (Draft Report). Research Triangle Park, N.C.: Research Triangle Institute, August 1979.

Read, F. L. Initial evaluation of the development and effectiveness of open space elementary schools (Doctoral dissertation, United States International University, 1973). *Dissertation Abstracts International,* 1973, *33,* 3221A. (University Microfilms No. 73–1312)

Reisner, E. H. *The Evolution of the Common School.* New York: Macmillan, 1930.

Reiss, S., & Dydhalo, N. Persistence, achievement, and open space environments. *Journal of Educational Psychology,* 1975, *67,* 506–513.

Remacle, L. F. A comparative study of the differences in attitudes, self-concept, and achievement of children in graded and nongraded elementary schools (Doctoral dissertation, University of South Dakota, 1971). *Dissertation Abstracts International,* 1972, *31,* 5948A. (University Microfilms No. 71–12, 649)

Reudi, J., & West, C. K. Pupil self-concept in an "open" school and in a "traditional" school. *Psychology in the Schools,* 1973, *10,* 48–53.

Rhodes, F. Team teaching compared with traditional instruction in grades kindergarten through six. *Journal of Educational Psychology,* 1971, *62*(2), 110–116.

Rivlin, L. G., & Rothenberg, M. The use of space in open classrooms. In H. M. Proshansky, W. H. Ittelson, & L. G. Rivlin (Eds.), *Environmental Psychology: People and Their Physical Settings* (2nd ed.). New York: Holt, Rinehart & Winston, 1976.

Sackett, J. W. A comparison of self-concept and achievement of sixth-grade students in an open-school, self-contained school, and departmentalized school (Doctoral dissertation, University of Iowa, 1971). *Dissertation Abstracts International,* 1972, *32,* 2372A. (University Microfilms No. 71–30, 486)

Santrock, J. W. Affect and facilitative self-control: Influence of ecological setting, cognition, and social agent. *Journal of Educational Psychology,* 1976, *68*(5), 509–535.

Schwebel, A. I., & Cherlin, D. L. Physical and social distancing in teacher-pupil relationships. *Journal of Educational Psychology,* 1972, *63,* 543–550.

Seyforth, J. I., & Canady, R. I. Team teaching: Indicators of expectations and sources of satisfaction. *Clearing House*, 1973, *47*, 420–422.

Shane, H. G. Grouping in the elementary school. *Phi Delta Kappan*, 1960, *41*(7), 313–319.

Shaplin, J. T. Description and definitions of team teaching. In J. T. Shaplin & H. F. Olds (Eds.), *Team Teaching*. New York: Harper & Row, 1964.

Sheridan, A. B. (Project Director). Estimates of school statistics, 1979–80. *National Education Association Research Memo.* Washington, D.C.: National Education Association, 1980.

Slater, B. Effects of noise on pupil performance. *Journal of Educational Psychology*, 1968, *59*, 239–243.

Spigel, J. *Open Area Study: Final Report*. Mississauga, Ontario: Peel Board of Education, 1974. (ERIC Document Reproduction Service No. ED 091 850)

Stearns, M. S.; Greene, D.; & David, J. L. *Local Implementation of P.L. 94-142* (Draft Year 1 Report). Menlo Park, Calif.: SRI International, 1979.

Sterns, H. N. Student adjustment and achievement in a team teaching organization (Doctoral dissertation, University of Michigan, 1968). *Dissertation Abstracts International*, 1969, *30*(1A), 116. (University Microfilms No. 69–12, 244)

Townsend, J. W. A comparison of teacher style and pupil attitude and achievement in contrasting schools: Open space, departmentalized, and self-contained (Doctoral dissertation, University of Kansas, 1971). *Dissertation Abstracts International*, 1972, *32*, 5679A. (University Microfilms No. 72–11, 719)

Traut, H. C. An in-depth study of six United States history classes utilizing team teaching (Doctoral dissertation, Ball State University, 1971). *Dissertation Abstracts International*, 1971, *32*, 845A. (University Microfilms No. 71–20, 705)

U.S. Bureau of Census. *Statistical Abstract of the United States: 1980* (101st ed.). Washington, D.C.: U.S. Government Printing Office, 1980.

Warner, J. B. A comparison of students' and teachers' performances in an open area facility and in self-contained classrooms (Doctoral dissertation, University of Houston, 1970). *Dissertation Abstracts International*, 1971, *31*, 3851A. (University Microfilms No. 71–4372)

Weinstein, C. S. Modifying student behavior in an open classroom through changes in the physical design. *American Educational Research Journal*, 1977, *14*(3), 249–262.

Weinstein, C. S. The physical environment of the school: A review of the research. *Review of Educational Research*, 1979, *49*(4), 577–610.

Weinstein, C. S., & Weinstein, N. D. Noise and reading performance in an open space school. *Journal of Educational Research*, 1979, *72*(4), 210–213.

Wilson, B. J., & Schmitz, D. W. What's new in ability grouping. *Phi Delta Kappan*, 1978, *59*(8), 535–536.

Wilt, H. J. A comparison of student attitudes towards school, academic achievement, internal structures, and procedures: The nongraded school versus the graded school (Doctoral dissertation, University of Missouri, 1971). *Dissertation Abstracts International*, 1972, *31*, 5105A. (University Microfilms No. 71–8406)

Winett, R. A.; Battersby, C. D.; & Edwards, S. M. The effects of architectural change, individualized instruction, and group contingencies on the academic performance and social behavior of sixth graders. *Journal of School Psychology*, 1975, *13*(1), 28–40.

Wren, S. J. P. A comparison of affective factors between contained classrooms and open area classrooms (Doctoral dissertation, University of Houston, 1972). *Dissertation Abstracts International*, 1972, *33*, 1397A. (University Microfilms No. 72–27, 509)

Wright, R. J. The affective and cognitive consequences of an open education elementary school. *American Educational Research Journal*, 1974, *12*(4), 449–468.

Yarborough, B. H., & Johnson, R. A. The relationship between intelligence levels and benefits from innovative nongraded elementary schooling and traditional, graded schooling. *Educational Research Quarterly*, 1978, *3*(2), 28–38.

Zifferblatt, S. M. Architecture and human behavior: Toward increased understanding of a functional relationship. *Educational Technology*, 1972, *12*(8), 54–57.

EMOTIONAL DEVELOPMENT

This review focuses on emotional development from young childhood (beginning at age 3) to adolescence. It relies primarily on three sources, to which the reader may refer for more details: articles by Charlesworth and Kreutzer (1973), by Hoffman (1975), and by Harter (1979). It may come as a surprise to the reader that the vast majority of research on emotional development was done in daycare and nursery school settings in the 1920s and 1930s, long before the sophisticated techniques of modern psychological and developmental research had been discovered. Because the few studies that have been done in the recent past have not been replicated, definitive knowledge about emotional development in children will have to be delayed until more systematic studies have been carried out.

Definition of Emotion. There are almost as many definitions of "emotion" as there are scholars of the emotional process. William James, one of the founding fathers of modern psychology, defined emotion as the "visceral" or bodily changes that follow a particular event and the feeling of those changes within the person (James, 1890). Some believe that emotion is purely an internal process involving feelings of good and bad, attraction and repulsion (Young, 1961). Others believe that emotions are not the visceral responses themselves, but rather the cognitive evaluations that we make in relation to these feelings: the same heightened arousal may be evaluated by one individual as exciting and by another as fearful, depending upon past experience, temperament, and situational factors (Schacter & Singer, 1962). A third view of emotion sees feelings not as passive, visceral responses, but as motives that are dynamic and adaptive. In this view, emotions are the "primary motivational system" (Izard, 1978): emotions give meaning to behavior. For example, a child's approach to a rabbit can be understood in terms of the interest or excitement that the rabbit stimulates. Similarly, if the rabbit bites the child, the child's withdrawal can be understood in relation to the surprise, pain, and fear that the child might be feeling.

Emotion and Personality. Another important issue concerns the role emotion plays in the total makeup of the individual. It is generally believed that emotions come in discrete, qualitatively distinct packages, referred to as the "basic affects": interest, excitement, surprise, fear, distress, enjoyment, shame, disgust, and anger. There are other states, called "moods," which are thought to be made up of combinations of these basic affects. Examples of moods are aggression, anxiety, affection, and concentration. An individual's "temperament," or personality, can be thought of as a function of the kinds of moods the individual usually experiences, as well as the relative tendency to change moods. Studies of mood in relation to personality have found some moderate correlations, at least in adults (Nowlis, 1965).

Development of Emotion in the Child. The emotional development of children over the age of 3 is an area that has received relatively little attention from psychologists. There are many studies of emotional development between birth and the age of 3, and there are many studies of emotion in adults. One of the reasons for this paucity of research on the middle years of childhood is that by age 3, the child is capable of experiencing all of the basic affects that are found in adults (Sroufe, 1979). Researchers have evidently assumed that, because of this fact, there is little or no reason to study emotional development after infancy.

By analogy to Piaget's stages of cognitive-intellectual functioning, one might say that by the age of 3, children have completed the sensorimotor stage of emotional development: they can experience each of the emotions, but they cannot conceptualize their own emotional experiences nor the emotional experiences of others. One might therefore expect that the child's cognitive understanding of his or her own emotional experiences and those of others is a more difficult developmental task than the cognitive understanding of the world of objects, space, and time (Harter, 1979).

One of the most notable aspects of emotions is that they are not concretely observable like nesting cups, pencils of different lengths, written words, or numbers. Our own emotions are experiences, not objects; the emotions of others are purely abstractions. Genuine emotional maturity, the awareness of one's own capacities and limitations and the ability to anticipate those of others, must therefore require the ability for abstract, or formal operational thinking (Hoffman, 1975).

There are a number of detailed and excellent works on the development of emotional expression in infants (Charlesworth & Kreutzer, 1973; Sroufe, 1979). The general pattern of infant emotional development is development from a relatively simple, one-dimensional emotional system at birth (feelings of pleasantness versus unpleasantness) that gradually matures in correspondence with the infant's sensorimotor development. The emotion of fear, for example, only begins at the age of 8 months, when infants can remember past experiences and compare them to their current ones. The emotions of shame and guilt can only appear after children are able to form a representation of the self. Knowledge of one's self and one's actions as *belonging* to one's self are required in order to feel pride, guilt, or shame. These cognitive achievements do not occur until after the second year of life, when children begin to develop skills for forming mental representations as well as linguistic skills that provide labels for the self and the self's actions.

Development of Emotional Expression. The overall pattern of findings on emotional expression seems to indicate that younger children are more expressive than older children or adults. This finding reflects the fact that younger children use more of their bodies—arms, legs, torsos—to express an emotion, whereas older children and adults rely on fine motor movements of the face and body. Older children also become more capable of supressing their emotions, as social situations or their own developing needs for self-control may warrant it. The development of specific expressions follows, using Charlesworth and Kreutzer's review (1973), unless otherwise noted.

Distress. In general, crying decreases and laughter increases with age. Children over the age of 3 only cry about five times per month in nursery school. Crying, as one might expect, tends to occur in stressful situations. It also seems to serve as an important social signal, since 78 percent of observed instances of crying occurred during social interaction. The use of crying for instrumental purposes or for manipulation of others, the incidence of crying in role play (pretended crying), the control of distress by means other than crying, and the awareness of social norms about crying have not been subjected to systematic research. There is very little known about the development of verbal expressions of distress.

Enjoyment. The data on the relation of laughter to age are inconclusive. Results show that nursery school children laugh about two to four times per hour. The tendency to laugh may be a stable personality trait, although this supposition is inconclusive. One study found that those children who laughed during free play also laughed during routine activity. Laughter, like crying, is a social response, occurring 94 percent of the time during interaction. Neither the relation of laughter to intelligence, social competence, or success in school nor the relation of any of these subtleties of smiling and laughter to specific social situations has been investigated. The only exception has been a study of coy behavior as used by nursery school children (Marvin & Mossler, 1976).

Anger. Like crying, anger has been shown to decrease with age. Physical expressions of rage—yelling, kicking, biting, and so on—are replaced by verbalizations. Older children may show anger in symbolic ways; they may even laugh as a way of annoying or irritating others. Older children are also more likely to settle their conflicts by negotiation and compromise. Between $2\frac{1}{2}$ and $3\frac{1}{2}$ years of age, children show anger primarily to adults, while 4-year-olds are more likely to become angry with other children.

Studies of anger have been done under the label "aggressive" behavior. Children 3 to 5 years of age tend to use aggression *instrumentally*, in order to achieve a goal, whereas 6-to-7-year-olds may use *hostile* aggression toward others in the form of criticism, ridicule, tattling, or verbal disapproval. While both boys and girls in the preschool years show the same amount of instrumental aggression, boys are more likely to display hostile aggression (Hartup, 1974).

Most of the research on aggression has dealt with how it is socialized by the family, the media, and the schools, and on effective ways to control aggression. This research has been reviewed by Hetherington and Parke (1979). In general, aggressive behavior by adult role models begets aggression in children. Aggression has been shown to be effectively controlled by a variety of techniques.

Fear. Overt expressions of fear—momentary stoppage of breathing, screaming, stiffening of the body, whitening of the face—are rarely observed in children over 3 years of age. Older children are usually able to avoid potentially fearful situations. Older children tend to develop a whole catalog of fears, such as fear of the dark, fear of dogs, fear of ghosts.

Fear is one of the few emotions that has been systematically studied in children over the age of 3. Barnett (1969) studied 228 girls 7 to 12 years of age and found that the same number of fears were found at each age, but the types of fear expressed by the children changed. Fears of imaginary creatures and for personal safety declined with age while fears related to school and social relationships increased as the child approached adolescence. Similar findings are reported by Angelino, Dollins, and Mech (1956). In a more recent study, the most common fears expressed by elementary school children were found to be bodily harm, robbers, kidnappers, death, and animals (Eme & Schmidt, 1978). This study also reported that individual children were likely to list the same specific fears on a follow-up interview one year later.

Other Data of Emotional Expression. One other study is worth mentioning in this context. Doris Gilbert (1969) asked 4-to-6-year-old children to verbalize their awareness of their own affective state, and she asked the children's teachers to rate each child on ability to verbalize affect (affect-awareness), maturity, empathy, and imagination. Gilbert found three basic patterns of expressiveness. *Affect-aware* children were highly verbal, did not try to hide their feelings, expressed a range of emotions, and were not reluctant to express joys and delights. *Unhappy* children were those who experience fear intensely, were often sad and disappointed, and were easily upset. *Restrained* children were not impulsive, did not get excited and avoided confrontation. The children who were highly *affect-aware* tended to be more imaginative in their play and more empathic with others, suggesting that awareness of own and others' emotions may be related.

Development of the Ability to Recognize Facial Expressions. Some research has been done on the ability to recognize facial expressions. However, the methods have been criticized on a number of grounds (Charlesworth & Kreutzer, 1973). As one might expect, older children recognize a broader range of expressions than younger children. Younger children are particularly sensitive to contextual factors. A study by Honkavaara (1961) found that 3- and 4-year-old children mistakenly referred to a sad girl as happy, if she was pictured wearing a red dress. Honkavaara also found that children from 3 to 6 years of age correctly labeled the expression (laughing, crying), but incorrectly identified the person's emotional state. This finding may relate to the abstract quality of another's emotional experience indicated earlier.

Odom and Lemond (1972) asked 5- and 10-year-olds to match pictures of similar facial expressions, and to match pictures of expressions and descriptions of a situation. The situation "eating a piece of candy" had to be matched with one of a list of facial expressions including joy, sadness, anger, and others. Then the children were asked to "make a face" like an adult modeling a particular expression. At both ages children could match expressions better than they could produce them, and the older children were more accurate in both matching and production.

Development of Emotional Concepts. How do children of different ages conceptualize emotion? Do they think that emotions can only be felt one at a time? Can the child's mind comprehend simultaneous, or even conflicting emotions? Piagetian theory suggests that ambivalence and other multi-emotional states can only be understood by formal operational children. Bruno Bettelheim (1977), in his analysis of children's stories, suggests that young children see the world as either all good or all bad. When mother is mean, she is a wolf or a wicked witch. When she is nice, she is the fairy godmother. But the young child cannot conceptualize the mother as both good and bad at the same time. One commonplace observation bears this point out. An adult can express a good deal of anger to a child, yet several minutes later, the child may approach the adult as if nothing had occurred. The child sees the "good" adult, even though the adult may still be steaming inside.

Research by Harter (1979) has confirmed these suppositions. She asked children between the ages of 3 and 13 to name as many emotions as they could. Three-year-olds were able to name "happy," "sad," "mad," and sometimes "scared." Children under 5 years of age did not have a clear understanding of the emotions of pride, shame, anxiety, and jealousy, even though their behavior demonstrated that they had felt those emotions. Harter found that older children not only were able to name more emotions, but could also generate a variety of composite emotional states or moods. The 10-to-13-year-olds often reported feelings of being annoyed, disappointed, relieved, discouraged, or anxious. Similar findings are reported by Farmer (1967).

As for the question of whether children can conceptualize more than one emotion at one time, Harter found that after the age of 7, children talked about one emotion following another in sequence, but only after the age of about 9 could children begin to conceive of having more than one emotion at the same time.

Harter's study bears out the Piagetian point of view that emotions are treated as abstract entities in the thought process. This view makes it difficult to reason with a 5-year-old, for example, about how it is normal to feel good sometimes and bad at other times. Again, the question of socialization—finding the most appropriate way to handle children's understanding of the self and the other through their feelings—begs for further research.

Another aspect of the conceptualization of emotions is the ability to tell whether emotional states have their source "inside" or "outside" the self. Wolman, Lewis, and King (1971) found that children do not systematically think of emotions as originating from inside themselves until 10 years of age. Before this time children are likely to "blame" their emotional states on external events, situations or persons.

Development of Understanding of Other's Emotions.   The development of empathy in young children is a steadily growing field of research, perhaps the most active of any of the aspects of emotional development that have been mentioned. The details of these recent findings take us far beyond the scope of this article. The most comprehensive theory of the development of children's empathy is that of Hoffman (1975). Hoffman suggests that there is both an emotional and a cognitive component to understanding another's emotions. His work dovetails nicely with that of Harter. As older children begin to conceive of the simultaneity of emotions in themselves, they also develop the awareness that other people feel emotions and that the emotions of others are independent of their own emotional state. According to Hoffman, the development of empathic understanding is but one manifestation of emotional maturity and the consolidation of a stable sense of personal identity. These are developmental issues that only begin to coalesce fully during adolescence.

The recent reports of empathic behavior of nursery-school-aged children can be explained without assuming that the child understands the other's feelings. Another person's distress may trigger a latent distress reaction within the child, who then responds to the other as a way of comforting the self. It often happens that the child provides just the kind of aid that the self requires in such a situation, regardless of the appropriateness of the aid to the distressed individual (Hoffman, 1975).

Children may also be influenced by the other's emotions. Lewis and Michaelson (1982) found that preschool children were more willing to approach a stranger if their mothers greeted the stranger warmly than they were when their mothers were hostile or negative to the stranger. Children also seem to rely on the other's emotions to learn verbal labels for emotional states or to learn when it is appropriate to express particular emotions.

These findings show that even young children are aware of the other's emotional expressions, but the children are not necessarily aware of the adult's emotional experience.

The Interface between Emotion and Education.   Until we have more specific research on children's emotions and on the role of emotion in learning and in social interaction, there is little that we can say that is definitive. In an earlier paper, I argued that there are three basic ways in which emotion can enter the educational process (Fogel, 1980).

First, emotion is inseparable from the learning process and may even provide the motivational control of learning. Emotions result anytime we attempt to solve a problem (interest, excitement), fail to solve it (frustration, anger, determination), and succeed in solving it (enjoyment, satisfaction). The emotions that result from a particular learning task depend in part on the child's abilities, in part on the situation in which the problem is presented, and in part on the teacher's ability to match the task to the child's abilities and provide the appropriate supports. The growing emotional sophistication of children influences the kinds of things teachers need to do at each age or grade in order to maintain interest and to deal with frustration.

Second, emotion enters the classroom via the teacher-child relationship. Any human interaction involves the mutual expression of emotion. Children develop strong attachments to teachers, as well as certain kinds of dependencies. Teachers likewise develop different emotional responses to each child. The success of the teaching-learning process may depend, in part, on the nature of the emotional relationship between teacher and child.

Finally, emotion is part of the content of classroom activities. Role play, children's films and stories, jokes, discussions of love and death are all ways in which emotion becomes a thing to be learned about. Direct discussions of feelings may also be a successful method, but the nature of the discussion has to take into account the child's conceptual limitations at each developmental stage.

Alan Fogel

See also Affective Education; Mental Health; Personality Assessment; Personality Theory; Psychological Services.

REFERENCES

Angelino, H.; Dollins, J.; & Mech, E. Trends in the "fears and worries" of school children. *Journal of Genetic Psychology,* 1956, *89,* 263–267.

Barnett, J. *Development of Children's Fears: The Relationship between Three Systems of Fear Measurement.* Unpublished M.A. thesis, University of Wisconsin, 1969.

Bettelheim, B. *The Uses of Enchantment.* New York: Random House, 1977.

Charlesworth, W., & Kreutzer, M. Facial expressions of infants and children. In P. Ekman (Ed.), *Darwin and Facial Expression.* New York: Academic Press, 1973.

Eme, R., & Schmidt, D. The stability of children's fears. *Child Development,* 1978, *49,* 1277–1279.

Fogel, A. The role of emotion in early childhood education. *Current Topics in Early Childhood Education*, 1980, *3*, 1–14.

Gilbert, D. The young child's awareness of affect. *Child Development*, 1969, *40*, 629–640.

Harter, S. *Children's Understanding of Multiple Emotions: A Cognitive-Developmental Approach.* Paper presented to the ninth annual symposium of the Jean Piaget Society, Philadelphia, 1979.

Hartup, W. Aggression in childhood: Developmental perspectives. *American Psychologist*, 1974, *29*, 336–341.

Hetherington, M., & Parke, R. *Child Psychology: A Contemporary Viewpoint.* New York: McGraw Hill, 1979.

Hoffman, M. L. Developmental synthesis of affect and cognition and its implications for altruistic motivation. *Developmental Psychology*, 1975, *11*, 607–622.

Honkavaara, S. The psychology of expression. *British Journal of Psychology Monograph Supplements*, 1961, *32*, 1–96.

Izard, C. On the ontogenesis of emotions and emotion-cognition relationships in infancy. In M. Lewis & L. Rosenblum (Eds.), *The Development of Affect.* New York: Plenum Press, 1978.

James, W. *Principles of Psychology.* New York: Henry Holt, 1890.

Lewis, M., & Michaelson, L. The socialization of affect. In T. Field and A. Fogel (Eds.), *Emotion and Early Interactions.* Hillsdale, N.J.: Lawrence Erlbaum Associates, 1982.

Marvin, R., & Mossler, D. A methodological paradigm for describing and analyzing complex non-verbal expressions: Coy expressions in pre-school children. *Representative Research in Social Psychology*, 1976, *7*, 133–139.

Nowlis, V. Research with mood adjective check list. In S. Tomkins & C. Izard, *Affect, Cognition, and Personality.* New York: Springer, 1965.

Odom, R., & Lemond, C. Developmental differences in the perception and production of facial expressions. *Child Development*, 1972, *43*, 359–370.

Piaget, J., & Inhelder, B. *The Psychology of the Child.* New York: Basic Books, 1969.

Schacter, S., & Singer, J. Cognitive, social and physiological determinants of emotional state. *Psychological Review*, 1962, *69*, 379–399.

Sroufe, L. A. Socioemotional development. In J. Osofsky (Ed.), *Handbook of Infant Development.* New York: Wiley, 1979.

Wolman, R.; Lewis, W.; & King, M. The development of the language of emotions: Conditions of emotional arousal. *Child Development*, 1971, *42*, 1288–1293.

Young, P. *Motivation and Emotion.* New York: Wiley, 1961.

EMOTIONAL DISTURBANCE

See Behavior Problems; Behavioral Treatment Methods; Mental Health; Psychological Services; Truants and Dropouts.

ENGINEERING EDUCATION

Engineers are an essential component of a modern industrialized economy. Landis (1980), using the technique of dynamic analysis, has shown that the United States engineering education "system" will be able to produce sixty to seventy thousand baccalaureate-level engineers (with B.S.E. degrees) each year during the 1980s, and that this is about the number required to sustain approximately a 3 percent annual growth in the gross national product. At the same time, the system must provide master's level education (M.S.E. degrees) for about twenty thousand engineers, and doctoral-level education (Ph.D., Sc.D., or D. Eng. degrees) for about three thousand. Because of the rapid rate of change of technology, there is also a requirement for a very large component of continuing engineering education. Klus and Jones (1978) have estimated that in a five-year period over 50 percent of engineers are involved in at least one formal continuing education course.

The demands placed on the undergraduate engineering system are complex. At the absolute minimum, the B.S.E. graduate must be able to perform adequately in an entry-level engineering position, usually in industry. Efforts to make a master's degree a requirement for an entry-level job in industry have been unsuccessful. In addition, the B.S.E. degree must provide a foundation for advanced formal graduate study by one-third of its recipients, and a basis for less formal continuing education by one-half. An additional complication arises from the fact that a small percentage of each year's B.S.E. graduates are welcome candidates for places in medical, law, and business schools. Finally, since each engineer must live as a person and a citizen as well, a substantial component (about 15 to 20 percent) of the undergraduate curriculum must be reserved for instruction in the liberal arts and social sciences. Indeed, recent social concerns about the impact of modern technology are reflected in even greater stress on the non-technical aspects of the engineering curriculum (Olmsted, 1968); Florman, 1976). It should also be noted that approximately 40 percent of B.S.E. engineering graduates leave the active practice of engineering between ten and twenty years after graduation to assume management positions, and a substantial fraction of B.S.E. graduates choose to take advanced education in a graduate school of business, leading to the Master of Business Administration (M.B.A.) degree.

The Engineering Manpower Commission (EMC) issues annual reports of engineering enrollments and degrees (EMC, 1980a) and also publishes time series of this data (EMC, 1980b). This information is particularly valuable because it presents separate data on trends in about twenty different engineering specializations, including students' sex, ethnic groups, and countries of origin. Schools are now admitting about one hundred thousand freshmen per year, and since most schools are also limiting enrollments, it appears that this is the maximum that the "system" can handle.

History. Engineering in the United States springs from two roots: self-educated canal builders in New York and New England, and European-educated (mostly French) engineer-officers who joined Washington's staff during the American Revolution. Although the Erie Canal was frequently referred to as "the first American engineering school," it is now generally accepted that engineering education in the United States really began with the establishment of a school at the Military Academy at West Point in 1802. The history of this early period is thoroughly documented in McGivern (1960) and in Rezneck (1968). A brief but accurate discussion of the entire span of American engineering education is given in Grayson (1977). Because of the close link between early French and American engineering education, the development of the former (Artz, 1966) is an important reference. In fact, the first engineering textbooks used in American schools were translations from the French.

Engineering education did not at first find a place in the universities, either in the United States or abroad. In France there arose the Ecole des Ponts at Chausées and the *école polytechnique,* in Germany, the *technisch Hochschule,* and in the United States and Great Britain the polytechnics. The formidably rational education required by the engineer was in conflict with the speculative and theological bent of the postrevolutionary universities, and it caused less strife to establish separate institutions. Things began to change in the decades surrounding the U.S. Civil War, particularly with the passage of the Morrill Act of 1862, which supported the establishment of universities to provide instruction in "agriculture and the mechanic arts." The early days of the fledgling land grant universities, complete with engineering schools, are well documented in biographies and histories by Cooley (1947), Havemeyer and Dudley (1959), and Condit (1962), Knoll (1963), Mandel and Shipley (1966), Gilbey (1968), among others. These describe, respectively, early engineering education at Michigan, Colorado, Purdue, Iowa State, Yale, and Princeton. In the 1980s many engineering schools will celebrate their centennials, and we may expect a new surge of engineering school history and biography.

Two major theories of engineering education—theoretical versus practical—struggled for supremacy in the post–Civil War period. The conflict stemmed from the earliest days of the mutual disdain of the canal builders and the military engineers. Calvert (1967) describes this conflict in terms of the "shop" culture versus the "school" culture, and traces of this concern remain in engineering education even today. Brittain (1977) traces the influence of the dispute in the founding of the Georgia Institute of Technology in 1884. Prior to the Civil War many, if not most, persons practicing engineering in the United States were self-taught, although a few (Fulton, Rumford, Latrobe) received at least some education in Europe. The Morrill Act also made the public universities a major partner in engineering education with the privately owned universities and polytechnics. As the West was opened, the largest schools of engineering developed in the land grant universities. In 1980 there were 248 institutions with accredited schools of engineering.

American Society for Engineering Education. With no long tradition to serve as a guide, there was a pressing need for communication among the leaders of engineering

education. At the World's Engineering Congress in Chicago in 1893, a session on engineering education resolved to form a new national society devoted entirely to its advancement, and at the close of the congress some seventy members created the Society for the Promotion of Engineering Education, electing as president Professor DeVolson Wood. The first meeting was held at Brooklyn Polytechnic Institute in August 1894. From the very beginning the society has sought, through its publications and conferences, to be the leader in theoretical and practical research on engineering education. Now called the American Society for Engineering Education (ASEE), it has been the principal repository of research results—as well as opinions, dialogue, and even invective—on all matters concerning engineering education in the United States.

The ASEE also has organized the formal structure for interaction between schools: its Engineering College Council and Technology College Council are basically organizations of school deans, and are entitled to representation on the ASEE's board of directors. The ASEE has also provided a U.S. focus for a continuing dialogue with engineering education activities in foreign countries and regions. Recently the ASEE sponsored a World Congress on the contributions of engineering education to the development process, with its proceedings edited by Collins and English (1976). International comparisons of systems of engineering education have been recorded by the European Society for Engineering Education (SEFI) in a volume edited by Comina (1978) describing systems in seventeen European countries, and by UNESCO (1976) in a volume covering the countries of Africa, Asia, and Latin America. Such international comparisons have taken on additional meaning since the countries of the European Common Market have begun to rationalize the exchange of the privileges of international professional practice.

Curriculum. General consensus on the content of an appropriate education for an entry-level engineer (B.S.E.) has been greatly aided by a series of reports, at approximately ten-year intervals since 1920, which sought comment and discussion from broadly representative segments of the engineering profession. The most influential of these reports include those by Mann (1918), Wickenden (1929), Hammond (1944), Grinter (1955), and Walker (1968). Although none are "official," in any legal sense, their recommendations have been widely adopted, and have provided a basis for approval of criteria applied in the accreditation process.

Engineering education is one of the most demanding curricula at the undergraduate level. Nominally it takes four years to get a B.S.E., but experience shows that about 50 percent of the candidates take four and a half to five years. Good secondary school preparation is essential in English, physical science, and mathematics. The student who only pursues three years of high school mathematics is severely handicapped, as a first course in calculus is an essential starting point in an engineering curriculum. In fact, a modern engineering curriculum will have a strong core of mathematics extending through at least six semesters, and the required engineering sciences (dynamics, thermodynamics, fluid mechanics, electronics, and so on) are usually positioned in the curriculum at points where the student's mathematical sophistication is adequate to the demands of the science.

Most engineering curricula provide a more or less common lower division (first two years), followed by a more specialized upper division (last two years). In the upper division specialization proceeds rather rapidly, as the student's interest is focused on a particular field such as civil, electrical, or mechanical engineering. These specializations, together with mining, industrial, and chemical engineering, constitute about 85 percent of the B.S.E.'s granted each year. The remaining 15 percent are made up of more than thirty other specializations, often serving a regional need: for example, petroleum engineering in the Southwest or ceramic engineering in Ohio. Engineering education has always included a substantial component of laboratory experience, and has thus been a rather expensive form of higher education. This has limited its availability in some ways, since less than two hundred and fifty of some two thousand American colleges and universities offer it.

Even among the former, some curricula differ substantially from the norm. Harrisberger (1976) explores six examples of experiential approaches to engineering education, and will soon publish results of a follow-up study of the graduates of these unique programs. There have also been several attempts to formally lengthen the course to five or more years, but these have generally failed. Some critics have urged a basically scientific education at the undergraduate level (Havemeyer & Dudley, 1959), with all engineering subjects to be taught at the graduate level. There have also been conflicts between the highly theoretical approach, which is really required by the amount of material to be covered in a modern curriculum, and the more practical, hands-on approach. As the level of theoretical instruction has risen, the field of "engineering technology" education—which retains more of the practical bent and surrenders the theoretical level—has flourished. Grinter (1972) chaired a committee that did an extensive study of engineering technology education and its relationship to engineering education.

Undergraduate engineering education provides the majority of engineers for the national economy, but the schools must also make provision for the approximately one-third who go on for advanced education. This advanced-level component (with M.S.E.'s or Ph.D.'s) is particularly important to the research-and-development segment of industry, which itself is an essential component in national industrial growth. The ASEE publishes an annual directory of research and graduate study, which provides up-to-date information, both financial and descriptive, of all the research being carried on by engineering schools. A by-product of this research is, of course, the development of a highly educated research-oriented frac-

tion of the total engineering population. It should be noted that some engineers disagree with this approach, believing that this highest level of education should be concentrated on the function of "design," rather than "research," and as a result a few programs leading to a M.Eng. or D.Eng. have evolved. This tendency does not appear to be growing rapidly.

Cooperative education. A unique contribution of engineering education to the national scene may be the concept of "cooperative education." Begun by Dean Herman Schneider at the University of Cincinnati in 1906, it provides a program that alternates classroom study with industrial employment, optimally with some linkage between the two activities. Such a program, of course, stretches the usual four-year curriculum to five years, but its supporters, who are many, believe the added experience and maturity brought to the student more than offsets the added time. Approximately 50 of the 248 accredited colleges of engineering offer cooperative education to some or all of their undergraduate students. A few schools have extended this principle to graduate studies in engineering, but the number is not large. In recent years, the U.S. Department of Education has supported efforts to induce additional schools to begin cooperative education programs in fields other than engineering.

Accreditation. In 1932 the several specialized engineering societies existing in the United States began to accredit undergraduate engineering curricula. The accreditation process is fairly conventional, beginning with an institutional self-study, followed by a visit from a team of representatives of the professional societies (half from education and half from industry), and ending with an advisory report to the institution's administration. The accreditation action, taken and by the Accreditation Commission of the Accreditation Board for Engineering and Technology (ABET), results in a three-year or six-year term of accreditation, or a show-cause order when accreditation is to be withdrawn. There are provisions for appeal and due process. The annual accreditation workload is heavy. In 1980, 57 visits resulted in 243 accreditation actions. A 1977 survey by the ASEE showed that more than 90 percent of the schools visited that year rated the accreditation process as good or better.

The accreditation process is still under development. Among the issues that have been debated in the last few years, without successful resolution, are the extension of the process to include accreditation of (1) dual-level (both B.S.E. and M.S.E.) programs, (2) continuing-level programs, and (3) engineering-related programs such as surveying and construction.

Although not strictly a part of the accreditation process, it should be noted that completion of the undergraduate program may be immediately put to the test—particularly by the Graduate Record Examination, for those who plan to enter graduate school, and the Fundamentals of Engineering Examination of the National Council of Engineering Examiners, for those who seek state registration prior to entering private practice. Coordination among the examining groups is achieved primarily by movement of individual examiners from one group to another.

Teacher Preparation. Prior to about 1900, there was no formal expression of interest in the preparation of engineering teachers. Indeed, this was one of the prime objectives of the founders of the Society for the Promotion of Engineering Education. Initially, engineering teachers moved directly from the ranks of practitioners into the schools. Much of early engineering education was a codification of current engineering practice, and graduates were expected to move directly from school to practice. However, as the technical content of engineering grew and became more specialized, graduate schools of engineering were organized in the 1930s, and it soon became imperative to seek new faculty who had been exposed to the higher education of the graduate schools. An excellent record of this transition period is given in Timoshenko's autobiography (1968). The graduate schools expanded further in the 1950s, primarily as a result of the lessons of World War II, and by 1970 it was almost a requirement that the young aspiring teacher should hold a Ph.D., or its equivalent, from one of the distinguished graduate schools.

This procedure has been severely criticized on two grounds. Many believe that the emphasis of the research-oriented Ph.D. leaves the younger teacher disassociated from the large areas of engineering practice that do not involve research, and the claim is made that modern students require a year or two of supplemental education within industry before they are ready for practice. Many industries, particularly the larger ones, have in fact developed such courses.

An additional criticism is that the Ph.D. program offers little guidance in the art of instruction, and completely ignores the contribution of psychology to modern learning theory. To help fill this latter gap, the ASEE has organized Effective Teaching Institutes and summer courses for engineering teachers, which have moved from campus to campus. A good survey of the materials presented is given in Lancaster's treatise (1974), based on courses given at Pennsylvania State University. The National Science Foundation has supported many of these efforts. The ASEE Educational Research and Methods Division has conducted sessions on major educational concepts, such as self-paced instruction, applications of technology, and theories of cognition, at ASEE annual conferences, and has cooperated each fall with the Institute of Electrical and Electronic Engineers in holding the Frontiers in Education Conference on similar topics. It must be admitted, however, that Ph.D-oriented graduate programs, followed by years of intense concentration on research required for progress toward promotion and tenure, make it difficult for most young faculty to focus on improvement in teaching technique.

Evaluation. As mentioned earlier, the profession has sponsored broadly based reviews of engineering education

approximately every ten years since 1920, the most recent being the study directed by Walker (1968). Each of these reports has had a significant impact on engineering education. In 1978, after discussing the timeliness of another study, covering the 1970s, the profession asked the ASEE to first determine the fate of various recommendations made in earlier studies. A preliminary report was published by the ASEE Long Range Planning Committee, chaired by Hancock (1979), resulting in a number of specific recommendations that were assigned to various segments of the society for implementation.

In addition to the national reports, several of the professional societies hold periodic review conferences on engineering education from the viewpoint of their specialization. Examples of these were reported in a monograph by Jones (1977), and another report was published in *Mechanical Engineering* (Fletcher & Marlowe, 1981).

The various efforts at comparative ratings of university departments have paid little attention to engineering, and in any case are usually regarded as opinion polls. Within the profession, Glower (1980) published a study of engineering schools based on entries in *Who's Who in Engineering*, and on research and publication levels. The methodology, and hence the results, are not universally accepted, but in any case do not differ substantially from the "opinion polls." Only about 10 percent of the schools are rated.

Current Issues. As recently as thirty years ago, economists had paid little attention to the contribution of technology to the national economy. However, since 1970 this issue has been studied with some intensity, and some economists now attribute as much as 35 percent of the annual growth of the gross national product to new technology. Although such economic modeling is in its infancy (EMC, 1972), it is clear that a regular input of highly educated engineers is an essential component for the sustenance of a healthy national economy. Concern that the national system of engineering education was not producing the number or quality of graduates required to enable the country to maintain a competitive position in international trade surfaced first in Great Britain. This concern led to the establishment of a Royal Committee of Inquiry in July 1977, and its report, submitted by the chairman, Sir Montague Finniston (1980), recommended widespread changes in the British system of teaching and granting degrees.

In February 1980, President Carter expressed concern that the United States system of science and engineering education might prove inadequate to the country's future requirements. This concern resulted in a recommendation (Hufstedler & Langenberg, 1980) for federal support of programs assisting engineering schools in the areas of facilities, equipment, graduate fellowships, and research. The report envisages an imminent decline in quantity or quality (or both) of engineering graduates of the late 1980s, preceded by a precipitous decline in qualified faculty. The American Society for Engineering Societies (Marlowe,

1980) participated in the preparation of this report and urged even stronger recommendations. There was also a valuable set of comments from Boley (1980).

As a result, a number of initiatives planned to address these problems were included in the budget of the National Science Foundation (NSF). Although the Reagan administration also resolved to retain and restore America's engineering competitiveness, the NSF's initiatives drew little support. This dilemma awaits resolution.

Donald Marlowe

See also Licensing and Certification; Professions Education.

REFERENCES

Artz, F. B. Development of Technical Education in France, 1500–1850. Cambridge, Mass.: MIT Press, 1966.

Boley, B. Issues in Engineering Education. Washington, D.C.: National Academy of Engineering, 1980.

Brittain, J. H. Engineers and the New South culture. Technology and Culture, 1977, 18, 175–201.

Calvert, M. A. Mechanical Engineers in America, 1830–1910. Baltimore: Johns Hopkins University Press, 1967.

Collins, W. L., & English, J. M. Educating Engineers for World Development. Washington, D.C.: American Society for Engineering Education, 1976. (ERIC Document Reproduction Service No. ED 121 623)

Comina, C. Guide to Engineering Education in Europe. Liège, Belgium: Ordina Editions, 1978.

Condit, K. H. History of the Engineering School of Princeton University. Princeton, N.J.: Princeton University Press, 1962.

Cooley, M. E. Scientific Blacksmith. New York: American Society of Mechanical Engineers, 1947.

Engineering Manpower Commission. The Demand for Engineers. New York: American Association of Engineering Societies, 1972.

Engineering Manpower Commission. Engineering and Technology Degrees, 1980. New York: American Association of Engineering Societies, 1980. (a)

Engineering Manpower Commission. Engineering Degree Statistics and Trends. New York: American Association of Engineering Societies, 1980. (b)

Finniston, M. Engineering the Future. London: Her Majesty's Stationery Office, 1980.

Fletcher, L., & Marlowe, D. E. The future of mechanical engineering education. Mechanical Engineering, 1981, 104.

Florman, S. C. Existential Pleasures of Engineering. New York: St. Martin's Press, 1976.

Gilbey, H. Arson Marston, Iowa State's First Dean of Engineering. Ames: Iowa State University, 1968.

Glower, D. R. A rational method for ranking engineering programs. Engineering Education, 1980, 70, 788–693.

Grayson, L. P. A brief history of engineering education in the United States. Engineering Education, 1977, 68, 246–264.

Grinter, L. E. Report on evaluation of engineering education. Journal of Engineering Education, 1955, 62, 40–66.

Grinter, L. E. Final Report: Engineering Technology Education Study. Washington, D.C.: American Society for Engineering Education, 1972.

Hammond, H. P. Engineering education after the war. Journal of Engineering Education, 1944, 34, 589–614.

Hancock, J. C. Review of Engineering and Engineering Technology Studies (REETS). Engineering Education, 1979, 70, 163–174.

Harrisberger, L. Experiential Learning in Engineering Education. Washington, D.C.: American Society for Engineering Education, 1976. (ERIC Document Reproduction Service No. ED 158 689)

Havemeyer, L., & Dudley, S. W. Engineering Heritage of Yale. New Haven, Conn.: Yale University Press, 1959.

Hufstedler, S., & Langenberg, D. N. Science and Engineering Education for the 1980s and Beyond. Washington, D.C.: U.S. Government Printing Office, 1980. (ERIC Document Reproduction Service No. ED 193-092)

Jones, R. C. Ethics, Professionalism, and Maintaining Competence. New York: American Society of Civil Engineers, 1977.

Klus, J. P., & Jones, J. A. Survey of Continuing Education Activities. Madison: University of Wisconsin, 1978. (ERIC Document Reproduction Service No. ED 167 805)

Knoll, H. B. Story of Purdue Engineering. Lafayette, Ind.: Purdue University, 1963.

Lancaster, O. Effective Technology and Learning. New York: Gordon Press, 1974.

Landis, F. A dynamic simulation model of engineering manpower needs. Engineering Education, 1980, 67, 218–225.

Mandel, H., & Shipley, J. Proud Past—Bright Future. Boulder: University of Colorado, 1966.

Mann, C. R. Study of Engineering Education. New York: Carnegie Foundation for the Advancement of Teaching, 1918.

Marlowe, D. E. Engineering Education: Issues and answers. Mechanical Engineering, 1980, 102, 24–27.

McGivern, J. C. First Hundred Years of Engineering Education in the United States. Spokane, Wash.: Gonzaga University Press, 1960.

Olmsted, S. W. Liberal learning for the engineer. Journal of Engineering Education, 1968, 59, 303–342. (ERIC Document Reproduction Service No. ED 028 705)

Rezneck, S. Education for a Technological Society. Troy, N.Y.: Rensselaer Polytechnic Institute, 1968.

Timoshenko, S. P. As I Remember. New York: Van Nostrand, 1968.

UNESCO. Directory of Engineering Education Institutions: Africa, Asia, Latin America. New York: Unipub, 1976.

Walker, E. A. Goals of Engineering Education. Washington, D.C.: American Society for Engineering Education, 1968. (ERIC Document Reproduction Service No. ED 029 798)

Wickenden, W. E. Report of Investigation of Engineering Education. Pittsburgh, Pa.: Society for the Promotion of Engineering Education, 1929.

ENGLISH LANGUAGE EDUCATION

"English language education" is but one of several umbrella labels that are applied to this complex field of teaching and learning. Variation both in terminology and in what that terminology denotes seems largely related to the ages of students served by a program. Elementary educators most often use the term "language arts" in reference to the skills of listening, speaking, reading, and writing that children learn as a means for sharing feelings, ideas, or information. The term "English," on the other hand, has traditionally been used at the secondary and college levels to describe a content subject or discipline that includes language, literature, and composition. Fortunately, one can find in the professional literature definitions, if not terms, that are sufficiently broad to accommodate professionals at any level. Judy (1981), for example, defines "English" as "*all* uses of language, from informal chatter to formal discussion, from short memos to long examination papers, from the 'language' of television to the language of computers" (p. 56); a program that is diffused throughout the school and the school day; and "a way of perceiving, knowing, learning, and becoming. English is not simply a matter of mastering the language, for language is a part of all aspects of human experience" (p. 57).

History. The history of English language education is a chronology less of its research than of significant dates marking its movements, conferences, publications, and thus its leaders. Though its roots span hundreds of years, the notion of English as a daily school subject at all educational levels derives in the main from the twentieth century. This section will first, then, describe a youthful profession, concentrating on its rise at the close of the nineteenth century through its curricular movements in the 1960s. The discussion of history will conclude with observations on the state of English language education at the writing of the fourth edition of this encyclopedia (Ebel, 1969).

Wars, economic crises, political changes, technological revolutions, and social reforms are reflected in this history. Perennial questions (e.g., "What is English?") dot it, right along with cyclical questions (e.g., "Why can't students read and write?") and contemporary queries (e.g., "How can computer technology be best applied to English language arts programs?"). The profession is not only young but restless as well. Its history records continuous stretching to meet new demands and growth toward the solution of lingering problems.

The history of English language education is revealed through dozens of dissertations, countless unpublished records, out-of-print reports, and numerous published articles, all of which explore segments of the profession's past. Those interested in such study will find their way made immeasurably easier because of the systematic and detailed work of Applebee (1974) and Hook (1979). Though Applebee focuses on the high school and on literature, the epochs he discusses are germane in most instances to all instructional levels and to all of English education. Hook's review encompasses much of the history of the profession, beginning with the founding of the National Council of Teachers of English (NCTE) in 1911 and continuing through 1978. The book describes the Council's beginnings, discusses its efforts to improve the teaching of English over the decades, explores its concern with and response to national problems, and speculates about its future. The importance of the NCTE to the general field of English education is that it is an umbrella organization, one that counts among its members individuals at all levels of instruction and one whose diverse publications respond to the general as well as the specialized interests of those in the field.

A final source of importance to historians is *English Journal,* the secondary school journal of the NCTE, first published in 1912. Two annotated indexes published in 1964 and 1972 guide the researcher to specific articles and two special issues (Judy, 1979a, 1979b) provide a historical overview.

Prior to the last decade of the nineteenth century, three instructional traditions vied for dominance in shaping English as a subject taught in schools: (1) an ethical tradition that placed its emphasis on moral and cultural development, (2) a classical tradition of intellectual discipline and close textual study, and (3) a nonacademic tradition largely concerned with enjoyment and appreciation (Applebee, 1974).

In 1892 the National Education Association appointed a Committee of Ten to arrange subject area conferences in nine fields—conferences intended to consider secondary school problems caused by college entrance requirements. Helping to establish the place of English in the schools was its designation as one of the nine fields and the subsequent *Report of the Committee of Ten . . .* (1894) which unified views about the teaching of English and brought together its many component parts.

A professional identity and independence for English teachers began to emerge with the appearance of early books (Hinsdale, 1896; Chubb, 1902; Carpenter, Baker, & Scott, 1903) and journal articles. Professional identity was further abetted by the formation of English clubs, the first being the New England Association of Teachers of English in 1901.

The NCTE was founded in 1911 by James Fleming Hosic and others "to create a representative body, which could reflect and render effective the will of the various local associations and of individual teachers, and, by securing concert of action, greatly improve the conditions surrounding English work" (NCTE, 1912, p. 30). Early meetings resulted in three decisions that remain in effect today: to work actively to sponsor local affiliate organizations, to form working committees on varied topics, and to establish an official journal, the *English Journal.*

A report by Hosic (1917) brought to a close a long-standing battle by high school teachers against college entrance examinations as a controlling influence on their courses. It declared the independence of the high school, stating that a range of course content should be provided to meet the needs of varied students, and that preparation for life, not for college, was the function of the high school.

The NCTE Committee on the Place and Function of English in American Life (Clapp, 1926) surveyed 22,000 people in a variety of social positions to determine the uses to which they were putting skills learned in English classes. The committee's report was reflective of its time in that it emphasized the functional uses of English in its definitions, content, scope, aims, and recommendations for curriculum. It endorsed such activities as interviewing, conversing, public speaking, writing, reading, and listening.

A pattern curriculum educators could follow as they tailored kindergarten through college English programs to the experiential needs of students was provided by Hatfield (1935). This synthesis of the best in current practice urged that units be carefully developed and socially useful, that they provide not only the kinds of experience people have in life but desirable experiences that they might otherwise miss. The widely used report was followed in 1939 by examples of classroom practices (Broening).

In 1945 a thirty-one-member NCTE Commission on the English Curriculum was organized to design a curriculum from preschool through graduate school. The Commission, between the years 1954 and 1963, issued five volumes. The third volume (1956), for example, reflects postwar concern that curriculum be derived from the needs of students in their local communities. Standing in stark contrast to the emphasis on experience was Warriner's text (1951), which emphasized the "basic" structure of English and remains pervasive in its influence.

In 1958 twenty-eight teachers met and defined thirty-five basic issues in the teaching of English. They called for a sequential and cumulative curriculum from kindergarten through graduate school (Stone, 1961). In radical opposition to the progressives, they declared English a discipline, a body of specific knowledge to be preserved and transmitted. A curriculum, therefore, was to be based on subject matter rather than on the needs and interests of individual students.

Beginning in 1960, the NCTE extended its long record of involvement with research in English language education by establishing a Research Foundation. In 1963 it inaugurated a research monograph series and the David H. Russell Distinguished Research Award. In 1967 its Standing Committee on Research founded the journal *Research in the Teaching of English*. Finally, in 1970, the Council bestowed its first Promising Researcher Awards.

Publication of *The National Interest and the Teaching of English* (Committee on National Interest, 1961) spurred federal interest in English by arguing the importance of English to the national welfare and documenting the need for reform in English instruction. Subsequent federal support for research, teaching, summer institutes, and curriculum study centers was provided under the U.S. Office of Education Cooperative Research Program's "Project English" in 1961 and the National Defense Education Act in 1964. Project English, a network of research and demonstration centers, enabled its participants to explore all aspects of English curriculum and to emerge with a variety of "new English" programs. From 1965 to 1967 the NDEA provided materials, equipment, supervision, and stipends for teachers attending summer and year-long institutes administered by colleges and universities and focusing on various facets of English.

In the mid-sixties, a report of the College Entrance Examination Board (see Commission on English, 1965) proposed standards of achievement in English and ways to meet them. It recommended a curriculum based on language, literature, and composition; devoted considerable attention to the training and working conditions of English teachers; and reflected much of the curriculum work developed under Project English.

Fifty specialists in the teaching of English at the elementary, secondary, and college levels in both American and British schools met at Dartmouth College in 1966 to discuss common problems. At the month-long seminar, the British exerted considerable influence on their American colleagues, largely through their concern for the language of the child, emphasis on informal discussion in instruction, use of improvisational drama, and encouragement of imaginative writing (Dixon, 1967; Muller, 1967).

Though the fourth edition of the *Encyclopedia of Educational Research* contained seven articles relating to subsets of English language education ("English Composition," "English Literature," "Handwriting," "Listening," "Reading," "Speech," and "Spelling"), no article addressed the field as a whole. Nevertheless, one can identify generic ideas about the state of the profession in 1969 from a survey of its component parts.

Within the entries one finds expression of a continuing confusion in terminology (e.g., "English," "grammar," "composition") and a struggle among ideologies. Issues mentioned then remain today: teaching load, evaluation, and teacher preparation and certification. Emergent research projects, such as the National Assessment of Educational Progress and the International Educational Achievement Studies, and even emergent research fields, such as radio, television, and film, appear far more mature now. In the entries are calls for research in English education which the seventies began to address, including establishment of interdisciplinary liaisons and explorations of the contributions of computers. Finally, the 1969 encyclopedia entries made it clear that the potential for research in English education was limited in numerous ways; in some measure those limitations remain.

Theory. Education in English language arts borrows its theories from a range of disciplines, from numerous theorists, and from innumerable translators of theory. It has been affected by theoreticians inside and outside of education whose overlapping concerns are the nature of human development, of language, and of learning and teaching. Representing that full range of theoretical influence and the intricacies of its interrelationships is beyond the scope of this discussion; it touches only on the highlights, and the categories used here are artificial.

Human development. Piaget (1973) was concerned with general questions about the nature of knowledge and of human intellectual development. His broad, highly influential, and routinely cited theories are linked with language education programs involving process or activity, rather than product or content, language programs emphasizing the act of writing, informal discussions, dramatic play, and exploratory responses to books. In Piaget's view, knowledge does not come to us ready-made from the outside; we must construct it. We do so slowly, over many years, not simply by reacting to our environment but by acting on it as well. A hallmark of Piaget's theory is the course of continuous development he describes, a series of fixed stages through which human beings progress at variable rates. Human growth means the ability to deal with progressively wider environments, to think about that which is more and more remote, to be less and less egocentric. As we grow, we both assimilate (incorporate new information within an existing framework) and accommodate (adapt our behavior to the environment). Though Piaget concedes that language becomes increasingly important as intelligence develops, he does not view language as the source of thought. For him, thought originates in action.

L. S. Vygotsky, a Russian-born psychologist and educator, paid tribute to Piaget but differed from him in at least two important ways. First, he had a greater interest in the relationship between instruction and development. He viewed learning as, optimally, a cooperation between adult and child: "What the child can do in cooperation today he can do alone tomorrow" (1962, p. 104). Second, more than Piaget, with his focus on child egocentricity, Vygotsky considered speech as communication, as a social event, not only for adults but for very young children as well. Vygotsky's theories rest on observations of children learning to talk and to solve problems. He studied interrelationships among language components, concluding, for example, that the development of writing does not repeat the development of speaking—which he considered a separate linguistic function—but helps children rise to a higher level of speech development.

Vygotsky's theory of the relationship of thought and language is also a theory of intellectual development and a theory of education. His analysis concludes that "thought and language . . . are the key to the nature of human consciousness. Words play a central part not only in the development of thought but in the historical growth of consciousness as a whole. A word is a microcosm of human consciousness" (p 153). Understanding others' thoughts means understanding their motivations—their desires, needs, interests, and emotions.

Luria (1976) describes research conducted in collaboration with Vygotsky. Both stressed that mental development must be viewed as a historical process in which the child's social and nonsocial environment induces the development of higher mental functions—historical in the sense that for Luria word meanings provide the child with the distilled results of the history of society. Luria saw language as a support for higher cognitive functions, and writing, particularly, as a unique way of learning.

Linguistics. Noam Chomsky was not the first to recognize that language is based on a system of rules that determines the interpretation of its many sentences. But it was he who revolutionized the scientific study of language with the publication of *Syntactic Structures* in 1957. His construction of a system of generative grammar for describing natural languages developed out of an interest in mathematics and modern logic. Though there exist today many schools of linguistics, and though not everyone accepts Chomsky's theory of transformational generative grammar, his influence extends to all disciplines concerned with the human capacity for language. This influence is as evident in esoteric publications on theoretical linguistics as it is in language arts textbooks for elementary school children. Chomsky emphasizes the ability of children to derive structural regularities (grammatical rules) from the utterances of those around them and then to make use of those same regularities to construct utterances they have never heard before. The implication for educators is clear: bathe children in a language-rich environment.

The major impetus for a cognitive approach to linguistics came from generative transformational linguistics. Two significant aspects of the approach are (1) its two-level conception of language—its physical manifestation, or "surface structure," and its meaning, or "deep structure"—and (2) its stress on the creative aspects of language, grammar being a finite set of rules for generating an infinite number of sentences. A major and continuing influence of transformational linguistics is its focus on meaning.

Of the many branches of linguistics, psycholinguistics for the past three decades has become progressively more significant to English educators. By combining insights from both psychology and linguistics, psycholinguistics offered a new way to view language processes. Particularly prevalent has been its application to reading, with the consequence that all manner of reading instruction programs now carry the descriptor "psycholinguistic."

Miller (1965), in a classic article, cites seven aspects of human language anyone should understand before doing psycholinguistic research: (1) not all physical features of speech are significant for vocal communication, and not all significant features of speech have a physical representation; (2) the meaning of an utterance should not be confused with its reference; (3) the meaning of an utterance is not the linear sum of the meanings of the words that constitute it; (4) the syntactic structure of a sentence imposes groupings that govern the interactions between the meanings of the words in that sentence; (5) there is no limit to the number of sentences or the number of meanings that can be expressed; (6) a description of a language and a description of a language user must be kept distinct; and (7) there is a large biological component to the human capacity for articulate speech (pp. 15–20).

Since the early 1960s linguists have repeatedly acknowledged that many important questions related to language change, education, and public policy could not be answered without information on the social factors affecting speech. Sociolinguistics, the study of language in its social setting, or the study of the social basis for verbal communication, is yet another branch of linguistics that affects English language education. Scholarly interest manifests itself through sustained empirical research into the myriad ways by which environment influences language. This interest continues a trend noted ten years ago, when Gumperz and Hymes (1972) cited a growing number of conferences, interdisciplinary symposia, and monographs attempting to stimulate behavioral research on stylistics and expressive speech, intrasocietal diversity of language, attitudes about language, and language politics and policy. Today, learning the conventions of communication is considered to be at least as important as learning the conventions of grammar. Hymes (1974) is credited with elaborating a concept of "communicative competence"—competence in those ways of interacting with others that are culturally acceptable. Labov drew upon sociology, anthropology, and psychology to develop creative techniques for studying linguistic variation among individuals (1972b). He argues, for example, that black vernacular exists as a separate and independent dialect of English (1972a).

The field of linguistics has changed radically since the work of such structuralists as Fries (1952) and Francis (1958), whose method was to sample language as spoken and to describe its phonological and grammatical patterns. The structuralists' belief that language is a set of habits acquired from the learner's social group and their lack of interest in semantics, or the meanings speakers intend to convey, has shifted to a view that holds meaning to be central. Theoretical linguists like Fillmore (1968) on case grammar and Chafe (1970) on meaning-structure grammar declared semantics as basic to any theoretical model of language. With the emphasis on semantics, pragmatics has become more important, since meaning is seen as being dependent in large measure on the situations in which speech acts occur. Research on language acquisition has also emphasized the centrality of semantics. Brown (1973) found the early utterances of children to be more readily explicable in terms of "semantic roles," such as agent, action, instrument, patient, and experiencer. Others, such as Halliday (1975), emphasize language functions and analyze utterances accordingly as instrumental, regulatory, interactional, personal, heuristic, imaginative, representational, and ritual.

Learning and teaching. In opposition to Chomskian notions of language learning is the behaviorist theory of Skinner (1957, 1974), which posits that language is acquired through a form of conditioning dependent on reinforcement or reward. (For Chomsky's view of the limitations of behaviorism, see his review of Skinner's *Verbal Behavior* published in 1959.) Papers by this influential and controversial psychologist began to influence English language education over fifty years ago, when he first demonstrated the success of behaviorist psychology in explaining, predicting, and modifying animal behavior—success based on an experiment involving the bar-pressing activity of a rat placed in a so-called Skinner box. Food bar experiments with rats led to a theory of human learning involving behavioral control through operant conditioning meth-

ods. Skinnerian influence can be seen in those aspects of the English curriculum in which program developers can define or have defined content convergently, have isolated curriculum components into subskills, have created variants of programmed instruction, and/or have developed behavioral objectives. Subskill approaches can be found, for example, in which writing is reduced to editing skills and reading to phonics skills. Undoubtedly, there are areas of human behavior to which the behaviorist model applies. But many English educators, as well as their parent organization, the National Council of Teachers of English, have vigorously opposed inflicting the model on instructional areas for which objectives cannot be specified in behavioral terms or evaluated by direct observation and measurement of student behavior.

Gagné (1970) has identified eight hierarchically arranged orders of learning that must be taken into account in any full description of learning: signal learning, stimulus-response learning, chaining, verbal association, discrimination, concept learning, rule learning, and problem solving. He urges that instruction be governed by the kind of learning to be accomplished, and he requires that learning be characterized by a "change in performance." His work has permitted teachers to break complex components of English language education into successively simpler components, to present the parts in an orderly way, and to reinforce appropriate responses.

Rogers represents a radical departure from those who advocate the imposition of learning from without. In his chief work on education, Rogers (1969) disparages teaching, stating that all learning comes from within; since it is self-directed, another person may only facilitate its acquisition. Rogers was especially popular in the 1960s, when educators and lay critics of the schools banded together in the name of affective education to rail against the traditional school curriculum, which they regarded as being pseudoscientific and antihumanistic. The British further popularized his views in 1966 at the Anglo-American Conference at Dartmouth. There Americans learned that the British were less concerned with the subject matter than with students' being able to use language to respond to their life experiences.

Of current import to English language learning is the work of neuropsychologists, neurophysiologists, and biochemists. Ornstein (1972), for example, studied the structure of the brain and the specialized functions of its left and right sides; Steiner (1975) studied learning associated with changed patterns of protein synthesis in particular portions of the cortex; and Gardner (1975) studied, among other matters, how the site of brain injury affects the ability of aphasics to write. Determining the role of hemisphericity in learning has most concerned English language educators during the last decade, with some regarding Ornstein's work as established fact and others as useful metaphor (Lloyd-Jones, 1978). Many hold hope that understanding of human neuropsychology and anatomy will someday provide insights into the language functioning not only of the mentally impaired but also of those whose language develops normally.

Among instructional theorists, English curriculum developers have turned for more than two decades to Bruner for answers to problems of sequence. His 1960 book contains the now familiar quote: "We begin with the hypothesis that any subject can be taught effectively in some intellectually honest form to any child at any stage of development" (p. 13). A Brunerian curriculum would include the structure of English, and that structure would be developed "spirally"—that is, central ideas would recur again and again at progressively higher levels of complexity. Through inductive thinking, students would progress from an initial intuitive knowledge to an explicit formulation of basic principles.

Bloom (1976) sets forth his theory and research for the concept of mastery learning, yet English educators know him best by his explicit formulation of ways students are expected to be changed by the educative process. Bloom's *Taxonomy of Educational Objectives* (1956) is a device for classifying educational goals for students in kindergarten through grade 12. Six major classes of objectives are ordered from simple to complex: knowledge, comprehension, application, analysis, synthesis, and evaluation.

Three other theorists continue to influence curriculum workers today. Havighurst (1948) affected curriculum development in many fields, including English. His work outlines major stages of life from preschool through graduate school, identifying for each stage important and appropriate characteristics, needs, learning outcomes, and activities. Tyler (1950) reduced decisions about curriculum planning to four basic questions: What educational purposes should the school seek to attain? What educational experiences can be provided that are likely to attain these purposes? How can these educational experiences be effectively organized? and How can we determine whether these purposes are being attained? Finally, Taba (1932), strongly influenced by Gestalt psychologists, antedated Bruner in insisting that the curriculum be concerned with large organizing ideas—ideas she termed more powerful because they subsumed many small discrete elements.

Recent Trends. Squire (1977) observed, "Language and literature inevitably reflect the values of a culture, and the teaching of language and literature inevitably reflects the conflicts and complexities of the culture in which the teaching occurs" (p. xvi). It is the cultural values, conflicts, and complexities that shaped English language education during the 1970s, the professional response to those forces, and the research strands carried into, through, and beyond the decade that are the subjects of this discussion of recent trends.

Influences on curriculum. The major concerns of the English language arts curriculum today are reflected in such recurring topics as the impact and use of television; international studies (Australia, Canada, Denmark, England, India); special populations (women, physically handicapped, ethnic minorities); media studies; textbooks (de-

pendence on, censorship of); teacher workload; middle schools; doublespeak and officialese; parents as educators; behavioral objectives; electives/mini-courses; back-to-basics; minimum standards and competency testing; standard English issues; teaching grammar; integrating language arts; career education; computer applications; film; gifted and talented; and accountability. Elements of this list can be related to the politics of the 1970s. Watergate, for example, led to an examination of curriculum content on several fronts. Two resolutions passed by the membership of the NCTE in 1971 urged the Council to "study dishonest and inhumane uses of language and literature by advertisers" and to "study the relation of language to public policy, to keep track of, publicize and combat distortion by public officials, candidates for office, political commentators, and all those who transmit through the mass media." Member interest in language and politics led to the formation of an NCTE Committee on Public Doublespeak.

Economic conditions during the 1970s also affected the profession. Undoubtedly, legislation such as California's Proposition 13 and Massachusetts's Proposition 2.5 is increasingly affecting the teaching of English language arts by closing school libraries and cutting budgets for supplies and support services for teachers.

From a content analysis of the ten volumes of *Language Arts* published in the 1970s, Jensen (1979) derived two key topics, reformation and accountability: "If there is doubt that the early 70s reflected a desire for reformation, this journal can provide necessary documentation. Dozens of articles demonstrated federal interest and efforts to support change in the nation's schools. Between 1970 and 1975 more authors touched on the elimination of illiteracy among the economically disadvantaged and on equal opportunity for all than on any other themes. Paralleling in the 1970s the rhetoric of reformation was the rhetoric of accountability, which provided a clear example of how changing times affect language instruction; of how the school and the language are social entities directly related to the conditions, values, and politics of the society. From the decade's beginning to its twilight the pages of this journal have been splattered with the words *accountability, behavioral objectives, performance contracting, voucher systems, national assessment, standardized tests, PERT charts, teaching modules, systems approaches, C/PBTE, management systems, subskills,* and (what else?) *back to basics*" (p. 601).

The topics of reformation and accountability reflect concern for the failure of students to learn essential skills, a concern grounded in the professional literature, which abounds with figures on illiteracy reported by testing organizations, polling companies, government agencies, and educational institutions.

By 1972 the popular press began to publicize a decline in Scholastic Aptitude Test (SAT) scores. This decline, first observed in 1963, was taken by the public as an objective index of the declining performance of schools. Forces outside the schools, aroused by the media, responded *en masse* with a call for still another back-to-basics movement.

Kaestle (1981) provides an instructive review of the history of literacy. He reminds us that widespread functional illiteracy is nothing new in America, that authors such as Copperman (1978) merely rediscovered illiteracy in the tradition of numerous others.

One positive thread is the progressively narrowing gap in literacy between social groups. For example, results from the National Assessment of Educational Progress released in 1981 show that the population of black 9-year-olds reduced the difference between themselves and the population as a whole by 9.9 percentage points. On the test of literal and inferential comprehension plus reference skills, 9-year-olds, in general, improved 3.0 percentage points after 1971. Nonetheless, as Kaestle reminds us, part of the challenge of today's illiteracy is that it remains disproportionately a problem of those who are poor, nonwhite, or immigrants.

Beginning at mid-decade and continuing today, public concern over declining test scores has affected the teaching of English. Smith (1979) places these effects into four categories: demands by the public to return to fundamentals and tradition; demands in some communities for fundamental schools (in 1975/76 there were no more than a dozen public fundamental schools in the country; by 1978/79 there were over a thousand); legislation in at least three-fourths of the states requiring some form of "competency testing" in basic skills; and a return to textbooks of an earlier era.

Glatthorn (1980) presents seven developments in the profession that deserve consideration by anyone making decisions about the English language arts curriculum today: (1) the increasing power of a stable teaching profession, (2) a shortage of discretionary funds in school district budgets, (3) continuing technological change (e.g., home and school computers, video-cassettes/discs), (4) the importance of the state's role in curriculum development (e.g., mandated courses and tests), (5) the increasing body of knowledge about the processes of teaching and learning, (6) continuing dissatisfaction with the schools expressed by parents and the general public, and (7) the growing divergence between what we think is happening in the classroom and what is actually taking place.

Response of the profession. English language arts teaching in the 1970s was changed less by internal forces than by forces from without. The profession was nudged to respond to parental pressures for reform and forced to respond to legislation and court orders. The response consumed considerable professional concentration and energy.

Congress has shown concern for school dropouts and has financed the Great Cities Improvement Program, Title I of the Elementary and Secondary Education Act, and Head Start, which were intended to increase the likelihood that students would stay in school longer. Congress also funded the Job Corps, established in 1964 under the Eco-

nomic Opportunity Act for the purpose of increasing the employability of disadvantaged youth. The major focus of the Job Corps was teaching basic skills—defined as handwriting, spelling, letter writing, composition, grammar, punctuation, vocabulary, usage, and reference skills—to its 90 percent male clientele. Through taxes, citizens supported Project 100,000, begun in 1966 by the Department of Defense because of the influx into the armed services of men with poor language and reading skills. Tax money funded Right to Read, initiated because of the numbers of children having difficulty learning to read, many of whom were from lower socioeconomic and minority groups. Established by the United States Office of Education, Right to Read set the goal of 99 percent literacy by 1980 for people 16 and under and 90 percent literacy for people over age 16. Federal assistance was implemented through state and local school boards for staff development, program analysis, information dissemination, and establishing pilot programs and regional Right to Read sites. Finally, and more recently, state boards of education, expressing concern over the failure of schools to teach minimal competencies, have financed statewide competency-testing programs. Maryland, California, Oregon, Florida, New York, and Texas, among other states, are now stipulating the abilities students must have acquired before being graduated from high school.

Some of the recent history of English language education has been written by the courts. The 1968 Bilingual Education Act, for example, caused far-reaching developments during the decade. The HEW Office of Civil Rights determined that compliance with the Supreme Court's 1974 *Lau* decision requires schools to adopt bilingual education—the use of both the child's native language and English as media of instruction.

Court decisions have related not only to language differences but also to differences among varieties of English. The judge in an Ann Arbor, Michigan, schools decision found that teachers' attitudes toward home language caused a psychological barrier to learning; he ordered the school district to develop a plan for sensitizing and training teachers to reduce this barrier.

Taxpayers' rebellions, worries about test scores, and fault-finding with schools have been answered by efforts to define literacy, to identify levels of competence one needs to communicate effectively, and to identify basic skills—with a proportion of the profession thinking such efforts are nothing less than presumptuous and foolhardy.

In 1978 twelve professional associations expressed their collective interest in "a renewed commitment to a more complete and more fulfilling education for all" (Organizations for the Essentials of Education). Their brief report is a reasoned response both to those who simplistically call for a return to the basics, and to those with simplistic responses to that call. A central concept within the statement is that skills cannot develop in isolation from content.

One of the most widespread manifestations during the 1970s of a curriculum based on student needs and principles of language growth was the elective English program in the secondary school. A wide range of short courses replaced English I, II, III, and IV, with their common course content of language, literature, and composition intended for all students. The revolution was never complete, however; electives were discussed at conventions and on the pages of professional journals, while Warriner's text (1951) remained in many classrooms. Hillocks (1972) surveyed English elective programs, finding that few featured systematic evaluation but that their effects on teacher and student attitudes were positive. He concluded, nevertheless, that electives provided no advantage over traditional programs in terms of student growth in measurable cognitive areas and that many courses paralleled traditional offerings and appeared to reflect teacher rather than student interests. Meanwhile, as negative public reaction to declining SAT scores reached the schools, educators were being forced to concern themselves with efficiency, assessment, quantification, and behavioral objectives— concepts not well suited to a "new English."

There remain educators who have not retreated to conservatism, who do not blame "new English" for test score declines, who readily point to the success of new methods of teaching writing or to paperback book programs. Here and there one can find residue of innovations from the 1960s, such as a revived interest in the gifted and talented and a fuller curriculum, including contemporary and adolescent literature, science fiction, creative drama, film study, and humanities. But generally, now is not a time for emphasis on experimentation, personal growth, classroom creativity, or curricular breadth.

The seventies closed in a conflict of opposing forces: the cognitive emphases of Bruner, the behaviorist influence of Skinner, and the personal growth curriculum that grew out of Dartmouth and was later recommended in the much-quoted Bullock report from Britain (1976). Of considerable significance was the work of Moffett (1968a, 1968b), who articulated the relationships between theory and practice and produced perhaps the closest approximation of a unified theory of teaching English. Moffett urged educators to look to the structure of the student rather than the structure of the subject matter. His texts, widely used in teacher education, are student-centered and based on a developmental theory of discourse and a commitment to language interaction and production.

Recent research. If curriculum, classroom, and text were less than dynamic during the 1970s, the research community can be looked to for some measure of consolation. Despite the bureaucratic imposition of movements that constrained the profession, there were those who thought and wrote expansively about what English language arts teaching and research can be; who saw commonalities in all learners; who recognized students' vast untutored talents; and who valued such immeasurable qualities as those found in imaginative expression and fine literature. Seeds planted in the 1970s, and in some cases long before, continue to be nourished in the 1980s.

Among such seeds are a growing focus on the learner, an appreciation of children's varied language skills, and a recognition of the need to know both students and language. Researchers have begun to document the language abilities of students. They have visited their subjects' homes, listened to classroom conversations, and recorded language on the playground and the street. They have verified, for example, children's mastery during the preschool years of thousands of words, the sounds, and the basic sentence patterns of the native language. A focus on language-in-process, which took hold in the 1960s, drew attention to the uses of language and resulted during the 1970s in many informant-based language studies, studies involving minimal disturbance of the transaction between user and process.

Recognition grows that the roots of language lie outside the school; that the classroom is but one place where language continues on its lifelong course of development; that teachers should be more concerned with language experience than with language study; that language knowledge grows from language use.

One can find a measure of interest in language learning in other cultures. The observation of the International Year of the Child in 1979 provided opportunities for American researchers and practitioners to become informed about how students meet reading, writing, and other language arts in England, Denmark, New Zealand, Australia, and elsewhere.

Educators have become increasingly aware of how the theories and methods of linguists, neuroscientists, psychologists, philosophers, anthropologists, and sociologists, among others, illuminate the ways in which language is learned and used. Other linkages of continuing interest are those among the language arts themselves as well as those between English language arts and the rest of the school curriculum. Listening, speaking, reading and writing are indeed not independent skills, are not used in isolation in social contexts. So too is there realization that language constitutes a significant part of the school day. Inasmuch as human beings do not talk about talking, read about reading, or write about writing, language cannot be learned or researched in an environment void of content.

One can also find evidence of growing interorganizational cooperation in solving problems related to language learning. In 1977, for example, the Interorganizational Committee, composed of representatives from seven national professional organizations, produced a statement of concerns and recommendations about reading before the first grade. The statement expresses dismay with the growing number of highly structured reading programs in prekindergarten and kindergarten classes and the extent to which achievement measures dictate program content and goals.

The following appear to be among the continuing themes of the 1980s: the curriculum should reflect a multimedia environment; theory building and subsequent curriculum building can be undertaken through small sample observational studies; what in the past was regarded as error may be untutored attempts to seek systems; process is as important as product; language learning is intradisciplinary and interdisciplinary; language learning extends from birth to death; and meaning is at least as important as form.

O'Donnell (1981) analyzed recent research in English language arts by surveying the articles published in *Research in the Teaching of English* from 1967 to 1977. He reported that 30 percent of the articles dealt with teaching English at the secondary level, 17 percent with college English, and 21 percent with elementary and preschool English. The remainder was unclassifiable or dealt with multiple grade levels. Thirty-nine percent of the studies were concerned with pupil characteristics (abilities, attitudes, etc.), 14 percent with teaching method, and 12.5 percent with curriculum and materials. Nine percent investigated evaluation procedures and an equal number research methods. Twenty-nine percent of the articles focused on composition, 24 percent on language, and 15 percent on literature. Twelve percent were concerned with reading. Only one study dealt with media and only one with drama. Almost half the studies were descriptive (including six case studies); one in seven was quasi-experimental. Only six of 176 articles published were true experimental studies and only one was a historical study. Ninety percent of the authors were associated with colleges or universities.

An ongoing contribution to the research community is a monograph series begun in 1963 by the NCTE. Most of the twenty volumes published to date deal directly or indirectly with aspects of language development or language analysis. Loban's *The Language of Elementary School Children* (1963) was an impressive first volume. Using a variety of original analytic procedures, he studied the oral and written language of over 300 children as that language changed from the time they entered kindergarten through their first six years of elementary school. In 1976 Loban followed his subjects' language development through grade 12. Other reports in the series that have had a demonstrable effect on the nature of research in English language education are on the subjects of response to literature, grammatical structures in writing, language attitudes, oral English, the effect of transformational grammar study on writing, transformational analysis of children's syntax, sentence combining, drama, forecasting the future of English education, the composing process, teaching a second language, children's poetry preferences, children's categorization of speech sounds, and understanding the appeal of fairy tales.

The most recent report in the series is by Purves (1981). His subjects were public school students aged 10, 14, and 18, teachers of English, and school administrators. Students took tests of reading comprehension and completed questionnaires on their backgrounds, interests, and opinions. Information on teachers was derived from a questionnaire.

The analysis, based upon data from a study by the International Association for the Evaluation of Educational Achievement published in 1973, reported that American students, as a group, performed creditably in comparison with other nationalities. Purves's aim was to secure profiles of students and teachers who achieve in the classroom, as well as those who fail to realize their potential, so that he could trace relationships with significance for teachers, curriculum planners, and teacher educators. The study yielded findings such as these:

1. The context students bring to school learning of reading and literature (through access to stimulating books and adult language at home) strongly influences their ability to benefit from existing school English programs.
2. A significant number of school English programs are unimaginative, consisting largely of busywork. They keep low achievers quiet but do not develop their ability to reason, make connections, analyze, or actively involve themselves in reading, writing, and other sustained uses of language.
3. A disturbing number of teachers of English appear to regard teaching as a temporary activity, do not keep up with new knowledge in their field, and, in their classroom practices, follow the line of least resistance.

These findings are reminiscent of a major study by Squire and Applebee (1966) of 158 high schools that seemed to have outstanding English programs. The researchers reported that more than one-half of class time was consumed by the teaching of literature, with little effort being made by teachers to integrate the English language arts. Lecture and recitation predominated; small-group activities and use of audiovisual aids were seldom observed. Though the authors reported evidence of much sound teaching in college preparatory programs, they also noted obvious weaknesses in programs for terminal students.

Research Problems. Just as English language education shares a theoretical base with other curriculum areas, so does it share a number of research problems. The field lacks a general, unifying theory; must contend with a slow-growing, multifaceted, context-bound phenomenon called language; depends upon assessment tools that are less than adequate; counts a small segment of the profession among its community of researchers; and disseminates its research findings to consumers in ways that leave a continuing gap between theory and practice.

English educators have nevertheless held high respect for the promise of research, even when they have found its manifestations wanting. Henry (1966) asked: "Why all this reliance on research in the improvement of English teaching . . . ? Education, like politics or religion or economics, must have recourse to some form of authority to lend stability to it as an institution. Education at present has no Supreme Court, no Vatican Council" (p. 230).

Theoretical base. In an age of increasingly sophisticated analytical tools and revolutionary possibilities for computer applications, a major problem of research in English education is less its execution or its reporting than its conception. Henry's harsh assessment (1966) was that until a major unifying theory of the field is developed within which various research tasks in teaching may be conducted, research in English teaching will have no real importance. Indeed, the call for practice deriving from a comprehensive theory appears timeless. Lyman (1929) wrote: "The objectives of instruction in English are as yet vague, uncertain, and far from agreed upon" (p. 69).

Yet, thanks to federal largess from the fifties to the late seventies, research and program development has proceeded at a frantic pace, as though there were theories being applied. For example, though no agreement exists on a hierarchical construct of skills, "management systems" are widely used in the teaching of reading. Pearson and Johnson (1975), in a review of several systems, termed them naive psycholinguistically; too concerned with skill at the expense of interest; unsupported by theory in their advocacy of sequenced, separable reading skills; deplorable in their assembly-line underpinnings; of questionable validity; and absurd in their notion of "mastery."

The nature of language. At least three characteristics of language itself add to the difficulty of undertaking research in English language education: language growth occurs slowly; language is a complex of interrelated components; and language is context-bound.

Changes in the significant abilities associated with achievement in English language arts occur slowly. Experimental studies, therefore, with treatments lasting only a few weeks or months are likely to result in conclusions of no significant difference.

A blend of science and art, skills and aesthetics, the multiple interrelated parts of English present a challenge for researchers, but less so than do the unpredictable behaviors of the human users of language. A curriculum field with many interrelated parts presents a problem to any researcher and a danger to the one who attempts to isolate one component for study. One can find in the research ample precedent for studies that artificially fragment language use, focus upon a single component as though it existed apart from others, or are undertaken without an effort to examine the influence of related disciplines. The researcher can avoid duplication and advance knowledge only through a broad perspective of the discipline and a perspective on related disciplines.

The components of the English language are qualitatively diverse, and one would expect resulting research to reflect this diversity. But there exist also great differences in the *quality* of scholarly attention devoted to the different segments of the field. While no single area could be called "overresearched," some areas clearly evidence neglect. The skill of decoding and syntactic aspects of linguistic development have been heavily studied. Identifying and teaching "basics," the importance of creative drama, and multimedia approaches to teaching are generously represented in the literature but in a testimonial vein, without research to back up claims. The effects of and response to instructional technology, handwriting, listening, and speaking have received scant attention recently.

Finally, English education research is made more difficult by the reality that language is context-bound and therefore subject to multiple influences. Complete control of the variables that can affect outcomes of research is clearly impossible. While many designs could be made tighter, excessive efforts to tighten operational plans yield studies that produce only trivial results. Language arts may, in fact, be even more subject to environmental contamination than other subjects. How does a researcher, for example, control for television exposure in answering a question such as "How are nonprint media affecting mastery of language?"

To be valid, research should measure the attainment of language-related goals in natural linguistic contexts. The success of a person's effort to write or speak is subject to the demands of a specific audience in a specific setting. Writers should address their thoughts to a known audience; readers should be provided passages of sufficient length to establish a context. Yet most traditional measures of language growth fail in the difficult task of accounting for context.

Schools are only one environment for observing and assessing students' language. Added to their artificiality as a context is the overwhelming number of complex interacting relationships in the classroom: students, teacher, subject matter, setting, instructional resources, and so on. In experimental studies, especially methods comparisons, a popular way to manage these factors systematically has been to focus only on treatment differences. This approach to the complexities of research on classroom instruction has tended to yield inconsistent or contradictory results when studies have been replicated in even slightly different contexts.

Researchers, finally, must take into account the prevailing skills, attitudes, and methods of English teachers, as well the pressures being exerted on them. If, for example, the dominant curricular emphasis in a school is that of "covering the basics," research carried on in a classroom governed by this priority must take the controlling principle into account.

Assessment tools. The results of some research in language education are suspect because of inadequate efforts to develop valid and reliable measuring instruments. As Squire (1969) reported, "Until better instruments become available, studies with clear implications for teaching are not likely to emerge" (p. 466).

Concern continues to be expressed that present instruments often have built-in sociocultural biases, that they reflect middle-class standards of language rather than the diversity of society, and that insufficient effort has been expended to create culture-fair instruments.

The many components of English require several kinds of measures. Formal assessment methods, such as standardized tests, have received far more attention in the literature than informal methods, such as naturalistic observation, though the latter are becoming increasingly popular, most notably in studies of the writing process. The problem with formal measures is that they have traditionally focused on the simplest and least subtle aspects of English instruction. The Task Force on Measurement and Evaluation in the Study of English of the NCTE (1975) listed sixteen facets of English. Only six of those facets are even partially included on standardized English tests: grammar and language facts, editing in writing and spelling, listening skill, study skills, reading skill, and understanding of literature. The ten facets not included are appreciation of literature, composing in writing, style and expression in writing, speaking skill, speaking effectiveness, production in media, understanding and appreciation of media, listening in various situations, development of values, and reading interests.

Clearly, there is no one English language arts test— one that is culture-fair, one that can account for the range of contexts in which language occurs, one that spans the boundaries of the field. Some of the reasons have been cited in earlier sections of this paper: assessing language in an uncontrived variety of contexts is difficult, and theoretical underpinnings of the field are incomplete and/or contradictory. Until an adequate conceptual foundation is in place, instrument development will continue to occur in a vacuum.

The researcher. Who is the English language education researcher? The researcher represents a small segment of the profession, largely university professors and graduate students (O'Donnell, 1981). What does that mean? In the case of dissertation research, much does not get beyond the supervisory committee, except for an occasional interlibrary loan. Though a few journal articles may result, authors of dissertations, by and large, do not proceed to establish national reputations as researchers. This largest body of research may also suffer from its need to be conducted within a reasonable period of time and within the researchers' financial means. Longitudinal studies, therefore, which are likely to require funding and the investment of many years of effort, tend to be avoided not only by graduate students but also by professors seeking promotions. Experimental studies—usually dealing with materials, methods, or curricula—have likewise been plagued with problems. Among these problems have been those cited earlier: the slow-growing nature of language, the complex context in which language occurs, and the difficulty of building strong experimental designs. These limitations may account for the relative scarcity of experimental research in English language education and the abundance of cross-sectional analyses, descriptive surveys, correlational studies, content analyses, and to an increasing extent, case studies. Blount (1973) made the reasonably safe assumption that professors and graduate students not only produce the most research but also constitute its major reading audience.

With teachers as neither willing consumers nor willing producers, the influence of research findings on classroom instruction is at best indirect and delayed. It seems obvious that research would have a greater effect on language learners if teachers were involved in its planning and execution. Though not a total solution, teachers as researchers would help to resolve a major problem facing English language education research: dissemination.

The consumer. Disseminating research findings in a way that influences classroom practice is a long-standing problem not unique to English education. An element of the problem is skepticism, particularly on the part of practitioners, about the worth of educational research.

In discussions of its effects on the nature and quality of American education, research gets mixed reviews. Squire (1976) believes that "on the long, hard, never-ending trail to improvement of education, research does play an important role" (p. 63). He urges educators to look not for immediate changes but for the long-range impact of an entire body of research, since changes lie less in single studies than in the continued influence of large numbers of related studies. Pointing to research strands related to basal readers, reading interests, response to literature, and reading and writing processes, Squire concludes that "research then has made a difference, does make a difference, and will make a difference" (1976, p. 65).

Though we may know that from conception to realization it took fifty-six years for heart pacemakers, sixty-three years for television, and thirty years for zippers (Berger, 1978), disillusionment about the gap between theory and practice comes easy for educators. Large-scale and radical changes in classroom practice are unlikely to occur in the short term, whether motivated by research findings or by any other force on the schools. Change, when it involves so many people, so many social variables, so many practices, and so many contexts is unlikely to be anything but slow-moving.

Research is criticized for failing to exhibit the kind of cumulative progression encouraged by Squire. It has been called duplicative, isolated, and fragmentary. Henry (1966), for example, bemoaned research that was at that time steered by a kind of science that resulted in "discrete, packaged, 'rigorous' studies unrelated to a large context or comprehensive frame, the sum of which . . . can lead to no advance in the discipline because no one is capable of synthesizing such studies *ad hoc;* and so these 'studies' lie by the hundreds, unused and unread, on the shelves of every state university library" (pp. 232–233). Other critics have pointed to research findings that are contradictory; to the pace of change, which quickly makes the results of some research obsolete; and to the often abstruse and dull style in which reports of research are written.

If research in the teaching of English has had little effect on classroom practice, it may be because researchers forget that classrooms are practical, ongoing operations headed by teachers who must make countless decisions daily about how to organize instruction. Studies of minute aspects of language undertaken by researchers removed from all the complexities involved in teaching a particular classroom of students are unlikely to have immediate import for teachers, no matter how much we might wish that instructional decisions were influenced by research findings.

Despite the adverse criticism parts of it have received, the total body of research in English education has not been labeled dated, fragmented, dull, unreliable, and insignificant, even by its harshest critics. Perhaps we need a more realistic estimate of the difficulties of doing research related to language teaching and learning. Perhaps we should celebrate the profession's commitment to research and the exponential rise in efforts to conduct research, even in the face of radically diminished financial support. Perhaps we should more strongly applaud those rare researchers who undertake long-range programs of coordinated studies, ground their studies in theory, imaginatively build upon methodological advances, utilize a range of research designs to support diverse purposes, develop sophisticated measuring instruments, and address their research questions to problems teachers face in classrooms. Perhaps we can do more to encourage research conducted cooperatively by graduate students, professors, agencies, career researchers, businesses, and most of all, classroom teachers. Among such a group one can find mastery of a discipline, knowledge of research design and data analysis, a sense of the significance of research questions, and a drive to find solutions to the unsolved problems of those who teach and those who learn English language arts.

Julie M. Jensen

See also Bilingual Education; Handwriting; Language Development; Listening; Literature; Reading; Speech Communication; Spelling; Writing, Composition, and Rhetoric.

REFERENCES

Applebee, A. N. *Tradition and Reform in the Teaching of English: A History.* Urbana, Ill.: National Council of Teachers of English, 1974. (ERIC Document Reproduction Service No. ED 097 703)

Berger, A. *Dimensions of Progress in the Teaching of English.* Unpublished paper, University of Pittsburgh, 1978.

Bloom, B. (Ed.). *Taxonomy of Educational Objectives.* New York: McKay, 1956.

Bloom, B. *Human Characteristics and School Learning.* New York: McGraw-Hill, 1976.

Blount, N. S. Research on teaching literature, language, and composition. In R. M. W. Travers (Ed.), *Second Handbook of Research on Teaching.* Chicago: Rand McNally, 1973.

Broening, A. M. (Chair). *Conducting Experiences in English.* New York: Appleton-Century, 1939.

Brown, R. *A First Language.* Cambridge, Mass.: Harvard University Press, 1973.

Bruner, J. S. *The Process of Education.* New York: Random House, Vintage Books, 1960.

Bullock, A. (Chair). *A Language for Life.* Palo Alto, Calif.: Pendragon House, 1976.

Burton, D. L. Research in the teaching of English: The troubled dream. *Research in the Teaching of English,* 1973, *7,* 160–189.

Carpenter, G. R.; Baker, F. T.; & Scott, F. N. *The Teaching of English in the Elementary and the Secondary School.* New York: Longmans, Green, 1903.

Chafe, W. L. *Meaning and the Structure of Language.* Chicago: University of Chicago Press, 1970.

Chomsky, N. *Syntactic Structures.* The Hague: Mouton, 1957.

Chomsky, N. Review of B. F. Skinner's *Verbal Behavior. Language,* 1959, *35,* 26–58.

Chubb, P. *The Teaching of English in the Elementary and Secondary School.* New York: Macmillan, 1902.

Clapp, J. M. *The Place of English in American Life.* Chicago: National Council of Teachers of English, 1926.

Commission on English. *Freedom and Discipline in English.* New York: College Entrance Examination Board, 1965.

Committee on National Interest. *The National Interest and the Teaching of English: A Report on the Status of the Profession.* Urbana, Ill.: National Council of Teachers of English, 1961.

Committee of Ten of the National Education Association. *Report of the Committee of Ten on Secondary School Studies, with Reports of the Conferences Arranged by the Committee.* New York: American Book, 1894.

Conference on College Composition and Communication. Students' right to their own language. *College Composition and Communication,* 1974, *25.*

Copperman, P. *The Literacy Hoax.* New York: Morrow, 1978.

Dixon, J. *Growth through English.* Reading, England: National Association for the Teaching of English, 1967.

Ebel, R. L. (Ed.). *Encyclopedia of Educational Research* (4th ed.). New York: Macmillan, 1969.

Educational Policies Commission. *Education for All American Youth.* Washington, D.C.: National Education Association, 1944.

Fillmore, C. J. The case for case. In E. Bach & R. Harms (Eds.), *Universals in Linguistic Theory.* New York: Holt, Rinehart & Winston, 1968.

Francis, W. Nelson. *The Structure of American English.* New York: Ronald Press, 1958.

Fries, Charles C. *The Structure of English.* New York: Harcourt, Brace & World, 1952.

Gagné, R. M. *The Conditions of Learning.* New York: Holt, Rinehart & Winston, 1970.

Gardner, H. *The Shattered Mind: The Person after Brain Damage.* New York: Knopf, 1975.

Glatthorn, A. A. *A Guide for Developing an English Curriculum for the Eighties.* Urbana, Ill.: National Council of Teachers of English, 1980.

Gumperz, J. J., & Hymes, D. (Eds.). *Directions in Sociolinguistics: The Ethnography of Communication.* New York: Holt, Rinehart & Winston, 1972.

Halliday, M. A. K. *Learning How to Mean: Explorations in the Development of Language.* London: Edward Arnold, 1975.

Hatfield, W. W. (Chair). *An Experience Curriculum in English.* New York: Appleton-Century, 1935.

Havighurst, R. J. *Developmental Tasks and Education.* Chicago: University of Chicago Press, 1948.

Henry, G. H. English teaching encounters science. *College English,* 1966, *28,* 220–235.

Hillocks, G. *Alternatives in English: A Critical Appraisal of Elective Programs.* Urbana, Ill.: ERIC Reading and Communication Skills, 1972.

Hinsdale, B. A. *Teaching the Language Arts: Speech, Reading, Composition.* New York: Appleton, 1896.

Hook, J. N. *A Long Way Together: A Personal View of NCTE's First Sixty-seven Years.* Urbana, Ill.: National Council of Teachers of English, 1979.

Hosic, J. F. *Reorganization of English in Secondary Schools* (Bureau of Education Bulletin No. 2). Washington, D.C.: U.S. Government Printing Office, 1917.

Hymes, D. *Foundations in Socio-linguistics: An Ethnographic Approach.* Philadelphia: University of Pennsylvania Press, 1974.

Interorganizational Committee. Reading and pre-first grade: A joint statement of concern about present practices in pre-first grade reading instruction and recommendations for improvement. *Language Arts*, 1977, *54*, 459–461.

Jensen, J. M. Dear readers. *Language Arts*, 1979, *56*, 601–603.

Judy, S. N. (Ed.). An historical primer on the teaching of English. *English Journal*, 1979, *68*, entire issue. (a)

Judy, S. N. (Ed.). English since Sputnik. *English Journal*, 1979, *68*, entire issue. (b)

Judy, S. N. *Explorations in the Teaching of English.* New York: Harper & Row, 1981.

Kaestle, C. F. Perspectives: Literacy and mainstream culture in American history. *Language Arts*, 1981, *58*, 207–218.

Labov, W. *Language in the Inner City: Studies in the Black English Vernacular.* Philadelphia: University of Pennsylvania Press, 1972. (a)

Labov, W. *Sociolinguistic Patterns.* Philadelphia: University of Pennsylvania Press, 1972. (b)

Lloyd-Jones, R. Sources of knowledge about literacy. In R. Beach & P. D. Pearson (Eds.), *Perspectives on Literacy.* Minneapolis: University of Minnesota College of Education, 1978.

Loban, W. *The Language of Elementary School Children.* Urbana, Ill.: National Council of Teachers of English, 1963.

Loban, W. *Language Development: Kindergarten through Grade Twelve.* Urbana, Ill.: National Council of Teachers of English, 1976.

Luria, A. R. *Cognitive Development: Its Cultural and Social Foundations.* Cambridge, Mass.: Harvard University Press, 1976.

Lyman, R. L. *Summary of Investigations Relating to Grammar, Language, and Composition* (University of Chicago Supplementary Educational Monographs No. 36). Chicago: University of Chicago, 1929.

Miller, G. A. Some preliminaries to psycholinguistics. *American Psychologist*, 1965, *20*, 15–20.

Moffett, J. *A Student-centered Language Arts Curriculum, Grades K-13: A Handbook for Teachers.* Boston: Houghton Mifflin, 1968. (a)

Moffett, J. *Teaching the Universe of Discourse.* Boston: Houghton Mifflin, 1968. (b)

Muller, H. J. *The Uses of English.* New York: Holt, Rinehart & Winston, 1967.

National Council of Teachers of English. Proceedings of the first annual meeting. *English Journal*, 1912, *1*, 30–45.

National Council of Teachers of English Commission on the English Curriculum. *The English Language Arts in the Secondary School.* New York: Appleton-Century-Crofts, 1956.

O'Donnell, R. C. Needed research in the teaching of English. In R. B. Shuman (Ed.), *Education in the Eighties: English.* Washington, D.C.: National Education Association, 1981.

Organizations for the Essentials of Education. *The Essentials of Education.* Urbana, Ill.: National Council of Teachers of English, 1978.

Ornstein, R. *The Psychology of Consciousness.* San Francisco: Freeman, 1972.

Pearson, P. D., & Johnson, D. D. Skills management systems: A critique. *Reading Teacher*, 1975, *28*, 757–764.

Piaget, J. *The Language and Thought of the Child.* New York: World, 1973.

Purves, A. C. *Reading and Literature: American Achievement in International Perspective.* Urbana, Ill.: National Council of Teachers of English, 1981.

Rogers, C. R. *Freedom to Learn.* Columbus, Ohio: Merrill, 1969.

Skinner, B. F. *Verbal Behavior.* New York: Appleton-Century-Crofts, 1957.

Skinner, B. F. *About Behaviorism.* New York: Knopf, 1974.

Smith, V. H. Beyond flax and Skinner: A personal perspective on teaching English, 1954 to the present. *English Journal*, 1979, *68*, 79–85.

Squire, J. R. English literature. In R. Ebel (Ed.), *Encyclopedia of Educational Research* (4th ed.). New York: Macmillan, 1969.

Squire, J. R. Research can make a difference. *Research in the Teaching of English*, 1976, *10*, 53–65.

Squire, J. R. (Ed.). *The Teaching of English.* Chicago: National Society for the Study of Education, 1977.

Squire, J. R., & Applebee, R. K. *A Study of English Programs in Selected High Schools Which Consistently Educate Outstanding Students in English* (Cooperative Research Project No. 1994). Urbana: University of Illinois, 1966.

Steiner, G. *After Babel: Aspects of Language and Translation.* New York: Oxford University Press, 1975.

Stone, G. W. *Issues, Problems, and Approaches in the Teaching of English.* New York: Holt, Rinehart, 1961.

Taba, Hilda. *The Dynamics of Education: A Methodology of Progressive Educational Thought.* London: Kegan Paul, Trench, Trubner and Co., 1932.

Task Force on Measurement and Evaluation in the Study of English. *Common Sense and Testing in English.* Urbana, Ill.: National Council of Teachers of English, 1975. (ERIC Document Reproduction Service No. ED 108 218)

Tyler, R. *Basic Principles of Curriculum and Instruction.* Chicago: University of Chicago Press, 1950.

United States Postal Service, and National Council of Teachers of English. *All about Letters.* Washington, D.C.: U.S. Government Printing Office, 1979. (ERIC Document Reproduction Service No. ED 181 463)

Vygotsky, L. S. *Thought and Language.* Cambridge, Mass.: MIT Press, 1962.

Warriner, J. E. *English Grammar and Composition.* New York: Harcourt, Brace, 1951.

ENVIRONMENTAL EDUCATION

When human beings discovered agriculture and gained a relative abundance of food, they stopped wandering and settled into villages that gradually became cities. With the beginnings of civilization, technology, surplus food, and relative security, humans grew in numbers and influence and began to alter the environment more rapidly than nature could repair it. Although we now have sufficient scientific and technological knowledge to solve many environmental problems, decisions regarding the use of our environment are not based on science and technology alone; they are based on customs, economic feasibility, political expediency, social desirability, and religious beliefs. It is impossible to make wise decisions about the environment without an understanding of economics, anthropology, political science, sociology, history, and the humanities, as well as the natural and physical sciences.

The realization that the relationship of human beings to the environment is a complex one and that human welfare hinges upon all other things in the environment made it apparent that systematic environmental education is necessary. This led eventually to the passage of the Environmental Education Act of 1970, which stimulated master plans for environmental education in many states.

In 1969, President Nixon formed the Environmental Quality Council, which advanced the idea of harmony between human beings and their environment as national policy. A number of national and state environmental education organizations were subsequently formed, and in 1971, the National Association for Environmental Education was created.

At the present time environmental educators seem to agree on two main principles for the development of environmental education programs in the schools. The first is that ecology constitutes the basis for environmental education: there can be no understanding of the relationship between human beings and the environment without understanding how nature works. The second is that environmental education is not a single discipline; it calls for a way of thinking that pertains to the social sciences and humanities as much as it does to the natural sciences. Humans learn about their relationship to their environment throughout their lives. Environmental education, then, must take place from preschool age through adulthood.

The literature of environmental education is broad, and most of it is observational and descriptive. Hendee (1974) noted a lack of rigorous empirical research in the area of environmental education, in part because the field of environmental education needs expertise from many disciplines, and those who call themselves environmental educators have not been able to develop a common ground (Disinger, 1979).

Concepts and Principles. Defining "environmental education" is not an easy task. Unlike other curriculum areas, the specific content of environmental education has never been well defined. It is universally agreed, however, that environmental education should be interdisciplinary, drawing from biological, sociological, anthropological, economic, political, and humanistic sources. It is also agreed that a conceptual approach to teaching environmental education is best.

Since 1971 a number of studies have dealt with the identification of concepts to be included in environmental education. Roth, Pella, and Schoenfeld (1970), with the cooperation of a national panel representing 40 disciplines, developed a taxonomy of 111 concepts appropriate for inclusion in environmental-management education. The concepts were divided into the following 12 categories: environmental management techniques, economics, environmental problems, environmental ecology, adaptation and evolution, natural resources, sociocultural environment, culture, politics, the family, the individual, and psychological factors.

Jeter, Jordan, and Ingison (1976), using the concept learning and development (CLD) model developed by Klausmeier, Ghatala, and Frayer (1974), created a conceptual framework for a program in environmental education. The CLD model describes conceptual development, beginning with the earliest discrimination of objects during the preschool years and extending through attainment of concepts at the level of the expert. Noted scholars from the disciplines of ecology, biology, economics, anthropology, environmental education, and curriculum and instruction helped develop a selection of central concepts following several guidelines: (1) the concepts should present a total view of the environmental situation, balancing the biological and social sciences; (2) the concepts should be reasonably nonoverlapping; and (3) the concepts should remain manageable in number. Nine concepts—ecosystem, human beings, values, technology, culture, cultural institution, energy, cycle, and population—were selected.

Program Development. Childress (1978) attempted to identify, describe, and analyze general curricular characteristics of a selected national sample of public elementary and secondary school environmental-education programs and project curricula with respect to grade level, justification, objectives, personnel involved in content selection, factors influencing content selection, curriculum organization, sources of content and subject matter, sources of instructional materials, instructional strategies, and curriculum-development constraints. He concluded that involvement in environmental education programs is greatest at grades five, six, ten, eleven, and twelve, and lowest in kindergarten. Student interest, the needs of the students, and teacher interest were the factors exerting the most influence on the selection of curriculum content. State-adopted environmental education textbooks and legislative mandates had the least influence. Materials developed by the teaching staff made up most of the instructional materials. Small group projects, class discussions, and field trip–community resource visits were the most frequently used instructional strategies. Multidisciplinary and interdisciplinary curricular organizations were in effect in a majority of programs and projects. Developing an appreciation of the environment was considered of more importance in a majority of programs than was helping students actually solve environmental problems and develop problem-solving skills. Finally, inadequate funding at all levels and insufficient time were seen as the greatest constraints on the development of environmental education curricula.

Hungerford, Peyton, and Wilke (1980) present goals for curriculum development in environmental education, the assumptions made in developing the goals, a comparison between the goals and the Tbilisi objectives for environmental education, and the results of an assessment of the goals by a panel of five nationally recognized scholars in environmental education. The researchers concluded that their goals for curriculum development in environmental education are valid and provide a suitable framework for guiding curriculum development at all levels in environmental education. Further, they recommended that instructional objectives be formulated in relation to each goal during curriculum development.

The studies reported in the area of curriculum development represent a significant movement toward achieving definition, structure, and organization for teaching environmental education concepts and principles.

Instructional materials. Many instructional materials have been produced by commercial publishing companies; in addition, many locally developed materials emphasize outdoor education. Games and simulations have attracted much attention because of their usefulness in developing decision-making skills.

Sibley (1974) compared the effectiveness of a simulation exercise, a simulation game, and conventional classroom instruction for the teaching of ecological facts and concepts and problems of population and pollution. He tried to determine if the attitudes of 163 sixth-graders about the environment were changed as a result of participating in four simulation games. He concluded that the students did have favorable attitudinal changes as a result of having participated in the games.

Bazan (1976) points out two problems with games and simulations in environmental education: limited player participation and lack of consideration of economic relationships. He provides a descriptive framework for evaluating games and describes four games. A systems approach that emphasizes the principal ecological variables of energy, space, time, resources, and diversity provides the framework. The four games—the externalities game, the agricultural policy game, the location game, and the environmental management game—have since been used profitably with entry-level undergraduate classes of up to forty students.

Social studies textbooks served as the focus of a study by Barnes et al. (1978–1979). The purpose of the study was to determine the extent to which environmental generalizations are included in widely used social studies series in grades 4, 5, and 6. The authors concluded that the treatment of environmental topics is extremely uneven and that many important concepts are not covered in the various series. They recommended that teachers locate and use appropriate supplementary materials to provide a comprehensive, global, socially oriented environmental program.

Values and attitudes. Environmental educators are concerned with a highly diverse, complex subject matter spanning many disciplines. In implementing environmental education conceptual frameworks, environmental educators attempt to enable students to become not only knowledgeable about environmental concepts and principles, but also active in solving problems in ways that reflect a value system harmonious with this knowledge. The emphasis is now on social needs and values as they relate to human activities in our ecosystem.

Harshman (1978–1979) suggests that environmental educators can profit from reviewing value-clarification processes, values analyses, and moral-development processes for use in their instruction. Baer (1980) warns, though, that the process of values clarification should be thoroughly researched by environmental educators. He states that before environmental educators advocate values-clarification methodology as a component of environmental education, they should familiarize themselves with the professional literature critical of that methodology. Baker, Doran, and Sarnowski (1978) developed an instrument to produce a profile of an individual's environmental values, the Environmental Value Inventory. They suggest that the Environmental Value Inventory be used as a tool to aid the teacher in determining the dominant values of a class, in monitoring the effects of instructional materials, and in assessing changes in students' values after instruction. They suggest, too, that further research is necessary if curricular decisions are going to be influenced. In an effort to look at the relationship between environmental knowledge and environmental attitudes, Kinsey and Wheatley (1980) developed the Environmental Issues Attitudes Defensibility Inventory (EIADI) to measure the defensibility of environmental attitudes. Defensibility relates to the amount of information a person brings to bear on a decision relating to an environmental problem. The EIADI is a research instrument, but its format allows its use as a classroom activity. The authors suggest that discussion or even role playing could evolve from using this instrument.

Many people believe that environmental problems are simply biological, physical, and chemical problems that will be solved by technological advancement. Environmental educators, however, recognize that in many ways the disruptions in our ecosystem are merely symptoms of underlying social beliefs and values. The challenge is to find ways to integrate values education successfully into environmental education. Further research is needed in this important area.

Teacher education. Teacher education programs must prepare teachers to understand the basic concepts of the philosophy of living in harmony with our environment and to develop appropriate teaching methods for environmental education. Teacher education, both preservice and in-service, is critical to environmental education programs (Stapp, 1975).

Ritz (1978) suggests that a program in in-service environmental education should have the following characteristics:

- The program should deal with basic science as needed, but it should not be science-dominated.
- It should be appropriate for teachers with a wide variety of backgrounds and interests.
- It should provide training in the methods of environmental education, as well as its content.
- It should have a strong motivational impact on the participants.
- It should encourage teachers to environmentalize their teaching.
- It should bring teachers into direct involvement with the particular environments under consideration.
- It should make a serious effort to engage teachers in exploring their personal assumptions, values, and feelings about society and self, and the relationship of these to the natural world. (p. 18)

Some research does exist in the area of teacher education dealing with the development of guidelines for model programs and attitude assessment. However, there is not much data from which strong inferences can be drawn (Roth, 1976). Inconclusive studies indicate a need for more extensive and rigorous research in this important area of teacher education.

Teacher education programs have been described by Brice (1973), S. Vogl (1973), R. Vogl (1973), Akenson (1970), and Ritz (1978). In all cases, follow-up of participants indicated both an attitude change and positive action regarding environmental matters. Fischer (1979–1980) trained college science students, rather than teachers, to work in elementary school classrooms as part of their course requirements. The elementary classroom thus became a place of learning for the college students and the elementary students, and a demonstration program for the elementary classroom teacher. Fischer reports that teachers increased their environmental knowledge and formed more positive attitudes toward environmental education. Further investigations of teacher attitudes toward environmental education would be worthwhile.

Bowman (1978) reports relatively little interest among surveyed state coordinators in teacher certification for environmental education. State coordinators apparently believe that environmental education is basically interdisciplinary and feel that it should be incorporated into all subject areas. The suggestion to include environmental education concepts in all educational methodology courses has received considerable support, but very few recommendations for implementation have been made.

Evaluation. A large number of environmental materials have been produced by commercial publishing companies, and there are ever-increasing numbers of locally developed materials, curricula, and programs. According to Doran (1977), "very few schools and material developers obtained 'hard' evaluative data regarding the effects of their programs and materials" (p. 21). Many, in fact, based their evaluations on qualitative data collected by the program or project staff. Swan (1971) noted previously that adequate tools for evaluating the effectiveness of environmental education programs and materials do not exist.

Doran (1977) states that it should be obvious that before the effects of any environmental education program can be evaluated, one must have not only valid, reliable measurement devices, but also a clear statement of the expected outcomes of the program. It appears that this has not happened yet in this field. Despite the great interest in the area of environmental education, relatively few tests have been developed to measure outcomes. Two available instruments (Herried & Haier, 1970; Gardner & Kleinke, 1972) are designed to assess instructional effects but are of dubious reliability (see Wheatley (1974) for a review of instruments assessing environmental values).

The state of the art in regard to evaluation in environmental education is best described as embryonic (Doran, 1977). Doran recommends that experts from the field of environmental education work with scholars from such fields as psychology and sociology to improve evaluation; he cites the work of Swan (1971) and Bennett (1974) as examples. He says that environmental educators must agree upon conceptual schemes, tables of specification, and even behavioral objectives. Then, he believes, one could make statements about an instrument's validity or its relationship to objectives. The entire area of evaluation in environmental education is indeed a challenge, but it is essential to the discipline.

Agency Activity. One of the most interesting facts about environmental education is that so many agencies, institutions, and organizations have become actively involved. Because environmental education cuts across so many disciplines, people have both professional and personal interests (Disinger, 1978).

Forest Service. The research and management programs of the Forest Service have compiled an extensive library of factual material on all aspects of environmental management. This material is distributed to the public through the mail and to field offices, cooperating agencies, and organizations. In addition, there are seminars, training sessions, and workshops held nationwide to disseminate this information.

In order to help educators, an integrated program of teacher education was begun around 1970; the program includes a wide variety of lesson plans and teaching aids. In addition, workshops have been held throughout the country. Both the materials and the workshops are designed to be open-ended and to encourage the active participation of teachers and students in the collection and evaluation of environmental data, the formulation and testing of hypotheses, and their application to existing environmental problems. The Smokey Bear and Woodsy Owl programs are treated as basically separate entities, although both have missions in the area of environmental education.

Soil Conservation Service. Support for environmental education as an integral part of school curricula is part of Soil Conservation Service policy. Professional staff members are asked to provide assistance at all levels of education. Some support takes the form of on-site help to schools and teachers in planning outdoor classrooms, consultative services to help professors and students with the design of studies and the gathering and analysis of data, assistance to schools and other organizations in conducting environmental education workshops to help teachers design programs and use outdoor teaching opportunities, and various kinds of publications.

Department of Energy. At the national level, teaching materials are developed and disseminated, and national conferences on energy are sponsored from time to time. In addition, all Department of Energy field offices provide educational programs at the state and regional levels.

A wide variety of teaching materials are developed, including manuals, sourcebooks, lesson plans, reference materials, informational booklets, films, and exhibits. Among the techniques used are faculty institutes, faculty workshops, conferences, and visiting lecturers.

Office of Environmental Education. Activities have been directed at identification and exploration of approaches to local needs, research on problems and issues related to environmental quality, development of contextual frameworks, and design, exploration, and assessment of learning systems. A number of competitive general grants and minigrants have been awarded to public and private agencies, organizations, and institutions to develop resource materials, personnel to work in this area, elementary and secondary programs, and community education.

National Park Service. Environmental education programs of the National Park Service are national in scope, regional in administrative direction, but local in nature. The major contribution of the National Park Service to environmental education has been the National Environmental Education Development (NEED) program, integrating materials for school grades kindergarten through 8. The program is multidisciplinary, and all its materials were published by Silver Burdett Company.

Other federal agencies involved in environmental education include, but are not limited to, the National Sea Grant Program, the Office of Coastal Zone Management, the Center for Population Research, the National Institute of Environmental Health Sciences, the Fish and Wildlife Service, the Environmental Protection Agency, and the National Science Foundation.

In the early 1970s the Conservation Education Association combined with similar organizations to identify ways to strengthen the growing environmental education movement. The Alliance for Environmental Education links thirty-two nongovernmental organizations whose purpose is to encourage development, implementation, and coordination of dynamic environmental education programs, not only among its members but also with other groups in the field of environmental education. Activities and accomplishments of the alliance include planning and conducting national conferences to identify and implement a national strategy for environmental education and publishing a newsletter, *Alliance Exchange*, which reports on developments in the field of environmental education. The membership includes groups representing youth organizations, professional education organizations and civic, conservation, and industry and labor organizations.

American Federation of Teachers. The American Federation of Teachers, an international union representing over 500,000 teachers and other education employees, has focused on developing an awareness of the need for environmental education, sending out information on environmental issues, urging accrediting associations to include environmental education programs in school evaluations, and conducting in-service workshops.

The American Federation of Teachers will continue to highlight the importance of environmental education, offer support in terms of lobbying, and disseminate information, and this information will be passed on to students of all ages.

American Forest Institute. Three major thrusts of the American Forest Institute lie in the area of environmental education: participation in professional organizations within the field of environmental education; publication and dissemination of materials for teachers; and dissemination of an environmental education supplementary curriculum, entitled Project Learning Tree, for educators in grades kindergarten through 12. Project Learning Tree is an attempt to provide balanced activities for teachers to use in the classroom to create an awareness of and knowledge about forest resources. The program describes situations for teaching critical thinking and problem-solving skills.

National Association for Environmental Education. The National Association for Environmental Education has as its mission the improvement of environmental education in all educational institutions. The primary goal of the association is "to develop, promote, and encourage vigorous support for educational programs that will produce an environmentally literate citizenry which lives in harmony with the ecosystem and possesses the skills, attitudes, and knowledge necessary to identify and solve environmental problems" (Roth, 1969, p. 91).

The activities of the association include an annual spring conference and a variety of publications, including a newsletter. The association also has an awards program that recognizes persons and groups that have made significant contributions to environmental education.

National Wildlife Federation. Environmental education efforts of the National Wildlife Federation take a variety of forms. The federation issues a number of publications on nature-related topics. Among those publications is one called *Environmental Discovery Units*, a teacher's guide to ecology containing twenty-four units covering kindergarten through twelfth grade. The federation also supports National Wildlife Week and issues National Wildlife Week materials to teachers. The federation intends to produce more environmental education curriculum materials to help teachers teach students about wildlife and environmental problems.

Soil Conservation Society of America. The Soil Conservation Society of America is dedicated to advancing good use of land. The society's environmental improvement concerns and competencies, though, extend beyond soil to include all natural resources. In education endeavors, the society stresses teaching and learning about and from the environment beginning in kindergarten and extending through postgraduate studies. Individual society members often serve as consultants in helping elementary and secondary schools design environmental education programs and outdoor learning activities. They assist in curriculum development at all levels and serve on environmental education advisory committees, editorial boards, and so on. In many states, society chapters conduct teacher institutes and student workshops in environmental studies. The Soil Conservation Society of America fully intends to remain an active participant in environmental education at the local, state, and national levels.

Other members of the Alliance for Environmental Education include, but are not limited to, the American Association of State Colleges and Universities, Boy Scouts of America, Girl Scouts of America, League of Women Voters, American Institute of Architects, Edison Electric Institute, United Auto Workers (Conservation Department), and Zero Population Growth.

Conclusions. The United States has made significant progress in the development and implementation of environmental education programs, but reliable assessment of program effectiveness is badly needed. In most instances, far more emphasis seems to be placed on program development than on researching program effectiveness. Research on attainment of objectives, acquisition of concepts, attitude changes, acquisition of skills, and methodology is also urgently needed. Roth (1969) identified the following areas in which research efforts should be concentrated:

1. Development of longitudinal national assessment techniques to document shifts in environmental perception and awareness, knowledge, and behavior exhibited by various age groups throughout the United States and abroad;
2. Initiation of baseline and longitudinal cognitive evaluative studies of teaching methodology, interpretive techniques, and learning strategies in relation to both formal and non-formal learning environments;
3. Determination of the effectiveness of various communication techniques and media in relation to selected environmental issues and audiences;
4. Comparison of alternative program models in relation to the development of competent professionals in environmental/resource management/education; and
5. Analysis of environmental program models in relation to citizen participation in environmental decision making. (p. 9)

Continued progress in environmental education programs depends upon the sophistication of empirical research. We must obtain data regarding the effects of the programs and materials that have been developed.

Jan Jeter

See also Citizenship Education; Recreation.

REFERENCES

Akenson, J. E. *Environmental Quality and a Humanistic Approach to Teacher Education.* Paper presented at the annual meeting of the National Council for the Social Studies, November 1970. (ERIC Document Reproduction Service No. ED 046 796)

Baer, R. A., Jr., A critique of the use of values clarification in environmental education. *Journal of Environmental Education,* 1980, *12*(1), 13–16.

Baker, M. R.; Doran, R. L.; & Sarnowski, A. A. An analysis of environmental values and their relation to general values. *Journal of Environmental Education,* 1978, *10*(1), 35–40.

Barnes, B.; Rivner, R.; Smith, M.; & Waln, L. Environmental education generalizations in middle-grade social studies series. *Journal of Environmental Education,* 1978–1979, *10*(2), 12–17.

Bazan, E. J. Environmental simulation games. *Journal of Environmental Education,* 1976, *8*(2), 41–51.

Bennett, D. B. Evaluating environmental education programs. In J. Swan & W. Stapp (Eds.), *Environmental Education.* New York: Wiley, 1974.

Bowman, M. L. State certification of environmental educators: A survey. *Journal of Environmental Education,* 1978, *9*(4), 51–54.

Brice, R. A. A procedural model for developing environmental education programs for teachers of young children (Doctoral dissertation, University of Georgia, 1973). *Dissertation Abstracts International,* 1974, *34,* 7. University Microfilms No. 73-31, 859)

Childress, R. B. Public school environmental education curricula: A national profile. *Journal of Environmental Education,* 1978, *9*(3), 2–11.

Disinger, J. F. *Environmental Education Activities of Federal Agencies.* Columbus: ERIC Information Analysis Center for Science, Mathematics, and Environmental Education, Ohio State University, 1978. (ERIC Document Reproduction Service No. ED 152 481)

Disinger, J. F. The literature of environmental education. *Journal of Environmental Education,* 1979, *10*(4), 2–3.

Doran, R. L. State of the art for measurement and evaluation of environmental objectives. *Journal of Environmental Education,* 1977, *9*(1), 50–63.

Fischer, R. B. The college and the classroom: Bringing the two together. *Journal of Environmental Education,* 1979–1980, *11*(2), 46–48.

Gardner, E. F., & Kleinke, D. J. *Syracuse Environmental Awareness Tests: Level III, Final Report on Construction and Norming.* Albany: New York State Department of Education, Division of General Education, 1972. (ERIC Document Reproduction Service No. ED 110 327)

Harshman, R. Value education processes for an environmental education program. *Journal of Environmental Education,* 1978–1979, *10*(2), 30–34.

Hendee, J. C. Challenging the folklore of environmental education. *Journal of Environmental Education,* 1974, *6*(2), 14–18.

Herried, C. E., & Haier, R. Ecology test (State University of New York at Buffalo). *Spectrum,* 1970.

Hungerford, H.; Peyton, R. B.; & Wilke, R. J. Goals for curriculum development in environmental education. *Journal of Environmental Education,* 1980, *11*(3), 42–47.

Jeter, J.; Jordan, A.; & Ingison, L. *Environmental Education: Needs and Specifications* (Working Paper No. 150), University of Wisconsin, Research and Development Center for Cognitive Learning, 1976.

Kinsey, T. G., & Wheatley, J. H. An instrument to inventory the defensibility of environmental attitudes. *Journal of Environmental Education*, 1980, *12*(1), 29–35.

Klausmeier, H.; Ghatala, E. S.; & Frayer, D. A. *Concept Learning and Development: A Cognitive View*. New York: Academic Press, 1974.

Ritz, W. C. Involving teachers in environmental education. *Journal of Environmental Education*, 1978, *9*(3), 15–18.

Roth, R. E. Fundamental concepts for environmental management education (K–16) (Doctoral dissertation, University of Wisconsin, 1969). *Dissertation Abstracts International*, 1970, *31*. (University Microfilms No. 69–22, 468)

Roth, R. E. *A Review of Research Related to Environmental Education, 1973–1976*. Columbus: ERIC Information Analysis Center for Science, Mathematics, and Environmental Education, Ohio State University, 1976. (ERIC Document Reproduction Service No. ED 135 647)

Roth, R. E.; Pella, M.; & Schoenfeld C. *Environmental Concepts: A List*. Madison: University of Wisconsin, Research and Development Center for Cognitive Learning, 1970. (ERIC Document Reproduction Service No. ED 045 376)

Sibley, W. A. Effect of simulation games on attitudes of sixth graders toward the environment (Doctoral dissertation, University of Virginia, 1974). *Dissertation Abstracts International*, 1974, *35*, 4. (University Microfilms No. 74-23, 251)

Stapp, W. B. Preservice teacher education. In N. McInnis & D. Albrecht (Eds.), *What Makes Education Environmental?* Louisville, Ky.: Data Courier, 1975.

Swan, J. A. Formation of environmental values: A social awareness. In Cook & O'Hearn (Eds.), *Processes for a Quality Environment*. Green Bay: University of Wisconsin at Green Bay Press, 1971.

Vogl, R. L. Selected Illinois high school superintendents' assessments of citizen action roles for seniors seeking environmental reforms (Doctoral dissertation, University of Michigan, 1973). *Dissertation Abstracts International*, 1974, *35*, 1. (University Microfilms No. 74-15, 887)

Vogl, S. M. W. Attitude change in inservice teachers toward the great lakes region in response to lectures or individualized inquiry and retrieval (Doctoral dissertation, University of Michigan, 1973). *Dissertation Abstracts International*, 1974, *35*, 1. (University Microfilms No. 74-15, 888)

Wheatley, J. *Affective Instruments in Environmental Education*. Columbus: ERIC Information Analysis Center for Science, Mathematics, and Environmental Education, Ohio State University, 1974.

EQUITY ISSUES IN EDUCATION

Busing, mainstreaming of handicapped students, and equivalent funding of athletics for girls and boys are just three of the many issues in educational equity that have surfaced in both public and educational arenas in the past few years. Although the issues are dissimilar, the controversy that surrounds them and other issues comes from different answers to the same basic questions: "What should or should not be done in the name of fairness?" and "Who should be helped at whose expense?" Although there is no one answer to either question, an analysis of possible answers and some of the assumptions and definitons that make up different answers can help provide a better understanding of educational equity.

The article begins with a summary of the role that government, particularly the federal government, has played in educational equity. It goes on to cover some definitions of educational equity and the assumptions behind those definitions. Finally it examines the question of to whom educational equity applies.

Legal Aspects. The Platonic ideal of equality of opportunity through education has been an important part of America and the American educational system (Walberg and Bargen, 1974). The creation of the common school system of public education has been equated with a national conviction that educational opportunity must be made universal. Thus the mythology of public education has historically been based on a "benevolent portrayal of constantly expanding opportunity" (Weinberg, 1977, pp. 1–2).

The importance of the concept of universal educational opportunity is based on the value ascribed to education. Throughout the nineteenth and, indeed, the twentieth century, there has been a strong belief in American education. Education has been seen as the route out of poverty and discrimination to full participation in the rewards of American society. For example, nineteenth century reformers advocated free public education as a way of "Americanizing" the increasing numbers of non–Anglo-Saxon immigrants. Education has been seen as an integral part of the American melting pot and the major way of transforming immigrant children into "good, productive, citizens" (Current, Williams, & Freidel, 1964).

As shown by Tocqueville's *Democracy in America* (1835) and Myrdal's *An American Dilemma* (1944), no country has continuously taken the ideal of educational opportunity more seriously or with greater anguish than the United States (Walberg & Bargen, 1974). The ideal of universal opportunity, however, has never been realized. Characteristics such as race, ethnicity, sex, and physical handicap have been accepted as inevitable limitations on educational opportunity (Weinberg, 1977; Flexner, 1974).

The history of this country is filled with examples of educational inequity including, for example, "compulsory ignorance" laws which forbade the teaching of writing to slaves (Sellers, 1950), dual educational systems for blacks and Mexicans (Rangel & Alcala, 1972), the denial of higher education to women (Flexner, 1974), and the isolation of handicapped learners (National Education Association, 1978). Yet along with a history of educational discrimination and inequity, there is also a history of governmental efforts to increase educational equity. For example, in 1912 when New Mexico became a state, its constitution (Article VIII) required that teachers be equally proficient in both Spanish and English and that "children of Spanish descent in the state of New Mexico shall never be denied the right and privilege of admission and attendance in the public schools or other public educational institutions of the State and they shall never be classed in separate schools, but shall forever enjoy perfect equality with other children in all public schools and educational institutions of the State" (Article X, Section 10).

There has been government involvement in educational equity in all three branches: the judiciary, the executive, and the legislative. Although at various times one branch has been more influential than others, the judiciary, particularly the Supreme Court, may indeed be considered the primary architect of educational equity as it currently exists. Court decisions such as *Brown* v. *Board of Education* (1954, 1955), *Lau* v. *Nichols* (1974), *Adams* v. *Richardson* (1972; subsequently cited as *Adams* v. *Bell*), and *Regents of California* v. *Bakke* (1978) and related legislation have laid down the design for equity.

In 1954 the Supreme Court, in a landmark decision, ruled that "in the field of public education, the doctrine of 'separate but equal' has no place. Separate educational facilities are inherently unequal" (*Brown* v. *Board of Education,* 1954). One year later, however, the Court ruled that desegregation of schools should take place, not by a specific deadline, but rather "with all deliberate speed" (*Brown* v. *Board of Education,* 1955). "All deliberate speed" meant that ten years after *Brown,* only 1.2 percent of black children in the deep South attended desegregated schools (Weinberg, 1977). Further, between 1955 and 1963 the Supreme Court refused to review all cases involving states' efforts to circumvent the *Brown* decision (Weinberg, 1979). *Brown,* nevertheless, had a tremendous influence. The outlawing of segregated school systems began the process of destroying dual elementary and secondary public school systems that continues today. Much of the success that process has had is directly related to the passage of the Civil Rights Act of 1964. Title IV of the Act authorized the U.S. Commissioner of Education to help school districts to desegregate and empowered the Attorney General to institute lawsuits to bring about desegregation (Weinberg, 1977). Perhaps more importantly, this act "prohibited discrimination in programs financed by federal grants, loans, and contracts; required each department to establish rules for implementing the Title; and gave agencies authority to cut off funds from recipients who failed to comply with the rules" (Mosher, Hastings, & Wagoner, 1979, p. 4). As well as prohibiting discrimination and encouraging desegregation, it also provided schools with technical assistance in their efforts to desegregate and to deal with the situations that came about as a result of desegregation. Title IV of the Civil Rights Act, which provided technical assistance and enforcement provisions for desegregation, covered more groups than did Title VI. Title VI prohibited discrimination on the basis of race, color or national origin while Title IV defined desegregation as "the assignment of students to public schools and within such schools without regard to their race, color, religion, sex or national origin." Prohibitions against discrimination in programs or activities receiving federal financial assistance were expanded to include dis-

crimination on the basis of sex (Title IX of the Education Amendments of 1972) and handicapping condition (Section 504 of the Vocational Rehabilitation Act Amendments of 1973 and P.L. 94-142, the Education for All Handicapped Children Act of 1975).

The Civil Rights Act of 1964 was the model for much of the newer legislation. In fact Title IX of the Education Amendments of 1972 prohibiting sex discrimination in education repeats most of the same language as Title VI of the Civil Rights Act which prohibited race, color, or national origin discrimination in programs or activities receiving federal financial assistance. The Civil Rights Act was also the basis of a major Supreme Court decision on educational equity, *Lau* v. *Nichols* (1974).

In this case the courts decided that "failure to offer instruction in the native language of children who are not fluent in English, denies them the opportunity to participate meaningfully in the educational process, a violation of the Civil Rights Act of 1964" (U.S. Commission on Civil Rights, 1979, p. 188). Although the court decided that "imposition of a requirement that before a child can effectively participate in the educational program, he must already have acquired those basic [English] skills is to make a mockery of public education" (*Lau* v. *Nichols,* 1974), it did not rule that individuals had a constitutional right to bilingual education, nor did it state what must be done by schools in order to be in compliance (U.S. Commission on Civil Rights, 1976).

As with *Brown,* much of the effort to attain the goals of *Lau* came from legislation rather than from the court decision. Although the Bilingual Education Act (Title VII of the Elementary and Secondary Education Act of 1962) was already in existence, after *Lau* it was greatly expanded in both focus and funding. Also *Lau* was the impetus for the Equal Educational Opportunity Act of 1974, which extended the Court rulings to all public schools regardless of whether they received federal funds, and led to the passage of new laws allowing or mandating bilingual education in some states (Mosher, Hastings, & Wagoner, 1979).

There are no landmark cases similar to *Lau* or *Brown* in higher education. Indeed "the constitutional law of higher education opportunity could hardly be said to exist" (Weinberg, 1977, p. 31). One exception to this is the case of *Adams* v. *Bell.* In this case the Court of Appeals found that higher education was also covered under Title VI of the Civil Rights Act of 1964 and ordered ten states to submit comprehensive plans for the desegregation of their higher education systems (Southern Education Foundation, 1974). This case, which was expanded in 1974 to include sex as well as race, is still in the courts.

A second major court case with ramifications for educational equity in higher education was the *Regents of California* v. *Bakke* (1978). The Supreme Court held "that it was impermissible for a university to set aside a fixed number of places for minority group members, but that race might be treated as one relevant factor in admissions decisions" (Greenawalt, 1979, p. 1). While the *Bakke* decision was very well publicized, there has been little data to document its effect on educational equity in higher education.

The court cases and legislation covered have focused on educational equity for racial and linguistic minorities. There are, however, two other groups for whom federal legislation pertaining to educational equity has been passed: women and handicapped persons.

In 1972, Title IX of the Education Amendments of 1972 was signed into law. Title IX mandated that "no person in the United States . . . shall, on the basis of sex, be excluded from participation in, be denied the benefits of, or be subjected to discrimination under any education program or activity receiving federal financial assistance." Although there is some question as to the degree to which Title IX is being enforced, the law has, to date, survived continued attempts on the part of Congress and the courts to abolish or neutralize it (Mosher, Hastings, & Wagoner, 1979).

Federal funds from the U.S. Office of Education to facilitate compliance with Title IX became available in 1976 from Title IV of the Civil Rights Act and from the Women's Educational Equity Act of 1974 (Klein and Goodman, 1980). Also the sex equity provisions of the 1976 Vocational Education Amendments encouraged the Office of Education to fund and provide for sex equity activities in vocational education.

Civil rights legislation for the handicapped followed a similar pattern. Section 504 of the Vocational Rehabilitation Act Amendments of 1973, like Title VI of the Civil Rights Act and Title IX, is a basic civil rights statute which (in this case) makes it illegal to discriminate against an "otherwise qualified handicapped individual . . . solely by reason of his handicap . . . under any program or activity receiving federal financial assistance."

The Education of All Handicapped Children Act of 1975 (P.L. 94-142) provides federal funds to assist state and local governments in providing free public education to handicapped students. It also is similar to Section 504 in requiring a free appropriate public education for handicapped students who receive funds from this Act. This law requires that handicapped children receive this education in the least restrictive educational environment based on a written, individualized education program (IEP) (Ballard, 1978).

Historically government's role in educational equity has been an important but confusing one. Laws have been made forbidding educational equity and laws have been made mandating it. Court decisions demanding equity have been promulgated, but frequently with neither deadlines for compliance nor power for enforcement. Moreover, laws and programs have been developed and implemented that conflict based on different definitions of equity. For example, much legislation and case law forbids the segregation within or between schools of students from different racial or ethnic groups; this is, however, what has happened in implementing bilingual education mandates and programs. These apparent contradictions occur in part because of a lack of agreement on the definition of educational equity.

Definitions of Equity. Educators, researchers, advocacy groups, and policy makers have all come up with "suggested" definitions of educational equity which are frequently varied and sometimes in conflict. For example, the answer to the question of whether the Chicago schools provide educational equality varies with the definition. "If equality means racial integration, the answer is no. If it means equal expenditures, the answer is yes. If it means equal resources . . . and reading achievement, the answer is no" (Walberg & Bargen, 1974, p. 24). Even more general definitions of educational equity can also be in conflict. For example, some women's groups and some school finance experts define equity as the same, yet bilingual advocates argue that the same treatment of English-speaking and non–English-speaking students would result not in equity but in the denial of equity (Mosher, Hastings, & Wagoner, 1979).

Most definitions of educational equity focus only on a singular aspect of equity, that is, either equity in access to, the process of, or the outcomes from, schooling (Hyman & Schaaf, 1981). Definitions that focus on access are almost exclusively devoted to higher education and professional schools. The existence of compulsory education laws and the *Brown* v. *Board of Education* Supreme Court decisions have made the question of access in elementary and secondary education somewhat moot (Hyman & Schaaf, 1981).

In higher education, some define educational equity as equal opportunity to gain entry and recommend different admissions or applications procedures (Bane & Winston, 1980). Others define educational equity as equal access to learning and advocate differential treatment for admissions and in the schooling itself (Adolphus, 1980).

Process definitions of educational equity, as expected, focus on the schooling itself. For example, some define educational equity as the elimination of separate but equal treatment and the mainstreaming of diverse groups of students into school classes and activities (National Education Association, 1978). Another process definition states that equity is a state beyond nondiscrimination which is characterized by fair and just, but not necessarily identical, treatment (Bornstein, 1981).

Outcome definitions of educational equity include: "real educational equity means that all students are provided educational experiences that ensure the achievement of certain uniform goals and objectives" (Green, Parsons, & Thomas, 1981, p. 282) and educational equity is "an equitable share of the benefits of schooling" (Mosher, Hastings, & Wagoner, 1979, p. 1). Some outcome-oriented definitions also include reference to potentially different starting points of the various groups. For example, Graham (1978) defined equity as reducing the predictive value of race, sex, and social class in determining educational achievement.

There is some question of the value of any of these definitions which focus on a single aspect of equity because of the lack of independence among access, process, and outcome. As Martel (1980, p. 3) comments, "the question of equal access is moot if what is accessed is of little value or is disproportionately unequal." Bornstein (1981, p. 10) agrees that the areas are related and goes on to suggest that "equal participation rates tend to produce equal success rates which provide an equal range of benefits and rewards." She has developed an equity continuum based on the belief that equity access, process, and outcomes definitions are all part of a process that begins at stage one (discrimination) and continues through stages such as fair rules/equal treatment (stage four) to culminate at equal success rates (stage seven).

The definitions of equity presented above are based on some common assumptions in each of the following dimensions: (1) views of the *attributes of learners* with a common social (or equity) group affiliation; (2) ways of structuring the educational *process* for the specified equity groups; and (3) desired goals, benefits, or *outcomes* for the equity groups. An analysis of the assumptions made under these dimensions and how these assumptions influence definitions of educational equity may assist individuals to formulate more complete definitions as well as to better understand the definitions of others.

Attributes of learners. The first dimension of a definition of educational equity describes how educators view the attributes of groups of learners. Learners are frequently described by their "ascribed" attributes or social group affiliation (i.e., sex, race, age, handicap, or socioeconomic status) rather than their achievements. Assumptions about learners based on their ascribed attributes tend to fall into two areas:

1. There are no educationally relevant differences between ascribed groups such as females and males, blacks and whites, Hispanics and Anglos. Based on this assumption, educators should be color-blind and gender-blind in their treatment of students. The within-group differences are of much greater importance than the between-group differences.

2. Learners in ascribed groups have educationally relevant attributes common to their group, but different from learners in other groups. Assumptions of causations of these differences include (a) cognitive or other educationally relevant differences are due to genetic or other innate factors and are not easily changed (Jenson, 1980; Benbow & Stanley, 1980); (b) cognitive or other educationally relevant differences are due to learned differences or are the result of socialization and have potential to be changed (Maccoby & Jacklin, 1974; Mayeske et al., 1973; Baratz & Baratz, 1970); and (c) cognitive or other educationally relevant differences include both learned differences and innate differences and thus some differences are likely to be malleable and others not (Bronfenbrenner, 1979; Scarr, 1968).

The educational process. A second component of any definition of educational equity is based on assumptions about the role of equity in the educational process. Assumptions in this dimension tend to fall into three areas:

1. The educational process has no role in promoting educational equity for groups. Differential treatments should be allowed based on the qualifications of individuals involved. This assumption tends to support the current status hierarchy and foster social selection among groups (Bordier, 1981).

2. Learners, regardless of ascribed group, should receive the same opportunities and resources, and should be judged by the same rules, expectations, and standards. This assumption is called horizontal equity because identical treatments are expected to help learners increase in parallel ways (Hyman & Schaaf, 1981). It is reflected in legislation such as Title VI of the Civil Rights Act and Title IX which forbid the denial of equal participation in federally assisted programs because of sex, race, and national origin. Providing equitable access or opportunities means that no societal barriers are deliberately left in place so that individuals can receive equal treatment. Although it may appear simple to determine if this is being implemented, subtle differences in these educational processes frequently make it difficult (Wirtenberg et al., 1981).

3. Learners from ascribed groups should be provided differential treatment as needed. This assumption is called vertical equity because, although learners (and perhaps groups) may start at different points, additional help is provided to those who have the greatest needs with the expectation that they will catch up to or surpass those who started ahead of them (Hyman & Schaaf, 1981). This assumption is the basis of legislation such as Title I of the Elementary & Secondary Education Act (ESEA), which provides compensatory education for children from poverty areas, and the 1976 Vocational Education Amendments, which provide moneys for states to support programs to overcome sex stereotyping in vocational education.

Desired learner goals. A third component of a definition of educational equity is based on assumptions of desirable goals, outcomes, or benefits. Assumptions in this dimension tend to fall into three areas:

1. Existing differences in ascribed groups should be maintained. This assumption implies, for example, that ethnic groups should retain their own language and customs or that sex differences in areas such as aggression, dependence, or verbal and mathematical skills should be maintained.

2. Nondominant groups (i.e., women, minorities, handicapped) should attain parity with the dominant group. This assumption implies that, for example, language minorities should learn standard English or that the deaf should learn to lip read and speak orally rather than learn sign language. Tests or standards of minimal educational competency are partially based on this assumption (Campbell & Scott, 1980).

3. Dominant and nondominant groups should become more similar in desirable attributes. For example, English speakers should learn Spanish while Spanish speakers learn English; females and males should learn leadership skills with a caring dimension (Gilligan & Langdale, 1980). De-

termining which attributes are desirable, is, of necessity, a major concern in this area. Adherents to this equity goal assumption should favor multicultural education programs, which help groups understand and value the attributes of other groups.

Assumptions related to one dimension will influence the choice of assumptions in another dimension. For example, one who believes in innate ascribed group differences is unlikely to believe that decreasing group differences is a viable educational outcome, but may or may not believe in equal treatment during the education process.

Analysis of the dimensions and assumptions should help clarify both definitions of educational equity and the basis for those definitions. There is however, one other component implicit in definitions of educational equity which has not yet been mentioned. For what group, or groups, should educational equity be attempted?

Educational Equity for Whom? In an ideal world, the response to the questions of educational equity for whom would be, "Why, for everyone, of course." But in the 1980s there are significant social and economic realities affecting public education. Enrollments are declining, costs are increasing, and taxpayer willingness to pay education bills is decreasing. Additional costs brought on by demands for educational equity "cannot be met within existing or lowered levels of school expenditures, unless services to some other clienteles are curtailed" (Mosher, Hastings, & Wagoner, 1979, p. 1). This is true regardless of the definition of equity. For example, treating girls and boys equally in athletics requires a great increase of money spent on girls' athletics or a decrease in boys' athletic opportunities (Matthews & McCune, 1976). Developing special programs for language minorities or the handicapped also costs money that must come from somewhere (National Education Association, 1978). A very real, very major equity issue in education in the face of fiscal realities becomes: Who should receive equitable treatment and at what cost?

Until the 1970s minority groups (specifically blacks) were the major concern of advocates for educational equity. With the 1970s came demands for educational equity for large numbers of other students who had suffered past educational discrimination, specifically girls and women, nonblack minorities, linguistic minorities and the handicapped. This trend is growing. Cloud (1980) listed thirty-eight different categories that could relate to educational equity issues. These included not only those listed earlier, but others such as age, religious preference, height, and income level. He also indicated that these thirty-eight did not constitute a comprehensive list.

Groups demanding educational equity are expanding within categories as well. In 1978 the National Education Association listed eighteen different handicapped subgroups, each with special educational needs, including emotionally disturbed, hearing impaired, orthopedically impaired, and educable and trainable mentally retarded.

Each of these numerous groups and subgroups has suffered in an inequitable educational system. Studies abound

indicating the results of an inequitable educational system on minorities (U.S. Commission on Civil rights, 1976; Weinberg, 1979; Chun, 1980), women (Harway & Asten, 1977; Fitzpatrick, 1976; Frazier & Sadker, 1973), and the handicapped (National Education Association, 1978; Weintraub et al., 1976). Analyses of classroom interaction, the allocation of resources, and previous laws indicate that there has been and continues to be inequitable treatment of students based on membership in ascribed groups (Berke, 1974; Sadker & Sadker, 1981).

Nationally about two out of every three black and Hispanic students still attend schools with over 50 percent minority enrollment (Green, Parsons, & Thomas, 1981), and in urban areas the trend toward desegregation is decreasing, with segregation becoming worse in northern states and integration stagnating in the Midwest (Price-Curtis, 1981). The problems of educational inequity are real and they are still with us.

Public awareness of the numbers of people whose educational needs are not being met is increasing. The effects of this awareness—the efforts of group members and advocates to gain educational equity—have had both positive and negative consequences. Many of the positive consequences were summarized earlier, in the laws and court cases whose goal was to open up educational opportunity to groups that had previously experienced discrimination. Other positive consequences include: increased awareness by educators of the needs of various groups, the development and use of multicultural, nonsexist materials, and, in general, an increased responsiveness to educational equity concerns.

There are negative effects to the expansion of the concept of educational equity as well. The large number of frequently conflicting, educational equity definitions has caused a great deal of confusion among legislators and educators alike as to what should be done to achieve equity. Moreover, different priorities and concerns have led advocates of educational equity to fragment into special interest areas focusing on equity for "their group" rather than working together for equity for all.

Another concern is that the proliferation of the number of groups recognized to be in need of educational equity has caused less attention to be paid to the "truly inequitable." If there is only a set amount of resources available for promoting educational equity, then every dollar spent on making schools more equitable for middle-class gifted students is not spent on, for example, lower-class black boys. While appropriate responses to this situation may be to work for more resources or to determine ways of using resources to help both groups, a more frequent response is for the groups and their advocates to go into competition for available resources.

The increasing number of groups recognized to be in need of educational equity may also be causing a competition between those students and "regular students." For example, Stearns and Cooperstein (1981) found that some school personnel felt that by providing handicapped children with individually appropriate education and related services, they were treating handicapped children as "more equal" than others. As one teacher commented, "I really believe in mainstreaming, but . . . the regular student gets the short end of the stick" (p. 325).

Underlying some of these issues is a concern that the focus on educational equity for specific groups may be leading to an emphasis on equality rather than on quality. While on one side there are scholars who believe educational policy should promote equity by providing special services to some (Bane & Winston, 1980), there are others who feel that providing special programs to the handicapped or disadvantaged and not to regular or gifted students is using policy to disadvantage advantaged students (Stearns & Cooperstein, 1981) and that the deemphasis on meritocracy is leading to mediocrity.

Mosher, Hastings, and Wagoner (1979) call the effort to actualize a national commitment to equality of opportunity "perhaps the longest-running game in the history of American public education" (p. 1). It is indeed the game with the most players and the most frequently changing sets of rules. It is also the game in which everyone (government, educators, parents, "concerned citizens," and even students) has been involved and in which all have a stake.

Patricia B. Campbell

Susan Klein

See also Bilingual Education; Black Education; Culture and Education Policy; Handicapped Individuals; Individual Differences; Legislation; Multicultural and Minority Education; Racism and Sexism in Children's Literature; Women's Education.

REFERENCES

Adams v. *Richardson*, 356, F. Supp. 92 (1972).

Adolphus, S. H. The pragmatics of higher education equity. In D. Martel (Ed.), *The Itinerary of the Concept Equal Educational Opportunity.* Syracuse, N.Y.: Center for a Human Future, 1980.

Ballard, J. *Public Law 94-142 and Section 504: Understanding What They Are and Are Not* (Rev. ed.). Reston, Va.: Council for Exceptional Children, 1978. (ERIC Document Reproduction Service No. ED 146 764)

Bane, M. J., & Winston, K. I. *Equity in Higher Education.* Cambridge, Mass.: Harvard Graduate School of Education, 1980.

Baratz, J., & Baratz, S. Early childhood intervention: The social scientific basis of institutionalized racism. *Harvard Educational Review,* 1970, *39,* 29–50.

Benbow, C. P., & Stanley, J. C. Sex differences in mathematical ability: Fact or artifact? *Science,* December 1980, *210*(4475), 1262–1264.

Berke, J. S. *Answers to Inequity: An Analysis of the New School Finance.* Berkeley, Calif.: McCutchan, 1974.

Bordier, N. *Evaluating the Implementation of Federal Educational Equity Policy: Title IX and Sex Equity Technical Assistance.* Paper presented at the annual meeting of the American Educational Research Association, Los Angeles, April 1981.

Bornstein, R. *Title IX Compliance and Sex Equity Definitions, Distinctions, Costs, and Benefits.* Paper presented at the annual meeting of the American Educational Research Association, Los Angeles, Calif., April 1981.

Bronfenbrenner, U. *The Ecology of Human Development: Experiments by Nature and Design.* Cambridge, Mass.: Harvard University Press, 1979.

Brown v. *Board of Education,* 347, U.S. 483 (1954).

Brown v. *Board of Education,* 349, U.S. 294 (1955).

Campbell, P. B., & Scott, E. Non-biased tests can change the score. *Interracial Books for Children Bulletin,* 1980, *11*(6), 7–9.

Chun, K. The myth of Asian-American success and its educational ramifications. *Information Retrieval Center on the Disadvantaged Bulletin,* Winter-Spring 1980, *15*(1 & 2), 1–12.

Cloud, S. *Equity Self-assessment in Post-secondary Education Institutions.* Boulder, Colo.: National Center for Higher Education Management Systems, 1980. (ERIC Document Reproduction Service No. ED 192 657)

Current, R. N.; Williams, T. H.; & Freidel, F. *American History: A Survey.* New York: Knopf, 1964.

Fitzpatrick, B. *Women's Inferior Education.* New York: Praeger, 1976.

Flexner, E. *Century of Struggle.* New York: Atheneum, 1974.

Frazier, N., & Sadker, M. P. *Sexism in School and Society.* New York: Harper & Row, 1973.

Gilligan, C., & Langdale, S. *The Contribution of Women's Thought to Developmental Theory: The Elimination of Sex Bias in Moral Development Research and Education.* Washington, D.C.: National Institute of Education, 1980.

Graham, P. A. *Address to the American Association of School Administrators Convention.* Atlanta, Ga.: February 17, 1978.

Green, R. L.; Parsons, M. A.; & Thomas, F. S. Desegregation: The unfinished agenda. *Educational Leadership,* 1981, *38*(4), 282–285.

Greenawalt, K. The implication of *Regents of California* v. *Bakke* for university admission and hiring. *Equal Opportunity Review,* February 1979.

Harway, M., & Asten, H. S. *Sex Discrimination in Career Counseling and Education.* New York: Praeger, 1977.

Hyman, J. B., & Schaaf, J. M. *Educational Equity: Conceptual Problems and Prospects for Theory.* Washington, D.C.: National Institute of Education, 1981.

Jenson, A. R. *Bias in Mental Testing.* New York: Free Press, 1980.

Klein, S. S., & Goodman, M. A. *Federal Funding to Promote Sex Equity in Education.* Washington, D.C.: U.S. Department of Education, 1980. (ERIC Document Reproduction Service No. ED 195 483)

Lau v. *Nichols,* 414 U.S. 563 (1974).

Maccoby, E. E., & Jacklin, C. N. *The Psychology of Sex Differences.* Stanford, Calif.: Stanford University Press, 1974.

Martel, D. (Ed.). *The Itinerary of the Concept Equal Educational Opportunity.* Syracuse, N.Y.: Center for a Human Future, 1980.

Matthews, M., & McCune, S. *Complying with Title IX: Implementing Institutional Self-evaluation.* Washington, D.C.: U.S. Department of Health, Education, and Welfare, 1976. (ERIC Document Reproduction Service No. ED 125 468)

Mayeske, G. W.; Beaton, A. E., Jr.; Cohen, W. M.; Okada, T.; & Wisler, C. E. *A Study of the Achievement of Our Nation's Students.* Washington, D.C.: U.S. Government Printing Office, 1973. (ERIC Document Reproduction Service No. ED 085 626)

Mosher, E. K.; Hastings, A. H.; & Wagoner, J. L. *Pursuing Equal*

Educational Opportunity: School Policy and the New Activists (Urban Diversity Series, No. 64). New York: ERIC Clearinghouse on Urban Education, 1979. (ERIC Document Reproduction Service No. ED 179 625)

Myrdal, G. *An American Dilemma: The Negro Problem and Modern Democracy.* New York: Harper & Brothers, 1944.

National Education Association. *A Study Report: Education for All Handicapped Children—Consensus, Conflict, and Challenge.* Washington, D.C.: National Education Association, 1978.

Price-Curtis, W. Black progress toward educational equity. *Educational Leadership,* 1981, *38*(4), 277–280.

Rangel, J. C., & Alcala, C. M. *De jure* segregation of Chicanos in Texas schools. *Harvard Civil Rights–Civil Liberties Law Review,* 1972, *7*, 310–321.

Regents of California v. *Bakke,* 483 U.S. 265 (1978).

Sadker, M., & Sadker, D. *Between Teacher and Student: Overcoming Sex Bias in Classroom Interaction.* Newton, Mass.: Education Development Center, 1981.

Scarr, S. Environmental bias in twin studies. *Eugenics Quarterly,* 1968, *15*, 34–40.

Sellers, J. B. *Slavery in Alabama.* University: University of Alabama Press, 1950.

Southern Education Foundation. *Ending Discrimination in Higher Education.* Atlanta, Ga.: The Foundation, 1974. (ERIC Document Reproduction Service No. ED 100 238)

Stearns, M. S., & Cooperstein, R. A. Equity in educating the handicapped. *Educational Leadership,* 1981, *38*(4), 324–325.

Tocqueville, A. de. *Democracy in America.* London: Saunders & Otley, 1835. Reprint, New York: Knopf, 1946.

U.S. Commission on Civil Rights. *Puerto Ricans in the Continental United States: An Uncertain Future.* Washington, D.C.: U.S. Government Printing Office, 1976. (ERIC Document Reproduction Service No. ED 132 227)

U.S. Commission on Civil Rights. *Toward an Understanding of Bakke* (Clearinghouse Publication No. 58). Washington, D.C.: U.S. Government Printing Office, 1979. (ERIC Document Reproduction Service No. ED 128 514)

Walberg, H. J., & Bargen, M. Equality: Operational definitions and empirical tests. In A. Kopan & H. Walberg (Eds.), *Rethinking Educational Equity.* Berkeley, Calif.: McCutchan, 1974, pp. 11–26.

Weinberg, M. *Minority Students: A Research Appraisal.* Washington, D.C.: U.S. Government Printing Office, 1977. (ERIC Document Reproduction Service No. ED 137 483)

Weinberg, M. *A Chance to Learn: A History of Race and Education in the United States.* Cambridge, England: Cambridge University Press, 1979.

Weintraub, F. J.; Abeson, A.; Ballard, J.; & LaVon, M. L. *Public Policy and the Education of Exceptional Children.* Reston, Va.: Council for Exceptional Children, 1976. (ERIC Document Reproduction Service No. ED 116 403)

Wirtenberg, J.; Klein, S.; Richardson, B.; & Thomas, V. Sex equity in American education. *Educational Leadership,* January 1981, pp. 311–319.

ETHNIC DIFFERENCES

See Culture and Education Policy; Equity Issues in Education; Individual Differences; Multicultural and Minority Education.

ETHNOGRAPHY

Historically, the term "ethnography" has referred to the set of field-research methods used by anthropologists in the scientific study of primitive, nonliterate cultures (Conklin, 1968). As such it might be contrasted with the laboratory experiment, which has been the prototypical psychological method, or the social survey, which has been the defining methodology of much of sociology. In professional education, as in the disciplines of anthropology and sociology, adaptations, extensions, and new syntheses have arisen in response to an ever changing agenda of problems, cross-disciplinary efforts, and realignments of research communities. At the present moment one of the most fundamental observations about the concept of ethnography, as used in education, is that it is evolving rapidly. This seems related to an explosion of activity from several research communities that are only partially in communication with each other. Delamont and Atkinson (1980), Hammersley (1980), and Smith (1979) summarize some of this diversity. Accompanying this rapid increase in research is a proliferation of conceptual distinctions, with accompanying labels, that contain ethnography as the root concept. Table 1 presents a list of terms and their recent exponents or commentators.

Although these variants of ethnography present their own diversity, it is important to realize that ethnography itself is only one label for several social science methodologies, used by different disciplines and in different research communities, that have a number of fundamental similarities. Quasi synonyms of "ethnography" include "case study," "field study," "naturalistic methods," "participant observation," "responsive evaluation," and "qualitative methods." Wax (1971) sees a continuity both historically and conceptually among ethnography, participant observation, and field study. She titled her own book *Doing Fieldwork* (1971). Within educational ethnography, Wolcott (1975, 1980) is the most vigorous exponent for careful delineation of labels and restriction of the term "ethnography" to a type of fieldwork whose problems, methods, and results are empowered by and illuminated through anthropological concepts. In contrast, one of the earliest and most influential educational ethnographers, Spindler (1981), is arguing now for a more differentiated conception—anthroethnography, psychoethnography, and socioethnography—reflecting the multiple disciplines and theoretical positions now allied with ethnography. Any inquirer surveying the literature in the general domain is advised to check indexes for all the variants and quasi-synonyms.

Exemplars of Methodology. When a field is in such zesty disarray it seems useful to present several exemplars, from different times and places, that have implicitly served as models for several generations of researchers. These exemplars are drawn from the ranks of the more classical anthropological practitioners—Malinowski, Whyte, and Geertz—rather than from current educational research-

TABLE 1. *Recent variants of "ethnography" among educational researchers*

Variant	Researcher(s)
Anthroethnography	Spindler, 1981
Anthropological educational ethnography	Delamont and Atkinson, 1980
Anthropological ethnography of schooling	Spindler, 1981
Anthropopedagogy	Morin, 1980
Blitzkrieg ethnography	Rist, 1980
Classical ethnography	Mehan, 1980
Classroom ethnography	Hammersley, 1980
Constitutive ethnography	Mehan, 1978
Contract ethnography	Wolcott, 1975
Cooperative ethnography	Hymes, 1980
Educational ethnography	Spindler, 1981
Educational ethnology	Hymes, 1980
Ethnographic approach	Fitzsimmons, 1975
Ethnographic case studies	Herriott, 1977
Ethnographic methods	Lutz, 1980
Ethnographic monitoring	Hymes, 1980
Ethnographies of classroom life	Hamilton, 1981
Ethnography and policy making	Mulhauser, 1975
Ethnography of schooling	Wolcott, 1975
Ethnopedagogy	Burger, 1971
Evaluation ethnography	Rist, 1980
Focused ethnography	Erickson, 1977
Macroethnography	Lutz, 1980
Microethnography of the classroom	Smith, 1967
Neoethnography	Bullivant, 1978a
New ethnography	Erickson, 1973
Psychoethnography	Spindler, 1981
Socioethnography	Spindler, 1981
Sociological educational ethnography	Delamont and Atkinson, 1980

ers. Each has done a major ethnographic study, and each has written articulately and influentially about his use of methodology.

Any students, whether neophytes or experienced scholars, pursuing the concept of ethnography cannot go far wrong by beginning with Malinowski's classic introduction to *The Argonauts of the Western Pacific* (1922). He comments: "One of the first conditions of acceptable Ethnographic work certainly is that it should deal with the totality of all social, cultural, and psychological aspects of the community, for they are so interwoven that not one can be understood without taking into consideration all the others" (p. xvi). So Malinowski states his holistic and functionalist position. He argues that ethnography depends on real scientific aims, on living right among the natives, and on using a variety of special methods of collecting, manipulating, and fixing evidence. In elaborating these ideas, Malinowski provides distinctions, images, and metaphors that have rallied anthropologists for six decades, and educational theorists more recently. These include (1)

foreshadowed problems versus preconceived solutions; (2) methods of statistical documentation by concrete evidence, charts, and synoptic tables; (3) collecting concrete data on real cases, drawing inferences for oneself, and pursuing the data relentlessly and completely; (4) blending observation, constructive work (analysis and writing), and empirical checking; (5) focusing on the imponderables of everyday life; and (6) penetrating the mental attitude of the subjects. The ultimate goal, if it needs stating in a simple final form, is "to grasp the native's point of view, his relation to life, to realize *his* vision of *his* world" (p. 25). Although the idealism of this has been tarnished a bit by Malinowski's diary (Malinowski, 1967; Geertz, 1967; Wax, 1972), the ethnographic model remains. Educational researchers approaching communities, schools, and classrooms remain well served by his ideas and ideals.

Two decades later William Foote Whyte, working in the unusual context of the Society of Fellows at Harvard University and under the tutelage of more behavioristically oriented anthropologists (Arensberg, Chapple, and

Kimball), began *Street Corner Society: The Social Structure of an Italian Slum*, the first of a series of his investigations into contemporary society and its institutions. Later he published a major methodological statement, "On the Evolution of *Street Corner Society*" (1955). Much of that essay was an attempt to give one account of the actuality of field research as he experienced it, which, he hoped, when compared with other such accounts, would lead to a theory of research methodology. As he said: "I am convinced that the actual evolution of research ideas does not take place in accord with the formal statements we read on research methods. The ideas grow up in part out of our immersion in the data and out of the whole process of living" (p. 280). A careful reading of Whyte's account suggests several major ideas about ethnography as he practiced it. First, the problem of his research evolved from an undifferentiated "vague idea" of studying a slum community into a set of ideas linking intensive analyses of small social groups to broader issues in the larger community. The micro-macro problem became the issue. Second, the evolution was facilitated by such factors as the comments of his colleague John Howard on the theme of leadership (p. vii); the kinds of relationships he had developed, especially with "Doc," a leader of an informal group in Cornerville (pp. 291–292); the participatory style of his involvement with his subjects (pp. 302–303); and the preponderance of the kinds of data he was accumulating (p. 308). Finally, Whyte presents an image of one kind of criterion for ethnographic research: "It was Henderson [senior fellow and professor of biochemistry] who was easily the most imposing figure for the junior fellows. He seemed particularly to enjoy baiting the young social scientists. He took me on at my first Monday night dinner and undertook to show me that all my ideas about society were based on soft-headed sentimentality. While I often resented Henderson's sharp criticism, I was all the more determined *to make my field research stand up against anything he could say*" (p. 288, italics added). If we generalize this comment, good ethnographic research should interrelate issues, data, ideas, and conclusions so as to withstand the most critical assaults of an analytical father figure.

If Malinowski's position can be categorized as "functionalist," and Whyte's as "behavioral" or "social interactionist," Geertz (1973) falls into another theoretical tradition: that of an interpretive perspective. In his sequence of ideas, anthropology's mode of inquiring is ethnography; ethnography is "thick description"; thick description is the untangling of knotted nets or webs of meaning; the webs of meaning are culture; and culture is the subject matter of anthropology. In his own words: "From one point of view, that of the text book, doing ethnography is establishing rapport, selecting informants, transcribing texts, taking genealogies, mapping fields, keeping a diary, and so on. But it is not these things, techniques and received procedures, that define the enterprise. What defines it is the kind of intellectual effort it is: an elaborate venture in, to borrow a notion from Gilbert Ryle, 'thick description'"

(p. 6). In its simplest form, the argument of Geertz uses an illustration of Ryle's notion that understanding culture is much like distinguishing the involuntary twitching of an eyelid from winking, from parodying a wink, and from practicing a wink or a parody of a wink. "Contracting your eyelids on purpose when there exists a public code in which so doing counts as a conspiratorial signal *is* winking. That's all there is to it: a speck of behavior, a fleck of culture, and—voilà!—a gesture" (1973, p. 6).

Thick description is the ascertaining of these multiple levels and kinds of meaning. If that seems too simple, follow Geertz in his brief account of Cohen and the Moroccan sheep raid (1973), the deep play of the Balinese cock fight (1973), his analysis of common sense (1975a), or the nature of art (1976). Quattrocento painters who write mathematical treatises on "gauging" and Islamic poets who engage in "agonistic interpersonal communication" exemplify and enlarge, according to Geertz, the complex webs of cultural meaning. The purpose of all this activity, in the search for meanings in the historical or contemporaneous world in which one's subjects live, is to be able to "converse with them." As one penetrates more and more deeply into a culture, the language one develops expresses finer and finer shades of meaning. The theoretical abstractions one creates then are reapplied to the reality one is investigating to develop further insightful thick description. The play of this kind of science into the more general problems of mankind and into a special view of the human condition is seen in Geertz's summary comment: "The essential vocation of interpretive anthropology is not to answer our deepest questions, but to make available to us answers that others, guarding other sheep in the valleys, have given, and thus to include them in the consultable record of what man has said" (1973, p. 30). In Kluckhohn's distinguished phrasing, "Anthropology holds up a great mirror to man and lets him look at himself in his infinite variety" (1949, p. 11).

In sum, ethnography as presented and rationalized by Malinowski, Whyte, and Geertz, in their substantive contributions and in their autobiographical and methodological accounts, accents several major perspectives and orientations: (1) living for an extended time in the community or with the group being studied, which permits the researcher as a person in his or her direct participation, observation, and note taking to become the major source of data; (2) a concern for the small, mundane, day-to-day events as well as the esoteric or "important" events in the lives of individuals living, working, and playing together; (3) a particularistic focus on these individuals' perspectives, meanings, and interpretations of their world; (4) an attempt to build a synthetic and contextualized if not holistic view of life in the community, organization, or group; (5) a tendency to intentionally view the interpretive or conceptual structures in the research as evolving, being discovered, or being construed throughout the course of the research from the first statement of the problem to the final report; (6) reporting through a conscious

TABLE 2. *Exemplars of educational ethnography*

	Community		School level				School position			Curriculum			Educational process				
	Mainstream	Minority	Elementary	Secondary	Tertiary	Professional	Student	Teacher	Administration	Formal	Informal	Hidden extra	Curriculum development	Evaluation	Innovation	Socialization	Teaching–learning
Becker et al., *Boys in White* (1961)	X					X	X			X	X	X				X	
Bullivant, *Tradition* (1978b)		X		X			X	X		X						X	X
Cusick, *High School* (1973)	X			X			X			X						X	
Hamilton, *Structure* (1976)	X		X					X	X	X	X		X	X			
Henry, "Attitude" (1957); "Spontaneity" (1959)	X		X					X	X	X						X	
Mehan, *Lessons* (1980)		X	X				X			X							X
Peshkin, *Growing up American* (1978)	X			X			X	X		X	X	X				X	
Rist, *Urban School* (1973)		X	X				X			X							X
Smith and Geoffrey, *Complexities* (1968)		X	X				X			X						X	X
Wax et al., *Indian Community* (1964)		X	X				X		X	X					X		
Willis, *Learning to Labor* (1978)		X		X			X			X						X	
Wolcott, *Principal* (1973)	X		X						X	X						X	

and creative blending of storytelling or narrating with more abstract conceptualizing or theorizing. These three major investigators, in their reports and methodological accounts, implicitly and explicitly differ in their theoretical perspective and metatheoretical assumptions—in what Sanday (1979) has called "the style of ethnographic paradigm(s)." Beyond the holistic, semiotic, or behavioral styles, differences exist in breadth (miniature versus middle range versus grand theory), in abstraction (substantive versus formal), in form (coherent versus eclectic), and in purpose (practical versus basic). Such distinctions go beyond ethnography, and perhaps beyond social science, into the foundation of Western thought (Pepper, 1942; Toulmin, 1972).

Exemplars of Educational Ethnography. In the genre and style of Malinowski, Whyte, and Geertz, and illustrating the six generalizations made about their work, educational ethnographers, from several parts of the world, from several substantive disciplines, and from varied theoretical perspectives have opened almost every facet of education to inquiry. Studies abound of communities (mainstream and minority), of schools (elementary, secondary, tertiary, and professional), of school positions (students, teachers, principals), of programs and curricula (formal, informal, extra, hidden), and of educational processes (curriculum development, evaluation, innovation, socialization, and teaching–learning) (Smith, 1979). For the ethnographer, each variation represents a solution to a complex, interrelated set of issues regarding problem, setting, procedure, focus, theoretical perspective, and research purpose. Table

2 illustrates this diversity and indicates how educational settings have been approached ethnographically. The dozen studies shown in the table provide a set of models for the neophyte and for the experienced researcher who desire a view of educational ethnography in action.

New Directions. Anyone who engages in predictions about the directions of creative scientific effort strains the credulity of the critical reader. Be that as it may, several kinds of activity seem to be in the offing. First, the flow of other social scientists and educational researchers into the provinces once claimed more exclusively by anthropologists will continue. The University of Chicago sociologists doing symbolic interactionist research and the Columbia University functionalists have had a long claim to descriptive-interpretive methods in communities, in organizations, and in life histories. Delamont and Atkinson (1980) vividly describe both sociologically oriented and anthropologically oriented ethnographic work in education in Britain; the former, they say, is "more lively and active." But the group that has overrun the territory recently are the educationists, especially the educational evaluators and educational psychologists, who have found that their tools (tests and statistical procedures), their conceptual structures (trait and behavioral theory), and their settings (laboratories) cannot deal adequately with the interactional, political, contextual, and cultural problems of schools and classrooms. As these workers have abandoned, altered, and adapted their perspectives, both concrete and abstract, they have left the educational research community in disarray over problems, methods, and standards. As they have adopted the "case study approach," they have accented the kind of synthetic and holistic activity, careful descriptive-narrative accounts, and participant perspectives represented by the several major anthropological positions (Hamilton et al., 1977; Smith, 1979).

A second prediction is that efforts to move analytically with constitutive ethnography, focused ethnography, or microethnography on selected issues in schooling and education will continue (Erickson, 1977; McDermott, 1978; Mehan, 1980; Stubbs & Delamont, 1976). In part this will involve increasing use of technology: videotapes of interaction, audio recording of interviews, and computerization of data analysis. Although theoretical accents will vary among neofunctionalism, neobehaviorism, neo–symbolic interactionism, and neo-Marxism, the general movement will collide—productively, it is hoped–with earlier and technically similar traditions of time sampling in child development, systematic observation in social psychology, and quantitative classroom analysis in education (Weick, 1968; Dunkin & Biddle, 1974).

Third, although focal groups, settings, and issues will always be highlighted by ethnographers, educational researchers, with ethnography as a main component, will be arguing for two kinds of context: the larger system or culture in which the educational event is embedded and the historical stream of which the contemporary event is a part. Microethnographers, conservative or radical, will debate among themselves as well as with exponents of macroanalysis; synthesizers will move toward codification (Smith, Prunty, & Dwyer, 1981; Hammersley, 1980; Hamilton, 1976; Eickelman, 1978; Berlak & Berlak, 1981).

Fourth, the perspectives of multiple actors in the educational drama will be presented more frequently than in the past. Pluralism and politics are here to stay. Moreover, the extension of the multiple perspectives to include the researcher, emic versus etic orientations, will continue to occur and continue to be debated. Perhaps it will resolve itself into concepts such as "experience-near" and "experience-distant" raised by Geertz and defined with devastating illustrations: "How, in each case, should they [the concepts] be displayed so as to produce an interpretation of the way a people live which is neither imprisoned within their mental horizons, an ethnography of witchcraft as written by a witch, nor systematically deaf to the distinctive tonalities of their existence, an ethnography of witchcraft as written by a geometer?" (1975b, p. 48). In professional education, which is intrinsically a normative domain, according to some philosophers (Peters, 1965; Scheffler 1971), educational ethnographers not only must phrase the experience-near perspectives of teachers, pupils, administrators, and parents and the experience-distant concepts of researcher-theorists, but must also phrase the more Jovian "experience-good" conceptions—not so light a task.

Finally, in keeping with the differentiated thinking of Spindler (1981), there will surely be an "educational ethnography," whose basic and derived concepts, ideas, and interpretations belong to education rather than to one or another of the social sciences.

In conclusion, educational ethnography in the early 1980s encompasses a domain of great vitality, controversy, and multiple referents. Even among the most highly regarded anthropologists, such as Malinowski, Whyte, and Geertz, the conception of anthropological theory and method, and the interdependence of theory and method, have been evolving as one would expect in any scientific domain. As indicated in Tables 1 and 2, multiple voices suggest that a diverse range of drummers will continue to call to and for ethnographic marchers. Perhaps the strongest benefit will be long-term, in the development of mirrors enabling the multiple participants in the schooling enterprise to see more clearly, think more creatively, converse more empathically, and decide more wisely about their educational lives.

Louis M. Smith

See also Anthropology; Culture and Education Policy; Sociology of Education; Systematic Observation.

REFERENCES

Becker, H. S.; Geer, B.; Hughes, E. C.; & Strauss, A. L. *Boys in White: Student Culture in Medical School.* Chicago: University of Chicago Press, 1961.

Berlak, A., & Berlak, H. *Dilemmas of Schooling: Teaching and Social Change.* London: Methuen, 1981.

Bullivant, B. Towards a neo-ethnographic method for small group research. *Australian and New Zealand Journal of Sociology,* 1978, *14,* 239–249. (a)

Bullivant, B. *The Way of Tradition: Life in an Orthodox Jewish School.* Hawthorn, Victoria: Australian Council for Education Research, 1978. (b) (ERIC Document Reproduction Service No. ED 170 202)

Burger, H. *"Ethno-pedagogy": A Manual in Cultural Sensitivity.* Kansas City: University of Missouri, 1971. (ERIC Document Reproduction Service No. ED 091 109)

Conklin, H. Ethnography. In D. L. Sills (Ed.), *International Encyclopedia of the Social Sciences.* New York: Macmillan and Free Press, 1968.

Cusick, P. *Inside High School.* New York: Holt, Rinehart & Winston, 1973.

Delamont, S., & Atkinson, P. The two traditions in educational ethnography: Sociology and anthropology compared. *British Journal of Educational Sociology,* 1980, *1,* 139–152.

Dunkin, M., & Biddle, B. *The Study of Teaching.* New York: Holt, Rinehart & Winston, 1974.

Eickelman, D. F. The art of memory: Islamic education and its social reproduction. *Comparative Studies in Society and History,* 1978, *20,* 485–516.

Erickson, F. What makes school ethnography "ethnographic"? *Council on Anthropology and Education Newsletter,* 1973, *4,* 10–19.

Erickson, F. Some approaches to inquiry in school community ethnography. *Anthropology and Education Quarterly,* 1977, *8,* 58–69.

Fitzsimmons, S. J. The anthropologist in a strange land. *Human Organization,* 1975, *34,* 183–196.

Geertz, C. Under the mosquito net. *New York Review of Books,* September 14, 1967, *9,* 12–13.

Geertz, C. *The Interpretation of Cultures.* New York: Basic Books, 1973.

Geertz, C. Common sense as a cultural system. *Antioch Review,* 1975, *33*(1), 5–26. (a)

Geertz, C. On the nature of anthropological understanding. *American Scientist,* 1975, *63,* 47–53. (b)

Geertz, C. Art as a cultural system. *Modern Language Notes,* 1976, *91,* 1473–1499.

Hamilton, D. *In Search of Structure: Essays from an Open Plan School.* Edinburgh: Scottish Council for Research in Education, 1976.

Hamilton, D. Generalization in the educational sciences: Problems and purposes. In T. Popkewitz & R. Tabachnick (Eds.), *The Study of Schooling: Field-based Methodologies in Educational Research.* New York: Praeger, 1981.

Hamilton, D., D. Jenkins, C. King, B. MacDonald, & M. Parlett (Eds.). *Beyond the Numbers Game.* Berkeley, Calif.: McCutchan, 1977.

Hammersley, M. Classroom ethnography. *Educational Analysis,* 1980, *2,* 47–74.

Henry, J. Attitude organization in elementary school classrooms. *American Journal of Orthopsychiatry,* 1957, *27,* 117–133.

Henry, J. Spontaneity, initiative, and creativity in suburban classrooms. *American Journal of Orthopsychiatry,* 1959, *29,* 266–279.

Herriott, R. Ethnographic case studies in federally funded multidisciplinary policy research: Some design and implementation issues. *Anthropology and Education Quarterly,* 1977, *8,* 106–115.

Hymes, D. *Language in Education: Ethnolinguistic Essays.* Washington, D.C.: Center for Applied Linguistics, 1980.

Kluckhohn, C. *Mirror for Man: The Relation of Anthropology to Modern Life.* New York: McGraw-Hill, 1949.

Lutz, F. W. Ethnography: The holistic approach to understanding schooling. In J. L. Gree & C. Wallat. *Ethnography and Language in Educational Settings.* Norwood, N.J.: Ablex, 1980.

Malinowski, B. *The Argonauts of the Western Pacific.* London: Routledge, 1922.

Malinowski, B. *A Diary in the Strict Sense of the Term.* New York: Harcourt, Brace & World, 1967.

McDermott, R.; Gospodinoff, K.; & Aron, J. Criteria for an ethnographically adequate description of concerted activities and their contexts. *Semiotica,* 1978, *24,* 246–275.

Mehan, H. Structuring school structure. *Harvard Educational Review,* 1978, *48,* 32–64.

Mehan, H. *Learning Lessons: Social Organization in the Classroom.* Cambridge, Mass.: Harvard University Press, 1980.

Morin, A. An anthropological model of evaluation applied to a media course in an open system of learning. *Media Message,* 1980, *9,* 16–23.

Mulhauser, F. Ethnography and policy making: The case of education. *Human Organization,* 1975, *34,* 311–315.

Pepper, S. *World Hypotheses: A Study in Evidence.* Berkeley: University of California Press, 1942.

Peshkin, A. *Growing Up American: Schooling and the Survival of Community.* Chicago: University of Chicago Press, 1978.

Peters, R. S. Education as initiation. In R. D. Archambault (Ed.), *Philosophical Analysis and Education.* London: Routledge & Kegan Paul, 1965.

Rist, R. C. *The Urban School: A Factory for Failure.* Cambridge, Mass.: MIT Press, 1973.

Rist, R. C. Blitzkrieg ethnography: On the transformation of a method into a movement. *Educational Researcher,* 1980, *9,* 8–10.

Sanday, P. R. The ethnographic paradigm(s). *Administrative Science Quarterly,* 1979, *24,* 527–538.

Scheffler, I. Philosophical models of teaching. In R. T. Hyman (Ed.), *Contemporary Thought on Teaching.* Englewood Cliffs, N.J.: Prentice-Hall, 1971.

Smith, L. M. The micro-ethnography of the classroom. *Psychology in the Schools,* 1967, *4,* 216–221.

Smith, L. M. An evolving logic of participant observation, educational ethnography, and other case studies. In L. Schulman (Ed.), *Review of Research in Education.* Chicago: F. E. Peacock, 1979.

Smith, L. M., & Geoffrey, W. *The Complexities of an Urban Classroom.* New York: Holt, Rinehart & Winston, 1968.

Smith, L. M.; Prunty, J.; & Dwyer, D. A longitudinal nested systems model of innovation and change in schooling. In S. Bacharach (Ed.), *Organizational Analysis of Schools and School Districts.* New York: Praeger, 1981.

Spindler, G. General introduction. In G. Spindler (Ed.), *Doing Ethnography of Schooling.* New York: Holt, Rinehart & Winston, 1981.

Stubbs, M., & Delamont, S. (Eds.). *Explorations in Classroom Observation.* New York: Wiley, 1976.

Toulmin, S. *Human Understanding* (Vol. 1). Princeton, N.J.: Princeton University Press, 1972.

Wax, M. Tenting with Malinowski. *American Sociological Review,* 1972, *37,* 1–13.

Wax, M.; Wax, R.; & DuMont, R. V., Jr. *Formal Education in an American Indian Community.* Supplement, *Social Problems,* 1964, *11*(4).

Weick, K. E. Systematic observational methods. In G. Lindsay & E. Aronson (Eds.), *The Handbook of Social Psychology* (2nd ed.). Reading, Mass.: Addison-Wesley, 1968.

Whyte, W. F. *Street Corner Society* (Rev. ed.). Chicago: University of Chicago Press, 1955.

Willis, P. *Learning to Labor.* Westmead, England: Saxon House, 1978.

Wolcott, H. *The Man in the Principal's Office: An Ethnography.* New York: Holt, Rinehart & Winston, 1973.

Wolcott, H. Criteria for an ethnographic approach to research in the schools. *Human Organizations,* 1975, *34,* 111–128.

Wolcott, H. How to look like an anthropologist without really being one. *Practicing Anthropology,* 1980, *3,* in press.

EVALUATION OF PROGRAMS

Many disciplines lay claim to program evaluation as an area for scholarly investigation and as an applied field. Each discipline lends a particular perspective to the interplay between theoretical and analytical work in program evaluation and the practice of evaluation in natural settings. This creates a dynamic relationship; knowledge gained in one area of endeavor modifies and refines the other discipline. The purpose of this article is to review the most salient contributions of various disciplines to the evaluation of educational programs in order to understand the range of diverse positions and issues designated by the subject.

Seven topics are discussed. The first section examines causes of the mercurial rise of program evaluation as a field of study. The second section discusses the various definitions of evaluation, research, evaluation research, and program evaluation, and distinguishes among them. Section three explores three areas of philosophy that influence program evaluation and further define it. Assumptions about epistemology, values, and praxis are embedded in all evaluation issues and have direct bearing on two major issues—methodology and politics of program evaluation—discussed in the fourth section. The fifth section looks at the many ways in which evaluators attempt to bring order to the field of evaluation through classification of evaluation approaches, both conceptual and applied. The last two sections discuss topics relatively new in program evaluation, resulting directly from evaluators' work in applied settings: utilization of evaluation findings and standards for conducting evaluations.

Among the topics for discussion, specific program evaluations of prominent intervention studies and longitudinal studies are not included. A recitation of large-scale educational intervention studies (such as Head Start and Follow Through) is detailed in other publications, and reference to such studies will be made only to illustrate a point (see Williams & Evans, 1969; Trismen, Waller, & Wilder, 1975; McDill, McDill, & Sprehe, 1969; Cicirelli, Evans, & Schiller, 1969; Ball & Bogatz, 1970). Research involving data base and longitudinal studies also are treated in depth elsewhere—by Tyler (1966), Merwin, (1966), and Ebel (1966) in the *Journal of Educational Measurement* on the National Assessment of Educational Progress; by Husén, (1967) on the International Study of Achievement; and by Flanagan (1966, 1978) on Project Talent and the fifteen-year follow-up. Although health care programs, welfare programs, and other social intervention programs undergo evaluation, this article focuses upon evaluation of education programs.

Growth and Development

Program evaluation, as a field for scholarly study and as an applied professional endeavor, has undergone enormous changes over the past decade. No entry exists in the fourth edition of the *Encyclopedia of Educational Research* (Ebel, 1969) for evaluation research. The entry "curriculum evaluation" (Heath, 1969) and the accompanying bibliography illustrates the narrow perspective of the field a little over a decade ago. Examination of the descriptors for evaluation used in *Education Index* from 1957 through 1979 documents the emphasis on evaluation as measurement, research designs, and curriculum evaluation; the descriptor "evaluation research" does not make an appearance until 1974, along with "social action programs." Such topics as "utilization" and "politics of evaluation," so critical to contemporary program evaluation, first

appear in the 1976–1977 listings. Other signs of the enormous growth of the field evaluation research are the number of journals and yearbooks devoted to evaluation since 1973 (*Evaluation Studies Review Annual*, Volume 1, 1976; *Educational Evaluation and Policy Analysis*, Volume 1, 1979; *Evaluation Review*, Volume 1, 1977; *Evaluation and Change*, Volume 1, 1973, formerly called *Evaluation; Evaluation News*, Volume 1, 1980) and the new scholarly associations emphasizing evaluation, such as the Evaluation Research Society and Division *H* of the American Educational Research Association. The best indicator of growth in a field is fiscal allocation. The annual budget of the Office of Planning, Budgeting, and Evaluation of the U.S. Office of Education grew 1,650 percent from 1968 to 1977 (McLaughlin, 1980).

Evaluation Programs. Availability of government moneys provided the impetus for much of the growth of evaluation research and its shaping of program evaluation. These funds were earmarked for two distinctly different purposes at two slightly overlapping points in time: massive curriculum development efforts preceding social intervention programs. Curriculum development of the 1950s and 1960s, responding to the *Sputnik* scare, served to modernize science and mathematics content and methods. Government funds provided for new curricula to upgrade the education programs of students who would become the nation's future technological leaders. The monies, especially National Science Foundation grants and private foundation funds, brought about the proliferation of new science, mathematics, and social studies curricula and supporting instructional materials. Evaluation of these product development efforts opened up one area of evaluation of educational programs, along with the attendant dialogue concerning definitions, models, and problems in evaluation (Welch, 1979). Evaluators of curriculum products had their roots mainly in educational research and educational psychology, and their approaches to program evaluation reflected the state of the art of evaluation in their respective disciplines at that time.

Moneys for social action programs, emanating from the War on Poverty legislation in the 1960s and early 1970s, served an egalitarian purpose. The social action programs of the 1960s included the range of antipoverty programs as well as large-scale educational intervention programs. Social scientists, active in conceptualizing social and economic amelioration projects, took the lead in designing and conducting evaluations of these programs in the light of their respective research traditions (Marris & Rein, 1973; Hyman & Wright, 1967). The history of these programs, the legislation that brought them into being, and their impact upon evaluation research are covered by Anderson and Ball (1978) and McLaughlin (1976).

Evaluators of curriculum development efforts and those engaged in evaluation of social intervention programs soon recognized the limitations of their respective research traditions in addressing pertinent evaluation questions. Curriculum product evaluation, conducted in field settings, presented previously unforeseen evaluation problems. Educational psychologists, drawing upon their strong experimental design tradition, found it difficult to randomly assign subjects to groups, obtain data, and otherwise intrude upon life in the classroom. Similarly, sociologists and political scientists engaged in evaluation of social intervention programs found critical limitations in applying their research approaches in naturalistic or field settings. Interdisciplinary consultation was frequently lacking. As designers of large-scale educational intervention programs brought together evaluation specialists from education and psychology as well as from the fields of sociology, political science, economics, anthropology, and policy research, evaluation took on an eclectic character. Today evaluators from education or psychology reference the evaluation literature from sociology, economics, anthropology, and policy analysis, and evaluators in these other disciplines show an awareness of their counterparts in education and psychology. This was not the case in the late 1950s and early 1960s. The various perspectives of different disciplines enriched each other, bringing about a reconsideration of research methodology in evaluation design beginning in the late 1960s.

In summarizing the decade of the 1970s, Cronbach et al. (1980) identify three central developments in program evaluation: (1) realization by policy analysts that field research would enhance planning; (2) recognition that politics and science are integral to evaluation; and (3) promotion of experimental methodology in order to avoid the criticisms of the early, large-scale intervention evaluations. The first and second developments have now become common knowledge among evaluators from the various disciplines. However, the place of experimental methodology among evaluation techniques is still a subject of dispute among evaluators. Moreover, it involves not only methodological issues, since its roots are embedded in epistemological issues and in questions of value and utility.

Definition

A definition of program evaluation derives its meaning from such terms as "evaluation," "research," "experimental research," and "evaluation research." In order to clarify the meaning of these terms, the differences between evaluation and research are discussed, and a working definition of research, experimental research, and evaluation research is formulated. Then, the different ways of defining evaluation are examined in terms of its various purposes.

Evaluation and Research. Distinctions between evaluation and research have received thorough treatment by Hemphill (1969), Worthen and Sanders (1973), Popham (1975), and Suchman (1967). Hemphill identified six areas that distinguish between research and evaluation: type of problem selected and how it is defined; use of hypotheses; role of value judgments in the development and implementation of design; replicability of the study; specification of data to be collected; and randomization. Worthen and

Sanders (1973) presented a list of twelve properties distinguishing research and evaluation. They add several other distinguishing characteristics to those mentioned by Hemphill: laws versus description, autonomy of inquiry, criteria for judging the activity, disciplinary base, and the training of evaluators. Contrary to Hemphill, Worthen and Sanders regard the salience of value questions as one of degree rather than kind. Popham's list (1975) corresponds in most instances with that of Worthen and Sanders, and many of the same points are identified by Suchman (1967) and by Caro (1977). Boruch (1976) and Boruch, McSweeny, and Soderstrom (1978) take strong exception to the assertion by Hemphill that randomization is neither feasible nor used frequently in evaluation studies. These references identify many social intervention studies in which subjects were randomly assigned to treatment and control groups; only a few of these, however, can be called educational studies.

To avoid the pitfalls of definitional disputes, for our discussion the term "research" will be used broadly to describe any form of systematic inquiry that seeks explanation of phenomena. "Experimental research" can then be defined as hypothesis-testing under controlled conditions, with careful attention to internal validity issues (Cook & Campbell, 1979), validation through replication, and generalizability. Evaluation research studies usually lack replicability because the system, program, or phenomenon being studied is dynamic; that is, it is in operation, changeable, and taking place in a naturalistic or field setting. Whereas the canons of scientific rigor are applied to evaluation research as far as possible, it is necessary to augment the study with descriptions of contextual variables, and to utilize the methodologies and perspectives of various disciplines in order best to understand the processes and functioning of the system, program, or phenomenon under study. The leaves the root term "evaluation" as yet undefined.

Evaluation Purposes. Three purposes appear most frequently in definitions of evaluation: (1) to render judgment on the worth of a program; (2) to assist decision makers responsible for deciding policy; and (3) to serve a political function. These purposes are not mutually exclusive; most evaluation researchers include rendering judgment and assisting decision makers in defining their tasks. And under different circumstances, definitions shift from one to another purpose. The political function, for example, is a recent addition that grew out of evaluators' experiences with educational intervention programs. As evaluators faced the realities of politically embedded social intervention programs, the political constraints imposed upon their design execution, and utilization of the evaluation became increasingly evident.

Valuing or assessing worth of a program is at the root of the concept of evaluation; judgment has historically been associated with the term. Judgment about the worth of a program generally refers to the degree to which an education program meets its intended outcomes, as R. M.

Wolf (1979) and Gowin (Gowin & Green, 1980) maintain. The objectives of a program, as measured by its outcomes, establish the criteria for rendering judgment. Popham (1975) and Scriven (1967) refer to these as "intrinsic criteria." The standards for determining the worth of a program are set by the program's intent. "Extrinsic criteria," as pointed out by Scriven (1967), are concerned with the quality of the program goals. The evaluator should not take these goals as given; rather, they should be assessed and their worth established. Extrinsic criteria also should be applied to curriculum products such as educational materials and program designs. An appropriate evaluation question would ask: Is this a "good" reading series, not as compared to some other reading series, but in its own right? Such an evaluation question returns us to the philosophical issues of criteria for establishing worth.

Gowin (Gowin & Green, 1980) offers some assistance in circumventing the philosophical dilemma by raising five evaluation questions that are responsive to the values issue in defining evaluation: (1) Is this thing any good?—an intrinsic value question; (2) What is it good for?—an instrumental value question; (3) Is it better than something else?—a comparative value question; (4) Can I make it better?—an idealization value question; and (5) Is this the right thing to do?—a decision question. These questions help to pinpoint value issues while avoiding the pitfalls inherent in one sweeping judgment about the worth of a program.

The second purpose of evaluation separates the roles of evaluator and decision maker. The responsibility for making a judgment about a program's worth resides in the decision maker; the evaluator's task is to provide the decision maker with sufficient information for arriving at a decision. The decision about a program involves judgment of the value or worth of the program to the user. The purpose of evaluation to provide information grew out of the problems encountered in evaluating social intervention programs, especially in regard to the political nature of these programs. Alkin (1969), Patton (1978), C. H. Weiss (1975), Stufflebeam and Webster (1980), and Cronbach et al. (1980) provide working definitions of evaluation from this perspective. Rather early in the short history of evaluation research, Alkin distinguished evaluation from rendering judgments. To Alkin (1969), evaluation is ". . . the process of determining the kinds of decisions that have to be made; selecting, collecting, and analyzing these decisions; and reporting this information to appropriate decision-makers" (p. 2). Definitions by Patton, Stufflebeam, and Webster reinforce the idea of separating the evaluative process from the decision-making process. To Patton (1978), evaluation research "is the systematic collection of information about the activities and outcomes of actual programs in order for interested persons to make judgments about specific aspects of what the program is doing and affecting" (p. 26). Stufflebeam and Webster (1980) offer a similar definition: "educational evaluation study is one that is designed and conducted

to assist some audience to judge and improve the worth of some audience to judge and improve the worth of some educational object" (p. 6).

The third purpose of evaluation is political. An outgrowth of evaluation as providing information, the political view of evaluation alerts evaluators to the political nature of evaluation and cautions them to be realistic in designing studies. Most evaluators concerned with the politics of evaluation draw on their experiences with social intervention programs and the political demands made by federal and state agencies primarily concerning the use of their findings but also concerning conduct of the study. As Freeman states, "evaluation is now a political tool" (1975). Gowin and Green (1980), C. H. Weiss (1975), Cronbach et al. (1980), and Cohen (1970) all refer to the political nature of evaluation. In his review of the literature on evaluating social action programs in education, Cohen concludes, "evaluating social action programs is only secondarily a scientific enterprise. First and foremost it is an effort to gain politically significant information on the consequences of political acts. To confuse the technology of measurement with the real nature and broad purposes of evaluation will be fatal" (pp. 236–237). Hill (1980), commenting upon the lessons learned from the National Institute for Education's compensatory education studies, draws the following conclusion: "Although evaluation results are essentially technical, their ultimate use is political. Without some appreciation for the politics of a decision, evaluators are unlikely to serve the decision making process well" (p. 76). (For an extensive treatment of evaluation and politics, see Sroufe, 1977.)

An authoritative definition of program evaluation remains elusive because of the lack of consensus about evaluation purposes. There is no single, right definition of evaluation. Rather, program evaluation involves all three purposes—judgmental, decision-making, and political—with different emphasis upon each purpose in different studies. Nevertheless, a concise definition of a program suggested by Cronbach et al. (1980) will serve the purpose of formulating our definition: it is "a standing arrangement that provides for social services." Adding the term "educational" to "program" narrows the range of services considered in this discussion of educational program evaluation. Evaluation of educational programs is one area of evaluation under the rubric of evaluation research; it involves all three designated purposes and applies the full range of evaluation research activities from initial design and planning through program implementation and institutionalization.

Philosophical Assumptions

Underlying the definitions of evaluation derived from its purposes are philosophical assumptions about epistemology and value. Program evaluation is an applied discipline, and it must confront the real world of people and institutions as well as social, economic, and political pressures. Thus we must consider practical assumptions (the world of praxis) in order to understand the nature of program evaluation.

Epistemological Issues. Every discipline must think through its particular way of knowing or establishing truth, a concern central to educational program evaluation. Kerlinger (1965) categorizes ways of knowing from the most holistic-inductive to the hypothetico-deductive, the latter being the epistemological basis of the scientific method. The hypothetico-deductive approach has served the natural sciences well throughout the twentieth century, despite the intrusion of the subjective nature of many decisions in the conduct of scientific investigation. As the social sciences (mainly psychology, sociology, economics, and education) emerged as separate disciplines apart from philosophy, they based their methodologies upon the hypothetico-deductive approach to seeking truth—if not truth in the purest sense, then at least establishing certainty within acceptable limits. Disciplines embedded in a social context presented problems different from disciplines in the natural sciences; however, even in the latter field, complex, interactive physical properties have exposed the limitations of the scientific method (Ziman, 1980). Concerns about what constitutes acceptable evidence and the problems of measuring complex, interactive social phenomena have challenged the "infallibility" of the hypothetico-deductive approach to answering questions in the social sciences (Polanyi, 1958; Hamilton et al., 1977; Guba, 1978).

In order to shake the hypothetico-deductive hold upon the methodologies of various social science disciplines, attacks have been extreme. The literature is filled with arguments concerning the idiosyncratic nature of knowing, abetted by the insights of existential philosophy and phenomenological psychology (Sartre, 1963; Merleau-Ponty, 1962; Deutscher, 1970). Researchers within these disciplines have tended to line up along humanistic/behavioral, qualitative/quantitative universalistic/particularistic, naturalistic/experimental continua. Program evaluation has been greatly affected by the schism: what is considered "acceptable" evaluation research often depends upon the position taken regarding one or another of these continua. However, to tenaciously hold to one extreme at the expense of the other ignores the magnitude of the problem of establishing certainty. An eclectic position recognizes the value of the scientific method in ferreting out new knowledge and establishing truth (until otherwise disproved), but it is also concerned with multiple perceptions and their effect upon defining what constitutes data (C. H. Weiss, 1979; and McLaughlin, 1980). It is not only a question of *how* to measure something, but of *what* should be measured in representing a phenomenon. House (1980) and Haney (1977) trace the bitter history of evaluating the Follow Through program on just this issue. Evaluation models that specify relationships between inputs and outputs within an experimental design without benefit of community questions and concerns may be incapable of

providing the type of data that permits meaningful evaluation. Thus, the context and perceptions of constituencies play an integral role in obtaining and interpreting meaningful data. A methodology that does not take context and varying perceptions into account, no matter how rigorously it applies the scientific method, has little value as an evaluation approach. Cronbach et al. (1980) sum up the eclectic position: "The evaluator will be wise not to declare allegiance to either quantitative-manipulative-summative methodology or a qualitative-naturalistic-descriptive methodology. He can draw on both styles at appropriate times and in appropriate amounts. Those who advocate an evaluation plan devoid of one kind of information or another carry the burden of justifying such exclusions" (p. 233).

Value Issues. Ultimately evaluation is concerned with value or worth. Whether it is the role of the evaluator to establish the worth of an educational program or whether this is a decision of the policy maker is not the concern here, although it is important in defining the term "evaluation." In this section, "value" is examined from two perspectives: (1) the political-economic roots of the value concept used in evaluation; and (2) social values in terms of costs and benefits.

Political-economic perspective. The political-economic perspective on value issues has its historical roots in eighteenth-century political philosophy and nineteenth-century economics. Prior to the mid-1960s, a generally unstated position on what society values characterized discussions about worth in program evaluation. House (1978) traces this position to J. S. Mill's principle of utilitarianism and views it as a hidden value assumption in education, one carried over into educational evaluation. The value of utility emanates from the principle of the greatest good for the greatest number, or as expressed by Bentham (1948), the "greatest happiness principle"; accordingly, the maximum good for the greatest number becomes the criterion of value. People are considered in the aggregate, and individual needs or special conditions are lost (House, 1976). A program that benefits the greatest number of students (benefit is typically associated with academic achievement, but does not necessarily have to be confined to it) is the program of most worth, or of the greatest utility.

Social intervention programs challenged the utility assumption by selecting for maximization a subgroup within the population. But these programs did not challenge the underlying principle of aggregation in determining utility. That is, even within a subgroup, some percentage of the total subgroup will not benefit, whereas others will benefit more than the general number; the "greatest happiness principle" as a criterion of value is predicated on an aggregated average. Shapiro (1981) offers five alternative criteria in addition to the utility principle of distribution: "equity," "Pareto-optimality," "majority," "minimax," and "dominance." The equity principle of distribution would view equalization of outcome as the criterion for evaluating the worth of an educational program by "minimizing differences across the individuals" (Shapiro, 1981). Pareto-optimality places its criterion of distribution on raising the outcome for every individual regardless of the degree of gain for any one individual; everyone gains, even though the average gain may be less than in a program in which few show gains but the average value of the gain is higher. The majority-distribution criterion modifies the Pareto-optimality criterion by looking at the numbers of those who actually show positive gains. Thus, if the majority of students showed even minimal gains, the program would satisfy the criterion of majority distribution. The minimax distribution criterion is predicated upon raising the level of those at the bottom, the worst off. Many social intervention programs select their subjects from this population, but revert to the utility criterion for analyzing outcomes and for determining the worth of the program. The dominance criterion of distribution matches the entry position of individuals and compares their performance in two different programs. The preferred program is the one with the greatest number of individuals who perform better than their counterpart in the second program. Shapiro illustrates through hypothetical examples how assessment of program outcomes will differ and decisions about the value of programs change depending upon distribution criteria. The outcomes that society values determine the focus of program evaluation and resulting decisions about the program's worth.

Benefit-cost perspective. The second way of considering the concept of worth or value when establishing a program's worth focuses upon social values in terms of costs and benefits. Examining costs and benefits transcends distribution of resources and its outcomes for a designated group; it explores the interactive consequences of distribution of resources and evaluates them in determining the worth of a program. Methodology from the field of economics provides a way of converting social values to costs and benefits. Benefit-cost analysis is intended as a way to assign monetary value to alternative choices. Cost, then, is the criterion (Haller, 1974).

Society has limited resources, and any shift in the assignment of resources has a cost factor and a benefit factor. The cost of installing a new program not only includes all the costs associated directly with the program (materials, personnel, physical plant, disruption to ongoing programs, administration, student time), but also opportunities foregone (those resources and current benefits that must be given up) and negative short-run and long-run consequences. Who receives what benefits from a program, from whose perspective is it a benefit, and who bears the brunt of the costs are fundamental social issues. Evaluation of the worth of an educational program to society (or local community) puts a premium on agreed-upon educational goals. Glennan (1969) suggests weighting the gains of one group (say the slow learners) against the gains and losses of another group (the gifted learners). Differential weighting of costs and benefits for different subgroups

in society, however, carries with it deep-seated philosophical implications about equality, equal distribution of resources, and equity.

In practice, applying benefit-cost analysis to socially embedded programs highlights the problems of obtaining consensus on philosophical issues underlying program goals, or for that matter, on the goals per se. Rossi (1972) raised a number of questions related to this issue. Reviewing the work of Wholey et al. (1970) on attempting a benefit-cost analysis to evaluate child health programs, he concludes that "the application of the cost-benefit analysis model . . . highlighted the difficulties involved in empirical application" (p. 29). Rothenberg (1975) also expressed reservations about assigning program worth on the basis of benefit-cost analysis. (For a general discussion of benefit-cost analysis see Haller, 1974; Rothenberg, 1975; Levin, 1975; and Thompson, 1980.)

Benefit-cost analysis, utilitarianism, and other criteria for evaluation such as those proposed by Shapiro (1981) do not resolve the underlying issue of the role of social values. However, the question of values is circular, returning us to epistemological considerations. Is there an ultimate criterion of worth? Does it reside in the social, political, or economic nature of man singularly or man generally? How do we establish with certainty the ultimate worth of the criterion? It may well be that the search for the single, right value system or the single best educational program is an unproductive activity, for program evaluation is basically a matter of praxis; thus we need to distinguish between intrinsic worth and pragmatic worth.

Practical Issues. Value may reside not so much in a statement of worth about a program but in the usefulness of the evaluation to the decision maker. This pragmatic perspective has been fair game for the field of evaluation; and sides are clearly drawn on whether the intent of evaluation is to render a value judgment. Scriven (1967), Boruch and Riecken (1975), R. M. Wolf (1979) and many others come down on the side of value judgments as the critical attribute of evaluation. C. H. Weiss (1977a, 1977b), Patton (1978), Edwards and Guttentag (1975) and others consider the rendering of value judgments to be beyond the role of the evaluator. To the latter group, the value of evaluation resides in its utility to the decision maker. The evaluator is placed squarely in the political arena and in the world of decision making.

If evaluation's role is to assist decision makers, then evaluators must consider the nature of decision making. Political science, especially in the areas of legislative decision making, conflict resolution, and policy making, offer models of decision making that apply to evaluation. Allison (1971) suggests three conceptual models for explaining decisions: the classical, organizational, and bureaucratic models.

Decision-making models. The classical model views human behavior as rational, purposive, and goal-directed. This view of human behavior also applies to classical economics, statistical decision theory, and game theory. The underlying concepts of the model include goals, alternatives, consequences and choice, and utility or benefit as well as their interrelationships. There is a conscious rationality in making a choice, given the objectives and consequences of alternatives. Most evaluations of programs before the 1970s assumed this view of human behavior; given the program goals, comparative data on alternative programs, and some information on consequences, the decision maker or evaluator could make a choice or render a value decision.

The second decision model derives from organizational theory (March & Simon, 1958; March, 1965; Simon, 1957). A network of semi-autonomous small organizations exists within a large organization. Each organization is primarily responsible for specific tasks and functions within a fixed set of procedures. According to Allison (1971), few large-scale decisions are made; rather most decisions must work through the procedures within each network, resulting in incremental changes that are less disruptive to large systems. Braybrooke and Lindbloom (1963) refer to this model of decision making as "disjointed incrementalism"; only crises precipitate dramatic decisions. This view of decision making leads to parochial priorities and perceptions. For example, evaluations that are designed to make "go/no go" decisions based upon the worth of a program have limited value to the decision maker; according to this model, only incremental changes are tolerable. Information about program functioning is of greater utility than recommendations requiring extensive changes, based upon the worth of the total program. By knowing the structure of the organization and its standard operating procedures, evaluators can build an evaluation design that takes the decision constraints of the rational-actor model into consideration.

The third model described by Allison (1971) is predicated on the role of power, or the political game played to keep the leader on top. Decisions are arrived at by the "pulling and hauling that is politics" (p. 144). Since, players within the shared power structure have their own constituencies to satisfy, decisions are the results of bargaining. Evaluation of programs in a large school system would need a design that is responsive to the individual players, their power base, and the factors determining the players' stand. The game of decision making involves negotiation, bargaining, and compromise.

Given one or another of these models, programs are conceived differently and the problems for evaluation formulated differently. The worth of the evaluation is contingent upon how well it reflects the prevailing model under which the decision maker functions.

If value is pragmatic and not absolute, a value decision cannot be arrived at without consideration of competing social demands and environmental stress. Regardless of whose definition of evaluation takes precedence, program evaluators must be alert to the political, social, and economic implications of the values expressed in the program (whether explicit or implicit) as well as the values held by the evaluator (Rosenthal, 1966). Sjoberg (1975) cautions evaluators that they may be functioning as "captives in a bureaucratic structure" unless they are alert to the ethical and political assumptions in a program. Cronbach (1978) resolves the value issue by withdrawing the evaluator from the fray: "It is not the task of the evaluator to determine whether a program is worthwhile, or what decision is 'right.' The evaluator cannot properly judge what conclusion is sound for someone else." (p. 14).

Methodological and Political Issues

Critical issues emerge from the positions taken by evaluators on evaluation methodology and politics. These issues are embedded in philosophical assumptions regarding epistemology, values, and praxis, and are integral to program evaluation design and the role of the evaluator. Methodological approaches are presented first, although the reader must bear in mind that they are influenced by political issues.

Methodology. The methodological principles governing measurement and design in social science inquiry also pertain to educational program evaluation (Caro, 1977). However, problems unique to evaluating programs present methodological issues that challenge traditional principles of measurement and design. These issues concern the nature of evidence for establishing certainty, the need for alternative methodologies to experimental and quasi-experimental designs, questions of criteria of value, and the impact of the real world of practice upon designing evaluation studies.

Training programs or limited intervention programs usually have fixed, agreed-upon goals, identifiable program features, recognizable procedures for carrying out a program, and measurable outcomes in terms of an acquired skill or a quantitative count. Education intervention programs, however, lack most of the above attributes. First, there is a lack of consensus on goals, or if consensus exists, attainment of goals is so removed from immediate participation in the program that the treatment is confounded many times over by intervening events. Second, the program never remains fixed, and if a clearly defined program is laid out, implementation varies considerably from one setting to another. Third, international organizational forces and external pressures act upon the program and the participants in ways that further modify or alter the treatment, for better or for worse. Fourth, what variables are identified, who makes the identification, who collects the data, and how the data are collected all shape the nature and, consequently, the validity of the evidence. R. S. Weiss and Rein (1972), Patton (1980), House (1978), Hamilton et al. (1977), Guttentag (1971), and others treat one or another of these issues. Thus, many evaluation researchers question the efficacy of what they call "traditional methodology," or the logico-deductive form of inquiry as applied to evaluation of intervention programs.

Glass and Ellett (1980) are cautious about such standards of science as objectivity, experimentation, and generalization. They conclude: "A large part of scientific judgment is knowing which circumstances are important and which are not. Such forms of knowing are largely tacit and qualitative, based on experience and involving assumptions of regularity, order, and stasis that are never formally checked as a part of science itself" (p. 244).

The problem reaches beyond experimental design. The evaluator's objectivity is called into question, as is the overemphasis on input-output variables to the neglect of process and context variables as well as reliance on measurable variables such as achievement, using instruments that obscure true performance. For convenience, we can divide evaluation researchers into four groups along methodological lines: experimentalists, eclectics, describers, and benefit-cost analysts.

In the first group are researchers engaged in "strong" research designs. Experimentalist evaluators focus upon establishing causal links between program and outcomes. This position is most prominently represented by Cook and Campbell (1979), Boruch and Riecken (1975), the RMC group (Horst, Tallmadge, & Wood, 1975), and Rivlin and Timpane (1975). Suchman (1967, 1970) serves as an early link between the experimentalists and the second group, the eclectics. The second group takes an eclectic position by drawing upon experimental designs that make possible causal statements along with methods that describe the process of program implementation as well as contextual variables effecting the program; in this way an evaluation design can search for multiple causality or generate plausible explanations that approximate reality. Cronbach (1980), R. S. Weiss and Rein (1972), and C. H. Weiss (1972b, 1972c) represent this position. The third group rejects experimental designs as inappropriate methodology for understanding socially embedded programs and their effects upon participants. To this group, meaningful data are only possible through in-depth descriptions of the program in context and through the personal testimony of participants. (See Stake, 1975; Patton, 1980; and Parlett & Hamilton, 1977 on descriptive evaluation.) The fourth group brings to evaluation research a methodological approach borrowed from economics, benefit-cost analysis (Thompson, 1980; Levin, 1975; Rothenberg, 1975; Haller, 1974). Another group of commentators rejects all forms of these methodological orientations. This group questions the social, political, and economic system that produces the need for intervention programs and attempts to search for roots that penetrate deeper into the structure of the social system (Apple, 1978; Baratz & Baratz, 1970). Table 1 identifies the four methodological orientations and compares their characteristics on ten dimensions. Although the distinctions among the groups appear sharp, in practice there is considerable overlap; differences fade in the course of conducting evaluations. In all cases, designs shift to accommodate what is politically feasible.

Experimentalist approach. The experimentalist approach can be characterized as positivist, utilizing experimental and quasi-experimental designs from agriculture and psychology to establish cause and effect relationships between dependent (output) and independent (input) variables. A comparison group is mandatory if randomization of subjects to treatment is not possible. Participants have no role in the evaluation process other than as respondents. There is little or no interaction between the evaluator and the program or the evaluator and internal and external forces operating on the program. The evaluation researcher stands above the politics of program evaluation.

To make a "go/no go" decision, the evaluation study should document strong causal links between the program and the outcomes. Riecken and Boruch (1974) acknowledge that there are a number of ways to establish effect but find the experimental approach "not only leads to clearer causal inferences, but the very process of experimental design helps to clarify the nature of the social problem being attacked" (p. 6). Where true experiments are not possible, then Campbell and Stanley (1963), Cook and Campbell (1979), and others propose quasi-experimental designs such as interrupted time-series, control-series design, regression discontinuity, and multiple group pre-post comparisons. Suchman (1969) raised the question of multiplicity of causes and interdependence of events that necessitate an evaluation design that transcends simple causal inferences. He stated that "no program is an entity unto itself but must be viewed as part of an ongoing social system" (p. 16). To Suchman, an analysis of a program's process should be as much a part of the design as measurement of the end results.

An alternative proposed by some experimentalists is termed "natural experiments," sometimes referred to as "planned variations." Outcomes related to variations in intervention programs with common goals are compared. The Follow Through programs represent planned variations (Rivlin & Timpane, 1975).

Eclectic approach. The second group of evaluators, the eclectics, do not reject experimental design but, like Suchman, regard process and context as critical components of an evaluation design. This group seriously questions the value of large-scale experimental studies of intervention programs. The reasons typically given include the difficulty of selecting satisfactory criteria, uncontrollable situations that preclude replication, lack of standard treatments across similar programs, that experimental studies yield only limited information, and, that the client-evaluator relationship influences the program (Cronbach, 1975).

A central concern of the eclectics is the overemphasis upon achievement as the single most important outcome. Not only is achievement criticized as too narrow a program goal (Cooley & Lohnes, 1976; Astin & Panos, 1971), but achievement testing is criticized as culturally biased (Perrone, 1977; Weker, 1974; Hoffmann, 1972). On the other hand, school personnel and many state and federal project officers maintain that achievement is the primary goal of

TABLE 1. *Four methodological approaches in program evaluation*

	Experimentalists Cook and Campbell (1979) Riecken and Boruch (1974) Rivlin and Timpane (1975)	*Eclectics* Bryk (1978) Cronbach and Associates (1980) R. S. Weiss and Rein (1972)	*Describers* Parlett and Hamilton (1977) Patton (1980) Stake (1975)	*Benefit-Cost Analyzers* Haller (1975) Levin (1975) Thompson (1980)
Philosophical base	Positivist	Modified positivist to pragmatic	Phenomenological	Logical/Analytic
Disciplinary base	Psychology	Psychology; sociology; political science	Sociology; anthropology	Economics; accounting
Focus of methodology	Identify causal links	Augment search for causal links with process and contextual data	Describe program holistically and from perspective of the participants	Judge worth of program in terms of costs and benefits
Methodology	Experimental and quasi-experimental designs	Quasi-experimental designs; case studies; descriptions	Ethnography; case studies, participant observation; triangulation	Benefit-cost analysis
Variables	Predetermined as input-output	Predetermined plus emerging	Emerging in course of evaluation	Predetermined
Control or comparison group	Yes	Where possible	Not necessary	Yes
Participants' role in carrying out evaluation	None	None to interactive	Varies (may react to field notes)	None
Evaluator's role	Independent of program	Cooperative	Interactive	Independent of program
Political pressures (internal-external)	Controlled in design; or ignored	Accommodated	Describe	Ignore
Focus of evaluation report	Render "go/no go" decision	Interpret and recommend for program improvement	Present holistic portrayal of program in process	Render judgment

educational intervention programs. Cohen (1970) questions the use of achievement as a proxy for social mobility (improving adult economic and social status) in social intervention programs inasmuch as causal relationships between school achievement and later social and economic status are lacking. Use of multiple criteria that represent a range of objectives and diverse value positions should overcome, in good measure, the limitations of evaluation studies that use academic achievement as the sole criterion. In addition to multiple criteria, evaluators now emphasize multiple input variables as well as context and process variables. Suchman (1970) suggested separating immediate, intermediate, and ultimate outcomes and proposed appropriate alternative methods for measuring these different outcomes, such as case studies, survey designs, and panel designs.

Bryk (1978) sums up the position of the eclectics as follows: "we should attempt to draw on the strengths of each approach—the objectivity of quantitative data, the richness of qualitative information—to create an integra-tive view of program impact" (p. 40). Where possible, causal links should be established and tied to program factors and to context and process variables.

From Table 1 we can extract a profile of the eclectic approach. It is based on a pragmatic philosophy and draws its evaluation designs from psychology, sociology, and political science. Eclectic evaluators find quasi-experimental designs more realistic than true experiments. Since evaluations are seldom conducted outside a political area, tradeoffs in internal and external validity are feasible within quasi-experimental designs. Descriptive data are necessary to augment the quantitative data base. Descriptions of the process of implementing the program as well as the sociopolitical context in which the program takes place are important in interpreting the quantitative data. Although random assignment to treatment and a control group are desirable, these may not be possible to arrange. The variables are predetermined, but the design is flexible enough to accommodate variables not predetermined. The evaluator assumes a nonthreatening stance and includes the program staff and participants in the evaluation process whenever it is possible. Cronbach et al. (1980) consider evaluators to be educators, since they interact with program participants. The evaluation report should assist in identifying specific elements in the program that require modification.

Describers. The epistemological orientation of the third group, the describers, rejects the positivist premises by which the experimentalists justify use of experimental designs in program evaluation as well as the eclectics' pragmatism, which may jeopardize the evaluator's independence. The describers regard their purpose, like that of the eclectics, as providing information to the decision maker. But phenomenologically based information, to the describer group, has greater validity than data obtained from traditional, structured measurement instruments (Stake and Easley, 1978). Generalizability is not the critical purpose of description, although, according to Guba (1978), naturalistic inquiry "strives for confirmability" (p. 17).

The describer evaluators can be characterized as philosophically attuned to phenomenology, and utilizing the methodology of social anthropologists and sociologists. Their tools are ethnography, case studies, participant observation, and triangulations. (Filstead, 1970; McCall & Simmons, 1969; Sindell, 1969; Smith, 1974.) Variables are not preselected but emerge in the process of describing the operation of the program in its naturalistic setting. As people interact in the program, the evaluation portrays a holistic picture of the total milieu. The evaluator moves in and out of the scene without involving the participants directly in the evaluation process. In some cases the evaluator's notes are shared with participants to check perceptions. The evaluator neither controls nor ignores internal and external political pressures but describes them.

Stanley (1972) takes issue with the describers. He refutes the charge that experimentation misses the essence of events because of its highly structured design. "Despite straw men to the contrary, educational experimentation can be as on-going, flexible, and sequential as the cleverness of the evaluator allows it to be. Inflexibility is more in the minds of planners, researchers, and critics than in the methodology itself. . . . Recent attempts to rule experimentation inapplicable because other methods are useful, too, seem misguided" (p. 70).

Benefit-cost studies. The fourth methodological orientation is based on distributional theory borrowed from economics and from accounting procedures. Benefit-cost evaluation studies are designed to determine how to choose between anticipated costs and anticipated benefits among alternatives. They are predicated on clear goal statements about what society values; the outputs are converted into monetary values. The difficulty of applying benefit-cost analysis resides in the specification of social goals. It is difficult enough to get consensus on educational goals, let alone converting human goals into market values (Rothenberg, 1975). Benefit-cost analysts look for payoffs in terms

of costs (to whom) both direct and foregone, and benefits (for whom). This means weighing the gains and losses of one group against those of another group (Coleman, 1972).

Cost effectiveness is an offshoot of benefit-cost analysis. In place of monetary values as the outcomes, cost effectiveness designates physical, cognitive, and psychological values. Levin (1975) distinguishes between cost effectiveness and benefit-cost analysis in the following way. "When the effectiveness of programs in achieving a particular goal (rather than their monetary values) is linked to costs, the approach is considered to be a cost-effectiveness rather than a cost-benefit analysis" (p. 93). Both types of cost studies can be incorporated as one facet of evaluation in an eclectic design. Their purpose is to assist the decision maker in making a "go/no go" decision based on cost factors.

Politics. Regardless of the methodological orientation of one or another group of evaluation researchers, none can escape the political forces that intrude on designing evaluation studies. Evaluation provides one set of data for subsequent decisions on allocation and distribution of resources. Resource management and assignment are policy decisions; hence, evaluation is a handmaiden of politics (Williams & Evans, 1969; C. H. Weiss, 1977a, 1977b; Rossi & Williams, 1972). Cohen (1970) articulates this position: "Decision-making . . . is a euphemism for the allocation of resources—money, position, authority. . . . Thus, to the extent that information is an instrument, basis, or excuse for changing power relationships within or among institutions, evaluation is a political activity" (p. 214). With the advent of large-scale intervention programs, such as Title I of the Elementary and Secondary Education Act, decisions about distribution of large resources and their subsequent redistribution could bring about shifts in power arrangements. Thus federally mandated evaluations of Title I programs placed evaluation in an active political dimension that it had not previously encountered. C. H. Weiss (1970) speaks to this problem: "The evaluator, unaccustomed to the political spotlight, finds old difficulties exacerbated and new problems burgeoning" (p. 59). Whether evaluators recognize the political nature of evaluation or not, internal and external politics impinging on evaluation studies have persistently exerted both constraints and influence on evaluations.

External and internal forces. External political forces at the federal and state level exert an influence on evaluation through specification of requests for proposals (RFPs); formulation of evaluation guidelines (Wholey et al., 1970; Levine & Williams, 1971); specification of methodology (Horst, Tallmadge, & Wood, 1975); and dissemination and utilization of evaluation data (Haney, 1977). Legislation of community input in social intervention program development and evaluation represents another form of political intrusion into the evaluation process. Many evaluation studies gained as a result of community input (Talmage, 1975; Talmage & Haertel, 1981; Grant, 1979); but for many program evaluations, the evaluation process became a battleground for contending parties (Caro, 1977). Teacher Corps and bilingual program evaluations were especially prone to power issues. C. H. Weiss (1970) expresses the evaluators' concern with government regulation of evaluation: "Government agencies may seek only to enforce standards of relevance and research quality, but they almost inevitably become suspect of political pressure, pressure to vindicate the program and justify its budget" (p. 61).

The same comment applies to the influence of internal forces upon evaluation. The program staff exhibits sensitivity to evaluation. At the local level a staff confronts the same consequences of resource allocations whether it is involved in a large-scale intervention program or a locally funded program. Since jobs and status are at stake, the substance of the evaluation report and release of the data become major political concerns in the life of the program staff and the immediate central officer responsible for approving the program. Talmage (1973) reported on an educational intervention program that had desegregation implications. The harried administrator insisted on using the lowest achieving school in the district as the control group, implying that the experimental school would look better.

Criticism. With external and internal personnel and constituencies perceiving evaluation as either a threat or a rallying point, the evaluation process is subject to criticism as one line of defense or attack. Evaluation methodology is the first target of attack, including the design, measurement instruments, and statistical analysis. This is followed by criticism of the evaluator, and misconstruing the goals of the program (Rossi, 1966; R. S. Weiss & Rein, 1972). Cohen (1970) pointed out that since social concerns are not stable but shift over time, original goals and issues differ by the end of the experimental period. The evaluator who is not intimately involved in program development and implementation may end up with a well-designed evaluation study addressing inappropriate goals.

Other criticisms also have some basis in reality. R. S. Weiss and Rein (1972) identified areas tending to producing tension between the evaluator and program administrators. Many evaluators show more concern for their evaluation design than for the well-being of the program. Evaluators want the program to hold still, whereas effective administrators insist upon adjusting the program as the need arises. Second, evaluators are dependent upon archival records and "uncommitted record keepers" and call into question the reliability of information. Third, as program goals are operationalized, they may assume an importance not originally intended and, consequently, not built into the evaluation design. Finally, evaluators may be less informed about the program than the project staff. Sjoberg (1975) is especially concerned with the ethical and political orientation that evaluators maintain as part of their evaluation assumptions. Working within the context of the power structure, evaluators are subject to bureaucratic values. Since the evaluators' role is tied to this structure and to sustaining the social order, their design and measurement procedures reflect this bias. Kuhn (1970) and

Petrie (1972) also consider the effects of previous visual-conceptual experiences in influencing what is seen.

The role of the evaluator comes into question once the political nature of evaluation is fully appreciated. The type of relationship between the program staff and the evaluator differs from that of the researcher; role relationships need to be restructured. Cronbach et al. (1980) and Cohen (1970) call for evaluators to also be educators. Talmage (1975) and Talmage and Haertel (1981) suggest collaborative relationships to avoid what Sjoberg sees as the evaluator's myopia. Caro (1971) suggests six ways that evaluators can contribute to program development. Inherent in most of his suggestions is the need for political astuteness on the part of the evaluator and the importance of assuming an educator role.

Whereas some researchers may lament the constraints placed on them by the political arena in which evaluation is conducted, others recognize this as the real world of evaluation. Campbell (1969) decried the political milieu in which evaluators function: "Trapped administrators have so committed themselves in advance to the efficacy of the reform that they cannot afford honest evaluation. For them, favorably biased analyses are commended, including capitalizing on regression, grateful testimonials, and confounding selection and treatment" (p. 428). On the other hand, Cohen (1970) recognizes the need to learn to function in the political setting: "The evaluation of social action programs is nothing if not an effort to measure social and political change. That is a difficult task under any circumstances, but it is impossible when the activity is not seen for what it is" (p. 232). The political nature of program evaluation is well-documented. The art and science of program evaluation need to be refined in order to function with integrity in the political world.

Classifying Evaluation Approaches

Given the range of positions evaluators can formulate from underlying philosophical assumptions, the proliferation of models for conceptualizing program evaluations should come as no surprise. According to Boruch and Wortman (1979), there is no one generalized model for conducting evaluations. Variations in program evaluation models result from differences in the purpose of evaluations, the types of evaluations, the methodology used in the conduct of evaluation, and the questions asked (Levine & Williams, 1971; C. H. Weiss, 1972b, 1972c; Alkin & Fink, 1974).

Before discussing schema for classifying evaluation models, we need to identify (1) the phases of a program undergoing evaluation; (2) the methodological spectrum from which evaluators choose to build evaluation designs; and (3) specific approaches or models that characterize evaluation designs. Then, six classification schema are presented that attempt to bring order to the many disparate models.

Program Phases and Types. Programs undergo evaluation at a number of phases in their development. The phases range from initial conceptualization through final implementation and on to institutionalization and maintenance. Scriven (1967) classified evaluation into two types: formative and summative. Formative studies are those conducted during the planning and implementation phases of program development. The purpose of formative evaluation is to provide the developer with useful information for ongoing adjustments during program development. (For a thorough review of the literature on formative evaluation, see Sanders & Cunningham, 1973.) Summative evaluation involves decisions about the worth of the program some time following the adjustment period. Although these distinctions prove helpful, they are not necessarily mutually exclusive. As Scriven himself recognizes, both types of evaluation do take place at various phases in a program's development, implementation, and final installation. During the formative phase of program evaluation, summative decisions are made about various parts of the program. At the conclusion of summative studies, the information is used to further modify programs. According to Cronbach et al. (1980), summative evaluation has no place in evaluation of intervention programs; it is more appropriate in such studies as the evaluation of drug control programs.

Alkin (1969) identified five types of program evaluations; the first three can be labeled "formative" and the last two "summative." Each evaluation is identified with a particular phase of a program's development. The first type, "systems assessment," is associated with the preplanning phase of program development, also called "needs assessment." It answers questions such as the following: Is there a need for a new program? What type of program? Can the system support a new program? How will it be received? How will it fit into the ongoing education program? "Program planning," the second type of evaluation mentioned by Alkin, is concerned with designing the program; evaluation looks at the internal "fit" among the various components of the program. "Program implementation," the third type, is frequently referred to as "process evaluation" (Stufflebeam & Guba, 1970; Provus, 1971; Worthen & Sanders, 1973), although Stake (1967) uses the term "transactions." Evaluation of program implementation concerns the process of carrying out the program, and involves not only program activities but how an organization puts the program into action.

The two summative evaluation types are designated by Alkin as "program improvement" and "program certification." In the former, the focus of evaluation is upon program effects. Program comparison, compliance review, and audit studies would fall into the category of program certification.

Several other types of evaluation are more difficult to arrange according to Alkin's schema; these include "service delivery assessment" and "evaluability." The Office of Service Delivery Assessment of the Department of Health and Human Services has developed a type of evaluation to assess the delivery services of federally funded programs (*Service Delivery Assessment*, n.d.). Its purpose is to provide information to government policy makers. Although it is summative in evaluating a program in place, its purpose is not to render decisions of worth but to keep government officials apprised of the current status of federally funded programs in order to assist them in decision making. Evaluability is a preassessment type of evaluation; prior to expending large sums of money on an evaluation, it attempts to determine if it is feasible to undertake, in terms of cost and utility. Evaluability is described by Horst et al. (1974), Wholey (1977), Rutman (1977), and Datta (1978).

Methodological Spectrum. Methodologies are classified along a continuum. The bipolar labels frequently used include soft and hard research (Cronbach & Shapiro, 1978), quantitative and qualitative research (Patton, 1980), objective and subjective epistemologies (House, 1978), conventional and naturalistic research (Guba, 1978), and behavioristic and humanistic research. These polarities leave the impression that one end of the continuum is more thorough, demanding, and empirical than the other end. The distinctions, however, are indicative not of scholarly rigor but proximity to or distance from the methodology of experimental research. Regardless of the methodological approach, good research is good research (Cronbach et al., 1980; Bryk, 1978). The method must fit the evaluation question.

Selected Evaluation Models. The function of a model in evaluation is to provide a conceptual framework or a rationale for designing evaluation studies. Although the term "approach" is more accurate than "model," the latter term is so widely used in the literature that we will accept it. By means of a model, the epistemological and evaluation criteria, assumptions and definitions, and the interrelationships among elements of an evaluation design are either explicitly stated or implied. Thus the model gives direction to an evaluation design (House, 1980). Some models lay out the procedures for conducting evaluations without explicitly specifying contingencies or the theoretical orientation upon which the model is based. Examples of models whose assumptions are implied include the CIPP model of Stufflebeam and Guba (1970), the discrepancy model of Provus (1971), and the RMC models of the United States Office of Education (Horst, Tallmadge, & Wood, 1975). The CIPP model is not so much a model as a way of correlating the phases of program development with types of evaluation. CIPP stands for "context, input, process, and product." The discrepancy model compares a program's plan with its actual functioning. RMC models aim to find out exactly how much students learn as a result of participating in Title I projects. These models indicated the approach to evaluation encouraged by the former U.S. Office of Education.

Other models are predicated on explicit assumptions about interactive client-evaluator behavior, facilitating value decisions or establishing causal links. Models predicted on distinct assumptions calling for specific approaches in the conduct of the evaluation include the transactional evaluation model (Rippey, 1973), connoisseurship model (Eisner, 1979), utilization model (Patton, 1978), responsive evaluation (Stake, 1975), adversary model (Owens, 1973; Levine, 1974), illumination model (Parlett & Hamilton, 1977), decision-theoretic approach (Edwards, Guttentag, & Snapper, 1975), among others. For discussion of the various models see Hamilton et al. (1977), House (1980), Guba (1978), Popham (1975), and Worthen and Sanders (1973).

Classification of Models. Model building in evaluation is so extensive that a classification schema is required in order to discuss the models systematically. Ross and Cronbach (1976), Guba (1978), Popham (1975), and Stufflebeam and Webster (1980) classify models according to a few categories to distinguish among them. Each schema is discussed briefly.

Ross and Cronbach (1976), in their critique of the *Handbook of Evaluation Research,* divide the models into two categories: mainstream and alternative models. In mainstream evaluation, tasks are evaluator-oriented. In the alternative models, both the evaluator and participants play active roles in the evaluation process.

Similarly, Guba (1978) uses a two-category system to differentiate among models. The categories are based on the forms of inquiry employed, either conventional or naturalistic. Conventional inquiry stems from a logical-positivist epistemology and naturalistic inquiry from a phenomenological epistemology. Having established the philosophical basis of the two categories, Guba contrasts the models on thirteen dimensions. Conventional models include systems models, Stufflebeam and Guba's CIPP model, the discrepancy model of Provus (1971), RMC models proposed by Horst, Tallmadge, and Wood (1975) for the United States Office of Education (USOE) the cause-effect linkage model (Suchman, 1967, 1969), and all other objective-driven models, including the benefit-cost analysis approach. Naturalistic models, represented by descriptive and ethnographic evaluations, include the judicial model proposed by R. L. Wolf (1975) (see also Thurston, 1978; Popham and Carlson, 1977). For participant models, see Rippey (1973), Talmage (1975), and LaBelle, Moll, and Weisner (1979); for connoisseurship, or the application of art criticism to evaluations, see Eisner (1979), Kelly (1978), and others such as the Service Delivery Assessment (n.d.) proposed by the U.S. Department of Health and Human Services.

Popham suggested three classifications of models: goal attainment models; judgmental models, further classified in terms of intrinsic and extrinsic judgments; and decision-facilitation models. Examples of goal attainment models are the objective-driven models exemplified by the work of Tyler (1966) and Metfessel and Michael (1967). Accreditation, such as that established by the National Study of School Evaluation (1978), would fall into the intrinsic category of judgmental models. Popham places the models of Scriven (1972, 1976) and Stake (1967) in the extrinsic

category. Scriven is associated with such approaches as "modus operandi" and "goal-free evaluations," and Stake with an approach called the "countenance model." The models of Stufflebeam and Guba (1970) and those of Stufflebeam (1971), Alkin (1969), and Provus (1971) are classified by Popham as decision-facilitation models.

Stufflebeam and Webster (1980) suggest that evaluation models can be classified according to one of three approaches: politically oriented studies that they call "pseudo-evaluations"; question-oriented studies that they label "quasi-evaluations"; and value-oriented studies, or "true evaluations." The first studies are politically controlled and inspired by public relations—hence pseudo-evaluations. The second approach asks questions and applies suitable methodologies, but may not be appropriate for assessing value or worth. Within this class of models Stufflebeam and Webster include objective-based studies, accountability studies, experimental research studies, testing studies, and management-oriented studies. Only evaluation studies that permit judgment fall into the category of true evaluation. These include accreditation studies, cost-benefit analyses, decision-oriented studies that use evaluation information continuously and systematically in arriving at decisions, consumer-oriented studies that identify social values before the fact, client-oriented studies in which the participants involved in the program evaluate it, and, lastly, connoisseur-based studies in which judgments are based upon expertise and "refined insights." True evaluations are not synonymous with "true experiments" as defined by Campbell and Stanley (1963) but refer to a definition of evaluation that focuses upon making a judgment, or assessing the value of a program.

House (1980) developed a comprehensive classification system for comparing and contrasting prominent models. His taxonomy relates the models to the ethics, epistemology, and political implications inherent in the philosophy of liberalism. The eight categories of models include systems models, behavioral objective models, decision-making models, goal-free, criticism, accreditation, adversary, and transaction models.

All the classification schema attempt to distinguish among the models regarding research methodology for establishing truth or at least making confirmatory statements; values from which criteria are derived for assessing worth; and the role of the evaluator in relation to the clients and the system in the evaluation process (praxis).

Use of Evaluation Data

If the primary purpose of evaluation is to provide information for action, as C. H. Weiss (1972c) states, then the degree to which evaluation data are of use to the policy maker determines the worth of an evaluation study. To understand evaluation use or nonuse, we need to be aware of the political milieu in which evaluation takes place and decisions are made. According to Patton (1978) and others, evaluations are used or ignored for political reasons from which evaluators cannot disassociate themselves. Patton states that "evaluation research is and necessarily will be political in conceptualization, design, implementation, and utilization" (p. 80). Just as evaluation must be viewed within the political context in which it functions, so too must utilization of evaluation data.

Three topics on use emerge from the literature. The first takes a negative approach: what are the reasons for the low use of evaluation findings by decision makers? The second topic concerns the circumstances that appear to be associated with utilization. The third involves recommendations to enhance utilization. Regardless of the topic, political pragmatism looms in the background.

Reasons for Low Use. In the late 1960s and early 1970s evaluators assumed that evaluation information was not typically used in the decision process. Regardless of the negative tone of an evaluation, programs were seldom discontinued on the basis of the evaluation report (Alkin & Daillek, 1979). Reasons given for low or no use include organizational inertia, methodological weakness, design irrelevance, and lack of dissemination (Wholey et al., 1970). C. H. Weiss (1972c) adds to this list the current state of evaluation practice. Caplan (1977), however, directly confronts the political issue. Politically, unfeasible implications of information doom utilization because data in and of themselves cannot override compelling political consequences. He attributes low use, aside from political implications, not to technological problems, such as slow flow of information or level of knowledge production, but to factors involving values, ideology, and decision-making style. The problem, according to Caplan, is in the policy maker's perspective.

What appears to be a lack of use of evaluation information may result more from the way we identify use than from the actual level of use. We need to understand the decision-making processes within an organizational context. The positions of Simon (1957), March (1965), Braybrooke and Lindbloom (1963), and Allison (1971) point out the shift in thinking about the role and authority of the decision maker. When use is tied to the classical decision maker model, evaluators are bound to be disappointed (Alkin, Daillak, & White, 1979; Patton et al., 1977). On the other hand, according to Boruch (1976), when decisions are viewed as disjunctive and incremental, or as a "sequential process with multiple decision points" rather than all-or-nothing decisions, then there is evidence of use. Boruch and Wortman (1979) document such evidence and conclude: "This larger view of decision-making as a continuous process suggests considerable utilization of evaluation findings" (p. 349).

C. H. Weiss (1977c) suggests "enlightenment" as an alternative approach to decision making and as a rationale for utilization. An "enlightenment" rationale for utilization is educative in purpose. The evaluator should assist decision makers in giving precedence to issues and should help the decision makers to better understand the relationship among issues. Use of evaluation data is not immediate or direct. Rarely can policy makers cite social science research findings that influence their decisions; influence is indirect and diffuse and comes through unexpected channels. Patton's definition (1978) of utilization comes close to Weiss's enlightment. "Utilization is a diffuse and gradual process of reducing decisionmakers' uncertainty within the existing social context." Knorr (1977) introduces the term "instrumental utilization" to describe how evaluation information is used. Similar to Weiss's enlightenment, Knorr describes instrumental utilization as indirect, diffuse, difficult to identify the level of utilization (local, state, federal) and a delayed process. She concludes: "The low visibility of this kind of utilization and the far too high expectations contribute to the popularity of the thesis that little utilization takes place. Its plausibility should be reexamined in the light of the present data and arguments" (p. 180).

C. H. Weiss (1979) attributes the conceptual confusion about research utilization to the many meanings of the term. She identifies seven models for conceptualizing utilization: knowledge-driven model, problem-solving model, interactive model, political model, tactical model, enlightenment model, and intellectual enterprise model. The various models broaden our conceptualization of use which may lead to identifying ways where research and evaluation are utilized that presently go unacknowledged. Patton et al. (1977) found this to be the case. Since the prevailing views of utilization were too narrow, they failed to designate the many uses of evaluations.

Attributes of Use. Several recent studies to determine the extent of use of evaluation findings identify a number of attributes associated with utilization. Alkin and Daillak (1979) and Alkin, Daillak, and White (1979) report on five in-depth case studies, in which there was gradual, incremental impact. They identified a number of factors related to the use of the evaluation information some time subsequent to the report. These factors included preexisting limitations on the evaluation, pertinent evaluation information, the evaluator's approach in encouraging use of the information, the evaluator's credibility, the evaluation recommendations suitable to organizational, budget, and other constraints, extent of external influence on data use, appropriateness of reporting procedures, and administrative style. Patton et al. (1977) report on a study of twenty randomly selected health program evaluations. Reinforcing Alkin's findings, they also found no large-scale implementation of evaluation recommendations, but evaluations were utilized and found to make a difference in unexpected ways. In keeping with nonclassical organizational models of decision making, Patton et al. found that evaluations were used as one major source of information. From this study the following factors were extracted as important for utilization. (1) Evaluators cannot disassociate themselves from the politics surrounding the program. (2) Evaluation designs should be oriented toward future decisions. (3) Key organizational decision makers should be active in defining the purpose, content, and methods of the evaluation study. (4) Utilization does not center around the final report. (5) Continuous evaluation feedback is more useful than the lengthy one-shot report. (6) Evaluators should plan for utilization before data are collected. (7) The evaluator personalizes the evaluation-reporting procedures to fit the intended audience. The personal factor emerges again and again in the Patton study. The study concludes: "It is in consciously working with such decision-makers to answer their questions that the utilization of evaluation research can be enhanced" (p. 161). In their article on utilization, Davis and Salasin (1975) reaffirm the evaluator/decision maker relationship; it is one of accommodation, not manipulation.

Hayman et al. (1979) add another factor influencing utilization that they call a "cross-level hypothesis of utilization"; the more proximate the data set is to the decision maker, the greater the utility. For example, at the federal level the most useful unit of analysis for the Department of Education is the state education level. Data on students at the classroom level, aggregated into one large data set, have little value for policy at the national level. However, at the school district level, data on the school level are more useful than data on individual students or the class as the unit of analysis. Wholey et al. (1972) support this position; they suggest placing responsibility for evaluation at the appropriate decision-making level.

To understand the type of information that influences decision makers, Florio et al. (1979) reported on a survey they conducted with decision makers. Individual student achievement data were rated by decision makers as the most important program effect, but unexpected outcomes and multiplier effects rated lower than other types of information. Public opinion polls were rated as having the highest influence upon decision makers, followed by state legislators, and then the media. Low on the list were the local education association and school personnel.

We can conclude that evaluation information does get used, but not in a global way; rather, data are acted upon piecemeal in the light of the decision maker's perception of the political context.

Enhancing Utilization. Based upon review of the literature, the few empirical studies of evaluation use to date, and their own views of the purpose of evaluation, Caplan (1977), C. H. Weiss (1972c), and Patton (1978) offer their recommendations for enhancing research and evaluation use; Caplan's suggestions are more academic than the pragmatic recommendations of Weiss and Patton. Caplan proposes the setting up of a group, composed of people with a combination of skills and insights into the practical aspects of production and use of knowledge, to work within an institutional setting. Their tasks would include (1) appraising the merits of research information; (2) bridging the gap between theoretical information and its practical use; (3) formulating policy issues into research questions; (4) differentiating between science and extrascientific needs; (5) working through value issues; and (6) gaining the trust of policy makers in order that social

science knowledge can be introduced at important junctures.

C. H. Weiss and Patton consider utilization to be within the framework of the evaluation process. C. H. Weiss (1977b) offers four procedures that hold promise for evaluation use: (1) early identification of users of evaluation results and selection of issues of concern to them; (2) participation of program personnel in the evaluation process; (3) prompt completion and release of the study; and (4) effective presentation of findings. Patton (1978) proposes a number of following steps to ensure use of evaluation data. The first two parallel Weiss's procedures. The next three steps involve clarifying program goals, framing evaluation questions in terms of the goals, and arranging goals in order of their usefulness. Patton proposes a causal-link design augmented by alternative designs; the utilization-focused evaluation, according to Patton, is an active-re-active-adaptive process.

Whether use should be the focus of evaluation, an integral component of an evaluation design, or a conscious concern of the evaluator, evidence indicates that use does not depend merely on the quality of the report or the tightness of its methodology. Decision makers must be helped to see the potential for using the evaluation information within the political context in which decisions are made.

Professional Standards

Lange (1974) pronounced evaluation a fad, with too many would-be experts taking on the evaluator's mantle. He does not quarrel with the solid theoretical base of evaluation. Educational practitioners, however, expect too much from evaluation, and some evaluators will agree to deliver what is not possible. In common with many applied fields of study, there are effective and ineffective professionals: those who are well trained and the inadequately trained, those who possess the interpersonal skills to work with practitioners and those who do not. There are several ways for a profession to guard against poor practice. One way involves setting up standards that mark excellence and serve as guides; the other way is through certification of professionals. For example, medicine takes both routes: the Hippocratic oath lays down standards of behavior; and professional certification, through approved programs and examinations, determines mastery of the requisite medical skills or competencies. Standards, guidelines, and competencies are attractive restraints on poor professional practice; however, these very restraints can curtail academic freedom, inhibiting exploration of new knowledge and techniques.

Criteria for Evaluation Research. A number of evaluators suggest criteria for evaluating programs, and some offer skills and competencies for carrying out evaluation studies. In his seminal work in evaluation research, Suchman (1967) identified five categories of criteria to evaluate a program's success or failure: effort, effectiveness, impact, cost effectiveness, and process. "Effort" considers the quality and quantity of program activities as they relate to input and output. "Effectiveness" separates the results of effort from effect. "Impact" refers to the adequacy of the outcome in terms of need. The other two categories are self-explanatory. Scriven (1974) reported on standards specifically selected to evaluate educational programs and products rather than evaluation *per se*. The thirteen standards serve as a checklist, with items ranging from determination of need and market to nine standards on product performance. The last two checklist items deal with cost effectiveness and extended support services, such as post-marketing services and in-service. Product performance standards include such checklist items as field trial, long-term performance, side effects, statistical and educational significance tests.

Taking a somewhat different approach, the American Educational Research Association assigned a Task Force on Research Training to identify the competencies needed by educational researchers and evaluators. The reports included lists of skills (Worthen & Gagné, 1969), a revised paper on the competencies omitted in the first report (Glass & Worthen, 1970), and a task analysis of research and evaluation activities (Anderson et al., 1971). Worthen (1975) integrated the three reports, summarizing the research and evaluation tasks and their related competencies. He identified twenty-five tasks and the abilities and knowledge associated with each of them. The list of competencies show a definite bias in terms of research orientation drawn from psychology. Worthen acknowledges that the list may require revision as evaluators draw on other disciplines in the future, namely, anthropology, economics, linguistics, history, and philosophy.

Standards. Improving the credibility of evaluators borders on establishing standards. Millman (1979) based the credibility of an evaluation report upon the role of the evaluator. To meet Millman's standards of a credible report, the evaluator needs a competent team, needs to involve the decision maker in the evaluation, be aware of and deal with the concerns of different constituencies, report directly to the group funding the study (rather than to a project director), and clearly separate fact from opinion in the report.

Of most interest are the standards for evaluation developed by the Joint Committee on Standards for Educational Evaluation (1981). The joint committee members were appointed to represent twelve organizations that saw the necessity of ensuring quality in evaluation. Since the organizations included both research associations and practitioner organizations, both producers and users of evaluation studies jointly worked out the standards. The initial work began in 1975 and was not without internal dissent; several original members withdrew because they questioned the value of setting down standards and saw the potential for negative consequences. The joint committee took a somewhat ambiguous position regarding the purpose of evaluation in an effort to encompass a range of

positions. They defined evaluation as "the systematic investigation of the worth or merit of some object." Since worth and judgment go undefined, the definition is broad enough to accommodate the position of most evaluators. Standards are defined as "principles commonly agreed to by people engaged in the professional practice of evaluation for the measurement of the value or the quality of education" (p. 112).

The joint committee incorporated thirty standards under one of four attributes that are necessary and sufficient for sound evaluation. Eight standards are subsumed under utility, which is defined as "evaluations responsive to the needs of the client group." These standards are the same as many of the items mentioned previously regarding evaluation use: audience identification, evaluator credibility, report clarity, and timeliness. The three standards under feasibility refer to the cost-effective and workable evaluation designs conducted in natural settings. These standards speak to practicability of design, political viability, and cost effectiveness. The eight standards under propriety are concerned with the rights of persons affected by the evaluation. Lastly, eleven standards are listed under accuracy; these are concerned with the technical aspects of evaluation that produce sound information.

The standards are presented according to the same format. The standard is defined, followed by (1) an overview presenting a short discussion of the standard, (2) guidelines or steps to follow in carrying out the standard, (3) potential pitfalls, (4) caveats, (5) in illustrative case, and, finally, (6) an analysis of the case.

The standards are sure to raise both favorable and unfavorable responses. The key issues revolve around whether or not program evaluation needs an external set of guidelines for conducting evaluation, the negative effects of externally imposed standards on a scholarly field of study, and whether or not standards improve the quality of evaluations. If standards become more than guidelines, is certification far behind?

Conclusions

The coming of age of program evaluation should not imply definitive answers to persistent issues. Rather, it means that a store of methods, techniques, and alternative ways of approaching problems from many perspectives have been examined and tested in practice. From this storehouse, evaluators must select and further shape their designs to fit the exigencies of a particular program. To design program evaluations, the evaluator must take into account the limitations of any single methodology, the constraints imposed by the program's political and social context, and the relationship between the evaluator and the many program constituencies.

As the field of program evaluation sharpens its tools, comes to understand the philosophical assumptions underlying a given evaluation design, and finds ways to make the evaluation useful to government agencies as well as to the local practitioner, program evaluation will establish itself as a field of study in its own right and as an area of professional practice.

Harriet Talmage

See also Curriculum Research; Experimental Methods; Experimental Validity; Federal Influence on Education; Qualitative Curriculum Evaluation; Statistical Methods.

REFERENCES

Alkin, M. C. Evaluation theory development. *Evaluation Comment*, 1969, *2*(1), 2–7.

Alkin, M. C., & Daillak, R. H. A study of utilization. *Educational Evaluation and Policy Analysis*, 1979, *1*(4), 41–50.

Alkin, M. C., Daillak, R.; & White, P. *Using Evaluations: Does Evaluation Make a Difference?* Beverly Hills, Calif.: Sage, 1979.

Alkin, M. C., & Fink, A. Evaluation within the context of product development: A user orientation. In G. Borich (Ed.), *Evaluating Educational Programs and Products*. Englewood Cliffs, N.J.: Educational Technology Publications, 1974, pp. 98–119.

Allison, G. T. *Essence of Decision: Explaining the Cuban Missile Crisis*. Boston: Little, Brown, 1971.

Anderson, R. B.; Soptick, J. M.; Rogers, W. T.; & Worthen, B. R. *An Analysis and Interpretation of Tasks and Competencies Required of Personnel Conducting Exemplary Research and Research-related Activities in Education* (Technical Paper No. 23). Boulder, Colo.: American Educational Research Association Task Force on Research Training, Laboratory of Educational Research, 1971.

Anderson, S. B., & Ball, S. *The Profession and Practice of Program Evaluation*. San Francisco: Jossey-Bass, 1978.

Apple, M. W. Ideology and form in curriculum evaluation. In G. Willis (Ed.), *Qualitative Evaluation: Concepts and Cases in Curriculum Criticism*. Berkeley, Calif.: McCutchan, 1978.

Astin, A. W., & Panos, R. J. The evaluation of educational programs. In R. L. Thorndike (Ed.), *Educational Measurement* (2nd ed.). Washington, D.C.: American Council on Education, 1971, pp. 733–751.

Ball, S., & Bogatz, G. A. *A Summary of the Major Findings in "The First Year of Sesame Street: An Evaluation."* Princeton, N.J., Educational Testing Services, 1970. (ERIC Document Reproduction Service No. ED 122 799)

Baratz, S., & Baratz, J. Early childhood intervention: The social science basis of institutionalized racism. *Harvard Educational Review*, 1970, *40*, 29–50.

Bentham, J. *An Introduction to the Principles of Morals and Legislation*. New York: Hafner, 1948.

Boruch, R. F. On common contentions about randomized experiments. In G. V. Glass (Ed.), *Evaluation Studies Review Annual*, 1976, *1*, 158–194.

Boruch, R. F.; McSweeny, A. J.; & Soderstrom, J. Bibliography: Illustrative randomized field experiments. *Evaluation Quarterly*, 1978, *2*, 655–695.

Boruch, R. F., & Riecken, W. H. (Eds.). *Experimental Testing of Public Policy*. Boulder, Colo.: Westview, 1975.

Boruch, R. F., & Wortman, P. M. Implications of educational evaluation for evaluation policy. In D. C. Berliner (Ed.), *Review of Research in Education*, 1979, *7*, 309–361.

Braybrooke, D., & Lindbloom, C. E. *A Strategy of Decision*. Glencoe, Ill.: Free Press, 1963.

Bryk, A. S. Evaluating program impact: A time to cast away stories, a time to gather stories together. In S. B. Anderson & C. Coles (Eds.), *New Directions for Program Evaluation: Exploring Purposes and Dimensions* (No. 1). San Francisco: Jossey-Bass, 1978.

Campbell, D. T. Reforms as experiments. *American Psychologist*, 1969, *24*, 409–429.

Campbell, D. T., & Stanley J. Experimental and quasi-experimental designs for research on teaching. In N. L. Gage (Ed.), *Handbook of Research on Teaching*. Chicago: Rand McNally, 1963.

Caplan, N. A minimal set of conditions necessary for the utilization of social science knowledge in policy formulation at the national level. In C. H. Weiss (Ed.), *Using Social Research in Public Policy Making*. Lexington, Mass.: Heath, Lexington Books, 1977.

Caro, F. G. Issues in the evaluation of social programs. *Review of Educational Research*, 1971, *41*, 87–114.

Caro, F. G. (Ed.). *Readings in Evaluation Research* (2nd ed). New York: Russell Sage Foundation, 1977.

Cicirelli, V. G., Evans, J. L.; & Schiller, J. *The Impact of Head Start: An Evaluation of the Effects of Head Start on Children's Cognitive and Affective Development* (Vol. 1), (Report to the U.S. Office of Education by Westinghouse Learning Corporation and Ohio University). 1969.

Cohen, D. K. Politics and research: Evaluation of social action programs in education. *Review of Educational Research*, 1970, *40*, 213–238.

Coleman, J. C. *Policy Research in the Social Sciences*. Morristown, N.J.: General Learning Press, 1972.

Cook, T. D., & Campbell, D. T. *Quasi Experimentation: Design and Analysis Issues for Field Settings*. Chicago: Rand McNally, 1979.

Cooley, W. W., & Lohnes, P. R. *Evaluation Research in Education*. New York: Wiley, 1976.

Cronbach, L. J. Beyond the two disciplines of scientific psychology. *American Psychologist*, 1975, *30*, 116–127.

Cronbach, L. J.; Ambron, S. R., Dornbusch, S. M.; Hess, R. D.; Hornik, R. C.; Phillips, D. C.; Walker, D. T.; & Weiner, S. S. *Toward Reform of Program Evaluation*. San Francisco.: Jossey-Bass, 1980.

Cronbach, L. J., & Shapiro, K. *Designing Educational Evaluations* (Preliminary Version). Stanford, Calif.: Stanford University, 1978.

Datta, L. Front-end analysis: Pegasus or shank's mare? In S. B. Anderson & C. D. Coles (Eds.), *New Directions for Program Evaluation: Exploring Purposes and Dimensions* (Vol. 1). 1978, 13–30.

Davis, H. R., & Salasin, S. E. The utilization of evaluation. In E. L. Struening & M. Guttentag (Eds.), *Handbook of Evaluation Research* (Vol. 1). Beverly Hills, Calif.: Sage, 1975, pp. 621–666.

Deutscher, I. Words and deeds: Social science and social policy. In W. J. Filstead (Ed.), *Qualitative Methodology*. Chicago: Markham, 1970.

Ebel, R. L. Some measurement problems in a national assessment of educational progress. *Journal of Educational Measurement*, 1966, *3*, 11–18.

Ebel, R. L. (Ed.). *Encyclopedia of Educational Research* (4th ed.). New York: Macmillan, 1969.

Edwards, W., & Guttentag, M. Experiments and evaluations: A re-examination. In C. Bennett & A. Lumsdaine (Eds.), *Evaluation and Experiment: Some Critical Issues in Assessing Social Programs*. New York: Academic Press, 1975.

Edwards, W.; Guttentag, M.; & Snapper, K. A decision-theoretic approach to evaluation research. In E. L. Struening & M. Guttentag (Eds.), *Handbook of Evaluation Research* (Vol. 1). Beverly Hills, Calif.: Sage, 1975, pp. 139–182.

Eisner, E. W. The use of qualitative forms of evaluation for improving educational practice. *Educational Evaluation and Policy Analysis,* 1979, *1*(6), 11–19.

Filstead, W. J. (Ed.). *Qualitative Methodology.* Chicago: Markham, 1970.

Flanagan, J. C. Evaluating educational outcomes. *Science Education,* 1966, *50,* 248–251.

Flanagan, J. C. (Ed.). *Perspectives on Improving Education: Project TALENT's Young Adults Look Back.* New York: Praeger, 1978.

Florio, D. H.; Behrmann, M. M.; Mason, G.; & Goltz, D. L. What do policy makers think of educational research and evaluation? Or do they? *Educational Evaluation and Policy Analysis,* 1979, *1*(6), 61–87.

Freeman, H. E. Evaluation research and public policy. In G. M. Lyons (Ed.), *Social Research and Public Policy.* Hanover, N.H.: Dartmouth College, Public Affairs Center, 1975.

Glass, G. V., & Ellett, F. S. Evaluation research. *Annual Review of Psychology,* 1980, *31,* 211–228.

Glass, G. V., & Worthen, B. R. *Essential Knowledge and Skills for Educational Research and Evaluation* (Technical Paper No. 5). Boulder, Colo.: American Educational Research Association Task Force on Research Training, Laboratory of Educational Research, 1970.

Glennan, T. K., Jr. *Evaluating Federal Manpower Programs: Notes and Observations.* Santa Monica, Calif.: Rand Corporation, 1969. (ERIC Document Reproduction Service No. ED 041 111)

Gowin, D. B.; & Green, T. F. Two philosophers view education. *Educational Evaluation and Policy Analysis,* 1980, *2*(2), 67–70.

Grant, C. A. (Ed.). *Community Participation in Education.* Boston: Allyn & Bacon, 1979.

Guba, E. G. *Toward a Methodology of Naturalistic Inquiry in Educational Evaluation.* Los Angeles: UCLA, Center for the Study of Evaluation, 1978.

Guttentag, M. Models and methods in evaluation research. *Journal of Theory in Social Behavior,* 1971, *1,* 75–95.

Haller, E. J. Cost analysis for educational program evaluation. In W. J. Popham (Ed.), *Evaluation in Education.* Berkeley, Calif.: McCutchan, 1974.

Hamilton, D.; MacDonald, G.; King, C.; Jenkins, D.; & Parlett, M. (Eds.). *Beyond the Numbers Game.* Berkeley, Calif.: McCutchan, 1977.

Haney, W. *A Technical History of the National Follow Through Evaluation.* Cambridge, Mass.: Huron Institute, 1977.

Hayman, J.; Rayder, N.; Stenner, A. J.; & Modey, D. L. On aggregation, generalization, and utility in educational evaluation. *Educational Evaluation and Policy Analysis,* 1979, *1*(4), 31–39.

Heath, R. W. Curriculum evaluation. In R. L. Ebel (Ed.), *Encyclopedia of Educational Research* (4th ed.). New York: Macmillan, 1969.

Hemphill, J. K. The relationship between research and evaluation studies. In R. W. Tyler (Ed.), *Educational Evaluation: New Roles, New Means: Sixty-eighth Yearbook of the National Society for the Study of Education.* Chicago: University of Chicago Press, 1969, pp. 189–220.

Hill, P. T. Evaluating educational programs for federal policy makers: Lessons from the National Institute of Education compensatory education study. In J. Pincus (Ed.), *Educational Evaluation in Public Policy Setting* (R-2502-RC). Santa Monica, Calif.: Rand Corporation, May 1980, pp. 48–76. (ERIC Document Reproduction Service No. ED 191 179)

Hoffmann, B. *The Tyranny of Testing.* New York: Crowell Collier & Macmillan, 1972.

Horst, D. P.; Tallmadge, G. K.; & Wood, C. T. *A Practical Guide to Measuring Project Impact on Student Achievement* (No. 1, Monograph Series on Evaluation in Education). Washington, D.C.: U.S. Department of Health, Education, and Welfare, 1975. (ERIC Document Reproduction Service No. ED 106 376)

Horst, P.; May, J. N.; Scanlon, J. W.; & Wholey, J. Program management and the federal evaluator. *Public Administration Review,* 1974, *34,* 300–308.

House, E. R. Justice in evaluation. In G. V. Glass (Ed.), *Evaluation Studies Review Annual* (Vol. 1). Beverly Hills, Calif.: Sage, 1976, pp. 75–99.

House, E. R. Assumptions underlying evaluation models. *Educational Researcher,* 1978, *7*(3), 4–12.

House, E. R. *Evaluation with Validity.* Beverly Hills, Calif.: Sage, 1980.

Husén, T. (Ed.). *International Study of Achievement in Mathematics: A Comparison of Twelve Countries.* New York: Wiley, 1967.

Hyman, H. H., & Wright, C. R. Evaluating social action programs. In P. F. Lazarsfeld, W. H. Sewell, & H. L. Wilensky (Eds.), *The Uses of Sociology.* New York: Basic Books, 1967, pp. 741–782.

Joint Committee on Standards for Educational Evaluation. *Standard for Evaluation of Educational Programs, Projects, and Materials.* New York: McGraw-Hill, 1981.

Kelly, E. F. Curriculum criticism and literacy criticism: Comments on analogy. In G. Willis (Ed.), *Qualitative Evaluation.* Berkeley, Calif.: McCutchan, 1978.

Kerlinger, F. N. *Foundations of Behavioral Research.* New York: Holt, Rinehart, 1965.

Knorr, K. Policy makers' use of social science knowledge: Symbolic or instrumental? In C. H. Weiss (Ed.), *Using Social Research in Public Policy Making.* Lexington, Mass.: Lexington Books, 1977.

Kuhn, T. *The Structure of Scientific Revolutions.* Chicago: University of Chicago Press, 1970.

LaBelle, T. J.; Moll, L. C.; & Weisner, T. S. Context-based educational evaluation: A participant research strategy. *Educational Evaluation and Policy Analysis,* 1979, *1*(3), 85–94.

Lange, R. R. A search for utility in new evaluation thought. *Theory into Practice,* 1974, *13*(1), 22–30.

Levin, H. M. Cost-effectiveness analysis in evaluation research. In M. Guttentag & E. L. Struening (Eds.), *Handbook of Evaluation Research* (Vol. 2). Beverly Hills, Calif.: Sage, 1975, pp. 89–122.

Levine, M. Scientific method and the adversary model. *American Psychologist,* 1974, *29,* 661–677.

Levine, R. A., & Williams, A. P., Jr. *Making Evaluation Effective: A Guide* (Report Prepared for the Department of Health, Education, and Welfare, No. R-788-HEW/CMU). Santa Monica, Calif.: Rand Corporation, May 1971.

March, J. G. (Ed.). *Handbook of Organizations.* Chicago: Rand McNally, 1965.

March, J. G., & Simon, H. *Organizations.* New York: Wiley, 1958.

Marris, P., & Rein, M. *Dilemmas of Social Reform.* Chicago: Aldine, 1973.

McCall, G. J., & Simmons, J. L. *Issues in Participant Observation.* Reading, Mass.: Addison-Wesley, 1969.

McDill, E. L.; McDill, M. S.; & Sprehe, J. T. *Strategies for Success in Compensatory Education: An Appraisal of Evaluation Research.* Baltimore: Johns Hopkins University Press, 1969.

McLaughlin, M. W. Implementation as mutual adaptation. In W. Williams & R. F. Elmore (Eds.), *Social Program Implementation.* New York: Academic Press, 1976, pp. 167–180.

McLaughlin, M. W. Evaluation and alchemy. In J. Pincus (Ed.), *Educational Evaluation in Public Policy Setting* (R-2502-RC). Santa Monica, Calif.: Rand Corporation, 1980, pp. 41–47. (ERIC Document Reproduction Service No. ED 191 179)

Merleau-Ponty, M. *Phenomenology of Perception.* London: Routledge & Kegan Paul, 1962.

Merwin, J. C. The progress of exploration towards a national assessment of educational progress. *Journal of Educational Measurement,* 1966, *3,* 5–10.

Metfessel, N. S., & Michael, W. B. A paradigm involving multiple criterion measures for the evaluation of the effectiveness of school programs. *Educational and Psychological Measurement,* 1967, *27,* 931–943.

Millman, J. On improving the credibility of evaluation. *Educational Evaluation and Policy Analysis,* 1979. *1*(6), 58–60.

National Study of School Evaluation. In *Evaluative Criteria* (5th ed.). Arlington, Va.: National Study of School Evaluation, 1978.

Owens, T. Education evaluation by adversary proceeding. In E. R. House (Ed.), *School Evaluation: The Politics and Process.* Berkeley, Calif.: McCutchan, 1973.

Parlett, M., & Hamilton, D. Evaluation as illumination: A new approach to the study of innovatory programs. In G. V. Glass (Ed.), *Evaluation Studies Review Annual* (Vol. 1). Beverly Hills, Calif.: Sage, 1977, pp. 140–157.

Patton, M. Q. *Utilization-focused Evaluation.* Beverly Hills, Calif.: Sage, 1978.

Patton, M. Q. *Qualitative Evaluation Methods.* Beverly Hills, Calif.: Sage, 1980.

Patton, M. Q.; Grimes, P. S.; Guthrie, K. M.; Brennan, N. J.; French, B. D.; & Blyth, D. A. In search of impact: An analysis of the utilization of federal health evaluation research. In C. Weiss (Ed.), *Using Social Research in Public Policy Making.* Lexington, Mass.: Heath, Lexington Books, 1977, pp. 141–164.

Perrone, V. *The Abuses of Standardized Testing.* Bloomington, Ind.: Phi Delta Kappa, 1977. (ERIC Document Reproduction Service No. ED 141 399)

Petrie, H. G. Theories are tested by observing the facts: Or are they? In L. G. Thomas (Ed.), *Philosophical Redirection of Educational Research: The Seventy-first Yearbook of the National Society for the Study of Education* (Part 1). Chicago: University of Chicago Press, 1972, pp. 47–73.

Polanyi, M. *Personal Knowledge.* Chicago: University of Chicago Press, 1958.

Popham, W. J. *Educational Evaluation.* Englewood Cliffs, N.J.: Prentice-Hall, 1975.

Popham, W. J., & Carlson, D. Deep dark deficits of the adversary evaluation model. *Educational Researcher,* 1977, *6*(6), 3–6.

Provus, M. *Discrepancy Evaluation for Educational Program Improvement and Assessment.* Berkeley, Calif.: McCutchan, 1971.

Riecken, H. W., & Boruch, R. F. *Social Experimentation: A Method for Planning and Evaluating Social Intervention.* New York: Academic Press, 1974.

Rippey, R. M. (Ed.). *Studies in Transactional Evaluation.* Berkeley, Calif.: McCutchan, 1973.

Rivlin, A. M., & Timpane, P. M. (Eds.). *Planned Variation in Education: Should We Give Up or Try Harder?* Washington, D.C.: Brookings Institute, 1975. (ERIC Document Reproduction Service No. ED 114 986)

Rosenthal, R. *Experimenter Effects in Behavioral Research.* New York: Appleton-Century-Crofts, 1966.

Ross, L., & Cronbach, L. J. (Eds.). Essay on the handbook of evaluation research. *Educational Researcher,* 1976, *5*(10), 9–19.

Rossi, P. H. Boobytraps and pitfalls in the evaluation of social action programs. In *Proceedings of Social Statistics Section.* Washington, D.C.: American Statistical Association, 1966, pp. 127–132.

Rossi, P. H. Testing for success and failure in social action. In P. H. Rossi & W. Williams (Eds.), *Evaluating Social Programs: Theory, Practice, and Politics* New York: Seminar Press, 1972, pp. 11–65.

Rossi, P. H., & Williams, W. *Evaluating Social Programs: Theory, Practice, and Politics.* New York: Seminar Press, 1972.

Rothenberg, J. Cost-benefit analysis: A methodological exposition. In M. Guttentag & E. L. Struening (Eds.), *Handbook of Evaluation Research* (Vol. 2). Beverly Hills, Calif.: Sage, 1975, pp. 55–88.

Rutman, L. Formative research and program evaluability. In L. Rutman (Ed.), *Evaluation Research Methods: A Basic Guide.* Beverly Hills, Calif.: Sage, 1977.

Sanders, J., & Cunningham, D. A structure for formative evaluation in product development. *Review of Educational Research,* 1973, *43,* 217–236.

Sartre, J. P. *Search for a Method.* New York: Knopf, 1963.

Scriven, M. The methodology of evaluation. In R. W. Tyler, R. M. Gagné, & M. Scriven (Eds.), *Perspectives of Curriculum Evaluation* (American Educational Research Association Monograph Series on Curriculum Evaluation, No. 1). Chicago: Rand McNally, 1967.

Scriven, M. Pros and cons about goal-free evaluation. *Evaluation Comment: The Journal of Education Evaluation,* 1972, *3*(4), 1–7.

Scriven, M. Standards for the evaluation of educational programs and products. In G. D. Borich (Ed.), *Evaluating Educational Programs and Products.* Englewood Cliffs, N.J.: Educational Technology Publications, 1974.

Scriven, M. Maximizing the power of causal investigation: The modus operandi method. In G. V. Glass (Ed.), *Evaluation Studies Review Annual* (Vol. 1), Beverly Hills, Calif: Sage, 1976.

Service Delivery Assessment. Washington, D.C.: Office of Inspector General, Department of Health and Human Services, n.d. (Mimeo)

Shapiro, J. *Extending the Evaluation Meta-theory: Alternative Criteria for the Assessment of Programmatic Outcomes.* (Unpublished paper, 1981)

Simon, H. A. *Administrative Behavior.* New York: Macmillan, 1957.

Sindell, P. Anthropological approaches to the study of education. *Review of Educational Research,* 1969, *39,* 593–607.

Sjoberg, G. Politics, ethics, and evaluation research. In M. Guttentag & E. L. Struening (Eds.), *Handbook of Evaluation Research* (Vol. 2), Beverly Hills, Calif.: Sage, 1975, 29–51.

Smith, L. (Ed.). *Anthropological Perspectives on Evaluation* (American Educational Research Association Monograph Series in Education, No. 7). Chicago: Rand McNally, 1974.

Sroufe, G. E. Evaluation and politics. In J. D. Scriber (Ed.), *The Politics of Education: Seventy-sixth Yearbook of the National Society for the Study of Education* (Part 2). Chicago: University of Chicago Press, 1977.

Stake, R. E. The countenance of educational evaluation. *Teachers College Record,* 1967, *68,* 523–540.

Stake, R. E. *Evaluating the Arts in Education: A Responsive Approach.* Columbus, Ohio: Merrill, 1975.

Stake, R. E., & Easley, J. *Case Studies in Science Education.* Urbana: University of Illinois, Center for Instructional Research and Curriculum Evaluation, 1978.

Stanley, J. C. Controlled field experiments as a model for evaluation. In P. H. Rossi & W. Williams (Eds.), *Evaluating Social Programs: Theory, Practice, and Politics.* New York: Seminar Press, 1972, pp. 67–71.

Stufflebeam, D. L. The relevance of the CIPP evaluation model for educational accountability. *Journal of Research and Development in Education,* 1971, *5*(1), 19–25.

Stufflebeam, D. L., & Guba, E. *Strategies for Institutionalization of the CIPP Evaluation Model.* Address delivered at the Eleventh Annual Phi Delta Kappa Symposium on Education Research, Columbus, Ohio, June 24, 1970.

Stufflebeam, D. L., & Webster, W. J. An analysis of alternative approaches to evaluation. *Educational Evaluation and Policy Analysis,* 1980, *2*(3), 5–20.

Suchman, E. A. *Evaluative Research: Principles and Practice in Public Service and Action Programs.* New York: Russell Sage Foundation, 1967.

Suchman, E. A. Evaluating educational programs. *Urban Review,* 1969, *3*(4), 15–17.

Suchman, E. A. The role of evaluative research. *Proceedings of the 1969 Invitational Conference on Testing Problems,* 1970, pp. 93–103.

Talmage, H. A case study of an evaluation. In R. M. Rippey (Ed.), *Studies in Transactional Evaluation.* Berkeley, Calif.: McCutchan, 1973.

Talmage, H. Evaluation of school/community social action programs: A transactional approach. *Journal of Research and Development in Education,* 1975, *8*(3), 32–41.

Talmage, H., & Haertel, G. D. Cooperative evaluation: A parent, teacher, and evaluator partnership. In S. Sharon, P. Hare, C. D. Webb, & R. Hertz-Lazarowitz (Eds.), *Cooperation in Education.* Provo, Utah: Brigham Young University Press, 1981.

Thompson, M. S. *Benefit-Cost Analysis for Program Evaluation.* Beverly Hills, Calif.: Sage, 1980.

Thurston, P. Revitalizing adversary evaluation: Deep dark deficits on muddled mistaken musings. *Educational Researcher,* 1978, *7*(7), 3–8.

Trismen, D. A.; Waller, M. I.; & Wilder, G. *A Descriptive and Analytic Study of Compensatory Reading Programs.* Princeton, N.J.: Educational Testing Service, 1975. (ERIC Document Reproduction Service No. ED 064 294)

Tyler, R. W. The objectives and plans for a national assessment of educational progress. *Journal of Educational Measurement,* 1966, *3,* 1–4.

Weiss, C. H. The politicization of evaluation research. *Journal of Social Issues,* 1970, *26*(4), 57–68.

Weiss, C. H. Evaluating educational and social action programs: A tree-ful of owls. In C. W. Weiss (Ed.), *Evaluating Social Action Programs: Readings in Social Action and Evaluation.* Boston: Allyn & Bacon, 1972. (a)

Weiss, C. H. *Evaluation Research: Methods of Assessing Program Effectiveness.* Englewood Cliffs, N.J.: Prentice-Hall, 1972. (b)

Weiss, C. H. Utilization of evaluation: Toward comparative study. In C. H. Weiss (Ed.), *Evaluating Social Action Programs: Readings in Social Action and Evaluation.* Boston: Allyn & Bacon, 1972. (c)

Weiss, C. H. Evaluation research in the political context. In M. Guttentag & E. L. Struening (Eds.), *Handbook of Evaluation Research* (Vol. 1). Beverly Hills, Calif.: Sage, 1975, pp. 13–26.

Weiss, C. H. Research for policy's sake: The enlightenment function of social research. *Policy Analysis,* 1977, *3,* 531–545. (a)

Weiss, C. H. (Ed.). *Using Social Research in Public Policy Making.* Lexington, Mass.: Heath, Lexington Books, 1977. (b)

Weiss, C. H. The many meanings of research utilization. *Public Administration Review,* 1979, *39,* 426–431.

Weiss, R. S., & Rein, M. The evaluation of broad-aim programs: Difficulties in experimental design and an alternative. In Weiss, C. H. (Ed.), *Evaluating Social Action Programs: Readings in Social Action and Evaluation.* Boston: Allyn & Bacon, 1972, pp. 236–249.

Weker, G. *Uses and Abuses of Standardized Testing in the Schools.* Washington, D.C.: Council on Basic Education, 1974.

Welch, W. W. Twenty years of science curriculum development: A look back. D. C. Berliner (Ed.), *Review of Research in Education,* 1979, *7,* 282–306.

Wholey, J. S. Evaluability assessment. In L. Rutman (Ed.), *Evaluation Research Methods: A Basic Guide.* Beverly Hills, Calif.: Sage, 1977.

Wholey, J. S.; Duffy, H. G.; Fukumoto, J. S.; Scanlon, J. W.; Berlin, M. A.; Copeland, W. C.; & Zelinsky, J. G. Proper organizational relationships. In C. H. Weiss (Ed.), *Evaluating Social Action Programs: Readings in Social Action and Evaluation.* Boston: Allyn & Bacon, 1972, pp. 118–122.

Wholey, J. S.; Scanlon, J. W.; Duffy, H. G.; Fukumoto, J. S.; & Vogt, L. M. *Federal Evaluation Policy: Analyzing the Effects of Public Programs.* Washington, D.C.: Urban Institute, 1970.

Williams, S. W., & Evans, J. The politics of evaluation: The case of Head Start. *Annals of the American Academy of Political and Social Science,* 1969, *385,* 113–132.

Wolf, R. L. Trial by jury. *Phi Delta Kappan,* 1975, *57,* 185–187.

Wolf, R. M. *Evaluation in Education: Foundations of Competency Assessment and Program Review.* New York: Praeger, 1979.

Worthen, B. R. Competencies for educational research and evaluation. *Educational Researcher,* 1975, *4*(1), 13–16.

Worthen, B. R., & Gagné, R. M. *The Development of a Classification System for Functions and Skills Required of Research and Research-Related Personnel in Education* (Technical Paper No. 1). Boulder, Colo.: American Educational Research Association Task Force on Research Training, Laboratory of Educational Research, 1969.

Worthen, B. R., & Sanders, J. R. (Eds.). *Educational Evaluation: Theory and Practice.* Worthington, Ohio: Charles A. Jones, 1973.

Ziman, J. *Teaching and Learning about Science and Society.* New York: Cambridge University Press, 1980.

EVALUATION OF TEACHERS

A great deal of the abundant rhetoric about teacher evaluation is designed to rally teachers to its support. Claims are made that teacher evaluation is not an event but a process; it is ongoing and continuous; its primary purpose is the improvement of instruction; and it involves teachers directly as full-fledged partners. These claims, however, are almost never reflected in current practice. By and large, evaluation happens to teachers once a year, with evaluators who are sometimes students and frequently administrators, making use of rating sheets that have been nominally approved for general use in the school by a committee of teachers. Teachers tend to view the process with some apprehension—accepting praise as obvious, well-deserved, and beside the point; and perceiving criticism aimed at improving their practice as subjective, unfair, irrelevant, or simply wrong-headed. Finally, there is very little evidence that teachers who receive evaluations are better teachers for it.

In this article the purposes meant to guide the formulation and implementation of teacher evaluation processes are delineated. Next, current practices in the field are described. The final section deals with issues and problems inherent in teacher evaluation. (As an aside, readers interested in the history of teacher evaluation might look to accounts available in Monroe & Clark, 1924; Beecher, 1949; and Barr & Jones, 1958.)

Goals. Bolton (1973) ascribes to teacher evaluation the following general goal: to safeguard and improve the quality of instruction received by students. Bolton acknowledges this overarching purpose can be achieved through programs giving varying emphases to the following functions: (1) improving teaching through the identification of ways to change teaching systems, teaching environments, or teaching behaviors; (2) supplying information that will lead to the modification of teachers' assignments, such as placements into other positions, promotions, and terminations; (3) protecting students from incompetence and teachers themselves from unprofessional administrators; (4) rewarding superior performance; (5) validating the school system's teacher selection process; and (6) providing a basis for teachers' career planning and professional development.

Although the purposes Bolton cites are important, they are quite modest when compared to the unrealistic and unwarranted expectations that some hold for teacher evaluation (Redfern, 1980). For instance, to believe that any teacher evaluation system will guarantee that children will learn what is taught is, in Redfern's term, "nonsense."

Two diverse functions are included in the list of goals described above. The first is termed "summative" (Scriven, 1967) and calls for making an overall judgment of the teacher's effectiveness. Judgments of this order lead to teachers being fired, reassigned, promoted, or given the teacher-of-the-year award. The second function, called "formative," is to contribute to the improvement of teaching by identifying areas of strengths and weakness. Here, as a rule, overall judgments are avoided and instead supervisors and administrators work to share with teachers information concerning improvements that might be made. The difficulty in separating these two functions apparently accounts for a large measure of the cynicism or fear that the concept "teacher evaluation" evokes in most teachers.

Finally, two important attributes of our society impinge upon the conceptualizations of the teacher evaluation process. The first is an increasingly sensitive view of justice. Because of our heightened awareness of the demands of justice in making evaluations and an accompanying litigious spirit that characterizes our society, we view teacher evaluation with increased wariness. Thus it is not sufficient merely to discern that a teacher is weak, it is also important that the bases of such a judgment appear to be objective and fair. Eisner (1976) made the distinction between appreciation and disclosure. The first has to do with identifying aspects of teaching that are worthy of notice and making judgments about them; the second deals with communicating to teachers what those judgments are and attempting to justify them. It appears the latter is more difficult in practice than the former.

The second attribute is the high esteem attributed in the American culture to the scientific method. The social sciences in general and education in particular developed during a time when the natural sciences were increasing their influence in society. It was reasonable to believe that the methods of science accounted for its successes and that those methods were also appropriate for the social sciences in general, and for teacher evaluation specifically. There is an expectation that the procedures and outcomes of social science should match the standards of the physical sciences in their objectivity and power. Thus, we have been trained to accept natural science metaphors in the field of teacher evaluation; for example, teaching is to be "measured," one would believe, with the precision scientists use to measure the speed of light. Clearly, teacher evaluation efforts fall far short of such standards. Soon, perhaps, a consensus will arise that indeed they are the wrong standards to apply to teacher evaluation methodology. In the meantime, the press for justice and the value attributed to "scientific" approaches seriously affect teacher evaluation practices.

Grading Teachers

The proponents of teacher evaluation insist that effective practice is more than simply rating and grading teacher performances (ASCD, 1950). Nothing in this entry should serve to deny this assertion. Although the goals of teacher evaluation transcend the mere grading of teachers, at the heart of any teacher evaluation system is the step in which the teacher's work is judged as excellent, satisfactory, or in need of improvement. Although labels such as these may be only implicit in the process, it is at the point of grading that the supervisor plans with the teacher to bring about changes in teacher behavior; that the assistant superintendent for public relations prepares copy for the newsletter bringing to the public's attention the work of outstanding teachers in the school; or that the assistant superintendent for personnel takes steps to initiate dismissal proceedings against a teacher deemed "inefficient" as a result of an evaluation process. All of these actions are congruent with the goals of evaluation cited above, and rely to some extent on the "grades" assigned to teachers through evaluation procedures.

For the most part, the process of teacher evaluation

found in the schools is guided by formal policy statements (Reavis, 1975). Increasingly, the negotiated agreements that bind school boards and collective bargaining groups of teachers contain language that addresses issues in teacher evaluation (Shahly, 1979). At the same time, researchers report that in spite of the fact that descriptions of evaluation policies and processes are in place, teachers appear confused about the purposes of the evaluation process (Zelenak, 1973) and about the criteria used (Thompson, Dornbusch, & Scott, 1975).

Hodel (1979) classified various approaches to the evaluation of teachers at the elementary level. The predominant mode of evaluation (found in 34 percent of the twenty-six schools he surveyed) was characterized as "joint assessment" in which the teacher and the principal talk over the extent to which pre-established goals were met. The second most frequent style, however, was for the principal to observe teachers, confer with them, and then to make unilateral ratings of their performance. The results of a number of surveys indicate that by and large principals are chiefly responsible for evaluating teachers and in the main they use rating scales or checklists that are completed primarily on the basis of classroom observations (Hodel, 1979; Shea, 1977; Reavis, 1975).

The visits that principals make to classrooms vary in frequency and length. Tomhave's study of elementary and secondary school districts in Iowa indicates that 31 percent of the 324 teachers he surveyed had not been supervised in a formal manner. Twenty-one percent reported they had been visited officially only once. The duration of the formal visits was usually brief, with 51 percent of the observations being for a half hour or less (Tomhave, 1978). In his study of the documentation that accompanied the implementation of teacher evaluation policies, Gosling (1978) noted that 54 percent of the records and reports of observation were dated either May or June, suggesting that teacher evaluation is essentially an end-of-the-year activity.

As part of his research, Gosling characterized the comments and evaluative statements entered onto the forms that principals and supervisors were required to complete. Of 2,202 comments that were subjected to analysis, 82 percent were positive while only 6 percent were of the "needs improvement" kind. According to Gosling, principals seemed wont to find reasons outside of the teaching context to account for any observed weaknesses, presumably with the sentiment that things will improve when circumstances external to the school change.

For reasons of history, tradition, and obscure notions of academic freedom, instructors in higher education are rarely observed by administrators for the purposes of teacher evaluation. Instead, data are collected from students who assess the quality of the instruction they have received on rating forms or check sheets, not unlike those utilized in public schools by principals. This approach to teacher evaluation has an interesting history, with discussions of its efficacy found as early as 1905 (Book). But, in contrast to the usual practice in public schools, rarely are follow-up conferences held to discuss the feedback received by the instructor. As a rule, the students' judgments are reduced to means and standard deviations, and assigned percentile rankings. Since there is some evidence that class size and the subject area of the course influence the ratings an instructor receives, separate norms are often established for these subgroupings for comparison purposes (Centra, 1980). The consensus of scholars who have reviewed studies of the psychometric properties of student ratings is that they provide reliable and useful information for carrying out the goals of the evaluation of teaching (Costin, Greenough, & Menges, 1971; Cohen, 1980). This is not to suggest that the use of student ratings is without controversy. A number of educators object to the process (Machlup, 1979), and even its advocates recognize limitations in the process (Centra, 1980).

Given these procedures, including the confusions, the limited periods of observations, and the apparently inadequate feedback, it is surprising that as many as half the teachers in most surveys find the process "adequate" (Shea, 1977; Tomhave, 1978). In the main, both teachers and evaluators are concerned about the effect of the process. Some doubt that it really makes a difference in improving teaching (Shahly, 1979). Further, there are many who feel that the process itself interferes with the "helping relationships" principals work hard to establish with their teachers. Judging and helping seem to be incompatible processes (Hodel, 1979). Hodel's survey led him to conclude that as evaluation practices become more formalized, principals are less able to improve instruction.

Ratings Scales and Checklists.   Surveys of teacher evaluation practice suggest that a central aspect of the vast majority of procedures is the use of the rating scale and checklist. One might imagine that these instruments were introduced for several reasons: (1) they give the appearance and promise of being objective, and therefore might serve to help teachers avoid the excesses and injustices of autocratic administrators; (2) the instruments have a "scientific" look about them, making the process seem more respectable, more professional; and (3) they serve the purpose of reducing the complexity of the teaching process thus making it more amenable to evaluation. Most evaluators assume that the global approach to teacher evaluation is not effective. Guidelines taken from *Teacher Evaluation to Improve Learning,* published by the Ohio Commission on Public School Personnel Policies, purport to reflect the judgments of experts in the field (Oldham, 1974). One guideline insists that "the teaching act must be broken down into specific skills which can be evaluated and an appropriate instrument and technique to measure each skill must be used." According to these guidelines, teaching is to be treated not as a thing which is, but as a process that is constituted (Schwab, 1960). Practices reflecting this reductionist view are dominant in the field.

Selecting Dimensions of Teaching.   Whether data are to be collected from observers using a checklist or from students utilizing a rating form of some sort, the first issue to be addressed in constructing a teacher evaluation process is that of selecting those dimensions to be included in an instrument. Generally, committees of teachers, consultants, parents, and citizens analyze the teaching task for the purpose of identifying dimensions suitable for rating. These dimensions almost always include such things as knowledge of subject matter and appropriateness of methods; they relate to such things as students, colleagues and administrators, professional attitudes, and other similar items. There is no known basis for limiting such a list; that is, most people can almost without fail think of a new dimension to add to a collection of dimensions that is putatively "complete." This problem is reflected in the findings of Kirk (1978), who surveyed 127 school systems in Alabama to critique the evaluation forms used to assess teacher performance. She reported that the dimensions included in the 85 forms she studied ranged in number from 4 to 111 with a median of 27. This curious situation brings to mind the difference between a collection of dimensions and a set of dimensions. A set of encyclopedia, for instance, is more than a collection: if one of its volumes is misplaced, the entity itself is affected. The same goes for a set of chess pieces or even a set of china. On the other hand, a collection of books remains a collection even if several volumes are lost or a few others are added. In this sense, in almost every case of the use of rating forms in teacher evaluation, the dimensions can best be characterized as collections rather than sets. This factor makes the fashioning of evaluation instruments a chancy affair—with politics, parochial views of teaching, and similar factors playing key roles in determining which dimensions of teaching are to be included and which are not.

The following list conveys the scope of dimensions found on evaluation instruments: organization, discipline, atmosphere for learning, handling of routine procedures, sense of humor, conduct and character, physical health and vitality, appearance, enthusiasm, communication skills, initiative, tact, judgment, lesson planning, clarity, task orientation, rapport, cooperation, wisdom, spark, drive, charisma, doubt, heart, vision, use of blackboard, vocal delivery, consistency, success in problem solving, success in management, leadership, communication skills, ability to build morale, preparational competencies, instructional skills, ability to motivate, and punctuality.

One particular kind of item that is included on many evaluation forms calls for the evaluator to make an "overall" assessment of the teacher's performance. Thus, the item does not represent a component of teaching, but instead requires the evaluator to make an evaluation on a holistic basis. Often the holistic evaluations are the ones used to make critical decisions about teachers—to promote them, to fire them, or to reassign them to other responsibilities. Although overall judgments are not helpful in a formative sense in giving direction to the improvement of teaching, they apparently correlate more highly with student learning than do ratings of specific instructional behavior (Centra, 1980; Shavelson & Dempsey-Atwood, 1976).

Grading Labels. A central aspect of most teacher evaluation plans is the affixing of descriptive labels to the various teaching behaviors of teaching that have been selected for scrutiny (Urmson, 1969). Following Urmson's advice, we can refer to the process of assigning teacher behavior to a particular classification as "grading" and the adjective used to describe the classification as a "grading label." Almost always, labels are selected in groups which imply an order of "goodness" from the most desirable to the least. The groups of labels found in wide use in the grading of teachers in the United States *circa* 1980 include the following: superior, good, satisfactory, weak; excellent, good, fair, needs improvement, poor; outstanding, above average, satisfactory, below average, requires improvement; extensive quality, moderate quality, negligible quality; outstanding, excellent, good, fair, unsatisfactory; and satisfactory, unsatisfactory.

A variant of the grading process is to include on the form declarative sentences describing some component of teaching behavior, such as "the teacher plans well." Label groups assigned to items such as these include almost always, often, some of the time, seldom, almost never; strongly agree, disagree, strongly disagree; yes, no; and involves all or nearly all pupils and is consistent, involves most of the pupils and few opportunities are missed, involves some pupils but falls short of involving most pupils and of being consistent, is inconsistent and reaches few pupils.

Few of the labels taken out of the context of the group in which it is embedded signal very much about the absolute quality of the teacher's behavior. Thus, someone who is rated "good" might be in the second highest classification in one system but in the third category in another. Apparently in attempts to soften the evaluation process, grading labels are selected to inflate the normal connotations of words. This approach to grading is seen in supermarkets as well: the smallest box of soap flakes offered in some brands is "giant size."

Judgments as data. Some writers distinguish between standards and criteria in the following fashion. A criterion is a statement that describes or designates a variable of interest or an attribute of a person that is to be considered. A standard denotes the amount of the variable or attribute required to receive a specific grade. Thus, if height were a criterion for becoming a policeman, a standard might be 60 inches. If a candidate for the police force met the height criterion at a standard of 60 inches or more, he would be graded "eligible." If he fell below the standard of 60 inches, he would be graded "ineligible." Ideally, evaluators would like to be able to specify both the criteria and the standards as clearly as was done in this example. Certainly, it would be helpful if the data to which the criteria and standards were applied could be specified as explicitly as in this illustration, however, this is almost never the case in teacher evaluation. Consider the logical and highly valued criterion "knowledge of subject matter." What is the evidence that bears on this criterion? And if we knew which evidence was relevant, what would be the standard? Because we are unable to treat the process of teaching as objectively or as analytically as our choice of language would suggest, we essentially fall back upon using judgments as data (Stake, 1970). We trust principals or students to make judgments about a teacher's knowledge of subject matter and we treat those judgments as evidence of a teacher's competence. How the judgments were rendered, on what basis they were formulated, what assumptions or implicit theories of teaching and learning they encompass are generally not known. Since these judgments are usually converted to numerical values, they are often treated as though they were precise measures of teacher effectiveness (Centra, 1980, p. 44).

In summarizing this section, it seems important to cite several practices that are not found in current practice with a great deal of frequency. Very few school systems make use of "gain" or test scores of students as measures of teacher efficacy. In spite of the logic that seems to inhere in such an approach and the advocacy of the use of student test performance that attended the recent accountability movement, teachers generally reject this form of evaluation. (Shahly, 1979; Jenkins & Bausell, 1974). Evidently there is a strong sense that poor results in the classroom as measured by student test performances may be due as much to situational constraints as to the performance of the teacher (Kowalski, 1978, p. 9).

Second, only rarely are teachers called upon to evaluate their colleagues. Kowalski (1978) reported that peer evaluations of classroom teachers takes place in 3.2 percent of the elementary schools, 3 percent of the junior high schools, and 3.5 percent of the senior high schools within a national sample of approximately 1,975 school districts surveyed in the United States. Even though teachers might be thought of as more knowledgeable and sympathetic to the constraints fellow teachers were experiencing, this approach appears to be unused and is generally undesired by teachers themselves.

Finally, as noted above, the selection of dimensions upon which to rate teachers is subject to a variety of pressures, since there is no firm and final consensus concerning what dimensions a rating scale ought to include. It is interesting to note how prominent a concern was manifest in the rating forms current 40 or so years ago for a teacher's taking care to advance the ideals of democracy and democratic living. Very few, if any, of the forms currently in use that were reviewed in the process of preparing this entry included items of this genre. It suggests that schools have in some sense abandoned the teaching of "democracy," or at least, have lowered the priorities assigned to teaching these ideals. This inference, if correct, seems quite serious and worthy of study.

Problems with Current Practices

The teacher evaluation process as practiced is flawed in many ways. Four central and well-known problems with it will be reviewed here: the first has to do with the ethical questions embedded in the process; the second with the methods through which data are collected; the third deals with the connection between the summative and formative roles of evaluation, and the last discusses interferences with the administrator-teacher relationship.

Ethical Questions. Much has been made in this entry of the lack of consensus dealing with the components of the teaching act that should be subject to scrutiny in the evaluation process. It is interesting to ask the basic question: For what should teachers be held accountable? McIntyre (1977) advanced five levels of responsibility to which suggested components might be assigned:

1. *The teacher's own behavior.* Is the teacher punctual? Does the teacher cover the material in the syllabus? Does the teacher show up for class? Does the teacher follow school rules and procedures?

2. *Pupils' in-class behavior.* Do students listen attentively? Do they behave according to the rules of the school? Do they initiate ideas and participate in discussions? Do they spend their in-class time "on-task"?

3. *Pupils' in-class mental activity.* Are the pupils interested in what the teacher is presenting? Do they understand what the teacher is saying? Are they curious about the subject matter presented in class? Are they motivated to learn?

4. *Pupil's in-class learning.* Have the students mastered the goals of instruction? Can they demonstrate at the close of the class or the term that they have learned what was intended for them to learn?

5. *Pupil's out-of-class activity.* Do the students spell words correctly on job applications? Do they vote and behave in other ways as good citizens? Do they apply critical thinking skills acquired in school to solving practical problems out of school?

In making use of this schema, it is important to recognize that a teacher might well accept goals properly classified at the higher levels without being willing to accept responsibility for their attainment; that is, a teacher might strive to have his students spell words correctly on job applications, but he also might resent criticism directed his way if it were to happen that one of his students made egregious errors on an application. This view is consistent with analogous situations found in other areas of our culture. Rarely does our society hold persons responsible for the behaviors of others in their care; we are that committed to the notion that people are or should be generally autonomous. Thus, as parents are almost never held responsible in a judicial sense for the crimes committed by their own children, neither should teachers be held accountable for the out-of-school behaviors of their students. If there existed a consensus in the profession as to what behaviors or actions on the teachers' part constituted good practice, then an evaluation could focus on those. If those practices were manifest, then the teacher would be free from negative evaluations that might accrue in instances when accepted practice fails. The problem is, of course, that no such consensus exists. In sum, it seems reasonable to hold teachers responsible for their own behaviors—the questions they ask, the assignments they give, the comments they make on students' papers, and so on. According to this framework, it is less reasonable to hold them responsible for motivating students or for attaining certain levels of student performance on tests.

Sources of data.   The process of making classroom observations is a central aspect of almost all teacher evaluation procedures. It certainly lends credibility to the process, for how else can evaluations be made without watching the teacher teach? And yet, the process is obviously fraught with problems. Scriven (1980) opines that evaluating teaching for summative purposes through classroom visits is not only incorrect, "it is a disgrace" (p. 11). First, as he points out, the visit itself alters the teaching, so what the evaluator is observing is not likely representative of the day-to-day teaching found in the classroom. Further, every observer brings to his tasks a set of implicit and explicit assumptions about teaching that influence the interpretations he places on what he sees. No matter how well the procedures are designed to control such biases, the interpretations of observers affect the process.

Efforts to diminish the subjective aspects of evaluation have led to the identification of "low inference" rating scales which are presumably more objective. Further, attempts to describe what a teacher is doing rather than how well he does it defeats the principal purposes of evaluation—assessing the worth of the teaching that is taking place. Once pure descriptions are taken, an evaluator presumably must still make judgments about them, a step that reintroduces bias into the process. To demonstrate the susceptibility of observers to variations in classroom teaching behaviors that presumably have little to do with efficacy, lecturers were trained to be slick, enthusiastic, and dynamic while they were teaching gibberish. In a number of replications, these "teachers" were able to generate high marks from students and peers who rated their performances (Ware & Williams, 1975). Called the "Dr. Fox Effect," the bias evident in the ratings is judged to be present in almost any situation in which a teacher is being assessed. To be fair about it, research findings suggest that the very qualities that the "lecturers" were trained to manifest are often associated with good teaching—and perhaps in spite of the worthless content of the lectures the lecturers merited good marks for their teaching.

Formative and Summative Evaluation.   The goals of formative and summative evaluation appear in practice to be incompatible. Often the implied threats and sanctions that may result from summative evaluations cloud efforts to improve teaching through formative evaluations.

It seems evident in the literature that too often the same persons using identical procedures perform both functions, often simultaneously. There is a growing consensus that the two functions must be made discrete. Thus, school systems might make use of a peer supervisory model for improving teaching and a more formal inspectorial model for making summative decisions. In any event, a separation seems warranted.

The relationship between formative and summative evaluation is made even more complicated by the fact that there is apparently no direct link between the two. Teachers who have received low "summative" ratings might try to improve their status by making changes in the various components of their teaching that have been deemed weak through a process of formative evaluation. It is likely that such efforts may result in higher ratings on the components so addressed, but very often the overall rating will remain unchanged. Thus, if a teacher who is rated summatively as mediocre and told his examinations need improvement, tries to write better tests, he will probably be rewarded by higher ratings in subsequent semesters; it is unlikely, however, that his overall rating will change. This eventuality is a serious dilemma which deserves the attention of teacher educators and evaluators.

Administrator-Teacher Relationships.   One of the most difficult aspects of teacher evaluation is the relaying to teachers the judgment that there are areas in which they "need improvement." Principals and supervisors often feel confident that they can discern what is called for in the evaluation process, however, disclosing those observations in helpful ways to teachers is the more difficult task. To someone not close to schools, this may seem to reflect the ineptness of school administrators. Indeed, there are administrators who reflect traits and dispositions that make it difficult for them to communicate effectively with their teachers; however, there are teachers, too, who seem to bristle at the slightest suggestion that there is anything in their performances about which they might make changes. The hard work of administrators to establish helping and cooperative relationships with teachers can be dashed by the process of evaluation, even when it is carried out in a fairly sophisticated manner. Often, principals and department heads wonder if the entire process is worth doing, given the side effects it can generate and the damage it can do. This problem may in part account for the high ratings that teachers tend to receive in teacher evaluation practice.

Summary.   The scientific bent of most of the teacher evaluation efforts described suggests that a key to a successful effort is getting accurate information into the hands of teachers—either in the form of judgments or descriptions of teacher behaviors as perceived by students or supervisors. Doubts have been raised, however, about the efficacy of feedback (McKeachie, 1976). Whether the problem is merely a technical one, a need to find a more efficient and effective way of coping with the problems of teacher evaluation, or whether we are facing a serious conundrum that cannot be transcended simply by better methods or techniques is not clear. Glass (1975) has offered the following paradox (paraphrased here) for us to consider: *Excellent teaching appears to emerge when teachers feel that they are not being judged and evaluated and when they feel that their worth as teachers is not contingent on how they score on an administrator's grading scale. And yet, it appears that teachers approach excellence in their profession to the extent that they respond to evaluations of their teaching.*

On the whole, we have not adequately thought through this apparent paradox. There is much to be done.

James Raths

See also Competency-Based Teacher Education; Faculty Development; Supervision of Teachers; Systematic Observation; Teacher Certification; Teacher Effectiveness; Teacher Selection and Retention.

REFERENCES

Association for Supervision and Curriculum Development. *Better than Rating: New Approaches to Appraisal of Teaching Services.* Washington, D.C.: The Association, 1950.

Barr, A. S., & Jones, R. E. The measurement and prediction of teacher efficiency. *Review of Educational Research,* 1958, *28,* 256–264.

Beecher, D. E. *The Evaluation of Teaching.* Syracuse, N.Y.: Syracuse University Press, 1949.

Bolton, D. L. *Selection and Evaluation of Teachers.* Berkeley, Calif.: McCutchan, 1973.

Book, W. F. The high school teachers from the pupil's point of view. *Pedgogical Seminary,* 1905, *12,* 239–288.

Centra, J. A. *Determining Faculty Effectiveness.* San Francisco: Jossey-Bass, 1980.

Cohen, P. A. A meta-analysis of the relationship between student ratings of instruction and student achievement (Doctoral dissertation, University of Michigan, 1980). *Dissertation Abstracts International,* 1980, *41,* 2011A. (University Microfilms No. 80-25, 666)

Costin, F.; Greenough, W. T.; & Menges, R. J. Student ratings of college teaching: Reliability, validity, and usefulness. *Review of Educational Research,* 1971, *41,* 511–535.

Eisner, E. W. Educational connoisseurship and criticism: Their form and functions in educational evaluations. *Journal of Aesthetic Education,* 1976, *10,* 135–150.

Glass, G. V. A paradox about excellence of schools and the people in them. *Educational Researcher,* 1975, *4,* 9–13.

Gosling, A. W. Teacher evaluation: An examination of formal expectations and actual content (Doctoral dissertation, Indiana University, 1978). *Dissertation Abstracts International,* 1979, *39,* 5228A. (University Microfilms No. 79-06002)

Hodel, G. J. A study of formal and informal teacher evaluation practices of selected elementary school principals (Doctoral dissertation, Northwestern University, 1979). *Dissertation Abstracts International,* 1979, *40,* 3020A. (University Microfilms No. 79-27386)

Jenkins, J. R., & Bausell, R. B. How teachers view the effective teacher: Student learning is not the top criterion. *Phi Delta Kappan,* 1974, *55,* 572–573.

Kirk, E. T. A critical analysis of teacher evaluation instruments in use in Alabama school systems (Doctoral dissertation, Auburn University, 1978). *Dissertation Abstracts International,* 1978, *40,* 583A. (University Microfilms No. 79-13687)

Kowalski, J. P. *Evaluating Teacher Performance.* Arlington, Va.: Educational Research Service, Inc., 1978.

Machlup, F. Poor learning from good teachers. *Academe,* October 1979, pp. 376–380.

McIntyre, D. *What Responsibilities Should Teachers Accept?* (Department of Education Seminar Papers No. 1). Sterling, England: University of Sterling, 1977.

McKeachie, W. J. Psychology in America's bicentennial year. *American Psychologist,* 1976, *31,* 819–833.

Monroe, W. S., & Clark, J. S. Measuring teaching efficiency. *University of Illinois Bulletin,* 1924, *21* (22, Circular No. 25).

Oldham, N. (Ed.). *Evaluating Teachers for Professional Growth: Current Trends in School Policies and Programs.* Arlington, Va.: National School Public Relations Association, 1974. (ERIC Document Reproduction Service No. ED 091 846)

Reavis, R. G. Evaluation practices in selected Texas public high schools (Doctoral dissertation, North Texas State University, 1975). *Dissertation Abstracts International,* 1975, *36,* 7978A. (University Microfilms No. 76-13, 188)

Redfern, G. B. *Evaluating Teachers and Administrators: A Performance Objectives Approach.* Boulder, Colo.: Westview Press, 1980.

Schwab, J. J. What do scientists do? *Behavioral Science,* 1960, *5,* 1–27.

Scriven, M. The methodology of evaluation. In *Perspectives of Curriculum Evaluation* (American Educational Research Association Monograph Series in Curriculum Evaluation No. 1). Chicago: Rand McNally, 1967.

Scriven, M. The evaluation of college teaching. In *Inservice.* Syracuse, N.Y.: Syracuse University, National Council of States of Inservice Education, 1980.

Shahly, G. L. The effects of collective bargaining on teacher evaluation (Doctoral dissertation, Wayne State University, 1979). *Dissertation Abstracts International,* 1979, *40,* 1805A. (University Microfilms No. 79-21721)

Shavelson, R., & Dempsey-Atwood, N. Generalizability of measures of teaching behavior. *Review of Educational Research,* 1976, *46,* 553–611.

Shea, N. P. A study of the teacher evaluation process in the junior high schools of the twenty largest school districts in Kansas (Doctoral dissertation, University of Kansas, 1977). *Dissertation Abstracts International,* 1977, *38,* 3868A. (University Microfilms No. 77-28, 910)

Stake, R. B. Objectives, priorities, and other judgment data. *Review of Educational Research,* 1970, *40,* 181–212.

Thompson, J. E.; Dornbusch, S. M.; & Scott, W. R. *Failures of Communication in the Evaluation of Teachers by Principals.* Stanford, Calif.: Stanford University, 1975. (ERIC Document Reproduction Service No. ED 607 077)

Tomhave, W. K. An exploratory study of teacher evaluation practice in selected Iowa schools (Doctoral dissertation, Iowa State University, 1978). *Dissertation Abstracts International,* 1978, *39,* 4607A. (University Microfilms No. 79-04025)

Urmson, J. O. On grading. In B. Bandman & R. S. Guttchen (Eds.), *Philosophical Essays on Teaching.* New York: Lippincott, 1969.

Ware, J. E., Jr., & Williams, R. G. The Dr. Fox effect: A study of lecturer effectiveness and rating of instruction. *Journal of Medical Education,* 1975, *50,* 149–156.

Zelenak, M. J. Teacher perceptions of the teacher evaluation process (Doctoral dissertation, University of Iowa, 1973). *Dissertation Abstracts International,* 1973, *34,* 2944A. (University Microfilms No. 73–31, 001)

EXPERIENTIAL EDUCATION

If education is the facilitation of learning by teachers or institutions, experiential education is education that incorporates a substantial component of experiential learning into its programming. In this article "experiential learning" is defined as learning in which the learner is in direct touch with the realities being studied. It is contrasted with learning in which the learner reads, hears, talks, or writes about those referents or realities but never comes into contact with them as part of the learning process (Keeton & Tate, 1978).

This article examines the varied uses of the terms "experiential education" and "experiential learning," reports diverse theories for their implications as to what is best learned experientially, treats the varieties and extent of experiential education and learning, discusses the programs of assessment and crediting of experiential learning outside of collegiate auspices, and reflects on the problems of assuring quality in experiential education.

A widespread but confusing usage equates experiential learning with "off-campus" or "nonclassroom" learning. Although on-campus classes in critical thinking or writing may consist entirely of lectures, teacher demonstration, and discussion *about* these subjects, a class may also incorporate periods of learner practice in critical thinking or writing.

Similarly, a theater course is quite likely to include actual enacting of scenes from the plays being studied, and there may be a theater on campus that provides further experiential material for the courses. Art programs on campus often emphasize studio work. Education programs commonly include a practicum or internship component.

A corollary usage treats external degree programs as if they were experiential education. Actually, some degree programs (e.g., the Regents of New York External Degree Program) include options that are purely credentialing services; that is, the learner claims to have already learned what the degree requires, and the program simply assesses this claim and either refuses or awards the degree. Other external degree programs provide educational services as well as crediting, but their courses may be purely lecture series or lecture-discussion experiences accompanied by the traditional writing and reading assignments. Still other external degree programs combine experiential with theoretical components and qualify as both experiential and off-campus (Keeton, 1979).

Experiential education typically involves not merely observing what is being studied but also doing something with it, such as testing the dynamics of the phenomenon (e.g., experimenting with pressure, heat, and mass in a physics laboratory) or applying the theory to achieve some desired result (e.g., using accurate empathy as an element of a crisis intervention strategy in an inner city internship in social work). The uses of the experiential component differ: to test a theory, to improve skills, to seek clues to a new theory, to achieve a social objective by applying a theory, and so on. In each instance, however, the learning process involves an experience of the particular process, object, or phenomenon being studied. Every educational activity is an experience for the learner, of course, but only a limited proportion of programs include experiences of the referent of the study.

Some definitions of experiential learning (and of education that uses it heavily) incorporate sentiments of commendation or approbation into the definition. For example, a definition that stipulates that experiential education fosters a more freely expressive personality and requires greater learner independence than other education forecloses an open investigation into whether educational strategies requiring hands-on experience are indeed more successful in eliciting habits of free expression and whether such expressiveness is best elicited through tactics using high levels of learner independence. While John Dewey uses descriptive language in contrasting the "new education" with the traditional, he appears at times to know by definition that these linkages are surely at work (e.g., Dewey, 1963).

Diverse Theories. The historical roots of experiential education are deep (Keeton & Associates, 1978, chap. 2, 1977). They go back beyond Aristotle, who studied biological phenomena at first hand, to Gautama Buddha, who counseled his followers to leave their habitual ways of life in order to try the Eightfold Path in actual daily life. Doubtless they also go beyond Buddha to the primitive hunter whose son learned to track and kill game in actual hunts. In this section some of the leading theories, instead of being surveyed chronologically, are treated in terms of the different functions or learning tasks to which they are addressed.

Learning how. To learn how to do a task or play a role is normally best done through hands-on experience or as close a simulation of the actual task or role as can be managed safely and economically. Thus, learning to type with great speed and accuracy requires extensive practice, preferably on the types of machines that the learner will use later. Even more important, no one wants to be operated upon by a surgeon who has merely read about surgery and heard the most learned surgeons explain and demonstrate how they do their work. At the same time unsupervised surgical practice is hardly to be recommended, and no airline entrusts fledgling pilots with supersonic aircraft until they have proven themselves in simulators. In the late nineteenth century, Oster of Johns Hopkins University wanted to be remembered for having been the first medical educator who taught his students on the wards. Gilbert Ryle, a British philosopher, makes much of the distinction between "knowing how" and "knowing that" and emphasizes that one can know how without at all being able to describe or explain the performance adequately or can grasp the descriptive theory of a field without being able successfully to apply it (Ryle, 1949, especially chap. 2).

Reformulating knowledge. Far more fundamental than learning how to do something is the creation of new knowledge or the transformation of oneself although learning how to perform a new role borders on self-reconstruction. It was John Dewey who contributed most to the awareness of this more basic function of experiential learning and education. For decades he and his interpreters and successors have been the leading advocates and analysts of experiential learning. For Dewey, experience is a cycle of "trying" and "undergoing." One senses a problem, gets an idea, tries it out in its arena of applicability, undergoes or experiences the consequences, and confirms or reinterprets theory in the light of those consequences. In the best cases, this process results in a "reconstruction" of experience (as in the adoption of Newtonian laws of motion), a recodifying of habits (as when one overcomes personal or racial bias), and an ongoing, active questioning through further experimentation (thus, a habituation toward learning to learn experientially). Buchler spoke of this activity as "proceptive" or initiatory in style. Thus, experiential learning so pursued actually transforms the individual at the same time that it revises and enlarges knowledge and alters practice. This learning affects the aesthetic and ethical commitments of individuals as well as altering their perceptions of the world and their interpretations of its nature. If education is to foster this learning, it will devise ways of inducing the questioning and the reshaping of both self and ideas that make these effects possible.

Dewey tended at times to treat experiential learning as consisting only of experiences that have these salutary effects but at other times to acknowledge that some experiences are "miseducative" or at least unproductive. He also wrote at times as if all experiential learning had to be cast in the mold of experimenting, after the model of modern science, thus excluding the possibility that one might unexpectedly (without planning) undergo an experience that precipitated a reexamination of values, a new perception of how things fit together, or a significant reshaping of one's own life and commitments.

Affective and cognitive insights. A tradition of thinking that has developed along relatively independent lines from the preceding two has been that about emotional or mental health. Psychological therapy, like medicine, has often provided "cures" and "treatment" before there was agreement as to why the treatment was successful. Jung, Erikson, Rogers, Perls, and Maslow are among the theorists who have both advocated new approaches to therapy and sought explanatory theories to account for successes and failures in treatment. In their theories there is an emphasis upon the interplay of the affective and cognitive aspects of the human person and upon the powerful role played by affect and emotion in determining behavior. Since becoming able to function in a way that integrates these aspects of oneself is a matter of learning new patterns of acting, thinking, and feeling, and since talking or reading about such change is relatively powerless to induce the change, learning in an experiential mode—that is, practicing the new feelings and behaviors and perspectives as an aid to learning them—is an emerging trend. Teachers and administrators of educational institutions have typically drawn a sharp contrast between teaching and therapy; yet learning to love learning, cherishing inquiry more than holding to established beliefs, and believing theory in the sense of acting upon it are all tasks that engage the affective and volitional side of human nature. A few thinkers, such as Rogers, Erikson, and more recently Chickering (1981), have noted the relevance of psychological theories of human development and health to educational theories, but the relationships between these two fields of practice are still relatively unexplored.

Action research. Yet another line of inquiry pointing toward the potency of experiential education is the work of Kurt Lewin and his successors in group dynamics and action research. Their thinking emerged from work on improving the effectiveness with which organizations function. Efforts were made, especially in corporations seeking to achieve greater productivity and efficiency, to improve the working environment and to improve the effectiveness of individuals in unimproved working environments. Seminars, lectures, and readings had proved relatively ineffective. So "laboratory training" events and "T-groups" (training groups) were tried, with dramatic and at times traumatic results.

This tradition was also concerned with the irrelevance of much social science research to the improvement of human society. A search for applicable research led to the idea of active interventions in which participant observers bring diverse perceptions of the resulting phenomena together for interpretation, for the "reconstruction" of theory, and for the rethinking of what is appropriate behavior when productivity is the goal. Part of the thinking underlying this work was the idea that a "democratic" environment can be more productive than either an authoritarian or a laissez-faire one. In addition, a "caring" environment was hypothesized to enhance morale and productivity. The impetus behind this work was not at all a search for a theory to explain the merits of experiential learning but rather a trial-and-error search for ways to improve productivity with a resulting interest in theory that would make it possible to continue to get such gains reliably in new situations. Lippitt, McGregor, and Bennis are in this tradition. Knowles, a thinker who has been highly influential in adult and continuing education, draws upon both Dewey and Lewin and their followers. Knowles has made a distinctive contribution on the function of learner self-directedness in eliciting new knowledge, insight, and behavioral competence in human interactions. The learner in this context takes charge of learning, using needed experts as supporting resources.

Developing of Cognition. A different source of theoretical understanding of experiential education is the work of Piaget and his followers. In the course of assisting Binet in the development of intelligence tests, Piaget became interested in how children reach their answers to particular questions (a concern with learning theory). After reviewing his descriptive notes, he distinguished among three modes of thinking that he saw as occurring in young children in a specific chronological sequence. Those modes are the enactive, the ikonic, and the symbolic. In the first or enactive stage, the child acts out ideas and experiences consequences. As the avoidance of painful experiences becomes an interest and the effort to leap ahead continues, a semisymbolizing phase (the use of partially corresponding images, or ikons) begins and improves the child's capacity to manipulate things and ideas. Finally, the use of symbols that are devoid of correspondence to their referents completes the growth to the level of thinking. Piaget saw this progression as one of emerging power and capability, or intelligence. He seemed to treat the earlier modes as inferior to, or more primitive than, the later modes.

Bruner, seeking to develop a theory of instruction (a normative rather than a descriptive enterprise), believed that some learning tasks are best performed through instruction that requires original inquiry. Learning the joys of discovery, developing the motivation to learn, and acquiring a belief capable of triggering action are tasks of this sort. Such learning is necessarily experiential but may move quickly from an enactive to an abstract mode. It is similar to the learning that a scientist does making a new discovery (note the difference between the laboratory as experience in original discovery and the laboratory as repitition of a known procedure to demonstrate a known theory or develop skill in laboratory processes). In the scientist's case, no one ever "knew" this thing before. In the case of Bruner's fifth-grader learning mathematics, this particular learner never grasped or became committed to the use of the idea before.

In his work on learning through gaming and simulation, Coleman makes a distinction between "information assimilation" and "experiential learning" (cited in Keeton & Associates, 1977, chap. 5). Coleman builds upon Bruner's theory of instruction, which dealt with such questions as how to implant a predisposition toward learning, how to structure a body of knowledge for learning, and how to sequence materials and to select and time rewards and punishments in such a way as to induce learning. Coleman hypothesizes that the nature of what is being learned may be important to the choice between the pattern of information assimilation and that of experiential learning. Information assimilation, as Coleman sees it, begins with receiving information, moves to assimilating the general principle, then to inferring particular applications of it,

and finally to applying it. Experiential learning proceeds in almost the reverse order, as Coleman defines this mode: first an action is carried out and its effects are observed; then comes the expectation that repetition of the same action in the same circumstances would have similar consequences; there may follow a grasp of a general principle, and finally that principle is used in new circumstances in anticipation of predicted results. After exploring whether the same or different things are learned through the two patterns, Coleman concludes by recommending a search for instructional strategies that combine the two approaches to learning in complex educational endeavors.

Social Critique. A quite different line of inquiry arose out of social criticism of western cultures. This philosophical movement can be traced to diverse sources, including Karl Marx, the antinomian theologies, John Dewey. Two of its most prominent contemporary adherents are Paolo Freire and Ivan Illich (e.g., Illich, 1971, 1973). Freire argued against teaching as a process of depositing the teacher's information and ideas and biases in the learners, who thus "bank" the learning. He argued on the grounds that the content so taught is false and is used to keep the poor and victims of racial and class discrimination in subjection and on the ground that the learners are kept in ignorance of how to find out the truth for themselves. He advocated a form of education that would raise the "critical consciousness" of learners through experiential encounters with the realitites of their own culture and society. Illich, likewise seeing in the prevailing forms of schools an instrument of conservatism and oppression, made a passionate case for "de-schooling" and for substituting freer forms of learning in more direct touch with the surrounding society.

Explication of Meaning. Underlying most of the theories cited thus far is a long tradition in western philosophy in which were argued the functions of concepts (a theoretical component) and experience (an experiential component) in the meaningfulness of terms and in what is now called the truth value of concepts or hypotheses about matters of fact. Plato distinguished between the highest knowledge, which is knowable by reason alone, and true opinion of daily affairs, which has to be checked against firsthand experience of those matters in order to be trusted. The continental rationalists, including Leibniz and Spinoza, defended the deliverances of reason as the only certain source of knowledge, and British empiricists such as Locke, Berkeley, and Hume pleaded the case for impressions of the senses as the necessary source of probable truth about the domain of science and practical affairs. Immanuel Kant sought to save science from skepticism by presenting a theory of knowledge that sees the mind as imposing its categories of organization and interpretation and the senses providing the necessary material of knowledge. In his view, both are essential to knowing. The outcome of this historical effort is that hypotheses of the kind that scientists commonly investigate can be confirmed or disconfirmed only by reference to experiences of their referents ("the realities") but that the framework of concepts within which those hypotheses are formed and tested is either an unavoidable lens or a convenient generative tool of the knowing intelligence.

In the light of this history, a theory of education that seeks to transmit from generation to generation not only the symbols of past understanding but also its substance and to pass on not only the outcomes of the earlier search for knowledge but also the processes and methods by which the search can be pursued must surely continue to search for pedagogies that mix theoretical study with experiential learning.

Optimal learning style. Kolb, drawing on the traditions of both Dewey and Lewin, has made an original contribution to the understanding of experiential learning in his work on learning styles. Using the concept of a learning cycle that circles from a basis of concrete experience to observations and reflection, which are assimilated into the formation of abstract concepts and generalizations, which lead to the drawing and testing of implications of the concepts in new situation, and thence back again to concrete experience, Kolb found that different learners function best by entering this cycle at different points. He finds each of these four styles correlating best with the frequency of learners in different academic majors. He hypothesizes that the ablest learners would strengthen themselves in the parts of the cycle in which they are weakest but might well enter into difficult studies by learning methods that draw upon their strengths at the outset. Kolb has also sought in theories such as those cited here, as well as others, elements of convergence that might disclose a more fundamental pattern in all of the processes of learning (Kolb, 1981).

A number of thinkers who eschew the radical reformers' prescriptions have nevertheless stressed that most learning occurs outside of schooling or education (Tough, 1971). Boud and Pascoe (1978) have sought evidence of ways in which the effects of experiential education can be enhanced. They have identified three variables for special attention: (1) the degree of learner control over learning process, (2) the degree of involvement of the learner's self, and (3) the degree of correspondence between the learning environment and the "real environment" (i.e., the environment in which the learning is meant to be applied).

Achieving a Liberal Education. Smythe (1978) has argued that in the domain of political and ethical understanding and action, the exposure of the student to the actual arena of political action and ethical choice is essential for teachers who would avoid both indoctrination and vapidity in their instruction. Reasoning that learning of these kinds is an essential and substantial component of liberal education, Smythe contends that a more serious exploration of the potential of experiential learning for liberal education is an urgent priority for advocates of both. A beginning of such an exploration appears in two books on experiential education and the liberal arts (Brooks & Althof, 1979; Loacker & Palola, 1981).

Smythe has also performed one of the most thoughtful efforts to date in the clarification of usages of the term "experiential learning" (1978).

Uses of Experiential Education. Peterson (1979) estimates the "learning force" (head count) in the United States as some 116 million deliberate learners in organizational settings. Of these, some 70 million are estimated to be in the school and college sector and some 46 million (40 percent) in nonschool organizations. At the postsecondary level, only 18 million of the estimated 64 million participants are enrolled in colleges or universities. Since the nonschool participants are largely part-time students, the total learning hours or learning effort of the two sectors is seen as similar in magnitude. In addition to this deliberate learning within organizations (Peterson prefers this terminology to "formal learning"), studies based on the work of Tough (1971) and others suggest that as much as 80 percent of all adults engage in self-directed projects using 100 hours or more of effort in a given year. Peterson speaks also of a domain of unintentional learning that "is a concomitant of living" and which has extensive implications and a frequency of unknown dimensions.

How much of this education, whether teacher-directed in formal organizations, self-directed in individually arranged projects, or unintentional, is properly considered experiential? Bearing in mind that experiential learning occurs in class and in school as well as outside but that being outside of institutional sponsorship does not guarantee what is here defined as "experiences of the referents of study," no documented estimate of this proportion has come to the author's notice. Unintentional learning is almost by definition experiential: it arises, unplanned, out of the impact of events that are sufficiently noteworthy to elicit reflection upon those specific experiences. Individually planned and directed learning is more likely than organized, teacher-directed, organizationally sponsored learning to include a substantial experiential component. The nonschool varieties of deliberate learning in organizational contexts are likely to be laced with more substantial experiential elements than are those provided by schools. For example, learning in the military services and employer-arranged instruction are more frequently oriented toward learning how to perform tasks, toward behavior modification, and toward productivity than is school learning, and those learning objectives dictate, in the light of the review of theories just provided, an emphasis upon experientially enriched and practice-laden education.

Within the experiential education movement of the 1970s and 1980s two distinctions are widely used—that between collegiate and noncollegiate experiential education and that between sponsored and nonsponsored experiential learning. Noncollegiate experiential education includes all genuinely experiential instruction that takes place outside of schooling institutions. Learning or education is, in this usage, "sponsored" if and only if it occurs under the aegis of an institution of higher or precollegiate education in which the learner is officially registered and the activity is an accepted part of the student's program of studies. In its policy documents, the American Council on Education has referred to nonsponsored learning as "extrainstitutional." The disadvantage of this usage is that the nonschool organizations providing the creditable learning in fact are "institutions" but ones whose primary missions are other than educational (Task Force on Educational Credit and Credentials, 1978).

Sponsored Experiential Education. The most familiar varieties of sponsored experiential education include clinical studies (medicine, teaching, clinical psychology, child development, and, recently, law); studio (the plastic and graphic arts); field experience and internship (many professional programs, Peace Corps and VISTA work, experience-abroad programs, service learning assignments education (jobs in industry, government, and nonprofit agencies of all kinds either alternating with full-time study periods or "parallel" with academic studies in residence), laboratory work of a discovery type or skill-practice type (the physical sciences, the "harder" social sciences), drill in academic skills (reading, writing, foreign language speaking, listening, reading, and writing, especially when done with native informants or in indigenous settings), apprenticeship (doctoral studies, student research and teaching assistantships, applied political science, occupational training, some legal studies), learning resource center activities (computer sciences, mathematics laboratories), studio (fine arts, architecture), and occupational training and education (paraprofessional and skilled occupations studies), and role playing, gaming, and simulations (economics, psychology, public policy).

As the listing of this variety indicates, experiential learning pervades the curriculum at the postsecondary level. Yet much contemporary discussion among academics treats it as "nontraditional" and "outside the mainstream." In a 1979–1980 survey at Michigan State University for the Council for the Advancement of Experiential Learning and the University, it was found that over seven thousand students in the fall term were participating in field experience in 172 programs (69 at graduate level, 103 at undergraduate) (Duley, 1978). The finding was a surprise to the academic administrators and even to the faculty members, who were generally unaware of the magnitude of the aggregate use of experiential education, but who were using it themselves for reasons deriving from the particular nature of the disciplines or professions being taught. There is still no comprehensive survey of sponsored experiential learning in the United States. Informed estimates as recently as 1980 were that one in seven college students participates in some form of sponsored experiential learning and that the proportion was rising.

Surveys of participation in collegiate programs with major experiential learning components show growing interest. A survey of cooperative education programs reported in 1975 estimated student participation at more than 170,000 in 968 institutions (institutions rose to 1,100 at a later date) and awarding of academic credit as occurring

in 304 programs in more than 125 curriculum areas (Wilson, 1978; Keeton & Tate, 1978).

The number of students studying abroad was estimated in 1980 to be over 50,000 a year, lagging far behind the numbers from other countries studying in the United States (263,938 in 1978–1979) (Flack in Neff, 1981, p. 13). Although Neff and his colleagues bemoaned the rarity with which leaders of cross-cultural learning programs exploited the cultural environment for learning, the students reported significant unintentional as well as deliberate learning from the host cultures.

Service learning and field experience education are formally sanctioned in no fewer than 1,000 institutions of higher education (Keeton & Tate, 1978, p. 6). Occupational and technical education with significant shop, apprenticeship, internship, and laboratory components is found in most community colleges and in some land grant institutions and other four-year universities.

These well-established uses include doctoral research, language laboratories, arts studios, education practica, composition and other writing practice courses, teaching assistantships, and science laboratories. These forms of experiential education are virtually universal in the relevant programs. The most traditional forms of sponsored experiential education are rarely included in discussions of the topic. The reluctance to include these techniques in discussions of experiential learning is usually rationalized on the grounds that these familiar uses are established practice and are of assured quality because of their entrenched position within ordinary instruction. Yet issues as to the optimal timing, quantity, design, and evaluation of these endeavors are still inadequately researched.

Among so-called experiential education programs receiving most public attention within the past six years one must list "prior learning" or, as it is more properly called, nonsponsored experiential learning and programs to assess and credit college-level learning so achieved. The objection to calling this activity "prior learning" is twofold: many students, after registering in colleges, choose to pursue experiential learning (on summer jobs, abroad, on part-time jobs during academic terms) that is not sponsored by their colleges but for which they later seek recognition either through waiver of prerequisites for more advanced work or in the form of academic credit. The evaluation of such learning presents the same technical problems as if it had occurred prior to matriculation. A second limitation of the label is that it makes the school, rather than the timing and design of the student's lifelong education, the central focus in thinking about the student's education.

In addition to voluntary learning in off-duty hours, individuals on active duty in the military have received education for work-related purposes in the United States for over fifty years. The volume of this activity continues to increase. While some of this instruction is in the mode of information transmission and indoctrination, the overwhelming pattern is one of a mixture of hands-on experience and instruction on needed generalized understanding of the tasks and phenomena being studied.

A further domain of enormous cope and increasing significance is that of formal instruction provided by employers in the governmental, private profit-making, and private nonprofit sectors. The corporate profit-oriented sector alone is estimated to spend between $20 billion and $40 billion per year on in-house training and education programs (Lynton, 1981), a sum of money comparable to the combined state appropriations for higher education in all fifty states (including financial aid).

In summary, although no comprehensive survey is available that distinguishes the scope of distinctively experiential learning programs from that of all deliberate and unintentional learning among people viewed as lifelong learners, it is clear that the volume of such education and learning is far larger than was imagined a decade ago.

The Assessment and Crediting of Nonsponsored Experiential Learning. Stimulated by recommendations of the Commission on Non-Traditional Education, Educational Testing Service invited nine (later ten) colleges and universities to join in the formation in March 1974, of the Cooperative Assessment of Experiential Learning Project (the early CAEL). An initial survey by Project staff and the Implementation Committee found some 45 institutions of higher education that then provided a comprehensive, individualized service of assessment of pre-enrollment nonsponsored college-level learning. The American Council on Education (ACE), the pioneer agency developing credit recommendations for noncollegiate instruction, had for decades provided such recommendations on credit awards for formal learning within the military services. It has more recently done so for corporate employers' educational programs. Guides embodying these recommendations are published regularly by the Council. In addition, the Regents of New York publish a similar *Guide to Educational Programs in Noncollegiate Organizations*, which in 1977 reported almost 800 courses of 70 organizations in New York. Also of long standing has been the College Level Examination Program (CLEP) of the College Entrance Examination Board, which provides written examinations nationwide for individuals to use in demonstrating learning equivalent to that of selected subject matter courses or curricular areas. Some 388,000 CLEP tests were taken in 1977–1978 and about 288,000 in 1979–1980. ACE, the Regents, and CLEP do not, however, award academic course credits. Credit awards are made by colleges and universities using the guides and the test results as evidence. Also none of these services is designed to examine the whole of an individual's relevant college-level learning for crediting or advanced standing. The CAEL Project was intended to fill this gap.

By 1977 the CAEL Project had developed a statement of "Principles of Good Practice in the Assessment of Experiential Learning" and had published workbooks for faculty assessors and instructors, guides to students, and aids to higher education administrators with respect to the installation of assessment programs and the monitoring of their quality. In that year CAEL (renamed the Council for the Advancement of Experiential Learning) was independently incorporated as an association of colleges and universities and set out to stimulate expansion of the number of providers of this service and to foster stronger efforts to assure the quality of both assessment services and the effective use of both sponsored and nonsponsored experiential learning. Among its services have been surveys in 1978 and in 1980 of the providers of assessment services and the publication of directories annotating these services. These directories are the best available evidence as to the conditions under which such assessment can be obtained. As of June 1981, the directories annotated over 525 institutions of higher education holding accredited or candidate-for-accreditation status that provide the service. A fall, 1980, survey by the Office of Credit and Credentials of the American Council on Education tallied over 1,000 institutions answering "Yes" to a question as to whether they offered credit awards on the basis of "portfolio" assessment (the "learning portfolio" is a CAEL-developed tool for facilitating assessment but is not used by all institutions with assessment programs). Assuming that some respondents may have misunderstood the question but that some others of the 1,000 institutions not replying to the ACE questionnaire (about 2,200 of the more than 3,100 replied) have a qualifying service, the probable number of institutions currently meeting the CAEL standard for listing is between 800 and 1,200. The principle underlying the assessment service is that if a person has achieved the learning and the competence objectives required for successful completion of a given course or curriculum, the person deserves recognition and appropriate placement in further education programs regardless of where that learning was acquired. The phenomenal growth in provision of such service since 1974, doubtless encouraged by the institutions' search for new clienteles in a time of threatened enrollment declines, suggests that the pedagogical principle of appropriate and equitable placement is firmly established in the United States. Some Canadian institutions of higher education have also been providing this service during recent years, and a group of British educators are actively at work to apply the guiding concepts to both entrance, placement, and sponsored learning (there called "sandwich courses" in the polytechnics).

Although informally good teachers have accelerated their students toward graduation with both advanced placement and waivers of requirements from time immemorial, the recent phenomenon of "prior learning assessment" has provoked much controversy. The Council on Postsecondary Accreditation issued a statement expressing both alarm and qualified support in 1977. It has subsequently joined the American Council on Education and the American Association of Collegiate Registrars and Admissions Officers in endorsing the principle and advising that strong quality assurance provisions be made, using guidelines such as the CAEL *Principles* (1977, reprinted 1979, 1980) for that purpose. The concern, shared by responsible critics and advocates alike, is twofold: first, that commercial ventures have sought to exploit learners with quick and easy degrees; and second, that well-intentioned but uninformed or inadequate providers seeking to serve unserved learners have actually done them a disservice.

Quality Assurance in Experiential Education. The concerns about quality assurance in programs crediting nonsponsored experiential learning are matched by concern among the advocates of sponsored experiential learning about the limited efforts of teachers and administrators to assure that the varieties of internship, cooperative education, apprenticeship, and other forms of sponsored experiential learning are adequately planned, designed, prepared for, and evaluated in comparison to other forms of instruction. As efforts by proponents of experiential learning have discovered, a primary obstacle to comparison is the relative dearth of available materials and research on the actual and intended learning outcomes of traditional, classroom-based programs. In fields in which machine-scorable paper and pencil tests are available, such measures are relatively easy to obtain, but, with increases in the complexity and sophistication of what the learner is to know and do, the difficulty also grows of finding publishable statements of outcomes sought or realized and of obtaining consensus among educators as to appropriate standards.

In a joint study sponsored by the regional accrediting associations, the Council on Postsecondary Accreditation recognized the need for increased emphasis by its member associations upon the actual learning outcomes of both traditional and nontraditional programs. To achieve this emphasis, it was pointed out, would require supplementing the traditional measures of quality based upon "inputs" and processes with assessment efforts making comparison among traditional and nontraditional programs feasible (Keeton & Tate, 1978, pp. 44–47).

A variety of efforts have been under way during the past decade to introduce more effective provisions for quality assurance than have previously been available. These efforts have included research on the usefulness of nontraditional degrees, the use of program reviews and educational audits using teams of qualified outside evaluators as part of the self-study process for accreditation, the development and publication of statements of intended outcomes of specific degree programs and of "program maps" charting the prerequisite learning competencies and knowledge for each stage of advancement toward the final objectives of the programs, the development of files of products (essays, art works, performance records, etc.) that permit accrediting examiners and other regulatory authorities to monitor results, and the training of faculty and of accrediting and supervisory personnel in the monitoring of program quality (Keeton, 1980).

Morris T. Keeton

See also Adult Education; Affective Education; Distance Education; Games and Simulations; Nontraditional Higher Education Programs.

REFERENCES

Boud, D., & Pascoe, J. *Experiential Learning: Developments in Australian Post-secondary Education.* Australian Consortium on Experiential Education, 1978.

Brooks, S., & Althof, J. *Enriching the Liberal Arts through Experiential Learning.* San Francisco: Jossey-Bass, 1979.

Chickering, A. *The Modern American College.* San Francisco: Jossey-Bass, 1981.

Dewey, J. *Experience and Education.* New York: Collier Books, 1963. (Originally published, 1938)

Duley, J. *Survey of Current Practices in Field Experience Education* (Paper #78). East Lansing, Mich.: Learning and Evaluation Service, Michigan State University, 1978.

Keeton, M. Building experiential learning into external degree programs. *Peabody Journal of Education,* 1979, *56*(3), 239–247.

Keeton, M., Ed. *Defining and Assuring Quality in Experiential Learning.* San Francisco: Jossey-Bass, 1980.

Keeton, M., & Associates. *Experiential Learning: Rationale, Characteristics, Assessment.* San Francisco: Jossey-Bass, 1977.

Keeton, M., & Tate, P. (Eds.). *Learning by Experience—What, Why, How.* San Francisco: Jossey-Bass, 1978.

Kolb, D. *Experience, Learning, and Development: The Theory of Experiential Learning.* Englewood Cliffs, N.J.: Prentice-Hall, 1981.

Loacker, G., & Palola, E. (Eds.). *Clarifying Learning Outcomes in the Liberal Arts.* San Francisco: Jossey-Bass, 1981.

Lynton, E. A. "Colleges, universities, and corporate training: Commonalities and contradictions." In *New Alliances with Business and Industry.* San Francisco: Jossey-Bass, 1981.

Minor, J. L., & Boldt, J. *Outward Bound USA.* New York: Morrow, 1981.

Neff, C. B., Ed. *Cross-cultural Learning.* San Francisco: Jossey-Bass, 1981.

Peterson, R. E. *Lifelong Learning in America.* San Francisco: Jossey-Bass, 1979.

Ryle, G. *The Concept of Mind.* London: Hutchinson, 1949.

Smythe, O. *Practical Experience and Liberal Education.* Unpublished manuscript, Harvard Graduate School of Education, 1978, available from author, College of Santa Fe, Santa Fe, New Mexico 87501.

Task Force on Credentialing Educational Accomplishment. *Recommendations on Credentialing Educational Accomplishment.* Washington, D.C.: American Council on Education, 1978. (ERIC Document Reproduction Service No. ED 159 958)

Tough, A. *The Adult's Learning Prospects.* Toronto: Ontario Institute for Studies in Education, 1971.

Wilson, J. W. *Developing and Expanding Cooperative Education.* San Francisco: Jossey-Bass, 1978.

EXPERIMENTAL METHODS

The variety of topics included in this work testifies to the breadth of the field of educational research. The primary purpose here is to familiarize the reader with the more orthodox forms of experimental methods, which remain the cornerstone of scientific research, as well as with modifications of orthodox designs into quasi-experimental methodologies. A secondary purpose is to consider preexperimental designs as they set the stage for their more appropriate experimental counterparts, as well as some issues of statistical analysis of experimental designs and selected ethical issues associated with experimentation in education.

To begin, it is necessary to indicate what constitutes an experiment and why experimental methodology is viewed as being powerful. When educational research is properly described as "experimental" the researcher has specified a finite set of researchable hypotheses and has established a systematic program of data gathering, under precisely defined conditions, in an effort to test those hypotheses. The hypotheses provide a network of statements relating the impact of an independent variable or a set of independent variables on some outcome variable or dependent variable(s). A hypothesis may be presented as a direct statement describing the impact of one variable upon another such as, "Students who are trained in word analysis skills are less likely than those who have not received such training to make spelling errors during composition writing." Or it may be stated in the form of a question, "What is the effect of training students in word analysis skills on their spelling error production during composition writing?" As Kerlinger (1973) notes, the fundamental weakness of many new researchers is their failure to make a satisfactory statement of the research question. Although this failure is especially common among new researchers, experienced researchers often have the same difficulties.

A well-formulated research question sets the stage for the specification of the elements that make up the structured experimental design (Kempthorne, 1961). On the basis of the question, the researcher must offer a clear definition of the population to be studied. Note that in the foregoing sample research question the population is vaguely defined as "students." The actual target population may be much more narrowly defined; for example, it may be seventh- and eighth-grade students. The selection process may further narrow the target population by specific constraints that the researcher wishes to impose.

The researcher must also offer a clear specification of the alternative experimental (or instructional) treatments that are to be applied to the population of concern. The specification should be precise enough to permit another, independent researcher to replicate the experiment in another setting. In addition, the researcher must specify how the various treatments are to be assigned to those who participate in the study. In experimental methodologies the assignment decision is tied to random assignment of subjects (persons or objects) to the alternative experimental conditions. In some instances, however, a researcher may introduce methodological controls on sam-

pling, such as blocking or matching, which constrain random sampling but improve the clarity of the research question and the interpretation of data. And the conditions under which the experiment is to be conducted must be defined, as well as the research materials or stimuli that are intended to create the treatment effects.

Further, the researcher must define valid and reliable measures of the outcome variable. And finally, the researcher must consider the analytic methods that are to be used to make inferences about the data that are collected. That is, the researcher must identify appropriate statistical tools for specifying real versus apparent, but false, differences in performance.

Campbell and Stanley (1963) define "experimentation" as "research in which variables are *manipulated* and their effect upon other variables observed." Their definition reflects the orthodox image of experimental methods that presumes the researcher has direct control over the application of a finite set of experimental treatments to samples of subjects randomly selected from a more general parent population. Experiments are structured within design constraints following the traditions established by Fisher (1935) and his students. In a controlled experiment, Fisher argued, the researcher has direct control over the variability of a precisely defined set of experimental conditions. Uncontrolled variation that occurs over "replicates" (or subjects) is subjected to random dispersion across treatment conditions, effectively negating its impact. Any systematic differences in the means of the samples thus can be attributed to the controlled variation in treatment conditions.

An experiment should not be seen as a single study that answers questions to the satisfaction of all. It should be repeated (replicated) and extended over several studies. Each replication should be independent of previous studies but should be conducted under similar conditions. Successive replicates not only provide confirmation of previous results, but offer refinements and extensions, and these in turn clarify the theory from which the research is derived. A recent review of the role of replication in educational research (Shaver & Norton, 1980) suggests that replication is a little used strategy. This implication is particularly bothersome because replication is a critical element in the progress of the science of education. In his statement on "strong inference" procedures Platt (1964) describes replication as a recycling process through which successive experiments reduce the number of plausible alternative hypotheses. Experimental research in education should become a recursive system in which the outcome of one experiment is the input to a subsequent experiment. The recursive system then becomes self-refining with each recursion, thus helping to reduce uncertainty. In the image of Hofstadter (1979), research becomes an "eternal braid."

Not all writers accept the characteristic of manipulation as a necessary prerequisite for a study to be called an experiment. In his definition Cattell (1966) carefully avoids the restriction of manipulation. He describes "an experiment" as "a recording of observations, quantitative or qualitative, made by *defined* and *recorded* operations and in *defined* conditions, followed by examination of the data by *appropriate* statistical and mathematical rules, for the existence of significant relations" (p. 20, italics added).

Although Cattell avoids the term "manipulation," he does emphasize definition. The issue of definition of terms in experimental research must not be taken lightly. Cattell directs researchers' attention to a critical dimension. The point of emphasizing definition, he says, is not to resurrect the excesses of the logical positivists but to foster clearer conceptualizations of input and output variables and intervening processes. As Moe (1979) notes, the most sophisticated experimental design will fail to yield significant results if it is based on a faulty or inadequate definition of constructs. Educational research is particularly vulnerable in this regard since many of the terms that enter the literature are speculative and ill defined. Given these limits it is the responsibility of the researcher to define precisely the manner in which theoretical constructs are to be assessed and treatments established.

A researcher may use experimental designs to provide a direct test of the causal impact of an independent variable on a dependent variable. Causality is demonstrated through a set of logical premises about the nature of differences and similarities in data derived from different experimental conditions. These premises derive directly from postulates outlined by John Stuart Mill (1848) more than a century ago and, as Tatsuoka (1969) comments, are surprisingly current. In an earlier edition of this encyclopedia, Tiedeman (1960) provided a useful analysis of the elements of Mill's scheme. If the assumptions of the experimental model are met, the researcher is able to state with some confidence that, all other things being equal, independent variable X causes a change in dependent variable Y.

Preexperimental Designs. There are research designs that are neither experimental nor quasi-experimental but are useful for study primarily because of their weaknesses. Some authors refer to these designs as preexperimental. Such designs might be of some benefit in exploratory or pilot studies but in general they offer the researcher very limited inferential power and should be avoided.

The first of these preexperimental designs is called a one-shot posttest-only design. In this design a researcher may apply some treatment (X) to a group of subjects and then measure their performance according to some outcome (O). The design may be diagrammed as follows:

One-shot Posttest-only Design

$$X \quad O$$

This kind of research might fall under the rubric of case studies in which a teacher or researcher reports success with a given instructional technique in a specific class.

For example, suppose an art teacher wants to assess the effect on spatial ability of practicing with a puzzle (Chinese tangram). The teacher gives the puzzles to a class of sixth-grade students to play with for several weeks. At the end of the year, upon testing the children with a standard test of spatial ability, the teacher that they score somewhat higher than do average sixth-grade students. May the teacher conclude that the use of tangrams caused an improvement in spatial ability? Well, not really.

The study suffers seriously from a variety of logical problems. Campbell (1957), Campbell and Stanley (1963), and Cook and Campbell (1979) refer to the class of logical errors that surround research designs as threats to internal or external validity.

Internal factors reflect the degree to which alternative explanations of results are plausible. Hence in the simplified one-shot posttest design one might suggest any number of plausible alternative explanations for the higher spatial ability of the sixth-graders. What the study fails to control is the element of history, or other events outside the province of the researcher, that may have led to the improved performance—as well as the factor of maturation in the sixth-graders. Nor does the study eliminate the possibility that the group performance is the result of a few exceptionally talented students in the sample. Inference from one-shot designs is weakened because it cannot legitimately counter such objections.

External validity refers to the degree to which the results of a given study may be generalized to a broader target population. For the most part, threats to generalizability result from sampling and ecological errors and will be addressed later.

To offset some of the alternative explanations and threats to internal validity, a pretest might be included. For example, the art teacher might give the students the spatial ability test at the beginning of the school year *(Oa)*, introduce the tangram treatment *(X)*, and measure outcome performance at the end of the year *(Ob)*. This design may be diagrammed as follows:

One-shot Pretest-Posttest Design

$$Oa \quad X \quad Ob$$

If the teacher were to demonstrate that the students scored on the pretest as average entering sixth-graders there might be some counterargument to the objection that they were atypical. However, the study still fails to counter the remaining objections. Indeed the introduction of the pretest may introduce a new threat—it may influence the students' posttest behavior. Also, as the time between the pretest and posttest increases there is the increased risk that the sample will be altered by the loss of some participants. Hence, although the one-shot pretest-posttest design offers some advantage over the first design, it is still unsatisfactory.

There is one other preexperimental design that is encountered in educational research. This design compares the outcome performance *(O)* of an intact group of students who happened to experience some treatment *(X)* with another group who did not.

Posttest-only Intact-group Design

$$\frac{X \quad O}{O}$$

As an example, suppose one wanted to assess whether a specific television program altered student attitudes. After the appearance of, say, a program on the Nazi treatment of Jews during World War II, a researcher distributes an attitude questionnaire intended to measure anti-Semitism. The researcher then compares the anti-Semitic attitudes of students who watched the program with the attitudes of those who did not. May the researcher attribute any observed differences in attitudes between the two groups to the telecast? Again, the answer is no. There is a very real risk that there were substantial differences in the preexposure attitudes of those who watched the program versus those who chose not to watch.

Experimental Designs. When a research design is considered experimental there is a clear implication that the researcher has established treatment groups through a process of random assignment *(R :)* of subjects to alternative treatments. In the simplest version of this design the researcher randomly assigns subjects to two groups. One group is considered the experimental group and receives the experimental treatment *(X)*. The second group serves as a control comparison group and receives no treatment. Both groups are assessed on the outcome variable using the same measure *(O)*.

Two-group Posttest-only Design

$$R: \quad X \quad O$$
$$R: \qquad \quad O$$

For example, consider a researcher who wants to assess the impact of training in question-asking techniques on teachers' classroom question-asking behavior. To accomplish this end, the researcher randomly assigns teachers to two groups. One group is trained in question-asking techniques; the other either is given no training or (preferably) training in some instructional technique that is not relevant to question-asking. The researcher then observes the teachers in their classrooms and compares the proportion of higher-order questions to lower-order questions. At this point, the researcher may reasonably conclude that any differences in teacher performance result from the experimental intervention. However, interpretation is not totally free of contamination because the presence of the observer may alter the teachers' behavior in ways favorable to the researcher's hypotheses. Ignoring the problem of experimenter obtrusiveness (see Webb et al., 1966), this

simple design is a direct application of Mill's (1848) method of differences. That proposition states that if all elements but one are the same in two settings, any differences may be attributed to the single, different element. Because the two groups are randomly assigned, it is reasonable to presume that they were equivalent prior to training. Training then becomes the element that differentiates the experimental from the control group. The researcher may conclude that, all other things being equal, training in the experimental technique produced the observed differences in performance.

In some cases a researcher wants assurance that the experimental and control groups were truly equivalent prior to experimental intervention. This is typically less of a problem in true experimental designs if the random samples are large enough (Campbell and Stanley, 1963). However, if samples are small, the researcher who has reason to question the preexperimental equivalence of the groups may opt to include a pretest. In this experimental design the researcher randomly assigns subjects to experimental and control conditions and gives both groups a pretest *(Oa)* and a posttest *(Ob)*.

Two-group Pretest-Posttest Design

$$R: \quad Oa \quad X \quad Ob$$
$$R: \quad Oa \qquad \quad Ob$$

As indicated, the use of a pretest in a true experimental design is unnecessary when samples of adequate size are randomly assigned to groups. However, this design may be used to control statistically the impact of some exogenous variable that is known will affect the outcome variable. Control of that exogenous variable permits more precise determination of the effects of the experimental treatment.

In some instances the researcher may suspect that the presence of a pretest affected the outcome variable or that the pretest interacted with the treatment to produce different results. That issue may be addressed through the use of what is called a Solomon four-group design.

Solomon Four-group Design

$$R: \quad Oa \quad X \quad Ob$$
$$R: \quad Oa \qquad \quad Ob$$
$$R: \qquad \quad X \quad Ob$$
$$R: \qquad \qquad \quad Ob$$

In this design four groups are assigned randomly: two parallel the two-group pretest-posttest design and two the two-group posttest-only design. The design thus allows the researcher to assess the presence or absence of the treatment and the effect of a pretest or no pretest. It also may be seen as a factorial design where one treatment (the experimental condition) is crossed with another treatment (a pretest or no pretest), and thus may be diagramed as follows:

	Training	*No Training*
Pretest	R:	R:
No Pretest	R:	R:

The term "crossed" means that every level of one experimental treatment occurs at every level of a second experimental treatment. When treatments are crossed, the researcher is able to test multiple hypotheses simultaneously. Included in those hypotheses is a new type of question regarding the unique joint contribution of the two treatments, referred to as an interaction. Where it is impossible to cross treatments—that is, a treatment group may only be found under one condition—the new treatment is said to be nested within a higher-order treatment condition.

The designs described earlier are built on two groups; however, the Solomon four-group design indicates that as the complexity of the research questions increases, the complexity of the design necessary to answer the questions increases as well.

Dimensions of Experiments. Cattell (1966) identifies six dimensions that underlie experimentation.

1. *The number of observed or measured variables.* In the simplest of experiments described above this dimension is reduced to the impact of a single independent variable on a single dependent variable. The researcher may choose to introduce a set of alternate independent variables that are crossed in factorial designs or nested in hierarchical designs and choose multiple outcome variables measured at a given time or across several instances.

2. *Manipulation.* Traditionally, the implicit, if not explicit, assumption has been that in what is to be considered an experiment the researcher must have direct control over independent variables through manipulation (see Campbell and Stanley's definition reported earlier). But Cattell notes that experimentation may imply other than direct control. Once again, Cattell prefers to use the term "defined" condition rather than "controlled" condition.

3. *Time sequence.* In cases where multiple outcome measures are assessed, the measurement of those variables may occur either simultaneously with the experimental manipulation or subsequent to it. As the length of time between manipulation and outcome measurement increases, time becomes a contaminating factor.

4. *Situational control.* In the laboratory experiment the researcher has a great deal of situational control. Alternative, contaminating sources of variation are controlled or held constant. The advantage to the researcher is that

the question of concern is more susceptible to analysis when the influence of these contaminants is removed. As the researcher moves outside the laboratory into classrooms or into uncontrolled natural settings, the clarity of the question becomes muddled by uncontrolled and uncontrollable conditions. The researcher who conducts experiments in natural settings gains ecological validity at the cost of internal validity. Conversely, the laboratory researcher gains control over internal validity at the cost of ecological validity.

5. *Choice of variables.* Some choices must be made concerning those variables that will and will not be included for study in a given experiment. A researcher simply cannot assess all possible permutations and combinations of potential independent variables on all possible outcomes. Were such a design possible to construct, the results would be uninterpretable.

6. *Choice of subjects.* Kempthorne (1961) provides an important distinction between the hypothetical reference population and the available population from which the researcher actually selects samples. Ideally, the researcher has access to the reference population from which random samples may be drawn. Once the experiment is completed, the results are generalizable back to the reference. In practice, however, the available population and the reference population are not the same. The researcher usually presumes the two are sufficiently similar to allow generalization not only from the samples back to the available population but also to the reference population. As the accessible population is subjected to constraints on sampling, its comparability to the parent population is jeopardized and hence generalizability is limited. Such factors as geography, administrative problems, legal constraints, and ethics may lead to constraints on the actual, accessible population. Accessibility of a population from which true random samples may be drawn is the most likely reason for a researcher to draw upon the quasi-experimental designs described in the following. First, however, some additional comments should be made on randomization.

Randomization. Orthodox experimental design is built on the premise that assignment of subjects to alternative treatments is independent and random. Logically, this allows the researcher to presume that all exogenous factors that have a known or unknown influence on the outcome variables are equally distributed across all groups. Randomization is thus the fundamental control process that allows the researcher to make a qualified conclusion: "All other things being equal . . . *X* causes *Y.*" As Meier (1975) emphasizes, it is precisely when hidden exogenous variables influence the outcome variable that randomization is most important. Statistically, the assumption of randomization allows the researcher to establish unbiased estimates of treatment and error variances. Where, however, those rare instances are found in which the impact of a randomly controlled exogenous variable is not linear and additive but interacts with the independent variable, randomization may serve to mask some of the casual contributions of a given experimental condition (Cronbach & Snow, 1977).

In practice true randomization may be impractical or impossible. This limitation is no small matter. Whereas internal validity refers to the integrity of conclusions reached within the context of a specific experiment, external validity refers to the generality of the results beyond the confines of the groups on which the study was conducted. The degree to which the sample of subjects used in the experiment is representative of a larger population, the greater the generality, and the greater the external validity. Once again, Kempthorne's (1961) distinction between the hypothetical parent population and the available population is relevant. The more closely related the two, the greater the ability of the researcher to generalize broadly.

Too often, researchers overlook the fact that the same constraints may apply to the materials used in the application of treatments. That is, if a single set of experimental materials is used in a study of teacher effects, there is no assurance that the same results will generalize to similar teachers using other materials. This is often seen where results are clearly observed in one content area but are ambiguous in another.

Quasi-experimental Designs. Campbell and Stanley (1963), and more recently Cook and Campbell (1979), point to the disenchantment and pessimism with which many educational researchers view orthodox experimental methods. The constraints of experimental methodology, it is argued, create a serious risk to ecological validity. There is, of course, value in such criticism. Educational researchers who adhere solely to the use of orthodox designs run the risk of overestimating their generality and underestimating the usefulness of other, less constrained designs.

Ultimately, it is not the orthodoxy of an experimental design that allows a researcher to make causal inferences, but the adequacy of the theoretical statements that underlie the design decisions. As Tufte (1974) warns, "All the logical, theoretical, and empirical difficulties attendant to establishing a causal relationship persist no matter what type of statistical analysis [or research design] is applied" (p. 5). Simply, the most sophisticated and rigorous of orthodox experimental and/or statistical methods are worthless in the absence of solid theory. Conversely, an adequate statement of theoretical propositions often reduces the need for overly complex designs.

Campbell and Stanley do not present quasi-experimental designs as a panacea or even a preferred alternative to experimental designs. As they point out, quasi-experimental designs should be used "where better designs are not feasible" (p. 34). The decision as to whether to rely on orthodox experimental designs or to use quasi-experimental design is usually related to the ability of the researcher to meet the demands of random assignment of subjects to groups. Where true randomization is not reasonable or possible, the educational researcher may find quasi-experimental designs useful.

The most common application of quasi-experimental designs is what Campbell and Stanley refer to as the nonequivalent control group design. This design uses two intact, nonrandomly selected groups; one is given an experimental treatment and the other serves as a control. Both groups are studied in parallel and given a pretest *(Oa)* and a posttest *(Ob)*. Only the experimental group is given the experimental treatment *(X)*.

Nonequivalent Intact-group Design

$$\frac{Oa \quad X \quad Ob}{Oa \qquad Ob}$$

A second quasi-experimental design that may be particularly useful in educational research is the time series design. Researchers use this design to make repeated assessments of the outcome variable over an extended period of time. At some point in the sequence of measures the experimental treatment is introduced. Any significant impact of the treatment may then be observed in a sudden shift in group or individual performance associated with the introduction of the treatment:

Time-series Design

$$Oa \quad Ob \quad Oc \quad Oe \quad X \quad Of \quad Og \quad Oh \quad Oi$$

An additional outcome that may be observed in the time series design is the decay in performance that may result as the time between experimental treatment and assessment increases. Although a version of this design has been used extensively in behavior modification research, it is less widely used in other educational research.

A third quasi-experimental design is a modification of the second preexperimental design and may be particularly useful when ethics demand that all participants be given an experimental intervention but there is a serious risk that pretesting will contaminate interpretation of the outcome measure. Suppose, for example, that a school system decided to institute a drug education program for its students and wanted to avoid the cueing effect the pretest might provide. In this case a random sample of students would be given the pretest and the experimental program but would not be given the posttest. A second randomly selected group would not be given the pretest, but would be given the experimental treatment and the posttest. This design may be diagramed:

Separate-sample Pretest-Posttest Design

$$\begin{array}{llll} R: & Oa & (X) & \\ R: & & X & Ob \end{array}$$

Following the posttest, the researcher compares pretest performance of the control group with the posttest performance of the experimental group. While the design is not ideal, it does offer some advantage over the preexperimental designs. It does not, however, rule out other intervening events that might equally have led to the change in performance.

Campbell and Stanley offer additional quasi-experimental designs that are not discussed here. Their 1963 report of research is considered by most educational researchers to be "must reading" for any serious student of educational research. Further, many of the ideas outlined in that report have been elaborated upon and refined in Cook and Campbell's newer volume (1979). Particularly useful in the latter volume are suggestions for analytic techniques for quasi-experimental designs.

Statistical Analysis. The reader who desires an in-depth consideration of statistics and experimental design is referred to sources such as Box, Hunter, and Hunter (1978), Edwards (1968), Ferguson (1976), Glass and Stanley (1970), Hays (1973), and Winer (1971). These sources provide descriptions of statistical and experimental designs with reference to social research.

A caveat about statistical analyses as they relate to experimental design is in order. Too often naive researchers generate designs that are so complex that analysis of results is difficult for the most experienced of researchers. New researchers should use experimental designs that are not so complex that they extend beyond their ability to interpret the results. The fact that a design is simple does not diminish its importance if it is wellformulated. Path analysis, multivariate analysis of variance, ridge regression, or other techniques may appear intriguing, but they should be attempted only after researchers have had considerable data analytic experience. Most questions may be asked in simple terms and inferences may be drawn from statistical analyses thought to be exploratory (Tukey, 1977).

Ethics of Experimental Research. Previous comments have alluded to ethical restrictions that may have an impact on the researcher's ability to meet the demands of randomization of subjects to treatment groups. There are cases in which the random assignment of subjects to an experimental or control group may be viewed as a breach of professional ethics. Further, the application of certain experimental treatments may be such that the treatments put the subject at risk to physical, psychological, or social stress. The educational researcher is obligated to weigh the ratio of risk to benefit in any experiment. Because previous research in education, medicine, and social sciences has sometimes fostered a somewhat cavalier attitude toward the rights of human subjects and the ethical responsibility of a researcher, considerable pressure has been placed on the research community to ensure that the rights of those who agree to participate in research be protected, in laboratory-based experiments, and in field-based nonexperimental designs as well.

Any subject should have the right to refuse to participate in a research study without being penalized. There should be no element of coercion in recruiting subjects. Participation of college or university students, for example, should not be seen as a mandatory component of a given course. While participation as a research subject may be one way in which a student might meet course requirements, students should be permitted to select an alternative mode of satisfying the requirements without jeopardy.

Prior to agreeing to participate in a research study, the prospective subjects should be informed in clear, precise terms about the purpose of the experiment and what they will be expected to do. This does not mean that the researcher must outline the research hypotheses, but it does mean that subjects have a right to know the general purpose of the study and to what use the data are to be put. If there are known risks, the subjects must be informed of those risks. The subjects should also be allowed to withdraw from participation at any time without jeopardy.

If the research participants are minors, then the researcher must also gain informed consent from their parents or guardians. Both parent and child should have the right to refuse.

Finally, all data gathered in an experiment should be considered confidential. Although this may seem obvious when data are sensitive, the requirement applies to all studies. Subjects should also be told that they may examine summaries of the group data once the study is complete.

Recent federal guidelines have reduced demands for stringent adherence to requirements such as these in studies that employ normal curricular procedures in the schools. Nonetheless, most universities and larger school districts maintain committees that review proposals for research that uses human subjects, and prospective researchers should query those committees for local guidelines.

Conclusions. In the view of Campbell (1957), the optimal experiment is one that is valid both internally and externally. The more precisely the researcher is able to define the conditions for sampling, application of treatments, assessment of outcomes, and analysis of data, the more likely the study is to meet these requirements. That is not to say that a researcher can generate valid experimental designs for every question. Some questions simply do not lend themselves to the constraints of orthodox experimental or quasi-experimental designs.

There is a common misconception that for an experimental design to be seen as competent, it must be complex. In reality, complexity and competency are only partially related. The most sophisticated experimental designs will not yield significant data if they are based on faulty theory. Rigorous designs cannot compensate for inadequate hypotheses or inappropriate definition of conditions. On the other hand, competent theory and appropriate hypotheses often reduce the need for complex designs and the risk of Type II errors.

Finally, beyond the discipline of design construction,

there is, as Brody and Brownstein (1975) comment, a degree of art to the effective design of experiments and the specification of experimental conditions. This "art" develops with experience. However, even experienced researchers understand the benefit of feedback and criticism during the early stages in the formulation of an experiment. Both new and experienced researchers can avoid many errors in logic and application by requesting colleagues who have no vested interest in an experiment to evaluate the adequacy of the statement of hypotheses and formulation of an appropriate design before data are gathered. In the short run such feedback is often discouraging. But in the long run it often saves researchers from committing serious mistakes.

Gary M. Ingersoll

See also Evaluation of Programs; Experimental Validity; Research Integration.

REFERENCES

Box, G. E. P.; Hunter, W. G.; & Hunter, J. S. *Statistics for Experimenters.* New York: Wiley, 1978.

Brody, R. A., & Brownstein, C. N. Experimentation and simulation. In F. I. Greenstein & N. W. Polsby (Eds.), *Handbook of Political Science* (Vol. 7). Reading, Mass.: Addison-Wesley, 1975.

Campbell, D. T. Factors relevant to the validity of experiments in social settings. *Psychological Bulletin,* 1957, *54,* 297–312.

Campbell, D. T., & Stanley, J. C. Experimental and quasi-experimental designs for research on teaching. In N. L. Gage (Ed.), *Handbook of Research on Teaching.* Chicago: Rand McNally, 1963.

Cattell, R. B. The principles of experimental design and analysis in relation to theory building. In R. B. Cattell (Ed.), *Handbook of Multivariate Experimental Psychology.* Chicago: Rand McNally, 1966.

Cook, T. D., & Campbell, D. T. *Quasi-experimentation.* Chicago: Rand McNally, 1979.

Cronbach, L. J., & Snow, R. E. *Aptitudes and Instructional Methods.* New York: Irvington, 1977.

Edwards, A. L. *Experimental Design in Psychological Research.* New York: Holt, Rinehart & Winston, 1968.

Ferguson, G. A. *Statistical Analysis in Psychology and Education* (4th ed.). New York: McGraw-Hill, 1976.

Fisher, R. A. *The Design of Experiments.* Edinburgh: Oliver & Boyd, 1935.

Hays, W. L. *Statistics for the Social Sciences* (2nd ed.). New York: Holt, Rinehart & Winston, 1973.

Hofstadter, D. R. *Gödel, Escher, Bach: An Eternal Golden Braid.* New York: Random House, Vintage Books, 1979.

Kempthorne, O. The design and analysis of experiments with some reference to educational research. In R. O. Collier & S. M. Elam (Eds.), *Research Design and Analysis: Second Annual Phi Delta Kappa Symposium on Educational Research.* Bloomington, Ind.: Phi Delta Kappa, 1961.

Kerlinger, F. N. *Foundations of Behavioral Research.* New York: Holt, Rinehart & Winston, 1973.

Meier, P. Statistics and medical experimentation. *Biometrics,* 1975, *31,* 511–529.

Mill, J. S. *System of Logic.* New York: Harper & Brothers, 1848.

Moe, T. M. On the scientific status of rational models. *American Journal of Political Science,* 1979, *23,* 215–243.

Platt, J. R. Strong inference. *Science,* 1964, *146*(3642), 347–353.

Shaver, J. P., & Norton, R. S. Randomness and replication in ten years of the *American Educational Research Journal. Educational Researcher,* 1980, *9,* 9–15.

Tatsuoka, M. M. Experimental methods. In R. L. Ebel (Ed.), *Encyclopedia of Educational Research* (4th ed.). New York: Macmillan, 1969.

Tiedeman, D. V. Experimental methods. In C. W. Harris (Ed.), *Encyclopedia of Educational Research* (3rd ed.). New York: Macmillan, 1960.

Tufte, E. R. *Data Analysis for Politics and Policy.* Englewood Cliffs, N.J.: Prentice-Hall, 1974.

Tukey, J. W. *Exploratory Data Analysis.* Reading, Mass.: Addison-Wesley, 1977.

Webb, E. B.; Campbell, D. T.; Sechrist, L.; & Schwartz, L. *Unobtrusive Measures: Nonreactive Research in the Social Sciences.* Chicago: Rand McNally, 1966.

Winer, B. J. *Statistical Principles in Experimental Design* (2nd ed.). New York: McGraw-Hill, 1971.

EXPERIMENTAL VALIDITY

Experiments are used by educational researchers both in building theories (often about narrowly circumscribed processes like reading or problem solving) and in evaluating the outcomes of more complex treatments or programs (as when tightly structured teaching in basic skills is compared to an "open" or child-centered approach). The validity of laboratory experiments for the former purpose touches on a somewhat different set of concerns than the validity of field experiments for the latter purpose. An experimenter building a theory worries a great deal about refining and purifying an experimental treatment; consider, for example, a succession of experiments on mediating processes in learning from written text (Anderson, 1970). In field experiments, one worries less about treatments (e.g., "mainstream" versus resource-room placement) that are necessarily complex and multifaceted. Attention is limited in this article to concerns about the validity of field experiments where the purpose is to assess the value of choosing to do A rather than B.

The "internal validity" of an experiment refers to the truth of a claim that an intervention or treatment caused a change in an outcome variable (Campbell & Stanley, 1963). This language suggests a simple sequence of operations in which a characteristic is observed, a treatment is then applied, and the characteristic is observed again to determine whether change has occurred. Experimental design remains this simple in some of the better understood and controlled areas of the physical and natural sciences. But the design of experiments in education is a more elaborate matter that typically involves the simultaneous comparison of treated and untreated units (persons or groups) that have been equated within the limits of chance by randomly designating which units will be treated and which not. Furthermore, to "untreat" someone is merely an imprecise way of indicating that units are treated in different ways (e.g., treatment A and treatment B) and the possibly different outcomes of this difference in treatment are observed. So the prototype of an educational field experiment is an arrangement of random assignment, differential treatment, and observation of outcomes of the following form:

$$R \quad X_A \quad O$$
$$R \quad X_B \quad O$$

Various personal experiences, imperfect variants of this basic design, and convenient comparisons of data usually lack the validity on which one can establish a defensible causal claim that A is responsible for increasing (or decreasing) the level of outcomes. The weaknesses of these "preexperimental" and quasi-experimental designs have been systematically described and discussed for over two decades (Campbell & Stanley, 1963; Cook & Campbell, 1979). The sources of internal invalidity include such familiar notions as history effects (events that intervene between preobservation and postobservation and merely coincide with the treatment), regression artifacts (the drift of formerly extreme observations toward the center of a distribution), selection biases (nonrandom differences between the group treated with A and the group treated with B), and effects of testing, maturation, instrumentation, mortality, and other influences.

The "external validity" of an experimental finding refers to the truth of its application in circumstances other than those in which it was originally established. "To the extent . . . [that] the results of an experiment can be generalized to different subjects (persons), settings, experimenters, and possibly tests, the experiment possesses external validity" (Bracht & Glass, 1968, p. 438). Program A outperforms B for Jones, but can it be expected to do so for Smith as well? Next to knowing whether A was in fact better than B for Jones or whether its superiority was an illusion created by a weakness in design or execution (the question of internal validity), what question could be more important about the finding than whether it can be reliably applied elsewhere?

Methodologists have given many reasons why experimental findings may not generalize. They can be classified broadly into factors of population invalidity, ecological invalidity, and historical invalidity. Population invalidity refers to differences among groups of persons. When an experiment is conducted with Jones's students, who are unlike Smith's, the finding might not generalize to Smith's students. The ecology referred to in "ecological invalidity" is the tiny ecology of the experiment itself: the personality of the experimenter, the nature of the measuring instruments, the attitude that subjects take toward the experiment *qua* experiment. If A outperforms B merely because B is familiar to the subjects and A is novel and amusing,

then the finding would not be observed in an environment that provides a steady diet of A. In another example, experimenter Brown may find repeatedly that his therapy for learning disabilities is effective, but the therapy may fall flat when executed by others who do not share Brown's confidence and belief. Historical invalidity refers to the fact that yesterday's experiment may no longer be true today. Clearly something changed overnight; time itself is marked by things happening, like hands circling the face of the clock. But when what once was true is no longer so, and no explanations are apparent, one says that the finding failed to generalize over time.

These abstract features of experiments—the truth of a finding and the scope of its generalization—can be used to help one think about designing better field experiments. But they merely assist and cannot replace the much more complex task of judging whether a particular finding is valid either internally or externally. Shortly after the publication of Campbell and Stanley's classic paper on internal and external experimental validity in 1963, the story circulated that an enthusiast had written a computer program that received a schematic diagram of experimental designs in terms of *R*'s and *O*'s and *X*'s and printed out whether or not the design was valid. The story is too believable to be funny; and it illustrates an important point ignored by whoever caused such a program to be written. The validity of an experiment can be judged no more satisfactorily by examining superficial characteristics of design than a psychometric test can be judged valid through inspection of its length and format. Like test validity, which researchers have come to appreciate as a characteristic of a particular use in a particular context (Cronbach, 1971), the validity of an experiment—either internal or external—is an assessment based on empirical facts. Not even the much maligned "pretest versus posttest" design is invalid; depending on the circumstances of its application, the pretest versus posttest design can be as reliable a guide to valid findings as the most elaborate and complicated design is in other circumstances. Thus it becomes a matter of some interest to inquire into the empirical facts concerning internal and external experimental validity.

Judgment of Internal Validity. Gavin Andrews, an Australian psychiatrist, compiled the findings of experiments in which various treatments for stuttering were evaluated (Andrews, Guitar, & Howie, 1980). Each experiment was a pretest versus posttest design without untreated control groups. Such a design is a valid assessment of treatment impact if the pretest level of performance (in this instance, judges' ratings of recorded segments of speech) accurately estimates the level of performance one would have observed on the posttest if the subjects had not been treated. Andrews judged that this condition was likely to have held in these studies. Stuttering among adults like these subjects is a stable pattern, not given to unaccountable shifts in severity. Adults who have stuttered since childhood will continue to stutter not only at nearly the same rate but in the same style unless some drastic intervention is made. Such was Andrews's judgment; and he is very likely right, because the pattern of findings of the forty-two experiments was eminently sensible. For example, certain clusters of treatments (the prolonged speech and the rhythm methods) were consistently superior to others. Moreover as time elapsed after treatment was terminated, subjects slowly lost most of the benefits of the treatment. Consider how various sources of internal invalidity could be judged immaterial in this case. Historical explanations of pretest-posttest gains (events in the home such as marriage, divorce, or the death of a relative) were implausible both because the experimenters would have recognized them and because stuttering is quite resistant to such external events. Posttest gains could not have been due solely to exposure to a pretest since both tests involved recorded speech segments that couldn't possibly have taught a subject how to speak articulately. Regression effects might have operated if subjects had sought treatment at a particularly severe point in their personal history of stuttering; they then might improve even without treatment. (Tautologically, one is slightly less sick the day before and the day after the sickest day in one's life.) But regression probably was not a serious threat because the daily fluctuations in severity of stuttering are known to be quite small, and the pretest to posttest improvement in the experiments was quite large. Perhaps this is sufficient to make the point that Andrews's and his colleagues' judgment of the internal validity of the experiments they studied was well founded and based on thorough experience with the phenomenon studied.

A pretest versus posttest design or any other design is not internally valid or invalid as such. Its validity depends on the circumstances of its use. Nonetheless some experimental designs can be preferred to others on the grounds that they leave fewer questions open to be resolved by judgments that may be fallible. Of course, it would have been preferable to evaluate stuttering therapies with wait-list control group designs; and the experimenters who are now designing the next evaluation of biofeedback treatment of stuttering would do well to give serious thought to using such a design. But one's attitude toward the experiment he is about to perform and toward a completed experiment that must be interpreted can be different without being irrationally inconsistent. Poorly done experiments may be internally valid in spite of their weaknesses. Their findings must not be fobbed off as invalid; rather, they must be interpreted and judged. Even the finest experimental design will leave open a broad field for exercise of judgment in its interpretation.

There are no experimental designs that guarantee the validity of causal claims resulting from their use. Even the "true experimental designs" in the taxonomy of Campbell and Stanley (1963) are no guarantee that findings will be internally valid. The interpretation of any experiment is ultimately a judgment informed by a variety of facts. Even in perfectly randomized designs, treatments may not be applied as intended or may not be applied at all.

Drug researchers learned long ago that it was necessary to check on whether the drug "taken" was actually swallowed. Moreover treatments A and B can become contaminated when pupils studying under one treatment collaborate on homework with students studying under the other. When experiments involve the assignment of intact groups of subjects to treatments, proper analysis and interpretation of levels of statistical confidence entails complex judgments about processes for which often few hard facts are available. Even the vaunted process of random assignment itself does not transcend the exercise of human judgment. Statisticians will admit that if random assignment to groups A and B results in an initial (pretest) difference that is uncommonly great—suppose, for example, that in a large third-grade reading experiment, group A contained 80 percent girls and group B only 30 percent—then it would be wise to put all subjects back in the proverbial urn and randomly assign again. When one is staring a Type I error in the face, one ought to do the sensible thing.

Conversely where experimental design and experimental validity are concerned, there is no *sine qua non*. "Bad" designs may yield valid findings. Yet it is eminently sensible to say that some designs are better than others.

Which facts help in judging the internal validity of experiments? In the case of the stuttering therapies, they were the specific facts about stuttering: its onset, its day-to-day consistency, its course over a lifetime. Will such specific facts be available generally for use in judging the internal validity of experiments? Probably not, particularly in educational research that encompasses such an enormously variegated and complex range of persons, activities, and actions. During the 1970s the U.S. federal government invested much time and research attention in attempts to determine the typical patterns of growth in basic skills achievement of elementary school pupils. Such knowledge if verified could be used to support the validity of simple pretest versus posttest designs for evaluating the benefits of government-sponsored compensatory education programs. The success of this effort to support the internal validity of a crude experimental design with a large collection of empirical facts remains to be seen.

Judgment of External Validity of Experiments. Cronbach (1980, p. 101) observed that "interpretation projects beyond the research operations and external validity are at issue." Although his subject was test validity, Cronbach's observation applies to experimental validity as well. Indeed, questions of validity of empirical claims are all one at the most fundamental level, and "in a sense all is construct validation" (Cronbach, 1980, p. 99).

Almost by definition, the judgment of the external validity of an experimental finding will be more difficult and less certain than the judgment of internal validity, for the question of external validity concerns the truth of a claim under conditions not observed in the experiment. How would the comparison of treatments A and B come out, if the experiment were conducted elsewhere under different conditions, by different researchers, or at another time? Not surprisingly, one seldom knows the answers to such questions with the same confidence that one knows whether A outperformed B in *this* experiment. It is unlikely that one possesses any reliable knowledge about the influences that mediate the comparative performance of treatments A and B when one has had to perform an experiment in the first place to determine whether A or B was superior.

This much is known fully. The outcomes of educational experiments are enormously variable across the conditions of the world in which experiments are performed and in which one would like to use their findings. A huge experimental field evaluation of a dozen or so models of primary school compensatory education revealed that the average differences among models in basic skills achievement were insignificantly small compared to the differences among different experimental sites evaluating the same model. On measures of reading achievement, the variance among the experimental effects, $(\overline{X}_T - \overline{X}_C) / s_x$, for thirteen different models was one-tenth as large as the average variance of experimental effects across experimental sites within models (.012 versus .144). (See table 5 in House et al., 1978, p. 149.)

The confusing complexity of educational programs contributes, no doubt, to the highly variable character of experimental findings. One imagines that simpler areas of research find more consistent results. This may not be so. Gilbert, McPeek, and Mosteller (1977) tallied the findings of 100 experiments in which an innovative surgical technique was compared to a traditional surgical technique for the same problem on such outcomes as survival, recovery time, complications during surgery, and the like. Sometimes the innovative technique was superior to the traditional technique; sometimes the experiments showed the reverse; and on the average, half the experiments favored innovative techniques and half favored traditional techniques. No pattern in the findings could be discerned.

The question of the generalization of an experimental finding comparing A and B is the question of whether the A versus B difference changes across other conditions: ritalin (A) is superior to coffee (B) for calming hyperactive 8-year-olds, but is it likewise superior with hyperactive 15-year-olds? The question is readily recognized as a question of interaction (in the factorial ANOVA sense) of an experimental factor (A v. B) with other factors (e.g., age). Experimenters who explicitly examine the interaction of A versus B with other factors in their experimental designs contribute to the appreciation of just how interactive experimental comparisons are; and by implication their findings suggest what problems might be encountered in generalizing main effect (i.e., marginal A v. B comparisons) findings to conditions not represented in their experiments. In the behavioral and social sciences and their neighboring areas of application, we have come to expect that interactions are prevalent and strong. Cronbach (1975) selected seventeen factorial experiments from four consecutive volumes (approximately 1971–1974) of the *Journal of Personality and Social Psychology*. He calculated the variability in means due to main effects (i.e., A v. B differences) and compared it to the variability in means due to interactions (i.e., A v. B for condition 1 as compared to A v. B for condition 2). The resulting tally revealed that the variability due to interactions was 60 percent as large as the variability due to main effects.

Highly interactive systems would be tolerable to the scientific temperament if they were interactive in ways that could be understood and anticipated. That is, if one possessed a richly appointed collection of constructs with a supporting collection of facts, then experimental findings could be generalized and extrapolated with confidence. To date, educational research is in no such agreeable position. The variability of experimental findings is by and large unpredictable. Two examples will clarify this claim.

Glass and Smith (1979) compiled studies that encompassed over 700 comparisons of pupil achievement in larger versus smaller school classes. In this body of data, the odds that a smaller class would outperform a larger class were only 55 to 45. (This was quite close to the finding by Gilbert, McPeek, & Mosteller (1977) of 50–50 odds "favoring" innovative surgical techniques). On the average, the smaller class had about twenty-three pupils and the larger class had about forty-two pupils. If comparisons were chosen wherein classes of fifteen were compared with classes of thirty, the odds that an experiment would favor the smaller class were hardly better than 60 to 40. But the ensuing analyses speak more directly to the point to be made here. Regardless of which of many characteristics was used to divide the experiments into special types, the odds that an experiment would show smaller classes superior to larger classes remained virtually the same: 60 to 40. For example, when experiments on class size in elementary school were compared with experiments in secondary school, the odds of finding smaller classes superior were roughly 60 to 40 in each group. The same pattern occurred when the experiments were distinguished by school subject taught, months of instruction, intelligence of pupils, experience of teachers, method of measuring achievement, and many other factors. An experiment comparing achievement in classes of fifteen and thirty pupils has only about six chances in ten of favoring the smaller class, and it is virtually impossible to improve on these odds knowing everything about the study that can be read in or inferred from a knowledge of the conditions under which it is conducted.

Smith, Glass, and Miller (1980) compiled the findings of nearly 500 experiments on the efficacy of psychotherapy. These 500 experiments encompassed more than 1,700 experimental findings, each expressed in the form of a mean comparison of psychotherapy and control groups divided by within-group standard deviation: $\Delta = (\overline{X}_p - \overline{X}_c) / s_x$. Although these 1,700 values of Δ averaged 0.85, indicating a fairly large effect for psychotherapy, the standard deviation of the Δ's was 1.25: the experimental findings were 150 percent more variable than they were large!

Although psychotherapy was thus demonstrated to be effective, its effectiveness varies greatly depending on other conditions. The question of what these conditions are and how well they predict the value of Δ that one could expect to observe in an experiment is the question of external validity. For each experiment, Smith, Glass, and Miller (1980) observed and recorded a large number of descriptive characteristics: when the experiment was done, by whom, with clients of what particular type, with therapists of what particular type, how outcomes were measured, when, and the like. In all, more than thirty characteristics of the experiments were coded. The correlations of these characteristics with Δ establish the empirical facts about generalizability of the experimental findings. Suppose, for example, that Δ was found to correlate .80 with years experience of the therapist (experienced therapists showing larger main effects than inexperienced ones) and .60 with the neurotic versus psychotic client distinction, and imagine further that the experience of therapist and the neurotic versus psychotic client distinction was uncorrelated in the 1,700 findings. Then the multiple correlation of these two descriptors and Δ would be +1 and a simple system of generalization would have been discovered; the outcome of a psychotherapy experiment could be perfectly predicted from a knowledge of the therapists' experience and the diagnosis of the clients. The possibility of highly externally valid experimental findings would have become a reality. The facts of the analysis by Smith, Glass, and Miller (1980) contrast sharply with this aspiration. None of the thirty or so characteristics—including most of the characteristics typically mentioned as the important factors of external validity by Campbell and Stanley (1963), Bracht and Glass (1968), Cook and Campbell (1979)—had any important correlation with the experimental findings. Date of the experiment and Δ correlated .07, client IQ and Δ correlated .08; and the correlation of Δ with other experimental characteristics was likewise tiny: .00 with client age, −.05 with length of therapy, .00 with therapist experience, −.01 with degree of "blinding" of the subjects and the experimenter. The highest correlate of Δ was "reactivity of measurement," $r = +.18$, accounting for 3 percent of the variance of Δ (see Smith, Glass, & Miller, 1980, pp. 206–207). When characteristics of the experiments were combined in multiple regression equations in attempts to predict Δ, the best results did no better than an accounting of 20 percent of the variance of Δ (Smith, Glass, & Miller, 1980, pp. 101–105).

Thus the results of the experiments were extremely variable, and their variability could not be effectively reduced by all the distinctions one typically draws among experiments (even when one is well informed about experimental external validity). In short, a single experiment on the efficacy of psychotherapy cannot be generalized. Indeed, the information it conveys beyond the narrow context in which it was conducted is extremely limited. This conclusion applies as well to nearly every other set of experiments on educational concerns that has been stud-

ied in the same way as the psychotherapy literature (Glass, McGaw, & Smith, 1981). Cronbach put it thus: "A laboratory generalization, once achieved, may not be a good first approximation to real-world relationships" (1975, p. 121). And then, adding pain to disappointment, he observed succinctly: "Generalizations decay" (1975, p. 122).

Educational researchers are incapable, by and large, of predicting the consequences of the applications of experimental findings. The knowledge that A excelled B in circumstance 1 gives little reason to expect that A will similarly excel B in circumstance 2. Educational researchers have little—indeed, scarcely any—systematic knowledge about how changes in any of several conditions relate to changes in the outcomes of the experimental treatments they evaluate. And there is reason to believe that the way in which they conceive of experimental findings being mediated (namely, by experimental bias, by aptitude treatment interaction [ATI], by decay of effects over time) is insufficient for coping with the complexity of the systems they attempt to study. Perhaps the "conditions of success" are unlikely combinations of known factors of experimental validity that have yet to be evaluated; perhaps success is conditioned by the private motives of the human beings who are the actors in these little experimental dramas. What works best? It all depends, and it depends on a number of conditions that we scarcely understand and cannot now describe.

Summary. The internal validity of an experimental finding cannot be judged solely in terms of the properties of the experimental design (whether randomization was used, whether control groups were measured simultaneously). Internal validity of a causal claim is a complex judgment that ultimately rests on a large number of empirical facts that necessarily extend beyond the context of the single experiment.

The external validity of an experimental finding rests similarly on judgment and a network of empirical facts. But in contrast to internal validity, the facts are more numerous and are less well established. Educational researchers have few solid facts to guide them in generalizing the findings of experiments.

Gene V Glass

See also Evaluation of Programs; Experimental Methods; Research Integration.

REFERENCES

Anderson, R. C. Control of student-mediating processes during verbal learning and instruction. *Review of Educational Research*, 1970, *40*, 349–369.

Andrews, G.; Guitar, B.; & Howie, P. Meta-analysis of the effects of stuttering treatment. *Journal of Speech and Hearing Disorders*, 1980, *45*, 287–307.

Bracht, G. H., & Glass, G. V. The external validity of experiments. *American Educational Research Journal*, 1968, *5*, 437–474.

Campbell, D. T., & Stanley, J. C. Experimental and quasi-experimental designs for research on teaching. In N. L. Gage (Ed.),

Handbook of Research on Teaching. Chicago: Rand McNally, 1963.

Cook, T. D., & Campbell, D. T. *Quasi-experimentation: Design and Analysis Issues for Field Studies.* Chicago: Rand McNally, 1979.

Cronbach, L. J. Test validation. In R. L. Thorndike (Ed.), *Educational Measurement.* Washington, D.C.: American Council on Education, 1971.

Cronbach, L. J. Beyond the two disciplines of scientific psychology. *American Psychologist,* 1975, *30,* 116–127.

Cronbach, L. J. Validity on parole: How can we go straight? In *New Directions for Testing and Measurement* (Vol. 5). Princeton, N.J.: Educational Testing Service, 1980, 99–108.

Gilbert, J. P.; McPeek, B.; & Mosteller, F. Statistics and ethics in surgery and anesthetics. *Science,* 1977, *198,* 684–689.

Glass, G. V., & Smith, M. L. Meta-analysis of research on the relationship of class size and achievement. *Educational Evaluation and Policy Analysis,* 1979, *1,* 2–16.

Glass, G. V.; McGaw, B.; & Smith, M. L. *Meta-analysis of Social Research.* Beverly Hills, Calif.: Sage, 1981.

House, E. R.; Glass, G. V.; McLean, L. D.; & Walker, D. F. No simple answer: Critique of the Follow Through evaluation. *Harvard Educational Review,* 1978, *48,* 128–160.

Smith, M. L.; Glass, G. V.; & Miller, T. I. *The Benefits of Psychotherapy.* Baltimore: Johns Hopkins University Press, 1980.

EXTRACURRICULAR ACTIVITIES

See Elementary Education; Recreation; Secondary Education.

F

FACTOR ANALYSIS

"Factor analysis" is a generic term associated with a number of multivariate statistical methods that model sets of manifest or observed variables in terms of linear functions of other sets of latent or unobserved variables. In many respects factor analysis methods are logical extensions of the idea of multiple regression. Whereas in multiple regression dependent variables are manifest (observed) variables linearly dependent upon a set of manifest independent variables, in factor analysis models dependent variables are manifest or observed variables linearly dependent on a set of latent, unobserved independent variables.

Factor analysis models are of two kinds: determinate models, in which the latent variables are determined uniquely by linear functions of the manifest or observed variables; and indeterminate models, in which the latent variables are not uniquely determined by linear functions of the manifest or observed variables. Determinate models are usually referred to as component analysis models. Indeterminate models include both the common factor analysis model, which seeks to account for the covariation between the manifest or observed variables in terms of latent common factor variables, and the classical measurement model, which regards each manifest or observed variable as the sum of two latent variables—a true score variable and an error variable.

Factor analysis methodologies also vary depending upon whether their aim is exploratory or confirmatory. Exploratory methods seek to discover the important latent variables of a new domain of variables. Confirmatory methods, on the other hand, seek to confirm hypotheses about the structural composition of manifest variables.

Exploratory Factor Analysis

History of Applications. Spearman (1904) is credited with having first formulated the idea of exploratory common factor analysis in 1904 when he sought to show that the correlations among a set of tests of scholastic achievement and of cognition could be accounted for by a single common factor, which he called g or "general intelligence." He hypothesized that each test of intellectual functioning would contain a component, g, common to all such tests and a specific component unique to each. By 1919 attempts to extend Spearman's g-factor model of the intellect to other tests had produced evidence for common factors other than simply a single factor common to all tests, leading researchers to develop methods for the discovery of other common factors. By the 1930s British psychologists had arrived at a hierarchical concept for the structure of the intellect. According to this concept, the intellect consists of numerous abilities, whose relative importance depends on their place in a hierarchy of abilities. At the peak of this hierarchy is general intelligence, which, it was believed, is involved in most intellectual activities. Just below this peak, according to this concept, are general abilities such as verbal/academic ability and spatial/mechanical ability, each of which was said to influence broad domains of intellectual functioning. Under these are even less general abilities concerned with special classes of tests. Finally, at the bottom of the hierarchy are specific abilities found only by individual tests (Vernon, 1961).

In the latter half of the 1930s a U.S. school of factor analysts developed under the influence of L. L. Thurstone and his students at the University of Chicago. Thurstone rejected the British view that the intellect is structured hierarchically with general intelligence at the top. He believed that the intellect consists of a number of primary mental abilities that combine to produce the varied forms of cognitive functioning in a manner analogous to the way the eye combines responses to mixtures of primary colors to produce various hues. To discover these primary mental abilities Thurstone was led to postulate the idea of a simple structure—that not every primary ability will be found in any given test of cognitive functioning. He implemented the simple structure concept mathematically by the procedure of factor rotation, which involved transforming the initial solution for the latent common factors (usually a principal factor solution or an approximation thereof) into a rotated solution that tended to align each factor with a distinct cluster of highly similar variables. Factors found by the rotation process were usually correlated among themselves unless the researcher forced the rotated factors to be uncorrelated. Thus, when the correlations among Thurstone's primary ability factors were themselves factor analyzed to obtain second-order factors, the resulting second-order factors were often recognized as similar to those reported by British psychologists as major group factors. In fact, higher-order factoring often produced a general factor common to all lower-order factors, and Spearman in particular identified this general factor with his *g* factor. The process of rotation was usually carried out manually by a graphical procedure, which in the 1930s and 1940s often took many weeks, and even months, to complete.

During World War II exploratory factor analysis along the lines developed by Thurstone was used extensively by the military in the development of tests for the selection of personnel for training. And after the war a number of psychologists continued these factor analytic studies of the intellect. Guilford (1967), for example, extended Thurstone's primary mental abilities concept to include some 120 potential factors, which he organized into a three-way scheme that classified a factor according to the mental operation involved, the content operated on, and the product produced by the operation. However, Guilford's resulting structure of the intellect model has been criticized because it requires the factors to be mutually uncorrelated variables and thus fails to recognize adequately the considerable correlational overlap that exists between all of his manifest tests, and which is better dealt with by a hierarchical model.

More recently Cattell (1963, 1971) and Horn (1968) described a factor analytic theory of intelligence involving two general factors: fluid intelligence and crystallized intelligence. These factors appear to function as second-order factors. Fluid intelligence is the capacity to perceive relationships and to discover correlates without the benefit of prior experience and education and is thus essentially equivalent to Spearman's conception of general intelligence. Crystallized intelligence is the general ability to solve problems in diverse content areas by relying on a fundamental core of broadly applicable learned abilities such as verbal comprehension, formal reasoning, and general knowledge.

Recent trends in the study of intelligence have shown an interest in reconciling the approach and theories of cognitive psychologists with factor analytic theories of intellectual performance. Until recently, cognitive psychologists were interested mainly in describing the processes used by the individual in problem solving, whereas differential psychologists, using factor analysis, have been con-

cerned primarily with discovering ways in which individuals vary in their problem-solving behavior. Cognitive psychologists have also approached their subject behavioristically and experimentally, whereas factor analytically oriented differential psychologists have focused on the trait as the conceptual paradigm of their work and have emphasized correlational methods. This difference in focus, which is basically concerned with whether the primary locus of causation of behavior is external or internal, traditionally has kept these two groups in separate camps. But now, Carroll (1976) has used an information-processing model to categorize the content of behavior involved in factor analytically derived tests of problem-solving behavior. And Sternberg (1977) has conducted experiments using a "componential analysis" method to evaluate various information-processing models of the processes used in solving verbal analogy problems, which have often been closely identified with general intelligence. Future research will likely involve confirmatory factor analyses designed to test information-processing models of individual differences in intellectual functioning.

The other major area in which factor analysis has been applied is personality. Guilford (1959) began work in the 1930s on a hierarchically organized model of personality based on factor analyses of personality traits. Eysenck (1947, 1967) used factor analysis to confirm his views that personality differences mainly involve the two dimensions of extraversion-introversion and neuroticism-stability, which he derived from Pavlov's theory of individual differences in cortical excitation and inhibition and a theory of individual differences in the responsivity of the autonomic nervous system but he also used experimentation to support his theory. Cattell, however, is perhaps the best-known factor analytically oriented personality theorist (Cattell, 1946, 1950, 1957, 1966). Basically a trait theorist, he believes that the manifest or surface traits of personality such as friendliness, assertiveness, and cooperativeness are determined by more fundamental source traits. These source traits may be discovered by factor analyzing the correlations among the ratings of traits within persons. The factors that account for the co-occurrences of traits are the source traits in question.

However, factor analytic studies of personality using trait ratings have been given a new interpretation as a result of another application of factor analysis. Osgood and Suci (1958) used factor analysis to chart the major dimensions of meaning among words. In this application similarity in meaning between two word scales is measured by the degree to which the word-scale ratings are correlated across objects rated. When the correlations among numerous word scales are factor analyzed, the resulting dimensions are interpreted as dimensions of meaning. Osgood and Suci (1958) describe three major dimensions of meaning, evaluation, potency, and activity, but report additional dimensions of lesser importance as well. After their work became known, others (Mulaik, 1964; Norman, 1963; Passini and Norman, 1966) noted the equivalence of the methodology used by Cattell to find source traits and the methodology used by Osgood to find dimensions of meaning. They also noted the similarity of the Osgood dimensions of meaning to various personality factors of Cattell and others. Thus the new interpretation of factors of personality trait ratings is that they are response dimensions within raters that mediate the linkage of trait words to the stimulus features of people and not causes within the persons rated of their manifest behavioral characteristics, which was Cattell's earlier interpretation (Cattell, 1950, p. 27). Similar interpretations are also applicable to factors obtained from analyses of other sign or verbally mediated responses of subjects to items found in attitude, interest, self-description, and organizational-climate inventories.

By the 1970s exploratory common factor analysis had reached methodological maturity and had been applied not only to studies of the structure of the intellect and of personality but also to studies of attitudes, interests, learning, organizations, and meaning. Factor analysis was even used in such nonpsychological applications as chemistry, geology, and biological taxonomy.

The Algebra of Exploratory Factor Analysis. The fundamental model equation of common factor analysis is given by

$$Z_i = f_{i1}x_1 + \cdots + f_{ir}x_r + u_i V_i, \; i = 1, \ldots, n, \quad (1)$$

where Z_i = the ith observed variable in a set of n observed variables,

f_{ij} = the common factor pattern loading or coefficient (analogous to a regression coefficient) indicating the weight to be attached to the jth common factor X_j in determining Z_i,

u_i = the unique factor pattern coefficient,

and V_i = the unique factor variable unique to variable Z_i.

In words, the ith observed variable Z_i is a weighted linear combination of r common factor variables and a unique factor variable. (For convenience, and without any loss of generality, in this discussion we assume that, unless otherwise stated, all variables have means of zero and variances of unity, which means that all variables are in standard-score form.)

In the model equation (1) for common factor analysis the common factor variables x_j, $j = 1, \ldots, r$, and the unique factor variable V_i are latent variables, that is, they are not directly observed but are inferred. The common factor model also places restrictions on the relations between these latent variables: the correlation $\rho(X_j, V_i)$ between any common factor variable X_j and any unique factor variable V_i must equal zero. Furthermore, the correlation $\rho(V_g, V_h)$ between any two unique factors V_g and V_h also must equal zero.

Because for each observed variable Z_i there exists a linear equation relating Z_i to the r common factors X_1, . . ., X_r and a corresponding unique factor V_i, we have n simultaneous linear equations in $n + r$ unknowns, where

the unknowns are the n unique factors and the r common factors. Because the number of unknowns (the latent factors) is greater than the number of equations and observed variables with which to determine them, the solution for the latent factors cannot be unique. Hence the latent factor variables are indeterminate. This indeterminateness for the latent variables of the common factor model is fundamental, and in exploratory factor analysis implies that more than one interpretation for the factors may be consistent with the model.

Model equation (1) also implies several important results. For example, the variance σ_i^2 of the ith observed variable may be derived from (1) as

$$\sigma_i^2 = \sum_{j=1}^{r} \sum_{k=1}^{r} f_{ij} f_{ik} \rho_{jk} + u_i^2, \quad (2)$$

where f_{ij} and f_{ik} are common factor pattern coefficients for variable i on factors j and k, respectively; ρ_{jk} is the correlation between factors j and k; and u_i^2 is the variance in Z_i to be attributed to the ith unique factor variable. Factor analysts usually denote the portion of variable i's variance attributable to the common factors as the communality of the variable and the portion due to its unique factor as the unique variance of variable i. Equation (2) thus may be rewritten as

$$\sigma_i^2 = h_i^2 + u_i^2, \quad (3)$$

where h_i^2 is the communality and u_i^2 the unique variance of variable i, respectively.

Of greater significance is the correlation between two variables Z_i and Z_h implied by model equation (1):

$$\rho_{ih} = \sum_{j=1}^{r} \sum_{k=1}^{r} f_{ij} f_{hk} \rho_{jk}. \quad (4)$$

Equation (4) implies that the correlation between two observed variables is only a function of its common factors, since any terms due to the unique factors of these observed variables vanish because of the assumptions about the correlations among unique and common factors in the common factor model.

An Example of Exploratory Factor Analysis. The performance of a factor analysis with data may be regarded as a process with five steps.

Step 1. Selecting variables. Although some researchers choose variables by using a haphazard selection of measures of some domain, this is not a recommended practice because "doublet factors" (underdetermined factors associated with but two variables) may result. Further, because of factor indeterminancy, the interpretations to be given any resulting factors will be largely guesswork. Thurstone (1947) regarded the variable-selection process as almost as time consuming as the later factor analysis, which in the 1940s could last a month. Thus the researcher should define the domain in terms of some hypothetical factors and select measures the researcher believes are determined by these factors for analysis. Then for each expected factor there should be in the set of variables to be analyzed

TABLE 1. *Correlations[1] among thirty-two group tests*

```
—1 Block counting
42 —2 Paper puzzles
50 37 —3 Cards
37 32 76 —4 Figures
21 08 34 33 —5 Hands
43 42 39 36 18 —6 Copying
39 24 35 37 41 28 —7 Bolts
47 42 47 47 16 47 29 —8 Gottschaldt figures
23 19 14 18 12 20 19 27 —9 Street pictures
24 19 18 23 18 25 23 28 36 —10 Mutilated words
38 31 37 40 22 45 25 49 17 25 —11 Designs
32 22 25 21 05 27 27 23 17 16 18 —12 Memory for pictures
14 14 22 17 03 16 18 23 02 08 18 25 —13 Visual memory
43 42 37 35 10 38 37 41 15 18 26 29 19 —14 Mechanical movements
54 58 54 45 27 50 38 53 21 20 35 28 15 56 —15 Surface development
41 33 62 60 25 39 32 46 20 25 44 20 07 29 49 —16 Reversals and rotations
49 40 58 57 38 39 43 48 17 25 40 27 17 45 58 55 —17 Lozenges
44 39 52 40 27 31 27 35 19 15 25 16 12 34 57 41 55 —18 Cubes
39 31 36 36 17 40 30 34 29 28 39 31 10 19 37 39 37 31 —19 Identical forms
42 28 36 30 11 33 25 31 26 25 29 29 15 25 41 36 34 32 39 —20 Mutilated pictures
28 25 29 32 13 29 13 25 16 10 27 18 09 14 27 28 26 25 30 12 —21 Jigsaw pieces
35 21 33 26 13 37 31 29 14 24 20 51 17 30 29 26 27 15 22 22 10 —22 Memory for geometric design
28 14 19 21 08 16 06 23 23 24 21 19 19 08 19 25 25 25 34 30 19 16 —23 Picture squares
47 37 37 32 12 44 33 40 15 36 35 23 15 39 43 32 42 41 38 37 21 25 27 —24 Letter series
47 35 38 35 17 45 36 45 18 30 34 20 11 36 42 33 43 33 40 34 20 28 26 68 —25 Letter grouping
45 31 33 33 13 43 31 44 17 22 35 28 12 33 46 32 46 36 39 32 20 30 22 54 54 —26 Figure analogies
42 34 32 34 06 32 22 36 21 31 30 22 05 30 38 35 30 28 41 25 25 25 21 38 42 34 — 27 Figure grouping
48 48 41 36 19 42 44 48 26 23 30 21 18 63 62 41 49 43 35 30 16 26 12 40 41 36 38 —28 Mechanical comprehension
34 36 53 54 18 31 34 37 15 16 23 25 14 36 49 46 47 43 26 28 31 24 18 31 37 27 27 36 —29 Rotation of solid figures
53 44 32 30 09 39 26 44 18 20 28 30 25 40 47 26 37 32 28 33 26 25 22 42 41 35 32 45 45 —30 Block assembly
30 34 23 22 02 19 27 26 19 12 13 18 09 50 39 16 27 30 17 21 10 16 06 05 06 14 19 51 31 29 —31 Mechanical experiences
23 32 26 18 01 22 26 24 18 13 12 25 10 49 47 13 26 29 16 24 09 24 00 16 20 27 18 57 28 26 55 —32 Electrical experience
```

[1] Decimal points have been omitted.

SOURCE: Thurstone, 1951.

at least three variables that the researcher believes are determined by it. This will ensure the expression of the factor as a well-defined common factor, if the researcher's hunches are correct.

To illustrate a common factor analysis we have selected a study of mechanical aptitude originally reported by Thurstone (1951) and have reanalyzed the correlations from that study using maximum likelihood estimation methods not available at the time it was made. At the outset of this study Thurstone hypothesized that mechanical ability is a cognitive ability involving some of the primary mental abilities, in particular, spatial ability and the ability to visualize movement in space, inductive reasoning, and speed and flexibility of closure. He also considered speed of perception and visual memory as component abilities of mechanical aptitude. Thus he used old tests from earlier analyses of the primary mental abilities, or constructed new tests when necessary to measure these hypothesized abilities, and included with them a number of tests of mechanical knowledge, skill, and experience. In all, Thurstone analyzed the correlations among 32 test variables. The correlations, which were based on responses to the tests by 350 high school boys, are shown in Table 1.

Step 2. Determining communalities and number of factors. Whereas Thurstone used the centroid method to determine the number of factors after provisional estimates of the communalities were placed in diagonal positions on the correlation matrix, to reanalyze Thurstone's data we used the maximum likelihood method, which first determines a provisional estimate of the number of common factors and then iterates to obtain estimates of the communalities and factor pattern coefficients (Jöreskog, 1969). At this stage the result of the analysis is the unrotated factor pattern matrix, which is derived from the weighted eigenvectors and reduced eigenvalues of the variance-covariance matrix obtained by dividing each correlation by the square roots of the respective variables' estimated unique variances. It is characteristic of unrotated solutions that the first factor is correlated with almost all the variables, whereas subsequent factors are related to fewer and fewer of the variables. The unrotated solution is obtained because it provides for the best fit to the variables of a common factor space with the specified number of factors.

There are a number of ways to estimate the number of common factors with which to begin the iterations to the final solution. One can do a principal components analysis of the correlation matrix and retain those factors with eigenvalues greater than unity. (The eigenvalues correspond to variances of linear combinations of the variables so chosen as to have maximum variance under the proviso that the sum of the squares of the weights attached to each variable in the respective linear combination equals unity and previous principal components have been partialed from the variables.) This criterion only establishes a lowest bound to the number of common factors; however, it is popular because the number of factors it provides usually leads to the retention of factors that are interpretable and to the exclusion of those that are not or have minimal influence. Another criterion to use is Cattell's scree test. In this test the eigenvalues of the original correlation matrix or of the variance-covariance matrix of the weighted variables (each variable being multiplied by the reciprocal of the square root of its estimated unique variance) are plotted against their ordinal value in order of descending magnitude. If a point is found at which the eigenvalues start to diminish in nearly a straight-line fashion after a noticeable drop from the value of the preceding eigenvalue, this point determines an estimate of the number of common factors. There is also a statistical test (Jöreskog, 1962, 1967) for the number of common factors but it is not used very often because the test statistic is only asymptotically distributed as chi square, meaning that we know it is distributed as chi square only when it is applied to situations with many observations. Unfortunately, when using this statistic, the power of the test that the number of common factors is no greater than some specified number also increases with the number of observations. And so just as one is able accurately to establish critical values of the test statistic for some specified probability level of making a Type I error, the test almost always rejects the null hypothesis because of minor and nearly negligible sources of common variance resulting from lack of fit of the model, thus leading to a search for more common factors. In the present study we decided on the basis of these various criteria to retain ten factors, as Thurstone (1951) had. The unrotated factor pattern matrix for the present analysis of Thurstone's thirty-two tests is given

in Table 2 and displays ten orthogonal common factors.

Step 3. Rotating the factors. Almost all factor analysts today "rotate" the factors to "simple structure" after obtaining the initial "unrotated solution." In simple structure solutions each factor tends to be associated with a distinct, nonoverlapping subset of the variables. The factors of simple structure solutions are thus easier to interpret because one has only to determine what is common to a small subset of the variables not found in the other variables. However, a major issue is whether to obtain "orthogonal" (uncorrelated) factors or correlated factors when one obtains the simple structure solution. Thurstone implemented rotation to simple structure using a reference vector technique, which sought to identify subspaces of the total common factor space that totally contained subsets of the variables. A reference vector would be positioned in common factor space so that as many variables as possible would be orthogonal to it. These variables would thus occupy a subspace of the common factor space that excluded the dimension occupied by the reference vector. The common factors were seen to be vectors at the intersections of these subspaces orthogonal to the various reference vectors. This had the practical effect of positioning each factor among the variables of the subset of variables to which it is most related. Presumably such factors would behave more like real variables and thus would be less ambiguous to interpret. However, factors obtained in this way are frequently correlated.

Correlated factors are often the result of other common influences that are confounded with the influences common only to the distinct subsets of variables that define the factors. For example, for children who are learning arithmetic, tests of addition and of multiplication may define two distinct common factors: addition and multiplication. These will be distinct common factors in a battery of several addition and multiplication tests insofar as the learning of one operation is independent of learning the other. On the other hand, although tests of addition and multiplication, respectively, may among themselves be homogeneous and highly correlated, they may still show moderate correlations with tests of the other operation. In this case it may be that performances on both addition tests and multiplication tests depend on the ability to memorize tables, or on abilities to distinguish number symbols. Thus the correlations among these common factors may reflect the presence of other common factors confounded with the original common factors, which might be isolated only after factor analyzing the correlations among the original common factors. Thus we may speak of first-order factors, second-order factors, and so on.

In the present reanalysis the ten factors were transformed to ten simple structure factors using the direct oblimin method (Jennrich & Sampson, 1966). This method yields correlated factors, although typically the correlations among them are not high. There are numerous other methods of rotating factors to simple structure, and, in fact, discovering better methods of rotating factors seems

TABLE 2. *Unrotated factor pattern matrix with communalities (h^2) based on analysis of correlations among thirty-two group tests using maximum-likelihood estimation*

Tests	Factors										h^2
	1	2	3	4	5	6	7	8	9	10	
1 BLOCKCN	.70	.12	.09	.06	−.05	.03	.07	−.07	−.03	.03	.53
2 PAPERPZ	.59	.20	−.09	−.02	.01	−.11	.11	−.04	−.13	−.09	.45
3 CARDS	.74	−.35	−.08	−.26	−.03	−.02	−.10	−.08	−.01	.01	.76
4 FIGURES	.70	−.42	−.05	−.33	−.07	−.01	−.09	.13	.07	−.01	.82
5 HANDS	.36	−.59	−.05	.55	−.15	.04	.00	.02	.00	−.01	.80
6 COPYING	.61	.08	.14	.03	.07	.07	.08	.09	−.26	−.08	.50
7 BOLTS	.54	−.12	−.08	.27	.04	.17	−.16	.11	.10	.00	.45
8 GOTSHFI	.67	.05	.06	−.08	.02	−.02	.11	.18	−.18	.10	.55
9 MUTFIGS	.31	.05	.01	.07	.06	.15	.33	.13	.24	−.05	.32
10 MUTWRDS	.37	.00	.20	.11	.11	.15	.15	.20	.22	.02	.33
11 DESIGNS	.53	−.10	.18	−.04	.05	.04	.21	.21	−.23	.14	.48
12 MEMPICS	.41	.17	.04	−.05	−.07	.61	−.08	−.20	−.02	−.01	.63
13 VISMEM	.26	.08	.02	−.06	−.15	.16	−.09	−.01	−.05	.34	.25
14 MECHMOV	.62	.25	−.29	.06	.13	.01	−.19	.10	−.04	.10	.62
15 SURFDEV	.78	.08	−.20	.08	.08	−.11	.08	−.16	−.17	−.09	.75
16 REVROT	.64	−.28	.02	−.22	.06	−.02	.15	.02	−.07	−.03	.57
17 LOZENGE	.73	−.19	−.04	.04	.04	−.05	−.01	−.10	−.02	.11	.60
18 CUBES	.62	−.08	−.10	.04	.08	−.22	.11	−.38	.10	.08	.63
19 IDENTFM	.54	−.02	.21	−.02	.12	.16	.29	.02	.10	−.09	.47
20 MUTPICS	.51	.07	.10	−.03	.05	.11	.16	−.11	.11	.04	.34
21 JIGSAW	.38	−.06	.09	−.11	−.11	.00	.17	−.03	−.03	−.12	.22
22 MEMGEO	.44	.06	.04	.00	.02	.49	−.15	−.04	−.10	−.06	.47
23 PICSQRS	.32	.00	.26	−.06	−.02	.10	.27	−.12	.21	.18	.35
24 LETSER	.63	.17	.44	.10	.21	−.13	−.17	−.05	.08	.06	.73
25 LETGPNG	.63	.12	.40	.11	.19	−.10	−.18	.07	.07	−.09	.69
26 FIGANAL	.59	.12	.24	.06	.19	.02	−.05	−.06	−.06	−.01	.46
27 FIGGPNG	.51	.11	.15	−.07	.12	.02	.12	.10	.07	−.16	.37
28 MECHCMP	.70	.23	−.30	.15	.15	−.07	.00	.15	.02	.03	.71
29 ROTSOLD	.62	−.06	−.10	−.18	−.17	−.07	−.10	−.08	.12	−.14	.52
30 BLKASM	.63	.39	.10	.05	−.51	−.09	−.01	.04	.02	−.01	.83
31 MECHEXP	.42	.26	−.55	.00	.03	.05	.09	.08	.16	.05	.59
32 ELECEXP	.44	.31	−.47	.06	.18	.08	−.07	.00	.09	−.07	.57

to be a favorite pastime for some factor analytic methodologists. However, the most popular methods, in addition to the direct oblimin method, are the varimax method for orthogonal simple structure (Kaiser, 1958), the Harris-Kaiser method (Harris & Kaiser, 1964), the promax method (Hendrickson & White, 1964), and maxplane (Cattell & Muerle, 1960; Eber, 1966). In the present analysis the direct oblimin solution for the factor pattern matrix of regression weights of the observed variables regressed on the common factors is given in Table 3. The corresponding matrix of correlations among the factors is given in Table 4.

Step 4. Interpreting the factors. Factor interpretation is certainly made easier if the researcher has selected vari-

ables for analysis to represent certain hypothetical factors. But for most researchers the interpretation of factors in an exploratory factor analysis depends on examining the factor pattern loadings and the correlations among the factors. Variables whose factor pattern coefficients on a given factor are large are then associated together, and the interpretation of the factor depends on the ingenuity (and subjectivity) of the researcher to identify something common to these variables that is absent in variables with near-zero coefficients on the same factor. This is the way in which most factors are interpreted, but one problem arises with this method. The indeterminacy of the factors that results when there are more factor variables (both common and unique) to determine than there are ob-

TABLE 3. *Rotated factor pattern matrix for ten factors obtained using direct oblim rotation*

Tests	Factors									
	1	2	3	4	5	6	7	8	9	10
1 BLOCKCNT	.15	−.02	−.08	.10	−.25	.13	.07	−.17	.17	.05
2 PAPERPZL	.26	−.02	−.25	−.03	−.24	.03	−.04	−.17	.07	−.10
3 CARDS	.04	−.73	−.03	.08	.05	.08	−.09	−.14	.04	.05
4 FIGURES	.03	−.90	−.00	.05	.03	−.02	.03	.10	.01	.06
5 HANDS	.01	.00	.12	.92	−.02	−.02	.02	−.05	−.10	−.03
6 COPYING	.44	.00	−.04	.06	−.12	.20	−.03	−.01	.16	−.08
7 BOLTS	−.06	−.10	−.22	.39	.01	.16	.07	.10	.18	.04
8 GOTSHFIG	.45	−.17	−.13	−.01	−.14	−.02	.06	.01	.09	.12
9 MUTFIGS	.04	.02	−.14	.05	−.04	.03	.51	.01	−.06	−.07
10 MUTWRDS	.03	−.02	−.04	.09	.01	.02	.43	.12	.20	.02
11 DESIGNS	.55	−.11	.04	.07	−.00	−.01	.13	.02	.03	.13
12 MEMPICS	−.07	.04	.01	−.02	−.03	.79	.05	−.04	−.07	.08
13 VISMEM	.07	−.04	−.04	−.01	−.09	.13	−.03	−.01	−.02	.40
14 MECHMOV	.11	−.07	−.59	.01	−.05	.06	−.11	.02	.20	.13
15 SURFDEV	.26	−.05	−.34	.15	−.14	.10	−.13	−.34	.07	−.13
16 REVROT	.27	−.51	.01	.03	.07	.03	.09	−.13	−.02	−.04
17 LOZENGE	.12	−.29	−.13	.24	.00	.02	−.01	−.24	.14	.11
18 CUBES	−.05	−.16	−.18	.14	−.02	−.08	.01	−.58	.14	.01
19 IDENTFM	.17	−.09	.04	.01	.00	.17	.39	−.11	.11	−.11
20 MUTPICS	.04	−.06	−.05	−.02	−.06	.15	.24	−.21	.11	.04
21 JIGSAW	.12	−.20	.12	.00	−.19	.07	.09	−.08	−.06	−.10
22 MEMGEO	.05	−.05	−.03	.05	.04	.64	−.03	.10	.05	.02
23 PICSQRS	−.01	−.03	.15	−.04	−.05	.04	.41	−.24	.07	.17
24 LETSER	.01	−.01	.04	−.02	−.07	−.01	.05	−.12	.77	.07
25 LETGPNG	.03	−.08	.03	.03	−.11	.02	.06	.04	.72	−.07
26 FIGANAL	.16	.01	−.03	.01	−.01	.16	.02	−.13	.44	−.01
27 FIGGPNG	.13	−.15	−.07	−.10	−.09	.07	.23	.03	.22	−.16
28 MECHCMP	.18	−.01	−.63	.11	−.10	−.07	.06	−.03	.16	.02
29 ROTSOLDS	−.17	−.51	−.09	.01	−.28	.06	−.04	−.07	.06	−.07
30 BLKASM	−.00	.05	−.03	.04	−.88	.00	.00	.05	.08	.12
31 MECHEXP	−.03	−.07	−.72	−.03	−.09	−.01	.16	−.04	−.21	.05
32 ELECEXP	−.06	.01	−.71	−.04	.02	.15	.01	−.06	.02	−.07

served variables to determine them with makes possible the existence of more than one distinct set of variables whose relationships with the observed variables would be that given by the factor pattern matrix and the matrix of correlations among the factors. Thus the factor pattern coefficients do not determine uniquely the meaning of the factors. Normally, however, this does not discourage most factor analysts because they feel that the likelihood of alternative interpretations, given our general knowledge about the world and the variables, will be small.

In the present reanalysis of Thurstone's thirty-two variables most of the same ten factors appeared as he reported (Thurstone, 1951). There were some minor exceptions, however. These factors are described briefly as follows:

(1) C_2: ability to perceive figures against a distracting background.
(2) S_1: ability to visualize a rigid configuration when moved into different positions.
(3) S_2: ability to visualize a configuration in which there is movement or displacement among the parts of the configuration as found in mechanical devices.
(4) K: kinesthetic imagery (not well determined).
(5) M_3: block assembly performance.
(6) M_2: memory for visual figures.
(7) C_1: ability to fuse a perceptual field into a single percept.
(8) S_3: ability to identify a point on a reoriented figure (topological invariance, another spatial visualization ability).

TABLE 4. *Correlations among rotated factors*

	Factors									
	1	2	3	4	5	6	7	8	9	10
Factor 1	1.00	−.46	−.21	.23	−.37	.33	.32	−.26	.44	.03
Factor 2	−.46	.100	.28	−.39	.40	−.36	−.26	.40	−.35	−.06
Factor 3	−.21	.28	1.00	−.19	.35	−.31	−.11	.18	−.23	−.00
Factor 4	.23	−.39	−.19	1.00	−.12	.20	.17	−.13	.26	.04
Factor 5	−.37	.40	.35	−.12	1.00	−.38	−.25	.35	−.37	−.10
Factor 6	.33	−.36	−.31	.20	−.38	1.00	.29	−.20	.36	.20
Factor 7	.32	−.26	−.11	.17	−.25	.29	1.00	−.21	.28	.02
Factor 8	−.26	.40	.18	−.13	.35	−.20	−.21	1.00	−.24	−.03
Factor 9	.44	−.35	−.23	.26	−.37	.36	.28	−.24	1.00	.06
Factor 10	.03	−.06	−.00	.04	−.10	.20	.02	−.03	.06	1.00

(9) *I:* Induction.
(10) (Uninterpretable).

From both our and Thurstone's (1951) analysis one can conclude that tests of mechanical experience related primarily to the second spatial visualization factor, S_2, involving the visualization of moving parts.

Step 5. Using factor scores. At this point some researchers would like to have more direct measures of the factors. Unfortunately, again because of factor indeterminacy, there is no unique solution for scores on the factors (see McDonald & Mulaik, 1979). Still, some researchers have used predicted scores derived from the observed variables by regression, utilizing the correlations among the observed variables and correlations between the variables and the common factors (the latter correlations derived from the factor pattern coefficients and the correlations among the factors) to determine the regression coefficients. However, there is some danger in using such factor scores, especially when the squared multiple correlation for estimating the factor in question from the observed variables is below .50. If one were to use the predicted factor scores in lieu of having the actual scores on the factor in question it would be quite possible for the predicted factor scores to be correlated .71 with some external variable, whereas the variable conceived to be the factor could have (if measured directly) but zero correlation with the same external variable.

Confirmatory Factor Analysis

If one has a hypothesis that specifies exactly the values of the coefficients of the factor pattern matrix F, the correlations among the common factors in the matrix C_{XX}, and the diagonal elements of the diagonal unique variances matrix U^2, then by the fundamental theorem of common factor analysis this hypothesis determines a specific correlation matrix for the observed variables given by the matrix equation $R = FC_{XX}F' + U^2$, which can be compared with an actual sample correlation matrix $\hat{R}$ for the same variables to evaluate the hypothesis. When one proceeds to test hypotheses about the common factors among a set of observed variables in the manner just described, one performs confirmatory factor analysis.

However, most factor analytic hypotheses are so vaguely formulated that only certain elements of the matrices F, C_{XX}, and U^2 are specified. For example, a researcher may be able to specify from a hypothesis only the zero elements of the factor pattern matrix F, which indicate what variables are *not* influenced by what factors. The researcher may also be able to specify that the factors are to be mutually uncorrelated, fixing C_{XX} to an identity matrix. The remaining unspecified or "free" elements of the factor pattern matrix and the diagonal elements of the unique variances may then have to be estimated from sample data conditional on the specified parameters being fixed at certain values, using, say, least squares, maximum likelihood, or generalized least squares estimation. In general, the researcher must specify enough (usually greater than r^2, where r is the number of hypothetical factors) independent parameters (elements) of the matrices F and C_{XX} so that the specified and conditionally estimated free parameters of these matrices determine a unique solution for $R = FC_{XX}F' + U^2$ not obtainable from any other values for F, C_{XX}, U^2 having the same specified parameters. When this condition is satisfied, the model generated by the hypothesis is said to be identified. Identified models make possible unambiguous tests of hypotheses as well as consistent estimates of free parameters.

As in exploratory factor analysis, factor indeterminacy resulting from the fact that there are more latent variables to determine than there are manifest variables with which to determine them can introduce a degree of ambiguity into the interpretation of the results of a confirmatory factor analysis. Although it is quite possible clearly to reject a hypothetical factor analytic model in a confirmatory factor analysis because it does not fit the data acceptably, it is not possible to confirm the model unambiguously when it does fit the data, unless certain stringent conditions, difficult to attain in practice, are met. These conditions are that either all the common factors in the sample of variables selected for analysis are determinate (almost impossible to attain) or all of the common factors of the domain of variables to which one will generalize one's inferences from the analysis are represented as common factors in the sample of variables selected. If at least two common factors of the domain are not represented as common factors of the sample of variables analyzed, then there exist infinitely many transformations of the common factors of the domain that would yield distinct variables whose relationships with the sample of variables are consistent with the factor pattern loadings and correlations among the factors obtained in the analysis of these variables. Hence if one's model is consistent with the data, it may be so because of factors in the domain other than those of one's model. This need not be regarded as a fatal shortcoming of common factor analysis, but rather as a problem of most inductive methods that seek to infer general laws beyond those particular instances used to establish them.

Jöreskog (1969) developed the statistical theory behind confirmatory factor analysis and provided the first computing algorithm for its practical implementation. He also supplied statistical tests for the goodness of fit of a sample correlation matrix to a hypothetical factor analytic model. Since then others have provided related computing algorithms, some allowing for more elaborate restrictions to be placed on the parameters of the model matrices than those given by Jöreskog. In the meantime confirmatory factor analysis has been shown to be a special case of other more general methods for testing models concerning the covariance structures of variables, such as analysis of covariance structures (Jöreskog, 1970) and linear structural equations models (Wiley, 1973; Jöreskog, 1973). A major drawback of these confirmatory methods at this time is their expensive consumption of computing time, even on large, high-speed computers. However, such methods do encourage the researcher to develop theories about the basis for relationships among variables and to test such theories. For further introductory discussion of confirmatory factor analysis and its applications see Mulaik (1972, 1975).

Stanley A. Mulaik

See also Aptitude Measurement; Intelligence Measurement; Multivariate Analysis; Personality Assessment; Statistical Methods.

REFERENCES

Carroll, J. B. Psychometric tests as cognitive tasks: A new "structure of intellect." In L. B. Resnick, *The Nature of Intelligence.* Hillsdale, N.J.: Lawrence Erlbaum Associates, 1976.

Cattell, R. B. *Description and Measurement of Personality.* Yonkers-on-Hudson, N.Y.: World Book, 1946.

Cattell, R. B. *Personality: A Systematic Theoretical and Factual Study.* New York: McGraw-Hill, 1950.

Cattell, R. B. *Personality and Motivation: Structure and Measurement.* Yonkers-on-Hudson, N.Y.: World Book, 1957.

Cattell, R. B. Theory of fluid and crystallized intelligence: A critical experiment. *Journal of Educational Psychology,* 1963, *54,* 1–22.

Cattell, R. B. *Scientific Analysis of Personality.* Chicago: Aldine, 1966.

Cattell, R. B. *Abilities, Their Structure, Growth, and Action.* Boston: Houghton Mifflin, 1971.

Cattell, R. B., Muerle, J. L. The "maxplane" program for factor rotation to oblique simple structure. *Educational and Psychological Measurement,* 1960, *20,* 269–290.

Eber, H. W. Toward oblique simple structure maxplane. *Multivariate Behavioral Research,* 1966, *1,* 112–125.

Eysenck, H. J. *Dimensions of Personality.* London: Kegan Paul, 1947.

Eysenck, H. J. *The Biological Basis of Personality.* Springfield, Ill.: Thomas, 1967.

Guilford, J. P. *Personality.* New York: McGraw-Hill, 1959.

Guilford, J. P. *The Nature of Human Intelligence.* New York: McGraw-Hill, 1967.

Harris, C. N., & Kaiser, H. F. Oblique factor analytic solution by orthogonal transformation. *Psychometrika,* 1964, *Z9,* 347–362.

Hendrickson, A. E., & White, P. O. PROMAX: A quick method for rotation to oblique simple structure. *British Journal of Statistical Psychology,* 1964, *17,* 65–70.

Horn, J. L. Organization of abilities and the development of intelligence. *Psychological Review,* 1968, *75,* 242–259.

Jennrich, R. I., & Sampson, P. F. Rotation for simple loadings. *Psychometrika,* 1966, *31,* 313–323.

Jöreskog, K. G. On the statistical treatment of residuals in factor analysis. *Psychometrika,* 1962, *27,* 335–354.

Jöreskog, K. G. Some contributions to maximum likelihood factor analysis. *Psychometrika,* 1967, *32,* 443–482.

Jöreskog, K. G. A general approach to confirmatory maximum likelihood factor analysis. *Psychometrika,* 1969, *34,* 183–202.

Jöreskog, K. G. A general method for analysis of covariance structures. *Biometrika,* 1970, *23,* 121–145.

Jöreskog, K. G. A general method for estimating a linear structural equation system. In A. S. Goldberger & O. D. Duncan (Eds.), *Structural Equation Models in the Social Sciences.* New York: Seminar Press, 1973, pp. 85–112. (ERIC Document Reproduction Service No. ED 051 257)

Kaiser, H. F. The varimax rotation for analytic rotation in factor analysis. *Psychometrika,* 1958, *23,* 187–200.

McDonald, R. P., & Mulaik, S. A. Determinacy of common factors: A nontechnical review. *Psychological Bulletin,* 1979, *86,* 297–306.

Mulaik, S. A. Are personality factors raters' conceptual factors? *Journal of Consulting Psychology,* 1964, *28,* 506–511.

Mulaik, S. A. *The Foundations of Factor Analysis.* New York: McGraw-Hill, 1972.

Mulaik, S. A. Confirmatory factor analysis. In D. J. Amick and H. J. Walberg (Eds.), *Introductory Multivariate Analysis.* Berkeley, Calif.: McCutchan, 1975, pp. 170–207.

Norman, W. T. Toward an adequate taxonomy of personality attributes: Replicated factor structure in peer nomination personality ratings. *Journal of Abnormal and Social Psychology,* 1963, *66,* 574–583.

Passini, F. T., & Norman, W. T. A universal conception of personality structure? *Journal of Personality and Social Psychology,* 1966, *4,* 44–49.

Osgood, C. E., & Suci, G. J. *The Measurement of Meaning.* Urbana: University of Illinois Press, 1958.

Spearman, C. E. "General intelligence" objectively determined and measured. *American Journal of Psychology,* 1904, *15,* 201–293.

Sternberg, R. J. *Intelligence, information processing, and analogical reasoning: The componential analysis of human abilities.* Hillsdale, N.J.: Lawrence Erlbaum Associates, 1977.

Thurstone, L. L. *Multiple Factor Analysis.* Chicago: University of Chicago Press, 1947.

Thurstone, L. L. *An Analysis of Mechanical Aptitude* (Psychometric Laboratory Report No. 62). Chicago: University of Chicago, 1951.

Vernon, P. E. *The Structure of Human Abilities* (2nd ed.). London: Methuen, 1961.

Wiley, D. E. The identification problem for structural equation models with unmeasured variables. In A. S. Goldberger & O. D. Duncan (Eds.), *Structural Equation Models in the Social Sciences.* New York: Seminar Press, 1973.

FACULTY DEVELOPMENT

Professional development for faculty is not a new phenomenon in the history of higher education. Leaves for the purpose of advancing scholarship and financial support to attend the meetings of professional associations are among the most frequent types of activities taken for granted by faculty members in most colleges and universities. During the past decade, however, professional development for faculty has expanded so that it now includes a much broader range of concerns than the improvement of scholarship. "Faculty development" is the term most commonly used today to refer to programs, activities, practices, and strategies that aim both to maintain and to improve the professional competence of individual faculty members in fulfilling their various obligations to a specific institution. Although professional and staff development activities are common at all levels of schooling, faculty development typically refers to the recent movement in postsecondary education toward total development of faculty members and their competence in professional activities. Faculty development interests range from research and scholarship in a discipline and teaching in a formal classroom to the informed management of one's professional career over time. Faculty development is defined in one recent report (Crow et al., 1976) as "the total development of the faculty member—as a person, as a professional, and as a member of the academic community" (p. 3).

Faculty development emerged as a significant movement in higher education at the conclusion of the 1960s. Three major factors have stimulated an expanding literature in this area of study. Student protests in postsecondary institutions during the 1960s were diverse in form and motivated by a wide range of dissatisfactions. Many students attempted to negotiate with faculty and administrators for the reform of an educational process that they felt was remote and unresponsive. This issue was of special concern to undergraduates in large universities emphasizing research and graduate training. The specific reforms sought by the student movement were not always realistic or practical; nevertheless, the call for effective teaching and a more demonstrable commitment by faculty members to the improvement of educational programs was an obvious theme. Riesman (1980) discusses this change from a tradition of faculty hegemony in past years to the present emergence of a consumerist emphasis. He notes that higher education has become more diverse in its objectives, less committed to the perpetuation of an elitist class in society, and more attentive to a broader age range among its clientele. Faculty development represents one response to these changes, although Riesman expresses some skepticism about the current thrust of faculty development programs and their ability to realize all the expectations set for them.

The second factor to influence the emergence of these programs has been the decline in the number of students expected to attend postsecondary institutions during the 1980s and 1990s. The reality that growth in college enrollments is finite and essentially controlled by birthrates has not been changed by creating new programs for older adults. Centra (1980a) points out that the 1980s will witness the end of the growth years in higher education. The academic community, having been sensitized to such issues as renewal, reassessment, realignment, and retrenchment, is now faced with the prospect of fewer students, higher costs, decreased job opportunities for young Ph.D.'s, increases in the average age of faculty, and a concentration on maintenance rather than growth. The prospect of a steady-state universe in higher education has led to the consideration of topics such as financial exigencies, managing reductions-in-force, and reallocation strategies that heretofore have not been prominent in the literature of higher education (Mortimer & Tierney, 1979).

Glenny (1980), in an analysis of demographic data, offers the following conclusions about the future of postsecondary education in the United States:

1. The decrease in the number of college-age persons in the population will have a sizable effect on most institutions of higher education by the end of the 1980s.
2. The effect of enrollment declines will be experienced differently depending upon the type of institution involved. Prestigious private colleges and distinguished research universities will be least vulnerable. Small private colleges (many of which are denomination-related), state colleges and universities, and emerging private and public universities that are not research-oriented will be most affected by enrollment declines.
3. By the end of the 1980s, college-age persons should begin to react to potential shortages in several major fields of specialization and in some professions. This

could increase enrollment rates, especially at prestigious institutions.

4. The enrollment loss sustained by a decrease in the number of persons 18 to 24 years old will not be offset by increases in adults entering college. Although postsecondary institutions, especially community colleges, will expand their offerings to attract adults to noncredit, nondegree courses, the majority of colleges and universities will continue to maintain curricula designed for persons seeking degrees. The competition for adult learners will be more difficult because of educational programs available from sources other than postsecondary institutions (television, industry, government).

5. Postsecondary educational opportunities will continue to expand through nonprofit organizations other than colleges and universities. Business, industry, and government will provide attractive alternatives to formal participation in a degree program at a college or university.

6. Social factors not related to enrollment decline will further complicate the ability of colleges and universities to attract students. Among these factors are the loss of meaning for the college degree as a way of assuring socioeconomic mobility, collective bargaining by faculty and its tendency to restrict change, and the growth of certification and licensing procedures that do not depend on postsecondary programs as the essential element in the procedure.

Glenny concludes that institutions that survive until the mid-1990s will have a better sense of their missions and goals, faculties who are better prepared in their discipline and better able to teach it, and stronger curricula for student learning. Students will have a wider range of opportunities to satisfy their needs.

The third factor to stimulate the emergence of faculty development programs has been the changing nature of careers in higher education (Shulman, 1979). Even in those research universities where scholarship still determines advancement, faculty members are being made to feel more conscious of responsibilities for maintaining and improving the quality of educational programs. The evaluation of teaching has become common in most postsecondary institutions (Centra, 1980b), thus heightening the concern about accountability for excellence in teaching. Many institutions use evaluation results in making decisions about retention, tenure, and advancement. Central to many faculty development programs are activities that respond to the results of evaluations of teaching (Smith, 1976). Career opportunities for those who aspire to faculty positions have decreased dramatically during the last decade, and the possibility of completing one's career at the same institution where one started is greater (Furniss, 1981a, 1981b). Diversity in the nature and goals of institutions has increased dramatically, with its attendant diffusion of the traditional career structure for academics (Martin, 1978–1979).

Faculty development efforts address the need to remain productive in an environment where new colleagues are few and the motivational effects of change are diminished. The increasing average age of faculty presents problems of vitality for institutions where tenure is assured. According to the Carnegie Council on Policy Studies in Higher Education (1980), approximately 40 percent of tenured faculty in four-year colleges and universities were between the ages of 36 and 45 in 1980. This statistic is projected to change to approximately 46 percent between the ages of 46 and 55 by 1990, and approximately 45 percent between the ages of 56 and 65 by 2000. The trend is obviously in the direction of older faculty who will need support and assistance to provide the quality and diversity of education appropriate for institutional survival during this twenty-year span. Faculty development is a major response to this change in the nature of career patterns for academicians.

Models. Many models for faculty development programs have been proposed during the past ten years. Bergquist and Phillips (1975) projected a frequently cited conceptualization that addresses the need to improve teaching and the quality of educational efforts in postsecondary institutions. According to these authors, the piecemeal efforts of the past to improve college teaching have not been effective. The hope of advancing the quality of higher education through traditional instructional improvement strategies fails to take into account the necessity for change in faculty members themselves and the impact of change on their institution. Bergquist and Phillips contend that effective faculty development must become an interactive process among three dimensions: (1) organizational, representing structural components; (2) instructional, representing the process of education; and (3) personal, representing the attitudes, beliefs, and values of individual faculty members.

Within the organizational dimension, such activities as departmental administration, departmental team building, departmental conflict management, and departmental decision making are critical for the creation of appropriate organizational climates to support effective teaching and scholarship. The instructional dimension includes such factors as instructional evaluations, classroom diagnosis, educational methods and technology, and curriculum development. The personal dimension includes procedures such as personal-growth workshops, life-planning workshops, interviews with faculty, and interpersonal skill training as well as supportive and therapeutic counseling.

Berquist and Phillips point out that the kind of comprehensive faculty development they propose for postsecondary institutions must involve full-time professionals to succeed. They suggest that appropriate entry points for the initiation of such a program are faculty interviews, evaluations (both self and student), and management development. Program planning should also put components into priority order to allow movement across dimensions; for example, one would use personal-growth workshops to initiate the consideration of educational methods and curriculum development, and then move from curriculum development activities into the area of departmental decision making.

Another model that has some elements in common with that of Bergquist and Phillips has been described by Toombs (1975). He points out that faculty development programs need to be built around the comprehensive nature of professional roles for faculty if they are to increase the probability of success. Faculty development must address not only the practical issues but also the conceptual issues of the profession. This comprehensive approach should include professional, curricular, and institutional dimensions. Faculty development programs should reflect the differentiated nature of participants' careers and recognize, at a minimum, differences between the inexperienced faculty member, the newly experienced, and the established experienced. The basic matrix that emerges from Toombs's model posits three dimensions on a vertical axis: professional and career issues, curricular and instructional issues, and institutional and organizational issues. The horizontal axis represents career stages: preservice, new and inexperienced, new and experienced, established and experienced, and nonteaching academics.

A model proposed by Simerly (1977) has as its central theme the degree of potential impact a faculty development program can have on the institution it serves. Six levels of involvement for faculty are delineated, ranging from program elements that would have the least impact on institutions to elements that would have greatest impact. The first approach is faculty development as individual freedom. Here no program elements are in place. Those in control assume that faculty, because of their prior academic preparation, will actively work to realize the goals of their institutions. At this level, little if any impact is anticipated because of the laissez-faire nature of institutional attitudes about faculty development. The second level of Simerly's model consists of activities to introduce and initiate the new faculty member to the institution, but does not provide for follow-up after this person has gotten beyond his or her first year. The third level, with potentially increased institutional impact over the first two levels, represents faculty development as career development. Here the typical concerns of the program are built around expectations for tenure and promotion and the institutional culture that sets the standards for career success. The fourth level of impact is faculty development built around instructional improvement and curriculum reform. Linking instructional improvement with curriculum change broadens the potential for impact beyond the single element of the individual course and its instructor. At the fifth level, faculty development efforts attempt to integrate the individual and the organization so that the goals and objectives of the institution and those of the faculty member can be made to reinforce each other. Faculty development programs that attempt a synthesis between faculty needs and institutional needs usually have elements typical of the first four levels. Programs that attempt to meld the individual and the institution generally view the faculty member in relation to his or her personal needs and concerns, professional roles and demands, and the expectations and rewards of the institution. The sixth level, the one with the greatest potential impact on the institution, defines faculty development as an organizational goal for the institution. This goal becomes operational through deliberate planning at all levels within the organization. The theme for planning is the effective use of faculty in a way that represents the best interests of both the faculty member and the institution. At this level, faculty development becomes an institutionalized commitment built into the organization through its governance and administrative configurations. Planning, maintaining, and improving the quality of the educational process become a central feature of programs.

Francis (1975) discusses a model that puts less emphasis on the nature of program elements and instead concentrates on their characteristics at several stages of growth. The most elemental stage is program activity directed toward attracting the attention of faculty, stimulating their thinking, and presenting information to them. This stage of consciousness raising implies no commitment to implementation and deemphasizes risk taking for the participants. The second stage of focal awareness moves from the abstractions of the first stage to a more practical and concrete consideration of specific issues in ways that imply commitment by faculty to do something as a result of their involvement. The third stage of subsidiary awareness emerges as a new climate for change is created. This stage is a natural outgrowth of stages 1 and 2, but now different kinds of activities are appropriate. Francis provides examples of the evolution of characteristics for faculty development efforts as they emerge from one stage to the next. If one faculty development element, for example, has to do with changes in policy and programs about the importance of teaching within the institution, an initiative at stage 1 might be a faculty-senate resolution about the importance of teaching effectiveness. This same initiative at stage 2 could be represented by grants to improve teaching for a small number of individuals and groups. At stage 3 the same concern could be represented by the establishment of moderate awards to support the teaching of large numbers of faculty.

Other models and strategies for faculty development programs and activities have been presented. Bergquist and Shoemaker (1976) provide case study examples of comprehensive programs. Instructional development agencies and their activities were surveyed by Alexander and Yelon (1972). A list of appropriate activities is available (Brown & Hanger, 1975). The faculty member as teacher dominates considerations of specific professional roles that faculty development strategies support (Axelrod, 1973; Centra, 1972; Davis, 1979; Eble, 1976; Ericksen & Cook, 1979; Kozma, 1978; Lindquist, 1978; Mathis, 1980a, 1980b; McKeachie & Kulik, 1975; Menges, 1980, 1981; Milton

& Associates, 1978). Adult development and the personality of the faculty member have been the focus of activities that view professional growth as essentially an expression of the beliefs, values, and attitudes of the person in the role of teacher and scholar (Freedman, 1973; Freedman et al., 1980). Faculty development as a specific instance of adult development, translated into stages of career development, is an additional use of adult development theory in higher education (Baldwin, 1979; Hodgkinson, 1974; Martin, 1975; Mathis, 1979; Weathersby & Tarule, 1980).

Studies. The rapid expansion of faculty development programs in community colleges, liberal arts colleges, and universities during the 1970s was stimulated by support from major philanthropic foundations and federal agencies. Many of the reports of faculty development efforts that abound in the literature are the result of the need to report to funding agencies about the results of grants given for a specific faculty development program. One of the first of these efforts was jointly sponsored by the American Association of University Professors and the Association of American Colleges, and was supported by a grant from the Carnegie Corporation. The Project to Improve College Teaching sponsored a series of conferences throughout the United States that attempted to ascertain the dimensions of effective, and ineffective, teaching as practiced in colleges and universities. Two reports were prepared by the director of the project and his associates (Eble, 1971a, 1971b). One report analyzed career development in college teaching with an emphasis on the effective college teacher. The other dealt with recognizing and evaluating effective teaching in the many institutional contexts in which it appears. These reports spoke to the need for more realistic assessments of the importance of teaching in higher education. They called attention to policies and practices in many institutions that clearly did not encourage faculty members to assume responsibility for maintaining effective teaching or for improving teaching practices that did not contribute to the quality of educational efforts. Credibility for the project was assured by its two sponsors. The Project to Improve College Teaching provided a stimulus for interest in faculty development activities to improve teaching (Eble, 1972). It did much to underscore the central role of the teaching function in maintaining institutional vitality. Prior to this project, foundation support was available for professional development activity, but the majority of it was directed toward increasing competence in a discipline through grants available for leaves and awards for the completion of research programs. One major exception in this history of support only for scholarship is the Associates Program, established by the Danforth Foundation in 1941. It seeks to improve the quality of human relations in colleges and universities through the recognition of talented teachers and their spouses. The Danforth Foundation maintains a fund that provides an opportunity for associates to receive some financial assistance to support individual educational projects.

The Exxon Foundation funded a study by Gaff (1975) that identified postsecondary programs designed to improve the quality of teaching and learning; described the range and variety of these programs; and discussed their place in the context of current trends and reforms in higher education. More than two hundred institutions with instructional improvement programs and/or centers for the in-service education of college teachers were identified. In analyzing the content of these programs, Gaff concluded that many could be characterized as focusing their efforts on faculty members. These programs were built on a philosophy that emphasized professional and personal development for faculty over the life span. A second type of effort emphasized instructional development with a focus on the design of courses, the use of specific methodology in instruction, and the manipulation of conditions of learning to produce more effective instructional impact. A third type of program concentrated on the organizational environment that provides a context for academic work. Gaff observed that the most successful programs included elements of all three approaches in some kind of comprehensive plan. He states: "From being virtually unheard of before 1970, the idea of professional development for the sake of better teaching and learning has become a social force within higher education that in many ways has a life of its own" (1975, p. 175). The following conclusions that Gaff made from his study have implications for decision making and the development of policy in all postsecondary institutions.

1. Although few colleges and universities had instructional improvement programs at the time of the study, the trend toward growth was pronounced.

2. Institutions should establish policies for broadening the participation of faculty members in professional development activities that examine and improve teaching. Voluntary participation is not a sufficient incentive to attract those faculty who may be most in need of assistance.

3. Budget allocations for the improvement of teaching should be expanded. Reliance on grant moneys to support faculty development does not produce the anticipated improvements needed for maintaining the quality of educational programs.

4. Involvement in faculty development activities should be rewarded if it is to be viewed as an integral part of a faculty member's commitment to his or her institution.

5. Many of the projects undertaken by faculty development programs are of short duration. Faculty, instructional, and/or organizational development programs should include efforts that go beyond the semester, quarter, or academic year.

6. Preparing faculty members for roles as consultants with their colleagues is essential if strategies for the improvement of teaching are to have a home in departments and in disciplines.

At the time of Gaff's study, very little was being done to evaluate the outcome of faculty development efforts. Evaluation strategies should become an essential part of program development and implementation. Gaff points out that in the final analysis, the effect of faculty development programs will be judged in terms of their effect on student learning. At the time of his study, students had little involvement in the activities of the programs reviewed. Gaff believes that students should become more centrally involved in faculty development programs since they are the recipients of the changes stimulated by such efforts.

During 1974, the Group for Human Development in Higher Education, a group of scholars who share a concern for improving the effectiveness of colleges and universities, published a monograph entitled *Faculty Development in a Time of Retrenchment* (1974). Its recommendations focused again on teaching as a major element in the movement to reform higher education.

The results of a major study of faculty development practices in colleges and universities in the United States were reported by Centra (1976). Centra's research, funded by the Exxon Foundation, identified 1,044 institutions with programs and/or practices for faculty development and/ or instructional improvement that were under way on campus. Questionnaires were sent to the program coordinators at each of these institutions, and 756 usable responses were received and analyzed. Four types of development programs were identified: (1) those with high faculty involvement, (2) those with an emphasis on instructional assistance practices, (3) those with traditional practices, and (4) those with an emphasis on assessment.

Examples of practices with high faculty involvement include workshops, seminars, or programs to introduce faculty to the goals of the institution; close cooperation of senior faculty with new faculty; use of faculty consultants to work with other faculty on improving teaching; and workshops or programs to help faculty improve their academic advising skills. Instructional assistance practices include the use of specialists to assist individual faculty in developing teaching skills, new courses, and evaluations of student performance. Traditional practices involve annual awards for excellence in teaching, leaves, seminars to help faculty improve research and scholarship skills, and summer grants for projects to improve course offerings. Practices that emphasize assessment include systematic ratings of instruction by students, formal assessments by colleagues for teaching or course improvement, and periodic reviews of the performance of all faculty members.

Centra's analysis of the effectiveness ratings of these practices indicated that a number of practices were regarded by the respondents as being more effective than others for attaining the goals of faculty development programs. Among instructional assistance practices, the use of specialists was rated high, as was the use of instructional technology. Workshops and seminars on teaching and the evaluation of student performance, assistance for faculty to improve their research and scholarship skills, and activities to acquaint faculty with the goals of their institution

were perceived as effective. Travel funds were assessed as an effective way to promote professional development. Formal assessments by colleagues through class visits and systematic ratings of instruction by students were also considered effective. Among traditional practices, faculty exchange programs with other institutions and courses offered to faculty by colleagues had a high rating. Among the practices viewed as least effective were annual awards to faculty for excellence in teaching, newsletters and articles, and periodic reviews of the performance of all faculty members.

During 1978, the Association of American Colleges initiated a project, funded by the Andrew W. Mellon Foundation, to evaluate faculty development programs at twenty colleges that had undertaken comprehensive faculty renewal efforts during the five years prior to 1979 (Nelsen, 1979; Nelsen & Siegel, 1980). The project director visited all twenty colleges and interviewed selected faculty, administrators, and students. The conclusions reached by the study were based on interviews with more than five hundred persons from these campuses. The colleges in the study could all be classified as liberal arts institutions concentrating essentially on undergraduate preparation. All had received grants from a foundation to support their faculty renewal efforts. These grants had been awarded for a wide range of initiatives representing faculty development needs as perceived by the institution. Although the major sources of data were focused interviews with faculty development participants at each institution, two interviewers on each campus also recorded independent judgments about the impact of the program. For purposes of classification, faculty development activities were divided into four categories: (1) professional development, (2) instructional development, (3) curricular change, and (4) organizational development. Each category represented specific kinds of activities that served as an operational definition for the category. The results of the evaluation were as follows (Nelsen & Siegel, 1980).

1. The most frequent approaches were efforts that involved professional development for individuals. Such activities included traditional professional growth options such as study leaves for individuals, support for attendance at professional meetings, and research and publication activities in a faculty member's discipline. More innovative approaches included study and preparation outside of one's own discipline, activities that helped faculty attain new research competencies, and the participation of faculty as learners in a colleague's course. Although individual professional development activities were in the majority, other types of initiatives included campuswide discussions of educational issues and workshops aimed at faculty attainment of competencies such as computer skills and writing skills.

2. Efforts to include instructional development opportunities as part of faculty development initiatives were not viewed by the interviewees as having the same level of success as individual professional development activities. They were skeptical about some activities, especially workshops, to help improve teaching. Instructional development projects perceived as most successful were those organized to provide specific, usable skills for faculty.

3. Projects that focused on curriculum innovation and change were perceived as more successful than instructional development projects but less successful than individual professional development efforts. The use of discussions about curriculum as a way of breaking down disciplinary boundaries was viewed quite favorably.

4. Organizational development was found to be a neglected area of faculty development activities. In the twenty institutions surveyed, only six projects were identified in which organizational development was the central theme. Only one of these was judged to be successful. The investigators concluded that organizational development represents the most critical dimension of faculty development because it includes the manipulation of the reward structure for faculty.

5. In the twenty institutions studied, the interviewers identified what they perceived to be two major inadequacies in faculty development programs: a lack of attention to questions of faculty advising of students and a neglect of the use of faculty evaluation strategies for improving the educational climate.

6. Effective management was characteristic of most successful faculty development programs. The investigators concluded that effective management is absolutely essential for program success. The study identified as components of effective management the presence of a decision-making unit consisting of either a faculty committee or a group of administrators that has a clear charge and an unambiguous structure, some linkage of faculty development activities to the reward structure of the institution, and flexible decision making that supports various approaches to faculty development. The investigators also found that effective management includes open communication with the campus about the existence of the faculty development program and the terms that govern an individual faculty member's ability to become involved in its activities. They concluded that open communication of successes and failures for ongoing projects is essential for credibility within the institution.

Although this particular evaluation can be criticized for sampling procedures and the manner in which data were collected, it does focus on a sample of those types of institutions—undergraduate liberal arts colleges—that have received a significant portion of private foundation support to initiate faculty development activities.

A more comprehensive assessment of faculty development programs in a wider sample of institutions was initiated by the Center for the Study of Higher Education at the University of Michigan in 1978 (Blackburn et al., 1980). This project was supported by the Fund for the Improvement of Postsecondary Education. It was designed to include three major efforts: (1) to develop instruments to assess the success of faculty development programs; (2) to provide data relating to formative and summative evaluation for the programs of twenty-four participating institutions; and (3) to explore the effectiveness, or ineffectiveness, of a range of strategies used to promote faculty growth in different institutional settings. The first part of the project consisted of a rating of potential program goals by expert respondents. These ratings indicated that instructional improvement goals had clear priority in the judgment of experts. These experts expressed little concern for other aspects of a faculty member's professional life.

The study by Centra (1976) provided the basis for the selection of the twenty-four institutions studied in depth. His classification of institutional programs into four groups—those representing high faculty involvement, instructional assistance practices, traditional practices, and an emphasis on assessment—formed the basis for the selection of a sample of community colleges, four-year colleges, and universities. Site visits were arranged at these institutions, and individuals on each campus who were directly concerned with faculty development activities were interviewed. These included deans, presidents, faculty development directors, committee members, and faculty who either favored or were critical of program elements.

The third phase of the project involved the design and administration of seven survey instruments. After a pilot effort that provided information for their modification, the instruments were mailed to a stratified random sample of faculty at each institution. The analysis of returns indicated that faculty value their teaching role very highly in all the institutional types surveyed. All faculty believed that they valued teaching more highly than did their colleagues. Faculty appeared to have a highly internal set of criteria by which they judged their own classroom performance. They felt that these criteria were supported by personal experience with students. They also felt that their classroom performance was not influenced by colleagues' or supervisors' opinions.

Within each institutional type, faculty underscored the importance of knowledge about their discipline in determining the effectiveness of their teaching. The investigators point out that the academic as expert dominates the responses from faculty. The image of the professor as one who transmits knowledge is a primary characteristic of faculty role, and the dominant method for transmitting this knowledge is the lecture. As one might expect, teaching was perceived as a basis for reward in those institutions in which teaching is the major activity for faculty. Faculty in research universities reported that publication and obtaining research funds were the most rewarded activities. Participants in faculty development efforts tended to be younger faculty from both tenured and nontenured ranks, and women appeared to be more likely to have engaged in faculty development activities than men.

Among the most frequently mentioned types of program activities in which faculty participated were on-campus workshops, although this type of activity received the lowest productivity rankings. Leaves were judged by faculty to be the most productive faculty development activity. Faculty indicated that increased interaction with peers represented a highly effective program outcome, as did support or confirmation of already established ideas and practices.

Blackburn et al. (1980) concluded that the tendency for faculty improvement programs to concentrate on the faculty member's instructional role may have been overemphasized and misdirected. Faculty did not indicate, in their responses to the questions asked of them in this study, the belief that higher education is infected by poor teaching. Although faculty may support instructional improvement programs, they do so generally because they believe their colleagues need such activities and not themselves. The major concerns that faculty have about teaching relate to needs to keep up in one's discipline. This represented the single most important factor in superior teaching as judged by the faculty studied. Although faculty rate workshops as helpful in stimulating awareness about teaching, they feel consultation with colleagues or experts to be superior for initiating attitudinal changes. According to these investigators:

Faculty development experts tend to equate faculty development with enhancing faculty instructional skills to the exclusion both of content specialization and attention to other aspects of the faculty role. It is here that faculty most profoundly disagree. Faculty perceive their professional development needs to be far broader than those accommodated by most faculty development programs. For example, concern for increasing one's skill in the area of research and scholarship seems to be particularly acute at this time. This probably reflects both a natural desire on the part of faculty to broaden their professional lives as well as a realistic response to changing pressures within their institutional reward structures.

From the perspective of faculty, then, it is the other professional development needs—as well as some personal ones—that faculty development programs need to focus on more. (Blackburn et al., 1980, p. 48)

Additional studies of faculty development programs abound in the literature on higher education. Support from private foundations such as the Exxon Foundation, Lilly Endowment, Danforth Foundation, Andrew W. Mellon Foundation, W. K. Kellogg Foundation, and Bush Foundation has provided project reports, many of which are available through the Educational Resources Information Center (ERIC). The Fund for the Improvement of Postsecondary Education (FIPSE) has been the major federal source of funds for faculty development programs. Bunting (1980) reports on the lessons learned from FIPSE funding. The activities of the W. K. Kellogg Foundation are delineated in reports edited by Lindquist (1978, 1979). The PIRIT Project, sponsored by the Society for Values in Higher Education and funded by FIPSE, is discussed by Gaff (1978).

Development and Faculty Careers. A number of authors who write about faculty development focus on career patterns as a mechanism for analyzing appropriate strategies and interventions to stimulate effective faculty behaviors (Baldwin, 1979; Mathis, 1974). These authors point out that professional development for academicians should begin at the time individuals are preparing for careers in higher education. Interventions during the graduate preparation of a future faculty member have received some attention in the literature. Carroll (1977, 1980) summarizes much of the research on the effects of training programs for teaching assistants. He concludes that most studies demonstrate a positive relationship between some form of preteaching preparation experience for teaching assistants and the effectiveness of their later activities in the classroom. He also points out that many of the studies merely describe training programs for teaching assistants and that few empirical investigations are available to assess the effects of training on specific teaching behaviors at a later point in time. Little attention has been given to cognitive or affective gains in teaching assistants as a result of in-service training experiences. Many universities now offer formal training experiences for credit available to anyone pursuing a Ph.D. Such experiences help prepare prospective academicians for their teaching responsibilities in a first academic appointment.

A second point of intervention for professional development of faculty is during the initial years of a faculty member's first appointment, or subsequent appointments, before tenure has been acquired. Faculty development activities designed to improve instructional competence tend to be sought more frequently by young faculty. An increasing mode of development activity for first-year faculty is an opportunity to become aware of the expectations that the institution sets for professional advancement and how these expectations might best be met through the resources that the institution has to offer. Growth contracts and professional development plans constitute one strategy that is finding increasingly frequent use, not only for faculty at all ages but especially for young faculty members who are in need of specific guidance (Pfnister, Solder, & Verroca, 1979). Hodgkinson (1974) has discussed the importance of a mentor for younger faculty members. Research by Cooper (1980) on the socialization of graduate students in political science departments underscores the importance of sponsorship as a way of shaping the attitudes of graduate students. Hodgkinson points out that the availability of a mentor who can help younger faculty develop priorities about the direction of their careers is an important variable in determining later productivity.

Faculty development during the middle and later years of one's career has not received the attention it deserves. The career goals of a nontenured faculty member are different in many ways from those of a person who needs to maintain a productive career after the security of tenure has been attained. Incentives that were important when the faculty member initiated a career may no longer be motivating forces for maintaining that career. The future of higher education, at least for the next ten years, indicates that faculty members will change jobs less frequently and that the membership of individual faculties will change less often than in the past. This steady-state pool of workers in higher education will be essential elements in an institution's ability to maintain vitality and productivity during periods of transition from a time of growth to a time of maintenance and retrenchment. The midcareer problems of established faculty are faculty development issues of a different order from those that interest graduate students and younger faculty. Established faculty members have demonstrated some degree of productivity in establishing their careers. Their needs relate to finding ways for maintaining motivation and productivity in a context that limits the possibility for new experiences. Faculty development efforts for midcareer personnel should include mechanisms for permitting them to have new and different experiences for limited periods of time as they approach retirement.

One aspect of faculty career patterns that is only now beginning to receive attention relates to those individuals who are preparing for retirement. These faculty seek professional development experiences to help them make the change from active participation in an academic community to either limited participation or commitment to an entirely different life-style. The increasing attention given in the literature to early retirement programs and to faculty development activities that include retirement counseling attests to the increasing significance of older faculty in institutions of higher education (Oi, 1979; Patton, 1979).

Another area of intervention for professional development concerns the responsibility of professional associations to help members who are academicians realize that the role of a faculty member includes obligations for effective teaching as well as creative scholarship. A number of projects in professional associations address this issue of assisting members of these associations who are involved in educational activities to become more effective teachers. Many disciplinary associations maintain divisions or sections that relate to the teaching of that discipline (Marty, 1976; Mauksch, 1980).

Of increasing interest is the responsibility of institutions to provide professional development programs for faculty members who are the victims of staff reduction or who may wish to change careers but have no mechanism to develop strategies for such a change. A study by the American Association for Higher Education (1981) provides a guide for campus activities relating to new options in career planning. A recent publication of the American Council on Education also addresses this issue (Furniss, 1981a, 1981b).

The relationship of faculty development to faculty productivity over time has not received the attention it deserves. Assessments of the effectiveness of faculty development strategies using faculty productivity as a criterion have not as yet been attempted. Faculty productivity is difficult to define and evaluate in ways that capture the multivariate nature of faculty role behaviors and how they interact relative to the quality of educational and scholarly efforts. If one seeks to relate faculty behaviors to educational outcomes for students, few studies have attempted to assess the wide range of outcomes suggested by Bowen (1977), Heath (1976, 1977), Pace (1979), Solmon and Ochsner (1978), or Wilson et al. (1975). The diverse beliefs, values, and attitudes that faculty have about a wide range of concerns and interests have been documented substantially (Ladd, 1979; Ladd & Lipset, 1975), but the relationship of these characteristics to productivity has not been effectively demonstrated. Ladd (1979) asserts that the model for academe that views faculty primarily as scholars and researchers, and rewards them accordingly, is seriously out of touch with the teaching model in which most faculty perceive teaching and educational activities as the dominant role attribute. Studies of faculty attributes suggest that role conflict, such as that between research and teaching, is a major issue that faculty development programs should address (Zacharias, 1981).

Investigations of faculty productivity by Blackburn (1979) underscore the central role of the institution in determining what is meant by productivity. He concludes that the productivity of faculty is predictable when one takes into consideration differences across types of institutions and between disciplines, differences that result from the nature of academic work, and differences between men and women. The effective use of time, says Blackburn, can influence productivity. Change in the nature of work over an entire career can have a motivational effect that stimulates productivity. A popular misconception about faculty productivity is that academicians are more productive during their younger years. Blackburn has found that productive faculty tend to remain productive. He has also found that the distance between productive and nonproductive faculty tends to increase over time. In addition, he points out that mentorship and sponsorship are important factors in initiating a productive career in higher education. Cooper (1980) has also found that sponsorship is a critical factor in determining the direction of an academic career. According to Blackburn, intrinsic rewards appear to have more value than extrinsic rewards in stimulating productivity. This relationship between rewards and productivity in higher education has not been ignored by researchers (Lewis & Becker, 1979). The results of a wide range of studies, however, leave much to be desired in providing answers that encompass the vast domain of institutional differences represented by postsecondary education in the United States and other developed countries.

Those responsible for the development of policies in higher education relating to the quality and diversity of educational and research efforts should give professional development for faculty a high priority during the years ahead. Faculty development has become an accepted fact in all the institutional types classified as postsecondary. The goals for faculty development range from focused concern with teacher-student interactions in community colleges (O'Banion, 1977) to the conflict in reward systems in research universities that favor scholarship and research in a climate that also demands effective teaching (Baldwin, 1979). To this diversity of needs and expectations can be added the wide range of issues in the forefront of research on higher education. These emphasize, as never before, the interactions between personal dimensions (teacher, student, administrator), curricular dimensions, and organizational dimensions as solutions are sought to maintain and improve quality (Chickering & Associates, 1981).

The conditions in higher education that stimulated the growth of faculty development programs during the 1970s will not disappear during the 1980s (Mortimer & Tierney, 1979). Policy issues in the postsecondary sector will increasingly be concerned with faculty productivity, the quality of educational programs, and the management of steady-state environments. Faculty development programs should continue to provide a context in which opportunities for professional growth are available for faculty. It is hoped that the 1980s will witness an expansion of research in this area.

B. Claude Mathis

See also Academic Freedom and Tenure; Evaluation of Teachers; In-Service Teacher Education; Supervision of Teachers; Teacher Centers; Teacher Selection and Retention; Teaching Styles.

REFERENCES

Alexander, L. T., & Yelon, S. L. (Eds.). *Instructional Development Agencies in Higher Education.* East Lansing: Michigan State University, Educational Development Program, 1972.

American Association for Higher Education. *Faculty Careers, New Options: A Guide to Campus Activities.* Washington, D.C.: The Association, 1981.

Axelrod, J. *The University Teacher as Artist.* San Francisco: Jossey-Bass, 1973.

Baldwin, R. Adult and career development: What are the implications for faculty? In *Current Issues in Higher Education* (No. 2). Washington, D.C.: American Association for Higher Education, 1979.

Bergquist, W. H., & Phillips, S. R. Components of an effective faculty development program. *Journal of Higher Education,* 1975, *46,* 177–211.

Bergquist, W. H., & Shoemaker, W. A. (Eds.). A comprehensive approach to institutional development. In *New Directions for Higher Education* (No. 15). San Francisco: Jossey-Bass, 1976.

Blackburn, R. T. Academic careers: Patterns and possibilities. In *Current Issues in Higher Education* (No. 2). Washington, D.C.: American Association for Higher Education, 1979.

Blackburn, R. T.; Pellino, G. R.; Boberg, A.; & O'Connell, G. Are instructional improvement programs off-target? In *Current Issues in Higher Education* (Vol. 2, No. 1). Washington, D.C.: American Association for Higher Education, 1980.

Bowen, H. R. *Investment in Learning.* San Francisco: Jossey-Bass, 1977.

Brown, D. G., & Hanger, W. S. Pragmatics of faculty self-development. *Educational Record,* 1975, *56,* 201–206.

Bunting, C. I. Funding quality improvement: Lessons for FIPSE experiment. In *Current Issues in Higher Education* (Vol. 2,

No. 2). Washington, D.C.: American Association for Higher Education, 1980.

Carnegie Council on Policy Studies in Higher Education. *Three Thousand Futures.* San Francisco: Jossey-Bass, 1980.

Carroll, J. G. Assessing the effectiveness of a training program for the university teaching assistant. *Teaching of Psychology,* 1977, *4,* 135–137.

Carroll, J. G. Effects of training programs for university teaching assistants: A review of empirical research. *Journal of Higher Education,* 1980, *51,* 167–183.

Centra, J. A. *Strategies for Improving College Teaching* (ERIC/ Higher Education Research Report No. 8). Washington, D.C.: American Association for Higher Education, 1972. (ERIC Document Reproduction Service No. ED 071 616)

Centra, J. A. *Faculty Development Practices in U.S. Colleges and Universities.* Princeton, N.J.: Educational Testing Service, 1976. (ERIC Document Reproduction Service No. ED 141 382)

Centra, J. A. College enrollments in the 1980s: Projections and possibilities. *Journal of Higher Education,* 1980, *51,* 18–39. (a)

Centra, J. A. *Determining Faculty Effectiveness.* San Francisco: Jossey-Bass, 1980. (b)

Chickering, A. W., & Associates. *The Modern American College.* San Francisco: Jossey-Bass, 1981.

Cooper, E. P. *An Examination of the Multiple Influences Affecting the Development of Faculty-Student Sponsorship Relationships in Two Elite Political Science Departments.* Unpublished doctoral dissertation, Northwestern University, 1980.

Crow, M. L.; Milton, O.; Moomaw, W. E.; & O'Connell, W. R., Jr. *Faculty Development Centers in Southern Universities.* Atlanta: Southern Regional Education Board, 1976. (ERIC Document Reproduction Service No. ED 129 132)

Davis, R. H. A behavioral change model with implications for faculty development. *Higher Education,* 1979, *8,* 123–140.

Eble, K. E. *Career Development of the Effective College Teacher.* Washington, D.C.: American Association of University Professors, 1971. (a) (ERIC Document Reproduction Service No. ED 089 630)

Eble, K. E. *The Recognition and Evaluation of Teaching.* Washington, D.C.: American Association of University Professors, 1971. (b) (ERIC Document Reproduction Service No. ED 046 350)

Eble, K. E. *Professors as Teachers.* San Francisco: Jossey-Bass, 1972.

Eble, K. E. *The Craft of Teaching.* San Francisco: Jossey-Bass, 1976.

Ericksen, S. C., & Cook, J. A. (Eds.). *Support for Teaching at Major Universities.* Ann Arbor: University of Michigan, Center for Research on Learning and Teaching, 1979. (ERIC Document Reproduction Service No. ED 180 312)

Francis, J. V. How do we get there from here? *Journal of Higher Education,* 1975, *46,* 719–732.

Freedman, M. (Ed.). Facilitating faculty development. In *New Directions for Higher Education* (Vol. 1, No. 1). San Francisco: Jossey-Bass, 1973.

Freedman, M.; Brown, W.; Ralph, N.; Shukraft, R.; Bloom, M.; & Sanford, N. *Academic Culture and Faculty Development.* Orinda, Calif.: Montaigne Press, 1980.

Furniss, W. T. New opportunities for faculty members. *Educational Record,* 1981, *62*(1), 8–15. (a)

Furniss, W. T. *Reshaping Faculty Careers.* Washington, D.C.: American Council on Education, 1981. (b)

Gaff, J. G. *Toward Faculty Renewal.* San Francisco: Jossey-Bass, 1975.

Gaff, J. G. (Ed.). Institutional renewal through the improvement of teaching. In *New Directions for Higher Education* (No. 24). San Francisco: Jossey-Bass, 1978.

Glenny, L. A. Demographic and related issues for higher education in the 1980s. In *Journal of Higher Education,* 1980, *51,* 363–380.

Group for Human Development in Higher Education. *Faculty Development in a Time of Retrenchment.* New Rochelle, N.Y.: *Change* Magazine Press, 1974.

Heath, D. C. What the enduring effects of higher education tell us about a liberal education. *Journal of Higher Education,* 1976, *47,* 173–190.

Heath, D. C. Academic predictors of adult maturity and competence. *Journal of Higher Education,* 1977, *48,* 613–632.

Hodgkinson, H. L. Adult development: Implications for faculty and administrators. *Educational Record,* 1974, *55,* 263–274.

Kozma, R. B. Faculty development and the adoption and diffusion of classroom innovations. *Journal of Higher Education,* 1978, *49,* 438–449.

Ladd, E. C., Jr. The work experience of American college professors: Some data and an argument. *Current Issues in Higher Education* (No. 2). Washington, D.C.: American Association for Higher Education, 1979. (ERIC Document Reproduction Service No. ED 184 406)

Ladd, E. C., Jr., & Lipset, S. M. *The Divided Academy: Professors and Politics.* New York: McGraw-Hill, 1975.

Lewis, D. R., & Becker, W. E., Jr. *Academic Rewards in Higher Education.* Cambridge, Mass.: Ballinger, 1979.

Lindquist, J. (Ed.). *Designing Teaching Improvement Programs.* Washington, D.C.: Council for the Advancement of Small Colleges, 1978.

Lindquist, J. (Ed.). *Increasing the Impact.* Battle Creek, Mich.: W. K. Kellogg Foundation, 1979.

Martin, W. B. Faculty development as human development. *Liberal Education,* 1975, *61,* 187–196.

Martin, W. B. The limits to diversity. *Change,* December–January 1978–1979, 41–45.

Marty, M. A. Disciplinary associations and faculty development. In D. W. Vermilye (Ed.), *Individualizing the System.* San Francisco: Jossey-Bass, 1976.

Mathis, B. C. *Persuading the Institution to Experiment: Strategies for Seduction.* Evanston, Ill.: Northwestern University, Center for the Teaching Professions, 1974. (ERIC Document Reproduction Service No. ED 158 683)

Mathis, B. C. Academic careers and adult development: A nexus for research. In *Current Issues in Higher Education* (No. 2). Washington, D.C.: American Association for Higher Education, 1979.

Mathis, B. C. Evaluating the effectiveness of teaching. In E. H. Loveland (Ed.), *Measuring the Hard-to-Measure: New Directions for Program Evaluation* (No. 6). San Francisco: Jossey-Bass, 1980. (a)

Mathis, B. C. What happened to research on college teaching? *Journal of Teacher Education,* March–April 1980, *31*(2), 17–21. (b)

Mauksch, H. O. What are obstacles to improving quality teaching? In *Current Issues in Higher Education* (Vol. 2, No. 1). Washington, D.C.: American Association for Higher Education, 1980.

McKeachie, W. J., & Kulik, J. A. Effective college teaching. In

F. N. Kerlinger (Ed.), *Review of Research in Education* (Vol. 3). Itasca, Ill.: F. E. Peacock, 1975.

Menges, R. J. Teaching improvement strategies: How effective are they? In *Current Issues in Higher Education* (Vol. 2, No. 1). Washington, D.C.: American Association for Higher Education, 1980.

Menges, R. J. Instructional methods. In A. W. Chickering & Associates, *The Modern American College.* San Francisco: Jossey-Bass, 1981.

Milton, O., & Associates. *On College Teaching.* San Francisco: Jossey-Bass, 1978.

Mortimer, K. P., & Tierney, M. L. *The Three "R's" of the Eighties: Reduction, Reallocation, and Retrenchment* (ERIC/Higher Education Research Report No. 4). Washington, D.C.: American Association for Higher Education, 1979. (ERIC Document Reproduction Service No. ED 172 642)

Nelsen, W. C. Faculty development: Prospects and potential for the 1980s. *Liberal Education,* 1979, *65,* 141–149.

Nelsen, W. C., & Siegel, M. E. (Eds.). *Effective Approaches to Faculty Development.* Washington, D.C.: Association of American Colleges, 1980.

O'Banion, T. Development staff potential. In *New Directions for Community Colleges* (No. 19). San Francisco: Jossey-Bass, 1977.

Oi, W. Y. Academic tenure and mandatory retirement under the new law. *Science,* 1979, *206,* 1373–1378.

Pace, C. R. *Measuring Outcomes of College.* San Francisco: Jossey-Bass, 1979.

Patton, C. V. *Academia in Transition: Mid-career Change or Early Retirement.* Cambridge, Mass.: Abt, 1979.

Pfnister, A. O.; Solder, J.; & Verroca, N. Growth contracts: Viable strategy for institutional planning under changing conditions? In *Current Issues in Higher Education.* Washington, D.C.: American Association for Higher Education, 1979.

Riesman, D. *On Higher Education.* San Francisco: Jossey-Bass, 1980.

Shulman, C. H. *Old Expectations, New Realities: The Academic Professions Revisited* (ERIC/Higher Education Research Report No. 2). Washington, D.C.: American Association for Higher Education, 1979. (ERIC Document Reproduction Service No. ED 169 874)

Simerly, R. Ways to view faculty development. *Educational Technology,* February 1977, *17*(2), 47–49.

Smith, A. B. *Faculty Development and Evaluation in Higher Education* (ERIC/Higher Education Research Report No. 8). Washington, D.C.: American Association for Higher Education, 1976. (ERIC Document Reproduction Service No. ED 132 891)

Solmon, L. C., & Ochsner, N. New findings on the effects of college. In *Current Issues in Higher Education.* Washington, D.C.: American Association for Higher Education, 1978.

Toombs, W. A three-dimensional view of faculty development. *Journal of Higher Education,* 1975, *46,* 701–717.

Weathersby, R. P., & Tarule, J. M. *Adult Development: Implications for Higher Education* (ERIC/Higher Education Research Report No. 4). Washington, D.C.: American Association for Higher Education, 1980. (ERIC Document Reproduction Service No. ED 191 382)

Wilson, R. C.; Gaff, J. G.; Dienst, E. R.; Wood, L.; & Bavry, J. L. *College Professors and Their Impact on Students.* New York: Wiley, 1975.

Zacharias, M. K. *Role Conflict in Academe.* Unpublished doctoral dissertation, Northwestern University, 1981.

FAMILY STUDIES

Scholars have only recently begun to focus systematically on the family as an educational institution. Education scholars, whether psychologists, sociologists, anthropologists, political scientists, historians, or statisticians, have traditionally focused on schools, giving only passing attention to the family as an educational setting (Cremin, 1974; Finkelstein, 1977). Similarly, scholars of the family have typically defined education as the work of schools rather than families. Although scholars have studied psychological, cognitive, or moral processes within the family and have explored the family as an economic, political, or cultural instrumentality and as an agency of child rearing, education has only been implicit in their awareness and in their descriptions of the family as an educational unit. Hence, present knowledge about the family as an educational institution has been derived only indirectly from such studies (Leichter, 1975).

In this article, "education" is defined as an interactive process by means of which teaching and learning take place, sometimes casually and simultaneously, sometimes not. Matters of teaching and learning might be technical, intellectual, or moral. They might be understood as attempts to transmit or transform culture, to allocate and distribute resources, to organize or reinforce structures of authority, to evoke sensibility and feeling, to inform consciousness and identity, and to transmit status. Whether they are understood to be psychologically, politically, or economically meaningful, educational encounters among family members and with agencies external to the family are ultimately interactive, dialectical, two-way exchanges, involving both teachers and learners, both teaching and learning (Finkelstein, 1979).

The following presentation of a literature of family studies reflects a belief that the systematic study of educational processes, rather than of intentions or results, should both convey the complexity of the family as an educational institution and reveal the nature and direction of family studies in education.

Strictly speaking, there are no comprehensive family studies in education. Instead, there are identifiable clusters of studies, each harboring different definitions of education and of the family, probing different problems, using various methodologies, drawing different conclusions, and identifying discrete aspects of family life to illuminate.

First, there are studies illuminating the variety of constraints and possibilities that organize and inform the very terms by which family members relate to one another, and through which educative influences are made manifest and educational processes proceed. Work in the history of the family is exemplary. Families might be organized in nuclear units, extended units, or household units. They might compose wide networks of extended kin, or simply the conjugal unit—mothers, fathers, and unmarried children. Family members might spend most of their time engaging together in the production, distribution, and con-

sumption of goods. They might come together only to eat or drink or play, rather than to work. Families might organize intense daily interactive environment, or they might exist primarily in order to produce children and transmit property and status. They might be more or less important agencies of moral nurture, more or less influential in the cultivation of sensibility, more or less powerful organizers of intellect, consciousness, belief, and meaning, or more or less responsible for child rearing and the completion of social tasks. Families might be more or less free to define their own experience and exercise choice. In short, the work of the family as an educational agency as complex as it is subject to change. Such, at any rate, is the burden of historical studies of the family.

Second, there are studies projecting the family as an autonomous unit in which human development is importantly shaped, molded, formed, or evoked. Focusing on the internal dynamics of the family, most particularly on relationships between nature and culture, family studies of this sort proceed on the assumption that the family is particularly powerful and therefore an independent educational institution.

Third, there are studies that view the family as a mediating agency—screening outside influences on the one hand, and contributing to educational and occupational achievement on the other. Studies of the family's contribution to outcomes of schooling are exemplary and regnant.

No matter which kind of study, what mode of investigation, or what normative framework, each cluster of studies provides only partial knowledge of the workings of the family. Each illuminates particular aspects of its functioning. Each assigns and weighs the importance of the family as an educational institution differently. Each necessarily reifies—that is, abstracts but objectifies in ways that tend to oversimplify the family's complexities and to obscure one or another of its educative dimensions. Finally, each cluster of studies contributes to the construction of what Geertz (1973) has called "templates or blueprints of experience," which may mystify at the same time as they may illuminate.

Historical Studies.   Since 1960, historians have joined in the general clamor over the fate of the family during the twentieth century. Evolving rapidly during the last twenty-year period, in which the imminent death of the family was simultaneously mourned, celebrated, predicted, and denied, the study of familial institutions in history promised new and important insights into the relative permanence of any of their features.

One of the more important emphases that has emerged in the last twenty years centers on relationships between parents and dependent children as they have evolved over time, a subject that had been typically ignored by historians of education (Cremin, 1970, 1974, 1980; Finkelstein, 1979).

The classic treatments of family history, reflected in the works of Calhoun (1918) Goodsell (1934), made no mention of fundamental changes in parent-child relationships, although they were abundantly attentive to the dynamics of relationships between men and women within the family. Enormously interested, as most family historians have been, in the effects of industrialization on modern life, they constructed a picture of family change that might be described as follows.

The preindustrial family was an undifferentiated sprawling, extended, patrilineal kinship network. It was distinguished by the power of its patriarchy and by its capacity to prepare rising generations for all the duties and requirements of life. Embedded in a lifelong matrix of daily face-to-face associations (on the land) where the boundaries between families and community were permeable, and the status of women and children was fixed and inferior, the family had been a large, hierarchical, authoritarian, partriarchal, self-contained unit of material production—an influential unit of cultural transmission and individual welfare.

As historians like Goodsell and Calhoun viewed it, the coming of industrialization changed all of that. Work moved the orbit of the household into factories controlled by outsiders. Undermining the influence of extended kinship networks, the rising industrial establishment increased the importance of small, mobile nuclear family units. As the family contracted into a nuclear core and households became smaller, the elaborate interpretation of family and work community disappeared. So, too, did hierarchical relationships between men and women, and personal associations in the marketplace.

The modern household, under the impact of industrialization, became a specialized agency. Family members in the new industrial order were bound together by natural bonds of affection rather than by material concerns. Built on a companionate base—a freely chosen voluntary arrangement of men and women—the nuclear family came to serve as an especially important historical focus of psychological devotion and loyalty. In the new industrial order, these historians implied, mothers and children acquired new status and authority. What is more, the family, through a process of structural functional differentiation, became a social unit specializing in love (Burgess, Locke, & Thomas, 1971). Since the family was unable to sustain the whole of the burden of initiating children into society, schools emerged, as eventually did welfare institutions and hospitals, to take up the social burdens once borne by the family (Parsons & Bales, 1955).

Assuming the universality of loving concern for the welfare and instruction of the young, historians did not examine either the attitudes of parents toward their children nor the character of instruction in families.

Parent-child relationships. A dramatic change in perspective has came about with the emergence of a veritable deluge of historical studies that both reflect and advance a certain skepticism about the universality of sentiment and nurture among parents and children, and most especially between mothers and their offspring. In a world where well-educated, affluent young people were turning their backs to their families, mothers of young children were leaving their homes in droves to go to work, and where the halls of academe were being breached by the sons and daughters of diverse immigrant and working-class groups, it made no sense to consider the nuclear family as fixed in its dynamic processes or to characterize it as free of tension, conflict, and ambiguity. Nor did it make sense to ignore its possibilities and limitations as an agency of instruction for the young. Hence, the travels of a new breed of historians into the unchartered waters of family relationships.

The matrix of daily associations in which family life is embedded has been an important focus and object of study for historians seeking to account for the fate of the nuclear family. No longer able to assume that close relationships between parents and children are inevitable and necessary, historians since 1960 have paid close attention to the capacity as well as the willingness of parents to persuade and to define the educational universe of their children.

In an imaginative and provocative work, *Centuries of Childhood*, Ariès (1962) concluded that the influence of parents over their children in matters of education was neither inevitable nor necessary, but provisional—dependent on ability to notice children as different from adults and in need of protection, restraint, and special vigilance. Concentrating his analysis on the character of family life in France as it was evolving over a long stretch of time from the twelfth century to the present, Ariès distinguished modern from medieval life in terms of, among other things, parents' roles in child rearing. In medieval society, the conjugal family ensured the transmission of property and name. But it did not involve parents in the careful nurture of their young, nor did it serve as a focus of devotion and loyalty for anyone. Nor was it differentiated, even in space, from the rest of society.

Sociability was the most representative characteristic of medieval society. Life proceeded in public, as a kind of polymorphous, undifferentiated collective endeavor, involving people of all ages and classes together in the business of life. After a period of relative neglect and indifferent nurture, children, starting around the age of 7, became part of this polymorphous tribe, living and working alongside adults, seeing, hearing, and observing what adults saw, heard, or said. Observing what he described as a precocious quality in the nature of their participation with adults, Ariès concluded that parents had no particular awareness of the nature of childhood, no detailed programs for the raising of children. They harbored no conception of childhood as a distinct and prolonged stage in the life cycle requiring isolation, protection, supervision, or special social arrangements. They did not seek to protect and instruct systematically. Childhood, in short, had not been discovered, nor, he might have added, had "parenthood" in the modern sense.

Gradually, over the course of several centuries, childhood was constructed, by human agency and human action. It involved the discovery of children as a class of people who were different from adults—vulnerable and in need of protection, restraint, and parental supervision. This discovery initiated a strategic retreat of conjugal families from the polymorphous world of medieval sociability. It initiated a reconstruction of schools, transforming them into regulatory agencies as well as Latin-learning centers. Ariès did not seek to detail the processes by which nuclear families became differentiated social units and the school became a disciplinary, regulatory, age-graded institution. But he did identify an emerging tendency to regulate the lives of the young and to control the networks of association in which they would develop. He perceived the dawn of a new era in which the family and other groups in society would vie with one another for the hearts and minds of the younger generation.

Ariès also created a new understanding of the modern nuclear family. It had emerged before industrialization, among "notabilities," as he called the emerging middle classes. Its emergence proceeded simultaneously with a massive internal reform of Catholic schools, which were fast becoming regulatory institutions. And, most important, it was distinguished from the traditional family, not only by its size and function, but by its insistence on privacy and by the quality, character, and intensity of relationships between parents and their children. Providing the means by which parents could watch over and guide their children, the modern family was distinguished by the totality of responsibility that it would assume for the moral, spiritual, and intellectual instruction of children. For Ariès, it was characterized as well by a kind of selfish privatism. The family, in his words, had seceded from public life. Its children had been quarantined, first by parents within the family and then by teachers in schools. The conscious regulation of life had begun.

Building on the pioneering work of Ariès, Stone (1977) described a similar pattern in England. Like the emerging middle-class family in France, the conjugal family of middling England was characterized by its ability to control and contain the influence on the young of village collectives, village customs, kin advice, and aristocratic patronage. Withdrawing into itself, the bourgeois family that emerged was not only a relatively self-contained unit of economic production and patriarchal authority, but in England, where Puritans and Protestants were powerful, a bastion of moral authority as well. If it did not entirely replace the church, the middling Protestant household had become a place in which character would be formed, morals molded, and literacy learned, and in which devotional piety would become a daily, ritually elaborated form of association between parents and children. Engaged in a "campaign to domesticate the holy spirit," Protestants generally, and Puritans in particular, defined the family rather than the village as a fundamental agent of spiritual nurture, literary education, and social control. To paraphrase Stone: The household replaced the parish . . . as a main agent of moral indoctrination. . . . It displaced

the church as a focus for communal activities and for the discipline of disobedient children and servants. The family head was the inheritor of the power of church.

Stone might have added that the child was the heir of a tutorial family and long periods of schooling as well (Finkelstein, 1979). In England and in France among bourgeois and high-born families, parents had become primary agents in the socialization of children, introducing them to basic forms of civilized living, shaping their values, forming their patterns of behavior, endowing them with manners and morals, and thus becoming the architects of childhood.

By 1700, the educative family was evident on American shores as well. It involved both fathers and mothers in close daily association with their offspring and with other families to whom children might be apprenticed. It was a family with primary authority and responsibility for child rearing. It was a family that provided fathers with near-dictatorial, if not toally unchallenged, power. It was a family that was legally responsible for moral, civil, occupational, technical, and intellectual matters of learning (Cremin, 1970; Demos, 1970; Axtell, 1974).

Profoundly different from traditional families that comprised the larger portion of humanity, the modern bourgeois family, as historians have told the tale, was seeking to disassociate itself and its children from the common mass of humanity and, in the process, to transform and "elevate," them from their less fortunate contemporaries.

Child-rearing advice. Engaging in what historians might describe as a form of domestic imperialism, bourgeois reformers created child-rearing manuals, tracts, and treatises that reflected their emerging concern with the young. Historians have traditionally studied an abundant and fascinating literature of advice in an attempt to understand the evolution of cultural traditions as they were mirrored in manuals of advice (Kuhn, 1947; Wishy, 1968).

During the 1970s, historians have attended to the "myth-making" possibilities of the child-rearing advice literature and its uses as an instrument of social control. An abundant and varied literature, it contained the injunctions of a varying group of domestic reformers. In the seventeenth century, advice to parents was rendered typically by Christian missionaries seeking to catechize native Americans or West African immigrants and their offspring (Cremin, 1974; Axtell, 1974). Or it was directed to fathers within the household when they seemed to fail in their responsibilities for the moral development of their children. In the nineteenth century, advice to parents was as likely to be written by moral reformers, evangelical Christians who, as they prescribed for and directed parents in the principles of domestic nurture, aimed to teach them how to prepare industrious citizens for an emerging nation (Kuhn, 1947, Wishy, 1968; Sklar, 1973). In the twentieth century, medical experts—social workers, psychoanalysts, psychologists, and pediatricians—entered the list of authorities advising parents how to bring up happy, healthy, high-achieving youngsters.

Over the past decade, historians have begun to define child-rearing advice literature as an ideological weapon, a powerful instrument of persuasion through which one group seeks to dominate another and fix their inferior status. Exploring nurture literature dynamically and functionally, they implicitly view it as a negative educational persuader—a source of myths and mystifications.

Badinter (1980), in an important study of French family policy from the eighteenth to the twentieth century, detects in the advice literature issuing from the French scientific establishment a myth of maternal instinct, which has fixed women in an inferior status. Stripped of economic power, and cast as the natural guardians of the young, women, she argues, were miscast as vessels of maternal instinct. Providing successive examples of feminine ambivalence toward children and of indifference, if not hostility, toward the young, Badinter seeks to demonstrate that maternal instinct is neither natural nor universal, but learned and historical, subject to manipulation, a tool in the subjugation of women.

Similarly, through a study of child-rearing advice in popular literature, historians have alluded to "a cult of true womanhood" emerging in the nineteenth century in the United States (Welter, 1966). Fixing women in an idyllic household, reformers articulated a norm of maternal perfection. By virtue of their inherent gentleness and moral superiority to men, women were held to be the only fit guardians for young children. The ideal household was projected as one that required the social isolation of mother and child and an intensification of their relationship. It was one in which mothers protected children from the contagions of unhealthful influence (Finkelstein, 1979; Mulligan, 1975). It placed mothers in a position of strategic importance for the developing sensibility of children. And it encouraged women to desist from seeking power in the marketplace or polling place, and even from cultivating their minds (Welter, 1966).

Studying a plethora of child-rearing advice issuing from physicians, psychologists, social workers, and social scientists in the twentieth century, Lasch (1979a, 1979b) saw in the advice of child counselors a justification and mystification of the fact that families had been transformed—from being relatively powerful institutions of economic production and cultural transmission to relatively impotent units of consumption in which children were being prepared to be consumers by becoming pleasure seekers. Through advice enjoining women to be attentive to the desires of their children and to minister conscientiously to their needs in the name of healthy personality development, twentieth-century child counselors misrepresented parents as omnipotent molders of personality, responsible for securing harmony and order within their household. Projecting a norm of family harmony, defining the home as a haven, counselors had in fact furthered the work of family disintegration in the name of parental omnipotence.

Coming to the relationships between child-rearing pre-scriptions and social change in a somewhat different manner, Donzelot (1979) has seen the hand of domestic reformers at work in two ways: in the construction of child-rearing norms and also in the forming of political coalitions and public policy.

Not content or comfortable with the view that families are the unwilling victims of social imposition, nor even with the assumption that they are coherent political units, Donzelot distinguished two channels of ideological diffusion: one voluntary, arising from within the family itself, and the other systematic and institutional, involving the construction of policies designed, at least initially, to police the lower orders of society.

Convinced by medical experts, or so Donzelot assumed, that their proper sphere was in the home, mothers heeded medical advice enjoining them to free children from the allegedly stifling grip of domestic servants and social promiscuities and construct around the children an educative model. Converts to the notion that children needed the exclusive guiding hand of their mothers in their early years, women willingly engaged children in what Donzelot described as a process of protected liberation.

As Donzelot sees it, the work of ideological diffusion proceeded along a different channel and through a different process for children of the urban lower classes. Unable to effect domestic reform among the lower orders of society, child-saving coalitions lent their influence to the construction of institutional stimulations and constraints. They helped to constitute public means of removing children from households, bringing them under the control of courts, which would then place them out. Using the emergence of the juvenile justice system to illustrate the process, Donzelot, like Schlossman (1977), Hawes (1971), and A. Platt (1969) before him, described the workings of the state acting *in loco parentis*. Abrogating in their own favor powers that families had hitherto exercised over the young, the courts justified the transfer of custody as serving the best interests of the child and society. And then they went on to treat their wards, not as prisoners in need of lawyers, but as juveniles in need of protection and supervision. In stripping away the right of counsel, they had completed an effective substitution of public for private control, installing judges as fathers and social workers as mothers.

The high wall of patriarchal authority that had enclosed the family in preindustrial eighteenth-century western Europe and America had been breached and then dismantled, to be replaced, in Donzelot's view, by the rise of a paternalistic state in the nineteenth and twentieth centuries (Glasser et al., 1978; Grob, 1979).

Institutionalization of childhood. Similar themes have punctuated the work of historians exploring the diffusion and institutionalization of ideas about childhood and child rearing in the nineteenth and twentieth centuries. The construction of what Donzelot called "tutelary complexes," those age-stratified, specialized institutions of child rearing have been the product of deliberate effort of child-savers to transfer control of children's lives from private to public authority, from parents to experts.

The hand of moral reformers and child-rearing experts was at work in successive attempts to restrict child labor and compel school attendance (Tyack, 1974; Kaestle & Vinovskis, 1978). It was made manifest when truancy became a punishable offense, justifying an intrusion of social workers and truant officers into family affairs (Tyack, 1974). It was evident in the construction of industrial schools in the early decades of the nineteenth century to house status offenders—boys and girls who had been picked up for prostitution, vagrancy, loitering, or vagabondage (Brenzel, 1980). It was evident in federally constructed boarding schools housing kidnapped native American boys and girls in need of detribalization, or, as federal legislators put it, "a primer and a hoe" (Finkelstein, 1977). It was evident in attempts by urban social reformers to organize children's play in the cities, in the period 1890–1920 (Cavallo, 1981). It was evident in the emergence of "delinquency" as a category and the juvenile court's acting in place of the parent (Schlossman, 1977). It was evident in the popularization and expansion of high schools in the progressive era, when "architects of adolescence" provided psychological justifications for extending and regularizing the period of dependency to include the teenage years (Kett, 1977). It was evident, as well, in the parent education movement in the 1970s (Schlossman, 1976; cf. Rothman, 1981).

There are studies proceeding from different assumptions about relationships governing parents and children in premodern societies, justifying an entirely different rendering of child-rearing exhortations, institutional arrangements, and public policies (Axinn, Glassberg, & Cenci, 1974). In an essay that has sent waves of discomfort through the historical profession, deMause (1974) explored modes of child rearing as they were reflected in relationships between parents and children from biblical times to the present. Using psychoanalytic concepts to interpret what he found, he characterized premodern Western culture as invariably abusive, neglectful, utterly without scruple in the treatment of children. Children were victims of murder, rape, incest, and debauchery. Free of regulatory restraints, the lives of the young were a nightmare from which they had only begun to emerge in the nineteenth and twentieth centuries.

Using this sort of perspective, other historians have been less quick to condemn attempts to exercise regulatory restraint on certain families. Exploring relationships between child abuse, public policy, and child rearing in America, Wyatt-Brown (1981), for example, distinguished three traditions of child rearing among Anglo-American and Celtic American families. Some were more violence-prone than others, using techniques of child nurture that were more or less likely to involve child beating. Implicitly making the point that experts and reformers might not have been wrong in their efforts to curb abuse, Wyatt-Brown seeks to correct critics of the paternalistic state,

while at the same time revealing the variability and complexity of American child-rearing practices within the family.

Perhaps formulating a few myths of their own, mainstream historians have proceeded on the assumption that the modern family is best understood as a besieged institution, mired willy-nilly in economic and political processes beyond its control and even its consciousness (Zuckerman, 1978; Finkelstein & Clignet, 1981). A few historians, not content to treat the family as a mere economic or political reflection or, as some have put it, a dependent variable, have begun systematically to explore whether, or in what ways, families might have been constrained by the force of political, economic, and ideological circumstances.

Family styles. There is an evolving corpus of historical literature suggesting that the family might be resistant and resilient—able through its educational processes to transform as well as reproduce economic relationships or, at the very least, not to fall apart under the impact of industrialization.

Studies of French-Canadian textile workers in New Haven in the period from 1800 to 1936 (Hareven, 1978), of Irish communities in urban America (Less & Modell, 1977), and of Buffalo's Italian community from 1880 to 1930 (McLaughlin, 1977) suggest that certain families not only survived the processes of industrialization, but importantly influenced who among members of the family would work, how they would work, and whether they would work at all under the systems of factory discipline that evolved (Gutman, 1976; Fox & Quitt, 1980).

Although he did not seek to explore the effects of economic transformation on the quality or processes of education within households, Cremin (1980) has nonetheless made mention of the persistence of traditional "modes of family pedagogy" on family farms and in developing factory towns where children and parents labored together. Indirectly, he has demonstrated that families were, even in this early state of capitalist development, important educators. As he put it: "The essential pedagogy was the oldest in the world—a combination of exemplification, demonstration, explanation, criticism, and suggestion on the part of the more experienced, and of imitation, observation, trial assistance, practice, inquiry, and listening on the part of the neophyte" (Cremin, 1980, p. 336).

More attentive to educational processes within the family, Laurie (1974), in a creative study of family styles among Philadelphia artisans, distinguished among groups of working men by the nature and timing of their family activities and the ages of entrance into school. Similarly, Wallace (1978) exercised a prodigious talent in the uses of psychological and ethnographic analysis in an attempt to reveal the daily processes of communal living as they proceeded in Rockdale, Pennsylvania, during the early years of industrialization.

Studying middle-class rather than laboring families in Chicago, Sennett (1977) presents a different picture. More in the mode of Ariès, Sennett represents the family as kind of a haven, a "utopian retreat from the cities" (Jeffrey, 1972). Alienated in the work place, men turned inward for solace, transforming the family from a public agency of technical learning to one in which moral matters of learning predominated. Not in decline, the emerging middle-class family became in fact a private and exclusive enclave for its members.

The vitality of cultural traditions is also a theme in studies exploring the relative durability and persistence of particular family styles. Not uncommonly focused on groups that have been the objects of systematic cultural imposition, historians have been exploring how various groups have adapted, resisted, or transformed cultural impositions, whether they came in the form of missionary efforts, as was common in the seventeenth, eighteenth, and early nineteenth centuries, or in the form of attempts by public school architects to use schools as deliberate instruments of civic education and character development in the nineteenth century, and to use Americanization programs in the twentieth century (Albin & Cavallo, 1981).

In an extraordinary study entitled *The Death and Rebirth of the Seneca*, Wallace (1970) explores the process by which Iroquois leaders adapted to a series of culture shocks following the American Revolution. An object of military conquest and of Quaker missionary efforts, the Seneca managed to create new educational strategies that preserved their cultural identities, even as their traditional life was destroyed.

Not as attentive as Wallace to transformations over time, nor to the variety of configurations characterizing the Afro-American experience (Berlin, 1980), historians have nonetheless described similar patterns of cultural adaptation among African and Afro-American families in slavery and freedom (Gutman, 1976; Genovese, 1976; Blassingame, 1972; Webber, 1978; Finkelstein, 1979; Levine, 1977). Focusing on the world the slaves made, historians have revealed the extraordinary power and vitality of African cultural forms and expressions. Each of them has recognized that the consciousness of slaves was being formed, molded, and expressed within a community that maintained solidarity and integrity by creating what Levine (1977) has called a "sacred world." It was a world that enabled slaves to transcend the environment in which they were forced to live, simultaneously creating a meaningful, richly expressive psychological and moral reality. In the world that the slaves made, culture was transmitted orally, reflected in song, dance, and religious ceremony. It was carried on through a series of informal relationships in household structures and configurations that were unique. The sacred world of Afro-Americans survived city life as well.

Like other immigrant families, black urban dwellers eased the way for incoming migrants during the 1920s and 1930s. With the aid of churches, newspapers, and community centers, black families helped to contain the shock of the new and at the same time maintain distinct aspects of Afro-American culture (Bond, 1972; Franklin, 1979).

Several historians have explored the educational process among perfectionistic families of one sort or another who had remained together on the land for several generations (Hostetler, 1974; Thomas, 1977). The very continuity of such families is testament to the vitality of traditional modes of association, even in the midst of relentless urbanization and industrialization. Henretta (1978), in an unusual study of mentalities, has made the interesting point that family characteristics are likely to remain stable on farms, suggesting that family migrations created cultural opportunities as well as cultural strains. Indeed, there is some reason to believe that separation—whether enforced or voluntary, whether urban or rural—has narrowed circles of associations for the young, thereby delegating to families comprehensive responsibilities (Finkelstein, in press).

There are a few studies exploring the effects of Americanization programs on family relations, but only a small number attend specifically to processes of education within households of immigrant groups in the cities (Handlin, 1971; Tyack, 1974). The subject has elicited more heat than light from educational historians (Ravitch, 1978) who are as yet more interested in arguing about the political and economic effects of public schooling than they are in exploring its effects on consciousness or on intergenerational relationships within families (Finkelstein, 1979).

A rich vein of literature exploring educational processes within households of middling and high-born families has, however, been developing. Focused on learners and learning processes, these historical studies attend to relationships between the transmission of culture and the acquisition of identity. As yet, these are discrete and particular studies, tied together only by a similarity of interest in the systematic study of human relationships within households across time, or in specific settings. They document an almost infinite variety of educational processes and possibilities evolving in no obvious linear sequence.

Using hitherto ignored sources of data—autobiographies, letters, diaries, art, and poetry—exploring the meaning of educational environments as they focus, advance, and extend relationships between parents and children and between children and the world outside the family, these process-oriented studies incorporate psychological, literary, and anthropological as well as sociological and economic frameworks into the analysis of educational processes within the family (McLuhan, 1962; Ong, 1977). These are histories that focus on the substance of adult-child relationships as they have been visually represented, philosophically and scientifically imagined by parents and experts, and psychologically organized within households (Plotz, 1979; Fishman, 1979; Beales, 1979; Finkelstein, 1979; Cohen, 1979).

Among these studies, those exploring the roots of revolutionary consciousness in family styles and child-rearing practices are among the more provocative (deMause, 1974; Platt, 1980). A monumental study entitled *The Protestant Temperament* by Greven (1977) identified at least three characteristic modes of cultural transmission operating among New English Protestants, anticipating three distinct political styles and sensibilities among the founders of the American Revolution. Similarly, Axtell (1974) explored educational processes within New English families, documenting, if not observing explicitly, that running away was an important effect of child-rearing practices among Protestant families in colonial New England. Through a three-generation study of the Tappan family, Wyatt-Brown (1975) traced the transformation of patriarchal religion into sexual repression, suggesting that the cult of domesticity had roots in preindustrial child-rearing traditions. In a study of child-rearing practices among Celtic Quakers living in the Delaware Valley in the eighteenth century, Levy (1978) has suggested that the commitment to soft nurture, to gentle measures of rearing the young, was not a postindustrial construction, nor necessarily an ideological weapon, but an intricate and a unique expression of Quaker consciousness and sensibility. Not removed from the mainstream of American life, Quakers, on the contrary, may have initiated some of its more characteristic educational ideals. Quoting Shelley, who called poets "the unacknowledged legislators of the world," Plotz (1979) sees in romantic poetry the roots of modern child-rearing prescriptions and beliefs. Finally, Perry (1980) has explored the life of Henry Clarke Wright in an attempt to understand the evolution of abolitionist sentiment and strategies of reform.

Yet another group of scholars explored the processes of sociability among women within households, seeking to understand the nature of "female sociability" in the nineteenth century (Smith-Rosenberg, 1975; Cott, 1977; Degler, 1980) and simultaneously to explore the particularities of Victorian domestic culture (Welter, 1976). In a different mode, Strickland (1973) has explored child-rearing practices in the Alcott household in an attempt to understand the sources and origins of Louisa May Alcott's literary output. Horn (1978) has studied the Blackwell family in an attempt to explore ways in which family life influenced occupational choice among its female members. Evolving a concept that they call educational biography, Lagerman (1979) and Cremin (1980) seek to explore patterns of mentorship and instruction as they are reflected in the life course of individuals and as they might distinguish one group or one educational configuration from another.

A few historical studies have explored continuities and discontinuities among members of the same household across generations, suggesting that the educational process might reflect an exchange of values between parents and children rather than a simple imposition. Such, at least, seems to have been true in the families of Cotton Mather (Hiner, 1979), the Adamses (Musto, 1980), and William James (Feinstein, 1980).

Attentive to transformations in human consciousness, sentiments, beliefs, and social organization, historians are in a unique position to explore the multiple ways in which families have resisted, adapted to, or succumbed to the force of historical circumstance. Without predictive value, the corpus of historical scholarship suggests that the family is not a single entity fixed in any of its capacities or possibilities. It is, in fact, *constructed* from inside and outside and also reconstructed from inside and outside. If it becomes extinct, it will be vanquished from inside and outside. Such is the burden of historical studies of the family.

Families as Autonomous Units. Less attentive to, or perhaps less interested in, the social, historical, political, and economic circumstances in which families happen to have found themselves, scholars have created a second cluster of studies projecting the family as a relatively autonomous agency of education in which human development is importantly shaped and molded. Focusing on the dynamics of parent-children interactions, three sorts of studies explore the processes by which children internalize the world of their families. First are those, still few in number, that examine the processes of community formation within households and seek to highlight the mechanisms by which children acquire a sense of the culture to which they belong. Second are the studies exploring patterns of cognitive growth and moral development. Third are the studies exploring the evolution of sensibility or feelings in the child. Finally, there is a developing literature exploring the family as educator.

Transmitters of culture. Even though historians and other social scientists postulate a decline in the capacity of parents to influence their children, the fact remains that parents, and particularly mothers, importantly inform the nature of various symbolic markers that children use to organize social life. An increasing number of anthropologists document the variety of ways in which mothers instill in their children a culture of eating, drinking, and cleaning. Lévi-Strauss (1964, 1968), for example, explores the determinants and consequences of distinctions between "raw and cooked" food. In a variant mode, Sahlins (1936) distinguishes one culture from another based on which animals are defined as edible or inedible. Some scholars explore the use of food as a mechanism of maternal/social control (Giard & Mayol, 1980). Fearful that children might make invidious comparisons of the culinary capacities of their mothers or, worse, reveal a lack of class in their table manners, some mothers discourage easy socializing. This phenomonon reflects, perhaps, the "privatization" of daily culture and an attendant fear of contamination from strangers (Sennett, 1977).

Social scientists are concerned not only with a diversity of table manners but also with the direct influence of mothers. Capitalizing on the work of Halbwachs (1950) exploring the social aspects of time, some researchers (Melbin, 1978) have also aimed to show how children "reproduce" the calendar and the timetables or schedules of their parents. They explore generational continuities and discontinuities between individuals within households and between public and private places, contrasting schedules of the day with schedules of the night.

Finally, all of these studies reveal how socialization processes within families distinguish nations from one another and regional, social class, or ethnic groups within a single nation. Although time studies emphasize continuity of cultural behaviors across generations, their authors do not explore how the transmission of these behaviors varies with stages and ages of children. There are other studies of the management of time that do (Bohen & Viveros-Long, 1981).

Cognitive and moral agencies. Intelligence is not only an unfolding of genetic possibilities; it is also influenced by the maturation of the body and brain and by the learning opportunities progressively offered by the environment. The work of Piaget (1926; 1932) is fundamental in any consideration of cognitive development. He delineates the stages through which the cognitive abilities of children evolve between birth and late adolescence, when young adults gain full control over their potential abilities and know how "to think about thinking." (1926, 1932, 1969) Showing how these stages are articulated around the appearance of language, Piaget was most interested in their universal characteristics. Hence, he did not examine family influences on the timing of language development.

Other psychologists and anthropologists have nevertheless suggested that the acquisition of reasoning is differentially patterned by the physical and linguistic milieus in which children grow up. Segall, Campbell, and Herskovitz (1966) have demonstrated the effects of age, culture, and physical environment on visual perception. Greenfield (1966) has also suggested that the way in which children learn to classify objects depends upon the linguistic properties of language and the opportunity that particular languages provide to symbolize numbers, colors, or concepts of number and color. For example, he found differences in patterns of cognitive development between Senegalese children who attended western schools and those who did not. Bernstein (1963) and Entwistle (1968) have associated different linguistic codes in use among the children of different social classes.

Whereas Piaget defined age as the primary source of variation in the processes of cognitive growth, other social scientists have insisted on the importance of the natural and cultural spaces that are occupied by family groups. Indeed, educational psychologists such as Bruner (1966) have attempted to show how families can use the findings of Piaget in order to stimulate the development of intelligence in their offspring.

Stressing the social nature of intelligence, Piaget also identified what he believed to be similarities in the social rules governing cognitive and moral activities and in the mechanisms underlying the development of moral judgments among children. Once again, he emphasized the universality of these mechanisms. Other social scientists, such as Kohlberg (1963, 1969), have explored the consequences of convergences and divergences in the moral demands made by the increasingly large social circles in which children participate. These scholars have suggested that patterns in the development of moral judgment are contingent upon the opportunities for role playing that are offered to children. Parents who seek their children's views, and elicit comparisons of their own views with those of their offspring, accelerate the internalization of moral rules.

Thus, in the case of both moral and cognitive growth, the successors of Piaget have distinguished cultural variability in the timing, number, and sequence of the corresponding stages. More important, they have also identified strategies that they believe can reduce variabilities and enhance the potential development of all children (Bruner, 1960).

Architects of sensibility. Piaget tried to identify the stages through which the cognitive and moral activities of children evolve, Freud (1962 [1930]), Jung (1968 [1961]), and later Erikson (1979) attempted to delineate the variety of phases through which human feelings evolve, from infancy to adolescence to adulthood. The concept of stage has different meanings in the two schools of inquiry. For Piaget, the appearance of language creates discontinuities in the development of cognitive and emotional activities. For Freud, basic instinctual impulses rather than language constitute the invariant driving force of human emotional life. For Piaget, cognitive development implies emotional progress. For the students of feelings, the properties of emotional growth induce pessimism. They insist upon the possibility of regression. Indeed, in traumatic situations, adults tend to reenact conflicts that they did not resolve during childhood. These conflicts correspond to the successive ordeals to which all people are subject as they mature. Emotional development might wither if there were no incentives to progress further, or it might not proceed at all if the severity of the "teaching techniques or demands" used by parents prevents children from mastering early conflicts.

Theories about emotional development continue to inspire contemporary social scientists in several distinct ways. First, psychoanalytic concepts have informed the work undertaken by social psychologists who study the distribution of power among adult family members and its effect on children. When, for example, children perceive that their fathers are stingy with their mothers or withhold emotional support, they will identify negatively and do their best to adopt opposite attitudes and behaviors. Further, forms of identification vary across cultural contexts. Where parents approach their children with a highly structured set of cultural prescriptions or proscriptions, identification patterns become role-bound. When parents' relations with children are governed by imprecise norms and prescriptions, children tend to reproduce and replicate emotional patterns and relationships (Winch, 1966).

Historians and anthropologists have also used psychoanalytic concepts to explore continuities and discontinuities in families over time and across cultures. As they study the evolution of sexual practices (Flandrin, 1980) or feeding styles or toilet-training practices (Badinter, 1980; de-

Mause, 1974), they take psychoanalytic theories to be truths about emotional development. So, too, do anthropologists like LeVine (1968), who concluded that childhood experience varies from one culture to another, giving particular shape to adult fears and aspirations.

Medical practice—the definition and treatment of diseases—has also been subject to psychoanalytic interpretation. A universal source of anxiety, diseases are assumed to "replicate" the particular frustrations experienced during childhood (Whiting & Child, 1956).

Psychoanalytic concepts also abound in studies exploring the effects of divorce and custodial arrangements on the timing, intensity, and character of relationships between children and separated parents. Observing an increase in the number of patients with narcissistic disorders, Kohut (1971) and others have looked beyond the simple family for explanations of psychological processes within the family. Still other scientists have challenged the importance initially assigned by psychoanalysts to the triangle of passions developed by men, women, and their sons. Feminist scholars like Chodorow (1978) suggest, for example, that female identity is not necessarily fixed in a universal Oedipal conflict, nor must mothers inevitably reproduce mothers. That they do might be a social construction rather than a biological necessity. As scholars focus their attention on the monopoly that women have on childbearing, some attribute the reproduction of mothering to natural and invariant forces, whereas others attribute it to the particular patterns of division of labor that go with "rampant patriarchalism."

Finally, certain social scientists have undertaken even more devastating and more encompassing criticisms of psychoanalytic theories. For them, it is the fundamental tenet of psychoanalysis that should be challenged—that self-doubt and interpersonal conflicts are internally wrought. Some social psychologists like Lemert and Dill (1978) and psychiatrists like Laing (1971) and Szasz (1974) have argued that mental disorders are social constructs and correspond to labels that significant individuals or agencies impose upon those whom they consider to be deviant. Arguing therefore that psychoanalytical theories contribute to a further atomicization of psychological or social life, they see mental disorders as a property of inter-individual modes of interaction rather than of individuals per se. Correspondingly, they seek to create new forms of bonds between the so-called patients and the so-called normal segments of the population through the creation of new forms of therapy. It is in this context that "family therapies" have developed.

Educators. A small but increasingly influential group of scholars has begun the monumental task of exploring the family as an educational agency. These historians, sociologists, economists, anthropologists, and psychologists have, under the leadership of Hope Jensen Leichter at Teachers College, brought a multidisciplinary focus to the problem of distinguishing educational aspects of family

processes. As they label the activities of the family, they use traditional educational categories—teaching and learning, memory, evaluation, labeling. In *The Family as Educator,* Leichter (1975) and her colleagues examined the variety of ways in which teaching and learning occurs within households. Parents teach children, children teach parents, children teach each other, grandparents teach parents, children learn from grandparents. Family members learn from friends. Families organize, mediate, refract, and transform information as it is represented on television and through other media of communication. Some teaching and learning are deliberate, and some learning occurs, as Leichter puts it, "at the margins of awareness."

Focusing on a multiplicity of educational transactions occurring within households, Leichter is attentive to the complexity, range, and variability of educational possibilities, and configurations within households. Incorporating themes from communications theory, interaction theory, role theory, labeling theory, and the like, she seeks to use dynamic process models of human interaction. The work is just beginning, and it is enormously promising.

Rich in their capacity to identify and reveal the complexity and multiplicity of relationships among members of the conjugal family, these studies have not focused primarily on the family as a link in a chain of institutions through which education also proceeds. Other studies have.

Families as Mediating Agencies. Another way of exploring the family as an educational agency is to focus on the performance of children outside the home—in schools, in the marketplace, and in the social and political arena of the real world. A long tradition of scholarly inquiry focuses on how members of various kinds of families fare in the social order and why they fare in different ways.

Inquiries are most often focused on external indicators of performance, namely, school achievement; occupational, economic, social, and political position; and indices of social adjustment (Lavine, 1965). A few studies explore relationships between the behavioral world of the family and the world outside familial boundaries by attending to the ways in which values are transmitted in the daily processes of living.

Socializing agencies. Reflecting an interest in intervention strategies, school performance studies focus on the relative willingness or unwillingness, ability or inability, of families to prepare their children to use schooling as an avenue of social mobility. In the process, they have created a corpus of scholarship defining certain classes of family as deficient on the one hand, or oppressed on the other (Musgrove, 1966a, 1966b).

Many studies of this sort evolve conclusions about family educative styles by assessing the number of years children spend in school and their achievements as measured by grades and standardized test scores. Harboring implicit definitions of what is important about families and how families ought to be defined and understood, various researchers seek different interpretations from the same kinds of data.

Some studies implicitly define the family as a cultural unit that transmits a set of prescriptive and proscriptive strategies for dealing with the outside world. Such studies, of course, expose the value-laden nature of educational experiences within the family. Thus, they suggest that schools as educative agencies cannot be considered value-free but must be viewed in terms of their explicit and implicit values and how these values are interfaced with the values of families served by schools within the context of the values of the social and political order.

A number of studies, analyzed *inter alia* by Scarr and Weinberg (1978), explore the extent of similarities in the cognitive and emotional outlook of homozygotic or heterozygotic twins reared together or in different environments and of siblings subjected to the same environmental variations. Although these studies are intended to deal with the issue of how modifiable nature may be to environmental circumstance, they have tended to oversimplify the complexity of interaction between nature and culture. In addition, the results of such studies have been misused to explain IQ differences between black and white children in biological rather than cultural, environmental, or educational terms.

Still other studies focus on family structure and how it affects children's ability to perform in school. An abundant literature, summarized by Anastasi (1956), has concluded that there is a negative relationship between family size and school achievement. Children from large families are not so successful in school as those from small families, leading researchers to conclude that a small family is better than a large family in its capacity as an educative agency.

Research is not limited, however, to generalizations about the family *per se*. Indeed, considerable attention has been given to the individual in reference to other members of the family and to how membership position affects individual school performance.

Some of the sociological literature suggests that the academic performance of last-born children is enhanced when their older siblings are attending academic institutions. First-born and only children are most likely to succeed in school. The influence of sib-rank, far from being absolute, seems to vary with the gender of both the child and the older siblings. Youngest daughters for example, embrace a wider range of university studies than their older sisters whose academic careers reflect what their mothers expect from them. Similarly, last-born sons seem to fare academically better when they have an older female sibling than when they have to conform to the model of an older brother (Brim, 1958).

Other researchers have focused on parental power structure and its influence on children's performance in school. Thus, children from families where wives-mothers are dominant are more likely to be achievers. Achievement gains have been studied in reference both to previous generations and to current surroundings. Further, such studies have sought to distinguish between the power held by such actors in their conjugal relations and in their relations toward children. Research indicates that high-achieving children come from families in which wives dominate their husbands and exercise authority over educational decisions concerning their offspring.

Such research, of course, defines the family as a sole source of influence and socialization, both formal and informal. A broader concept of the family as an educative agency is reflected in the conclusion of other researchers, who analyze school achievement data in relationship to the socialization processes.

Indeed, all these analyses suggest that individual differences in academic performance result from differences in the economic status of the families from which children originate; differences in the cultural capital provided to children; discrepancies between family and official school values; and the relative political powers of families.

In studies that implicitly define the family as a financial resource, researchers focus on the amount of money families can or will spend to pay tuitions, to provide nutrition, and to purchase clothes and educational materials for the education of their children (Eicher & Garbona, 1979). At the same time, these researchers also assess the relative capabilities of families to purchase schooling for their children, thus forgoing the income of their children.

Extending economic modes of analysis to cultural themes, another group of researchers explores culture as capital, discovering that individual differences in academic performances might reflect cultural as well as economic differences among social classes. As they analyze differences in performance, these researchers interpret such differences as reflections of the cognitive and emotional behaviors of parents, which are class-bound. Thus, the assumption seems to be that oppression is fixed by cultural as well as economic inequalities among families, regardless of the nature of the larger political order (Bourdieu & Passeron, 1968).

Extending that line of argument, Bernstein (1963) distinguished between the language codes of more or less privileged classes. Noting that teachers tend to use syntactic elaborated codes, researchers have observed a fit between the linguistic code of the school and that of middle-class or upper-class families. Their less privileged counterparts are disadvantaged by the more restricted codes used in their families.

Taking into consideration ethnic and social class variations in the richness of the symbols used by differing children, television producers have organized educational programs, such as "Sesame Street" and "The Electric Company," in order to accelerate and/or facilitate individual adaptation to the essential stimuli of the school world. Studies that evaluate the impact of educational television on school performance suggest that educational intentions can be sabotaged by families who choose, for one reason or another, not to watch.

Similarly, attempts by professional educators may also fail if there is a disjunction of values between children and school authorities. Thus, the person-oriented value system of the Italians of the West End of Boston might be at odds with the object-oriented value system of the schools. Hence, Italian parents might not encourage academic aspirations or exert tight controls over their children's academic progress (Gans, 1963). Differences in value systems derive not only from ethnicity but also from religion. In an attempt to account for differences in school achievement among Jewish, Catholic, and Protestant children, sociologists have often explained the differences in terms of the relative importance placed on self-reliance and autonomy (Lensky, 1961; Greeley, 1978). Indeed, Catholics seem to be at an academic disadvantage, or so the researchers imply, because Catholic children are excessively dependent on external authorities.

Sociologists have identified a variety of advantages and disadvantages that accrue to children from different homes. Middle-class children, for example, are highly advantaged relative to their less privileged counterparts—the beneficiaries of a hidden curriculum stressing school achievement, professional aspirations, and individual striving (Miller & Swanson, 1958; Strodtbeck, 1974).

Labeling certain classes of families as more or less useful educational agencies for their children, some analysts have also distinguished among families in terms of their capacity to deal with the emotional needs of children. Thus, the academic failures of black children are commonly imputed to the matrifocal nature of the households from which they come. As sociological researchers construct a picture of the black family, they commonly project it as essentially fatherless and therefore lacking in role models for male children.

Prolonged parental absence, whether it is caused by divorce, occupational necessity, abandonment, or death, seems to have academically deleterious effects. Coleman (1961) has suggested that separations between families and children render children more vulnerable to peer influence. Such influence may complement or sabotage the influence of the family or the school educative agencies, depending on the values of the peer culture—whether they are oriented toward academics, fun, or delinquency.

Children might be further disadvantaged by the perceptions of teachers and counselors who are susceptible to the mirages of social appearance. Both teachers and counselors inadvertently tend to harbor different expectations for children from different social classes and so fail to set the same standards for all (Cicourela & Kitsuse, 1963; Lightfoot, 1978; Coleman et al., 1966).

Even though schools might be intended to provide opportunity for upward mobility, their success depends on the elimination of economic, social, and cultural differences or, as some researchers have suggested, on a transformation of economic, political, and social inequality in the society (Jencks, 1972; Musgrove, 1966a, 1966b; Turner, 1963).

Although schooling may not produce dramatic social, political, or economic revolutions, there is some suggestion in the sociological literature that prolonged school attendance may result in transformations in family patterns and in the relative power of families to exercise authority over their children.

There is a rich literature exploring the effects of educational attainment on matrimonial choices, conjugal relations, and childbearing and child-rearing activities (Goode, 1963; Cochrane, 1979). And there is, as well, a corpus of work similarly constructed, exploring political socialization (Goode, 1963; Elder & Bowerman, 1964; Hess & Torney, 1969; Merelman, 1971).

In general, sociological studies exploring the family as a socializing agency use global and indirect measures of the influence of the family as an agency of social placement and/or as a structure of opportunity. Their definitions of family situations arise not from naturalistic observations of the family, but from the theoretical perspectives they seek to develop, whether they are theories of social change (Goode, 1963; Demos & Boocok, 1978) or the analyses of immutable political or economic laws (Bourdieu & Passeron, 1968).

A kind of impatience with grand theory has motivated some scholars to begin the difficult process of exploring the family from the inside, seeking often to dispel what they believe to be a corpus of myths issuing from the social science literature (Erikson, 1964).

Families on their own terms. Lightfoot's *Worlds Apart* (1978) and Stack's *All Our Kin* (1975) seek specifically to demystify the notion that black mothers are inadequate as parents, and that black families are educationally deficient. Impatient with rigid categories and fixed and static views of social processes, they seek to develop what Lightfoot calls "a kaleidoscopic vision of family-school interactions" (p. 17), exploring what she describes as a "complex and multi-dimensional reality." To put it in the manner of Laing (1971), human beings relate not only externally, like two billiard balls, but relate two worlds of experience when they meet. To treat them otherwise will create violence and mystification.

Robert Coles, a most impatient critic of grand theory and of reification, has created an enormous corpus of work exploring the lives of children and parents from the inside looking out (Coles, 1964, 1967a, 1967b, 1977a, 1977b). As an observer of and a participant in the lives of hundreds of families, he has created a grand and systematically atheoretical testimony to the complexity and variety of educational encounters within families. He has, in his own words "paid attention to children from all parts of the country: rural and urban; from each of the major racial and cultural groups," and from all the so-called socioeconomic strata or classes (1977a, p. viii).

Notwithstanding his distaste for theory, Coles has nonetheless attended to the multiple ways by which children learn who they are, how they ought to behave, what they might believe, and how they can expect to fare in the world. The range of mentalities is nothing less than dazzling in his presentations of family life, and he is a careful analyst of processes of political and economic socialization, attending, as few others have, to the human relationships through which social learning occurs (Coles, 1975, 1977b; Looff, 1971).

Combining a commitment to theory with a commitment to naturalistic observation, Leichter (1978) has attempted to explore relationships between the behavioral world of the family and the communities to which it is bound, using education as an overall focus in her studies. Distinguishing two kinds of research—that which defines the family in relationship to theoretically derived categories and that which takes as a point of departure the family's view of itself—she threads her way through an enormous body of literature in search of ways to wed theory to sensitive interpretation of families and communities as educators. Recognizing the problem of reification and distortion, she summarizes this huge volume of literature, revealing a tendency to reduce complexity: "the new behavioral biologists look at human families as a reflection of instinctual imperatives; the psychoanalytically-oriented psychologists examine the dynamics of the resolution of psychological needs and dependencies in the family; the interactionists look at the family as an arena of interpersonal encounters; the economists consider family behavior in relation to outside economic forces or as a determinant of outside opportunities for its members; and the cultural and symbolic analysts look to the symbolic organization of family behavior and the meaning of family terms as components of broader symbolic systems" (pp. 575–576).

Policy Implications. Leichter (1978) has identified one of the more intractable problems besetting scholars who seek to understand the family and to inform public policy responsibly. Most approach the study of the family through distorted disciplinary lenses. Something like single-issue political campaigners, they define the world of the family in relationship to a particular epistemological reality, taking a particular intellectual screen, laying it over the family, and producing a partial portrait of family reality, too often taking it for the whole or most compelling truth.

Historians and sociologists, for example, commonly proceed on the assumption that families are ultimately passive conduits of political and economic realities. They treat the family as if it were simply a delegate of social status, an unwitting creation of political and economic arrangements and ideological constructions. Uninterested, typically, in educational processes within families, or in the course of nurture and daily activity, they have implicitly analyzed the evolution of the family as it reveals economic and political changes, rather than as it might illuminate the whole of relationships between men and women or parents and children within a household. For historians and sociologists, the family is not uncommonly defined in mutually contradictory terms; we see the family as being in decline at the very moment in time when we see it portrayed as an autonomous nuclear unit with specialized functions and educated possibilities. It is understood by scholars to be simultaneously omnipotent and helpless—a powerful source of alienation on the one hand, a dismantled fortress of invulnerability on the other. It is described as both oppressive and liberating, freeing women and children from the yolk of patriarchal authority, while at the same time exposing the harshness of the world of production outside of the household. Unable to provide the kind of intimacy thrust upon it, the family has failed to civilize, even as it nurtures systematically. In short, the family has been understood to be both the victim and the cause of modern alienation and community failures, both the symptom and the disease (Finkelstein and Clignet, 1981).

Yet another portrait of the family emerges from scholars seeking to observe the processes of human development rather than the evolution of family arrangements. For cognitive psychologists, the family is implicitly portrayed as a nursery of intellect or stupidity. For medical specialists, the family portrait is often one of disease and contagion. For still other scholars, the family appears as a place in which community is formed or deformed and in which consciousness is raised, directed, or suppressed. And, in the hands of certain education professionals, the family portrait has commonly taken on a rosy or dark hue depending on the capacity of family offspring to appreciate and use schools in the service of political, economic, or personal mobility. Through the lenses of child advocates, we see the family evaluated in relationship to the developmental requirements of childhood—defined and understood, of course, by parent-rearing experts. Through the lens of feminist consciousness, we commonly see women as faced with impedimentive children, husbands, and other constraining realities.

Family scholars are frequently called upon to submit testimony in behalf of one or another course of public action. Indeed, scholarly expertise and technical know-how have been placed in the service of an amazing diversity of family concerns—from children's health to genetic planning, to family poverty, to mothers' needs, to children's requirements. Experts have informed the decision of the courts on behalf of parents, children, teachers, cousins, grandparents, boys, girls, mothers, and fathers. Never neutral or objective, scholarly testimony evolves on a shifting ideological terrain, among intellectual fads, fashions, and arguments. Always wrapped in a cloak of scholarly objectivity, experts have been likely to advance myths as well as realities, value judgments as well as technical expertise.

Family studies in education are not, as we have seen, typically the territory that professional educators have inhabited. But the family has become an object of new and more impassioned speculation and anxiety on the part of educators. One can only hope that family studies in education will flourish with collaboration among experts representing the entire range of human understanding and sensibility. One can only hope that educators will be able to distinguish myths from reality, benevolence from politics, and ambition from objectivity. If they can, they will abide by the canons of scholarly tradition.

Barbara Finkelstein

See also Anthropology; History of Education; Sociology of Education; Women's Education.

REFERENCES

Albin, M., & Cavallo, D. *Family Life in America, 1620–2000.* St. James, N.Y.: Revisionary Press, 1981.

Anastasi, A. Intelligence and family life. *Psychological Bulletin,* 1956, *53,* 187–209.

Aries, P. *Centuries of Childhood: A Social History of Family Life* (Robert Baldick, Trans.). New York: Knopf, 1962.

Axinn, J.; Glassberg, E.; & Cenci, M. *The Century of the Child: Progress and Retreat.* Philadelphia: University of Pennsylvania Press, 1974.

Axtell, J. *The School upon the Hill: Education and Society in Colonial New England.* New Haven, Conn.: Yale University Press, 1974.

Badinter, E. *L'amour en plus: Histoire de l'amour maternel, 17ème–20ème siècles.* Paris: Flammarion, 1980.

Beales, R. W. Anne Bradstreet and her children. In B. Finkelstein (Ed.), *Regulated Children, Liberated Children: Education in Psychohistorical Perspective.* New York: Psychohistory Press, 1979.

Berlin, I. Time, space, and the evolution of Afro-American society on British mainland, North America. *American Historical Review,* 1980, *85*(1), 44–78.

Bernstein, B. Social class and linguistic development: A theory of social learning. In A. H. Halsey, J. Floud, & C. A. Anderson (Eds.), *Education, Economy, and Society.* New York: Free Press, 1963.

Blassingame, J. W. *The Slave Community: Plantation Life in the Antebellum South.* New York: Oxford University Press, 1972.

Bohen, H. H., & Viveros-Long, A. *Balancing Jobs and Family Life: Do Flexible Work Schedules Help?* Philadelphia: Temple University, 1981.

Bond, H. M. *Black American Scholars: A Study of Their Beginnings.* Detroit: Balamp, 1972.

Bourdieu, P., & Passeron, J. C. *La reproduction.* Paris: Editions de Minuit, 1968.

Brenzel, B. M. Domestication as reform: A study of the socialization of wayward girls, 1856–1905. *Harvard Educational Review,* 1980, *50,* 196–214.

Brim, O. Family structure and sex-role learning of children. *Sociometry, 1,* 1958, 1–16.

Bruner, J. *The Process of Education.* Cambridge, Mass.: Harvard University Press, 1960.

Bruner, J. *Toward a Theory of Instruction.* Cambridge, Mass.: Harvard University Press, 1966.

Burgess, E. W.; Locke, H. J.; & Thomas, M. M. *The Family: From Tradition to Companionship* (4th ed.). New York: Van Nostrand, 1971.

Calhoun, A. H. *A Social History of the American Family* (2 vols.). Glendale, Calif.: Clark, 1918.

Cavallo, D. *Muscles and Morals: Organized Playgrounds and Urban Reform, 1880–1920.* Philadelphia: University of Pennsylvania, 1981.

Chodorow, N. *The Reproduction of Mothering.* Berkeley: University of California Press, 1978.

Cicourel, A., & Kitsuse, J. *The Educational Decision-makers.* Indianapolis: Bobbs-Merrill, 1963.

Cochrane, S. *Fertility and Education: What Do We Really Know?* Baltimore: Johns Hopkins University Press, 1979.

Cohen, S. In the name of the prevention of neurosis: The search for a psychoanalytic pedagogy in Europe, 1905–1938. In B. Finkelstein (Ed.), *Regulated Children, Liberated Children: Education in Psychohistorical Perspective.* New York: Psychohistory Press, 1979.

Coleman, J. C. *The Adolescent Society.* New York: Free Press, 1961.

Coleman, J. C.; Campbell, E. Q.; Hobson, C. J.; McPartland, J.; Mood, A. M.; Weinfeld, F. D.; & York, R. L. *Equality of Educational Opportunity.* Washington, D.C.: U.S. Government Printing Office, 1966. (ERIC Document Reproduction Service No. ED 012 275)

Coles, R. *Children of Crisis: A Study of Courage and Fear* (Vol. 1). Boston: Little, Brown, 1964.

Coles, R. *Children of Crisis: Migrants, Sharecroppers, Mountaineers* (Vol. 2). Boston: Little, Brown, 1967. (a)

Coles, R. *Children of Crisis: The South Goes North* (Vol. 3). Boston: Little, Brown, 1967. (b)

Coles, R. Children and political authority. In *The Mind's Fate: Ways of Seeing Psychiatry and Psychoanalysis.* Boston: Little, Brown, 1975.

Coles, R. *Children of Crisis: Eskimos, Chicanos, Indians* (Vol. 4). Boston: Little, Brown, 1977. (a)

Coles, R. *Children of Crisis: Privileged Ones* (Vol. 5). Boston: Little, Brown, 1977. (b)

Cott, N. F. *The Bonds of Womanhood: Woman's Sphere in New England, 1780–1835.* New Haven, Conn.: Yale University Press, 1977.

Cremin, L. A. *American Education: The Colonial Experience, 1607–1783.* New York: Harper & Row, 1970.

Cremin, L. A. The family as educator: Some comments on the recent historiography. In H. J. Leichter (Ed.), *The Family as Educator.* New York: Teachers College Press, 1974.

Cremin, L. A. *American Education: The National Experience, 1783–1876.* New York: Harper & Row, 1980.

Degler, L. N. *At Odds: Women and the Family in America from the Revolution to the Present.* New York: Oxford University Press, 1980.

deMause, L. The evolution of childhood. In L. deMause (Ed.), *The History of Childhood.* New York: Psychohistory Press, 1974.

Demos, J. *A Little Commonwealth: Family Life in Plymouth Colony.* New York: Oxford University Press, 1970.

Demos, J., & Boocock, S. (Eds.). *Turning Points: Sociological and Historical Essays on the Family.* Chicago: University of Chicago Press, 1978.

Donzelot, J. *The Policing of Families.* New York: Pantheon Books, 1979.

Eicher, J. C., & Lévy-Garboua, L. *Economique de l'éducation.* Paris: Economica, 1979.

Elder, G., & Bowerman, C. Adolescent perception of family power structure. *American Sociological Review,* 1964, *29,* 551–567.

Entwistle, D. Developmental socio-linguistic abilities of inner city children. *American Journal of Sociology,* 1968, *74*(3), 37–49.

Erikson, E. H. *Childhood and Society.* New York: Norton, 1964.

Erikson, E. H. *Identity and the Life Cycle.* New York: Norton, 1979.

Feinstein, H. Words and work: A dialectical analysis of value transmission between three generations of the family of William James. In M. Albin (Ed.), *New Directions in Psychohistory*. Lexington, Mass.: Lexington Books, 1980.

Finkelstein, B. The twain shall meet: The history of childhood and the history of education in documents. *Journal of Psychohistory*, Spring 1977, *4*, 553–591.

Finkelstein, B. Uncle Sam and the children: A history of government involvement in child rearing. *Review Journal of Philosophy and Social Science*, 1977, *3*(2), 139–153.

Finkelstein, B. Introduction and chapter 6. In B. Finkelstein (Ed.), *Regulated Children, Liberated Children: Education in Psychohistorical Perspective*. New York: Psychohistory Press, 1979.

Finkelstein, B. *Casting Networks of Good Influence: Moral Education in Nineteenth- and Twentieth-century America*. Paper presented at the Charles Riley Armington Seminar on Moral Education, Case Western Reserve University, April 1981. (a)

Finkelstein, B. Exploring community in urban educational history. In D. Ravitch (Ed.), *Community in Urban Educational History*. New York: Holmes & Meier, forthcoming.

Finkelstein, B., & Clignet, R. The family as inferno: The dour visions of four family historians. *Journal of Psychohistory*, 1981, *8*.

Fishman, S. The double-vision of education in the nineteenth century: The romantic and the grotesque. In B. Finkelstein (Ed.), *Regulated Children, Liberated Children: Education in Psychohistorical Perspective*. New York: Psychohistory Press, 1979.

Flandrin, J. L. Repression and change in the sexual life of young people in medieval and early modern times. In R. Wheaton & T. Hareven (Eds.), *Family and Sexuality in French History*. Philadelphia: University of Pennsylvania Press, 1980.

Fox, V. C., & Quitt, M. H. (Eds.). *Loving, Parenting, and Dying: The Family Cycle in England and America, Past and Present*. New York: Psychohistory Press, 1980.

Franklin, V. *The Education of Black Philadelphians*. Philadelphia: University of Pennsylvania Press, 1979.

Freud, S. *Civilization and Its Discontents* (J. Strachey, Ed. and Trans.). New York: Norton, 1962. (Originally published, 1930)

Gans, H. *The Urban Villagers*. New York: Free Press, 1963.

Geertz, C. *The Interpretation of Culture*. New York: Basic Books, 1973.

Genovese, E. J. *Roll Jordan Roll: The World the Slaves Made*. New York: Pantheon Books, 1976.

Giard, L., & Mayol, P. *Habiter, cuisiner*. Paris: Union Générale d'Editions, 1980.

Glasser, I.; Gaylin, W.; Rothman, D.; & Marcus, S. *Doing Good: The Limits of Benevolence*. New York: Pantheon Books, 1978.

Goode, W. *World Revolution and Family Patterns*. New York: Free Press, 1963.

Goodsell, W. *A History of Marriage and the Family*. New York: Macmillan, 1934.

Greeley, A. *The American Catholic: A Portrait*. New York: Basic Books, 1978.

Greenfield, P. On culture and conservation. In J. Bruner, R. Oliver, & P. Greenfield (Eds.), *Studies in Cognitive Growth*. New York: Wiley, 1966.

Greven, P. *The Protestant Temperament: Patterns of Child-rearing, Religious Experience, and the Self in Early America*. New York: Knopf, 1977.

Grob, G. Doing good and getting worse: The dilemma of social policy. *Michigan Law Review*, January–March 1979, *77*, 761–783.

Gutman, H. G. *The Black Family in Slavery and Freedom, 1750–1925*. New York: Pantheon Books, 1976.

Halbwachs, M. *La mémoire collective*. Paris: Presses Universitaires de France, 1950.

Handlin, O. *Children of the Uprooted*. New York: Grosset & Dunlap, 1971.

Hareven, T. K. The dynamics of kin in an industrial community. *American Journal of Sociology*, 1978, *84*(Suppl.), S151–183.

Hawes, J. M. *Children in Urban Society: Juvenile Delinquency in Nineteenth-century America*. New York: Oxford University Press, 1971.

Henretta, J. A. Families and farms: Mentalité in pre-industrial America. *William and Mary Quarterly*, 1978(3rd series), *35*, 29–32.

Hess, R., & Torney, J. *The Development of Political Attitudes in Children*. Chicago: Aldine, 1969.

Hiner, N. R. Cotton Mather and his children. In B. Finkelstein (Ed.), *Regulated Children, Liberated Children: Education in Psychohistorical Perspective*. New York: Psychohistory Press, 1979.

Horn, M. E. *The Effect of Family Life on Women's Role Choices in Nineteenth-century America*. Unpublished manuscript, 1978.

Hostetler, J. A. *Hutterite Society*. Baltimore: Johns Hopkins University Press, 1974.

Jeffrey, K. The family as a utopian retreat from the city: The nineteenth-century contribution. *Soundings*, 1972, *55*, 21–41.

Jencks, C. *Inequality*. New York: Basic Books, 1972.

Jensen, A.; Kagan, J.; McHunt, J.; Crow, J.; Bereiter, C.; Elkind, D.; Cronbach, L.; & Brazziel, W. Environment, heredity, and intelligence. *Harvard Educational Review* (Reprint Series No. 2), 1969.

Jung, C. G. *Man and His Symbols*. New York: Dell, 1968.

Kaestle, C. F., & Vinovskis, M. A. From apron strings to ABCs: Parents, children, and schooling in nineteenth-century Massachusetts. In J. Demos & S. S. Boocock (Eds.), *Turning Points: Historical and Sociological Essays on the Family*. Chicago: University of Chicago Press, 1978.

Kett, J. F. *Rites of Passage: Adolescence in America, 1790 to the Present*. New York: Basic Books, 1977.

Kohlberg, L. The development of children's orientations toward a moral order: I. Sequence in the development of moral thought. *Vita Humana*, 1963, *6*, 11–33.

Kohlberg, L. Stage and sequence: The cognitive-developmental approach to socialization. In D. A. Goslin (Ed.), *Handbook of Socialization Theory and Research*. Chicago: Rand McNally, 1969.

Kohut, H. *The Analysis of the Self*. New York: International Universities Press, 1971.

Kuhn, A. L. *The Mother's Role in Childhood Education: New England Concepts, 1830–1860*. New Haven, Conn.: Yale University Press, 1947.

Lagerman, E. C. *A Generation of Women: Education in the Lives of Progressive Reformers*. Cambridge, Mass.: Harvard University Press, 1979.

Laing, R. D. *Politics of the Family*. New York: Pantheon Books, 1971.

Lasch, C. *The Culture of Narcissism: American Life in an Age of Diminishing Expectations*. New York: Norton, 1979. (a)

Lasch, C. *Haven in a Heartless World: The Family Besieged*. New York: Basic Books, 1979. (b)

Laurie, B. G. Nothing on compulsion: Lifestyles of Philadelphia artisans, 1820–1850. *Labor History*, 1974, *15*, 337–366.

Lavine, D. *The Prediction of Academic Performance*. New York: Russell Sage, 1965.

Leichter, H. J. Some perspectives on the family as educator. In H. Leichter (Ed.), *The Family as Educator*. New York: Teachers College Press, 1975.

Leichter, H. J. Families and communities as educators: Some concepts of relationship. *Teachers College Record*, May 1978, *79*(4), 563.

Lemert, E., & Dill, F. *Offenders in the Community*. Lexington, Mass.: Lexington Books, 1978.

Lenski, G. *The Religious Factor*. New York: Doubleday, 1961.

Less, L. H., & Modell, J. The Irish countryman urbanized: A comparative perspective on the famine migration. *Journal of Urban History*, 1979, *3*, 391–408.

Levine, L. W. *Black Culture and Black Consciousness: Afro-American Folk Thought from Slavery to Freedom*. New York: Oxford University Press, 1977.

LeVine, R. *Dreams and Deeds in African Cultures*. Chicago: University of Chicago Press, 1968.

Lévi-Strauss, C. *Le cru et le cuit*. Paris: Plon, 1964.

Lévi-Strauss, C. *L'origine des manières de table*. Paris: Plon, 1968.

Levy, B. Tender plants: Quaker farmers and children in the Delaware Valley, 1681–1735. *Journal of Family History*, June 1978, *3*, 116–133.

Lightfoot, S. L. *Worlds Apart: Relationships between Families and Schools*. New York: Basic Books, 1978.

Looff, D. H. *Appalachia's Children: The Challenge of Mental Health*. Lexington: University Press of Kentucky, 1971.

McLaughlin, V. Y. *Family and Community: Italian Immigrants in Buffalo, 1880–1930*. New York: Cornell University Press, 1977.

McLuhan, M. *The Gutenberg Galaxy: The Making of Typographic Man*. Toronto: University of Toronto Press, 1962.

Melbin, M. Night as frontier. *American Sociological Review*, 1978, *43*, 3–22.

Merelman, R. *Political Socialization and Educational Climates*. New York: Holt, Rinehart & Winston, 1971.

Miller, D., & Swanson G. *The Changing American Parent: A Study in Detroit*. New York: Wiley, 1958.

Mulligan, J. S. *The Madonna and Child in American Culture*. Unpublished doctoral dissertation, University of California at Los Angeles, 1975.

Musgrove, F. *The Family, Education, and Society*. Boston: Routledge & Kegan Paul, 1966. (a)

Musgrove, F. *Youth and the Social Order*. Boston: Routledge & Kegan Paul, 1966. (b)

Musto, D. F. Continuity across generations: The Adams family myth. In M. Albin (Ed.), *New Directions in Psychohistory*. Lexington, Mass.: Lexington Books, 1980.

Ong, W. J. *Interfaces of the Word*. Ithaca, N.Y.: Cornell University, 1977.

Parsons, T., & Bales, R. F. The American family: Its relations to personality and social structure. In *Family, Socialization, and Interaction Process*. New York: Free Press, 1955.

Perry, L. *Childhood, Marriage, and Reform: Henry Clarke Wright, 1797–1870*. Chicago: University of Chicago, 1980.

Piaget, J. *The Language and Thought of the Child*. New York: Harcourt, 1926.

Piaget, J. *The Moral Judgment of the Child*. New York: Harcourt, 1932.

Platt, A. *The Child Savers: The Invention of Delinquency*. Chicago: University of Chicago Press, 1969.

Platt, G. M. Thoughts on a theory of collective action: Language, affect, and ideology in revolution. In M. Albin (Ed.), *New Directions in Psychohistory*. Lexington, Mass.: Lexington Books, 1980.

Plotz, J. The perpetual messiah: Romanticism, childhood, and the paradoxes of human development. In B. Finkelstein (Ed.), *Regulated Children, Liberated Children: Education in Psychohistorical Perspective*. New York: Psychohistory Press, 1979.

Ravitch, D. On the history of minority group education in the United States. In D. Warren (Ed.), *History, Education, and Public Policy*. Berkeley, Calif.: McCutchan, 1978.

Rothman, D. *The Child, the Family, and the State: Past Realities and Future Prospects* (Working Paper No. 1). College Park: University of Maryland, Center for the Study of Education Policy and Human Values, 1981.

Sahlins, M. *Culture and Practical Reason*. Chicago: University of Chicago Press, 1936.

Scarr, S., & Weinberg, R. Influence of family background on intellectual attainment. *American Sociological Review*, 1978, *43*(5), 674–692.

Schlossman, S. L. Before home start: Notes toward a history of parent education in America, 1897–1927. *Harvard Educational Review*, August 1976, *46*, 436–468.

Schlossman, S. L. *The American Delinquent: The Theory and Practice of Progressive Juvenile Justice, 1825–1920*. Chicago: University of Chicago Press, 1977.

Segall, M.; Campbell, D.; & Herskovitz, M. *The Influence of Culture on Visual Perception*. Indianapolis: Bobbs-Merrill, 1966.

Sennett, R. *The Fall of Public Man*. New York: Random House, Vintage Books, 1977.

Sklar, K. K. *Catharine Beecher: A Study in American Domesticity*. New Haven, Conn.: Yale University, 1973.

Smith-Rosenberg, C. The female world of love and ritual: Relations between women in nineteenth-century America. *Signs*, 1975, *1*(1), 1–29.

Stack, C. *All Our Kin: Strategies for Survival in a Black Community*. New York: Harper & Row, 1975.

Stone, L. *The Family, Sex, and Marriage in England, 1500–1800*. New York: Harper & Row, 1977.

Strickland, C. A transcendentalist father: The child-rearing practices of Amos Bronson Alcott. *History of Childhood Quarterly*, 1973, *1*(1), 4–51.

Strodtbeck, F. Family interaction, values, and achievement. In R. Winch & J. Goodman (Eds.), *Selected Studies in Marriage and the Family*. New York: Holt, Rinehart & Winston, 1974.

Szasz, T. *The Myth of Mental Illness: Foundation of a Theory of Personal Conduct*. New York: Harper & Row, 1974.

Thomas, R. D. *The Man Who Would be Perfect: John Humphrey Noyes and the Utopian Impulse*. Philadelphia: University of Pennsylvania, 1977.

Turner, R. Modes of social ascent through education: Sponsored and contest mobility. In A. H. Halsey, J. Floud, & C. L. Anderson (Eds.), *Education, Economy, and Society*. New York: Free Press, 1963.

Tyack, D. *The One Best System: A History of American Urban Education*. Cambridge: Harvard University Press, 1974.

Tyack, D. Ways of seeing: An essay on the history of compulsory schooling. *Harvard Educational Review*, 1976, *46*, 355–390.

Wallace, A. F. C. *The Death and Rebirth of the Seneca*. New York: Knopf, 1970.

Wallace, A. F. C. *Rockdale: The Growth of an American Village in the Early Industrial Revolution*. New York: Knopf, 1978.

Webber, T. L. *Deep Like the Rivers: Education in the Slave Quarter Community, 1831 to 1865*. New York: Norton, 1978.

Welter, B. The cult of true womanhood, 1820–1860. *American Quarterly*, 1966, *18*, 151–174.

Welter, B. *Dimity Convictions: The American Woman in the Nineteenth Century.* Athens: Ohio University Press, 1976.

Whiting, J., & Child I. *Child Training and Personality.* New Haven, Conn.: Yale University Press, 1956.

Winch, R. *Familial Determinants of Psychological Identification.* Indianapolis: Bobbs-Merrill, 1966.

Wishy, B. *The Child and the Republic: The Dawn of Modern American Child Nurture.* Philadelphia: University of Pennsylvania Press, 1968.

Wyatt-Brown, B. Three generations of Yankee parenthood: The Tappan family, a case study of antebellum nurture. *Illinois Quarterly*, Fall 1975, *38*, 12–28.

Wyatt-Brown, B. *Child Abuse, Public Policy, and Child Rearing in America: An Historical Approach* (Working Paper No. 2). College Park: University of Maryland, Center for the Study of Education Policy and Human Values, 1981.

Zuckerman, M. Dreams that men dared to dream: The role of ideas in Western modernization. *Social Science History*, Spring 1978, *2*, 932–945.

FEDERAL INFLUENCE ON EDUCATION

The involvement of the national government in the educational enterprise of the United States is peripheral to the tasks for which thousands of subnational governments and independent institutions are primarily responsible. Educational services reach the American public through many channels; there are, for example, separate ways of providing for pre–school-age children; for formal elementary, secondary, and postsecondary schooling, under both public and private auspices; for military and technical training; and for research and development. Unlike countries in which a central ministry of education establishes relatively uniform policies and practices on a national scale, the United States operates its educational programs in a highly decentralized fashion. The vast public education enterprise is firmly rooted in American federalism and its distinctive forms of intergovernmental relations (Mosher, 1977).

From this complex, shifting, and often bewildering milieu of educational policy making and practice, a few trends—which will be described in the following sections—have emerged over several decades: (1) Significant national governmental influence in education is a relatively recent development. (2) Federal funding of education has been justified on the basis of its instrumental value for the accomplishment of goals other than the advancement of the educational process. (3) Changes in established policy and procedures have been incremental rather than associated with sudden shifts or reversals. (4) A highly fragmented structure for educational policy making has produced a patchwork of national policies and programs. (5) Educational policy making has attained a prominent and

controversial position on the national domestic policy agenda.

Funding. The influence of the national government on the educational enterprise may be examined from several perspectives—constitutional, legal, ideological, programmatic, or fiscal—but it is useful initially to show the nature and extent of the federal financial investment in education. These data provide concrete evidence of policy trends, and, even more cogently, are grist for debates about the appropriate federal role which tend ultimately to revolve around issues of finance (Halperin, 1980).

Table 1 presents the "big picture" of current federal investment in education, broadly defined, from the vantage point of the funding government. As of 1978, the latest year for which firm fiscal data are available, the price tag was nearly $29 billion, composed of major allotments from several federal departments and agencies: Health, Education, and Welfare (HEW); Agriculture; Defense; Labor; and the Veterans Administration. Table 1 also shows the amounts and proportional share of the total federal funding allocated to elementary and secondary education; higher education; vocational, technical, and continuing education; and other education-related programs.

It is notable that HEW paid only slightly more than one-third of the total federal bill, with expenditures divided about evenly between the elementary-secondary and the higher education programs. Not allocated to either category are the child nutrition programs administered by the Department of Agriculture and the manpower-training programs of the Department of Labor which together amounted to 27.5 percent of total expenditures. Higher education received more than one-third of all the federal funding, with more than half its share coming from subventions for veterans' education paid out by the Veterans Administration and for mission-oriented research-and-development activities that are underwritten by all the federal agencies. About half these federal outlays for research and development (R & D) in colleges and universities are categorized as related to educational purposes, but not as direct subventions to higher education.

Table 2 puts federal fiscal contributions to education over the past twenty years in sharper focus from the recipients' point of view, since it presents data on federal support for education in educational institutions. It also distinguishes between grants and loans as methods of funding and shows levels of spending since 1960 in the specific programs that have claimed the major share of federal funds. The sizable contributions by the Department of Agriculture's school nutrition programs are here included in the amounts allocated to elementary and secondary schools, and the shares of higher education and precollegiate education thus appear as nearly equivalent during the twenty-year period. It should be noted that between 10 and 25 percent of total federal funding reported in Table 2 is "not classifiable by level" and that all amounts in Table 2 are shown in current dollars, which do not reflect monetary inflation since 1960.

TABLE 1. *Federal funds for education by agency, fiscal year 1978 (in millions of dollars)*

Departments or agencies	Elementary and secondary education	Higher education	Vocational, technical, and continuing education	Other education	Amount	Percentage of federal funds
Health, Education, and Welfare	$4,820	$ 4,780	$ 169	$ 243	$10,012	34.5%
Agriculture	112	12	—	2,912	3,036	10.5
Defense	318	1	3	994	1,316	4.5
Labor	—	—	4,918	—	4,918	17.0
Veterans Administration	—	2,697	498	—	3,195	11.0
All agencies—research and development in colleges and universities	—	2,542	—	2,614	5,156	17.8
All other agency funding	476	145	118	610	1,349	4.7
Total	$5,726	$10,177	$5,706	$7,373	$28,982	100.0%
Percentage of federal funds	19.7%	35.2%	19.7%	25.4%	100.0%	

SOURCE: Adapted from Grant & Eiden, 1980, table 159.

The trend for support of all programs has been upward, with the exception of loans for the construction of college facilities. The two most heavily funded programs since 1972 are those for educationally deprived children in the elementary and secondary schools (Title I, ESEA) and for grant and loan assistance to students in postsecondary institutions, which were estimated to account for about 36 percent of total federal funding in fiscal year 1980. The programs with the longest history of federal support—vocational education, impact aid (grants to school districts affected by the presence of federal governmental installations), and basic research in colleges and universities—continue to receive substantial amounts, with a marked upward trend in funding for vocational education since 1972. The new generation of programs that emerged during the 1970s—education for the handicapped, bilingual education, and emergency aid for school districts under court order to desegregate their schools—have all had rapid funding increases, amounting in fiscal year 1980 to an estimated 12 percent of the federal funds for elementary and secondary education.

Table 3 shows the relative contribution of the federal government to the total expenditures of all the country's educational institutions. Elementary and secondary schools expended 64 percent of the total outlay of $166.2 billion, and 81 percent of all expenditures were by public institutions. However, the relative share of expenditures by public and private institutions differed at each level, with private institutions accounting for a much higher percentage of the total outlays for higher education (32 percent) than for elementary and secondary education (11 percent).

The federal government's share in institutional costs also varies by level of education and type of institution.

It makes no direct contribution to private institutions for elementary and secondary education; but with regard to higher education, it provides a higher proportion of the outlays of private institutions (17.7 percent) than it does for public ones (11.8 percent). Although the total amounts of federal funds expended at the elementary-secondary and postsecondary levels are not greatly disparate ($9.1 billion and $8.1 billion, respectively), federal contributions to higher education represent a relatively higher share of the total higher education outlays, especially those of private institutions. Federal funds are distributed very unevenly among the roughly three thousand institutions of higher education, and a relatively small number receive a disproportionate share of the total. For example, among the twenty-two campuses that the Carnegie Commission classifies as "Research Universities I," federal funds supplied 34 percent of their "educational and general" revenues in 1973/74 (Finn, 1978, p. 37).

Federal support of public elementary and secondary education takes the form of "grants-in-aid" to both states and localities, a strategy for transfer of funds employed throughout the intergovernmental structure. Table 4 provides data, in constant dollars, on total revenues of public elementary and secondary schools and on the percentage changes in their revenue receipts from federal, state, and local sources from 1946 to 1978. Total revenues from all sources rose from $10.5 billion to $80.9 billion, and concurrently the state share of revenues rose by about 10 percent and the local share decreased by 16 percent. The federal share rose from 1.4 percent in 1946 to 8.1 percent in 1978, with the most notable increases between 1946 and 1954 and between 1962 and 1966. The proportionately small contribution from the federal government is widely distributed among the country's approximately sixteen thou-

TABLE 2. *Federal funds supporting education in educational institutions and related activities; selected years, 1960–1980 (in millions of dollars)*

Level, type of support, program area	1960	1966	1972	1978	1980[a]
Elementary & secondary education (grants)					
Educationally deprived children (Title I, ESEA)	—	$ 746	$ 1,570	$ 2,346	$ 3,011
Impact aid	$ 258	410	649	766	619
Education for the handicapped[1]	.01	5	68	294	762
Basic vocational education	45	118	371	403	568
Emergency school aid[2]	—	5	92	232	321
Bilingual education	—	—	26	107	149
School lunch & milk program	306	422	1,213	2,665	2,963
Other elementary & secondary programs	186	753	1,064	1,567	1,660
Total, all elementary & secondary programs	$ 795	$2,459	$ 5,053	$ 8,380	$10,053
Higher education (grants)					
Basic research	407	941	1,192	2,111	2,642
Facilities & equipment	1	304	576	600	582
Student assistance	408	845	3,112	6,201	5,937
Other higher education grant programs	14	183	292	473	578
Higher education (loans)					
Student loans[3]	40	235	287	748	1,246
College facilities	200	376	62	55	−20
Total, all higher education grants & loans	$1,070	$2,884	$ 5,521	$10,188	$10,965
Other grant programs (not classifiable by level)[4]	173	923	2,421	5,703	7,563
Total, all grant & loan programs, all levels	$2,038	$6,266	$12,994	$24,271	$28,581

[a] Estimated.   [1] Amounts for teacher training not included.   [2] Also includes civil rights services and training.   [3] Includes National Defense Education Act and insured student loans.   [4] Includes vocational, technical, and work training; veterans' education; general continuing education; training of state, local, and federal civilian personnel.

SOURCE: Adapted from Grant & Eiden, 1980, tables 160 and 163.

TABLE 3. *Estimated expenditures of educational institutions by level of institution, public or private control, and share of federal funds, 1979/80 (in billions of dollars)*

Type of institution	Elementary and secondary education		Higher education		Total	
	Amount	Percent	Amount	Percent	Amount	Percent
Public	$ 95.4	89.0	$39.9	68.0	$135.3	81.0
Private	11.7	11.0	19.2	32.0	30.9	19.0
Total	$107.1	100.0	$59.1	100.0	$166.2	100.0
	Share of federal funds					
Public	$ 9.1	9.5	$ 4.7	11.8	$ 13.8	80.0
Private	—	—	3.4	17.7	3.4	20.0
Total	$ 9.1	9.5	$ 8.1	14.0	$ 17.2	100.0

SOURCE: Adapted from Grant & Eiden, 1980, table 16.

TABLE 4. *Revenue receipts of public elementary and secondary schools, by source, in percentage of constant 1977/78 dollars; selected years, 1946–1978*

Year	Total revenues (billions)	Percentage distribution			
		Federal	State	Local[1]	Total
1946	$10.5	1.4%	34.7%	63.8%	100%
1950	14.4	2.9	39.8	57.3	100
1954	18.3	4.5	37.4	58.1	100
1958	26.7	4.0	39.4	56.6	100
1962	36.5	4.3	38.7	56.9	100
1966	49.7	7.9	39.1	53.0	100
1970	66.8	8.0	39.9	52.1	100
1974	78.2	8.5	41.7	49.8	100
1978[a]	80.9	8.1	44.1	47.8	100

[1] Includes intermediate.   [a] Estimated.

SOURCE: Adapted from Dearman & Plisko, 1979, table 4.3.

sand school districts. Only 6 percent are not involved in any program, whereas 53 percent participate in two or more programs (Goor et al., 1978–1979, p. 10).

The federal government has assumed very little responsibility for the direct operation of either precollegiate-level schools or institutions of higher education. Exceptions are overseas schools for military dependents, schools on military bases, and schools for American Indians and for inmates of federal penitentiaries. The government also operates undergraduate-degree-granting institutions for each of the military services and the Coast Guard and provides advanced graduate study opportunities for government employees. It makes appropriations for the support of two institutions of higher education located in Washington: Howard University and Gallaudet College, a school for the deaf.

Legislation. Historians emphasize that federal aid to education began with the Land Ordinance of 1785, which authorized grants of public domain for educational purposes, but this farsighted legislation was only a small step on a "long road to federal admission of responsibility" (Miles, 1974). Proposals for various forms of federal involvement surfaced periodically on the congressional agenda during the nineteenth century, but despite frequently intensive efforts, legislative successes were rare. Sustained financial support did not come about until basic changes occurred in American society, stemming from the Depression of the 1930s, World War II, rapid technological advances, the baby boom of the 1950s, and the postwar surge of civil rights activism. Moreover, extensive federal grants-in-aid to education were not authorized until a quarter-century after they had become a well-entrenched feature of intergovernmental programs in transportation, welfare, and health.

A number of more or less detailed historical accounts are available concerning the legislation enacted before

1960 (Advisory Commission on Intergovernmental Relations, 1981; Conrad & Cosand, 1976; Miles, 1974; Milstein, 1976; Munger & Fenno, 1962; Pierce, 1964; Rivlin, 1961; Tiedt, 1966). A chronology of the major laws includes the first and second Morrill Acts in 1862 and 1890, providing aid to the states for establishing and operating land grant colleges; the Smith-Hughes Act (1917) and the George-Barden Act (1946), supporting vocational education; impact aid legislation (amendment of the Lanham Act of 1940, and P.L. 81-815 and P.L. 81-874, 1950); the Servicemen's Readjustment Act, or GI Bill (1944), providing educational benefits for veterans of World War II and subsequently those of the Korean War; the National School Lunch Act (1946) and the School Milk Program (1954); the Cooperative Research Act (1954); and the National Defense Education Act (1958). (See the reference list for sources of information concerning the detailed provisions of the education legislation. The National Center for Education Statistics provides a convenient legislative chronology and brief summaries in the annual *Digests of Educational Statistics*. Also the Department of Education publishes annually an indexed guide to all the federal assistance programs that cites the specific legislative authority for each program.)

Each of these laws set precedents for marginal forms of federal assistance to both higher education and elementary and secondary education through general purpose and special category grants, loans, contracts, subventions to students, and commodities, but their uses were circumscribed. Localism and institutional autonomy were barriers to federal influence on educational policy, as was widespread public resistance to utilization of federal tax revenues for supporting private schooling at precollegiate levels or segregated school systems in the southern states. The financial needs of educational institutions became increasingly severe after World War II, but they were considered to be state and local or private-sector responsibilities and not a concern of the national government. The National Defense Education Act of 1958 is perhaps the best example of the congressional policy that finally prevailed: namely, to justify the federal government's assistance to education, under its constitutional power to advance the general welfare, as instrumental to ameliorating a specific national social need or crisis.

This rationale continued to apply even at the height of the Great Society initiatives taken during President Johnson's tenure from 1963 to 1968. The intent to advance social justice and conduct a national "war on poverty" was made explicit by the passage in 1964 of the Economic Opportunity Act and the Civil Rights Act, both of which had important side effects on educational policy. Moreover, they presaged a political climate favorable to the passage of educational legislation targeted to disadvantaged clienteles that expanded existing programs, created many new programs, and dramatically increased the levels of federal financial support. The major enactments during 1963 were the Higher Education Facilities Act (P.L. 88-204) and the Vocational Education Act (P.L. 88-210). Next followed in 1965 the passage of the Elementary and Secondary Education Act (ESEA) and the Higher Education Act (HEA), which are generally regarded as dramatic legislative breakthroughs. Diehard opponents of federal aid found it hard to resist the "omnibus" of benefits these acts provided (Bailey & Mosher, 1968; Eidenberg & Morey, 1969; Meranto, 1967; Sundquist, 1968; Thomas, 1975). They established a basic framework based on categorical grants for delimited clienteles, and the programs they supported have survived congressional expansions, modifications, and reauthorizations during the 1960s and 1970s. Education grant-in-aid programs now account for one hundred of the total of five hundred throughout the federal government.

Further important legislative initiatives in the ensuing decade were the International Education Act (P.L. 89-698, 1966); the Education Professions Development Act (P.L. 90-35, 1967); the Environmental Education Act (P.L. 91-516, 1970); the Bilingual Education Act (Title VII of the ESEA Amendments of 1968, P.L. 90-247); the authorization of the National Institute of Education (NIE), the Emergency School Aid Act, and the Basic Educational Opportunity Grants (Pell grants) in the Education Amendments of 1972 (P.L. 92-318); and the Education for All Handicapped Children Act (P.L. 94-142, 1975).

After 1968, however, the focus of congressional activity began gradually to shift from almost exclusive preoccupation with authorizing programs to obtaining, in the annual appropriations contests, funding for programs already on the books. Congress also undertook more intensive oversight activities and began to incorporate into the reauthorizations of the ESEA and HEA various regulatory requirements to deal with what it perceived as problems of implementing the federal assistance programs, such as closer adherence to legislative intent by educational offi-

cials at federal, state, and local levels; better reporting and evaluation of program operations; and reduction of the procedural and reporting tasks of aid recipients (Dershimer, 1976; Finn, 1978; Gladieux & Wolanin, 1975; Hughes & Hughes, 1972; Institute for Educational Leadership, 1976a, 1976b, 1978; Kirst, 1972, 1978; McLaughlin, 1975; Murphy, 1971; Summerfield, 1974; Timpane, 1978).

Purposes of Programs. No master plan for framing federal legislation or expanding educational funding has evolved through historical experience or contemporary agreement. According to Halperin, there is "no coherent, widely shared, or clearly understood 'national policy' for supporting and strengthening the abstraction called the nation's 'educational system'" (1980, p. 28). Instead, Congress has enacted a series of categorical programs that vary in practically every way: in scope, in eligibility requirements, in methods of funding, in administrative arrangements, in recipient responsibilities, and in the constraints placed on the use of funds.

The minutiae of legislation and program operations make analysis difficult, but according to Timpane (1978), the "basic settlement" has not changed since 1960 and five distinct federal purposes are discernible: (1) promoting equal educational opportunity; (2) stimulating educational reforms; (3) supporting educational research; (4) promoting educational preparation for employment; and (5) providing limited general support (pp. 4–7). In 1977 the Congressional Budget Office classified the major purposes of the elementary and secondary education programs as follows, showing the relative share of federal appropriations each received: (1) for support of selected curricula, resources, and services for specified types of students, 44 percent; (2) for general student populations, 8 percent; (3) for auxiliary services, 33 percent; (4) for specified types of school districts, 12 percent; (5) for research, change, and evaluation, 4 percent.

Somewhat duplicatory but more expansive summaries of federal purposes are offered by Halperin (1980), Kirst (1972), and the National Academy of Education (1979). All stress the primacy of two objectives at the precollegiate level: advancing equal opportunity and elevating the quality of educational services. At the higher-education level, equity concerns justify the provision of loans and grants directly to students, and encouragement of a broad range of research activities is the next most important priority. The National Academy (pp. 2–4) also identified some additional areas in which the "legitimacy of federal concern and action has been sanctioned": (1) providing the nation with a broad view of the purposes and possibilities of education in our society; (2) assisting in meeting training needs created by new federal initiatives, and working with other levels of government to provide for the development of personnel whose skills are deemed essential to the national interest; and (3) determining and publicizing the condition of education in the United States.

Policy Making at the National Level. The federal arena for educational policy making is crowded with an extraordinary number of participants: those with authority to make official decisions and outsiders who wish to influence the decisions. The first group includes the president and the White House staff, especially the Office of Management and Budget; executive agencies, such as the departments of education, health and human services, labor, justice, and agriculture, as well as the Veterans Administration and the National Science Foundation; federal courts of varying jurisdiction; the Senate and the House of Representatives, each with its own authorizing, appropriations, and budget committees and subcommittees and a cadre of individual members and staff aides who specialize in education-related issues.

Persons in or out of the federal government who wish to understand and influence the interplay of relationships among this cast of characters face a formidable task. However, there are some useful guidelines. By rule and precedent, policy making proceeds by definable stages from formulation through implementation, and under the provision for separation of powers, the requisite tasks are performed at different stages by identifiable networks of specialists. They focus their efforts selectively; that is, policy priorities vary from time to time and at various stages of the process. Official documentation and journalistic reporting of national governmental activities is extensive, and since 1965 information about the federal educational policy apparatus from scholarly and operational sources has proliferated. As is the case with other federal domestic programs, many educational professionals in both the governmental and private sectors now disseminate policy-oriented data, conduct legislative liaison, and provide expertise in the art of grantsmanship.

The American governmental system of checks and balances provides knowledgeable persons with many opportunities to introduce policy proposals, changes, compromises, and delays. It is extremely difficult and onerous to bring novel, complex, and costly measures unscathed from the proposal stage to the point of authorization, so that the leaders of the executive branch and Congress tend to settle for less ambitious, less contentious, and incremental forms of change.

In general, presidents anticipate more political risks than advantages from active support of federal assistance to education, and they have limited the leadership resources they are willing to expend (Finn, 1977). President Johnson was an exception in the high priority he gave to educational concerns and in his record of obtaining congressional support. By contrast, his successors, Presidents Nixon and Ford, engendered enduring congressional hostility when they tried to cut back the Great Society educational assistance programs. Between 1968 and 1980, veteran congressional committee chairmen like Senator Claiborne Pell (D., R.I.) and Representative Carl D. Perkins (D., Ky.) seized the initiative, and with much bipartisan support extended the benefits of federal aid to new clienteles and also devised statutory controls on the actions

of executive branch officials (*Education Laws*, 1978). Once in motion, congressional activism and independence are difficult to curb and channel, even for incoming administrations with strong electoral support, such as that of President Reagan in 1981. The Reagan proposals sharply to reduce levels of federal funding for education and to modify the structure for its distribution confront endemic congressional resistance to the loss of visibility for "its own" programs, to actions that alienate beneficiaries in the members' states and localities, and to procedural changes that increase bureaucratic discretion in spending federal funds.

The important influence of judicial decisions on educational matters is discussed elsewhere in this work. It is noteworthy that many recent actions of congress and the executive branch were taken in response to, or anticipation of, litigation over educational policy (Orfield, 1978; Wise, 1979). Issues such as busing, for example, brought education, once almost a negligible concern on the national scene, into the spotlight as an arena of continuous conflict between the branches and levels of government.

Numerous participants from outside the federal establishment make an essential contribution to shaping the actions of the insiders. Among the most influential are the spokespersons for the subnational governments: governors, mayors, legislators, school superintendents, school board members, and college and university trustees and presidents. Also working to advance their own views are parents, teachers, students, taxpayers, and advocates for or against a wide range of educational and social issues (Saxe, 1981). Some of these protagonists are highly organized and well financed on a national scale, with an extensive grass-roots membership and networks of representation at state and local levels of government. Other groups have only a few members and a limited number of specialized concerns. Table 5 provides a typology of the educational interest groups, with examples to illustrate each category. Bailey (1975, p. 6) estimated that in 1975 there were between two hundred fifty and three hundred headquarters of associations in Washington that purported to speak for more than 70 million people who were deeply involved in the country's educational enterprise.

Despite their diversity, the interest groups have some fairly basic similarities. One is their need for a Washington-based operation to monitor policy-making activities at close range and to provide timely, action-oriented information to their members. Virtually all the associations have tax-exempt status and wrestle with a lobbying dilemma: how to press effectively for desired legislative or funding objectives without jeopardizing their standing as "nonpolitical" organizations. This problem, together with the reluctance of many grass-roots members to align themselves with overt and aggressive forms of political activity, gives rise to the designation of the interest groups as "low-key" lobbyists (Bailey, 1975; King, 1975; *Washington Lobby*, 1971). On the other hand, the two major teachers'

TABLE 5. *Typology of Washington-based education representation, with examples*

Type	Examples
I. Umbrella organizations	American Council on Education Committee for Full Funding of Education Programs
II. Institutional associations	American Association of Community and Junior Colleges Association of Independent Colleges and Schools
III. Teachers' unions	National Education Association of the United States American Federation of Teachers American Association of University Professors
IV. Professions, fields, and disciplines	Music Educators National Conference American Political Science Association Association of American Medical Colleges
V. Librarians, suppliers, and technologists	American Library Association National Audio-Visual Association, Inc. College Entrance Examination Board
VI. Religion, race, sex	National Catholic Educational Association Washington Research Project Action Council American Association of University Women
VII. "Lib-lab" (liberal, labor) lobbies	AFL-CIO National Farmers Union
VIII. Institutions and institutional systems	Pennsylvania State University New York State Education Department
IX. Administrators and boards	American Association of School Administrators National School Boards Association Association of Governing Boards of Universities and Colleges Council of Chief State School Officers
X. Miscellaneous	Council for Basic Education National Committee for Citizens in Education National Student Lobby

SOURCE: Adapted from Bailey, 1975, p. 9.

groups, the National Education Association (NEA) and the American Federation of Teachers (AFT), officially registered their liaison personnel as lobbyists and became very active during the 1970s in election politics, endorsing favored candidates and making campaign contributions.

This major defection from the ranks of the educational groups is symptomatic of the difficulties the public and the professionals have in reaching agreement on policy goals and strategy and in forming coalitions. They typically react to proposals made by noneducators, rather than developing their own initiatives. Factional infighting erupts particularly over policies or funding provisions that benefit one sector, such as research-oriented universities, but disadvantage another, such as community colleges. Competition for favorable treatment, which becomes more intense at times when funding cutbacks are threatened, gives rise to ambivalent positions. For example, when contesting the fiscal stringencies advocated by Republican administrations during the 1970s and 1980s, many of the advocates of local governmental and institutional autonomy tempered their previous opposition to federal controls and lobbied Congress to continue the aid programs in their existing forms.

These tendencies of interest groups are especially counterproductive in dealing with Congress, whose members are more likely to comprehend and to treat seriously policy positions that are unequivocal and broadly supported. Until fairly recently, Congress watchers considered the lobbying of educators to be comparatively ineffective. Since the late 1960s, however, the leading education associations have had some successes in building cohesive arrangements, such as the Committee for Full Funding of Education Programs, and in achieving common legislative goals. Moreover, Congress has heard from many quarters a drumbeat of concerns and complaints about the problems state and local education officials, administrators of colleges and universities, and individual citizens experience in trying to implement, or benefit from, the federal assistance programs; complaints also abound about difficulties in complying with federal regulations relating to equal employment opportunity and equal access to facilities, occupational health and safety, and freedom of information.

Several prestigious study commissions (underwritten, for example, by the Carnegie and Sloan foundations), independent advisory groups mandated by legislation, and major research organizations such as the Brookings Institution and the Rand Corporation have produced periodic analyses of federal educational assistance programs and recommendations for their improvement, modification, or elimination (Ashworth, 1972; Berman & McLaughlin, 1978; Breneman & Nelson, 1980; Carnegie Commission on Higher Education, 1968, 1970, 1972; Carnegie Council on Policy Studies in Higher Education, 1975, 1979, 1980; Docksai, 1980; Hill, 1979; Hill & Rettig, 1980; Hughes, 1975; National Advisory Council, 1980; President's Commission for a National Agenda for the Eighties, 1980; Rivlin & Timpane, 1975; Sloan Commission, 1980; Williams, 1978). The evidence is persuasive that high costs, frustration, and inefficiency derive from narrowly focused and overlapping programs, complex and detailed regulations, lack of coordination among federal officials, and delays and reverses in budgetary and appropriations decisions. Unfortunately, these problems appear to derive from the workings of a highly complex, tradition-laden, and improvisational system for educational policy making, and they elude easy solutions.

Issues of Federal Programming. Federal legislation typically contains disclaimers of intent to control the country's educational enterprise, but it is clear that federal policies, programs, regulations, and funding have a significant influence on the ways in which nearly sixteen thousand school districts and three thousand institutions of higher education carry out their respective missions. Some effects of the growing federal presence since 1965 are apparent all across the country—in, for example, the observance of the new intergovernmental fiscal procedures, in the numerous federally funded employees of recipient agencies, in the numbers and types of students receiving federal assistance, or in the vast array of reports of ongoing program activities. Other effects are more long-range, less obvious, and more in dispute, so that comprehensive and unbiased conclusions about the impact of federal activities are problematical and likely to remain so (Radin, 1978).

One reason for this situation is the sheer number and diversity in size and capacity of the implementing agencies. Another is that federal policy makers have concentrated on achieving a variety of broadly defined, sometimes conflicting goals and have been unwilling or unable to anticipate the problems of implementing federal programs at the grass-roots level. Another reason is the tendency of recipient agencies to resent and resist external mandates, especially those relating to equal educational opportunity and improvement of educational services, which, presumably, would not have been invoked if Congress, the courts, or individual litigants had perceived pre-

viously existing situations to be satisfactory. Moreover, the meaning of the goals of equity and reform in operational terms is subject to a wide range of interpretations. What follows is a brief summary of some of the particular areas in which the nature and extent of federal influence remain at issue.

Definition of responsibility. Beginning with the U.S. Supreme Court ruling on school desegregation in 1954, federal requirements relating to equal educational opportunity produced a shift in power relationships in the educational establishment. However, this has been an evolutionary readjustment, with all the affected agencies exerting pressures and counterpressures on one another, instead of operating in well-defined areas of responsibility and influence. For example, federal policy for education has two contrary thrusts: regulatory strategies to prohibit certain actions on the part of subnational agencies; and financial incentives to stimulate desired improvements. Each strategy requires different modes of implementation. For the first, federal officials must prepare regulations for publication in the *Federal Register,* which spell out in detail the intent of the legislative enactments; and their approach is typically to incorporate measures to forestall every potential infraction of the regulations they can think of. The success of the second strategy requires, on the other hand, building relationships of trust and shared responsibility with the recipient agencies. In practice, however, the two strategies are confounded when the detailed regulations imposed on many of the financial assistance programs restrict the ability of the recipient agencies to make program innovations, and when funding is not terminated in cases of flagrant violations of federal requirements.

In utilizing discretionary federal funds and designing the funded program services, state and local educational agencies tend to steer a middle course, following as much as possible the strategies and methods to which they are accustomed (Berke & Kirst, 1972; Murphy, 1974). Implementation studies indicate that with the possible exception of Title I of ESEA, the administration of the intergovernmental education programs derives as much from "bottom-up" interpretations and actions as it does from "top-down" directives (Berman & McLaughlin, 1978; Datta, 1980; Farrar, DeSanctis, & Cohen, 1980; Kirst & Jung, 1980; Timpane, 1978).

Nonetheless, the recipient agencies, which provide the bulk of educational funding, consider that the federal constraints are costly, intrusive, and inappropriate. They argue that federal objectives—both regulatory and programmatic—could be better attained by giving them maximum authority to make policy and fiscal adjustments to meet their highly variable needs and circumstances (Cronin, 1976). This alternative raises questions from those with a stake in the federal programs as to how or whether accountability for carrying out national purposes could be ensured. These are the basic issues in the protracted debate about the relative desirability of "block grants," which would aggregate separate program funds and provide greater decision-making authority to grant recipients, in comparison with a system of numerous "categorical grants," each with its own set of federally monitored requirements (Halperin, 1976).

Program evaluation. An innovation of the ESEA in 1965 was the requirement that local, state, and federal agencies evaluate and report on program effects, and this evaluation mandate spread to nearly all subsequent federal programs (House, 1979). Emphasis on evaluation was part of a general shift in policy and administrative emphasis from measuring program inputs in terms of money, facilities, and personnel to outputs in terms of quality and efficacy of services provided. Program evaluation was not a new undertaking for educators, but the federal influence dramatically heightened its priority and visibility, and more significantly, the commitment of financial resources to its performance. Consequently, during the ensuing years evaluation has been a "growth industry" for personnel coming both from the ranks of educational agencies and from private companies working under government contract. The area of evaluation, in which the professional literature has burgeoned, has attained status as a methodological subfield.

There is some consensus about the policy effects of the buildup of federal evaluation activities, such as the focusing of public and policy makers' attention on measures of pupil achievement as criteria of program effectiveness; the perennial tensions that develop between program evaluators and program operatives; and the occasional use of evaluation findings as weapons in the federal educational assistance wars. However, evaluation professionals are themselves at variance over many technical and utilization issues, and the potential contributions that program evaluations might make to better-informed educational policy decisions remain debatable (Abert, 1979; Abt, 1976; House, 1973; Hyde & Shafritz, 1979; Weiss, 1972; Zweig, 1979). With the notable exception of the NIE study (1978) of Title I, experience to date indicates that federal policy makers have preferred to rely on other resources (Andringa, 1976).

Extension of benefits. The major thrust of federal policy making during the late 1960s and the 1970s was the further extension of educational assistance to disadvantaged populations, so that by 1980 benefits for large numbers of economically deprived school-age children, college students, and handicapped youth represented the predominant federal investment in education. Compensatory services on a smaller scale were also made available to bilingual and gifted children. In line with the national interest in ensuring equal educational opportunity, affirmative action programs were mandated for women, and subnational governments were encouraged to undertake reforms of school finance (Mosher, Hastings, & Wagoner, 1979). Among other, but as yet unsuccessful, proposals to extend federal benefits is provision of federal income tax deductions for partial costs of tuition at private schools or colleges. The rationale offered is that the financial burdens

of public and private school patrons would thereby be more equitable.

The expansion of federal assistance, frequently in response to strenuous lobbying by specific groups of beneficiaries, has raised some troublesome problems and dilemmas for the educational community and the general public. One relates to rising costs, especially those for the education of handicapped children, which have intensified opposition to educational expenditures across the board. Another is the question of feasible limits for equalization; groups who are ineligible for present benefits come to see themselves as the victims of "affirmative discrimination," disadvantaged by the government's policies for remedying past inequities. Perhaps the most basic concern relates to the educational mission of schools and colleges. The federal emphasis on equity is perceived as distorting priorities and absorbing resources essential to maintain balanced and coherent educational programs. Moreover, local constituencies that have been the principal supporters of public education in the past have become concerned that emphasis on compensatory services will lower its standards and quality to unacceptable levels.

Strategies for reform. The strategies that the federal government has used to influence, and hopefully improve, educational practice have been indirect and varied. The beginnings of sustained interest and funding date back to the passage of the Cooperative Research Act in 1954, but many subsequent efforts have been episodic and short-lived. The most important undertaking has been the support of educational research, which is presently most evident in the activities of the Bureau of Educational Research and Improvement in the Department of Education. Funding for research is also included in appropriations for vocational education and the education of handicapped children. Although it might seem that a national interest in research, as the least intrusive of federal purposes, would be the most acceptable and least controversial, it has in fact been the most vulnerable to attack by congressional and executive branch critics, who value practical, immediate payoff from public expenditures rather than what they consider to be, at best, very uncertain results in the distant future. Furthermore, educational research lacks a large, well-organized constituency. In comparison with other fields, such as health, energy, and space technology, in which federal funding for basic research has been generous, educational research has had modest support, with a higher proportion of resources devoted to statistical, developmental, and dissemination activities. Since 1965 the ERIC system for research information retrieval has become a widely used professional resource.

In addition to its own Washington-based activities, the federal government has supported, by grants and contracts, a network of regional research organizations, as well as projects undertaken by private organizations and individual researchers; and it has also encouraged state departments of education to upgrade their own research capabilities. Since the federal government is presently the leading patron of educational research, the vagaries of its funding provisions and the research priorities that it establishes are of crucial importance in the field. Educational researchers chafe under this dependency, but it must be conceded that federal investment is responsible for the great expansion and enrichment of the field since 1965.

Federal strategies aimed more directly at improving educational practice at the operating level cover a wide spectrum. They include targeting of funds to instruction in specific curriculum areas, such as science, reading, or area studies (this includes support of curriculum development, and training and retraining of teachers); subventions and technical assistance to state departments of education for upgrading their planning and management activities; imposing requirements and earmarking funds for support of public and parental participation in educational affairs; underwriting programs, such as Head Start, for pre–school-age children; subventions for instructional materials and library resources and for teacher-run "resource centers"; heavy investment in evaluation activities; and initiation of small-scale experimental and demonstration programs, with varying degrees of federal direction and involvement.

Duration of programs has varied from a few months to several years. Some flourished for a time in the limelight and then slipped from view when educators objected or leadership support waned. A few experiments, like the small-scale experimental voucher plan, received wide publicity and aroused much controversy. Nearly all have been extensively documented, and conclusions are mixed as to both their immediate and long-range impacts on the far-flung educational enterprise—which, it is widely recognized, is typically slow to adopt innovations.

Summary. The involvement of the federal government in education is not large in comparison with its other functions, or with the responsibilities carried out by subnational governments and private institutions, but discourse about its influence is, in 1981, a chorus of disharmony in professional circles and in the public arena. This extends to every aspect of present policy, large or small: laws and regulations that provide expressions of national purpose and financial support; vagaries of the federal policy-making process; problems of implementing diverse programs; gains achieved or losses suffered by individual students and by the interest groups and institutions involved in their education—even basic changes in established patterns of intergovernmental relations.

The potential role of the federal government in education has long been a contentious topic, but historically support was actually given only to a few scattered forms of educational assistance as a means to furthering various national purposes. In the early 1960s, however, the purpose of advancing equal educational opportunity gained ascendancy, accompanied by far higher levels of federal funding, gradual extension of benefits to clienteles considered disadvantaged under existing practice, and new procedures for accountability on the part of educational agencies. The methods for formulating policies and programs

to accomplish these ends were designed more with a view to winning congressional support than to accommodating the readiness or capability of recipient agencies to implement them. The subsequent uncertainties and conflicts were predictable, as will be the continuing efforts to bring some order into the present disarray. In sum, the federal government has established an enduring and important, but as yet emerging, influence on American education.

Edith K. Mosher

See also Governance of Schools; Judicial Decisions; Legislation; Research Laboratories and Centers; U.S. Department of Education.

REFERENCES

Abert, J. G. (Ed.). *Program Evaluation at HEW: Research versus Reality* (Part 2: Education). New York: Marcel Dekker, 1979.

Abt, C. C. (Ed.). *The Evaluation of Programs.* Beverly Hills, Calif.: Sage, 1976.

Advisory Commission on Intergovernmental Relations. Intergovernmentalizing the classroom: Federal involvement in elementary and secondary education. In *The Federal Role in the Federal System: The Dynamics of Growth* (Vol. V). Washington, D.C.: U.S. Government Printing Office, 1981.

Andringa, R. C. Eleven factors influencing federal legislation. In *Federalism at the Crossroads: Improving Educational Policymaking.* Washington, D.C.: George Washington University, Institute for Educational Leadership, 1976, pp. 79–80.

Ashworth, K. H. *Scholars and Statesmen.* San Francisco: Jossey-Bass, 1972.

Bailey, S. K. *Education Interest Groups in the Nation's Capital.* Washington, D.C.: American Council on Education, 1975.

Bailey, S. K., & Mosher, E. K. *ESEA: The Office of Education Administers a Law.* Syracuse, N.Y.: Syracuse University Press, 1968.

Berke, J. S., & Kirst, M. W. *Federal Aid to Education: Who Benefits? Who Governs?* Lexington, Mass.: Lexington Books, 1972.

Berman, P., & McLaughlin, M. W. Implementing and sustaining innovations. In *Federal Programs Supporting Educational Change* (Vol. 8). Santa Monica, Calif.: Rand Corporation, May 1978. (ERIC Document Reproduction Service No. ED 159 289)

Breneman, D. W., & Nelson, S. C. Education and training. In J. A. Pechman (Ed.), *Setting National Priorities: Agenda for the 1980s.* Washington, D.C.: Brookings Institution, 1980.

Carnegie Commission on Higher Education. *Quality and Equality: New Levels of Federal Responsibility for Higher Education.* New York: McGraw-Hill, 1968; revised recommendations, 1970.

Carnegie Commission on Higher Education. *Institutional Aid: Federal Support to Colleges and Universities.* New York: McGraw-Hill, 1972.

Carnegie Council on Policy Studies in Higher Education. *The Federal Role in Postsecondary Education: Unfinished Business, 1975–1980.* San Francisco: Jossey-Bass, 1975.

Carnegie Council on Policy Studies in Higher Education. *Next Steps for the 1980s in Student Financial Aid: A Fourth Alternative.* San Francisco: Jossey-Bass, 1979.

Carnegie Council on Policy Studies in Higher Education. *Three Thousand Futures: The Next Twenty Years for Higher Education* (Final Report). San Francisco: Jossey-Bass, 1980.

Congressional Budget Office, Congress of the United States. *Budget Issue Paper on Elementary, Secondary, and Vocational Education: An Examination of Alternative Federal Roles.* Washington, D.C.: U.S. Government Printing Office, January 1977.

Conrad, C., & Cosand, J. *The Implications of Federal Education Policy* (ERIC/Higher Education Research Report No. 1). Washington, D.C.: American Association for Higher Education, 1976. (ERIC Document Reproduction Service No. ED 124 066)

Cronin, J. M. The federal takeover: Should the junior partner run the firm? In *Federalism at the Crossroads: Improving Educational Policymaking.* Washington, D.C.: George Washington University, Institute for Educational Leadership, 1976, pp. 67–70.

Datta, L. E. Changing times: The study of federal programs supporting educational changes and the case for local problem solving. *Teachers College Record,* 1980, *82,* 101–116.

Dershimer, R. A. *The Federal Government and Educational R & D.* Lexington, Mass.: Lexington Books, 1976.

Docksai, R. F. The Department of Education. In C. L. Heatherly (Ed.), *Mandate for Leadership: Policy Management in a Conservative Administration.* Washington, D.C.: Heritage Foundation, 1980.

Education Laws 1978. Arlington, Va.: National School Public Relations Association, 1978. (ERIC Document Reproduction Service No. ED 168 155)

Eidenberg, E., & Morey, R. D. *An Act of Congress: The Legislative Process and the Making of Educational Policy.* New York: Norton, 1969.

Farrar, E.; DeSanctis, J. E.; & Cohen, D. K. Views from below: Implementation research in education. *Teachers College Record,* 1980, *82,* 77–100.

Finn, C. E., Jr. *Education and the Presidency.* Lexington, Mass.: Lexington Books, 1977.

Finn, C. E., Jr. Federal patronage of the universities: A rose by many other names? In S. Hook, P. Rurtz, & M. Todoronch, *The University and the State: What Role for Government in Higher Education?* Buffalo, N.Y.: Prometheus Books, 1978.

Gladieux, L. E., & Wolanin, T. R. *Congress and the Colleges: The National Politics of Higher Education.* Lexington, Mass.: Lexington Books, 1976.

Goor, J.; Moore, M.; Demarest, E.; & Farris, E. *School Districts Participating in Multiple Federal Programs.* Washington, D.C.: National Center for Education Statistics. Fast Response Survey System (FRSS), Report No. 7, Winter 1978/79.

Grant, W. V., & Eiden, L. J. *Digest of Education Statistics, 1980.* Washington, D.C.: National Center for Education Statistics, U.S. Government Printing Office, 1980.

Halperin, S. Block grants or categorical aids? What do we really want: Consolidation, simplification, decentralization? In *Federalism at the Crossroads: Improving Educational Policymaking.* Washington, D.C.: George Washington University, Institute for Educational Leadership, 1976, pp. 67–70.

Halperin, S. The educational arena. *Educational Evaluation and Policy Analysis,* 1980, *2,* 27–36.

Hill, P. T. *Do Federal Education Programs Interfere with One Another?* (Paper Series P-6416). Santa Monica, Calif.: Rand Corporation, September 1979. (ERIC Document Reproduction Service No. ED 192 445)

Hill, P. T., & Rettig, R. A. *Mechanisms for the Implementation of Civil Rights Guarantees by Educational Institutions.* Santa Monica, Calif.: Rand Corporation, January 1980.

House, E. R. (Ed.). *School Evaluation: The Politics and Process.* Berkeley, Calif.: McCutchan, 1973.

House, E. R. The objectivity, fairness, and justice of federal evaluation policy as reflected in the Follow Through evaluation. *Educational Evaluation and Policy Analysis,* 1979, *1,* 28–42.

Hughes, J. F. (Ed.). *Education and the State.* Washington, D.C.: American Council on Education, 1975.

Hughes, J. F., & Hughes, A. O. *Equal Education: A New National Strategy.* Bloomington: Indiana University Press, 1972.

Hyde, A. C., & Shafritz, J. M. (Eds.). *Program Evaluation in the Public Sector.* New York: Praeger and Holt, Rinehart & Winston, 1979.

Institute for Educational Leadership. *Federalism at the Crossroads: Improving Educational Policymaking.* Washington, D.C.: George Washington University, Institute for Educational Leadership, 1976. (a) ERIC Document Reproduction Service No. ED 132 721)

Institute for Educational Leadership. *Perspectives on Federal Educational Policy: An Informal Colloquium.* Washington, D.C.: George Washington University, Institute for Educational Leadership, 1976. (b) (ERIC Document Reproduction Service No. ED 129 150)

Institute for Educational Leadership. *Educational Policy in the Carter Years.* Washington, D.C.: George Washington University, Institute for Educational Leadership. 1978. (ERIC Document Reproduction Service No. ED 187 154)

King, L. R. *The Washington Lobbyists for Higher Education.* Lexington, Mass.: Lexington Books, 1975.

Kirst, M. W. *The Growth and Limits of Federal Influence in Education* (Occasional Paper 72-9). Stanford, Calif.: Stanford University, School of Education, September 1972.

Kirst, M. W. The changing politics of education: Actions and strategies. In E. K. Mosher, and J. L. Wagoner, Jr., *The Changing Politics of Education: Prospects for the 1980's.* Berkeley, Calif.: McCutchan, 1978.

Kirst, M., & Jung, R. The utility of a longitudinal approach in assessing implementation. *Educational Evaluation and Policy Analysis,* 1980, *2,* 17–34.

McLaughlin, M. *Evaluation and Reform: The Case of ESEA, Title I.* Cambridge, Mass.: Ballinger, 1975.

Meranto, P. *The Politics of Federal Aid to Education in 1965: A Study in Political Innovation.* Syracuse, N.Y.: Syracuse University Press, 1967.

Miles, R. E., Jr. Education. In *The Department of Health, Education, and Welfare.* New York: Praeger, 1974.

Milstein, M. M. *Impact and Response: Federal Aid and State Education Agencies.* New York: Columbia University, Teachers College Press, 1976.

Mosher, E. K. Education and American federalism: Intergovernmental and national policy influences. In J. D. Scribner (Ed.), *The Politics of Education: The Seventy-sixth Yearbook of the National Society for the Study of Education.* Chicago: University of Chicago Press, 1977.

Mosher, E. K.; Hastings, A. H.; & Wagoner, J. L., Jr. *Pursuing Equal Educational Opportunity: School Politics and the New Activists* (ERIC/CUE Urban Diversity Series, No. 64). (ERIC Document Reproduction Service No. ED 179 625) New York: ERIC Clearinghouse on Urban Education; Institute for Urban and Minority Education; Columbia University, Teachers College, 1979.

Munger, F. J., & Fenno, R. F., Jr. *National Politics and Federal Aid to Education.* Syracuse, N.Y.: Syracuse University Press, 1962.

Murphy, J. T. Title I of ESEA: The politics of implementing federal educational reform. *Harvard Educational Review*, 1971, *41*, 35–63.

Murphy, J. T. *State Education Agencies and Discretionary Funds: Grease the Squeaky Wheel.* Lexington, Mass.: Lexington Books, 1974.

National Academy of Education. *The Appropriate Federal Role in Education: Some Guiding Principles* (Report of a Committee). Washington, D.C.: National Academy of Education, 1979.

National Advisory Council on the Education of Disadvantaged Children. *The Office of Education Administers Changes in a Law: Agency Response to Title I, ESEA Amendments of 1978* (Report to the President prepared by E. R. Reisner, NTS Research Corporation). Washington, D.C.: The Council, May 1980. (ERIC Document Reproduction Service No. ED 191 936)

National Institute of Education. *The Compensatory Education Study: Final Report to Congress.* Washington, D.C.: National Institute of Education, 1978. (ERIC Document Reproduction Service No. ED 161 996)

Orfield, G. *Must We Bus? Segregated Schools and National Policy.* Washington, D.C.: Brookings Institution, 1978.

Pierce, T. M. *Federal, State, and Local Government in Education.* New York: Center for Applied Research in Education, 1964.

President's Commission for a National Agenda for the Eighties. An education agenda for the 1980s. In *Government and the Advancement of Social Justice: Health, Welfare, Education, and Civil Rights in the Eighties.* Washington, D.C.: U.S. Government Printing Office, 1980.

Radin, B. A. Equal educational opportunity and federalism. In M. W. Williams (Ed.), Government in the Classroom: Dollars and Power in Education. *Proceedings of the Academy of Political Science*, 1978, *33*, 77–86.

Rivlin, A. M. *The Role of the Federal Government in Financing Higher Education.* Washington, D.C.: Brookings Institution, 1961.

Rivlin, A. M., & Timpane, P. M. *Planned Variation in Education.* Washington, D.C.: Brookings Institution, 1975.

Saxe, R. W. (Ed.). Interest groups. *Education and Urban Society*, 1981, *13*.

Sloan Commission on Government and Higher Education. *A Program for Renewed Partnership.* Cambridge, Mass.: Ballinger, 1980.

Summerfield, H. L. *Power and Process: The Formulation and Limits of Federal Educational Policy.* Berkeley, Calif.: McCutchan, 1974.

Sundquist, J. L. *Politics and Policy: The Eisenhower, Kennedy, and Johnson Years.* Washington, D.C.: Brookings Institution, 1968.

Thomas, N. C. *Education in National Politics.* New York: McKay, 1975.

Tiedt, S. W. *The Role of the Federal Government in Education.* New York: Oxford University Press, 1966.

Timpane, M. (Ed.). *The Federal Interest in Schooling.* Cambridge, Mass.: Ballinger, 1978.

U.S. Department of Health, Education, and Welfare; National Center for Educational Statistics. *Problems Stemming from Children's Eligibility for Multiple Federal Programs.* 1979.

Washington Lobby. Washington, D.C.: Congressional Quarterly, 1971.

Weiss, C. *Evaluating Action Programs: Readings in Social Action and Education.* Boston: Allyn & Bacon, 1972.

Williams, M. F. (Ed.). Government in the classroom: Dollars and power in education. *Proceedings of the Academy of Political Science*, 1978, *33*, 1–160.

Wise, A. E. *Legislated Learning: The Bureaucratization of the American Classroom.* Berkeley: University of California Press, 1979.

Zweig, F. M. (Ed.). *Evaluation in Legislation.* Beverly Hills, Calif.: Sage, 1979.

FIELD EXPERIENCES IN TEACHER EDUCATION

Field experiences are among the elements of the preservice education of teachers grouped under the label "clinical experiences." Warner, Houston, and Cooper (1977) note that the *Dictionary of Education* includes forty-six uses of the terms "clinic" and "clinical" and go to specify clinical experiences as opportunities for the trainee to learn in actual client settings. Smith (1970) states: "All direct and simulated activities in both the laboratory and practicum phases of a modern program of teacher education are in this view clinical experiences" (p. 1). The *Forty-first Yearbook of the Association of Student Teaching* defines professional laboratory experiences as "all those contacts with children, youth, and adults (through observation, participation, and teaching) which make a direct contribution to the understanding of individuals and their guidance in the teaching/learning process" (Schunk, 1962, p. 131). The term "field experience" is here used synonymously with "clinical experience." Turns (1970) reported that 380 of 482 institutions approved by the National Council for Accreditation of Teacher Education provided field experiences prior to student teaching. Varieties of field experiences and their effects are the concerns of this article.

Accreditation. In 1948 the American Association of Colleges of Teacher Education enunciated nine principles of field experience, five of which focused on pre–student teaching (Beach & Reinhartz, 1978). During the late 1960s and throughout the 1970s, early and extensive field experiences became an article of faith supported by college-based teacher educators, classroom teachers, professional associations, and potential employers. Pre–student-teaching field experiences have been required by the National Council for the Accreditation of Teacher Education's Standard 2.3.3, Teaching and Learning Theory with Laboratory and Clinical Experiences (*Standards for the Accreditation of Teacher Education*, 1979), and by the National Association of State Directors of Teacher Education and Certification's Standard 2.8, School-Institutional Relationships (*Standards for State Approval*, 1979). The inclusion of such experiences is also endorsed by the National Student Education Association (Allen, 1971). Recently Ohio has specified that all certification candidates have field experiences in urban, suburban, and rural schools (*Standards for Colleges*, 1975).

Proponents hold that students who work with master teachers acquire knowledge and skills necessary to become effective teachers, whereas critics insist that classroom teachers do not have the knowledge, skills, or time necessary to train neophytes (Elmore, 1979). At the beginning of the 1980s, the definition, value, and role of pre–student-teaching field experiences continued to be a topic of intense interest.

Program Description. Field experiences are designed to test and shape attitudes about students, teaching, and learning (*Elementary TEAM Program*, 1975; "TEAM" refers to "Teacher Education Access Model"); help students make career decisions (Ishler, Lee, & Wilhoyte, 1978; Freeland, 1978; Finley, 1975); provide exposure to the variety of environments in which education takes place (Beach & Reinhartz, 1977; Otto, 1976); give opportunities to practice specific teaching techniques (Knight, 1975); apply ideas associated with a particular curricular area (Kulm, 1975; Melograno, 1976); or assist neophytes in role acquisition (Reitman, 1973; Henry & Glasheen, 1972). On occasion such experiences may also be used to support delivery of community services (*Vocational Clarification*, 1971; *Union University*, 1975).

Experiences usually take one of five generic forms: observation, participation, tutoring, small-group instruction, and short-duration–large-group instruction. Observation varies widely among programs reported. Perhaps the least organized are those that require students to report a specified number of hours of observation in educational settings prior to admission to the professional preparation sequence. Settings often include day care programs, nursery schools, and church or Sunday schools as well as public school classrooms. Site selection and logistical arrangements often are the student's responsibility. Emphasis is on the student's presence and the assumption that exposure will assist the individual to determine whether to pursue education as a career. However, the outcome of such exposure is difficult to evaluate. Students who complete the requirement and enter the sequence (as opposed to others, who leave the population) may be assumed to have confirmed a career choice. But it is not known why they have done so.

Once students have entered the preservice program, observation requirements become more systematic. When associated with education course work, observation is focused on their seeing what they have been learning about. Students in human development courses observe the linguistic, physical, cognitive, and social abilities of children in particular classrooms. The student is a passive member of the environment learning from the interaction of children and teacher.

Participation adds a new dimension to the experience: active involvement. Generally, the participating preservice student functions as an aide in the classroom. Duties may include preparation and distribution of instructional materials and supervision of noninstructional activities. In these situations the emphasis is on getting the feel of the social system, the organization of school.

Tutoring is a logical extension of aiding in which the education student accepts responsibility for one or two learners. Activity follows a plan established by the classroom teacher or subject-matter specialist. Tutorial experiences are often part of courses in reading instruction.

Small-group instruction and short-duration–large-group instruction are also associated with methods courses. In these situations the student plans the activity, selects materials, carries out the instruction, and evaluates the lesson.

These five types of experience progress logically from initial encounters with the schools through practice that would prepare the student to accept the responsibilities of full-time student teaching. It is, therefore, interesting to note that relatively few of the nation's teacher-preparation institutions require that preservice students participate in a full sequence of pre–student-teaching field experiences.

There seem to be two major reasons why such experiences have not become universally required: governance and logistics. Descriptions of existing programs stress the importance of collaborative relationships between college faculty and host teachers. This collaboration implies full participation in the development of the experience, from goal setting to evaluation. It also implies the involvement of practitioners in the full preservice program. Such shared governance often proves to be an insurmountable obstacle, because, in most instances, no special fiscal resources are available, programs are voluntary in nature, students usually provide their own transportation, and faculty accept supervisory responsibility as part of regular instruction. Thus the level of risk taking necessary to support long-term involvement is low. It is acknowledged that field experiences at any point in the preservice program create extra demands for all concerned. When alternatives are available, the less demanding programs tend to draw the students.

Program Models. Those institutions that have adopted a full sequence present interesting variations on the theme. At Southern Illinois University, the sequence consists of (1) September experience, (2) teacher-aide experience, (3) elementary block program, and (4) secondary laboratory experience prior to student teaching (Verduin & Heinz, 1970). Edgecliff College (Finley, 1975) requires a five-phase program. An initial two-semester experience combines the study of education with observation in school classrooms. Phases 2 and 3 combine on-campus course work with tutoring and then aiding in an elementary school. During phase 4, students study teaching methods and practice the teaching of specific skills in schools. Phase 5 consists of one semester of full-time teaching.

The University of Georgia requires prospective secondary English teachers to serve as teacher aides during their general education sequence (*Secondary English Teacher Preparation*, 1977). This experience leads to the Advanced Professional Education Sequence (APES), which lasts two quarters. Students enrolled in professional education courses are placed in schools where they assist by doing clerical tasks and progress through observation and tutoring to small-group and occasional large-group instruction en route to solo teaching with a full load. Optional peer teaching is also included.

Those institutions that require a less extensive sequence also vary the point in the student's program at which field experiences occur. Some institutions prefer a sophomore experience (*Union University*, 1975), whereas others delay the experience until the junior year (*Undergraduate Experimental Program*, 1972; MacNaughton, 1978). The critical factor in each program is the integration of field work with on-campus course work.

Evaluation. The most common approach to evaluation of pre–student-teaching field experiences focuses on the perceptions of students and their attitudes. Students who have completed a field experience often perceive the role of teacher more realistically, exhibit significant concern about their own adequacy in performing that role, and express faith in the efficacy of the experience (Uhlenberg & Holt, 1975). Among participants, field experiences have produced more positive attitudes about students, teaching and learning, and the teacher-preparation program than are found among participants in traditional programs (Crowl & Alsworth, 1976; Knoll, 1973).

In a volunteer program in an inner-city school, participants' experiences "favorably increased their attitude toward teaching and students; led them to rate more highly their senior education block courses, to consider teaching in slum-poverty type schools, to feel more sure of their decision to teach or not to teach; and made them feel more prepared to be a teacher" (Marso, 1971, p. 198). Experiences focusing on specific subject areas, such as science teaching (Knoll, 1973), have been shown to have similar positive effects.

In an interesting experiment, Clark (1974) added a field experience to an introductory educational psychology course and evaluated participants and a control group on measures of achievement, educational philosophy, and attitudes. Her results revealed that adding the field experience did not affect performance but did affect attitudes and philosophical values positively.

Measures of performance are less common than those of perceptions and attitudes. However a five-year study of graduates of the University of Washington's teacher education program reported that graduates with field experience rated higher on eleven categories of teaching performance (*1979 Distinguished Achievement*, 1979). Student teachers at Bowling Green State University who had completed prior field experiences rated themselves higher on twelve items and were rated higher on performance by both university supervisor and cooperating teacher (Marso & Reed, 1971). Gantt and Davey (1972) reported that students who completed a field-supplemented methods course exhibited strong feelings of confidence when compared to students who did not have such an experience.

Bartos (1973) experimented with four variations of the classroom–field experience mix in examining perceptions of prospective teachers. He suggests that such experience (1) can be inserted much earlier in the student's program;

(2) must be continually redesigned to allow for practical applications of theory-related ideals; and (3) in most beneficial when field and classroom components are concurrent.

A most interesting variation is reported by Newlove (1969), who arranged for students to teach one fifteen-minute lesson to an unfamiliar class of an unfamiliar teacher. Students were filmed and a feedback session was held. Results showed increased respect for the teaching profession and increased concern with student achievement.

Criteria. Clearly, those field experiences that are well thought out, adequately supported, and thoroughly evaluated appear to have positive effects. Examination of successful experiences in teacher education and similarly successful experiences of preparation programs in other professions suggests some logical criteria. Warner, Houston, and Cooper (1977) suggest that the individual should be engaged in actual observation and treatment of clients in a natural setting in which there is the opportunity to manipulate instructional variables. Performance expectations are explicit and public, and feedback is systematic and supportive, encouraging the trainee to assume increasing responsibility for further professional growth.

Research Concerns. When host teachers are asked to rate a student's performance during or immediately after the experience, they report positive results. However, three characteristics of the experiences reported remain bothersome.

First, voluntary participation remains the rule. Thus the population studied is self-selected. When reports indicate that these individuals are more committed to teaching, perceive that they have more to learn about their profession, and appear to be more proficient than their peers who did not opt for the field experience, the results follow predictable patterns.

Second, the adequacy of the samples studied is a problem. Research to date has focused on relatively small groups of students, for example, fourteen students in a methods class, twenty-four sophomores in a particular program, students in a special urban education program. Moreover, the studies tend not to be replicated. Reports leave the impression that some experiences were developed with an eye to the completion of the research rather than as an ongoing part of the program. Conversely, when the experience was clearly an ongoing part of the program, evaluation tended to be downplayed. Such statements as "Evaluation is an ongoing process" or "Because of the experimental nature of the program and its short duration, evaluation is incomplete" abound.

Masked effects of pre–student-teaching field experiences pose the third problem. Often these experiences are lumped together as part of a field-based teacher education program. The entire program is evaluated and reported without differentiating among constituent parts. Thus the effect of a particular component, such as a tutorial experience, may be hidden amid data gathered regarding the whole program.

It is worth noting that studies comparing the effectiveness of field-bases versus campus-based programs tend to compare variations of a single program within a college or university rather than distinctly different programs within the institution or programs from several institutions. Again the distinguishing characteristics include the voluntary nature of participation in the field-based curriculum. Moreover, although the perceptions of students, host teachers, and teacher educators reported are positive, criterion-referenced data regarding performance are at best inconclusive. When attempts have been made to follow graduates of field-based programs into employment settings, results of supervisors' ratings after one year tend to show no difference when compared to ratings of graduates of campus-based programs.

Conclusions. Data reported suggest positive effects of field experiences on characteristics that are essential to the professional educator. However, the voluntary nature of programs reported, the generally small sample size, the masking of the effect of these experiences in studies of whole field-based programs, and the paucity of longitudinal studies indicate the strong need for additional research.

Thomas F. Ryan

See also Laboratory Experiences in Teacher Education; Laboratory Schools; Student Teaching; Teacher Education Programs.

REFERENCES

Allen, M. R. Early and continuous direct experience with children. *Contemporary Education,* April 1971, *42*(5), 226–228.

Bartos, R. B. *A Study of Field Participation and Classroom Experiences and Their Effects upon the Perceptions of Prospective Teachers.* Paper presented to the American Educational Research Association, New Orleans, February 1973. (ERIC Document Reproduction Service No. ED 075 381)

Beach, D. M., & Reinhartz, J. *An Experimental Program in Field-based Prestudent Teaching Experiences.* Unpublished manuscript, University of Texas at Arlington, 1977. (ERIC Document Reproduction Service No. ED 135 746)

Beach, D. M., & Reinhartz, J. Relating theory to practice: Establishing a field-based program. *Kappa Delta Pi Record,* December 1978, *15*(2), 35–38.

Clark, A. T. *The Effect of a Public School Field Experience upon Student Achievement, Educational Philosophy, and Attitudes in an Introductory Educational Psychology Course.* Unpublished manuscript, University of North Dakota, 1974. (ERIC Document Reproduction Service No. ED 098 171)

Crowl, T. K., & Alsworth, P. L. *School-based Teacher Education: An Empirical Investigation.* Staten Island, N.Y.: City University of New York, Richmond College, 1976. (ERIC Document Reproduction Service No. ED 121 789)

Elementary TEAM (Teacher Access Education Model) *Program.* Philadelphia: Temple University, College of Education, 1975. (ERIC Document Reproduction Service No. ED 117 072)

Elmore, R. Field-based teacher education: How far do we go? *Education,* 1979, *99*(4), 378–380.

Finley, J. R. *Progressive Field Experience Program of Edgecliff College, Cincinnati, Ohio.* Cincinnati, Ohio: Edgecliff College, 1975. (ERIC Document Reproduction Service No. ED 117 077)

Freeland, K. *Assessing the Practicum Experience.* Unpublished manuscript, University of Iowa, 1978. (ERIC Document Reproduction Service No. ED 156 670)

Gantt, W. N., & Davey, B. *Pre–Student Teachers React to Field-supplemented Methods Courses.* Unpublished manuscript, University of Maryland, 1972. (ERIC Document Reproduction Service No. ED 084 241)

Henry, P. M., & Glasheen, P. *A Program for Pre-service Education Field-based Sequential Role Development and Differentiated Staffing.* Paper presented at the Association for Supervision and Curriculum Development Annual Conference, Philadelphia, March 1972.

Ishler, R. E.; Lee, C. M.; & Wilhoyte, R. L. Planned field experiences: The key to career decisions. *Action in Teacher Education,* 1978, *1*(1), 38–43.

Knight, L. B. *The Evaluation of an Early Experience in Science Teaching.* Paper presented at the Forty-eighth Annual Meeting of the National Association for Research in Science Teaching, Los Angeles, March 1975. (ERIC Document Reproduction Service No. ED 108 870)

Knoll, G. C. *Do Pre–Student Teaching Experiences Change Attitudes toward Teaching?* Unpublished manuscript, 1973. (ERIC Document Reproduction Service No. ED 087 775)

Kulm, G. *The Effects of Practicum Experience on the Opinions of Secondary Mathematics Teachers.* Paper presented at the Annual Meeting of the American Educational Research Association, Washington, D.C., March 1975. (ERIC Document Reproduction Service No. ED 111 691)

MacNaughton, R. H. *Partnership in Spirit and in Fact: A Description of the Parma Teacher Education Project.* Unpublished manuscript, 1978. (ERIC Document Reproduction Service No. ED 164 441)

Marso, R. N. Project Interaction: A pilot study in a phase of teacher preparation. *Journal of Teacher Education,* 1971, *22*(2), 194–198.

Marso, R. N., & Reed, R. L. *Observable Changes in Student Teacher Behavior following Field-oriented Elementary Education Programs.* Unpublished manuscript, 1971. (ERIC Document Reproduction Service No. ED 085 395)

Melograno, V. J. *Changes in Selected Characteristics of Pre-service Teachers following Variable, Semi-variable, and Non-variable Field Experiences.* Unpublished manuscript, Cleveland State University, 1976. (ERIC Document Reproduction Service No. ED 126 010)

Newlove, B. W. *The Fifteen-minute Hour: An Early Teacher Experience* (Report series No. 23). Austin; Texas University, Research and Development Center for Teacher Education, 1969.

1979 Distinguished Achievement Award Entry: University of Washington Teacher Education Program. Seattle: University of Washington, 1979.

Otto, P. B. *A First Course in a Competency-based–Field-based Teacher Preparation Program.* Paper presented at the Annual Conference of the Association of Teacher Educators, 1976. (ERIC Document Reproduction Service No. ED 121 795)

Reitman, S. W. An alternative field work model for prospective teachers. *Interchange,* 1973, *4*(2–3), 61–77.

Schunk, B. (Ed.) The outlook in student teaching. *Forty-first Yearbook of the Association of Student Teaching.* Dubuque, Iowa: William C. Brown, 1962.

Secondary English Teacher Preparation Program: University of Georgia. Athens: Georgia University, Department of Language

Education, 1977. (ERIC Document Reproduction Service No. ED 180 943)

Smith, E. B. (Ed.). *A Guide to Professional Excellence in Clinical Experiences in Teacher Education*. Washington, D.C.: Association for Student Teaching, 1970. (ERIC Document Reproduction Service No. ED 043 560)

Standards for Colleges or Universities Preparing Teachers. Columbus: Ohio Department of Education, 1975.

Standards for State Approval of Teacher Education (Revision of U.S. Office of Education). Circular No. 351. Salt Lake City: Utah State Board of Education, 1979.

Standards for the Accreditation of Teacher Education. Washington, D.C.: National Council for the Accreditation of Teacher Education, 1979.

Turns, T. J. The determination and evaluation of professional laboratory experiences prior to student teaching (Doctoral dissertation, University of Oklahoma, 1970). *Dissertation Abstracts International*, 1970, *31*, 2780A.

Uhlenberg, D., & Holt, L. *The Influence of an Early Field Experience on Student Attitudes in a Traditional Program of Teacher Education*. Unpublished manuscript, University of Utah, 1975. (ERIC Document Reproduction Service No. ED 106 255)

Undergraduate Experimental Program. Charlottesville: Virginia University, School of Education, 1972. (ERIC Document Reproduction Service No. ED 083 249)

Union University "Early Bird" Internship Program in Teacher Education. Jackson, Tenn.: Union University, 1975. (ERIC Document Reproduction Service No. ED 117 095)

Verduin, J. R., Jr., & Heinz, C. R. *Pre-student Teaching Laboratory Experiences*. Dubuque, Iowa: Kendall-Hunt Publishing Co., 1970.

Vocational Clarification, Community Involvement, and Curricular Change through a Student-initiated and Student-led Field Experience Program. Seward, Nebr.: Concordia Teachers College, 1971. (ERIC Document Reproduction Service No. ED 066 426)

Warner, A. R.; Houston, W. R.; & Cooper, J. M. Rethinking the clinical concept in teacher education. *Journal of Teacher Education*, 1977, *28*(1), 15–18.

FINANCIAL AID TO STUDENTS

This article begins with the historical development of student aid, giving major attention to the types that originated after World War II. Current student aid programs are enumerated in Table 1. The goals of these programs are described; then research on student aid is presented.

Financial aid to college students is as old as higher education itself. The rulers of early Egypt, in the process of educating their own sons, provided student space in their courts for the sons of good families (Graves, 1929). The fees charged by Greek sophists depended greatly upon the "breadth of the sophist's reputation and the depth of the student's, or student's father's purse" (Walden, 1970). Fees were graduated according to a student's means and were completely ignored in cases of the poorest students (Walden, 1970).

With the organization of higher education into institutions, the financing of students of lesser means was accomplished through subsidized or discounted tuition, room and board, clothing, bedding, and parchment. Undergraduate students came to be admitted to late-medieval universities in part so that graduate students could collect tutorial fees to offset their own education (Cobban, 1975).

Low tuition always has been the major kind of student aid. In American colonial colleges, tuition could be kept low largely because of private donations and low salaries paid to professors. Still, colleges offering financial aid to students often found themselves in the student-loan business because tuition did not have to be prepaid and very often was late in forthcoming. Thirty-three of Dartmouth's thirty-nine graduates of 1806 owed the college money when diplomas were awarded. At Thomas Jefferson's University of Virginia, promising poor students were awarded senatorial scholarships, and for a time the state Assembly even paid board costs. Across the new nation, college agents often were authorized to offer free tuition in perpetuity to the designee of donors who had contributed a fixed sum.

A major student-aid role for government was not in evidence until much later. State student aid in the 1860s consisted of free tuition for some Civil War veterans attending state universities; federal aid probably began with the establishment of the Reserve Officer's Training Corps in 1917. In 1935 the Social Security Act was passed and although it was insignificant for higher education at the time, the survivor's benefits of that act amounted to over $1.5 billion in 1980. Between 1933 and 1943, the National Youth Administration made payments under the Student Work Program with some 620,000 students and $93 million being involved (Axt, 1952; Rivlin, 1961). During World War II a few war loans were made to students, but not until the postwar GI Bill did the federal role reach major proportions.

Various GI bills, after World War II and the Korean War, aided about 8 million veterans in what remains as the most significant student aid program ever. Roughly half of all college-level students were veterans in the immediate postwar years. Living expenses were paid directly to students and tuition and fees directly to institutions; by 1950, $4 billion and $1 billion had been expended accordingly. The Korean GI Bill discontinued direct payments to institutions, instead awarding flat grants to students—a change favoring lower-cost public institutions.

Although GI Bill programs continue today, the modern era of federal student assistance may be said to have begun with the passage of the National Defense Education Act (NDEA) in 1958. The NDEA, which probably would not have been passed had it not been for the Russian *Sputnik*, was a loan program requiring modest matching of institutional funds. By 1967, over $1 billion had been borrowed by more than 1 million students, 70 percent of whom were from low-income families, the target of the NDEA (Nash

TABLE 1. *Estimated major student-aid expenditures in millions of dollars for 1980*

Programs	Amount
Federal	
Basic Educational Opportunity Grants	$ 2,400
Supplemental Educational Opportunity Grants	370
College Work-Study	550
State Student-Incentive Grants	77
National Direct Student Loans[1]	300
Guaranteed Student Loans[2]	1,000
GI Bill	1,877
Social Security (educational)	1,509
State[2]	1,000
Institutional[2]	1,800
Total	$10,883

[1] Interest and insurance subsidies only.
[2] Estimated.

SOURCES OF DATA: U.S. government documents.

& Lazarsfeld, 1968). Now entitled the National Direct Student Loan (NDSL) Program, it calls for a 4 percent interest rate. It accounted for $300 million in federal subsidies in 1980.

Other federal programs soon followed; most have persisted. The College Work-Study (CWS) Program originated in 1964 and amounted to $550 million in 1980. CWS continues to be need-based and requires some matching of institutional funds. The Educational Opportunity Grant (EOG) Program was established by the Higher Education Act of 1965, which also authorized the Guaranteed Student Loan (GSL) Program. The EOG Program later gave way to the Supplemental Educational Opportunity Grant (SEOG) Program, but GSLs continue. GSL interest subsidies and insurance alone amounted to more than $1 billion in 1980. Interest rates now are 9 percent, and the GSL Program no longer is limited to low-income groups. Under the GSL, dependent students may borrow up to $25,000 and parents $15,000. In 1966 a new GI Bill, patterned after the Korean War Bill, was passed by Congress. Peak spending was over $3 billion per year in the middle 1970s and totaled about $1.9 billion in 1980. More than 6 million Vietnam-era veterans have been aided.

The landmark federal student aid legislation was the Education Amendments of 1972. The amendments established Basic Educational Opportunity Grants (BEOGs), which became the cornerstone of the federal effort and amounted to $2.4 billion in 1980. BEOGs are need-based, limited to low-income and middle-income students. If plans are followed, by 1985 they will permit students to receive annually grants for up to 70 percent of their educational costs but not more than $2,600. Also established by the amendments were State Student-Incentive Grants (SSIGs), which provide for federal matching of increases in state student aid awards based upon need. In 1980, SSIGs amounted to $77 million and were heavily targeted

on students attending independent colleges and universities. Supplemental Educational Opportunity Grants (SEOGs) evolved in this legislation from EOGs. SEOGs, which amounted to $370 million in 1980, are seen as "supplemental" to the basic grants and are heavily concentrated upon students in independent institutions. Additionally, state financial-aid programs contributed roughly $1 billion in 1980; institutional programs are estimated to have contributed $1.538 billion in 1976/77 (Gomberg & Atelsek, 1979). Total student-aid expenditures now are roughly $12 billion with almost $11 billion coming from these major programs.

Of major influence in expanding funding for these programs were national policy studies by the Committee for Economic Development (1973) and the Carnegie Commission on Higher Education (1973). These studies urged the expansion of need-based student-aid programs in part through raising public college tuitions and converting the saved institutional-aid monies to student aid funds.

Goals. Although the central aim of student aid has never varied greatly, emphases and refinements have occurred periodically. From the earliest days of higher education, expanding opportunities to low-income students has been the central goal of student aid; the interacting consideration of student academic potential, however, has been variously applied. In earlier years the necessary but insufficient condition for receiving student assistance was to demonstrate academic promise. Awards were made to students of high scholarship, provided in most cases that they could demonstrate financial need. Although some smaller aid programs still reward scholarship (a very few require *only* scholarship), most student financial assistance now is based almost purely upon need.

In recent years "opportunity" has become more liberally defined and applied. Now the goals of student financial assistance are considered to be student access, choice, and retention and completion. Implicitly, access is defined as actual enrollment in college, not mere opportunity to enroll. The reason is that achievement of "opportunity" is far too difficult to measure and because actual enrollment is a far more acceptable policy goal. Choice is defined to mean opportunity to enroll at any institution to which the student can gain admittance. The policy perspective is that not only should student aid assure access but it should be sufficient to permit student freedom to choose institutions that may be more expensive. A major contributing reason for this national policy goal—though due to political and legal constraints largely an unofficial one— is the desire by elected officials to assist independent colleges and universities, many of which in the 1970s experienced financial difficulty. Finally, it is held that student aid should assist students in staying in college until they graduate. The former two of these student opportunity goals have received major research attention whereas the retention and completion goal has been studied very little, at least in the context of student aid.

Research. The assumption fundamental to the above section is that student aid will promote the listed goals. Specifically, it is assumed that demand theory applies to higher education; that is, demand for (enrollment in) a higher education institution will vary with such factors as the potential student's (or family's) money income, the "price" of enrollment, and the price of alternative enrollments. Although it is known that such economic considerations are only one set of factors, and probably not a very important set, clearly these factors are the easiest and most politically acceptable to manipulate; thus they are key instruments of public policy. (For a discussion of the research regarding the relative potency of economic and noneconomic factors affecting higher education access see Fife, 1975, pp. 21–32.)

Student aid as a means of promoting access, choice, retention and completion, and enrollment at independent institutions has given rise to considerable research. Early studies simply queried students as to the effects of aid on their attendance decision or they asked nonstudents about their reasons for nonattendance. Although criticized for their obvious potential bias, these studies did measure student-aid impacts directly. Employing the former model, Fredericksen and Schraeder (1951) found that of several thousand veterans attending college, only about 10 percent identified the GI Bill as the determining factor. Similarly, Cole (1957) reported that 90 percent of 1,600 rejected scholarship applicants attended college anyway, and Berdie's highly regarded study (1954) of 25,000 Minnesota high school seniors concluded that only about 400 more superior students would have enrolled in college if aid had been granted. A parallel study in New Mexico specified 1 percent as the portion of sufficiently able and motivated students who also lacked the financial means to attend (Smith, Mathany, & Milfs, 1960). In contrast more recent data show that among recipients of state student aid, from about one-third to one-half specified aid as the

determining factor in their decision to attend college (Leslie & Fife, 1974). Analyzing these and other data, Carlson (1974) reported that 20 percent of high-income and 60 percent of low-income students identified aid as the critical element.

Much recent research has sought to avoid the possible bias resulting from questioning students about the effects of aid by analyzing actual student behaviors. This research has been categorized as student demand studies which connect student aid to impacts upon access and choice by assuming that aid can be viewed as a reduction in net price. The student demand framework and accompanying multiple regression approach were first applied by Campbell and Siegel (1967), who aggregated enrollment and corresponding family income and tuition data for 1927 to 1963. Campbell and Siegel estimated that income and tuition increases (a net price increase) of 1 percent resulted in enrollment changes of 1.20 and −0.44 percent, respectively. From the same data Hight (1970) estimated the varying effects upon public and independent colleges, noting 0.977 and 1.701 percent enrollment increases, respectively, per 1 percent income increase and 1.058 and 0.641 enrollment decreases, respectively, per 1 percent tuition increase. Thus, independent college enrollments were seen to be more dependent upon the student's (family) income and less sensitive to tuition increases than was true of public college enrollments. Hoenack (1967), using cross-sectional data for the University of California, estimated comparable 0.70 and −0.85 percent enrollment increase and decrease, respectively, per 1 percent income and tuition increase. Later Hoenack, Weiler, and Orvis (1973) estimated, from time series data, enrollment decreases ranging from 0.533 to 1.811 percent for each percentage point increase in tuition for four colleges of the University of Minnesota. Corrazzini, Dugan, and Grabowski (1972) combined cross-sectional Project Talent and Massachusetts data to show that enrollments at public universities are more than twice as sensitive as enrollments at junior colleges and private universities. Carlson, Farmer, and Weathersby (1974) manipulated 1966 data obtained by Radner and Miller (1970) from four states and concluded that sensitivity to tuition price changes for low-income students was nearly three times greater than for middle-income students and more than four times greater than for high-income students; variation, however, was slight among institutional classifications when family income was held constant. Jackson and Weathersby (1975) rendered these and other student demand studies comparable by constructing a "typical" student faced with a $100 tuition increase in a college cost of $2,000 in 1974. Synthesizing the results, Jackson and Weathersby concluded that a $100 price increase would reduce the college-going rate by from 0.06 to 1.9 percentage points or a 1974 average enrollment decrease of about 3.8 percent. Hyde (1978) applied similar techniques to conclude that in 1978 a $100 tuition increase would be associated on average with about a 3 percent enrollment decrease and that the

FINANCIAL AID TO STUDENTS

aid subsidy necessary to attract one additional student was roughly $3,400.

The single, notable experiment to assess the effects of tuition price changes was conducted at two two-year centers of the University of Wisconsin. In 1973, when tuitions were reduced by $331, head-count enrollments at the two centers grew by 23.1 and 47.0 percent, respectively, while the increase was only 7 percent at twelve nonexperimental centers. In 1976, when tuition was again raised (by $377), enrollments at the two centers declined by 21.9 percent compared to a 0.4 percent increase in the nonexperimental centers (American Association of State Colleges and Universities, 1977).

In sum, every major study has concluded that college attendance rises with increases in income and declines with price increases. A good estimate is that enrollments decline by an average of about 3 percent for each $100 tuition increase in 1978 constant dollars. In the absence of offsetting student aid, however, low-income students are roughly three times as sensitive to price increases as are middle-income students, and enrollments at public institutions are roughly twice as sensitive to price changes as are independent institution enrollments (Hyde, 1978). (Student aid reduces the impact of price increases; that is, especially for low-income students, price increases must be "netted out" for student aid in order to estimate the tuition effect.) The inference is that in reducing the "net" price of higher education, student aid almost certainly expands educational opportunity, particularly for low-income students. One estimate is that largely because of student aid, net costs (amount met by student's personal means) of higher education for the lowest-income students are 31 percent of total costs compared to 46 percent for middle-income and 26 percent for the highest-income students (Hyde, 1979). One group that is heavily low-income—minorities—seems to be doing extremely well under student aid programs: minorities receive a disproportionate share of student aid, and their freshman enrollment rates may roughly equal those of majority students (Leslie, 1977).

Although the implications for the goal of increasing enrollments at independent institutions and thereby enhancing institutional choice cannot be drawn directly from available research, it is clear that independent colleges are assisted more by student aid than are public institutions, principally because student aid is targeted upon those students in greatest need, and need is greatest where prices are highest. Further, the existence of aid tends to entice students away from public and into independent institutions. Leslie and Fife (1974) estimated that 31.8 percent of state aid recipients represent enrollment gains for the independent sector compared to 11.0 percent for the public sector. Leslie (1978) estimated that more than 11 percent of all independent sector enrollments could be related to public student aid for an overall public subsidy of $1.262 billion and a net gain of $370 million for independent institutions in 1975. Thus, the institutional choice

goal is advanced through student aid as well as the implicit goal of assisting independent colleges.

At the other end of the college-cost continuum, public two-year colleges fare least well under student-aid programs (Leslie, Martorana, & Fife, 1975). Nelson (1979), upon examining the major public programs of student aid, concluded that community college students receive their fair share of BEOG awards but are slighted by most other aid programs. This was clearly so in the case of the campus-based programs and was most dramatically true of state-aid programs.

Studies relating student aid to retention in and completion of college are much more scarce. Astin (1975) has shown that loans tend to be correlated with dropping out whereas grants and work-study are associated with persistence. Astin concludes that one major reason for dropping out is financial need. It is known that retention and completion are more elusive student aid goals than is mere access. For example, blacks, who are a major target of student aid programs, are more likely to drop out than are nonblacks (U.S. Bureau of the Census, 1975; American Council on Education, 1967).

A special set of studies concerns student loans. Johnstone, Wackman, and Ward (1972), who interviewed 937 students on ten campuses, reported a preference for conventional over variable-term loans and a desire to minimize the amounts repaid. Wing (1973) reported a borrower desire to limit the period of loan amortization, whereas Brugel, Johnson, and Leslie (1977), from intensive interviews with 200 student borrowers, reported (1) a possible doubling of present debt before the debt level would become burdensome; (2) a desire for more repayment options; (3) delay of repayment method selection until after graduation; (4) up to 13 percent of income to be devoted to repayment; (5) ten-year repayment for small debt levels but twenty-five–year repayment for higher debt levels; and (6) favoring of loan programs that tie repayment to earnings but strong disapproval of subsidizing low earners by other borrowers.

A national probability sample of the high school class of 1972 was examined to assess the role of student aid in paying for the costs of higher education (Leslie, 1980). During the four collegiate years studied, student aid rather uniformly met about 27 percent of college expenses although figures varied tremendously by student subset. For part-time students, senior-year student aid met only about 9 percent of student expenses; women met slightly more of their expenses through aid than did men; student aid to minorities as a share of total expenses far exceeded aid to the majority group, as did aid to low-income students in comparison to aid to higher-income groups.

Recently, attention has been drawn to several new groups previously treated inequitably by student aid. Partially because of the higher net costs and a corresponding decline in their higher education participation rates, middle-income students were the object of the Middle-Income Student Assistance Act (MISAA) of 1978. Principal changes under MISAA were to remove the income eligibility ceiling from GSLs and to raise the ceiling for BEOGs to $25,000. Ceilings were reintroduced or lowered again by the Reagan Administration. The Education Amendments of 1980 extended the eligibility of several student aid programs to part-time students and mandated that the financial needs of independent students be treated similarly to those of students who are dependent upon their families.

Other issues associated with student aid concern the inflationary effects of student aid upon tuition prices and loan defaults. As the federal government shifted its financial support from institutions to students, the former became aware that they could capture more federal money by raising their prices. One estimate was that in 1976/77 roughly one-fourth to one-third of federal student aid went to pay for tuition increases brought on by that aid (Leslie, 1979). The default issue reached near-crisis proportions in the mid-1970s as many former students, particularly those who had attended proprietary schools, found they could avoid loan repayment by declaring bankruptcy. This legal loophole was mended through federal legislation.

Student aid will continue for some time to be the major federal vehicle for fulfilling the national policy goals of student access, choice, and retention and completion. States, too, increasingly will rely upon this financing mode as a means of shifting more of the burden to students and their families and supporting independent institutions indirectly. Beyond the cuts made recently by the Reagan Administration, student aid developments in the near future will involve some fine-tuning of existing programs with an eye to increasing efficiency and holding burgeoning costs down. The rapid growth of recent years has been greatly slowed. Tax credits for higher education expenses will gain in favor, but their passage is at this writing problematic.

Larry Leslie

See also Financing Colleges and Universities; Legislation.

REFERENCES

American Association of State Colleges and Universities. *Wisconsin Low Tuition Experiment Ends: Tuitions Up, Enrollments Down.* (AASCU Special Report). Washington, D.C.: The Association, 1977.

American Council on Education. *The American Freshman: National Norms for Fall 1967.* Washington, D.C.: The Council, 1967.

Astin, A. W. *Preventing Students from Dropping Out.* San Francisco: Jossey-Bass, 1975.

Axt, R. G. *The Federal Government and Financing Higher Education.* New York: Columbia University Press, 1952.

Berdie, R. F. *After High School What?* Minneapolis: University of Minnesota Press, 1954.

Brugel, J. F.; Johnson, G. P.; & Leslie, L. L. The demand for student loans in higher education: A study of preferences and attitudes. In *Research in Higher Education.* New York: APS Publications, 1977, *6*(1), 65–83.

Campbell, R., & Siegel, B. The demand for higher education in the United States: 1919–1964. *American Economic Review,* June 1967, pp. 482–494.

Carlson, D. *Student Price Response Coefficients for Grants, Loans, Work-Study Aid, and Tuition Changes: An Analysis of Student Surveys.* Paper presented to the Policy Development Group, Assistant Secretary of Education Office, Department of Health, Education, and Welfare, Washington, D.C., November 1974.

Carlson, D.; Farmer, J.; & Weathersby, G. *A Framework for Analyzing Post-secondary Education Financing Policies.* Washington, D.C.: U.S. Government Printing Office, 1974.

Carnegie Commission on Higher Education. *Higher Education: Who Pays? Who Benefits? Who Should Pay?* New York: McGraw-Hill, 1973.

Cobban, A. B. *The Medieval Universities: Their Development and Organization.* London: Methuen, 1975.

Cole, C. C., Jr. Scholarship applicants today. *College Board Review,* 1957, *32,* 17–20.

Committee for Economic Development. *The Management and Financing of Colleges.* New York: The Committee, 1973.

Corrazzini, A. S.; Dugan, D. J.; & Grabowski, H. G. Determinants and distributional aspects of enrollment in U.S. higher education. *Journal of Human Resources,* Winter 1972, 39–59.

Fife, J. D. *Applying the Goals of Student Financial Aid* (ERIC/Higher Education Research Report No. 10). Washington, D.C.: 1975.

Fredericksen, N., & Schraeder, W. B. *Adjustment to College: A Study of 19,000 Veteran and Non-veteran Students in Sixteen American Colleges.* Princeton, N.J.: Educational Testing Service, 1951.

Gomberg, I. L., & Atelsek, F. J. The institutional share of undergraduate financial assistance, 1976–1977. In *Research in Education* (American Council on Education Panel Report No. 42). November 1979. (ERIC Document Reproduction Service No. ED 172 624)

Graves, F. P. *A History of Education before the Middle Ages.* New York: Macmillan, 1929.

Hight, J. *The Supply and Demand of Higher Education in the U.S.: Public and Private Institutions Compared.* Paper presented to the Econometric Society, December 1970.

Hoenack, S. *Private Demand for Higher Education in California.* University of California, Office of Analytical Studies, 1967. (Mimeo)

Hoenack, S.; Weiler, W.; & Orvis, C. *Cost-related Tuition Policies and University Enrollments.* University of Minnesota, Management Information Division, 1973. (Mimeo)

Hyde, W. D. (Ed.). *Issues in Postsecondary Education Finance: Summaries of Six Issues.* Denver, Colo.: Education Commission of the States, 1978.

Hyde, W. D. (Ed.). *The Equity of the Distribution of Student Financial Aid* (Report No. F79-2). Denver, Colo.: Education Commission of the States, 1979.

Jackson, G. A., & Weathersby, G. B. Individual demand for higher education: A review and analysis of recent empirical studies. *Journal of Higher Education,* November-December 1975, *46,* 623–652.

Johnstone, D. B.; Wackman, D. B.; & Ward, S. Student attitudes toward income contingent loans. *Journal of Student Financial Aid,* 1972, *2,* 11–27.

Leslie, L. L. *Higher Education Opportunity: A Decade of Progress*

(ERIC/Higher Education Research Report No. 3), Washington, D.C.: 1977.

Leslie, L. L. *The Role of Public Student Aid in Financing Private Higher Education.* Tucson, Ariz.: University of Arizona, Center for the Study of Higher Education, 1978.

Leslie, L. L. *The Impact of Federal Need-based Student Aid on Postsecondary Tuition.* Testimony to the Subcommittee on Postsecondary Education, Committee on Education and Labor, U.S. House of Representatives, May 9, 1979.

Leslie, L. L. *Student Financing.* Boulder, Colo.: National Center for Higher Education Management Systems, 1980. (Mimeo)

Leslie, L. L., & Fife, J. D. The college student grant study: The enrollment and attendance impacts on student grant and scholarship programs. *Journal of Higher Education,* December 1974, *1055*(9), 651–671.

Leslie, L. L.; Martorana, S. V.; & Fife, J. D. Financing postsecondary education through students: Windfall profit or recession for community colleges? *Community College Review,* March 1975, *2*(4), 14–34.

Nash, G., & Lazarsfeld, P. F. *New Administrator on Campus: A Study of the Director of Student Financial Aid.* College Entrance Examination Board, 1968.

Nelson, S. C. *Community Colleges and Their Share of Student Financial Assistance.* Washington, D.C.: Brookings Institution, 1979.

Radner, R., & Miller, L. S. Demand and supply in U.S. higher education: A progress report. *American Economic Review,* May 1970.

Rivlin, A. *A Role of the Federal Government in Financing Higher Education.* Washington, D.C.: Brookings Institution, 1961.

Smith, S. E.; Mathany, H. V.; & Milfs, M. M. *Are Scholarships the Answer? A Report on a Scholarship Program for Students of Limited Means.* Albuquerque: University of New Mexico, 1960.

U.S. Bureau of the Census. *Current Population Reports, School Enrollment: Social and Economic Characteristics of Students, October 1974* (Series P-20, No. 286). Washington, D.C.: U.S. Department of Commerce, 1975.

Walden, J. W. H. *The Universities of Ancient Greece.* Freeport, N.Y.: Libraries Press, 1970.

Wing, C. W., Jr. *Duke's Deferred Tuition Program and a Plan for the Future* (Report to the Sloan Foundation). 1973. (Mimeo)

FINANCING COLLEGES AND UNIVERSITIES

Research and study in higher-education finance most recently have centered upon the following areas: (1) declining resources, (2) indicators of financial health, (3) special problems of financing independent colleges, (4) special problems of financing community colleges, (5) costing, (6) financing facilities, (7) financial implications of collective bargaining, and (8) student aid (discussed elsewhere).

Revenue Source and Expenditure Categories. American colleges and universities are financed in an eclectic manner varying greatly by type of institution. Tables 1 and 2 present institutional financing data. Together, public

and independent institutions had income of almost $41 billion in 1979. Public institutions received 59 percent of their educational and general (E & G) funds in the form of state and local appropriations and 15 percent equally from tuition and from government grants and contracts. Independent institutions, on the other hand, relied far more heavily on tuition and fees (50 percent) and private gifts and grants (20 percent); 19 percent came from government grants and contracts.

Regarding expenditure categories, instruction accounted for 44 percent of public, and 37 percent of independent E & G budgets. As one would expect, public institutions spent more for public service; and, because of a proportionately larger resident-student population, independent institutions devoted a larger share of their budgets to the "Other" category, which included auxiliary enterprises such as dormitories and food service.

Declining Resources. At the beginning of the 1970s, higher-education leaders were in a state of high anxiety. Several studies had proclaimed a financial crisis in college and university finance (Jenny & Wynne, 1970; Cheit, 1971; Jellema, 1971, 1973). Several national reports were produced (Committee for Economic Development, 1973; Carnegie Commission, 1973) describing the perceived crisis and possible remedies. A major new financing policy resulted (student assistance), which indirectly infused billions of new dollars into higher-education institutions.

As the 1970s ended, the state of anxiety was still high. The higher-education share of state budgets was on the decline (although real per student revenue continued to increase in most years), and the anticipated enrollment decline caused great concern among many institutions, particularly about such issues as deferred maintenance, the backlog of facilities needs, high fixed costs, decline in faculty earning power, increased institutional reliance on tuition income, and the maintenance of educational quality.

Indicators of Financial Problems. Financial difficulties have created a need for reliable indicators of institutional financial conditions and future prospects. Using reduction in quality or service as a criterion, Cheit (1971) identified private and urban institutions, regional universities, and those with high student aid and high faculty salary costs as being in greatest financial difficulty. In a controversial work, Lupton, Augenblick, and Heyison (1976) asked a panel of finance experts to review the financial and related documents of fifty-five institutions and place them in various categories of financial health. A subsequent discriminant analysis produced sixteen variables the experts held to be financial-health indicators. The variable set included control (public, private) and type of institution; enrollment and expenditure trends; plant additions; and numerous financial ratios that combined various measures of revenue, expenditures, assets, enrollments, and degrees conferred. Dickmeyer and Hughes (1979a) and Dickmeyer (1980) derived financial indicator norms that related thirteen categories of income and expenditures to enrollment

TABLE 1. *Revenue sources for U.S. public and independent higher-education institutions: Percentage contribution from each source (1979)*

	Public	Independent
State and Local Appropriations	59%	2%
Tuition and Fees	15	50
Private Gifts and Grants	4	20
Government Grants and Contracts	15	19
Other	7	9
Total Educational and General	100	100
	($28,281,000,000)	($12,614,000,000)

for community and junior colleges. The same authors (Dickmeyer & Hughes, 1979b) constructed indicators for small colleges. Measures were structured around a framework consisting of financial strength, estimated risk, and changes affecting financial and nonfinancial resources. Jenny (1979) focused on cash flows, capital charges, and revenue and expenditure structures to construct yet another indicator set. The National Center for Higher Education Management Systems has begun an ambitious and long-term project to build norms for twenty-five indicators in five higher-education areas: students, research, public service, organizational character, and institutions. Eight indicators describe institutions; four of these bear directly on financing.

Financing Independent Colleges. A special concern of research in financing independent colleges is their uncertain financial future. A broad treatment of this problem is provided by Breneman and Finn (1978). The critical issues for independent institutions are enrollments, the gap between public and independent college tuitions, student aid, and institutional closings.

Jenny and Wynne (1970), Cheit (1971), and Jellema (1971, 1973) documented the financial stress on independent institutions in the late 1960s and early 1970s. Pace's report (1972), one of three for the Carnegie Commission, painted a picture of cautious optimism for the financing of Protestant colleges, whereas Greeley's essay (1969) on Catholic colleges concluded that their "financial problems . . . are probably no more acute than the problems of

American private higher education in general, and, in some respects are less acute" (pp. 70–71), and Astin and Lee's report (1972) on so-called invisible colleges (the 494 small, private colleges with limited resources) stated that the issue is one of survival—how to get enough students to keep the doors open. Nevertheless, more recently, the annual reports by Bowen and Minter (1975–1980) on the state of private higher education indicate that the late 1970s became years of near stability.

Because of the importance of tuition income, the key to the financial health of independent institutions is found in enrollments. The independent sector, which enrolled about one-half of all college students in 1950, enrolled only about one-third in 1966 and only about one-fifth in 1980. Nevertheless, the 2,662,000 independent-college students enrolled in 1980 represented an absolute increase for private institutions of some 38 percent over 1965, and annual percentage increases for independent institutions during the 1970s generally were larger than the corresponding public-institution percentage increases. The absolute number of students attending college increased during these years, and although the growth in absolute numbers was slower for independent institutions, proportional increases (year by year) were larger for these institutions than for public institutions.

The tuition-gap issue is seen by independent colleges as pivotal for maintaining their enrollments and thus their financial health. This gap between the independent and public sectors overall was about $1,509, representing a

TABLE 2. *Categories of expenditure for public and independent higher-education institutions: Percentage allocation for each category (1979)*

	Public	Independent
Instruction	44%	37%
Academic Support	9	8
Research	11	12
Public Service	5	2
Other	31	41
Total Educational and General	100	100
	($27,088,000,000)	($12,341,000,000)

SOURCE OF DATA: National Center for Educational Statistics.

3:1 tuition ratio in 1980; the ratio was about 4:1 for four-year institutions. However, student aid effectively was closing this gap somewhat, and the enrollment record of the 1970s suggested that a near equilibrium in percentage enrollment growth rates had been achieved.

Although forecasts in the early 1970s predicted the closing of many private colleges and a net loss of 65 independent institutions was claimed between 1970 and 1978 by the National Association of Independent Colleges and Universities (1978), the number of private colleges listed in the Education Directory grew from 1,520 in 1970 to 1,644 in 1978. It appears that disparate methods of counting explained some or all of this decline. Most of the schools that have closed are recently established colleges; rarely have old-line, traditional independent colleges closed their doors.

Financing Community Colleges. High-quality studies of community college financing have been scarce. One exception is the study done by Breneman and Nelson (1981). Their book treats essentially all of the major financial issues facing community colleges, including efficiency and equity, general issues of institutional funding and budgeting, and future prospects. Another useful work is the community college finance-research review written by Hyde and Augenblick (1980).

Major financial issues facing community colleges concern general methods of financing, specifically the role served by state governments, the related question of state equalization funding, and tuition. The most common pattern of government support of community colleges is mixed state and local funding, which is found in about 60 percent of states; the remaining 40 percent essentially are totally state-supported (Wattenbarger and Stepp, 1979). Most state funding is based on enrollment and is usually a flat grant per student, often with an adjustment by program or area of study. A few states make general institutional grants. The trend is in the direction of additional shares being paid by state governments, particularly where state initiatives or referenda have restricted local property-tax collections.

Equalization funding concerns intrastate equity in financial support among community college districts. Augenblick (1978) utilized data from four states to show the magnitude of variations in expenditure per student. Intrastate coefficients of variation (a measure of dispersion or range) ranged from .320 in California to .119 in Mississippi, although variations in district property-tax wealth and local district revenues were much greater.

Finally, community colleges always are concerned with tuition prices. Their enrollments hinge in large part upon the relatively low tuition prices charged. Carlson (1975) estimated from 1967–1972 data that community college enrollments declined by 4.75 percent per $100 tuition increase (estimated from an average $302 tuition base).

Costing. As income has been squeezed, states and institutions have looked for ways to allocate resources effectively. One major related area of emphasis has been "costing," that is, identifying the expenses associated with various educational activities.

Several noteworthy costing studies have been conducted. The broadest and most complete to date has been the Adams, Hankins, and Schroeder four-volume work (1978) documenting the experiences of institutions in producing cost information and its usefulness in administrative decision making. The National Center for Higher Education Management Systems early in the 1970s developed *Information Exchange Procedures* that established standards, procedures, and definitions for collecting and comparing cost information. The National Association of College and University Business Officers (NACUBO) long has been interested in higher-education costing and for a number of years has maintained a Costing Standards Committee. Through the Committee, NACUBO has published several costing papers, one of the more significant being *Fundamental Considerations for Determining Cost Information in Higher Education* (1975).

Empirical costing studies probably began when Russell and Reeves (1935) wrote of enrollments and cost per student, scope of programs and cost per student, and excellence and expenditures—three relationships that remain at the heart of costing research today. A major difference is that Russell and Reeves's correlations have given way to multivariate analysis. The next major study was the California and Western Conference Cost and Statistical Study (1956), which described production relationships (e.g., programs, students, faculty costs) on a unit-cost basis for several major universities. The purpose was to develop comparative cost information. Carlson's excellent and unique study (1972) employed "frontier analysis" to identify how the lowest-cost institutions managed to be so efficient. Verry and Davies (1976) conducted perhaps the most extensive and careful cost analysis, estimating marginal costs and considering various economy-of-scale issues in British universities. A recent U.S. study examined reasons for cost variations among major research universities (Brinkman, 1981).

Financing Facilities. Again and again, studies have shown that among the first expenses to be cut during periods of financial stress are those for maintenance and building improvements. By the end of the 1970s, the amount deferred in maintenance and delayed construction, remodeling, and refurbishing was in the tens of billions of dollars. Deferred maintenance alone has been estimated at $35 billion (Kaiser, 1979). A survey in Nebraska estimated deferred maintenance costs for the entire state university system at $21 million (Kaiser, 1979). The estimate for Syracuse University was $18 million (Kaiser, 1979). Clearly, deferring needed repairs, failing to convert facilities to meet new needs, and delaying necessary construction projects are actions that ultimately will severely strain higher-education resources.

Implications of Collective Bargaining. The financial implications of collective bargaining are a new topic in college and university finance. The topic is considered important because it is widely held that institutional financial flexibility will be reduced greatly by the need to satisfy the terms of collective bargaining agreements. Birnbaum (1974) matched eighty-eight pairs of union and nonunion institutions and reported a $777 salary advantage for unionized faculties. Brown and Stone (1977) found no significant impacts on salary, compensation, and promotions; however, Morgan and Kearney (1976), using a more carefully controlled design, concluded that unionized faculty received salaries $1,200 higher in 1974. Leslie and Hu (1977) confirmed the findings of Morgan and Kearney but detected a declining union salary advantage. Leslie and Hu also found that unionism appears to be associated with higher tuition and fee charges and increased government appropriations. In the most extensive work completed to date, Guthrie-Morse, Leslie, and Hu (1981) concluded that the early compensation gains of union over nonunion faculties at least partially dissolved with time. Furthermore, merit as a basis for setting faculty salaries was greatly reduced in importance under collective bargaining agreements.

Summary. Major public policy questions surround these several financing topics. How will the integrity of higher education be maintained during a period of relative enrollment and financial decline? What indicators are valid and reliable measures of institutional financial status? What special financial problems are being faced by independent and community colleges? What role can be played by cost analysis in the reallocation of institutional resources? What is the magnitude of costs of deferred maintenance and delayed construction, and how can this problem be met? What are the financial implications of collective bargaining? These are the higher-education policy questions that have been addressed by research and study in the finance of higher education.

Larry Leslie

See also Financial Aid to Students; Financing Schools; Higher Education; Legislation; Organization and Administration of Higher Education; Philanthropic Foundations; State Influences on Education.

REFERENCES

Adams, C. R.; Hankins, R. L.; & Schroeder, R. G. Study of Cost Analysis in Higher Education. Unpublished manuscript, University of Minnesota, Graduate School of Business Administration, Management Sciences Department, 1978.

Astin, A. W., & Lee, C. B. T. The Invisible Colleges: A Profile of Small Private Colleges with Limited Resources. Highstown, N.J.: Carnegie Commission on Higher Education, and McGraw-Hill, 1972.

Augenblick, J. Issues in Financing Community Colleges. Denver; Education Commission of the States, 1978. (ERIC Document Reproduction Service No. ED 164 020)

Birnbaum, R. Unionization and faculty compensation. Educational Record, Winter 1974, pp. 29–33.

Bowen, H. R., & Minter, W. J. Private Higher Education: Annual Report on Financial and Educational Trends in the Private Sector of American Higher Education (6 vols.). Washington, D.C.: Association of American Colleges, 1975–1980.

Breneman, D. W., & Finn, C. E. (Eds.). Public Policy and Private Higher Education. Washington, D.C.: Brookings Institution, 1978.

Breneman, D. W., & Nelson, S. C. Financing Community Colleges: An Economic Perspective. Washington, D.C.: Brookings Institution, 1981.

Brinkman, P. T. Factors affecting instructional costs in major research universities. Journal of Higher Education, 1981, 52, 265–279.

Brown, W. W., & Stone, C. C. Academic unions in higher education. Economic Inquiry, 1977, 15, 385–396.

California and Western Conference Cost and Statistical Study for the Year 1954–1955. Berkeley, Calif.: Fund for the Advancement of Education, University of California, Printing Department, 1956.

Carlson, D. The Production and Cost Behavior of Higher Education Institutions (Paper p-36, Ford Foundation Program for Research in University Administration). Berkeley: University of California, 1972. (ERIC Document Service No. ED 081 375)

Carlson, D. Estimated Demand Functions for Higher Education. Unpublished manuscript, University of California at Davis, 1975.

Carnegie Commission on Higher Education. Higher Education: Who Pays? Who Benefits? Who Should Pay? New York: McGraw-Hill, 1973.

Cheit, E. F. The New Depression in Higher Education: A Study of Financial Conditions at Forty-one Colleges and Universities. Highstown, N.J.: Carnegie Commission on Higher Education, and McGraw-Hill, 1971.

Committee for Economic Development. The Management and Financing of Colleges. New York: The Committee, 1973. (ERIC Document Reproduction Service No. EC 090 829)

Dickmeyer, N. Comparative Financial Statistics for Community and Junior Colleges: 1978–79. Washington, D.C.: National Association of College and Business Officers, 1980. (ERIC Document Reproduction Service No. ED 194 141)

Dickmeyer, N., & Hughes, K. S. Comparative Financial Statistics for Community and Junior Colleges: 1977–78. Washington, D.C.: National Association of College and Business Officers, 1979. (a)

Dickmeyer, N., & Hughes, K. S. Self-assessment of Financial Condition: A Preliminary Edition of a Workbook for Small Independent Institutions. Washington, D.C.: National Association of College and Business Officers, 1979. (ERIC Document Reproduction Service No. ED 175 322) (b)

Greeley, A. M. From Backwater to Mainstream: A Profile of Catholic Higher Education. Highstown, N.J.: Carnegie Commission on Higher Education, and McGraw-Hill, 1969.

Guthrie-Morse, B.; Leslie, L.; & Hu, T. Assessing the impact of faculty unions: The financial implications of collective bargaining. Journal of Higher Education, 1981, 52, 237–255.

Hyde, W., & Augenblick, J. Community College Students, Costs, and Finances: A Review of Research Literature. Denver: Education Commission of the States, 1980. (ERIC Document Reproduction Service No. ED 192 841)

Jellema, W. W. The Red and the Black: Special Preliminary Report on the Financial Status, Present and Projected, of Private Institutions of Higher Learning. Washington, D.C.: Association of American Colleges, 1971. (ERIC Document Reproduction Service No. Ed 058 837)

Jellema, W. W. Redder and Much Redder: A Follow-up Study

to "The Red and the Black." Washington, D.C.: Association of American Colleges, 1973. (ERIC Document Reproduction Service No. ED 058 838)

Jenny, Hans H. "Specifying Financial Indicators: Cash Flows in the Short and Long Run," *New Directions for Higher Education, 7*(2), pp. 15–30, 1979.

Jenny, H. H., & Wynne, R. G. *The Golden Years.* Wooster, Ohio: College of Wooster, 1970.

Kaiser, H. H. *Mortgaging the Future: The Cost of Deferring Maintenance.* Washington, D.C.: Association of Physical Plant Administrators of Universities and Colleges, 1979. (ERIC Document Reproduction Service No. ED 175 096)

Leslie, L. L., & Hu, T. W. The financial implications of collective bargaining. *Journal of Education Finance,* Summer 1977, *3*(1), 32–53.

Lupton, A.; Augenblick, J.; & Heyison, J. The financial state of higher education. *Change,* September 1976, *8*(8), 21–35.

Morgan, D. R., & Kearney, R. C. Collective bargaining and faculty compensation: A comparative analysis. *Sociology of Education,* 1977, *50,* 28–39.

National Association of College and University Business Officers. *Fundamental Considerations for Determining Cost Information in Higher Education.* Washington, D.C.: NACUBO Administrative Service, 1975. (ERIC Document Reproduction Service No. ED 118 003)

National Association of Independent Colleges and Universities. *Openings, Closings, Mergers, and Accreditation Status of Independent Colleges and Universities.* Washington, D.C.: NAICU, 1978. (ERIC Document Reproduction Service No. ED 165 681)

Pace, C. R. *Education and Evangelism: A Profile of Protestant Colleges.* Highstown, N.J.: Carnegie Commission on Higher Education, and McGraw-Hill, 1972.

Russell, J. D., & Reeves, F. *Finance.,* Vol. 7 of *The Evaluation of Higher Institutions.* Chicago: University of Chicago Press, 1935.

Verry, D., & Davies, B. *University Costs and Outputs.* Amsterdam: Elsevier, 1976.

Wattenbarger, J. L., & Stepp, W. F. *Financing Community Colleges.* Gainesville: University of Florida, Institute of Higher Education, 1979. (ERIC Document Reproduction Service No. ED 175 518)

FINANCING SCHOOLS

The finance of elementary and secondary education in the United States is largely in the domain of *public* finance. Approximately 90 percent of total expenditures on elementary and secondary education in the United States during the academic year 1978/79 ($97 billion) were derived from federal, state, or local governments, and more than 93 percent of the pupils attending elementary and secondary schools were enrolled in public schools during the fall of 1978 (Grant & Lind, 1979, tables 2 and 18). A discussion of educational finance, therefore, must involve the study of public finance in general and the public finance of education in particular.

It is almost taken for granted that elementary and secondary (hereafter, E & S) education is a public responsibility. The major issues involve the what, how, who, and for whom questions: what programs should be supported; which level of government is responsible for what proportion of the total support; in what manner should aid to education be distributed, and what strings should be attached (if any); and which groups in society should pay what portion of the educational costs relative to the benefits that the public school system provides them. Such a view is relatively modern. Less than a century and a half ago, debate raged in this nation, as in many others, about whether education was a public or private concern. "The idea that education was a function of the state obtained in only one western nation—the kingdom of Prussia. . . . In America [in the eighteenth century], education continued to be regarded as a private or semiprivate enterprise, a responsibility left by government to the church and the parents" (Meyer, 1967, p. 121).

The support of free public schools in America gained strength during the 1820s and 1830s, sparked by the leadership of such visionaries as Horace Mann, Gordon Carter, and Henry Barnard. The initial movement—"the free school movement"—gained momentum, and the modern era of school finance began.

The early methods of school finance included the sale of land and the institution of state lotteries for education. As the number of schools and students grew, however, the need for additional revenue prompted local authorities to seek other sources, and the tax on real property was selected. The property tax continues to support the bulk of local educational expenditures to this date.

Americans believed for a long time that education is the responsibility of local governments. This is consistent with the notion of *subsidiarity,* that decisions should be made at the level closest to the decision situation. If a situation can be handled sufficiently by local governments, then the state or federal governments should not interfere (Coons, Clune, & Sugarman, 1970). In time, however, it appeared that local financing of education is inadequate. The works of Cubberley (1905), Strayer and Haig (1923), and Mort (1933) characterize the nature of the dissatisfaction with local finance. Their main objection was the unequal education that resulted from exclusive reliance on local sources, giving rise to substantial discrepancies in educational expenditures among schools within each state. Although their views differed, their essential argument was that the state must intervene in order that every locality can spend a reasonable minimum amount on education. Morrison (1930) went further, advocating full state funding of education.

As a result of the state-aid movement, legislation was passed in every state providing at least some state aid to local schools. But the type and extent of state aid was considered by many to be woefully inadequate, giving rise to the reform movement of the 1970s and 1980s. Although the issue is in the domain of economics, the great push forward was achieved mainly as a result of legal and constitutional considerations. The most celebrated work, with far-reaching impact on school finance, was the study by Coons, Clune, & Sugarman (1970), who argued that the existing arrangements of school finance violated the Fourteenth Amendment to the U.S. Constitution, because the rights of minors (pupils) were not protected. Since the "quality" of education a child receives (measured by the per pupil expenditures on education) varies greatly from district to district, and since a child is powerless to determine where he or she resides, the rights of children to quality education are infringed. And although the United States Supreme Court rejected the argument in the *Rodriguez* v. *San Antonio* case, asserting that equal educational opportunity is not guaranteed under the U.S. Constitution, many state courts held that unequal educational expenditure is unconstitutional under the states' constitutions, forcing significant reforms of the states' educational finance systems.

Major Issues. The foregoing paragraphs have briefly outlined the historical development of the finance of E & S schools. Underlying the development of educational finance systems are a number of important and controversial issues.

Equity. Educational "equity" or "fairness" is usually interpreted to mean that all children, regardless of social class, race, creed, or economic status, should have equal access to quality education. The equity issue, no doubt, has been the most persistent cause of educational reform. The idea of a free public school may be defended by the notion that children of the poor could not afford to pay for schooling and that equity criteria demand that they obtain access to schooling. The argument for state aid is also based on the argument that exclusive local finance of schools create inequities among schools and school districts. The wealthier districts can pay more for schooling, so pupils in such districts can obtain a better education than those in poorer school districts. The introduction of state aid, in inverse relation to local wealth, would help reduce interdistrict variations in educational resources.

Even if the equity argument is accepted, several questions remain. Should equity be defined in terms of expenditures or other school resources (i.e., inputs) or in terms of educational outcomes (i.e., outputs), such as achievement on tests? Although the vast majority of studies, court cases, and arguments center on inputs, the real issue concerns outputs. But the state of the art is such that much less is known about interdistrict and interschool variations in educational outcomes than about inputs. Furthermore, if equity is to be achieved, should attention be confined to school districts, or should we also consider equity among schools in the same district, classes in the same school, and students in the same class? As we move successively closer to the pupil, the task of guaranteeing equity becomes progressively more difficult. Moreover, the notion of equity is far from clear, and it is difficult to get consensus about its ultimate meaning. Some argue that equity considerations require equality of *opportunity;* others demand

complete equality of *outcomes.* In addition, some argue for less emphasis on equity so that competing criteria (such as efficiency) will not suffer, whereas others argue for complete equity no matter what the consequences.

Efficiency. Economic efficiency implies the achievement of maximum output per unit of input. If the children of poor families are discouraged from attending school, by financial and other causes, total performance of the economy might suffer. Some intervention by government to spur investment in schooling may therefore be justified. Moreover, there is the "externality" argument, which states that education bestows benefits not only on the person being educated but also on others: peers, family, coworkers, employees, employers, and society at large (Weisbrod, 1962). For example, when children are at school, parents are free to pursue their careers and are freed from child care chores. Since such external benefits are not included in an individual's private demand for education, there will be a discrepancy between the social and private demand for education, resulting in underinvestment in education. Government intervention (such as financial aid to students or schools or both) may therefore be justified.

What is less well understood, however, is that the existence of external benefits—and even the equity criteria— does not necessarily justify government *operation* of schools. Most people take it for granted that E & S education belongs in the public schools. As noted above, this is a relatively recent phenomenon, propelled in large measure by the desire to promote the Americanization of the diverse nationalities migrating to the United States. As West (1970) points out, the arguments for public operation of schools rest on seriously questionable premises.

The search for efficiency often appears to conflict with the search for equity. For example, it has been argued that complete equality of per pupil expenditures in a state would eliminate the existence of "lighthouse districts," where innovation is expected to occur at an accelerated pace. Considering that long-run efficiency requires experimentation and innovation, some argue that a little equity should be given up to insure continued inventiveness. And to the extent that complete equalization is achieved by bringing high-spending districts down to a lower state standard (rather than bringing all districts up to the standards of the highest-spending districts, a move that in all likelihood would cost a state more than it is willing to pay), the loss in educational excellence in the high-spending districts may have serious repercussions for developing the future leaders of America.

Need. Another issue in educational finance is concerned with the "needs" of various segments of the student body. (The word "needs" is placed in quotation marks because it does not represent unambiguous requirements but is more closely related to desires or wants. The education finance literature, however, fails to make the important distinction between actual needs and mere wants.) Even complete equalization of funding is flawed when some students require more resources than others. Since some pupils are physically, mentally, or culturally disadvantaged (relative to the average pupil), equal resources per pupil would imply unequal educational outcomes to the disadvantaged. Programs and formulas to account for such needs have mushroomed in recent years, greatly complicating state aid to education. Aside from obvious special needs, such as those of physically and mentally disabled students, additional need areas have received attention, such as relative sparsity of student population (resulting in higher transportation costs), and cost-of-living differences among communities (resulting in higher educational costs in some areas). Also, districts with declining enrollments are sometimes considered to have a special need, because state aid funds are disbursed on per-pupil basis, whereas short-run costs of education are less sensitive to enrollment changes: for example, when enrollments decline by 10 percent, state aid funds will decline by 10 percent, but the district may not be able to reduce the number of classes and schools by 10 percent. School closure, in particular, is subject to intense political pressure. Thus, the savings to a school district from declining enrollments are almost certainly less than proportional to the reduction in enrollments (Abramowitz & Rosenfeld, 1978).

Inflation. State aid formulas almost universally employ dollar figures per pupil, per classroom, or per teacher. As prices increase, so too do educational costs, and in the absence of appropriate state legislation, state aid funds provide fewer educational resources. This is especially acute in states where the legislature meets only biannually, but high rates of inflation cause severe problems in most states. Although proposals have been made for indexing state aid funds to the cost-of-living (or cost-of-education) index, legislators have been reluctant to transfer discretionary decision-making power to a formula.

Equity, efficiency, need, and other considerations have affected the development of state aid to education. Because educational finance remains in the domain of state and local governments, there are considerable variations among the states in educational finance. These variations are explored further in a subsequent section. But in all cases (with the exception of Hawaii, which has full state funding), a state-local partnership exists in the finance of education, with local revenues largely dependent on the real property tax and with state aid used for correcting interdistrict differences in wealth, need, and other considerations.

Federal Aid. Federal aid to elementary and secondary education may be direct or indirect. Direct aid includes funds that are specifically earmarked for local school districts. Three categories of direct aid are usually recognized: (1) aid for children of poor families (commonly known as "educationally disadvantaged"), given through provisions of Title I of the Elementary and Secondary Education Act (ESEA) of 1965 and subsequent amendments; (2) aid for schools located in "federally impacted areas" (where large federal installations, such as military bases, are located); and (3) other "categorical" aid, consisting of

vocational and other grant programs mandated by ESEA and the Vocational Education Act of 1963 (with subsequent amendments). Examples of discretionary (categorical) aid programs include school library resources, textbooks, and other instructional materials for school children; education of the handicapped; and dropout prevention programs.

Indirect aid is given through federal grants to the states, portions of which are passed on to school districts. Also, programs such as the Revenue Sharing Act of 1972, funneling federal funds to the states, which in turn are required to pass them on to local governments (excluding school districts), relieve the states from using funds for nonschooling purposes, thus making it possible for them to provide additional funds for the support of schools.

In 1978–1979, $7.9 billion, or approximately 8.1 percent of elementary and secondary expenditures, came from federal sources. This contrasts with only 3.9 percent in 1955–1956, and represents more than a doubling of the role of the federal government. Nevertheless the federal role remains quite limited, focused mainly on special purpose programs and special needs (such as students from poor families). Moreover many federal programs require state or local matching funds, creating an inertia against use of federal funds. It is too early to speculate at this time what effect changes proposed by the Reagan administration may have on direct or indirect federal aid to schools, although initial proposals indicate a significant reduction of such aid.

State Aid Formulas. A large portion of state aid to local school districts is funneled through "general" or "basic support" programs, distributed by means of a formula. With the exception of Hawaii (where a single, unified school system exists, fully funded by the legislature, with executive control by the governor) and North Carolina (where state aid is given on a per teacher basis without regard to local wealth), all states use a formula containing an element of equalization: state aid is given in inverse relation to some measure of community wealth, most frequently real property valuation per pupil. A brief discussion of the major state aid formulas is provided here. For more detail consult the works of Cohn (1974, 1979); Benson (1978); and Garms, Guthrie, and Pierce (1978).

The Foundation plan. Major features of the plan include the following: F, the foundation level, which supposedly reflects the minimum expenditures necessary to support a reasonably sound educational program; r, the mandated local tax rate, representing the effort required by the local government to support education under the state-local partnership concept; V_i, the assessed valuation of property per pupil in the ith district, representing local wealth; and $WADA_i$, weighted average daily attendance, representing the local student count adjusted for different student needs (grade level, physical or mental disability, etc.). If EA_i is defined as equalization aid to the ith school district, then the general Foundation plan calls for the computation of state equalization aid as follows:

$$EA_i = WADA_i \ (F - rV_i). \tag{1}$$

In words, equalization aid to the ith district is the difference between the foundation level, F, and the local share, rV_i, multiplied by the adjusted student count. Generally only positive differences are considered. When rV_i exceeds F, EA_i is zero.

Variations of the plan abound. For instance, the number of classrooms or teachers might be used instead of the adjusted student count (as in South Dakota). Or ADM (average daily membership) might be substituted for ADA (average daily attendance). And various methods may be used to account for grade differences and other need areas in the weights applied to $WADA_i$. Also, alternative measures of wealth may be used, although V_i is the most popular by far. Possible wealth measures include community income, revenue from sales or income taxes or both, and indexes of wealth based upon a combination of these and other factors.

Opponents of the Foundation plan find fault with each of the plan's main features. The fixed foundation level, F, is regarded as too inflexible, requiring periodic action by legislatures to bring it up to date with changing educational costs, technology, and public demand for improved services. Many critics oppose the plan because of its reliance on the real property tax, a revenue source considered by many to be extremely inequitable, because its burden is alleged to vary inversely with income. Although the contention that the property tax is regressive has been challenged, it continues to be the least popular tax (Netzer, 1966; Musgrave & Musgrave, 1980, chap. 21). It has also been argued that the property tax is an "ugliness tax": it allegedly discourages owners of real property from improving their property, since such improvements increase the assessed valuation of the property and hence the tax liability. Also, the property tax is considered "revenue inelastic," that is, that revenues from the tax increase proportionately less than increases in community income. For these and other reasons, critics prefer a school finance system free of the disadvantages of the real property tax.

Perhaps the strongest attack on the Foundation plan was launched by Coons, Clune, and Sugarman (1970). They contend that the plan is inconsistent with what they believe is the correct definition of equity, which they term "wealth neutrality." A plan would be wealth neutral if expenditures per pupil in a given district were totally unrelated to community wealth. Even if V_i is accepted as the proper definition of community wealth, the Foundation program, in this view, fails the wealth neutrality test unless F is set equal to the highest level of educational spending in the state or unless any negative differences between F and local effort (rV_i) are refunded to the state (the "recapture" clause). Since no state satisfied either of these conditions in 1970, wealth neutrality was not achieved. In practice the achievement of absolute wealth neutrality is rarely expected, with courts allowing a reasonable deviation ("permissible variance") from the ideal. But a cursory review of state plans indicates quite clearly that most states do not even come close to wealth neutrality, permitting substantial variations in per-pupil expenditures among school districts.

The guaranteed valuation plan. Also known as the resource equalizer plan, this plan is a variation on the Foundation plan. Instead of setting a foundation level, F, the legislators select an assessed property valuation per pupil that the state is willing to guarantee each district. Denote this guaranteed level by V_g. Now the local share remains rV_i, as in the Foundation plan, and equalization aid is calculated according to the following:

$$EA_i = WADA_i \ (rV_g - rV_i). \tag{2}$$

Note that if V_g is simply F/r, then $rV_g = F$, and equations (1) and (2) are algebraically equivalent. The administration of the two systems, however, might be quite different, so that the practical effect of the two formulas on the allocation and distribution of educational resources may be quite different. Again, equation (2) is generally used only when rV_g (the guaranteed yield) exceeds rV_i (the local share). When rV_i exceeds rV_g, equalization aid is usually zero.

Since the Foundation and the guaranteed valuation plans are extremely similar, the objections leveled against the former also apply in large measure to the latter.

The percentage equalizing plan. The additional objection to both the Foundation and the guaranteed valuation plans is that neither encourages increased tax effort by local governments beyond the mandated tax rate. Imposition of a matching aid formula is believed to remedy such disincentives. This is achieved by the percentage equalizing plan.

If a statewide standard for property valuation, call it V_s, is promulgated, if the legislature selects a scalar x, whose value varies inversely with the state's share of educational funding, and if local expenditures per pupil are designated by the symbol EXP_i, then equalization aid is calculated according to equation (3):

$$EA_i = WADA_i \ (1 - xV_i/V_s)EXP_i . \tag{3}$$

The choice of V_s is a matter of discretionary policy, with larger values of V_s resulting in increased state aid, and vice versa. For example, if V_i/V_s is ½ for district i, and if x is 0.25, then EA_i is $0.875EXP_i$, or 87.5 percent of local expenditures. If $V_1 V_s$ increases to 2, and x remains at 0.25, EA_i is reduced to $0.5EXP_i$. If V_i/V_s is, again, 2, but x increases to 0.4, EA_i will be reduced to only $0.2EXP_i$. When x is set equal to 0.5, districts for which V_i/V_s is equal to or greater than 2 will receive no state aid.

The percentage equalizing plan has been endorsed by Feldstein (1975). Feldstein argues that only such a plan could meet the conditions of wealth neutrality, when the latter concept is interpreted properly. Others disagree, because the plan does not guarantee equal resources regardless of community wealth. Also, a major deficiency of the percentage equalizing plan is the tendency of adopting states to set limits on the level of local expenditures that the state will support (New York is one such example).

The district power equalizing plan.   Originally proposed by Coons, Clune, and Sugarman (1970), the district power equalizing plan (DPE) is supposed to eliminate community wealth as a determinant of educational expenditures. The original plan called for the development of a schedule of revenue entitlement (denoted here by *RE*), based upon a district's tax effort. Equalized aid per weighted pupil is simply the difference between *RE* and actual tax yield (or the local share), $r_i V_i$, where r_i is the real property tax rate chosen by the ith district. Total equalized aid in a district is given by equation (4):

$$EA_i = WADA_i \ (RE - r_i V_i). \qquad (4)$$

An important provision of the original DPE plan is that equation (4) must be applied for *all districts*, even if $r_i V_i$ exceeds *RE*. In the latter case, the difference between a district's tax yield and its revenue entitlement would be turned over to the state. Under such a plan, all districts selecting the same r_i will have identical per pupil expenditures, regardless of community wealth.

If tax effort is independent of community wealth, then a DPE plan, with a recapture clause, will satisfy the wealth neutrality requirement. To the extent that tax effort and community wealth are positively correlated, as suggested from an investigation of the plan in some areas of Florida, wealthier communities will select a higher tax rate and therefore receive a larger entitlement. One method to deal with this problem would be to set upper limits for the allowable tax rate. When this method was applied in Utah, virtually all districts chose the maximum tax rate, and the practical effect was to transform the property tax from a local to a statewide tax.

Critics of the DPE plan argue that its reliance on the property tax is undesirable. They also argue that tax effort should not be a determinant of educational expenditures, any more than community wealth should be—even if the two are unrelated. Why should a child suffer just because he happens to live in a community where residents choose to minimize their tax efforts? Finally, political realities are such that it is unlikely that a recapture clause can be passed by a legislature. Without the recapture clause, the DPE plan is nothing but a slight variation of the Foundation or the guaranteed valuation plans.

Flat grants.   Not long ago, state school finance systems relied largely or even exclusively on flat grants. These are state funds given to school districts on the basis of (weighted or unweighted) pupil, teacher, or classroom count, regardless of community wealth and local tax effort. At present, only North Carolina relies exclusively on flat grants, but in many states flat grants supplement the equalized aid (based on one of the plans described earlier). Although flat grants do not appear to be equalizing, they do in fact equalize resources to some extent. Tax contributions to the state (principally sales or income taxes) vary proportionately with community wealth. Poorer communities contribute less per person to such taxes but receive the same educational aid per pupil (which generally translates to relatively more aid *per capita*, because in poorer communities there are more children per family and fewer children are enrolled in private schools), whereas the opposite is true in wealthier communities. It follows that the tax-transfer system does result in a redistribution from wealthier to poorer communities. In fact, a flat grant that is sufficiently high is likely to be far more equalizing than a Foundation plan with a low foundation level *(F)*. It should be recognized, however, that a given degree of equalization can be achieved at much less cost to the state through one of the equalization plans than through flat grants.

Encumbering provisions.   This discussion cannot be concluded without some comments on the encumbering legislation that accompanies many educational finance programs. Most bothersome are the minimum, maximum, and save-harmless (or grandfather's clause) aspects of the various programs. In some states, maximum amounts or percentages of total funds are fixed, and even more states have minimums—amounting to a flat grant. A save-harmless clause is quite common, allowing a district to choose between the funds to which it is entitled under the present formula or an amount to which it was entitled at some previous year, whichever is larger. All too often, unfortunately, such provisions sap, in the name of practical politics, any strength the educational finance program might have.

Specific-purpose funding.   In addition to the basic support program, state funds are channeled for support of specific needs, especially transportation, textbooks, vocational education, capital outlays, and special education. Since the treatment of these categorical grants varies so much among the states, it is difficult to describe these funding areas in the limited space allowed here. A complete description of the states' programs for 1978–1979 is contained in Tron (1980), and a series of annual updates has been provided by the Education Commission of the States, for example, McGuire, Augenblick, and Hammond (1980).

State Aid: Current Status.   Only a brief description of the current status of educational finance in the states is possible here. For the sake of brevity, the latest available information (for 1979–1980) is compressed into Table 1.

Note that a majority of the states (twenty-seven) employ the Foundation plan, and only two employ versions of the DPE plan. The wide discrepancy among the states in the relative importance of state aid and the basic support program is also apparent. The variations in per pupil expenditures are also considerable.

Missing from the table are the wide variations in per pupil expenditures *within* the states, and the idiosyncrasies of the various finance plans. No two plans are alike, even if the same label (e.g., Foundation) is used to describe them. Wide variations are found in the foundation level, required local effort, measure of community wealth, and encumbering provisions. A more complete description of

TABLE 1. *General characteristics of state education finance systems, 1979–1980*

State	Basic support program	State aid as a percentage of total expendi- tures 1978–1979	Basic support programs as a percentage of state aid 1978–1979	Estimated total expenditures per pupil 1979–1980
Alabama	Foundation	75%	87%	$1,503
Alaska	Percentage Equal.	86	55	4,779
Arizona	Foundation	43	90	2,236
Arkansas	Foundation	61	77	1,502
California	Guaranteed Val.	68	76	2,000
Colorado	Guaranteed Val.	45	87	2,085
Connecticut	Guaranteed Val.	29	65	2,757
Delaware	Percentage Equal.	74	65	2,664
Florida	Foundation	61	85	1,886
Georgia	Foundation	64	79	1,331
Hawaii	Full-state fund.	100	53	1,855
Idaho	Foundation	67	70	1,542
Illinois	Found. and G. V.	54	71	2,483
Indiana	Foundation	53	89	1,849
Iowa	Foundation	52	97	2,506
Kansas	Guaranteed Val.	47	83	2,310
Kentucky	Found. and G. V.	78	96	1,722
Louisiana	Foundation	65	86	1,797
Maine	Found. and G. V.	52	100	1,859
Maryland	Foundation	34	41	2,319
Massachusetts	Foundation	31	74	2,757
Michigan	Guaranteed Val.	43	79	2,349
Minnesota	Foundation	67	66	2,428
Mississippi	Foundation	70	88	1,613
Missouri	Foundation	39	76	1,836
Montana	Dist. Power Equal.	61	97	2,247
Nebraska	Foundation	18	76	2,076
Nevada	Foundation	40	100	1,806
New Hampshire	Foundation	5	46	1,515
New Jersey	Guaranteed Val.	43	53	2,893
New Mexico	Foundation	78	90	1,855
New York	Percentage Equal.	41	91	3,041
N. Carolina	Flat Grants	73	91	1,800
N. Dakota	Foundation	64	82	1,652
Ohio	Guaranteed Val.	43	56	1,918
Oklahoma	Found. and Perc. Equal.	57	96	2,070
Oregon	Foundation	30	86	2,459
Pennsylvania	Percentage Equal.	42	74	2,499
Rhode Island	Percentage Equal.	42	87	2,538
S. Carolina	Foundation	61	68	1,581
S. Dakota	Foundation	18	90	1,793
Tennessee	Foundation	52	89	1,611
Texas	Foundation	57	99	1,701
Utah	Dist. Power Equal.	71	66	1,609
Vermont	Percentage Equal.	41	66	1,810

TABLE 1. *General characteristics of state education finance systems, 1979–1980 (cont.)*

State	Basic support program	State aid as a percentage of total expenditures 1978–1979	Basic support programs as a percentage of state aid 1978–1979	Estimated total expenditures per pupil 1979–1980
Virginia	Foundation	37	75	1,927
Washington	Foundation	68	76	2,256
W. Virginia	Foundation	65	94	1,882
Wisconsin	Guaranteed Val.	38	81	2,459
Wyoming	Found. and G. V.	32	73	2,343

SOURCES OF DATA: Tron, 1980; McGuire, Augenblick, & Hammond, 1980.

the various finance plans is contained in the sources for Table 1.

Summary. The discussion of school finance in the foregoing pages is necessarily sketchy and does not provide a full account of the wide-ranging variations in school finance theory and practice. A glimpse of the main features of school finance has been provided, however, and the list of references includes a number of studies to which the interested reader may turn for a fuller account.

Educational finance has progressed from a system dominated by church and private schools to a public school system where a large share of revenue is supplied by the states, with local revenues derived almost exclusively from real property tax levies. The states' share in public school finance has increased steadily over the years, and phenomena such as Proposition 13 in California (where voters approved significant reductions in property taxes) increase the probability that the states' share will increase further. Educational finance legislation, moreover, has become much more complicated and sophisticated, incorporating the results of economic analysis, such as the relation between school costs and school size (Cohn, 1968). Other areas, such as cost-of-education indexes (Chambers, 1980) and the modern theory of income distribution (Hickrod, Chaudhari, & Lundeen, 1980), are likely to be incorporated in future school finance legislation. But the issue of efficiency has remained relatively unexplored, both independently and in relation to school finance reform (one exception is Cohn, 1981). As one observer remarked, the interface between equity and efficiency and its repercussions on school finance are likely to become the focus for school finance research in the 1980s. Such a belief is strengthened by the observation that federal and state funds for social services are becoming scarce, and therefore local schools must find ways to improve efficiency, that is, produce more for each dollar of available resource.

Elchanan Cohn

See also Administration of Educational Institutions; Business Administration of Schools; Financial Aid to Students; Financing Colleges and Universities; Local Influences on Education; School Boards; State Influences on Education.

REFERENCES

In addition to the works listed here, the reader may wish to explore current and past issues of periodicals in this area (especially the *Journal of Education Finance, Economics of Education Review,* and *Journal of Human Resources*), publications of the Education Finance Center, Education Commission of the States, and publications of the United States Department of Education, particularly the Federal School Finance Project.

Abramowitz, S., & Rosenfeld, S. (Eds.). *Declining Enrollment: The Challenge of the Coming Decade.* Washington, D.C.: National Institute of Education, 1978. (ERIC Document Reproduction Service No. ED 150 708)

Benson, C. S. *The Economics of Public Education* (3rd ed.). Boston: Houghton Mifflin, 1978.

Chambers, J. G. The development of a cost of education index: Some empirical estimates and policy issues. *Journal of Education Finance,* 1980, *5,* 262–281. (ERIC Document Reproduction Service No. ED 176 368)

Cohn, E. Economies of scale in Iowa high school operations. *Journal of Human Resources,* 1968, *3,* 422–434.

Cohn, E. *Economics of State Aid to Education.* Lexington, Mass.: Lexington Books, 1974.

Cohn, E. *The Economics of Education* (Rev. ed.). Cambridge, Mass.: Ballinger, 1979.

Cohn, E. Combining efficiency and equity: Optimization of resource allocation in state school systems. In W. W. McMahon & T. G. Geske (Eds.), *Financing Education: Overcoming Inefficiency and Inequity.* Urbana: University of Illinois Press, 1982.

Coons, J. E.; Clune, W. H., III; & Sugarman, S. D. *Private Wealth and Public Education.* Cambridge, Mass.: Belknap Press, Harvard University Press, 1970.

Cubberley, E. P. *School Funds and Their Apportionment* (Contributions to Education, No. 2). New York: Columbia University, Teachers College, 1905.

Feldstein, M. S. Wealth neutrality and local choice in public education. *American Economic Review,* 1975, *65,* 75–89.

Garms, W. I.; Guthrie, J. W.; & Pierce, L. G. *School Finance: The Economics and Politics of Public Education.* Englewood Cliffs, N.J.: Prentice-Hall, 1978. (ERIC Document Reproduction Service No. ED 154 481)

Grant, W. V., & Lind, G. C. *Digest of Educational Statistics, 1979.*

Washington, D.C.: U.S. Government Printing Office, 1979. (ERIC Document Reproduction Service No. ED 172 458)

Hickrod, G. A.; Chaudhari, R. B.; & Lundeen, V. Progress toward school finance equity goals in Indiana, Iowa, and Illinois. *Journal of Education Finance*, 1980, *6*, 176–200.

McGuire, K.; Augenblick, J.; & Hammond, J. *School Finance at a Fifth Glance*. Denver: Education Commission of the States, 1980.

Meyer, A. E. *An Educational History of the American People* (2nd ed.). New York: McGraw-Hill, 1967.

Morrison, H. C. *School Revenue*. Chicago: University of Chicago Press, 1930.

Mort, P. R. *State Support for Public Education*. Washington, D.C.: American Council on Education, 1933.

Musgrave, R. A., & Musgrave, P. B. *Public Finance in Theory and Practice* (3rd ed.). New York: McGraw-Hill, 1980.

Netzer, D. *Economics of the Property Tax*. Washington, D.C.: Brookings Institution, 1966.

Strayer, G. D., & Haig, R. M. *The Financing of Education in the State of New York*. New York: Macmillan, 1923.

Tron, E. O. (Ed. and Comp.) *Public School Finance Programs, 1978–1979*. Washington, D.C.: U.S. Government Printing Office, 1980. (ERIC Document Reproduction Service No. ED 188 341)

Weisbrod, B. A. Education and investment in human capital. *Journal of Political Economy* 1962, *70* (Suppl.), 106–123.

West, E. G. *Education and the State* (2nd ed.). London: Institute of Economic Affairs, 1970.

FOREIGN LANGUAGE EDUCATION

The field of foreign language education entered the 1970s with rising expectations. The 1960s had seen solid governmental support for foreign language programs, primarily through the National Defense Education Act (NDEA) of 1958. NDEA funding had had far-reaching effects, contributing to teacher training as well as curriculum and materials development. Enrollments grew, materials and methodology had come together in the dominance of the audiolingual approach to foreign language instruction, and language laboratories had been installed in schools and universities everywhere. As the 1970s progressed, however, the situation deteriorated rapidly until foreign language education found itself once more in a battle for survival. The struggle persisted on several fronts: in the schools, in the universities, and in the minds of the public. The forces that brought about this change were both internal and external. Research in second language learning raised questions about the validity of the psychological basis of the audiolingual approach; laboratories lacked stimulating materials; and the new, longer curricular sequences were unable to retain students. Developments in general education such as the back-to-basics movement in the public schools, student antagonism toward college requirements, and fiscal pressures at all levels of education combined to weaken programs.

In numbers, foreign language enrollments dropped during the 1970s, although they seemed to have bottomed out as of this writing. The latest enrollment surveys show that in 1978, 17.8 percent of public secondary students were enrolled in a foreign language course (Hammond and Scebold, 1980); this compares with the 27.7 percent enrolled in 1968. The state of Connecticut has the highest enrollment, with 39.2 percent, but the range includes Mississippi, which has only 4.5 percent of its students involved in a foreign language course. Thus even with the strength of NDEA funding in the 1960s, foreign languages have reached at best only one-fourth of the high school population.

At the university level, the picture is not much brighter. Although the number of students in college has risen steadily since 1960, the peak enrollment in foreign language courses occurred in 1968. The 1977 registration survey reported that only 8.9 percent of all college students were taking a foreign language course. Between 1968 and 1977 the percentage of growth was negative for French (−36.6 percent), German (−37.4 percent), and Russian (−31.7 percent). There were slight increases for Italian (9.8 percent) and Spanish (3.2 percent). Among the less commonly taught languages, registrations have increased continuously in Arabic and Japanese, and Chinese has held steady (Association of Departments of Foreign Languages, 1978). The early 1980s have seen scattered reports of reinstated language requirements and successful elective programs, but there is not yet any statistical confirmation of rising numbers.

Issues for the 1980s. The plight of foreign language study became so bad that it led to U.S. vulnerability in complying with the Helsinki Agreement of 1975. The Final Act requires signers to agree "to encourage the study of foreign language and civilization as an important means of expanding communication among peoples." In recognition of this country's lack of accomplishment with respect to that goal, Jimmy Carter, in September 1978, appointed a President's Commission on Foreign Language and International Studies. In its report, *Strength through Wisdom: A Critique of U.S. Capability (1979)*, the commission stated that "Americans' incompetence in foreign languages is nothing short of scandalous, and it is becoming worse" (p. 5). The commission claimed to have found "a serious deterioration in this country's language and research capacity, at a time when an increasingly hazardous international military, political and economic environment is making unprecedented demands on America's resources, intellectual capacity and public sensitivity" (p. 1).

The year in which the commission gathered testimony was one of unprecedented political and professional involvement for foreign language educators and for international specialists in business and government; a chronicle of the events of that year is provided by Geno (1981). The recommendations of the commission have set the tone for the 1980s. However, a different president is in office and the responsibility for converting recommendations into action becomes the task of the profession in conjunction with government and the public. The issues for the 1980s have been explored in two volumes of the Foreign Language Education Series issued by the American Council of Teachers of Foreign Languages (ACTFL) (Phillips 1980, 1981). These issues include institution of a massive public awareness campaign; implementation of model programs in elementary schools, secondary schools, and higher education; and creation of a link with global education and international studies.

An initial effort at defining priorities for and by the foreign language profession took place in November 1980 at the National Priorities Conference, an invitational meeting sponsored by the ACTFL and several publishers. Leaders in the profession presented papers on curriculum and materials development, evaluation, research, teacher education, and global education. Publication of these papers (Lange, 1981) should set the stage for concentrated action and reaction by the profession, particularly in the curriculum and testing fields.

The major shift anticipated in foreign language curriculum is toward the development of minimal communicative ability, as defined by Valdman (1978). Indeed, communication has become the focus of goals, activities, and testing in newer materials and in many classrooms. Whereas the audiolingual era of foreign language instruction was built upon pattern drills aimed at mastery of the structure of the target language, communicative approaches attempt to define the essentials of a meaningful exchange between speakers or writers. Learners advance from survival-level language to more standard forms. Success must often be measured in a global fashion, based upon whether meaning was transferred or not and to what degree. Thus, a desperate need exists for the development of proficiency tests appropriate for various levels of communication and in the several skills.

With a focus upon communicative ability, curriculum will also need to diversify. A communication event involves much more than language, and culture takes on a new and expanded role in this instance. Instead of a curriculum that has concentrated almost totally on linguistic elements, as has been the case with both audiolingual and grammar syllabi, portions of classroom time must be devoted to the cultural context of the target language community (e.g., Stern & Cummins, 1981). Topics such as gestures, semantics, sociolinguistics, and pragmatics are all receiving renewed attention because of the light they shed on what makes a communication event successful. The next decade will see more research in these fields as well as attempts to transform that information into classroom materials.

Psychological-Sociological Foundations. The major shift in theory affecting foreign language instruction was the abandonment by the early 1970s of audiolingual methods that were based on behaviorist psychology and a habit-formation assumption about language learning. In the field of learning psychology, cognitive approaches to language

acquisition and development were gaining prominence and establishing a theoretical basis very different from that of stimulus-response; the tenets supporting audiolingualism were being shaken or refuted. For example, the natural order of skills—listening, speaking, reading, writing,— had mandated the sequence for classroom teaching under the audiolingual approach. Pattern drills, dialogue memorization, and inductive presentations of grammar were also part of the package. However, cognitive psychologists such as Ausubel (1968) made strong arguments demonstrating the incompatibility of audiolingual techniques for adolescents and adults. What was natural for the child was not necessarily natural or effective for the adult. Children learned in a "natural skill" sequence because that was the only order available to them. The contrast between features of language learning expounded by cognitive psychologists and by audiolingualists (see Table 1) was the basis for much debate in foreign language circles.

Comparison of teaching methods. Even as cognitive psychologists were discovering new explanations for the language-learning process, many classroom teachers were beginning to feel doubts about the efficacy of the method in which they had been trained by NDEA institutes and teacher preparation courses. Students could show off and recite dialogues with appropriate pronunciation, intonation, and fluency, but could they use line 4 if it was not preceded by lines 1–3? They manipulated their pattern drills with 90 percent accuracy, but they were not necessarily any more accurate in expressing their own ideas than previous students who might have translated each word rather painfully.

In an effort to assess the effects of the new methods on student achievement, a large comparative study was carried out. The Pennsylvania Project, as it was popularly known (Smith, 1970), included 104 teachers of French and German in 61 intact classes in 58 Pennsylvania school districts.

Three approaches to foreign language instruction were compared: "traditional," which unfortunately was not well defined and thus included a variety of methods; "functional skills," a rigid audiolingual method; and "functional skills with grammar," a modified audiolingual approach. If the researchers had a bias at the outset, it was that the audiolingual method would prove to be superior, as had been evidenced by several smaller studies (e.g., Scherer & Wertheimer, 1964). The expected failed to happen. Audiolingual students did not do better than traditionally trained ones on most measures and in most skill areas; indeed the latter did better in reading and as well as the audiolingual ones in speaking.

At the time, the results of the Pennsylvania Project received criticism from several sources and for various reasons. The design of the study was attacked, as were the accuracy and reliability of the tests and the degree to which teachers adhered to their randomly assigned strategies. And it must be remembered that the government had gone to great expense to train large numbers of teach-

TABLE 1. *Comparison of audiolingual and cognitive views of foreign language learning*

Audiolingual theory and features	Cognitive theory and features
1. Direct learning of second language meanings and syntactical functions is preferable; much use of visuals; classes conducted in foreign language.	1. Learner already has store of concepts, vocabulary, and code of one language; needs only to acquire an additional set of symbols for old, familiar meanings.
2. Rote learning of phrases, patterns, dialogues dominated.	2. Pattern practice must be meaningful for learner to achieve knowledge of syntactic and semantic contribution of words, phrases. Only then can comparable phrases or recombinations be made.
3. Inductive learning of grammatical generalizations achieved by pattern practices, drills, followed by generalizations.	3. An adult is capable of understanding complex relationships, of transferring and applying rules.
4. Presentation of spoken forms must be mastered before written ones. Prereading phases were a common practice.	4. For literates, reading can be a tool. Older learner uses written language as a prop to recognize word boundaries, appreciate structure for transfer purposes, and reduce stress.
5. Natural speed rendition of language was recommended.	5. Gain is achieved over time with practice. Artificial simplification is justifiable at early stages.

ers in audiolingual methods. From the perspective of the 1980s, however, it is generally acknowledged that no single way to teach a foreign language is best for all students in all situations. Audiolingualism was not the answer, and the foreign language profession will probably hesitate to ever again endorse a single methodology. In fact, it is impossible in this article to describe foreign language teaching today, since it is marked by diversity, eclecticism, and an individuality grounded in the preferences of a particular teacher, the demands of a specific school department or system, or the needs of individual students. An important contribution of the audiolingual movement, and one that remains regardless of preferred methodology, has been the emphasis on oral skills. Consequently, many audiolingual techniques are widely used to develop communication skills in today's classrooms.

Before further consideration of classroom practices, it is important to look at other areas that psycholinguists and second language researchers have been investigating. Some of their findings have been implemented in programs, materials, or methodologies. Others persist as theory.

A model of school learning. Since language is a skill requiring a continuous sequence of learning as well as control of prerequisites, it lends itself to programs of mastery learning. Carroll's model (1963, 1974) of school learning has been applied with success in learning a foreign language. His model consists of five elements: (1) the learner's aptitude (as a function of time needed to achieve a task; (2) the learner's general intelligence; (3) the learner's perseverance (time allowed by the learner; (4) the quality of instruction (sequence order); and (5) the opportunity for learning (time allowed by the school).

Many language teaching practices are predicated upon these assumptions. Certainly the programs in individualized foreign language instruction, which peaked in the mid-1970s, drew heavily upon the Carroll model. These programs manipulate the time variable in the Carroll model as follows:

1. *Aptitude:* Given sufficient time, almost any learner can master a learning task. Individualization provides for variance in the amount of time required.
2. *General intelligence:* Instruction is modified to meet the needs of the individual's capacity to understand.
3. *Perseverance:* Time varies with the learner's degree of satisfaction. Individualized instruction consists of those factors identified as contributing to satisfaction— achievement, recognition, learning itself, responsibility, advancement.
4. *Quality of instruction and opportunity for learning:* Mastery is possible when each student receives treatment best suited to his learning needs. Individualization provides for various sequences and circumstances. Its purpose is to enlarge the opportunity for learning.

A review of individualization in teaching foreign languages can be found in Phillips (1974). Although full-fledged individualized programs are no longer as numerous as formerly, many individualized instructional techniques have filtered into everyday classroom practices so that mastery learning, sequence, and attention to individual learning strategies are built into many current materials and approaches. The current interest in intensive language classes and immersion programs also derives from their ability to increase significantly the time devoted to language instruction, thus affecting aptitude, perseverance, and opportunity for learning.

Theories of language acquisition. Even as Carroll (1974) described a cognitive-code learning theory, he did not totally reject the habit-formation basis of audiolingualism. Rather, he suggested that acquisition involved both reasoning and habit formation, with efficacy and predominance depending upon the stage of learning, the language elements involved, and differences in the learner's aptitude and preferred learning style. This fusion of learning processes as well as the complexity of language learning may also account for the fact that broad methodological comparisons, such as the Pennsylvania Project, may not result in the clear-cut superiority of any one method.

A promising area of research has focused upon the contrast between receptive skill learning (listening and reading) and productive tasks (speaking and writing). There is mounting evidence that a sequence requiring receptive mastery before proceeding to productive skills is preferable. A study by Postovsky (1971) compared students who were required to listen to Russian sounds without pronouncing them with others who heard and spoke from the outset. Those with the receptive concentration performed equally well or better on pronunciation tests at the end of the unit of instruction. This confirmed the "listening before speaking" sequence of audiolingualism, but perhaps for different reasons. Cognitive explanations are based upon associations established in the brain that require underlying templates to store the sounds before they can be recalled and uttered.

Models of second language learning. A comprehensive review of various second language learning models was written by Stern and Cummins (1981). Although their work concentrates upon Canadian research, it is applicable to any second language theory; indeed, it should be recognized that much research in language learning is being conducted in Canada under the auspices of the Ontario Institute for Studies in Education (OISE). For this article, concentration on a few models of the language learning process will be sufficient.

The first model is entitled the "L1–L2 Connection" by Stern and Cummins (1981). It presents the major issue over which methods have traditionally clashed: should learners use their native language to learn a foreign one ("cross-lingual" learning) or should all classroom work be done in the foreign language, with no reference to the first ("intralingual" learning)? Proponents of both processes abound, and there are even those who suggest an intermediate model (Corder, 1978) in which an "interlanguage" process is used by the learner. According to this view, instances in which the student consciously reconstructs the second language on the basis of the first are balanced by others in which the second language samples are practiced and used directly. The teacher might thus decide upon the language elements best learned by reference to the first language and those elements that would benefit from extensive target language drill. Students, as they gain fluency, would decrease their dependency on interlanguage. In the final analysis, this conflict, like many other conflicts, may be resolved in the mind of the learner by the choice of his or her most efficient and preferred learning style.

A second problem identified by Stern and Cummins (1981) is what they call the "explicit-implicit option": the choice between deliberate, conscious, cognitive approaches to the task and automatic, subconscious, intuitive ones. Krashen (1978) has developed a Monitor Model for second language acquisition based upon the interrelationship between language *learning,* which he defines as a conscious, explicit process, and *acquisition,* the more subconscious, implicit one. The Monitor hypothesis suggests that acquisition is responsible for fluency in second language performance. When conscious learning is at work it functions as an editor, a monitor that corrects and applies rules as one speaks or writes. Acquisition is the preferable process, for use of the monitor would tend to impede fluency. The implications of this theory for classroom instruction and curriculum design are far-reaching; at the extreme, proficiency would be practically impossible to achieve if language is "learned," and designing school programs in which language can be "acquired" would preclude almost anything but an immersion experience. Research into the Monitor Model continues to assess how formal and informal linguistic environments contribute to language competency.

Individual learning strategies. From an emphasis on teacher behavior, research has recently turned to observing more closely how the learner as an individual processes new information. In place of the probably futile search for the one best method, many researchers are observing successful learners in order to identify the strategies they use. Hosenfeld (1975) encourages students to "think aloud" as they complete grammatical exercises or read in a second language. She has been able to discover the successful strategies of good learners as well as the ineffective strategies of poor ones. Rubin (1975) drew up a list of learning strategies after observing language classes, listening to student self-reports, analyzing herself, and questioning second language teachers. Sperry (1972) summarizes problems that arise from some of the bipolar dimensions of cognitive style, such as field-dependence or independence, breadth or categorizing, tolerance or intolerance of ambiguity. These characteristics are particularly significant for the second language learner. For example, field-independent learners can focus on the relevant linguistic elements of a task and disregard irrelevant ones. On the other hand, the field-dependent learner approaches the task in a more global fashion and is often unable to separate an element from its context. As these dimensions of cognitive style are probed for their influence on the language learner, more appropriate approaches can be developed for the individual student, or where possible, the student may be taught more useful strategies. Some of this research has begun to have an impact on classroom practices. For instance, Birckbichler and Omaggio (1978) have developed a guide to assist teachers in the diagnosis of learning problems and the prescription of specific classroom activities to remediate them.

The final words on research into the language learning–language teaching process have yet to be written. With each development comes a batch of new questions; much has been learned and advances have been made. A theoretical foundation that would translate into a prescriptive methodology is no longer an issue, however. If anything is known for certain, it is that human beings learn a second language in a multifaceted, complex process that involves variables in learning strategies and styles, in the linguistic units themselves, and in the sociolinguistic factors involved in communication. As Stern and Cummins (1981) write: "The aim of such research remains to better understand L2 [second language] learning under different conditions at different age or maturity levels and at different levels of proficiency" (p. 237). Jarvis (1981) also rejects the usefulness of broad comparative studies in favor of more descriptive research. His use of the term "descriptive" is not traditional, emphasizing, instead, close observation and analysis of the many classroom behaviors that make up the teaching-learning process.

Curriculum planners can evaluate and implement research findings in terms of students, teachers, and available resources, but the research does not prescribe a curriculum. Current issues in teacher training, at the preservice and in-service levels, also arise from the lack of a dominant methodology. It was much easier in the era of audiolingualism to instruct teachers in the techniques mandated by the theory. Tomorrow's teachers must know the language, the culture, the language-learning process, and the language learner before they can attempt to map out a plan to bring them together. And all this takes place as new knowledge continues to be generated.

Trends. The dominant trend in foreign language teaching is toward greater concentration on developing communication skills. It may seem surprising to the lay person that this has not been a primary emphasis all along. One need only recall, however, the many people who acknowledge an exposure to two years of studying a language even as they testify to the fact that "I can't speak a word of it." Several forces have contributed to this communicative orientation, but it was the report of the President's Commission (*Strength through Wisdom,* 1979) that brought the issue to the attention of the government and the public.

The commission reported that the United States suffers from a lack of foreign language "proficiency," meaning communicative ability, on all fronts; for example, many foreign service jobs with language requirements have been filled without the desired proficiency simply because candidates were not available. Also, the cultural aspect of language use and cross-cultural contacts needs to be expanded if better international performance by government and business personnel at home and abroad is to be achieved. In the final analysis, the commission recommended that all possible support be given to increase foreign language enrollment, but it is in the classroom that the goal of communicative ability must be fostered. Research and curriculum must henceforth provide the language learner with a real world context, that is, linguistic content in its full cultural environment.

Communicative language approaches. A major development in communicative course design was achieved by the Council of Europe (Van Ek, 1977). Known as the "Threshold-Level Syllabus," it bases course content on speech acts, functional categories, and semantic notions and discourse rather than on grammatical sequences, as do traditional syllabi. Wilkins (1976) has designed a functional-notional syllabus for second languages that includes a comprehensive list of "notions," or meanings, commonly expressed in English. The "functions" refer to what people choose to *do* with those meanings: for example, they may wish to persuade, to inform, to lie. A syllabus thus designed establishes a communication goal from the outset and operates in a cyclical fashion as the learner progresses from relatively simple utterances to more complex ones. It is doubtful that this model can be directly implemented into general purpose courses, for it is not possible to anticipate exactly which notions and functions a student might need to express. However, by fusing some of the common purposes of language onto the grammatical syllabus in use in most schools, communicative goals can be reached. Instead of practicing language in pattern drills or in isolated exercises, the student would work within a meaningful context for some imagined, yet realistic, language purpose (Guntermann, 1979; Guntermann & Phillips, 1981; Valdman, 1978).

The functional-notional syllabus is a promising one for the many new classes grouped under the label "special purpose language courses." These courses are most commonly found in higher education and/or adult education programs. When individuals have clearly defined needs and purposes for language study, the notions and functions they want to be able to express are narrower and therefore easier to identify for teaching. The medical technician, social worker, and police officer in special purpose Spanish courses learn quite rapidly the content relevant to their job needs. Numerous colleges are revising required sequences as well as elective courses so that students move from basic language courses into the more specialized ones emphasizing limited skills (oral language, reading) and content. Formerly, advanced language led to literature; now becoming a proficient user of language is an equally important objective. Whatever the educational level, Rivers (1979) emphasizes that special purpose or career-preparation language courses must be built on a general four-skill sequence. She also sees these classes as being particularly appropriate for community colleges and continuing education programs in which the role, or even the need, for a foreign language curriculum had never been firmly established.

Intensive instruction. Experiments with immersion programs were begun in Canada as early as 1965, but the numbers of students and schools involved in this approach have grown steadily during the 1970s. Immersion programs are characterized by the fact that they really are not a language curriculum at all. Mainly developed for elementary and middle schools, they "immerse" the entering youngster in a second language environment in which new knowledge and content in most disciplines are taught in the foreign language. Communication is not some long-range goal; the foreign language is used for communication from the start. The content and activities involved in studying subjects are the main objectives, and the proficiency "acquired," in Krashen's sense (1978) of the term, is a by-product. Most of the Canadian immersion experiments began with elementary school-age native speakers of English learning French. These projects, some now over fifteen years in operation, have undergone extensive observation and evaluation. The achievement scores of immersion students in their academic subjects have been impressive. Students have not suffered academically because they were learning in a second language; indeed, they have outperformed monolingual children on many tests. (See Lambert & Tucker, 1972, for a case study of one program.)

The United States has successfully emulated some of the Canadian models. One program that has achieved high visibility in the popular press and broadcast media is the Montgomery County, Maryland, French (and now Spanish) immersion experience at the Four Corners Elementary School. In a 1978 article Gabriel Jacobs, the principal, shared implementation procedures with administrators and foreign language educators. Four Corners is a public school, and all students are eligible to enroll, but participation in the program is by parental choice. Students follow the regular district curriculum; the only difference is that they use foreign language materials. The purchase of these materials is the only additional cost to the system. Standardized achievement tests confirm that the immersion students are comparable to their peers. Other schools across the country are exploring this option. Immersion is particularly appropriate for large school systems, where it can be one alternative school program among many. Some of the newer bilingual magnet schools in cities like Cincinnati and Pittsburgh are similar to an immersion program. These bilingual schools are attracting native speakers of English and developing proficiency in a foreign tongue, and should not be confused with bilingual classes for children from linguistic-minority groups.

"Intensive language instruction" escapes clear definition, and the label has been applied to a spectrum of courses ranging from the doubling up of classes, two semesters in one, to full terms devoted to language instruction. There are intensive summer programs, camp programs, interim programs (usually in January), even immersion or intensive weekends. Generally, the courses do provide a higher than normal number of contact hours with the language. A team of instructors is often available, the target language is used exclusively, and extracurricular activities are an important element. Often these classes are conducted outside the typical school setting, in a language house or wing of a building in which some isolation from the "English-speaking world" can be achieved.

Advantages of immersion or intensive programs rest on the fact that formal, analytical study of a foreign language is not a sufficient condition, either in terms of time or approach, to acquire fluency. The learner requires a more total exposure to the speech community, or in its absence, a simulated one, so that cultural and social interactions can be practiced along with developmental skills. The curricular design of these programs substitutes for the experience of actually living in a foreign country, and students learn the language in a more natural way. Indeed, such programs may improve upon an experience abroad for novice learners, because they bring some necessary structure and cognitive organization to the language-learning situation.

Foreign language and global education. The last few years have seen concentrated efforts by professional organizations to build connections between teachers of foreign languages and of social studies. The objective of developing global perspectives in schoolchildren must be an interdisciplinary task, and these two subject areas could assume major responsibility for this dimension of the curriculum. Strasheim (1981) pinpoints the middle school as the ideal place for cooperation by foreign language and social studies faculty in developing global education content. This is not a limiting statement, however, for culture and content units in global education touch upon many, if not most, parts of the curriculum. Strasheim calls these units "curricular complements"; an example would be a unit on food or hunger in the world. Several subject areas could be involved in simultaneous studies:

- Foreign languages: food, meals at home and in restaurants, table settings, customs and traditions in the target culture and/or language
- Home economics: the preparation of foods from the cultures represented in the foreign language program
- Social studies: the food chain, calorie consumption around the world, global food quality, and related matters

Under this model, middle school language classes would devote from 20 to 25 percent of instructional time to language skills with a cultural dimension.

At the university level, foreign languages need to be tied more closely to international or area studies programs. Rivers (1979) encourages language teachers to assign collateral readings in other disciplinary areas so that students can see the usefulness of bringing their knowledge of the original language to that content. Similarly, students should be stimulated to apply knowledge from other areas to the foreign language classroom, particularly as it relates to international events and their implications. Rivers also recommends double majors in foreign language and international studies; indeed, no specialist in either field should be able to avoid competency in the other. It might be noted that testimony before the President's Commission revealed the existence of area studies programs in which proficiency in the language of the region was not a requirement.

The international high school. The ultimate merger of foreign language proficiency and an international perspective can be found in the international high school. There are presently some twenty public schools and eight private or parochial ones that offer the International Baccalaureate (IB). These schools all follow the same set of syllabi, and their students submit to examinations sanctioned by the International Baccalaureate Office in Geneva, Switzerland. Recipients of this degree in the United States join a worldwide group of young people fluent in several languages and well-schooled in a rigorous academic program. For a description of one such program, that of the Washington International School in the nation's capital, see Goodman and Scott (1981).

In addition to those offering the IB, other public school systems are experimenting with a school-within-school concept. An international high school is housed in a wing, or on a floor, of the regular building, and its students follow a special program of studies with concentration on foreign languages and subjects that have an international focus. This model is particularly useful when late entry—beyond elementary or middle school—into the program is desired.

Experimental methodologies. Whereas the general trend is toward communicative courses and a cultural emphasis in language study, this direction alone does not mandate a method. The concepts are integrated into various courses and are accommodated by many approaches to teaching. There do exist, however, a number of more narrowly defined methods that claim success in teaching foreign languages. It must be noted that the majority of these methods have been developed and implemented by individuals or teams of researchers and may have an idiosyncratic component that underlies their effectiveness. For the most part, the techniques that define the successful approach are detailed and prescriptive; the method works only as described; and the student population tends to be rather specialized in goals, attitudes, or abilities. Most of these methods have not yet undergone rigorous examination or evaluation by outsiders; this is not to say that an approach may not be effective, only that it may not have the same results when generalized to a more varied and typical school population.

The Total Physical Response method is based upon a series of classroom experiments by Asher (1969, 1977) and Asher, Kusudo, and de la Toore (1974). They developed a method of teaching that utilized commands as the core of instruction. Students demonstrated listening comprehension by carrying out the instructions as they heard and understood them. Basic tenets of this approach include (1) understanding precedes speaking; (2) understanding is developed by use of the imperative in order to manipulate student behavior; (3) speaking is never forced, and a readiness to express oneself in the foreign language comes when the student has cognitively internalized the language code. This system has been gaining ad-

herents in many college classes; it has yet to be extrapolated to reading-writing or reading as the primary mode. It is based on the cognitive principle of receptive learning serving as a prerequisite for productive skill development. Introducing psychomotor-level involvement might provide another important learning ingredient. In any case, this method is a topic for further research, particularly as pertaining to adult learners who seem especially insecure with speaking at early stages of instruction.

Community Language-Learning; sometimes called "a Counseling-Learning Model" appeals strongly to the affective dimension in its attempt to develop cognitive skills. The innovator of this approach, Curran (1976), was a priest with a background in psychology, and many counseling techniques are incorporated into his method. Students sit in a circle; the teacher remains outside and acts as a resource by providing language translations for ideas, thoughts, and feelings that individuals wish to express. Students pass through stages as they gain independence from the teacher-counselor as the source of language samples and correction. The only specimens of language learned are those initiated by members of the group. The method has been particularly effective with adults, and it certainly focuses on communication objectives and a functional-notional, yet personalized, syllabus.

Gattegno, a British psychologist, uses a set of colored wooden rods, called "Cuisenaire rods," of varying lengths to represent sounds, words, and structures of the language. The combinations of sizes and colors demonstrate patterns in the language and trigger responses from students. Only the foreign language is used in the classroom, and the teacher strives to become less and less dominant in directing the lesson. To be successful with this method, students must be able and willing to reason inductively and to take responsibility for correcting their own errors; that is, they must monitor their speech carefully. Proponents of "The Silent Way" tend to support it wholeheartedly. (See Karambelas, 1971, for further description of the method.)

The Lozanov method, or "Suggestopedia," has received attention in the popular press, perhaps because of the exotic nature of some of its procedures. Its basic approach is an appeal to the subconscious by means of a suggestive, positive environment. Techniques common to yoga, use of baroque music, breathing exercises, soft lighting, and voice modulation by the teacher serve to relax learners and take them through a cycle of (1) review by means of games, role play, and conversation; (2) new material presented in creative, interesting dialogues; and (3) the "séance," the original feature in which the language units are "absorbed." (See Bancroft, 1978, for a description of the method.)

Future Research. Having learned some lessons from the past, researchers in second language learning have been revising their methods and focus in an effort to improve their contributions to new knowledge and thereby to better teaching. Whereas theoretical research had once supplied the basis of language teaching methods (audiolingualism, transformational grammar), neither theory nor methods held up to the rigors of time and evaluation. Teachers began to mistrust research findings and concentrated on doing what worked, regardless of theoretical or applied research confirmation. Generally, what was becoming successful in the classroom was an increased emphasis on communication as objective and activity. In the research field, investigators were also considering the communicative aspect of language use and the means of achieving proficiency. Instead of comparing method A to method B, topics such as error analysis, tolerance for error (as evidenced by native speakers in regard to second language users), interlanguage, and all the components of the communicative process dominate the newer studies. It seems as if, at this point, researchers and teachers are sharing the same interests; it is time that a dialogue take place and that once again they also communicate with one another.

Only a dent has been made in understanding the second language learning process. Continued work will deal with the "acquisition versus learning" dichotomy. Even if it is ascertained that acquisition—language learning in a natural state—is superior, it does not negate the need to study the most effective means of conducting classroom instruction. Since learning a language will always remain for most a formal mode, knowledge about learner characteristics and behaviors in the classroom will continue to be important. Questions still exist regarding optimal age for language learning, differences the age factor brings to the task, and cognitive factors such as risk taking and motivation. Research into linguistic factors crucial to the development of foreign language proficiency must be pursued, and this includes developing instruments to evaluate proficiency in reading, writing, speaking, and listening; identifying elements that affect comprehensibility of an imperfect message; and defining functional-notional categories. Most crucial perhaps is the replacement of achievement and discrete-point tests with measures of proficiency, such as scales and ratings, that adequately describe the learner's communicative ability and development. The theoretical task will require more studies about the sequence of language learning—particularly whether the natural order that seems to exist in the learner's first language or the natural order of the second language predominates in the second language situation. It is also possible that the L1–L2 connection produces its own best sequence, which differs from that in either language. More investigative efforts will continue with the Monitor Model and other variations of input-output models. Certainly, the evidence for maximum exposure to receptive language samples is compelling. If further experimentation confirms this, major changes in materials and teaching practices should result. Extensive listening and reading practice will replace the current emphasis on productive skills. Language laboratories will take on new functions as listening centers and reading rooms, with collections of tapes and magazines for "input" practice instead of the tedious drills and repetitions that are the essence of current materials. Finally, the entire field of modern technology has yet to be breached by foreign language educators in any significant way. As new information is gained on how learners apply rules and how they communicate more freely, researchers can utilize computers and technology for maximum achievement. Many aspects of the rule-governed, formal language syllabus could be programmed, freeing the teacher to fulfill the role of counselor, or facilitator of communication.

Stern and Cummins (1981) have outlined several approaches that foreign language researchers might pursue in place of the broad methodological comparisons prevalent in the last two decades. Jarvis (1981) concurs, cautioning particularly against the action research that proliferates in the literature. His concern is that untrained people with inadequate research expertise and misdirected purposes are thwarting the generation of new knowledge about the teaching-learning process that is the only legitimate goal. Research that inquires into a theory of second language learning and its implications for pedagogy is a desirable area of investigation. Because theory failed the practitioner in former times is no reason to belittle the importance of having a theoretical basis for language learning. Also, Jarvis, Stern, and Cummins support strongly descriptive studies focusing on the many aspects of student and teacher behaviors and interactions, including interview data gathered by probing mental processes and otherwise unobservable student strategies. A third approach would utilize small-scale studies and comparisons of single variables to assess their impact on learning. Ideally, these would evolve from the theoretical or descriptive studies. Finally, results of small-scale investigations would lead to large-scale attempts to discover what happens when different conditions, different circumstances, and different learners are brought together.

The President's Commission on Foreign Language and International Studies launched the foreign language profession into the 1980s with renewed hope for recognition of its contribution to American education. Some fundamental changes have already occurred at a professional level. A consensus on the major goal for foreign language instruction, communicative proficiency, has been reached. Government and business seem to now realize that the United States can no longer bear the burden of monolingualism. A public opinion survey (Eddy, 1979) has revealed that positive attitudes toward foreign language instruction are a reality. It remains to be seen how this translates into the acts—the acquisition of skills and cross-cultural awareness—that can transform this country from linguistic dependence on others' knowledge of English to multilingual global interdependence.

June K. Phillips

See also Bilingual Education; Language Development; Second Language Acquisition.

REFERENCES

Asher, J. J. The total physical response approach to language learning. *Modern Language Journal*, 1969, *53*, 334–341.

Asher, J. J. *Learning Another Language through Actions: The Complete Teacher's Guidebook.* Los Gatos, Calif.: Sky Oaks Productions, 1977.

Asher, J. J., Kusudo, J.; & de la Torre, R. Learning a second language through commands: The second field tests. *Modern Language Journal*, 1974, *58*, 24–32.

Association of Departments of Foreign Languages. Personal communication, 1978.

Ausubel, D. P. *Educational Psychology: A Cognitive View.* New York: Holt, Rinehart & Winston, 1968.

Bancroft, W. J. The Lozanov method and its American adaptations. *Modern Language Journal*, 1978, *62*, 167–175.

Birckbichler, D. W., & Omaggio, A. C. Diagnosing and responding to individual learner needs. *Modern Language Journal*, 1978, *62*, 336–345. (ERIC Document Reproduction Service No. ED 146 806)

Carroll, J. B. A model of school learning. *Teacher's College Record*, 1963, *64*, 723–733.

Carroll, J. B. Learning theory for the classroom teacher. In G. A. Jarvis (Ed.), *The Challenge of Communication* (American Council of Teachers of Foreign Languages Foreign Language Education Series, Vol. 6). Skokie, Ill.: National Textbook Company, 1974.

Corder, S. P. Language-learner language. In J. C. Richards (Ed.), *Understanding Second and Foreign Language Learning: Issues and Approaches.* Rowley, Mass.: Newbury House, 1978.

Curran, C. A. *Counseling-Learning in Second Languages.* Apple River, Ill.: Apple River Press, 1976.

Eddy, P. A. Foreign languages in the U.S.A.: A national survey of American attitudes and experiences. In *President's Commission on Foreign Language and International Studies: Background Papers and Studies* (Stock No. 017-080-02070-0). Washington, D.C.: U.S. Government Printing Office, 1979. (ERIC Document Reproduction Service No. ED 179 117)

Geno, T. H. A chronicle: Political, professional, and public activities surrounding the President's Commission on Foreign Language and International Studies. In T. H. Geno (Ed.), *Foreign Language and International Studies: Toward Cooperation and Integration.* Middlebury, Vt.: Northeast Conference, 1981.

Goodman, D. B., & Scott, G. The international high school: A challenge for scholars. In J. K. Phillips (Ed.), *Action for the Eighties: A Political, Professional, and Public Program for Foreign Language Education* (American Council of Teachers of Foreign Languages Foreign Language Education Series). Skokie, Ill.: National Textbook Company, 1981. (ERIC Document Reproduction Service Nos. ED 197 604 and ED 197 596)

Guntermann, G. Purposeful communication practice: Developing functional proficiency in a foreign language. *Foreign Language Annals*, 1979, *12*, 219–225.

Guntermann, G., & Phillips, J. K. Communicative course design: Developing functional ability in all four skills. *Canadian Modern Language Review/Revue canadienne des langues vivantes*, 1981, *37*, 329–343.

Hammond, S. B., & Scebold, C. E. *Survey of Foreign Language Enrollments in Public Secondary Schools* (Final Report, Grant No. Goo7901693). Washington, D.C.: U.S. Department of Education, Office of International Education, 1980.

Helsinki Agreement, Conference on Security and Cooperation in Europe, Final Act, 1975. (Department of State Publication 8826, General Foreign Policy Series 298).

Hosenfeld, C. The new student role: Individual differences and implications for instruction. In G. A. Jarvis (Ed.), *Perspective: A New Freedom* (American Council of Teachers of Foreign Languages Foreign Language Education Series, Vol. 7). Skokie, Ill.: National Textbook Company, 1975.

Jarvis, G. A. Action research versus needed research. In D. L. Lange Ed.), *Proceedings of the National Conference on Professional Priorities.* In preparation, 1981.

Karambelas, J. Teaching foreign languages "The Silent Way". *Association of Departments of Foreign Languages Bulletin*, 1971, *3*(1), 41.

Krashen, S. D. The Monitor Model for second language acquisition. In R. Gingras (Ed.), *Second Language Acquisition and Foreign Language Teaching.* Arlington, Va.: Center for Applied Linguistics, 1978.

Lambert, W. E., & Tucker, G. R. *Bilingual Education of Children: The St. Lambert Experiment.* Rowley, Mass.; Newbury House, 1972. (ERIC Document Reproduction Service No. ED 082 573)

Lange, D. L. (Ed.). *The Proceedings of the National Conference on Professional Priorities.* New York: American Council of Teachers of Foreign Languages Materials Center, 1981.

Phillips, J. K. Individualization and personalization. In G. A. Jarvis (Ed.), *Responding to New Realities*, Foreign Language Education Series, Vol. 5). Skokie, Ill.: National Textbook Company, 1974.

Phillips, J. K. Imperatives for the eighties. In J. K. Phillips (Ed.), *The New Imperative: Expanding the Horizons of Foreign Language Education* (American Council of Teachers of Foreign Languages Foreign Language Education Series). Skokie, Ill.: National Textbook Company, 1980.

Phillips, J. K. (Ed.). *Action for the Eighties: A Political, Professional, and Public Program for Foreign Language Education* (American Council of Teachers of Foreign Languages Foreign Language Education Series). Skokie, Ill.: National Textbook Company, 1981. (ERIC Document Reproduction Service No. ED 197 596)

Postovsky, V. Effects of Delay in Oral Practice at the Beginning of Second Language Learning. *Modern Language Journal*, 1974, 229–239.

Rivers, W. M. Educational goals: The foreign language teacher's response. In W. C. Born (Ed.), *The Foreign Language Learner in Today's Classroom Environment.* Middlebury, Vt.: Northeast Conference, 1979. (ERIC Document Reproduction Service Nos. ED 185 836 and ED 185 834)

Rubin, J. What the "good language learner" can teach us. *Teachers of English to Speakers of Other Languages Quarterly*, 1975, *9*, 41–51.

Scherer, A. C., & Wertheimer, M. *A Psycholinguistic Experiment in Foreign Language Teaching.* New York: McGraw-Hill, 1964.

Smith, P. D., Jr. *A Comparison of the Cognitive and Audiolingual Approaches to Foreign Language Instruction.* Philadelphia: Center for Curriculum Development, 1970.

Sperry, L. (Ed.). *Learning Performance and Individual Differences.* Glenview, Ill.: Scott, Foresman, 1972.

Stern, H. H., & Cummins, J. Language teaching/learning research: A Canadian perspective on status and directions. In J. K. Phillips (Ed.), *Action for the Eighties: A Political, Professional, and Public Program for Foreign Language Education*

(American Council of Teachers of Foreign Languages Foreign Language Education Series). Skokie, Ill.: National Textbook Company, 1981. (ERIC Document Reproduction Service No. ED 197 596)

Strasheim, L. Broadening the middle school curriculum through content: Globalizing foreign languages. In J. K. Phillips (Ed.), *Action for the Eighties: A Political, Professional, and Public Program for Foreign Language Education* (American Council of Teachers of Foreign Languages Foreign Language Education Series). Skokie, Ill.: National Textbook Company, 1981. (ERIC Document Reproduction Service No. ED 176 599)

Strength through Wisdom: A Critique of U.S. Capability (Report to the President from the President's Commission on Foreign Language and International Studies, Stock No. 017-080-02065-3). Washington, D.C.: U.S. Government Printing Office, 1979. (ERIC Document Reproduction Service No. ED 176 599)

Valdman, A. Communicative use of language and syllabus design. *Foreign Language Annals*, 1978, *11*, 567–578.

Van Ek, J. A. *The Threshold Level for Modern Language Learning in Schools*. London: Longman, 1977.

Wilkins, D. A. *Notional Syllabuses*. London: Oxford University Press, 1976.

G

GAMES AND SIMULATIONS

The simulation of technological systems became relatively familiar to many Americans in the late 1960s when television broadcasts presented simulations of spacecraft maneuvers simultaneously taking place millions of miles away. The reading public became informed, too, at about that time, of the extensive use of war games made by the military and diplomatic corps during and after World War II. The utilization of simulation and games, however, has not been limited to demonstration of the operation of technological systems or to exercises in international relations. Since the early 1960s, the technique has spread to schools of business, to college and adult education classes, and to elementary and secondary school classes. In these contexts games and simulations are employed in teaching about such diverse topics as addiction, gender roles, health-care problems, environmental protection, and city politics. Horn and Cleaves (1980), Belch (1973), and Stadsklev (1979) provide documentation of several thousand published games and simulations on a wide range of topics (Becker, 1980).

Newcomers to the field will encounter not simply an extensive array of materials but also considerable terminological confusion, for the terms "game," "simulation," and some variant of "gaming simulation" are frequently used interchangeably, depending upon the predilections of the author. Let us begin, therefore, with some definitions.

A "simulation" is a form of model, but one that differs from the more traditional models used in education—verbal, graphic, mathematical, and physical—in that it is dynamic rather than static (Greenblat, 1975; Raser, 1969); that is, a simulation illustrates not simply the state of the system at any given moment but also the way it changes. For example, a diagram of the solar system (a graphic model) is static, whereas the operating model of the system one sees in a planetarium (a simulation) is dynamic. A "simulation," then, displays functions and dynamic processes, as well as elements and their relationships.

Simulation entails abstraction and representation from the referent system. Central features must be identified and simplified, and less important ones are omitted. Once the components have been put together, the simulation can be operated by a computer; it may operate through a combination of computer and human players (Greenblat & Uretsky, 1977; Anderson, 1980), or all operations may be generated by and calculated by human players. The first of these (those operated by computer) is a "computer simulation"—a form that will not be considered here. The second and third are properly referred to as "gaming simulations," "game simulations," or "simulation games," but sometimes are abbreviated as "games" or "simulations."

The term "gaming simulation" takes into account two central dimensions. "Game" is used because the environment and activities of participants have the characteristics of games: players have goals, sets of activities to perform, constraints on what can and cannot be done, and payoffs (good and bad) as consequences of their actions. The term "simulation" is also employed, since the elements are patterned from real life; that is, the roles, goals, activities, constraints, and consequences—and the linkages among them—simulate or model those elements of reality. A gaming simulation, then, is a hybrid form, entailing the performance of gamelike activities in a simulated environment.

As was suggested earlier, several terms are often used interchangeably. One can, however, distinguish between related examples of interest here by considering the possible intersections of teaching-training techniques, simulations, and games.

As Figure 1 suggests, in addition to the "pure" forms (A, B, and C), there are gaming simulations *not* used for teaching (D)—for example, some realistic commercial games played primarily for recreational purposes. There are also nonsimulation games used for teaching (E); samples from this category include mathematics games such

713

FIGURE 1. *Simulations, games, and teaching techniques*

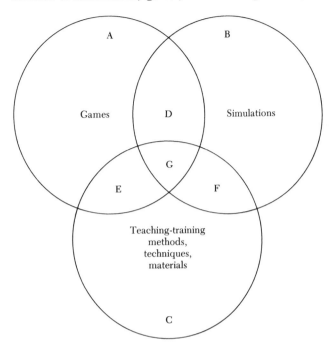

as "Equations" and some word games. Category F includes simulations used for teaching that do not have the game characteristics; examples include flight simulators for training pilots, simulation exercises in which disasters are simulated to teach medical and paramedical personnel to deal with real-world disaster conditions when they arise, and a laboratory for architects to learn design through simulation (Lawrence, 1980). Finally, there is category G: gaming simulations for teaching and training. In this category, one currently finds the largest number of examples in a wide variety of subject fields. The remarks that follow deal primarily with categories E, F, and G.

Games, Simulations, and Role Playing. Despite some obvious similarities, gaming simulations differ from role-playing exercises and from such endeavors as mock congresses. Although role playing is an element of gaming simulations, in the latter, roles are defined in interacting systems; that is, emphasis is on the role as it interacts with other roles. The model creates the dynamic interaction, the constraints, the rewards, and the punishments. Gaming simulations differ from role-playing exercises in the degree of structure or formalization they entail and in their emphasis on interaction processes rather than on the playing of individual roles. Further, in many instances of classroom role playing, several students participate while the remainder of the class watches. In a gaming simulation, all participate; none are passive outsiders.

Even limiting our attention to those materials that fall in categories E, F, and G, we encounter considerable variety in such characteristics as form and complexity of materials; time, money, and personnel needed for game opera-

tion; and types of learning for which the materials are appropriate. Games and simulations also differ considerably in the degree of specificity versus abstraction of components, and in the extent to which parameters are determined by the designer versus the participants (Ruben, 1973; Heap, 1971; Degnan & Harr, 1971).

The movement of games into the schools in the early 1960s was primarily in the fields of business (Cohen & Rhenmann, 1961; Graham & Gray, 1969) and social science. Within a short time the technique spread to other subject areas, and it enjoyed a meteoric rise for several years (Boocock & Schild, 1968). As educators pointed out that games and play have long served as models of socialization (Anderson & Moore, 1968) and urged that teachers recognize the value of play as an aid to learning (Bruner, 1966), the potential of gaming was recognized.

Furthermore, as Coleman et al. (1961), Coleman (1966), and Sarason (1971) pointed out, an effective argument could be made that in most schools too little attention was paid to the ways that students can learn from one another. Gaming-simulation advocates noted that gaming takes advantage of the important contributions of group dynamics, peer learning, and peer pressure in the learning process. Yet others (Anderson & Moore, 1968) stressed the importance of each student having an *active* role in his or her learning process; those experimenting with the technique pointed out that games provided for this, allowing the learner to be both recipient and agent at various times.

The initial and somewhat uncritical enthusiasm of the early 1960s was tempered as increasing demands were made for evidence of the power, rather than statements of the potential, of gaming simulations. To use these new materials required not only money, but time to locate, obtain, and learn to administer them. Effective use demanded their thoughtful integration into the curriculum; administrators often had to be convinced to permit the innovation. Such costs, it was recognized, had to be weighed against the benefits that could be expected, not theoretically but in terms of empirical data derived from serious analysis of prior usage.

Given the wide range of materials and the vast differences between them, it is scarcely suprising that evaluation has proved a tricky problem. Owing to the diversity, results from studies with a particular game or games cannot be generalized to learning from games in general. The quality of evaluative research is still limited by severe methodological problems (Greenblat, 1973; Inbar & Stoll, 1972; Orbach, 1977; Pierfy, 1977), including the fact that most teachers who employ gaming simulations are those who believe in the efficacy of the technique, thereby creating a contamination effect (Remus, 1981).

There are numerous claims about the results of teaching with games and simulations (Greenblat, 1973), but the central hypotheses concern increases in motivation and interest, affective learning (about oneself and about others, i.e., empathy), and cognitive learning. In recent years there has been a substantial growth in hard data to supplement the voluminous anecdotal material attesting to the power of games to increase motivation, interest, and affective learning (Dukes & Seidner, 1978; Williams, 1980; Rosen, 1981).

Although there is evidence that cognitive learning takes place, most studies have revealed little difference in the amount of cognitive learning with games as compared to more traditional techniques (Szafran & Mandolini, 1980). It should be noted, however, that students do not appear to learn significantly *less* cognitive material while showing the other gains already mentioned. Findings of nonsignificant differences in cognitive learning have often been accompanied by caveats that gaming teaches systemic understanding, which is difficult or impossible to measure with traditional pen-and-pencil short-answer tests of the sort that have often been used to measure comparative learning with different techniques, and that it provides referents for concepts already known (Bredemeier, 1978).

Finally, limited evidence is available to substantiate the claims that gaming helps to develop general skills, problem-solving abilities, and interpersonal-relations skills, although these appear to be frequent outcomes (Duke, 1977).

Although the state of evaluation has improved, a number of unanswered questions must be addressed in the years to come. Some preliminary research exists, as has been indicated, but much more must be learned to answer such questions as the following.

1. What harm is done by materials that contain poor simulation components? If gaming simulations are as compelling as some argue, then we must ask about the effects of utilizing models that *distort* reality (Shirts, 1970).

2. What are the effects of teaching with materials that contain bad gaming components—for example, those that foster excessive competition?

3. What are the effects of being on a losing team or in losing roles? How are self-esteem and attitudes toward the winners affected (Greenblat, 1980)?

4. How do variations in teacher behavior and attitude affect game operation and learning from the experience?

5. What kind of game is useful for what kind of learning? This, too, has not been adequately addressed, despite the fact that games vary in their complexity, length, degree of abstraction, and type of model.

6. How do we understand the asymmetrical learning experiences of students who participate in the same game? Some roles are more complex or more challenging; thus the problem of differential learning is to some degree structured into the experience. Furthermore, players are not only in simulated roles, but are players in a game and students in a class. They are simultaneously playing not only the simulated role but real ones as well, and it is often difficult to disentangle these influences.

7. Who doesn't like games and who doesn't learn from them? The little that is known about this limits our capability in terms of knowing the conditions under which games

should and should not be employed, or under what circumstances they are appropriate (Pratt, Uhl, & Little, 1980; Remus, 1977).

8. How *many* games can effectively be utilized with a given group?

It appears that we have now entered a more stable period. Games and simulations have proven to be valuable pedagogical tools. In the future, in addition to new games and simulations being produced and marketed, we can expect improvements in our understanding of their impacts.

Cathy S. Greenblat

See also Affective Education; Computer-Based Education; Experiential Education; Individualized Systems of Instruction; Laboratory Experiences in Teacher Education; Nontraditional Higher Education Programs.

REFERENCES

Anderson, A. R., & Moore, O. K. Some principles for the design of clarifying educational environments. In D. A. Goslin, *Handbook of Socialization Theory and Research.* Chicago: Rand McNally, 1968.

Anderson, R. E. Computer simulation games. In R. E. Horn & A. Cleaves, *The Guide to Simulation/Games for Education and Training.* Beverly Hills, Calif.: Sage, 1980.

Becker, H. A. The emergence of simulation and gaming. *Simulation and Games,* June 1980, *11.*

Belch, J. *Contemporary Games* (Vol. 1). Detroit: Gale, 1973.

Boocock, S. A., & Schild, E. O. *Simulation Games in Learning.* Beverly Hills: Sage, 1968.

Bredemeier, M. Providing referents for sociological concepts: Simulation gaming. *Teaching Sociology,* July 1978, *5,* 409–421.

Bruner, J. *Toward a Theory of Instruction.* Cambridge, Mass.: Harvard University Press, 1966.

Cohen, K., & Rhenmann, E. The role of management games in education and research. *Management Science,* January 1961, *11,* 131–166.

Coleman, J. *Equality of Educational Opportunity.* Washington, D.C.: U.S. Department of Health, Education, and Welfare, Office of Education, 1966. (ERIC Document Reproduction Service No. ED 012 275)

Coleman, J., et al. *The Adolescent Society.* New York: Free Press, 1961.

Degnan, D. A., & Harr, C. M. Computer-assisted simulation in urban legal studies. *Journal of Legal Education,* 1971, *23,* 353–365.

Duke, R. D. *Gaming: The Future's Language.* Beverly Hills, Calif.: Sage, 1977.

Dukes, R., & Seidner, C. *Learning with Simulations and Games.* Beverly Hills, Calif.: Sage, 1978.

Graham, R. G., & Gray, C. F. *Decision Games Handbook.* New York: American Management Association, 1969.

Greenblat, C. S. Teaching with simulation games: A review of claims and evidence. *Teaching Sociology,* October 1973, *1.*

Greenblat, C. S. Seeing forests and trees: Gaming-simulation and contemporary problems of learning and communication. In C. S. Greenblat & R. D. Duke, *Gaming-Simulation:*

Rationale, Design, and Applications. Beverly Hills, Calif.: Sage, 1975.

Greenblat, C. S. Group dynamics and game design: Some reflections. *Simulation and Games,* March 1980, *11.*

Greenblat, C. S., & Uretsky, M. Simulation in social science. *American Behavioral Scientist,* 1977, *20,* 411–426.

Heap, R. The student as resource: Uses of minimum-structure simulation games in teaching. *Simulation and Games,* 1971, *3.*

Horn, R., & Cleaves, A. *The Guide to Simulations/Games for Education and Training* (4th ed.). Beverly Hills, Calif.: Sage, 1980.

Inbar, M., & Stoll, C. *Simulation and Gaming in Social Science.* New York: Free Press, 1972.

Lawrence, R. The simulation of domestic space: Users and architects participating in the architectural design process. *Simulation and Games,* September 1980, *11.*

Orbach, E. Some theoretical considerations in the evaluation of instructional simulation games. *Simulation and Games,* 1977, *8,* 341–360.

Pierfy, D. A. Comparative simulation game research: Stumbling blocks and stepping stones. *Simulation and Games,* June 1977, *8,* 255–268.

Pratt, L. K.; Uhl, N. P.; & Little, E. R. Evaluation of games as a function of personality type. *Simulation and Games,* September 1980, *11,* 336–346.

Raser, J. *Simulation and Society.* Boston: Allyn & Bacon, 1969.

Remus, W. E. Who likes business games? *Simulation and Games,* March 1977, *8,* 64–68.

Remus, W. E. Experimental designs for analyzing data on games: Or even the best statistical methods do not replace good experimental control. *Simulation and Games,* June 1981, *12.*

Rosen, D. METRO-APEX as a course. *Simulation and Games,* June 1981, *12.*

Ruben, B. *The What and Why of Gaming.* Paper presented at the twelfth annual meeting of the National Gaming Council and the International Simulation and Gaming Association, 1973.

Sarason, S. *The Culture of the School and the Problem of Change.* Boston: Allyn & Bacon, 1971.

Shirts, R. G. Games students play. *Saturday Review,* May 16, 1970, *53,* 81–82.

Stadsklev, R. *Handbook of Simulation Gaming in Social Education, Part 2: Directory of Noncomputer Materials.* University: University of Alabama, Institute of Higher Education Research and Services, 1979.

Szafran, D., & Mandolini, A. Test performance and concept recognition: The effect of a simulation game on two types of cognitive knowledge. *Simulation and Games,* 1980, *11,* 326–335.

Williams, R. H. Attitude change and simulation games: The ability of a simulation game to change attitudes when structured in accordance with either the cognitive dissonance or incentive models of attitude change. *Simulation and Games,* June 1980, *11*(2), 177–196.

GENERAL EDUCATION

See Curriculum and Instruction in Higher Education; Higher Education; History and Philosophy of Higher Education; Junior and Community College Education; Undergraduate Instruction.

GENIUS

See Creativity; Gifted Persons; Intelligence.

GEOGRAPHY

Before the American Revolution, geography was excluded from the formal curriculum of most American schools; it was taught by tutors as a practical subject, largely by rote (Dunbar, 1970; Graves, 1975). After the Revolution a number of nationalistic geographies were written, and some colleges included geography in entrance examinations (Rumble, 1946; Antonelli, 1970; Vuicich & Stoltman, 1974). In about 1850, Guyote's text established physical geography as a secondary school subject (Mayo, 1964; Vuicich & Stoltman, 1974). Graves (1975) has attributed growth of geography to efforts of lobbies. By 1889, thirty-two of the thirty-eight states required instruction in geography, usually as a science. In 1894, the Committee of Ten of the National Education Association (NEA) emphasized physical geography, and it was almost universally required; but in 1916, the NEA's Commission on Social Studies directed that social aspects of geography be integrated with other social sciences. Professional geographers identified with science and refused to cooperate, with the result that geography began to decline (Vuicich & Stoltman, 1974). Educators adopted the expanding horizons sequence, integrated disciplines, and liberalized teaching methods (Kennamer, 1970; Vuicich & Stoltman, 1974). After *Sputnik,* curriculum theory emphasized concepts and process as content, and several curriculum projects were initiated (Kennamer, 1970; Vuicich & Stoltman, 1974). However, in the fourth edition of the *Encyclopedia of Educational Research* geography was represented as a neglected subject (Skretting & Sundeen, 1969), and only two of the five projects were judged to be encouraging in conception. Several area studies projects were classified as culture studies.

Social Foundations. Erasmus, Sir Thomas Elyot, and Kant regarded geography as a prerequisite to understanding history (Graves, 1975). A number of recent essays similarly place emphasis on knowledge of location as an aid to understanding current events (Schallert, 1968; Wise, 1975; Walter & Bernard, 1978; McKenzie, 1980; Owen & Manson, 1980). An early advocate of geographic education, Morse, argued that such understanding was necessary for all classes in a republic (Antonelli, 1970).

Moralistic and nationalistic geographies were written to induce patriotism and national identity (Rumble, 1976; Antonelli, 1970). This nationalistic function may help to explain the persistence of the environmental determinism noted by Jackson (1976). Studies of attractive children in other countries probably socialize, but according to a different frame of reference.

New spatial association theories are useful in understanding and solving problems of business, social, environmental, and urban planning (e.g., Krumme, 1970; Saarinen, 1976; Harrison, 1977; Broek et al., 1980; Lawton, 1980). However, geographers have generally appealed for funding on the basis of academic and achievement needs and major geography proposals have not stressed international studies or population, environmental, and energy problems.

Psychological foundations. Since the Progressive era, elementary geography has been dominated by G. S. Hall's theory of mental evolution (Hunt, 1961) as elaborated by Piaget (Hunt, 1961; Flavell, 1963) and applied by Progressives. It is widely assumed that young children learn best from concrete experience and that abstract ideas should not be emphasized until adolescence (e.g., Rousseau, 1911; Barton, 1953; Towler & Nelson, 1968; McCartin, 1970; Meyer, 1973; Houghton & Morgan, 1974; Graves, 1975; Stoltman, 1971, 1976).

A substantial body of current research describes errors in spatial reasoning of uninstructed children and generally confirms the findings of Piaget and Inhelder (1956). Primary school children rarely conceive of perspectives other than their own, whereas intermediate grade pupils can do so with concrete models but not with Euclidean concepts (Laurendau & Pinard, 1970; Towler, 1970; Massey, 1971; Hart & Moore, 1973; Pufall & Shaw, 1973; Eliot & Salkind, 1975; Rand, Towler, & Feldhusen, 1976). On the other hand, some studies that vary in methodology and task suggest that practical map understandings develop rather early (Blaut, McCreary, & Blaut, 1970; Feldman, 1971; Blaut & Stea, 1971, 1974; Cobb, 1977; Cox, 1977); generalizations are therefore difficult to make. Studies also suggest that children learn place concepts by observing a local scene and overgeneralizing features to entire countries (Stoltman, 1971; 1976; Graves, 1975; Olivera, 1976; Towler & Price, 1976).

A similar line of descriptive research reports patterns in environmental perception and cognitive maps (Lynch, 1960). In most studies, subjects describe an area from memory without instruction, and fairly predictable types of landmarks, pathways, and boundaries are mentioned by subjects of similar age, social class, and setting (Wood, 1973; Dueck, 1974, 1976; Rothwell, 1974; Downs & Meyer, 1978). Perceptions differ according to residence and social class (Mauer & Baxter, 1972; Calland, 1973; Orleans, 1974; Dueck, 1974, 1976). Dueck (1974, 1976) and Matthews (1980) found that the number of elements mentioned differs across age-groups, that the number of landmarks increases and that the type of elements mentioned develops from the egocentric to the conventional with age. In a training study, Herman (1980) demonstrated that cues directing attention and construction activity improved children's cognitive maps, Mauer and Baxter (1972) did not detect differences correlated with age but did find differences correlated with race. Others have studied attitudes toward regions and neighborhoods (e.g., Gould

& White, 1974; Ermuth & Mercer, 1975; Dueck, 1976).

Since the advent of information-processing theory (e.g., Bruner, 1960; Ausubel, 1963; Gagné, 1965), some researchers have asserted that young children can be taught geographic ideas to enhance reasoning. Rice and Cobb (1978) concluded from an excellent review that even young children can learn most kinds of geographic ideas and skills if they are instructed, and that it is not necessary to delay teaching ideas. McKenzie and Henry (1979) taught third-graders to deduce large or small amounts of rainfall from an abstract principle, contradicting the belief of Ward (1972) and Graves (1975) that children in Piaget's stage of concrete operations cannot do so. In two excellent studies, Crabtree successfully taught abstract concepts to first-graders and second-graders (1968) and later demonstrated vertical transfer of these ideas to solving problems of spatial analysis (1974). If children can be taught ideas to facilitate reasoning, information-processing theory provides a viable alternative to traditional ontogeny as a foundation for geographic education.

Projects and Studies. Three projects deserve particular mention in this period. Crabtree's U.S. Office of Education project not only produced effective instructional materials but also provided support for a basic theoretical model (Crabtree, 1968). This work has received altogether too little attention from educators, as Rice and Cobb have stated (1978). Similarly, Rice's Geography Curriculum Project has been only modestly supported by the University of Georgia and occasional U.S. Office of Education grants, but it has produced eight units with instructional materials (Bettis, 1977) and a number of studies that go beyond evaluation to test generalizable hypotheses involving elementary school subjects (Steinbrink, 1970; Imperatore, 1970, 1971; Dale, 1972; Keach & Pierfy, 1972; Pierfy, 1972; Pelletti, 1973; Jones, 1974). Again, the accomplishments of the project exceed the amount of recognition received.

Undoubtedly the High School Geography Project, sponsored by the Association of American Geographers (Association of American Geographers, 1970) and initially funded by the Ford Foundation, is the best supported and publicized of the projects of the 1960s. The intact program has not been widely adopted (Beyer & Herbert, 1968; Patton, 1970; Dumas & Guenther, 1971), but it may have had an impact on the study of geography in college (Richburg, 1970; Hill, 1970; Kinerney, 1975), as well as important effects in England (Graves, 1975). Generally, program evaluations reflect gains in achievement on concepts taught and emphasize positive attitudes of students and teachers (e.g., Womack, 1969; Carswell & Kurfman, 1971; Richburg, 1971), although fewer differences in achievement were detected from programs with complementary content (Womack, 1969; Richburg, 1971). Deemphasis of global coverage and the rationale behind it have been criticized (Beyer & Herbert, 1968; Marsh, 1973; Vuicich & Stoltman, 1974). Vuicich & Stoltman (1974) provide a fascinating account of the project's evolution.

A number of descriptive studies in this period report that knowledge of geographic concepts is limited among students (Lanegran, Snowfield, & Laruent 1970; Nisser, 1970; Hromyk, 1972; Bettis & Manson, 1975). Knowledge of map skills is mixed but more encouraging in some cases (Rushdoony, 1968; Blaut & Stea, 1974; Giannagelo & Frazee, 1977; Schneider, 1976). And knowledge of locations is generally disappointing (Wise, 1975; Bettis & Manson, 1975; National Assessment of Educational Progress, 1975). The Bettis and Manson study (1975) is a model for research of this type. Hubbard and Stoddard (1978) report vague but positive attitudes toward geography, but McTeer (1979) found that geography was the least popular of all social sciences among high school students.

Trends. There have been distinct increases in enrollment in geography courses in high school and colleges since 1965 (Cotton, 1968; Glowacki, 1970; Briavel, 1974; Snaden, 1978; Burke, 1979), with a reduction in uniformity of required courses and a tremendous increase in course titles (Briavel, 1974; Snaden, 1978; Burke, 1979). There is considerable variation in the education of cartographers (Dhalberg, 1977; Kent, 1980). Geography is not consistently required in the education of high school teachers, including social studies specialists (Groenhoff, 1970). Environmental conservation courses have greatly increased (Vining, 1980). A number of colleges have instituted community internships for undergraduates (Heiges, 1977, 1979; Corey & Stewart, 1973; Brown, 1978; Rossman, 1978).

Curriculum. In curriculum, Pattison's four traditions (1964) are mentioned often: study of physical phenomena; interactions between man and land; description of unique regions; and generalizations about spatial relationships (e.g., Robinson, 1976). The bulk of essays continue to emphasize concepts and process skills (Peters, 1969; Kennamer, 1970; Vuicich & Stoltman, 1974; Salyer, 1975; Roiley, 1978; Bacon, 1979, Steinbrink & Jones, 1979, Brock et al., 1980). On the other hand, teachers continue to stress factual information (Bloomer, 1971; Abdi, 1979; Elliott & Kennedy, 1979; Shaver, Davis, & Helbrun, 1979), which Shaver, Davis, and Helbrun suggest may be quite appropriate. Again, some essays recommend more attention to location facts. Hawkins (1977) noted omission of some map skills in texts published in the early 1970s, and Milburn (1972) noted that texts often failed to define critical concepts. Most elementary texts compare cultures (Kennamer, 1970), to show different ways of satisfying similar needs.

Teaching methods. In methodology, there has been a dramatic increase in suggestions for simulation games, but relatively little research on their effects in geography. Croft (1971) and Stubbles (1974) showed gains in achievement after simulations; and Pierfy (1972) also found that a simulation group reported positive attitudes and outscored a control group on retention and recognition of analogies. Ellinger and Frankland (1976) found no significant differences between several simulations and a lecture

control, however. More controlled research is needed to discover when simulations are effective and what aspects of the simulations produce effects, before the method becomes reliably generalizable.

Little new support was detected in this period for superiority of inductive-discovery teaching strategies. Ellis (1974) found no difference in achievement when experiences were sequenced from enactive to symbolic or vice versa. Dale (1972) found no difference between a questioning mode of instruction and an expository text. And Lahnston (1972) found no difference in retention between an expository and a discovery method. On the other hand, a number of studies suggested effects of variables associated with expository teaching, and are mentioned in the following paragraphs.

Glowatski (1973) reported favorable effects of behavioral objectives on student attitudes, and Khoynejad (1980) found facilitative effects on intentional and incidental learning. These studies seem consistent with studies outside the field of geography (Duchastel & Merrill, 1976; Melton, 1978). Allen (1969), Steinbrink (1970), Oppong (1978), and Morganett (1980) all found positive effects of advance organizers. Khoynejad (1980) also found effects of prequestions on intentional learning. Again, findings are consistent with other research (Hartley & Davies, 1976).

Three studies (Rosenshine, 1968; Hadman, 1972; Simpson, 1975) suggest more care in providing clear definitions, rule-example discourse, and frequent repetition. The findings are consistent with general trends (Markle, 1975; Tennyson & Park, 1980). There is some indication that reading may facilitate learning of map skills (Stoltman & Goolsby, 1973), but it is not clear that maps or illustrations necessarily facilitate learning of information from text (Davis & Hunkins, 1968; Davis, 1971; King, 1972).

Two studies point out that college students do not necessarily participate in small-group tutorials, and that a few students do most of the talking (Hollis & Terry, 1977; Webb, 1980). Four studies suggest positive effects on achievement when students are required to make overt responses to testlike commands or questions at frequent intervals during instruction (Savage, 1972; Collins & Adams, 1978; McKenzie & Henry, 1979; McKenzie & Schadler, 1980). Again, these findings are consistent with other research (Faw & Waller, 1976).

Bass (1980) evaluated an in-service program that trained experienced teachers to use a preinstructional strategy, to provide information directly, and to require frequent responses of pupils to testlike questions. Teachers changed methods of planning, student achievement increased, and level of achievement correlated with the number of elements of direct instruction used by the teacher. Research on teacher behaviors and pupil achievement outside geography suggests similar findings (e.g., Brophy, 1979).

Methodological Problems. The typical problems of sampling systematically from some larger population to enhance generalizability, of variations in testing procedure, and of the absence of appropriate control groups plague research in geography education. A peculiar type of problem also occurs when different researchers study native ability of students, or ability after some but poorly defined instruction, as in the case of developmentalist studies; if performance is lower than mastery, some researchers assert that pupils did learn or displayed potential, whereas others assert that the findings imply lack of readiness. Another serious problem is that many studies evaluate effects of a complex treatment, and it is impossible to determine what specific variables accounted for or produced effects. Ideally, studies of instruction using several comparable treatment groups should be designed to measure effects of discrete variables as well as interactions between combinations of variables.

Too much important information (facts about locations and regions; concepts of types of features, areas, or distributions; and generalizations about relationships), and the need to teach map and analytic skills burden the curriculum and the time allotted to teaching geography. The problem is exacerbated by the inefficiency of typical instructional methods and by competition among specialists to advance particular branches of work. Tough decisions about what knowledge is of most worth to citizens will help, but not solve, the problem.

Clearly, many environmental, population, energy, and urban problems have implications for geography curricula, but research on spatial and environmental perception also has implications for social policy. As Gould and White (1974), Graves (1975), and Saarinen (1970, 1976) suggest, what people perceive in their environment varies according to education and cultural emphasis. Before crowding and resource problems become impossibly acute, society must inform its members of the concepts that enable citizens to perceive and understand the importance of subtle features affecting the quality of life.

Gary R. McKenzie

See also Social Studies Education.

REFERENCES

Abdi, E. G. *The Teaching of Selected International Relations Concepts in Georgia Public High Schools.* Unpublished doctoral dissertation, Georgia State University, 1979.
Allen, D. I. *Effects on Learning and Retention of Written Social Studies Material of the Use of Advance Organizers with Memory Level or Higher Order Questions.* Unpublished doctoral dissertation, University of California at Berkeley, 1969.
Antonelli, M. Nationalism in early American geographies: 1784–1845. *Journal of Geography*, 1970, *69*, 301–305.
Association of American Geographers. *Geography in an Urban Age.* New York: Macmillan, 1970.
Ausubel, D. P. *The Psychology of Meaningful Verbal Learning.* New York: Grune & Stratton, 1963.
Bacon, R. S. Building a curriculum in introductory geography through core concepts. *Journal of Geography*, 1979, *78*, 152–156.
Barton, T. F. Geography for children six to eight. *Journal of Geography*, 1953, *52*, 281–291.
Bass, J. S. *Effects of an Inservice Program on Teacher Planning and Pupil Achievement with Middle School Social Studies Teachers.* Unpublished doctoral dissertation, University of Texas at Austin, 1980.
Bettis, N. C. The Geography Curriculum Project. *Journal of Geography*, 1977, *76*, 69–70.
Bettis, N. C., & Manson, G. An assessment of the geographic learning of fifth-grade students in Michigan. *Journal of Geography*, 1975, *74*, 16–24.
Beyer, B. K., & Herbert, F. D. Implementing curriculum change in geography: An approach and an appraisal. *Journal of Geography*, 1968, *67*, 423–428.
Blaut, J. M.; McCreary, G. F.; & Blaut, A. S. Environmental mapping in young children. *Environment and Behavior*, 1970, *2*, 335–349.
Blaut, J. M., & Stea, D. Studies in geographic learning. *Annals of the Association of American Geographers*, 1971, *61*, 387–393.
Blaut, J. M., & Stea, D. Mapping at the age of three. *Journal of Geography*, 1974, *73*, 5–9.
Bloomer, F. E. *Social Studies Teachers' Perception of Topics in Geography.* Unpublished doctoral dissertation, Ohio State University, 1971.
Briavel, H. Geography in the competitive academic marketplace. *Journal of Geography*, 1974, *73*, 40–43.
Broek, J.; Hunker, H.; Mussig, R.; & Cirrincione, J. *The Study and Teaching of Geography.* Colombus, Ohio: Merrill, 1980.
Brophy, J. E. Teacher behavior and its effects. *Journal of Educational Psychology*, 1979, *71*, 733–750.
Brown, E. L. *Internships for the Undergraduate Major in the Liberal Arts College.* Paper presented at the meeting of the National Council for Geographic Education, Milwaukee, Wis., October 1978. (ERIC Document Reproduction Service No. ED 161 818)
Bruner, J. *The Process of Education.* Cambridge, Mass.: Harvard University Press, 1960.
Burke, J. D. Undergraduate geography programs: Contemporary characteristics and changes. *Journal of Geography*, 1979, *78*, 172–177.
Calland, A. R. *An Investigation of the Images Held by a Small Sample of Primary School Children in Their Local Environment.* Unpublished master's thesis, University of London, 1973.
Carswell, R. V., & Kurfman, D. G. *Differential Effects of Self-contained Teacher Education Kits on Pre- and Inservice Social Studies Teachers.* Paper presented at the annual meeting of the American Educational Research Association, New York; February 1971. (ERIC Document Reproduction Service No. ED 049 957)
Cobb, R. L. *The Effects of Varying Verbal Instructions on the Ability to Coordinate Viewpoints and on Map Conceptualization.* Unpublished doctoral dissertation, University of Georgia, 1976.
Cobb, R. L. Perspective ability and map conceptualization in elementary-school children. *Journal of Social Studies Research*, 1977, *1*, 9–19.
Collins, A., & Adams, M. J. Effectiveness of an interactive map display in tutoring geography. *Journal of Educational Psychology*, 1978, *70*, 1–7.
Corey, K. E., & Stewart, A. W. *Community Internships for Undergraduate Geography Students.* Washington, D.C.: Association of American Geographers, 1973.

Cotton, J. V. *The Status of Public Senior High School Geography in Maryland, 1964–1965.* Unpublished doctoral dissertation, Pennsylvania State University, 1968.

Cox, C. W. *Children's Map-reading Abilities with Large-scale Urban Maps.* Doctoral dissertation, University of Wisconsin at Madison, 1977. (Publication No. 78-4, University of Georgia, Geography Curriculum Project, 1978)

Crabtree, C. *Teaching Geography in Grades One through Three: Effects of Instruction on the Core Concept of Geographic Theory* (Final Report, Project No. 5–1037, U.S. Office of Education). University of California at Los Angeles, 1968. (ERIC Document Reproduction Service No. ED 021 869)

Crabtree, C. Some factors of sequence and transfer in learning the skills of geographic analysis. Part 1 of *Children's Thinking in the Social Studies.* Unpublished manuscript, University of California at Los Angeles, Graduate School of Education, 1974.

Croft, J. D. *The Development and Evaluation of a Geographical Simulation Game Involving the Arkansas River Project.* Unpublished doctoral dissertation, University of Tulsa, 1971.

Dale, J. R. *The Effects on Achievement of Using the Forced Inferential Response Mode on an Intermediate Grade Population-Geography Unit.* Unpublished doctoral dissertation, University of Georgia, 1972.

Davis, O. L., Jr. The usefulness of a map with geographic text: A reanalysis of experimental data. *Journal of Geography,* 1971, *70,* 303–306.

Davis, O. L., Jr., & Hunkins, F. The usefulness of a map with geographic text. *Journal of Geography,* 1968, *67,* 362–366.

Dhalberg, R. A. Cartographic education in U.S. colleges and universities. *American Cartographer,* 1977, *4,* 348–350.

Downs, R. M., & Meyer, J. Geography of the mind: An exploration of perceptual geography. *American Behavioral Scientist,* 1978, *2,* 59–77.

Duchastel, P. C., & Merrill, P. The effects of behavioral objectives on learning: A review of empirical studies. *Review of Educational Research,* 1976, *49,* 53–71.

Dueck, K. G. *The Image of a Neighborhood.* Unpublished doctoral dissertation, University of Texas at Austin, 1974.

Dueck, K. G. Imageability: Implications for teaching geography. *Journal of Geography,* 1976, *75,* 135–148.

Dumas, W., & Guenther, J. *The National Social Studies Projects: A Survey of Curriculum Implementation in Missouri and Kansas.* Unpublished manuscript, University of Missouri, 1971. (ERIC Document Reproduction Service No. ED 160 516)

Dunbar, G. S. Geographic education in early Charleston. *Journal of Geography,* 1970, *69,* 348–350.

Eliot, J., & Salkind, N. J. (Eds.). *Children's Spatial Development.* Springfield, Ill.: Thomas, 1975.

Ellinger, R., & Frankland, P. Computer-assisted and lecture instruction: A comparative experiment. *Journal of Geography,* 1976, *75,* 109–201.

Elliott, M. J., & Kennedy, K. J. Australian impressions of social studies theory and practice in secondary schools. *Social Education,* 1979, *43,* 291–296.

Ellis, A. K. Concept and skill development in a primary geography unit utilizing alternate learning progressions. *Journal of Geography,* 1974, *73,* 20–26.

Ermuth, F. E., & Mercer, J. Student images of urban concepts. *Journal of Geography,* 1975, *74,* 144–150.

Faw, H. W., & Waller, T. G. Mathemagenic behaviors and efficiency in learning from prose materials: Review and critical reactions. *Review of Educational Research,* 1976, *46,* 691–720.

Feldman, D. H. Map understanding as a possible crystallizer of cognitive structures. *American Educational Research Journal,* 1971, *8,* 845–502.

Flavell, J. H. *The Developmental Psychology of Jean Piaget.* Princeton, N.J.: Van Nostrand Reinhold, 1963.

Gagné, R. M. *The Conditions of Learning.* New York: Holt, Rinehart, 1965.

Giannangelo, D. M., & Frazee, B. M. Map-reading proficiency of elementary educators. *Journal of Geography,* 1977, *76,* 63–68.

Glowacki, W. M. The status of geography in the secondary schools of Connecticut. *Journal of Geography,* 1970, *69,* 434–436.

Glowatski, E. A. Behavioral objectives for geography facilitate communication and increase test performance. *Journal of Geography,* 1973, *72,* 36–45.

Gould, P. R., & White, R. R. *Mental Maps.* Baltimore: Penguin Books, 1974.

Graves, N. J. *Geography in Education.* London: Heinemann Educational Books, 1975.

Groenhoff, E. L. Geography in the preservice education of high school teachers. *Journal of Geography,* 1970, *69,* 351–353.

Hadman, L. E. Geographic concepts need to be explicit. *Journal of Geography,* 1972, *71,* 520–525.

Harrison, J. D. What is applied geography? *Professional Geographer,* 1977, *29,* 297–300.

Hart, R. A., & Moore, G. The development of spatial cognition. In R. M. Downs & D. Stea (Eds.), *Image and Environment.* Chicago: Aldine, 1973.

Hartley, J., & Davies, I. K. Preinstructional strategies: The role of pretests, behavioral objectives, overviews, and advance organizers. *Review of Educational Research,* 1976, *46,* 239–265.

Hawkins, M. Map and globe skills in elementary school textbooks. *Journal of Geography,* 1977, *76,* 261–265.

Heiges, H. E. Progress and development of a student internship program in geography. *Journal of Geography,* 1977, *76,* 147–149.

Heiges, H. E. Development of a geographical student internship programme: A mini-manual. *Journal of Geography in Higher Education,* 1979, *3,* 29–39.

Herman, J. F. Children's cognitive maps of large scale spaces: Effects of exploration, direction, and repeated experience. *Journal of Experimental Child Psychology,* 1980, *29* 126–143.

Hill, D. A. Strategies of the high school geography project for the colleges: A new heresy. *Journal of Geography,* 1970, *69,* 544–551.

Hollis, G. E., & Terry, P. Learning about small-group teaching. *Journal of Geography in Higher Education,* 1977, *1,* 73–76.

Houghton, D. M., & Morgan, V. M. Children's reasoning about their environment. *Journal of Geography,* 1974, *73,* 5–10.

Hromyk, W. J. *An Evaluation of High School Seniors' Knowledge of Anglo-American Geographic Concepts.* Unpublished doctoral dissertation, University of Oregon, 1972.

Hubbard, R., & Stoddard, R. *High School Images of Geography: A Search for Interpretation.* Paper presented at the annual meeting of the Association of American Geographers, New Orleans, April 1978. (ERIC Document Reproduction Service No. ED 156 576)

Hunt, J. M. *Intelligence and Experience.* New York: Ronald Press, 1961.

Imperatore, W. *Evaluation of a Conceptual Geography Unit for Kindergarten.* University of Georgia, Geography Curriculum Project, 1970.

Imperatore, W. Geography at the kindergarten level. *Journal of Geography,* 1971, *70,* 296–302.

Jackson, R. H. The persistence of outmoded ideas in high school geography texts. *Journal of Geography*, 1976, 75, 399–408.

Jones, F. G. *The Effects of Mastery and Aptitude on Learning, Retention, and Time*. Unpublished doctoral dissertation, University of Georgia, 1974.

Keach, E. T., Jr., & Pierfy, D. A. *The Effects of a Simulation Game on Learning of Geographic Information at the Fifth-Grade Level* (Final Report, Project No. 2-D-060, U.S. Office of Education). University of Georgia, 1972. (ERIC Document Reproduction Service No. ED 068 889)

Kennamer, L., Jr. Emerging social studies curriculum: Implications for geography. In P. Bacon (Ed.), *Focus on Geography: Key Concepts and Teaching Strategies*. Washington, D.C.: National Council for the Social Studies, 1970.

Kent, R. B. Academic geographers/cartographers in the United States: Their training and professional activity in cartography. *American Cartographer*, 1980, 7, 59–66.

Khoynejad, G. *The Effects of Behavioral Objectives, Prequestions, and a Combination of Both on Intentional and Incidental Learning from Written Text by Secondary School Students*. Unpublished doctoral dissertation, University of Texas at Austin, 1980.

Kinerney, E. J. *The High School Geography Project in Relation to Instructional Practices in Introductory College Geography: An Upward Dissemination of Educational Innovation*. Unpublished doctoral dissertation, University of Maryland, 1975.

King, F. L., III, *A Study of Selected Variables Involved in the Use of Illustrations with Geographic Text*. Unpublished doctoral dissertation, East Texas State University, 1972.

Krumme, G. Location theory. In P. Bacon (Ed.), *Focus on Geography: Key Concepts and Teaching Strategies*. Washington, D.C.: National Council for the Social Studies, 1970. (ERIC Document Reproduction Service No. ED 048 042)

Lahnston, A. T. *Comparison of Directed Discovery and Demonstration Strategies for Teaching Geographic Concepts and Generalizations*. Unpublished doctoral dissertation, University of Washington, 1972.

Lanegran, D. A.; Snowfield, J. G.; & Laurent, A. Retarded children and the concepts of distance and direction. *Journal of Geography*, 1970, 69, 157–160.

Laurendau, M., & Pinard, A. *The Development of the Concept of Space in the Child*. New York: International Universities Press, 1970.

Lawton, R. Career opportunities for geographers. *Geography*, 1980, 65, 236–244.

Lynch, K. L. *The Image of the City*. Cambridge, Mass.: MIT Press, 1960.

Markle, S. They teach concepts, don't they? *Educational Researcher*, 1975, 4, 3–9.

Marsh, C. The rationale behind HGSP: An outsider's view. *Journal of Geography*, 1973, 72, 37–39.

Massey, D. L. *A Study of Children's Spatial Stages and Temporal Concepts*. Unpublished doctoral dissertation, University of Kansas, 1971.

Matthews, M. H. The mental maps of children: Images of Coventry's city centre. *Geography*, 1980, 65, 169–179.

Mauer, R., & Baxter, J. C. Images of the neighborhood and city among black, Anglo, and Mexican American children. *Environment and Behavior*, 1972, 4, 351–388.

Mayo, W. L. *The Development and Status of Secondary School Geography in the United States and Canada*. Ann Arbor, Mich.: University Publishers, 1965.

McCartin, R. The cognitive and affective learning of children.

In P. Bacon (Ed.), *Focus on Geography: Key Concepts and Teaching Strategies*. Washington, D.C.: National Council for the Social Studies, 1970. (ERIC Document Reproduction Service No. ED 048 042)

McKenzie, G. R. The importance of teaching facts in elementary social studies. *Social Education*, 1980, 44, 494–498.

McKenzie, G. R., & Henry, M. Effects of questions on attention, test anxiety, and achievement in a classroom rule-learning task. *Journal of Educational Psychology*, 1979, 71, 370–375.

McKenzie, G. R., & Schadler, A. *Effects of Three Practice Modes on Attention, Anxiety, and Achievement in a Classroom Association Learning Task*. Paper presented at the annual meeting of the American Educational Research Association, Boston, April 1980.

McTeer, H. J. High school students' attitudes toward geography. *Journal of Geography*, 1979, 78, 55–56.

Melton, R. F. Resolution of conflicting claims concerning the effects of behavioral objectives on student learning. *Review of Educational Research*, 1978, 48, 291–302.

Meyer, J. W. Map skills instruction and the child's developing cognitive abilities. *Journal of Geography*, 1973, 72, 27–35.

Milburn, D. Children's vocabulary. In N. Graves (Ed.), *New Movements in the Study and Teaching of Geography*. London: Temple Smith, 1972.

Morganett, L. L. *The Effects of Testing and Level of Knowledge of an Advance Organizer on Learning and Retention of Social Studies Content*. Unpublished doctoral dissertation, Indiana University, 1980.

National Assessment of Educational Progress. *Social Studies Technical Report: Summary Volume* (Report No. 03–55–21). Denver: National Assessment of Educational Progress, 1975. (ERIC Document Reproduction Service No. ED 117 019)

Nisser, M. F. *A Study to Determine the Degree to Which Selected Elementary Education Majors at the University of Southern Mississippi Have Acquired Certain Concepts and Knowledge in Geography*. Unpublished doctoral dissertation, University of Southern Mississippi, 1970.

Olivera, L. The concept of territorial decentration in Brazilian schoolchildren. In J. Stoltman (Ed.), *Spatial Stages Development in Children and Teacher Classroom Style in Geography: International Research in Geographical Education*. Kalamazoo: Western Michigan University, 1976.

Oppong, J. E. *A Study of the Advance Organizer and Its Effects on Achievement of Ninth-grade Social Studies Students*. Unpublished doctoral dissertation, University of Georgia, 1978.

Orleans, P. Differential cognition of urban residents: Effects of social scale on mapping. In R. Downs & D. Stea (Eds.), *Image and Environment*. Chicago: Aldine, 1974.

Owen, E. E., & Manson, G. P. The most visible countries and cities in the world revisited. *Journal of Geography*, 1980, 79, 186–191.

Pattison, W. P. The four traditions of geography. *Journal of Geography*, 1964, 63, 211–216.

Patton, D. J. *From Geographic Discipline to Inquiring Student: Final Report of the High School Geography Project*. Washington, D.C.: American Association of Geographers, 1970.

Pelletti, J. C. *The Effects of Graphic Roles on Learning Geography Materials in the Middle Grades*. Unpublished doctoral dissertation, University of Georgia, 1973.

Peters, W. *Perceptual Agreement of Social Studies Teachers and Professional Geographers on Aspects of a Cognitive Geographic Paradigm*. Unpublished doctoral dissertation, University of Minnesota, 1969.

Piaget, J., & Inhelder, B. *The Child's Conception of Space* (F. Langdon & J. Lunzer, Trans.). New York: Humanities Press, 1956.

Pierfy, D. A. *The Effects of a Simulation Game on the Learning of Geographic Information of the Fifth-grade Level.* Unpublished doctoral dissertation, University of Georgia, 1972.

Pufall, P. B., & Shaw, R. E. Analysis of the development of children's spatial reference systems. *Cognitive Psychology,* 1973, *5,* 151–175.

Rand, D.; Towler, J. O.; & Feldhusen, J. Geographic knowledge as measured by Piaget's spatial stages. In J. Stoltman (Ed.), *Spatial Stages Development in Children and Teacher Classroom Style in Education.* Kalamazoo: Western Michigan University, Department of Geography, 1976.

Rice, M. J., & Cobb, R. L. *What Can Children Learn in Geography? A Review of Research.* Boulder, Colo.: ERIC Clearinghouse for Social Studies/Social Science Education and Social Science Education Consortium, Inc., 1978. (ERIC Document Reproduction Service No. ED 166 088)

Richburg, R. W. *An Assessment of the Impact of HSGP.* Memorandum to the High School Geography Project Steering Committee, June 1970. (ERIC Document Reproduction Service No. ED 125 960)

Richburg, R. W. *An Application of Item Sampling Procedures to the Evaluation of an Innovative Geography Curriculum.* Unpublished doctoral dissertation, University of Colorado, 1971.

Riley, J. M. *Teacher Competencies in Secondary-education School Geography: A Validated Perception Model.* Unpublished doctoral dissertation, University of Maryland, 1978.

Robinson, J. L. A new look at the four traditions of geography. *Journal of Geography,* 1976, *75,* 520–530.

Rosenshine, V. B. *Behavioral Predictors of Effectiveness in Explaining Social Studies Material.* Unpublished doctoral dissertation, Stanford University, 1968.

Rossman, M. *Internships for Social Science Majors: Development and Longitudinal Evaluation of a Model Program.* Paper presented at the annual meeting of the Eastern Psychological Association, Washington, D.C., March 1978.

Rothwell, D. C. *Cognitive Mapping of the Home Environment.* Unpublished doctoral dissertation, University of British Columbia, 1974.

Rousseau, J. J. *Emile* (B. Foxley, Trans.). London: J. M. Dent & Sons, 1911.

Rumble, H. E. Early geography instruction in America. *Social Studies,* 1946, *37,* 266–268.

Rushdoony, H. A. A child's ability to read maps: A summary of the research. *Journal of Geography,* 1968, *67,* 213–222.

Saarinen, T. F. Environmental perception. In P. Bacon (Ed.), *Focus on Geography: Key Concepts and Teaching Strategies.* Washington, D.C.: National Council for the Social Studies, 1970. (ERIC Document Reproduction Service No. ED 048 042)

Saarinen, T. F. *Environmental Planning: Perception and Behavior.* Boston: Houghton Mifflin, 1976.

Salyer, G. M. *Geography in the Elementary School As Portrayed by the "Journal of Geography."* Unpublished doctoral dissertation, Ohio University, 1975.

Savage, T. V., Jr. *A Study of the Relationship of Classroom Questions and Social Studies Achievement of Fifth-grade Children.* Unpublished doctoral dissertation, University of Washington, 1972.

Schallert, R. E. Toward structuring geography: What should be memorized? *Journal of Geography,* 1968, *67,* 211–213.

Schneider, D. O. The performance of elementary school teachers and students on a test of map and globe skills. *Journal of Geography,* 1976, *75,* 326–332.

Snaden, J. N. Geography in Connecticut revisited, *Journal of Geography,* 1978, *77,* 84–86.

Shaver, J. D.; Davis, O. L.; & Helbrun, S. The status of social studies education: Impressions from three N.S.F. studies. *Social Education,* 1979, *43,* 150–153.

Simpson, J. D. *The Effects of Critical Property Identification and Form of Instance Presentation on Children's Concept Attainment in the Social Studies.* Unpublished doctoral dissertation, University of Washington, 1975.

Skretting, J. R., & Sundeen, J. E. Social studies education. In R. L. Ebel (Ed.), *Encyclopedia of Educational Research* (4th ed.). New York: Macmillan, 1969.

Steinbrink, J. E. *The Effectiveness of Advance Organizers for Teaching Geography to Disadvantaged Rural Black Elementary Students.* Unpublished doctoral dissertation, University of Georgia, 1970.

Steinbrink, J. E., & Jones, R. M. Confluent curriculum development in geographic education. *Journal of Geography,* 1979, *78,* 94–97.

Stoltman, J. P. *Children's Conceptions of Territory: A Study of Piaget's Spatial Stages.* Unpublished doctoral dissertation, University of Georgia, 1971.

Stoltman, J. P. Territorial concept development: A review of the literature. In J. Stoltman (Ed.), *Spatial Stages Development in Children and Teacher Classroom Styles.* Kalamazoo, Mich.: University Department of Geography, 1976.

Stoltman, J. P., & Goolsby, T. M., Jr. Developing map skills through reading instruction. *Journal of Geography,* 1973, *72,* 32–36.

Stubbles, R. L. *Enhancing the Learning of Topographic Map Use through a Simulation Game.* Unpublished master's thesis, Texas A & M University, 1974.

Tennyson, R., & Park, O. The teaching of concepts: A review of instructional design literature. *Review of Educational Research,* 1980, *50,* 55–71.

Towler, J. O. The elementary-school child's concept of reference systems. *Journal of Geography,* 1970, *69,* 89–93.

Towler, J. O., & Nelson, L. D. The elementary-school child's concept of space. *Journal of Geography,* 1968, *67,* 24–28.

Towler, J. O., & Price, D. The development of nationality and spatial relationship concepts in children: Canada. In J. Stoltman (Ed.), *Spatial Stage Development in Children and Teacher Classroom Style in Geography: International Research in Geographical Education.* Kalamazoo: Western Michigan University, 1976.

Vining, J. W. The status of conservation courses: An analysis of enrollments. *Journal of Geography,* 1980, *79,* 28–32.

Vuicich, G., & Stoltman, J. *Geography in Elementary and Secondary Education: Tradition to Opportunity.* Boulder, Colo.: ERIC Clearinghouse for Social Studies Education and Social Science Education Consortium, 1974.

Walter, B. J., & Bernard, D. E. Ashpile or rising phoenix? A review of the status of regional geography. *Journal of Geography,* 1978, *77,* 192–196.

Ward, E. H. *Conceptual Thinking in Geography: An Enquiry into the Development of Understanding of Climate Concepts.* Unpublished master's thesis, University of Nottingham, 1972.

Webb, G. Student participation in tutorials. *Journal of Geography in Higher Education,* 1980, *4,* 16–22.

Wise, J. Student deficiency in basic world knowledge. *Journal of Geography,* 1975, *74,* 477–88.

Womack, James A. *An Analysis of Inquiry-oriented High School Geography Project Urban Materials.* Unpublished doctoral dissertation, University of Colorado, 1969.

Wood, D. *I Don't Want to But I Will.* Unpublished doctoral dissertation, Clark University, 1973.

GIFTED PERSONS

Throughout recorded history in all cultures there has been keen interest in persons who have displayed superior abilities. As early as 2200 B.C., the Chinese had developed an elaborate system of competitive examinations to select outstanding persons for government positions (DuBois, 1970); in the fourteenth century, the Ottoman Turks assigned leadership responsibilities to young men who met prescribed standards of physical beauty and stamina (Laycock, 1979). The behaviors or performance areas that were rewarded in particular societies were to a great extent a function of the needs and values of the prevailing culture.

Scholars of the 1900s were discontented with the haphazard selection of "the gifted" through arbitrary standards and sought to define "giftedness" in more precise, systematic, and empirical terms, which have brought some clarification along with controversy to the definition and identification of human accomplishment. However, the precise definition of giftedness remains a question with no universally accepted answer.

The proposed definitions of giftedness tend to isolate those individuals who have proven high competence in particular fields of aptitude or performance. At the conservative end of the definition continuum is Terman and Associates' definition (1926) of the gifted as being "the top one percent level in general intellectual ability, as measured by the Stanford-Binet Intelligence Scale or a comparable instrument" (p. 43). In this definition, restrictiveness appears in terms of both the type of performance specified (i.e., intelligence test tasks) and the level of performance required for one to be designated gifted (i.e., the top 1 percent).

At the other end of the continuum might be found more liberal definitions, such as the following one developed by Paul Witty (1958): "There are children whose outstanding potentialities in art, in writing, or in social leadership can be recognized largely by their performance. Hence, we have recommended that the definition of giftedness be expanded and that we consider any child gifted whose performance, in a potentially valuable line of human activity, is consistently remarkable" (p. 62). Although Witty's definition expands the concept of giftedness, it opens up ambiguity by introducing a values issue—that is, by mentioning "potentially valuable lines of human activity." Also, reliability of subjective measurement becomes an issue with this more liberal definition, as one must rely upon human judgment when determining "consistently remarkable" performance.

In recent years, the values issue has been largely resolved. However, there are very few educators who cling to a "straight IQ" definition or purely academic criteria for identifying giftedness. "Multiple talent" and "multiple criteria" are almost the bywords of the present-day interest in the gifted.

The problem of subjectivity in measurement has not been as easily allayed. As the definition of giftedness extended beyond those abilities that are reflected in tests of intelligence, achievement, and academic aptitude, it has become necessary to place less emphasis on precise estimates of performance and potential and more emphasis on the opinions of qualified human judges.

In recent years the definition of gifted children set forth by the U.S. Office of Education (USOE) has grown in popularity as it has been adopted by numerous states and school districts throughout the nation (Marland, 1972, p. 2):

Gifted and talented children are those identified by professionally qualified persons who by virtue of outstanding abilities are capable of high performance. These are children who require differentiated educational programs and/or services beyond those normally provided by the regular school program in order to realize their contribution to self and society.

Children capable of high performance include those with demonstrated achievement and/or potential in any of the following areas, singly or in combination:
1. General intellectual ability.
2. Specific academic aptitude.
3. Creative or productive thinking.
4. Leadership ability.
5. Visual and performing arts.
6. Psychomotor ability.

The USOE definition identifies a wider variety of abilities that should be included in a definition of giftedness, but at the same time it presents two major problems. The first problem is the failure to include motivational factors as a component of giftedness. A second problem relates to the nonparallel nature of the six categories included in the definition. Two of the six categories (specific academic aptitude and visual and performing arts) are general performance areas in which talents and abilities are manifested. The remaining four categories are processes that can be applied to performance areas. For example, a person can apply creativity to chemistry or photography. In fact, processes such as creativity and leadership do not exist apart from a performance area to which they can be applied.

The USOE definition can be misinterpreted and misused by practitioners. It is common to find educators developing entire identification systems based on the six USOE categories and in the process treating the categories as if they were mutually exclusive. It is also distressing that many educators who acknowledge the above six categories continue to rely on a relatively high intelligence or aptitude test score as a minimum requirement for identifying gifted children for special programs.

Three Components of Giftedness. An alternative approach to defining giftedness is to identify individuals who have some measure of three traits: above-average ability, creativity, and task commitment. Research on "creative-productive" individuals has shown consistently that although no single criterion can be used to determine giftedness, persons who have achieved recognition because of their unique accomplishments and creative contributions possess these traits.

In the material below, the role of each trait is discussed with respect to research that has been conducted. Attention will be focused on the nonintellective factors of task commitment and creativity. The general goal here will be to argue for a definition of giftedness that places equal emphasis on each of the three major traits.

Above-average ability. One of the most consistent mistakes made in the identification of the gifted has been to confuse proficiency (usually measured by test scores and grade point averages) with creative productivity. The fact that a person performs well on tests, learns lessons well, and generally pleases his or her teachers is no guarantee that this individual possesses the other characteristics necessary for creative-productive accomplishment. Terman (1959) states in his later writings that high intelligence and giftedness are not necessarily synonymous.

A definition of giftedness must begin by clearly distinguishing between proficiency in lesson learning and test taking on the one hand and innovative behavior and creative-productive accomplishments on the other. In a review of research that examined the predictive strength of tests measuring intellectual aptitude and academic achievement, Wallach (1976) found that the power of intelligence and achievement tests to identify future creative producers is greatly diminished when one achieves scores in the upper ranges. He suggests that test scores be used only to screen out persons who score in the lower ranges and that beyond this point decisions be based on samples of professional competence.

Cox (1926) conducted a comprehensive biographical study of 300 of the most eminent men of history. A variety of procedures was used to estimate the IQ of her subjects, the mean IQ being 155 in a range of 100–200. Cox concluded that the genius is one whom intelligence tests would have identified as gifted in childhood but she also warned that not every child who tests high will become eminent. In his own longitudinal study of 1,300 subjects scoring 140 or higher on the Stanford-Binet Intelligence Scale, Terman found adults who pursued a wide range of occupations "as humble as those of policeman . . . seaman . . . typist and filing clerk" (Terman, 1970, p. 39). He concluded that intellect and later life achievement are far from perfectly correlated (Terman, 1975).

The absence of a strong relationship between assessments of intellectual ability as measured by school grades and tests of achievement and intelligence on the one hand

and later-life professional contributions on the other has been well documented in a variety of professional fields. In a study of the relationship between the contributions of physicists and biologists (based on such criteria as patents granted and number of publications), Harmon (1963) found that individuals receiving high ratings as professional scientists could not be predicted from any of the academic proficiency information. In fact, the correlations between these traditional measures of academic success and professional accomplishments were frequently negative. In two studies of professional mathematicians, Helson (1971) and Helson and Crutchfield (1968) found no significant IQ differences between mathematicians judged by their peers as performing particularly good research and a control group of mathematicians of low productivity. Similar results have been reported in studies of chemists and mathematicians (Bloom, 1963), psychologists (Marston, 1971), research scientists (MacKinnon, 1968), artists (Barron, 1963), and architects (MacKinnon, 1968). It seems apparent that for individuals whose intellectual ability exceeds a minimum or threshold level for entry into the particular field, professional attainments are a function of abilities other than those measured by tests of academic achievement or intelligence.

In a review of occupational studies dealing with traditional indicators of academic success and postcollege performance, Hoyt (1965) concluded that traditional assessments of academic success have at best a modest correlation with various indicators of success in the adult world. The review included forty-six studies in seven occupational areas, including business, teaching, engineering, medicine, scientific research, journalism, government, and the ministry. The criteria for determining the level of accomplishment varied from salary level to numbers of publications to behavioral performance ratings. Although a number of the studies suffered from experimental measurement or statistical weaknesses, Hoyt concluded that "academic achievement (knowledge) and other types of educational growth and development are relatively independent of each other" (p. 73). Similar conclusions were reached in analogous studies conducted by Ghiselli (1973), Creagar and Harmon (1966), and Baird (n.d.).

Given the inadvisibility of relying on grades or objective measures of intelligence and academic achievement to predict adult accomplishment, other studies have attempted to establish the validity of additional indicators. Wallach (1976) suggested that the emphasis be shifted from test scores to actual accomplishments as a measure of above-average ability. Other studies have explored ratings of extracurricular academic accomplishments. Parloff et al. (1968) found that ratings of the novelty and effectiveness of high school students' research projects conducted independently of course work were uncorrelated with intellectual aptitude test scores or grades. Mednick (1963) reported similar findings when college faculty evaluated independent research projects for imaginativeness and the degree to which they represented a contribution to knowledge in the field. Wallach and Wing (1969) found that students' accomplishments outside the classroom in the areas of literature, science, art, music, dramatics, political leadership, and social services were reported as frequently for students in the lower third of score ranges on the Scholastic Aptitude Test as for students in the upper third.

These findings assume greater importance when one takes into consideration the results of a study conducted by the American College Testing (ACT) Program (Munday & Davis, 1974).

The ACT study focused on the accomplishments of over 2,200 adults two years after college. The participants had completed a "Student Profile Section" as high school seniors. The adult followup questionnaire consisted of checklists of accomplishments in seven areas ranging from leadership to art to science. Test-retest reliabilities were considered adequate (from .79 for science to .93 for leadership). Moreover, the authors reported that the scales were highly independent of one another (e.g., a person high in leadership did not also tend to score highly in drama).

Median correlations for comparable high school and adult accomplishments were +.22, a finding that the authors considered significant, considering the overall limitations of the research. They conclude that nonacademic accomplishments should be considered in college admissions, and that educators should consider ways in which talents other than the academic might be nurtured by public schools.

Holland and Astin (1962) also found a positive relationship between high academic performance and out-of-school accomplishments. For their sample of 953 high-aptitude students, whom they assessed over intervals of one to four years, college achievement (defined as grades, unusual accomplishments in art and science, and election to student office) was best predicted by simple self-ratings of past similar achievements in high school. This finding was consistent for three of the four areas of achievement assessed (leadership, scientific, and artistic). Only in the area of academic achievement did grades play a significant role in the prediction model.

As part of their interest in broadening the definition of talent, Baird (1976) reported that the National Merit Scholarship Corporation and the American College Testing Program have developed scales of nonacademic accomplishments in science, writing, art, music, speech drama, and leadership (see also Munday & Davis, 1974) that have proved to be reliable and are not subject to faking. In every study reported, the accomplishment scales had very low correlations with grades and the ACT academic-ability test scores and are thus considered to be independent.

In summary, there is a substantial body of evidence that suggest the use of measures of intellectual or academic potential for initial screening purposes only. The same research points to the need for greater use of creative thinking scales, ratings of past accomplishments, and ratings of creative production for the prediction of adult achieve-

ment. Wallach (1976) strongly supports placing more emphasis on work samples as evidence of creative productivity. Hoyt (1965) suggests that greater reliance be placed on "profiles of student growth and development" rather than traditional means of determining academic success.

Creativity. Gifted persons are usually characterized as being creative. In much of the research cited previously, persons selected for intensive study were identified by creative accomplishments (or products) rather than by test scores. MacKinnon (1964) used such an approach when he asked panels of judges (professors of architecture and editors of major American architectural journals) first to nominate and later to rate the work of a pool of new architects using the following dimensions of creativity:

1. Originality of thinking and freshness of approaches to architectural problems.
2. Constructive ingenuity.
3. Ability to set aside established conventions and procedures when appropriate.
4. A flair for devising effective and original fulfillments of the major demands of architecture—namely, technology (firmness), visual form (delight), planning (commodity), and human awareness and social purpose. (p. 360)

Panel members were also asked to write summary evaluations of the architect's work, indicating the basis for their nomination.

MacKinnon's analysis of the creative-productive process of architects has important implications for defining giftedness as behavior. First, the criteria for creative accomplishment were formulated within a specific performance area (e.g., architecture) by persons who have specialized expertise in the particular area. Second, the judgment of qualified persons (including peers) was the major procedure for identification. Finally, and perhaps most important, judgments were based on the actual performance (or products) of the nominees rather than traditional predictors of performance such as test scores or grade point averages. Likewise, Nicholls (1972) prefers the discussion of "creativity" to involve the analysis of products rather than the delineation of certain personality traits or factors. Citing the lack of evidence correlating specific skills, abilities, or predisposing components of creative production with adult accomplishments, he applies the term "creativity" to the "evidence of achievements that are original and make a meaningful contribution to culture" (p. 717). The identification of creativity, then, if delegated to a score on a test of divergent thinking or ideational fluency, circumvents the real-world documentation of creativity as creative production.

Albert (1975), in his search for a behavioral definition of genius, refers to Galton's determination of eminence as an objective attribute—that is, something that is known because of its influence on a large number of people over many years.

If creativity is manifest in inventions, ideas, and compositions, how does one document such propensities in youngsters who have not yet been alive long enough to exhibit such behaviors? Various tests of divergent thinking and checklists of creativity have been suggested for use in identifying elements of creative production in children but these tests do not always relate to other accomplishments. The empirical problems of construct validity, criterion-related validity, and reliability affect the accuracy with which creativity can be identified in children.

Two major problems continue to cast doubt on the construct validity of creativity tests. (1) There is no unified theory of creativity and no operational definition on which to base instruments (Treffinger, Renzulli, & Feldhusen, 1971); definitions of creativity permeate research literature with both detailed and broad interpretations that do not clearly establish whether creativity is a process, a product, or a combination of the two. (2) There is not sufficient evidence that current creativity tests tap a different set of abilities from those measured by tests of intelligence (Crockenberg, 1972; Ward, 1975); creativity tests have failed to prove that they measure a distinct component of human activity.

In fact, ideational fluency (i.e., the ability to produce many ideas about a given topic, problem, or question) is the only form of creative-thinking ability that differs significantly from intellectual aptitude (Singer & Whiton, 1971; Wallach, 1976; Wallach & Wing, 1969; Wallbrown & Huelsman, 1975).

Criterion-related validity issues include problems of possible criterion bias (Brogden & Taylor, 1950) and the lack of a substantial relationship between performance on creativity tests and "real-world" creativity (Crockenberg, 1972; Treffinger & Poggio, 1972; Treffinger, Renzulli, & Feldhusen, 1971). Unfortunately, very few tests have been validated against real-life criteria of creative accomplishments, and in cases where such studies have been conducted the creativity tests have fared poorly (Crockenberg, 1972) or the research has suffered from methodological problems preventing definitive conclusions. Baird (n.d.) alluded to the tenuous relationship between divergent-thinking measures and nontest creative problem solving: "There is a large difference between a child's ability to think of twenty uses of a red brick and the publication of an article in a scientific journal" (p. 1). In addition, by their very nature tests of creativity eliminate an essential component of creative problem solving: that of a problem definition (Getzels & Csikszentmihalyi, 1975).

And although some validation studies have reported limited relationships between measures of divergent thinking and creative-performance criteria (Dellas & Gaier, 1970; Guilford, 1964; Shapiro, 1968; Torrance, 1969; Torrance, 1972; Torrance, Bruch, & Morse, 1973), the research evidence for the predictive validity of such tests is not very strong, as evidenced by the inability of ideational fluency tests to predict overall extracurricular activities and accomplishments assessed upon high school graduation (Kogan & Pankove, 1974).

After conducting a comprehensive review of validation and prediction studies of divergent-thinking tests, Nicholls (1972) concluded that divergent thinking is characteristic of highly creative persons; however, he urged caution in the uncritical acceptance of these tests as definitive measures of creativity. He suggested that whenever possible an analysis of creative products would be preferable to the trait-based approach in making predictions about creative potential (p. 721).

Wallach (1976) reached a similar conclusion in his extensive review of creative studies. A number of the studies he analyzed found correlations between ideational fluency and such variables as out-of-school attainments in literature and science (Wallach & Wing, 1969), ratings of expressiveness in children's drawings (Singer & Whiton, 1971), and clay products (Wallbrown & Huelsman, 1975). However, he suggested that "it is difficult to describe measurable relationships between creativity and eminence" (p. 60) and recommended that work samples and verifiable signs of creative potential be provided by qualified judges. The procedure recommended by Wallach would involve having candidates for special programs submit examples of their best written work or reports on scientific projects they have conducted (p. 60). Wallach also suggests that student self-reports about creative accomplishments are sufficiently accurate to provide a usable source of data. He cites Maxey and Ormsby's (1971) study in which a high level of agreement was found between student reports on out-of-school accomplishments and information provided by the school (p. 58).

Task commitment. Creative-productive individuals are often characterized as having high levels of refined or focused form of motivation known as task commitment. Gifted persons are repeatedly described as involving themselves totally in a specific problem or area for an extended period of time.

Sir Francis Galton, considered to be both the father of modern psychometrics and the first person to carry out scientific studies of genius, was a strong proponent of the hereditary basis for what he called "natural ability." He nevertheless subscribed heavily to the belief that hard work was characteristic of a gifted person.

The studies of Lewis Terman undoubtedly represent the most widely recognized and frequently quoted research on the characteristics of gifted persons. When Terman began his studies in 1911, he used as his selection criterion the top 1 percent level in general intellectual ability as measured by the Stanford-Binet Intelligence Scale (Terman & Associates, 1926). The comprehensiveness of his research design, which included a detailed follow-up of his subjects, gained widespread attention among educators and psychologists.

Although Terman never suggested that task commitment should replace intelligence as a definition of giftedness, he did state that "intellect and achievement are far from perfectly correlated." To identify the internal and external factors that help or hinder the fruition of exceptional talent and to measure the extent of their influence are among the major problems of our time (Terman, 1954, p. 230).

The legacy of both Galton and Terman indicates clearly that task commitment is an important part in the development of a gifted person. Galton believed strongly that intrinsic motivation and the capacity for hard work were necessary conditions for superior accomplishment. And if three decades of intensive research caused Terman to take a second look at what makes giftedness, then perhaps the time has come for us to apply his results and conclusions to a reconsideration of our present-day definition.

In addition to the work of Galton and Terman, several more recent research studies have shown that creative-productive persons are far more task-oriented and involved in their work than are people in the general population. Perhaps the best known of these studies is the work of Roe (1952) and MacKinnon (1964, 1968). Roe conducted an intensive study of the characteristics of sixty-four eminent scientists. Although the intellectual ability range of her subjects was wide, "the group as a whole was characterized by high average intelligence" (p. 23). The following summary statement, however, points out that *all* of her subjects had a high level of commitment to their work: "The one thing that all of these 64 scientists have in common is their driving absorption in their work. They have worked long hours for many years, frequently with no vacations to speak of, because they would rather be doing their work than anything else" (Roe, 1952, p. 25).

What is perhaps an even more significant result of Roe's study was that many of her subjects showed interests in particular areas at an early age. This finding certainly has implications for the feasibility of building task commitment into identification procedures.

MacKinnon's (1964) study of highly creative architects lends additional support for placing greater emphasis on the role played by task commitment and other nonintellectual characteristics in identifying gifted persons. MacKinnon and his coworkers found that creativity and eminence in architecture do not require IQs beyond those of most college graduates. Tests of intelligence did not distinguish between his most and least creative groups.

In a review of studies dealing with the characteristics of creative-productive individuals Nicholls (1972) found patterns that were consistently similar to the research findings reported by Roe and MacKinnon.

Clearly, the consideration of task commitment as a factor in the production of real-world accomplishments must play a part in any definition of giftedness that purports to be research-based.

Summary: The three-ring conception of giftedness. Although the studies reviewed thus far used different research procedures and dealt with a variety of populations, there is a striking similarity in their major conclusions. First, academic ability (as traditionally measured by tests or grade point averages) showed limited relationships to creative-productive accomplishment. Second, nonintel-

lectual factors, and especially those related to task commitment, consistently played an important part in the cluster of traits that characterized highly productive people. Task commitment is not as easily and objectively identifiable as general cognitive abilities, but it appears to be a major component of giftedness and should therefore be reflected in a definition.

Although no single statement can effectively integrate the many ramifications of the research studies described above, the following definition of giftedness is proposed in an attempt to incorporate the major conclusions and generalizations resulting from this review of research: "Giftedness is composed of three basic characteristics: above average general abilities, high levels of task commitment, and high levels of creativity. Gifted and talented children are those possessing or capable of developing this composite set of traits and applying them to any potentially valuable area of human performance. Children who manifest or who are capable of developing an interaction among the three clusters require a wide variety of educational opportunities and services that are not ordinarily provided through regular instructional programs."

Programming for Gifted. The studies reviewed above provide sufficient evidence for the inclusion of creativity and task commitment in any operational definition of giftedness. It seems to follow that any scheme used to identify children as gifted would include these traits. However, even cursory examination of many identification designs will show the overemphasis on academic aptitude and achievement, usually at the expense of the nonintellective traits.

Giftedness should not be considered a pervasive quality. The research scientist, for example, is not expected to be a renowned poet, nor is the design engineer expected to master chemical equations. Likewise, children in programs for the gifted will not perform equally well in all curricular or extracurricular areas. Research and common sense tell us that the behavior of the gifted is both topical and temporal in nature. That is, it emerges in response to interest and operates at maximum efficiency during given periods of time. It is when a strong interest emerges and the child is unquestionably eager to put forth maximum creative effort that supplementary services and resources should be made available to the child. It goes without saying that an important part of overall programming is the encouragement (indeed, the creation) of task commitment and creativity. But if we restrict our efforts for such encouragement to students who have been preselected (on the basis of test scores) for a special program, we may fail to "turn on" the child who has the greatest potential for benefiting from interest-development and creativity-producing activities.

The Revolving Door Identification and Programming Model (RDIM) (Renzulli, Smith, & Reis, 1981) represents a significant new approach to selecting students for participation in programs for the gifted. In contrast with traditional methods of programming for the gifted, RDIM assumes that giftedness *is* both temporal and topical and is exhibited in behaviors rather than existing as a set of personality and intellectual traits. Through RDIM, students are recognized for the degree to which their abilities were brought to bear upon a particular topic area rather than for the mere attainment of a particular test score. In essence, RDIM provides the mechanism for bright pupils to receive special services at the time and in the performance areas in which such services have the highest potential for doing the most good for a particular youngster.

To implant this model, services in programs for the gifted are provided for a numerical percentage of the general pupil population rather than for a percentage based on IQ. Program size is indicated as a specific number of "slots" available for pupils rather than as a set of preselected pupils. The program involves irregular periodic changes among the students attending the resource room during a given time block. This means establishing a "talent pool" consisting of a percentage (usually 15 to 25 percent) of the general student population.

If a talent pool member displays certain traits in a particular area of study, and if we are reasonably certain the student has above-average ability in the area of interest, then the student pursues that topic under the resource teacher for a given time. One child goes to the resource room until the project is completed and then steps aside for another child. If, however, the student displays new creative ideas or task commitment in another area of interest, or if the student would like to do more advanced research on the original topic, we must determine whether to continue that child in the resource room at that point in time.

The essence of the Revolving Door Model is in making entrance decisions through use of "status information" (objective and/or subjective knowledge about a child that can be gathered and recorded for deciding on entrance into a talent pool) *plus* "action information" (dynamic interactions that take place when a student is "turned on" by an area of study). Action information cannot be pregathered and recorded, but it gives the teacher reason to believe that a child might like to pursue an area in greater depth. This type of information (coupled with status information) helps identify the youngsters with the highest potential for benefiting from supplementary services.

This model also provides for exit criteria, through a form that helps students formulate their objectives, focus on a problem in relation to a particular area of study, locate and organize appropriate resources, and identify relevant outlets and audiences for their creative work. The form is like a contract, and, once fulfilled, it offers a rationale for concluding a child's time in the program. It can also be used for evaluation and reporting to parents.

The Revolving Door Model can help overcome many problems associated with programs for the gifted and talented. This approach allows the program to serve more students, to avoid the IQ cutoff game, to place the rationale for advanced-level services on characteristics that are un-

equivocally supported by research literature, and to shift the emphasis of special programs from lesson-oriented, whole-group activities to the development of individual strengths and interests. This approach will also help in accountability and program evaluation.

Research Directions. The ultimate value of the definition of giftedness offered in this article can be assessed in its impact in two major areas: development and further refinement of theory relating to conception of giftedness; and pragmatic applications in the areas of identification and program practice. Suggestions are offered for further research in these areas, and, although the list is by no means exhaustive, it is hoped that the suggestions will indicate areas for high-priority research. Issues in need of research attention include the following:

1. Exploration of possible age and/or sex differences in manifestations of the three traits.
2. Assessment of home and school influences on the development of task commitment.
3. Definition of the relationships among the three traits and various styles of learning.
4. Identification of the indicators of superior performance in specific performance areas.
5. Development and/or further refinement of alternative instruments (e.g., self-report checklists) appropriate for younger as well as culturally diverse populations (Renzulli et al., 1976).
6. Exploration of additional sources of identification information such as parents (White, 1978) and peers (Jenkins, 1978).
7. Investigation of "nonconventional" systems for identification (Renzulli & Smith, 1977).
8. Development of program-evaluation instruments and techniques sensitive to the proposed definition.
9. Assessment of the effects of particular program provisions on later life accomplishments.
10. Implementation of programming options for the academically capable that are based upon the enhancement of individual pupils' interests and abilities.

It is hoped that the conception and definition of giftedness developed in this chapter will be employed in improving the effectiveness and the efficiency of the educational process and that the identification of children for programs for the gifted will consider the topical and temporal nature of the production of gifted behaviors.

Joseph S. Renzulli
James R. Delisle

See also Creativity; Individual Differences; Intelligence.

REFERENCES

Albert, R. S. Toward a behavioral definition of genius. *American Psychologist*, 1975, *30*, 140–151.

Baird, L. L. *Using Self-reports to Predict Student Performance.* New York: College Entrance Examination Board, 1976.

Baird, L. L. *The Relationship between Academic Ability and High*

Level Accomplishment: Academic Intelligence and Creativity Re-examined. Princeton, N.J.: Educational Testing Service, undated.

Barron, F. *Creativity and Psychological Health.* Princeton, N.J.: Van Nostrand, 1963.

Bloom, B. S. Report on creativity research by the examiner's office of the University of Chicago. In C. W. Taylor & F. Barron (Eds.), *Scientific Creativity: Its Recognition and Development.* New York: Wiley, 1963.

Brogden, H. E., & Taylor, E. K. The theory and classification of criterion bias. *Educational and Psychological Measurement,* 1950, *10,* 159–186.

Cox, C. C. *The Early Mental Traits of Three Hundred Geniuses.* Vol. 2 of L. M. Terman (Ed.), *Genetic Studies of Genius.* Stanford, Calif.: Stanford University Press, 1926.

Creagar, J. A., & Harmon, L. R. *On-the-Job Validation of Selection Variables* (Technical Report No. 26). Washington, D.C.: National Academy of Sciences—National Research Council, 1966.

Crockenburg, S. B. Creativity tests: A boon or boondoggle for education? *Review of Educational Research,* 1972, *42,* 27–45.

Dellas, M., & Gaier, E. L. Identification of creativity: The individual. *Psychological Bulletin,* 1970, *73,* 55–73.

DuBois, P. H. *A History of Psychological Testing.* Boston: Allyn & Bacon, 1970.

Getzels, J. W., & Csikszentmihalyi, M. From problem-solving to problem-finding. In I. A. Taylor & J. W. Getzels (Eds.), *Perspectives in Creativity.* Chicago: Aldine, 1975, pp. 90–116.

Ghiselli, E. E. The validity of occupational selection tests. *Personnel Psychology,* 1973, *26,* 1–36.

Guilford, J. P. Some new looks at the nature of creative processes. In N. Fredrickson & H. Gilliksen (Eds.), *Contributions to Mathematical Psychology.* New York: Holt, Rinehart & Winston, 1964.

Harmon, L. R. The development of a criterion of scientific competence. In C. W. Taylor & F. Barron (Eds.), *Scientific Creativity: Its Recognition and Development.* New York: Wiley, 1963, pp. 44–52.

Helson, R. Women mathematicians and the creative personality. *Journal of Consulting and Clinical Psychology,* 1971, *36,* 210–220.

Helson, R., & Crutchfield, R. S. Creative types in mathematics. *Journal of Personality,* 1968, *36,* 589–607.

Holland, J. L., & Astin, A. W. The prediction of the academic, artistic, scientific, and social achievement of undergraduates of superior scholastic aptitude. *Journal of Educational Psychology,* 1962, *53,* 132, 133.

Hoyt, D. P. *The Relationship between College Grades and Adult Achievement: A Review of the Literature* (Research Report No. 7). Iowa City: American College Testing Program, 1965.

Jenkins, R. C. W. *The Identification of Gifted and Talented Students through Peer Nomination.* Unpublished doctoral dissertation, University of Connecticut, 1978.

Kogan, N., & Pankove, E. Long-term predictive validity of divergent thinking tests: Some negative evidence. *Journal of Educational Psychology,* 1974, *66*(6), 802–810.

Laycock, F. *Gifted Children.* Glenview, Ill.: Scott, Foresman, 1979.

MacKinnon, D. W. The creativity of architects. In C. W. Taylor (Ed.), *Widening Horizons in Creativity.* New York: Wiley, 1964.

MacKinnon, D. W. Selecting students with creative potential. In P. Heist (Ed.), *The Creative College Student: An Unmet Challenge.* San Francisco: Jossey-Bass, 1968.

Marland, S. P. *Education of the Gifted and Talented: Report to the Congress of the United States by the U.S. Commissioner of Education, and Background Papers Submitted to the U.S. Office of Education.* Washington, D.C.: U.S. Government Printing Office, 1972.

Marston, A. R. It is time to reconsider the Graduate Record Examination. *American Psychologist,* 1971, *26,* 653–655.

Maxey, E. J., & Ormsby, V. J. *The Accuracy of Self-report Information Collected on the ACT Test Battery: High School Grades and Items of Non-academic Achievement* (ACT Research Report No. 45). Iowa City: American College Testing Program, 1971.

Mednick, M. T. Research creativity in psychology graduate students. *Journal of Consulting Psychology,* 1963, *27,* 265–266.

Munday, L. A., & Davis, J. C. *Varieties of Accomplishment after College: Perspectives on the Meaning of Academic Talent* (ACT Research Report No. 62). Iowa City: American College Testing Program, 1974.

Nicholls, J. C. Creativity in the person who will never produce anything original and useful: The concept of creativity as a normally distributed trait. *American Psychologist,* 1972, *27,* 717–727.

Parloff, M. B.; Datta, L.; Kleman, M.; & Handlon, J. H. Personality characteristics which differentiate creative male adolescents and adults. *Journal of Personality,* 1968, *36,* 528–552.

Public Law 95-561, Title IX, Part A. *The Gifted and Talented Children's Education Act of 1978,* Section 902.

Renzulli, J. S., & Smith, L. H. Two approaches to identification of gifted students. *Exceptional Children,* 1977, *43,* 512–518.

Renzulli, J. S.; Smith, L. H.; & Reis, S. M. Identifying and programming the gifted student. *Education Digest,* 1981, *47,* 45–47.

Renzulli, J. S.; Smith, L. H.; White, A. J.; Callahan, C. M.; & Hartman, R. K. *Scales for Rating the Behavioral Characteristics of Superior Students.* Mansfield Center, Conn.: Creative Learning Press, 1976.

Roe, A. *The Making of a Scientist.* New York: Dodd, Mead, 1952.

Shapiro, R. J. Creative research scientists. *Psychologia Africana,* 1968, Supplement No. 4.

Singer, D. L., & Whiton, M. B. Ideational creativity and expressive aspects of human figure drawing in kindergarten-age children. *Developmental Psychology,* 1971, *4,* 366–369.

Terman, L. M. The discovery and encouragement of exceptional talent. *American Psychologist,* 1954, *9,* 221–230.

Terman, L. M. *Genetic Studies of Genius: The Gifted Group at Mid-life.* Stanford, Calif.: Stanford University Press, 1959.

Terman, L. M. Psychological approaches to the biography of genius. In P. E. Vernon (Ed.), *Creativity.* Baltimore: Penguin Books, 1970.

Terman, L. M. The discovery and encouragement of exceptional talent. In W. B. Barbe & J. S. Renzulli (Eds.), *Psychology and Education of the Gifted* (2nd ed.). New York: Halsted Press, 1975, pp. 6–20.

Terman, L. M., and Associates. *Genetic Studies of Genius: Mental and Physical Traits of a Thousand Gifted Children.* Stanford, Calif.: Stanford University Press, 1926.

Torrance, E. P. Prediction of adult creative achievement among high school seniors. *Gifted Child Quarterly,* 1969, *13,* 223–229.

Torrance, E. P. Career patterns and peak creative achievements of creative high school students twelve years later. *Gifted Child Quarterly,* 1972, *16,* 75–87.

Torrance, E. P.; Bruch, C. B.; & Morse, J. A. Improving predictions of the adult creative achievement of gifted girls by using autobiographical information. *Gifted Child Quarterly*, 1973, *17*, 91–95.

Treffinger, D. T., & Poggio, J. P. Needed research on the measurement of creativity. *Journal of Creative Behavior*, 1972, *6*, 253–267.

Treffinger, D. T.; Renzulli, J. S.; & Feldhusen, D. J. Problems in the assessment of creative thinking. *Journal of Creative Behavior*, 1971, *5*(2), 104–112.

Wallach, M. A. Tests tell us little about talent. *American Scientist*, 1976, *64*, 57–63.

Wallach, M. A., & Wing, C. J., Jr. *The Talented Student: A Validation of the Creativity-Intelligence Distinction*. New York: Holt, Rinehart & Winston, 1969.

Wallbrown, F. H., & Huelsman, C. B., Jr. The validity of the Wallach-Kogan creativity operations for inner city children in two areas of visual art. *Journal of Personality*, 1975, *43*, 109–126.

Ward, V. S. Basic Concepts. In W. B. Barbe & J. S. Renzulli (Eds.), *Psychology and Education of the Gifted*. New York: Irvington, 1975.

White, A. J. *Construction and Validation of an Instrument to Identify Selected Dimensions of Giftedness*. Unpublished doctoral dissertation, University of Connecticut, 1978.

Witty, P. A. Who are the gifted? In N. B. Henry (Ed.), *The Fifty-seventh Yearbook of the National Society for the Study of Education, Part II: Education of the Gifted*. Chicago: University of Chicago Press, 1958.

GLOBAL EDUCATION

See International Education.

GOVERNANCE OF SCHOOLS

"Governance" is a relatively new concept in educational research and analysis. The term rarely appeared in scholarly journal indexes or doctoral dissertation titles before the 1970s. Since 1970, however, several dozen books, nearly two hundred doctoral dissertations, and more than two thousand journal articles and reports have been devoted to this topic. It is not surprising, therefore, that no entries on school governance or politics appear in the fourth edition of the *Encyclopedia of Educational Research* (1969). At that time governance was generally understood to be merely a subtopic of the sociology of education.

History. It is instructive to consider briefly the reasons for the recent emergence of the concept of educational governance. At first glance, scholarly neglect of educational politics during the first six decades of the twentieth century is doubly surprising. Neither education scholars nor political scientists took a serious interest in the topic, despite the fact that school districts are the most numerous governmental units in the country and education commands the lion's share of state and local taxes. Political

scientists with an interest in tax or expenditure policies generally bypassed schools to concentrate on municipal, county, state, or federal governmental activities. And education researchers, despite an obvious interest in factors affecting the quality and quantity of education, almost invariably adopted psychological or administrative perspectives instead of seeking political interpretations of school performance.

The problem cannot be attributed to either a lack of adequate theoretical frameworks or a paucity of effective research techniques. The foundations of political theory were laid well before the beginning of the twentieth century—long before either psychological or organizational analysis of human behavior were adequately formulated. And the techniques of effective political research were being applied to political parties, state governments, and the organization of municipal government long before they were applied to schools.

One might argue that school governance was neglected because neither educators nor political scientists wanted to encroach on territory that seemed to belong to the other. Iannaccone (1967) offers a different and more convincing explanation, however. He argues that educational governance was ideologically defined as "nonpolitical" during the early part of the twentieth century by leaders of the progressive-urban reform movement who were seeking to free the schools from the widespread abuses and distortions of nineteenth-century patronage politics. According to Iannaccone, progressive reformers tended to confuse analysis of the politics *of* education with problems created by politics *in* education. In an effort to get patronage politics *out* of the schools, the reformers adopted the highly effective—and essentially political—strategy of declaring that education policy should be made by professional educators who are politically neutral, highly trained experts in matters of organization and pedagogy. This reform ideology produced a rapid and massive shift in political power away from lay citizens and elected public officials to the hands of professional educators. Thus, according to Iannaccone, the separation of politics and education is itself a highly political act, but one that must be interpreted and supported in nonpolitical terms. The reform ideology was so successful that it led educators and political scientists, as well as the lay public, to believe that politics plays little or no role in shaping educational policy and school operations.

Recent historical scholarship not only supports Iannaccone's general line of argument but suggests that the foundation for this development was laid during the middle years of the nineteenth century. Katz (1975), for example, documents the rise of a public-bureaucratic conception of schools that gradually overpowered conceptions based on private-corporate, philanthropic, and neighborhood-service models. As public bureaucracies, schools were vulnerable to abuse at the hands of urban political machines. As political abuses spread, reform by professional experts looked more and more attractive. Real change, however, awaited the development of public revulsion and outrage at political interference, insensitivity to child welfare, and economic inefficiency. Muckraking journalism during the 1890s created the needed climate of public opinion. The work of Joseph Mayer Rice (1893) focused that opinion on the schools, resulting in sweeping reforms and a virtually complete masking of the political basis of educational policy.

No doubt, the resurgence of widespread and explicit interest in school governance reflects the demise of the progressive reform movement. Cremin's history of the Progressive Education Association describes the transforming impact of progressivism on the schools and highlights its demise as a vital force in American education (Cremin, 1964). The Progressive Education Association collapsed and disappeared in 1955, about a decade before governance became an important issue in educational research. The link between these two events is even closer. An essay by Eliot in 1959 is widely recognized as a major turning point in the development of political interest in education (Eliot, 1959, see also Rosenthal, 1969).

Definition. It is difficult to specify precisely what is meant by the term "governance." The thesaurus of the Educational Resources Information Center (ERIC) offers the following definition: "The policy-making, objective-setting, and exercise of authority in an organization, institution, or agency—includes administrative or management functions to the extent that they relate to the execution of policy and authority" (1980, p. 97). This definition suggests three aspects of schooling encompassed in the concept of governance. First, governance is concerned with the "remote control" of school operations by means of regulatory policies, the establishment of educational goals and objectives, or the exercise of political and administrative authority. Interest in indirect control over education was stimulated in large measure by the recognition that there is a substantial gap between public expectations for schools and their actual performance. In the provocative phrase coined by Weick (1976), school operations have been found to be only "loosely coupled" to the intentions and explicit expectations of citizens, elected officials, and even professional educators. How and why this gap between expectation and performance arises has been a subject of continuing interest to students of school governance.

Second, schools are (and must be) *political* institutions. Although educators may emphasize economic efficiency or client interest in day-to-day school operations, the ultimate source of their authority—and of the educational objectives they are required to pursue—lies in the legal machinery of government. Thus the study of school governance is concerned with how the power and authority of the state are used to organize and control the educational system.

Third, school governance spans the boundary between the political and the managerial or administrative aspects of schooling. As the power of educators to influence, rede-fine, or simply ignore politically formulated policy mandates has become more obvious, scholarly and public concern has expanded from a relatively narrow focus on formal governmental structures to a rather broad interest in governance processes and mechanisms. Thus, the ERIC definition requires that governance analysis include a study of any aspect of administration or management that affects the execution of policy or the establishment of authority.

Early Governance Issues. Throughout the first half of the twentieth century, school governance was largely concerned with developing and supporting a rapidly expanding public school system. "Professionalization," "expansion," and "reorganization" are the central terms in any summary of major issues during this period.

Professionalization was encouraged by the adoption of teacher tenure laws and the promulgation of a doctrine of academic freedom. It was enhanced by the emergence of the school superintendent as chief executive officer and primary policy maker for local districts, and was supported by the rapid expansion of teacher training and licensure programs. Professionalization was a natural expression of the progressive ideology. Progressives believed that governmental services would respond adequately to client interests only if strong executive managers insulated them from political opportunism and corruption. Kaufman (1956) describes this as the domination of the democratic values of representation and participation by organizational commitments to strong executive leadership and neutral technical expertise. Callahan (1962) describes the ideology influencing this bureaucratization and professionalization as a "cult of efficiency," in order to highlight the quasi-religious fervor with which it was pursued during the early decades of this century.

Expansion as an early theme in educational governance touched many facets of school policy and operations. Schooling expanded to cover nearly all children, 6 to 13 years old. As Tyack (1974) reports, over 99 percent of this group were in school by 1960. A rapid expansion also occurred in the number of years children spend in schools. Kindergartens were added to bring 5-year-olds into the system, mandatory attendance ages were raised to keep adolescents in school longer, and massive public commitments were made to the development of low tuition colleges and universities. Curricular expansion was also undertaken during this period. Vocational education, enacted into federal law in 1917, encouraged the schools to become involved in the preparation of craft and technical workers; art, music, hygiene, social studies, and science offerings expanded rapidly; and special education programs were developed to serve both handicapped and gifted children.

Reorganization was the third major governance theme during this period. The most dramatic evidence of this reorganization theme is seen in the reduction of the total number of school districts from 110,000 in 1900 to around 26,000 by 1960. This consolidation of school districts took place while the total population in the country was expanding from 72 million to over 179 million. As a result, the typical school board member who represented 138 people in 1900 had a constituency nearly twenty times larger by 1970. This political reorganization was accompanied by massive changes in the institutional character of public education. School superintendents became chief executives in what is frequently the largest business enterprise in a community. The bureaucratic mechanisms of budgetary control, rational planning, and extensive regulation were embraced and elaborated.

Although professionalization, expansion, and reorganization were the dominant governance themes prior to 1950, a number of other issues lurked beneath the surface, threatening to disrupt the progressive reformers' grand design for what Tyack (1974) calls "the one best system." Religious conflict—between Protestants and Catholics, between fundamentalists and liberals, between sectarian groups and mainstream churches—repeatedly surfaced. It surfaced in arguments over curriculum materials (e.g., creationism versus evolutionary theory); prayers, religious symbols, and holidays; the place of religious instruction in school curricula; and the use of tax money to support educational services for parochial school children. Racial and ethnic strife also threatened the prevailing progressive definition of schooling. Exclusion of minorities, suppression of non-English languages, and systematic inequities in the funding for minority schools were widespread, if not extensively debated, during this period. As the first half of the twentieth century came to an end, another subordinate issue came into view. Suburban migration by the middle class left urban centers crowded with poor and minority citizens attracted to the cities by job opportunities. At the same time, the postwar "baby boom" brought unprecedented pressure on the schools to expand services rapidly. The result was an exacerbation of tensions among competing rural, urban, and suburban interests over scarce tax dollars and teaching talent.

Critical Events of the 1950s. Although serious, these subordinate issues might have been handled fairly comfortably within the progressive framework if three critical events had not occurred during the 1950s. Progressivism was stretched to the breaking point, and school governance was dramatically altered by (1) the *Brown* decisions on school desegregation by the Supreme Court (1954, 1955); (2) the launching of the *Sputnik* satellite by the Russians (1957); and (3) the unionization of teachers in New York (culminating in a strike in 1960). Dramatizing previously unrecognized fundamental issues, these events challenged basic tenets of the progressive vision. Not only were these problems ignored by progressives; they were also exacerbated and made more intransigent by the very ideological commitments that gave progressivism its power.

In the case of court-mandated desegregation, for example, education professionals repeatedly asserted that they were (or at least should be) totally "color blind" in the

management of schools (Crain, 1968; and Kirby, Harris, & Crain, 1973). As a result, school officials resisted court intervention while simultaneously refusing to accept responsibility for the pernicious effects of racial isolation on minority students. It is little wonder, then, that many minority leaders began to equate professionalism with racism in the schools. This issue, which simmered throughout the 1950s, exploded in the 1960s as it merged with the other two basic challenges to an established progressive ideology.

If the race question challenged the political responsibility of school officials, the launching of *Sputnik* raised questions about their competence. The ability of a totalitarian regime with meager resources to achieve a technological breakthrough of such magnitude came as a disquieting shock to the American public and their elected leaders. Could professional educators have been asleep on the job? Were school programs "soft" and students "mollycoddled"? Could it be that educators, freed from political surveillance, had lost their commitment to educational excellence—and drifted into comfortable, self-serving mediocrity?

For its part, the profession responded to *Sputnik* with the proclamation that it "proved" the need for more money and more thoroughgoing professional control over curriculum. Had *Sputnik* been the only crisis, this response might have been convincing, but the professional reaction heightened the sense of crisis without overcoming the underlying fear that professional educators were unable or unwilling to adequately meet public expectations. Thus, while Congress rushed to adopt and fund the National Defense Education Act (1958), it also set in motion a fundamental reexamination of school programs, decision-making processes, and overall effects.

Even before reactions to the *Brown* decisions and the *Sputnik* launching became visible, the third critical event took place. New York City teachers, under the leadership of Albert Shanker, visibly portrayed a growing conflict between teacher and administrative interests within seemingly well-organized school bureaucracies. New York was not the first place where teachers sought and received the right to form unions and bargain collectively with school boards. As early as 1959, Wisconsin had adopted a collective bargaining statute requiring the recognition of teacher unions. The New York strike did, however, attract widespread public attention, making tensions within the education profession unmistakably obvious. Again, the problem was not simply that such tensions were disruptive to the education of children. Teacher unionization became a profound crisis for the schools because it challenged the progressive assumption that educators are politically neutral experts serving their clients, rather than self-interested workers battling over control of the terms and conditions of their employment. Many school board members initially reacted to collective bargaining as a direct challenge to their sovereignty as the sole legitimate agency of school governance. Unionization forced them to recognize as untenable the naive assumption that school policy decisions, formulated in close collaboration with school superintendents, were being enthusiastically and routinely accepted and implemented by teachers and principals. As the progressive vision of a monolithic bureaucracy with a unified command structure proved inadequate, the basic structure of scientific management and professional service delivery was called into question.

New Issues. Reaction to the challenges of the 1950s radically transformed school governance during the 1960s. Three broad clusters of school policy issues surfaced and became the basis for highly visible and frequently volatile school politics throughout the 1960s and 1970s. These three issue clusters are best identified by their major slogans: "equality of educational opportunity," "improving student achievement (or outcomes)," and "access to (or participation in) policy making." Each of these slogans has given symbolic significance to a number of specific policy issues, and each is linked to one of the three catalytic events of the 1950s.

Equality of educational opportunity was, of course, the battle cry of desegregation advocates. The *Brown* decisions were argued and decided on the grounds that racial separation has an inevitably damaging effect on educational opportunities for minority children. And the argument was subsequently expanded to cover *de facto* racial segregation created by either housing patterns or student "tracking" systems within school programs.

Once the equity argument had been successfully applied to racial segregation, it was brought to bear on a whole series of new educational policy issues. The earliest and most substantial expansion of the equity issue involved sweeping reforms in school finance. Armed with research and development work sponsored largely by the Ford Foundation, civil rights advocates and educational reformers pressured state legislatures and the courts to revise school funding systems and to eliminate massive interdistrict inequities in support. These efforts reached their zenith in the *Serrano* decision (1971) in California and the *Cahill* decision (1973) in New Jersey. The movement was seriously and probably premanently weakened by the Supreme Court's *Rodriquez* decision (1973), which effectively declared that school finance inequities are not subject to the protection of the federal Constitution.

In addition to finance, the equity argument was applied to (1) cultural and linguistic minorities (especially Hispanics), (2) due process rights for individual students, (3) women, and (4) students with mental or physical handicaps. The equity rights of each of these groups were addressed by substantial federal policy actions as well as by fairly widespread state and local agitation and accommodation. Equality for minorities was pursued through the adoption of the 1978 amendments to Title VII of the Elementary and Secondary Education Act. The rights of students, addressed in the *Wood* (1975), *Tinker* (1969), and *Goss* (1975) cases before the Supreme Court, stimulated the adoption of a substantial number of student due pro-

cess laws and regulations by states and local school districts. Equity for female students and staff members was encouraged through adoption of Title IX of the Civil Rights Act of 1974. Equality of educational opportunity for mentally and physically handicapped students was endorsed in the adoption of the Education for All Handicapped Children Act (P.L. 94-142) in 1975.

Student achievement issues were stimulated by reaction to the *Sputnik* launching. The earlier emphasis on expanding educational services rapidly gave way to controversy and concern over declining test scores and inadequate reading and writing performance by high school graduates. The student achievement issue stimulated a wave of curriculum revisions. The so-called new math came to symbolize both the goals and the weaknesses of these new programs. Anxiety over achievement also created support for revisions in teacher preparation and licensure laws and curriculum adoption policies, for a back-to-basics movement at the grass roots level, and for widespread adoption of some form of minimum competency testing for high school students.

Achievement issues sometimes merged with equity issues, as when minority leaders demanded new textbooks, better qualified teachers, and greater flexibility in programs for ghetto schools. Just as frequently, however, achievement was seen as diametrically opposed to equity, as when whites resisted desegregation on the grounds that it would damage quality school programs or when minorities argued that tests aimed at assessing quality were culturally biased.

Although stimulated by intraprofessional tensions surrounding collective bargaining, access or participation issues reflect a broad-based reexamination of the presuppositions of the progressive vision. During the 1940s and 1950s, research in the field of mananagement began to challenge central tenets of "scientific management" as well as classical bureaucratic theories. What came to be known as the "human relations" school of management argued that middle managers and workers embrace and pursue organizational goals more fully when they have a voice in selecting and defining them. Moreover, it was argued, centralized decision making in large organizations is not flexible enough to accommodate unique situational factors encountered in different locations throughout the system. As research evidence supporting this human relations approach to management began to accumulate, it fueled demands by teachers for a voice in school management. It also encouraged advocates for parent and citizen groups to believe that participation in school policy making is administratively sound as well as politically appropriate. Hence, by 1970, widespread demands for "administrative decentralization" and "community control" had precipitated major revisions in the administrative structures of many school districts.

A client-participation approach to public policy closely paralleled the emergence of the human relations school of management. A series of federal laws, beginning with the Housing Act of 1949, steadily expanded the concept of citizen rights in the formation of public policy. The high-water mark for this view was reached when "maximum feasible participation of the poor" was required by the Economic Opportunity Act of 1964. Since that time, there has been a continued commitment to increasing the influence of lay citizens in many public policy arenas. The schools have been no exception to this trend. Title I of the Elementary and Secondary Education Act (1965) required that citizen advisory councils be created to review school plans for this program. By 1980 citizen advisory groups became a routine (though not very important) part of most school systems. Several states have even adopted some form of public access or disclosure provisions in their collective bargaining statutes. Florida, for example, has required that all bargaining sessions be open to the public. California law now requires that schools receiving school improvement grants create formal school-site councils, with balanced teacher and community representation to plan for the use of these funds, and New York has required public disclosure of tests used to evaluate student achievement.

Concern with issues of access and participation has stimulated extensive research into the selection and decision-making behavior of local school board members. The behavior of state and federal policy makers has also been subjected to substantial research in recent years. As research into the formation of school policy has matured, however, it has become painfully obvious that school governance is both complex in operation and uncertain in outcomes. It has also become evident that different theoretical frameworks can be used to organize governance research. Moreover, as different frameworks are used to gather and interpret data, dramatically different conclusions are drawn regarding the ability of public schools to guarantee equality of educational opportunity, ensure high levels of achievement, or provide for democratic access to educational goal setting and policy formation. Four essentially different theoretical frameworks—or paradigms—can be identified among the most important of these recent research studies. Distinguishing among these four paradigms greatly facilitates summarizing and interpreting the state of available knowledge about school governance issues.

Four Research Paradigms. Kuhn (1970) used the term "paradigm" to describe the fundamental presuppositions used by scientists in constructing theories of the natural world. He argued that scientists are able to develop meaningful theories only as they adopt the overall perspective (or world view) presupposed by a particular paradigm. In adopting such a perspective, Kuhn argued, scientists are led to concentrate on certain aspects of their experience and to neglect, ignore, or perhaps even repress others.

By applying Kuhn's framework to recent research on school governance, four paradigms can be identified.

These four paradigms, shown in Table 1, can be used to interpret most recent work by both political scientists and sociologists. Comparison among the better studies provides helpful insights into the general direction of recent educational politics research and helps to clarify many of the divergent findings related to equity, achievement, and participation. Each paradigm makes distinctive assumptions about (1) how the basic units of any sociopolitical system are organized or defined; (2) what causal linkages bind these basic units together into a meaningful system of action; (3) what sort of generative metaphor or underlying analogy can be used to elaborate our understanding and interpretation of the overall system; (4) what primary social control mechanism is responsible for guiding actions within the system; and (5) how best to conceptualize the motivations that drive the actions of individuals and groups within the system.

Structural. Research based on the paradigm labeled "Structural" in Table 1 assumes that sociopolitical systems are defined by the formal structures that exist within them. This paradigm is easily recognized in the writings of the American Federalists, who judged the legitimacy of a government by its form. They argued that liberty is guaranteed by properly structuring an internal division of powers among the executive, legislative, and judicial branches of government. Grodzins (1966) offers a sophisticated contemporary interpretation of the structural paradigm. This paradigm has been applied to school district elections by such scholars as Kimbrough (1964), Minar (1966), and Zeigler and Jennings (1974). These researchers have shown that school board policy decisions are strongly influenced both by the way board members are selected and by the nature of their interactions with professional educators and community power groups. Since school elections are generally separated from regular partisan politics, boards are susceptible to domination by either professional interests or informal community elites.

When interpreting the actions of the various governmental subunits with formal responsibility for shaping educational policy, structural theorists assume that political action springs directly from conflicts of interest among individuals and groups competing for access to and control over scarce and valued goods in society. They view society as a kind of machine, in which every part of the social structure works in accordance with its own intrinsic character and is linked with others in a dynamic balance of tension and conflict. Hence, for this paradigm, politics is equated with the exercise of power, and individuals are assumed to pursue various interests with a level of intensity directly proportional to the priority they have attached to each different interest.

In an essay widely recognized as the beginning of contemporary political interest in education, Eliot (1959) illustrates possible uses for each of the four paradigms described in Table 1. He began the first of four proposals for expanding political research with the reminder that,

TABLE 1. *Characteristics of the four school governance paradigms*

| | Paradigms | | | |
	Structural	Functional	Interaction	Exchange
Basic units	Formal structures	Functional structures	Persons acting purposefully	Agents acting rationally
Assumed causal linkage	Conflicts of interest	Cooperative goal pursuits	Creation of symbolic cultures	Bargaining over scarce valuables
Underlying analogy	A machine	An organism	A conversation	A marketplace
Primary control mechanism	Power	Authority	Persuasion	Exchange
Motive force for action	Interest (priority)	Need (prerequisite)	Meaning (felt significance)	Desire (utility)

in public education, "the formal structure is based on state constitutions and statutes" (Eliot, 1959, p. 1032). In this section of his essay he formulated a structural interpretation of school politics, noting the ways in which conflicts between local and state agencies or between lay and professional interests are given form and direction by these structural arrangements. Having set out this structural analysis, he then called for researchers to undertake studies of the institutions that control educational policy by examining the "voting behavior, ideological predispositions, the clash of interests, decision-making, and the impact of individuals" (p. 1035). Such terms capture effectively the central thrust of all structural theories: politics is identified with conflict, and governance is equated with shaping and controlling conflicts so that they are kept within acceptable bounds.

Functional. Research based on the functional paradigm also involves close scrutiny of social structures. In this case, however, structures are recognized by their functional contributions to sociopolitical goals, rather than by their formal specification in constitutions or statutes. Functional theories emphasize collaborative and cooperative aspects of political behavior rather than conflicts of interest. Theorists adopting this paradigm envision social systems as being like organisms. Stabilizing and goal-directed organismic processes are assumed to arise naturally as individuals and groups interact with each other in order to fulfill mutual needs. Rather than power, functional theories emphasize the importance of social authority. They highlight the fact that governments are created out of the mutual consent of the governed in order to realize goals that require cooperative action.

Functionalist conceptions of political action include both the positive view of cooperation set forth by theorists such as Parsons (1951) and Almond and Powell (1966), and the more negative view set forth by analysts like Ag-

ger, Goldrich, and Swanson (1964) and Koerner (1968). Iannaccone's analysis (1967) of state politics and Thomas's interpretation (1975) of federal policy making both draw upon the functional paradigm.

Interaction. Research based on the interaction paradigm looks at individual actors rather than the structural arrangements that link them together. Interactionist theories assume that groups of individuals are brought together through the creation of cultural symbols and value systems. Groups sharing a common set of cultural meanings interact with each other and with members of other groups on the basis of these shared symbolic meanings.

Theorists utilizing the interaction paradigm presume that social action systems are analogous to conversations. It is impossible to predict the future course of a conversation without knowing the perceptual frameworks and basic value systems of the participants. Actions by one person stimulate reactions from another, but those reactions depend on how the second person interprets the gestures of the first and what purposes he or she maintains at the time. Interaction theories emphasize the importance of persuasion as a control mechanism. Through symbolic communication, individuals acquire a system of meanings and are motivated to act in accordance with the "felt significance" of these meanings.

Lutz and Iannaccone (1978) elaborate an interaction theory of local school governance that they call a "dissatisfaction" theory of democracy. They argue that school district politics are deeply influenced by the ideologies and value systems of school district citizens. Mitchell and Badarak (1977), Iannaccone and Lutz (1970), and Pois (1964) represent other examples of research using the interaction paradigm. Mitchell's work (1981) on legislative decision making offers a detailed interactionist paradigm for interpreting the complexities of state legislative politics.

TABLE 2. *How the four paradigms interpret contemporary school governance issues*

| | Paradigms | | | |
	Structural	Functional	Interaction	Exchange
Assessing legitimacy of governance systems	Adequate and informed competition	Appropriate action	Citizen satisfaction	Payoff equity
Criteria of adequate democratic legitimacy	Proper distribution/ separation of powers	Proper response to issues	Political quiescence	Fair exchange
Mechanisms for resolving issues	Assignment to proper agency	Value-based debate/ agreement	Replacing or redirecting policy makers	Manipulation of incentives
Pivotal issues addressed	Equality of opportunity	Achievement of results	Participation and access	Freedom of choice

Exchange. Research based on the exchange paradigm shares in common with interactionist theories an emphasis on the importance of individual actors. Where the interactionist emphasizes purposeful action, however, exchange theorists insist that actions are based on some form of rational cost-benefit calculation. Some exchange theorists assume that all important social exchange involves an identifiable currency or token system. Others come closer to the interactionists by accepting psychological rewards and incentives as media of exchange.

Whatever the exchange medium, however, exchange theorists envision social and political action as a metter of bargaining over scarce and valued goods. The exchanges are competitive in that all of the participants are motivated to improve their own "net worth" by bartering less valuable for more valuable tokens. Thus the marketplace is seen as the underlying metaphor in this paradigm; individual desires and utility functions are assumed to control the overall pattern of social exchange. Dahl's classic study (1961) of school policy formation in New Haven illustrates effective use of the exchange paradigm. And House's work (1974) on the politics of educational innovation applies the exchange framework to the behavior of educators and school district citizens.

When Eliot (1959) examined the pluralistic pressure groups affecting school policy, he implicitly embraced the exchange paradigm. He identified the political resources of lay groups and professional educators and described differences in how they interact in the local, state, and federal policy-making arenas. He summarized the relationship by saying, "As to what should be taught, generally the professionals are dominant." This tendency, he argued, is probably appropriate, because "their financial dependence on public approval makes them somewhat responsive to reasonable public demands" (p. 1048). That is, an exchange of professional service for financial support creates a policy system with shared control.

Interpretation of contemporary governance issues. As indicated in Table 2, each of the four paradigms directs attention to different aspects of school governance.The legitimacy of any particular governance system is viewed differently by theorists utilizing the different paradigms. Structural analysts, for example, assess legitimacy by asking if there are (1) adequate and informed competition among citizens for control of formal governance structures, and (2) if there is a proper distribution or separation of powers among the various formal structures. If, as Zeigler and Jennings (1974) assert, there is little competition for seats on the local school board, the winning candidates are poorly informed, and most decisions are preempted by the school superintendent or the state legislature, then one must conclude that school boards are not structurally legitimate expressions of democratic governance.

By contrast, functional theorists assess the legitimacy of particular governance mechanisms in terms of (1) whether the governing agency takes necessary and appropriate actions to achieve collective goals, (2) whether the mechanisms respond directly to the demands made by citizen or client groups. If, as the research reported by Wirt (1975) suggests, school boards are largely controlled by brute social forces, and if they resist explicit demands for policy change made by citizen groups and are unable to change the performance of professional educators significantly, we can conclude that they are not functionally legitimate vehicles for democratic governance.

In contrast to the generally negative conclusions regarding school board legitimacy growing out of structural and functional research, interaction and exchange theorists see school boards as relatively legitimate governance mechanisms. Lutz and Iannaccone (1978), for example, argue that school board legitimacy depends on citizen satisfaction and political quiesence. They argue that dissatisfied citizen groups can and do dramatically alter school board governance systems. And using an exchange theory, Dahl

(1961) argues that, despite substantial variations in the political resources of different citizen groups, school governance systems are forced to provide equitable payoffs to most citizens through explicit exchanges of political support for specific policy decisions.

As indicated in Table 2, each of the four political research paradigms focuses on a different mechanism for resolving school governance issues. Hence each is compatible with a different conception of the most important issues to be resolved.

Structural analysts assume that issues are to be resolved by having them assigned to the proper formal agency for decision. Thus they emphasize the importance of handling local education issues at the local level and of separating legislative from executive and judicial questions. This emphasis on turning issues over to the proper authorities for action leads structuralists to be most sensitive to questions regarding the protection of minority interests. If the agency with proper jurisdiction cannot or will not provide equal treatment, structualists seek the development of new structures with adequate power to intervene on behalf of disadvantaged citizens. It is not surprising, therefore, that equity issues have stimulated direct involvement of federal agencies in many formerly local school district decisions.

Functionalist theories call attention to political deliberation and debate as vehicles for resolving governance issues. Because society's goals, rather than group conflicts, are seen as the primary focus of governance in this paradigm, theorists using it are much more likely to study issues related to student achievement. By studying factors correlated with student achievement, functionalist researchers hope to provide information needed to guide political debates and shape appropriate responses.

The interaction paradigm calls attention to the importance of altering the beliefs and commitments of formal policy makers in resolving governance issues (often by replacing key personnel). From the interactionist perspective, official policy makers incorporate the values and beliefs of constituents and/or clients by creating systems of open access and communication. Thus, it is not surprising that interactionist theories are most often used to interpret the recent participation issues in education.

Exchange theories emphasize the importance of manipulating incentive systems in order to resolve political issues. By changing who gets what (and when they get it), exchange theorists argue, we can reduce political conflict and realize "the greatest good for the greatest number" of citizens. Such a point of view is expressly endorsed in recent proposals for a system of educational vouchers (Coons & Sugarman, 1978) and tuition tax credits. Exchange theories may well come to dominate education policy during the 1980s.

Summary. Research on school governance can be interpreted from two different perspectives. First, dramatic redefinition of the central issues in the politics of education has occurred as a result of reactions to the *Brown* decisions,

the *Sputnik* launching, and the New York teacher strike. Equality of educational opportunity, excellence in student achievement, and participation in school policy formation have emerged as the most important contemporary school governance issues because of these three events. Second, four different paradigms have been used to design and interpret most recent political research in education. An examination of how these paradigms are applied to school governance issues reveals that each concentrates attention on a different set of governance issues and highlights different strategies for their resolution.

Douglas E. Mitchell

See also Collective Negotiations; Federal Influence on Education; Judicial Decisions; Legislation; Local Influences on Education; School Boards; State Influences on Education.

REFERENCES

Agger, R. E.; Goldrich, D.; & Swanson, B. E. *The Rulers and the Ruled: Political Power and Impotence in American Communities.* New York: Wiley, 1964.

Almond, G. A., & Powell, G. B. *Comparative Politics: A Developmental Approach.* Boston: Little, Brown, 1966.

Brown v. Board of Education, 347 U.S. 483 (1954).

Brown v. Board of Education, 349 U.S. 294 (1955).

Callahan, R. E. *Education and the Cult of Efficiency* Chicago: University of Chicago Press, 1962.

Coons, J. E., & Sugarman, S. D. *Education by Choice: The Case for Family Control.* Berkeley: University of California Press, 1978.

Crain, R. *The Politics of School Desegregation: Comparative Case Studies of Community Structure and Policy-making.* Chicago: Aldine, 1968.

Cremin, L. A. *The Transformation of the School.* New York: Random House, Vintage Books, 1964.

Dahl, R. *Who Governs? Democracy and Power in an American City.* New Haven, Conn.: Yale University Press, 1961.

Educational Resources Information Center. *Thesaurus of ERIC Descriptors.* Phoenix, Ariz.: Oryx Press, 1980.

Eliot, T. Toward an understanding of public school politics. *American Political Science Review,* 1959, *52,* 1032–1051.

Goss v. Lopez, 419 U.S. 565 (1974).

Grodzins, M. *The American System: A New View of Government in the United States.* Chicago: Rand McNally, 1966.

House, E. *The Politics of Educational Innovation.* Berkeley, Calif.: McCutchan, 1974.

Iannaccone, L. *Politics in Education.* New York: Center for Applied Research on Education, 1967.

Iannaccone, L., & Lutz, F. W. *Politics, Power, and Policy.* Columbus, Ohio: Merrill, 1970.

Katz, M. B. *Class, Bureaucracy, and Schools.* New York: Praeger, 1975.

Kaufman, H. Emerging conflicts in the doctrine of public administration. *American Political Science Review,* 1956, *50*(4), 1057–1073.

Kimbrough, R. *Political Power and Educational Decision-making.* Chicago: Rand McNally, 1964.

Kirby, D. J.; Harris, T. R.; & Crain, R. L. *Political Strategies in Northern School Desegregation.* Lexington, Mass.: Lexington Books, 1973.

Koerner, J. D. *Who Controls American Education? A Guide for Laymen.* Boston: Beacon Press, 1968.

Kuhn, T. *The Structure of Scientific Revolutions* (2nd ed.). Chicago: University of Chicago Press, 1970.

Lutz, F. & Iannaccone, L. *Public Participation in Local School Districts.* Lexington, Mass.: Heath, 1978.

Minar, D. The community basis of conflict in school systems politics. *American Sociological Review,* 1966, *31*(6), 822–835.

Mitchell, D. E. *Shaping Legislative Decisions: Education Policy and the Social Sciences.* Lexington, Mass.: Heath, 1981.

Mitchell, D. E., & Badarak, G. Political ideology and school board politics. *Urban Education,* 1977 *12*(1), 55–83.

Parsons, T. *The Social System.* Glencoe, Ill.: Free Press, 1951.

Pois, J. *The School Board Crisis: A Chicago Case Study.* Chicago: Educational Methods, 1964.

Rice, J. M. *The Public School System and the United States.* New York: Century, 1893.

Robinson v. *Cahill,* 62 N.J. 473 303A 2d 273 (1973).

Rosenthal, A. (Ed) *Governing Education: A Reader on Politics, Power, and Public School Policy.* Garden City, N.Y.: Doubleday, 1969.

San Antonio Independent School District et al. v. *Rodriquez et al.,* 411 U.S. 1 (1973).

Serrano v. *Priest,* 5 Cal. 3d 584, 487 P. 2d 1241 (1971).

Thomas, N. C. *Education in National Politics.* New York: McKay, 1975.

Tinker v. *Des Moines Community School District #21,* 393 U.S. 503, 89 S. Ct. 733, 21 L. Ed 2d F31 (1969).

Tyack, D. *The One Best System.* Cambridge, Mass.: Harvard University Press, 1974.

Weick, K. Educational organizations as loosely coupled systems. *Administrative Science Quarterly,* 1976, *21*, 1–19.

Wirt, F. (Ed). *The Polity of the School: A New Research in Educational Politics.* Lexington, Mass.: Lexington Books, 1975.

Wood v. *Strickland,* 420 U.S. 308 (1975).

Zeigler, L. H.; Jennings, M. K.; with Peak, G. W. *Governing American Schools.* North Scituate, Mass.: Duxbury Press, 1974.

GRADING PRACTICES

See Marking Systems; Undergraduate Instruction.

GRADUATE EDUCATION

When Bernard Berelson (1960) wrote his book on the subject, graduate education in the United States was about eighty-five years old. By now its history covers more than one hundred years. The National Research Council (NRC, 1978) of the National Academy of Sciences published a volume entitled *A Century of Doctorates* that provides an exhaustive analysis of the doctoral (Ph.D.) population during the first one hundred years of graduate education in this country.

Among other publications that examine the history of graduate education are *The Beginnings of Graduate Education in America* (Storr, 1954) and *Academic Degree Structures: Innovative Approaches* (Spurr, 1970).

In his *Prologue-Reminiscences-Epilogue* of the proceedings of the twentieth annual meeting of the Council of Graduate Schools in the United States, Arlt (1981) summarizes the origins of graduate education in the United States by giving the following highlights. The first American Ph.D. was awarded by Yale University in 1861; the first true graduate school was established at Johns Hopkins University in 1876, followed by graduate schools at Columbia, Chicago, and California. To quote from Arlt: "In the next two decades these five universities considered themselves as the custodians of the value of the Ph.D. degree and the course of study that led to it" (p. 2). By 1900 nine additional universities were engaged in graduate education in a major way: Harvard, Pennsylvania, Princeton, Clark, Cornell, Catholic University, Stanford, Michigan, and Wisconsin. In 1900 this group of fourteen universities awarded approximately 90 percent of all doctoral degrees. Another 110 institutions were engaged in master's degree education, with one-third of them committed to doctoral study.

A gradual expansion of graduate education occurred in the first half of the 1900s. However, a dramatic change occurred in the 1960s; graduate education experienced unprecedented growth in terms of enrollments, graduate degrees awarded, and level of research participation. Approximately 75,000 master's degrees and 10,000 doctorates were awarded in 1960; the numbers for 1970 are 230,000 master's degrees and 32,000 doctorates!

The Master's Degree.   Two characteristics of the master's degree that have remained constant throughout its history are change and durability. While the value and meaning of the degree have been debated, it is an academic standard that has commanded greater or lesser respect for 800 years. The word "master" comes from the Latin *magister,* which means "teacher," and from the time of its origin the master's degree has been strongly associated with pedagogy.

Perennial controversies and questions surround this degree. The intellectual worth of a given master's degree can be ascertained only by consulting the holder's undergraduate transcript and graduate school record. There is no consensus on the experiences that a master's degree program should offer; there is no agreement on the skills and abilities that a person who has completed a master's degree should be expected to have.

The first Master of Arts was granted at the University of Paris in the twelfth century. It was the highest degree offered by the arts faculty, and it served as a credential for becoming a member of that faculty. The holder could also study toward a doctorate in medicine, law, or theology.

Gradually the master's degree fell into disuse in continental Europe or was granted as an adjunct to the baccalaureate with little or no additional scholarly labor. As the highest earned degree in England and subsequently in America, it retained greater prestige for a time. In 1642, when Harvard graduated its first class, the master's degree indicated rigorous academic achievement—three years of study beyond the bachelor's level. However, by the early nineteenth century the master's degree at Harvard, as well as at all other universities in the United States, had diminished in significance.

The University of Michigan is often credited with reviving the master's degree. In 1858 its regents resolved that the master's degree be conferred on holders of a baccalaureate, provided that they pursued two courses each semester for one year, passed an examination in at least three of the studies, and presented a thesis. The state universities of North Carolina and Georgia adopted these requirements soon thereafter. By the beginning of the twentieth century, variations on these requirements characterized master's degree programs in most institutions.

The master's degree achieved its own identity, separate and apart from that of the doctorate, when colleges and universities began to expand their offerings in education and to admit women to graduate study. In 1939 it was estimated that three-fourths of liberal arts master's degrees were earned by public school teachers. During the next two decades, the growth of master's degree education was clearly related to the growth of primary and secondary education.

The neglected state of the master's degree was addressed at the first annual meeting of the Council of Graduate Schools in the United States, held in December 1961.

At the council's annual meetings throughout the early 1960s speakers proposed ways to return the master's degree to a respected level of learning. Most programs were directed toward education and training of teachers for junior colleges.

By the mid-1960s, the master's degree was coming to be regarded as the final degree in fields other than education. The "practitioner" master's degree was the fully acceptable credential for social work (Master of Social Work), planning (Master of Urban Planning), and business (Master of Business Administration). Groups and associations within these professions exercised considerable influence over requirements as they shaped master's degree programs according to their concept of what individuals who practice these professions should know.

During the late 1960s and early 1970s, the "New Left" claimed that graduate schools were guilty of processing students for a dehumanizing technological system. This criticism fostered new expressions of concern about social problems by all sectors of higher education. Some new master's degree programs were intended specifically to address such problems as urban studies, ecology and environmental studies, black studies, and women's studies. Because these were new disciplines, sometimes fashioned from old ones using new terminology, they tended to refuel the long-standing controversy about "quality" and master's-level education. In 1975 the Council of Graduate Schools in the United States issued a policy statement, entitled "The Master's Degree," that set forth the quality standards by which graduate programs leading to master's degrees may be judged.

The final report of the National Board on Graduate Education (NBGE, 1975) commented on master's degree graduate education as follows: "Master's level work with an applied, career-oriented focus is likely to increase. . . . Many of the innovations in graduate education should be attempted initially at the master's level and thus the degree warrants a resurgence of attention (p. 59).

The National Center for Education Statistics of the U.S. Department of Education, which has conducted surveys annually since 1947/48 on the number of degrees conferred by U.S. colleges and universities by level of degree (bachelor's, master's, and doctoral), sex of student, and major field of study, reports in (1980) that the number of master's degrees conferred in the United States in the last two decades rose rapidly, peaking in 1976 and 1977. During the twelve months ending June 30, 1978, the number of master's degrees awarded was 311,700 compared with 317,200 in 1976/77. The small decrease (1.7 percent) might be attributable to the decline in degrees conferred in the field of education; 7,800 fewer master's degrees were conferred in the field of education in 1977/78. A comparison of the number of master's degrees conferred upon men and women in selected fields in the United States in 1972/73 and 1977/78 is shown in Table 1.

The Doctoral Degree. Among the doctoral degrees associated with graduate education, the Doctor of Philosophy (Ph.D.) is dominant. Other doctoral degrees are awarded in graduate education; for the most part, they are professionally oriented, as their titles suggest. Among them are Doctor of Education (Ed.D.), Doctor of Business Administration (D.B.A.), Doctor of Social Work (D.S.W.), Doctor of Nursing (D.N.), and Doctor of Psychology (D.Psych.). In the United States, the Doctor of Science (D.S.) is usually awarded as an honorary degree.

About 100 years ago, in the late 1870s, the number of Ph.D.'s awarded was about 40; by 1900 the figure was 300; by 1925 it was 1,200; and in the early 1970s the number ranged between 33,000 and 34,000. These facts, together with a wealth of other information, are presented in a volume entitled *A Century of Doctorates—Data Analyses of Growth and Change,* a report from the Board on Human Resource Data Analyses of the Commission on Human Resources of the NRC (NRC, 1978). This volume is the seventh in a series of publications by the National Academy of Sciences having to do with doctorates granted in the United States, the baccalaureate origins of the doctorate recipients, and some of their educational and employment characteristics. (The term "Ph.D." is used generically in the report and refers to all third-level (doctoral) degrees except the M.S., D.D.S., D.V.M., and J.D.). It is a comprehensive compilation of data and analyses of the Ph.D. population in the United States.

In the early 1960s a new doctoral degree, the Doctor of Arts (D.A.), was introduced for "a doctoral program of at least three years in length which emphasizes in its recruitment and requirements the preparation for a career as college teacher and which accepts an expository thesis

TABLE 1. *Master's degrees conferred upon men and women in selected fields: United States, 1972/73 and 1977/78*

1972/73		1977/78	
Men	*Women*	*Men*	*Women*
Education 28.5%	Education 56.2%	Business and management 25.0%	Education 53.4%
		Education 23.7%	
Business and management 19.2%			
	Library science 5.5%		Health professions 6.7%
Engineering 10.6%		Engineering 9.6%	
	Public affairs and services 4.7%		Public affairs and services 6.3%
Social sciences 8.1%		Public affairs and services 6.5%	
	English and literature 4.5%		Business and management 5.4%
Public affairs and services 3.8%		Social sciences 6.1%	
	Health professions 4.4%		Library science 3.7%
All other fields 29.8%		All other fields 29.1%	
	All other fields 24.7%		All other fields 24.5%

SOURCE: U.S. Department of Education, National Center of Education Statistics, *Digest of Education Statistics, 1980.*

in lieu of the conventional research dissertation" Spurr (1970, p. 145).

The first D.A. programs were offered in mathematics, English, history, and the fine arts at Carnegie-Mellon University in 1967. Encouragement for the development of additional programs was provided by grants from the Carnegie Corporation. Several institutions developed D.A. programs; however, the majority were not attracted to this new degree. Most argued that Ph.D. programs accomplished what the D.A. degree was designed to accomplish. Several comprehensive studies have been published on the D.A., for example, *Proceedings of the Wingspread Conference on the Doctor of Arts Degree* (Eastman, 1970) and publications by Dressel and Thompson (1974, 1977, 1978).

The Ph.D. degree has been the subject of considerable study as an increasing number of institutions have offered programs leading to this degree and the environment for learning has changed.

In 1964 the Association of Graduate Schools of the Association of American Universities, and the Council of Graduate Schools in the United States (CGS) issued a statement on "The Doctor of Philosophy Degree." The statement describes the characteristics of a good-quality program.

More recently, the CGS has issued two documents that describe characteristics of quality doctoral programs: *The Doctor of Philosophy Degree* (CGS, 1977) and *Requirements for the Ph.D.* (CGS, 1979).

More than 300 institutions are regionally accredited in the United States to award the Ph.D. The number of doctoral degrees awarded since 1875, at five-year intervals through 1975, is shown in Table 2. Since 1975 the number of Ph.D.'s conferred has decreased; in 1980 approximately 31,000 were granted.

In addition to changes in the total population of doctor-

ate holders, there has been a shift in the numbers of Ph.D. recipients within major subject areas. The number of doctorates awarded in the humanities has decreased dramatically since 1974. Fewer doctorates are being awarded in physical sciences and engineering while the number of Ph.D.'s in social sciences and education has increased slightly.

The low representation of minority group members in graduate education, particularly of blacks at the doctoral level, is a continuing problem. During the last several years there has been little increase in the number of blacks holding Ph.D.'s, in the sciences and in engineering.

Postdoctoral Education. An important form of education for many talented scientists and engineers is postdoctoral education. Postdoctoral appointments made by universities, serve as a period of transition between the completion of the Ph.D. and entrance into a professional career in research. This format of concentrated effort and experience in advanced research has been highly successful in advancing knowledge as well as providing an environment that encourages the development of talent. In 1977 there were approximately 14,000 postdoctoral students in U.S. universities. Demographic circumstances in graduate education, as well as major constraints on funding of research and development projects, have reduced postdoctoral opportunities.

Graduate Schools. The governance of graduate education at an institution is shared by the academic departments and interdepartmental committees, on the one hand, and the graduate faculty and a chief graduate administrative officer, on the other. The title of Dean of the Graduate School was used almost exclusively for the chief graduate administrative officer in the first half of this century. Today various alternative titles are employed, such

TABLE 2. *Doctorates granted annually by U.S. universities, 1875–1974, at five-year intervals*

Year	Ph.D. total	Year	Ph.D. total
1875	23	1935	2,529
1880	54	1940	3,277
1885	77	1945	1,634
1890	149	1950	6,535
1895	272	1955	8,905
1900	382	1960	9,998
1905	369	1965	17,110
1910	443	1970	31,489
1915	611	1975	33,146
1920	562	1975	33,146
1925	1,206	1980	30,982
1930	2,075		

as Vice President for Graduate Studies and Research, Dean for Graduate Studies and Research, Coordinator of Graduate Education, and others. The graduate dean (or the chief graduate administrative officer, by whatever title) usually has the responsibility for supervising the administration of all graduate programs in the institution and maintaining the central office for information on all matters of graduate education. In many, but not all, institutions, the chief graduate administrative officer is also responsible for the research program and, hence, has an expanded title such as Vice President for Graduate Studies and Research.

The chief graduate school officer. The chief graduate school officer is in a strategic leadership position in which the responsibilities are broad and comprehensive. Some of the duties and responsibilities that characterize the office and illustrate the central role performed by its holder are the following: participation on major university committees concerned with resources; admission of students and certification of their progress, including completion of degree requirements; program initiation, consolidation, and termination; program evaluation and governance; and representation of the graduate school at meetings of professional associations.

The structure of graduate education. The CGS has summarized the patterns of administrative organization for graduate education in universities and colleges (CGS, 1981a) as shown in Figure 1. The predominant format of organization is one that centralizes the authority in a graduate school (or graduate studies) office. A few institutions have elected to decentralize the administration to the various colleges or schools of the institution. Examples A–D in Figure 1 show various administrative arrangements of the former type, while example E illustrates a decentralized scheme. Here authority and administrative control are decentralized to the deans of colleges and schools.

A highly decentralized administrative structure for graduate education has several potential weaknesses. For example, programs may become isolated from each other; an institutional data base for all of graduate education is more difficult to maintain; standards of quality are more likely to fluctuate; and representation of graduate education to the president's office is fractionated.

Changes in the scope and character of graduate education in the decades ahead are likely to encourage changes in organization and administration.

An Agenda for Graduate Education. At the beginning of the 1980s, graduate education finds itself in an uncertain and changing environment. The steady increase in enrollment by traditional full-time students is over. Federal support for graduate students, in terms of fellowships and traineeships, has all but disappeared. New faculty positions are few and far between, and almost nonexistent in some disciplines.

According to Storr (1953), it was discontent with the state of American colleges that led to the opening of the country's first graduate schools. In those days, critics claimed that higher education was too conservative and was out of step with the spirit of the age. Storr's work is a reminder that graduate education is embedded in its times, rather than standing apart from them. Detachment is critical to scholarly work—but scholarly work is done in a context, a period of history that may repress or encourage it but always influences it.

William D. McElroy, former chancellor of the University of California, San Diego, in his keynote address to the eighteenth annual meeting of CGS, stated that "our society, and indeed the world, requires more, not less, of the highest quality people from our graduate schools." The CGS has identified five objectives as important goals for graduate education in the decades ahead: (1) expansion of diversity in graduate education and research; (2) continued growth of the nation's knowledge capital through research and graduate education; (3) access to opportunity for all qualified people; (4) development of effective partnerships with government and industry; and (5) improvement of the quality of graduate programs, together with development of a more objective methodology to assess the quality of programs.

Reviews of Graduate Education. A comprehensive analysis of graduate education was undertaken in 1971 when the Conference Board of Associated Research Councils (the American Council on Education, the Social Science Research Council, the American Council of Learned Societies, and the National Research Council) established the National Board on Graduate Education. The board published a series of reports between 1972 and 1976 that reviewed and assessed aspects of graduate education: *Graduate Education: Purposes, Problems, and Potential* (NBGE, 1972); *Doctorate Manpower Forecasts and Policy* (NBGE, 1973); *Federal Policy Alternatives toward Graduate Education* (NBGE, 1974); *Science Development, University Development, and the Federal Government* (NBGE, 1975); *Outlook and Opportunities for Graduate*

742 GRADUATE EDUCATION

FIGURE 1. *Examples of organization and administration of graduate education in U.S. universities and colleges*

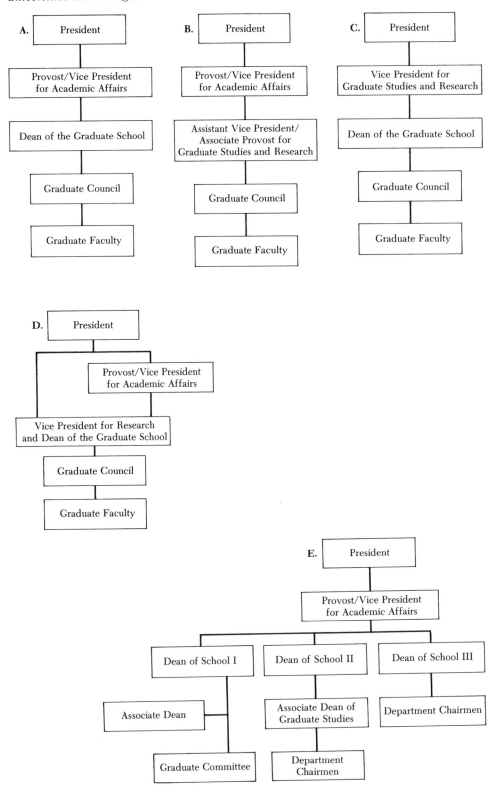

SOURCE: Council of Graduate Schools in the United States, 1981a.

Education (NBGE, 1975); and *Minority Group Participation in Graduate Education* (NBGE, 1976).

An extensive report on the philosophy and future of graduate education (Frankena, 1978) is contained in a report from an international conference on this subject held at the University of Michigan.

Michael J. Pelczar, Jr.

See also Higher Education; History and Philosophy of Higher Education; Organization and Administration of Higher Education; Professions Education.

REFERENCES

Arlt, G. O. *The First Twenty Years: Prologue—Reminiscences—Epilogue* (Proceedings of the twentieth annual meeting of The Council of Graduate Schools in the U.S.). Washington, D.C.: The Council, 1981.

Berelson, B. *Graduate Education in the United States.* New York: McGraw-Hill, 1960.

Council of Graduate Schools in the United States. *The Master's Degree.* Washington, D.C.: The Council, 1975.

Council of Graduate Schools in the United States. *The Doctor of Philosophy Degree.* Washington, D.C.: The Council, 1977. (ERIC Document Reproduction Service No. ED 153 546)

Council of Graduate Schools in the United States. *Requirements for the Ph.D.* Washington, D.C.: The Council, 1979. (ERIC Document Reproduction Service No. ED 187 280)

Council of Graduate Schools in the United States. *The Organization and Administration of Graduate Schools in the U.S.* Washington, D.C.: The Council, 1981. (a)

Council of Graduate Schools in the United States. *Proceedings of the Annual Meetings* (Vol. 20). Washington, D.C.: The Council, 1981. (b)

Dressel, P. L., & Thompson, M. M. College teaching: Improvement by degrees. *American College Testing Program Monograph,* 1974, *13.*

Dressel, P. L., & Thompson, M. M. *A Degree for College Teachers. The Doctor of Arts.* Berkeley, Calif.: Carnegie Council on Policy Studies in Higher Education, 1977.

Dressel, P. L., & Thompson, M. M. The doctor of arts: A decade of development, 1966–1977. *Journal of Higher Education,* 1978, *49,* 329–336.

Eastman, A. M. *Proceedings of the Wingspread Conference on the Doctor of Arts Degree.* Washington, D.C.: Council of Graduate Schools in the U.S., 1970. (ERIC Document Reproduction Service No. ED 055 089)

Frankena, W. K. *The Philosophy and Future of Graduate Education.* Ann Arbor: University of Michigan Press, 1978.

National Board on Graduate Education. *Graduate Education: Purposes, Problems, and Potential.* Washington, D.C.: National Academy of Sciences, November 1972. (ERIC Document Reproduction Service No. ED 070 413)

National Board on Graduate Education. *Doctorate Manpower Forecasts and Policy.* Washington, D.C.: National Academy of Sciences, November 1973. (ERIC Document Reproduction Service No. ED 084 983)

National Board on Graduate Education. *Federal Policy Alternatives toward Graduate Education.* Washington, D.C.: National Academy of Sciences, March 1974. (ERIC Document Reproduction Service No. ED 089 599)

National Board on Graduate Education. *Science Development, University Development, and the Federal Government.* Washington, D.C.: National Academy of Sciences, June 1975. (ERIC Document Reproduction Service No. ED 108 968)

National Board on Graduate Education. *Outlook and Opportunities for Graduate Education.* Washington, D.C.: National Academy of Sciences, December 1975. (ERIC Document Reproduction Service No ED 199 568)

National Board on Graduate Education. *Minority Group Participation in Graduate Education.* Washington, D.C.: National Academy of Sciences, 1976. (ERIC Document Reproduction Service No. ED 125 494)

National Center for Education Statistics. *Digest of Education Statistics.* Washington, D.C.: U.S. Government Printing Office, 1980. (ERIC Document Reproduction Service No. ED 172 458)

National Research Council, Commission on Human Resources, Board on Human-Resource Data and Analyses. *A Century of Doctorates.* Washington, D.C.: National Academy of Sciences, 1978. (ERIC Document Reproduction Service No. ED 156 064)

Spurr, S. H. *Academic Degree Structures: Innovative Approaches.* New York: McGraw-Hill, 1970.

Storr, R. J. *The Beginnings of Graduate Education in America.* Chicago: University of Chicago Press, 1953.

U.S. Department of Health, Education, and Welfare, National Center for Education Statistics. *Earned Degrees Conferred, 1977–78.* Washington, D.C., 1980.

GROUP PROCESSES

A group that gets things done is more than a mere collection of individuals. In this article, we begin by telling what we mean by a "group." Second, we discuss "influence," which we view as the medium through which work gets done and norms are maintained. Third, we turn to "roles and expectations," through which we anticipate the behavior of others in groups. Fourth, we turn to a particularly important pattern of influence—"cooperation"—and describe its effects and uses in classrooms and among faculty. Fifth, we turn to a particularly important task for groups—"solving problems." Sixth, we discuss "friendship" and some of its effects in classrooms. Seventh, because effective groups cannot be brought into being by fiat, nor do they appear full-blown from the void, we describe the "stages of their development." Finally, we list some books that have had special importance in the "history" of research on groups in the United States. As research goes on, researchers lose interest in some features of life in groups and become interested in others. Sometimes the shift is faddish, but more often, we think, it occurs because researchers find new conceptions of how groups function that are more useful than the older ones. We have chosen topics for this article that have been, we think, the important lines of research during the last decade.

Groups. More and more researchers are coming to think of groups as social systems—as "living systems," to use Miller's phrase (1978). Living systems show interdependence among their parts and act with purpose. By a "group," we mean a living system in which (1) there is more than one individual (most working groups contain more than two or three; (2) members are face to face, or can be; (3) every member can communicate with every other without much trouble; and (4) if there is a leader, authority, or boss (there need not always be one), there are no subleaders, authorities, or bosses. If there are subgroups with subleaders, we would speak of the system as an "organization," even though it might be a small one. In this article, of course, we shall be dealing mostly with groups that occur in schools. And because this is an article on happenings within groups, we shall say little about relations between groups and nothing about the interactions that arise in complex organizations.

The first important feature of a group is the interdependence of its members. They depend on one another to accomplish their task. The members of a curriculum committee depend on one another in generating ideas, seeking information, compiling portions of reports, and so on. Indeed, if only one person does all the work, people say the committee is "not really" a committee, or is one "in name only," by which they mean that the committee does *not* have interdependent members and is not a group in our sense.

The second important feature of a group is its purposiveness. All groups take on certain tasks in preference to others. They do not act randomly, without purpose, nor do they take on tasks and purposes randomly. They come into being with one or more purposes, and new purposes grow out of old ones. Groups are often named by their purposes: the curriculum committee, the administrative cabinet, the history class, the science department, and so on.

The third important feature is communication. Groups in our sense always have denser communication within themselves than they have with other groups. For example, it is easy for every member of the curriculum committee to communicate with every other member at its regular meetings, but it is more difficult for them to communicate with every member of the assembly committee, because the two committees do not have joint meetings. Indeed, some groups are recognizable by the density of communication within themselves and by little else—that is what people usually mean by a "clique." When people say that someone "belongs to" or "hangs out with" a certain group, the most obvious thing they mean is that the person spends more time communicating with members of that group than with members of other groups. When we find pairs of people who communicate very little or not at all, we have found the "boundary" between one group and another.

We can think of those three features of groups—interdependence, purposiveness, and dense communication—as the soil from which the other features of group life can grow: norms such as cooperation, problem-solving style, influence patterns, friendship and cohesiveness, and so on.

Groups make use of interdependence, purpose, and communication, in one way or another, to develop their own unique ways of doing things.

Two pairs of ideas about groups are found again and again in the literature. One is the distinction between the formal and informal relations among members. The formal relations are those legitimated by written documents or by established custom. The relation between the chairperson and the other members is an example. So is the relation between the chairperson and the recorder. In a classroom, much of the deportment of student toward teacher is formal, because it is specified by long custom understood both by teacher and student.

The informal relations are those regularized by the group itself for its own purposes. Maintained by mutual understanding and often not much verbalized, they are "the way we do things around here." They include the patterns of interaction each individual chooses for himself or herself. Sometimes the informal relations are in conflict with the formally specified relations, but often they supplement them. Friendship cliques among faculty or students exemplify informal relations. When teachers get help from one another outside formal committees or in-service training programs (though these may have been established for the purpose), they are using informal links.

The other pair of ideas found repeatedly in the literature is the distinction between task and process—that is, between working on the task and working on the procedures or the interpersonal relations through which the task can get done. Because groups usually come together (convene) with a particular task in mind and then discover that some matters of procedure or personal interrelationships emerge to demand attention, the terms "convening task" and "emergent task" are sometimes used instead of "task" and "process." By working on task, we mean doing those things that are a direct part of the convening task. In a cooperative arithmetic game in a classroom, students are working on the task when they are doing the arithmetic problems, keeping score, and the like. They are working on process when they encourage one another, tutor one another outside the game, cheer at a high score, sympathize with a member who gets a wrong answer, and so on. Working on process is also called "maintaining" the group and dealing with "socio-emotional" matters.

Influence. The last decade has seen a remarkable convergence of research findings and interpretations of these findings among investigators of social influence. The overlaps among their proposals encourage us to believe that they have gotten hold of some important and reliable features of the way we humans influence one another.

At least two writers have revised Maslow's (1954) theory of developmental stages in the salience of needs, which ran from a concern with physical security through a concern with one's social relations to a concern with "self-actualization"—that is, exercising one's capacities to the fullest. Alderfer (1969, 1972), for example, has conducted experimentation that shows different ages and circumstances that bend one's concern to matters of existence, relatedness to others, or the growth of one's capacities. Harrison (1979) describes influence as operating through three facets. His facet of "level" contains the stages of sustenance, self-definition, and generativity, the first and last of which are very like the first and last stages of Maslow and Alderfer. Self-definition overlaps with the middle stages of those two authors because we always "define" ourselves to a considerable degree by our relations with others. Alderfer and Harrison, like Maslow, put forward their developmental categories as needs that can become salient at certain times, and can therefore open the individual to influences that promise to answer those needs. Harrison makes the useful point that the individual's time perspective at the earliest stage is relatively short, and predicting the effects of influence is relatively easy, whereas time perspective at the latest stage is long and prediction is more difficult.

Boulding (1978) says we deal with one another in three domains: the "polity" (which operates chiefly through threat), the "economy" (which operates chiefly through exchange), and the "integry" (which operates chiefly through integrative processes such as affection, trust, cooperation, and coordination of roles). Obviously, one can influence another by threat, by offering the exchange of goods and services, and by offering (or withholding) affection and trust. Harrison's second facet (1979), that of "needs," overlaps somewhat with Boulding's categories; Harrison's categories are political-economic, social, and competence needs. Foa and Foa (1974), after a great deal of research, cut the pie somewhat differently. They say that we exchange six interpersonal resources with one another: goods, money, information, status, love, and services. We gain influence or power over another by giving (or offering to give) or withholding (or threatening to take away) one or more of those six resources.

McClelland's three categories of need—achievement, affiliation, and power—have influenced much research. (For exposition, see McClelland 1958 or McClelland et al., 1953.) The category of power has the flavor of control over one's own life. DeCharms (1968 and 1976, for example) introduced the concepts of being a "pawn" (being pushed around at the will of others) or an "origin" (being confident of the desirable results of initiating one's own actions). Among schoolchildren, DeCharms has shown strong correlations between being an origin and succeeding academically. He has also demonstrated that children can be trained to be origins.

Harrison (1977) has also proposed four "styles," or methods, of influence. One way to exert influence (or control or coordination) is to use charisma, which Harrison calls "common vision" and which means, to use Berlew's definition (1974) instead of Harrison's, (1) expressing for the others their values and aspirations, (2) enabling them to see that it is within their power to take action, and (3) convincing them that the time to act is *now*. A second way to

exert influence is to encourage participation of all members by (1) showing them that their contributions are valued, (2) exposing one's own resources, desires, and emotions, and (3) putting trust in others' abilities and intentions. A third way is to use assertive persuasion—to argue for and against proposals. The fourth way is that of reward and punishment; that includes setting standards for others and bargaining with competitors. The four styles of influence have been validated through use in a great many training programs.

In his 1979 article, Harrison offers two more categories: (1) separation, meaning a desire to act alone, and (2) unification, meaning a desire to act in concert with others. "Separation" overlaps with McClelland's "power." We shall mention the overlaps of "unification" with categories of other writers below.

Two older sets of categories should be mentioned. Longabaugh (1963), after experiments with children, offered the three categories of dominance-submission, love-hostility, and activity-passivity. French and Raven (1959) proposed five categories that enable one to exert power or influence over others: having information, exerting coercion or reward, being a member of a reference group, being an expert, and possessing legitimized power.

We find six threads running through the various categories. A category of one writer is rarely identical with that of another, but we think there are strong overlaps. We list below the categories that seem to us to lie along each of the six threads. One category sometimes appears under two headings.

1. *Existence:* Maslow's security; Alderfer's existence; Foa and Foa's goods, money, and services; Boulding's economy; Harrison's sustenance and political-economic need.
2. *Role and status:* French and Raven's legitimate power; Foa and Foa's status; Harrison's common vision and self-definition.
3. *Information:* French and Raven's information and expertness; Foa and Foa's information; Harrison's assertive persuasion.
4. *Cohesiveness and affection:* Maslow's social relations; McClelland's affiliation; French and Raven's reference-group power; Longabaugh's love-hostility; Alderfer's relatedness; Foa and Foa's love; Harrison's participation with trust, social and unification needs; Boulding's integry.
5. *Competence and growth:* Maslow's self-actualization; McClelland's achievement; French and Raven's expertness; Longabaugh's activity-passivity; DeCharms's origin or pawn; Alderfer's growth; Harrison's generativity, competence, and separation.
6. *Reward and punishment:* McClelland's power; French and Raven's coercion or reward; Longabaugh's dominance-submission; DeCharms's origin or pawn; Harrison's reward-and-punishment and political-economic need; Boulding's polity.

What methods of influence appear most in schools? Teachers generally have strong influence over students through their ability to use coercion, their superior status, and their presumed monopoly of information. Teachers can exert little power through controlling the satisfaction of existence needs, for obvious reasons. Though most teachers influence their students now and then through intuitive use of cohesiveness and affection, they rarely do it systematically. To judge by many recent criticisms of schools, competence and growth, in the large sense meant by the authors cited above—developing the whole range of human capacities—are paid much less attention than many teachers and parents would prefer.

Students use a great deal of reward and punishment among themselves. They also achieve status among their peers for reasons their teachers may or may not approve. And also among themselves, they influence one another (probably more often than teachers influence them) through the resource of information (about nonacademic as well as academic matters), through cohesiveness and affection, and through mutual aid in achieving competence and growth.

The teacher's power can be significantly undermined when overt conflict occurs frequently with high-power students. Since quite often the power of students is based on their being attractive (referent power), and teacher power is based primarily on legitimacy, high-power students have more influence over the peer group than the teacher does. When teachers face overt conflict with students in the classroom, they cannot achieve influence and increase student learning by simply resorting to their legitimate authority or by using punishment. Coercion may gain short-term, overt compliance, but punishment will reduce the students' longer-term interest and lessen the likelihood of their reaching important academic goals. Direct, open encounters between students and teacher—those that recognize the right of students to have some power over their own classroom procedures—can be used as a means for developing plans and procedures acceptable to both parties. The teacher who learns the skill of sharing decision making with students will generally achieve some degree of referent power and will, in fact, have fewer instances of overt power struggles.

Students who feel powerful and influential tend to feel secure in the classroom and to be happy, effective, and curious there. Students who are powerless tend to possess poor images of themselves. They feel negative about school and do not perform at levels consonant with their abilities. Powerlessness induces anxiety; the classroom becomes a threatening and insecure place. Although shared power and influence are difficult to establish, a teacher can begin by distributing part of the legitimate power to students and by arranging for students to participate actively in classroom leadership positions.

Unequal power relationships between teachers and students may induce alienation in the form of powerlessness. The pitfalls of student powerlessness were delineated very well by Herndon (1965), Kohl (1967), Kozol (1967), and Silberman (1970). And the "alternative school" movement represents a response on a large scale to the desire of students to have more of a say in relation to classroom procedures and their own learning goals.

In a critical review of the literature on power in public schools, Tjosvold (1976) summarized some ways in which the authority hierarchy of administrators and teachers can pose important problems for group processes in the classroom. Tjosvold pointed out several factors. (1) School personnel often use their status to control unilaterally much student behavior unrelated to academic achievement, and by doing so fail to facilitate the objective of creating skillful, self-directed, responsible adults. (2) Confronted with students they believe are uncommitted to classroom procedures and academic goals, educators may use their power in ways that backfire. For example, the use of isolation or expulsion may enhance educators' power but usually will not encourage academic learning. (3) People who occupy unequal social status usually have interpersonal relationships characterized by inaccurate communications, deception, competition, and ineffective conflict resolution. For example, students in trouble will not seek the advice or assistance of educational authorities. Tjosvold concluded his summary by arguing for the need for structural change in schools, along with the behavioral changes pointed to in the studies of democratic leadership. He suggested cooperative structures to decrease the inevitably superior social status of school administrators and teachers and to increase student participation in school-related problem solving and decision making.

As shown in studies by both Bonney (1971) and Lilly (1971), planned efforts at modifying peer group power structures are very difficult to launch and also very difficult to maintain so that the changes become self-sustaining. Bonney focused on the efforts of teachers to aid students who were rejected by their classmates. Bonney's teachers gave special attention, special assignments, and special roles to rejected students. Although a few students made some gains in their status among their peers, the gains lasted for only a few days to a week. Lilly experimented with ways of improving the interpersonal acceptance of unpopular, powerless, low-achieving elementary students by having them participate in a special moviemaking project. They worked closely with highly popular peers and were given permission to leave the regular classroom to engage in this highly valued project. The treatment was successful in improving the acceptance of the low-status peers—but again, as in Bonney's results, for only a short time.

Changing the power structure of a classroom group requires keen diagnosis, constructive action, and continual and persistent efforts over a long period of time. Such change cannot be brought about by simply attempting to modify personal characteristics of certain individual students. Attempts at helping low-power students learn skills for wielding interpersonal influence may meet with some short-term success, but only normative and structural changes in the day-to-day group life in the classroom can assure major changes in classroom leadership patterns.

Deci (1971) found that when a tangible external reward such as money was used, the subjects being studied gave up their intrinsic motivation for pursuing the rewarded activity. In contrast, Deci found that when verbal reinforcements were used as the external rewards, subjects' intrinsic motivations seemed to increase. Concrete rewards such as money or candy may add to the helpless orientation of students as studied by Dweck and Rapucci (1973) or to the pawn-like orientation suggested by the work of DeCharms.

DeCharms (1972) argues that students learn to act as pawns (helpless) or origins (self-initiators) because of the way they are taught by their teachers. Teachers who receive special training in facilitating more origin-like student behavior are more successful than untrained teachers in establishing classrooms where students are likely to be classified as origins. The trained teachers learn how to help students set their own goals, pursue those goals in their own ways, and take personal responsibility for their classroom actions. DeCharms found, moreover, that while the students were acting more origin-like they were improving in their academic achievement as well.

Paula Johnson (1976) provides specific examples of the way power is used differently by boys and girls. Johnson hypothesizes that expert power, reward power, and coercive power are used differently by boys and girls because of their different experiences during early socialization. With regard to expert power, girls learn early that they should not display their expertise and knowledge openly—especially when in the company of boys. The classic bind girls face is, "If I do too well in school, who will ask me to the senior prom?"

The stereotypic female orientation in relation to males is one of helplessness. Girls who behave helplessly in relation to boys eventually come to believe they are less competent than boys. In Patricia Schmuck's studies of women administrators in public schools (1976), she found that women who were asked to take on a task of influence and responsibility often responded, "Who me?"—implying both their own sense of incompetence and their self-perception of low worth in relation to others.

Reward and coercion are used differently by boys and girls. Girls tend to use them less directly than boys do; that is, girls disguise them with threats of anger or tears, or with ingratiation. In fact, the uses of rewards and coercion have been designated as stereotyped by sex: girls who use rewards and coercion overtly and directly are considered to be masculine, and boys who maneuver indirectly are labeled "feminine" or "sissy."

People who use legitimate power must believe they have the right and responsibility to wield influence, and the persons being influenced must feel obligated to comply. Women do not hold many legitimate power positions in American society, except in the field of public education.

Their legitimate power positions in education, however, are typically in relation to students—not in relation to adult professionals, as evidenced by the minuscule numbers of women in administrative positions within the public schools.

In an effort to see if female and male teachers differed in the ways they behaved toward girls and boys, Brophy and Good (1970) summarized a large number of relevant studies. They were unable to uncover any significant differences between teachers of the two sexes. Men and women teachers, alike, treated boys and girls differently and consistently so. Boys interacted with teachers more frequently, and the interactions tended to be more negative than interactions between teachers and girls.

We often think of formally appointed leaders as having more influence or power than others. Perhaps we are usually more attentive to signs of influence from them than to signs from others. Conversely, when our attention is drawn by someone's influential act, we are likely to say that the person is showing a sign of leadership. In schools, we attribute leadership in varying degrees to students, teachers, and administrators, though it is leadership of different sorts.

The classic experiment on leadership in a semieducational setting was that of Lewin, Lippitt, and White. The study was reported in several journals as early as 1939. The findings were summarized by Lippitt and White (1947) and expanded by White and Lippitt (1960). Boys in three small clubs, with adult leaders, carried out tasks such as making masks and toy airplanes. The boys with the authoritarian leader showed more hostility and more submissiveness than boys in the other two groups. The boys with the democratic leader showed more creativity, friendliness, and group-mindedness. The groups with the authoritarian and democratic leaders were about equally effective in their tasks and more effective than the laissez-faire group. Work slowed down or stopped when the authoritarian leader left the room, but continued when the democratic leader left.

Stogdill (1974) summarized thirty-eight studies on the relationships between participative or authoritarian leadership, on the one hand, and group productivity, satisfaction, and cohesiveness on the other. He concluded that though satisfaction and cohesiveness are probably associated with participative leadership, group productivity does not vary consistently with the different styles of leadership.

Stogdill's summary gives rise to the following sorts of thoughts about teachers' leadership. Authoritarian teachers often do accomplish a great deal with their students, particularly when they are able to communicate a sense of openness and accessibility. But even though the highly respected authoritarian teacher exerts successful influence and may even lead students effectively through the maze of academic learning, other outcomes are possible. It is likely that the actions of such teachers also encourage feelings of dependency, competition, and some powerlessness, and at times make students feel alienated from the subject matter.

Teachers who try to hold on to power and responsibility for student learning and behavior may well have orderly, quiet, and even pleasant classrooms—provided the students as a group are not "uncontrollable." In contrast, classrooms with teachers who share leadership with their students will often *not* be so neat and orderly; the problems that do arise will quickly come into the open, and the routines of group life will be analyzed frequently through discussions about immediate interpersonal concerns. Since teachers who share leadership will be allowing their students to learn about self-control and individual responsibility, they must expect, in turn, that students will experience some difficulty in learning to control their own behavior, just as the students sometimes have trouble understanding a mathematical concept. What students do learn about their abilities to control their own behavior and to be responsible for themselves can also have direct implications for their academic performance. Self-control and self-responsibility are not only concerns related to classroom discipline, but are integrally tied to behavior required for pursuing academic objectives.

Even though students do not hold legitimate authority, they do have significant power in the classroom. They can get their peers to do things by rewarding them with smiles, gifts, or other inducements. They can also wield influence by coercing peers through threats of physical punishment or exclusion. Some students are influential because they are charismatic; i.e., others find them attractive and can identify with them. Still others are able to get their peers to follow them because they are viewed as experts.

Several empirical studies have systematically explored the characteristics of students with high power in formal group or classroom settings (Polansky, Lippitt, & Redl, 1950; Gold, 1958). Such studies as these have shown generally that influential students possess attributes that are valued by members of the peer group. Students who hold positions of high power are good at doing things (expert power) and have a cluster of highly valued personal characteristics (referent power) such as strength, good looks, friendliness, and helpfulness in interpersonal relations. Moreover, the actions of powerful students are typically observed more closely by their peers than the actions of others in the classroom. Thus, they can either measurably enhance or inhibit effective classroom group processes by their actions.

Students too often can exert influence for unproductive ends. For example, Polansky, Lippitt, and Redl (1950) studied the attempts at influence by problem campers—the kind of peer-group influence about which teachers have nightmares. Even though the powerful youths in this study had severe emotional problems, their behaviors were not unlike those that might occur in average classrooms. Students with high emergent influence initiated lewd songs, threw food in the lunchroom, and generally disobeyed rules of the camp. Other less powerful students tended

to imitate and follow them. The counselors were powerless to stop the misbehavior. In many classrooms, teachers have experienced students seizing power and leading the class, however momentarily, in such games as "Drop your pencil every five minutes," "Sharpen pencils, everyone, at 3:00 P.M.," or "Everybody cough at 2:15 P.M."

There is no doubt that leadership exists; in many groups, that is, members look to one person to exert influence and are more ready to accept influence from that person than from others. The leader may be formally appointed (as in the case of teachers and administrators) or may emerge (as informal leaders do). The point is sometimes forgotten, however, that *all* members of a group exert some influence, ranging from very little to very much. By definition, therefore, all members partake of leadership to some degree at one time or another. The trick, in classrooms or elsewhere, is to marshal as much of the influence as possible toward productive ends.

There is also no doubt that the phenomenon of leadership is complex. We showed earlier that researchers are beginning to think in very similar ways about influence, and that convergence may make it easier during the coming years for them to help one another in sorting out the kinds of leadership that are effective for different purposes, and the ways leaders (including teachers and administrators) can be effectively trained. At the moment, although we can state a few things about leadership with some confidence, as we did above, many important details remain perplexing.

A book edited by McCall and Lombardo (1978), for example, examined the complexities and frustrations in research on leadership. In it, Pfeffer (1978) reviewed concepts of leadership; he found them to be ambiguous and to use a multitude of different dimensions. He reviewed research on whether different kinds of leadership had predictable effects; he found the results equivocal. He hunted for research on the *magnitude* of effects and found none. Pfeffer concluded that "if one is interested in understanding the causality of social phenomena as reliably and accurately as possible, then the concept of leadership is probably a poor place to begin" (p. 30). He went on to say that we like to feel that we have control over our environment, and hence we often attribute outcomes to persons—especially to those officially named as leaders—rather than to context.

In the same book, Weick (1978) argues that the effective leader is a docile leader; that is, the effective leader discerns where the followers want to go and then hurries to get just a little bit in front of them. Merei reported the same conclusion after a study (1949) with children.

Vaill (1978) asked what it is that the leader is leading. He offered forty-seven hypotheses about characteristics of high-performing systems. Two of them follow:

One can observe a great deal of experimentation and rehearsal in a high-performing system. Various ways of operating the system are tried. There seems to be only temporary fixation (if at all) on "the one best way" to operate the system.

Communication from members to outsiders about how and why the high-performing system operates as it does will tend to be in platitudes and generalities, or by means of showing rather than telling. Members will feel and often say, "There's no way I can explain it to you."

Vaill makes it clear that the effective leader is not one who has discovered a simple formula or a magical prescription. He or she must deal constantly with ambiguity and change.

Roles and Expectations. Although human behavior is often hard to predict in detail, all of us do succeed, after some acquaintance, in predicting some of the behavior of others. After a while, we do find that some of our predictions about others are borne out, and we come to have *expectations* about their behavior. We expect others to act in certain ways because we have seen them act in those ways several times before.

Roles have powerful effects on behavior. People in certain jobs, in certain socioeconomic classes, in certain subcultures, and in other stereotyped relations to others such as patient-to-doctor or student-to-teacher show regularities of behavior. Through acquaintance with persons in special roles, we come to expect similar behavior from other persons in the same roles. That is another way we develop predictions about the behavior of others.

It often happens that our expectations about others cause us not to wait to find out more about a particular person, but to act as if we already know how that person will act. The other person then sometimes reacts to our action in a way that confirms our expectations. If we expect a person to be cheerful, we are likely to greet the person cheerfully, and that is more likely to draw a cheerful response than a glum one. The effect is called the "self-fulfilling prophecy." The effect of the prophecy is to influence others to act in such a way that we ourselves are subsequently influenced to continue acting the way we began. In cybernetic language, the pattern is called "positive feedback." In common language, it is called the "vicious circle," though the effect can be happy as well as vicious. This circular self-maintaining process is very common in human life. Indeed, it exists wherever there is a continuing pattern of human interaction. It exists in schools as elsewhere. Here, we shall limit ourselves to an important circular process in classrooms—namely, Rosenthal and Jacobson's (1968) "Pygmalion effect."

It has long been noticed that many teachers, when they initiate interaction with students in the classroom, use different styles with different students. On the face of it, that seems desirable, since every student is unique and might benefit from particularized attention. The suspicion can arise, however, that the teacher may be choosing a method of influence on the basis of mistaken stereotype rather than on the basis of the actual and particular abilities and needs of the student. In particular, it has long been noticed that students begin to be characterized by teachers as high performers and low performers early in grade school, and then rarely move from one category to the

other. They move more rarely, that is, than other facts we know about children, teachers, and the measurement of academic ability would lead us to expect.

Schmuck and Schmuck (1979, p. 72) tell of a teacher whose class of students in a junior high school had been designated as mentally retarded. Through careful mental testing, the teacher discovered that fewer than half the students could be properly so classified. Yet she had great difficulty in convincing the school's administrators that the students should be treated differently. Could it be that the expectations (predictions) that some teachers have about low-performing and high-performing students help to hold the students in those categories despite their potential abilities?

That question and questions related to it have been the subject of hundreds of empirical studies. In the mid-1970s, Rosenthal (1976) used meta-analysis to integrate more than 300 studies. Overwhelming any possible attribution of the results to chance, the studies gave strong evidence consistent with the hypothesis that teachers often act as part of a circular process that makes it very difficult for low-performing and high-performing students to move out of those categories.

Studies have turned up many ways in which teachers behaved differently toward students they believed to have high academic capability and those they believed to have low capability. When teachers believed they were interacting with bright, high-performing, or "good" students, they smiled, nodded approvingly, leaned toward the students, looked them in the eyes, spoke in a friendly manner, gave them opportunities to learn new material, taught them difficult material, waited for them to come up with the right answer to a question, gave clues or rephrased a question to help them answer it, paid close attention to what they said, and praised them for correct responses to questions—all more often or more strongly than when the teachers believed they were interacting with "poor" students. Some of those actions on the part of the teacher can have direct effects on academic performance—for example, giving students only easy material to learn or failing to give them enough time to come up with a right answer. The effects of other actions are more indirect.

Cooper (1979) has described the way the circular process is probably maintained. It starts with the desire of teachers to maintain control. The next part of the circle is the expectation teachers have, on the average, that control will be easier when they, rather than the student, initiate interaction and when they deal with the student "privately" rather than "publicly." "Privately" means a condition in which the teacher gives little attention to other students and in which other students give little attention to the teacher's interaction with the one student. That condition can come about, for example, when all students are doing seat work and the teacher and the one student can have a quiet talk.

The desire of teachers to maintain control affects "good" and "poor" students differently. For students whom teachers expect to be good students, the effects are straightforward. The teacher encourages the students with favorable attention, the students find their efforts to perform well rewarded by that attention, and they continue to try to do well. For students whom teachers expect to be poor students, however, the train of effects is more subtle. The teacher gives attention to the presumably poor student not when the student is (or is not) trying to perform well, but *when the teacher is expecting to have to exert control.* The presumably poor student gets the same behavior from the teacher whether the student is struggling to perform well, giving an irrelevant but polite answer, or making a discourteous remark; that is, the teacher acts to increase control. The student finds that trying to do well has no more likelihood of bringing favorable attention than any other action, and the student's motivation to do well decreases.

If students for whom the teacher has low expectations are rewarded or punished depending on the teacher's anticipation of the need for control and not on the student's academic achievements, then those students will perceive their efforts to have no effect on their academic success. They will lose motivation to put effort into academic matters. The less effort they expend, of course, the more evidence the teacher has to support the expectation that the students cannot be expected to do very well, and we are back full circle. Cooper (1979) cites many studies that give evidence to support the pattern he describes.

To recapitulate, teachers want to maintain control. When working with the class as a whole, teachers anticipate that interacting with students for whom they have low expectations will threaten their control of the class. Therefore, they discourage class participation by those students so that they can work with them singly, one-to-one. Those students find that their effort is not rewarded by signs of approval from the teacher, and they reduce their effort. Therefore, they do not do well, and the teacher's original perception of them is reaffirmed. Thus the circle is completed. It is a circle difficult to break, as we illustrated with the case of the teacher's "mentally retarded" class.

Cooperation. The beneficial features of cooperation have probably been noted ever since some primeval human first became aware of social pattern. Cooperation is a special subform of influence in which participants in a task gain benefits for themselves when they all act so as to maximize the performance of the common task. Cooperation typically brings out the kind of influence noted by the authors we cited in item 4, "cohesiveness and affection," in our listing under the heading "Influence." A classic analysis of cooperation and competition is that of Deutsch (1949).

So powerful are the effects of cooperation that Sherif et al. (1961) were able to produce competition between groups of boys and then to produce cooperation between the same groups—one of the very few instances in social science when an effect was produced and then reversed. Many researchers have been investigating the effects of cooperation in education during the last decade. If the length of this section were to reflect the amount of recent attention to cooperation in education, it would be one of the longer sections. The agreement among the research studies, however, especially as shown in a couple of careful recent reviews, enables us to present the important points briefly.

D. W. Johnson et al. (1981) recently published a meta-analysis of 122 studies comparing the effectiveness of cooperation, cooperation with intergroup competition, interpersonal competition, and individual (independent) work. They used three methods of meta-analysis: voting, effect size, and z-score. Comparing cooperation and competition, they found an effect size of 0.78 favoring cooperation. That is, the academic achievement of the average student in the cooperative condition was as good as that of students at the 78th percentile in the competitive condition. The achievement of the average student in the cooperative condition was also as good as that of persons at the 78th percentile in the individualistic condition. Similarly, though not as strongly, the achievement of the average student in the condition of cooperation with intergroup competition was as good as that of students at the 64th percentile in the interpersonal competitive condition and as good as that of students at the 69th percentile in the individualistic condition. Johnson et al. found no significant difference between cooperation with and without intergroup competition and none between competition and individualistic work. The voting and z-score methods of meta-analysis confirmed the analysis by effect size.

Those are strong findings. They argue that the use of cooperation in classrooms instead of competition can make a great difference in academic achievement. They also found some evidence, however, that cooperation was less effective with tasks of simple rote decoding and correcting. The benefits of cooperation showed most strongly with tasks of concept attainment, verbal problem solving, categorization, spatial problem solving, retention and memory, motor learning, and guessing, judging, or predicting.

Slavin (1980) reviewed twenty-eight projects lasting at least two weeks conducted by teachers in elementary or secondary classrooms. He assessed the effects not only on academic achievement but also on race relations and mutual concern among students. Because he examined the projects against a detailed theoretical analysis of (1) the kinds of communication possible in cooperative and competitive groups and (2) the bearing of the communication upon different sorts of tasks, Slavin was able to set forth some unusually detailed conclusions:

1. Cooperative learning techniques produced poorer academic achievement in only one of the twenty-eight projects; in most of them, cooperation produced significantly superior learning.
2. Cooperative learning techniques did better for low-level learning (such as rote knowledge or calculation) when the techniques were well structured, made it

clear that there was individual accountability for performance, and used a clear reward system for the groups.

3. Cooperative learning techniques did better for high-level learning (such as analyzing problems and making judgments) when the techniques made use of "high student autonomy and participation in decision making" (p. 337).
4. Cooperative learning techniques showed strong favorable effects on racial relations.
5. Cooperative learning techniques showed fairly consistent favorable effects on friendship and liking among students.
6. In some of the studies, cooperative learning techniques seemed to increase students' self-esteem.
7. Students in classes using cooperative learning generally reported liking school better than did students in traditionally taught classes.

Sharan (1980) also reviewed studies on cooperation, many of them the same studies reviewed by Slavin (1980), and reached reasonably similar conclusions.

The findings on the effects of cooperation in classrooms are especially dramatic when one considers the rarity with which cooperative learning methods are used in schools. All investigators urge teachers to use cooperative methods more often than they do now. On the other hand, no one recommends giving up other methods entirely. Johnson and Johnson (1975) and Schmuck and Schmuck (1979) are explicit in recommending cooperative, competitive, or individualistic methods according to their suitability for different tasks.

Problem Solving. In addition to solving cognitive problems in groups as a form of achievement or performance, students can also be thought of as working together to reduce social and organizational problems among themselves or in the school as a whole. Notable beginnings on the latter topic were the books by Fox, Luszki, and Schmuck (1966) and Schmuck, Chesler, and Lippitt (1966). Since those writings, some empirical literature has accumulated, but not yet enough to justify confident statements about what might be done.

Group problem solving among faculty is another matter. In schools as in industry, government, and the military, formal and informal groups constantly make plans and try to solve problems, and psychologists, sociologists, and other social scientists have been studying the functioning of groups since the late 1800s. The amount of research grew rapidly after World War II. (Mills, 1979, tells insightfully of the advances and confusions.) Nevertheless, a good deal of mystery remains about efficacious or successful problem solving in groups.

Hare (1976) summarizes what is known about the productivity of groups. The productive groups are well organized, systematically carry out the steps in the problem-solving process, have a large number of friendships within the group, have members who are aware of the characteristics of the group that bear upon productivity, and have

high cohesiveness. Groups can be trained to be more productive. In addition to the factors just mentioned, productivity is also affected by members' personalities, their social characteristics, group size, kind of task, communication network, leadership style, rules for decisions, and type of feedback about process. That seems like a lot of knowledge, but almost all the studies Hare cites were done in laboratories or industry, and he cites only a few studies to back up some of his conclusions. Processes in groups are strongly affected by the norms of the organizations in which they are embedded, and very few studies have been conducted of the detailed processes in groups embedded in schools.

There is a good deal of practical lore about using systematic problem solving in groups to get work done in schools and to bring about changes in the school organization's way of doing things—see, for example, chapter 7 of Schmuck et al. (1977). And some studies have shown greater organizational efficacy among faculties who have made conscious use of systematic group problem solving. For example, in elementary schools where more staff members underwent longer practice in systematic problem solving and had active support from their principals, Schmuck et al. (1975) found that, compared to other schools, those faculties (during two years) formed strong structures for team teaching (pp. 160–161), made greater progress toward personal goals (p. 168), increased more in their feelings of influence on how the school was run (pp. 182, 322), increased more in the positive results they saw from their own efforts (p. 318), and increased more in their collaboration with others in deciding teaching methods and subject matter for their classes (pp. 328, 329), among other outcomes.

Similarly, Runkel et al. (1980) found that faculties in elementary and junior high schools that had undergone training in problem solving, compared to other schools, were more responsive to one another's requests for help; sought consultation or made joint decisions with colleagues more often about teaching methods, curriculum, or student conduct; more often succeeded when they tried to establish team teaching; and dealt with innovations with greater dispatch, either bringing them to fruition more rapidly or deciding sooner not to go forward with them (p. 133).

Though the two studies just cited, along with others in the literature, encourage the belief that systematic problem solving in groups in schools can have useful results, they tell little about the extent to which the outcomes are due to the problem-solving discussions themselves (in comparison, for example, to the general marshaling of energy that occurs when a new, special project is undertaken), and they also tell us little about how necessary or sufficient are the particular steps and techniques used in the problem-solving discussion. Meanwhile, a dramatic portrayal of one way problem solving can go wrong is given by Janis (1972), who has described "groupthink" at high levels of the U.S. government: groups can sometimes be led by their high *esprit de corps* and their strong self-confidence to overlook realistic obstacles to their plans and to overlook alternative plans that seem at first less appealing but are realistically more feasible.

Some useful discussions of organizational change in schools and some instructive case studies appear in Baldridge and Deal (1975). Some theories about solving problems in schools and some proposals for sequencing the work appear in Runkel et al. (1979).

Friendship. Evidence mounts that friendship among students not only makes school a more pleasant place for them but also aids academic learning. The effects of the opposite of friendship—hostility—are obvious. We have visited schools in which many students are so fearful of other students that they cannot concentrate even when they are in class under the protection of the teacher. But even in relatively peaceful schools, friendship makes a difference.

Unfortunately, we could find no review of recent research on the subject. We mention here a few studies to indicate what we think is the trend in findings. Schmuck (1963, 1966) found that students who can name accurately the other students who name them as friends but who are named by few others tend to use their academic abilities at a lower level and have less favorable attitudes toward self and school than students who are similarly accurate but are named by more other students. Moreover, in classrooms where friendship choices are rather evenly distributed throughout the class, students often think of themselves as being liked at least by a few others, use their abilities more highly, and have more favorable attitudes toward themselves and the school. This occurs even among those who actually hold lower status in the classroom than others.

These findings were essentially corroborated in an important study by Lewis and St. John (1974), which dealt with the achievement of black students within classrooms having a majority of whites. To study the dynamics of racially integrated classrooms, Lewis and St. John collected extensive data from 154 black sixth-graders in twenty-two majority-white classrooms in Boston. Their results showed that a rise in the achievement of the blacks depended on two factors: (1) norms stressing achievement in the classrooms and (2) acceptance of black students into the classroom peer group. The second factor was shown to be especially important. The mere presence of academically achieving white students was not sufficient to raise achievement levels of black students. The performance of blacks was strongly influenced by the whites' acceptance of them as friends.

It is also important to note once again that some research evidence indicates that girls are affected more by an absence of friends than boys. According to a review by Hoffman (1972), affective relationships are paramount for girls, and much of their achievement is motivated by a desire to please others. Thus, Hoffman argues, in school situations where excellence in academic performance might threaten affiliation, girls may very well sacrifice performance to maintain friendships.

One clue as to how the needs for friendship and achievement might be integrated and formed into an enhancing relationship comes from a study by Lucker et al. (1976). This action research compared the academic performance of fifth- and sixth-graders (including both girls and boys as well as Anglos and minorities) working in small, interdependent learning groups with their performance in traditional, teacher-focused classrooms. In the small interdependent learning groups, students taught one another the material to be covered. Though the Anglos performed equally well in both types of classes, the minorities performed significantly better in interdependent classes than in traditional ones.

Group Development. Effective groups are not born, but made. Every new group, no matter how individually skillful the members have shown themselves to be in other groups, must go through stages in which the members discover how to work together. At least one of the stages is bound to be stressful.

The traditional classroom of students, in which the interaction goes chiefly from the teacher to each student, with little interaction among the students, has not yet entered the first stage of development. When teachers first try to marshal the power of the group for educational purposes, they often misinterpret the conflicts and disorders that arise as meaning that something is going wrong. On the contrary, groups in formation find a stage of that sort necessary.

Though most of the research was done with adults, several researchers (Parsons and Bales, 1955; Schutz, 1958, 1966; Gibb, 1964; and Tuckman, 1965) have brought out important features of group development. Schmuck and Schmuck (1979) brought together the ideas of these researchers and others into a scheme suitable for guiding the teacher in the classroom. Their four stages are (1) facilitating psychological membership, (2) establishing shared influence, (3) pursuing academic goals, and (4) recognizing the conditions of self-renewal.

In the first stage, that of exploring membership, students accustomed to traditional classrooms will have difficulty understanding the idea that the teacher wants them to become what we have been calling a "group" in this article. (And we are not saying that the cohesive student group is the best vehicle for all kinds of learning in schools.) To begin building a group, the teacher will do best to take time for experiences and exercises that use the kinds of influence that build ties among students: those we have classified as "cohesiveness and affection" in the section on "Influence" and the methods we described under "Cooperation." Influence styles, such as those under "Reward and punishment," often produce divisiveness and should be avoided at this early stage.

In the second stage, that of establishing shared influence, conflict and discord are likely to arise. Most students have been taught to be competitive during their years in school, and working together will require them to learn new skills. Cooperative games, used early, will give them the concept of collaboration and some practice in mutually helpful behavior. In this stage, the teacher can make explicit the influence techniques of cohesiveness and affection and encourage their use by students with one another. In addition, the use of the influence techniques of "role and status" can help organize the group work in the class. Judicious use of rewards, well distributed among the students and not limited to a few, can also be useful. During this stage, too, it is important that the teacher look for the kind of circular process that contains the self-fulfilling prophecy we described under "Roles and Expectations." The teacher should seek ways to break such destructive processes and support constructive ones.

In the third stage, that of pursuing academic goals, the work done earlier will pay off. The organizing work will enable students to solve their own problems better, and mutual helpfulness will make it easier for them to pursue work with less supervision. The friendships that result from cooperation and the influence methods of cohesiveness and affection will support academic work. This is not to say that this stage will be one of sweetness and harmony. Every group must recycle the developmental stages to some extent when the task changes. As the class moves more heavily into academic work, some recycling must occur. There will be conflicts, for example, over assignments and over shirking by some students. The teacher will need to use some time to recycle the earlier methods. If the first two stages have not been hurried, however, the recycling should go rather easily, and it should provide further social learning for the students.

In the fourth stage, that of recognizing the conditions for self-renewal, students will be in a position to appreciate the stages of group development themselves. After some months of productive work together, they should know not only how to organize tasks for successful group work (something many students in some schools never learn), but also how to organize *people*. They will have come to understand the methods of influence in groups and will be able to talk about these methods, to plan with them, and to use them appropriately.

History of Research. We could start with Aristotle, but we won't. Scholars in Europe and America began writing about empirical investigations of interpersonal relations around the turn of the present century, but studies of group processes increased dramatically in frequency after World War II. Given limited space, our selection of works to mention must be arbitrary, but the following books in psychology and sociology seem to us noteworthy: Homans (1950), Thibaut and Kelley (1959), Hare, Borgatta, and Bales (1965), McGrath and Altman (1966), Cartwright and Zander (1968), Shaw (1971), Steiner (1972), Triandis (1977), and Miles (1981). Books written with application to education are Henry (1960), Charters and Gage (1963), Schmuck, Chesler, and Lippitt (1966), Johnson (1970), Schmuck and Schmuck (1974), Johnson and Johnson (1975), Bar-Tal and

Saxe (1978), Johnson (1979), Rutter et al. (1979), Schmuck and Schmuck 1979), McMillan (1980), and Sharan et al. (1980).

Philip J. Runkel
Richard A. Schmuck

See also Classroom Organization; Sociology of Education.

REFERENCES

Alderfer, C. P. An empirical test of a new theory of human needs. *Organizational Behavior and Human Performance,* 1969, *4,* 142–175.

Alderfer, C. P. *Existence, Relatedness, and Growth.* New York: Free Press, 1972.

Aronson, E. *The Jigsaw Classroom.* Beverly Hills, Calif.: Sage, 1978. (ERIC Document Reproduction Service No. ED 160 576)

Baldridge, J. V., & Deal, T. E. *Managing Change in Educational Organizations.* Berkeley, Calif.: McCutchan, 1975.

Bar-Tal, D., & Saxe, L. (Eds.). *Social Psychology of Education.* Washington, D.C.: Hemisphere, 1978.

Berlew, D. E. Leadership and organizational excitement. In D. A. Kolb, I. M. Rubin, & J. M. McIntyre (Eds.), *Organizational Psychology: A Book of Readings* (2nd ed.). Englewood Cliffs, N.J.: Prentice-Hall, 1974, pp. 265–277. (Also in *California Management Review,* 1974)

Bonney, M. E. Assessment of efforts to aid socially isolated elementary school pupils. *Journal of Educational Research,* 1971, *64,* 359–364.

Boulding, K. *Ecodynamics.* Beverly Hills, Calif.: Sage, 1978.

Brophy, J., & Good, T. Teachers' communication of differential expectations for children's classroom performance: Some behavioral data. *Journal of Educational Psychology,* 1970, *61,* 365–374. (ERIC Reproduction Service No. ED 041 838)

Cartwright, D., & Zander, A. *Group Dynamics: Research and Theory* (3rd ed.). New York: Harper & Row, 1968.

Charters, W. W., Jr., & Gage, N. L. *Readings in the Social Psychology of Education.* Boston: Allyn & Bacon, 1963.

Cooper, H. M. Pygmalion grows up: A model for teacher expectation communication and performance influence. *Review of Educational Research,* 1979, *49*(3), 389–410.

DeCharms, R. *Personal Causation.* New York: Academic Press, 1968.

DeCharms, R. Personal causation training in the schools. *Journal of Applied Social Psychology,* 1972, *2*(2), 95–113.

DeCharms, R. *Enhancing Motivation: Change in the Classroom.* New York: Irvington, 1976.

Deci, E. L. Effects of externally mediated rewards on intrinsic motivation. *Journal of Personality and Social Psychology,* 1971, *18,* 105–115.

Deutsch, M. A theory of cooperation and competition. *Human Relations,* 1949, *2,* 129–152.

Dweck, C. S., & Rapucci, N. D. Learned helplessness and reinforcement responsibility in children. *Journal of Personality and Social Psychology,* 1973, *25*(1), 109–116.

Foa, U. G., & Foa, E. B. *Societal Structures of the Mind,* Springfield, Ill.: Thomas, 1974.

Fox, R.; Luszki, M.; & Schmuck, R. *Diagnosing Classroom Learning Environments.* Chicago: Science Research Associates, 1966.

French, J. R. P., & Raven, B. H. The bases of social power. In D. Cartwright (Ed.), *Studies in Social Power*. Ann Arbor: University of Michigan Press, 1959, pp. 150–167.

Gibb, J. Climate for trust formation. In L. Bradford, J. Gibb, & K. Benne (Eds.), *T-group Theory and Laboratory Method*. New York: Wiley, 1964, pp. 279–309.

Gold, M. Power in the classroom. *Sociometry*, 1958, *21*, 50–60.

Hare, A. P. *Handbook of Small Group Research* (2nd ed.). New York: Free Press, 1976.

Hare, A. P.; Borgatta, E. F.; & Bales, R. F. *Small Groups: Studies in Social Interaction* (2nd ed.) New York: Knopf, 1965.

Harrison, R. Materials for a training program in personal power and influence. Plymouth, Mass.: Situation Management Systems, 1977.

Harrison, R. A practical model of motivation and character development. In J. W. Pfeiffer & J. E. Jones (Eds.), *1979 Handbook for Group Facilitators*. San Diego, Calif.: University Associates, 1979, pp. 207–220.

Henry, N. B. (Ed.). *The Dynamics of Instructional Groups*. Fifty-ninth Yearbook (Part 2). Chicago: National Society for the Study of Education, 1960.

Herndon, J. *The Way It Spozed to Be*. New York: Bantam Books, 1965.

Hoffman, L. W. Early childhood experiences and women's achievement motives. *Journal of Social Issues*, 1972, *28*(2).

Homans, G. C. *The Human Group*. New York: Harcourt Brace, 1950.

Janis, I. L. *Victims of Groupthink*. Boston: Houghton Mifflin, 1972.

Johnson, D. W. *The Social Psychology of Education*. New York: Holt, Rinehart & Winston, 1970.

Johnson, D. W. *Educational Psychology*. Englewood Cliffs, N.J.: Prentice-Hall, 1979.

Johnson, D. W., & Johnson, F. P. *Learning Together and Alone: Cooperation, Competition, and Individualization*. Englewood Cliffs, N.J.: Prentice-Hall, 1975. (ERIC Document Reproduction Service No. ED 104 868)

Johnson, D. W.; Maruyama, G.; Johnson, R.; & Nelson, D. Effects of cooperative, competitive, and individualistic goal structures on achievement: A meta-analysis. *Psychological Bulletin*, 1981, *89*(1), 47–62.

Johnson, P. Women and power: Toward a theory of effectiveness. *Journal of Social Issues*, 1976, *32*(3), 99–109.

Kohl, H. R. *Thirty-six Children*. New York: New American Library, 1967.

Kozol, H. R. *Death at an Early Age*. Boston: Houghton Mifflin, 1967. (ERIC Document Reproduction Service No. ED 023 766)

Lewis, R., & St. John, N. Contribution of cross-racial friendship to minority group achievement in desegregated classrooms. *Sociometry*, 1974, *37*(1), 79–91.

Lilly, M. S. Improving social acceptance of low-sociometric-status, low-achieving students. *Exceptional Children*, January 1971, 341–347.

Lippitt, R., & White, R. K. An experimental study of leadership and group life. In T. M. Newcomb & E. L. Hartley (Eds.), *Readings in Social Psychology*. New York: Holt, 1947, pp. 315–330.

Longabaugh, R. A category system for coding interpersonal behavior as social exchange. *Sociometry*, 1963, *26*, 319–344.

Lucker, G. W.; Rosenfield, D.; Siker, J.; & Aronson, E. Performance in the interdependent classroom: A field study. *American Educational Research Journal*, 1976, *13*(2), 115–123.

Maslow, A. J. *Motivation and Personality*. New York: Harper & Row, 1954.

McCall, M. W., Jr., & Lombardo, M. M. (Eds.). *Leadership: Where Else Can We Go?* Durham, N.C.: Duke University Press, 1978.

McClelland, D. C.; Atkinson, J. W.; Clark, R. A.; & Lowell, E. L. *The Achievement Motive*. New York: Appleton-Century-Crofts, 1953.

McClelland, D. C. Methods of measuring human motivation. In J. W. Atkinson (Ed.), *Motives in Fantasy, Action, and Society*. New York: Van Nostrand, 1958, pp. 7–42.

McGrath, J., & Altman, I. *Small Group Research*. New York: Holt, Rinehart & Winston, 1966.

McMillan, J. *Social Psychology of School Learning*. New York: Academic Press, 1980.

Merei, F. Group leadership and institutionalization. Human Relations, 1949, *2*, 23–39. (Reprinted in G. E. Swanson, T. M. Newcomb, & E. L. Hartley (Eds.), *Readings in Social Psychology* (Rev. ed.). New York: Holt, 1952, pp. 318–328).

Miles, M. B. *Learning to Work in Groups: A Practical Guide for Members and Trainers* (2nd ed.). New York: Columbia University, Teachers College, 1981.

Miles, M. B., & Charters, W. W., Jr. *Learning in Social Settings: New Readings in the Social Psychology of Education*. Boston: Allyn & Bacon, 1970.

Miller, J. G. *Living Systems*. New York: McGraw-Hill, 1978.

Mills, T. M. Changing paradigms for studying human groups. *Journal of Applied Behavioral Science*, 1979, *15*(3), 407–423.

Parsons, T., & Bales, R. F. *Family Socialization and Interaction Process*. New York: Free Press, 1955.

Pfeffer, J. The ambiguity of leadership. In M. W. McCall, Jr. & M. M. Lombardo (Eds.), *Leadership: Where Else Can We Go?* Durham, N.C.: Duke University Press, 1978, pp. 13–34.

Polansky, N.; Lippitt, R.; & Redl, F. An investigation of behavioral contagion in groups. *Human Relations*, 1950, *3*, 319–348.

Rosenthal, R. *Experimenter Effects in Behavioral Research* (2nd ed.). New York: Irvington, 1976.

Rosenthal, R., & Jacobson, L. *Pygmalion in the Classroom*. New York: Holt, Rinehart & Winston, 1968.

Runkel, P. J.; Schmuck, R. A.; Arends, J. H.; & Francisco, R. P. *Transforming the School's Capacity for Problem Solving*. Eugene, Oreg.: Center for Educational Policy and Management, 1979. (ERIC Document Reproduction Service No. ED 168 206)

Runkel, P. J.; Wyant, S. H.; Bell, W. E.; & Runkel, M. *Organizational Renewal in a School District: Self-help through a Cadre of Organizational Specialists*. Eugene, Oreg.: Center for Educational Policy and Management, 1980.

Rutter, M.; Maughan, B.; Mortimore, P.; & Ouston, J. *Fifteen Thousand Hours*. Cambridge, Mass.: Harvard University Press, 1979.

Schmuck, P. A. *Sex Differentiation in Public Schools Administration*. Washington, D.C.: National Council of Administrative Women in Education, 1976. (ERIC Document Reproduction Service No. ED 126 593)

Schmuck, R. A. Some relationships of peer-liking patterns in the classroom to pupil attitudes and achievement. *School Review*, 1963, *71*, 337–359.

Schmuck, R. A. Some aspects of classroom social climate. *Psychology in the Schools*, 1966, *3*, 59–65.

Schmuck, R. A.; Chesler, M.; & Lippitt, R. *Problem Solving to Improve Classroom Learning*. Chicago: Science Research Associates, 1966.

Schmuck, R. A.; Murray, D.; Smith, M. A.; Schwartz, M.; & Runkel, M. *Consultation for Innovative Schools: OD for Multiunit Structure.* Eugene, Oreg: Center for Educational Policy and Management, 1975. (ERIC Document Reproduction Service No. ED 102 724)

Schmuck, R. A., & Schmuck, P. A. *A Humanistic Psychology of Education: Making the School Everybody's House.* Palo Alto, Calif.: National Press Books, 1974. (ERIC Document Reproduction Service No. ED 091 813)

Schmuck, R. A., & Schmuck, P. A. *Group Processes in the Classroom* (3rd ed.). Dubuque, Iowa: Brown, 1979. (ERIC Document Reproduction Service No. ED 137 166)

Schutz, W. *FIRO: A Three-dimensional Theory of Interpersonal Behavior.* New York: Holt, Rinehart & Winston, 1958.

Schutz, W. *The Interpersonal Underworld.* Palo Alto, Calif.: Science and Behavior Books, 1966.

Sharan, S. Cooperative learning in small groups: Recent methods and effects on achievement, attitudes, and ethnic relations. *Review of Educational Research,* 1980, *50*(2), 241–271.

Sharan, S.; Hare, A. P.; Webb, C.; & Lazarowitz, R. H. (Eds.). *Cooperation in Education.* Provo, Utah: Brigham Young University Press, 1980.

Shaw, M. E. *Group Dynamics.* New York: McGraw-Hill, 1971.

Sherif, M.; Harvey, O. J.; White, B. J.; Hood, W. R.; & Sherif, C. W. *Intergroup Conflict and Cooperation: The Robbers Cave Experiment.* Norman. University of Oklahoma, Institute of Group Relations, 1961.

Silberman, C. *Crisis in the Classroom.* New York: Random House, 1970.

Slavin, R. E. Cooperative learning. *Review of Educational Research,* 1980, *50*(2), 315–342.

Steiner, I. D. *Group Process and Productivity.* New York: Academic Press, 1972.

Stogdill, R. M. *Handbook of Leadership: A Survey of Theory and Research.* New York: Free Press, 1974.

Thibaut, J. W., & Kelley, H. H. *Social Psychology of Small Groups.* New York: Wiley, 1959.

Tjosvold, D. *The Issue of Student Control: A Critical Review of the Literature.* Paper presented at the annual meeting of the American Educational Research Association, April 1976. (ERIC Document Reproduction Service No. ED 125 113)

Triandis, H. C. *Interpersonal Behavior.* Monterey, Calif.: Brooks-Cole, 1977.

Tuckman, B. W. Developmental sequence in small groups. *Psychological Bulletin,* 1965, *63*, 384–399.

Vaill, P. B. Toward a behavioral description of high-performing systems. In M. W. McCall, Jr. & M. M. Lombardo (Eds.), *Leadership: Where Else Can We Go?* Durham, N.C.: Duke University Press, 1978, pp. 103–125.

Weick, K. The spines of leaders. In M. W. McCall, Jr. & M. M. Lombardo (Eds.), *Leadership: Where Else Can We Go?* Durham, N.C.: Duke University Press, 1978, pp. 37–61.

White, R. W., & Lippitt, R. *Autocracy and Democracy.* New York: Harper & Brothers, 1960.

H

HANDICAPPED INDIVIDUALS

A remarkable feature of recent policies and practices relating to special education has been the increasing emphasis on the individual. Despite the continued use of such undifferentiated terms as "the handicapped" and "the disabled," social institutions in general and schools in particular have started looking at the people so classified as individuals. Most special educators always have held this view of their clients when they got down to teaching processes, but now it is pervading the entire educational establishment. Indeed, it may be that the day is not far off when every student, whether handicapped or no, will be regarded as an individual rather than as a member of a cohort for whom predictions and judgments are made according to age-grade or other group norms.

To delineate some of the developments undergirding the view of the handicapped student as an individual, this article discusses issues related to individual versus group identities and strategies, traditional concepts of categories of exceptionality and how they are being altered, recent changes in the preparation of classroom teachers, and changes in decision processes that give more independence to handicapped persons.

Emphasis on the Individual. Although most states in the United States have had compulsory school attendance laws for many decades, usually for children aged about 7 to 16, only in the last decade has "compulsory" been applied to schools as well as children and youth. In earlier periods it was common for students who were difficult to teach or control in classrooms simply to be expelled from or permitted to drop out of school. During the 1970s a number of significant adjudications not only established the right of all children and youth to a free public education, but also enunciated the obligation of all schools to provide such an education and not to demit any student from school for whatever reason without the observance of due process procedures. In addition, the courts ex-

tended the right to education to every disabled child and youth, no matter how severely handicapped, and laid down some principles to ensure that this right was observed. These principles were summarized in a remarkable piece of federal legislation enacted in 1975: Public Law 94-142, the Education for All Handicapped Children Act. The states were mandated to find and enroll in school every child, including even those with the most extreme handicaps, and to provide a "free appropriate public education" for all those between the ages of 3 and 21. (In Summer 1981 the U.S. Congress considered but rejected legislation to repeal Public Law 94-142. The future of the law is uncertain. It seems likely, however, that the salient principles in the law will continue to apply to school programs for the handicapped no matter what the Congress does.)

The requirement that the schools provide to each handicapped student an appropriate education means that each such student must be provided with a program tailored to his or her specific needs. Simply enrolling students with exceptional needs in standard school programs and allowing them to sink or swim—a practice sometimes known as "dumping"—is not compliance with the law. An educational program, based on what is officially called an Individualized Educational Plan (IEP), must be developed for each handicapped child on the basis of evaluations conducted by a team of experts, and subsequently negotiated with the student's biological or surrogate parents.

American society's notion of what kinds of children are worth educating has changed radically over the past few decades. Until recently schools were expected to act as crude sorters of children—running elimination contests that shunted aside those with special needs—and to use assessment procedures that were oriented mainly toward predicting academic achievements and the place of students in the business-industrial economy. Now every child is enrolled in school and no premature demission may be made for any student. Although schools continue to prepare students for jobs in industry and business, schooling itself is now supposed to enhance the development of each individual. Tyler (1978) succinctly stated the current function of the school as follows: "The task of the educational system is no longer one of screening and sorting; what it is expected to do is to stimulate maximum learning in persons of all ability levels, a much more difficult task" (p. 236). The dominance of *vertical* measurements of individual differences—that is, orientation toward "how high a level an individual has attained or should be able to attain" (p. 236)—has been superseded by orientation to helping each student learn as much as possible. "In schools teachers are being challenged to find out how each individual learns most readily rather than just how much he or she learns in a standard situation" (p. 237).

Sources of Change.   What has caused this remarkable shift in focus? A reading of the testimony before the courts and Congress prior to the articulation of the various mandates suggests that vested interest groups, mostly parents of handicapped children, were the immediate precipitants. Indeed, the National Association for Retarded Citizens, the Association for Children with Learning Disabilities, and similar groups were strong advocates for more inclusive and individualized arrangements in the schools. However, additional factors were involved, including a variety of research and scholarly achievements in the 1950s and 1960s that established the rationality of making changes in the schools, and, especially, massive changes in the structures of programs for handicapped students.

Behavioral psychologists, for example, invented applications of the principles of applied behavior analysis, which were first developed by B. F. Skinner, to the education of handicapped students. Bijou and Baer (1961), Haring (1974), Lindsley (1964), Lovitt (1970, 1976), and Wolf, Risley, and Mees (1964), among others, developed techniques for studying single subjects, and despite many difficulties and resistance from other scientists, made experimentation with single subjects an acceptable research design.

Behaviorists developed methods of ascertaining baseline data on a single child's behavior—for example, a child's rate of being out-of-seat, inattentive, or interfering with others in the classroom (Deno & Mirkin, 1977)—and then introducing a treatment program and observing the resulting new rates of behavior in the same categories of interest. The treatment undertaken by a teacher might be any systematic procedure for reinforcing the child's on-task behavior to see if that would bring about direct gains in desired attentiveness and simultaneously reduce the rates of off-task, out-of-seat, or disturbing behaviors. If A represented the preliminary baseline period and B the period of intervention, it would be possible to return to the A condition (no treatment) to see if the rates for undesirable behavior increased. By means of such ABA designs and other, more complicated procedures, as well as by use of behavior rates (noting both accelerations and decelerations in certain behaviors within designated time periods), it became possible to accurately assess the effec-

tiveness of various instructional interventions for each pupil. Work of this kind, and especially its applications to severely handicapped children, provided part of the documentation on which judges and legislators could establish the principle that schools must enroll all children and conduct their education according to explicit individualized plans.

Other developments of importance included the work of Cronbach and associates on aptitude-treatment interactions (Cronbach & Gleser, 1965; Cronbach & Snow, 1977). This line of thinking was first given prominence in Cronbach's presidential address at the annual convention of the American Psychological Association in 1957; he appealed for the joining together in common endeavor of the "two psychologies": the correlational psychologists, on the one hand, who tend to be interested in the measurement of individual differences and correlations of the measurements, and the experimental psychologists, on the other hand, who tend to be interested in the effects of different treatments but who regard individual differences as part of the error factors. Cronbach urged a broader effort to seek understanding of individual differences in ways that make effective treatment decisions possible. In a statistical sense, this notion called for research that explored the possibilities of interactions (the most powerful case being disordinal interactions) between aptitudes reflecting individual differences and alternative instructional treatments. This line of work reclaimed for the concept of aptitude its relation to the individual: how does he or she learn best? (Hunt & Sullivan, 1974). It also undermined the notion of a single or simple expectancy level for children's achievements. Increasingly, what one expected of a pupil was seen as the function of how he or she was taught, her or his life situation in general, and the inherent characteristics of each. Notions of fixed capacity for learning were seen as such only if treatments also were fixed. These ideas were basic to an enlarging and more open view of human potentialities.

The review of research on the modifiability of human intellectual abilities, particularly the encouraging results of early intervention studies reviewed by Hunt (1961), opened new approaches to intensive educational efforts on behalf of high-risk children. Work by Kirk (1958) and Heber et al. (1972), among others, further encouraged more open views of the modifiability of human intelligence through educational efforts.

Robert Glaser's seminal thinking on criterion-referenced testing (Glaser, 1963) and the developmental work of Popham and associates (e.g., Popham & Husek, 1969) on relating measurement procedures to specific curriculum goals and objectives were of fundamental importance. The rapid development of prosthetic devices, particularly those relating to communication problems (e.g., the Bliss Symbol Board, individual electronic hearing aids, and low-vision aids), also was extremely important in changing the attitudes held by professionals and society at large about the educability of many handicapped persons.

A distinction is sometimes made between a "disability" (the loss or absence of a physical, sensory, neurological, intellectual, or bodily function) and a "handicap" (the prevention or restriction of the ability to function efficiently in the world). Not all disabled persons are handicapped. The effective use of prosthetic devices or techniques may prevent a disability from becoming a handicap; so, too, may expertise provided by teachers, and encouragement to achieve competence and independence by family members, school personnel, and community leaders.

Many other research and technical developments could be cited as part of the silent background of the advocacy activities and the judicial and legislative imperatives of the 1970s—all of them leading to emphasis on the individual handicapped person. The major point, however, is that at the time, it became evident that a person's handicap needed to be understood in a broad ecological sense. A disability became a handicap or not partly on the basis of the disabled person's links with the external community.

Effect of New Policies. The effects of the new policies in the schools can be seen in the approximately 4 million IEPs that have been written each year since 1977/78 (Wright, 1980). The figure has been increasing slowly but shows no sign of soon reaching the 8 million mark anticipated at congressional hearings during the early 1970s. Nevertheless, even 4 million IEPs are sufficient to have an effect on the nation's schools. Almost all teachers, principals, psychologists, and other school staff members of the nation are engaged in carrying out the regulations that have been adopted by federal and state legislatures to guarantee the educational rights of handicapped students.

Issues in Classification. An ironic and complicating aspect of the new developments in special education has been the conflict over the traditional handicap classifications and labels. On the one hand, children must be classified as handicapped, usually according to some category, in order for the local school district to qualify for the financial supports provided under state and federal laws; on the other hand, there is a rising tide of resentment and resistance by parents to some of the categories, especially those that seem to demean and stigmatize children: for example, EMR (educable mentally retarded) or ED (emotionally disturbed).

When persons are categorized there is a tendency to organize data according to what is true for the group. Researchers establish the "group rates" and textbook writers prepare chapters that summarize these "rates." For example, persons in the mentally retarded category may be described as relatively low achievers, socially backward, rigid in personality, destined for low-level occupations, and so on. Such group characterizations are crude, undemocratic, and often wrong when applied to *individuals*. We should avoid dipping into group rates when we take that first look at individuals; but the great difficulties of quickly assessing the many individuals we meet frequently cause us to take the convenient group-rate approach. This

stereotyping is much resented by increasing numbers of handicapped students and their families.

The importance of classification issues was highlighted by a special study led by Nicholas Hobbs. This investigation, the Project on Classification of Exceptional Children, was undertaken at the request of Elliot L. Richardson, then U.S. secretary of health, education, and welfare, to look into "a serious national problem: '[t]he inappropriate labeling of children as *delinquent, retarded, hyperkinetic, mentally ill, emotionally disturbed,* and other classifications [which] has serious consequences for the child'" (Hobbs, 1975, p. ix). At the beginning of the report (p. 1), Hobbs stated: "Nothing less than the futures of children is at stake" as the consequence of appropriate or inappropriate classification.

Systems of special education categories are not entirely consistent from one state to another. For example, the "brain-injured" category used in Texas does not have a counterpart in most other states; and Minnesota's program for SLBP (Special Learning and Behavior Problems) is probably a unique designation. In general, the categories found around the country do not all "carve nature at its joints"; rather, they show the influences of political, demographic, and economic pressures on the intent to respond to the characteristics and needs of children. It is not surprising, therefore, that programs so constructed should be restructured in response to changes in political and economic pressures.

During the 1960s and 1970s, many educators were forced into awareness of the excessive rates at which minority group children had been classified and labeled for school purposes as EMR or ED. Court cases, such as that of *Larry P.* v. *Riles* (1972) and *Isaac Lora* v. *Board of Education* (1979), were initiated by minority group parents to combat discriminatory classification and placement practices.

The *Larry P.* case centered on the use of certain intelligence tests in the California school system to classify black children and place them in EMR classes. The court ruled against the use of traditional intelligence tests (except under very special court-approved conditions) to assess black students. Thereupon the California State Department of Public Instruction decided not to use such tests in assessing any child, which has resulted in a massive decline in enrollment in EMR classes in California schools. The case, heard in federal court, was followed throughout the nation and has had widespread effects, particularly after the appeal to a higher federal court, which strongly reaffirmed the initial determination and directives.

The issue in the *Isaac Lora* case was the referral, classification, and placement of supposedly emotionally disturbed students in the New York City public schools. The courts found the schools' procedures to be inadequate; among the remedies ordered was a large-scale, two-year in-service training program for the city's seventy thousand teachers and all other educational professionals. This order led to what was probably the largest single in-service education project ever undertaken anywhere. It was conducted co-operatively by staff members of the Graduate Center of the City University and New York public schools.

Litigation like *Isaac Lora, Larry P.,* and many other cases has become part of a general onslaught against all forms of simplistic special education classification, labeling, and placement systems. Resistance is particularly strong against systems that are stigmatic and ascribe to pupils such general predispositions that teachers expect little achievement from them. For example, the EMR label suggests that a child is inherently less educable (i.e., less capable of academic achievement) than a learning-disabled (LD) child; the LD label suggests that vigorous efforts in instruction may be fruitful and worthwhile. The distinguishing diagnostic variable between EMR and LD is the presumed difference in educability, which is often based on doubtful tests, or so the argument goes.

Much of the growing controversy over classification and labeling can be viewed as part of the social policy that looks to the individual rather than to categories of persons as the basis of planning, organization, and accountability. But what is involved is not a total assault upon classification systems. After all, education in schools does not happen in a one-to-one situation, with an instructor and a pupil on opposite ends of the proverbial log; it happens in complex group situations. Thus it is necessary to follow some rational system of grouping pupils. Age-grade grouping is still common. What is in doubt, then, is not the organization of schools as such but some of the functional classifications of mildly and moderately handicapped children. Specifically, the EMR, LD, and ED categories are doubtful bases for child placement.

The schools are in a predicament. On the one hand, parents and the courts are challenging the traditional classification of handicapped children by category; on the other hand, federal legislation mandates such classification for children who receive special education services in order for the states and local schools to be eligible for compensatory funding. One accommodation to the situation is a general erosion in the attention given to categories and labels. For example, when different categories of pupils are commingled in the same special education resource room, teachers usually find that labeling is not necessary for instruction; perfunctory estimates of how many children are in what category, therefore, should be sufficient to satisfy state and federal regulations. For these reasons, the traditional classification practices are likely to be considerably revised in the future.

Categorical teacher preparation. During the nineteenth century, when the practice arose of classifying and placing children according to their handicaps, the teachers who worked with these children were given the same classifications. Indeed, until recently most states offered about eight or nine different kinds of special education teacher certifications or licenses. The common categories are: speech-language pathologist; teacher of learning-disabled children; teacher of the educable mentally retarded; teacher of the trainable mentally retarded; teacher of the visually impaired; teacher of the deaf and hard-of-hearing; teacher of the emotionally disturbed; and teacher of children with orthopedic or other health impairments.

Now that special education programs are being decentralized according to the principle of the least restricted environment, it has become increasingly difficult to maintain many categorized programs in their narrowest versions. The principle of the least restrictive environment or least restrictive alternative was written into many court decisions and laws of the 1970s. It requires that special education be delivered to handicapped children in places that least interfere with their lives—that is, while the children remain in their maternal homes and attend neighborhood schools. As a result, there has been a rapid development of resource rooms or special education programs that cut across the traditional categorical boundaries (Deno, 1975). Correspondingly, there has been a surge in noncategorical preparation programs for special education teachers.

In 1973, Reynolds conducted a national Delphi Survey for the Council for Exceptional Children that detected the trend toward cross-categorical teacher certifications. Data were collected from a national sample of state directors of special education and of teacher certification; college administrators; college faculty in speech and hearing and in special education; graduate and undergraduate students in special education; and public school general administrators, special education administrators, regular and special education teachers, and speech and hearing therapists.

In one item respondents were asked to predict how many different kinds of special education certificates would be issued by the states in 1978 and 1983. They were informed that seven or eight different kinds were being offered by most states in 1973.

On the first round of the survey, the results for the group as a whole were, for 1978, 6.7 different kinds and, for 1983, 6.4. Second-round results were, for 1978, 6.5, and, for 1983, 5.8. These data show that most respondents expected the number of kinds of certificates to be reduced in the late 1970s and early 1980s.

They were then asked how many different kinds of certificates would be offered if they had the power to control the situation. Results (second round) were: for 1978, 5.1; for 1983, 4.9. These responses showed the desirability of a still fewer kinds of specialized certification. On the average, respondents thought there could and should be only about five different kinds of certificates rather than seven or eight. State directors of special education, state directors of teacher certification, and leaders in the field of special education held even stronger than average expectations that the number of kinds of certificates should and would be reduced. Of all the groups surveyed, only the regular teachers expected an increase. They believed that there should be specialists to attend effectively to all the problems of children that they themselves had difficulty meeting, and this would mean more and more teaching specialties.

General results of the survey showed that the kinds of special certificates most likely to persist were the following: Speech-language therapy; hearing handicaps; visual handicaps; severe and profound handicaps (a generic certificate); and a generic special education certificate for children showing mild and moderate handicaps. It appears that the Delphi Survey of 1973 was accurate in its predictions: many states are moving in the directions outlined (Barresi & Bunte, 1979; Gilmore & Argyros, 1977). At least one state (Louisiana) moved rapidly to change all its programs for mildly and moderately handicapped students, and their teachers, to a noncategorical base (Nix, 1980).

The new policies regarding education for the handicapped have also had major implications for changes in the preparation of regular classroom teachers; inasmuch as the majority of children with special needs evidence mild to moderate handicaps, the least restrictive placement for them tends to be the regular classroom. Unfortunately, at the time the Education for All Handicapped Children Act of 1975 became effective in 1977, few regular classroom teachers had the necessary training or experience for working with such children. Although the law included financial support for in-service programs to acquaint teachers already in the schools with the characteristics and needs of the handicapped children who would be entering their classrooms, no attention was given to the preparatory training of prospective classroom teachers.

In order to encourage the revision of teacher-preparation programs in colleges and departments of education, the Bureau of Education for the Handicapped (later, the Office of Special Education in the Department of Education) initiated the Deans' Grant program of support to develop a reconceptualization of teacher-preparation curricula. (Behrens & Grosenick, 1978). By 1981 more than two hundred colleges and universities had undertaken important changes in their regular teacher education programs with support by Deans' Grants; many others undertook changes without special financial aid. The general direction of the changes in regular teaching preparation have been summarized by Reynolds (1979) in terms of ten "clusters of capability."

Instructional needs classification. The fact that some of the traditional classification systems have given way and children are being grouped according to less narrowly framed criteria gives rise to the question of how they are to be classified. Much as we may dislike categorizations that have no functional purpose, we must have some way of distinguishing pupils with specific educational needs. In general, therefore, the answer to the question is that the orientation should be toward instructional classifications. For example, in the schools "blindness" has been defined quite strictly in accordance with instructional needs for some time: a student is blind for purposes of

schooling when he or she cannot use sight as the medium for reading and must use braille and/or other reading systems that do not depend upon sight. Such an approach to classification is appropriate and valid for purposes of schooling even though it is very different from procedures used in other contexts and for different purposes. Similarly, a child is "deaf" only when the auditory channel, after all prosthetic devices have been considered and applied, is not functional for purposes of the teaching and learning of language. The classification in school is made distinctly for educational purposes.

Likewise, the approaches used in special education resource and other programs that break out of the old categorical modes are modeled according to instructional needs. Children who might have been classified as EMR or LD are, instead, assessed and taught according to each individual's relation to the curriculum structure. What does he or she know in reading, arithmetic, social skills, and the like? What are the sensible next steps in teaching this particular child?

The aptitude-treatment-interaction concept advanced by Cronbach and Gleser (1965) is useful in this context. Reynolds and Balow (1962) outlined general methods by which aptitude variables can be considered in allocating students to appropriate instructional systems. Similarly, the data-based system developed by the behavior analysts is extremely useful in providing precise objectives and procedures for meeting the needs of individuals (e.g., Deno & Mirkin, 1977).

Systems for the detailed analysis of intra-individual variation in presumed underlying psychological traits, such as the Illinois Test of Psycholinguistic Abilities (Kirk, McCarthy, & Kirk, 1968), also are being widely used in instructional planning for individuals rather than categories. However, these methods involve very difficult technical issues, as in use of nonregressed measures in profile analysis, and many serious questions of validity for purposes of instructional planning (Ysseldyke & Salvia, 1974; Kavale, 1981; Arter & Jenkins, 1979).

Shift to Common Concerns. The strong focus on the individual during the 1970s was broader, of course, than concern with handicapped students or their schooling. It was a period in which individuals pitted themselves against the system politically and culturally as an outgrowth of the civil rights movement of the 1960s. In a summary essay on the 1970s, "Epitaph for a Decade," Morrow (1980) observed: "The American gaze turned inward. . . . Social critic Tom Wolfe called it the Me decade, a term that caught the epoch's dreamily obsessive self-regard. The 70s were given over to building private, not public morale" (pp. 38–39).

Today, however, attention clearly is beginning to turn not necessarily away from the individual but certainly to a consideration of common concerns, to what must be created and supported broadly in the community in order to provide adequately for individuals. As early as 1950 Childs spoke of the necessity of teaching children to work and play together, to create a sense of community: "The public school has been expected to nurture this basic moral consciousness (human brotherhood), not simply by its instruction of the young in the history, the laws, the political processes and the social ideals of our democratic way of life, but also by the provision of actual opportunity for the children of the various component groups—economic, religious, and racial—to grow to respect one another by living, studying, working, and playing together" (p. 241).

The work of Johnson and Johnson (1975) illustrates the emergence of a new conception of group or social structure in classrooms that recognizes the needs of individuals but also the necessity for mutual respect and decency so that individuals can learn and prosper (see also Gottlieb & Leyser, 1981; Slavin, 1978). The investigators suggest, at least for parts of the school curriculum, that students be organized into heterogeneous groups to work toward goals which have been structured to require cooperative social behavior for their achievement. This deliberate management of the social structure stimulates students to recognize and accept individual differences and to deal with them constructively and amiably. Thus children learn gradually to help set policies for their communities (particularly those of classrooms and schools) that will benefit all the members. The supporting argument for the cooperative classroom is that even in a highly competitive society children must learn to work together to achieve common ends. For example, the Apollo mission in 1981, in which a vehicle was launched into orbit and then returned to dry land, required a remarkable degree of cooperation from the moment of its conception to its successful completion; nevertheless, the event was heralded internationally as a competitive achievement.

Responsibility for Decision Making. Students today are expected to share responsibility not only for their particular social environments but also for managing their schools and making decisions that affect their lives. In this way they help to solve what would otherwise be very difficult management problems in their classes, and also learn gradually to operate with personal independence. All too often, handicapped persons have been expected to live a life of dependence, but that, too, is changing and is an important aspect of the growing respect for the individual person.

A specific line of study with handicapped persons focuses on the locus of control in decision making, a concept that was generated by Rotter's social-learning theory (1954). The basic premise of the idea is the attribution of one's "good luck" or "bad luck" to forces external or internal to oneself. For example, students who fail an important test may attribute their poor performances to the teacher's not liking them (an external cause) or to insufficient study (an internal cause). Tyler (1978) noted that persons who attribute responsibility to internal sources ("internals") have an advantage over those who attribute responsibility to external sources ("externals"). However, "research has demonstrated that one's orientation can be shifted toward internality by appropriate educational procedures" (Tyler, 1978, p. 218).

Research has shown that handicapped persons appear to be depressed in their performances by their expectations that the probability of success will be low (Bryan & Pearl, 1979; Cromwell, 1963). Such expectations are reinforced according to the theory, by frequent failure experiences in general, and in the specific behavioral domain being considered. Expectations and experiences interact to produce increasingly low concepts of self and efficiency in behavior. Persons who have experienced much success in life tend to use failure as a stimulus for increased effort, but this is not so for those whose expectations have been attenuated by frequent failure. The latter have little reason to see the locus of control in their lives as internal (Chan & Keogh, 1974; Piersel & Kratochwill, 1979).

Fortunately, it appears that efforts by educators to establish internality in locus of control and independence in general aspects of life by individual handicapped persons can be fruitful. Indeed, some would say that the drive for independent living has reached the proportions of a major social movement (DeJong, 1979). Motivation has come partly from handicapped persons themselves. For example, the Center for Independent Living (CIL) in Berkeley, California, has become a strong force for orientation and training of the handicapped, and has also been a strong advocacy center for governmental policies that support the independent living movement (Brown, 1978). A second major source of energy in support of the movement has been federal legislation, in particular the 1973 Rehabilitation Act. Legislation relating to transportation, architectural barriers, housing, and education also has been important.

A variety of programs that teach handicapped children (and the nonhandicapped, too) to be more responsible is now developing. Wang and Stiles (1976), for example, have demonstrated the application of systems procedures in elementary schools, with curricular components designed explicitly to teach students to be increasingly responsible for curriculum decisions. Their work involves the mainstreaming of many handicapped students, so that they as well as other students acquire experience in internalizing controls and taking on larger personal responsibilities.

Similarly, many schools have developed systems in which students measure and record their own performance as parts of instructional processes. Behavior analysts, for example, have demonstrated procedures, even in elementary grades, in which children record their daily progress on learning tasks and link the data to curricular decisions and behavior controls (see Lovitt, 1973).

Summary. Deep structural changes are occurring in school programs for handicapped children. The move is away from simple categorization and labeling, institutionalization, assumed dependence, isolation, and infantilization, and toward more consideration of what is unique about each individual, mainstreaming, independent living, broad community understanding, acceptance of the handicapped as persons, and training for adulthood. This is more than a minor pendulum swing or a temporary enthusiasm. It is a basic and long-standing change. The primacy of the concept of individuality is perhaps the central feature of the change, but it is important to note the complementary changes occurring in the community as well. Even in the community represented in the classroom there is growing awareness of the broadly shared responsibility—by everyone, literally—to help create social structures that are decent in every way and that specifically help to foster the development of handicapped individuals.

Maynard C. Reynolds

See also Attitudes toward the Handicapped; Deinstitutionalization of the Handicapped; Equity Issues in Education; Learning Disabilities; Mental Retardation; Preschool Education for the Handicapped; Special Education.

REFERENCES

Arter, J. A., & Jenkins, J. R. Differential diagnosis-prescriptive teaching: a critical appraisal. *Review of Educational Research,* 1979, *49*(4), 517–555.

Barresi, J., & Bunte, J. *Special Education Certification Practice: A National Survey, December 1979.* Reston, Va.: Council for Exceptional Children, 1979. (ERIC Document Reproduction Service No. ED 189 800)

Behrens, T., & Grosenick, J. K. Deans' grant projects: Supporting innovations in teacher-education programs. In J. K. Grosenick & M. C. Reynolds (Eds.), *Teacher Education: Renegotiating Roles for Mainstreaming.* Reston, Va.: Council for Exceptional Children, 1978, 1–5. (ERIC Document Reproduction Service No. ED 159 156)

Bijou, S. W., & Baer, D. M. *Child Development: A Systematic and Empirical Theory.* New York: Appleton-Century-Crofts, 1961.

Brown, B. M. Second generation: West coast. *American Rehabilitation,* July–August 1978, *3*, 23–30.

Bryan, T., & Pearl, R. Self-concepts and locus of control of disabled children. *Journal of Clinical Child Psychology,* 1979, *8*(3), 223–226.

Chan, K. S., & Keogh, B. K. Interpretation of task interruption and feelings of responsibility for failure. *Journal of Special Education,* 1974, *8*(2), 175–178.

Childs, J. *Education and Morals.* New York: Appleton-Century-Crofts, 1950.

Cromwell, R. L. A social learning approach to mental retardation. In N. R. Ellis (Ed.), *Handbook of Mental Deficiency.* New York: McGraw-Hill, 1963, pp. 41–91.

Cronbach, L. J. The two disciplines of scientific psychology. *American Psychologist,* 1957, *12*, 671–684.

Cronbach, L. J., & Gleser, G. C. *Psychological Tests and Personnel Decisions* (2nd ed.). Urbana: University of Illinois Press, 1965.

Cronbach, L. J., & Snow, R. E. *Aptitudes and Instructional Methods.* New York: Irvington, 1977.

DeJong, G. *The Movement for Independent Living: Origins, Ideology, and Implications for Disability Research.* Lansing, Mich.: University Center for International Rehabilitation, 1979. (ERIC Document Reproduction Service No. ED 175 217)

Deno, E. (Ed.). *Instructional Alternatives for Exceptional Children.* Reston, Va.: Council for Exceptional Children, 1975. (ERIC Document Reproduction Service No. ED 074 678)

Deno, S. L., & Mirkin, P. K. *Data-based Program Modification: A Manual.* Reston, Va.: Council for Exceptional Children, 1977. (ERIC Document Reproduction Service No. ED 144 270)

Gilmore, J. T., & Argyros, N. S. *Special Education Certification: A State of the Art Survey.* Albany: New York State Department of Education, Office of Education of Children with Handicapping Conditions, 1977. (ERIC Document Reproduction Service No. ED 158 447)

Glaser, R. Instructional technology and the measurement of learning outcomes: Some questions. *American Psychologist,* 1963, *18*, 519–521.

Gottlieb, J., & Leyser, Y. Facilitating the social mainstreaming of retarded children. *Exceptional Education Quarterly,* 1981, *1*(4), 57–69.

Haring, N. G. *Behavior of Exceptional Children.* Columbus, Ohio: Merrill, 1974.

Heber, R.; Garber, H.; Harrington, S.; Hoffman, L.; & Falender, C. *Rehabilitation of Families at Risk for Mental Retardation* (Progress Report). Madison, Wis.: Rehabilitation Research and Training Center in Mental Retardation, 1972. (ERIC Document Reproduction Service No. ED 087 142)

Hobbs, N. *The Futures of Children.* San Francisco: Jossey-Bass, 1975.

Hunt, D. E., & Sullivan, E. V. *Between Psychology and Education.* New York: Dryden, 1974.

Hunt, J. M. *Intelligence and Experience.* New York: Ronald Press, 1961.

Isaac Lora v. *Board of Education, New York City.* 75 Civ. 917 (E.D. N.Y. 1979).

Johnson, D. W., & Johnson, R. T. *Learning Together and Alone: Cooperation, Competition, and Individualization.* Englewood Cliffs, N.J.: Prentice-Hall, 1975.

Kavale, K. Functions of the Illinois Test of Psycholinguistic Abilities (ITPA): Are they trainable? *Exceptional Children,* 1981, *47*(7), 496–510.

Kirk, S. A. *Early Education of the Mentally Retarded: An Experimental study.* Urbana: University of Illinois Press, 1958.

Kirk, S. A.; McCarthy, J. J.; & Kirk, W. *Illinois Test of Psycholinguistic Abilities.* Urbana: University of Illinois Press, 1968.

Larry P. v. *Riles.* 343 F. Supp. 1306 (N.D. Cal. 1972).

Lindsley, O. R. Direct measurement and prosthesis of retarded behavior. *Journal of Education,* 1964, *147*, 62.

Lovitt, T. C. Behavior modification: The current scene. *Exceptional Children,* 1970, *37*, 85–91.

Lovitt, T. C. Self-management projects with children with behavioral disabilities. *Journal of Learning Disabilities,* 1973, *6*(3), 138–150.

Lovitt, T. C. Applied behavior analysis techniques and curriculum research: Implications for instruction. In N. G. Haring & R. L. Schiefelbusch (Eds.), *Teaching Special Children.* New York: McGraw-Hill, 1976.

Morrow, L. Epitaph for a decade. *Time,* 1980, *115*, 38–39.

Nix, J. K. *Louisiana Standards for State Certification of School Personnel* (Bulletin No. 746, rev.). Baton Rouge: State of Louisiana, Department of Education, 1980.

Piersel, W. C., & Kratochwill, T. R. Self-observation and behavior change: Applications to academic and adjustment problems through behavioral consultation. *Journal of School Psychology,* 1979, *17*(2), 151–161.

Popham, J., & Husek, T. Implications of criterion-referenced measurement. *Journal of Educational Measurement*, 1969, *6*, 1–9.

Reynolds, M. C. *Delphi Survey: A Report of Rounds I and II*. Reston, Va.: Council for Exceptional Children, Committee on Professional Standards and Guidelines, 1973. (ERIC Document Reproduction Service No. ED 087 734)

Reynolds, M. C. *A Common Body of Practice for Teachers: The Challenge of Public Law 94-142 to Teacher Education*. Washington, D.C.: American Association of Colleges for Teacher Education, 1979. (ERIC Document Reproduction Service No. ED 186 399)

Reynolds, M. C., & Balow, B. Categories and variables in special education. *Exceptional Children*, 1962, *38*, 357–366.

Rotter, J. B. *Social Learning and Clinical Psychology*. Englewood Cliffs, N.J.: Prentice-Hall, 1954.

Slavin, R. E. Student teams and achievement decisions. *Journal of Research and Development in Education*, 1978, *12*, 39–49.

Tyler, L. E. *Individuality*. San Francisco: Jossey-Bass, 1978.

Wang, M. C., & Stiles, B. An investigation of children's concept of self-responsibility for their school environment. *American Educational Research Journal*, 1976, *13*(3), 159–179.

Wolf, M. M.; Risley, T.; & Mees, H. L. Application of operant conditioning procedures to the behavior problems of an autistic child. *Behavior Research and Therapy*, 1964, *1*, 305–312.

Wright, A. R. *Local Implementation of PL 94-142: Second-year Report of a Longitudinal Study* (Stanford Research International Project H 7124). Menlo Park, Calif.: SRI International, 1980.

Ysseldyke, J. E., & Salvia, J. Diagnostic-prescriptive teaching: Two models. *Exceptional Children*, 1974, *41*, 181–186.

HANDWRITING

Numerous surveys of research and literature related to handwriting are available (Andersen, 1966a, 1966b; Brown, 1977; Herrick, 1960; Horn, 1967; Huitt, 1972; Otto & Andersen, 1969; Petty, 1966; Shane & Mulry, 1963). In response to some of these surveys, Herrick and Okada (1963) identified various directions that handwriting research might take. These suggestions for future research formed the basis for subsequent reviews of research conducted during the 1960s (Askov, Otto, & Askov, 1970) and the 1970s (Peck, Askov, & Fairchild, 1980) and are the basis for the presentation of research findings here.

In the interest of brevity, research studies discussed by Otto and Andersen in the previous edition of the *Encyclopedia of Educational Research* (4th ed., 1969) are not reexamined here or are mentioned only briefly. For a historical perspective on handwriting research, readers should consult earlier editions of the encyclopedia.

Legibility. Research on the legibility of letters produced during writing has proceeded in three directions. The first approach has involved examining illegible letters to determine which forms are most difficult to produce (Horton, 1970; Lewis & Lewis, 1964; Newland, 1932; Pressey & Pressey, 1927).

A second approach to the study of letter-form production and legibility has concerned the modifications of letters as written by students. Seifert's study (1959) revealed that one-third of the children in grades 6 through 9 exhibited personal, but legible, handwriting styles that deviated from the standard taught. In a related study involving college students, Schell and Burns (1963) concluded that initial handwriting instruction should emphasize simplified letter forms to preclude the possibility of idiosyncratic letter modifications in later years. However, Epstein, Hartford, and Tumarkin (1961) found that female college seniors who retained letter forms taught in elementary school tended to be less educated, bright, and mature than their female classmates who modified letter forms. Taken together, these studies indicate that handwriting instruction might incorporate simplified letter forms without loss of legibility.

A third direction taken in the study of letter formations has used factor analysis to ascertain commonalities among letter shapes. Some studies have isolated factors common to capital letters (Kuennapas, 1966, 1967) or to lower case letters (Kuennapas & Janson, 1969). However, Stennett, Smithe, and Hardy (1972) report that no clear-cut patterns emerged when uppercase and lowercase manuscript letters were analyzed in their study.

Instructional Techniques. The most common instructional technique for teaching new letter forms has been copying based on traditional practices rather than research evidence. Several studies (Askov & Greff, 1975; Hirsch, 1973; Hirsch & Niedermeyer, 1973) have recently compared copying to other techniques, especially tracing. All studies demonstrated the superiority of the copying method. Williams (1975), on the other hand, found that visual discrimination training for preschool subjects from low-income families apparently does transfer to new letters, but that learning from copying does not transfer to new letters. Handwriting training must therefore focus on all letters, since young children apparently cannot generalize from a learned letter to new letters. Søvik (1976, 1979) found that verbal instruction combined with demonstration improved copying performance. Furthermore, he found some tentative evidence that copying a close model produces better performance than copying a model at some distance. Further research is needed to determine whether distance (for example, copying material on the chalkboard as opposed to copying material on the desk) is a factor influencing success in copying a model letter form. A series of studies (Helwig, 1976; Johns, 1977; Trap, 1977) have successfully used transparent overlays to teach correct letter formation, although some difficulty occurs in generalizing strokes to unfamiliar letters.

Some research has focused on techniques for improving handwriting instruction. These techniques include educational television (Forster, 1971), computers (Teulings & Thomassen, 1979), animated flip books (Wright & Wright, 1980), programmed workbooks (Olson, 1970), direct instruction in eye-hand coordination (Fairchild, 1979), teaching handwriting as a perceptual as well as a motor task (Furner, 1969a, 1969b, 1970), and rule-based instruction (Kirk, 1978).

Clear correlates of handwriting skill do not emerge from the research literature. Intelligence has not been shown to be a significant correlate, especially after subjects have been instructed in handwriting (Lewis, 1964; Lindell, 1964). Perceptual-motor abilities appear to be important in beginning instruction (Chapman & Wedell, 1972; Poteet, 1970), especially for learning distinctive features of letters (McCarthy, 1977; Wheeler, 1972). Lack of clearly established hand dominance, however, does not seem to affect copying ability (Shimrat, 1970).

Body-part Positions. Much of the literature on body-part positions during writing has compared the performance of right-handed and left-handed subjects. Neither Reed and Smith (1962) nor Lewis (1964) found significant differences in writing due to handedness after instruction. As suggested by Askov, Otto, and Askov (1970), these studies contradict earlier conclusions advanced by Guilford (1936) that right-handed writers are superior in legibility and speed. Enstrom (1962) determined that fifteen altered hand positions were used by 1,103 left-handed writers in grades 5 through 8. Judgments of writing quality, neatness, speed, and "healthful" body positions were made. Interestingly, the position receiving the highest overall rating was not the one taught as an adjustment for left-handed students. Drawings of adapted positions for left-handed writers were given. Croutch (1969) also gave suggestions for correct positions of the body and paper for left-handed and right-handed students.

Callewaert (1963) gave a detailed description of an alternative handwriting grip. However, results of a study comparing this modified grip and the traditional grip indicated that twenty right-handed college students found the traditional grip to be more comfortable (Otto et al., 1966). More recently, Mendoza, Holt, and Jackson (1978) reported on a successful method to teach proper pencil grip to 4-year-old children. Kao (1973) found that extensive hand-finger exercise appeared to accelerate the pace of adults' writing without impeding tracing accuracy.

Regarding the effect of body position upon handwriting, Lurçat (1968) found that posture was the most important factor affecting the slant of handwriting.

Stress and Speed. Using unique methodology and instrumentation to measure stress, Herrick and Otto (1961) found widely varying pressure exerted on the barrel of a special transducer pen by students in grades 4 and 6 and in college. The data revealed that, in general, high point-pressure accompanies high grip-pressure and low point-pressure accompanies low grip-pressure.

New handwriting speed norms were created by Groff (1969) for grades 4, 5, and 6. These new norms have substantially reduced speeds as compared to the older Ayres norms. Rarick and Harris (1963) found that bright and average sixth-graders produced their fastest writing sample under the condition requiring fast writing. The slowest

writing resulted from the condition demanding the "best" writing. Writers termed generally superior produced the most legible samples across all writing conditions.

Jackson (1970) found that intermediate students using manuscript writing wrote significantly faster than students using cursive writing. However, no significant differences were shown for legibility between the two experimental groups. The superiority of manuscript writing with respect to speed supports Andersen's earlier suggestions (Andersen, 1966b).

Rice (1976) concluded that handwriting rate was a significant predictor of language achievement and assignment completion for 199 sixth-grade students. He suggested that teachers employ a writing-rate test accompanied by achievement expectation norms in order to anticipate students' general language and written assignment levels.

Instructional Sequences. Various surveys of instructional practices (Addy & Wylie, 1973; Herrick & Okada, 1963; Noble, 1963) have indicated that most elementary schools have separate handwriting instruction of approximately fifteen to twenty minutes per day in grades 1 to 4 and several times per week in grades 5 to 8. Although some research (Boyle, 1963; Newland, 1932; Tagatz et al., 1969) suggests the advantages of individualized diagnostic-prescriptive procedures, generally instruction is provided for the class as a whole. Manuscript writing is taught in first grade, and cursive writing usually in the latter half of the second or third grade.

The question of manuscript writing versus cursive writing has been debated at great length. Now that manuscript writing is commonly taught as an initial form of writing in the United States, the question seems to be why children are taught to use cursive writing so soon after having learned manuscript writing. Research pertaining to this issue is discussed by Otto and Andersen (1969). Herrick (1960) and Andersen (1966b), in separate surveys of earlier research, concluded that manuscript writing should be retained beyond the primary grades, because it is more legible and more easily learned, and it can be written at least as fast as cursive writing. Some research evidence (Templin, 1963; Weinert, Simons, & Essig, 1966) suggests that instruction in manuscript writing creates ease and produces better-quality writing. Jackson's study (1970) indicates that intermediate-grade students using manuscript writing wrote faster than comparable students taught to use cursive writing in the third grade. No differences were found in legibility, however. Up-to-date large-scale studies are needed to validate or refute the present practice of switching primary children from manuscript to cursive writing. One must question the wisdom of this practice, especially since manuscript writing is generally accepted in the adult world (Groff, 1964; Templin, 1963).

A solution to the dilemma of manuscript writing versus cursive writing has been proposed by the proponents of italic writing. Analyzing the teachings of seven Renaissance writing masters, Osley (1979) concludes that modern systems of italic handwriting are closest to those principles of good writing. Lehman (1976), reporting the results of a three-year study in one school district, measured the writing of primary-grade children by four criteria. Subjects who were taught italic writing deviated one-half as much from their letter models as did the comparison group, who were taught manuscript writing followed by cursive writing. On a speed test at the end of third grade, the italic group produced more letters in a two-minute time period than the comparison group. Results cannot be considered conclusive until large-scale comparisons can be made. Long-term effects, measured some time after initial instruction, also need to be considered. Although adoption of italic writing would create tremendous changes for inservice teachers, administrators, and parents—and it is unlikely that such groups would welcome these changes when concern focuses primarily on other basic skills—the advantages and disadvantages of italic handwriting instruction are worth exploring as an alternative to the current practice of teaching two systems to beginning writers.

Graves (1979), describing a two-year case study of the development of the writing of primary school children, notes that handwriting is influenced by the stage of the writer's development. Like early speech patterns, early handwriting lacks organization. When children have opportunities to choose their own writing topics, language, and format, handwriting improves. Handwriting has been found in this study to be a critical index to teachers of how to help children with composition.

Suggestions, as well as research, concerning handwriting instruction for various categories of special education children can be found in Block (1978), Carter and Synolds (1974), Enstrom (1966), Fauke et al. (1973), Gerard (1978), Graham and Miller (1980), Green (1967), Harrison (1968), Haworth (1971), Lahey et al. (1977), Linn (1968), Macleod and Procter (1979), McElravy (1964), and Parres (1969). Although some writers (Joseph & Mullins, 1970; Mullins et al., 1972) have proposed cursive handwriting instruction for learning-disabled students, research is needed to demonstrate its superiority for this group.

Instruments and Paper. Use of beginner's pencils do not appear to produce significantly better handwriting in nursery to first-grade subjects (Parker, 1973). Children also appear to prefer adult pencils (Herrick, 1961). Third-grade subjects produced more letters in a story-writing task using felt-tip and ball-point pens than those subjects using pencils (Krzesni, 1971).

Although Halpin and Halpin (1976) found no significant differences in handwriting quality of kindergarten children using paper with lines of different widths, Kau-To Leung et al. (1979) found that first-grade subjects produced significantly more accurate letter strokes using large-spaced paper. However, differences in the results may be due to different evaluation procedures.

Evaluation. The history and development of handwriting scales in the United States has been summarized by Otto and Andersen (1969). Fischer (1964) has analyzed handwriting characteristics in Germany and identified size and slant as two of five factors to be evaluated. In a related study, Craig (1965) found that height and uniformity of small letters, uniformity of tall and capital letters, and alignment were the important factors affecting both teachers' ratings of legibility and sixth-grade students' ability to read their peers' writing. Apparently, teachers tended to equate readability with legibility.

Attempts to develop and assess techniques for measuring letter formation have been described by Helwig et al. (1976) and Jones, Trap, and Cooper (1977). Both studies have involved the use of transparent overlays to measure the range of deviations in handwritten letters from given model letters. As Otto, Askov, and Cooper (1969) have shown, once teachers are adept at using a scale to rate handwriting samples, they can rate samples without the use of such scales.

Conclusions. The recent interest in handwriting research, guided by Herrick and Okada's suggested directions, has been encouraging (Herrick & Okada, 1963). The realization that handwriting is more than a motor task, since it also involves perception and discrimination, has made it an attractive subject for researchers. Cognitive abilities also come into play as children learn to judge their productions against models (Harris & Herrick, 1963).

In short, handwriting is a vehicle for studying processes of learning in easily measured, concrete ways. The use of new methodologies to measure characteristics of handwriting as well as the effects of particular instructional treatments is also encouraging. More tightly controlled studies are being conducted, with some replications occurring, to validate findings of other investigators. We have recently found fewer surveys of existing practices and increased emphasis on experimental research as the vehicle for answering questions about handwriting instruction.

And yet, current practices in handwriting instruction, perhaps more than in any of the other basics taught in elementary school, are guided by traditional wisdom and commercial materials. Federal money for large-scale studies of handwriting instruction has not been available as it has been for studies of reading. Given our increasingly impersonal world, concerned primarily with efficiency, one wonders why any interest has been shown in such a form of personal expression. Precisely because handwriting is a form of personal expression, it needs to be preserved, researched, and taught effectively as well as efficiently. And, since it involves a form of personal expression, a child's success or failure in handwriting instruction influences how he or she feels about other school learning. We hope that this review will encourage researchers to respond to the challenge of applying quantitative methods to an essentially qualitative experience and personal form of expression.

Eunice N. Askov
Michaeleen Peck

See also English Language Education.

REFERENCES

Addy, P., & Wylie, R. E. The "right" way to write. *Childhood Education,* 1973, *49,* 253–254.

Andersen, D. Handwriting research: Movement and quality. In T. Horn (Ed.), *Research on Handwriting and Spelling.* Champaign, Ill.: National Council of Teachers of English, 1966. (a) (ERIC Document Reproduction Service No. ED 089 362)

Andersen, D. Handwriting research: Style and practice. In T. Horn (Ed.), *Research on Handwriting and Spelling.* Champaign, Ill.: National Council of Teachers of English, 1966. (b) (ERIC Document Reproduction Service No. 089 362)

Askov, E., & Greff, K. Handwriting: Copying versus tracing as the most effective type of practice. *Journal of Educational Research,* 1975, *69,* 96–98.

Askov, E.; Otto, W.; & Askov, W. A decade of research in handwriting: Progress and prospect. *Journal of Educational Research,* 1970, *64,* 100–111.

Block, J. Teaching reading and writing skills to a teenaged spastic cerebral palsied person: A long-term case study. *Perceptual and Motor Skills,* 1978, *46,* 31–41.

Boyle, M. C. An experimental study of a diagnostic-remedial program in handwriting in the fourth, fifth, and sixth grades (Doctoral dissertation, Fordham University, 1963). *Dissertation Abstracts,* 1963, *24,* 642. (University Microfilms No. 63–5584)

Brown, G. Handwriting: A state of the art research paper. Manitoba, Canada: Winnipeg School Division Number 1, 1977, 1–53.

Callewaert, H. For easy and legible handwriting. In V. Herrick (Ed.), *New Horizons for Research in Handwriting.* Madison: University of Wisconsin Press, 1963.

Carter, J., & Synolds, D. Effects of relaxation training upon handwriting quality. *Journal of Learning Disabilities,* 1974, *7,* 236–238.

Chapman, L., & Wedell, K. Perceptual-motor abilities and reversal errors in children's handwriting. *Journal of Learning Disabilities,* 1972, *5,* 321–326.

Craig, M. An analysis of the relationships between the ease of reading sixth grade handwritten papers by peers and teacher evaluation of the handwritten papers with selected handwriting factors. (Doctoral dissertation, Ball State University, 1965). *Dissertation Abstracts,* 1966, *27,* 325-A. (University Microfilms No. 65–13, 035)

Croutch, B. Handwriting and correct posture. *Academic Therapy,* 1969, *4,* 283–284.

Enstrom, E. The relative efficiency of the various approaches to writing with the left hand. *Journal of Educational Research,* 1962, *55,* 573–577.

Enstrom, E. Out of the classroom; handwriting for the retarded. *Exceptional Children,* 1966, *32,* 385–388.

Epstein, L.; Hartford, H.; & Tumarkin, I. The relationship of certain letter form variants in the handwriting of female subjects to their education, I.Q., and age. *Journal of Experimental Education,* 1961, *29,* 385–392.

Fairchild, S. The effect of sequenced eye-hand coordination experiences on the young child's ability to reproduce printed symbols (Doctoral dissertation, Pennsylvania State University, 1979). *Dissertation Abstracts International,* 1979, *40,* 1856A (University Microfilms No. 7922285)

Fauke, J.; Burnett, J.; Powers, M.; & Sulzer-Azaroff, B. Improvement of handwriting and letter recognition skills: A behavior modification procedure. *Journal of Learning Disabilities,* 1973, *6,* 25–29.

Fischer, G. Zur faktoriellen Struktur der Handschrift (Factorial structure of handwriting). *Zeitschrift für Experimentelle und Angewandte Psychologie,* 1964, *11,* 254–280.

Forster, R. An experiment in teaching transitional, cursive handwriting by educational television with teacher attitude toward the teaching of handwriting as a factor (Doctoral dissertation, Ohio University, 1971). *Dissertation Abstracts International,* 1971, *32,* 1184A–1185A. (University Microfilms No. 71–22, 959)

Furner, B. The perceptual-motor nature of learning in handwriting. *Elementary English,* 1969a, *46,* 886–894.

Furner, B. Recommended instructional procedures in a method emphasizing the perceptual-motor nature of learning in handwriting. *Elementary English,* 1969b, *46,* 1021–1030.

Furner, B. An analysis of the effectiveness of a program of instruction emphasizing the perceptual-motor nature of learning in handwriting. *Elementary English,* 1970, *47,* 61–69.

Gerard, J. An investigation into the efficacy of a task analysis model for the diagnosis and remediation of handwriting problems of the learning disabled (Doctoral dissertation, Boston College, 1978). *Dissertation Abstracts International,* 1978, *39,* 1474A. (University Microfilms No. 7813775)

Graham, S., & Miller, L. Handwriting research and practice: A unified approach. *Focus on Exceptional Children,* 1980, *13* (2), 1–16.

Graves, D. Let children show us how to help them write. *Visible Language,* 1979, *13*(1), 16–28.

Green, M. I. An introductory study of teaching handwriting to the brain injured child. *Exceptional Children,* 1967, *34,* 44–45.

Groff, P. New speeds in handwriting. In W. Otto & K. Koenke (Eds.), *Remedial Teaching: Research and Comment.* Boston: Houghton Mifflin, 1969.

Groff, P. Preference for handwriting style by big business. *Elementary English,* 1964, *41,* 863–864, 868.

Guilford, W. *Left-handedness: Its Effects upon the Quality and Speed of Writing of Pupils in the Fifth and Sixth Grades.* Unpublished master's thesis, College of Puget Sound, 1936.

Halpin, G., & Halpin, G. Special paper for beginning handwriting: An unjustified practice? *Journal of Educational Research,* 1976, *69,* 267–269.

Harris, T. L., & Herrick, V. E. Children's perception of the handwriting task. In V. E. Herrick (Ed.), *New Horizons for Research in Handwriting,* Madison: University of Wisconsin Press, 1963.

Harrison, E. M. The brain damaged child and writing problems. *Academic Therapy,* 1968, *4,* 13–21.

Haworth, M. The effect of rhythmic-motor training and gross-motor training on the reading and handwriting abilities of educable mentally retarded children (Doctoral dissertation, University of Nebraska, 1970). *Dissertation Abstracts International,* 1971, *31,* 3991A–3992A. (University Microfilms No. 71–2890)

Helwig, J. Measurement of visual-verbal feedback on changes in manuscript letter formation (Doctoral dissertation, Ohio State University, 1975). *Dissertation Abstracts International,* 1976, *36,* 5196A. (University Microfilms No. 76–3448)

Helwig, J. J.; Johns, J. C.; Norman, J. B.; & Cooper, J. O. The measurement of manuscript letter strokes. *Journal of Applied Behavior Analysis,* 1976, *9,* 231–236.

Herrick, V. E. Handwriting and children's writing. *Elementary English,* 1960, *37,* 248–258.

Herrick, V. E. Handwriting tools for children. *National Education Association,* 1961, *50,* 49–50.

Herrick, V. E., & Okada, N. The present scene: Practices in the teaching of handwriting in the United States. In V. E. Herrick (Ed.), *New Horizons for Research in Handwriting*, Madison: University of Wisconsin Press, 1963.

Herrick, V., & Otto, W. Pressure on point and barrel of a writing instrument. *Journal of Experimental Education*, 1961, *30*, 215–230.

Hirsch, E. The effects of letter formation practice and letter discrimination training on kindergarten handwriting performance (Doctoral dissertation, University of California, Los Angeles, 1973). *Dissertation Abstracts International*, 1973, *33*, 6648A–6649A. (University Microfilms No. 73–13, 143)

Hirsch, E., & Niedermeyer, F. C. The effects of tracing prompts and discrimination training on kindergarten handwriting performance. *Journal of Educational Research*, 1973, *67*, 81–83.

Horn, T. D. Handwriting and spelling. *Review of Educational Research*, 1967, *37*, 168–177.

Horton, L. Illegibilities in the cursive handwriting of sixth graders. *The Elementary School Journal*, 1970, *70*, 446–450.

Huitt, R. Handwriting: The state of the craft. *Childhood Education*, 1972, *48*, 219–223.

Jackson, A. A comparison of speed and legibility of manuscript and cursive handwriting of intermediate grade pupils (Doctoral dissertation, University of Arizona, 1970). *Dissertation Abstracts International*, 1971, *31*, 4383A–4384A. (University Microfilms No. 71–6811)

Johns, J. The effects of training, self-recording, public charting, and group contingencies on manuscript handwriting legibility (Doctoral dissertation, Ohio State University, 1976). *Dissertation Abstracts International*, 1977, *37*, 4824A. (University Microfilms No. 77–2425)

Jones, J.; Trap, J.; & Cooper, J. Technical report: Students' self-recording of manuscript letter strokes. *Journal of Applied Behavior Analysis*, 1977, *10*, 509–514.

Joseph, F., & Mullins, J. A script to supplant cursive writing or printing. *Teaching Exceptional Children*, Arlington, Va.: Council for Exceptional Children, 1970.

Kao, H. The effects of hand-finger exercise on human handwriting performance. *Economics*, 1973, *16*, 171–175.

Kau-To Leung, E.; Treblas, P. V.; Hill, D. S.; & Cooper, J. O. Space, size, and accuracy of first-grade students' manuscript writing. *Journal of Educational Research*, 1979, *73*, 79–81.

Kirk, U. Rule-based instruction: A cognitive approach to beginning handwriting instruction (Doctoral dissertation, Columbia University Teachers College, 1978). *Dissertation Abstracts International*, 1978, *39*, 113A–114A. (University Microfilms No. 7810888)

Krzesni, J. S. Effect of different writing tools and paper on performance of the third grader. *Elementary English*, 1971, *48*, 821–824.

Kuennapas, T. Visual perception of capital letters: Multidimensional ratio scaling and multidimensional similarity. *Scandinavian Journal of Psychology*, 1966, *7*, 189–196.

Kuennapas, T. Visual memory of capital letters: Multidimensional ratio scaling and multidimensional similarity. *Perceptual and Motor Skills*, 1967, *25*, 345–350.

Kuennapas, T., & Janson, A. Multidimensional similarity of letters. *Perceptual and Motor Skills*, 1969, *28*, 3–12.

Lahey, B. B.; Busemeyer, M. K.; O'Hara, C.; & Beggs, V. E. Treatment of severe perceptual-motor disorders in children diagnosed as learning disabled. *Behavior Modification*, 1977, *1*, 123–140.

Lehman, C. L. *Handwriting Models for Schools*. Portland, Oreg.: The Alcuin Press, 1976.

Lewis, E. An analysis of children's manuscript handwriting (Doctoral dissertation, University of California, 1964). *Dissertation Abstracts*, 1964, *25*, 1786–1787. (University Microfilms No. 64–9832)

Lewis, E., & Lewis, H. Which manuscript letters are hard for first graders? *Elementary English*, 1964, *41*, 855–858.

Lewis, E., & Lewis, H. An analysis of errors in the formation of manuscript letters by first-grade children. In W. Otto & K. Koenke (Eds.), *Remedial Teaching: Research and Comment*. Boston: Houghton Mifflin, 1969.

Lindell, E. *The Swedish Handwriting Method*. Copenhagen, Denmark: Ejnar Munksgaard, 1964.

Linn, S. Remedial approaches to handwriting dysfunction. *Academic Therapy*, 1968, *4*, 43–46.

Lurçat, L. Etude de la succession des mots et du contrôle de leur alignement dans une epreuve de dictée (Study of the succession of words and of control of their alignment in a dictation test). *Journal de Psychologie Normale et Pathologie*, 1968, *65*, 209–231.

Macleod, I., & Procter, P. A dynamic approach to teaching handwriting skills. *Visible Language*, 1979, *13*(1), 29–42.

McCarthy, L. A child learns the alphabet. *Visible Language*, 1977, *11*, 271–284.

McElravy, A. Handwriting and the slow learner. *Elementary English*, 1964, *41*, 865–868.

Mendoza, M.; Holt, W.; & Jackson, D. Circles and tape: An easy teacher implemented way to teach fundamental writing skills. *Teaching Exceptional Children*, 1978, *10*, 48–50.

Mullins, J.; Joseph, F.; Turner, C.; Zawadyski, R.; & Saltzman, L. A handwriting model for children with learning disabilities. *Journal of Learning Disabilities*, 1972, *5*, 306–311.

Newland, T. An analytical study of the development of illegibilities in handwriting from the lower grades to adulthood. *Journal of Educational Research*, 1932, *26*, 249–258.

Noble, J. K. Handwriting programs in today's schools. *Elementary English*, 1963, *40*, 513–517.

Olson, G. *The Effectiveness of a Programmed Method of Instruction for Teaching Handwriting Skills to Migrant Children*. Tallahassee: Florida State Department of Education, 1970. (Eric Document Reproduction Service No. ED 039 062)

Osley, A. S. Canons of Renaissance handwriting. *Visible Language*, 1979, *13*(1), 70–94.

Otto, W., & Andersen, D. Handwriting. In R. Ebel (Ed.), *Encyclopedia of Educational Research* (4th ed.). New York: Macmillan, 1969.

Otto, W.; Askov, E.; & Cooper, C. Legibility ratings for handwriting samples: A pragmatic approach. In W. Otto & K. Koenke (Eds.), *Remedial Teaching: Research and Comment*. Boston: Houghton Mifflin, 1969.

Otto, W.; Rarick, G.; Armstrong, J.; & Koepke, M. Evaluation of a modified grip in handwriting. *Perceptual and Motor Skills*, 1966, *22*, 310.

Parker, T. The developmental nature of children's ability to use varying diameter writing instruments (Doctoral dissertation, University of Virginia, 1972). *Dissertation Abstracts International*, 1973, *33*, 3399A–3400A. (University Microfilms No. 72–33, 250)

Parres, R. M. The body midline as a psychoeducational variable affecting the handwriting habits of mentally retarded children (Doctoral dissertation, Wayne State University). *Dissertation Abstracts*, 1969, *29*, 3468A–3469A. (University Microfilms No. 69–6079)

Peck, M.; Askov, E. N.; & Fairchild, S. H. Another decade of research in handwriting: Progress and prospect in the 1970's. *Journal of Educational Research*, 1980, *73*(5), 283–298.

Petty, W. T. Handwriting and spelling: Their current status in the language arts curriculum. In T. A. Horn (Ed.), *Research on Handwriting and Spelling*. Champaign, Ill.: National Council of Teachers of English, 1966.

Poteet, J. Identification, classification, and characteristics of first-grade students with learning disabilities in reading, writing and mathematics (Doctoral dissertation, Purdue University, 1970). *Dissertation Abstracts International*, 1971, *31*, 3994A. (University Microfilms No. 71-2669)

Pressey, S., & Pressey, L. Analysis of 3,000 illegibilities in the handwriting of children and adults. *Education Research Bulletin*, 1927, *6*, 270–273.

Rarick, G., & Harris, T. Physiological and motor correlates of handwriting legibility. In V. Herrick (Ed.), *New Horizons for Research in Handwriting*. Madison: University of Wisconsin Press, 1963.

Reed, G., & Smith A. A further experimental investigation of the relative speeds of left- and right-handed writers. *Journal of Genetic Psychology*, 1962, *100*, 275–288.

Rice, R. The use of handwriting rate for predicting academic achievement and suggesting curriculum modification (Doctoral dissertation, University of Akron, 1976). *Dissertation Abstracts International*, 1976, *37*, 1887A. (University Microfilms No. 76-21, 857)

Schell, L., & Burns, P. Retention and changes by college students of certain upper-case cursive letter forms. *Elementary English*, 1963, *40*, 513–517.

Seifert, E. Personal styles of handwriting in grades six, seven, eight, and nine (Doctoral dissertation, Boston University, 1959). *Dissertation Abstracts*, 1960, *20*, 3581. (University Microfilms No. 59-6594)

Shane, H. G., & Mulry, J. G. *Improving Language Arts Instruction through Research*. Washington, D.C.: National Education Association, Association for Supervision and Curriculum Development, 1963, 45–60.

Shimrat, N. Lateral dominance and directional orientation in the writing of American and Israeli children (Doctoral dissertation, Columbia University, 1970). *Dissertation Abstracts International*, 1970, *31*, 2267B. (University Microfilms No. 70–19, 698)

Stennett, R.; Smithe, P.; & Hardy, M. Developmental trends in letter-printing skill. *Perceptual and Motor Skills*, 1972, *34*, 183–186.

Søvik, N. The effects of different principles of instruction in children's copying performances. *Journal of Experimental Education*, 1976, *45*, 38–45.

Søvik, N. Some instructional parameters related to children's copying performance. *Visible Language*, 1979, *13*(3), 314–330.

Tagatz, G. E.; Otto, W.; Klausmeier, H. J.; Goodwin, W. L.; & Cook, D. M. Effect of three methods of instruction upon the handwriting performance of third and fourth graders. In W. Otto & K. Koenke (Eds.), *Remedial Teaching: Research and Comment*. Boston: Houghton Mifflin, 1969.

Templin, E. M. The legibility of adult manuscript, cursive, or manuscript-cursive handwriting styles. In V. E. Herrick (Ed.), *New Horizons for Research in Handwriting*. Madison: University of Wisconsin Press, 1963.

Teulings, Hans-Leo H. M., & Thomassen, A. J. W. M. Computer-aided analysis of handwriting movements. *Visible Language*, 1979, *13*(3), 218–231.

Trap, J. Manuscript proficiency as an indication of readiness for cursive handwriting and learner verification of evaluative overlays for transition cursive letter strokes (Doctoral dissertation, Ohio State University, 1977). *Dissertation Abstracts International*, 1977, *38*, 2547A. (University Microfilms No. 77–24, 722)

Weinert, F.; Simons, H.; & Essig, W. *Theorie und Praxis der Schulpsychologie*, band V: *Schreiblehrmethode und Schreibentwicklung* (Theory and Practice of the School Psychology, volume 5: The Teaching of Handwriting and Its Development). Weinheim, Germany: Verlag Julius Beltz, 1966.

Wheeler, M. Untutored acquisition of writing skill (Doctoral dissertation, Cornell University, 1971). *Dissertation Abstracts International*, 1972, *32*, 5503B. (University Microfilms No. 72–10, 533)

Williams, J. Training children to copy and to discriminate letter-like forms. *Journal of Educational Psychology*, 1975, *67*, 790–795.

Wright, D. C., & Wright, J. P. Handwriting: The effectiveness of copying from moving vs. still models. *Journal of Educational Research*, 1980, *74*(2), 95–98.

HARD-OF-HEARING

See Hearing Impairment.

HEALTH EDUCATION

Health education is "a process with intellectual, psychological, and social dimensions relating to activities which increase the abilities of people to make informed decisions affecting their personal, family and community well-being. This process, based on scientific principles, facilitates learning and behavioral change in both health personnel and consumers, including children and youth" (Report of the Joint Committee on Health Education Terminology, 1973, p. 28). For the purposes of this entry, the focus will be on published research relating to health education in schools, kindergarten through grade 12. This includes curricular models, techniques, methods and materials for instruction, content for instruction, factors influencing instruction, student knowledge and needs, evaluation, and teacher capabilities. The research reviewed is inclusive of the years 1967 through 1980. Although extensive, it represents "directions and trends which research has taken" (Mayshark, 1969, p. 579).

History. Social change has been influential in the pattern of development of health instruction in public schools in the United States. As early as 1889, state laws mandated that antialcohol teaching be part of the curriculum (Nolte & Brannan, 1979). At that point in time, the textbook was the curriculum and the hygiene text had specific sections on the effects of alcohol on the human body, as well as sections on bones, muscles, breathing, food, and the nervous system. The primary focus was on physical health.

Social change again influenced the teaching of hygiene at the turn of the century. The incidence of tuberculosis and influenza and the conditions in the larger city schools as the result of the influx of immigrants were factors. A primary focus in hygiene was on health habits such as proper breathing, sleeping with the window open, sleeping eight to ten hours a night, and keeping the hands clean. Memorization of health habits and recitation of these as a group within the class were typical patterns of instruction. The physiological basis for health was the essential organizing element for curricular content.

The teaching of hygiene (health) maintained its focus on the physical health of the individual. Units of instruction centered on disease concepts, the anatomy of the body, and habits people could develop that would protect them from disease or help them when they became ill.

Study of the nervous system became the springboard to mental health. An analysis of textbooks at the turn of the century reveals information on the need to exercise the brain and to rest the body so that the brain could function well. The primary belief about health was that it was physical, it was freedom from disease, and habits could be developed to keep one healthy.

Other factors influencing health education, in addition to disease, were World War I, with draftees in poor physical health; the development of voluntary health organizations, which focused on disease or illness of one part of the body; the Depression years; and World War II. The crises in the lives of people continued to be the substance for content in health education. This crisis orientation has continued to pervade the profession and has had variable influences on curricular direction. Such crises as smoking, drug abuse, teenage pregnancies, and circulatory problems have been but a few to give direction to health instruction.

In the late 1950s, with the advent of curricular innovations, a nationwide study of health education practices in schools was recommended by the Joint Committee on Health Problems in Education of the National Education Association and the American Medical Association (1959). This study, the School Health Education Study (SHES), commenced in 1960 and was the first nationwide research project in health education.

The SHES was initially funded by the Samuel Bronfman Foundation of New York City (Veenker, 1963). This research project produced three publications from 1960 through 1967: *Synthesis of Research in Selected Areas of Health Instruction* (Veenker, 1963), *School Health Education Study: A Summary Report* (Sliepcevich, 1964), and *Health Education: A Conceptual Approach to Curriculum Design* (School Health Education Study, 1967).

They are landmarks in the history of school health education—landmarks from the perspective that this was the first synthesis of research in health instruction, the first nationwide study on health instructional practices and health behavior of students in the public schools, and the first nationwide health education curriculum.

Concurrent with the SHES project, concern was demonstrated about the increase in morbidity and mortality from cigarette smoking. The surgeon general's report on smoking and health (U.S. Public Health Service, 1964) stimulated activity to determine the amount of smoking among school-age children and characteristics of school-age smokers. Subsequently, the focus shifted to the development of methods for use in the classroom for antismoking programs. The crisis brought action, and the emphasis was on illness. The need was to develop knowledge and actions that would prevent smoking and thus illness.

Additional health education activity at the national level began occurring. This activity was brought about through changes in the health of the American population as determined by the Office of the Surgeon General of the United States through data analysis and evaluation (U.S. Public Health Service, 1964; Horn, 1971).

Funding for curriculum development and research became available from the federal government, as well as from organizations such as the American Heart Association and the American Lung Association. Prior to the 1960s, federal funds had never been available for research on health instruction in public schools.

As a result of federal research and research conducted by the School Health Education Study, efforts were undertaken to initiate health education in states where it did not exist and to improve existing programs.

Although health education has continued with the vestiges of crisis orientation and a focus on illness prevention, a research trend is toward health promotion and wellness.

Research. The following topics provide an overview of the research efforts in school health education since 1967. Several other sources for evaluation in knowledge and attitudes in health education are Vincent (1978), who utilizes alternative approaches to measuring attitude change, and Fors and Devereaux (1979), who suggest evaluation designs for school health education.

Teaching techniques. Weber (1978) compared the values-clarification and lecture methods in health education. Six hypotheses were tested: values-clarification and lecture methods would be equally effective in generating and maintaining a positive change in (1) health knowledge, (2) health attitudes, (3) health behavior, (4) a flexible world orientation, and (5) four measures of self-actualization, and (6) in addition, students would evaluate both teaching methods similarly. From the results of this study, it was concluded that the objectives of health instruction are equally served by both methods. Knipping and Chandler (1975) examined behavioral modification techniques in the classroom. They compared rational self-counseling and transactional analysis. These two techniques were used to corroborate the hypothesis that if attending school becomes a mind-expanding experience, the students are less likely to use mind-expanding chemicals.

Herold (1978) studied the production and use of an attitudinal film in birth control education. A film, *It Couldn't Happen to Me*, was produced, focusing on teenagers' motives for not using birth control. Pretest and posttest measures indicate that the film was effective in making viewers more aware of the psychological factors involved in not using birth control; preliminary results seem to indicate that this birth control film can change attitudes toward birth control without increasing attitudes of acceptance of sexual permissiveness.

Evans (1973) performed a study linking research in the social psychology of persuasion and behavior modification with its relevancy to school health education. The study examined the value of fear in causing individuals to develop or change their attitudes when introduced to persuasive messages or educational materials, and the relationship between such attitude changes and behavior change. The results suggest that with careful programming of motivation and reinforcement with students over a protracted period of time, by not depending too heavily on fear appeals but using positive messages as well, and by employing very specific instructions and almost daily training, effective, permanent health habits may be instilled. This will be particularly so if the mechanisms for shifting from "external" to "internal" reinforcement are more precisely developed, so that effective health skills are increasingly exercised in the home with increasingly less supervision in the school setting.

Osman (1974) examined the feasibility of using selected value-clarifying strategies in a health education course for future teachers. The study was further designed to develop, modify, describe, and evaluate the selected strategies. The results led to the conclusion that the use of selected values-clarifying strategies in a health education course for future teachers is not only feasible but also personally satisfying and professionally edifying.

Behavior modification and values clarification were analyzed by Greenberg (1975a). In particular, he defined and described conditions under which they are best conducted, drew contrasts and similarities, and suggested potential research pertaining to the two methodologies. Suggested research areas include (1) the establishment and evaluation of the effectiveness of a program that combines behavior modification with values clarification; (2) the recidivism rate for health-related behaviors; (3) the potential for developing decision-making skills via behavior modification; (4) the transferability of a student's learning from a controlled environment to a natural one; (5) values confusion and drug abuse; (6) the permanence of any behavior change resulting from values clarification; and (7) the process by which health-related values are established.

Textbooks. Because of an explosive influx of scientific terminology and vocabulary in the health science fields, educational textbooks, specifically those structured for health education, have become burdened with complex jargon. The net result of this has been less understanding of this style of writing, less readability with respect to educational level. Since a study by McTaggart (1964), little if any research on the readability of health science textbooks has been conducted. Two studies evidenced in research literature in the 1970s serve to substantiate the previous claim.

Using the standardized revised Dale-Chall formula for reading level determination, Miller, Schur, and Miller (1974) selected four current series of seventh-grade and eighth-grade health textbooks for analysis of estimated readability level. The formula evaluates two criteria: sentence complexity (length) and vocabulary difficulty. The results were fourfold. Of the four eighth-grade books, none had a strong eighth-grade placement level; one of the seventh-grade textbooks had an overall fifth-grade readability equivalent; the remaining seventh-grade books had readability levels at about a sixth-grade to seventh-grade level; and for all four series, the eighth-grade book had a statistically higher readability level than its seventh-grade counterpart, although one series had no significant difference. The greatest variation in readability occurred in topic areas such as mental health, nutrition, personal health, physiology and anatomy, and disease. The topic area of human sexuality had the lowest levels of readability, and the most difficult material related to public health issues. The recommendations from this study were that some consideration should be given to raising the reading level of all books designed for eighth-grade students and maintaining seventh-grade readability levels.

Contrary to this study is a second study also utilizing the Dale-Chall readability formula. The study by Merki and Morris (1972) was to determine the reading grade level of supplementary materials in drug education available for grades 5 through 12 in the Texas public schools. The findings showed that 53 percent of drug education materials analyzed were proper to respective grade level and 47 percent were outside stated test limitations. Of the 47 percent, 45 percent were indicated as being college-level reading material. The conclusions from this study support the need for supplementary drug education materials to be written at the appropriate reading level. The recommendations suggest that health agencies should be concerned with rewriting the drug education materials that they produce to meet the readability levels of various grades. Curriculum personnel should direct efforts at evaluating this material so that classroom teachers will have a readability index from which to choose. Classroom teachers should consider level of readability to serve as a corollary to other learning experiences, and should be provided with materials that correspond in readability level with the wide range of reading abilities typically found in classroom settings.

These studies indicate the need for similar studies on high school health textbooks and elementary textbooks, and in addition, an analysis of supplementary health materials in relation to readability level and grade level.

Student evaluation. Student evaluation for determining the effectiveness of school health education classes or curriculum can be attained through a multitude of designs. Evaluators must realize that data from an evaluation tool indicating that a program is ineffective may stem from inadequate learning theory at the base of the program, poor teaching processes, or the evaluation design utilized. Adhering to the basic principles and rules of research design will assure evaluation data that truly reflect the school health education program.

Archer and Arendell (1978) described studies using the McLeod High Risk Inventory, an instrument designed to test the statistical relationship between a number of psychological states and pro-drug attitudes or frequent drug use. This instrument originated from two surveys at a drug education center in 1972 and 1974. The inventory is also designed to measure the impact of a primary prevention program on those psychological states that have been demonstrated to be correlated to pro-drug attitudes.

Since its inception, results from the inventory have illustrated the psychological states conducive to pro-drug attitudes. In order of decreasing effect, they included rebelliousness; poor family relationships; poor feelings toward school, expecially toward teachers; a poor sense of well-being; and inadequate coping skills. Peer pressure, feelings of acceptance and self-esteem, personal values, and a sense of a locus of control were states that had very little affect on attitudes toward drug use.

Numerous evaluation instruments have been developed to examine attitudes in various content areas of health. In the conceptual area of mood-modifying substances, the Drug Perception Scale is used to clarify some of the drug-related issues and misconceptions concerning substance use and abuse. Students review their perceptions about listed drugs on the scale, and classroom discussion serves to resolve information discrepancies (Tow, 1978).

An instrument for evaluating attitudes toward drinking was designed at Southern Illinois University in a course called Healthful Living. The instrument ascertains attitudes toward behavioral situations such that they are deemed acceptable, unacceptable, or ambiguous. In addition to its value as an attitudinal research tool, the instrument may function in a variety of ways as a teaching aid (Smith, 1971). Parcel (1975) conducted a study to develop an instrument to measure attitudes toward the personal use of premarital contraception. He specifically dealt with an instrument to measure the degree of favorableness or unfavorableness toward the personal use of contraception during premarital sexual activity. The instrument, termed the Premarital Contraceptive Attitude Evaluation Instrument, has a high degree of reliability and validity. Literature concerning premarital contraceptive attitudes and behavior indicate an absence of objective and systematic measurement of attitudes toward personal use of contraception. The development of the instrument in this study demonstrated that contraceptive attitudes can be measured effectively.

Death education has become an integral aspect of school health education. If health educators are to be concerned with education about death, they must also become cognizant of attitudes toward death. Hardt's (1975) study was designed to provide a valid and reliable measure to assess attitudes toward death. The attitude scale developed was the Thurstone Equal-Appearing Interval Attitude Scale. Results of the study indicate that age, sex, social position, church attendance, and recency of death experience contribute little to one's attitude toward death. The results provide a valid, reliable means to determine mean, range, and standard deviation of the attitudes of potential learners and change that has occurred after the educational experience.

In the past it has been customary to develop a scale to measure specific attitudes. Vincent (1974) has developed a scale with alternate forms to measure attitudes toward any health practice. The particular scales are equal-interval scales. When the health practice to be measured is inserted on the scale and reproduced, the attitude respective to that particular health practice can be attained.

Because of new curricular approaches in health education, new testing instruments are needed for evaluating both instructional programs and student achievement. The study conducted by Seffrin and Veenker (1972) was to develop a valid testing instrument to assess health instruction outcomes among high school students who have completed their last high school course in health science. The final standardized achievement test for measuring selected health education objectives in the cognitive domain was a reliable, internally consistent instrument and met standards for curricular validity. The test can be used to ascertain needs of students in the cognitive domain of health education and provides a means of evaluating curricular results at the high school level. This instrument is valuable for further health education research.

Solleder (1972, 1979) has produced two valuable resources in student evaluation in health education. The first illustrates techniques for the development of items in the cognitive domain. The second is an annotated bibliography of knowledge, attitude, behavior, and school health program evaluation instruments for elementary, junior high, senior high, college, and nonstudent groups.

Content instruction. Most of the research in content areas of health education has been done as the result of major health problems in society. In a study focusing on teaching human sexuality to junior high students, using an interdisciplinary approach, Kapp, Taylor, and Edwards (1980) found that there was a statistically significant increase in student knowledge. The approach presented a comprehensive view of young people as sexual beings.

Another approach to sex education curriculum development was based on questions submitted by students. Kleinerman et al. (1971) found this approach to teaching sex education in a ghetto school to be valuable in the documentation of student needs. It was also facilitative of the educational process.

Two studies have examined the status of sex education in California and Illinois. A voluntary six-year program developed in Anaheim, California, on family life and sex education appeared to have family, student, and teacher support. However, the program was discontinued after three years under pressure of representatives of the John Birch Society (Cook, 1972).

Ready (1973) found that in the public schools of Illinois,

family life and sex education programs are not meeting the needs of students. Time is not being allocated to the subject, it needs to be integrated into all areas of the curriculum, state guidelines need to be developed, and teachers should receive more and better training in the subject area.

Greenberg (1975b) studied the effects of teaching a unit on homosexuality to high school students. It was found that the unit did not affect faith in people, acceptance of others, and levels of perceived masculinity and femininity. It was concluded that the students who participated found the unit to be interesting and informative and felt that their attitudes toward different life-styles became more open.

Fitzmahan (1977) studied the activities of the Washington State Office of Public Instruction in its efforts to prevent venereal disease through education. School and community workshops were designed, using five major objectives. At least one workshop was planned for each of the twelve Educational Service Districts of Washington. In an evaluation it was determined that one of the primary benefits expected to occur was the information dissemination to more than 11,000 students.

Two basic trends in alcohol education were identified by Blane (1976). These focused on personal control and society in which alcohol is morally neutral, its use is integrated into activities that reflect social solidarity, and it is not associated with a social hazard.

In a similar review of smoking education programs, Thompson (1978) found that most of the methods used in programs to change smoking behavior have shown little success. She reviewed sixteen years of research programs, which included antismoking campaigns, youth-to-youth programs, a variety of message themes, and teaching methods by instructors, groups, peers, and media.

Stone (1978) found that the School Health Curriculum Project fifth-grade unit had an effect on students' reported attitudes toward smoking. In using the Perceived Vulnerability and Smoking Test, she found that significant differences existed between males and females. These differences may have implications for locating high-risk students.

Chen and Thompson (1980) studied junior high level students regarding smoking behavior and knowledge about smoking. Results showed that the majority of parents did not approve of their children's smoking; the mother's smoking practices were not associated with the children's smoking, and students who were smokers were not as knowledgeable about the harmful effects of cigarette smoking on health as nonsmokers. Also studying junior high students, Rabinowitz and Zimmerli (1974) found that a special educational program significantly increased knowledge about smoking and caused a positive change in attitude toward personal responsibility for tobacco use. Participants in this program also showed significant reduction in smoking compared with a control group. The researchers concluded that several distinct approaches to

health education should be explored for social subgroups with different backgrounds of exposure, involvement, and motivation in order to achieve comparable outcomes.

Eng et al. (1979) studied a method of increasing students' knowledge of cancer and cardiovascular disease prevention. They found that participation in a risk-factor screening program alone or in combination with a formal curriculum on cancer and cardiovascular disease is effective in improving students' knowledge about these two health problems.

Teacher capabilities. Research in the capabilities of the health education teacher has ranged from national studies examining the preparation of the teacher to the effects of teacher expectations on students in the classroom.

Pigg (1976) looked at competency-based professional-preparation programs nationwide. The findings indicated that there was a lack of consensus among health educators as to what constitutes competency-based health education. Competency-based education is a method of education and may not be philosophically appropriate in all situations.

Banks (1980) surveyed health educators nationally to determine whether there was consensus in the belief that one dimension of health was spiritual and that this dimension should be included in the preparation programs for health educators. Affirmative answers to both questions were supported by her study. The survey also assisted in the development of a definition of the spiritual dimension of health. The definition was based on four aspects: a unifying force within individuals, meaning in life, a common bond between individuals, and individual perceptions of faith.

Utilizing the School Health Curriculum Project as a performance-based education for teachers, Caramancia, Feiler, and Olsen (1974) studied the effects of the preparation on the health knowledges and attitudes of fifth-grade students. The results of this performance-based education of the teacher indicated that there was a positive influence on the health knowledge and attitudes of students, specifically in relationship to cigarette smoking.

Similar results were found by Pierce and Byrne (1979) in their study of the effects of in-service workshops on dental health for teachers. They studied the personal hygiene performance and dental cognition in kindergarten, second grade, and fifth grade. Teacher participation in the workshops significantly affected these factors positively.

Teacher and administrator perceptions and expectations influence the performance of students in health education. These qualities also affect socially sensitive areas of the curriculum.

Kohn (1973) utilized a teacher self-reporting system to study the expectations of teachers and the performance of students. It was found that improved school performance might have been related to the teachers' increasing demands of underestimated students and decreasing demands of overestimated ones. The teachers' attitudes and evaluations of students and their expression of these appeared to vary with their preconceptions of students' abilities.

Reed (1973) analyzed the perceptions of high school principals in public and Catholic schools in Illinois about the importance of sex education in the curriculum. It was concluded that this group of administrators considered it as an integral part of the high school curriculum and a majority offered this content area within their programs.

Two other studies on attitudes and readiness of teachers examined the attitudes of Arizona educators toward specific content areas in sex education (Shuck, 1972) and the readiness of teachers for roles in family life education (Kent, Abernathy, & Middour, 1971).

Reed and Munson (1976) studied the preparation of teachers of sexuality and found that an important first step was the resolution of one's sexual self. Positive attitudes or feelings toward one's own sexuality were essential to teaching in this often highly sensitive area. Workshops used to achieve these qualities were organized around the concepts of knowledgeability, trustability, acceptability, possibility, movability, changeability, and authenticity.

Chen and Rakip (1975) studied the effect of the teachers' smoking behavior on their involvement in smoking education in schools. They found that ex-smokers were the most active group in attempting to initiate change in student smoking behavior, while the smokers were the least active in this respect.

Student knowledge needs. In an assessment of the health education knowledge of public school seniors in Colorado, Stephens (1971) found that many of the students were accepting of health misconceptions. As the size of the school increased, however, there were fewer misconceptions. The areas of most incorrect responses were consumer health and nutrition. Several predictors of health misconception scores were identified. In order of importance were mother's education and father's education and occupation.

Nutrition misconceptions of secondary school youth were studied by Tifft and Stanton (1972). They found that there was widespread belief in these and that more boys than girls subscribed to them, but there was not a significant difference.

Three studies focused on the knowledge needs of students in family life and sex education. Decker and Caetano (1977) examined variations in natal knowledge among high school students. There was significant difference in levels of knowledge of different racial and ethnic groups. Whites scored highest, followed by blacks and Mexican-Americans. Males in all groups were significantly less knowledgeable.

Sherriffs and Dezelsky (1979) did a comparative study of adolescents' perceptions of sex education needs in 1972 and 1978. It was found that topics of preparation for marriage and parenthood, birth control methods, and strategies designed to assist adolescents in understanding them-

selves were considerably more important in 1978 than they were in 1972. It was felt by both groups that accurate information and improved understanding of sexuality were definite needs of adolescents.

Vacalis (1974) polled physicians and teachers to determine what knowledge was important for the public in order for them to utilize the health care delivery system effectively. There was a large discrepancy between the two groups, which indicated a need to develop a convergence of priorities and thinking. Knowledge of health care delivery systems is basic in public school health education programs.

Factors influencing instruction. A mixture of curiosity, poor information, poor parent models, and rejection of authority figures appeared to be etiologic to drug taking and influenced teaching about drugs, according to a study by Grant (1971).

Dearden and Jekel (1971) established a pilot program in high school drug education utilizing nondirective techniques and sensitivity training. Although at that reporting too few data were available, it was the impression of the authors that there had been a positive change in the attitudes and behavior of those students involved. It was also believed that a greater long-term impact might come from changes in teachers and the school system in the direction of more openness of communication.

Pethel (1971) used two methods of presenting the subject of drug abuse to ninth-grade students. One method was student-oriented, with students planning, developing, and presenting their own program. The other method was traditional, with the teacher planning the students' work. The findings showed no differences between the methods. It appeared also that neither method could produce appreciable increases in knowledge or more favorable attitude change, perhaps because both units were only eight hours long.

Jones, Nowack, and Heindel (1972) also examined the use of two methods of instructing about venereal disease to eighth-grade and tenth-grade students. The methods were arbitrarily labeled "conventional" and "programmed." The study revealed that students had a limited knowledge of venereal disease and that they could learn about venereal disease from either teaching method equally as well. Again, time may have been a factor, since the unit was three days in length.

Curricular models. Two nationwide curricular models have emerged that provide direction for school health education. The School Health Education Study (SHES) is the initial model, having been started in 1964. A framework of concepts was developed for the kindergarten-through-grade-12 program. This framework was then translated into instructional materials consisting of long-range goals, behavioral objectives, content, learning activities, student evaluation activities, and teacher-student resource materials.

The instructional materials were pilot-tested in four school systems in the United States: Great Neck–Garden

City, New York; Evanston, Illinois; Tacoma, Washington; and Alhambra, California. Allen and Holyoak (1972, 1973) evaluated the results of this conceptual approach to teaching health education. The purposes of the research were (1) to determine if students, instructed by means of the conceptual approach, showed a significant difference in self-reported health behavior compared with students involved with a more traditional teaching approach, and (2) to determine if the students' self-reported health behavior changed significantly within each of the schools after a period of instruction. The findings indicated that the conceptual approach was equal to or superior to the more traditional approach with regard to self-reported health behaviors of students. Students' self-reported health behavior patterns can be changed through instruction in selected areas. Significant behavioral changes were reported at each educational level.

In the second part of the study, published one year later, the results were (1) the conceptual approach to teaching health education appeared to be an important factor in the development of understanding related to the positive health behavior of elementary students; (2) the conceptual approach to teaching health education had no appreciable positive effect on the reported health behavior patterns of junior high school students; and (3) the conceptual approach to teaching health education produced a senior high school student who was as knowledgeable regarding positive health behavior as the average senior high school student.

The second nationwide model is the School Health Curriculum Project, which was also initiated in the 1960s. It was developed from a sixth-grade classroom program and now exists in a form for kindergarten through grade 7. This program used the human body and its structure and functioning for the curricular framework. The federal government contracted with several agencies and organizations for the production of the teaching materials as well as for in-service training of teachers.

Olsen, Redican, and Krus (1980) have summarized the research that has accompanied the evolution of this curricular model. The research has been extensive, but it has focused on individual units rather than the value of the curricular model.

Research Needs. Research in school health education has increased considerably since 1970. A primary question is whether this research has given leadership to the field. Much of the research has occurred as the result of federal and state monies available for categorical activities. However, the complexities of school health education have created difficulties in research.

Creswell (1971) has provided an overview of needed research in school health education:

1. An applied behavioral science research for the purpose of improving school health education, including the whole school-age population, kindergarten through college.
2. Research that is oriented toward the promotion of health through the education process.

3. Research involving the cognitive, affective, and overt behavioral aspects of health learning.
4. Research concerning the sociological aspects of health education and health behavior.
5. Research concerning the health problems and health behavior characteristics of the school-age group.
6. Research on the study and analysis of health instruction, including curriculum, methods, motivational factors, teacher role, and peer group influence.
7. Research concerning the evaluation of school health education programs and practices. (p. 3)

Following the trend in the development of health education, much of the recent research has focused on categorical areas such as smoking and health, alcohol and health, cardiovascular disease and health. The health problems and characteristics of children involved with these issues have generated much research, and there has also been complementary research on curriculum, methods, materials and peer group influence. Thus, the pattern for health education research has been that first there is a health problem affecting the school-age population, then knowledge about the problem is gathered, materials and methods focusing on the health problem are developed, the materials are distributed, and research is initiated.

Kolbe and Iverson (1980) have very succinctly summarized the needs for school health education research:

1. Research is needed to address school health education programs which are comprehensive in nature with respect to the integration of content areas and impacts, in contrast to addressing categorical programs and isolated effects.
2. Research needs to address school health education programs which are integrated within comprehensive health education delivery mechanisms.
3. Research needs to concomitantly increase our understanding of biophysical relationships among human behavior, health, and disease *and* increase our understanding of relevant psychosocial phenomena. Without the latter, the utility of the former can only remain potential.
4. Research needs to address organizational theories and practices related to the implementation and maintenance of school health education programs.
5. Research needs to address the establishment of acceptable and appropriate objectives for school health education programs, as well as acceptable measurement strategies. (p. 7)

Research in school health education will continue to escalate. Quality control is an essential and much needed element.

Ann E. Nolte

See also Drug Abuse Education; Home Economics Education; Nutrition Education; Parent Education; Sex Education.

REFERENCES

Allen, E., & Holyoak, J. Evaluating the conceptual approach to teaching health education: A summary. *Journal of School Health*, 1972, *42*, 118–119.
Allen, E., & Holyoak, J. Evaluation of the conceptual approach

to teaching health education: A second look. *Journal of School Health*, 1973, *43*, 293–294.

Archer, E., & Arendell, R. A measuring instrument for use in drug education: Development of the McLeod High Risk Inventory. *Journal of Drug Education*, 1978, *8*, 313–325.

Banks, R. Health and the spiritual dimension: Relationships and implications for professional preparation programs. *Journal of School Health*, 1980, *50*, 195–205.

Blane, T. Recent trends in alcohol education. *Health Education*, 1976, *1*(3), 36–37.

Caramancia, V. P.; Feiler, E. G.; & Olsen, L. K. Evaluation of the effects of performance-based teacher education on the health knowledge and attitudes of fifth-grade students. *Journal of School Health*, 1974, *44*, 449–454.

Chen, T. L., & Rakip, W. R. The effect of the teachers' smoking behavior on their involvement in smoking in schools. *Journal of School Health*, 1975, *45*, 455–461.

Chen, T. L., & Thompson, L. A study of smoking behavior and smoking education at the junior high level. *Health Education*, 1980, *11*(3), 7–9.

Cook, R. W. A great experiment in sex education: The Anaheim story. *Journal of School Health*, 1972, *42*, 7–9.

Creswell, W. Research relationships and relevancy. *School Health Review*, 1971, *2*(4), 2–11.

Dearden, M., & Jekel, J. A pilot program in high school drug education utilizing non-directive techniques and sensitivity training. *Journal of School Health*, 1971, *41*, 118–124.

Decker, D., & Caetano, D. F. Variations in natal knowledge among high school students. *Journal of School Health*, 1977, *47*, 286–288.

Eng, A.; Bitvin, G.; Carter, J.; & Williams, C. Increasing students' knowledge of cancer and cardiovascular prevention. *Journal of School Health*, 1979, *49*, 505–507.

Evans, R. I. Research in the social psychology of persuasion behavior modification: Relevant to school health education? *Journal of School Health*, 1973, *43*, 110–113.

Fitzmahan, D. L. Venereal disease prevention education in Washington state. *Health Education*, 1977, *8*(1), 13–14.

Fors, S. W., & Devereaux, M. J. Suggested evaluation designs for school health education. *Health Education*, 1979, *10*(4), 26–29.

Grant, J. A. Drug education based on a knowledge, attitude, and experience study. *Journal of School Health*, 1971, *41*, 383–385.

Greenberg, J. Behavior modification and values clarification and their research implications. *Journal of School Health*, 1975, *45*(2), 91–95. (a)

Greenberg, J. A study of personality change associated with the conducting of a high school unit on homosexuality. *Journal of School Health*, 1975, *45*, 394–398. (b)

Hardt, D. V. Development of an investigatory instrument to measure attitudes toward death. *Journal of School Health*, 1975, *45*, 96–99.

Herold, E. S. The production and use of an attitudinal film in birth control education. *Journal of School Health*, 1978, *48*, 307–310.

Horn, D. Educational aspects of smoking research. *School Health Review*, 1971, *2*, 15–18.

Joint Committee on Health Problems in Education of the National Education Association and the American Medical Association. *Minutes of the Annual Meeting.* Unpublished manuscript, American Medical Association, Department of Health Education, 1959.

Jones, H.; Nowack, D.; & Heindel, J. Which methodology for vene-

real disease education? *School Health Review*, 1972, *3*(2), 8–9.

Kapp, L.; Taylor, B.; & Edwards, L. Teaching human sexuality in junior high school: An interdisciplinary approach. *Journal of School Health*, 1980, *50*, 80–83.

Kent, R.; Abernathy, J.; & Middour, R. C. Teacher readiness for roles in family life education: An exploratory study. *American Journal of Public Health*, 1971, *61*, 586–599.

Kleinerman, G.; Grossman, M.; Breslow, J.; & Goldman, R. Sex education in a ghetto school. *Journal of School Health*, 1971, *41*, 29–33.

Knipping, R., & Chandler, L. A classroom comparison of behavioral modification techniques. *Journal of School Health*, 1975, *45*, 34–36.

Kohn, R. M. Relationships between expectations of teachers and performance of students (Pygmalion in the classroom). *Journal of School Health*, 1973, *43*, 498–503.

Kolbe, L., & Iverson, D. Research in school health education: A needs assessment. *Health Education*, 1980, *11*(1), 3–7.

Mayshark, C. Health education. In R. L. Ebel (Ed.), *Encyclopedia of Educational Research* (4th ed.). New York: Macmillan, 1969.

McTaggart, A. C. Measuring the readability of high school health texts. *Journal of School Health*, 1964, *34*, 434–443.

Merki, D., & Morris, E. A study of readability of drug education materials. *School Health Review*, 1972, *3*(6), 6–7.

Miller, D.; Schur, J.; & Miller, K. The readability of junior high school health textbooks. *Journal of School Health*, 1974, *44*, 382–385.

Nolte, A., & Brannan, J. Through the looking glass: Health education curriculum. *Health Education*, 1979, *10*(6), 5–11.

Olsen, L. K.; Redican, K. J.; & Krus, P. H. The school health curriculum project: A review of research studies. *Health Education*, 1980, *11*(1), 16–21.

Osman, J. D. The use of selected value-clarifying strategies in health education. *Journal of School Health*, 1974, *44*, 21–25.

Parcel, G. S. Development of an instrument to measure attitudes toward the personal use of pre-marital contraception. *Journal of School Health*, 1975, *45*, 156–160.

Pethel, D. L. Comparisons of two approaches to instruction on drug abuse. *School Health Review*, 1971, *2*(2), 9–11.

Pierce, P., & Byrne, J. Effect of teacher in-service workshops on student dental health. *Journal of School Health*, 1979, *49*, 400–403.

Pigg, R. M., Jr. A national study of competency-based programs. *Health Education*, 1976, *7*(4), 15–16.

Rabinowitz, H., & Zimmerli, W. Effects of a health education program on junior high school students' knowledge, attitudes, and behavior concerning tobacco use. *Journal of School Health*, 1974, *44*, 324–330.

Ready, J. The current status of family life and sex education in the public schools of Illinois. *Journal of School Health*, 1973, *43*, 49–51.

Reed, C. E. An analysis of the perceptions of high school principals in public and Catholic schools relative to the importance of sex education in the curriculum. *Journal of School Health*, 1973, *43*, 198–199.

Reed, D. A., & Munson, H. E. Resolution of one's sexual self: An important first step for sexuality educators. *Journal of School Health*, 1976, *51*, 31–36.

Report of the Joint Committee on Health Education Terminology. *School Health Review*, 1973, *4*(6), 25–30.

School Health Education Study. *Health Education: A Conceptual Approach to Curriculum Design.* St. Paul: 3M Education Press, 1967.

Seffrin, J. R., & Veenker, C. H. A standardized achievement test of health education objectives in the cognitive domain. *Journal of School Health*, 1972, *42*, 43–46.

Sherriffs, J., & Dezelsky, T. Adolescent perceptions of sex education needs: 1972–1978. *Journal of School Health*, 1979, *49*, 343–346.

Shuck, R. F. Attitudes of Arizona educators toward specific content areas in sex education. *Journal of School Health*, 1972, *42*, 122–124.

Sliepcevich, E. M. *School Health Education Study: A Summary Report*. Washington, D.C.: School Health Education Study, 1964.

Smith, D. R. An instrument for evaluating attitudes toward drinking. *Health Education Review*, 1971, *2*(2), 12–13.

Solleder, M. K. Evaluation in the cognitive domain. *Journal of School Health*, 1972, *42*, 16–20.

Solleder, M. K. *Evaluation Instruments in Health Education* (3rd ed.). Washington, D.C.: American Alliance for Health, Physical Education, Recreation, and Dance, 1979. (ERIC Document Reproduction Service No. ED 179 550)

Stephens, G. E. Prevalence of harmful misconceptions in Colorado high school seniors. *Journal of School Health*, 1971, *41*, 161–162.

Stone, E. The effect of a fifth-grade health education curriculum model on perceived vulnerability and smoking attitudes. *Journal of School Health*, 1978, *48*, 667–672.

Thompson, E. L. Smoking education programs, 1960–1976. *American Journal of Public Health*, 1978, *68*, 250–259.

Tifft, J., & Stanton, J. B. Nutrition misconceptions of secondary school youth, *School Health Review*, 1972, *3*(6), 8–11.

Tow, P. K. One way to ascertain drug perceptions. *Health Education*, 1978, *9*(2), 41.

U.S. Public Health Service: Smoking and Health. *Report of the Advisory Committee to the Surgeon General of the Public Health Service* (U.S. Public Health Service Publication No. 1103). Washington, D.C.: U.S. Government Printing Office, 1964.

Vacalis, D. T. Determination of vital areas of knowledge needed for wise consumer use of health care systems. *Journal of School Health*, 1974, *54*, 390–394.

Veenker, H. *Synthesis of Research in Selected Areas of Health Instruction*. Washington, D.C.: National Education Association, 1963.

Vincent, R. J. New scale for measuring attitudes. *School Health Review*, 1974, *5*(2), 19–21.

Vincent, R. J. An alternative approach to measuring attitude change. *Health Education*, 1978, *9*(6), 22–23.

Weber, C. A comparison of values clarifications and lecture methods. *Journal of School Health*, 1978, *48*, 269–274.

HEALTH SERVICES

See Psychological Services; Rehabilitation Services.

HEARING IMPAIRMENT

The first school for the hearing impaired (deaf and hard-of-hearing) was opened in the United States in 1817. The early schools were primarily residential in nature. According to recent information, there are approximately 541 schools and classes serving about 44,000 hearing-impaired children from preschool age through high school. Approximately 40 percent of these children are educated in private and public residential schools, and the remaining 60 percent are educated in day schools and day classes. These figures are representative of the numbers of children attending special schools for the hearing impaired, but are not conclusive. Hearing-impaired children of school age who are not served in special programs are not included in this census. It is estimated that the prevalence rate for hearing loss is approximately 2 per 1,000 population (Schein and Delk, 1974). These figures serve to indicate the need for educational and vocational planning for a sizable population of hearing-handicapped people.

Some of the major issues in the education of the hearing impaired concern modes of communication, language training, and the efficacy of early identification and intervention.

Modes of Instruction.   In school programs for hearing-impaired children, the modes of instruction have been manual (signs and finger spelling) and oral (speech reading and use of residual hearing). Common to the different modes as a means of expressing English forms is writing. It appears that there are at least two basic systems within the manual approach. American Sign Language (ASL) is a formal language structure distinct from spoken English, but it translates into English forms. Sign symbols express ideas and concepts. Some variations of ASL have been classified as manual English.

In manual English, new signs have been developed to represent more faithfully English morphology in a visual mode. These systems are referred to as the Linguistics of Visible English (LOVE), Signed English (Siglish), Seeing Essential English (SEE[1]), and Signing Exact English (SEE[2]). Theoretically the aural-oral modality is an exact replication of English forms; it attempts to utilize visual cues (speech reading) to supplement information received by a faulty auditory-discriminating system.

In recent years these two modes have been refined and expanded. During the late 1960s and early 1970s, total communication was introduced as the mode combining manual-oral modalities (Holcumb, 1972). Total communication is viewed by its proponents as a philosophy rather than a method. The philosophy combines aural-oral-manual modes and is used according to the expressive-receptive needs of the hearing-impaired individual. Total communication incorporates appropriate manual, aural, and oral modes of communication in order to ensure effective communication with and among hearing-impaired persons (Garretson, 1976).

Research on the efficacy of these various modalities has been anecdotal and after the fact. Longitudinal research, which examines the effects of transfer from one of the many visual modes into an English mode is notably lacking in the literature. Wilbur (1979) states the case most succinctly.

There is not enough current, objective research and evaluation to reach a truly informed decision, in addition to which it must be recognized that no decision, method, or program is right for every child. There are some guidelines for choosing and some warnings to heed, but the renewed interest in sign language-based programs for deaf children has not been met with a renewed interest in assessing its effectiveness. Too often a decision is made, followed by an ever-increasing feeling of the need to defend it. This does not lead to objectivity, which is badly needed. (p. 229)

Language Training and Acquisition. The language skills of hearing-impaired children will vary with the age of the onset of hearing loss, the amount of the hearing loss, and ecological factors affecting language acquisition. The development of a fluent language system is the primary teaching target for teachers of the hearing impaired. Language development in all children involves the recognition and comprehension of syntax, semantics, and pragmatics.

The most commonly used systems for teaching language to the hearing impaired are grammar-based and require practice in vocabulary development, phrase and sentence patterning, as well as a great deal of memorization. Examples of these systems are the Fitzgerald Key (1949), Barry Five Slates (1899), and Wing Symbols (1887). An extension of these systems appears to be a more cognitively based approach called "patterning" (Buckler, 1968). The essence of this procedure is the use of command forms that vary with the construction that follows the verb. Seven basic sentence patterns are used in this approach. Language exposure is achieved in a natural situation as opposed to a contrived drill-teaching situation.

A more recent linguistic-based approach is described by Blackwell et al. (1976). Language is developed in the context of a spiraling curriculum, as part of a systematic method of language teaching within the total curriculum. However, this approach is criticized for using five basic sentence patterns based on adult models of language rather than a developmental approach to acquiring language.

The issue of whether the language of hearing-impaired students is deviant or delayed (Byrne & Shervanian, 1977) confounds the instructional approach used in the acquisition and development of language. Many of the early approaches automatically assume that hearing-impaired students must be taught all of the structures of English. In some of the more recent linguistic-based language programs, however, language is assumed to be generative in nature, capable of being taught according to the rules of normal language acquisition and development. Longitudinal, systematic studies are needed to address the question, "What is the best or better method of teaching language to hearing-impaired students?"

Normal language acquisition has been studied extensively (Bloom, 1970; Brown, 1973; Clark & Clark, 1977). Only in recent years have investigators begun systematic studies of the language of the hearing-impaired. Most of these studies have been descriptive, tending to demonstrate differences between normally hearing subjects and hearing-impaired subjects; or differences between hearing-impaired subjects on such variables as age of onset of the hearing loss, the amount of the hearing loss, and the pathology of the hearing loss.

The Office of Demographic Studies at Gallaudet College, Washington, D.C., has provided a wealth of descriptive information on the education of hearing-impaired children. For example, in one publication (1971), educational achievement data from a standardized test were reported on 16,815 students ranging in age from under 6 to over 20 years of age. In the batteries, the subtest testing paragraph meaning reported the average scores across batteries to be from 2.33 to 7.83, with an average of all batteries at 4.36. These data are an indication of the educational lag between hearing-impaired children in special or self-contained programs and normally hearing children. It is apparent from most descriptive studies that delayed acquisition of language skills is the most common factor underlying delayed educational skills.

Initial and ongoing assessment of language skills should receive a high priority in the overall assessment of hearing-impaired children. The hearing-impaired child's educational success in reading, mathematical reasoning, and other school subjects is highly correlated with an ability to comprehend and express English language structures.

Comprehensive language assessment should involve at least two sets of data, one derived from formal and another from informal tests of language functioning. The information gleaned from formal, standardized language tests will provide data related to age norms of a general population of students. These data provide teachers and clinicians with a general picture of weaknesses and strengths in various areas of language functioning. Concerns about validity and reliability need to be raised since most language tests are standardized on normally hearing populations. A recent exception to this is the Test of Syntactic Ability (TSA), which does provide a good data base from a hearing-impaired population (Quigley, 1978). One problem with standardized tests, however, is the tendency to focus on special grammatical structures within the confines of basic syntax.

Informal tests of language function devised by teachers and clinicians provide a more complete picture of the student's total language skills. For a number of reasons, hearing-impaired students present splinter skills in areas of language comprehension and production that are not always sampled in formal testing sessions. A spontaneous sampling of language over time provides additional information regarding syntactic, semantic, and pragmatic areas of language functioning. Many hearing-impaired children function at levels significantly below their processing abilities. Analysis of language needs to be an ongoing process to determine progress and to keep the goals of an IEP current and relevant.

Effects of Identification and Intervention. Early identification and intervention has been a priority objective of educators of the hearing impaired for many years. For a number of years early education was provided by preschool programs. These programs tended to accept children in the age range of 4 to 5 years old. As educational philosophy changed, so did the concept of preschool education. The age limits for educational services changed to a point where nursery-preschool programs begin as early as 2 years of age. The real effects of good early education programs have been obscured by the type of research produced. As a result, the efficacy of early programming has been primarily demonstrated by its end product—namely, the progress students make in preschool programs. From a stratified sample of subjects relating to the age of entry to school, it appears that those students starting school earliest tend to complete more grades in school. One out of five persons who began school before age 5 completed one or more years of college. These data are age-based and not necessarily causal (Schein & Delk, 1974).

Another aspect of early intervention is parent education and training. At the time of identification of hearing loss, the infant or toddler can be provided services indirectly through parent education. The major goals of a parent-training program were summarized by Horton (1975): (1) to teach parents to optimize the auditory environment for their child; (2) to teach parents how to communicate with their child; (3) to teach parents strategies of behavior management; (4) to familiarize parents with the principles, stages, and sequences of normal development, including language development; and to apply this frame of references in stimulating their child; and (5) to apply effective support to aid parents in coping with their feelings about their child and to reduce the stresses that a handicapped child places on the integrity of the family.

The effects of early identification and preschool intervention on subsequent educational progress have not been empirically demonstrated. However, retrospective analysis demonstrates that the earlier an intervention program begins, the more likely will the hearing-impaired child succeed in using a hearing aid, in general educational achievement, and in better social and emotional adjustment.

Rollie R. Houchins

See also Deinstitutionalization of the Handicapped; Handicapped Individuals; Language Development; Preschool Education for the Handicapped; Rehabilitation Services; Speech Language Services.

REFERENCES

Academic Achievement Test Results of a National Testing Program for Hearing-impaired Students: United States, Spring, 1971. Washington, D.C.: Gallaudet College, Office of Demographic Studies, 1972. (ERIC Document Reproduction Service No. ED 067 802)

Barry, K. *The Five-slate System: A System of Objective Language Teaching.* Philadelphia: Sherman & Company, 1899.

Blackwell, P. M.; Engen, E.; Fischgrund, J. E.; & Zarcadoolas, C. *Sentences and Other Systems.* Washington, D.C.: Alexander Graham Bell Association for the Deaf, Inc., 1978.

Bloom, L. *Language Development: Form and Function in Emerging Grammars.* Cambridge, Mass.: MIT Press, 1970. (ERIC Document Reproduction Service No. ED 038 418)

Brown, R. *A First Language: The Early Stages.* Cambridge, Mass.: Harvard University Press, 1973.

Buckler, M. S. Expanding language through patterning. *Volta Review,* 1968, *70,* 89–96.

Byrne, M. C., & Shervanian, C. C. *Introduction to Communicative Disorders.* New York: Harper & Row, 1977.

Clark, H., & Clark, E. *Psychology and Language.* New York: Harcourt Brace Jovanovich, 1977.

Fitzgerald, E. *Straight Language for the Deaf.* Washington, D.C.: Alexander Graham Bell Association for the Deaf, Inc., 1949.

Garretson, M. D. Total communication. *Volta Review,* 1976, *77,* 88–95.

Holcomb, R. K. Three years of the total approach: 1968–1971. *Proceedings of the Forty-fifth Convention of American Instructors of the Deaf,* 1972, pp. 522–530.

Horton, K. B. Early intervention through parent training. *Otolaryngological Clinics of North America,* 1975, *8,* 143–157.

Quigley, S. P.; Steinkamp, M. W.; Power, D. J.; & Jones, B. W. *Test of Syntactic Abilities.* Beaverton, Oreg.: Dormac, Inc., 1978.

Schein, J. D., & Delk, M. T. Jr. *The Deaf Population of the United States.* Silver Springs, Md.: National Association of the Deaf, 1974. (ERIC Document Reproduction Service No. ED 101 517)

Wilbur, R. B. *American Sign Language and Sign Systems.* Baltimore, Md.: University Park Press, 1979.

Wing, G. The theory and practice of grammatical methods. *American Annals of the Deaf,* 1887, *32,* 84–92.

HIGH SCHOOL

See Secondary Education.

HIGHER EDUCATION

This article, which provides an overview of the field of higher education, is divided into two main parts. The first part presents one approach to depicting the context in which the field can usefully be considered, including the size and scope of the enterprise, its purposes and goals, and environmental characteristics that affect it. The second part discusses three major features characterizing higher education in the United States—diversity, quality, and access—and current issues related to each. Attention is given to major policy statements of nationally recognized commissions as well as to empirical research findings.

The Carnegie Commission on Higher Education and its successor body, the Carnegie Council on Policy Studies in Higher Education, have produced thirty-seven major reports and numerous research and technical documents. Collectively they constitute the most important current review of higher education. Their policy recommendations, as well as the results of their commissioned research, are available in summary form (Carnegie Commission, 1972a; Carnegie Commission, 1975; Carnegie Council, 1980a). A summary and analysis of the commission's work was prepared by Mayhew (1974).

Context

The Domain of Higher Education.   Higher education, as defined by the National Center for Education Statistics, (NCES), includes study beyond the secondary school level at an institution that offers programs terminating in an associate degree (two-year), baccalaureate degree (four-year), or higher graduate or professional degree (NCES, 1980a). It thus includes nondegree programs offered in such institutions, but excludes programs of advanced study increasingly located in business, industry, and other non-collegiate settings.

As of fall 1979, there were 3,142 institutions of higher education that enrolled 11.9 million students, a number equal to 39 percent of the 18-year-old to 24-year-old age cohort (NCES, 1981). In 1978 these institutions employed 1.86 million persons in professional and nonprofessional positions (44 percent of whom were members of the instructional staff), and expended (in 1977/78) 46.0 billion dollars for current operations (NCES, 1980b).

The system of higher education in the United States is the largest and most complex in the world. Institutions are commonly differentiated on a number of characteristics, among which are control, level of degree, and size. In 1978 there were 1,474 public institutions under the control of federal, state, or local governmental units, or some combination thereof; and 1,660 institutions considered as private and organized either as independent and nonprofit (788) or affiliated with a Protestant, Catholic, or other religious group (742). In addition, this group of private institutions included ninety-six classified as profit making, a recently recognized category of degree-granting institution. Institutions are also frequently categorized according to highest level of degree offered, with 1,193 offering programs of two but less than four years in length (most of these institutions are public community colleges); 1,471 offering a baccalaureate or master's degree, but less than a doctorate; and 427 offering doctoral programs. The range in campus size in this country is enormous. Although there are more private than public colleges, the latter tend to be larger on the average and so enroll 78 percent of the student body. Of 3,131 campuses reporting in 1978, 286 (almost all private) enrolled less than 200 students and 25 (almost all public) enrolled 30,000 or more (NCES, 1980b).

Numerous classification schemes have been created to establish typologies of institutions that could be useful in research (e.g., Astin, 1962; Baldridge et al., 1978; Bowen & Minter, 1976; Ladd & Lipset, 1975; Lazersfeld & Thielens, 1958). The most widely employed of these (Carnegie Council, 1976) divides institutions into six major categories and nineteen subcategories based upon several criteria, including level of federal financial support, degree level, undergraduate selectivity, curriculum, and institutional size. The six major categories include (1) doctorate-granting institutions (subdivided into four groups based on level of federal support and number of degrees awarded); (2) comprehensive universities and colleges (subdivided into two groups based on program and enrollment); (3) liberal arts colleges (subdivided into two groups based on their admissions standards or the number of graduates later earning the doctorate); (4) two-year colleges or institutes; (5) professional schools and other specialized institutions (subdivided into nine groups based on program); and (6) institutions for nontraditional study. The most well-known and prestigious institutions in the United States are likely to belong to only two of the nineteen subgroups (Research Universities I, a subcategory of the doctorate-granting institutions includes the fifty institutions with the greatest federal financial support of academic science; and Liberal Arts Colleges I, a subcategory of liberal arts colleges with selective admissions policies). It is important to note, however, that they constitute only a small minority of institutions in the United States.

Purposes and Goals.   The purposes of the earliest colleges in this country were to transmit and preserve classical culture, provide moral training, and prepare young men for positions of clerical and lay leadership. The changing purposes of higher education over the past 345 years since the founding of Harvard College are traced in the standard histories of the field (Brubacher & Rudy, 1976; Rudolph, 1962; Veysey, 1965) and reviews of educational purposes and goals (Bowen, 1977, Trivett, 1973). Higher education in the United States has always served the needs of the larger society, and earlier consensus about the purposes and goals of colleges and universities has been replaced, particularly since the end of World War II, with diversity and conflict mirroring the complex interests and objectives of a pluralistic society.

The Carnegie Commission (1973c) suggested that there are five major purposes served by contemporary higher education and rated the performance of American colleges and universities on achieving each: (1) the provision of opportunities for intellectual, aesthetic, ethical, and skill development of individual students and the provision of campus environments that can constructively assist students in their more general developmental growth (rated as "generally adequate"); (2) the advancement of human capability in society at large (rated as "superior"); (3) the enlargement of educational justice for the postsecondary age-group (rated as "unsatisfactory but improving"); (4) the transmission and advancement of learning and wisdom (rated as "superior"); (5) the critical evaluation of society—through individual thought and persuasion—for the sake of society's self-renewal (rated as "quite uneven in the past and uncertain for the future"). Stated in these general terms and related to the entirety of the higher education system rather than to individual institutions, these purposes probably enjoy universal support and approval. It is when attempts are made to define specific goals and programs in institutions that the ambiguities, inconsistencies, and contradictions inherent in these abstractions begin to appear. For example, two studies of faculty and administrative perceptions of forty-seven specific goals at eighty institutions (Gross & Grambach, 1968, 1974) suggest that most of those goals are considered to be important. Even though research has proposed ways of structuring higher education goals (Lenning et al., 1977) and processes for linking institutional goals to specific outcomes (Romney, 1978), the difficulty of obtaining agreement on definition and measurement remains. The ambiguity that results from the simultaneous embracing of large numbers of diverse goals is one of the characteristics of academic institutions that define them as organized anarchies (Cohen & March, 1974).

The purposes of higher education consists of more than merely the aggregated goals of individual institutions, however. The influence of colleges and universities upon societal values, redistribution of income, economic development, social mobility and equity, and related issues has made them a critical instrument of public policy.

A major purpose from this policy perspective was presented immediately after World War II by a presidential commission that stated that the strengthening of democracy required free and universal access to higher education for all qualified students. The commission recommended elimination of all financial, racial, and religious barriers to higher education as well as development of community colleges and establishment of extensive programs of adult education (President's Commission on Higher Education, 1947). Rapid expansion of the system during the next two decades was reflected in a more diverse student body, bigger institutions, and a proportionately larger public sector (Hodgkinson, 1971), and was accompanied by an "academic revolution" (Jencks & Reisman, 1968) characterized by increased professionalization of the faculty and general acceptance throughout the system of meritocratic academic values.

Concern that diversification of the student body had not been accompanied by new academic programs and approaches adequate to meet their needs led to numerous studies and recommendations concerning the development of higher education. The controversial and influential Newman Report (1971) argued a need for new types of colleges, new missions, and new patterns of college-going to meet the needs of new students. The report noted and criticized high college attrition rates, lockstep curricula, decreasing diversity, depersonalization, bureaucratization, insensitivity to minority students and women, and credentialism. It presented a number of recommendations, including the need to develop new academic enter-

prises that offer alternatives to the "academic mode" of learning (particularly as they integrate education and experience), increased opportunities for adults to continue their education, establishment of regional examining universities and television colleges, state and federal institutional grants that students could use at any institution and which would therefor encourage institutional competition, and diversification of the faculty through appointment of experienced nonacademics. Several contemporaneous policy studies shared the same perspectives (Carnegie Commission, 1971c, 1972b, 1973b).

More recently, an increasingly diverse student body has led to a broader conception of postsecondary education that includes proprietary schools, employers, community service agencies, unions, and other organizations. As a consequence, policy recommendations are now more likely to include higher education with other educating institutions. The Carnegie Commission report *Toward a Learning Society* (1973d) recommended opening up more collegiate and noncollegiate options for young people; creating opportunities for adults to participate in postsecondary education of various kinds; mixing education, work, and service as part of a postsecondary program for young people; and mixing age-groups in educational institutions. At the same time, a national commission gave impetus to the use of nontraditional methods in higher education and called for a commitment to lifelong learning, a focus upon the learner rather than credentials, training of faculty in nontraditional instructional models, use of educational technology, and better systems of information collection and dissemination concerning educational opportunities (Commission on Non-Traditional Study, 1973). Without specifying the roles of colleges and universities, the commission urged that institutions shift their emphasis from degree granting to service to learners.

Expanded opportunities in postsecondary education were envisioned for young people as well as for adults by the Carnegie Council. In *Giving Youth a Better Chance* (1979b), the council called for community colleges to accept responsibility for providing job training for high school dropouts, to emphasize cooperative education and apprenticeship programs, and to develop closer cooperative relationships with high schools.

Environment. As a system connected to the political, social, economic, and cultural developments of the larger society, higher education has been in the past (Henry, 1975) and will continue in the future to be dramatically affected by changes in its environment. Current trends related to recent changes include the rise of the public sector, transition from free sector to regulated industry, increased reliance on public funding, increased role of larger institutions, reduction of public confidence, changing rate of growth, an older faculty, more defensive reactions internally, a new generation of students (many ill prepared for academic work), and more pressure to serve the student market (Carnegie Council, 1980b).

The future of higher education will be largely dependent upon economic conditions, international crises, scientific breakthroughs, shifts in public ideology, social movements, and other important events that are not only outside the control of higher education but are also for the most part unpredictable. Of all these factors, a dramatic decrease in enrollments between 1978 and 1997 is one of the few environmental constraints that can now be predicted with reasonable assurance. Even here, however, caution must be observed, since enrollment projections of the past have proven to be highly unreliable (Carnegie Commission, 1971d). The major cause of the decline will be the 23 percent reduction by 1997 of persons in the 18-to-24-year-old age-group (Carnegie Council, 1980b; NCES, 1980a), the age-group from which institutions have traditionally drawn the greatest proportion of their students.

Some factors that may further contribute to the enrollment decline, including the decreasing economic value of a college degree, decreases in high school graduation rate, and increased opportunities for education outside the higher education system (Dresch, 1975; Freeman, 1976; Glenny, 1980; NCES, 1980a) may be offset at least in part by projected increases in the participation rates of women, part-time students, and older students (Carnegie Council, 1980b). Enrollment estimates for the mid-1990s range from decreases of up to 40 percent (Carnegie Foundation, 1975; Dresch, 1975); to the possibility of an increase under certain conditions (Bowen, 1974; Frances, 1980). However, the Carnegie Council's "most likely case" prediction of a 5 to 15 percent decline in undergraduate enrollment between 1978 and 1997 appears to reflect current consensus (Carnegie Council, 1980b).

When enrollment predictions for the entire system are disaggregated, they are expected to affect different categories and institutions in different ways, depending upon such factors as program, prestige, location, and capacity for planning. In general, research universities, selective liberal arts colleges, and public community colleges are expected to maintain enrollments, whereas less selective liberal arts colleges and private two-year colleges will be the most vulnerable to enrollment pressures. Institutions in the declining population centers of the East and Midwest will be at higher risk than those in areas experiencing population growth, such as the South, Southwest, and West (Carnegie Council, 1980b; Carnegie Foundation, 1975). Since almost all institutions are heavily dependent either directly or indirectly upon enrollment for income, the predicted enrollment trends are likely to have dramatic effects upon the programs, staffs, and structures of most institutions in some ways and to drive a small number of them out of existence (Carnegie Council, 1980b; Cartter, 1976; Glenny et al., 1976; Leslie & Miller, 1974; Mortimer & Tierney, 1979; Shulman, 1979; Stadtman, 1980).

In addition to changes related to demography, the political environment is likely to have a major influence on higher education. Expanded roles of states in the regula-

tion, oversight, and control of institutions under their jurisdiction have been related to the increasing scope of the higher education enterprise in terms of enrollments and budgets, growing public concern for accountability, competing fiscal demands of other social service activities, and the perceived need to coordinate growth during the past two decades (as well as to coordinate decline during the next two).

Thoughtful policy statements have suggested principles by which both legitimate state interests can be protected and the erosion of institutional independence can be halted (Carnegie Commission, 1971a; Carnegie Foundation, 1976; Education Commission of the States, 1980). The Carnegie Council (1980b) has explicitly warned against attempts by the states to place systems of higher education under increased control and the use of enrollment projections as a justification for reducing institutional budgets to harmful levels—both trends that have been seen in the past and may be seen in the future.

The planning, funding, and program approval functions of the states are likely to affect institutions in direct and visible ways, but the influence of the federal government is likely to be more indirect through support of student-aid programs and academic research and through the large number of legislative acts and agency regulations related to various aspects of institutional operations (Bender, 1977). Although federal regulations all relate to public policy objectives, they require institutional funds to administer (Van Alstyne & Coldren, 1977), and the issue of whether the costs justify the benefits was widely debated (American Association of University Women, 1978; Carnegie Council, 1975; Carnegie Council, 1980b; Edwards, 1980; Grant, 1977; Hobbs, 1978; Lester, 1974).

The highly controversial recommendations of the Sloan Commission on Government and Higher Education (1980) endorsed federal goals in the area of nondiscrimination and equal opportunity, but suggested that undue duplication of effort and confusion can be eliminated by creating a single consolidated agency for enforcing all equal opportunity regulations affecting higher education. The commission also recommended that federal regulations concerning financial accountability be revised to support university research goals.

Major Features

Diversity. Differing needs of various interest groups, lack of any formal mechanisms for coordinating higher education policy at the national level, and academic autonomy of private institutions have led to a level of institutional diversity in the United States unparalleled in the world. This diversity has been considered responsible both for the high level of performance of the higher education system and for its responsiveness to society (Ben-David, 1972; Carnegie Commission, 1973c). In addition to differences in source of control, program, size, and degree level already mentioned, institutions vary in terms of the clientele they serve and their educational and public policy objectives.

Among the special-interest institutions that have been developed to meet the needs of specific clienteles are those identified as historically or predominantly black (Bowles & DeCosta, 1971; Carnegie Commission, 1971b; Jencks & Riesman, 1968; McGrath, 1965; Willie & Edmonds, 1978); colleges for women (Carnegie Commission, 1973a; Jencks & Riesman, 1968); and colleges for particular religious groups (Greeley, 1969; Hobbs & Meeth, 1980; Jencks & Riesman, 1968; Pace, 1972).

Other institutions have been created or have evolved to meet implicit or explicit educational or public policy objectives. These include the regional state colleges and universities, many of which evolved from teacher-training institutions and which are now multipurpose in nature (Dunham, 1969; Harcleroad, Molen, & VanOrt, 1976); land grant universities (Anderson, 1976); community colleges (Medsker & Tillery, 1971); and small, special-interest private institutions (Astin & Lee, 1972; Jencks & Riesman, 1968; Jonsen, 1978; Keeton, 1971; Keeton & Hilberry, 1969).

According to some authorities, significant environmental pressures may currently be acting to reduce levels of diversity in higher education (Hodgkinson, 1971; Jencks & Riesman, 1968; Martin, 1969; Newman, 1971; Pace, 1974). Others have suggested that the level of diversity is either unchanged or in fact may have somewhat increased (Baldridge et al., 1978; Stadtman, 1980). There is as yet no accepted definition of "diversity" that would permit these competing views to be empirically resolved.

Although a number of issues still remain in dispute, concern about the future of the private sector in general is widely shared. Earlier doubts concerning the viability of the private sector (Cheit, 1971; Jellema, 1973) appear to have been premature, but future enrollment declines may have a disproportionate effect on the smallest and least selective institutions in this group as increasing tuition differentials with public institutions make them less competitive in the student marketplace. Some of these institutions have made strategic changes in their clientele and mission in an effort to maintain enrollments, but short-term enrollment gains may be offset in the long run by changes of institutional climate that make these private institutions less distinctive and attractive to students (Anderson, 1977). Twice as many private institutions (122) closed in 1969–1978 as during the preceding decade, even though the total number of private institutions increased during that period (NCES, 1980a). The future of at least part of the private sector may depend upon whether public policy adopts a market approach permitting institutions to survive or fail based on their ability to enroll students, or whether states or the federal government will intervene through direct grants or programs of student financial aid that provide assistance to these institutions (Benezet, 1976;

Breneman & Finn, 1978; Comptroller General, 1978; Education Commission of the States, 1977). The history and current status of state support of private higher education are presented by Howard (1977).

The Carnegie Council (1977b, 1980b) has stated that preserving and strengthening the private sector is in the public interest and recommends that public support be available in addition to increased efforts by the institutions themselves. To protect the autonomy of the institutions, the council suggests that state funds be channeled to colleges primarily through student financial aid and that each state develop long-range plans that include policies directly related to private higher education.

Access. The 1947 Presidential Commission recommendation for universal access to higher education marked the real start of a major transition to our present system of mass higher education and to acceptance of access as a central motif and premise of the system. Several major Carnegie Commission and Council reports have dealt with the issue of access at length (Carnegie Commission, 1968, 1970a, 1970b; Carnegie Council, 1977a).

Barriers to access in the United States still exist, although they are probably lower and less widespread than in any other country. Although financial problems have still not been fully resolved, contemporary concerns regarding access now focus for the most part upon barriers related to ethnic group and sex.

Studies of minority enrollments have documented the significant changes that have occurred over the past decade. Grossly underrepresented in the total higher education system a decade ago (Crossland, 1971), enrollment of black students increased dramatically from 522,000 in 1970 to 1.1 million in 1977 (*Black Enrollment*, 1979). Determining the actual level of minority enrollments is difficult because various studies use different bases for comparison and enrollment patterns between and within various ethnic groups differ so widely. Evidence to date suggests that minority students may be more likely to attend college than nonminority students of the same level of academic achievement and socioeconomic status, but that they are still somewhat underrepresented in total undergraduate enrollments and in many areas of study (Brown & Stent, 1977; Mingle, 1979; NCES, 1980a). The underenrollment of minorities is particularly apparent in highly selective institutions (Morris, 1979) and graduate and professional schools (National Board, 1976). Minority students are also less likely to earn both undergraduate and graduate degrees than their white contemporaries (*Data on Earned Degrees*, 1979; Gilford & Syverson, 1979) and are significantly underrepresented on college and university faculties (*Higher Education Staff Information Report*, 1977). Because the issue of access in many ways serves as a proxy for the questioning of definitions of social justice and institutional structures, the desegregation of American campuses has had major effects on all aspects of higher education, including the creation of new administrative roles, curriculums, resource allocation processes, and faculty and student relationships (Peterson et al., 1978).

Although in 1979 women outnumbered men as students in colleges and universities for the first time (Anderson, 1980), discrimination and subtle socialization processes have made sex a barrier to access in the past and continue to influence attendance patterns and selection of areas of study. Successive reduction in the percentage of women passing through each key point of advancement in higher education is now well documented (Carnegie Commission, 1973a). Contributing factors include discrimination in admissions to undergraduate and graduate programs; institutional rules and regulations that disproportionately disadvantage women; inadequate guidance, health, and related student services; and persistent socialization into sexual stereotypes (Astin, Harway, & McNamara 1976; Furniss & Graham, 1974; Gappa & Uehling, 1979; Rossi & Calderwood, 1973). Female faculty and administrators are more likely to be in the lower ranks, to have lower salaries than their male counterparts, to be promoted more slowly, and in other ways to be disadvantaged in their academic careers (Bayer & Astin, 1975; Gappa & Uehling, 1979; NCES, 1980b; Van Alstyne & Withers, 1977). Some progress is being made, however. The number of women heading colleges and universities rose from 148 in 1975 to 177 in 1978, for example (Anderson, 1980).

Quality. The definition of "quality" in American higher education is elusive. To some it refers to excellence in academic research at the graduate level, to others it is related to increased selectivity in undergraduate admissions, and to still others it implies the maintenance of integrity and distinctiveness among institutions offering programs suitable to students with varying interests and measured ability levels. Whatever the meaning of the term, many authorities fear that the level of quality of students, faculty, programs, and institutions built up over the years may be eroding. Comparing higher education in the 1960s with higher education in the 1980s and 1990s, the Carnegie Council (1980b) concluded, "Excellence was the theme. Now it is survival." (p. 30).

Studies of undergraduate institutions have used selectivity as a proxy for quality (Astin & Henson, 1977; Astin & Solomon, 1979), and "reputational" studies of quality at the graduate and professional levels have been undertaken by Cartter (1966), Roose and Anderson (1970), Blau and Margulies (1974–1975), and Cartter and Solomon (1977). Such studies assume that the reputation of a school's faculty closely reflects its educational worth. As critics have pointed out, however, faculty research and productivity may occur at the expense of undergraduate education, may decrease diversity, and may reinforce unwarranted anonymity of the vast majority of institutions in this country (Lawrence & Green, 1980).

State planning agencies have accepted responsibility for maintaining and enhancing program quality in the public sector, but have little authority over private institutions (Halstead, 1974). Their quality-control function depends upon establishment of regulations governing institutional functioning and review of both new and existing programs (Barak & Berdahl, 1978). The Sloan Commission (1980) recommended that states control quality through periodic and published peer program reviews of all public institutions, with private institutions invited but not required to participate. The Carnegie Council (1980b) has expressed reservations about state-mandated program reviews as an intrusion into academic affairs and has suggested that such reviews should be conducted directly by institutions and accrediting agencies and indirectly through market pressures by students as they make their enrollment choices.

Quality in academic institutions is to some extent assessed and maintained through the activities of state government, regional, and program accrediting bodies in addition to program review (Harcleroad, 1980). The accrediting bodies have recently been criticized, however, for failing to properly sanction weaker institutions and for approving institutions and programs that meet only minimal quality standards (Carnegie Council, 1979a; Sloan Commission, 1980).

Current social and economic conditions related to intensified competition for new students have already begun to affect institutional quality. Evidence of deterioration at some institutions includes increased student cheating, abuse of financial aid, theft and destruction of academic property, grade inflation, awarding credits for inadequate work, misleading advertising, admission of unqualified foreign students, and inadequate support services. Entering students have lower test scores than in the past; large numbers of students need remedial work; admissions requirements are being lowered; students are being retained regardless of performance; and quality of product as measured by scores on tests taken before entering graduate work has deteriorated significantly (Carnegie Council, 1979a; Carnegie Council, 1980b; Carnegie Council, 1980b; Levine, 1980).

Recommendations for improvement are easier to articulate than to implement. Although suggesting in *Three Thousand Futures* that each institution in the nation has an opportunity to help shape its own future, the Carnegie Council (1980b) indicated that the prospects for the system as a whole are not bright. In reviewing projections for the future, the council said, "Most of these factors support the old and static more than the new and dynamic. . . . Some of the drama of the next two decades will center around the natural and strong efforts of many within the academic community, and particularly among faculty members, to hold on to what they cherish most from the past, and the necessity, felt more strongly by administrators and trustees, to adapt to new realities of the student market" (p. 31).

Those who attempt to make use of research about higher education should keep clearly in mind that the processes, systems, structures, and dynamics that have been the subject of investigation in the past may only poorly reflect the realities toward which we are now heading.

Robert Birnbaum

See also Admission to Colleges and Universities; Curriculum and Instruction in Higher Education; Graduate Education; History and Philosophy of Higher Education; Junior and Community College Education; Organization and Administration of Higher Education; Undergraduate Instruction.

REFERENCES

American Association of University Women. *But We Will Persist.* Washington, D.C.: The Association, 1978.

Anderson, C. J. *1980 Fact Book.* Washington, D.C.: American Council on Education, 1980.

Anderson, C. L. *Land Grant Universities and Their Continuing Challenge.* East Lansing: Michigan State University Press, 1976.

Anderson, R. E. *Strategic Policy Changes at Private Colleges.* New York: Teachers College Press, 1977.

Astin, A. W. An empirical characterization of higher education. *Journal of Educational Psychology,* 1962, *53*(5), 224–235.

Astin, A. W., & Henson, J. W. New measures of college selectivity. *Research in Higher Education,* 1977, *6*, 1–9.

Astin, A. W., & Lee, C. B. T. *The Invisible Colleges: A Profile of Small, Private Colleges with Limited Resources.* New York: McGraw-Hill, 1972.

Astin, A. W., & Solomon, L. C. Measuring academic quality: An interim report. *Change,* 1979, *11*, 48–51.

Astin, H.; Harway, M.; & McNamara, P. *Sex Discrimination in Education: Access to Post-secondary Education.* Los Angeles: Higher Education Research Institute, 1976.

Baldridge, J. V.; Curtis, D. V.; Ecker, G.; & Riley, G. L. *Policymaking and Effective Leadership.* San Francisco: Jossey-Bass, 1978.

Barak, R. J., & Berdahl, R. G. *State-level Academic Review in Higher Education.* Denver: Education Commission of the States, 1978.

Bayer, A. E., & Astin, H. S. Sex differentials in the academic reward system. *Science,* May 1975, *188*, 796–802.

Ben-David, J. *American Higher Education: Directions Old and New.* New York: McGraw-Hill, 1972.

Bender, L. W. *Federal Regulation and Higher Education.* Washington, D.C.: American Association for Higher Education, 1977.

Benezet, L. T. *Private Higher Education and Public Funding.* Washington, D.C.: American Association for Higher Education, 1976.

Black Enrollment in Higher Education: Trends in the Nation and the South. Atlanta: Southern Regional Education Board, 1979.

Blau, P. M., & Margulies, R. Z. The reputations of American professional schools. *Change,* Winter 1974–1975, *6*, 42–47.

Bowen, H. R. Higher education: A growth industry? *Educational Record,* 1974, *55*(3), 147–158.

Bowen, H. R. *Investment in Learning: The Individual and Social Value of American Higher Education.* San Francisco: Jossey-Bass, 1977.

Bowen, H. R., & Minter, W. J. *Private Higher Education: Second Annual Report on Financial and Educational Trends in the Private Sector of American Higher Education.* Washington, D.C.: Association of American Colleges, 1976.

Bowles, F., & DeCosta, F. A. *Between Two Worlds: A Profile of Negro Higher Education.* New York: McGraw-Hill, 1971.

Breneman, D. W., & Finn, C. E., Jr. (Eds.). *Public Policy and Private Higher Education.* Washington, D.C.: Brookings Institution, 1978.

Brown, F., & Stent, M. D. *Minorities in U.S. Institutions of Higher Education.* New York: Praeger, 1977.

Brubacher, J. S., & Rudy, W. *Higher Education in Transition* (3rd ed.). New York: Harper & Row, 1976.

Carnegie Commission on Higher Education. *Quality and Equality: New Levels of Responsibility for Higher Education.* New York: McGraw-Hill, 1968.

Carnegie Commission on Higher Education. *A Chance to Learn: An Action Agenda for Equal Opportunity in Higher Education.* New York: McGraw-Hill, 1970. (a)

Carnegie Commission on Higher Education. *The Open-door Colleges: Policies for Community Colleges.* New York: McGraw-Hill, 1970. (b)

Carnegie Commission on Higher Education. *The Capitol and the Campus: State Responsibility for Post-secondary Education.* New York: McGraw-Hill, 1971. (a)

Carnegie Commission on Higher Education. *From Isolation to Mainstream: Problems of the Colleges Founded for Negroes.* New York: McGraw-Hill, 1971. (b)

Carnegie Commission on Higher Education. *Less Time, More Options: Education beyond the High School.* New York: McGraw-Hill, 1971. (c)

Carnegie Commission on Higher Education. *New students and New Places.* New York: McGraw-Hill, 1971. (d)

Carnegie Commission on Higher Education. *A Digest and Index of Reports and Recommendations, December 1968–June 1972.* Berkeley Calif.: The Commission, 1972. (a)

Carnegie Commission on Higher Education. *Reform on Campus: Changing Students, Changing Academic Programs.* New York: McGraw-Hill, 1972. (b)

Carnegie Commission on Higher Education. *Opportunities for Women in Higher Education: Their Current Participation, Prospects for the Future, and Recommendations for Actions.* New York: McGraw-Hill, 1973. (a)

Carnegie Commission on Higher Education. *Priorities for Action: Final Report of the Carnegie Commission on Higher Education.* New York: McGraw-Hill, 1973. (b)

Carnegie Commission on Higher Education. *The Purposes and the Performance of Higher Education in the United States.* New York: McGraw-Hill, 1973. (c)

Carnegie Commission on Higher Education. *Toward a Learning Society: Alternative Channels to Life, Work, and Service.* New York: McGraw-Hill, 1973. (d)

Carnegie Commission on Higher Education. *Sponsored Research of the Carnegie Commission on Higher Education.* New York: McGraw-Hill, 1975.

Carnegie Council on Policy Studies in Higher Education. *Making Affirmative Action Work in Higher Education: An Analysis of Institutional and Federal Policies with Recommendations.* San Francisco: Jossey-Bass, 1975.

Carnegie Council on Policy Studies in Higher Education. *A Classification of Institutions of Higher Education* (Rev. ed.). Berkeley, Calif.: Carnegie Foundation for the Advancement of Teaching, 1976.

Carnegie Council on Policy Studies in Higher Education. *Selective*

Admissions in Higher Education. San Francisco: Jossey-Bass, 1977. (a)

Carnegie Council on Policy Studies in Higher Education. *The States and Private Higher Education: Problems and Policies in a New Era.* San Francisco: Jossey-Bass, 1977. (b)

Carnegie Council on Policy Studies in Higher Education. *Fair Practices in Higher Education: Rights and Responsibilities of Students and Their Colleges in a Period of Intensified Competition for Enrollments.* San Francisco: Jossey-Bass, 1979. (a)

Carnegie Council on Policy Studies in Higher Education. *Giving Youth a Better Chance: Options for Education, Work, and Service.* San Francisco: Jossey-Bass. 1979. (b)

Carnegie Council on Policy Studies in Higher Education. *The Carnegie Council on Policy Studies in Higher Education: A Summary of Reports and Recommendations.* San Francisco: Jossey-Bass, 1980. (a)

Carnegie Council on Policy Studies in Higher Education. *Three Thousand Futures: The Next Twenty Years for Higher Education.* San Francisco: Jossey-Bass, 1980. (b)

Carnegie Foundation for the Advancement of Teaching. *More than Survival: Prospects for Higher Education in a Period of Uncertainty.* San Francisco: Jossey-Bass, 1975.

Carnegie Foundation for the Advancement of Teaching. *The States and Higher Education: A Proud Past and a Vital Future.* San Francisco: Jossey-Bass, 1976.

Cartter, A. M. *An Assessment of Quality in Graduate Education.* Washington, D.C.: American Council on Education, 1966. (ERIC Document Reproduction Service No. ED 016 621)

Cartter, A. M., *Ph.D.'s and the Academy Labor Market.* New York: McGraw-Hill, 1976.

Cartter, A. M., & Solomon, L. C. The Cartter report on the leading schools of education, law, and business. *Change,* 1977, *9,* 44–48.

Cheit, E. F. *The New Depression in Higher Education: A Study of Financial Conditions at Forty-one Colleges and Universities.* New York: McGraw-Hill, 1971.

Cohen, M. D., & March, J. G. *Leadership and Ambiguity: The American College Presidency.* New York: McGraw-Hill, 1974.

Commission on Non-Traditional Study. *Diversity by Design.* San Francisco: Jossey-Bass, 1973.

Comptroller General of the United States. *Problems and Outlook of Small, Private Liberal Arts Colleges.* Washington, D.C.: United States General Accounting Office, 1978. (ERIC Document Reproduction Service No. ED 117 984)

Crossland, F. E. *Minority Access to College: A Ford Foundation Report.* New York: Schocken Books, 1971.

Data on Earned Degrees Conferred by Institutions of Higher Education by Race, Ethnicity, and Sex, Academic Year 1976–1977. (Vol. 2). Washington, D.C.: Office for Civil Rights, 1979. (ERIC Document Reproduction Service No. ED 176 636)

Dresch, S. P. Educational saturation: A demographic-economic model. *American Association of University Professors Bulletin,* Autumn 1975, *61*(3), 239–247.

Dunham, E. A. *Colleges of the Forgotten Americans.* New York: McGraw-Hill, 1969.

Education Commission of the States. *Final Report and Recommendations: Task Force on State Policy and Independent Higher Education.* Denver: The Commission, 1977.

Education Commission of the States. *Challenge: Coordination and Governance in the Eighties.* Denver: The Commission, 1980.

Edwards, H. T. *Higher Education and the Unholy Crusade against Governmental Regulations.* Cambridge, Mass.: Harvard University, Institute for Educational Management, 1980.

Frances, C. *College Enrollment: Testing the Conventional Wisdom against the Facts.* Washington, D.C.: American Council on Education, 1980.

Freeman, R. B. *The Over-educated American.* New York: Academic Press, 1976.

Furniss, W. T., & Graham, P. A. *Women in Higher Education.* Washington, D.C.: American Council on Education, 1974. (ERIC Document Reproduction Service No. ED 098 872)

Gappa, J. M., & Uehling, B. S. *Women in Academe: Steps to Greater Equality.* Washington, D.C.: American Association for Higher Education, 1979. (ERIC Document Reproduction Service No. ED 169 873)

Gilford, D. M., & Syverson, P. D. *Summary Report: Doctoral Recipients from United States Universities.* Washington, D.C.: National Academy of Sciences, 1979.

Glenny, L. A. Demographic and related issues for higher education in the 1980s. *Journal of Higher Education,* 1980, *51*(4), 363–380.

Glenny, L. A.; Shea, J. R.; Ruyle, J. H.; & Freschi, K. H. *Presidents Confront Reality: From Edifice Complex to University without Walls.* San Francisco: Jossey-Bass, 1976.

Grant, A. T. *The Impact of Federal Policies on Higher Education Institutions.* Tucson: University of Arizona, Higher Education Program, 1977.

Greeley, A. M. *From Backwater to Mainstream: A Profile of Catholic Higher Education.* New York: McGraw-Hill, 1969.

Gross, E., & Grambach, P. V. *University Goals and Academic Power.* Washington, D.C.: American Council on Education, 1968. (ERIC Document Reproduction Service No. ED 028 692)

Gross, E., & Grambach, P. V. *Changes in University Organization, 1964–1971.* New York: McGraw-Hill, 1974.

Halstead, D. K. *Statewide Planning in Higher Education.* Washington, D.C.: U.S. Government Printing Office, 1974. (ERIC Document Reproduction Service No. ED 096 914)

Harcleroad, F. F. *Accreditation: History, Process, and Problems.* Washington, D.C.: American Association for Higher Education, 1980.

Harcleroad, F. F.; Molen, T., Jr.; & Van Ort, S. *The Regional State Colleges and Universities in the Middle 1970s.* Tucson: University of Arizona, Higher Education Program, 1976.

Henry, D. D. *Challenges Past, Challenges Present: An Analysis of American Higher Education since 1930.* San Francisco: Jossey-Bass, 1975.

Higher Education Staff Information Report (EEO-6). Washington, D.C.: Equal Employment Opportunity Commission, 1977.

Hobbs, W. C. *Government Regulation of Higher Education.* Cambridge, Mass.: Ballinger, 1978.

Hobbs, W. C., & Meeth, L. R. *Diversity among Christian Colleges.* Arlington, Va.: Studies in Higher Education, 1980.

Hodgkinson, H. L. *Institutions in Transition: A Profile of Change in Higher Education.* New York: McGraw-Hill, 1971.

Howard, A. E. D. *State Aid to Private Higher Education.* Charlottesville, Va.: Michie, 1977.

Jellema, W. W. *From Red to Black: The Financial Status of Private Colleges and Universities.* San Francisco: Jossey-Bass, 1973.

Jencks, C., & Riesman, D. *The Academic Revolution.* New York: Doubleday, 1968.

Jonsen, R. W. *Small Liberal Arts Colleges: Diversity at the Crossroads?* Washington, D.C.: American Association for Higher Education, 1978. (ERIC Document Reproduction Service No. ED 154 680)

Keeton, M. T. *Models and Mavericks: A Profile of Private Liberal Arts Colleges.* New York: McGraw-Hill, 1971.

Keeton, M. T., & Hilberry, C. *Struggle and Promise: A Future for Colleges.* New York: McGraw-Hill, 1969.

Ladd, E. C., Jr., & Lipset, S. M. *The Divided Academy: Professors and Politics.* New York: McGraw-Hill, 1975.

Lawrence, J. K., & Green, K. C. *A Question of Quality: The Higher Education Ratings Game.* Washington, D.C.: American Association for Higher Education, 1980. (ERIC Document Reproduction Service No. ED 192 667)

Lazersfeld, P. F., & Thielens, W., Jr. *The Academic Mind: Social Scientists in a Time of Crisis.* Glencoe, Ill.: Free Press of Glencoe, 1958.

Lenning, O. T.; Lee, Y. S.; Micek, S. S.; & Serice, A. L. *A Structure for the Outcomes of Post-secondary Education.* Boulder, Colo.: National Center for Higher Education Management Systems, 1977.

Leslie, L. L., & Miller, H. F. *Higher Education and the Steady State.* Washington, D.C.: American Association for Higher Education, 1974. (ERIC Document Reproduction Service No. ED 091 965)

Lester, R. A. *Antibias Regulation of Universities: Faculty Problems and Their Solutions.* New York: McGraw-Hill, 1974.

Levine, A. *When Dreams and Heroes Died: A Portrait of Today's College Students.* San Francisco: Jossey-Bass, 1980.

Martin, W. B. *Conformity: Standards and Change in Higher Education.* San Francisco: Jossey-Bass, 1969.

Mayhew, L. B. *The Carnegie Commission in Higher Education: A Critical Analysis of the Reports and Recommendations.* San Francisco: Jossey-Bass, 1974.

McGrath, E. J. *The Predominantly Negro Colleges and Universities in Transition.* New York: Teachers College Press, 1965.

Medsker, L., & Tillery, D. *Breaking the Access Barrier: A Profile of Two-year Colleges.* New York: McGraw-Hill, 1971.

Mingle, C. R. *Black and Hispanic Enrollment in Higher Education, 1978: Trends in the Nation and the South,* Atlanta: Southern Regional Education Board, 1979.

Morris, L. *Elusive Equality: The Status of Black Americans in Higher Education.* Washington, D.C.: Howard University Press, 1979.

Mortimer, K. P., & Tierney, M. L. *The Three "R's" of the Eighties: Reduction, Reallocation, and Retrenchment.* Washington, D.C.: American Association for Higher Education, 1979. (ERIC Document Reproduction Service No. ED 172 642)

National Board of Graduate Education. *Minority Group Participation in Graduate Education.* Washington, D.C.: National Academy of Sciences, 1976. National Center for Education Statistics. *The Condition of Education* (1980 ed.). Washington, D.C.: U.S. Government Printing Office, 1980. (a) (ERIC Document Reproduction Service No. ED 188 304)

National Center for Education Statistics. *Digest of Educational Statistics, 1980.* Washington, D.C.: U.S. Government Printing Office, 1980.(b)

National Center for Education Statistics. *The Condition of Education* (1981 ed.) Washington, D.C.: U.S. Government Printing Office, 1981.

Newman, F. *Report on Higher Education.* Washington, D.C.: U.S. Department of Health, Education, and Welfare, 1971. (ERIC Document Reproduction Service No. ED 049 718)

Pace, C. R. *Education and Evangelism: A Profile of Protestant Colleges.* New York: McGraw-Hill, 1972.

Pace, C. R. *The Demise of Diversity: A Comparative Profile of Eight Types of Institutions.* Berkeley, Calif.: Carnegie Commission on Higher Education, 1974.

Peterson, M. W.; Blackburn, R. T.; Gamson, Z. F.; Arce, C. H.; Davenport, R. W.; & Mingle, J. R. *Black Students on White Campuses: The Impacts of Increased Black Enrollments.* Ann Arbor: University of Michigan, Institute for Social Research, 1978.

President's Commission on Higher Education. *Higher Education for American Democracy: A Report of the President's Commission on Higher Education.* New York: Harper, 1947.

Romney, L. C. *Measures of Institutional Goal Achievement.* Boulder, Colo.: National Center for Higher Education Management Systems, 1978.

Roose, K. D., & Anderson, C. J. *A Rating of Graduate Programs.* Washington, D.C.: American Council on Education, 1970. (ERIC Document Reproduction Service No. ED 046 345)

Rossi, A. S., & Calderwood, A. (Eds.). *Academic Women on the Move.* New York: Russell Sage, 1973.

Rudolph, F. *The American College and University.* New York: Knopf, 1962.

Shulman, C. H. *Old Expectations, New Realities: The Academic Profession Revisited.* Washington, D.C.: American Association for Higher Education, 1979. (ERIC Document Reproduction Service No. ED 169 874)

Sloan Commission on Government and Higher Education. *A Program for Renewed Partnership.* Cambridge, Mass.: Ballinger, 1980.

Stadtman, V. A. *Academic Adaptations: Higher Education Prepares for the 1980s and 1990s.* San Francisco: Jossey-Bass, 1980.

Trivett, D. A. *Goals for Higher Education: Definitions and Directions.* Washington, D.C.: American Association for Higher Education, 1973. (ERIC Document Reproduction Service No. ED 082 698)

Van Alstyne, C., & Coldren, S. L. *Financing Higher Education: Basic Facts Underlining Current Issues.* Washington, D.C.: American Federation of Teachers, 1977.

Van Alstyne, C., & Withers, J. S. *Women and Minorities in Administration of Higher Education Institutions: Employment Patterns and Salary Comparisons.* Washington, D.C.: College and University Personnel Association, 1977.

Veysey, L. R. *The Emergence of the American University.* Chicago: University of Chicago Press, 1965.

Willie, C. V., & Edmonds, R. R. (Eds.). *Black Colleges in America: Challenge, Development, Survival.* New York: Teachers College Press, 1978.

HISPANIC-AMERICAN EDUCATION

Hispanic Americans consist of several groups: primarily Mexican Americans, Puerto Ricans, Cubans, and others from Caribbean islands and Central and South Americans. In 1978 the U.S. Census Bureau estimated that there were more than 12 million Hispanics on the United States mainland. This figure represents 5.3 percent of the total population. It is generally agreed that Hispanics are the fastest-growing minority group in the United States, at 2.2 percent a year as compared to 1.3 percent for blacks. The largest subgroup is the Mexican Americans, who number

7 million, or 59 percent of all Hispanic Americans, or 3.2 percent of the total population. This group tends to be localized in the Southwest, and there are substantial numbers in the large industrial cities such as Chicago and Detroit (U.S. Bureau of the Census, 1979; National Center for Educational Statistics [NCES], 1980).

Puerto Ricans number 1.8 million, or 0.8 percent of the total population. This second largest group is unlike the other Hispanic-American groups in that its members have been United States citizens since 1917 (Puerto Rico enjoys commonwealth status within the United States government). Most Puerto Ricans who live on the mainland first migrated to New York City and then spread into surrounding states such as New Jersey, Connecticut, and Pennsylvania (NCES, 1980).

In recent years, the net migration rate of Puerto Ricans to the mainland has been a negative value. Puerto Rican records report that betwen 1970 and 1977, about one-fourth of the Puerto Ricans living on the mainland were born on the mainland. The other three quarters of the Puerto Ricans living on the mainland were born in Puerto Rico and will later return to Puerto Rico (NCES, 1980).

The next largest group of Hispanics in the United States is the Cubans, who number 700,000, or 0.4 percent of the total population. Most Cubans came to this country after the Cuban Revolution of the late 1950s; they are drawn largely from middle- and upper-class families with a higher than average level of education. Most of the Cuban population is concentrated in Florida, with others in New Jersey and New York.

The other Hispanic Americans, from Central and South America, number 900,000 (NCES, 1980).

Most Hispanic-Americans come from Spanish-speaking countries and use Spanish as their first language. In 1978 the Department of Education estimated that there were 3.5 million children in this country who could speak little or no English, 70 percent of them Hispanic.

Hispanics are younger on the average than the majority population. The median age for Hispanics in 1978 was 22.1 years, compared with 30.6 years for the majority groups. Among the Hispanic subgroups, Puerto Ricans have the youngest median age (20.3 years); the median ages of Mexican Americans and Cubans, respectively, are 24.2 years and 31.7 years (NCES, 1980; Brown & Stent, 1977).

Achievement and Attainment. The educational enrollment data for elementary and secondary students show three troublesome trends: (1) Hispanic children enroll in school at rates lower than those for non-Hispanic students; (2) they fall behind their classmates as they progress through school; and (3) their attrition rates are higher than those of non-Hispanic students (NCES, 1980).

School enrollment data for children aged 3 to 6 indicate that 64.6 percent of the majority group children are enrolled in schools, compared to 56.7 percent of Hispanic children. In 1976 there were approximately 3 million Hispanic children enrolled in elementary and secondary schools, representing 6 percent of the total public school enrollment in the fifty states and the District of Columbia. Mexican American children comprised 63 percent of the Hispanic enrollment, Puerto Rican children accounted for 15 percent, Cuban and Central or South American children each accounted for 5 percent, and the remaining 11 percent were "other Hispanics" (NCES, 1980).

A 1978 study by the Office for Civil Rights, U.S. Department of Health, Education, and Welfare, revealed that about two-thirds of Hispanic students attended schools composed predominantly of minority students. Over 30 percent attended schools in which minority students comprised 90 to 100 percent of the total enrollment, and another 30 percent attended schools where minority enrollment was between 50 and 89 percent. Regional comparisons showed that segregation of Hispanic students was highest in the Northeast but was increasing most rapidly in the Midwest (U.S. Department of Health, Education, and Welfare, 1978; NCES, 1980).

Achievement data from representative samples of young Hispanic Americans in the fall of 1971 and spring of 1975 collected by the National Assessment of Educational Progress (NCES, n.d. [a]) revealed that Hispanic students were significantly below the national average for the three age levels measured (9, 13, and 17) with respect to each of five subject-matter areas. The five subject areas were: social studies, science, mathematics, career and occupational development, and reading. The best showing by Hispanics was by 17-year-olds in career and occupational development, where they were about 7 percentage points below the national average for their age group. The poorest showing was by 17-year-olds in mathematics, where they were 14 percentage points below the national average. Scores for Hispanics in actual terms and relative to non-Hispanics decreased in mathematics, science, and social studies with increasing age (NCES, 1980, pp. 217–225).

NCES figures for 1980 also indicated that whereas 67 percent of the adult non-Hispanic population had completed high school, only 41 percent of Hispanic adults held a high school diploma. Although there was considerable intergroup variation, every Hispanic group trailed the non-Hispanic population. Hispanics aged 14 to 19 were twice as likely not to have completed high school as non-Hispanics in the same age bracket. It is also known that 22.1 percent of Puerto Ricans and 24.2 percent of Mexican Americans graduated from high school, and the Cuban population had a high school graduation rate of 43.9 percent (Brown & Stent, 1977). Cordasco and Bucchioni (1968) reported that in 1960, 84 percent of males and 97 percent of the females born in Puerto Rico left school before graduating.

About 5 percent of the participants in vocational programs in noncollegiate schools are Hispanic, almost half of whom are Mexican Americans. Twenty-four percent of the Hispanics and 6 percent of the non-Hispanics do not have a high school diploma. Also, Hispanics are more likely than others to be enrolled in trade and industrial programs, but less likely to be enrolled in health programs. Hispanics and non-Hispanics are similar in full-time versus part-time attendance patterns, with about one-fifth in each group enrolled full-time (NCES, 1980).

Hispanics account for about one-fifth of the total participants in federally funded adult basic education. This program includes instruction for a high school equivalency examination and instruction in English as a second language. In Arizona, California, and New Mexico, Hispanics constitute more than half of the total participants. There are somewhat more women than men enrolled in these programs (NCES, 1980).

Of those Hispanics who complete high school, a slightly higher percentage, 21.2 percent, are enrolled in college as contrasted with the 19.8 percent figure for majority group high school graduates (NCES, 1980).

Between 1970 and 1978, the numbers of Hispanic full-time undergraduate students doubled, while the percentage of all undergraduates enrolled full-time increased from 2.1 to 3.5. The number of Hispanics enrolled in graduate and professional schools more than doubled, and the percentage increased from 1.2 to 2.2. This increase in Hispanic enrollments occurred during a growth period when enrollments were increasing for both minority and majority students. Even so, Hispanics still constitute a very small component of full-time enrollment in higher education (NCES, 1980). In 1974, 2.8 percent of the college enrollment was Hispanic American. In 1971, Mexican-American freshman enrollment was 1.1 percent, compared to 1.5 percent in 1972 and 1.5 percent in 1974. In 1971, 2 percent of all freshmen were Puerto Ricans; the figure was 0.6 percent in 1972 and 0.6 percent in 1974 (Brown & Stent, 1977).

In the fall of 1978, a higher percentage of Hispanics than non-Hispanics were concentrated in the freshman and sophomore years of college: 81 percent versus 72 percent. Of particular note is the high percentage, 30 percent, of Hispanic students who were classified as "other first-year" rather than as "first-time freshman." This suggests that Hispanics take more than a year to complete their first year of college, possibly because of a lower rate of full-time attendance (NCES, n.d. [b]; NCES, 1980).

Forty-two percent of Hispanic full-time undergraduates were enrolled in two-year colleges, compared with 23 percent of non-Hispanics. About one-third of both groups attended full-time. A higher percentage of Hispanic than other undergraduates were part-time students. Among juniors and seniors, Hispanics were less likely to be attending universities, as opposed to other four-year colleges (NCES, n.d. [b]; NCES, 1980).

Another pattern that distinguishes Hispanic enrollments is the institutional concentration of undergraduates. Hispanic students are concentrated in a small number of institutions. Twenty-four percent of all Hispanic students on the United States mainland are enrolled in twenty-one institutions. Of these institutions, four could be classified as "historically Hispanic," since they were established spe-

cifically to serve Hispanic students and have bilingual curricula and Hispanic leadership. The four institutions are Boricua College, Colegio Cesar Chavez, Deganawida-Quetzalcoatl (D-Q) University, and Hostos Community College of the City University of New York. These institutions were established in the 1970s, and as of fall 1978 enrolled only 2,154 Hispanic students (NCES, 1980).

Another obvious pattern of Hispanic enrollments is the geographical distribution of the schools enrolling significant percentages of Hispanics. In 1978, only New Mexico, whose population is nearly 40 percent Hispanic, had a Hispanic enrollment of more than 10 percent at all three levels: undergraduate, graduate, and first-professional (that is, law and medicine). Hispanic undergraduate enrollment in Texas was 13 percent. No other state exceeded 10 percent in any of the three enrollment levels (NCES, 1980; U.S. Department of Health, Education, and Welfare, 1979).

Figures for Puerto Rican student migration and reverse migration show that in 1975, 4,547 of the students enrolled in colleges in the United States identified themselves as residents of Puerto Rico. This number represented 4 percent of all Puerto Rican residents who were enrolled in college. Over a thousand mainland United States residents attended college in Puerto Rico in 1975.

On the United States mainland, Hispanics earned 4.1 percent of all associate degrees, primarily in the arts and sciences; 2.0 percent of all bachelor's degrees, more frequently in social sciences and "foreign" languages; 1.9 percent of all master's degrees, more likely in education and "foreign" languages and less likely in the sciences and the fields of business, administration, or management; 1.6 percent of all doctoral degrees, mostly in education and "foreign" languages; and 1.7 percent of all first-professional degrees, concentrated in law but increasing in medicine (NCES, 1980).

The National Longitudinal Study (1979) of the high school class of 1972 shows that attrition rates for Hispanics began to exceed those of non-Hispanics in the first year of college. By 1974, both higher attrition rates and lower rates of transferring from two-year colleges to four-year colleges were evident for Hispanics. Hispanics left college more often for financial reasons or because of academic failure, whereas non-Hispanics more frequently said they found school to be irrelevant. By 1976, four years after enrolling in academic college programs, Hispanics showed higher attrition rates than their majority group counterparts. The data also showed correspondingly lower Hispanic graduation rates. Fifty-seven percent of college-enrolled Hispanic men and 54 percent of Hispanic women versus 34 percent of both Anglo men and women did not earn degrees.

Bilingual Education. Recent data (1978) indicate that between 3.5 and 5 million children of school age come from homes where a language other than English is spoken. To help these bilingual children, federal funds have been made available to schools since 1968 for demonstration projects in bilingual education through the Bilingual Education Act (Title VII of ESEA, the Elementary and Secondary Education Act of 1965).

With the United States Supreme Court Decision in 1974 in the case of *Lau* v. *Nichols,* an affirmative responsibility was placed on school districts throughout the United States to provide special attention and instruction to children with few English language skills so that they would have a fair chance to benefit from their schooling (Matute-Bianchi, 1979).

In 1975, the Office of Civil Rights issued the findings of a national task force, made up predominantly of educators, regarding Hispanic-American education. In the findings, bilingual education was recommended as one of the means of achieving educational equity.

The *Serna* v. *Portales Municipal School* decision *mandated* bilingual education as a means for fulfilling the federal rights of Chicano children living in Portales, New Mexico. Consistent with the above, the Aspira Consent Decree in 1974 specified several mandates to aid in the education of Puerto Rican youth. The mandates focused on language. For example, the decree called for an improved method of accurately and systematically identifying and classifying children who are Spanish-speaking or Spanish-surnamed. It asked that programs be developed to improve a child's ability to speak, understand, read, and write English. It also provided for instruction in substantive courses in Spanish, and it called for professional staff fluent in Spanish (Milan & Muñoz-Hernandez, 1977).

Two major types of bilingual programs have been implemented: transitional programs that utilize the native language until the child can communicate in English and maintenance programs that continue instruction in both English and the native language throughout the student's school years.

In 1974 the National Institute of Education contracted with the American Institutes for Research (AIR) to conduct an evaluation of the national impact of ESEA Title VII Spanish-English bilingual programs. The report indicated (1) that both Title VII and non–Title VII Hispanic student achievement in English language arts was at approximately the 20th percentile at pretest and posttest; (2) that non–Title VII Hispanic students had a higher mean score in English language arts, but this was not reported as a significant difference; (3) that Title VII Hispanic students generally performed better than non–Title VII Hispanic students in mathematical computation; (4) that Title VII Hispanic students made gains in Spanish reading from pretest to posttest; and (5) that participation in a Title VII project did not affect attitudes toward school-related activities (Golub, 1979, pp. 359–360). These findings have been cited to justify a decreased support for bilingual education among many groups. This lack of support has likewise affected both teacher training and materials development.

Sociocultural Variables. Hispanic-American education has been concerned with other variables besides language.

Sociocultural variables have been investigated. The heterogeneity of groups has been addressed. Socialization processes at the classroom level have been observed. Desegregation has also been of conern to some researchers. Classroom practices that have been addressed are tracking and ability grouping, interaction patterns between teachers and students, and student labeling and testing.

The research findings indicate that sociocultural variables are sometimes integrated into the curriculum. For example, history may be taught more effectively, and presented more accurately, if Hispanic participation is included. Sociocultural variables are also sometimes used to justify the failure of Hispanic students in academic work. For example, attributes such as fatalism, orientation to the present, and familialism may be viewed as contributing to such failure.

Hispanic researchers have attempted to acknowledge differences between the various Hispanic groups. Their research has, however, been confined to a particular group rather than expanded to include comparative studies between the groups.

Research also indicates that Hispanic groups are not socialized in the classroom in the same manner as other students. Rather, Hispanics may be segregated, tracked, or labeled as deficient. Teachers do not interact with Hispanic students in the same way as with others. Testing procedures continue as before, and Hispanics' achievement scores have not improved.

Overcoming Discrimination. Several organizations have emerged to speak and lobby for improved conditions in the education of Hispanic Americans. One of the most recent and effective is the Hispanic Higher Education Coalition. This organization is composed of a number of Hispanic individuals and organizations concerned with higher education in the United States. The coalition is interested in increasing the impact of Hispanics on the development of higher education policy and improving opportunities for Hispanics in postsecondary education. The coalition has centered its strategies and positions on issues of access to higher education, retention in higher education, and professional development. Through active involvement, the Hispanic Coalition has been able to increase Hispanic visibility in higher education, particularly at the federal level ("Hispanic Higher Education Coalition," 1980).

As shown in census data, Hispanic Americans are increasing at a rate that is affecting American society on a broad scale. Equally important is the fact that this group is younger on the average than the majority population, and thus its members will continue to require educational services. It follows that the critical issue is to develop an instructional program particularly suited for Hispanic Americans. Bilingual education has focused attention on the group and has identified certain problem areas, but has not been totally satisfactory. Language is a serious, pervasive problem with this group, but the most fundamental problem may be that particular instructional techniques have not yet been developed. These techniques should encompass recruitment, retention, and finally graduation processes.

Labor participation and career futures cannot be meaningful for this group without a minimal educational foundation. Youth initiative programs and school-to-work transitional programs have been successful to the degree that Hispanic youth have acquired basic skills and knowledge, in order that their personal resourcefulness can aid them even under adverse conditions.

Finally, serious attention must be directed at the continuing education of Hispanic Americans. Because of ever present immigration patterns, this group will continue to have members who require fundamental educational services. It cannot be assumed that everyone will eventually be absorbed into the majority. Also, the group's heterogeneity will continue to pose educational problems. First, its mixed composition of Mexican Americans, Puerto Ricans, Cubans, and other Hispanics must be taken into account when educational programs are designed. Second, each group consists of subgroups representing different levels of Americanization and social development. For example, some Mexican Americans have been in this country since the sixteenth century, whereas others have just arrived from Mexico. As stated before, Puerto Ricans may be born in Puerto Rico, reside in the United States temporarily, and return to Puerto Rico. These differences between and within Hispanic groups must be considered in the delivery of educational services to them. The challenge remains to prepare this group's members for active participation in our society.

Flora Ida Ortiz

See also Bilingual Education; Culture and Education Policy; Multicultural and Minority Education.

REFERENCES

Bilingual Education Act, Public Law 90-247, 81 Stat., 783,816 (January 2, 1968), as amended by the Education Amendments of 1974, Public Law 93-380, 88 Stat., 484,503 (August 21, 1974), and as amended by the Elementary and Secondary Education Amendment of 1978, Public Law 95-561, 92 Stat., 2268 (November 1, 1978).

Brown, F., and Stent, M. D. *Minorities in U.S. Institutions of Higher Education.* New York: Praeger, 1977.

Cordasco, F., and Bucchioni, E. (Eds.). *Puerto Rican Children in Mainland Schools.* Metuchen, N.J.: Scarecrow Press, 1968.

Golub, L. S. The impact of descriptive and evaluative research of bilingual education programs on federal, state, and local public policy. In R. V. Padilla (Ed.), *Ethnoperspectives in Bilingual Education Research;* vol. 1, *Bilingual Education and Public Policy in the United States,* pp. 349–366. Ypsilanti: Eastern Michigan University, 1979.

The Hispanic Higher Education Coalition. *Hispanic Higher Education News,* July 1980, *6,* 6.

Matute-Bianchi, M. E. The federal mandate for bilingual education. In R. V. Padilla (Ed.), *Ethnoperspectives in Bilingual Education Research;* vol. 1, *Bilingual Education and Public Policy in the United States,* pp. 18–38. Ypsilanti: Eastern Michigan University, 1979.

Milan, W. G., and Muñoz-Hernandez, S. The New York City Aspira Consent Decree: A mechanism for social change. *Bilingual Review,* September–December 1977, pp. 169–179.

National Center for Educational Statistics. *Hispanic Student Achievement in Five Learning Areas, 1971–75* (National Assessment of Educational Progress). Washington, D.C.: U.S. Department of Health, Education, and Welfare, n.d. (a) (ERIC Document Reproduction Service No. ED 138 414)

National Center for Educational Statistics. *Opening Fall Enrollment, 1978: Special Tabulations.* Washington, D.C.: U.S. Department of Health, Education, and Welfare, n.d. (b)

National Center for Educational Statistics. *The Condition of Education for Hispanic Americans.* Washington, D.C.: U.S. Department of Education, 1980. (ERIC Document Reproduction Service No. ED 188 853)

U.S. Bureau of the Census. *Persons of Spanish Origin in the United States, March 1978.* (Current Population Reports, Series P. 20, No. 339). Washington, D.C.: U.S. Department of Commerce, 1979.

U.S. Department of Health, Education, and Welfare, Office for Civil Rights. *State and National Summaries of Data Collected by the 1976 Elementary and Secondary Schools Civil Rights Survey.* Washington, D.C.: U.S. Department of Health, Education, and Welfare, 1978.

HISTORIOGRAPHY

Three major schools of thought are currently important in the research and writing of educational history in the United States. They have been aptly described as "pietism," "culturism," and "radicalism" in an article by Butts (1974). The first of the schools, pietism, dominated the field of educational history throughout the first half of the twentieth century. The most famous and representative pietist historian was E. P. Cubberley, who published a textbook (1919) that became the standard work in the field until well into the 1950s. Cubberley's work was characterized by its concentration on schooling as the proper province of educational history, its relative neglect of the early periods of American history in favor of a lengthy treatment of the common school and public school of the nineteenth and twentieth centuries, and its highly positive attitude toward the schools and their role in the development of American democracy.

Revisionist Approaches. In the late 1950s and 1960s, a revision of the study of educational history was begun, initially by scholars in history departments who thought that educational historians such as Cubberley, based in departments and schools of education, had conceived the field inappropriately, in terms of professional, not academic concerns. These cultural revisionists sought to broaden the definition of education to include institutions other than schools, such as the family, community, and the church, and to study this broadened concept of education in the early periods of American history as well as in more recent centuries. Bailyn's essay (1960) on colonial educational history developed an alternative approach to that of Cubberley, and Cremin (1965) explicitly elaborated the criticisms of Cubberley that had been implicit in Bailyn's book.

In the 1960s, another group of scholars undertook a revision of educational history that reflected explicitly radical social and political views. Radical revisionists agreed with cultural revisionists on the conceptual limitations of Cubberley's definition of education as schooling, but the radicals argued that both Cubberley and the cultural revisionists shared an unfounded optimism about American society, politics, and schools. The most notable early radical work was Michael Katz's book (1968) on Massachusetts common school reform in the mid-nineteenth century, which argued that the common school was biased in favor of the upper classes and imposed its values upon the lower orders. Katz continued his argument in another book (1975a) on the growth of bureaucracy in urban schools. Other notable radical revisionist works were produced by Spring (1972) and by Karier, Violas, and Spring (1973).

The trenchant criticism of the schools and their leaders by the radical revisionists has not gone unquestioned by other educational historians. Butts (1974), Greene (1973), and Urban (1975) have all criticized various aspects of radical revisionist analyses. In 1975, an entire issue of the *History of Education Quarterly* was devoted to rebuttals of radical revisionist critiques of John Dewey (Bourke, 1975; Eisele, 1975; Lawson, 1975; Zerby, 1975). Later that same year, both Karier (1975) and Feinberg (1975) defended their revisionist analyses against the charges of their critics. More recently Ravitch (1977, 1978) has devoted an entire volume to a criticism of radical revisionist scholarship, and it, in turn, has provoked responses from Feinberg et al. (1980).

Those interested in a lengthier account of the recent debates among the schools of educational historians should consult the article by Cohen (1976), collected, along with a number of valuable articles, in the volume edited by Warren (1978). Complete summaries of recent work in the field have been compiled in a review article by Clifford (1976) and in a bibliography by Cremin (1977). The historiographical debates and discussion provoked by revisionist scholarship has kept the field of educational history lively and controversial for the past two decades. Work has continued in the tradition of each of the three interpretive schools—pietist, cultural, and radical—but writers and researchers in each of these traditions have been forced to pay attention to the arguments of the other groups. Tyack (1976) has recently argued that the interpretive models in educational history have developed to the point that the historian now needs to combine interpretations not by an eclectic summing up of various positions, but by an "attempt to integrate them into a more complex understanding of social reality" (p. 389).

Comparative Approaches. Tyack's call for a new level of interpretive understanding has been echoed by Herbst (1980), who urged historians of education to get "beyond the debate over revisionism" by, among other suggestions, adopting a specifically comparative approach to historical studies of education. Herbst's own mastery of American educational history and his familiarity with German language and culture as well as the history of other European cultures is a model for scholars to emulate. His account of American educational policy in occupied Germany after World War II (Herbst, 1980) is sensitive to both German and American orientations and perceptions. Kaestle (1976) has also produced a comparative analysis of elite attitudes toward mass education in England and the United States. The British scholar, Harold Silver, has undertaken several comparative studies of educational developments in Britain and the United States in the twentieth century. Currently at work on a study of poverty reform in the 1960s in both countries, Silver (1980) has published a synthesis of his earlier studies of education in the two nations. Each of these studies has focused on a comparison between education in the United States and in one or another European country, certainly only a small part of the much larger universe that should be illuminated by sound comparative historical studies. Most of the work on educational history in non-American contexts, however, has been done by scholars who specialize in study of a particular nation or culture and avoid an explicitly comparative perspective. Thus, the dearth of genuinely comparative historical studies of education is due, in no small part, to the hesitancy of educational historians, like most other modern scholars, to undertake projects that call for mastery of more than one discrete field of study.

Comparative studies within the boundaries of American educational history have been undertaken, however, and they have been helpful in deepening interpretive perspectives. Kaestle and Vinovskis (1979) studied a number of Essex County, Massachusetts, rural and urban communities in the nineteenth century; Graham (1974) looked at schooling in four diverse geographical settings in the late nineteenth century; and Olneck and Lazerson (1974) compared the achievement levels of various immigrant groups in early twentieth-century American schools. Each of these studies emphasized the complexity of relationships underlying its interpretive model.

Biographical Approaches. Urban (1981) attempted to get educational historians to leave behind the debates over radical revisionism by urging a regional emphasis in historical studies in order to carefully test generalizations reached through study of national movements. Clifford (1975, 1978) urged the value of biographical and autobiographical approaches as a corrective to the excessive social emphasis of most work in educational history, particularly radical revisionism. Her own biography of Edward L. Thorndike (Joncich, 1968) is a good example of the value of her admonition, as are the biographies of G. Stanley Hall (Ross, 1972) and Catherine Beecher (Sklar, 1973). The British psychologist L. S. Hearnshaw (1979) has produced a critical biography of Cyril Burt that illuminates current controversies in educational psychology. Skinner's recent autobiography (1976, 1979) is of great interest to both educational historians and other educational researchers.

Quantitative Methodologies. A fairly recent methodological innovation in educational history is the development of quantitative techniques. Historical "quantifiers" share a commitment to their new methodologies that seems to enable them to overcome ideological barriers to communication such as those between radicals and other educational historians. Whereas Katz (1975b), perhaps the leading quantifier, works within an explicitly radical perspective, Troen (1975) utilized quantitative techniques in support of an analysis of the St. Louis schools that was explicitly antiradical. Quantitative studies from a variety of perspectives form a significant portion of the work in history of education undertaken at the Shelby Cullom Davis Center for Historical Studies over several years. The volumes of essays from the Davis center edited by Stone (1974, 1976) contain several quantitative analyses that sensitively explore numerous aspects of the educational history of the United States as well as several European Countries.

Psychohistory and Family History. At the opposite end of the methodological continuum from quantitative history, the field of psychohistory has not had as great an impact on the work of educational historians. Cohen (1976) notes the lack of attention paid to psychoanalytic techniques and concepts as tools for educational historians as well as the almost total absence of historical studies of the relations between the psychoanalytic movement and the educational enterprise. However, allied fields such as the history of childhood and family history are examples of the few areas within educational history where psychoanalysis has penetrated. Hiner (1978) reviewed the literature in the history of childhood, pointing out the contributions of psychohistorians to this field, as well as some of the more controversial aspects of their work. Greven (1977) used psychoanalytic concepts as part of his explanation of the colonial temperament several years after he had produced a largely quantitative study of colonial families (1970). Demos (1970) combined quantitative and psychoanalytic methods in his study of families in Plymouth colony, illustrating that the quantifiers and psychohistorians share with each other a willingness to borrow theoretical explanations and methods of analysis from the social sciences. Family history and the history of childhood have been vital sources of methodological innovation in educational history and will no doubt continue to produce novel analyses and interpretations.

History of Universities. One other topic within the history of education, the history of colleges and universities, deserves mention because of its wealth of material, exemplifying some of the major conceptual and methodological issues in the field. Analyses of student backgrounds by Almendinger (1975) and Potts (1977) used quantitative and other techniques to reopen debate on the vitality or morbidity of the early nineteenth-century "old-time college." Herbst (1982) studied the constitutional history of the colonial colleges, placing their charters in a comparative context that included several European countries. Hawkins (1972) and Storr (1966) produced studies of late nineteenth-century university presidents and their institutions that viewed them within the broader context of American intellectual and social development. Billington (1973) produced a life of the historian of the American frontier, Frederick Jackson Turner, which concentrated on Turner's career as a university professor, surely an approach worthy of emulation by historians studying professors in other disciplines. McLachlan (1978) argued that work in the history of higher education has developed to the point that a revision of the conventional wisdom generated by scholars such as Hofstadter and Metzger (1955), and later refined by Rudolph (1962) and Veysey (1965), is now in order. McLachlan's challenge has not been taken up, however; and his own use of later work by such scholars as Rudolph (1977) to criticize that conventional wisdom is an indication that the old paradigm is more likely to be modified and updated than replaced by new modes of interpretation.

This brief survey has slighted the work of numerous scholars in history of education in order to highlight the major interpretive works and methodological issues that now animate the field. To say that educational history is a fertile field, lively and controversial, is in many ways an understatement. Scholars are now in the process of resolving older interpretive debates and moving on to newer approaches, methods, and issues. The prospects for continued scholarly growth and development are excellent, as reflected, for example, by the award of the Pulitzer Prize to Cremin's most recent volume (1980).

Wayne J. Urban

See also Archives and Records Management; Curriculum History; History of Education; History and Philosophy of Higher Education.

REFERENCES

Almendinger, D. F., Jr. *Paupers and Scholars: The Transformation of Student Life in Nineteenth-century New England.* New York: St. Martin's Press, 1975.

Bailyn, B. *Education in the Forming of American Society: Needs and Opportunities for Study.* Chapel Hill: University of North Carolina Press, 1960.

Billington, R. A. *Frederick Jackson Turner: Historian, Scholar, Teacher.* New York: Oxford University Press, 1973.

Bourke, P. F. Philosophy and social criticism: John Dewey, 1910–1920. *History of Education Quarterly,* 1975, *15,* 3–16.

Butts, R. F. Public education and political community. *History of Education Quarterly,* 1974, *14,* 165–183.

Clifford, G. J. Saints, sinners, and people: A position paper on the historiography of American education. *History of Education Quarterly,* 1975, *15,* 257–268.

Clifford, G. J. Education: Its history and historiography. *Review of Research in Education,* 1976, *4,* 210–267.

Clifford, G. J. Home and school in nineteenth-century America:

Some personal history reports from the United States. *History of Education Quarterly*, 1978, *18*, 3–34.

Cohen, S. The history of the history of American education, 1900–1976: The uses of the past. *Harvard Educational Review*, 1976, *46*, 298–330.

Cremin, L. A. *The Wonderful World of Ellwood Patterson Cubberley: An Essay in the Historiography of American Education*. New York: Teachers College, Bureau of Publications, 1965.

Cremin, L. A. *Traditions of American Education*. New York: Basic Books, 1977.

Cremin, L. A. *American Education: The National Experience, 1783–1876*. New York: Harper & Row, 1980.

Cubberley, E. P. *Public Education in the United States*. Boston: Houghton Mifflin, 1919.

Demos, J. *A Little Commonwealth: Family Life in Plymouth Colony*. New York: Oxford University Press, 1970.

Eisele, J. C. John Dewey and the immigrants. *History of Education Quarterly*, 1975, *15*, 67–85.

Feinberg, W. On reading Dewey. *History of Education Quarterly*, 1975, *15*, 395–415.

Feinberg, W.; Kantor, H.; Katz, M.; & Violas, P. *Revisionists Respond to Ravitch*. Washington, D.C.: National Academy of Education, 1980.

Graham, P. A. *Community and Class in American Education*. New York: Wiley, 1974.

Greene, M. Identities and contours: An approach to educational history. *Educational Researcher*, 1973, *2*, 5–17.

Greven, P. J., Jr. *Four Generations: Population, Land, and Family in Colonial Andover, Massachusetts*. Ithaca, N.Y.: Cornell University Press, 1970.

Greven, P. J., Jr. *The Protestant Temperament: Patterns of Child-rearing, Religious Experience, and the Self in Early America*. New York: Knopf, 1977.

Hawkins, H. *Between Harvard and America: The Educational Leadership of Charles W. Eliot*. New York: Oxford University Press, 1972.

Hearnshaw, L. S. *Cyril Burt: Psychologist*. Ithaca, N.Y.: Cornell University Press, 1979.

Herbst, J. Beyond the debate over revisionism: Three educational pasts writ large. *History of Education Quarterly*, 1980, *20*, 131–145.

Herbst, J. *From Crisis to Crisis: American College Government, 1636–1819*. Cambridge, Mass.: Harvard University Press, 1982.

Hiner, N. R. The child in American historiography: Accomplishments and prospects. *Psychohistory Review*, 1978, *7*, 13–23.

Hofstadter, R., & Metzger, W. P. *The Development of Academic Freedom in the United States*. New York: Columbia University Press, 1955.

Joncich, G. *The Sane Positivist: A Biography of Edward L. Thorndike*. Middletown, Conn.: Wesleyan University Press, 1968.

Kaestle, C. F. "Between the Scylla of brutal ignorance and the Charybdis of a literary education": Elite attitudes toward mass schooling in early industrial England and America. In L. Stone (Ed.), *Schooling and Society: Studies in the History of Education*. Baltimore: Johns Hopkins University Press, 1976.

Kaestle, C. F., & Vinovskis, M. A. *Education and Social Change in Nineteenth-century Massachusetts*. New York: Cambridge University Press, 1979.

Karier, C. J. John Dewey and the new liberalism: Some reflections and responses. *History of Education Quarterly*, 1975, *15*, 417–443.

Karier, C. J.; Violas, P. C.; & Spring, J. H. *Roots of Crisis: American Education in the Twentieth Century*. Chicago: Rand McNally, 1973.

Katz, M. B. *The Irony of Early School Reform: Educational Innovation in Mid-nineteenth-century Massachusetts*. Cambridge, Mass.: Harvard University Press, 1968.

Katz, M. B. *Class, Bureaucracy, and Schools: The Illusion of Educational Change in America*. New York: Praeger, 1975. (a)

Katz, M. B. *The People of Hamilton, Canada West: Family and Class in a Mid-nineteenth-century City*. Cambridge, Mass.: Harvard University Press, 1975. (b)

Lawson, A. John Dewey and the hope for reform. *History of Education Quarterly*, 1975, *15*, 31–66.

McLachlan, J. The American college in the nineteenth century: Toward a reappraisal. *Teachers College Record*, 1978, *80*, 287–306.

Olneck, M. R., & Lazerson, M. The school achievement of immigrant children: 1900–1930. *History of Education Quarterly*, 1974, *14*, 454–482.

Potts, D. College enthusiasm as public response, 1800–1860. *Harvard Educational Review*, 1977, *47*, 28–42.

Ravitch, D. The revisionists revised: Studies in the historiography of American education. *Proceedings of the National Academy of Education*, 1977, *4*, 1–84.

Ravitch, D. *The Revisionists Revised: A Critique of the Radical Attack on the Schools*. New York: Basic Books, 1978.

Ross, D. *G. Stanley Hall: The Psychologist as Prophet*. Chicago: University of Chicago Press, 1972.

Rudolph, F. *The American College and University: A History*. New York: Knopf, 1962.

Rudolph, F. *Curriculum: A History of the American Undergraduate Course of Study since 1636*. San Francisco: Jossey-Bass, 1977.

Silver, H. *Education and the Social Condition*. London: Methuen, 1980.

Skinner, B. F. *Particulars of My Life*. New York: Knopf, 1976.

Skinner, B. F. *The Shaping of a Behaviorist: Part Two of an Autobiography*. New York: Knopf, 1979.

Sklar, K. K. *Catherine Beecher: A Study in American Domesticity*. New Haven, Conn.: Yale University Press, 1973.

Spring, J. H. *Education and the Rise of the Corporate State*. Boston: Beacon, 1972.

Stone, L. (Ed.). *The University in Society* (2 vols.). Princeton, N.J.: Princeton University Press, 1974.

Stone, L. (Ed.). *Schooling and Society*. Baltimore: Johns Hopkins University Press, 1976.

Storr, R. J. *Harper's University: The Beginnings*. Chicago: University of Chicago Press, 1966.

Troen, S. K. *The Public and the Schools: Shaping the St. Louis System, 1838–1920*. Columbia, Mo.: University of Missouri Press, 1975.

Tyack, D. B. Ways of seeing: An essay on the history of compulsory schooling. *Harvard Educational Review*, 1976, *46*, 355–389.

Urban, W. J. Some historiographical problems in revisionist educational history: Review of *Roots of Crisis*. *American Educational Research Journal*, 1975, *12*, 337–350.

Urban, W. J. History of education: A southern exposure. *History of Education Quarterly*, 1981, *21*.

Veysey, L. R. *The Emergence of the American University*. Chicago: University of Chicago Press, 1965.

Warren, D. R. (Ed.). *History, Education, and Public Policy*. Berkeley, Calif.: McCutchan, 1978.

Zerby, C. L. John Dewey and the Polish question: A response to the revisionist historians. *History of Education Quarterly,* 1975, *15,* 17–30.

HISTORY AND PHILOSOPHY OF HIGHER EDUCATION

Advanced study as conducted today within the formal structure of colleges, universities, and similar institutions can trace its origins and traditions in unbroken line to the medieval universities founded during the twelfth and thirteenth centuries. In several European cities—notably Bologna, Paris, Salerno, Salamanca, and Oxford—learned masters and their students gathered in communities similar in some respects to the merchants' and artisans' guilds of the Middle Ages. Like the guild apprentices, students strove to perfect their knowledge and skills in order to qualify for licensure to practice their craft, teaching. Vestiges of guild ceremonies can still be discerned in the marshall's baton, the vestments and hoods, and the degrees awarded in the modern university convocation.

Pre-Christian Origins.   In its broader aspect, however, higher education flourished in many parts of the ancient world long before the beginning of the Christian era. Undoubtedly, advanced study was carried on at some of the early centers of religious worship and learning. In the temples of ancient Egypt, training in sacerdotal functions was supplemented by instruction in record keeping and administrative skills essential to the vast enterprises favored by the rulers. Indeed, the tradition of the priest-scholar continues to this day in areas the world over. In India, important centers of learning grew up at Taxila and Nalanda (Nolanda). With their keen interest in legal and moral issues, the Hebrews also maintained places of worship and study; Jerusalem had a long history as a center of religious thought and speculation. With the emergence of Confucianism in China after the third century B.C., the scholar became the key man in the nation's civil service. In this tradition, which survived until the twentieth century, scholars who successfully completed certain rigorous examinations became privileged administrators and advisors to those in power.

As early as the sixth century B.C., the Greeks, to whose intellectual ideals the Western world has long paid homage, passed laws requiring the education of certain members of the citizen class. Institutions such as Plato's Academy, Aristotle's Lyceum, Zeno's Stoa, and Isocrates' School of Rhetoric drew the thinkers and scholars of the civilized world. Certain cities gained lasting reputations as centers of learning: Athens; Alexandria, with its great library and diadem of resident scholars; Rhodes; and in time, Rome and Constantinople. To them flocked logicians, dialecticians, rhetoricians, lawyers, physicians, and other men of learning to study with the masters.

The fall of Rome and the onset of the Dark Ages sent the Western world into a profound intellectual and cultural decline. Learning was kept alive by a few literate men toiling in isolated monasteries and in palace schools, such as that maintained for Charlemagne by the English monk, Alcuin. In the Islamic world, on the other hand, the lamp of learning burned brightly after the seventh century in cities such as Baghdad, Mecca, Damascus, and Cairo, and in Cordova, Seville, Toledo, and Granada, the strongholds of Moorish Spain. Here Western scholars were later to rediscover the knowledge of the ancient classical world: chemistry, mathematics, pharmacy, medicine, navigation; here, too, they would encounter the writings of the Muslim philosopher-physicians Avicenna and Averroës, both of them serious students of the works of Aristotle.

For centuries a close relationship existed between the functions of the scholar, priest, civil servant, and administrator, on the one hand, and those of the physician and lawyer, on the other. The man of learning was expected to possess many skills, including those of the healer and the advocate; full-time pursuit of scholarship purely for its own sake was probably rare.

Education in the western hemisphere at roughly this same period is less well documented, but it seems indisputable that centers of learning existed in the empires of the Incas, the Mayas, and the Aztecs. Few of their books or manuscripts survived the depredations of the European conquerors, but there is evidence that learned men, usually members of the priestly class, made significant discoveries, particularly in mathematics and astronomy.

European Universities.   By the fifteenth century, more than fifty European universities were in operation, among them, Uppsala, Copenhagen, Aberdeen, Louvain, Tübingen, Freiburg, St. Andrew's, Leipzig, and Basel. The first medieval institutions had few of the trappings of the modern university; for example, there were no admission requirements, and no degrees were awarded. Many of these institutions came into being as an indirect result of attempts to educate men for the church. Bishops, who were responsible for the education of priests within their bishoprics, established schools in the cathedrals; in time, some of the clerics who taught in these institutions extended instruction to persons with a taste for scholarly inquiry but with no immediate vocation for the priesthood.

One of the most renowned of these teachers was the philosopher-monk Abelard, who often flirted with heresy in his brilliant analyses of theological and philosophical questions. Using the techniques of the logician and disputant, Abelard won fame as a formidable debater; students in such great numbers flocked to Paris to hear him that in time the more advanced scholars had to be pressed into service to teach the newcomers. Eventually, teaching licenses were required of those undertaking to instruct the growing student body, and examinations, usually oral, were devised to assess the competence of applicants seeking licensure.

In Paris and elsewhere, universities gradually took shape as students and their masters organized themselves into loose confederations resembling the guilds and incorporating some of the guild usages. The students who gathered to debate, attend lectures, and study were known by a variety of names, including *studium generale*. In time, the term *universitas*—the group or the whole—was applied to these bodies of masters and scholars who banded together in the pursuit of knowledge.

Tacit approval of these groups by the church of Rome was essential to their survival. Fortunately, many popes not only tolerated but actively encouraged these centers of learning by means of land grants, preferments, and favorable rulings on a variety of disputes that flared between the university and the local church and citizenry. When these "town and gown" squabbles could not be settled by papal ruling, it was not uncommon for masters and students to leave in a great "dispersal" and establish the university elsewhere. The entire institution at Paris decamped on several occasions and remained away for some time. In these intervals new universities were spawned in nearby towns, which showed little reluctance to inherit the wealth and prestige as well as the inevitable problems that accompanied these institutions.

Students, some only 14 or 15 years old, prepared for their university studies by learning Latin, usually with the help of a local clergyman or tutor. Not until the fifteenth century were students in any great number prepared for university work by attendance at a Latin grammar school; not until the time of the Renaissance were students admitted with a required knowledge of Greek. For centuries the university remained a preponderantly masculine institution. From the fourteenth century onward, young women could be counted among the ranks of the well educated, but for the most part they were educated by tutors in the home and not exposed to the hazards of university life.

University attendance demanded substantial resources, and the sons of the poorer classes were at great disadvantage. The problem was approached in a disconcertingly pragmatic manner in Germany, where students were permitted to obtain licenses to beg from the townspeople. Fortunately, a few scholarships existed for impoverished but promising young men, most of whom were expected to repay this generosity by electing a life within the church upon completion of their studies.

As a measure of economy, students often banded together to share living expenses in residence halls and rented rooms; some of these communal living quarters later achieved official status as colleges within the university. Despite the rigors of the scholar's life, students were frequently a high-spirited, riotous lot. Games similar to rugby and soccer were popular, and there is ample evidence that some devoted an unseemly amount of time to less wholesome forms of amusement. Except for certain capital offenses, students were subject to punishment only at the hands of university officials, a circumstance that often exacerbated the already tense relationship that existed between town and gown. At a later period, some universities maintained a student prison—a *carcer*—in which to punish the unruly and the lawbreakers. Students confined there often carved or burned their names on wall or ceiling in proud acknowledgment of their transgressions.

On the other hand, many students were devoted scholars, and large numbers were headed for careers in the church. Study, discussions, prayer, recitation, disputation, lectures, and religious observances occupied much of their time. The disputation, or formal argument, was a particularly challenging and popular activity that contributed directly to the student's education by allowing him to practice his skills in logic and rhetoric and to demonstrate his knowledge of theology and the liberal arts. Sometimes a student defended a thesis against a single adversary; on other occasions, he took on several opponents before an interested audience.

The medieval curriculum. Within the university, the old classical world, the world of reason and debate—at least those parts of it that were known and not under interdict—existed in uneasy harmony with the new world of Christian faith, thanks, in part, to the writings and teachings of Thomas Aquinas and other theologian-philosophers. Consequently, university students and faculty were absorbed by the study of theology and the branches of philosophy appropriate to the analysis of religious questions. Theology and its handmaiden, philosophy (as it was regarded by many in medieval times), were the staples of the university curriculum until the Renaissance brought a resurgence of interest in classical languages and literature, especially Greek. Before the Renaissance, however, the medieval student espoused the curricular ideal of the seven liberal arts as set forth in the writings of Martianus Capella, Boethius, and others. These scholars maintained that certain studies—among them grammar, rhetoric, logic, music, arithmetic, astronomy, and geometry—were appropriate for the educated man. How many of the seven liberal arts each student was taught depended on the knowledge as well as the inclination of the teaching masters, but it is clear that ways were found to inject a religious element into all seven. Theology was sometimes referred to as the greatest of the liberal arts because it alone could liberate the human soul from its troubles.

His course work with the arts faculty completed in four years or so, the student might study for an additional period before taking an examination to acquire a license to teach. Or he might continue in one of the three professional schools of law, medicine, or theology. Canon law and a civil law based on summaries of the Code of Justinian were the staples of a legal education. The writings of Galen, Hippocrates, and other physicians and herbalists provided a medical background, but anatomical dissection was strictly prohibited in most places until the seventeenth century. Students who chose theology faced a long and tedious course of study that included canon law, church doctrine, and endless disputes on religious questions.

Most medieval universities were loosely organized, the pattern of governance taking different forms. A student's place of origin determined the particular unit or "nation" to which he belonged. At the University of Paris the arts masters were usually in control, whereas at Bologna, long famous for its law school, the older law students handled many of the administrative details, from renting rooms to paying the masters. At some universities, notably in Italy, the Low Countries, and in Scotland at a later date, trustees held the charter for the institution and were responsible for its affairs. Whether under the direct control of the masters, students, or a body of trustees, however, the universities were usually subject to the authority of Rome. Consequently, care had to be taken not to offend that awesome power.

When the Reformation and Counterreformation swept Europe, these same institutions were often whipsawed between the authority of Rome and that of local officials—either the Protestant clergy and city fathers or a prince or king bent on controlling the institution to further his own interests. The history of Oxford, for example, is riddled with intense religious disputes in which dons and masters disagreed on the proper object of the university's loyalties (Rowse, 1975).

Financial support for the universities came from many sources. Fees, of course, played a large part, as did monies and land from popes, princes, and other benefactors. The University of Edinburgh received the proceeds from the municipal rental of mourning clothing. It was common for university students and faculty to be exempted from paying certain taxes and fees.

The university's major purpose was to strengthen a student's character, especially in its Christian aspects, and to equip his mind to the fullest with the knowledge of Western culture. When universities permitted and even encouraged the disputation, however, students were exposed to a wide range of ethical, moral, social, and even political issues, and were given an opportunity, albeit a limited one, to question certain portions of revealed truth and authority. Although the church fathers and Aristotle remained unassailable in matters of religion and philosophy, the door had been opened a crack, permitting a glimpse of a broader world beyond. Serious students strained to secure that glimpse.

The Renaissance. As the fifteenth century advanced, the spread of classical humanism and other Renaissance ideals created a great hunger for knowledge of the languages, literature, and cultures of classical Greece and Rome. The works of ancient authors hitherto unknown to the Western world were dusted off and studied in the original or translated for wider dissemination. The search for classical antiquity even led to the ransacking of monasteries for old manuscripts that had been copied and exchanged among Christian monks for centuries. In this manner, the writing of the Roman orator and educator, Quintilian, came to light again in a Swiss monastery. Eventually, popes, princes, clergymen, wealthy citizens, and scholars were to join in the search for the knowledge of ancient Greece and Rome, a quest that led them to the writings of Islamic and Judaic scholars. The voyages of discovery by explorers in the fifteenth and sixteenth centuries brought a flow of riches and knowledge to European cities. Inevitably, man's intellectual focus began to shift away from the icy mansions of the next life to the world of contemporary human beings with their needs, strivings, and achievements. The scholars of the Renaissance and their allies found the ancient worlds that were the objects of their search, and in the process, transformed their own culture.

Universities played a vital part in the intellectual ferment of the day. Scholars learned new languages, analyzed better examples of the old Latin now available, and translated both pagan and Christian literature into European tongues. They were not alone in their intellectual activities, however; the educated classes, poets, artists, clergymen, and wealthy patrons of the arts, such as the Medici family in Florence, were all in the vanguard of the quest for a superior culture. Their goal was a better life through an appreciation of the past, a celebration of the best of the present, and, transcending all, a due regard for the will of the Almighty.

The Protestant Reformation gave further impetus to the study of Hebrew, Greek, and Latin, the languages in which Holy Writ was recorded. With the Bible available in translation, the common folk at last had access to it; first, however, more elementary schools were needed to meet the increased demand for literacy. Once the authority of the Roman church was cast off, responsibility for worshiping the Almighty and seeking his will shifted to the individual. The emphasis now was neither on the Greek ideal of individualism nor even on the desire to promote human excellence that characterized the Renaissance, but rather on the duty of every man to strive for salvation. Even if the universe were preordained, as some believed, it was still incumbent on the saved and the damned alike to determine the will of God in all the affairs of men.

The inevitable reaction to the Reformation—the Counterreformation, led by Ignatius Loyola's Society of Jesus—resulted in the establishment of some of Europe's finest schools. Ironically, many of the church's most effective critics in later times would be educated in these excellent Jesuit institutions.

Personal piety was of paramount importance to men of the Reformation, as well as to many scholars in the time of the Renaissance, among them that prototypical thinker, Erasmus. However, it was the fusion of classical ideals with the principles of Christian faith that brought to education, which was recognized as vital to an understanding of both, a sophistication it had not known since Greek times. When the philosophers and scientists of the Enlightenment appeared on the scene with their world-altering ideas, they encountered an educational philosophy that embodied this sophistication and an awareness of the human condition. Indeed, some would argue that the Enlightenment thinkers were the products of that educational philosophy.

During the wars of the Reformation, the universities were often caught in the middle and obliged to espouse one cause or another. Wracked by these religious disputes, in which faculty and students frequently played leading roles, the universities declined in prestige and influence. In earlier times, faculty members, especially those in the arts, theology, and law, had been called upon to help settle religious and legal disputes; now, forced into the role of partisans of a particular cause, they were subject to all the acrimonious charges and repressive measures that stalk the political combatant. It is ironic that the activists of the 1960s who demanded the "politicization" of the universities hoped by this means to solve many of society's ills, apparently unaware of the disastrous effects on the institution when it has become embroiled in current social controversies.

The year 1543 was marked by several significant events in the intellectual world: Copernicus published his revolutionary and controversial explanation of the workings of the solar system; and Vesalius brought out his superb book on human anatomy, for which contribution he was seized by the Inquisition and forced to make a pilgrimage to Jerusalem or face death for the crime of dissecting a human cadaver. In the same year, the mathematics of the great Greek mathematician Archimedes was rediscovered. Yet, nearly a century later, the astronomer and scientist Galileo would be forced to recant his statement in support of the Copernican hypothesis because his views and those of Copernicus conflicted with the natural philosophy expounded by the pagan Aristotle whose writings had long been accepted by the church as authority in such matters.

The Enlightenment and the nineteenth century. It was not until the onset of the scientific revolution of the seventeenth century, touched off by the work of such men as Bacon, Newton, Kepler, and Pascal and by the social and political writings of Locke, Rousseau, Voltaire, Diderot and others that the age of the Enlightenment dawned. Now at last mathematics, empirical science, reason, and experience were permitted to transform human knowledge of the world and of the nature of human society. Although many who contributed to these remarkable advances were based within the university, the institution itself was not always hospitable to the new ideas or to those who espoused them. Societies, such as the Royal Society of England, the French Academy of Science, and the Berlin Academy were more likely to welcome ideas and their advocates. Moreover, the universities too often preferred to cling to the classical languages and literatures that had been so liberating in centuries past and to the religious disputes that consumed so much time and energy. It was not until the founding of the University of Berlin in 1809 that the ideals of the modern university began to take shape.

In the nineteenth century, the universities of Berlin, Bonn, Munich, and Breslau joined the excellent institutions founded in the eighteenth century at Halle and Göttingen to make Germany an educational mecca for scholars the world over. Here students flocked in search of the new university ideal glorifying research and advanced scholarship with its emphasis on the elements of experiment, seminar, graduate study, and the faculty mentor. Here they encountered such seminal concepts as *Lernfreiheit*, the idea that the student should have freedom to choose his course of study; and *Lehrfreiheit*, the notion that the professor should be free to teach and study what he prefers. German thinkers also championed the separation of university and state on the grounds that the true interests of the state are most effectively served by a university operating under maximum freedom.

University founders followed students to nineteenth-century Germany to see the new university ideal in practice. From the United States came Daniel C. Gilman and Andrew D. White, who were soon to head, respectively, the Johns Hopkins University in Baltimore and Cornell University in New York. The former is regarded by many as the first true American university; the latter served as a model for many of the state universities and land grant colleges that arose in this country in the last half of the nineteenth century.

American Universities. At the time of the American Revolution there were nine colleges in the colonies, all but one of them founded by religious groups, predominantly Calvinist in persuasion. The exception was the College of Philadelphia (later the University of Pennsylvania) established by Benjamin Franklin and a group of businessmen, several of them Quakers. These institutions were heavily influenced in their curricular choices by medieval, Renaissance, and Reformation notions. Considered appropriate areas of study were classical languages and literatures, rhetoric, geometry, astronomy, mathematics, and natural and moral philosophy.

Admission to a college required that a student master enough Latin to be able to read a little Tully (Cicero), know some mathematics, and bring evidence of a "blameless life," usually attested to by a letter from a clergyman. Religion permeated every aspect of college life. It was common, for example, for the president of the college to teach moral philosophy to the senior class as the capstone of their educational experience. Moreover, the moral philosophy thus inculcated was not bland or neutral in tone; on the contrary, it was Protestant, and even more significant, it reflected the particular brand of Protestant zeal that flared in the hearts of the college's founders. Not surprisingly, about half the graduates of Harvard College in the seventeenth century entered the ministry; a much smaller number became public officials, physicians, teachers, merchants, planters, soldiers, and the like.

The recitation remained one of the favorite modes of instruction, but lectures, declamation, and disputation were also employed. Concerned as they were for the spiritual welfare of the students, all of these early colleges put heavy emphasis on matters affecting their moral well-being. Endless rules dealt with every aspect of student behavior, from the wearing of hats to regular church attendance and the mode of address toward seniors. Faculty members were likely to be young men waiting for a desirable pulpit to beckon; most often, they were recent graduates of the college.

The eighteenth century. In the eighteenth century, students organized literary and debating societies that met to consider religious and secular questions, both old and new. Some of these groups came to possess libraries more extensive than that of the college itself; some acquired other property holdings as well. Loyalty to the societies at times exceeded that accorded to the institutions, especially those with roots so firmly planted in the past that they were unwilling to address any contemporary questions.

The colleges were small; Harvard, for example, did not have a graduating class numbering one hundred until just before the Civil War (Rudolph, 1962). Most were on the brink of financial disaster and dependent on the good will of the founding denomination for funds as well as for students. In time, most of these colleges were governed by boards of trustees dominated by members from the founding church.

The master's degree was awarded in the eighteenth century, and a few candidates wrote master's theses to obtain it. For other recipients, conferral of the degree was contingent on paying a fee and staying out of jail for a specified length of time. As a rule, medicine and law were learned through apprenticeship although Philadelphia had a small medical school just before the Revolution. A few students such as the noted physician Benjamin Rush had gone to Europe to study; a few solitary professors of law and medicine were to be found in some of the colleges. Some of the professionals—the physicians, lawyers, and engineers—were immigrants from Europe. Although advanced study beyond that for the bachelor's degree was obtainable in Europe, a number of Americans, including George Washington, discouraged it, fearing that prolonged study abroad might imbue their young countrymen with noxious foreign ways.

After the Revolution when charters became easy to obtain, American higher education expanded dramatically. The number of colleges increased more than twentyfold between the Revolution and the Civil War. In addition to the many older religious groups interested in founding colleges, new ones such as the Catholics and Swedenborgians also took a hand. Furthermore, as a result of the Northwest Land Ordinances of 1785–1787, each new state entering the Union was required to set aside land for a university as well as for lower schools. In time, many states created state universities with the proceeds of these lands. After passage of the Morrill Act in 1862, which reserved for each state thirty thousand acres of public land per

U.S. representative and senator, many additional institutions were created.

As more states passed compulsory education laws after 1855, renewed interest arose in efforts to create educational opportunity for the young. Many more teachers were required, and several states met the challenge by creating teachers' colleges, which in time became four-year enterprises granting the bachelor's degree. Today, many of these institutions are state universities. Oberlin, a college originally restricted to the education of men, admitted women in 1836. Later a number of institutions devoted solely to educating young women were founded, among them, Emma Willard's Troy Female Seminary, Vassar, Mount Holyoke, Smith, Wellesley, Radcliffe, and Rockford College.

The nineteenth century. The Industrial Revolution of the 1830s created a need for engineers and technicians of several kinds. Rensselaer Polytechnic Institute had been founded in 1824 to meet this need, and West Point graduates were another source of civil-engineering knowledge and skill. However, the demand for engineers was so great that by the middle of the century, schools of engineering were being established at the universities. Among the most successful units of the land grant colleges, they turned out the educated professionals needed to build the railroads, factories, bridges, canals, and roads essential to a rapidly industrializing nation. A stimulated interest in science accompanied the proliferation of schools of engineering. The Smithsonian Institution, headed by its first secretary, Joseph Henry, opened its doors in 1846, and was soon followed by the Lawrence Scientific School at Harvard and the Sheffield Scientific School at Yale.

For most of the nineteenth century, the purpose of a college education was perceived as the shaping of the student's character and his initiation into the great classical tradition and intellectual achievements of the Western world. What was demanded of the college, the authors of the Yale Report of 1828 insisted, was that it "lay the foundation of a superior education." This was to be done through the "*discipline* and *furniture* of the mind; expanding its powers, and storing it with knowledge" (Quoted in Hofstadter & Smith, 1961, I, p. 278). It was important to exercise all the mental faculties and to provide the mind with a balanced curriculum of mathematics, the physical sciences, ancient literature, readings in English, logic and mental philosophy, written composition, discussion, oratory, and the like. With the mind properly exercised on the best knowledge and filled with the proper "furniture," the educated human would be able to meet and solve new problems of any kind. As for the practical subjects so dear to the heart of Benjamin Franklin and others, what could be more practical, it was argued, than proper exercising of the mind? A new skill—bookkeeping, for example—could be learned quickly on the job. The purpose of college was not to teach what could be more quickly learned in the marketplace; rather it was a place in which to train the mind. Unusually influential, the Yale Report has been called the most "important educational document written in America before the Civil War" (Hofstadter & Smith, 1961, p. viii).

About the time that Yale's president and faculty were expounding the principles that would shape the curriculum and aims of the institution at New Haven, the Supreme Court of the United States and its chief justice, John Marshall, issued a ruling in the Dartmouth College case. To the delight of Daniel Webster and his clients, the trustees of the college, the court upheld the right of private colleges, once in possession of a charter, to conduct business with a minimum of state interference. This celebrated case, which gave wide protection to incorporated businesses as well as to colleges, assured the place of private colleges in the American higher educational scheme, and, in the process, extended that shield to public institutions as well. As a result, private and public colleges exist side by side to this day in the United States, the one stimulating the other and both enjoying substantial freedom to conduct collegiate and university activities in a manner deemed suitable by those in charge. To be sure, state and federal authorities with the power over the purse and the right of legal enactment can exercise numbing control over public institutions; nevertheless, the existence of a lively private sector has placed some restraints on governmental interference in public university affairs and has provided an example for public officials to emulate whenever possible. Today, despite vast differences in tuition that place the private institutions at a severe disadvantage, they remain a vital part of American higher education, confounding those who have predicted their demise for the past one hundred years and more. Indeed, private institutions enrolled more than 50 percent of all college and university students in the country until the 1950s, when the public sector received massive infusions of public monies, both state and federal. Despite intense pressure emanating from the public sphere, private institutions are still among the most distinguished in the land. Increasingly, however, costs of attending a private institution threaten to prevent all but the wealthy or the most determined from matriculating.

If the Yale Report set the tone for collegiate institutions in the United States in the first half of the nineteenth century, it was the new Industrial Revolution with its technology, inventions, and emerging professions, as well as the social and intellectual forces it set in motion, that came to influence the second half. Radical change was forced on some of the institutions. At Harvard College in 1869, the new president, Charles Eliot, introduced the elective approach to curriculum by first abolishing all subject requirements for seniors in 1872; by 1894, even a freshman at Harvard was required to take only rhetoric and a single modern language (Rudolph, 1962). Other colleges followed suit, although only a few chose to go as far as Harvard in making almost the entire curriculum elective. James McCosh of Princeton was adamant in his opposition to the elective approach, insisting that free election of

courses was a bid for popularity, not a call to intellectual freedom. The purpose of college, he insisted, remained what it had always been—the training of the mind. Even Eliot's faculty at Harvard seems to have begun to harbor reservations about the elective approach after the turn of the century, and after his retirement in 1909, turned away from free election to a slight degree by requiring a certain number of courses in a major field.

Election was advanced as a means by which a student would prepare for maturity by choosing his own course of study; in so doing, it was argued, he would take a deeper interest in what he studied and would make decisions of a sort that promote mature judgment. Another excellent argument for the elective approach, although one seldom made by its advocates, was that professors had long since become restive at teaching boys the classical languages and literature. Professors who held a Ph.D. from Berlin or some other European university were especially disgruntled at having to teach undergraduates the classical curriculum when they longed to work with advanced students eager to grapple with physics, chemistry, or modern history. The elective approach gave such persons the opportunity to teach some of their specialties, and to do so at the graduate level.

McCosh may have been partially correct when he insisted that the elective approach was a bid for popularity. The Morrill Act of 1862, designating to each state thirty thousand acres per U.S. senator or representative, was certainly motivated by a desire to make colleges accessible to students who had never before had access to such institutions. The proceeds of these public lands were to be used "to promote the liberal and practical education of the industrial classes in the several pursuits and professions of life." Within eight years of passage of the act, thirty-seven states had authorized some form of educational enterprise affording instruction in the prescribed areas. The seventy-one land grant institutions in existence today constitute an integral part of the American higher education enterprise and provide education for the "industrial classes" as well as for the children of the affluent. For many years these institutions struggled to overcome criticism that not enough was being done to benefit the farmer. In response, the various defenders of the land grant college asserted that the colleges were not intended merely to turn out more efficient farmers but to give children of the working classes a chance to obtain a college education, and in some cases to prepare for a profession as well (Anderson, 1976).

A dedication to public service characterized the new institutions. At the University of Wisconsin under Charles Van Hise, for example, officials declared that the entire state constituted its campus, and proceeded to demonstrate their commitment to the public interest by research activities designed to benefit all the citizenry. One noteworthy contribution was the Babcock butterfat test so vital to the success of the state's dairy industry.

In this same period, a number of institutions were

founded with the aim of helping former slaves to become free men in fact as well as in law. Howard University in Washington, D.C., was created by the federal government in an effort to provide educational opportunity for freedmen; Fisk, Atlanta, Tuskegee, and Hampton Institute began with a similar purpose. A number of southern states founded not one but two land grant institutions in order to ensure separation of the races in higher education. Although such enterprises have been declared unconstitutional, full integration in higher education of the races has not yet been achieved.

American educational leaders of the latter half of the nineteenth century held that human understanding would be advanced through research and that superior teaching would be found in institutions that encourage scholarship and research activities of the highest order. Among those who had an opportunity to put their theories into practice were Daniel C. Gilman at the Johns Hopkins University, which opened in 1876; William Rainey Harper at the University of Chicago, founded in 1892, with financial support from John D. Rockefeller; Andrew D. White at Cornell University; and G. Stanley Hall at Clark University. Johns Hopkins and Chicago were the prototypes of the phenomenally successful institution that encompassed both the basic education of undergraduates and the advanced training of graduate and professional students, at the same time placing a premium on research and scholarship (Veysey, 1965).

The older institutions—Yale, Harvard, Columbia—responded to the challenge of these serious new rivals by organizing graduate faculties and encouraging advanced study and research. In the meantime, the ranks of state universities and land grant colleges continued to grow. Today, the fifty major institutions, private and public, comprising the American Association of Universities sponsor much of the research and grant most of the Ph.D. degrees awarded in the United States.

With the rise of the new universities came the establishment of many new professional societies, hundreds of which are now in existence. The American Association for the Advancement of Science (1848) and the American Philosophical Society (1743) were joined by the American Historical Association (1884), the American Mathematical Society (1888), and the American Psychological Association (1892). The American Association of University Professors, founded in 1915, enrolled all professors without regard to specialty and made vigilance on behalf of academic freedom one of its major causes. Late in the century, accrediting agencies, such as the New England Association, the Middle Atlantic States Association, the North Central Association, and the Southern Association were formed to raise standards, smooth the process of transfer between institutions, and recognize degrees.

The activities of the universities expanded rapidly to embrace many new specialities and professions. The three original professional schools—law, medicine, and theology—and engineering, a nineteenth-century addition,

were now augmented by schools of agriculture, home economics, dentistry, pharmacy, education, business, library science, and others. With the proliferation of areas of specialization, it is not uncommon for a modern university to include one hundred or more departments, institutes, and other subdivisions.

The twentieth century. The emphasis on free election in the late nineteenth century was succeeded in the twentieth century by demands for curricular cohesiveness as a means of averting chaos. At Harvard, students were required to declare a major, that is, to specialize in the offerings of a single department; later, a minor in a second area was added. In time, demands for broad comprehensive programs led to the development of year-long survey courses. The next few decades saw notable experiments in higher education at Amherst and in the Experimental College of the University of Wisconsin under Alexander Meiklejohn, at St. John's College, and at the University of Chicago, where general education emerged in its most highly developed form. Shaped by the educational philosophy of Robert M. Hutchins, the "Chicago Plan" prescribed the highly integrated undergraduate course of study, with the bachelor's degree attained in three years and specialization reserved for graduate school. The general education approach was based on the premise that advanced scholarship appropriate to the university should not deflect the undergraduate from the pursuit of the essential body of knowledge possessed by truly educated persons. As practiced at Chicago, Columbia, St. John's, and elsewhere from the 1930s to the 1950s, general education was the most sophisticated and thoughtful philosophy of education to emerge since the Renaissance humanists first infused Western culture with the ideals of classical Greece and Rome.

To keep Harvard College from being submerged in the great Harvard University, the faculty in 1945 published *General Education in a Free Society,* a plan for a program of studies with courses in the humanities and in the social and natural sciences. Less well developed than the Chicago or Columbia programs, the Harvard plan nevertheless enhanced the prestige of general education and encouraged many institutions to introduce some broad unifying elements into a curriculum that had grown increasingly diverse and more political than pedagogical in its structure.

General education is not without its critics, however; some view it as running counter to society's need for specialists, technicians, and professionals. Since it makes tremendous demands on the professor, others see it as impractical on pedagogical grounds in this era of large enrollments and widely varying student abilities. Unfortunately, misconceptions of what general education implies have prompted some institutions to tinker with the curriculum in a manner that appalled the movement's proponents. Since the decline of the general education movement in the 1950s, the collegiate curriculum has seen a proliferation of academic offerings at both the undergraduate and graduate levels, sometimes in response to societal demands and sometimes as a means of utilizing the talents of teaching assistants and junior faculty.

The prodigious growth of elementary education in the United States stimulated by the passage of compulsory attendance laws from 1855 to 1900 and the boom in secondary schools from 1900 to 1940 have been echoed in the decades since 1945, by the dramatic increase of higher education in this country and, indeed, the world over. Public Law 346—the "GI Bill"—enabled millions of American veterans to attend college after World War II. Successive wars have prompted legislation, similar to although perhaps less wisely drawn than the original bill. One effect of these laws was to increase educational opportunity for men at the expense of women. However, unprecedented female enrollments in recent years have restored the balance that had almost been achieved in the 1920s.

Early in the twentieth century, educational opportunity in the United States underwent a phenomenal expansion with the introduction of the junior or community college. Most of the institutions founded in this country in the past twenty-five years have been community colleges; only the present budget crises and the dwindling numbers of college-age students seem to have slowed their growth. Indeed, many states have succeeded in locating a community college within easy commuting distance of almost every student. California has long been a leader in the movement, and the idea has spread to many foreign countries, notably Japan. Offering the first two years of college and a variety of other programs, the community colleges may be specialized—technical, vocational, college-preparatory, for women only—or all-inclusive, and offer adult or evening programs as well. Tuition and fees are generally low, and every effort is made to meet the needs of the community.

The decades of the 1960s and 1970s were marked not only by expansion, but also by upheaval and unrest in the higher education establishment. On campus, officials were ill prepared to cope with burgeoning enrollments and the increasingly diverse student population that resulted. Relaxed social and sexual mores soon forced schools to abandon the last vestiges of their role *in loco parentis*. Major social changes only added to the tensions: the civil rights struggles of racial minorities, the first stirrings of the women's movement, increased demands for social welfare, and the growing disillusionment with American foreign policy in the Vietnamese conflict. By the end of the 1960s, universities and colleges in the United States and in Europe, Japan, and elsewhere were shaken to their foundations by students demanding politicization of the institutions as a means of attaining political and social reform.

The assaults against the university in the 1950s by reactionaries outside the academic setting had led to repressive measures against some faculty members, speakers, and groups suspected of Communist ties. In the 1960s and 1970s, on the other hand, the attacks came from within

as students, sometimes assisted by their mentors, engaged in antiauthoritarian behavior ranging from peaceful sit-ins to violent confrontations often requiring police intervention. This ugly train of events was climaxed after the invasion of Cambodia in 1971 by the tragedy at Kent State University, where four students fell before the rifles of national guardsmen called in to quell disorder.

With the end of the Vietnam War in 1973, campus tensions gradually relaxed, and students turned away from activism to resume serious academic pursuits. Recent years have seen continued expansion of schools of business, law, medicine, and engineering to meet increased demands for professional education. Racial minorities and women have enrolled in greater numbers than ever before as grants, loans, and scholarships have become more widely available, and social programs, such as affirmative action, have begun to make an impact. Special funding from private and governmental sources has been administered by the universities to further the education of the needy and the newly arrived immigrant.

Research, a primary goal of the university since the late nineteenth century, was given further impetus after World War II by funding and encouragement from business, industry, and state and federal governments. Today, only a few institutions annually receive more than $100 million in federal research monies; however, smaller amounts go to hundreds of other institutions, leading some observers to question whether the colleges and universities can long continue to retain their autonomy. There is no question, however, that this massive commitment has helped make the United States a world leader in research; over thirty-three thousand Ph.D.'s are awarded in this country each year, and American professors receive a significant proportion of the Nobel Prize awards. Foreign students gravitate to U.S. institutions as American students did to German universities in the nineteenth century.

In many parts of the world today, the university functions unabashedly as the handmaiden of the state. In the People's Republic of China, the universities are instruments of the state charged with turning out skilled professionals and technicians imbued with the proper state-approved ideals. In African countries, one of higher education's main responsibilities has been to prepare citizens for tasks associated with the advance from tribal and colonial societies to the world of modern technology. Soviet universities educate a much higher proportion of Russian citizens than ever before in the advanced technical and professional skills essential to any industrial society. Many institutions in the Middle East have cooperative working arrangements with American and European institutions to develop the educational and technical capacities of the suddenly oil-rich states.

Demands of increased educational opportunity have resulted in riots and sit-ins in France, Germany, and Italy in recent years. Higher education in Great Britain, long dominated by Oxford and Cambridge, has undergone unprecedented expansion in recent decades. Many new regional universities have sprung up, among them the so-called red-brick institutions, making educational opportunities more widely available. The University Grants Committee was set up after World War II in an effort to provide British higher education with funds from the central government while allowing it to remain free of paralyzing governmental control.

Serious problems now face higher educational enterprises the world over, and the expectations held for them by individuals and governments alike are at once a challenge and a threat. Although it may be settled fact in many countries that the university's prime object must be the betterment of the state, the means to this end are far from clear. Other societies take the view that the long-term and short-term interests of the state may not be identical and that since the university is primarily concerned with long-term goals, it can be of greatest service if permitted to foster free thought and inquiry rather than to inculcate the propaganda often favored by the state.

The age-old questions remain. Who can profit most from a higher education? What knowledge is of most worth? How can knowledge best be transmitted from one generation to the next? Where should the resources come from? What is the proper relationship between the colleges and the society of which they are a part? And, finally, who is to answer these questions?

David Madsen

See also Higher Education; History of Education; Philosophy of Education.

REFERENCES

Anderson, G. L. (Ed.). *Land Grant Universities and Their Continuing Challenge.* East Lansing: Michigan State University Press, 1976.

General Education in a Free Society: Report of the Harvard Committee. Cambridge, Mass.: Harvard University Press, 1945.

Hofstadter, R., & Smith, W. *American Higher Education: A Documentary History* (2 vols.). Chicago: University of Chicago Press, 1961.

Rowse, A. L. *Oxford in the History of England.* New York: Putnam, 1975.

Rudolph, F. *The American College and University: A History.* New York: Knopf, 1962.

Veysey, L. R. *The Emergence of the American University.* Chicago: University of Chicago Press, 1965.

HISTORY AS SUBJECT MATTER

The decade of the 1970s witnessed public and professional outcries about the endangered status of history in the schools. In 1976, the *New York Times* conducted a second national evaluation of knowledge of American history (the first was conducted in 1943) and concluded that Americans were uninformed about their past (*"Times* Test of College Freshmen," 1976). That survey, however, was only a reflection of an outpouring of public comment about the status of history (Kownslar, 1976). The public comment was paralleled by professional comment about history instruction. As early as 1967, Edgar Wesley called for the abolition of history courses. At the same time, Mortimer Smith (1966) claimed that the social studies were destroying history courses. By the early 1970s, these conflicting concerns were surfacing in the American Historical Association (Gorman, 1971), in social studies education periodicals (Ridgley, 1973), and in the professional education literature (Ward, 1971). Dire predictions were made that required courses in history at the college level would not exist by 1980 (Rojas, 1972). The debate over history continued for the remainder of the decade, as writer after writer predicted the demise of history as a separate subject (Hammet et al., 1977; Stearns, 1977; Weinland & Roberts, 1978; Fox-Genovese, 1979; Schumann, 1980).

The peak of professional concern, however, was expressed in a report by Richard Kirkendall (1975) of the Organization of American Historians (OAH). Kirkendall declared that history was in a grave state of crisis, precipitated by doubts about its usefulness for both individuals and society. An OAH survey found that a substantial number of respondents reported marked decreases in college history-course enrollments. Kirkendall (1976) suggested that the perception of lack of utility contributed to the decline of history in the curriculum. Lack of utility was echoed by Kownslar (1976), who claimed that history, as currently taught, was often not relevant to student needs. He also suggested that it was poorly taught, a contention that many have acknowledged, but few have actually investigated. McGee (1978), on the other hand, saw the current relaxation of academic requirements, emphasis on fads, and lack of structure and continuity as major culprits in the decline of history. The pressures of the job market were also noted as contributing to the decline (Fox-Genovese, 1979).

The New History.   The decline in history has not been linked, however, to a recognized change in history itself. In 1913, James Harvey Robinson and Charles A. Beard called for an end to what H. G. Wells called "the chronicle of wars and kings" (Pessen, 1977). That traditional approach has been challenged in the past decade and a half by British and American scholars, inspired by the Annales school in France. The new history being written is far more comprehensive, subjecting all human behavior and all segments of society to study and using contributions from sociology, anthropology, and economics (Greene, 1975). Pratt (1974) suggested that history should seek a new rationale. Hays (1974), in a plea for the new history, commented that history courses in college should emphasize people and their settings. Bullock (1978) described the impact of the new history and argued for a combination of old and new approaches.

Shenton and Jakoubek (1980), on the other hand, saw

the new approaches to history as American in origin. The historical descriptions of the United States prior to *Sputnik* and the tumultuous 1960s were exemplified by the consensus historians (Hofstadter, Boorstin, and Schlesinger), who viewed the American experience as devoid of fundamental conflict. *Sputnik* caused an erosion of confidence, which the civil rights movement reinforced. Accompanying the movement was black consciousness and an effort to discover its past, which in turn forced other Americans to look to their past. Women and minority groups began looking back, using new methodologies particularly suited for the nonvisible elements of our society. The result, according to Shenton and Jakoubek (1980), was a refocus of American history as a new social history.

Enrollments in History Courses. The actual research on the status of history is more limited than the rhetoric about its impending demise. Between 1971 and 1974, attendance at college-level history classes fell by 76,000 students (*American History Association Newsletter*, 1974). In grades nine through twelve during the period 1961–1973, student enrollment in world history reflected a 5 percent increase, in U.S. history, a 42 percent increase, while enrollments in economics, sociology, and psychology registered gains of 102, 175, and 321 percent respectively. The total percentage of students enrolled in U.S. history courses in grades nine through twelve lost only three percentage points during that twelve-year period, while enrollment in world history dropped from 18 to 12 percent (Carroll et al., 1979). The National Assessment of Educational Progress, in a comparison of the 1971/1972 and 1975/1976 school years, determined that the knowledge level of 17-year-olds had declined three percentage points, while the level of 13-year-olds had showed only slight decline and the level of 9-year-olds registered no statistical change (National Assessment of Educational Progress, 1978). The *New York Times* test showed little difference between 1976 scores and 1943 scores, although both were acknowledged to be low (Fiske, 1976).

History and the Social Studies Curriculum. At the elementary level, history is difficult to separate from social studies, which appears to be in danger of being crowded out of the curriculum. Social studies commands less instructional time than reading, mathematics, or language arts command, the same or slightly more than science and physical education, and more than the fine arts (Weiss, 1978; Joyce & Tucker, 1980). Hass (1979) found that social studies instruction in elementary schools has declined in a few districts to one or two hours a week, a view supported by Shaver, Davis, and Helburn (1979). More information may be forthcoming. A commission recently established by the Council for Basic Education is examining the current status of history in the nation's elementary schools (Marty, 1980).

Despite this trend, history continues to occupy a significant and traditional place in the social studies curriculum. Shaver et al. (1978) found most social studies curricula dominated by history and government. Project Span rein-

forced this view, noting a pattern of curriculum offerings in history virtually unchanged in the past sixty years (Morrissett, Hawke, and Superka, 1980).

The view of history as mortally wounded is also confounded somewhat by recent activity. The growing popularity of History Day suggests that history may be witnessing a revival. The American Historical Association (AHA) and Indiana University, in 1969, began a history-education project to improve the teaching of history. The AHA also created, in 1974, a teaching division to promote teaching as a central concern of the AHA. The rapid growth of the Society for History Education and its journal, *The History Teacher*, attest to the strong forces at work counteracting the decline of history.

Valuations of History. Teachers' perceptions of history as subject matter have only been tentatively investigated. One survey showed that 700 Missouri teachers ranked U.S. history second and world history fourth in a list of most important subjects in the social studies (Krakow, 1974). The investigator suggested that researchers should examine why history, especially non-Western history, is considered less important than other social sciences. Pulliam (1972) reported that teachers found world history to be suffering from a host of maladies: problems of definition, external organization, objectives, content, methodology, materials, and teacher preparation. A study of the teaching of history in Iowa examined both teacher and superintendent attitudes towards U.S. and world history, finding that these two groups agreed on the importance of U.S. history, but disagreed on the value of world history. Only 54 percent of the superintendents believed that students should take such a course, compared with 74 percent of the teachers (Carroll et al., 1979). Nevertheless, teachers continue to be at the heart of the teaching process in selection of text, content, methodology, and goals (Shaver et al., 1979).

Public attitudes toward history, meanwhile, remain curiously ambivalent. The Gallup poll reported in 1978 that social studies was less useful than English, mathematics, and other courses, yet the next year rated American history among the top four "essential subjects" (Gallup, 1979). Student attitudes appear largely negative, if history is subsumed under social studies, with reports of irrelevance and lack of usefulness predominating (Morrissett et al., 1980).

Critiques of Textbooks. History textbooks in the 1970s came under increasing attack from minority groups questioning portrayals of themselves, from conservative groups questioning values, and from reading specialists concerned about readability.

Depictions of women and ethnic groups. The role of women in U.S. history texts was questioned by several researchers (Trecker, 1971; Hahn, 1978), who suggested that women, when included, were often presented stereotypically. Later studies echoed these findings, arguing that texts portrayed "standard" women, while omitting others who fought for controversial issues (Julian, 1979), or arguing that the new, more equal treatment of women included white women, but limited inclusion of native, Mexican-American, or black women (Garcia & Woodrick, 1979). Hunkins et al. (1977), who reviewed the portrayal of women in the first half of the decade in both social studies and history texts, reported a growing body of literature focusing on bias against women.

Many of the studies of black representation in textbooks reflected the changes that the civil rights movement of the 1960s had produced in textbooks (Joyce, 1973). A study of recent textbooks and those published prior to 1960 (Turetsky, 1974) identified a consistent trend towards increased attention to black Americans, but noted a lack of depiction of blacks in white-collar positions. Perez (1979) exemplified the emerging focus on the treatment of the role of the Mexican American in textbooks. McDiarmid and Pratt (1971) conducted a massive study of prejudice, exploring bias against Jews, Moslems, blacks, American Indians, and immigrants. Gribskov (1973) was one of several researchers who examined textbook accounts of Indians. Hata and Hata (1974) represented growing concern with other minorities. Hunkins et al. (1977) provide an excellent review of textbook studies focused on ethnicity.

Treatments of political and cultural issues. Other studies of textbooks were concerned with the manner in which issues were presented, or systematically ignored. Herz (1978), examining how the cold war was depicted, concluded that none of the texts studied gave an overly favorable view of American foreign policy. Peiser (1973) tried to determine how populism was presented and found that texts typically reflected a traditional view, excluding revisionist or counter-revisionist positions and indeed failing to note that different interpretations exist. Friendlander (1973) criticized textbooks for their treatment of the holocaust. Another study determined that seven basal texts differ significantly in their treatment of two typical topics (the Civil War and the Great Depression) in American history (Smith, 1980). Anyon (1979) found that U.S. history texts reflect an ideology that serves the interests of particular groups to the exclusion of others. Silverstein (1970) described the inclusion of violence in recent texts, noting that certain forms of violence, such as American against non-American, seemed more likely to be described in a favorable light. Fitzgerald (1979), in a widely acclaimed interpretation, claimed that texts until recently depicted all Americans as Protestants. Even recent changes, which incorporated minorities, failed to eliminate a host of lunacies, including exaggeration and espousal of government orthodoxy.

The present and future of textbook critiques. Grambs (1980), in an extensive review that followed earlier work, commented that in 1968 she could find only 164 published studies of textbooks. A virtual explosion of interests has occurred since. She noted, however, a continuing lack of research on how teachers are depicted and few studies on the changing role of men and few trend studies. Even the readability of history textbooks came under scrutiny

during this decade. One study concluded that readability varied substantially both within and across texts and that passages were rarely placed in a systematic progression from easy to difficult (Bradley, Ames, & Mitchell, 1980). Hunkins et al. (1977) called sexual bias the most crucial topic for study in the years ahead. As other social movements gain importance, they too will call for increased attention to given portrayals. The shift in political values to the right may also galvanize textbook critics, who have recently been active in textbook-adoption proceedings around the country.

Despite all of these findings, little attention has been directed to determine the effect, if any, of bias and distortion in textual material used by students. The politics of adoption may serve as yet another research focus, as the adoption process becomes increasingly politicized. Whatever the future for research, the future for textbooks appears certain. According to Jantzen (1979), the textbooks of the 1980s will be thick, hard-covered, easy to read, and loaded with largely traditional content and some skills exercises. Variety of both form and content will likely decrease in the years ahead (Schneider & Van Sickle, 1979).

Methods. Many studies report that the dominant styles of instruction continue to be lecture and discussion-recitation (Morrissett et al., 1980). Nevertheless, some professional educators have advocated the use of new approaches and techniques in history instruction (Hollister, 1976). The Wingspread Conference called for an end to rote memorization, urging that history instruction be tied to the community (Scott, 1969). Encouraged by the television success of programs like "Roots," writers have urged the use of methods like oral history to help students create a personal past (Mehaffy, Sitton & Davis, 1979). Family history has become part of the history curriculum of more than 150 colleges in the United States (Fiske, 1977). Public history, a relatively new phenomenon of historical research in the community for public, not academic, benefit has been suggested as a viable approach for public school history instruction (Sitton, 1980). A growing body of literature attests to the possibilities of these new methods, although little research has accompanied these writings. Two researchers did find gains in factual knowledge with the use of dramatic play among elementary school children (McKinney & Golden, 1973). Another researcher compared the new concept of mastery learning with the more traditional lecture-discussion approach, concluding that the mastery approach was far more successful (Crotty, 1975). A third researcher investigated one historical antecedent to modern teaching techniques, the source-study method in Nebraska in the early part of the twentieth century (Smolens, 1970).

The author of a leading social studies methods text, noting at least six possible approaches to the teaching of history, suggested "postholing," a curriculum design which focuses on a few significant periods and studies them in great depth, as the recommended approach in the elementary grades, with special attention to social history. In junior high, the curriculum would shift to a study of the twenty or thirty significant decisions in American history, such as "Shall we add the Louisiana Territory?" Only in high school would the curriculum revert to the traditional narrative approach (Kenworthy, 1973). Recent evidence suggests that Kenworthy's approach is used at the high school level where history courses appear to be traditional, chronological, and political (Carroll et al., 1979). History teaching at the junior high and elementary level is also perhaps traditional in approach, although less evidence is available.

How and when textbooks are used has also become a subject for investigation. Weiss (1978) reported that most teachers rely on only one textbook. Kimball (1969) found textbooks to be the center of the course. One study suggested that teachers use commercially prepared materials 90 out of 100 instructional minutes ("Report on a National Study," 1976). Project Span, confirming earlier reports, found that 50 percent of teachers use one text and that 90 percent of homework comes from the text. Project Span called for increased attention to how textbooks are actually used in the classroom (Morrissett et al., 1980).

The rise and fall of the new social studies. One mode of instruction, inquiry, emerged from the proliferation of new social studies projects of the 1960s. The high point of the period for social studies was 1967, with more projects, more writing, and more discussion than before or since (Hass, 1979). The Amherst Project, the only project to focus directly on history, became the focus of study of one investigator (Samec, 1976). Some of the energy of the new social studies was directed towards the teaching of history. Several studies attempted to demonstrate that inquiry techniques could be taught to teachers (Zevin, 1973). Simultaneously, however, the danger signals were being sounded about acceptance of the new social studies. Guenther and Dumas (1973) found only a minority of classes using new social studies materials in Kansas and Missouri. Tucker (1972) found methods teachers equated new social studies with the new curriculum projects and complained that the new approach was overly academic. As early as 1974, Kownslar was calling for a synthesis of the old and new social studies approaches. Shaver, Davis, and Helburn (1979) noted clear evidence that the curriculum projects growing out of the new social studies had left few remnants, if indeed they had even penetrated the majority of public school classrooms. Inquiry, in particular, witnessed a spectacular failure, prompted by teacher concerns about potential loss of classroom control. Even some of the few schools that had adopted new social studies materials were in the process of abandoning them (Marker, 1980).

Adoption and rejection of new materials. Another area of research that touched history instruction was the study of adoption and rejection of new materials. The new social studies projects spawned a decade of research on the nature of the adoption process of new curriculum materials. Hahn (1974) found little correlation between per-

ceptions, attitudes, and subsequent adoption of new material. She did find that potential adoptors tended to come from urban and suburban communities, a distinction that supported later analyses of the professionalization of rural and urban teachers (Carroll et al., 1979). In another study, Hahn (1977) urged further research to determine what particular attributes were most important at different stages in the adoption process. That study found positive correlation between potential observers' attitudes and observable benefits, with relatively little positive correlation between potential adoptors' attitudes and actual adoption. Both Hahn studies and a later replication (Kissock & Falk, 1978) called for research attention to other attributes of innovations and other variables to help understand the process of adoption. In an extension of these studies, Marker (1980) studied the process of abandoning new materials. He found that loss of an innovation's major advocate, unrealistic expectations, and misapplication were major factors in the abandonment decision. All of these findings seem applicable to new materials in history.

Directions for research. Gross (1972) complained that doctoral research in the social studies continued to be fragmented, with studies often not being reported in the literature and demonstrating little agreement on conclusions. Those complaints can certainly be extended to the subject of history, yet some preliminary work has been done. The study by Carroll (et al., 1979) should be highlighted, for its thoroughness and emphasis on needed areas of research. The impact, for example, of the teacher-coach on history instruction requires attention, as does the difference between large and small school districts. The massive National Science Foundation survey (Shaver et al., 1979) of the status of the social studies should also be noted, as well as the follow-up study, Project Span (Morrissett et al., 1980). These investigations have stimulated much needed discussion and hopefully will stimulate more research. Despite the many calls for new teaching techniques, little research has been directed towards ideal modes of instruction for the teaching of history. Textbook studies need to examine new dimensions of presentation, but more importantly must begin to focus on the impact of bias on student learning. Student attitudes toward history should be more clearly elaborated. More information on enrollments and curriculum patterns also appears necessary. Perhaps the most fundamental need, however, is to move inside classrooms, recasting teachers and researchers in new and different roles. Shaver, Davis, and Helburn (1979) urged that new research paradigms, employing ethnographic techniques, might form a productive pattern for future efforts. Perhaps the model for research in the decade to come will combine a variety of research techniques, as recently exemplified by Carew and Lightfoot (1979). More thorough research, combining both objective and subjective measures, will be necessary to describe more fully the status of history and to recreate more fully the complexities of the modern classroom.

George L. Mehaffy

See also Citizenship Education; Social Studies Education.

REFERENCE LIST

American Historical Association Newsletter, September 1974, *6*, 1.

Anyon, J. Ideology and United States textbooks. *Harvard Educational Review*, August 1979, *49*, 361–386.

Bradley, J. M.; Ames, W. S.; & Mitchell, J. N. Intrabook readability: Variations within history textbooks. *Social Education*, October 1980, *44*, 524–528.

Bullock, A. Is history becoming a social science? The case of contemporary history. *History Teacher*, August 1978, *11*, 549–561.

Carew, J. V., & Lightfoot, S. L. *Beyond Bias: Perspectives on Classrooms*. Cambridge, Mass.: Harvard University Press, 1979.

Carroll, W. E.; Jones, A.; Gelfand, L.; Heywood, W. C.; Fitch, R.; Kinter, P.; & Hawley, E. *The Teaching of History in the Public High Schools of Iowa*. Grinnell, Iowa: Grinnell College, 1979. (Available from first author, Cornell College, Mt. Vernon, Iowa 52314)

Crotty, E. K. An experimental comparison of a mastery learning and lecture discussion approach to the teaching of world history (Doctoral dissertation, State University of New York, Albany, 1975). *Dissertation Abstracts International*, 1975, *36*, 7150A–7151A. (University Microfilms No. 76-10,610)

Fiske, E. B. High schools cut priority for teaching U.S. history. *New York Times*, May 3, 1976, pp. 1, 43.

Fox-Genovese, E. The crisis of our culture and the teaching of history. *History Teacher*, November 1979, *13*, 89–101.

Friendlander, H. *On the Holocaust: A Critique of the Treatment of the Holocaust in History Textbooks Accompanied by an Annotated Bibliography*. New York: B'nai B'rith Anti-defamation League, 1973. (ERIC Document Reproduction Service No. ED 157 857)

Gallup, G. H. The tenth annual Gallup poll of the public's attitudes toward the public schools. *Phi Delta Kappan*, September 1978, *60*, 33–45.

Gallup, G. H. The eleventh annual Gallup poll of the public's attitude toward the public schools. *Phi Delta Kappan*, September 1979, 33–46.

Garcia, J., & Woodrick, C. S. The treatment of white and non-white women in U.S. textbooks. *Clearinghouse*, September 1979, *53*, 17–22.

Gorman, M. A. Letter to the editor. *American Historical Association Newsletter*, May 1971, *9*, 13–15.

Grambs, J. D. The study of textbooks and schoolbooks: A selective bibliography. In W. E. Patton (Ed.), *Improving the Use of Social Studies Textbooks* (Bulletin 63). Washington, D.C.: National Council for the Social Studies, 1980.

Greene, J. P. The "new history": From top to bottom. *New York Times*, January 8, 1975, p. 37.

Gribskov, M. E. A critical analysis of textbook accounts of the role of Indians in American history. (Doctoral dissertation, University of Oregon, 1973). *Dissertation Abstracts International*, 1973, *34*, 3301A. (University Microfilms No. 73-28,597)

Gross, R. E. A decade of doctoral research in social studies education. *Social Education*, May 1972, *36*, 555–560.

Guenther, J., & Dumas, W. Teacher familiarity with and use of Project Social Studies materials in the Midwest. *Educational Leadership*, April 1973, *30*, 641–643.

Hahn, C. L. *Perceptions of New Social Studies Projects and Their Adoption in Four States*. Paper presented at the annual meeting of the National Council for the Social Studies, Chicago, 1974. (ERIC Document Reproduction Service No. ED 098 141)

Hahn, C. L. Attributes and adoption of new social studies materials. *Theory and Research in Social Education*, April 1977, *5*, 19–40.

Hahn, C. L. Review of research on sex roles: Implications for social studies research. *Theory and Research in Social Education*, March 1978, *6*, 73–99.

Hammett, H. B.; Sidman, C. F.; Longin, T.; & French, H. P., Jr. Can the teaching of history survive 1984? *History Teacher*, February 1977, *10*, 229–248.

Hass, J. D. *The Era of the New Social Studies*. Boulder, Colo.: Social Science Education Consortium, 1967.

Hass, J. D. Social studies: Where have we been? Where are we going? *Social Studies*, July/August 1979, *70*, 147–154.

Hata, D., Jr., & Hata, N. I. *I Wonder Where the Yellow Went? Distortions and Omissions of Asian Americans in California Education*. Paper presented at the annual meeting of the American Educational Research Association, Chicago, 1974. (ERIC Document Reproduction Service No. ED 093 747)

Hays, S. P. History and the changing university curriculum. *History Teacher*, November 1974, *8*, 64–72.

Herz, M. F. *How the Cold War Is Taught: Six American History Textbooks Examined*. Washington, D.C.: Georgetown University, 1978. (ERIC Document Reproduction Service No. ED 161 816)

Hollister, C. W. Pulling history out of the doldrums. In *Report on Teaching: 1*. New Rochelle, N.Y.: Educational Change, Inc., 1976. (ERIC Document Reproduction Service No. ED 122 703) (Also published as *Change*, March 1976, *8*, 24–25.)

Hunkins, F. P.; Ehman, L. H.; Hahn, C. L.; Martorella, P. H.; & Tucker, J. L. *Review of Research in Social Studies Education: 1970–1975* (Bulletin 49). Washington, D.C.: The National Council for the Social Studies, 1977.

Jantzen, S. L. What textbooks will be like in 1985. *Media and Methods*, January 1979, pp. 70–72.

Joyce, W. W. Minorities in primary grade social studies textbooks: A progress report. *Social Education*, March 1973, *37*, 218–233.

Joyce, W. W., & Tucker, J. L. Toward a constructive plan of action in elementary social studies teacher education. *Social Education*, October 1980, *44*, 508–512.

Julian, N. B. *Treatment of Women in United States Textbooks*. Las Cruces: New Mexico State University, 1979. (ERIC Document Reproduction Service No. ED 178 371)

Kenworthy, L. S. *Social Studies for the Seventies*. Lexington, Mass.: Xerox College Publications, 1973.

Kimball, E. G. *A Survey of the Teaching of History and Social Studies in Secondary Schools*. Princeton, N.J.: Educational Testing Service, 1969. (ERIC Document Reproduction Service No. ED 075 277)

Kirkendall, R. S. The status of history in the schools. *Journal of American History*, September 1975, *62*, 557–570.

Kirkendall, R. S. What has happened to the teaching of history in the United States? *Social Education*, October 1976, *40*, 446–451.

Kissock, C., & Falk, D. R. A reconsideration of "Attributes and Adoption of New Social Studies Materials." *Theory and Research in Social Education*, September 1978, *6*, 56–70.

Kownslar, A. O. (Ed.). *Teaching American History: The Quest for Relevancy—Forty-fourth Yearbook of the National Council for the Social Studies*. Washington, D.C.: National Council for the Social Studies, 1974.

Kownslar, A. O. The status of history: Some views and suggestions. *Social Education,* October 1976, *40,* 447–449.

Krakow, J. L. *Which History Is Most Important? Views from Secondary History Teachers.* Unpublished manuscript, 1974. (ERIC Document Reproduction Service No. ED 159 128)

Marker, G. W. Why schools abandon "new social studies" materials. *Theory and Research in Social Education,* Winter 1980, *7,* 35–57.

Marty, M. A. Doing something about the teaching of history: Agenda for the eighties. *Social Education,* October 1980, *44,* 470–473.

McDiarmid, G., & Pratt, D. *Teaching Prejudice: A Content Analysis of Social Studies Textbooks Authorized for Use in Ontario.* Toronto: Ontario Institute for Studies in Education, 1971.

McGee, R. T. *Conference on the Teaching of History.* Denton: North Texas State University, 1978. (ERIC Document Reproduction Service No. ED 162 950)

McKinney, J. D., & Golden, L. Social studies dramatic play with elementary school children. *Journal of Educational Research,* December 1973, *67,* 172–176.

Mehaffy, G. L.; Sitton, T.; & Davis, O. L., Jr. *Oral History in the Classroom: How To Do It Series.* Washington, D.C.: National Council for the Social Studies, 1979.

Morrissett, I.; Hawke, S.; & Superka, D. P. Six problems for social studies in the 1980s. *Social Education,* November/December 1980, *44,* 561–569.

National Assessment of Educational Progress. *Changes in Social Studies Performance, 1972–1976.* Denver, Colo.: Education Commission of the States, 1978. (ERIC Document Reproduction Service No. ED 161 791)

Peiser, A. C. Populism in high school textbooks. *Social Education,* April 1973, *37,* 302–309, 316.

Perez, R. J. A quantitative analysis of the treatment of the Mexican American in state-adopted Texas history textbooks (Doctoral dissertation, University of Michigan, 1979). *Dissertation Abstracts International,* 1979, *40,* 730A. (University Microfilms No. 7916792)

Pessen, E. A discipline illuminating the lives of the dead. *New York Times,* April 17, 1977, p. 11.

Pratt, D. The functions of teaching history. *History Teacher,* May 1974, *7,* 410–425.

Pulliam, W. E. *The Status of World History Instruction in American Public Schools.* Boulder, Colo.: Clearinghouse for Social Studies/Social Science Education, 1972. (ERIC Document Reproduction Service No. ED 072 984)

Report on a National Study of the Nature and the Quality of Instructional Material Most Used by Teachers and Learners. (Educational Products Information Exchange Report No. 71). New York: EPIE Institute, 1976.

Ridgley, R. Will the history survey be salvaged? *Social Studies,* December 1973, *64,* 313–315.

Rojas, B. The end of history. *Social Studies,* March 1972, *63,* 118–124.

Samec, C. E. A history of the Amherst Project: Revising the teaching of American history (Doctoral dissertation, Loyola University of Chicago, 1976). *Dissertation Abstracts International,* 1976, *37,* 2699A. (University Microfilms No. 76-24,457)

Schneider, D. O., & Van Sickle, R. L. Status of the social studies: The publishers' perspective. *Social Education,* October 1979, *43,* 461–465.

Schumann, P. F. History and geography should be scrapped. *Educational Leadership,* 1980, *37,* 342, 364.

Scott, J. A. *New Dimensions for History Teaching in the Schools.*

Bloomington: Indiana University, 1969. (ERIC Document Reproduction Service No. ED 048 070)

Shaver, J. P.; Davis, O. L., Jr.; & Helburn, S. W. The status of social studies education: Impressions from three NSF studies. *Social Education,* February 1979, *43,* 150–153.

Shenton, J. P., & Jakoubek, R. E. Rethinking the teaching of American history. *Social Education,* October 1980, *44,* 461–469.

Silverstein, L. A critical analysis of the treatments given violence in leading eleventh-grade American history textbooks (Doctoral dissertation, Northwestern University, 1970). *Dissertation Abstracts International,* 1970, *31,* 3312A. (University Microfilms No. 71-1970)

Sitton, T. Public schools and public history. *Educational Forum,* March 1980, *44,* 277–283.

Smith, A. Are they all alike? History textbooks for poor readers. *Social Studies,* September/October 1980, *71,* 199–204.

Smith, M. (Ed.). *A Decade of Comment on Education.* Washington, D.C.: Council for Basic Education, 1966.

Smolens, R. The source-study method of teaching history in Nebraska (1891–1920) (Doctoral dissertation, Columbia University, 1970). *Dissertation Abstracts International,* 1970, *32,* 3741A. (University Microfilms No. 72-4188)

Stearns, P. N. Clio contra Cassandra. *History Teacher,* November 1977, *11,* 7–28.

Times test of college freshmen. *New York Times,* May 2, 1976, pp. 1, 65–66.

Trecker, J. L. Women in U.S. history high school textbooks. *Social Education,* March 1971, *35,* 249–260.

Tucker, J. L. Teacher educators and the "new" social studies. *Social Education,* May 1972, *36,* 549–555.

Turetsky, F. The treatment of black Americans in primary grade textbooks used in New York City elementary schools. *Theory and Research in Social Education,* December 1974, *11,* 25–49.

Ward, P. L. Why history? *High School Journal,* October 1971, *55,* 1–10.

Weinland, T. P., & Roberts, A. D. Clio at the crossroads. *Social Studies,* January/February 1978, *69,* 32–35.

Weiss, I. R. *Report of the 1977 National Survey of Science, Mathematics, and Social Studies Education: Final Report.* Durham, N.C.: Research Triangle Institute, 1978. (ERIC Document Reproduction Service No. ED 152 565)

Wesley, E. B. Let's abolish history courses. *Phi Delta Kappan,* September 1967, *44,* 3–8.

Zevin, J. Training teachers in inquiry. *Social Education,* April 1973, *37,* 310–316.

HISTORY OF EDUCATION

Changes in the history-of-education field during the twentieth century have occurred along two planes. Its scope has broadened beyond a focus on schools to include "the deliberate, systematic, and sustained effort," in Cremin's now familiar phrase, "to transmit or evoke knowledge, attitudes, values, skills, and sensibilities" (1970, p. xiii). In addition, unique and often critical perspectives on education goals, organizations, and outcomes as they affect women (Burstyn, 1974; Sklar, 1973), racial and ethnic minorities (Mohraz, 1979; Wollenberg, 1978), and working-class people (Gitelman, 1974; Grubb & Lazerson, 1975; Reese, 1981) have added to the field's depth and complexity. Its scope thus includes the institutions, processes, and influences—public and private, formal and informal—in and through which individuals and groups become educated. Cremin (1977) argued that defining educational effort as sustained intentionality saves the historian of education from biting off "more than anybody could chew" (Storr, 1976, p. 333). Agreement among his colleagues, however, is not universal (Eisele, 1980). The point is not merely that a fixed definition of education arbitrarily restricts the historian's interest and curiosity about possibly relevant phenomena, as Eisele suggested, or that a conception stressing "intentionality too easily blinds us to the educative effects of the law, literature, and the arts," a conclusion Cremin rejected (1976, p. 93). Unintentional teaching and incidental or serendipitous learning can provide otherwise unavailable critical distance on intentional education, and they may prove to have more lasting effects. Whether Cremin entertains either of these possibilities, he modified the statement, if not the spirit, of his definition of education. By 1977, it encompassed "effort to transmit, evoke, *or acquire* knowledge, attitudes, values, skills, *or* sensibilities, *as well as any outcome of that effort*" (Cremin, 1977, p. 134, italics added). Three years later he included among the outcomes of educational effort "any learning that results from the effort, direct or indirect, intended or unintended" (1980, p. ix). What the definition excludes remains imprecise, although apparently it expresses limited interest in making normative and critical distinctions among experiences that are educative, non-educative, or miseducative (Eisele, 1980; Katz, 1981).

In recent years, historians of education have devoted considerable energy to arguments about sources, perspectives, and the scope of their field (Butts, 1974; Clifford, 1975, 1976; Cohen, 1976, 1978; Cremin, 1965; Greene, 1973; Urban, 1975; Warren, 1978a). They have also managed to overstate the claim that the quality of contemporary historical research on education exceeds absolutely that produced by their nineteenth-century and twentieth-century predecessors, a strategy partly understood as an effort to gain respectability for the field within history departments (Butts, 1974; Clifford, 1976; Cremin, 1965). But few can deny that the critical content has broadened and deepened with the construction of histories of education in the United States that are complex, lively and life-like, and provocative. These results follow in part the more rigorous and specialized training of historians of education, a factor affecting the quality of historical research in general, and their commitment to keep education in context. The results are also due to mining of new or underutilized sources, availability of computers to help analyze masses of quantitative data, and, most important, willingness of some historians to question the efficacy of education, however defined.

Lay people and scholars viewing from without may see the history of education as a field in dynamic disarray, but they reap the benefit of the internal debate even if its fine points escape them. The field now encompasses historical case studies and survey histories of schools and school systems, libraries, higher education, the family, childhood and youth, child-rearing practices, professional organizations, legislation, court decisions, formal and informal curricula—almost every conceivable topic, even if only remotely connected to educational phenomena. In devising interpretive frameworks, historians of education borrow shamelessly from the social and behavioral sciences and to a lesser extent in recent years from the humanities. The result has been a growing, dynamic, complex literature that probes the major intellectual, social, cultural, and public policy questions and controversies of the twentieth century.

The extent to which this literature has been educational beyond the circle of historians remains unclear. One finds tacit, if crude, confirmation of history's utility in the prefaces or first chapters of dissertations and monographs treating a variety of topics, from education of the handicapped and bilingual education to the effect of particular curricula and education policies. These obligatory "history sections" suggest an author's need to take a running start on a topic. They tend not to reflect the expanded scope of the history-of-education field so much as commonsense notions about educational development, unquestioned assumptions about its value, and a preference for histories grounded in like-minded assumptions over those that would test these assumptions. Among social and behavioral scientists and policy analysts who uphold the most rigorous standards for their own fields, one still finds suggested that history, if useful, should offer a simple, sweet story to support or at least set the stage for their findings and recommendations.

The development and assessment of federal education policy in the United States illustrates the point. Herbert Hoover's National Advisory Committee on Education (1931) began its study by adopting a notion of education gleaned from the reports of the U.S. Bureau of Education. It expected to find a limited federal role in education of relatively recent vintage, but learned instead that federal educational activity began long before the bureau's founding in 1867 as the subcabinet Department of Education and extended beyond an interest in schools to involve programs of every cabinet department and several independent agencies as well. Lamenting what it called a regrettable development, the commission anticipated (and opposed) any expansion of federal interest in schools. Fifty years later advocates of the cabinet Department of Education likewise based their proposals on the history of federal educational activity. Their arguments echoed those of the proponents of the original department, adding that the new agency's principal task would be to coordinate the variety of federal involvements in education (U.S. Senate, 1978). They failed to anticipate that several programs proposed for transfer to the new department felt very much at home in other agencies. Those programs with aggressive, loyal, and politically well-connected constituencies tended to be left where they were.

Knowledge of the long, as over against recent, history of congressional treatment of federal service programs might have saved the staff and proponents of the National Institute of Education from considerable grief during the 1970s. A study of NIE's founding years by three social scientists repeated the error: they were apparently unaware that the agency's difficulties with Congress paralleled those of the departments of Agriculture and Interior and the original Department of Education a century earlier (Sproull, Weiner, & Wolf, 1978; Warren, 1974). Studying these historical analogies might have prepared the NIE staff to interact more effectively with Congress and its committees or at least alerted them to the possibility that increased NIE appropriations would follow, not precede, politically acceptable evidence of the agency's worth.

Proposals within the Reagan administration to abolish the Department of Education are equally innocent of historical knowledge. Presumably, the aim of such an action would be to improve education in the United States by relaxing federal influence over local and state affairs so that agencies at those levels could exercise greater authority over delivery of educational services. Prospects for realizing that objective might be brightened, or at least more openly assessed, if the dismantling of the original department in 1869 and the consequences of that action were examined. Federal education agencies of various sorts have existed in the United States since the 1830s. Historical research thus offers resources for identifying tested alternative organizations for federal involvement in education that might prove informative to both advocates and opponents of the Department of Education.

History alone is an inadequate basis for determining policy and for predicting what scholars in other fields will find through their research, but historical knowledge is not thereby incidental to social and behavioral science research in education or to education policy analysis and planning. To both it offers, first, the possibility of tested analogies to contemporary issues and questions; second, resources for longitudinal studies; and, third, analytical frameworks for identifying and weighing contextual variables that may influence research and policy outcomes. By way of illustration, the following discussion organizes an examination of recent research in the history of education around three broad topics, focusing on education in the United States.

Education and Its Publics.   One of the most persistent yet difficult to formulate issues in American education concerns the shape, focus, and origins of its popular support. That the support became widespread in the nineteenth century is common knowledge. Parents, in Kaestle's words, "voted with their children's feet" (1976, p. 393). He was referring to the extensive commitment to school attendance evident in several regions during the first half of the century. Other forms and levels of education also

gained currency: academies and colleges, libraries, museums, military training, industrial education, and professional schools and societies. In the case of academies, the institutions preceded significant increases in attendance. Common schools developed the other way around, at least in some states: attendance seems to have come before the institutions were re-formed as state-supervised systems. Other than attendance and the clamor to establish institutions, indications of popular support for education were ambiguous. Funding, for one, tended to be modest and unreliable, although it increased gradually. Thus, the critical question is not whether support materialized and eventually spread across the country but why it did so. Answers help explain the development of education goals and organizations.

One influence was the city, more precisely, its heterogeneity, size, and density. The mutually reinforcing bonds of family, church, work, and neighbors that sustained values and permitted personalistic, informal business transactions in homogeneous communities lost power in urban settings (Calhoun, 1973; Wade, 1959). Negotiating with outside influences could no longer be left to the preacher in part because he lacked the ability to understand or repulse them. Horace Mann, recalling his boyhood in a disintegrating Massachusetts community early in the nineteenth century, saw state reformatories, mental institutions, and especially common school systems as strategies to hold society together. They would serve as the new enabling institutions invented to replace the less formal social processes that were no longer effective (Messerli, 1972). The schools, as it turned out, were less invented than recovered from Massachusetts's colonial past. Although he rejected their theology, Mann wanted to revive the Puritans' commitment to systems of schools. Messerli (1972) saw overwhelming public support for Mann's school plan, a conclusion Kaestle (1976) disputed. Conflicts abounded between parents and schools, especially over centralization and teacher authority, Kaestle argued. Rather than a popular consensus existing on the value of systematized schooling, he suggested, support for the institutions drew from "trade-offs." However imperfectly, schools provided literacy and moral training for those needing such equipment (Kaestle, 1976; Calhoun, 1973). In cities, schools were not simply humanitarian gestures. Just as urban dwellers learned that volunteer police, firefighters, and garbage collectors failed to provide reliable services, so they determined the inadequacy of informal or private schooling. As Kaestle, Katz, and others showed (Kaestle, 1973; Kaestle & Vinovskis, 1980; Katz, 1968, 1975, 1976, 1980b), the result, and perhaps the aim, was not increased enrollment rates, greater literacy, or, initially, more schools, but in time standardized, centralized school systems that could offer efficient and effective basic education.

Urban boosterism also helps explain popular support for the establishment of schools, academies, libraries, newspapers, and other educational enterprises (Wade, 1959).

Here the influence was a mixture of civic pride and survival strategies. Like Samuel Bard, who wanted New York, not Philadelphia, to have the first American medical school, urban boosters across the country sought distinction for their cities by establishing institutions of learning and culture (Calhoun, 1973). Bard failed in his particular effort, but the New York–Philadelphia rivalry in the eighteenth century was illustrative of a long history of competition among cities vying for markets, industry, and population. Education was one of the lures.

One problem with the urban explanation is that it does not account for the higher and earlier school enrollment rates in rural communities that some historians have found. Rural schools were intertwined with the established web of enabling institutions (family, church, work, and neighbors). As Kaestle (1976) suggested, boredom may also have provided an incentive. What else, besides going to school, was a child to do during the winter? Rural support for public and private schools, churches, spelling bees, and other educational efforts was evident not only in Massachusetts and New York, where interest in education was traditionally high, but also in the newer states and territories (Church & Sedlak, 1976). Kansas farm children, immigrant and native whites together, attended sod-house schools in the mid-nineteenth century and paid for the privilege (Stratton, 1981). Using New York and Massachusetts data, Kaestle and Vinovskis (1980) offered three explanations for the higher enrollment rates they found in villages and rural communities during the years from 1790 to 1840, when the drive for state centralization began having noticeable effect: "First, the political literature of the Revolutionary period, and the excitement of nation building, added secular political reinforcement to traditional motives for widespread education . . . second . . . was the increasing provision of schooling for girls . . . [and] third . . . was the decentralization of the location and control of schools" (pp. 25–26).

These explanations pose questions of their own. The first seems to contradict the authors' earlier argument that plans and schemes for state and national systems of schools offered during the Revolutionary generation, which were very much a part of the political literature of the period, had little impact locally. Perhaps they did, at least to the extent of confirming education as a source of pride and social cohesion. Decentralization sounds better than it looked, if schools in rural Kansas after midcentury can be accepted as typical (Dick, 1954; Stratton, 1981). That leaves the accessibility of schools to girls as the surest explanation of rural school enrollment rates, beyond the obvious fact that schools formed an integral part of the rural social fabric. Further, women provided a multiplier effect. They attended schools as students and returned later as teachers. One of Joanna Stratton's pioneer women thought that "about two thirds of the women of Kansas have taught school" (p. 160).

The rural schools in Kansas shed light on the quantitative data examined by Kaestle and Vinovskis (Clifford,

1975; Finkelstein, 1975; Stratton, 1981). With the children came books, whatever they had at home. If a family possessed slates, the children brought those too. Otherwise, a hardened dirt floor and a long stick allowed lessons in writing and arithmetic. Equipment—maps, blackboards, desks, chairs—was virtually nonexistent. The teacher, almost always a woman, created the curriculum for the particular students confronting her. They ranged in age from 6 or 7 to early adolescence. Teachers "boarded around" and also received their salaries from parents either directly, a set amount per child, or indirectly from funds collected by school committees. Salaries ranged between $10 and $20 per month while the term was in session. School terms varied in length, usually three to four months; rarely overlapped planting and harvest times; and survived good weather and bad. Parent commitment was strong; enrollment rates were high and steady. The last was the point Kaestle and Vinovskis wanted to make. Further, they noted that the schools' holding power, measured by enrollment rates, did not increase noticeably in villages and rural communities after centralization set in. Following the examples of New England and Western Reserve states, Kansas joined that process in the second half of the nineteenth century. District schools merged into county and city school systems that were supervised, age graded, and tax supported. A political economics reading of the development emphasizes the instrumental role played by teachers and school administrators seeking improved working conditions and greater professional autonomy (Michaelsen, 1977; West, 1967). Tax-based, state-controlled schools seemed to promise less local interference with school operations and more reliable funding. If Kansas can be considered representative, however, no one, especially not parents, was completely happy with the rural district school, however romanticized in memory. Pearson, one of Stratton's sources, had little patience with the latter: "The miracle was that a love of learning ever survived the rigors of school days then. But it did, in some cases" (Stratton, 1981, p. 159). Kaestle and Vinovskis correctly challenged the notion that the late eighteenth and early nineteeth centuries represented something of an educational "Dark Ages" in the United States. Popular support for education, including schools, was strong. It remained strong after 1840, but the schools began to change dramatically.

Calhoun (1973) suggested the transformation came none too soon. In the period from 1750 to 1870, the economy became pervasively capitalistic, the mode of business and interpersonal transactions changed, and their complexity and number increased and became less susceptible to individual control. The population grew, rearranged itself, and admitted successive waves of immigrants. Early in the nineteenth century, gaps between British and American institutions became painfully clear, particularly with regard to professional training. Later, applications of knowledge focused on industry, war technology, and agricultural production, and population statistics developed as a means of communication and record keeping. In these altered circumstances, literacy became a minimum requirement for entering the complexities of the outside world.

It was no wonder that people resorted to systematized education, although one might speculate why they were so easily satisfied (Calhoun, 1973). By the late nineteenth century, children in schools were learning more and acquiring knowledge with what might be termed greater efficiency. Observers noted, however, an inability to apply learned ideas and techniques. Emphasis on different cognitive roles for males and females, one quantitative, the other verbal, interfered with development of problem-solving skills and ability to sustain connected discourse. Rote and superficial learning flourished. A growing barrier separated school from the outside world, skill from reality, and precision from intuition. Calhoun (1973) concluded: "There remained the strong possibility that Americans were thinking in ways less rigid than observation of school suggested. This possibility rested partly on the attitudes that children brought to school . . . yet partly also on the success that practical men scored in building a culture outside any schools" (p. 132).

Calhoun worried about the quality of American culture, the people's realized ability to chase problems not answered, not even anticipated, in schoolbooks. But what if formal education offered prospects of a different order? Some of the nation's early political strategists said it did, in language unfamiliar and quaint to twentieth-century ears: The national interest in education is larger than the sum of private and local interests. Butts's long advocacy of the idea of the public school derived from that formulation (Butts, 1974, 1978). He did not argue that schools evolved without conflict or that they succeeded in realizing the ideals set for them, only that they were employed to address a persistent problem. Even from the distance of two centuries, the fundamental American dilemma during the early national period can be appreciated. How was a political community to be built that was independent of Europe and stronger than private and regional loyalties?

Plans for school systems devised as an answer to the question apparently had little immediate effect, as several historians observed (Kaestle & Vinovskis, 1980; Katz, 1981). Kaestle and Vinovskis argued that early-nineteenth-century Americans seemed satisfied with local arrangements for schooling, but they also noted a growing nationalism that fed popular interest in schools and helped to shape them. This contradiction within public support for public schooling was confronted by the Massachusetts legislature in 1840 over the issue of whether to abolish the state board of education and the normal schools. The conflict was not between supporters and opponents of public schools, but rather focused on "the proper content of education as well as on the role of the state in its development and control" (Kaestle & Vinovskis, 1980, p. 230). Butts's point was that such issues arise when education is attached to public policies affecting a plurality of interests (Butts,

1974, 1978). They tend not to arise so long as education is viewed as essentially a private matter or entrusted to an evolving pattern of institutions and processes of the sort described by Cremin. In Butts's view the American public school was essentially a political idea, evolving from disparate sources, that connected national well-being to the development of free, public, accessible, and inclusive schools. Establishing government's guarantee of such education, if necessary apart from popular demand for it, was essential, Butts argued, to both modernization and the formation of democratic political community in the United States. He joined other historians, however, in admitting that the idea has never been fully tested (Butts, 1974; Clifford, 1975; Kaestle & Vinovskis, 1980; Katz, 1968, 1973).

Recent research in the history of education in the United States has focused considerable attention on the relation of education to its publics. That growing popular support particularly for schools has responded to discrete urban, economic, cultural, and political influences hardly comes as news. Clarity about the changing character of that support over time, on the other hand, its regional similarities and differences, and the complex interactions that have helped explain it represents a clear gain for the field and a resource for policy analysts and policy makers. Of special interest are suggestions that the public settled for forms of education perceived by some as not wholly attractive and useful, that the public schools sacrificed quality in pursuit of standardized learning, and that commitment to the need for education outweighed immediate effects when education was expected to serve public policy objectives. An ironic estrangement separating education from its publics may have evolved. Historians studying the control of education tended to think so.

Education and Control. Historians have employed several conceptions of control in examining the roles of public institutions and agencies (Kaestle, 1973; Karier, 1975; Tyack, 1974), churches and other private organizations (Lannie, 1968, 1976; Sanders, 1977), educational professionals (Bledstein, 1976; Callahan, 1962; Eaton, 1975; Mattingly, 1975), communities (Graham, 1974; Seller, 1978), and organizational forms (Calhoun, 1969; Katz, 1975) in determining education goals and outcomes. The most useful of these studies have attempted to correlate effects with sources of power, the former ranging from aims and policies to student achievement and the latter encompassing both formal authority and indirect influence. The research tended to be guided by a common assumption: Education is in part a political process that organizes and distributes various sorts of power. The assumption ignores the old chestnut about museums, churches, families, and other educational forms, especially schools and colleges, being "above" politics, hence innocent of conflict over power. Control of schools has received most of the attention.

Several trends in the form and mode of control over education can be identified. The construction of public school systems serving large and heterogeneous populations, in a state or large city, for example, has been accompanied by the removal of control from the constituents of particular schools (Tyack, 1974). An emerging profession of education in the nineteenth century helped to stimulate national uniformity among schools and in time a talent pool of university-trained education specialists (Callahan, 1962). If the founding of national and regional organizations and periodicals for school people can serve as a guide, professionalization of education began as early as the 1830s (Mattingly, 1975). Finally, there is evidence that the structure of institutions and systems served both to organize and to control them (Katz, 1975). As stated, these trends cloak considerable local variation. They are supported by numerous case studies, which together constitute a major strength of contemporary historical research on education. Comparative studies, however, are rare; thus, generalizations about the control of education remain necessarily tentative and hypothetical.

Changes in the form and mode of school control did not have direct or immediate payoffs in terms of enrollment rates and measured student achievement, although nineteenth-century data on the latter are neither widespread nor reliable (Kaestle, 1973; Kaestle & Vinovskis, 1980; Olneck & Lazerson, 1974). Rather, they accompanied such institutional and policy alterations as curriculum standardization, lengthened school terms, and increased school district size (and a corresponding decrease in the number of districts). By the twentieth century the vast majority of children and youth attended school. Conflict occurred throughout the process. Residents in rural areas and small towns, although not entirely pleased with their local schools, tended to oppose district consolidation and the concomitant curricular and administrative changes that placed them literally and figuratively at a distance from the schools their children attended (Tyack, 1974). Although typically lacking formal authority and staff, nineteenth-century state education agencies endorsed centralization in a movement that spread from the Northeast and Midwest throughout the country early in the twentieth century. The goals were to realize economies of scale and reduce local variation among policies and programs, but the effort came wrapped in reformist language and energy. State funding, however, did not function to equalize local education capability during the nineteenth century, nor was it intended to do so (Coons, Clune, & Sugarman, 1970).

A corresponding development occurred in cities as part of the progressive reform agenda in the late nineteenth and early twentieth centuries. School boards became smaller and tended to be composed of business and professional men elected or appointed at large rather than from urban subdivisions (Cronin, 1973). Their involvement in administration and supervision decreased as administrative staffs became larger, adopted hierarchical organizations, and increasingly prepared for their jobs at universities. With professionalization and bureaucratization came teacher organizations and the start of explicit labor-man-

agement tensions in the schools (Herrick, 1971). Although the conflicts typically pitted female teachers against male administrators, the fundamental issue concerned the locus and extent of professional control in schools.

Several historians have traced the origins of these developments to the early nineteenth century (Katz, 1968, 1975; Kaestle, 1973; Troen, 1975). Katz (1975) argued that alternatives to "incipient bureaucracy" were rejected and that these early decisions set the stage for the mature urban school bureaucracies that were in place before the close of the century. Criticism of his interpretation revolved around two arguments. One depicted nineteenth-century bureaucratization as a relatively natural evolution toward rational organization (Kaestle, 1976; Kaestle & Vinovskis, 1980). The other saw a misreading of nineteenth-century public education, which for the most part was not urban or bureaucratically organized (Tyack, 1976, 1978). Both criticisms missed Katz's central point that school bureaucracies assert values. Fundamentally, they represent choices that have had cumulative effects, not objective responses to such impersonal forces as urbanization (Callahan, 1962; Karier, Violas, & Spring, 1973; Katz, 1975; Wiebe, 1967).

Bureaucratization occurred elsewhere in education as well: among private schools and throughout higher education (Sanders, 1977; Veysey, 1965). Organizational forms differed, but a consistent result was distance separating institutional control from constituents. On the other hand, not all such alienation could be attributed solely or directly to bureaucratic organization. Eastern and southern European immigrant ethnic parishes complaining about cultural insensitivity in Roman Catholic school systems tended to blame Irish or German influence over church affairs, not the hierarchical structure itself (Sanders, 1977).

In the nineteenth century, local control of public schools began shifting to localism, control by locally situated elites, including education professionals. Systematic exercise of state authority over school districts began to occur in the twentieth century (Coons, Clune, & Sugarman, 1970). By the late 1960s, when debate focused on federal involvement in public education, the most striking development in school control had occurred at the state level. For the first time in the nation's history, the proportion of public school funds contributed from state sources approached 50 percent. That historians are only beginning to study state roles in public education is tacit confirmation of the often noted urban bias in recent education historiography (Clifford, 1975, 1976).

Historical research has identified changing forms and configurations of control over education. Within public and private schools, formal authority has on occasion been curtailed by voluntary associations and community groups having only the power to influence decisions. Education professionals have exercised control over aspects of programs and institutions regardless of formal delegations of authority to governing boards. National and regional associations of educators have influenced policy directly and indirectly, the latter by engendering a sense of profession among their members and developing professional consensus on program and policy proposals (Mattingly, 1975).

The record indicates diminishing local control over formal education, public schools in particular. Explanations of the process have spawned vigorous, often bitter debate among contemporary historians (Kaestle, 1976; Katz, 1968; Troen, 1975). The key questions revolve around the matter of imposition: Has education in the United States been a response to public demand and interest? Has it been imposed? The answer to both is yes. Convincing evidence from what Finkelstein called the "intentional literature" described how countless parents and communities in the nineteenth century labored to bring schools into being. (Clifford, 1975, 1976; Finkelstein, 1975). Once successful, they more or less grudgingly released the schools or their students to systems over which they had less influence. Troen (1975) argued that in St. Louis an urban school system evolved in response to the changing composition and needs of its constituents. Equally persuasive documentation noted the extent to which education development and reform emanated from the top down. Education in the United States seems to have been controlled dialectically, with resulting institutions and processes that were in but not exactly of society.

Education and Equity. Historians have examined inequity in American education from two broad orientations. Intellectual and cultural historians (Church & Sedlak, 1976; Cremin, 1980; Greene, 1965) emphasized the contradictions between policies and practices and education goals. Social historians (Kaestle & Vinovskis, 1980; Katz, 1976) speculated on the causes of inequity discovered from enrollment, attendance, and achievement data. In both cases, education inequity emerged as a producer of social dynamite. If education is necessary, whether for nation building, developing political community, or preparing citizens for differential roles in a capitalistic society, it becomes a matter for direct or covert enforcement. Exclusion from education threatens to produce marginal, potentially disruptive individuals or groups lacking requisite values, skills, and loyalties. Using quantitative data, social historians reached similar conclusions in correlating education variables with race, social class, ethnicity, or gender. If education is necessary, it must be inclusive. If it is not necessary, the rationale supporting the pervasive network of education in the United States, especially standardized, centralized, and compulsory public schools, loses its central argument. Inclusiveness, to be sure, can be given different meanings. It does not imply that, for example, all children in school should move through the same curriculum. On the other hand, arbitrary or systematic discrimination in schools, like other forms of exclusion, raises the specter of dysfunctional social outcomes. These hypothetical considerations help explain why historians treat inequity in education as a spectrum of issues. Federal or state constitutional questions or humanitarian concerns offer insufficient frameworks for analyzing its various forms and outcomes.

The most obvious form has been direct exclusion. At one time or another in various parts of the country, Americans have been denied access to education on the basis of race, gender, ethnicity, handicap, or age. Although the historical literature on direct exclusion from education often favors moral argument over critical analysis, it reveals complexities that caution against making hasty generalizations (Anderson, 1975; Franklin, 1973). The exclusion of black people from schools in the 1850s, for example, seems to have been equally systematic in northern and southern cities (Pessen, 1980; Wade, 1964). Although considerable regional variation has occurred relative to the victims and the duration of direct exclusion, violence, conflict, and protest have been common accompaniments (Tyack, 1974). Those who practiced exclusion have tended to be motivated as much by self-perceived status as by desire for long-term economic gain or political enhancement (Cash, 1941; McDonald & McWhiney, 1980). Negative economic correlations, particularly the social costs of exclusion by race, have been cumulative and difficult to contain geographically.

An equally potent form of education inequity, indirect exclusion has produced more ambiguous results than direct exclusion. In the late nineteenth and early twentieth centuries, racially segregated schools, an example of indirect exclusion, tended to have more black teachers than did integrated schools (Tyack, 1974). Black parents thus confronted a dilemma of choosing presumably better programs or attractive adult models for their children. Tyack reported that in many cases they opted for segregated schools. Several American Indian tribes found themselves excluded by virtue of being forcibly included in boarding and reservation schools that they correctly perceived as inimical to Indian cultures (Adams, 1971). During the 1840s, Roman Catholics faced a similar situation in New York City. They rejected the Public School Society's schools in favor of parish institutions because of the pan-Protestant tone and anti-Catholic curriculum of the public schools (Kaestle, 1973; Lannie, 1968). Turn-of-the-century immigrants in Buffalo, New York, discovered that Americanization classes failed to prepare them for American life as effectively as less formal educational programs they created for themselves (Seller, 1978). Barriers to positions of authority functioned as another form of indirect exclusion. Women found themselves welcomed in schools as teachers, but not as superintendents or, until the twentieth century, even as full members of the National Education Association (Tyack, 1974). Language also served to exclude some from education, although among non–English-speaking people older and newer immigrants of the same nationality group often disagreed about the wisdom of clinging to a native tongue. In the nineteenth century, German immigrants in several cities secured the establishment of bilingual programs in public schools, but in the early twentieth century German-American organizations tended to oppose such strategies (Tyack, 1974). By this time, the notion of the common school had given way to a differentiated curriculum intended to attract and hold more students (Krug, 1964). Curriculum specialization became a form of indirect exclusion.

Historians have also identified education inequities on the basis of policy outcomes and student achievement. Kaestle and Vinovskis (1980) found that school attendance in Massachusetts varied according to ethnicity. Somewhat independent of social class, urban and rural foreign-born children attended school at lower rates than their native-born counterparts. Olneck and Lazerson (1974) discovered considerable variation of achievement among immigrant children of different nationalities. Furthermore, the achievement of particular groups varied from city to city. Kaestle and Vinovskis also warned that their data reflected local conditions. In neither case did the authors argue that schools intended to produce inequities. They explained the results as an interplay of cultural and local economic factors. The significance of the findings was thereby enhanced, not mitigated. By relying on outcome data, rather than the traditional "rhetoric of intention," the "new" social history advocated by Kaestle and Vinovskis planted education inequity amid structural interactions in society. Katz (1980b, 1981) agreed that reworked goal statements promise modest changes in the effects of schooling but insisted that historians can go beyond balanced descriptions of structural complexities. They can understand the extent to which the complex patterns of interaction can be fundamentally just or fundamentally unjust.

When applied to effects of education on social classes, Katz's advice sparks strong disagreement among historians. The quarrels often focus on research methodology and design in the attempt to explain contradictory findings (Kaestle & Vinovskis, 1980; Katz, 1980a). Using quantitative and documentary evidence, Katz (1976, 1981) noted a significant shift in the rationale for public education between the early and middle nineteenth century, with the rise of industrial capitalism as the intervening variable. By the late nineteenth century, centralized school systems offered differential preparation for workers needed in the emerging economy. The effort was intentional, effective, and imposed by the middle class. Why, then, did Kaestle and Vinovskis ask, did workers acquiesce? Katz's point was that initially at least they did not (Katz, 1968). Witness their opposition to such innovations as the high school on the grounds that it promised little benefit to laboring people. That point, too, is in contention. Kaestle and Vinovskis found that support for the high school in Lynn, Massachusetts, cut across social classes. If anything, it was an imposition on the middle class.

The importance of such debates transcends methodological disputes (Warren, 1978b). At issue is the relation of education to social-class mobility and, more basically, the openness or rigidity of the American social structure. A major conceptual and methodological difficulty posed in much of the current research concerns the extent to which social-class characteristics can be isolated from religious, cultural, and racial factors (Shrader, 1980; Worthman, 1971). More local studies are needed, the "building blocks" that Thernstrom advocated (Hareven, 1971, p. xiv) as necessary to the development of general historical theory. The utility of such theory will be determined largely by how historians approach social-class phenomena. Quantitative data disaggregated in various ways can help define categories to which certain outcomes are attributed. They reveal little, however, about lived processes, relationships, and aspirations. Historians are likely to discover that social-class phenomena take on sharply different meanings, depending on whether they are viewed from afar or within.

General themes and trends in education history are easily identified, but recent research in the field issues a warning about their use and significance. They provide overviews, indications of where things headed. By collapsing time, they open for inspection both its linear and circular qualities. Immediate and long-term effects and correlations can be calculated; however, education has exhibited striking local variations. Losing or distorting this richness of detail drains life and texture from both history and education. The case studies completed by contemporary historians of education tend to avoid this risk while running others. Gaps and weaknesses in the case study literature limit its utility not only to historians but to other scholars and policy makers as well. The literature contains an urban bias that distracts attention from education in other settings while positing unreal urban-rural dichotomies. Parochial inclinations would be softened by a greater emphasis on cross-national and cross-cultural comparative case studies. Such research would be a major contribution to the policy field, given its often noted provincialism. Finally, a social science orientation that in Bender's terse judgment on the Kaestle and Vinovskis research was "so naively wary of ideology" (Bender, 1980, p. 1270) does not avoid interpretations; it only delivers them wrapped in objectivity. When historians dismiss ideas, Paul Mattingly argued, "as evidence with lesser authority than hard facts" (1975, p. xiv), the price is history that no one lived. Rigorously conducted intellectual history breathes life into case studies and brings the interpretive task out of the closet. It helps, in short, to put education in its place.

That may be education historians' most useful and continuing contribution to other scholars and policy makers: reminders in detail that education has been less important than old pieties pretended it to be and more powerful than anyone predicted.

Donald R. Warren

See also Archives and Records Management; Curriculum History; Historiography; History and Philosophy of Higher Education; Philosophy of Education.

REFERENCES

Adams, E. C. *American Indian Education: Government Schools and Economic Progress.* New York: Arno Press, 1971.

Anderson, J. D. Education as a vehicle for the manipulation of black workers. In W. Feinberg & H. Rosemont, Jr. (Eds.), *Work, Technology, and Education*. Urbana: University of Illinois Press, 1975.

Bender, T. Review of *Education and Social Change in Nineteenth-century Massachusetts* by C. F. Kaestle & M. A. Vinovskis. *American Historical Review*, 1980, *85*, 1269–1270.

Bledstein, B. J. *The Culture of Professionalism: The Middle Class and the Development of Higher Education in America*. New York: Norton, 1976.

Burstyn, J. N. Catharine Beecher and the education of American women. *New England Quarterly*, 1974, *47*, 386–403.

Butts, R. F. Public education and political community. *History of Education Quarterly*, 1974, *14*, 165–183.

Butts, R. F. *Public Education in the United States: From Revolution to Reform*. New York: Holt, Rinehart & Winston, 1978.

Calhoun, D. The city as teacher: Historical problems. *History of Education Quarterly*, 1969, *9*, 312–325.

Calhoun, D. *The Intelligence of a People*. Princeton, N.J.: Princeton University Press, 1973.

Callahan, R. *Education and the Cult of Efficiency*. Chicago: University of Chicago Press, 1962.

Cash, W. J. *The Mind of the South*. New York: Random House, Vintage Books, 1941.

Church, R. L., & Sedlak, M. W. *Education in the United States: An Interpretive History*. New York: Free Press, 1976.

Clifford, G. J. Saints, sinners, and people: A position paper on the historiography of American education. *History of Education Quarterly*, 1975, *15*, 257–272.

Clifford, G. J. Education: Its history and historiography. *Review of Research in Education*, 1976, *4*, 210–267.

Cohen, S. The history of the history of American education, 1900–1976: The uses of the past. *Harvard Educational Review*, 1976, *46*, 298–330.

Cohen, S. History of education as a field of study: An essay on the recent historiography of American education. In D. R. Warren (Ed.), *History, Education, and Public Policy*. Berkeley, Calif.: McCutchan, 1978.

Coons, J. E.; Clune, W. H., III; & Sugarman, S. D. *Private Wealth and Public Education*. Cambridge, Mass.: Belknap Press, 1970.

Cremin, L. A. *The Wonderful World of Ellwood Patterson Cubberley: An Essay in the Historiography of American Education*. New York: Teachers College, Bureau of Publications, 1965.

Cremin, L. A. *American Education: The Colonial Experience, 1607–1783*. New York: Harper & Row, 1970.

Cremin, L. A. *Public Education*. New York: Basic Books, 1976.

Cremin, L. A. *Traditions of American Education*. New York: Basic Books, 1977.

Cremin, L. A. *American Education: The National Experience, 1783–1876*. New York: Harper & Row, 1980.

Cronin, J. M. *The Control of Urban Schools: Perspectives on the Power of Educational Reformers*. New York: Free Press, 1973.

Dick, E. *The Sod-house Frontier, 1854–1890*. Lincoln, Nebr.: Johnsen, 1954.

Eaton, W. E. *The American Federation of Teachers, 1916–1961: A History of the Movement*. Carbondale: Southern Illinois University Press, 1975.

Eisele, J. C. Defining education: A problem for educational history. *Educational Theory*, 1980, *30*, 25–33.

Finkelstein, B. Pedagogy as intrusion: Teaching values in popular primary schools in nineteenth-century America. *History of Childhood Quarterly*, 1975, *2*, 349–378.

Franklin, V. P. Historical revisionism and black education. *School Review*, 1973, *81*, 477–486.

Gitelman, H. M. *Workingmen of Waltham: Mobility in American Urban Industrial Development, 1850–1890*. Baltimore: Johns Hopkins University Press, 1974.

Graham, P. A. *Community and Class in American Education*. New York: Wiley, 1974.

Greene, M. *The Public School and the Private Vision*. New York: Random House, 1965.

Greene, M. Identities and contours: An approach to educational history. *Educational Researcher*, 1973, *2*, 5–17.

Grubb, W. L., & Lazerson, M. Rally 'round the workplace: Continuities and fallacies in career education. *Harvard Educational Review*, 1975, *45*, 451–474.

Hareven, T. K. (Ed.). *Anonymous Americans: Explorations in Nineteenth-century Social History*. Englewood Cliffs, N.J.: Prentice-Hall, 1971.

Herrick, M. J. *The Chicago Schools: A Social and Political History*. Beverly Hills, Calif.: Sage, 1971.

Kaestle, C. F. *The Evolution of an Urban School System: New York City, 1750–1850*. Cambridge, Mass.: Harvard University Press, 1973.

Kaestle, C. F. Conflict and consensus revisited: Notes toward a reinterpretation of American educational history. *Harvard Educational Review*, 1976, *46*, 390–396.

Kaestle, C. F., & Vinovskis, M. A. *Education and Social Change in Nineteenth-century Massachusetts*. New York: Cambridge University Press, 1980.

Karier, C. J. (Ed.). *Shaping the American Educational State: 1900 to the Present*. New York: Free Press, 1975.

Karier, C. J.; Violas, P. C.; & Spring, J. H. *Roots of Crisis: American Education in the Twentieth Century*. Chicago: Rand McNally, 1973.

Katz, M. B. *The Irony of Early School Reform: Educational Innovation in Mid–nineteenth-Century Massachusetts*. Cambridge, Mass.: Harvard University Press, 1968.

Katz, M. B. Review of *Roots of Crisis* by C. J. Karier, P. C. Violas, & J. H. Spring. *Harvard Educational Review*, 1973, *43*, 435–442.

Katz, M. B. *Class, Bureaucracy, and the Schools: The Illusion of Educational Change in America* (Expanded ed.). New York: Praeger, 1975.

Katz, M. B. The origins of public education: A reassessment. *History of Education Quarterly*, 1976, *16*, 381–407.

Katz, M. B. Hardcore educational historiography. *Reviews in American History*, 1980, *8*, 504–510. (a)

Katz, M. B. Reflections on the purpose of educational reform. *Educational Theory*, 1980, *30*, 77–88. (b)

Katz, M. B. Review of *American Education: The National Experience, 1783–1876* by L. A. Cremin. *American Historical Review*, 1981, *86*, 205–206.

Krug, E. A. *The Shaping of the American High School*. New York: Harper & Row, 1964.

Lannie, V. P. *Public Money and Parochial Education: Bishop Hughes, Governor Seward, and the New York School Controversy*. Cleveland: Case Western Reserve University Press, 1968.

Lannie, V. P. Church and school triumphant: The sources of American Catholic educational historiography. *History of Education Quarterly*, 1976, *16*, 131–145.

Mattingly, P. H. *The Classless Profession: American Schoolmen in the Nineteenth Century*. New York: New York University Press, 1975.

McDonald, F., & McWhiney, G. The South from self-sufficiency to peonage: An interpretation. *American Historical Review,* 1980, *85,* 1095–1118.

Messerli, J. *Horace Mann: A biography.* New York: Knopf, 1972.

Michaelsen, J. B. Revision, bureaucracy, and school reform: A critique of Katz. *School Review,* 1977, *85,* 229–246.

Mohraz, J. J. *The Separate Problem: Case Studies of Black Education in the North, 1900–1930.* Westport, Conn.: Greenwood Press, 1979.

National Advisory Committee on Education. *Federal Relations to Education.* Washington, D.C.: National Capital Press, 1931.

Olneck, M. R., & Lazerson, M. The school achievement of immigrant children: 1900–1930. *History of Education Quarterly,* 1974, *14,* 454–482.

Pessen, E. How different from each other were the antebellum North and South? *The American Historical Review,* 1980, *85,* 1119–1149.

Reese, W. J. "Partisans of the proletariat": The socialist working class and the Milwaukee schools, 1890–1920. *History of Education Quarterly,* 1981, *21,* 3–50.

Sanders, J. W. *The Education of an Urban Minority: Catholics in Chicago, 1833–1965.* New York: Oxford University Press, 1977.

Seller, M. S. Success and failure in adult education: The immigrant experience, 1914–1924. In D. R. Warren (Ed.), *History, Education, and Public Policy.* Berkeley, Calif.: McCutchan, 1978.

Shrader, V. L. Ethnicity, Religion, and Class: Progressive school reform in San Francisco. *History of Education Quarterly,* 1980, *20,* 385–402.

Sklar, K. K. *Catharine Beecher: A Study in American Domesticity.* New Haven, Conn.: Yale University Press, 1973.

Sproull, L.; Weiner, S.; & Wolf, D. *Organizing an Anarchy: Belief, Bureaucracy, and Politics in the National Institute of Education.* Chicago: University of Chicago Press, 1978.

Storr, R. J. The role of education in American history: A memorandum. *Harvard Educational Review,* 1976, *46,* 331–354.

Stratton, J. L. *Pioneer Women: Voices from the Kansas Frontier.* New York: Simon & Schuster, 1981.

Troen, S. K. *The Public and the Schools: Shaping the St. Louis System, 1838–1920.* Columbia: University of Missouri Press, 1975.

Tyack, D. B. *The One Best System: A History of American Urban Education.* Cambridge, Mass.: Harvard University Press, 1974.

Tyack, D. B. Ways of seeing: An essay on the history of compulsory schooling. *Harvard Educational Review,* 1976, *46,* 355–389.

Tyack, D. B. The spread of schooling in Victorian America: In search of a reinterpretation. *History of Education,* 1978, *7,* 173–182.

Urban, W. J. Some historical problems in revisionist educational history (Review of *Roots of Crisis* by C. J. Karier, P. C. Violas, & J. H. Spring). *American Educational Research Journal,* 1975, *12,* 337–350.

U.S. Senate, Committee on Governmental Affairs. *Department of Education Organization Act of 1978* (Report No. 95-1078). Washington, D.C.: 95th Congress, 2nd Session, 1978. (ERIC Document Reproduction Service No. ED 161 150)

Veysey, L. R. *The Emergence of the American University.* Chicago: University of Chicago Press, 1965.

Wade, R. C. *The Urban Frontier.* Chicago: University of Chicago Press, 1959.

Wade, R. C. *Slavery in the Cities: The South, 1820–1860.* New York: Oxford University Press, 1964.

Warren, D. R. *To Enforce Education: A History of the Founding Years of the United States Office of Education.* Detroit: Wayne State University Press, 1974.

Warren, D. R. A past for the present. *Educational Theory,* 1978, *28,* 253–265. (a)

Warren, D. R. (Ed.). *History, Education, and Public Policy.* Berkeley, Calif.: McCutchan, 1978. (b)

West, E. G. The political economy of American public school legislation. *Journal of Law and Economics,* 1967, *10,* 101–128.

Wiebe, R. H. *The Search for Order: 1877–1920.* New York: Hill & Wang, 1967.

Wollenberg, C. *All Deliberate Speed: Segregation and Exclusion in California Schools, 1855–1975.* Berkeley: University of California Press, 1978.

Worthman, P. B. Working class mobility in Birmingham, Alabama, 1880–1914. In T. K. Hareven (Ed.), *Anonymous Americans: Explorations in Nineteenth-century Social History.* Englewood Cliffs, N.J.: Prentice-Hall, 1971.

HOME ECONOMICS EDUCATION

Home economics in its most comprehensive sense is the study of the relation between, on the one hand, the laws, conditions, principles, and ideals concerned with the immediate environment of human beings and, on the other hand, the social nature of human beings (Baldwin, 1949). It emphasizes such crucial aspects of family living as nutritional needs of individuals, responsibilities of parenthood, interpersonal relationships, and management of financial resources. It also addresses clothing design, selection, care, and construction; textiles for home and clothing; housing for the family; and art as an integral part of family life.

Some formal instruction in needlework and cookery was given as early as 1789 in New England schools, but it was not until the twentieth century that home economics was developed as a subject in the public school curriculum. A group of interested persons, gathered in a series of conferences at Lake Placid, New York, between the years 1899 and 1910, began broadening the concept of instruction in family living beyond that of teaching simple skills. These conferences established the home and family as the focus for study (Richards, 1908). By 1914, home economics programs were available in some schools in all states.

Through various acts of Congress, support and direction for home economics programs have been provided at all educational levels. The Morrill Act, for example, helped land grant colleges and universities to develop programs of home economics. By 1914, more than 250 institutions offered four-year courses leading to a baccalaureate degree. Other legislative acts provided for instruction, below college level, in occupations related to home economics and outreach programs for adults. Amendments in 1976 to vocational legislation emphasized that the content of programs should be shaped by current national and local economic, social, and cultural conditions and needs.

By the late 1960s, programs in home economics were provided through the formal school organization at all levels: elementary, secondary, postsecondary, college, and university. Home economics was taught in nearly all high schools in the country as preparation for homemaking. Education for gainful employment in occupations utilizing the knowledge and skills in home economics subject-matter areas had been instituted. A review of state reports showed rapid progress in this extension of home economics programs. Change in the leadership structure for home economics education was recognized as shifting from the U.S. Office of Education (USOE) to the major professional organizations.

A national survey (Coon, 1962) using data gathered from state education department reports of 1959 for 3,796 schools showed that 49 percent (about 2.35 million) of all girls in public secondary schools were enrolled in home economics courses as were slightly more than 1 percent (about 63,000) of all boys. No more recent data on enrollment were available as of 1968.

Research History. The report in the fourth edition of the *Encyclopedia of Educational Research* (1969) pointed out the paucity of research prior to 1940 and its slow growth up to 1963 (Nelson, 1969). This latter date marked the passage of the Vocational Education Act, which, among other directives, provided financial support for research. Ten percent of the total appropriation for vocational education each year was to be used for research-training programs and research, and an additional amount was allotted for development, improvement, and evaluation of programs. Two centers for research and leadership in vocational and technical education were established. It was noted that a large proportion of the research and study had concentrated on areas relating to the curriculum: trends and conditions in society that affect the lives of individuals in their homes, needs of learners, and organization of knowledge in home economics. The first of the conferences convened to define the cognitive content of the field and the first of a series to identify a basic framework of competencies and concepts for teacher education had been held. Numerous studies had provided information on needs, interests, values, beliefs, and attitudes of learners on which to base curriculum decisions. The use of programmed instruction had received some attention from researchers. Most research had dealt with factors related to effectiveness of teaching and preparation of teachers. Few answers were found to questions of teacher effectiveness. Grade point average was seen to be the best predictor of quality of teaching. College home economics curricula were examined in one study from opinions of administrators and alumnae; findings generally confirmed satisfaction with the curriculum. Another study evaluated the revision of a college core curriculum; constituents were satisfied with the resulting curriculum. One state evaluated its total vocational education program through questionnaires to teachers; a considerable number believed too little emphasis had been placed on preparation to teach family relations, child development, family economics and management, and consumer education. There were very few reports of program evaluation in occupational home economics. Home economics education research had produced tested techniques and instruments useful in classroom instruction, teacher preparation programs, and program evaluation.

Research Themes. Answers to basic questions about the content, policy, and student body of home economics were presented in three planning papers commissioned by the National Institute of Education. The first analyzes content of programs and audiences served and offers implications for research and program development (Hughes, 1979). The second discusses criteria for determining effectiveness of curricula in consumer and homemaking programs, identifying the major two criteria as meeting needs of targeted populations and developing homemaker competencies most essential for coping with current socioeconomic conditions (Cross, 1979). The third (Simpson, 1979) examines characteristics of the American family and relevant social issues having implications for home economics. From these analyses and the efforts of other researchers, recurring themes in home economics education have been identified.

Prominent among them is the recognition that homemaking functions are increasingly cognitive and complex and not likely to be learned in the contemporary home and family setting. Both men and women have been conditioned culturally to perceive homemaking as women's work. With about one-half of all adult women in the work force, however, an unprecedented need exists for education of both men and women in family responsibilities. It cannot be a mother alone who takes on the prudent management of the family ecosystem that is essential to the future of human life. It is the family that determines and shapes the values essential to maintaining harmony between people and resources. Today, as never before, the functioning family needs to be understood, because it is undergoing extreme pressure. The family has the potential and awesome responsibility to shape the future through its everyday decisions and actions (Paolucci, 1978).

Home economists believe that an understanding of the role of nutrition and its application to daily living can be regarded as preventive medicine and is essential to the future of everyone, especially children. Nutrition education has been a topic of discussion for decades. Its importance is not questioned, but its implementation and success seem to defy general agreement (Baird, 1979). Research indicates that a large proportion of citizens in the United States are ignorant of even the most basic nutritional principles and that their poor dietary practices are adversely affecting their health (Byrd-Bredbenner, 1980). New ways of addressing nutrition education are needed.

Essentially, secondary school presents the last universal opportunity for parenthood education. Home economics educators share society's concern for its need. Concern over the effects of continual inflation and related economic problems that affect consumers has strengthened the impetus for teaching consumer education.

A very evident theme concerns the need for outreach programs for the elderly, school-age parents and single parents, the economically disadvantaged, and inmates of correctional facilities, thus extending home economics beyond the classroom to the larger community. In addition to the need for outreach is the need to serve in an integrated classroom those learners who are handicapped emotionally, physically, or mentally.

Over all these is the concern that home economics provide a diversified program that addresses varied needs with emphasis on those of greatest importance to the populations served. And with this concern is the pressing need for evaluating programs to look at their outcomes and consequences.

Research and Development Sponsorship. Systematic efforts to organize the subject matter of home economics at the secondary level began in 1961 under sponsorship of the USOE. Over a period of four years, a series of workshops brought together hundreds of home economists from secondary classrooms, state departments of education, and colleges and universities to identify concepts and generalizations which define the structure of home economics (East, 1980).

Home economists at a workshop at Iowa State University, sponsored by the American Home Economics Association, identified professional competencies in five conceptual areas: educational philosophy, professional role, program planning, educative process, and research. The report was published as *Competency-based Professional Education in Home Economics* (1974).

The American Home Economics Association sponsored a national workshop where home economists identified criteria for reaching specified competencies in professional education in home economics, resulting in the publication *Competencies for Home Economics Teachers* (1978). Partial financial support for publishing the material was provided by J. C. Penney Company, Inc., and the National Association of Teacher Educators in Home Economics of the American Vocational Association.

Home economics teacher educators have recognized that Competency-Based Teacher Education (CBTE) is dependent on adequate means to assess student competency and that there must be sufficient quality in the instruments developed to ensure ample information for decisions. Instruments for measuring the competencies to be developed were evaluated at a national working clinic held in Kansas City, Missouri, in 1976 and sponsored by the USOE; these have been published as *Instruments for Assessing Selected Professional Competencies for Home Economics Teachers by Home Economics Teacher Educators* (1978).

Curricula developed under federal funding include a four-part guide entitled *Consumer Education Curriculum Modules: A Spiral Process Approach* (Murphy, 1974). Four modules, designed for use with learners ranging from ninth-graders to adults, address the processes of becoming a critical consumer. A six-step spiral approach is used to provide repeated exposure to the processes at different levels of complexity and to provide teacher flexibility in responding to the changing interests and increasing ability of learners to deal with abstractions. Pretests and posttests are included, as is an overall behavior inventory identifying consumer competence level.

Researchers from Indiana, Ohio, and New York, under USOE funding, collaborated to develop and test two courses preparing disadvantaged pupils for homemaker and wage-earner roles (Nelson, Lowe, & Dalrymple, 1975). One was oriented to homemaking, and the other to preparation for jobs in food service at the entry level; both included orientation to the possible dual role of homemaker–wage earner. A three-week workshop prepared the selected teachers and refined curriculum materials.

Consumer-homemaking teachers at the Choctau adult education demonstration project (*Choctau Adult Education*, 1975), in Philadelphia sponsored by the Bureau of Adult, Vocational, and Technical Education of USOE, developed microunits in basic nutrition, food purchasing, dieting, money management, obtaining credit, budgeting, life insurance, and taxes for a disadvantaged population.

Federal funds supplied the support under which Lowe (1978) and her colleagues developed ten nongraded modules of competency-based curriculum for occupational areas. Results of field testing indicate that the modules are effective and can be used in varied situations.

More home economics curriculum materials have been developed under state funding than under federal funding. Kohlman et al. (1977), working in Iowa, developed and tested instructional procedures and techniques for teachers working with mildly handicapped pupils mainstreamed into eighth-grade and ninth-grade home economics classes, where essential skills to be learned were those of consumer behavior. The researchers' plan incorporated the use of activity centers with modules of self-directed activities to meet needs of both typical and mildly mentally and/or physically disabled pupils working together in heterogeneous groups. New Jersey teachers developed a handbook to help those working with mentally retarded students (*Home Economics and the Exceptional Student*, 1976). Conditions and desired outcomes were identified for each concept within four basic areas: personal development, interpersonal relations, home management, and child care. Ford (1976), in Minnesota, developed a total of 205 miniunits for coeducational classes in the middle school and junior high designed to be free of sex bias. In New York, Farris (1978) devised materials for, implemented, and evaluated an in-service program to encourage reduction of sex stereotyping by home economics and other vocational teachers. The program was carried out as a six-hour workshop. Pretesting showed sex-stereotyped perceptions of students; posttest results indicated little change in attitude. As it became clear that a six-hour workshop did little in changing deeply held attitudes, project emphasis shifted to exploring alternative workshop designs. A source book for conducting and assessing effectiveness of programs was produced.

Funds have not been available for evaluation research on a national level, and systematic state-level evaluations of outcomes for learners generally have been lacking. However, evaluation studies supported by state funds were carried out in Illinois and New York. Fults (1972) evaluated the 147 consumer-homemaking education programs in Illinois. Replies to a questionnaire from administrators (106), teachers of consumer-homemaking programs (136), and previously enrolled students (1,328 males and 2,933 females) indicated that major objectives of the programs were being met. A study commissioned by the Illinois State Office of Education (*Comparative Assessment of Secondary Consumer and Homemaking Education Programs, 1974–1975*, 1975) examined the effectiveness of the consumer education component of home economics programs and identified program aspects to which effectiveness could be attributed. Programs in 128 schools serving disadvantaged populations were studied. Students enrolled in the home economics programs scored significantly higher on the measures used than did control groups. Three program characteristics were significantly related to test performance: average length of course (in days), number of units developed, and number of units implemented. The high-achieving group had an average of 30 percent more instructional time than the low-achieving group.

A formative evaluation of ten outreach programs of homemaking and consumer education tailored to needs of low-income adults and out-of-school youth was carried out in New York (Nelson, Jacoby, & Shannon, 1978). Techniques used to gather evidence of participant progress toward program objectives included interviews, ratings, recordings of critical incidents, systematic observations, and records of attendance and activities. Gains in knowledge and attitude were significantly higher for high-exposure participants than for those with low exposure in the area of clothing and textiles; significant gains in personal development were found for participants in eight of the ten centers. Teachers reported application of learning in all subject areas and increased use of community services.

Effect of Social Conditions. Curriculum development in home economics education continues to focus on the family as a continuing but changing social unit and on identified trends and conditions in society which impinge on it. The women's movement has been of influence. The period is one of rapid social change, newly developing values related to sexuality, blurring of male-female roles, and emphasis on self-fulfillment. Women have moved into the world of paid employment outside the home in increasing numbers. There is a need for teaching those skills necessary in operating a home while holding a job, and for providing education in sharing homemaking skills for males who have begun to express more interest in the fathering role and in their rights and responsibilities (Hughes, 1979).

Inflation has brought an intensified need, especially among young families and increasing numbers of families in retirement, for education in the skills crucial for resource management. Many American adults have been shown not to possess the consumer skills necessary to utilize resources efficiently in management of a family's economy (Northcutt et al., 1975). Results of studies by nutritionists and home economics educators have suggested that renewed efforts with new strategies are needed in nutrition education. There is mounting concern over the current degree of documented family violence, particularly child and wife abuse and child neglect. Although birthrates for the population at large have fallen, conception among teenage girls has increased dramatically. Of concern are the serious health difficulties faced by the pregnant teenager, frequent lack of prenatal care, danger of infant mortality, and possible ill effects of prematurity to the baby (Simpson, 1979).

Accountability for the effect home economics curricula and programs have on their learners has prompted program evaluation and development of competency-based teacher-preparation materials. The identification of the structure of knowledge of home economics subject matter and home economics teacher preparation begun in 1961 has continued as an important influence in curriculum development (Nelson, 1979).

Curriculum Development. Hughes (1969) developed a month-long curriculum unit, complete with all materials needed for implementation. It particularly emphasized management problems associated with the dual role of homemaker and wage earner and factors involved in deciding on employment, costs of employment, and provision for child care. Murphy (1974) developed a curriculum to teach consumers to question and evaluate purchases critically. Ford (1976) designed miniunits for use with boys and girls in middle-school classes.

Beavers (1979) identified common and unique competencies for postsecondary programs in fashion merchandising, fashion design, apparel services, and window-treatment services. White (1972) studied curricula of technical-level associate degree and certificate child-development programs to determine potential for incorporating a lattice-ladder concept of career mobility. Based on information from this study, she designed a broad curriculum to enhance flexibility on the job and the adaptability needed to work in related areas. Lowe (1978) devised competency-based teaching modules for home economics occupations.

Needs of learners. In an era where the concerns addressed by home economics are issues of national priority, needs of learners especially to be noted are those related to nutrition education, preparation for parenthood, and management of resources.

A statewide needs assessment mandated by the amendments to the Child Nutrition Act (Public Law 95-166) provided data on nutritional status, food habits, and nutrition-related health problems of a stratified random sample of

Oklahoma schoolchildren in grades K–12. Results of the survey provided a basis for the conclusion that Oklahoma children and adolescents need nutrition education. Nearly 20 percent of the students ate no breakfast on the survey day; their reports of food eaten indicated that two-thirds did not have adequate diets. There was no relationship between knowledge of the basic 4 food groups and adequate diet for students in the study (Baird, 1979). Research by Schwartz (1975) on a random sample of female graduates of randomly selected Ohio high schools indicated that these young women did not apply nutritional knowledge to their choice of food.

Because of increasing adolescent pregnancies and marriages, parenthood education programs for secondary school students are growing in numbers. Mentally disabled students are being mainstreamed into these programs. Adams (1980) reported perceptions of such students in randomly selected Iowa schools regarding the need for parenting information. Among needs mentioned, these students gave highest priority to information about the costs of raising children, the responsibilities of parents, and the nature of marriage.

Petrich, Henning, and Rodman (1972) attempted to determine the life skills graduates of vocational and technical programs in Wisconsin perceived as necessary. Survey responses from 1,300 graduates indicated that unfilled needs were those related to communication skills, consumer skills, combining work life and family life, and teaching children about reproduction and marriage. Findings from the Adult Functional Competency Study by Northcutt et al. (1975) indicated that some 34.7 million adult Americans were functioning with difficulty in coping with basic requirements related to consumer economics. Braun (1979) carried out an assessment of competency levels of elderly learners. Thirty-five percent of those studied who were 60 to 65 years of age were rated as functioning with difficulty in five areas of competency. Miller's study (1978) of elderly adults resulted in recommendations that programs for this population focus on problems related to home ownership, the practical and legal problems of earnings and retirement income, and consumer rights.

To develop a curriculum for teaching life skills to prepare incarcerated men and women for reintegration into society, researchers at Florida International University identified from inmates these most wanted skills: understanding personal and social relationships, understanding human sexuality and birth control, improving personal appearance, and managing money (Crabtree, 1980).

Special needs. Whiteford (1979) designed and adapted individualized instructional materials emphasizing nutrition and enhancement of self-image for students with special needs in junior high school home economics classes. Durr and Bell (1980) surveyed teachers who had handicapped students in their classes to identify problems and possible ways to deal with them. Teachers' contributions resulted in a manual describing services and materials. Curriculum developers at Florida State University

(Pestle, 1978; Wilcox & Pestle, 1980) prepared, tested, and found effective programmed units for secondary students dealing with needs of the elderly in relation to nutrition, food purchasing, food management, and housekeeping. Managing Independent Living, a program developed for adult female offenders in state residential correctional facilities designed to help with transition from a dependent life-style, was implemented by group and individualized instruction and use of community resources. The curriculum guide, developed over a period of eight years, presents activities and references appropriate for persons with less developed and more developed reading and cognitive skills. Emphasis is on decision making, communications skills, and management. In the correctional facility testsite, it was determined that the program could be carried out for less than the average cost of maintaining one woman for one year (Thomas, 1980).

Conway (1979) developed a course to prepare teachers for helping with reading problems of students in secondary school home economics classrooms by incorporating teaching of reading skills with presentation of home economics subject matter. Exploratory-study results indicated that such preservice help for teachers can make a beneficial difference in student learning. Krieger (1978) produced a multimedia learning experience to help teachers be responsive to and deal skillfully with visually impaired learners. From contributions of vocational home economics educators in Wisconsin, Dougherty (1977) compiled a volume of program procedures, educational strategies, and teaching materials useful in programs for the disadvantaged. Some curriculum materials were specifically designed for special-needs learners: those preparing disadvantaged pupils for homemaker and wage-earner roles (Nelson, Lowe, & Dalrymple, 1975) and the modules of self-directed activities by Kohlman et al. (1977).

Needs of teachers. Carpenter (1978) surveyed preparation of home economics teachers for working with mainstreamed children, finding that the majority lacked any preservice training for this responsibility, though most expressed themselves strongly as needing help. Redick (1974), studying the needs of teachers of the physically handicapped, identified these as developing and adapting curriculum, understanding needs of handicapped students, and individualizing instruction.

Program content and instrument development. A national study was initiated in 1978, designed and carried out by home economics educators to identify what was taught and who were served by home economics programs (Hughes, Rougvie, & Woods, 1980). The population for the study consisted of all public schools in states and territories agreeing to participate. A stratified sample with systematic selection within strata but with varying sampling rates was drawn; 1,662 schools in 41 states provided data. Coon (1962) had found earlier that about two-thirds of the periods in a typical program were devoted to foods and nutrition, and clothing and textiles. The 1980 report concluded that vocational consumer and homemaking programs in secondary schools in the United States included necessary content. Recommended adjustments within secondary programs were directed toward providing critical home economics content for greater numbers of students. Data from the study by Mears, Ley, and Ray (1981) confirmed the inclusion of nutritional knowledge and food use, parenthood education, management of resources, and consumer education in the sample of programs they examined.

Several measurement devices have been developed by home economics educators. Some were produced for use in specific research studies but appear to have broader applicability. Home economics education measurement specialists produced tests to assess children's achievement of nutrition concepts designated important by the 1969 White House Conference on Food, Nutrition, and Health (Fanslow, Brun, & Hausafus, 1979). The tests were used with 240 pupils in 16 schools across the United States at each grade level, K–6, representing low-, middle-, and high-socioeconomic groups. McCall (1973) produced two 100-item tests for use in grades 7–12 based on the guidelines for consumer education developed by the staff of the President's 1970 Committee on Consumer Interest. Weis (1979a) developed 6 criterion-referenced devices judged valid to measure student achievement of cognitive, affective, and psychomotor objectives of food service education. Field trials for 4 of them have demonstrated high reliability. McClelland (1980) developed a rating scale for parenting behaviors, assessing the parent's management of the physical environment, interaction with a baby, and an interview schedule focusing on parental behaviors and the reasons given for them.

Instruments have been developed for use in evaluating preservice home economics teachers' competencies. A series of studies by Gilbert (1974), Caputo (1975), and Fanslow, Caputo, and Hughes (1979) identified indexes useful and reliable in examining teacher effectiveness. Brun (1970) developed and tested a system featuring a structured tally sheet for observing, recording, and analyzing teacher behaviors occurring in a classroom setting that stimulate student cognitive responses. Murphy's spiral curriculum for consumer education included criterion-referenced assessment devices for each of its modules (Murphy, 1974). The Illinois Test of Consumer Knowledge (ITOCK) was developed for the Illinois Comparative Assessment of Secondary Consumer and Homemaking programs (*Comparative Assessment*, 1975).

Bias and sex stereotyping. The Vocational Education Act of 1976 called attention to the need for programs of vocational education that would overcome sex discrimination, encourage elimination of sex stereotyping, and deal with the changing roles of men and women. Bell and Durr (1980) studied responses from a sample of 4,033 male high school students enrolled in randomly selected schools throughout Texas. Data indicated that approximately two-thirds of the males encountered no problems related to attitudes toward enrollment in homemaking classes, to

suitable facilities, and to instructional materials. They perceived homemaking education as useful in the achievement of personal and career goals. Ott et al. (1980) gathered information from a sample of approximately 800 tenth-grade occupational students, their parents, and counselors in thirty-seven schools in New York State. Boys indicated only limited support for traditional "female" courses. Parents indicated sex-stereotyped attitudes, and students perceived these accurately.

Weis (1979b) reviewed home economics textbooks published between 1964 and 1974, still being used in classrooms, for sex bias and stereotyping. It was evident that clothing and textiles, and foods and nutrition texts were female-oriented. Human-development and family-relationship texts distributed orientations more equitably. Unroe's examination of textbooks currently used in home economics focused on subtle forms of sex bias (Unroe, 1977). Most of the texts did not appear to show women's role in a manner consistent with reality. There was little indication that the majority of women were not full-time homemakers, and none that they were also often heads of families. There was little allusion to the fact that often women work at a paid job and operate a household. Careers were seen as separate from homemaking and not as a major role to be correlated with household activities. Females were not shown as having a wide variety of employment possibilities. Analysis of home economics career texts found that women were not shown in careers involving authority, seniority, career commitment, or good wage scales. They were shown in low-status occupations.

Studies of effectiveness. A few large-scale studies examining program effectiveness are noted in the section on sponsored research (Fults, 1972; *Comparative Assessment*, 1975; Nelson, Lowe, & Dalrymple, 1975; Nelson, Jacoby, & Shannon, 1978).

Using naturalistic methods, seven secondary home economics programs identified as effective were examined through in-depth case studies (Mears, Ley, & Ray, 1981). Teachers appeared to be the key factor; students saw them as concerned about students, and teachers in turn cared about students and what they learned. Curricula provided relevant contemporary experiences.

Statewide follow-up studies of completers of secondary school child-care services programs gave evidence that comparatively few were employed in the occupation for which they had been trained. Respondents believed that their training had been good but generally felt that guidance counselors had not helped them in occupational choice and that neither child-care services teachers nor other school personnel had helped them find jobs (Butler, 1971; Gasper, 1977; Dennison, 1978).

Enrollment. USOE home economics enrollment data for 1975 showed a total of 3,283,857 students at secondary, adult, and postsecondary levels. Of this number, 926,241 (28 percent) were males. Enrollment data reported for the 1978/79 school year for a randomly selected national sample of secondary home economics programs indicated that 19 percent of students were male (Hughes, Rougvie, & Woods, 1980), an encouraging increase over the slightly more than 1 percent males in secondary home economics programs reported for 1959 (Coon, 1962). Data concerning statewide enrollment were available from two states: in Texas, for 1978/79, over one-quarter million persons were enrolled, with 31.2 percent of these males (Bell & Durr, 1980); in Iowa, data for 1976 indicated a total secondary and adult home economics enrollment of 84,042, with males making up 16 percent of this figure (Hughes, 1979). A survey of enrollment in Minnesota identified nearly 9 percent of females and over 14 percent of males in the sample of secondary home economics programs as having special needs (Whiteford, 1976). An estimated 590,000 students nationally (male and female) were enrolled in secondary occupational home economics programs in 1979 (Weis, Carlos, & Kreutzer, 1980). Membership in the Future Homemakers of America, an integral part of consumer-homemaking programs, was given in 1980 as more than 400,000 in 12,000 chapters (Walton & Howard, 1980).

Research Summaries. Home economics educators have regularly reviewed the research in home economics education. Early publications were those of Spafford and Amidon (Spafford & Amidon, 1959; Amidon & Spafford, 1960). Since 1966, a series of reviews have been published under the sponsorship of the National Center for Research in Vocational Education at Ohio State University (Chadderdon & Fanslow, 1966; Gorman & Magisos, 1970; Nelson, 1970; Bailey, 1971; Gorman & Manning, 1971; Nelson, 1979).

Special Problems. More research on the process of teaching home economics than on the results of teaching it has been possible with what limited funds have been available (Nelson, 1979). Longitudinal studies on completers of consumer-homemaking programs emphasizing behaviors that affect the quality of life are needed. Researchers have examined the impact of newly developed curricula, but not all have monitored or reported the adequacy or integrity with which the curricula were implemented. Home economics education researchers are only beginning to initiate the naturalistic, ethnographic studies that should allow close observation of variations among programs and offer learner perceptions of programs as well as a holistic view of outcomes.

There is a pressing need for leadership at the national level. A single home economics educator carries the responsibility for home economics in the U.S. Department of Education. Concern, stemming from this need, that broad and comprehensive research programs would not be undertaken led to the establishment of an Ad Hoc Committee on Research formed by the Policy and Planning Committee of the Home Economics Division of the American Vocational Association. Members of this committee have taken the initiative and responsibility for proposing a broad structure to indicate the scope of research needed in home economics education in order to describe accurately, evaluate, and give direction to programs. Priorities

in items of research that are needed, in terms of both chronological order and identifying basic structure necessary to support later research, have been considered. Efforts are currently under way to establish a network within home economics education for enhancing communication about research needs, research priorities, and collaboration in data collection and research. The National Census Study was the first research study sponsored by the Ad Hoc Committee (Hughes, Rougvie, & Woods, 1980). Others are under way.

Home economics is considered a field of service or action; its questions or problems are those that concern the home and family. Its subject matter derives from many disciplines, the selection and organization of such subject matter being determined by the problems the profession seeks to solve. In home economics education the entire focus of attention is on the concerns of the family and its social conditions. This special attention has been justified over the years on the grounds that the family, as a significant social institution in which most people participate for most of their lives, deserves at least as much thought and knowledge as other arenas of action in which people engage (Brown, 1980). Home economics programs contain subject matter that has been documented as needed by our society, most particularly by those who are least advantaged (Hughes, 1979).

Census data and reports of research document changes in form and style of family life. Divorce has doubled since 1960. Estimated on current trends, one of every three persons between the ages of 25 and 35 married for the first time in 1975 will be divorced; about two of every five of those who divorce and remarry will have their second marriage also end in divorce. Illegitimate births have increased since 1950. Households made up of unmarried men and women living together doubled from 1970 to 1976. Households headed by a female increased 33 percent whereas households of married couples increased only 9 percent (St. Marie, 1977).

Wives and mothers have moved into paid employment outside the home. Not only has a cumulative change occurred in women's involvement in the labor market, but the average work life expectancy of women has increased by more than one-half since 1950. A sense of seriousness about their occupational involvements is apparent among women. Greater importance is attached to education and counseling influences that affect life choices and career decisions (Weis, Carlos, & Kreutzer, 1980).

Essential competencies needed by both male and female homemakers include those related to responsibilities of parenthood and interpersonal relationships, management of resources, and attending to nutritional needs of individuals. Parenting is the most crucial of these (Cross, 1979). More than one-third of mothers of preschool children are in the labor force and one-half are the mothers of school-age children. An estimated two out of every five children born in the 1970s will live in a single-parent family for at least part of their childhoods. Kinship networks have weakened; brothers and sisters are increasingly scarce (the statistically average child has less than one). Increasing numbers of "latch key" children are growing up with no care in the hours after school except perhaps the electronic parent that occupies more waking hours of American children than any other single influence (Kenniston, 1976). In 1976, one girl in ten was a mother before her eighteenth birthday. Children are having children. Their biological readiness to parent has been called into question (Boss & Hooper, 1980).

Our societal setting has generated unprecedented nutritional problems. The myth of the excellence of the American diet has been debunked. The safety and nutritional value of our highly processed and quickly prepared food have been questioned. Nutritional ills of poverty and affluence have been pointed out. Obesity affects one-fifth or more of the population. Our characteristic dietary patterns have been linked to six of the ten leading causes of death: heart disease, stroke, cancer, diabetes, arteriosclerosis, and cirrhosis of the liver, with obesity a compounding variable in several. Specifically implicated as associative factors are our excessive consumption of fat, cholesterol, sugar, and salt. Prevention must become a major objective, with nutrition education providing programs synthesizing emphasis on prevention with the traditional focus on dietary adequacy. Educational strategies will necessarily be aimed at attitude and behavior change (Devine, 1977).

The 1970s reintroduced many people to the concepts of scarcity and economic uncertainty. It is likely that families will continue to be faced with increasing demands on their resources and increasingly complex economic decisions in the 1980s. Rapidly changing and unpredictable economic conditions bring substantial and devastating changes for many individuals and families because they threaten expectation of continuous improvement in level of living (Robinson, 1977). Employment of a second earner in the family is a change that brings money resources but reduces time and skill resources within the household. Studies have shown the inequity of an average seventy-hour work week for women combining paid work and homemaker roles when husbands and children "help" rather than share family responsibilities (Walker, 1976).

Home economics educators have such responsibilities as emphasizing socialization of children toward energy-efficient future lives; focusing studies on energy and the food system, from production to waste disposal; and exploring for clothing and housing the energy implications of production, retailing, maintenance, and product use (Maas et al., 1978). Such dramatic changes point to the necessity of teaching management processes: knowing values, setting goals, developing resources, making plans, and assessing progress.

Research Needs. Immediately needed in research are examination of the effect of home economics programs in the lives of learners and identification of criteria against which effectiveness is to be determined. Longitudinal studies of homemaking students are needed. Addressing such problems as the unique needs of teenage parents, management of the home after a workday spent in outside employment, management of single-parent households, impact on families of social policies relating to child care outside the home, school feeding programs, and health care delivery should be considered. New approaches to nutrition education are needed. Continuing development of curriculum and teaching materials is desirable, especially of those materials that meet the needs of today's homemakers and make a special effort to avoid a white, middle-class, female orientation. Systematic accounting of the extent to which home economics programs serve various targeted populations should be a part of record keeping. In school programs, these would include handicapped and otherwise disadvantaged students, teenage parents, and males; in outreach programs, they would include low-income families, the elderly, and single parents.

As of 1976, no studies had addressed the question of effectiveness at the national level; very few had been done on a regional or statewide basis. Funding for such research has not been available. In the Education Amendments of 1976 to the Vocational Education Act, Congress asked the National Institute of Education to undertake a "thorough evaluation and study of vocational education programs including those of consumer and homemaking." These studies are currently under way. Inquiry is directed toward the effectiveness of consumer homemaking programs, as well as toward the use of vocational education funds—what they buy, whom they serve—and their compliance with legislation that implicitly recognizes the changing roles of men and women, the unprecedented movement of large numbers of women into the labor force, and the changing nature of family life (Hendrickson & David, 1980).

Much of the research in the last decade has been devoted to teacher preparation. Home economics researchers have studied professional education and practices of teachers, learning processes, and teaching methods; and needs, characteristics, and interests of those to be taught. Many have focused on identification and attainment of teacher competencies and developed instruments for their testing. Others have produced and pilot tested curriculum and teaching materials.

Under the encouragement of the Ad Hoc Committee on Research, a surge of research has taken place in the last two years. Communication about research needs and research possibilities has been enhanced. Cooperative research projects have been initiated. Under way currently, in the planning, or the data-gathering, or the report-writing stages, are several projects: a study to determine effectiveness of parent education programs; one to determine outcomes for mildly handicapped students learning parent education, consumer education, and nutrition concepts; studies preliminary to longitudinal research on outcomes for homemaking education students; and pilot studies of program completers using ethnographic methods.

Helen Y. Nelson

See also Consumer Economics Education; Health Education; Nutrition Education; Parent Education; Vocational Education.

REFERENCES

Adams, D. U. *Parenting Needs of Iowa Minimally and Mildly Mentally Disabled Teenagers.* Unpublished master's thesis, Iowa State University, 1980.

Amidon, E., & Spafford, I. *Studies of Home Economics in High School and in Adult Education Programs, 1955–1958.* Washington, D.C.: United States Office of Education, 1960.

Bailey, L. C. *Review and Synthesis of Research on Consumer and Homemaking Education* (Information Series No. 33). Columbus: Ohio State University, Center for Vocational and Technical Education, 1971. (ERIC Document Reproduction Service No. ED 048 482)

Baird, J. *Nutrition Education: A Needs Assessment for Oklahoma.* Stillwater: Oklahoma State University, Division of Home Economics, 1979.

Baldwin, K. E. *The AHEA Saga.* Washington, D.C.: American Home Economics Association, 1949.

Beavers, I. *Standards for Postsecondary Programs in Textiles and Clothing.* Ames: Iowa State University, Department of Home Economics Education, 1979.

Bell, C. G., & Durr, G. E. *An Analysis of Problems Perceived by Male Students Enrolled in Vocational Homemaking Education: Final Report.* Austin: Department of Occupational and Technical Education, Research Coordinating Unit, 1980.

Boss, P. G., & Hooper, J. O. Teaching adolescents about parenthood. *Journal of Home Economics,* Summer 1980, *58,* 40–42, 58.

Braun, B. S. *Consumer Knowledge of Older Women.* Unpublished doctoral dissertation, University of Missouri, 1979.

Brown, M. M. *What Is Home Economics Education?* Minneapolis: University of Minnesota, Department of Vocational and Technical Education, 1980.

Brun, J. K. K. *An Observational Method for Studying Classroom Cognitive Processes.* Unpublished doctoral dissertation, Iowa State University, 1970.

Butler, S. E. *A Follow-up Study of New York State Child Care Services Graduates, 1966–1970.* Unpublished master's thesis, Cornell University, 1971.

Byrd-Bredbenner, C. *The Interrelationships of Nutrition Knowledge, Attitudes toward Nutrition, Dietary Behavior, and Commitment to the Concern for Nutrition Education.* Unpublished doctoral dissertation, Pennsylvania State University, 1980.

Caputo, C. C. *Validation of a Teaching Performance Device.* Unpublished doctoral dissertation, Iowa State University, 1975.

Carpenter, B. W. *Selected Educators' Perceptions toward the Study of Mainstreaming in Home Economics Programs.* Unpublished doctoral dissertation, Kansas State University at Manhattan, 1978.

Chadderdon, H., & Fanslow, A. M. *Review and Synthesis of Research in Home Economics Education.* Columbus: Ohio State University, Center for Research and Leadership Development in Vocational and Technical Education, 1966. (ERIC Document Reproduction Service No. ED 011 563)

Choctau Adult Education Demonstration Project: Final Report (Vol. 2, A 309 B). Washington, D.C.: Department of Health, Education, and Welfare, United States Office of Education, Bureau of Adult, Vocational, and Technical Education, 1975. (ERIC Document Reproduction Service No. ED 133 112)

Comparative Assessment of Secondary Consumer and Homemaking Education Programs, 1974–1975 (Final report). Durham, N.C.: IBEX, Inc. Springfield: Illinois State Office of Education, 1975. (ERIC Document Reproduction Service No. ED 126 285)

Competencies for Home Economics Teachers. Ames: Iowa State University Press, 1978.

Competency-based Professional Education in Home Economics. Washington, D.C.: American Home Economics Association, 1974. (ERIC Document Reproduction Service No. ED 109 480)

Conway, E. D. *The Development and Assessment of a Course on Teaching Reading Skills for Home Economics Preservice Teachers.* Unpublished doctoral dissertation, Cornell University, 1979.

Coon, B. *Home Economics in Public Secondary Schools: A Report of a National Study.* Washington, D.C.: U.S. Office of Education, 1962.

Crabtree, M. P. Home economists in correctional education: A new area to explore. *Journal of Home Economics,* Winter 1980, *72,* 42–44.

Crawford, G. C. *Impact of Iowa Secondary Vocational Home Economics Programs with Emphasis on Consumer Education.* Unpublished doctoral dissertation, Iowa State University, 1980.

Cross, A. A. Assessment of consumer and homemaking education. In *The Planning Papers on Consumer and Homemaking Education Programs* (Vocational Education Study Publication No. 2). Washington, D.C.: U.S. Government Printing Office, 1979. (ERIC Document Reproduction Service No. ED 171 960)

Dennison, L. B. *Factors Affecting Employment in Related Occupations of 1975–1976 Completers of Secondary Occupational Child-care Programs in Virginia.* Unpublished doctoral dissertation, Virginia Polytechnic Institute and State University, 1978.

Devine, M. M. Ecology of human nutrition: Systems and synergisms. In *Proceedings of a Conference on Living in America: Home Economics for the Third Century.* Ithaca: Cornell University, New York State College of Human Ecology, Department of Community Service Education, 1977.

Dougherty, B. *Wisconsin Consumer and Homemaking Programs: Compilation of Program Procedures, Educational Strategies, and Teaching Materials Related to Consumer and Homemaking Programs in Wisconsin* (Final report of Project No. 19-00-2151-527). Madison: Board of Vocational, Technical, and Adult Education, 1977. (ERIC Document Reproduction Service No. ED 151 554)

Durr, G. E., & Bell, C. G. *Mainstreaming the Handicapped Student in Vocational Home Economics: Final Report.* Austin: Texas Education Agency, Department of Occupational Education and Technology, Research Coordinating Unit, 1980.

East, M. *Home Economics: Past, Present, and Future.* Boston: Allyn & Bacon, 1980.

Fanslow, A. M.; Brun, J. K.; & Hausafus, C. *Nutrition Achievement Tests, Kindergarten to Sixth Grade.* Rosemount, Ill.: National Dairy Council, 1979.

Fanslow, A. M.; Caputo, C.; & Hughes, R. P. Reliable assessment of home economics teachers' behaviors. *Journal of Vocational Education Research,* Winter 1979, *4,* 1–2.

Farris, C. J. *A Pilot Project: Inservice for Reducing Sex Stereotyping in Vocational Education.* Albany: New York State Education Department, Bureau of Home Economics Education, 1978.

Ford, R. *Middle School/Junior High Coeducational Mini-units in Home Economics.* St. Paul: Minnesota State Department of Education, Division of Vocational and Technical Education, 1976.

Fults, A. C. *Evaluation of Special Consumer-Homemaking Programs in Illinois High Schools*. Carbondale: Southern Illinois University, School of Home Economics, 1972. (ERIC Document Reproduction Service No. ED 118 866)

Gasper, S. G. *A Study of Programs of Occupational Home Economics*. Unpublished doctoral dissertation, University of Kentucky, 1977.

Gilbert, A. L. *Changes over Time in Judged Competencies of Home Economics Student Teachers*. Unpublished doctoral dissertation, Iowa State University, 1974.

Gorman, A. M., & Magisos, J. H. *Bibliography of Research on Consumer and Homemaking Education*. Columbus: Ohio State University Press, 1970. (ERIC Document Reproduction Service No. ED 039 336)

Gorman, A. M., & Manning, D. E. *A Listing of Data Collection Devices for Use in Research in Home Economics Education, 1962–1969*. Columbus: Ohio State University, Center for Vocational and Technical Education, 1971. (ERIC Document Reproduction Service No. ED 050 275)

Hendrickson, G., & David, H. Vocational education study: A policy inquiry. *Journal of Home Economics*, Spring 1980, *72*, 14–16.

Home Economics and the Exceptional Student: A Handbook for Home Economics Teachers Working with Mentally Retarded Students. New Brunswick: Rutgers, State University of New Jersey, and New Jersey State Education Department, Division of Vocational Education, 1976. (ERIC Document Reproduction Service No. ED 128 602)

Hughes, R. P. Development and evaluation of a curriculum package on preparation for a dual role. *Journal of Home Economics*, 1969, *61*, 350–358.

Hughes, R. P. Consumer and homemaking education today: An analysis. In *The Planning Papers on Consumer and Homemaking Education Programs* (Vocational Education Study Publication No. 2). Washington, D.C.: U.S. Government Printing Office, 1979.

Hughes, R. P. Consumer and Homemaking education: Do we know the effects? *Voc Ed*, September 1980, *55*, 46–49.

Hughes, R. P.; Rougvie, B.; & Woods, B. *The National Census Study of Secondary Vocational Consumer and Homemaking Programs*. Ames: Iowa State University Research Foundation, Inc., 1980.

Instruments for Assessing Selected Professional Competencies for Home Economics Teachers by Home Economics Teacher Educators. Ames: Iowa State University Press, 1978.

Kenniston, K. The emptying family. *New York Times*, February 18, 1976.

Kohlman, E. L.; Rougvie, B. S.; Davison, J. A.; and Schultz, J. B. *Procedures for Teaching Skills for Living in Classes Where Mildly Handicapped Pupils Are Integrated with Nonhandicapped Pupils: Final Report*. Des Moines, Iowa: Department of Public Instruction, Career Education Division, 1977.

Krieger, M. M. W. *Selected Instructional Techniques to Create Change of Attitude toward Blindness of Pre- and In-service Vocational Home Economics Teachers*. Unpublished doctoral dissertation, University of Michigan, 1978.

Lowe, P. K. Curriculum development in occupational Home Economics: An AHEA/OE project. *Journal of Home Economics*, March 1978, *70*, 39–41. (EJ 180 843)

Maas, B.; Morrison, P. M.; Gladhart, J. J.; Zuiches, J. G.; Keith, D. K.; & Long, B. R. Energy and families: The crisis and the

response. *Journal of Home Economics*, Winter 1978, *5*, 18–21.

McCall, C. L. *Development of a Test for Assessing Competency in Consumer Education*. Unpublished doctoral dissertation, Pennsylvania State University, 1973.

McClelland, J. A. *Evaluation of Parenthood Education Components of Vocational Home Economics Programs in Iowa*. Doctoral dissertation, Iowa State University at Ames, 1980.

Mears, R. A.; Ley, C. J.; & Ray, E. M. *Dimensions of Home Economics Programs: Seven Case Studies*. University Park: Pennsylvania State University, Division of Occupational Vocational Studies, 1981.

Miller, N. H. *Consumer Behavior and Consumer Attitudes of the Elderly: A Descriptive Profile and Program Implications*. Unpublished doctoral dissertation, University of Wisconsin, 1978.

Murphy, P. D. *Consumer Education Curriculum Modules: A Spiral Process Approach*. Fargo: North Dakota State University, 1974. (ERIC Document Reproduction Service No. ED 095 267-271)

Nelson, H. Y. Home economics. In R. Ebel (Ed.), *Encyclopedia of Educational Research* (4th ed.). New York: Macmillan, 1969.

Nelson, H. Y. *Review and Synthesis of Research on Home Economics Education* (Research Series No. 57). Columbus: Ohio State University, 1970. (ERIC Document Reproduction Service No. ED 038 519)

Nelson, H. Y. *Home Economics Education: A Review and Synthesis of the Research* (Information Series No. 184). Columbus: Ohio State University, National Center for Research in Vocational Education, 1979. (ERIC Document Reproduction Service No. ED 179 768)

Nelson, H. Y.; Jacoby, G. P.; & Shannon, T. M. Evaluation of consumer and homemaking education programs for low-income adults. *Home Economics Research Journal*, March 1978, *6*, 223–241. (ERIC Document Reproduction Service No. ED 180 863)

Nelson, H. Y.; Lowe, P. K.; & Dalrymple, J. I. Preparing disadvantaged pupils for homemaker and wage-earner roles. *Home Economics Research Journal*, December 1975, *4*, 103–114.

Northcutt, N.; Selz, N.: Shelton, E.; & Nyer, L. *Adult Functional Competency: A Summary*. Austin: University of Texas, 1975.

Ott, M. D.; Carmichael, M. M.; Gallup, J. M.; Lewis, G. L.; Russ, A. J.; & Veres, H. C. *The Identification of Factors Associated with Sex-role Stereotyping in Occupational Education*. Ithaca, New York: Cornell University, Cornell Institute for Occupational Education, 1980. (ERIC Document Reproduction Service No. ED 186 671)

Paolucci, B. Energy decisions and quality living. *Journal of Home Economics*, Winter 1978, *70*, 22–23.

Pestle, R. E. *Adaptations of Homemaking Skills for the Aged: Curriculum Materials*. Tallahassee: State of Florida Department of Education, 1978.

Petrich, B.; Henning, J.; & Rodman, N. *Assessment of Felt Needs for Preparation in "Life Skills" of Graduates of Diploma and Associate Degree Programs in the Wisconsin Vocational, Technical, and Adult Education System*. Madison: University of Wisconsin, School of Family Resources and Consumer Sciences, Department of Home Economics Education and Extension, 1972. (ERIC Document Reproduction Service No. ED 151 728)

Redick, S. S. *Selected Characteristics of Home Economics Teachers and Programs for Physically Handicapped Students*. Unpublished doctoral dissertation, Iowa State University, 1974.

Richards, E. H. Ten years of Lake Placid conferences on "Home economics: Its history and aims." In *Proceedings of the Tenth Annual Lake Placid Conference on Home Economics,* 1908.

Robinson, J. R. Changing needs in financial management. In *Proceedings of a Conference on Living in America: Home Economics Education for the Third Century.* Ithaca: Cornell University, New York State College of Human Ecology, Department of Community Service Education, 1977.

Schwartz, N. Nutrition knowledge, attitudes, and practices of high school graduates. *Journal of the American Dietetic Association,* 1975, *66,* 28–31.

Simpson, E. J. Legislation for consumer and homemaking education: Social implications. In *The Planning Papers on Consumer and Homemaking Education Programs* (Vocational Education Study Publication No 2). Washington, D.C.: U.S. Government Printing Office, 1979.

Spafford, I., & Amidon, E. *Studies on the Teaching of Home Economics in Colleges and Universities.* Washington, D.C.: U.S. Office of Education, 1959.

St. Marie, S. S. Societal impacts on families of the future: Implications for home economics education. In *Proceedings of a Conference on Living in America: Home Economics Education for the Third Century.* Ithaca: Cornell University, New York State College of Human Ecology, Department of Community Service Education, 1977.

Thomas, R. G. *De-institutionalization: Managing Independent Living.* St. Paul: University of Minnesota, Division of Home Economics Education, 1980.

Unroe, J. D. *An Examination of Selected Aspects of Sexist Bias in Home Economics Textbooks.* Unpublished master's thesis, Florida State University, 1977.

Walker, K. E., & Woods, M. E. *Time Use: A Measure of Household Production of Family Goods and Services.* Washington, D.C.: American Home Economics Association, Center for the Family, 1976.

Walton, L., & Howard, P. The student connection. *Voc Ed,* November–December 1980, *55,* 40–43.

Weis, S. F. *Evaluation Materials for Food Service Instructional Programs in Pennsylvania.* University Park: Pennsylvania State University, Division of Occupational and Vocational Studies, 1979. (a)

Weis, S. F. Examination of home economics textbooks for sex bias. *Home Economics Research Journal,* 1979, *7,* 147–162. (b)

Weis, S. F. Home economics jobs: Undervalued, underpaid. *Omicron Nu Newsletter,* November 1980, *2,* 3.

Weis, S. F.; Carlos, A.; & Kreutzer, J. R. *Foundations of Occupational Home Economics.* Washington, D.C.: Home Economics Education Association, 1980.

White, J. G. *The Lattice-ladder Concept Applied to Child Development Programs in Technical Programs.* Unpublished doctoral dissertation, Ohio State University, 1972.

Whiteford, E. B. *Special Needs Students in Regular Home Economics Programs: 1976 Survey of Selected Minnesota Secondary School Teachers.* St. Paul: Minnesota State Department of Education, 1976. (ERIC Document Reproduction Service No. ED 131 277)

Whiteford, E. B. *Individualized Instructional Materials for Special Needs Students in Junior High School Home Economics Programs.* St. Paul: University of Minnesota, Division of Home Economics Education, 1979.

Wilcox, C. F., & Pestle, R. E. Secondary school usage of instructional materials on nutrition and aging. *Journal of Nutrition for the Elderly,* Spring 1980, *1,* 55–63.

HOME-SCHOOL RELATIONSHIPS

The home and school are dominant forces in the lives of most persons until young adulthood. Consistent with a long-standing belief in American society that children benefit if teachers and parents work together, much has been said and written exhorting teachers and parents to form harmonious relationships. Recent research has focused primarily upon three topics. The first topic is the current status of home-school relationships; the beliefs and opinions of parents and teachers regarding the frequency and manner of home-school interaction. The second topic concerns the problems that hamper the parent-teacher relationship, including the barriers to achieving effective relationships. The third topic considers the effectiveness of the various approaches in increasing quantity and improving quality of parent-teacher interaction, along with the anticipated consequences of changing or improving relationships. This article reviews the research on these three issues.

Status of Home-School Relationships. The need to foster good parent-teacher relationships frequently expressed by teachers and parents. The 1980 Gallup poll of attitudes toward the public schools asked persons to indicate their opinion of the most important elements of education. Good parent-teacher relationships were ranked fourth on a list of fourteen elements (Gallup, 1980). In a companion study, members of Phi Delta Kappa ranked good parent-teacher relationships third in importance (Elam & Gough, 1980). Another study of 1,272 superintendents reported parents' lack of interest ranked fifth of eighteen major problems facing the schools. The improvement of the parent-teacher relationship was ranked by the superintendents as the fifth of twelve needed improvements in the public schools (Duea & Bishop, 1980).

Even though the need for good relations between parents and teachers is generally endorsed, several studies indicate that parents and teachers prefer rather infrequent face-to-face interactions. Crotts and Goeldi (1974) found that most parents (65 percent) and teachers (80 percent) favored two or fewer conferences per year. In this study, all of the parents and 80 percent of the teachers preferred conferences to be twenty minutes or less in duration. The 1980 Gallup Poll (Gallup, 1980) reported similar results. Eighty-three percent of the parents approved of a plan for parent-teacher communication involving one conference at the beginning of each semester.

A number of studies of the actual amount of contact between parents and teachers have been reported, generally demonstrating that contact between parents and teachers is usually limited (McPherson, 1972; Lortie, 1975; Carew & Lightfoot, 1979). Each of these studies reported that teachers seek contact with parents only in crises or problem situations.

Perhaps of more importance than the amount of contact between parents and teachers is the manner in which they relate. A number of typologies for classifying the ways parents relate to educational personnel have been developed. The work of Verba and Nie (1972) on involvement of citizens in the political process influenced the typologies developed by Liechty (1979) and Salisbury (1980). Other taxonomies have been developed by Fantini (1980) and Jackson and Stretch (1976).

The Jackson and Stretch (1976) paper provides a good example of these typologies. Jackson and Stretch proposed five types of parental involvement: parents as recipients and supporters; parents as educators and learners; parents as noninstructional volunteers; parents as instructional volunteers; and parents as decision makers. In data collected in Canada, Jackson and Stretch (1976) found that parents, teachers, and administrators desired more parent involvement as noninstructional volunteers, instructional volunteers, and decision makers—all of which are the more intense and active forms of involvement. In each of the five types of parental involvement, however, teachers expressed a preference for more parental involvement than did the parents.

Jackson and Stretch's conclusions are in sharp contrast with findings by Salisbury (1980) and Lortie (1975). Salisbury (1980) reports on a study involving six suburban communities. He reported that "supportive activism" constituted the normal type of citizen involvement in the schools. Supportive activists have a positive attitude toward the schools and participate in a way that maintains the status quo. A similar finding is reported by Lortie (1975). Lortie's study of teachers in five cities found that teachers sought a relationship with parents that he characterized as "supportive nonintervention." Supportive nonintervention entails parental endorsement and reinforcement of teacher policies and practices at a distance (Lortie, 1975).

Since there were both instrumentation and geographic differences among the Jackson and Stretch, Salisbury, and Lortie studies, it is impossible to determine if the difference in findings about the preferred type of parental involvement in the schools reflects real differences among communities or merely is an artifact of different approaches to the collection of data.

Barriers to Cooperation.   It is not uncommon for researchers who have studied the parent-teacher relationship to offer a pessimistic assessment of it. In a classic book on the sociology of education written some time ago, Waller (1932) claimed: "Parents and teachers are natural enemies, predestined each for the discomfiture of the other" (p. 68). Waller saw the enmity between parents and teachers not as a consequence of personal malevolence but as a result of differences between the social structures of the home and school.

A number of investigations have described the problems of coordination and cooperation in terms of the social characteristics of home and school (Parsons, 1959; McPherson, 1972; Corwin & Wagenaar, 1976; Lightfoot, 1978; Lightfoot, 1980). These investigators have described the cultural and structural differences between the home and school and explained how these differences affect interaction.

As members of a school system, teachers are expected to adhere to the policies and norms of the system. Teachers are a part of a complex system of persons, each of whom is expected to function in ways defined as legitimate by authorities in the system. Warren's cross-cultural study (1973) of teachers in Germany and the United States shows how teachers are caught in the dilemma of adhering to belief in the value of parent-teacher cooperation while maintaining some semblance of professional autonomy. Warren (1973) found that teachers accept the need for cooperation between themselves and parents. Yet, "they are exhorted by the educational community (administrators, teachers' organizations, colleges of education) to be professional—to see themselves as specialized experts and members of a relatively autonomous collegial body with normative constraints on interaction with clients. The implication for structuring appropriate relations with parents are for the teachers not at all clear." (pp 287–288). In other words, a clear translation of the abstract belief in the need for parent-teacher cooperation into a role prescription for teachers is lacking.

McPherson (1972) discussed another important difference—the contrast in orientation of parents and teachers toward the child. Both parents and teacher may be concerned about the child's welfare, but the parents' relationship with the child is more personalized than is the teacher's. Although there are expressive differences among teachers, their concern for each individual pupil must be tempered by concern for their group of pupils. Thus, what should or can be done for each pupil is constrained by a teacher's sense of what is in harmony with the group's needs (McPherson, 1972).

An important aspect of a social system such as the school is its "boundary maintenance." Boundary maintenance refers to the procedures used to separate those who are in the system from those who are not. The stronger the boundaries of the school system, the less and more limited the participation of parents. The penetrability of its boundaries is an important structural dimension of an organization. Corwin and Wagenaar (1976) studied variables associated with "boundary maintenance" in forty schools. The amount of parent-teacher interaction found by Corwin and Wagenaar declined with school system formalization of rule, centralization of decision making, and solidarity of teacher organizations. Both formalization and centralization represent a constraint on teachers' ability to deviate from standard procedures. Thus, parents with complaints or concerns may be disinclined to bring them to teachers.

Hollister (1979) reanalyzed data collected in eighteen elementary schools in Detroit. He concluded that parental demands are factors in increasing school bureaucratization. Hollister defines "bureaucratization" as the use of rationalistic controls on the behavior of personnel. In this sense, bureaucratization serves to deflect parental demands and to ensure at least minimal performance levels for school personnel. Bureaucratization in a school system may be a response to parental pressure to ensure that certain things happen, but it may also serve as a basis for "passing the buck."

Improving Parent-Teacher Relationships. The most conspicuous approach to improving parent-teacher relationships has been the formation of various organizations. Prominent among these organizations are the National Congress of Parents and Teachers (PTA) and the National Committee for Citizens in Education (often referred to as the Parents' Network). These two organizations reflect different perspectives toward relationships between home and school.

The PTA was founded about the turn of the century. In 1981, the national PTA claimed approximately 6 million members. This organization has stressed the commonality of interest of parents and teachers and has maintained recognition of the limits of proper parent involvement. Prior to 1972, the national bylaws stipulated that local PTA units should cooperate in the improvement of education but should not interfere with the administration of the schools or attempt to control school policies. In 1972, the bylaws were changed to broaden the scope of PTA involvement. The revised section of the bylaws (Article III, d) reads as follows: "The Association shall work with the schools to provide quality education for all children and youth and shall seek to participate in the decision-making process establishing school policy, recognizing that the legal responsibility to make decisions has been delegated by the people to Boards of Education." (*National Parent-Teacher Association Handbook, 1979–1981*, p. 235). While broadening the scope of parental participation, the revised bylaws maintain the PTA's historic emphasis upon the cooperative mode of parent-teacher interaction.

A more adversarial stance is taken by the National Committee for Citizens in Education (Parents' Network). This organization was incorporated in 1973; in 1980, it claimed a membership of 250,000. It provides information on laws and policies affecting the educational rights of parents, assistance in organizing power bases, and training in negotiating skills. The Parents' Network attempts to equip parents with the skills they need to become agents for educational change and reform. The organization assumes that parents will need to use legal solutions and political pressure in order to protect the welfare of their children in the schools. Although there is some literature on the value of organizations such as the PTA (Popp, 1973; Farber & Lewis, 1975), there is little empirical information on the influence of such organizations in increasing the quantity or improving the quality of parent-teacher relationships.

Other Remediation Attempts. Belief in the need for a more cohesive relationship between parents and teachers has prompted a number of attempts to increase communication in ways other than face-to-face discussions. Various techniques have been investigated such as recorded telephone messages (Bittle, 1975); changing report cards (Giannangelo, 1975); use of letters to instruct parents on providing reinforcement for daily reports from their children (Karraker, 1972); and structured two-way communication programs using postcards and telephone calls (Lordeman, Reese, & Friedman, 1977). These studies usually indicate positive results. Since there is virtually no replication, it is difficult to estimate how effective these approaches would be in other sites.

Unfortunately, there has been little research with respect to ways of improving relationships based upon the social structure of the school system. However, Comer (1976) has provided an example of one such study, in which he reports a project undertaken to reduce the impersonality of teacher-parent relationships. He reports that sustained and intensive interactions between parents and teachers led to changes in attitudes and beliefs of parents, teachers, and students. Comer singles out the placement of students with the same teacher for two years as particularly helpful in providing the time needed to build relationships.

Another type of attempted remediation has come through court actions. The Family Rights and Privacy Act authorizes parents to inspect and challenge school records pertaining to their children. Public Law 94-142, for example, requires parental involvement in educational decision making for their children. Federal projects such as Follow Through, Title I, and Teacher Corps have contained requirements for community involvement in the administration and functioning of the programs. Some court orders involving desegregation have required school systems to develop procedures for parental and community involvement in the implementation of desegregation orders (Carol, 1977).

Research on the impact of legal mandates and court orders to increase parental involvement has not provided a clear understanding of the effect of these actions in increasing the quantity and quality of parental involvement in schools (Yoshida et al. 1978; Gordon, et al., 1979; Salett & Henderson, 1980). The logistical and fiscal problems involved in carrying out research on national programs such as Follow Through or Public Law 94-142 are coupled with design and methodological problems of large-scale field research.

Consequences. One of the important issues for research on this topic concerns the consequences of improving the parent-teacher relationship. Does increasing the amount of parental involvement or changing the ways in which parents interact with educational personnel lead to other educational improvements? Several reviews of literature have discussed the methodological and conceptual flaws in studies of the consequences of parental involvement (Filipczak, Lordeman, & Friedman, 1977; Davies et al., 1978; Fantini, 1980). They have concluded that few empirical data exist on the relationship between the amount and types of parent-teacher relationships and other outcomes such as student performance and behavior, teacher functioning, and citizen support for the schools.

Attempts to modify parent-teacher relationships are based upon the assumption that conflict between home and school is undesirable and harmful. However, Waller (1932) and Lightfoot (1980) contend that conflict between them may be beneficial. Lightfoot (1980) distinguishes between "creative conflict" and "negative dissonance," noting that creative conflict is "adaptive to development and socialization of children" (p. 67). Waller (1932) saw conflict as useful because he believed it represented the resistance of parents to accept the school's orientation toward the child. Since Waller felt teachers could not be as concerned about the individual welfare of the child as are the child's parents, he believed conflict was evidence of parents' continued efforts to protect the welfare of the child.

Conclusions. The research on parent-teacher relationships points to the following conclusions. (1) At the abstract or philosophical level, parents and teachers generally support the need for cooperation and coordination. (2) The actual amount of face-to-face contact between parents and teachers is limited. Contact is typically confined to infrequently scheduled conferences and meetings to discuss crises or problems. (3) The structural characteristics that affect interaction between parents and teachers are beginning to be understood. Such understanding helps us to recognize that the problems in communication and interaction between parents and teachers emerge from the social and organizational characteristics of the home and school. Even though a number of studies have focused upon the characteristics of schools that promote a xenophobic response of educators toward parents, it seems clear that parents are not lined up *en masse* at the school door struggling for entry. Indeed, Salisbury's research (1980) suggests that establishment of citizens groups within a community may inhibit responsiveness of educational personnel toward the parents who are critical of school programs or policies. A number of efforts directed to increasing parental participation have been initiated by school administrators and teachers. Not all of these can be ruled out as attempts to co-opt parental involvement or to provide the semblance of participation without substance. Forces impelling participation and barriers to participation can be found both within the school and the home. (4) Research on specific programs to achieve improved parent-teacher relationships has not yielded a consistent understanding of means for improving the situation. (5) There is inadequate information about the consequences of improved parent-teacher relationships. (6) The one-parent family entails special logistical and legal problems for the home relationship. There is little information on these problems in the literature.

The knowledge that can be teased out of the literature can serve as a sound basis for continued research and can assist those who seek to improve the ways in which parents and teachers relate. A good example of the use of current understandings of home-school relationships to develop recommendations is contained in a paper by Bridge (1976).

In this paper, Bridge defines various categories of decision problems for school administrators and explains the appropriate mode of parental involvement for each category. Bridge's work illustrates the value of increased understanding, through research, in guiding practice and policy.

Fifty years ago, Waller (1932) began his discussion of parents and teachers with a blunt criticism: "A marked lack of clear thought and plain speaking exists in the literature touching the relationship of parents and teachers" (p. 68). A considerable amount of the literature produced in the years following Waller's comment continues to be vulnerable to his criticism, but understandings are emerging that should be helpful to those concerned about parent-teacher relationships.

James Bosco

See also Attendance Policy; Discipline; Homework; Instruction Processes; Parent Education.

REFERENCES

Bittle, R. G. Improving parent-teacher communication through recorded telephone messages. *Journal of Educational Research*, 1975, *69*(3), 87–95.

Bridge, R. G. Parent participation in school innovations. *Teachers College Record*, 1976, *77*(33), 366–384.

Carew, J. V., & Lightfoot, S. L. *Beyond Bias*. Cambridge, Mass.: Harvard University Press, 1979.

Carol, L. N. Court-mandated citizen participation in school desegregations. *Phi Delta Kappan*, 1977, *59*(3), 171–173.

Comer, J. P. Improving the quality and continuity of relationships in two inner-city schools. *Journal of the American Academy of Child Psychiatry*, 1976, *15*(3), 535–545.

Corwin, R. G., & Wagenaar, T. C. Boundary interaction between service organizations and their publics: A study of teacher-parent relationships. *Social Forces*, 1976, *55*(2), 471–491.

Crotts, J. H., & Goeldi, J. T. An investigation of parent-teacher conferences in the elementary school. *Illinois School Research*, 1974, *11*(1), 18–27.

Davies, D.; Clasby, M.; Zerchykov, R.; & Powers, B. *Patterns of Citizen Participation in Educational Decisionmaking*. Boston: Institute for Responsive Education, 1978.

Duea, J., & Bishop, W. L. The PROBE results: Important differences in public and professional perceptions of the schools. *Phi Delta Kappan*, 1980, *62*(1), 50–52.

Elam, S. M., & Gough, P. B. Comparing lay and professional opinion on Gallup poll questions. *Phi Delta Kappan*, 1980, *61*(1), 47–48.

Fantini, M. D. Community participation: Alternative patterns and their consequences on educational achievement. In R. L. Sinclair (Ed.), *A Two-way Street: Home-School Cooperation in Educational Decision Making*. Boston: Institute for Responsive Education, 1980.

Farber, B., & Lewis, M. The symbolic use of parents: A sociological critique of educational practice. *Journal of Research and Development in Education*, 1975, *8*(2), 34–43.

Filipczak, J.; Lordeman, A.; & Friedman, R. M. *Parental Involvement in the Schools: Towards What End?* Paper presented at the annual meeting of the American Educational Research

Association, New York, 1977. (ERIC Document Reproduction Service No. ED 143 104)

Gallup, G. H. The twelfth annual Gallup poll of the public's attitudes toward the public schools. *Phi Delta Kappan*, 1980, *62*(1), 33–46.

Giannangelo, D. M. Make report cards meaningful. *Educational Forum*, 1975, *39*(4), 409–415.

Gordon, I. J.; Olmsted, P. P.; Rubin, R. I.; & True, J. H. How has Follow Through promoted parent involvement? *Young Children*, 1979, *34*(5), 49–53.

Hollister, C. D. School bureaucratization as a response to parents' demands. *Urban Education*, 1979, *14*(2), 221–235.

Jackson, R. K., & Stretch, H. A. Perceptions of parents, teachers, and administrators to parental involvement in early childhood programs. *Alberta Journal of Educational Research*, 1976, *22*(2), 129–139.

Karraker, R. M. Increasing academic performance through home-managed contingency programs. *Journal of School Psychology*, 1972, *10*(2), 173–179.

Liechty, T. A. *Patterns of Citizen Participation in Education.* Paper presented at the annual meeting of the American Educational Research Association, San Francisco, 1979. (ERIC Document Reproduction Service No. ED 172 373)

Lightfoot, S. L. *Worlds Apart: Relationship between Families and Schools.* New York: Basic Books, 1978.

Lightfoot, S. L. Exploring family-school relationships: A prelude to curricular designs and strategies. In Robert L. Sinclair (Ed.), *A Two-way Street: Home-School Cooperation in Educational Decision Making.* Boston: Institute for Responsive Education, 1980.

Lordeman, A.; Reese, S. C.; & Friedman, R. M. *Establishing and Assessing Two-way Communication between Parents and Schools.* Paper presented at the annual meeting of the American Educational Research Association, New York, 1977. (ERIC Document Reproduction Service No. ED 143 103)

Lortie, D. C. *School-teacher: A Sociological Study.* Chicago: University of Chicago Press, 1975.

McPherson, G. H. *Small Town Teacher.* Cambridge, Mass.: Harvard University Press, 1972.

National Parent-Teacher Association Handbook: 1979–1981. (Article III, d., 235). Chicago: The Association, 1979.

Parsons, T. The school class as a social system: Some of its functions in American society. *Harvard Educational Review*, 1959, *29*(4), 297–318.

Popp, L. A. PTA: Pathetically trivial alliance or potential teaching assistants? *Journal of Research and Development in Education*, 1973, *7*(1), 72–77.

Salett, S., & Henderson, A. *A Report on the Education for All Handicapped Children Act: Are Parents Involved?* Columbia, Md.: National Committee for Citizens in Education, 1980.

Salisbury, R. H. *Citizen Participation in the Public Schools.* Lexington, Mass.: Lexington Books, 1980.

Verba, S., & Nie, N. *Participation in America: Political Democracy and Social Equality.* New York: Harper & Row, 1972.

Waller, W. *The Sociology of Teaching.* New York: Russell & Russell, 1932.

Warren, R. L. The classroom as a sanctuary for teachers: Discontinuities in social control. *American Anthropologist*, 1973, 280–291.

Yoshida, R. K.; Schensul, J. J.; Pelto, P. J.; & Fenton, K. S. The principal in special education placement. *National Elementary Principal*, 1978, *58*(1), 34–38.

HOMEWORK

Homework is assigned to students at every level of schooling everywhere in America, yet a perusal of recent educational psychology textbooks (such as Biehler, 1978; Cronbach, 1977; Gage & Berliner, 1979) reveals that these authors say virtually nothing about this pervasive phenomenon. One might surmise from this finding that there is no research on the topic and, consequently, nothing to say about homework. However, a computer search of the ERIC data base using "homework" as the subject descriptor revealed 581 entries from 1966 to December 1980, and a search of the *Psychological Abstracts* data base revealed 127 entries from 1967 to November 1980. Admittedly, not all of the papers cited are directly relevant to homework as we normally construe it, but many of them are pertinent to the topic.

This dilemma is resolved after one reads the many articles. Although nothing definitive emerges on the role of homework in the schools, it is still important for teachers to have some sense of the literature on homework. What follows is not a comprehensive review, but rather a selective review of some of the more important papers on the topic.

Overall there are three types of articles dealing with homework: two types based on research and one type based on personal opinion. Most of the research papers are of the questionnaire or survey type; far too few are derived from experimental research in which students have been randomly assigned to an experimental group (such as a homework group) and a control group (such as a no-homework group). The personal opinion articles are nonempirical, speculative papers conveying the differing experiences and opinions of administrators, teachers, and/or parents.

Survey Research. The survey research by Check (1966) portrays quite well the typical findings of large-scale endeavors of this kind. Check distributed over one thousand questionnaires to six distinct populations, ranging from elementary and secondary school students to college students to parents. He found that parents and teachers alike strongly favor homework and that students at the elementary, junior high, and senior high school level all feel that homework is necessary. However, parents, teachers, and students are all concerned about the type of homework assignments being given.

The findings of a large-scale survey of seventy-seven New York school districts by Bond and Smith (1966) seem to shed light on what may be the source of some of this concern. In particular, these researchers found that teachers generally ignore individual differences in their pupils when making homework assignments. Also, such assignments often require reading, which most reading specialists do not advise. Furthermore, homework assignments usually are mere drill exercises, not "research and independent study," and assignments are not systematically corrected, graded, and returned to the students. Whereas this research was conducted about fifteen years ago, the problems it depicts are typical of those found today in schools throughout the United States (Lee & Pruitt, 1979). Further evidence that problems persist comes from Friesen's review of opinion polls taken from 1916 to 1977, in which sixty-one-year period he found little change in the attitudes of parents, teachers, and students (Friesen, 1978).

Some specific points from the Friesen review are worth mentioning, however. For example, although most homework assignments are teacher-dominated, students seem to prefer joint planning of such assignments (Smith, 1934). Students also like assignments to be thoroughly explained and to be more than busy work (Schiller, 1954). And finally, home environment (attitudes of parents toward school and parents' level of education) seems to have an important influence on students' views toward homework and, of course, toward school in general (Brooks, 1916).

Strang's work (1968, 1975) in this area is unusual in that it represents a review of all three types of articles: surveys, experimental investigations, and personal opinions. As such, her work is pivotal to the experimental research on homework. Strang's conclusions and recommendations regarding homework also relate well to the Bond and Smith report and to the Friesen review. Strang concludes that some homework is necessary and that it should be a logical extension of classwork, enriching the students' knowledge of ideas taught in the classroom. Students should be able to discern the purpose of their homework assignments, many of which should be done on a voluntary basis. Strang further contends that assignments should be tailored to the individual needs and interests of the student and that they should not be too long and involved. Finally, Strang argues that the teacher should "spend some class time helping students to get started on their homework" (1975, p. 27).

While these recommendations make a great deal of sense and are laudable in their own right, there is virtually no experimental evidence to support these or any other set of recommendations. As Strang observes, experimental research on homework is "limited and inadequate" (1968, p. 2). In her brief discussion of experimental research on homework, Strang (1968, 1975) relies almost exclusively on the Goldstein review (1960), which is one of the first thorough reviews of experimental research in this area.

Experimental Research. Goldstein (1960) examined all articles on homework listed in the *Education Index* for the thirty years preceding 1958 and found only 17 experimental investigations out of 280 papers in the index. An examination of the 17 studies reveals, however, that at least one (Cooke & King, 1939) is a correlational study and not an experiment, the latter involving manipulation of independent variables rather than the mere observation of a relationship between variables. Another one of the studies (Sutcliffe & Canham, 1937) involves a comparison of homework groups with supervised study groups,

wherein the supervised study groups were also given varying degrees of homework, and, in some instances, the same amount as the homework groups. Most of the experiments reviewed by Goldstein (1960) suggest that regularly assigned homework contributes to academic achievement and "a few of the best designed experiments show this quite clearly" (p. 221).

Hedges (1964) chose to examine what he considered to be the "most thorough" 40 of 292 studies published during the period between 1954 and 1964. He concluded that there was no "comprehensive and firm research evidence on the various facets of homework" (p. 45).

The next major review of research was conducted by Austin (1978), who focused on mathematics homework experiments that had been reviewed by Goldstein (1960) and on those published subsequently between 1960 and 1977. Austin contends that after 1960, mathematics homework experiments became more complex. Such experiments included students from different grade levels rather than just one grade level, and attitude measures rather than only achievement measures as dependent variables. Austin, combining across all experiments reviewed, found sixteen achievement comparisons significantly favoring the homework group and thirteen such comparisons showing no difference between the homework group and the no-homework group. One should bear in mind the problems associated with this "box score" approach to presenting results from many different experiments.

The most recent review of homework experiments has been done by Friesen (1979). He examines twenty-four research studies done between 1923 and 1976 in elementary and secondary schools, and contends that there has been improvement over the years in both the design and reporting of results of the experimental research on homework. In Friesen's review (1979), twelve experiments demonstrate positive effects of homework on achievement, while eleven experiments demonstrate no difference or negative effects. One experimenter (Hansen, 1972) found that the homework groups performed significantly better than the no-homework groups on two investigator-designed examinations, but equal to each other on standardized tests.

Of the twelve experiments yielding positive results, two (Anderson, 1946; Schain, 1954) showed that high-ability students profit less from homework than low-ability students, and one (Doane, 1973) showed the opposite effect, at least in terms of correlational data. Also, in one experiment (Di Napoli, 1937), fifth-graders given compulsory homework performed somewhat better than the no-homework group at this level, but the reverse occurred for the seventh-graders. Collectively, these results seem to suggest that grade level and ability level of students may interact with homework. More research is needed to ascertain the precise nature of this relationship.

Of the eleven experiments in the Friesen review (1979) yielding negative results, two (Hudson, 1956, Ten Brinke, 1967) involved achievement comparisons between homework and supervised study rather than between homework and no homework. In the Hudson experiment (1965), the supervised study group was given more time in school to complete the next day's assignment as well as one-fourth fewer problems than the homework group. A somewhat similar pattern existed in the Ten Brinke (1964) experiment. Under these conditions, it is hard to conceive of the homework group not feeling neglected and overworked. It is somewhat surprising that the supervised study groups did *not* outperform the homework groups in these experiments. In another investigation (Schroeder, 1960) that produced negative results, the same daily assignments were given to the homework and no-homework groups, but the homework group had to complete their assignments at home rather than in class. This study actually compares homework and no-homework conditions rather than unsupervised assignments done in school and those done at home.

The final noteworthy experiment is the Schmidt study (1973), comparing a compulsory homework group to a noncompulsory homework group. In this case, the noncompulsory group also received homework and was explicitly encouraged, although not required, to do the problems. The comparison thus involves required homework versus encouraged homework rather than homework versus no homework. Furthermore, the noncompulsory group was given weekly quizzes while the compulsory group was not given such quizzes. Such an experimental arrangement renders it impossible to have an unequivocal interpretation of the results. Schmidt should have examined these two variables (homework versus no homework and quizzes versus no quizzes) in a 2×2 analysis of variance rather than mixing them in the way he did.

For the reasons given, four of the eleven experiments "against" homework reviewed by Friesen (1979) did not actually test the basic homework hypothesis as it is normally understood. A test of homework effects necessarily involves the fundamental comparison between a homework group and a no-homework group. Whether or not homework is superior to supervised study is a different, but empirically answerable, question.

I am reasonably sure that homework of the right kind given under the right set of conditions positively influences academic achievement. What is needed is more well-designed and well-executed experimental research aimed at systematically examining different kinds of homework under different sorts of conditions. It could well be the case that some of the recommendations made target some of the important kinds and conditions of homework assignments.

However, uncovering all of the factors influencing homework and then unambiguously testing these factors in experimental settings will not be an easy task, for a wide variety of factors, some quite subtle, seem to affect the success or failure of homework. According to Holtzman (1969), a few of the most important factors are home environment, interest and educational background of par-

ents, precise nature of the assignment, and feedback procedures of the teacher.

Personal Opinion Articles. According to Strang (1975), a major problem of homework is the vast discrepancy between recommended procedures for homework assignments and those actually being used by teachers. However, rare indeed is the individual school or the school district that has an established policy regarding homework. In the absence of such a policy, teachers decide on their own what to do about homework.

Typically, there is no homework policy at all, a fact that causes little surprise, inasmuch as recommendations for homework are necessarily derived from personal opinion rather than from firm experimental evidence. There are, however, some intuitively appealing ideas about homework offered in some of the personal opinion papers. Perhaps one of the most interesting papers in this regard is one by Lee and Pruitt (1979).

A common problem with homework assignments is that they only require superficial understanding of concepts taught in school. Simple practice exercises frequently have this flaw. Worse still are mere busywork assignments. Lee and Pruitt (1979) present an interesting typology of homework assignments as a guideline for teachers in "prescribing and utilizing homework as a teaching tool" (p. 31). This homework typology allows teachers to understand the purpose of a particular assignment more clearly. The four types of homework are (1) practice—designed to drill or reinforce skills and information covered in class; (2) preparation—given to prepare students to profit from subsequent lessons; (3) extension—provided to ascertain if a student can extend the concept or skill learned in class to a new situation; and (4) creative—designed to require students to integrate many skills and concepts in producing some project. Lee and Pruitt argue that while practice exercises are useful when followed by a short quiz and corrective feedback, more emphasis needs to be placed on the other three types of assignments mentioned. For preparation assignments, there should be some systematic checkup, usually a quiz, as well as some classroom followup, but not in the sense of merely going over the same material in the same way. The use of extension and creative assignments is crucial, since they normally require higher mental processes than mere rote recall and simple comprehension, such as those involved in being able to define a concept in one's own words. According to Lee and Pruitt (1979), some allowance for and encouragement of divergent responses are critical in extension and creative assignments.

There are, of course, numerous other personal opinion papers on homework, many of which argue for or against homework. One argument for homework is that it extends the amount of time a student is learning (Yeary, 1978). It is also argued that homework assignments help develop initiative and a sense of responsibility in students and that certain kinds of learning are best done when done alone (Yeary, 1978). Hall (1972) contends that "home assignments can provide opportunities to use human and physical resources not available in the school" (p. 41).

Those against homework argue that much homework is just busywork and that supervised study is superior to homework, since "each student has an equal opportunity to get adequate assistance" (Gerry, 1970, p. 20). This latter point is especially important for weaker students who may make mistakes while doing homework, thereby reinforcing the very responses that should be avoided (Pope, 1978). Moreover, Pope argues that many family feuds are caused by homework and that students become confused and upset over vague assignments that require too long to complete and often go unchecked. Many of these complaints, however, could be remedied by following the suggestions of Lee and Pruitt (1979). Perhaps the major source of friction regarding homework is that it takes up students' time outside of class, time which could be spent for recreational, social, leisure, or family activities (Ehler, 1978; Kotnour, 1978; Shannon, 1970).

John P. Rickards

See also Home-School Relationships; Independent Study; Instruction Processes.

REFERENCES

Anderson, W. E. An attempt through the use of experimental techniques to determine the effect of home assignments upon scholastic success. *Journal of Educational Research*, 1946, *40*, 141–143.

Austin, J. D. Homework research in mathematics. *School Science and Mathematics*, 1978, *79*, 115–122.

Biehler, R. *Psychology Applied to Teaching* (3rd ed.). Boston: Houghton Mifflin, 1978.

Bond, G. W., & Smith, G. J. Homework in the elementary school. *National Elementary Principal*, 1966, *45*, 46–50.

Brooks, E. C. The value of home study under parental supervision. *Elementary School Journal*, 1916, *17*, 187–194.

Check, J. F. Homework: Is it needed? *Clearing House*, 1966, *41*, 143–147.

Cooke, D. H., & King, L. Should children study at home? *American School Board Journal*, 1939, *98*, 49–50.

Cronbach, L. J. *Educational Psychology* (3rd ed.). New York: Harcourt Brace Jovanovich, 1977.

Dinapoli, P. *Homework in the New York City Elementary Schools* (Teachers College, Columbia University, Contributions to Education, No. 719). New York: Columbia University, Bureau of Publications, 1937.

Doane, B. S. The effects of homework and locus of control on arithmetic skills and achievement in fourth-grade students (Doctoral dissertation, New York University, 1972). *Dissertation Abstracts International*, 1973, *33*, 5548A. (University Microfilms No. 73–8160)

Ehler, K. Does homework disrupt the home? *Teacher*, 1978, *96*, 24.

Friesen, C. D. *The Results of Surveys, Questionnaires, and Polls Regarding Homework*. Iowa City: University of Iowa, 1978. (ERIC Document Reproduction Service No. ED 159 174)

Friesen, C. D. *The Results of Homework versus No-homework Research Studies*. Iowa City: The University of Iowa, 1979. (ERIC Document Reproduction Service No. ED 167 508)

Gage, N. L., & Berliner, D. *Educational Psychology* (2nd ed.). Chicago: Rand McNally, 1979.

Gerry, H. The year that homework died. *Today's Education*, 1970, *59*, 20–21.

Goldstein, A. Does homework help? A review of research. *Elementary School Journal*, 1960, *1*, 212–224.

Hall, N. Homework that works. *Today's Education*, 1972, *61*, 41–42.

Hansen, D. W. An investigation of the effects of required homework on achievement in college mathematics (Doctoral dissertation, University of Denver, 1972). *Dissertation Abstracts International*, 1972, *33*, 2814A–2815A. (University Microfilms No. 72–19,031)

Hedges, W. Guidelines for developing a homework policy. *National Elementary Principal*, 1964, *44*(2), 44–47.

Holtzman, W. H. Homework and assignments. In R. L. Ebel (Ed.), *Encyclopedia of Educational Research* (4th ed.). New York: Macmillan, 1969.

Hudson, J. A. A pilot study of the influence of homework in seventh-grade mathematics and attitudes toward homework in the Fayetteville public schools. (Doctoral dissertation, University of Arkansas, 1965). *Dissertation Abstracts*, 1965, *26*, 906. (University Microfilms No. 65–8456)

Kotnour, J. No homework: A student's right. *Clearing House*, 1978, *51*, 278–81.

Lee, J., & Pruitt, K. W. Homework assignments: Classroom games or teaching tools? *Clearing House*, 1979, *53*, 31–35.

Pope, L. A new look at homework. *Teacher*, 1978, *96*, 94–95.

Schain, R. L. Another homework experiment in the social studies. *High Points*, 1954, *36*, 5–12.

Schiller, B. A questionnaire study of junior high school students' reactions to homework. *High Points*, 1954, *26*, 23–26.

Schmidt, G. E. The effectiveness of large lecture recitation sections versus small group classes and the influence of compulsory-homework-and-quizzes on the achievement and attitudes of calculus II students (Doctoral dissertation, Kansas State University, 1973). *Dissertation Abstracts International*, 1974, *35*, 222A (University Microfilms No. 74–14,371)

Schroeder, H. A. *Homework versus No-homework in Elementary Algebra*. Unpublished master's thesis, Mankato State College, 1960.

Shannon, E. Homework that works. *Today's Education*, 1970, *59*, 17–19.

Smith, W. R. Home study practices in the elementary schools of certain school districts in western Pennsylvania (Doctoral dissertation, University of Pittsburgh, 1934). *Dissertation Abstracts*, 1933–1934, *1*, 68.

Strang, R. S. Guided study and homework. In *What Research Says to the Teacher*. Washington, D.C.: National Education Association, 1968. (ERIC Document Reproduction Service No. ED 077 901)

Strang, R. S. Homework. In *What Research Says to the Teacher*. Washington, D.C.: National Education Association, 1975. (ERIC Document Reproduction Service No. ED 118 559)

Sutcliffe, A., & Canham, J. W. *Experiments in Homework and Physical Education*. London: J. Murray, 1937.

Ten Brinke, D. P. Homework: An experimental evaluation of the effect of achievement in mathematics in grades seven and eight (Doctoral dissertation, University of Minnesota, 1964). *Dissertation Abstracts*, 1967, *27*, 4176A. (University Microfilms No. 65–15,326)

Yeary, E. What about homework? *Today's Education*, 1978, *67*, 80–82.

I

INDEPENDENT STUDY

As with many concepts in education, "independent study" has a variety of definitions. Several terms in the literature are used almost synonymously with independent study—"self-directed learning" and "independent learning," for example. Other terms are referred to as forms of independent study: "homework," "study hall," "contracts," "learning modules," and "unsupervised study." Related terms such as "individualized study," "personalized systems," "computer-assisted instruction," and "self-instruction" are similar to, but not synonymous with, independent study. In an attempt to clarify the term, two different categories of independent study that are most prominent in the literature are defined. Also described are practices and benefits of the concept, research on effectiveness of independent study, barriers to independent study, theory building, stages and skills in independent study, independent study in relation to the curriculum, and future options for the concept. The article emphasizes independent study conducted under school auspices.

Definitions. Generally, the literature indexed under the term "independent study" reflects two broad and different categories of definitions. First, independent study is defined as a process or a goal of schooling and does not presume any specified body of knowledge. In this context, independent study is motivated primarily by the student's own aims, rewarded intrinsically by the student, conducted under the auspices of the school, and exists independently of regular classes (Alexander & Hines, 1967; Beeler, 1979; Dressel & Thompson, 1973; Rogge, 1965). It is not an isolated activity; students share their studies with those who might help in the learning process such as teachers, tutors, resource specialists, and peers. This view of independent study has been contrasted with teacher-directed or other-directed learning (Alexander & Hines, 1967; Gibbons & Phillips, 1978).

A second view of independent study is as a methodology for learning a body of content, with both methodology and content developed and structured by the teacher. The audio-tutorial mode of instruction is central to this definition. S. N. Postlethwait is credited with originally developing this methodology at Purdue University, he defined it as a program of learning organized so that students are able to proceed through a program at their own pace, filling in the gaps that they do not know and omitting what they do know. According to this view, independent study makes use of every educational device that will foster the learning desired, sequences the learning experiences effectively and efficiently, and integrates the learning experiences (Postlethwait, Novak, & Murray, 1969). Butzow (1977) defined it as a method of instruction in which there can be a more equal opportunity for achievement regardless of the student's previous achievement record. This definition of independent study emphasizes the learning of specific content defined by the teacher in addition to a variety of resources developed by the teacher; however, the student may choose some materials and may set his or her own pace.

Alexander and Hines (1967) stated that it may be advantageous that an official definition of independent study has not yet been accepted, since it has made possible more exploration of new practices. However, it was also suggested that lack of agreement concerning the meaning of independent study has hampered needed research and development of the concept (Alexander & Burke, 1972).

Some authors have made a clear distinction between "individualization" and independent study. For example, Alexander and Hines (1967), Della-Dora and Blanchard (1979), and Dressel and Thompson (1973) indicated that learning can be individualized without providing any degree of independence or responsibility for the student. Individualized instruction can be highly, or even entirely, teacher-controlled. Dressel and Thompson (1973) suggested that individualization can be a first step toward independent study, but that independence in learning

FIGURE 1. *Degrees of student responsibility and decision making about learning*

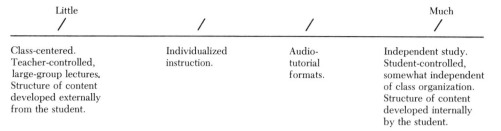

Little			Much
Class-centered. Teacher-controlled, large-group lectures. Structure of content developed externally from the student.	Individualized instruction.	Audio-tutorial formats.	Independent study. Student-controlled, somewhat independent of class organization. Structure of content developed internally by the student.

needs to progress beyond the stage of individualization.

Other authors pointed to a closer relationship between individualization and independent study or learning. For example, Macdonald (1967) identified three conceptualizations of independent learning. One conception emphasized the independence of students in learning the same material. A second conception, called individualized instruction, provides a variety of ways for students to achieve the same general goals; audio-tutorial methods exemplify this conception. The third conception of independent learning involves self-selection, whereby the student has a choice of activities as well as an independent choice of the learning task. The first two conceptions are largely teacher-controlled, whereas the third conception indicates greater responsibility and greater independence for the student.

The various definitions and forms of independent study can be placed along a continuum of student responsibility and control over the learning process (see Figure 1). At one end of the continuum is large-group instruction, which is teacher-directed and entails little or no student involvement in decision making. At the other end of the continuum is independent study, which is largely student-controlled learning. In between are different forms of individualization and controlled forms of independent study that vary with the amount of control held or shared by teacher and student. The work reviewed here concerns the concepts farther to the right on the continuum and excludes those to the left of center.

Independent Study Practices. Although Hubbell (1976) called independent study a product of the middle and late 1960s, the concept of self-directed inquiry has been traced back to colonial days (Bonthius, Davis, & Drushal, 1957; Long & Ahsford, 1976). Long and Ashford (1976) noted that the historical use of the concept has not been recognized because so many different terms have been used to refer to it (among them, "independent study"). For example, the American colonists employed the process because of the lack of opportunities to attend school.

Bonthius, Davis, and Drushal (1957) stated that by 1920 the idea of independent study as a method of instruction had been established. One of the earliest surveys of practice was conducted by Aydelotte in 1924 (Dressel & Thompson, 1973). He suggested that the combination of

student freedom and academically rigorous requirements hampered the growth of independent study. About the same time, Robinson was one of the earliest to experiment with the concept at Stanford University (Rogge, 1965). His program originally consisted of a few high-achieving juniors and seniors engaged in special work under the supervision of the faculty; but the program expanded from 1925–1928, and practices gradually became modified. Freshmen were eventually included; small group conferences replaced individual meetings with professors; and some departments reduced the amount of freedom available to the student. The earlier independent study practices often was restricted to honor students (Brown, 1968; Holtzman, 1969; Rogge, 1965). It was believed that only gifted and very bright students would have the necessary skills and motivation to engage in independent study.

Bonthius and others suggested that independent study be considered a goal of schooling rather than simply a learning process (Dressel & Thompson, 1973). This suggestion was based upon the contention that all students need the capability for independent study in order to continue learning after schooling ends. Bonthius, Davis, and Drushal (1957) conducted a survey of twenty colleges that offered independent study. The major goals of the programs reflected their suggestion. The goals most often reported were to enable the student to assume greater responsibility for education and to grasp the meaning of scholarship.

Later, the concept as a goal of schooling was given an endorsement by the so-called Trump plan in 1956 (Alexander & Hines, 1967; Brown, 1968). The Commission on the Experimental Study of the Utilization of Staff in the Secondary School recommended that instructional time in the secondary schools be divided according to three categories: 40 percent of the time should be spent in large-group instruction, 20 percent in small-group discussions, and 40 percent in independent study.

As indicated, Postlethwait developed the concept of the audio-tutorial mode of instruction in 1961 for a freshman botany class at Purdue University (Postlethwait, Novak, & Murray, 1969). The method originally was developed as supplementary lectures for students with limited backgrounds in botany, to enable them to keep up with the pace of the class. Reactions to the method were so favorable that the concept was extended to include the entire class in the second semester. In this format, independent study was used in conjunction with general assemblies, small assembly sessions, and other activities.

In recent years, independent study practices have expanded, and usage has been reported at all levels of schooling, from elementary school (Carpenter & Quiring, 1978) to college, in virtually all subject areas and with all types of students. Regardless of this increased interest, survey studies of practices have concluded that independent study remains more a concept than a practice at all levels of schooling. Although Dressel and Thompson (1973) proposed that no student be allowed to graduate from college with a baccalaureate degree until he or she showed the ability to plan and carry out one project through independent study, they concluded on the basis of a random sample of 372 colleges that it is a better concept in print than in practice (Thompson & Dressel, 1970). They also concluded the concept was more popular at small private colleges than large public institutions, and it was seldom available to all students.

Varieties of programs. Alexander and Hines (1967) conducted a survey of thirty-six secondary schools on independent study and reached similar conclusions as did Thompson and Dressel (1970) at the college level. In spite of considerable interest in the concept, only 1 percent or 2 percent of the schools actually had independent study programs. Programs involved the above-average student, even though respondents believed that they were useful for all students. The study was later updated (Alexander & Burke, 1972) through a review of the literature. On that basis, Alexander and Burke (1972) reported a greatly increased use of the label "independent study" and a markedly increased number of articles on the topic. The authors concluded that the use of independent study had been increased in the secondary schools; and the evidence, although still scant, was beginning to indicate its potential. They did have some question regarding the quality of growth in independent study practices.

Dressel & Thompson (1973) noted a variety of forms of independent study at the college level: independent projects, credit by examination, independent research, fieldwork, study abroad, work-study programs, interim terms, and group independent study that avoids isolating the student. Alexander and Hines (1967) identified five patterns of independent study in the secondary schools: (1) independent study privileges or options that provide choices for large numbers, if not all, students on a scheduled time basis; (2) individually programmed independent study, in which the student is guided, but not tutored, in a program based upon his or her needs and interests; (3) job-oriented independent study that prepares students for a particular job or career; (4) seminars in which students engaged in independent study come together on occasion to share their studies; and (5) quest-type programs designed to develop special aptitudes and talents of an individual not necessarily related to job or career interests. Independent study had also taken the form of a culminating activity, such as a final requirement for graduation;

correspondence courses (one of the oldest forms); and programmed instruction. The largest number of students (58 percent) were engaged in library research, followed by laboratory projects (13.7 percent), creative projects (18.6 percent), and field experiences (9.8 percent).

In the later study updating the first survey, Alexander and Burke (1972) concluded that research had not determined the merits of each of the five types of independent study. Of the five types, only the first two—independent study privileges or options and individually programmed but not prescribed independent study—were the most widely used. They noted that independent study as released time from regular classes was also found to be the most frequently used form by Poulson in his study of independent study practices in Pennsylvania. They observed that a variety of definitions were given to independent study, two of which were very different from theirs: (1) independent study time or scheduled time for study, and (2) individual study or individualized instruction through the use of prescribed programmed materials.

Danridge et al. (1979) and Brown (1968) described contract learning as another form of independent study: a written agreement signed by the student, the parent or guardian, and the certificated educator who will supervise the student's project. This form is often more structured than others because it may include specific objectives and evaluation procedures.

Bonthius, Davis, and Drushal (1957) concluded from their survey that the largest type of independent study program consisted of information gathering and analysis based upon library work, followed by field work, artistic creation, administrative activities, self-study, and designing or building a project.

Advantage and Benefits.   In spite of the rather limited practice of independent study, interest in the concept has remained high. Perhaps this is due to the potential benefits to the student who engages in the process of independent study.

The advantages of independent study as a process and goal of schooling cluster into two categories: (1) achievement and cognitive learning and (2) process and affective growth. In terms of achievement and cognitive learning, it has been noted that proactive students, supported by independent study, learn more and better than reactive students (Alexander & Hines, 1967; Gibbons & Phillips, 1979; Hubbell, 1976; Knowles, 1975; Stewart, 1980). Intrinsic motivation from this active role is thought to increase, and, as a result, learning becomes more personalized and meaningful (Brown, 1968; Henney, 1978). Self-directed learning emphasizes the development of higher cognitive behaviors (Henney, 1978) and offers opportunities to study topics beyond the regular curriculum (Alexander & Hines, 1967; Brown, 1968). Alexander and Hines (1967) concluded from their study that not only did students achieve in the area of independent study but they also achieved better in other courses in which no independent study was used and they showed better student achievement beyond high school. Also, students retained what they had learned longer and made better and longer use of it (Alexander & Hines, 1967; Knowles, 1975). Thus, independent study helps students become competent in many areas and expert in at least one field (Brown, 1968; Gibbons & Phillips, 1979). Independent study places responsibility for learning on the student (Alexander & Hines, 1967; Beggs & Buffie, 1965; Knowles, 1975) and thereby assists the student in developing important processes and affective learnings. Students acquire skills necessary to educate themselves, or learn how to learn and become self-directed learners (Alexander & Hines, 1967; Brown, 1968; Dressel & Thompson, 1973; Gibbons & Phillips 1978, 1979; Henney, 1978; Stewart, 1980; Thompson & Dressel, 1970). This self-direction allows the student to continue learning beyond the confines of the school and after formal schooling has ended. The ultimate model for this process was identified as the university scholar, who is very independent and persistent in his or her learning (Kolcaba, 1980). These skills would help assure that the second goal most often cited in the survey by Thompson and Dressel (1970), continuing curiosity, is encouraged in the students.

Students develop personal decision-making skills (Gibbons & Phillips, 1979; Henney, 1978; Stewart, 1980). Related to this, students learn a willingness to take risks, how to deal with the consequences of one's actions, and how to persevere in spite of obstacles. In addition, a sense of personal worth, independence, adequacy, accomplishment, and self-reliance is developed through independent study (Alexander & Hines, 1967). Independent study will help destroy the division between life and school that many students now experience (Henney, 1978) and will assist students in perceiving greater applicability of what they learn. Independent study also helps students break out of age groups (Brown, 1968; Gibbons & Phillips, 1979) and relate more effectively to a wide range of people.

Potential benefits have also been cited for independent study as a method of studying content; these involve instructional benefits, adaptability of the method, and process skills. In terms of instructional benefits, each student receives the benefit of being tutored by senior staff members (Postlethwait, Novak, & Murray, 1969) who have developed the materials. This helps to overcome two disadvantages that Case (1980) observed in the traditional lecture-laboratory approach: the quality of the material presented to students varied with instructors, and instructors repeated the same material in courses with a decreasing amount of enthusiasm. Tapes demand greater attention on the part of students, so they are not so easily distracted by other students in the learning environment (Postlethwait, Novak, & Murray, 1969). Students can receive more individual attention if desired, since the method provides the teacher with specific information about the difficulties a student may be having (Geisert, 1977; Postlethwait, Novak, & Murray, 1969; Sturges & Grobe, 1976). By placing responsibility for learning upon the student rather than upon the teacher's methodology (Postlethwait, Novak, & Murray, 1969), the method encourages the development of personal responsibility.

Flexibility of method is also considered to be a major benefit. The method is adaptable to the individual student's own pace, best study times, needs for institutional facilities, resources, and staff, and needs for specific information (Fisher & MacWhinney, 1976; Geisert, 1977; Moore, 1966; Morris, Surber, & Bijou, 1978; Postlethwait, Novak, & Murray, 1969; Struges & Grobe, 1976). This flexibility allows capable students to move faster, and gives slower students enough time to gain the information they need.

Process skills teach students to manage their own time, enabling them to more adequately plan completion of assignments from other courses (Morris, Surber, & Bijou, 1978). The self-pacing provision also emphasizes personal inquiry in learning (Geisert, 1977; Sturges & Grobe, 1976).

Effectiveness. There has been limited empirical research with respect to independent study as a process and goal of education. Both of the major survey studies based upon this definition (Alexander & Hines, 1967; Dressel & Thompson, 1973) cited a lack of research in this area. Both of these studies reported claims of effectiveness of independent study, but the claims were not supported by experimental research data. They were, rather, the beliefs and conclusions, perhaps opinions and observations, of knowledgeable people based upon survey data. Later, however, Alexander and Burke (1972) concluded that research indicated that independent study was at least equal to, if not better than, other forms of study in regard to student achievement and positive student attitudes.

Several authors, however, have cited the effectiveness of this form of independent study based upon empirical research. Holtzman (1969) reported experimental data from two studies on this form. One showed equal achievement for control groups and independent study students, and the second study showed increased achievement by the independent study students. Ward et al. (1977) studied the effects on student achievement and attitudes of training teachers through the use of a minicourse on how to use independent study. Student involvement was greater with those teachers using independent study, but no significant differences in achievement were found when measured by traditional achievement tests. Classes in which few (six) students engaged in independent learning systems had a higher-quality teacher instruction and guidance than did students in classes in which one-half or more of the students participated in independent learning.

The bulk of empirical research conducted on independent study has centered on the more structured approach designed to teach a body of content using some variation of the audio-tutorial methodology. These studies generally have examined the effectiveness of the audio-tutorial method in comparison to the traditional lecture-discussion method in three areas: (1) achievement and student activities toward course content and the audio-tutorial method;

(2) personality and motivational factors of students engaging in the audio-tutorial method; and (3) the economic efficiency of the audio-tutorial method. It is important to note that methodology used in these research studies varied greatly; different aspects of the method were assessed in various studies; and most of the studies were conducted with college students.

Student Achievement and Attitudes. Two major reviews of the literature summarized much of the research prior to 1977: Fisher and MacWhinney (1976) and Dawson (1977). In a review of eighty-nine studies, forty-four of which were experimental research studies conducted at the college level in courses using modular independent studies with a recorded audio component, Fisher and MacWhinney (1976) concluded that two hypotheses must be entertained: (1) the audio-tutorial method produces achievement gains; and (2) positive affective responses toward the method are reported from many students in many subject areas. They further concluded that the use of the audio-tutorial method seems particularly suitable for courses that have much factual content and specific skills, especially when the students are not all high achievers. There seemed to be no consistent effects determined by sex of the student on the value of the audio-tutorial method. Fisher and MacWhinney (1976) suggested that the most documented attribute of the audio-tutorial method is its favorable evaluation by students. In all cases, students reported that they liked it at least as well as other approaches and often favored it. The studies indicated that students enjoyed the freedom of the approach; believed that they learned more; considered the method to be more stimulating and more motivating; and reported greater ease of learning. These were positive attitudes about methodology and not course content.

Dawson (1977) summarized forty research studies on personalized, individualized, and self-paced teaching in college economics courses and concluded, as did Fisher and MacWhinney (1976), that this methodology is at least as effective as the traditional lecture-discussion approach. His conclusion about student attitudes was less firm, however; in his studies, student attitudes were often, but not always, positive toward the innovative approach.

A review of studies conducted after these two major summaries generally supported these conclusions: the audio-tutorial method is at least equal to or better than more traditional methods in fostering student achievement and positive attitudes. All of the following studies examined student achievement, but not all included attitudes toward the methodology as part of the research design.

Butzow (1977) used the audio-tutorial approach with an all-male chemistry class and found no significant difference in change of attitude toward chemistry, but found a slight improvement in attitude toward the audio-tutorial method. The best predictors of success in this type of instruction were measures of prior achievement and the grade point average (GPA). The scores of lower-achieving students with respect to attitudes toward the course had a somewhat greater negative change than did the scores of higher-achieving students. Attitudes toward course content were found not to be good predictors of achievement in audio-tutorial courses. Student achievement patterns were not altered much during the course and were the same as in traditionally taught courses. He concluded that student attitudes toward the audio-tutorial mode were not particularly positive.

Case (1980) used the audio-tutorial approach in a college biology course for nonbiology majors and compared student effects in this course to those of of the conventional lecture-laboratory format. Eighty percent of the students in the audio-tutorial approach said they had achieved the stated objectives of the course, and 61 percent of the students in the traditional approach said they had achieved course objectives even though no objectives were stated. Case (1980) concluded that the tutorial format promoted learning. Students in the experimental mode reported the laboratory exercises to be more stimulating and more relevant to their interests (77 percent) than did students in the conventional approach (42 percent), even though laboratories were identical. Responses of students also suggested that they were more stimulated by the method than by the content of the course.

Kahle conducted several general investigations using the audio-tutorial approach in biology classes. One investigation (Kahle, Douglass, & Nordland, 1976) suggested that disadvantaged college students may be handicapped by traditional group instruction and can learn more effectively and efficiently in the audio-tutorial mode; these students indicated a preference for the audio-tutorial method. A similar investigation was conducted with respect to disadvantaged urban high school students in a biology course with a high dropout rate (Kahle, Nordland, & Douglass, 1976). This method also was found to increase learning for these students when materials were carefully sequenced and structured in an individual learning format.

Mayes, Brigham, and McNeill (1977) studied student attitudes toward the audio-tutorial mode in a precalculus class. Responding to an attitude questionnaire in the final examination period, students indicated that they were satisfied with the course organization and believed the course requirements to be realistic. They rated the laboratory facilities and schedules for assistance as adequate. Generally, the students liked the audio-tutorial course about as well as any other course.

Morris, Surber, and Bijou (1978) found no difference in grade distributions between students in a self-paced child development class and those in an instructor-paced child development class. Different patterns of achievement were noted, however, in terms of when different modules of study were begun and completed. There was no significant difference in posttest achievement, retention scores (although the self-paced group scored somewhat better), withdrawal rate, course satisfaction, or in numbers of units completed by students in the two classes.

Renne and Blackhurst (1977) found a significant difference in achievement, favoring a programmed class with special education students moving at their own pace in comparison with two other types, a traditional one and a traditional one using programmed study guides. Students with a high grade point average (GPA) scored higher in achievement in all three sections. There was no significant difference among the groups with respect to student satisfaction.

Sturges and Grobe (1976) found no significant difference in achievement of students with high, middle, and low aptitude for botany classes taught by the audio-tutorial method or in the conventional way. The audio-tutorial class was at least equal to the conventionally taught class in fostering achievement.

Suter (1977) examined attitudes of students using the A-T method who were ill prepared for the study of organic chemistry. The students had low proficiency in English, low scores on entrance examinations, and difficulty in understanding presentations in lectures. She concluded that there was no change in the percentage of students making A's and B's; the attrition rate decreased from 35–55 percent range to the 20–35 percent range; and the students reacted very favorably to the use of taped units. The better students also estimated that this approach decreased their outside study time by 30 percent. It was noted that the students for whom the lessons specifically had been prepared did not use them as often as did the better students. She suggested that perhaps unprepared students were less successful because they did not take advantage of the study aids available, and that lack of motivation (in terms of the large amount of time necessary to overcome deficiencies in a subject) may also be a factor in the lower achievement.

Personality and Motivational Factors.   Devitt (1979) investigated the personality and motivational factors related to student choice of independent study in 250 high school juniors. The description of the study process, unfortunately, was not clearly described, but at least one of his groups appeared to be of the audio-tutorial type. In his work, Devitt developed a profile of characteristics separating students who chose independent study in three different settings: a resource center, a regular classroom, or a diagnostic achievement center. His conclusions indicated that intelligence played a weak role in separating the two groups of students and that a complex mix of motivational and personality variables was involved in most of the cases. From this work, he projected the possibility of developing a measure of personality and motivational factors to discriminate among students preferring dependent and independent study. He cautioned against offering independent study to only bright students since they may not want it.

Economic Efficiency.   Fisher and MacWhinney (1976) reported that economic advantages of the audio-tutorial method were often mentioned, but not demonstrated very rigorously. Most researchers indicated high initial costs, but these supposedly were recovered over the years.

In his review of forty research studies, Dawson (1977) concluded that programmed materials were less expensive than traditional programs and saved time for both students and teachers. Moore (1976) evaluated a media resource-based project and concluded that the costs of developing and operating such a program required a four-year period to match the costs of a program based on traditional classroom procedures. In the fifth and later years, the savings became significant.

As these research studies on effectiveness of independent study are reviewed, three cautions and generalizations appear warranted. First, most of the research has been conducted with college students, along with a few studies of high school students. Noticeably absent are studies at the elementary level and in adult education (Kotaska & Dickinson, 1975). Second, the research designs were usually different from study to study; some were better designs than others. Although all of the studies had some common characteristics, such as self-pacing or other aspects of self-regulation in the learning process, and were largely externally controlled, they differed in terms of other characteristics such as use of different media. Some studies examined the effects of the total audio-tutorial approach, whereas other studies examined effects of its parts, such as the study guide or reactions of students to the various components of the audio-tutorial method. Third, the definitions of independent study, self-paced learning, and even of the more carefully defined term, "audio-tutorial method," differed in some studies.

In spite of these differences, there is an impressive accumulation of related research on the topic that consistently supports the two generalizations noted by Fisher and MacWhinney (1976). First, variations of the audio-tutorial method studied present a clear message that student achievement is at least equal to, and in many cases superior to, traditional approaches in which the teacher imparts knowledge through a lecture. This generalization strongly suggests that the audio-tutorial method is a viable alternative that can be used in presenting information and skills to students. A second generalization is that students have a favorable opinion of independent study. The degree to which this favorable disposition will remain over years of experiencing the audio-tutorial method is not known. Some researchers cautioned that the audio-tutorial approach should not be the only teaching method in the course (Case, 1980; Geisert, 1977).

Barriers to Independent Study.   A number of authors discussed barriers that impede the development or blunt the benefits of independent study; these barriers relate to teachers, students, and institutions. Brew and McCormick (1979) identified as a barrier the view of learning held by students; if it is different from the organization of courses, it can impede learning. Some students, for example, view learning as a passive process of absorbing content, whereas others actively search out interrelationships among ideas. Lectures tend to foster the first view, and when students engage in independent study, they must adapt their study methods to the more active view of learning.

In their survey of independent study in thirty-six high schools, Alexander and Hines (1967) reported four student-related problems: (1) the need for more or different resources for learning; (2) need for work and study space; (3) need for adequate direction; and (4) the need for group experiences in independent study. Dressel & Thompson (1973) named one student-related problem: student apathy and discouragement in the face of deviation from easy and familiar course work. Two others were identified in an earlier report on the study (Thompson & Dressel, 1970): (1) some students found a combination of regular courses and independent study disconcerting; and (2) Students were frustrated with the bureaucratic procedures associated with the program. Brown (1968) emphasized that some students are not prepared for independent study and recommended that not all students should engage in it.

Although neither problem was viewed as serious, the two most frequently reported barriers with respect to teachers reported by Alexander and Hines (1967) concerned scheduling and finding planning time for teachers. Other related problems involved (1) providing adequate teacher preparation; (2) the need for a supervisor to take charge of the program; and (3) providing adequate evaluation.

Dressel and Thompson (1973) cited three obstacles relating to teachers in their study of colleges using independent study. Departmental autonomy contributes to a lack of control and irregularities in the program; objectives and goals for independent study are often unclear to the faculty; and faculties are resistant to work load. Thompson and Dressel (1970) noted additional barriers; the fear by faculty that any significant extension of independent study will lower academic standards and encourage student irresponsibility; and the faculty view of independent study as prescribed independence.

In their review of the research on audio-tutorial forms of independent study, Fisher and MacWhinney (1976) stated that faculty attitudes may be more critical than attitudes of students in deciding whether audio-tutorial methods will be used. The method must be satisfying to the faculty as well as manageable in work load. Henney (1978) cited the attitude of the teacher toward students as a potential barrier. The teacher must believe that (elementary) students can and do want to learn. Without this basic attitude, independent study cannot be very successful. Brown (1968) extended this potential barrier to include the attitudes of administrators toward students.

Gibbons and Phillips (1978) identified a problem that often develops as the teacher begins to use the more unstructured forms of independent study: the role of the teacher must change to deal more with process than content and with small groups or individuals rather than large groups. As a result, some teachers reported that they felt initially incompetent in their new roles. They even found their philosophy of education severely challenged, and some had problems finding personal gratification in their new roles.

Two institutional factors not related to students or teachers were also identified: the importance of the type of institutional environment supporting independent study as a goal (Dressel & Thompson, 1973); and cost of the program (Thompson & Dressel, 1970).

Kelly (1965) suggested other possible obstacles to independent study (Kelly referred to "nondirected, unsupervised independent study" and did not further define the process): (1) students may not be equipped to accept the necessary responsibility; (2) teachers and staff members may not be prepared to use independent study; (3) teachers are legally responsible to provide supervision when students are under school jurisdiction; (4) scheduling problems present obstacles, although data processing equipment might help; (5) facilities may not be designed to implement independent study on a mass basis; and (6) few high school libraries have the equipment and materials needed to enable large numbers of students to engage in independent study. Kelly predicted that students will show a lack of self-direction and fail to accept responsibility because of these barriers.

Theory of Independent Learning. M. G. Moore (1973) has begun to develop a unified theory of independent learning and teaching. His attempts focused on learning in which the teacher is physically separated from the student. Communication in this case must be by print or by electronic or other impersonal means. He has proposed three subsystems to his theory: a communication system; a learning system; and the teacher. The communication system must bridge the gap between student and teacher. In the learning system, the student must be an autonomous learner who has both the will and ability to use his or her learning powers, overcome obstacles, try difficult learning tasks, and resist coercion. The role of the teacher is to be a resource and helper, not a controller.

Skills and Stages. Kolcaba (1980) named six necessary skills for independent learning: (1) know how to set goals for learning; (2) know which skills to use to achieve goals; (3) focus attention upon what is to be learned; (4) understand where, when, and why to use each learning skill; (5) set standards for evaluating learning; and (6) apply evaluation methods.

Stewart (1980) outlined a series of steps that should occur in independent study. Initially, the teacher encourages students to define one or more objectives for learning. Then the teacher helps the student formulate a plan for meeting the aims or purposes of the project that have been defined. Next the teacher provides the student with related resources and the student becomes involved in learning activities. Finally, the student and teacher decide which evaluation methods to use in order to determine what progress toward the objectives has been made. Each student's progress may well differ from that of the others. It is possible that a student may not be able to complete the proposed independent study plan. When this becomes apparent, it is essential for the teacher and student to decide whether to modify the plan or to change the objectives or study topics.

Relation to the Curriculum. Perhaps part of the difficulty in defining the concept of independent study is related to the general difficulty in defining "curriculum." There are those who believe that the curriculum should be composed of well-defined behavioral objectives, tightly structured and sequenced learning activities, and some objective method of measuring student progress toward the objectives. This view of curriculum will lead students through a series of experiences that are essentially planned by others in order to learn more or less the same content. This type of curriculum usually emphasizes a correct answer and breaks a learning task into small sequential steps that the student learns one at a time. People who view the curriculum in this way tend to draw upon behaviorist psychology for principles of learning and teaching and usually are referred to as "behaviorists" (Klein, 1980).

There is another group of curriculum specialists, however, who view the curriculum quite differently. They view learning much more holistically, as highly personal and somewhat unpredictable. They reject the concept of behavioral objectives and believe that outcomes of learning can only be known after engaging in the learning activity, not prior to the activity. They are much more concerned with self-evaluation than with public, objective, standardized means to evaluate learning. The learner ought to be in charge of his learning, and the teacher should be a facilitator, not in control. Those with this view look to humanistic psychology for their learning principles (Klein, 1980).

It appears that these two conceptions of curriculum are compatible with, perhaps, to some degree, even responsible for the differing definitions of independent study included in this article. It is possible that some of the staunch supporters of each definition would reject the other definitions of independent study. Rather than vigorously defend one definition over another, however, each one should be examined (along with any others) to determine their usefulness to schooling and education processes. When this is done, a case can be made for each approach.

The more flexible, less structured approach to independent study can certainly foster some curricular goals very effectively. Many broad curricular plans will include goals such as developing the ability to learn, developing unique potentials of each student, understanding and valuing one's heritage, and accepting responsibility for one's own actions. These goals would seem to be most compatible with each student having considerable freedom and flexibility in choosing and setting his or her own learning topics and strategies. Other curricular goals emphasize the abilities to read, write, and compute, and attain knowledge of the world around us. When a student needs to spell words correctly, have mastery over basic processes in arithmetic, or know some specific body of content, the more structured, sequential approach to independent study would seem to be most compatible. These learning tasks are more easily designed and programmed than are some others. In a comprehensive curriculum, there is a need for both definitions, and each should be used to further the goals with which it is most compatible.

Future Perspectives. Thompson and Dressel (1970) were not very optimistic about the future of independent study as they defined it, nor were Alexander and Hines (1967). Three factors seem to favor the externally structured approach: the research being conducted, social pressures on education, and the availability of technology. First, research on independent study is biased in favor of the audio-tutorial approach. This definition seems to be receiving the most attention now and will be likely to in the future. The body of research in this area will undoubtedly grow, and it may become even more popular as it is shown to be more efficient and effective.

Kahle (1978) has pointed out the benefits to research that the audio-tutorial method can make. It helps to solve the problem of internal validity since it holds constant the instructor variable. It should help also in providing for external validity since it will allow researchers to use larger and more representative samples. Instruction is formulated as a package, and teachers cooperating in research studies using this method will have available individualized modules with different cognitive styles, intellectual levels, ethnic backgrounds, verbal abilities, or attitudes. These options would greatly increase the possible learning modes among which students and teachers may choose (Kahle, 1979). Similar reasons were proposed by Postlethwait, Novak, and Murray (1969); instruction can be standardized, and opportunities are increased for research on learning processes. More research on the audio-tutorial approach will occur in part because it is easier to conduct empirical research on this method than on the less structured one.

Second, the social pressures being exerted on American education favor the externally structured type of independent study. The curriculum is becoming more compressed and is expected to be efficient and to produce objective evidence of student learning in the form of achievement test scores. To the extent that these kinds of pressures continue to exist, the internally structured definition of independent study (as a goal, fostering a variety of outcomes, and favoring an evaluation method perhaps unique to each student), will remain a worthy ideal more than an essential practice in schools.

Third, the technological approach as employed in the audio-tutorial method will increase in the future as the availability of technology increases in schools. Calculators, computers, and audiovisual materials will become more common and will be used in this method to tutor a variety of students.

The audio-tutorial approach to independent study clearly is desirable and needed for certain kinds of learning in the curriculum. And yet, in their desire to use a good technique to foster certain kinds of learning, educators must guard against the use of only one approach to independent study to the exclusion of different types for other necessary goals, learnings, and skills. A variety of approaches is needed in a balanced curriculum.

If independent study is to be successfully implemented in any form, students and teachers must be helped to understand it, develop the necessary skills for engaging in it, and develop the necessary attitudes to encourage it. These understandings, skills, and attitudes will require careful nurturing during their developmental stages. Adequate facilities also must be provided. No teacher or student should be expected to engage in independent study without the proper preparation and facilities that are necessary for the process to be used effectively to achieve the desired outcomes.

M. Frances Klein

See also Distance Education; Homework; Individualized Systems of Instruction; Instruction Processes; New Technologies in Education; Nontraditional Higher Education Programs; Systems Design in Instruction.

REFERENCES

Alexander, W. M., & Burke, W. I. Independent study in secondary schools. *Interchange*, 1972, *3*(2–3), 101–113.

Alexander, W. M., & Hines, V. A. *Independent Study in Secondary Schools*. New York: Holt, Rinehart & Winston, 1967.

Beeler, K. D. Student self-directed learning: An essential goal in education (or let's have fewer "edward bears"). *Kappa Delta Pi Record*, October 1979, *16*(1), 20–22.

Beggs, D. W., & Buffie, E. G. (Eds.). *Independent Study: Bold New Venture*. Bloomington: Indiana University Press, 1965.

Bonthius, R. H.; Davis, F. J.; & Drushal, J. G. *The Independent Study Program in the United States: A Report on an Undergraduate Instructional Method*. New York: Columbia University Press, 1957.

Brew, A., & McCormick, B. Student learning and an independent study course. *Higher Education*, July 1979, *8*(4), 429–441.

Brown, B. F. *Education by Appointment: New Approaches to Independent Study*. West Nyack, N.Y.: Parker, 1968.

Butzow, J. W. A study of the interrelations of attitudes and achievement measures in an audio-tutorial college chemistry course. *Journal of Research in Science Teaching*, January 1977, *14*(1), 45–49.

Carpenter, M. Y., & Quiring, J. D. Using modular format in teaching health concepts to primaries. *Journal of School Health*, September 1978, *48*(7), 404–408.

Case, C. L. Impact of audio-tutorial laboratory instruction in biology on student attitudes. *American Biology Teacher*, February 1980, *42*(2), 121–123.

Dandridge, S.; Harter, J.; Kesster, R.; Myers, M.; & Thomas, S. *Independent Study and Writing*. Berkeley: University of California, 1979. (ERIC Document Reproduction Service No. ED 184 114)

Dawson, G. G. *A Summary of Research in Personalized, Individualized, and Self-paced Instruction in College Economics*. Old Westbury: State University of New York and New York Council on Economics Education, April 1977. (ERIC Document Reproduction Service No. ED 144 859)

Della-Dora, D., & Blanchard, L. J. (Eds.) *Moving toward Self-directed Learning*. Alexandria, Va.: Association for Supervision and Curriculum Development, 1979.

Devitt, T. O. Personality and motivational factors in student choice of independent study. *Educational Technology*, April 1979, *19*(4), 52–56.

Dressel, P. L., & Thompson, M. M. *Independent Study*. San Francisco: Jossey-Bass, 1973.

Fisher, K. M., & MacWhinney, B. AV autotutorial instruction: A review of evaluative research. *AV Communication Review*, Fall 1976, *24*(3), 229–261.

Geisert, P. Individualized instruction: Can A-T meet the challenge of the future? *American Biology Teacher*, January 1977, *39*(1), 51–52, 64.

Gibbons, M., & Phillips, G. Helping students through the self-education crisis. *Phi Delta Kappan*, December 1978, *60*(4), 296–300.

Gibbons, M., & Phillips, G. Teaching for self-education: Promising new professional role. *Journal of Teacher Education*, September–October 1979, *30*(5), 26–28.

Henney, M. Facilitating self-directed learning. *Improving College and University Teaching*, Spring 1978, *26*(2), 128–130.

Hubbell, J. W. An independent study that pays off—twice. *Journal of Physical Education and Recreation*, November–December 1976, *47*(9), 40–41.

Kahle, J. B. A-T instruction: A perspective and a prediction. *American Biology Teacher*, January 1978, *40*(1), 17–20.

Kahle, J. B.; Douglass, C. B.; & Nordland, F. H. An analysis of learner efficiency when individualized and group instructional formats are utilized with disadvantaged students. *Science Education*, April–June 1976, *60*(2), 245–250.

Kahle, J. B.; Nordland, F. H.; & Douglass, C. B. An analysis of an alternative instructional model for disadvantaged students. *Science Education*, April–June 1976, *60*(2), 237–243.

Kelly, E. T. Unsupervised study: Proceed with caution. *Clearinghouse*, October 1965, *40*(2), 100–101.

Klein, M. F. A curriculum perspective on the Beginning Teacher Evaluation Study (BTES). In *Time to Learn*. Washington, D.C.: National Institute of Education, 1980. (ERIC Document Reproduction Service No. ED 192 454)

Knowles, M. S. *Self-directed Learning: A Guide for Learners and Teachers*. Chicago: Follett, 1975.

Kolcaba, R. F. Independent learning skills: Keys to lifelong education. *Curriculum Review*, February 1980, *19*(1), 15–19.

Kotaska, J. G., & Dickinson, G. Effects of a study guide on independent adult learning. *Adult Education*, Spring 1975, *25*(3), 161–168.

Long, H. B., & Ashford, M. L. Self-directed inquiry as a method of continuing education in colonial America. *Journal of General Education*, Fall 1976, *28*(3), 245–255.

Macdonald, J. B. Independent learning: The theme of the conference. In G. T. Gleason (Ed.), *The Theory and Nature of Independent Learning*. Scranton, Pa.: International Textbook Company, 1967.

Mayes, V.; Brigham, L.; & McNeill, S. V. Student attitudes toward an audio-tutorial course in precalculus. *Mathematics Teacher*, March 1977, *70*(3), 229–231.

Moore, G. A. The evaluation of a media resource-based learning project and its modification of traditional classroom procedures. *Audiovisual Instruction*, February 1976, *21*(2), 36–40.

Moore, M. G. Toward a theory of independent learning and teaching. *Journal of Higher Education*, December 1973, *44*(9), 661–679.

Morris, E. K.; Surber, E. K.; & Bijou, S. W. Self-pacing versus instructor-pacing: Achievement, evaluations, and retentions. *Journal of Educational Psychology*, April 1978, *70*(2), 224–230.

Postlethwait, S. N.; Novak, J.; & Murray, H. T., Jr. *The Audio-tutorial Approach to Learning through Independent Study and Integrated Experiences* (2nd ed.). Minneapolis: Burgess Publishing Co., 1969.

Renne, D. J., & Blackhurst, A. E. Adjunct autoinstruction in an introductory special education course. *Exceptional Children*, January 1977, *43*(4), 224–225.

Rogge, W. M. Independent study is self-directed learning. In D. W. Beggs & E. G. Buffie (Eds.), *Independent Study: Bold New Venture*. Bloomington: Indiana University Press, 1965.

Stewart, W. J. Making use of independent study. *Education*, Summer 1980, *100*(4), 371–372.

Sturges, A. W., & Grobe, C. H. Audio-tutorial instruction: An evaluation. *Improving College and University Teaching*, Spring 1976, *24*(2), 81.

Suter, P. H. Using audio-tutorial study lessons to teach the unprepared student. *School Science and Mathematics*, March 1977, *77*(3), 247–250.

Thompson, M. M., & Dressel, P. L. A survey of independent study practices. *Educational Record*, Fall 1970, *51*(4), 392–395.

Ward, B. A.; Mortensen, E.; Trinchero, R.; Lash, A.; Lai, M.; Linn, R.; Fisher, C.; Stanton, G.; & Cahen, L. *The Effects of an Independent Learning System on Student Achievement and Attitudes*. (Final Research Report, Vol. 1). San Francisco: Far West Laboratory for Educational Research and Development, 1977.

INDIVIDUAL DIFFERENCES

Students differ. Within a given fifth-grade classroom, for example, students may differ in ability, motivation, attitude, personality, learning style, sex, ethnicity, and socio-economic status. Moreover, classrooms appear to be becoming more diverse rather than less diverse. The passage of Public Law 94-142, the increased attention to students with limited English-speaking ability, and the federal and state emphases on ensuring equal treatment of students have resulted in a situation in which teachers confront students with a wide range of characteristics within their classrooms.

This diversity presents a challenge to the average classroom teacher as well as to educators generally, whose goals are to optimize student achievement and to ensure that every student learns the basic skills necessary to function in our society. This diversity has also presented a challenge to psychologists whose goals are to develop generalizations that explain and predict human behavior. The purpose of this article is to outline dimensions of individual differences, to describe psychological approaches to the study of individual differences, and to discuss the implications of theory and research on individual differences for education.

Dimensions

Over the years psychologists have focused upon many dimensions of individual differences. Recent texts on individual differences address the following topics: intelligence, special abilities, creativity, cognitive styles, personal constructs, values, attitudes, and interests (Tyler, 1974; Messick, 1976; Tyler, 1978). A discussion of the dimensions of individual differences by Shuell (1981) divides individual differences into the two main categories of mental abilities and personality and then further subdivides personality differences into the categories of cognitive style, locus of control, achievement motivation, and anxiety. In addition, many discussions of individual differences now include a consideration of between-group differences, such as sex differences, race differences, ethnic differences, and cultural differences. For this reason, some educational researchers have suggested that the psychological term "individual differences" be replaced by the broader term "student diversity."

An exhaustive review of each of these dimensions of individual differences will not be attempted here, but rather an attempt will be made to highlight recent research and theory on these topics.

Intelligence. The dimension of individual differences that has received the most attention by psychologists is intelligence or general ability. Intelligence has typically been defined as a person's score on an intelligence test. Intelligence tests generally include a wide range of items, from those that test general knowledge (How many states are there in the United States?) to those that test verbal reasoning (Boy is to girl as man is to _____).

Intelligence or general ability has been of particular interest to educators because of its strong relationship to classroom learning and school achievement. Although intelligence is highly related to school achievement, psychologists have not yet determined which is cause and which is effect. As Tyler (1974) has pointed out, more intelligent children tend to get better grades in school, remain in school longer, and have more positive attitudes toward school; but it is also true that remaining in school is likely to increase one's level of general ability. Thus, the relationship is probably one in which intelligence affects classroom learning and classroom learning, in turn, affects intelligence.

In addition to receiving more research attention than any other individual difference variable, "intelligence" has probably been the focus of more controversy than any individual difference variable considered by psychologists. In the 1960s, the controversy centered around the origin of intelligence and the relative contribution of heredity and environment to intelligence (Jensen, 1969). In the 1970s, the controversy focused more on intelligence testing—the content of intelligence tests and whether intelligence tests should be given (Block & Dworkin, 1976). Criticism of intelligence testing became so strong that in many school districts such testing was discontinued. One argument against intelligence testing states that if teachers are aware of students' ability scores, then they are likely to treat high-ability students differently from low-ability students; this differential treatment may lead to a "self-fulfilling prophecy" whereby high-ability students do well in school because teachers believe that they will do so (Rosenthal & Jacobson, 1968). However, recent research by Brophy and Evertson (1981) suggests that although teachers show respect for students that they rank high in achievement and have good working relationships with them, they do not otherwise treat them preferentially. On the other hand, teachers do appear to behave differently towards students that they perceive as "cooperative" compared to students that they perceive as "uncooperative." Differences in cooperativeness seem to be more related to student personality than to student ability.

Personality. Individual differences in personality have been a major concern of psychologists. Psychologists have attempted to predict a person's behavior in social situations by measuring personality traits. Personality traits are defined as enduring characteristics or characteristic ways of responding across situations. Traits are considered as continuous dimensions on which individual differences are measured in terms of the quantity of a personality characteristic (Mischel, 1981). Personality traits are typically measured by a person's responses to a paper-and-pencil test or questionnaire. Two widely used personality tests are the Minnesota Multiphasic Personality Inventory (MMPI) and the California Psychological Inventory (CPI). The MMPI measures personality traits such as depression, masculinity-femininity, and social introversion, and the CPI measures such traits as sociability, responsibility, tolerance, and flexibility. When taking these tests, the respondent answers "true" or "false" to items such as "I am shy" or "I worry a lot." The degree to which the respondent possesses a given trait is then determined by his or her scores on the items that are keyed to that trait.

During the 1960s and 1970s, personality traits came under attack by many psychologists (e.g., Mischel, 1968). These psychologists argued that research showed that persons do not show consistent behavioral patterns or traits across time and situations. They argued that a person's behavior depended more on the situation than on an enduring characteristic of the individual. For example, an "honest" person may not cheat on a college test but may feel quite free to cheat on an income tax return. Bem and Allen (1974) proposed an interesting solution to this dilemma. They suggested that some people may be consistent in at least some areas of their behavior. In particular, they found that persons who identified themselves as being more consistent in personality traits tended to be more consistent than those who identified themselves as highly variable. Although the controversy among psychologists over the situational specificity of human behavior continues, many of the former critics of personality traits have come to acknowledge that there are certain consistencies in a person's behavior across situations, whether they are

called personality traits or "person variables" (Mischel, 1973, 1981). Two examples of personality dimensions will be discussed here. They appear to be related to school learning, and they have been the focus of much recent research. These are "cognitive styles" ("learning styles") and "locus of control."

Cognitive styles. Messick (1976) has defined cognitive styles as characteristic "ways of organizing and processing information and experience." Although cognitive styles are often classified as personality traits, they also reflect consistent differences in cognitive functioning and thus reflect both differences in abilities and personality (Cronbach & Snow, 1977). Cognitive styles are what many educators are discussing when they use the term "learning styles."

Under "cognitive style," Messick (1976) includes dimensions such as the following: field independence versus dependence (responding to the environment in analytical as opposed to global terms); cognitive complexity versus simplicity (the tendency to construe the world in a multidimensional or abstract way as opposed to a single dimensional or concrete way); reflection versus impulsivity (differences in the speed and adequacy with which alternative hypotheses are formulated and information is processed); risk-taking versus cautiousness (individual differences in a person's willingness to take chances to achieve a desired goal); and sensory modality preferences (individual differences in the relative reliance upon the kinesthetic, visual, or auditory sensory modalities).

Research suggests that cognitive styles may be importantly related to learning. For example, Witkin et al. (1977) have pointed out that although field dependence-independence is not significantly related to overall school achievement, it is related to achievement in specialized areas. The field-dependent person is one who, in perception, is less able to keep an item separate from its surrounding field or context than the field-independent person. Many studies have shown that relatively field-independent students perform significantly better in occupations that require analytical skills, such as mathematics, sciences, engineering, and architecture, than do field-dependent students. On the other hand, field-dependent persons are better at learning materials that have a social content than are field-independent persons. Field dependence-independence has also been found to be related to educational-vocational choices, with field-independent persons favoring domains such as science and engineering that require competence in cognitive articulation and field-dependent persons favoring domains such as social work and education that require perception of and attention to the social context.

Recently many educators have argued that learning can be improved by adapting teaching to a student's learning style (cognitive style) or by putting students with teachers who have similar learning styles (Dunn & Dunn, 1978; Fischer & Fischer, 1979; Reckinger, 1979). Unfortunately, these recommendations are based upon theory rather than upon research. Reviews of recent research by Cronbach & Snow (1977) and Witkin et al. (1977) indicate that attempts to adapt teaching to cognitive styles or to match teachers and students on cognitive styles have yielded inconsistent results. Thus, more research is needed before one can make recommendations about how educators can adapt to students' cognitive styles.

Locus of control. "Locus of control" refers to what individuals perceive as the cause or origin of their achievement. On this dimension, persons range from being external, at one end, to internal, at the other. Persons classified as more external in locus of control believe that their successes and failures are the result of factors external to themselves, such as luck, fate, the teacher, or the difficulty or ease of the task itself. In contrast, persons classified as more internal in locus of control believe that their successes and failures are due to factors internal to themselves such as their own ability or effort. (See Lefcourt, 1976.) Locus of control is typically measured by a person's responses to a paper-and-pencil test. A typical locus of control item would be the following: "When you don't do well on a test at school, is it (1) because the test was especially hard or (2) because you didn't study for it?" The first response would represent attributing achievement to external factors, whereas the second response attributes achievement to internal factors.

Research has concentrated upon students' attributions for success and failure not only in terms of whether the attributions are internal or external but also in terms of whether the attributions involve stable or unstable factors. As a result of this research, a new personality dimension has emerged that may be even more important in educational settings than locus of control. This personality trait has been called "learned helplessness" by Seligman (1975).

Learned helplessness. Helpless or failure-prone students tend to attribute their failures to a lack of ability and their infrequent successes to external factors such as luck or the ease of the task. They perceive ability as a relatively stable factor that is difficult to change; and they view external factors such as luck or the task as outside of one's control. Thus, the helpless students feel powerless because they perceive their successes and failures as due to factors outside their own control (Covington & Beery, 1976). In contrast, "mastery-oriented" students tend to attribute their successes to ability and effort and their failures to lack of proper effort. For these students, their successes give them confidence because successes are taken as evidence of ability to do well. Failure, on the other hand, is not threatening to these students because it merely signals the need for them to try harder next time (Covington & Beery, 1976).

Learned helplessness may be particularly important in educational settings because research has shown that mastery-oriented students are more likely to work harder and longer than helpless students, whereas helpless students are more likely to give up on difficult tasks (Dweck, 1975; Thomas, 1979). Research has also demonstrated that it is possible to change students' attribution for failure and, as a result, improve students' persistence on difficult tasks (Dweck, 1975). In most studies, attribution retraining has involved the experimenter telling students when they fail that it was because they need to try harder (Dweck, 1975; Thomas, 1979). More recently, however, researchers have employed direct attribution retraining strategies in which students, following failure, say to themselves, "I need to try harder next time" (Fowler & Peterson, 1981).

These results suggest that "learned helplessness" is an important personality characteristic among students that needs to be considered by educators. Moreover, the research also suggests that learned helplessness should not be regarded as a static personality trait that cannot be changed. On the contrary, research findings suggest that learned helplessness can be altered through appropriate educational interventions. They also indicate that there may be some individual differences for which remediation is an appropriate educational strategy. Learned helplessness would appear to be one of these individual differences.

Psychological Approaches

In his presidential address to the American Psychological Association, Cronbach (1957) described two psychological approaches to the study of individual differences. These two approaches—the correlational approach and the experimental approach—have their roots in the English and German traditions of nineteenth-century scientific psychology.

Correlational and Experimental Approaches. The "correlational" or "psychometric" approach was formulated in England during the last part of the nineteenth century and emphasized the description and measurement of human differences. This approach was represented by the work of Sir Francis Galton, who attempted to establish an inventory of human abilities and to document resemblances between large numbers of related and unrelated persons. His measures of individual differences included physical measures such as sensory acuity, reaction time, and strength of movement. In contrast, experimental psychologists such as Wundt and Ebbinghaus were working in their laboratories to formulate general laws of human behavior that would hold true across individuals. The "experimental" approach has attempted to manipulate variables and design treatments to control behavior. Thus, differences between individuals have been a source of irritation for experimental psychologists whose aims are to design treatments that are effective across individuals and to eliminate individual differences.

Over the years, both of these approaches have been reflected in educational practice. From its earliest beginnings, the psychometric approach has been intimately involved with education. For example, in the 1890s Alfred Binet developed the first intelligence test for the purpose of identifying children who were not able to be educated as part of the regular school curriculum and needed to be assigned to special schools. This procedure of testing individual students to gather information about individual differences, using the information about individual differences to predict success, and then selecting students for certain treatment, including curricula, methods, or classes, exemplifies the correlational approach. Today this approach is often referred to as "tracking." An assumption of "tracking" is that students are placed in one "track" rather than another because they would not be able to achieve educational objectives in the more difficult "track."

The experimental approach in psychology has also had an impact on education. The experimental approach attempts to improve student achievement by designing better learning environments, instructional materials, or instructional methods without regard to individual differences between students. For example, B. F. Skinner (1968) argued that using principles of operant conditioning, one could design a "technology of teaching" that would improve student learning and reduce individual differences between students. This technology of teaching would involve the teacher providing effective reinforcers to the student for appropriate responses. The experimental approach is also exemplified by "mastery learning" (Bloom, 1971). Bloom (1976) has argued that "what any person in the world can learn, almost all persons can learn if provided with appropriate prior and current conditions of learning" (p. 7). Mastery learning strategies have been designed to provide these appropriate conditions of learning. The assumption is that individual differences in students can be overcome or eliminated by an effective treatment.

The Aptitude-Treatment Interaction (ATI) Approach. Cronbach (1957) argued that neither the correlational nor the experimental approach to individual differences was as powerful in isolation as they would be in combination. He proposed merging the two approaches into an "aptitude-treatment interaction" (ATI) approach. The ATI approach involves assessing individual differences or aptitudes in students and then assigning the student to the treatment or method that maximizes the outcome for students of the aptitude level. The ATI approach is similar to the correlational approach because it includes assessment of individual differences or aptitudes in students. However, it is dissimilar because the correlational approach emphasizes selection of students who can and cannot achieve a given outcome, whereas the ATI approach involves adaptation of the treatment so that all students can achieve a given outcome. The ATI approach is similar to the experimental approach because it involves designing optimal treatments. However, the ATI approach assumes that there is no one best treatment for all students, and that the "best treatment" might differ for students of different aptitude levels.

Over the past two decades, research on aptitude-treatment interactions has burgeoned. This research has been reviewed by Bracht (1970), Berliner and Cahen (1973), Cronback (1975), Snow (1976), and Tobias (1981), but by far the most comprehensive review of the ATI literature has been conducted by Cronback and Snow (1977). One recurring theme in these reviews of ATI research is the difficulty of replicating ATI findings across studies and the small number of consistent ATI findings that have been obtained. However, some replicable ATI patterns have emerged for general ability (intelligence) and "constructive motivation."

Cronbach and Snow (1977) concluded that consistent aptitude-treatment interactions had been found with measures of general ability. Within this category they included intelligence, reading ability, scholastic aptitude, nonverbal reasoning, and grade point average. Based on the Cronbach and Snow review, Snow (1976) stated that students who were low in general ability did poorly and students who were high in general ability did well in treatments or teaching methods that (1) placed burdens of information processing on learners; (2) used elaborate or unusual explanations; (3) involved a "new" curriculum; (4) included discovery or inquiry methods; (5) encouraged learner self-direction; (6) were relatively unstructured or permissive; (7) relied heavily on words rather than pictures or other media; or (8) were rapidly paced. In contrast, students low on general ability did well in treatments or methods that (1) relieved the learners of information processing demands; (2) simplified or broke down the task to be performed; (3) provided redundant text information; (4) substituted other media such as pictures for words; and (5) used simplified demonstrations, models, or simulations.

Tobias (1981) reached similar conclusions for aptitude-treatment interaction studies in which the aptitude was prior achievement and the treatment was "instructional support." He defined prior achievement as a student's pretest score in a subject area. Instructional support was defined as the assistance given to the learner in organizing content, making provisions to maintain attention, providing feedback regarding the student's performance, and monitoring the student's achievement from one unit of instruction to another. Tobias concluded that research indicated that the lower the level of prior achievement, the more the student needed instructional support in order to master the instructional objectives.

Recently Peterson, Janicki, and Swing (1981) have reported evidence for the existence of a replicable aptitude-treatment interaction pattern for general ability when the treatments involve having a student work either alone or in a small mixed-ability group on seat-work problems assigned by a teacher following a teacher-taught lesson. High-ability and low-ability students benefited from small-group learning situations, whereas medium-ability students did slightly better working alone. The important classroom processes producing this aptitude-treatment interaction appeared to be those involved when students worked with other students in a small group. The picture that emerged was that children improved their own learning by teaching other students in the small group and that this teaching benefited the child who was the "teacher" more than the child who was the "student." High-ability students and low-ability students did more explaining than medium-ability students in the small group and thus "benefited from this approach." Medium-ability students, on the other hand, tended not to be involved in explaining to other students in the small group and thus were not particularly helped by this approach.

Cronbach and Snow (1977) also reported consistent aptitude-treatment interaction findings for "constructive motivation." They characterized the student who is high on constructive motivation as one who is highly motivated to achieve and tends to prefer to achieve by being independent rather than conforming. Cronbach and Snow concluded that the constructively motivated student responds better to teaching that provides freedom and challenge and requires the learners themselves to supply their own structure in the learning situation. Students low on constructive motivation, on the other hand, do not do well with teaching that places the burden of responsibility on the learners themselves. A similar pattern of findings for constructively motivated students has been reported by Peterson (1979).

Another aptitude considered in the Cronbach and Snow (1977) review was students' preferences for a given instructional approach. Recently, many educators have considered students' preferences to be a measure of "learning style" and have argued that students will do best if they are assigned to an approach that matches their own stated preference (e.g., Dunn & Dunn, 1978). Cronbach and Snow (1977) reported that in a few studies testing this strategy, the results indicated that basing instructional adaptations on students' preferences did *not* improve learning and tended to be detrimental. Research by Peterson & Janicki (1979) has supported this conclusion. These findings cast doubts upon the appropriateness of assigning students to their preferred instructional method.

In sum, contrary to the pessimistic conclusions of some reviewers, aptitude-treatment interaction research has yielded some consistent findings. These findings seem to have direct implications for educational practice, and these implications will be discussed below. Meanwhile, other psychologists and educational researchers have been exploring a new approach to merging the correlational and experimental traditions in psychology. This approach—the aptitude process approach—was suggested by Glaser (1972) and has been more fully explicated by Snow, Federico, and Montague (1980).

The Aptitude Process Approach. The "aptitude process approach" proposes to describe aptitudes or individual differences between students in terms of the cognitive processes that comprise these aptitudes. Proponents of this approach such as Federico (1980) argue that "instead of normatively based, psychometric measures of abilities and aptitudes with their static trait-like properties, what is needed are individually based, idiosyncratic indices of cog-

nitive processes with their dynamic, state-like properties. With them, instruction can be optimized by prescribing treatments to support mediational activity or to modify detrimental, interfering mediation activity" (p. 11).

The aptitude process approach merges the experimental and correlational approaches by combining the work on cognitive processes in experimental psychology with the psychometric work that has been done by correlational psychologists. In recent years, experimental psychologists have been increasingly concerned with cognitive processes involved in memory and learning. For them, learning involves the processes of perceiving, attending, encoding (converting the information into meaningful form), storing the information in memory, retrieving the information from memory, decoding, and generating information. The psychometric approach or correlational approach, on the other hand, has attempted to describe individual differences among persons by giving tests and then assigning scores that represent each person's place on the continuum for the variable being measured.

A major limitation of the psychometric approach is that although a person's score can be used to predict performance in various situations, one has no way of knowing the processes and strategies that the person used in taking the test. The aptitude process approach, on the other hand, attempts to analyze these processes. For example, the aptitude process researcher might ask individuals to take a vocabulary test and to "think aloud" as they take the test and respond to each item. In addition, the researcher might measure the time required for the person to respond to each item, and might also track the eye movements of the person during the test. This information would then be used to attempt to describe the cognitive processes or strategies that the test taker used in responding to the vocabulary test. The researcher could then describe, for example, how the processes of a high scorer on the vocabulary test differed from the processes of a low scorer on the vocabulary test (Snow, 1980).

The aptitude process approach to the study of individual differences appears to have important potential implications for education. If, for example, researchers discover the cognitive processes and strategies underlying the performance of a person who is high in verbal ability (scores high on a vocabulary test), then this information could be used effectively by educators to intervene in these processes and to improve students' verbal ability. Thus, individual differences such as ability would no longer be considered to be static, traitlike properties but rather would become dynamic, statelike properties that could be changed through education. Unfortunately, research on aptitude processes has just begun and has not yielded the rich descriptive information on individual differences that would be useful for educators. Perhaps when the next *Encyclopedia of Educational Research* is published in a decade, research on aptitude processes will have yielded sufficient information to contribute to a theory of learning and teaching as well as to educational practice.

Educational Implications

A number of educational implications can be drawn from the study of individual differences, the most obvious being that individual differences between students cannot be ignored and must be considered in any effective educational system. A number of systems of individualizing education have been proposed. Because they are described elsewhere in this encyclopedia, they will not be considered in detail here. Most of these systems are based either explicitly or implicitly upon psychological models of individualization. Thus, a brief review of these models seems appropriate.

Psychological Models of Individualization. Walberg (1975) has proposed a taxonomy of seven psychological models of individualization, including (1) selection, (2) enrichment, (3) acceleration, (4) diagonostic hierarchical, (5) diagnostic random, (6) multimodal, and (7) multivalent.

"Selection" involves using measures of individual differences to select those who are "unfit" for education. This approach is commonly used in higher education in Europe, where only the most able students are selected to go on to the university.

"Enrichment" and "acceleration" are similar in the sense that students move through the same course of instruction in the same sequence, with students having to repeat the entire sequence if they fail. According to Walberg (1975), in the enrichment model each student spends the same amount of time in learning, and individual differences are revealed in the normal distribution of test scores that are highly related to students' aptitudes; students who are more able tend to do better on the unit test at the end of the unit, whereas students who are less able tend to do worse. In contrast, in the acceleration model the time spent by each student is variable; students who are less able take more time to complete the unit, and students who are more able complete the unit quickly. If given enough time, all students eventually complete the unit and thus achieve the criterion score on the test at the end of the unit.

The two diagnostic models described by Walberg include the "hierarchical" and the "random" models. In the diagnostic model, student achievement is assessed before beginning instruction. The pretest scores are then used to place the student in the most appropriate point in the sequence of instruction. In the hierarchical model, the sequence of instruction is hierarchical so that the elements of one unit must be completed before going on to the next unit. The "random model" assumes that the units of instruction need not be completed in a particular sequence. In both diagnostic models, individual differences in prior achievement are measured and considered in order to assign the student to the appropriate unit of instruction.

The "multimodal" and "multivalent" models both involve multiple courses or types of instruction as means of individualization. The multimodal model consists of several courses of instruction that all lead to the same achievement goal. Individual differences in students are assessed, and then each student is assigned to the type or course of instruction that is best suited to the student's aptitude; this model reflects the aptitude-treatment interaction approach described above. The multivalent model also assumes different courses or types of instruction, but these different courses lead to different goals for different students. Individual differences are assessed at the beginning of instruction, and then these scores are used to assign students to different courses of instruction having different goals.

The taxonomy of psychological models of individualization is only one of many that have been developed. Rohwer, Rohwer, and B-Howe (1980) suggest the following models: (1) selection, (2) remediation, (3) diversified instruction, and (4) diversified instruction with multiple objectives. Other models have been suggested by Klausmeier (1977) and Glaser (1977).

Education for the Eighties. As described in the introduction, current educational policies have resulted in more diverse classrooms and schools. Barring major changes in educational policy, it appears that in the eighties, teachers will be dealing with increased diversity within their classrooms, and principals will be dealing with increased diversity within their schools.

In responding to student diversity, educators might consider the four models proposed by Rohwer, Rohwer, and B-Howe (1980). Of these four models, the model least likely to be used appears to be the selection model. The historic tradition in our country of education for all would appear to militate against selecting certain students as being "unfit" for learning. Moreover, the advent of mainstreaming appears to exemplify the trend against selection of students. The three most viable models for education of the individual in the eighties appear to be remediation, diversified instruction, and diversified instruction with multiple objectives. Educators' attempts to remediate individual differences will be informed by the continued research on aptitude processes. In addition, research on personality traits such as "locus of control" appears to be tending toward a process description of these personality variables. Thus, it seems likely that by the end of the eighties, educators may be able to use the results of research on aptitude processes and personality processes to develop educational interventions that would remediate individual differences in cognition and motivation. The greatest potential for educating individually different students appears to be through diversified instruction, having either a single objective or multiple objectives.

Results of aptitude-treatment interaction research. Although there are many ways in which aptitude-treatment interaction findings could be used to diversify instruction, we will describe only three examples here. First, classroom teachers might diversify instruction within their own classrooms. For example, the results of aptitude-treatment interaction research suggest that having students work on seat-work problems in small mixed-ability groups facilitates the achievement of high-ability and low-ability students, whereas having students work individually on seat-work problems is better for medium-ability students. These findings have direct implications for classroom teachers who seek to maximize the mathematics achievement of their students who vary in mathematics ability. They might teach the lesson to the whole class using a direct instruction approach but then vary the way in which students work on mathematical seat-work. Thus, within the classroom the teacher might have medium-ability students working individually on seat-work while high-ability and low-ability students work on seat-work in small groups. The research would suggest that the teacher will maximize the achievement of individually different students by such an arrangement.

Second, school principals might observe the teaching styles of teachers in their schools, assess relevant individual differences in students, and then assign students to teaching styles that would maximize their achievement based on their level of ability or personality. For example, most high schools have many teachers who teach the course called Introduction to Social Studies. Assignment of students to these courses is typically done in a semirandom manner by a counselor or a computer either separately or in combination. In contrast, the counselor or the administrator might use the aptitude-treatment interaction findings for constructive motivation to assign students to the sections of the course. In implementing this procedure, the administrator or counselor would give students a short paper-and-pencil questionnaire to assess their levels of constructive motivation. Then the counselor would either recommend or assign the student high on constructive motivation to teachers who had been observed to provide students a great deal of freedom and responsibility for their own learning. On the other hand, students low on constructive motivation would be recommended or assigned to teachers who provide most of the structure for their students and do not place burdens of responsibility on the learners themselves.

Such a strategy would not require individual teachers to change their teaching styles provided that the teachers already differed in their teaching styles. However, in many schools there may be so few teachers of a given course or section that it would be necessary for teachers to change their styles to adapt to student differences. Thus, a third strategy would be one in which teachers would change their teaching styles, and each teacher could teach with a different style to adapt to individual differences in students. For many administrators, it may appear to be a difficult task to get teachers to change their teaching styles. However, recent research on teaching effectiveness has shown that it is possible to change teachers' behavior with a minimal amount of training consisting of a short training manual plus one or two short meetings with the teachers (Anderson, Evertson, & Brophy, 1979; Good & Grouws, 1979).

Finally, educators might consider an additional model as a way of dealing with individual differences. This model, which might be called the "teaching as bowling" model, was described by Schulz in a 1976 "Peanuts" cartoon in which the following interaction occurred between Linus and Charlie Brown: Linus said to Charlie Brown, "Our teacher has an interesting theory. She says teaching is like bowling. All you can do is roll the ball down the middle and hope you touch most of the students." Charlie Brown replied very sagely, "She must be a terrible bowler!" One almost suspects that Charlie Brown had read the research on individual differences and aptitude-treatment interaction.

Penelope L. Peterson

See also Gifted Persons; Handicapped Individuals; Individualized Systems of Instruction; Intelligence; Measurement in Education; Psychology; Sex Differences.

REFERENCES

Anderson, L. M.; Evertson, C. M.; & Brophy, J. E. An experimental study of effective teaching in first-grade reading groups. *Elementary School Journal*, 1979, *79*, 193–223.

Bem, D. J., & Allen, A. On predicting some of the people some of the time: The search for cross-situational consistencies in behavior. *Psychological Review*, 1974, *81*, 506–520.

Berliner, D. C., & Cahen, L. S. Trait-treatment interaction and learning. In F. N. Kerlinger (Ed.), *Review of Research in Education* (Vol. 1). Itasca, Ill.: F. E. Peacock, 1973.

Block, N. J., & Dworkin, G. (Eds.). *The IQ Controversy: Critical Readings*. New York: Pantheon, 1976.

Bloom, B. F. Mastery learning. In J. H. Block (Ed.), *Mastery Learning: Theory and Practice*. New York: Holt, Rinehart & Winston, 1971.

Bloom, B. F. *Human Characteristics and School Learning*. New York: McGraw-Hill, 1976.

Bracht, G. H. Experimental factors related to aptitude-treatment interactions. *Review of Educational Research*, 1970, *40*, 627–645.

Brophy, J. E., & Evertson, C. M. *Student Characteristics and Teaching*. New York: Longman, 1981.

Covington, M. V., & Beery, R. G. *Self-worth and School Learning*. New York: Holt, Rinehart & Winston, 1976.

Cronbach, L. J. The two disciplines of scientific psychology. *American Psychologist*, 1957, *12*, 671–683.

Cronbach, L. J. Beyond the two disciplines of scientific psychology. *American Psychologist*, 1975, *30*, 116–127.

Cronbach, L. J., & Snow, R. E. *Aptitudes and Instructional Methods*. New York: Irvington, 1977.

Dunn, R., & Dunn, K. *Teaching Students through Their Individual Learning Styles: A Practical Approach*. Reston, Va.: Reston Publishing, 1978.

Dweck, C. S. The role of expectations and attributions in the alleviation of learned helplessness. *Journal of Personality and Social Psychology*, 1975, *31*, 674–685.

Federico, P. A. Adaptive instruction: Trends and issues. In R. E. Snow, P. A. Federico, & W. E. Montague (Eds.), *Cognitive Process Analyses of Aptitude*. Vol. 1 of *Aptitude, Learning, and Instruction*. Hillsdale, N.J.: Lawrence Erlbaum Associates, 1980.

Fischer, B. B., & Fischer, L. Styles in teaching and learning. *Educational Leadership*, 1979, *36*, 245–254.

Fowler, J. W., & Peterson, P. L. Increasing reading persistence and altering attributional style of learned helpless children. *Journal of Educational Psychology*, 1981, *73*, 251–260.

Glaser, R. Individuals and learning: The new aptitudes. *Educational Researcher*, 1972, *1*, 5–13.

Glaser, R. *Adaptive Education: Individual Diversity and Learning.* New York: Holt, Rinehart & Winston, 1977.

Good, T., & Grouws, D. The Missouri mathematics effectiveness project: An experimental study in fourth-grade classrooms. *Journal of Educational Psychology*, 1979, *71*, 355–362.

Jensen, A. R. How much can we boost IQ and scholastic achievement? *Harvard Educational Review*, 1969, *39*, 1–123.

Klausmeier, H. J. Instructional programming for the individual student. In H. J. Klausmeier, R. A. Rossmiller, & M. Saily (Eds.), *Individually Guided Elementary Education: Concepts and Practices.* New York: Academic Press, 1977.

Lefcourt, H. M. *Locus of Control.* Hillsdale, N.J.: Lawrence Erlbaum Associates, 1976.

Messick, S. (Ed.). *Individuality in Learning.* San Francisco: Jossey-Bass, 1976.

Mischel, W. *Personality and Assessment.* New York: Wiley, 1968.

Mischel, W. Toward a cognitive social learning reconceptualization of personality. *Psychological Review*, 1973, *80*, 252–283.

Mischel, W. *Introduction to Personality* (3rd ed.). New York: Holt, Rinehart & Winston, 1981.

Peterson, P. L. Aptitude x treatment interaction effects of teacher structuring and student participation in college instruction. *Journal of Educational Psychology*, 1979, *71*, 521–533.

Peterson, P. L., & Janicki, T. C. Individual characteristics and children's learning in large-group and small-group approaches. *Journal of Educational Psychology*, 1979, *71*, 677–687.

Peterson, P. L.; Janicki, T. C.; & Swing, S. R. Ability x treatment interaction effects on children's learning in large-group and small-group approaches. *American Educational Research Journal*, 1981, *18*, 453–473.

Reckinger, N. Choice as a way to quality of learning. *Educational Leadership*, 1979, *36*, 255–256.

Rohwer, W. D.; Rohwer, C. P.; & B-Howe, J. R. *Educational Psychology: Teaching for Student Diversity.* New York: Holt, Rinehart & Winston, 1980.

Rosenthal, R., & Jacobson, L. *Pygmalion in the Classroom: Teacher Expectation and Pupils' Intellectual Development.* New York: Holt, Rinehart & Winston, 1968.

Seligman, M. E. P. *Helplessness: On Depression, Development, and Death.* San Francisco: Freeman, 1975.

Shuell, T. J. Dimensions of individual differences. In F. H. Farley & N. J. Gordon (Eds.), *Psychology and Education: The State of the Union.* Berkeley, Calif.: McCutchan, 1981.

Skinner, B. F. *The Technology of Teaching.* New York: Appleton-Century-Crofts, 1968.

Snow, R. E. Research on aptitude for learning: A progress report. In L. S. Shulman (Ed.), *Review of Research in Education* (Vol. 4). Itasca, Ill.: F. E. Peacock, 1976.

Snow, R. E. Aptitude processes. In R. E. Snow, P. A. Federico, & W. E. Montague (Eds.), *Cognitive Process Analyses of Aptitude.* Vol. 1 of *Aptitude, Learning, and Instruction.* Hillsdale, N.J.: Lawrence Erlbaum Associates, 1980.

Snow, R. E.; Federico, P. A.; & Montague, W. E. (Eds.). *Cognitive Process Analyses of Aptitude.* Vol. 1 of *Aptitude, Learning, and Instruction.* Hillsdale, N.J.: Lawrence Erlbaum Associates, 1980.

Thomas, A. Learned helplessness and expectancy factors: Implications for research in learning disabilities. *Review of Educational Research*, 1979, *49*, 208–221.

Tobias, S. Adaptation to individual differences. In F. H. Farley & N. J. Gordon (Eds.), *Psychology and Education: The State of the Union.* Berkeley, Calif.: McCutchan, 1981.

Tyler, L. E. *Individual Differences: Abilities and Motivational Directions.* Englewood Cliffs, N.J.: Prentice-Hall, 1974.

Tyler, L. E. *Individuality: Human Possibilities and Personal Choice in the Psychological Development of Men and Women.* San Francisco: Jossey-Bass, 1978.

Walberg, H. J. Psychological theories of educational individualization. In H. Talmage (Ed.), *Systems of Individualized Education.* Berkeley, Calif.: McCutchan, 1975.

Witkin, H. A.; Moore, C. A.; Goodenough, D. R.; & Cox, P. W. Field-dependent and field-independent cognitive styles and their educational implications. *Review of Educational Research*, 1977, *47*, 1–64.

INDIVIDUALIZED SYSTEMS OF INSTRUCTION

Instruction is said to be individualized when it successfully takes into account the differences in learning aptitude found in students of a given age or grade. Critics have charged that conventional teaching ignores such differences and have often proposed replacing it with a more individualized approach. Some have recommended alternative forms of classroom organization, such as ability-grouped classes, nongraded classes, programs of rapid promotion, and open classrooms. Others have recommended extensive use of individualizing technological aids, such as programmed instruction, computer-based teaching, and audiovisual instruction. And still others have proposed use of individualized assignments, learning contracts, and individual projects. All of these alternatives can be, and have been, discussed under the broad rubric of "individualized instruction."

These approaches seem to be stepping-stones to other critics who have proposed more radical changes in teaching. Instead of recommending a single change in classroom organization, technology, or learner assignments, these more radical critics have called for changes in all of them through adoption of fully individualized systems of teaching. Within these systems, learners work individually on their studies using materials and procedures appropriate to their needs, and they complete their studies at individually appropriate rates. Individualized systems require overhaul of classroom organization, new roles for teachers and other school personnel, new formats for instructional and evaluation materials, and a new freedom from clock and calendar for learners. Among the best known of the individualized systems are Keller's Personalized System of Instruction (PSI); Postlethwait's Audio-Tutorial Approach (A-T); Individually Prescribed Instruction (IPI);

Program for Learning in Accordance with Needs (PLAN); Individually Guided Education (IGE); and Bloom's Learning for Mastery (LFM). This article focuses on such systems of individualized instruction rather than on individualized instruction in the broad sense.

Early Systems. For much of history, formal schooling has meant individualized teaching. Pupils were taught individually by Greek and Roman tutors in the first academies, and they continued to be taught individually in America until the middle of the nineteenth century. At that time, children of different ages still met in one-room schools with one teacher and progressed at their own rates through the few instructional materials available. With the establishment of the first graded school in 1848, however, classroom organization began changing in schools throughout the country. The administrative and economic efficiencies of grading were so great that lockstep progression became the norm everywhere, and by 1860 individualized schooling had virtually vanished from American education (Otto, 1950).

For one hundred years educators searched for ways to reintroduce individualization, and they achieved some notable successes. Three of these were especially important in preparing the way for the explosive development of individualized instruction in the 1960s: the development of grouping approaches during the late nineteenth century; the invention of self-paced unit approaches in the 1920s; and the programmed instruction revolution of the 1950s and early 1960s.

Individualization by grouping. The grouping plans established at the end of the nineteenth century were meant to break the educational lockstep established by the graded school (Otto, 1950). The Cambridge Plan of 1893, for example, required the same work of all pupils for the first three grades, but arranged the work of the last six grades into two parallel courses, a regular course requiring six years and a special course for brighter pupils requiring four. The Batavia Plan employed additional teachers to give special assistance to slow learners, while the North Denver Plan singled out the brighter pupils for special help. In the Santa Barbara Concentric Plan, students were separated into A, B, and C sections. All students covered the basic content set out for the C's, but the B pupils did more extensive work than the C's, and the A's did still more than the B's.

Such plans for grouping, acceleration, and enrichment have become a part of the landscape of American education. One hundred years after their introduction, they are still with us, and they still have the support of most teachers (National Education Association, 1968). The permanence and popularity of these plans in American education is perhaps an indication of their basic merit. Another indication of such merit comes from syntheses of evaluation findings on the effects of grouping. One recent statistical synthesis, based on more than forty studies, concluded that grouping makes a very small, but positive, contribution to student learning, as well as a somewhat larger, positive contribution to student attitudes (Kulik, 1981).

Grouping plans were also important historically in keeping the goal of individualized instruction alive until truly individualized systems were established during the 1920s. Like these true systems, the grouping plans take into account broad, stable individual differences in aptitude. But unlike individualized systems, the grouping plans cannot easily handle those pupils with uneven patterns of ability who are very strong in one subject and very weak in another. Even more serious, the grouping plans cannot handle momentary differences among learners in their reactions to instruction. Even very similar children differ from occasion to occasion in degree of concentration, amount of fatigue, and interest in a given subject. Grouping methods cannot make adjustments for such fluctuations; self-paced unit approaches can.

Self-paced unit approaches. Frederic Burk, who established the Concentric Plan at Santa Barbara, eventually came to see the shortcomings of grouping approaches and began to work out a new way to meet the needs of students of different aptitudes (Ward et al., 1925). Beginning in 1912, he established in the elementary school of the San Francisco State Normal School the first clear-cut plan for individual instruction and promotion. In Burk's Individual System, class recitations were abandoned and daily assignments were never given. Instead, Burk and his teachers divided school work into units, constructed self-instructional materials for each unit, and tested each pupil for mastery as the pupil completed the work outlined for a unit. Under Burk's system, children moved forward on an irregular front, subject by subject, according to the number of units satisfactorily completed.

Burk's student Carleton Washburne applied and refined Burk's system in the public schools of Winnetka, Illinois (Washburne, 1925). Under Washburne's leadership, the Winnetka Plan received international recognition and acclaim. At Winnetka, pupils spent half their time in individual work and half their time on group and creative activities. During the time devoted to individual instruction, they worked on their own tasks with the help of self-instructional materials. When self-testing showed that a pupil was ready to move from one unit to another, the child took a test to demonstrate mastery to the teacher. Tests were repeatable, but children had to demonstrate 100 percent mastery before beginning work on a new unit. The Winnetka plan called for no recitations. Teachers spent their time working with individuals or with small groups, encouraging and supervising. No child ever "failed" or "skipped a grade." Each child simply took up the next school year where he or she had left off the year before in a given subject.

In the *Twenty-fourth Yearbook of the National Society for the Study of Education* (Whipple, 1925), Washburne pulled together the work done on individualized instruction up to that time. Even today his treatment of this theme seems timely. The practices he described, the rationale he presented, and his evaluation results could almost fit into today's journals. Washburne may have hoped that this careful treatment would excite new interest in individualized systems of instruction, but the yearbook did not do this. It was to serve instead as a monument to an educational era that had come to an end. Although individualized systems of instruction did not die out entirely during the years of the great Depression and World War II (Washburne & Marland, 1963), they faded from view, and meaningful experimentation with them virtually stopped. When individualized systems reappeared in the 1960s, they seemed to be new and exciting inventions without roots in the past.

Programmed instruction. The impulse that led to the reinvention of individualized systems in the 1960s was basically a technological impulse, a desire to use machines to increase teaching efficiency. The impulse came from psychologist and inventor B. F. Skinner, who in 1954 called for a technological revolution in education (Skinner, 1954). In this classic article, "The Science of Learning and the Art of Teaching," he criticized conventional teaching methods and argued that mechanical devices could make teaching more effective. Skinner predicted that such devices would ensure student mastery of material to be learned and would reduce the amount of punishment, frustration, and boredom in schools. In Skinner's view, teaching machines would transform education; they would make teaching efficient and learning joyful.

B. F. Skinner was not the first person to develop a machine to assist teachers (Silberman, 1962). The history of automated instruction goes back at least to 1860 when Halcyon Skinner developed and patented a device to teach spelling. But this device and other early automated devices attracted little attention, and today such machines are remembered, if at all, simply as curiosities. B. F. Skinner's teaching machines, on the other hand, immediately received wide attention. A few years after Skinner's 1954 paper, articles on teaching machines and programmed instruction began appearing in journals with great frequency. In the early sixties, Skinner's programmed instruction seemed to be one of the most exciting and promising innovations in the entire history of education.

The basic idea underlying programmed instruction is that the learning of any behavior, no matter how complex, rests upon the learning of a sequence of less complex component behaviors. Theoretically, therefore, by breaking a complex behavior down into a chain of component behaviors and by having students master each link in the chain, teachers can ensure student mastery of even the most complex skills. In practice, Skinner's programmed instruction has three key characteristics. First, the programs present instructional materials in a sequence of brief presentations—"frames," or small steps of about a sentence or a paragraph in length. Second, they require learners to make an active response by correctly answering

a question or solving a problem presented in each frame. And third, Skinner's programs give learners immediate feedback about their mastery or nonmastery of the material presented in each frame. If an answer or solution is correct, learning is reinforced, and the learner goes on to the next frame. If an answer or solution is not right, the error is immediately corrected so that misunderstandings are not propagated.

Excitement about programmed instruction has died down in recent years, and today Skinner's machines and programmed texts are no longer a major focus of educational research or practice. One problem was that the premises of programmed instruction did not hold up well in experimental studies. Carefully sequenced frames, overt learner responses, and high rates of positive reinforcement—originally thought to be the key requirements for successful programs—turned out in practice to be unnecessary, or at least not always necessary (Gage & Berliner, 1979). Another problem was that the contributions of programmed instruction to school learning turned out to be less dramatic than originally expected. Hundreds of studies have compared the effectiveness of programmed and conventional instruction in school settings, and although just over half the studies come out in favor of programmed instruction, almost half come out in favor of conventional teaching (Ebeling, 1981; Kulik, Cohen, & Ebeling, 1980). Other alternative teaching methods have compiled more impressive records in the schools (Hartley, 1978; Kulik, Kulik, & Cohen, 1980).

Skinner's teaching machines and programmed texts still seem important today, however, because of the work that they inspired. For it was Skinner's programmed instruction that rekindled interest in individualized instruction in the 1960s. Skinner's emphasis on short units, step-by-step progress, learner activity, frequent evaluation, immediate feedback, and mastery led directly to the reinvention of individualized systems by his students and colleagues. The individualized systems in use in so many classrooms today may therefore be thought of as the children of Skinner's revolution.

Contemporary Individualized Systems. In the 1960s, individualized systems were developed for all levels of education. These systems were used in college classrooms for the first time, and they were used once again in elementary and secondary schools. Although many individualized systems were developed, only a few received wide publicity and became well-known models for instruction.

Keller's Personalized System of Instruction. Keller's Personalized System of Instruction (PSI) is an individually paced, mastery-oriented teaching method that has had a significant impact on college-level education. Its history goes back to 1964 when psychologist Fred Keller, along with his colleagues J. Gilmour Sherman, Rudolfo Azzi, and Caroline Bori, offered the first personalized course at the University of Brasilia in Brazil. In 1968, Keller published a paper entitled "Goodbye, Teacher" that described the plan in detail. In the years that followed, hundreds of papers were written about PSI, thousands of teachers offered courses using the method, and hundreds of thousands of students studied by it.

In his 1968 paper Keller describes the five features that distinguish PSI from conventional teaching procedures: (1) a mastery requirement for advance; (2) individual rates of progress through courses; (3) an emphasis on printed study guides for communication of information; (4) use of student proctors or tutors for individual evaluation of student performance; and (5) inclusion of only a few lectures in each course, not for transmitting information but for stimulation and motivation of students.

Work in PSI courses is divided into topics or units, often corresponding to chapters of a course text. A printed study guide directs the work on each unit. Although study guides vary, a typical one introduces the unit, states objectives, suggests study procedures, and lists study questions. A student may work anywhere—including the classroom—to achieve the objectives outlined in a study guide. Before moving from one unit to the next, the student must demonstrate mastery of the first unit by perfect or near-perfect performance on a short examination. Students are examined on the units only when they feel prepared, and they are not penalized for failure to pass a first, second, or later examination on a unit. Undergraduate proctors (or tutors) evaluate readiness tests as satisfactory or unsatisfactory, prescribe remedial steps for students who encounter difficulties, and inevitably offer support and encouragement to their fellow students.

Although Keller is a major interpreter of the principles of operant conditioning and an associate of B. F. Skinner, his approach differs from Skinner's in several major ways. First, Keller does not atomize instruction into the small frames of Skinnerian programs. Keller's units usually cover about a week's worth of work. Second, Keller does not control stimulus conditions for learning as completely as does Skinner. Instead, Keller gives learners a great deal of flexibility to study in their own ways on their own time. Keller's PSI recalls, more than anything else, the practices of the Winnetka Plan. What distinguishes it from the Winnetka model is the undergraduate proctor, and Keller himself has termed the proctor the one real innovation of his approach.

Among the best sources for information about PSI are *The Keller Plan Handbook* (Keller & Sherman, 1974); a volume of germinal papers on PSI (Sherman, 1974); and a volume on behavioral instruction (Johnson & Ruskin, 1977). The Center for Personalized Instruction at Georgetown University disseminates information on this teaching method and publishes the *Journal of Personalized Instruction.*

Postlethwait's Audio-Tutorial Approach. Like Keller's PSI, Postlethwait's Audio-Tutorial Approach (A-T) has been used primarily in college teaching. The method dates back to 1961, when biologist Samuel Postlethwait began developing audiotapes and other visual and manipulative materials for remedial instruction in his introductory botany course at Purdue University. When Postlethwait's initial efforts proved successful, he decided to convert his entire course to an audio-tutorial approach. The revised course had three major components: independent study sessions, in which students learned from audiotapes and other media in self-instructional carrels; general assembly sessions, held each week, which were used for guest lectures, long films, and major examinations; and weekly integrated quiz sessions, which were held for groups consisting of between six and ten students and an instructor. In 1969, Postlethwait and his colleagues developed an additional approach to audio-tutorial instruction called "minicourses," or self-contained instructional units that provided even greater individualization of the amount, nature, and sequencing of instruction. The basic source for information about A-T is *The Audio-Tutorial Approach to Learning* (Postlethwait, Novak, & Murray, 1972). The International Congress on Individualized Instruction (formerly the Audio-Tutorial Congress) publishes a newsletter *(One-to-One)* and holds an annual convention that gives special emphasis to A-T teaching.

Individually Prescribed Instruction and PLAN. There are two computer-managed individualized systems that have been used extensively in elementary and secondary education since their development in the 1960s. The first Individually Prescribed Instruction (IPI) materials were developed in 1964 at the Learning Research and Development Center at the University of Pittsburgh, under the leadership of Robert Glaser and John Bolvin. A regional laboratory of the United States Office of Education, Research for Better Schools, later became the principal developer of IPI for use in the public schools, and Appleton-Century-Crofts was the principal publisher of IPI materials. Program for Learning in Accordance with Needs (PLAN) was developed during the period from 1967 to 1971 under the leadership of John Flanagan and was a joint effort of the American Institutes for Research, the Westinghouse Learning Corporation, and fourteen cooperating school districts (Flanagan et al., 1975). Westinghouse Learning assumed responsibility for further development and dissemination of the system after 1971. A few years after their development, PLAN and IPI were each being used in about one hundred schools throughout the country.

At the heart of both systems are large sets of carefully formulated learning objectives. IPI's objectives are hierarchically and sequentially organized and cover such subjects as mathematics, reading, and science. Interrelated IPI objectives are first grouped together to form units, and units are then grouped together into levels. The students master the objectives in a basic sequence. PLAN's behavioral objectives cover all twelve grades in the areas of language arts, social studies, science, and mathematics. In all, PLAN includes to total of more than six thousand objectives, far more than any one student can handle during the school years, since each objective takes about two or three hours for an average student to master. Students and teachers therefore use the PLAN pool of objectives to design programs of study that fit individual tastes and needs.

Both IPI and PLAN follow a basic diagnostic-prescriptive teaching cycle. The teacher first finds out what the pupil knows and then provides learning materials that are appropriate for the pupil. After the pupil works individually with the materials, the teacher assesses progress and mastery and finally requires additional work and additional evaluation if the pupil has not reached the mastery level. Because this diagnostic-prescriptive cycle is basic to each system, each contains extensive provisions for student testing. IPI materials, for example, include placement tests, which the teacher uses to assign each child at the beginning of the year to a particular unit; unit pretests, which show whether a child can skip work on certain objectives; curriculum-embedded tests; and posttests, which the child uses to demonstrate mastery of an entire unit. Both systems also key lesson materials and methods to each instructional objective. The developers of PLAN list the commercial materials appropriate for each objective in learning activity packages referred to as Teaching-Learning Units. The developers of IPI, on the other hand, have created special learning materials to be used with IPI objectives.

Although the basic instructional model used in IPI and PLAN is simple, substantial changes in classroom organization are usually necessary to implement the systems. Because classrooms must be set up for continuous progress of students, grade designations lose some of their meaning. Teachers must assume new roles as managers and tutors, and often paraprofessional aides are necessary to help with the individual work. Computer management is also necessary for efficient handling of the vast amount of student data collected under the systems.

Major contributors to these plans describe them in a book on individualized systems edited by Talmage (1975). Glaser and Rosner's chapter provides basic references on IPI, and the chapter by Flanagan et al. provides similar sources on PLAN. A report from the Educational Products Information Exchange (1974) contains a comprehensive evaluation of each of the systems.

Individually Guided Education. Individually Guided Education (IGE) was initially developed in 1965/66 at the University of Wisconsin's Research and Development Center for Cognitive Learning under the direction of Herbert J. Klausmeier. IGE soon proved to be one of the most influential individualized systems, and by 1976 there were some three thousand IGE elementary and middle schools in the United States. Klausmeier defines IGE as a total system with seven interrelated parts. These include, among others, such features as a program of home-school communications and a program of continuing research and development. At the heart of the system, however, are instructional programming for individual students and the people who run IGE schools.

Teachers in IGE schools follow the basic diagnostic-pre-

scriptive approach used in IPI and PLAN. Using criterion-referenced tests, observation schedules, and work samples, teachers assess the level of achievement, learning style, and motivation level of each student. They then identify appropriate instructional objectives for each child to attain over a short period of time, and set up instructional programs for the children. Teachers may have pupils work on IGE resource materials keyed to specific objectives, or the teachers may draw on their own experience and materials in setting up a child's program. Finally, however, when instruction seems complete for a child or for a group of children, the teachers reevaluate pupil performance on specific objectives to determine whether children have attained the mastery level. Children who demonstrate mastery move on to the next sequence of skills; children who do not may be given alternative activities on the same skills.

IGE requires an extensive change in school organization. More than anything else, it is this change that makes IGE distinctive. A typical IGE school of 500, for example, is divided into four large multiage groupings of 100 to 150 pupils, called instructional and research units. Each unit includes a unit leader (who is also a teacher), the staff teachers, special teachers, and other personnel in some schools. A special committee composed of the principal and the unit leaders replaces the principal as the sole educational policy maker for each school; the unit leaders share decision making with the principal.

A book by Klausmeier, Rossmiller, and Saily (1977) provides a detailed description of the concepts and practices of IGE. The appendix of this volume contains a list of supplementary audiovisual and print material on the method. A shorter overview of IGE appears in Talmage's book (1975). A description and evaluation of IGE as an instructional system appear in a report by the Educational Products Information Exchange (1974).

Learning for Mastery. Benjamin Bloom's approach Learning for Mastery, differs from other systems in a number of respects. Not the least of them is its relationship to an explicit theory of individual differences. Bloom's practices derive from Carroll's model of school learning and pupil aptitude (Carroll, 1963). At the heart of this model is Carroll's premise—based on his studies of individual differences in second language learning—that scores on aptitude measures reflect differences in the amount of time needed for learning rather than differences in the amount that can be learned. Time needed for learning is the key variable in the model. In brief, the model states that learners will succeed in learning a given task to the extent that they receive proper instruction and that they spend the amount of time on the task that they individually need to learn it. According to Carroll, therefore, virtually all students can achieve mastery of any learning task if each is given enough time and if they all receive good instruction.

In an article entitled "Mastery Learning" first published in 1968 in UCLA's *Evaluation Comment,* Bloom (1968) drew some inevitable conclusions from Carroll's model. If students are normally distributed in aptitude for a subject and all receive exactly the same instruction for the same amount of time, then, he pointed out, the end result will be a normal distribution on achievement in the subject. The final differences in achievement will reflect the initial differences in aptitude. If, on the other hand, students are normally distributed in aptitude and each receives high-quality instruction for the amount of time that he or she needs, then almost all will achieve mastery of the subject. Initial differences in aptitude will not be reflected in final differences in achievement; time will vary, mastery will not. This was the same conclusion that Washburne had drawn nearly a half-century earlier (Washburne, 1925).

Bloom (1968) also described the procedures by which he incorporated these ideas into his own teaching at the University of Chicago. He first broke down the course into smaller units of learning, often corresponding to chapters in a textbook. He then constructed brief diagnostic-progress tests for each unit. These tests could be used to determine whether or not students had mastered the units. Finally, he devised prescriptions for further study by those who did not achieve mastery immediately. Prescriptions included work in small groups of two or three students; individual tutoring; rereading particular pages of the original or alternative instructional materials; assignments in workbooks or programmed texts; and use of selected audiovisual materials.

Unlike other individualized systems, Bloom's approach can be used in conventional classrooms where the teacher already has a course of study to cover in a fixed period of time, where time for diagnostic testing is limited, where extra aides are not available, and where student learning must be graded. Bloom's method can be used either in a group-based, teacher-paced format or in an individual-based, self-paced format. Since Bloom's method is a general approach to teaching rather than a set of materials or even an exact format for such materials, it is difficult to estimate precisely the extent of its adoption. However, writings by Bloom and his students (Block & Anderson, 1975; Block & Burns, 1976; Bloom, 1976) make it clear that this approach has been widely used both in this country and abroad. These writings also describe in detail the ideas and practices of mastery learning.

Assessment of Effectiveness. How effective are these systems of individualized instruction? No one study can answer this question. Systems of individualized instruction have been evaluated at different times, in different settings, and with different results. To determine how effective these systems are and to find the settings in which they are most effective, researchers have to synthesize findings from a variety of sources. Among the types of syntheses they have produced are narrative reviews, box score reviews, and meta-analyses.

Meta-analysis, introduced by Glass (1976), has definite advantages over narrative reviews and box score reviews.

First, it uses objective procedures for locating as many studies as possible on a given issue. Second, it uses quantitative or quasi-quantitative techniques for describing features and outcomes of these studies. Third, meta-analysis uses statistical methods to describe results and to relate study features to study outcomes. Compared to meta-analysis, narrative reviews are subjective and box score reviews are lacking in precision (Smitt & Glass, 1977).

This article therefore emphasizes meta-analytic findings, but it also reports conclusions from narrative and box score reviews where appropriate. Although it covers syntheses of findings both at the college level and at the elementary and secondary school level, it covers them separately. This is partly because teaching challenges in colleges are different from those in elementary and secondary schools. Another reason for the separate presentations derives from the distinctly different records of effectiveness of individualized instruction at the two different levels of teaching.

College level. Researchers have carried out a large number of outcome studies comparing results from PSI classes with results from conventional classes. They have also carried out many process studies designed to determine effects of specific PSI components. A number of different reviewers have summarized the findings of both types of studies, and they agree remarkably well in their overall conclusions about this teaching method.

Both narrative and box score reviewers have concluded that results from PSI courses are generally positive (e.g., Block & Burns, 1976; Johnson & Ruskin, 1977; Kulik, 1976; Robin, 1976). A typical box score review found, for example, that more than 95 percent of the studies reported better achievement results in PSI classes, and more than 80 percent of the studies reported significantly better achievement results (Kulik, 1976). Box score and narrative reviewers also pointed out that student ratings tend to be favorable in PSI classes, but some reviewers cautioned that course withdrawal rates may be higher in PSI classes.

Meta-analyses produced an even clearer indication of the effectiveness of PSI. Kulik, Kulik, and Cohen (1979a) reported the results from a meta-analysis of approximately seventy-five studies. They found that in the average study PSI is remarkably effective. It boosts student achievement on final examinations by one-half standard deviation, or from the 50th to the 70th percentile on a typical final examination. This effectiveness is clear in a variety of settings and with a variety of research designs. Studies carried out in psychology, however, reported stronger results than did studies from other disciplines, and studies in which a single teacher taught both experimental and control classes produced less clear results than did studies with different teachers in experimental and control classes.

This meta-analysis also examined the evidence on types of outcomes for which PSI is most effective. Achievement effects are clearest in studies using delayed measures of learning (with examinations administered weeks or even months after the completion of a college course); are next clearest on studies calling for integrative responses on final examinations; and are least clear on final examinations requiring simple recall of information. J. A. Kulik and his colleagues (Kulik, Kulik, & Cohen, 1979a) also reported that PSI has equal effects on the achievement of higher-aptitude and lower-aptitude students—contrary to predictions from Bloom's mastery model. Finally, they found that effects of PSI on student ratings of instruction are as clear and as positive as its effects on student achievement.

A comprehensive review (Kulik, Jaksa, & Kulik, 1978) of component or process studies of PSI concluded that the unusual effectiveness of the method is attributable primarily to four of its features: frequent testing of student performance; immediate feedback to students on their performance; the requirement that students redo work until test results show that they have reached a high level of performance; and the amount of review that is built into PSI courses. PSI courses drop significantly in effectiveness with reductions in the amount of testing, delays in test feedback, reduction in the mastery standard, or decreases in the amount of built-in review. The more distinctive and controversial features of PSI have apparently played a less important role in PSI's instructional success. Amount of tutorial help available from proctors, for example, seems unrelated to overall student achievement; restrictions can also be placed on self-pacing in PSI courses without affecting student achievement; and lectures may be used for transmitting information in PSI courses without negative or positive effects on student achievement.

Reviewers also reported generally favorable effects from Postlethwait's A-T, but the effects are not as strong as those from Keller's PSI. Kulik, Kulik, and Cohen (1979b), for example, reported results from a statistical synthesis of findings from forty-eight comparative studies of A-T. In the typical study, A-T raised examination performance from the 50th percentile to the 58th percentile—a small but statistically reliable amount—and A-T had no significant effect on student course ratings or on course completions. A narrative review of A-T evaluation findings by Mintzes (1975) reported a similar pattern of results.

Elementary and secondary schools. Reviews of evaluation findings at the elementary and secondary levels are far less consistent in their conclusions about individualized systems. Some reviews have reported clear learning gains from individualized systems; other reviewers have reported little or no effect or even negative effects on learning from individualized systems.

The reviews written by developers of individualized systems have generally reported favorable results. Reviews by Bloom and his co-workers (Block & Burns, 1976; Bloom, 1976), for example, have reported striking results from the use of mastery methods. In almost all studies cited by Block and Burns, for example, mastery-taught students outscored conventionally taught students on achievement tests, and in the typical study the mastery-taught students scored more than 0.8 standard-deviation units higher on achievement measures than students in nonmastery classes. In addition, Block and Burns reported that mastery approaches typically elicit more favorable affective responses.

This glowing picture of evaluation findings is counterbalanced by another picture of individualized systems that comes from reviews in the field of mathematics education. Mathematics is often considered the ideal subject for individualization since it is a hierarchically ordered field in which each skill builds on a foundation provided by lower-level skills. The reviews from mathematics, however, do not give a positive picture of the effects of individualization. Schoen (1976), for example, concluded that elementary school results are overwhelmingly against individualized instruction as measured by mathematics achievement. At the secondary level, only one of a dozen studies reviewed by Schoen reported improved mathematics achievement in individualized classes, whereas three researchers reported greater achievement in traditional programs. No secondary study reviewed by Schoen showed improvements in the affective areas attributable to individualization. Hirsch's findings (1976) were similar. Of thirty-three studies, five favored individualization, four favored group-based instruction, and twenty-four found no differences in results from individualized and group-based teaching. Miller's results, (1976), based on eighty-eight studies, are consistent with those of these other reviews.

Hartley (1977) carried out a meta-analysis of results of individually paced approaches to mathematics instruction in elementary and secondary schools. Included among the studies that Hartley examined are 51 on individualized systems. These 51 papers report results from a total of 139 separate comparisons. Hartley found that the average effect reported in these studies is small, and effects are negative in approximately 30 percent of all studies. Hartley also reported that studies using IPI materials show especially weak effects.

After literally hundreds of studies, therefore, the effectiveness of individualized elementary and secondary school teaching is still open to question. Some reviewers have painted a favorable picture of results; other reviewers have drawn more negative conclusions. Favorable effects may be restricted to certain methods, certain fields, or certain settings; or different reviewers may simply be familiar with selected parts of the literature. At any rate, future studies and syntheses will have to explain why different reviews disagree so sharply in their conclusions about elementary and secondary individualization, and why the picture at this level is so much less clear than the picture at the college level.

James A. Kulik

See also Computer-Based Education; Distance Education; Independent Study; Individual Differences; Media Use in Education; Systems Design in Instruction.

REFERENCES

Block, J. H., & Burns, R. B. Mastery learning. In L. S. Shulman (Ed.), *Review of Research in Education* (Vol. 4). Itasca, Ill.: F. E. Peacock, 1976.

Block, J. H., & Anderson, L. W. *Mastery Learning in Classroom Instruction.* New York: Macmillan, 1975.

Bloom, B. S. Mastery learning. *Evaluation Comment* (Vol. 1, No. 2). Los Angeles: University of California at Los Angeles, Center for the Study of Evaluation of Instructional Programs, May 1968.

Bloom, B. S. Mastery learning. In J. H. Block (Ed.), *Mastery Learning: Theory and Practice.* New York: Holt, Rinehart & Winston, 1971.

Bloom, B. S. *Human Characteristics and School Learning.* New York: McGraw-Hill, 1976.

Carroll, J. A model of school learning. *Teaching College Record,* 1963, *64,* 723–33.

Ebeling, B. J. *Meta-analysis of Programmed Instruction in Grades 7–12.* Paper presented at the meeting of the American Educational Research Association, Los Angeles, April 1981.

Educational Products Information Exchange. Evaluating instructional systems. *EPIE Educational Product Report,* 1974, *7*(58), 1–64.

Flanagan, J. C.; Shanner, W. M.; Brudner, H. J.; & Marker, R. W. An individualized instructional system: PLAN. In H. Talmage (Ed.), *System of Individualized Education.* Berkeley, Calif.: McCutchan, 1975.

Gage, N. L., & Berliner, D. C. *Educational Psychology* (2nd ed.). Chicago: Rand McNally, 1979.

Glaser, R., & Rosner, J. Adaptive environments for learning: Curriculum aspects. In H. Talmage (Ed.), *Systems of Individualized Education.* Berkeley, Calif.: McCutchan, 1975.

Glass, G. V. Primary, secondary, and meta-analysis of research. *Educational Researcher,* 1976, *5,* 3–8.

Hartley, S. S. Meta-analysis of the effects of individually paced instruction in mathematics (Doctoral dissertation, University of Colorado, 1977). *Dissertation Abstracts International,* 1978, *38*(7-A), 4003. (University Microfilms No. 77-29,926).

Hirsch, C. R. A review of research on individualized instruction in secondary mathematics. *School Science and Mathematics,* 1976, *76,* 499–507.

Johnson, K. K., & Ruskin, R. S. *Behavioral Instruction: An Evaluative Review.* Washington, D.C.: American Psychological Association, 1977.

Keller, F. S. Good-bye, teacher. *Journal of Applied Behavior Analysis,* 1968, 1, 79–89.

Keller, F. S., & Sherman, J. G. *PSI: The Keller Plan Handbook.* Menlo Park, Calif.: W. A. Benjamin, 1974.

Klausmeier, H. J. IGE in elementary and middle schools. *Educational Leadership,* 1977, *34,* 330–336.

Klausmeier, H. J.; Rossmiller, R. A.; & Saily, M. (Eds.). *Individually Guided Elementary Education: Concepts and Practices.* New York: Academic Press, 1977.

Kulik, C.-L. C. *The Effect of Ability Grouping on Secondary School Students.* Paper presented at the meeting of the American Educational Research Association, Los Angeles, April 1981.

Kulik, J. A. PSI: A formative evaluation. In B. A. Green (Ed.), *Personalized Instruction in Higher Education: Proceedings of the Second National Conference.* Washington, D.C.: Georgetown University, Center for Personalized Instruction, 1976.

Kulik, J. A.; Cohen, P. A.; & Ebeling, B. J. Effectiveness of programmed instruction in higher education: A meta-analysis of findings. *Educational Evaluation and Policy Analysis,* 1980, *2,* 51–64.

Kulik, J. A.; Jaksa, P.; & Kulik, C.-L. C. Research on component features of Keller's personalized system of instruction. *Journal of Personalized Instruction,* 1978, *34,* 307–318.

Kulik, J. A.; Kulik, C.-L. C.; & Cohen, P. A. A meta-analysis of outcome studies of Keller's personalized system of instruction. *American Psychologist,* 1979, *38,* 307–318. (a)

Kulik, J. A.; Kulik, C.-L. C.; & Cohen, P. A. Research on audio-tutorial instruction: A meta-analysis of comparative studies. *Research in Higher Education,* 1979, *11,* 321–340. (b)

Kulik, J. A.; Kulik, C.-L. C.; & Cohen, P. A. Instructional technology and college teaching. *Teaching of Psychology,* 1980, *7,* 199–205.

Miller, R. L. Individualized instruction in mathematics: A review of research. *Mathematics Teacher,* 1976, *69,* 345–351.

Mintzes, J. J. The A-T approach 14 years later: A review of recent research. *Journal of College Science Teaching,* March 1975, pp. 247–252.

National Education Association, Research Division. *Ability Grouping* (Research Summary 1968-S3). Washington, D.C.: National Education Association, 1968.

Otto, H. J. Elementary education. In W. S. Monroe (Ed.), *Encyclopedia of Educational Research* (2nd ed.). New York: Macmillan, 1950.

Postlethwait, S. N.; Novak, J.; & Murray, H. T., Jr. *The Audio-Tutorial Approach to Learning.* Minneapolis: Burgess, 1972.

Robin, A. R. Behavioral instruction in the college classroom. *Review of Educational Research,* 1976, *46,* 313–354.

Schoen, H. L. Self-paced instruction: How effective has it been in secondary and post secondary schools? *The Mathematics Teacher,* 1976, *69,* 352–357.

Sherman, J. G. (Ed.). *PSI: Forty-one Germinal Papers.* Menlo Park, Calif.: W. A. Benjamin, 1974.

Silberman, H. F. Characteristics of some more recent studies of instructional methods. In J. E. Coulson (Ed.), *Programed Learning and Computer-based Instruction.* New York: Wiley, 1962.

Skinner, B. F., The science of learning and the art of teaching. *Harvard Educational Review;* 1954, *24,* 86–97.

Smith, M. L., & Glass, G. V. Meta-analysis of psychotherapy outcome studies. *American Psychologist,* 1977, *32,* 752–760.

Talmage, H. (Ed.). *Systems of Individualized Education.* Berkeley, Calif.: McCutchan, 1975.

Ward, M. A.; Carter, G. E.; Holmes, H. M.; & Anderson, C. Individual system as developed in the San Francisco State Teachers College. In G. M. Whipple (Ed.), *The Twenty-Fourth Yearbook of the National Society for the Study of Education: Adapting the Schools to Individual Differences* (Part 2). Chicago: National Society for the Study of Education, 1925.

Washburne, C. W. Burk's individual system as developed at Winnetka. In G. M. Whipple (Ed.), *The Twenty-Fourth Yearbook of the National Society for the Study of Education: Adapting the Schools to Individual Differences* (Part 2). Chicago: National Society for the Study of Education, 1925.

Washburne, C. W., & Marland, S. P., Jr. *Winnetka: The History and Significance of an Educational Experiment.* Englewood Cliffs, N.J.: Prentice-Hall, 1963.

Whipple, G. M. (Ed.). *The Twenty-fourth Yearbook of the National Society for the Study of Education: Adapting the Schools to Individual Differences* (Part 2). Chicago: National Society for the Study of Education, 1925.

INDUSTRIAL ARTS EDUCATION

Industrial arts is entering its second century. It made its initial appearance under the name "manual training." Piecemeal instructional activities related to this subject were found in various communities and at various grade levels throughout the nineteenth century, but the first focused, continuous, and successful effort to develop and disseminate a program began with the opening of the three-year manual training high school in St. Louis on September 6, 1880. By the end of the decade, similar schools could be found in Boston, New Orleans, San Francisco, and St. Paul, and in most other large cities (Woodward, 1887).

The manual training high schools sought to provide a blend of rigorous academic studies with equally rigorous and varied technical studies. The typical student's program was about equally divided between language and social studies, mathematics and science, and shop and drawing. And all elements of the program were thought to make equally important contributions to the total education of youth facing life in an industrial democracy.

Throughout Europe, a similar educational revolution had been going on. Della Vos, an instructor at the Imperial Technical School in Moscow, brought an exhibit of instructional exercises (called the "Russian system" in the literature) to the 1876 Philadelphia Centennial Exposition (Bennett, 1937). When Woodward (1904) viewed this exhibit, he saw the means to an end he had sought for most of a decade. He recognized how graded exercises could be employed to systematically teach manipulative skills. Thus, earlier development in Europe influenced the nature of manual training here.

There was soon to be a further European influence. Cygnaeus, well acquainted with the writings of Pestalozzi and Froebel, had observed in Finland in the 1860s some of the same socioeconomic forces at work that Woodard later became aware of in the United States (Bennett, 1937). Youth were increasingly drifting away from traditional activities to stultifying factory employment and urban living. Cygnaeus therefore started an educational *sloyd* program of useful project-centered construction activities for all grade levels, and *sloyd* spread throughout Finland, Denmark, Norway, and Sweden.

Whereas Cygnaeus was trying to retain essential attitudes, knowledge, and skills that he saw slipping away, Della Vos's motivation was to develop an instructional program to train workers. The Russian system actually did not fit Woodward's purpose (which, like that of Cygnaeus, was cultural-liberal rather than vocational), but he could not identify an alternative. Others observed the advantages of *sloyd*, which itself made limited inroads in the United States through the efforts of Larsson, who came to Boston from Sweden to teach the system (Larsson, 1893). As a reaction against the authoritarian, lockstep, exercise method of teaching manual training, there was a movement away from throwaway exercise pieces, which re-

quired no problem solving and design considerations by the learners, to individualized and useful projects, which met these criteria. Early in the 1890s the name "manual arts" began to be substituted for "manual training" to indicate this evolution (Browski, 1969). Perhaps in this way the thrust of *sloyd* was parried, since it soon slipped into oblivion in the United States, at least as a unique entity.

Industrial arts advocates have not wanted for critics. The first group to harass them were the academicians. Steeped in the Greek tradition that considered anything directly useful unworthy of being included in the school program, they have often charged that there is little of value in the study of industrial arts. A second group, the vocationalists, created a schism that became sharply defined in 1910 and resulted in the passage of the first secondary school vocational education act in 1917 (Bennett, 1937). This group charged that industrial arts was not sharply enough focused or studied long enough each day to provide proper vocational education. At the same time as vocational education proponents were saying industrial arts was too broad, industrial arts advocates were saying it was too narrow. Snedden and Warner (1927) were prominent in a parade of authors who promoted a broadening of the scope of industrial arts subject matter.

During its first fifty years, industrial arts lacked an organization that had as its sole purpose the promotion and improvement of the field on a national basis. Such an organization, named the American Industrial Arts Association (AIAA), was founded in 1939 (Warner, 1939). At the 1947 AIAA national conference Warner presented a curriculum proposal entitled "The New Industrial Arts Curriculum," later renamed "A Curriculum to Reflect Technology" (Warner, 1965). This proposal probably has had a greater impact than any other upon industrial arts theory. It introduced subject-matter divisions of communications, construction, management, manufacturing, power, and transportation. Bits and pieces of the ideas and terminology of the proposal gradually filtered into the literature, but the proposal did not affect practice on a widespread basis. Yet, the proposal stimulated curriculum innovation in the 1960s, and today the basic proposal and its terminology are much like what is proposed in the curriculum guides of a number of states.

During the 1960s the first large-scale curriculum research and development projects were funded: the American Industry Project (Face, Flug, & Swanson, 1965) and the Industrial Arts Curriculum Project (Towers, Lux, & Ray, 1966).

Through all this, and despite the optimism of Hutchcroft (1960), two jarring status studies of national scope (Dugger et al., 1980; Schmitt & Pelley, 1966) confirmed that there is little factual basis for assuming that the field is capable of aggressively closing the continuing theory–practice gap. Despite the extensive development of the 1960s, in 1980 instruction in drafting, metalworking, and woodworking (essentially the 1880 program) still characterized what was taught in the name of industrial arts. The field uniformly claims it is providing technological literacy for the next generation. Its programs, in the main, appear to be incapable of delivering on this claim. It appears better suited to orienting youth to the tools, materials, and processes of craftspersons of the last century and their social impact rather than to the nature of modern industry and how it affects us (Lux, 1977).

Curriculum Development. Dewey (1899) advocated "a balance between the intellectual and the practical phases of experience" (p. 131) in designing desirable elementary school activities. His work at the turn of the century stimulated national interest in incorporating industrial arts activities into elementary school programs (Mayhew & Edwards, 1936). At midcentury, well-defined programs of elementary school industrial arts could be found from Los Angeles to Long Island, and in Cleveland every elementary school building had a full-time industrial arts specialist assigned to it. Large cities, such as Chicago and Cleveland, had full-time city supervisors of elementary school industrial arts.

Secondary school industrial arts has been successful almost despite itself. Even as the manual training high schools were developing in the major cities, existing high schools began to add manual training, manual arts, and then industrial arts programs. Some of these programs indeed were opened in basements, storerooms, and maintenance facilities, but other schools built new wings for them. Most new high schools provided extensive, costly laboratories for industrial arts, until the vast majority of high schools across the United States offered industrial arts in one form or another. Unfortunately, the programs usually reflected the blacksmith shop, drafting room, and cabinet shop of the nineteenth century rather than modern industry.

In 1914, when the junior high school movement began, industrial arts found strong allies. Since the new schools were to provide comprehensive orientation experiences for early adolescents, widespread support appeared for placing both the fine and applied arts prominently into their programs. The result has been to make junior high school industrial arts programs the strongest in the K–12 spectrum. Here also has been the strongest tendency to innovate. Although there has been some tendency to simply model junior high programs after their senior high counterparts, some have seen the need to view the developmental needs of the early adolescent as a consideration that dictates another approach (Householder, 1972).

Teacher education. Manual training no sooner got started than concern was expressed for ways of finding effective teachers. The temptation at first was to try tradesmen as teachers, but Woodward (1887) was probably among the first to express dissatisfaction with this source of supply. In any case, there seemed to be early and general agreement that an adequate manual training teacher must be both a craftsperson and a professionally educated teacher. Early in the 1880s existing normal schools began to add special courses to prepare manual training teachers (Bennett, 1937).

Many less than baccalaureate level programs continued to operate well into the twentieth century, but the baccalaureate became the universal standard for industrial arts teachers before midcentury. Today more than two hundred colleges and universities offer industrial arts teacher education programs (Dennis, 1980). Many of the programs also offer master's degrees, and more than a dozen offer Ph.D.'s in industrial arts education.

An Accreditation Committee (1977) also has been developed, and the American Council on Industrial Arts Teacher Education (ACIATE) has published standards and guidelines for undergraduate program evaluation in that field. Gallagher (1976) built upon teacher task inventories in industrial arts, and Devier (1981) built upon previous recruitment studies to assist colleges in more effectively recruiting so as to help end the continuing serious shortage of industrial arts teachers (Smith, 1974).

Adult and higher education. One could develop considerable evidence to support the claim that adults have not been able to keep abreast of industrial technological developments, leading to the assumption that there are many demands for and widespread offerings of industrial arts courses for adults. This assumption would not be warranted. Many communities do offer classes in traditional crafts, such as cabinetmaking and upholstering. However, more courses are needed that deal with energy problems, community construction problems including transportation alternatives, zoning and land-use regulations, urban renewal/revitalization problems, and recycling/resource alternatives. Such offerings would more nearly characterize the need to focus upon industrial technology and its cultural impact rather than on handicrafts and their effect upon society.

Although isolated introductory technology courses are being offered as humanities options at a few colleges and universities, there is no obvious well-defined program in industrial arts at this level.

Theoretical Foundations. Pestalozzi is credited in the industrial arts field with having been the "father of manual training" (Bennett, 1926, p. 106). He rebelled against the whole "bookish" nature of education, regardless of subject-matter area, and laid the foundation of educational theory based on learning by doing. Dewey (1899, 1901) did much to continue the experimentation and to popularize a theoretical framework with regard to the role of experience in education. Throughout the formative years of the concept of learning by doing, it was widely felt that an activity/experience had little value as an end in itself, as contributing to learning a body of practical subject matter. Thus, the usefulness of measuring and cutting something to a standard was thought by many to derive from its contribution to learning arithmetic. Similarly, the usefulness of handling and changing the form of natural resources was based upon its contribution to nature study.

Today, because industrial arts activities reinforce learning in other school subjects by showing practical applications of the latter's theories, these activities are widely acknowledged as methodology (Downs, 1969; Logan, 1973; Miller, 1977; Pershern, 1967; Pierson, 1974a, 1974b, 1974c; Thieme, 1965). The additional significance of industrial arts as one of the subject-matter components of a contemporary liberal education is still questioned, but the balance is slowly shifting toward an acceptance of it on both counts—as having method and subject-matter values. Also, there is considerable evidence of its unique significance for special students (Buffer, 1973; Gaulden, 1973; Wentz, 1969).

There is also reason to question whether conditions in the United States in the 1980s are sufficiently like those of ancient Greece to warrant using the Greek view of knowledge as a basis for structuring curriculum. Many industrial arts theorists (Brown, 1977; DeVore, 1980; Maley, 1973; Osburn, 1963; Ray, 1980) have observed how Americans have industrialized, urbanized, and experienced profound sociocultural changes. Even in the early years of this century young people commonly helped to build and repair, cook and sew, sow and harvest, and naturally learned how to be self-sufficient. Now they do not. Some would hold that this places added responsibilities upon the school. The subject matter of industrial arts, for most of humankind's history, has been learned naturally outside of the formal school. In the last century, sociocultural changes have erased the opportunities for this to occur naturally. As a result, young people are left without an adequate orientation to the world of work—especially the work of that one-third of the labor force engaged in the tens of thousands of different occupations in industry. They are left without an orientation to the tools, materials, and processes of production. They are left without a natural means to learn wise consumer, safety, and health knowledge, attitudes, and skills.

The little red schoolhouse could well afford to offer largely or even exclusively academic studies. Social analysts today have greater difficulty accepting its "basics" as being adequate to satisfy the educational needs of today's youth (Lux, 1979). Ample opportunities to study industrial arts subject matter can now be found only in the schools.

Research. In industrial arts, little sponsored research has been done. A tradition of research as a normal part of a professor's duties has not developed to any significant degree. The vast majority of research has been accomplished by graduate students in the completion of degree requirements. Only a small number of staff studies have been done, supported by small grants from state and federal agencies and private foundations. Most observers would probably agree that this condition is one of the greatest roadblocks to improving industrial arts.

The first bibliography of research in industrial arts covers the period 1920–1948 (*Studies in Industrial Education*, 1949). It lists more than fifteen hundred studies in industrial arts, as well as others in industrial vocational educa-

tion. The research listed can be characterized as being largely descriptive, contributing little to the evaluation or generation of theories, and making little substantive contribution to the advancement of the profession.

With regard to the identified need for a guide to future researchers, Suess (1969) reported a summary of forced-choice rankings of research needs in industrial arts and described a model of a systems analysis for classification of industrial arts. He also recommended specification of the network of critical variables that define the field of industrial arts education to provide a conceptual model for organizing and directing research in the field.

Porter (1964) observed that many classroom industrial arts teachers felt that the research done in colleges seemed somewhat removed from their problems. He proposed a handbook to guide teachers in setting up studies and analyzing the results that would outline typical problems, show how to set up a small research design, and show how to treat the data with selected nonparametric procedures. However, industrial arts classroom teachers generally remain weak in research design and methodology.

The situation is not all that much better in higher education. Evans (1966) listed six obstacles to the development of research in industrial arts, including shortage of trained personnel, failure to utilize personnel from related disciplines, disagreement on objectives, emphasis on teaching in higher education, use of the dissertation for instruction rather than research, and shortage of funds (pp. 14–17). He predicted that these problems would be ameliorated, but he felt that the most serious was the first one listed. The situation remains now much as it was then.

With the emergence and refinement of work on a taxonomy of the psychomotor domain (Harrow, 1972), industrial arts researchers should aggressively develop a research base with regard to teaching and learning in this domain. Nelson (1967) has, for example, developed a framework for research on motor learning.

The recent focus on hemispheric specialization within the brain (Wittrock, 1977) also probably has considerable implications for research in industrial arts, but relevant studies are just underway. Clearly some of Evans's concerns about lack of expertise and need for interdisciplinary teamwork (1966) take on special meaning.

Finally, with the pace of change so slow and the need for it so great, industrial arts researchers need to become much more knowledgeable about change phenomena. D'Ambrosio (1969) has shown a direction to go in developing comparative evidence of the new and the old, and Caron (1975) and Renken (1974) have studied the relevance of school organizational style and teacher attitudes, respectively, as they relate to change, but the field is amazingly short on this kind of research.

Public Policy Issues. Industrial arts is slowly maturing. But the process could be made less painful and perhaps even expedited with some assistance in the policy arena. Some academic advisers counsel students away from industrial arts. Also, administrators and curriculum directors often view studies in industrial arts as being of little value. Research does not support this conventional wisdom. A study of five college classes of about seventy-five hundred each, five years after their admission and without regard to their major fields of study, showed that having one or more units of industrial arts credit on their high school transcripts did not negatively affect their academic survivability (Bortz, 1971). According to Cook and Martinson, "It may be that the 'best' program for any student is simply to do his best work in all the courses he takes" (1962, p. 707). A review of the research would free counselors and others to create policies that give individuals a free choice in electing industrial arts.

Industrial arts programs in comprehensive and technical high schools also need strong support from both academicians and vocationalists. The record of our great technical high schools in starting students on careers in engineering, science, and technology strongly suggests that the present common alternative of an area vocational school or a largely academic high school is not meeting the needs of either today's students or the national self-interest. A well-balanced program of humanities, mathematics, science, and technology must be available to students. It often is not.

Finally, industrial arts are of special value to women. Clearly, if they wish to choose wisely from nontraditional, technical occupations they need adequate orientation to them. Also, today's technology-filled yard and home cannot be used to maximum advantage without some industrial arts background. All need special help in achieving technological literacy, but girls do especially, since tradition still provides them with less chance than boys to achieve it naturally. An assist in solving this problem is readily available. The federal and state legislatures have mandated the allocation of vocational monies to support the offering of "useful" home economics (courses not designed to prepare students for entry into payroll jobs). Industrial arts courses are no less useful, and the same provisions should be made for them as well. It is now optional whether the respective states fund industrial arts in the same way as they fund "useful" home economics.

Donald Lux

See also Junior High and Middle School Education; Metric Education; Secondary Education; Trade and Industrial Education; Vocational Education.

REFERENCES

Accreditation Committee. *Standards and Guidelines for Undergraduate Program Evaluation in Industrial Arts Teacher Education.* Washington, D.C.: American Council on Industrial Arts Teacher Education, 1977.

Bennett, C. A. *History of Manual and Industrial Education up to 1870.* Peoria, Ill.: Bennett, 1926.

Bennett, C. A. *History of Manual and Industrial Education, 1870–1917.* Peoria, Ill.: Bennett, 1937.

Bortz, W. R. The relationship of selected high school courses to success in college (Doctoral dissertation, Ohio State University, 1971). *Dissertation Abstracts International,* 1972, *32,* 3742A. (University Microfilms No. 72-04427)

Brown, K. W. *Model of a Theoretical Base for Industrial Arts Education* (Academy of Fellows Monograph No. 1, William E. Warner Series). Washington, D.C.: American Industrial Arts Association, 1977.

Buffer, J. J., Jr. *Review and Synthesis of Research on Industrial Arts for Students with Special Needs.* Columbus: Ohio State University, National Center for Research in Vocational Education, 1973. (ERIC Document Reproduction Service No. ED 090 394)

Bzowski, E. D. An analysis of some movements which may have influenced the growth and development of manual arts (Doctoral dissertation, University of Maryland, 1969). *Dissertation Abstracts International,* 1970, *30,* 5265A. (University Microfilms No. 70-10282)

Caron, M. A. Teacher professionalism and organizational style: Their effects on the adoption of the industrial arts curriculum project materials in junior high school industrial arts programs in Ohio (Doctoral dissertation, Ohio State University, 1975). *Dissertation Abstracts International,* 1975, *36,* 1348A. (University Microfilms No. 75-19420)

Cook, D. R., & Martinson, W. D. The relationship of certain course work in high school to achievement in college. *Personnel and Guidance Journal,* 1962, *60,* 703–707.

D'Ambrosio, V. C. Comparative psychomotor achievement in two industrial arts courses (Doctoral dissertation, Ohio State University, 1969). *Dissertation Abstracts International,* 1971, *30,* 4250A. (University Microfilms No. 70-06756)

Dennis, E. A. (Comp.). *Industrial Teacher Education Directory.* Cedar Falls: University of Northern Iowa, 1980.

Devier, D. H. *Industrial Arts Teacher Education Student Recruitment Practices and Their Effectiveness in the State of Ohio.* Unpublished doctoral dissertation, Ohio State University, 1981.

DeVore, P. W. *Technology: An Introduction.* Worcester, Mass.: Davis, 1980.

Dewey, J. *The School and Society.* Chicago: University of Chicago Press, 1899.

Dewey, J. The place of manual training in the elementary course of study. *Manual Training Magazine,* July 1901, *2,* 197.

Doty, C. R. The effect of practice and prior knowledge of educational objectives on performance (Doctoral dissertation, Ohio State University, 1968). *Dissertation Abstracts,* 1969, *29,* 3035A. (University Microfilms No. 69-04876)

Downs, W. A. The effect of constructional activities upon achievement in the areas of science and mathematics at the fifth-grade level (Doctoral dissertation, University of Missouri, 1968). *Dissertation Abstracts,* 1969, *29,* 2542A. (University Microfilms No. 69-03232)

Dugger, W. E., Jr.; Bane, E. A.; Pinder, C. A.; Miller, C. D.; Young, L. H.; Dixon, J.; Vanderveloe, J.; & Rider, L. Standards for industrial arts education programs: A project report. *Journal of Epsilon Pi Tau,* 1980, *6*(2), 13–22.

Evans, R. N. Introduction. In J. D. Rowlett (Ed.), *Status of Research.* Bloomington, Ill.: McKnight, 1966.

Face, W. L.; Flug, E. R. F.; & Swanson, R. S. Conceptual approach to American industry. In G. S. Wall (Ed.), *Approaches and Procedures in Industrial Arts: Fourteenth Yearbook of the American Council on Industrial Arts Teacher Education.* Bloomington, Ill.: McKnight, 1965.

Gallagher, J. V. A job analysis of Ohio secondary industrial arts teachers with implications for change in teacher education (Doctoral dissertation, Ohio State University, 1976). *Dissertation Abstracts International*, 1977, *37*, 7000A. (University Microfilms No. DBJ 77-10531)

Gaulden, C., Jr. Acquisition and retention of a psychomotor task in educable mentally retarded children as influenced by the presence or absence of action and terminal feedback (Doctoral dissertation, University of Missouri, 1973). *Dissertation Abstracts International*, 1974, *35*, 909A. (University Microfilms No. 74-18531)

Harrow, A. J. *A Taxonomy of the Psychomotor Domain*. New York: McKay, 1972.

Householder, D. L. *Review and Evaluation of Curriculum Development in Industrial Arts Education*. (Information Series No. 53, VT 014 273). Columbus, Ohio: Center for Vocational Education, 1972. (ERIC Document Reproduction Service No. ED 060 175)

Hutchcroft, C. R. Industrial arts. In C. W. Harris (Ed.), *Encyclopedia of Educational Research* (3rd ed.). New York: Macmillan, 1960.

Larsson, G. *Sloyd* for elementary schools contrasted with the Russian system of manual training. *National Education Association Proceedings*, 1893, *32*.

Lockette, R. E. (Ed.). *Industrial Arts for Senior High Schools: Twenty-third Yearbook of the American Council on Industrial Arts Teacher Education*. Bloomington, Ill.: McKnight, 1973. (ERIC Document Reproduction Service No. ED 078 133)

Logan, N. The effect of construction activity upon achievement at the third-grade level (Doctoral dissertation, University of Missouri, 1973). *Dissertation Abstracts International*, 1974, *35*, 942A. (University Microfilms No. 74-18580)

Lux, D. G. From heritage to horizons. *Journal of Epsilon Pi Tau*, 1977, *3*(1), 7–12.

Lux, D. G. Back to the basics won't work. *Man/Society/Technology*, 1979, *38*(8), 24–26.

Maley, D. *The Maryland Plan*. New York: Bruce, 1973.

Mayhew, K. C., & Edwards, A. C. *The Dewey School* (Introduction by John Dewey). New York: D. Appleton-Century, 1936.

Miller, P. W. The effects of selected industrial arts activities on educable mentally retarded students' achievement and retention of metric linear concepts. (Doctoral dissertation, Ohio State University, 1977). *Dissertation Abstracts International*, 1978, *38*, 4627A. (University Microfilms No. DDK77-31934)

Nelson, O. W. A framework for research in industrial arts motor learning (Doctoral dissertation, University of Minnesota, 1967). *Dissertation Abstracts*, 1968, *28*, 3568A. (University Microfilms No. 68-01636)

Ohio State Committee on Coordination and Development. *A Prospectus for Industrial Arts in Ohio*. Columbus: Ohio State Department of Education, 1934.

Osburn, B. N. *Industrial Arts Is for Human Beings* (Bulletin No. 2). Washington, D.C.: American Industrial Arts Association, 1963.

Pershern, F. R. The effect of industrial arts activities on science achievement and attitudes in the upper elementary grades (Doctoral dissertation, Texas A & M University, 1967). *Dissertation Abstracts*, 1967, *28*, 549A. (University Microfilms No. 67-09802)

Pierson, M. J. *Psychological Base for Education* (Monograph I).

San Marcos: Texas Industrial Arts Association Curriculum Study, 1974. (a)

Pierson, M. J. *Psychological Base for Education* (Monograph 2). San Marcos: Texas Industrial Arts Association Curriculum Study, 1974. (b)

Pierson, M. J. *Psychological Base for Education* (Monograph 3). San Marcos: Texas Industrial Arts Association Curriculum Study, 1974. (c)

Porter, C. B. (Ed.). *Classroom Research: Thirteenth Yearbook of the American Council on Industrial Arts Teacher Education*. Bloomington, Ill.: McKnight, 1964. (ERIC Document Reproduction Service No. ED 044 487)

Ray, W. E. Toward consensus regarding an industrial arts curriculum base. *Journal of Epsilon Pi Tau*, 1980, *6*(2), 8–12.

Renken, G. H. A study of the attitudes of Kansas industrial education teachers toward participation in innovative curricular programs (Doctoral dissertation, Kansas State University, 1974). *Dissertation Abstracts International*, 1975, *35*, 5076A. (University Microfilms No. 75-02533)

Schmitt, M. L., & Pelley, A. L. *Industrial Arts Education* (OE 33038, Circular No. 791). Washington, D.C.: U.S. Government Printing Office, 1966. (ERIC Document Reproduction Service No. ED 017 667)

Smith, D. F. Serious teacher shortages exist in industrial arts. *Man/Society/Technology*, March 1974, *38*, 12–15.

Snedden, D., & Warner, W. E. *Reconstruction of Industrial Arts Courses*. New York: Teachers College Bureau of Publications, 1927.

Studies in Industrial Education (Bulletin No. 4) Washington, D.C.: American Vocational Association, 1949.

Suess, A. R. *National Conference on Research Industrial Arts* (Leadership Series No. 20). Columbus: Ohio State University, Center for Vocational and Technical Education, 1969. (ERIC Document Reproduction Service No. ED 029 986)

Thieme, E. Pupil achievement and retention in selected areas of grade five using elementary industrial arts activities integrated with classroom units of work (Doctoral dissertation, Pennsylvania State University, 1965. *Dissertation Abstracts*, 1965, *26*, 2084. (University Microfilms No. 65-09830)

Towers, E. R.; Lux, D. G.; & Ray, W. E. *A Rationale and Structure for Industrial Arts Subject Matter*. Columbus: Ohio State University Research Foundation, 1966. (ERIC Document Reproduction Service No. ED 013 955)

Warner, W. E. *Industrial Arts Teacher Education: Invitation to a National Conference*. Columbus, Ohio: Epsilon Pi Tau, 1939.

Warner, W. E. *A Curriculum to Reflect Technology*. Columbus, Ohio: Epsilon Pi Tau, 1965.

Wentz, C. H. A study of industrial arts activities for educable mentally retarded junior high school youth with implications for guidelines in special industrial arts activities (Doctoral dissertation, Texas A & M University, 1969). *Dissertation Abstracts International*, 1972, *33*, 194A. (University Microfilms No. 70-11590)

Wittrock, M. C. (Ed.). *The Human Brain*. Englewood Cliffs, N.J.: Prentice-Hall, 1977.

Woodward, C. M. *The Manual Training School*. Boston: Heath, 1887.

Woodward, C. M. Addresses of welcome (stenographic notes). *Journal of Proceedings and Addresses of the Forty-third Annual Meeting*. Washington, D.C.: National Education Association, 1904, *43*, 45–46.

INDUSTRIAL TRAINING

Industrial training has been referred to as the shadow educational system (H. Goldstein, 1980). As with most shadows, the features are blurred and distorted. In the case of industrial training, the distortions come from general lack of knowledge about this extensive learning enterprise.

One purpose of this article is to clarify the nature and goals of industrial training, and the research and issues related to it, so that the field of education will be better able to support and scrutinize this growing instructional system. The importance of industrial training is reflected in several recent publications ("Education/Training," 1980; "Training in Industry," 1978), which suggest that private-sector training may replace military training as a major contributor to the advancement of learning theory and learning technology (Swanson, 1978). This forecast is based on economic considerations and their ultimate effect on training decision making in the private sector.

The case for industrial training, whether it involves on-the-job skills training or advanced seminars offered by prestigious universities for business executives, is grounded in the quest for increased profits. A correlate of increased profits is increased productivity. Increasing productivity, in its simplest sense, requires (1) improved equipment and processes or (2) gains in worker knowledge and skill (Jacobs, 1981; McDonnell, 1981). The latter implies training that will ultimately result in increased productivity.

Current industrial training practices are seldom described in research publications. Unlike public-sector industrial psychologists and educators who study the training process or who function as academic critics, industrial trainers are the primary participants in the private sector. Although their responsibilities may regularly demand the same rigorous analysis, synthesis, and evaluation behaviors found in published research, their accomplishments are typically disseminated informally to members of a work group or to management in the form of proposals or reports. Unfortunately, there is little time or encouragement to disseminate findings any farther than these immediate work settings. In fact, industrial training personnel are often discouraged from disseminating research and development data because of the sensitive or proprietary nature of the information. Thus much of what is occurring in industry cannot be easily evaluated.

The distinction between education and training has been debated among learning professionals and nonprofessionals for generations. However, it is generally conceded that intent to control the information the learner receives and establishment of specific performance criteria distinguish training from education. Controlled information is acceptable for training but constitutes an unacceptable educational experience. Education requires the review and evaluation of alternative positions on a given topic.

Within the industrial training profession there is no certification or degree program that prepares practitioners to enter it. University programs to prepare persons specifically for the private-sector industrial training profession are a recent development (McCollough, 1981). Furthermore, training is a secondary organizational goal that exists to support the production of selected goods or services. These conditions make it almost impossible for an outsider to predict the role, staffing, methods, or facilities devoted to training within any company. Each company independently determines its goals, content, and methods of training. The training function is directly affected by the inner workings of a specific industry or business. The major influences upon training are the financial and nonfinancial goals of the company involved. Training efficiency and training effectiveness are two additional important influences. Measures of these influences often serve as proxies for a company's financial goals.

The remainder of this article addresses the two major influences on training, the three principal types of training in use today, and the four job roles involved in providing training. The research and policy issues in each are presented and discussed.

Influences on Training. The question of means versus ends may initially appear to be a very elementary issue as related to industrial training. An analysis of the issue reveals that the research methods most widely possessed by professional trainers are particularly adaptable to studying questions of means rather than questions of ends (Copa, 1981). As a result, the questions of "how to do it" and the pressures of "getting it done" easily lead the industrial trainer away from the goals of the organization. Furthermore, these departures from the organization's goals lead to the criticism that training practices are fads which gain support through reported success that is seldom based on systematic data collection (Campbell, 1971).

Industrial training activities considered in isolation from the context of a firm's financial and nonfinancial goals are prime targets for this criticism. Therefore, it is important to understand these goals and their influence on training.

Financial goals. It is a simple truth that American industry exists to make money, not to train its employees. No goods-producing or service-producing industry would opt to have a training department if it were able to hire and retain fully competent employees at a fair market cost. Employees are trained because less than competent employees reduce the productivity of the organization and therefore reduce profits. Training, therefore, is an investment with an expected return. Training decisions made outside this context are destined to be short-lived (Douthat, 1970).

The investment-return perspective clarifies one's view of the private sector's training function. This perspective suggests that a $300 training program resulting in a $350 return is a bad investment compared to a $1 million training program resulting in a $2 million return. Within this framework, training is not a dispensable company frill. Rather, it is a tool for economic survival.

Research on the cost analysis of training is extremely

important to the vitality of industrial training. Limited empirical studies are reported in the literature. One such study has provided benchmarks for manufacturing industries in the training of semiskilled workers (Cullen et al., 1976). In comparing unstructured buddy-system training to structured training, questions such as time required to become competent, overall cost comparisons, break-even points, and projected savings were empirically answered. As one views the literature, it becomes obvious that this study is an exception (Antil, 1972; Zemke, 1978).

Profit, one of the two major driving forces behind industry, is a stepchild in much of the professional training literature, which emphasizes means rather than ends. The literature is inundated with evidence of "how to do it" rather than "did it get done." Even in this context, right or wrong, financial investment-return decisions about training are made. These decisions may be based on empirical data or subjective judgments; they may be made by training personnel and top management or by top management alone. The voids in the literature on the cost analysis of training are not totally representative of practices in the profession; some training cost analyses are methodologically rigorous (Cullen et al., 1978; Rosentreter, 1978). However, many of them represent informed and systematic estimates. These estimates are totally acceptable to the profit-seeking enterprise but unacceptable to academic scholars. Thus, most reports could never appear in the literature because of their lack of rigor and generalizability.

The primary research that appears to be guiding many locally adapted cost-analysis efforts is rooted in the quantitative sciences (Passmore, 1978; Thompson, 1980). Practical adaptations from the literature, with attention to the cost-accounting methods that exist within specific companies, characterize the methods typically used by trainers to analyze the cost of training.

Nonfinancial goals. Nonfinancial company goals are the second major influence on training. Often ignored in the training research literature, since they are overshadowed by the concern for profits, these goals can be stated or unstated, logical or illogical. For example, companies that establish a corporate personnel policy of hiring from within whenever possible establish parameters that affect the training function. Likewise, policies of companies committed to being the financial or technological leader in their field also influence the training function.

Since company goals and their effects on training are almost totally ignored in the training research literature, techniques for analyzing company goals, along with the training constraints and opportunities that would result, are nonexistent. Since the training profession does little to study these ends, it is not surprising that it is often dumbfounded when it hears of large training departments being suddenly eliminated or of highly touted training centers having little or no effect on the actual work performance of trainees.

In an effort to conform as closely as possible to company goals, trainers often rely on narrow measures of training efficiency and effectiveness, such as serving more trainees this year than last year with the same resources or increasing posttraining test scores. These measures are often used to satisfy management's concerns about training's contribution to the financial and nonfinancial goals of the company. Such measures are most satisfactory in companies that are fiscally sound, that have widely held nonfinancial goals, and that have an established and reasonable training function.

Types of Training. Of the many complicated forms of training that exist today, three principal types can be identified: skills and technical training, management and subject-matter training, and motivational training.

Skills and technical training. Skills and technical training is primarily concerned with worker-machinery interactions. This training is related to the production of goods, the sale of machinery and tools, and the maintenance of hard goods.

There has been abundant interchange of knowledge and practice among skills and technical training personnel in the military, in public-sector vocational and technical education, and in industrial training. Job and task analysis techniques have been researched for decades in all three fields and are widely accepted in each. It is interesting to note that recent regulatory agency pressures for fair employment practices have renewed the training profession's commitment to job and task analysis (Gordon, 1978).

Some of the recent modifications to job and task analysis have at times taken the analyst away from direct observation of competent workers as the data source (DeCaro, 1978; Folley, 1969; Rosenfeld & Thornton, 1976). Empirical evidence supporting the validity of these indirect methods for specific job settings is thin. Prien (1977) draws attention to the need to match particular methods of analysis to specific training problems or situations. In an effort to evaluate more systematically the importance of tasks within a job, efforts have been made to develop a task-scaling method (Ammerman, Essex, & Pratzner, 1974; Ammerman & Pratzner, 1974, 1975, 1977).

It should be noted that these more indirect efforts have come from public-sector vocational educators and that these persons are necessarily more concerned about transfer of training than their private-sector counterparts. Private-sector personnel are more likely to rely on traditional methods utilizing direct observation of a highly skilled worker and a detailed analysis of that person's behavior in order to identify tasks and their relative importance (Musick, 1981; Ridley, 1980). In addition to carefully selecting a skilled worker to analyze, researchers often observe multiple workers and record tasks in greater detail. Furthermore, information, such as learning difficulty (Mager, 1967) and classification of the domain of behavior required for task details, is analyzed (Gropper, 1974; Swanson & Poor, 1981).

Standard job and task analysis techniques are very effective for determining observable worker-machinery interactions of a procedural nature. For example, the details of setting up a machine, running it, and shutting it down can easily be determined. Another aspect of a machine operator's job that is not so easily understood is troubleshooting the equipment.

Whether troubleshooting a faulty production process (e.g., imperfections in extruded ten-inch-diameter plastic pipe) or a malfunction in the process equipment (e.g., inoperable plastic-pipe extrusion machines), the required know-how is complex. The oil-covered maintenance man of yesterday is more likely today to have a white shirt and an oscilloscope. Industry demands have changed. At present there are extremes in equipment size—massive to miniaturized—and equipment is very expensive; equipment is also more specialized, more difficult to keep running, and more difficult to repair once broken than it used to be; and there are lower on-site inventories of backup equipment and parts (Petzinger, 1981).

The financial consequences of using an unskilled work force within these conditions can be substantial. Because of this possibility, a recent study by Johnson (1980) is of interest. Within his computer-based troubleshooting-training program, he also teaches the cost-effectiveness considerations of diagnostic alternatives to specific equipment problems. In a more elementary mode, it should be noted that the analysis required to determine the knowledge and skills necessary to troubleshoot equipment goes beyond understanding procedures. Troubleshooting has largely been ignored by the private-sector training and development profession in the United States. It appears as though the majority of research and development in the area of industrial process and troubleshooting analysis is being done in Europe (Frank & Smith, 1969). Available research into the areas of process analysis and the use of process simulations (Roberts, 1976) points to an interesting public–private sector issue. The movement in engineering education away from applied studies and the concentration of public vocational schooling on procedural skills leave a void in the general work force. Since the industrial training profession draws from the engineering and production fields, there is an equivalent shortage of persons in training who are competent in the area of process and troubleshooting analysis. The nature of industrial technology and the problem of keeping it running demand greater attention by private-sector and public-sector trainers. The high degree of hardware standardization in the military has allowed it to stratify and proceduralize the troubleshooting behavior of its technical personnel and thus maintain efficiency and effectiveness with a minimum of worker training (Foley, 1978). It does not appear that private-sector skill and technical training will ever reach this point of sophistication, because of the diversity and competitive nature of industry and its hardware.

Management and subject-matter training. Management and subject-matter training deals with worker-worker and worker-idea interactions. Topics like organizational communication, employee appraisal, decision making, management by objectives, time management, and fiscal management are representative of management training programs. Management training, at face value, often appears luxurious when compared to skills and technical training. Managers making decisions about the training of managers tend to be more forgiving in respect to costs, immediacy of returns, and inclinations toward ceremony (Adams, 1976).

Before the emergence of the career development movement in the 1970s (Morgan, 1977; Walter, 1976), general management training helped to fulfill the implementation of career progression programs in large companies (Bright, 1976). The pattern was rather simple and effective, and still exists today. Promising managers are selected to attend one of a sequence of management courses at company headquarters. Here they are taught general job-related management information and are introduced to selected corporate operations and personalities. Participants are observed as much during out-of-class events as in the training sessions themselves. High-potential people from among the participants are noted by management and tagged for later promotion. The cycle of training and promotion continues, with each visit to headquarters becoming more selective. This cycle is usually capped off with intensive management seminars held at prestigious universities and lasting from one week to three months.

Almost nothing in the literature treats methods of analyzing specific subject matter dealing with management behavior. Research and literature on assessment of training needs have provided effective methods of determining whether training is necessary to solve a particular problem (Harless, 1975), and yet there are no equivalent methods for specifying the precise subject matter that should be covered within the particular area of need. For example, determining that training for first-line supervisors is needed is quite different from determining what content should be covered.

The issue, in a nutshell, is that the rather powerful job and task analysis tools that exist for skills and technical training do not exist for management and subject-matter training. This void results in a reliance on external consultants in the area of management and subject matter training who typically emphasize training programs that deal with general management topics. Furthermore, these programs are often the target of the criticism of training faddishness (Campbell, 1971).

As one might expect, consultant services are costly and encourage the organization to hire in-house persons with the same analysis and design competencies. At the same time, the direction in management training is away from general training to more specific knowledge and practice, with closer scrutiny of payoffs in respect to financial and nonfinancial goals. The additional design and development time required to produce these more specific programs has created a dichotomy of sorts. On the one hand, an increased number of companies are marketing their training programs on the outside, in order to gain a profit on their investment. On the other hand, there are efforts to limit competitors' knowledge of training programs in that they are perceived as proprietary and the source of a competitive edge. Training programs that have important financial consequences often end up being guarded just like new products, manufacturing processes, or raw-material formulations.

Motivational training. Motivational training is designed to influence human attitudes and beliefs. It might be tempting to equate such training with sales training, but that would clearly be a misrepresentation. For example, the intent and method of many safety-training efforts and management seminars can be classified as motivational training. Likewise, much of what goes on under the name of sales training can be best categorized as skills training or management training.

The relation of means to ends in motivational training is a critical ethical concern (Clement, Pinto, & Walker, 1978). Training with intent to manipulate someone to accept a predetermined position without that person's ever being made aware of the process or intent is considered unethical.

Sensitivity training as a method of motivational training gained much attention and was widely implemented in the late 1960s and early 1970s. However, the implications of efforts aimed at changing deep-rooted values so as to modify organizational behavior have been challenged from a number of positions (Campbell & Dunnette, 1968). I. L. Goldstein (1980) noted that sensitivity training lacks a theoretical base; Smith (1976) highlighted the lack of long-term effects; and Cooper (1975) reiterated that ethical concerns still appear to be the most significant issue surrounding sensitivity training. Newer methods of attitudinal training, such as organizational development and quality circles, although still largely unproven, do not rely on the revivalist type of techniques frequently found in sensitivity training. They appear to be grounded in both human and organizational needs and seem to rely on more straightforward methods to obtain desired changes (Miller, 1976; Yager, 1981).

Job Roles in Training. The four training job roles are instructor, media producer, designer, and manager. All four job roles are related to the three principle types of training: skills and technical training, management and subject-matter training, and motivational training.

In the past ten years, the learning professions have been very active in specifying learner outcomes in the form of competency statements (Storey, 1979). A logical extension of this activity is to apply the competency concept to the training profession itself. What are the important or necessary competencies of a trainer? This basic question has been addressed by several important research studies. One such study conducted by the American Society for Training and Development (Pinto & Walker, 1978) revealed the following fourteen areas of trainer competencies: (1) program design and development; (2) management of external resources; (3) job-related and

performance/related training; (4) individual development planning and counseling; (5) training research; (6) group and organization development; (7) material resources development; (8) professional self-development; (9) management of the training and development function; (10) management of internal resources; (11) management of working relationships with managers; (12) needs analysis and diagnosis; (13) conducting classroom training; and (14) determining appropriate training approaches.

Another way of viewing the job roles within this professional mélange is to match them with the typical phases of the training process. The five phases of a training program include analysis, design, development, implementation, and control (Swanson, 1980).

Training Phases	Job Roles
Analysis	Manager, designer
Design	Designer
Development	Media producer, designer
Implementation	Instructor
Control	Manager, instructor

Instructor. Some trainers only instruct. These persons provide one or more of the three types of training. A trainer's forte may be instruction skills quite independent of content, and thus he or she may be found teaching in all three areas: skills, management, and motivational training.

In large training organizations entry-level trainers are often hired into instructor positions. Furthermore, they may be restricted to one type of training (e.g., management training) and a limited number of specific courses. In some instances the situation parallels a military-training mode. This mode allows prospective instructors to take the courses they will teach and ultimately to teach these courses precisely as they had learned them. These conditions suggest that the designer of the training is pulling all the strings and that the instructor is relegated to robot status, but these jobs are usually enriched by adding design responsibilities once instruction skills are proven.

Recent training literature is almost void of research and development work on the selection of instructors, the process of instructing, and the evaluation of instructors. Extensive reviews of the training research literature by Campbell (1971) and I. L. Goldstein (1980) provide no evidence of inquiry in the profession on this topic.

Although not adequately reflected in the literature, instruction and communication skills are highly valued in industrial training. This is abundantly clear in the training profession when the issues of retention, promotion, and perceived program effectiveness are examined. It is interesting to note that the widely accepted, anecdotal evaluation methods that ask trainees how they like their experience are for the most part aimed at instructor effectiveness. The forty-eight industrial training methods indentified by Wenig (1978) require a complex repertoire of instructing skills that are apparently being taken for granted in the literature. Likewise, the extensive body of related knowledge and research in the area of teacher education, and specifically in vocational-industrial teacher education, is being ignored.

Trainers are expected to have adequate instruction skills, and those full-time trainers who prove to be deficient in these skills are often terminated. Attention to the development of instruction skills is often reserved for part-time trainers, who, in the area of skills and technical training, are often people with good interpersonal skills chosen from the ranks of supervisory or hourly workers. Their work experience provides face validity to the trainees, and, at times, job knowledge. The literature does report efforts at developing the instructor skills of supervisory and hourly workers (Murphy, 1981).

Media producer. Many persons back into the training profession as a result of media production skills. For example, a person trained as a photographer may be hired on a training staff to produce photographs used in training materials. This person may be viewed as a technician in one situation. Yet a similar person with expertise in producing slide and cassette programs may be catapulted to a training design or management position in a company that suddenly commits itself to training primarily through the use of these media. Artists, writers, movie producers, and video producers are some of the other personnel in this media production category.

It is also interesting to observe manufacturers of media hardware moving into software production. This is usually done as a means of marketing their primary hardware product. Media software and market interactions are particularly dynamic. The desire to accommodate a good client or to utilize available human talent and available production hardware at times guides nontraining enterprises into the training business (*Training in Industry and Business*, 1976).

In the balance, experimental research has shown various media to be effective, but not the key to learning. Media methods have been important components of many training innovations, but effectiveness is moderated by relatively high costs. However, rapid change in communications technology—from communications satellites to sophisticated low-cost home computers—and the resulting shifts in cost-effectiveness may shake the very roots of the training profession (Bonini, 1975).

Designer. Those who design industrial training are in a position to thoughtfully interpret and synthesize the many variables affecting training. Less is known about the design function than about the functions of instructing, producing media, and managing training. Training design is presently more of an art than a science. Training systems advocates often place "design" in their set of training flowchart boxes but know little about what the trainer actually does in conceptualizing an appropriate strategy. Concerns such as the goals of the company, training goals, delivery options, trainee characteristics, and time constraints must

all be taken into account in providing the best training strategy.

Areas of research related to design are presently being considered by the profession. Now that computer-assisted instruction (CAI) is proving to be cost-effective, training designers need computer knowledge. The computer allows the designer to rethink who gets training, how, where, and when (Bonini, 1975). CAI is freeing the designer from many long-established constraints and establishing a whole new set.

Modeling theory and research are now visible in the training literature (Goldstein & Sorcher, 1974; Latham & Saari, 1979; Smith, 1975). The behavior-modeling method requires presentation of principles, presentation of model behavior, role playing, and reinforcement. In some companies, management training has been significantly influenced by behavior-modeling theory. Although it has not been reported in the literature, one corporate management training group has established an elaborate evaluation scheme for selecting believable actors to perform as role models on videotapes (Sisson, 1979).

Manager. The person who manages training is ultimately held responsible for its contribution to the financial and nonfinancial goals of the company. In pursuit of these goals, he or she is required to orchestrate the instructors, media producers, designers, and other resources of the training department. The tools of general management are also the tools of people who manage training. Two unique and critical training management tasks are worth highlighting. They include assessment of training needs and evaluation of training effectiveness from cost and behavioral perspectives.

The major goal of training-needs assessment is to separate training-related from non–training-related problems. In addition, it is important to categorize training problems as (1) present sources of organizational pain, (2) nice improvements, or (3) considerations in future or long-term planning. Although there is need for continued research and development, several tested methods of training-needs assessment exist (Harless, 1975; *Successful In-Company Training Programs*, 1974). As one might expect, trainers regularly unearth non–training-related problems during needs-assessment work. Depending on the position of training in the structure of the organization, training managers may get involved in nontraining problems. The interface of training personnel and nontraining problems is usually organizational development (OD). OD solutions typically contain training and nontraining proposals. The nontraining proposals often deal with some form of work redesign (Murrell & Vaill, 1975).

The second unique and critical training management task is to evaluate training effectiveness in terms of cost and behavior change. The issue of cost analysis is the ultimate accountability problem for the manager. The same can be said of the behavioral effectiveness of training. The body of knowledge about evaluation far outstrips actual practice in the training field. This fact may be partially explained by a general belief that practice is an integral part of training and is in itself a good evaluation. Further, evaluation if often viewed with hostility, and thus training managers tend to deemphasize it in order to maintain cooperation in training programs, especially those not mandated by the company. The computer may provide a stimulus for redirection in the area of evaluation and other training management functions. Computer-managed training allows trainees to report individually and thus dictates a different means of monitoring behavior. One such management system goes beyond evaluation into a total record-keeping system (Murphy, 1980).

Summary.   Selected research and development issues in industrial training will be highlighted as a means of summarizing this article. Two overriding issues, stated in the form of questions, overlay training as a whole, including types of training and job roles in the training profession. This overlay allows one to extrapolate from the questions more specific issues within each of the categories.

The major issues that transcend all forms of training in industry pertain to financial and nonfinancial goals. Specific methods of inquiry to answer the following questions are high-priority issues. (1) What are the costs and benefits of training? (2) What are the goals of the organization? It is appropriate to raise these questions across the board, by type of training and by job role.

The selected issues within each of the types of training and job roles in training highlight the needs and future direction of the industrial training profession. These include (1) analysis of processes and troubleshooting behavior; (2) analysis and synthesis of subject matter; (3) ethics of attitudinal training; (4) development and evaluation of instructional skills; (5) new high-technology media-communications systems; (6) understanding of the training-design process; (7) needs-assessment methods; and (8) computer-managed training.

The vitality of industrial training will largely be a function of its ability to pay attention to the major issues confronting the profession. Distractions abound and have traditionally bled off much professional energy. Focus of purpose and method within the profession will need to be continually monitored by both researchers and practitioners.

Richard A. Swanson

See also Labor and Education; Trade and Industrial Education; Vocational Education.

REFERENCES

Adams, R. P. The ceremonial side of training: Of what value to first-line supervisors. *Training and Development Journal*, 1976, *30*(10), 34–37.

Ammerman, H. L.; Essex, D. W.; & Pratzner, F. C. *Rating the Job Significance of Technical Concepts: An Application to Three Occupations (Research and Development Series No. 105).* Columbus, Ohio: Center for Vocational Education, 1974. (ERIC Document Reproduction Service No. ED 114 593)

Ammerman, H. L., & Pratzner, F. C. *Occupational Survey Report on Business Data Programmers: Task Data from Workers and Supervisors Indicating Job Relevance and Training Criticalness* (Research and Development Series No 108). Columbus, Ohio: Center for Vocational Education, 1974. (ERIC Document Reproduction Service No. ED 126 278)

Ammerman, H. L., & Pratzner, F. C. *Occupational Survey on Automotive Mechanics: Task Data from Workers and Supervisors Indicating Job Relevance and Training Criticalness* (Research and Development Series No 110). Columbus, Ohio: Center for Vocational Education, 1975. (ERIC Document Reproduction Service No. ED 126 279)

Ammerman, H. L., & Pratzner, F. C. *Performance Content for Job Training* (Research and Development Series No. 121-125, Vols. 1–5). Columbus, Ohio: Center for Vocational Education, 1977. (ERIC Document Reproduction Service No. ED 146 369, ED 146 370, ED 146 371, ED 146 372, ED 146 373).

Antil, F. H. Training can be professional. *Training and Development Journal*, 1972, *26*(11), 14–17.

Bonini, C. P. *Computers, Modeling, and Management Education Technical Report No. 6.* Stanford, Calif.: Stanford University Graduate School of Business, 1975.

Bright, W. E. How one company manages its human resources. *Harvard Business Review*, 1976, *52*(1), 81–93.

Campbell, J. P. Personnel training and development. *Annual Review of Psychology*, 1971, *22*, 565–602.

Campbell, J. P., & Dunnette, M. D. Effectiveness of T-group experiences in managerial training and development. *Psychological Bulletin*, 1968, *70*, 73–104.

Clement, R. W.; Pinto, P. R.; & Walker, J. W. How do I hurt thee? Let me count the ways: Unethical and improper behavior by training and development professionals. *Training and Development Journal*, 1978, *32*, 10–12.

Cooper, C. L. How psychologically dangerous are T-groups and encounter groups? *Human Relations*, 1975, *28*, 249–260.

Copa, G. H. What should we do about research in vocational education? *Beacon-American Vocational Education Research Association* (Special ed.), 1981, *10*, 1–7.

Cullen, J. G.; Sawzin, S. A.; Sisson, G. R.; & Swanson, R. A. Training: What's it worth? *Training and Development Journal*, 1976, *30*(8), 12–20.

Cullen, J. G.; Sawzin, S. A.; Sisson, G. R.; & Swanson, R. A. Cost effectiveness: A model for assessing the training investment. *Training and Development Journal*, 1978, *30*(1), 24–29.

DeCaro, J. J. A methodology for determining skills needed in a technical career. *Journal of Studies in Technical Careers*, 1978, *1*(1), 1–10.

Douthat, J. Accounting for personnel training and development costs. *Training and Development Journal*, 1970, *24*(6), 2–6.

Education/training in business and industry. *Phi Delta Kappan*, January 1980, *61*, 311–333.

Foley, J. D., Jr. Determining needs of department store sales personnel. *Training and Development Journal*, 1969, *23*(7), 24–27.

Foley, J. D., Jr. Instructional materials for improved performance. *Journal of Industrial Teacher Education*, 1978, *15*(4), 30–44.

Frank, H. E., & Smith, P. J. A British impression of the American training scene. *Training and Development Journal*, 1969, *23*(1), 20–23.

Goldstein, A. P., & Sorcher, M. *Changing Supervisor Behavior.* New York: Pergamon Press, 1974.

Goldstein, H. *Training and Education by Industry.* Washington, D.C.: National Institute for Work and Learning, 1980.

Goldstein, I. L. Training in work organizations. *Annual Review of Psychology,* 1980, *31,* 229–272.

Gordon, S. R. The impact of fair employment laws on training. *Training and Development Journal,* 1978, *32*(6), 29–44.

Gropper, G. L. *Instructional Strategies.* Englewood Cliffs, N.J.: Educational Technology Publications, 1974.

Harless, J. H. *Ounce of Analysis (Is Worth a Pound of Objectives).* McLean, Va.: Harless Performance Guild, Inc., 1975.

Jacobs, B. A. Does Westinghouse have the productivity answer? *Industry Week,* March 23, 1981, pp. 95–98.

Johnson, W. B. *Computer Simulations in Fault Diagnosis Training: An Empirical Study of Learning Transfer from Simulation to Live System Performance.* Unpublished doctoral disseration, University of Illinois, 1980.

Latham, G. P., & Saari, L. M. The application of social learning theory to training supervisors through behavioral modeling. *Journal of Applied Psychology.* 1979, *64*(3), 239–246.

Mager, R. F., & Beach, K. M., Jr. *Developing Vocational Instruction.* Belmont, Calif.: Fearon, 1967.

McCollough, R. *American Society for Training and Development Directory of Academic Programs in Training and Development/Human Resource Development.* Washington, D.C.: ASTD, Society, 1981.

McDonnell, L. Efficiency/Tonka typical of U.S. concern with productivity. *Minneapolis Tribune,* February 8, 1981, pp. 1D–5D.

Miller, J. Motivational aspects of job enrichment. *Management International Review,* 1976, *16*(20), 37–46.

Morgan, D. C. Career development programs. *Personnel,* 1977, *59*(5), 23–27.

Murphy, B. P. *Designing a Computer-based Joint Apprenticeship Program Management System.* Paper presented at the National Conference on Computer-based Education-Control Data Corporation, St. Paul, Minn., September 1980.

Murphy, B. P. Professional development and performance strategies for line trainers. *Performance and Instruction,* 1981, *20*(5), 3–5.

Murrell, K. L., & Vaill, P. B. *Organizational Development: Sources and Applications.* Madison, Wis.: American Society for Training and Development, 1975.

Musick, C. *Loom Maintenance Training Package.* Graniteville, S.C.: Graniteville Company, 1981.

Passmore, D. L. Economics of training. *Journal of Industrial Teacher Education,* 1978, *15*(4), 66–67.

Petzinger, T., Jr. Out of order: Avoiding plant failure grows more difficult. *Wall Street Journal,* January 8, 1981, pp. 1, 14.

Pinto, P. R., & Walker, J. W. *A Study of Professional Training and Development Roles and Competencies.* Madison, Wis.: American Society for Training and Development, 1978.

Prien, E. P. The function of job analysis in content validation. *Personnel Psychology,* 1977, *30,* 167–174.

Ridley, F. R. *Job Analysis and Test Development Study for Mechanical Repairers-Helpers.* Washington, D.C.: Potomac Electric Power Company, Department of Human Resources, 1980.

Roberts, L. Simulation in training—Part 6: The use of process simulators, a case history. *Industrial Training International,* 1976, *11*(10), 318–320.

Rosenfeld, M., & Thornton, R. F. *A Case Study in Job Analysis Methodology.* Princeton, N.J.: Educational Testing Service, 1976.

Rosentreter, G. E. *Economic Evaluation of a Training Program* (Research Series Paper No. 1). Washington, D.C.: American Society for Training and Development, 1978.

Sisson, G. R. Personal communication, January 10, 1979.

Smith, P. B. Controlled studies of the outcome of sensitivity training. *Psychological Bulletin,* 1975, *82*(4), 597–622.

Smith, P. E. Management modeling training to improve morale and customer satisfaction. *Personnel Psychology,* 1976, *29*(3), 351–359.

Storey, W. D. *A Guide for Career Development Inquiry/State-of-the-Art Report on Career Development.* (Research Series Paper No. 2) Washington, D.C.: American Society for Training and Development, 1979.

Successful In-Company Training Programs. Chicago: Dartnell Corporation, 1974.

Swanson, R. A. Training in industry: Summary of the implications for industrial teacher education. *Journal of Industrial Teacher Education,* 1978, *15*(4), 78–80.

Swanson, R. A. Training technology: The system and the course. *Epsilon Pi Tau Journal,* 1980, *6*(2), 49–52.

Swanson, R. A., & Poor, G. W. *Analyzing Work Behavior: Techniques for Skills and Human Relations Development Trainers.* Paper presented at the Southern Minnesota American Society for Training and Development, Minneapolis, Minn., March 1981.

Thompson, M. S. *Benefit-Cost Analysis for Program Evaluation.* Beverly Hills, Calif.: Sage, 1980.

Training in Industry and Business: L. E. O'Neil and Associates, Inc. Bowling Green, Ohio: Bowling Green State University, WBGU-TV, 1976. (Videotape)

Training in industry and its implications for industrial education. *Journal of Industrial Teacher Education,* 1978, *15*(4).

Walter, V. Self-motivated personal career planning: A breakthrough in human resources management (Part 2). *Personnel Journal,* 1976, *55*(4), 161–167.

Wenig, R. E. Industrial training methods. *Journal of Industrial Teacher Education,* 1978, *15*(4), 45–65.

Yager, E. G. The quality control circle explosion. *Training and Development Journal,* 1981, *35*(4), 98–105.

Zemke, R. The systems approach: Is it really best? *Training,* 1978, *15*(8), 18.

INFANT DEVELOPMENT

The birth process marks a distinct developmental transition. The infant is suddenly thrust into a new world of experience and begins a process of growth clearly different from that of the previous nine months. The development of the infant over the next two years will be marked by rapid physical growth coupled with the ability to integrate and adapt to a complex external world. This article will focus on the process by which the infant develops strategies for dealing with the social world. It also examines the issue of infant day care and the nature of the environment capable of supporting optimal social development.

The fetal period is marked by enormous growth spurts

and the differentiation of various physical systems. In the last few months of prenatal life, the fetus begins to react to external stimulations of light and sound. These are, however, merely precursors. Following birth, the infant is engulfed in a new universe of stimulation including drastic temperature and nutritional changes, and visual, auditory, and tactile experiences. The infant, however, is not merely a reactive being in a world of stimulation but rather an active participant (Moss, 1967). Although the external world presents challenges to which the infant must adapt, the infant has various unique capabilities and characteristics that affect how this world will react and then interact. This mutuality of influences has been elaborated in a transactional model by Sameroff and Chandler (1975). The mutual accommodations made at one time are seen as affecting those that will occur later.

Early Cognitive Development. Infant development is treated here as the process of mutual adaptation through which the infant develops into the socially effective and somewhat independent toddler. As a starting point for this discussion, it is helpful to understand the limitations of the infant's capabilities. As these become elaborated, so does the way in which the infant experiences the world. The most detailed theoretical explanation of this process is contained in Piaget's description (1963) of the sensorimotor period. Initially, the infant experiences the world only through the actions he or she performs. With experience, the infant begins to differentiate objects from actions and then thought from action. Part of this developmental progression involves the infant's growing understanding that its actions affect objects and people (for example, shaking a rattle to produce a sound). This differentiation also involves the realization that objects exist independently and separately from the infant's own experience of them and that they continue to exist when no longer in sight. The end of this period occurs when the infant becomes capable of forming internal representations of objects or persons. Faced with a problem, the infant no longer physically acts out a solution, but uses internal symbols to plot a course of action.

The ability to use symbols marks a critical developmental transition. The capacity frees the child from the concrete, here-and-now orientation. For the purpose of this discussion, the infancy period will refer to the sensorimotor period, marked by egocentrism, a here-and-now orientation, and a developing process of differentiation of objects from their actions. Thus, infancy here refers to an orientation to the environment rather than to chronological age.

Maternal Attachment. The elaboration in mental capabilities is used by John Bowlby (1969, 1972) as a framework for describing the emergence of infants' initial social attachments. Bowlby's work focuses upon the primary social relationship, or attachment between the mother and infant, as the beginning of the process that eventually leads to ties with a larger social network. Evidence to support the primacy of the maternal attachment, or "monotro-

pism," comes from studies of institutionalized infants who were found to suffer a variety of mental disorders following separation from the mother (Spitz & Wolf, 1946; Robertson and Bowlby, 1952; Heinicke & Westheimer, 1965; Robertson and Robertson, 1971). The necessary primacy of the maternal relationship in contrast to the maintenance and use of several adult relationships, has been questioned (Belsky & Steinberg, 1978; Smith, 1980). Others have held that the infant's interaction patterns with the mother are unique, suggesting the preference for a principal adult care giver (Brazelton, Koslowski, & Main, 1974; Lamb, 1977).

Bowlby postulates that the infant's security in the initial relationship allows the mother to serve as a secure base for exploration. To picture this, imagine a circle around the infant and mother. When the infant is under stress, the circle becomes smaller and the child moves closer to the mother. Older children or infants in familiar surroundings will use a larger circle. Further, older children tolerate more distance since they can use distal signals to "check in" with the mother. The circle may contract under stress but not as severely as before. The functioning of the secure base system has been described in several ethological observational studies of infants (Anderson, 1972; Blurton-Jones & Leach, 1972).

Bowlby's theory of attachment as an organizational construct has received a good deal of research support, (Ainsworth, Bell, & Stayton, 1971; Waters, 1978). Earlier attempts to examine attachment as a trait through observation of discrete behaviors such as crying on separation failed to yield evidence of any individual consistency (Masters & Wellman, 1974).

Effects of mother-infant separation. Recent interest in the development of individual differences has been stimulated by the work of Mary Ainsworth (Ainsworth et al., 1978). Infants placed in a mildly stressful situation resulting from brief separations from the mother were found to display distinctive response patterns. The largest number of children reacted as would be predicted from the circle analogy described above, greeting the mother on her return and remaining close to her as long as reassurance was necessary. For the other two groups, the mother did not appear to offer a secure base. One group displayed avoidant, passive, repetitive play behaviors and ignored the mother's bids for social interaction. The other group was ambivalent, displaying a good deal of behavioral disorganization and need for comfort but an inability to obtain it successfully.

The stability and consistency of these behavioral patterns has been validated and extended in recent studies (Marvin, 1970; Waters, 1978). Behaviors consistent with laboratory classifications have been noted in naturalistic observations of separation and reunion episodes (Blanchard & Main, 1979; Cohen & Ambron, 1980). Bowlby's attachment paradigm holds that disruptions in the infant's relationship to the mother should also affect his or her ability to form other social relationships or to explore the environment in a manner likely to promote cognitive development. Recent research appears to offer support for this view. Security of attachment has been related to concurrent exploratory behavior and cognitive functioning (Ainsworth & Bell, 1970; Stayton, Hogan, & Ainsworth, 1971); effectiveness is a problem-solving situation at 2 years of age (Matas, Arend & Sroufe, 1978); peer interactions at 20 and 23 months (Pastor, 1981), measures of peer competence and ego strength during the preschool years (Lieberman, 1977; Waters, Wippman, & Sroufe, 1979), and teacher assessment of competence and ego resiliency at age 5 (Arend, Gove, & Sroufe, 1979).

Maternal effectiveness. Since the quality of early infant–care giver interactions affects the quality of the attachment bond and indirectly the development of social and cognitive abilities, factors that influence the course of these early interactions are of considerable interest. Qualities of the infant that have been found to influence interactions include the infant's temperament (Carey, 1970; Thomas & Chess, 1977), responsiveness and alertness (Moss, 1967; Brazelton, Koslowski, & Main, 1974; Osofsky & Danzger, 1974), and behavioral organization (Field, 1979; Vaughn, Taraldson, Crichton, & Egeland, 1980). Maternal characteristics that affect her relationship to her infant include family-related stress (Vaughn et al., 1979) and attitudes toward child rearing, (Davids & Holden, 1970; Beckwith, 1971). Both maternal responsiveness to infant cues and the effectiveness of her response during the first year have been related to the quality of the attachment (Ainsworth, Bell, & Stayton, 1971; Clarke-Stewart, 1973). This behavior on the part of the mother is felt to reinforce the infant's belief that his or her behavior can affect the environment and contribute to his or her feeling of competency (Yarrow & Pederson, 1972). Failure to gain this expectation may cause the infant to become disinterested or wary.

One measure of maternal effectiveness involves assessment of the pacing of interaction, or synchrony (Greenberg, 1971; Brazelton, Koslowski, & Main, 1974). Eliciting interactions and maintaining the interest of the infant involves sensitive monitoring of the infant's ability to cope with stimulation. Overstimulation results in the infant's withdrawal; whereas pacing (that is, disengaging briefly when the child does so), has been found actually to prolong the length of the interaction. The ability of the infant to respond to stimulation varies a good deal (Brazelton, Koslowski, & Main, 1974; Field et al., 1978). Infant health factors such as prematurity or birth size affect the difficulty that the mother encounters in monitering interactions with the infant (Field, 1979). Programs aimed at providing support to mothers of at-risk infants have noted long-term effects (Widmayer & Field, 1980).

Infant Day Care. Given the importance of early experience, the issue of infant day care assumes great significance. The concerns are twofold. First, does day care attendance affect intellectual development? Second, does attendance affect the development of social relationships, either the quality of the attachment bond to the mother or the ability of the infant to form affective bonds with peers or care givers? Given the importance of these issues, it is unfortunate that little research has been done with children under two years of age. Since few infants are in organized group care, identification of a sample with roughly similar histories is difficult. Most research dealing with infant center care has involved model university-based centers (Caldwell et al., 1970; Keister, 1970; Kagan, Kearsley, & Zelazo, 1978). Other studies have involved intervention programs aimed at providing enriching experiences or child development training for mothers (Gordon, 1975). When middle-class populations are involved, infant care has no effects. Kagan's study, in fact, revealed that when day care and non–day care infants from different ethnic backgrounds were compared, ethnicity accounted for more of the performance differences than did day care attendance. When the programs are aimed at enrichment, day care infants tend to perform better on standardized tests, but these effects tend to "wash out" at later ages. Longitudinal follow-up studies appear to indicate less direct benefits, such as lower dropout rates and fewer assignments to special education classes (Darlington et al., 1980).

Given the importance of the first years in the establishment of a secure attachment bond, a number of researchers have examined whether day care attendance affects the security of the mother-infant relationship. The initial study conducted by Mary Blehar (1974), reported that 36-month-old day care children were more avoidant and 46-month-old day care infants were more resistant on reunion with the mother than were their home-reared counterparts. Various attempts to replicate this study have failed (Roopnairene & Lamb, 1978; Portnoy & Simmons, 1978). However, in all these studies children over two years of age made up the study sample. The strange situation procedure is considered inappropriate for children in this age range since they no longer display heightened attachment behavior in response to brief separations from the mother.

Effects of Day Care on Mother Attachment. A number of recent studies of infants in child care have noted differences in their attachment behavior. Blanchard and Main (1979) reported that among infants 12 to 25 months of age, avoidance of the mother was related to length of center attendance. Infants who had just entered care displayed avoidant behaviors more frequently. Several other studies, however, appear to indicate that factors influencing the quality of mother-infant interactions, not separation or length of attendance, may account for observed differences. Schwartz (1978) examined attachment behaviors of 18-month-old full-time, part-time, and non–day care infants. The day care group had entered care before 6 months of age. When the three attendance groups were compared, 9 percent of the part-time day care infants were classified as anxiously attached, compared with 30 percent of the non–day care and 40 percent of the full-time day care infants. Further, the full-time day care infants displayed avoidant behaviors on reunion signficantly more frequently than did children in the other two groups. Thus, day care attendance did not affect the likelihood that an infant would develop an anxious attachment. In fact, it appears that brief daily separations may actually help to support the relationship. In a follow-up study, 90 percent of the working mothers interviewed felt that part-time employment offered the opportunity for out-of-home stimulation with fewer conflicts than full-time positions (Schwartz, 1980). Vaughn, Gove, and Egeland (1980) compared infants placed in care before one year of age; between one year and eighteen months; and home-reared controls. No differences were found in the number of secure and insecurely attached infants in these three groups. However, similar to Schwartz's finding, of the children in the early day care group, those who displayed an anxious attachment were more frequently found to display avoidant rather than ambivalent attachment patterns. Those mothers who worked, however, reported higher levels of life stress than did mothers who stayed home. Maternal life stress has been related to anxious attachment patterns (Vaughn et al., 1979). The results of these studies suggest that the critical issue may not be separation, especially given Schwartz's finding for part-time day care infants. Rather, the issue of maintaining a secure attachment bond despite daily separations may involve life and role satisfactions of the mother that allows her to maintain quality interactions with her infant during periods when they are together.

Day Care and Attachment to Others. Infants' ability to adjust to day care situations also involves their ability to form attachments to multiple care givers. Lamb (1977) suggests that the relationship with the father is formed early and appears to serve a different purpose than the one with the mother. Schaffer and Emerson (1964) noted a similar tendency among infants and siblings in their pioneering study. Infants have been found to be capable of forming useful relationships with adults in child care situations (Kagan, Kearsley, & Zelaz, 1978; Cohen & Ambron, 1980), but appear to continue to prefer the mother when she is available. For young infants, the presence of a single alternate care giver may prove more useful for maintaining the attachment to the mother than group care (Hock, 1976). Thus, the infant appears to be both flexible and active in his or her interactions with the social environment.

Further research is needed with respect to infant day care and its effects on social and cognitive development. Examinations should focus on three major areas: the impact of infant care arrangements on the family; the effects of various kinds of care, including the number of alternate care givers, group size, and organizational arrangements; and the impact of entry into care on infants at various developmental stages. Several promising studies are underway that will yield answers to some of these questions.

Pamela M. Schwartz

REFERENCES

Ainsworth, M. D., & Bell, S. M. Attachment, exploration, and separation illustrated by the behavior of one-year-olds in a strange situation. *Child Development,* 1970, *41,* 49–67.

Ainsworth, M. D.; Bell, S. M.; & Stayton, D. J. Individual differences in strange situation behavior of one-year-olds. In H. R. Schaffer (Ed.), *The Origin of Human Social Relations.* New York: Academic Press, 1971.

Ainsworth, M. D.; Blehar, M.; Waters, E.; & Wall, S. *Patterns of Attachment.* Hillsdale, N.J.: Lawrence Erlbaum Associates, 1978.

Anderson, J. W. Attachment behavior out of doors. In N. Blurton-Jones (Ed.), *Ethological Studies of Child Behavior.* London: Cambridge University Press, 1972.

Arend, R.; Gove, F. L.; & Sroufe, L. A. Continuity of individual adaptation from infancy to kindergarten: A predictive study of ego-resilliency and curiosity in preschoolers. *Child Development,* 1979, *50,* 950–959.

Beckwith, L. Relationships between attributes of mothers and their infants' IQ scores. *Child Development,* 1971, *42,* 1083–1097.

Belsky, J., & Steinberg, L. D. The effects of day care: A critical review. *Child Development,* 1978, *49,* 929–949.

Blanchard, M., & Main, M. Avoidance of the attachment figure and social-emotional adjustment in day care infants. *Developmental Psychology,* 1979, *15,* 445–446.

Blehar, M. C. Anxious attachment and defensive reactions associated with day care. *Child Development,* 1974, *45,* 683–692.

Blurton-Jones, N., & Leach, G. M. Behavior of children and their mothers at separation and greeting. In N. Blurton-Jones (Ed.), *Ethological Studies of Child Behavior.* Cambridge: Cambridge University Press, 1972.

Bowlby, J. *Attachment.* Vol. 1 of *Attachment and Loss.* New York: Basic Books; London: Hogarth Press, 1969.

Bowlby, J. *Separation.* Vol. 2 of *Attachment and Loss.* New York: Basic Books; London: Hogarth Press, 1972.

Brazelton, T. B.; Koslowski, B.; & Main, M. The origins of reciprocity: The early mother-infant interaction. In M. Lewis & L. Rosenblum (Eds.), *The Effect of the Infant on Its Caregiver.* New York: Wiley, 1974.

Caldwell, B.; Wright, C.; Honig, A.; & Tannenbaum, J. Infant day care and attachment. *American Journal of Orthopsychiatry,* 1970, *40,* 397–412.

Carey, W. B. A simplified method for measuring infant temperament. *Journal of Pediatrics,* 1970, *77,* 188–194.

Clarke-Stewart, K. A. Interactions between mothers and their young children: Characteristics and consequences. *Monographs of the Society for Research in Child Development,* 1973.

Cohen, M. C., & Ambron, S. R. *The Ecological Validity of a Laboratory Measure of Attachment.* Paper presented at the second International Conference on Infant Studies, New Haven, Conn., April 1980.

Darlington, R. B.; Royce, J. M.; Snipper, A. S.; Murray, H. W.; & Lazar, I. Preschool programs and the later school competence of children from low-income families. *Science,* 1980, *208,* 202–204.

Davids, A., & Holden, R. H. Consistency of maternal attitudes and personality from pregnancy to eight months following childbirth. *Developmental Psychology,* 1970, *2,* 364–366.

Field, T. M. Interaction patterns of pre-term and term infants. In T. M. Field (Ed.), *Infants Born at Risk.* New York: Spectrum, 1979.

Field, T. M.; Hallock, N.; Ting, G. T.; Dempsey, J. R.; Dabiri, J.; & Shuman, H. H. A first year follow-up of high-risk infants: Formulating a cumulative risk index. *Child Development,* 1978, *49,* 119–131.

Gordon, I. J. *Intervention in Infant Education.* Paper presented at the Texas Conference of Infancy, Austin, Texas, June 23, 1975.

Greenberg, N. H. A comparison of infant-mother interactional behavior in infants with atypical behavior and normal infants. In J. Hellmuth (Ed.), *The Exceptional Infant,* Vol. 2: *Studies in Abnormalities.* New York: Brunner/Mazel, 1971.

Heinicke, C. H., & Westheimer, I. *Brief Separations.* New York: International Universities Press, 1965.

Hock, E. *Alternative Approaches to Child Rearing and Their Effects on the Mother-Infant Relationship* (final report). Washington, D.C.: Office of Child Development, 1976.

Kagan, J.; Kearsley, R. B.; & Zelazo, P. R. *Infancy: Its Place in Human Development.* Cambridge, Mass.: Harvard University Press, 1978.

Keister, M. E. *The Good Life for Infants and Toddlers: Group Care of Infants.* Washington, D.C.: National Association for the Education of Young Children, 1970.

Lamb, M. E. Father-infant and mother-infant interaction in the first year of life. *Child Development,* 1977, *48,* 167–181.

Lieberman, A. F. Preschoolers' competence with a peer: Influence of attachment and social experience. *Child Development,* 1977, *48,* 1277–1287.

Marvin, R. S. *Attachment and Reciprocity in the Two-year-old Child.* Unpublished master's thesis, University of Chicago, 1970.

Masters, J. C., & Wellman, H. M. The study of human infant attachment: A procedural critique. *Psychological Bulletin,* 1974, *81,* 218–237.

Matas, J.; Arend, R. A.; & Sroufe, L. A. Continuity of adaptation in the second year: The relationship between quality of attachment and later social competence. *Child Development,* 1978, *49,* 547–556.

Moss, H. A. Sex, age, and state as determinants of mother-infant interaction. *Merrill-Palmer Quarterly,* 1967, *13,* 19–36.

Osofsky, J. D., & Danzger, B. Relationships between neonatal characteristics and mother-infant interaction. *Developmental Psychology,* 1974, *10,* 124–130.

Pastor, D. The quality of mother-infant attachment and its relationship to toddlers' initial sociability with peers. *Developmental Psychology,* 1981, *17,* 326–335.

Piaget, J. *The Origins of Intelligence in Children.* New York: Norton, 1963.

Portnoy, C. F., & Simmons, C. H. Day care and attachment. *Child Development,* 1978, *49,* 239–242.

Robertson, J., & Bowlby, J. Responses of young children to separation from their mothers (Part 2). *Courrier du Centre International de l'Enfance,* 1952, *2,* 131–142.

Robertson, J., & Robertson, J. Young children in brief separation: A fresh look. *Psychoanalytic Study of the Child,* 1971, *26,* 264–315.

Roopnairene, J. L., & Lamb, M. The effects of day care on attachment and exploratory behavior in a strange situation. *Merrill-Palmer Quarterly,* 1978, *24,* 85–96.

Sameroff, A. J., & Chandler, M. J. Reproductive risk and the continuum of caretaking causality. In F. D. Horowtiz, M. Hetherington, S. Scarr-Salapatek, & G. Siegel (Eds.), *Review of Child Development Research* (Vol. 4). Chicago: University of Chicago Press, 1975.

Schaffer, H. R., & Emerson, P. Patterns of response to physical contact in early human development. *Journal of Child Psychology and Psychiatry,* 1964, *5,* 1–13.

Schwartz, P. M. *The Effects of Separations Due to Child Care on Attachment Behaviors of Eighteen-month-old Infants.* Unpublished doctoral dissertation, University of Michigan, 1978.

Schwartz, P. M. Working mothers of infants: Conflicts and coping strategies. In D. G. McGuigan (Ed.), *Women's Lives: New Theory, Research, and Policy.* Ann Arbor: University of Michigan Press, 1980.

Smith, P. K. Shared care of young children: Alternative models to monotropism. *Merrill-Palmer Quarterly,* 1980, *26,* 371–389.

Spitz, R., & Wolf, K. Anaclitic depression. *Psychoanalytic Study of the Child* 1946, *2,* 313–342.

Stayton, D. J.; Hogan, R.; & Ainsworth, M. D. Infant obedience and maternal behavior: The origins of socialization reconsidered. *Child Development,* 1971, *42,* 1057–1069.

Thomas, A., & Chess, S. *Temperament and Development.* New York: Brunner/Mazel, 1977.

Vaughn, B. E.; Gove, F. L.; & Egeland, B. The relationship between out-of-home care and the quality of infant-mother attachment in an economically disadvantaged population. *Child Development,* 1980, *51,* 1203–1214.

Vaughn, B. E.; Taraldson, B.; Crichton, L.; & Egeland, B. Relationship between neonatal behavioral organization and infant behavior during the first year of life. *Infant Behavior and Development,* 1980, *3,* 47–66.

Vaughn, B. E.; Waters, E.; Egeland, B.; & Sroufe, L. A. Individual differences in infant-mother attachment at twelve and eighteen months: Stability and change in families under stress. *Child Development,* 1979, *50,* 971–975.

Waters, E. The reliability and stability of individual differences in infant-mother attachment. *Child Development,* 1978, *49,* 483–494.

Waters, E.; Wippman, J.; & Sroufe, L. A. Attachment, positive affect, and competence in the peer group: Two studies in construct validation. *Child Development,* 1979, *50,* 821–829.

Widmayer, S. M., & Field, T. M. *Brazelton Deomonstrations for Mothers: Their Effects on Preterm Infant Development at One Year.* Paper presented at the second International Conference on Infant Studies, New Haven, Conn., April 1980.

Yarrow, L., & Pederson, F. Attachment: Its origin and course. In H. Hartup (Ed.), *The Young Child.* Washington, D.C.: National Association for the Education of Young Children (NAEYC), 1972.

INFORMATION MANAGEMENT AND COMPUTING

Information management and computing are inseparable concepts. The development of the integrated circuit that is used in computers has so profoundly affected the means by which information is stored, retrieved, and manipulated that, for researchers in education, information management and computing can be usefully discussed together. Developments in computing are changing not only how information for research is acquired and used, but also what research is undertaken.

Within the last few decades, operational computers have progressed from virtual nonexistence to becoming a basic extension of human capability (not unlike the telephone). In 1944 the first operational digital computer was put into use at Harvard University. Six years later, in 1950, there were only twelve computers in the United States, but by 1960 there were 6,000. Today there are 50,000 general-purpose computers in the United States and another 40,000 in use around the world. These 90,000 machines are valued at over $35 billion (U.S. House of Representatives, 1978).

Numbers of computers alone do not tell the entire story of the growth in computing. Technological advances in electronic circuitry have enabled the development of computers with much greater capacity at mere fractions of the cost of earlier "generations" of computers. "An individual integrated circuit on a chip, perhaps a quarter of an inch square, now can embrace more electronic elements than the most complete piece of electronic equipment that could be built in 1950" (Noyce, 1977). As a result, today's computers are thousands of times faster, more reliable, and more cost-effective than those built three decades ago. The increasingly popular $300 microcomputer of today has a larger computing capacity than the first computer built and is twenty times faster and thousands of times more reliable.

These changes are enhancing our capabilities for conducting research in education. To appreciate the importance of information management and computing for educational research, however, it is becoming increasingly necessary to understand some of the more fundamental technical developments that have taken place and are likely to take place in the not-too-distant future. Despite its relatively recent impact on society, the computer as we know it traces its "ancestry" over centuries. The first part of this article briefly sketches those technical developments that were necessary predecessors to today's computer and speculates about future technical developments. The impact of these technical developments on research in education is then discussed, particularly development of data bases for research and techniques for data analysis. The computer has also fostered the emergence of relatively new areas of education-related research. Yet, problems inherent in the field of computing and information management persist and may worsen. These topics are discussed at the end.

Early Developments. Computers are a natural outgrowth of many earlier developments, some dating back hundreds of years. Goldstine, in his seminal work *The Computer from Pascal to von Neumann* (1972), provided a particularly thoughtful synthesis of the impact of early contributors to the field of computing.

The most widely recognized progenitor of the field is British mathematician Charles Babbage (1792–1871). After working on several calculator machines, Babbage conceived of his "analytical engine" in 1833 and devoted the rest of his life to its development. His machine was theoretically capable of executing any mathematical operation. It could store sequences of instructions and memory, use punch cards, and store mathematical tables in memory. Because Babbage's idea was developed at a time when there were no sophisticated electronic devices, much of his work was ridiculed by contemporaries. Nevertheless, Babbage's concept of the analytical engine is considered by some to be one of the great human intellectual achievements and to mark an introduction to the computer age (Sippl & Sippl, 1980).

Babbage's historical significance lies as much in the motivation for his work as in the work itself. For many years mathematicians were concerned about production of tables by means of mathematical calculations. Such tables were the means by which early scientists learned how to record their experiences so that others could benefit from them. When tables were produced by means of various mathematical principles, as in the case of a table of logarithms, numerous instances of human error arose, and these errors were the basis for irritation with the people who had done the work. It was the idea of replacing "fallible" people with "infallible" machines that appealed so strongly to Babbage.

The need for accurate yet not intellectually stimulating calculation has continued to foster development of refinements in computing. A notable instance relates to the taking of the census by the U.S. Department of Interior. From 1890 onward, two men who were prominent in this regard were Herman Hollerith (1816–1929) and John Billings (1839–1912). Hollerith, proceeding on Billings's suggestions used a system of punched holes to represent various census characteristics, such as male or female, black or white, native- or foreign-born, and age. He designed the system using a continuous roll of paper instead of individual cards. The roll of paper ran under a set of contact brushes that completed an electrical circuit if and only if a hole was present. The completed circuit activated counters that advanced one position for each hole counted; the counters were operated by an electrical mechanical relay. For the 1890 census, Hollerith used cards instead of the roll of paper because he realized that cards could be prepared by different people in different locations at different times and then assembled in one large deck for subsequent tabulation. He also saw that cards could be stored according to a given characteristic. Thus, in the analysis of population statistics, one could in a few sorts determine how many people out of a given population had characteristics A, B, C and how many did not. This work contributed greatly to the development of punch card equipment.

Digital computers. It was nearly fifty years before the limitations of punch card technology for scientific calculation were clearly understood and it was seen that Babbage's original concepts provided a more fruitful basis for future work. Two groups of major contributors in this regard were Howard Aiken of Harvard University and Claire Lake of International Business Machines Corporation, on one hand, and George R. Stiebitz and his colleagues at Bell Laboratories on the other. In 1937 Aiken indicated four points of difference between punch card accounting machinery and calculating machinery as required in the sciences: ability to handle both positive and negative numbers, to utilize various mathematical functions, to be fully automatic in operation without need for human intervention, and to carry out a calculation in the natural sequence of mathematic events (Goldstine, 1972). The basic idea underlying computers of this era, that of using telephone switching for computing purposes, was conceived of before World War I by Stiebitz and his colleagues. The Bell Telephone Company decided to test the idea on a small scale by building for its use a machine capable of performing addition, subtraction, multiplication, and division of complex numbers. Several important developments resulted from the approaches of Aiken, Stibitz, and others, the most lasting of which was a renaissance of interest in digital means for scientific computation. This method had lain dormant for a century because of the highly useful analog machines.

The primary differences between analog and digital computers that spelled a loss of interest in analog computers had to do with accuracy and the speed of analog equipment. Every machine is built out of parts having certain tolerances and capable of running at certain speeds. Not only is there an upper limit on engineering precision, but also, with age, a degradation sets in in which the parts become less accurate so that the precision of the total machine's responses diminishes. Moreover, the faster the mechanical device is driven, the less accurately it depicts the mathematical situation. A digital approach would be preferable if only it were very much faster. However, analog devices turned out in the ages of mechanical and electromechanical technologies were decisively faster than digital ones.

Electronic computers. Renewed interest in the digital machine in the late 1930s and 1940s coupled with its linking to electronics defined the nature of many new developments in computing. The advantages of purely electronic computers over electromechanical ones became apparent at this time. Digital machines are built on the possibility of remembering one of two possible states. These remembering devices can be achieved with either electromechanical relays or vacuum tubes. The fundamental difference between the electromechanical and electronic approaches is one of speed. A few years after the early work of Aiken and Stiebitz on electromechanical components for computing, a group at the University of Pennsylvania's Moore School of Electrical Engineering began to study the applications of vacuum tubes to computations. This group, which included John Mauchley and J. P. Eckert, were confronted with difficult development problems as they sought the use of electronic tubes in relays. Circuits for this application had to be developed, and the speeds that were sought were far above anything attempted in the computer field so far. Yet the potential

results warranted the effort. A relay takes anywhere from one to ten milliseconds (a "millisecond" is one one-thousandth of a second) to cause a relay physically to open or close. This "slow" time is due to the inertia of the mechanical parts.

Support for this work was provided largely through the U.S. Army Ballistic Research Laboratory, one of whose main functions was the production of firing and bombing tables and related gun control data. Automation of this calculation process was to be the *raison d'être* for the first electronic digital computer, ENIAC (Goldstine, 1972). The relay time for ENIAC was on the order of five microseconds (five one-millionths of a second), at least a thousand times faster than the electromechanical devices at Bell Labs and Harvard. In overall performance, then, it was several hundred times faster than the best of the relay machines. In addition to its 18,000 vacuum tubes, ENIAC contained about 70,000 resistors, 10,000 capacitors, and 6,000 switches. It was 100 feet long, ten feet high, and three feet deep. Its operation consumed 140 kilowatts of power. Completed in 1945, it was moved to Aberdeen Proving Ground, where it was used by the Ballistic Research Laboratory.

John von Neumann began work with the ENIAC staff at the Moore School and subsequently contributed in a major way to development of the second, much more advanced, electronic digital computer at the University of Pennsylvania, EDVAC. Chief among these advances was the stored-program facility, which exists in today's computers. A stored-program computer need not be oriented toward some particular computation and can carry out any calculation desired and defined by the user. Von Neumann also pressed successfully for binary representation of numbers in EDVAC, a departure from the digital representation in ENIAC.

After World War II leadership in the design development of computing shifted to the Institute for Advanced Study at Princeton, at least in part because von Neumann returned to the institute. In addition, Eckert and Mauchley left the University of Pennsylvania in 1946 to form their own company. They were successful in obtaining a contract with the National Bureau of Standards to build a machine designed on EDVAC principles for the Bureau of the Census. The machine, UNIVAC (Universal Automatic Computer), was started in 1947 and was operational in 1951. By this time the scientific importance of computers was realized by the university and government community, and commercial applications followed.

Contemporary Computers. Developments in computing over the last three decades are perhaps more spectacular because of the relatively short time span within which they have occurred. The major hardware developments of the computer have focused largely on increases in speed and memory capacity. Consequently many of the advances in information management and computing are traceable to advances in hardware. Information retrieval is measured in nanoseconds (billionths of a second) because of the near infinitesimal distance the signals must travel in such microminiaturized components as chips.

An electron-beam device, writing a pattern of bits on a small wafer of semiconductor material, can store about 100 billion bits, which is the digital equivalent of about 3 million pages of typewritten text or roughly 10,000 books of text. Magnetic bubble devices have even higher bit densities than the wholly electronic semiconductor devices. Communication satellites are opening up channels for computer-to-computer communication that will transmit 50 million bits per second. The channels of the nation-wide computer network with the highest information transmission rate (ARPANET) transmit 50 thousand bits per second. This recent increase by a factor of 1,000 in capability is accompanied by a very large decrease in cost per bit (Licklider, 1980). Optic fibers the diameter of a human hair will soon be able to carry more than 100 million bits of information per second, or the equivalent of ten books of text per second per fiber. Information can rapidly be dumped onto computer output microfiche. Laser printers, controlled by computers, can print several pages of high-quality text and graphics per second. The type fonts and graphic figures are under program control and therefore limited only by the imagination and skill of people. Digital videodiscs are being developed to hold about 10 million bits. Since videodiscs and other high-storage-capacity devices can store images as well as data, the potential for pictorial as well as numerical analysis is greatly enhanced. Hardware continues to undergo rapid development and modification (Ahl, 1981).

Although hardware is in a more advanced state of development than software, changes in software are more apparent to the educational researcher. Instructions to the computer (software) are of two general types: "systems software" (software that extends and augments the general capabilities of the hardware) and "applications software" (software that performs functions that are meaningful in the minds of the people who want to use the computer system for purposes specific to their field of work). As users of computers, educators treat systems software much as if it were hardware. Applications software, on the other hand, requires constant choices on the part of educational researchers and more directly affects the nature of information handling and analysis.

Many educational applications have existed for some time, and others will continue to be developed: computer-based drill and practice, computer-assisted instruction, computer-managed instruction, computer-assisted reasoning and problem solving, business games, computer-based testing, stand-alone teaching machines, stand-alone electronic games, and others. These and research-oriented applications were created through the development of applications software programs.

Information Management and Communications. Hardware and software developments not only have combined to enhance information management but, in combination with communications technology, have blurred the distinction between information management and communications. A noted scientist commented, "We will have one digital world in which transmission, processing, computing, storage, and switching of voice, pictures, and data will be inextricably intertwined both in communications facilities and in their use" (Pierce, 1980, p. 624). Communication is as much a part of computing as computing is of communication.

This confluence of computers and communications has important implications for the educational research community. It not only changes the way in which current research methods are implemented, but also expands the potential for research using data bases that have heretofore not been available. Portending this trend, the British some years ago developed an experimental television data base retrieval system called Teletext that provided automatic information, selectable by the television viewer but without cost and without interference with regular programs. Another system called New Data provided much more detailed data base information that allowed the users to use the television and the telephone to search for the displayed "menus" of information headings. The French developed a competing system called ANTIOPE, and the West Germans purchased the rights to the British systems and called their version of it BILDSCHIRMTEXT (Sippl & Sippl, 1980).

Increased use of networks of computers in communication and resource sharing will likely be one of the major developments in computers and information management during the 1980s (Chofatas, 1980; House, 1980; Fife, 1974). Many systems will likely be sold for data base retrieval use both in homes and among businesses, educational institutions, and government divisions. The exploding quantity of data available through these kinds of systems will increasingly provide an enticing alternative to researchers who heretofore have had little reason to consider existing data bases for research.

Information and Education Research. Trends in hardware and software development not only are expanding the number of ways in which research in education can be conducted, but also are creating researchable issues heretofore unexamined. Large amounts of data are daily being created, stored, and made available to the research community. Analytical techniques for data manipulation are increasing in power, number, and kind. Finally, fields of study within education have developed which are so intimately associated with computing that they were not even conceived of in previous decades.

Existing data bases. Although many data bases continue to be created solely for a single study, educational researchers are increasingly relying on existing data bases that have been created by others. No document better portrays this trend than the entry "Data Processing and Computing" (Cooley, 1969) in the fourth edition of the *Encyclopedia of Educational Research.* Cooley appropriately devoted a large amount of space to the problems associated with constructing instruments to collect and gather data and in converting these data to computer-usable form. Implicit in the discussion is the valid (at the time) assumption that the educational researcher is personally engaged in virtually all stages of the analytic process, including problem definition, development of research problems, development of instrumentation, administration of instruments, preparation of data, analysis, and reporting of findings. This "vertical integration" of research is still practiced by many, if not the vast majority of, educational researchers. The proliferation of data and ease of access, however, combined with the high costs of gathering original data, are causing many researchers to consider use of existing data bases. These alternative data are of three general types: administrative data bases, research data bases, and bibliographic data bases. Over the last several decades banks of information have been created within educational agencies (e.g., school districts, colleges and universities, state departments of education). In these institutions data are gathered largely in response to the regulatory or management functions of the organizations. Other data bases have been constructed specifically for research purposes, but these have been documented and made available for secondary analyses. Third, time-sharing and remote access have fostered the rapid growth of non-quantitative, bibliographic data bases that increasingly are being used for research.

A "data base" is a continuously updated collection of related records that are treated as a unit. Over the last several decades most educational agencies have computerized at least some of the data necessary for their organization to function. Very often an institution does not have a single file, but rather many data bases that overlap to varying degrees. In higher education, for example, there may be separate data bases for admissions, registration, grading, curricula, space utilization, payroll, ledgers, student affairs, and personnel. Each of these may have a separate file that may include a variety of data elements. Hamblen and Landis (1980) provided a particularly complete and recent survey of both data bases and computing in higher education. Barnette and Taffel (1973) provided a similar analysis for state departments of education.

These data bases have recently come to be appreciated as rich sources of information on a wide variety of important and current research questions. Furthermore, they provide a level of magnitude and detail that is often far beyond the ability of individual researchers to replicate (even with substantial external funding). Studies of career mobility of the twenty-five thousand teachers in the Chicago school systems, for example, were undertaken for a total cost for data collection of less than $500 (Hentschke & Cline, 1981).

Part of the impetus for development of some data bases has been the emergence of mandated state and federal reporting requirements for special programs. The Management and Information System for Occupational Education in the state of Massachusetts is an example (Massachusetts State Department of Education, 1974). This system collects and stores basic census data for all occupational programs in Massachusetts, primarily in order to meet all the current requirements of the federal government's Division of Occupational Education, including the Annual Federal Report. Data elements include descriptions of training programs, enrollments, costs, and job entry skills acquired by completers of the program.

Not only are data bases growing in number, size, and level of detail of information, but initial steps have been taken toward standardizing definitions and data collection procedures among educational institutions so that the data from different institutions will be comparable. Myers and Topping (1974) described the information exchange procedures developed by the National Center for Higher Education Management Systems (NCHEMS). The procedures include standard definitions and instructions for collecting information about disciplines, student degree programs, outcomes of instructional programs, and general institutional characteristics. These "institutional" data bases are designed primarily for management purposes but provide potentially useful sources of data for educational researchers. Numerous other data bases are being developed specifically with the educational researcher in mind.

Many of the costs inherent in generating a data base are increasing while the costs associated with storing and retrieving data are decreasing. Because of these shifts, more and more major research endeavors are being undertaken with the explicit purpose of providing data bases that can be used subsequently by additional researchers seeking to pursue a variety of related questions. Examples of these data bases include the National Institute of Education's *Safe School Study* (Leinwand, 1978) and the National Center for Educational Statistics' *National Longitudinal Study of High School Seniors* (Carroll & Morrison, 1976). The National Longitudinal Study (NLS) of the high school class of 1972 is perhaps the best example of a data base that not only was expensive to create but can provide a rich source of information for a variety of studies. Planning for the study began in the late 1960s, and data collection began in the spring of 1972. A baseline survey was conducted on a nationally representative random sample of 21,600 high school seniors drawn from 1,200 high schools. The first follow-up survey commenced in October 1973 and obtained data from 93 percent of students in the sample. A second follow-up, in the fall of 1974, obtained a 94 percent response. Subsequent follow-ups were initiated every two or three years thereafter.

Whether or not data bases emerge through the reporting mandates of individual organizations or as a result of large-scale research efforts, the number and kind of data bases in education are mushrooming. The survey conducted by Feller (1976) is indicative of this trend. In order to improve coordination among federal agencies concerned with collection and use of education data, the National Center for Education Statistics compiled a directory of federal agency educational data tapes covering a wide array of information, including those directly related to elementary-secondary education; postsecondary education; demographic, vital, health, and welfare data; labor supply and demand; libraries and media centers; and federal outlays for education. These and other data bases raise issues of accessibility, overlap, and quality that will increasingly concern the educational researcher in the future (Dodd, 1979). The rapidly expanding use of nonbibliographic data bases, coupled with the fact that information accessed from these data bases in many cases is not available in print, underscores the importance of the educational research community's becoming aware of the form and content of these sources (Wisdom & Houghton, 1977). Reviews by Wood (1977) and Autrey (1978) provided useful introductions to the growing field of education-related data bases.

Despite the widespread growth of data bases in education, their use is not without problems. Rules and regulations relating to privacy and the protection of individuals, as well as to access of researchers to data normally maintained by various agencies, have an impact upon the extent to which data can be collected and the extent to which data collection for one purpose can be made available to other researchers for other purposes. Powell (1977) outlined a variety of these problems and discussed issues that need to be addressed within the research community in order to ensure the availability of data for secondary analysis. From time to time *On-Line Review* publishes a directory of nonbibliographic (numeric) data bases. Entries are arranged alphabetically by name of data base, followed by name of data base producer, subject content, and online vendor ("Nonbibliographic Databases on Line," 1978). A more specialized dictionary was provided by Tyzenhouse (1978), who described data available from four vendors.

Bibliographic data bases have also proliferated and are increasingly used by researchers in education. Literally dozens of online data bases exist in addition to the Education Resources Information Center (ERIC), the *Current Index to Journals in Education* (CIJE), and *Dissertation Abstracts*. They range from *Abstracts of Instructional and Research Materials in Vocational and Technical Education*, to *Exceptional Child Education Abstracts*, to Medical Literature Analysis and Retrieval System, to the New York Times Information Bank, to *Resources in Education*, to Xerox Curriculum Materials Clearinghouse. A summary of the growth of federally supported bibliographic data bases was provided by the Comptroller General of the United States (1979). That report discussed management of scientific and technical bibliographic data bases by the federal government, the existence of overlapping and duplicative bibliographic information services, application of cost-recovery principles to bibliographic information services, and the need to manage information as a resource.

For the educational researcher, bibliographic data bases play an increasingly important role in at least two ways: they increase the speed with which researchers may discover relevant documents and, through an index of headings, enable the researcher to formulate search requests.

Most of these data bases function on a combination of features, such as connectors and limitors, which require carefully phrased search requests in order to be effective. Although computer time appears to be expensive, the amount of material generated in a short time makes it a relatively economical method of search. Furthermore, attempts are being made to make the data understandable and available to nonspecialists, for example, nonlawyers needing to examine case law (Rodgers & Barefield, 1979). Marcus and Reitjes (1976) described progress being made to enable the researcher to access multiple bibliographic retrieval systems simultaneously through networking.

Techniques of data analysis. The educational researcher is faced with options to consider in data manipulation as well as in data selection. The evolution of statistical packages has already been described. Five related trends in data analysis should be discussed: statistical methods, test scoring, simulation, graphic and pictorial representation, and bibliographic analysis.

1. *Statistical Methods.* Special-purpose algorithms, among the earliest means for aiding data analysis via computer, continue to be developed. (Apparently the current stock of library programs and statistical analysis packages is not sufficient for all research needs.) The titles of these are reflective of either the specific nature of the statistical analysis, the specific abilities of the programming language or the resulting statistical program, or the specific capabilities of a particular machine. As examples, consider the following titles that appeared in print in 1979: "A FORTRAN IV Program for Configural Frequency Analysis" (Schlattmann & Wildgrube, 1979), "Statistics with the TRS/80" (Heuer, 1979), "MULTICORR: A Computer Program for Fast, Accurate, Small-Sample Testing of Correlation Pattern Hypotheses" (Steiger, 1979), and "A Chi-Square Program for a Microcomputer Using a Tape Unit" (Dreger, 1979). These types of special-purpose computer programs continue to be generated and reported in such journals as *Educational and Psychological Measurement, Creative Computing, Journal of Educational Statistics, Psychometrika,* and *Applied Psychological Measurement,* among others.

2. *Test Scoring and Analysis.* Computers are being used directly in the process of testing and test scoring. Special programs have been written tailored to testing instruments (Aiken, 1978; Lund & King, 1978). Increasingly tests are constructed to use the ability of an auxiliary device to read optically the responses directly without converting them into punch tape, punch cards, or another intermediate format. Even more recently, the feasibility of interactive computer-assisted testing was being examined (Cartwright & Derevensky, 1978). These developments greatly reduce the time period between when a test is administered and when the results of the test are interpretable.

3. *Computer Simulation.* Computer simulation has become a widely used technique of data analysis. Applications in most major areas of social and behavioral sciences, including education, have been developed over the last

several decades. Perhaps the most ambitious survey of these developments is Holst's *Computer Simulation 1951–1976: An Index to the Literature* (1979). Specific applications are too numerous to mention, except to say that they range from very specific and relatively basic simulations of probability distribution (e.g., Fleischman, 1978) to simulations of specific problems or issues within education (e.g., Peterson & Thain, 1976) and very general models of educational systems (e.g., Grauer, 1976).

4. *Computer Graphics and Pictorial Images.* In many research endeavors a physical or pictorial representation of data represents potentially a powerful means of condensing and portraying research findings. Computers are capable of receiving graphics as input and of displaying output in graphic form. Devices exist that convert line drawings and other graphic representations into digital values that are processed and sent to the computer for analysis, storage, or computation. (For a comprehensive discussion of computer graphics, see Newman & Sproull, 1979.) Mapping is particularly useful when research calls for collection of vast amounts of data that require much synthesis before they can be interpreted. Examples of computer mapping have been reported in research in language development (Herrick, 1978) and in special education (Joiner, 1979), as well as in converting contingency table data to linear graph form (Paulhus, 1977). Videodisc applications in educational research are likely in the near future (Branson & Foster, 1979).

5. *Bibliographic Analysis.* Increasingly bibliographic data bases are providing important material for research. The techniques of nonnumeric data analysis include using the searching and sorting capabilities built into bibliographic data bases to identify findings. Research studies are sorted on the basis of various descriptors using such connectors as "and," "or," or "greater than." Resulting groupings of research studies are then further analyzed using more traditional statistical techniques. Representative of this type of work is that done by Dickson and Moskoff (1980). Using computer-based bibliographic data base search procedures, they located 66 reports involving 80 experiments, 114 referential tasks, and over 6,200 individuals. The studies were entered into a statistical software package system (SPSS) and analyzed for characteristics of the subjects, experimental designs, factors influencing referential communication performances, and changes in research over time. Dickson and Moskoff found that communication performance was strongly related to age but not to sex or verbal ability, and that the trends since 1960 in communication research have been to use younger children in the studies, to examine simpler communication tasks, and to use research designs in which the subjects talk to experimenters rather than to other subjects. Bibliographic sources themselves then become data bases, and the methods of analysis include those associated with both nonnumeric and numeric data bases.

Emerging uses of computers. Computer capabilities have not only influenced the ways in which data are analyzed but also influence what becomes an important research topic; for example, the growth of computer-based instruction has fostered inquiry into the ways in which students learn via computers. The ability of the computer to individualize instruction has then enabled researchers to monitor the ways students interact with the computer and, therefore, gain greater understanding about how individuals pursue problems on computers (a relatively new problem) and how this finding relates to how people learn in general (an old problem) (Splittgerber, 1979). Similar computer influences are found in communications research (Vallee et al., 1978), language research (Belmore, 1975), interpersonal communication (Fogel, 1978), and other education-related fields. Artificial intelligence is perhaps the most obvious example of a field of research that has depended upon the computer for its inception and continued growth. *Machines Who Think* (McCorduck, 1979) provided a review of the growth and development of artificial intelligence.

Pervasive Problems. Like any other field, information management and computing faces a set of challenges or critical factors that, if surmounted, would lead to improvement in the field. Rapid technological changes have caused a degree of instability and uncertainty that provides its own set of problems. Despite increases in productivity and decreases in cost, computers represent large capital investments for most organizations, and the range of choices available to purchasers and maintainers of computers is almost limitless. Furthermore, the arguments favoring a particular configuration or structure of data processing are potentially outdated within relatively short periods of time. Improvements in technology reduce costs and increase choices. The increasing popularity of microcomputers and minicomputers is a current manifestation of this trend. Leong-Hong and Marron (1978) described the problems inherent in administering data bases. Descriptions of problems associated with centralized versus decentralized (distributed) data processing abound (Bryson & Howard, 1979).

Some problems are more pervasive and persistent than others. Perhaps one of the most widespread problems affecting the use of information systems is the ever present possibility of deterioration in the quality of data. Errors in data can come about in a variety of ways. Hence, there is no simple adjustment for them. Errors can be made as a result of incorrect input, measurement, and collection methods; failure to follow correct procedures; loss or nonprocessing of data; incorrect recording or correcting of data; mistakes in processing procedures; and deliberate falsification. Because the problems are diverse, a variety of efforts to control data quality are required. The difficulties with errors may be partially overcome by internal controls to detect them: internal and external auditing of computer operations, addition of confidence limits to data, and instructions to users in measurement and processing procedures so they can evaluate possible error.

A second common problem associated with information

management and computers is accumulation and storage of data that have very little probability of being used. Given the ease and economy with which data can be collected, relatively little attention has been devoted to selectivity (Davis, 1974). In 1868 reports from town superintendents to the state superintendent of public instruction in New Jersey contained only twenty-six items. In 1973 the inventory of data items collected by the state department of education revealed that the total was in the neighborhood of twenty-six thousand items. If New York Department of Education files were to record information from the six hundred school districts and twenty-four hundred schools in the state, and these data were retained for a minimum of three years, the volume of data stored would be over fifteen million items from the school districts and over sixty million items from local schools, for a total of more than seventy-five million items per year, or just under a quarter of a billion data items for the three-year period (Maloney, 1975). Large quantities of data, however, do not necessarily imply useful information for decision making. Often school-district-level information is not sufficiently individualized and skill-specific to be useful to teachers at classroom instruction levels (Farber, 1974).

Many of the problems associated with computers and information systems are in fact problems of planning and control within organizations. Organization of work flows, proper staffing, anticipation of future needs, etc., can be done well or poorly in all undertakings, including operation of computers. The fact that these problems arise in computer operations does not necessarily imply that they are unique to computing (Topping, 1979).

Despite these other problems, computers and information systems are increasingly ubiquitous. Their use has already become so pervasive within the research community that they are in a sense disappearing into studies and communication systems: instead of being novel and unique pieces of equipment, they have become extensions of human analytic capability. And yet, the rapid developments of the past decade would indicate that the potential of computers in information management for educational research is far from being fully realized.

Guilbert C. Hentschke

See also Archives and Records Management; Computer-Based Education; Libraries; New Technologies in Education; Systems Design in Instruction.

REFERENCES

Ahl, D. H. Dateline: Tomorrow. *Creative Computing*, 1981, 7(5), 14.

Aiken, L. R. A general questionnaire analysis program. *Educational and Psychological Measurement*, 1978, 38(1), 167–169.

Autrey, P. *Publicly Available Numerical Data Base Systems Useful in Social Planning and Policy-making: A General Discussion and a Case Study.* Paper prepared for a library science course, University of Texas at Austin, Graduate School of Library Science, May 1978. (ERIC Document Reproduction Service No. ED 167 154)

Barnette, J. J., & Taffell, S. *The Status of Management Information Systems (MIS) in State Departments of Education.* Montgomery: Alabama State Department of Education, 1973. (ERIC Document Reproduction Service No. ED 192 750)

Belmore, N. F. *Language-teaching Research and the Computer.* Stockholm: Swedish Council for Social Science Research, 1975. (ERIC Document Reproduction Service No. ED 123 930)

Branson, R. K., & Foster, R. W. Educational applications research and videodisc technology. *Journal of Educational Technology Systems*, 1979, 8(3), 241–262.

Bryson, C. H., & Howard, R. D. A call for different styles of data management and institutional research: Centralized versus decentralized planning. *Cause/Effect*, March 1979, 2(2), 10–15.

Carroll, S. J., & Morrison, P. A. *National Longitudinal Study of High School Seniors: An Agenda for Policy Research.* Santa Monica, Calif.: Rand Corporation, 1976. (ERIC Document Reproduction Service No. ED 135 818)

Cartwright, G. R., & Derevensky, J. L. Interactive computer-assisted testing: A feasibility study. *Journal of Educational Technology Systems*, 1978, 6(3), 219–228.

Chorafas, D. N. *Computer Networks for Distributed Information Systems,* New York: Petrocelli Books, 1980.

Comptroller General of the U.S. *Better Information Management Policies Needed: A Study of Scientific and Technical Bibliographical Services.* Washington, D.C.: U.S. General Accounting Office, 1979. (ERIC Document Reproduction Service No. ED 179 191)

Cooley, W. Data processing and computing. In R. Ebel (Ed.), *Encyclopedia of Educational Research* (4th ed.). New York: Macmillan, 1969, pp. 283–291.

Davis, G. B. *Management Information Systems: Conceptual Foundations, Structure, and Development.* New York: McGraw-Hill, 1974.

Dickson, W. P., & Moskoff, M. *A Meta-analysis of Referential Communication Studies: A Computer-readable Literature Review.* Madison: Wisconsin University Research and Development Center for Individualized Schooling, May 6, 1980.

Dodd, S. A. Bibliographic references for numeric social science data files: Suggested guidelines. *Journal of the American Society for Information Sciences*, March 1979, 30(2), 77–82.

Dreger, R. M. A chi-square program for a microcomputer using a tape unit. *Educational and Psychological Measurement*, 1979, 39(3), 685–688.

Farber, I. J. *The Development and Implementation of a Multi-level Management Information Feedback System.* Paper presented at the annual meeting of the American Educational Research Association, Chicago, 1974. (ERIC Document Reproduction Service No. ED 090 993)

Feller, B. A. *Directory of Federal Agency Education Data Tapes.* Washington, D.C.: U.S. Government Printing Office, 1976. (ERIC Document Reproduction Service No. ED 120 232)

Fife, D. W. *Research Considerations in Computer Networking to Expand Resource-sharing* (NBS Technical Note 801). Washington, D.C.: National Bureau of Standards, 1974. (ERIC Document Reproduction Service No. ED 094 746)

Fleishman, A. I. A method for simulating non-normal distributions. *Psychometrika*, 1978, 43(4) 521–532.

Fogel, D. S. DYAD: A computer program for the analysis of interpersonal communication. *Educational and Psychological Measurement*, 1978, 38(1), 187–188.

Goldstine, H. H. *The Computer from Pascal to von Neumann*. Princeton, N.J.: Princeton University Press, 1972.

Grauer, R. T. On the modeling of educational systems, II. *Journal of Educational Technology Systems*, 1976, *4*(4), 281–298.

Hamblen, J. W., & Landis, C. (Eds.). *The Fourth Inventory of Computers in Higher Education: An Interpretive Report* (EDUCOM Series in Computing and Telecommunications in Higher Education). Princeton, N.J.: Inter-university Communications Council (EDUCOM), 1980.

Hentschke, G. C., & Cline, H. *Educational Career Mobility under Organizational Growth and Contraction*. Paper presented at the annual meeting of the American Educational Research Association, Los Angeles, April 1981.

Herrick, E. M. *Interactive Computer Programs for Sorting and Mapping Dialect Data*. Paper presented at the International Conference on Methods in Dialectology, London, Ontario, August 1978. (ERIC Document Reproduction Service No. ED 187 113)

Heuer, R. Statistics with the TRS-80. *Creative Computing*, December, 1979, *5*(12), 46–47.

Holst, P. A. *Computer Simulation 1951–1976: An Index to the Literature*. London: Mansell Ltd., 1979.

House, W. C. (Ed.). *Electronic Communications Systems*. New York: Petrocelli Books, 1980.

Joiner, L. M. When a map is worth one thousand ANOVAs: Applications of statistical cartography in special education research and planning. *Journal of Special Education*, Winter 1979, *12*(4), 421–432.

Leinwand Associates, Inc. *Data Files Documentation*. Vol. 3 of *Safe School Study*. Newton, Mass.: Leinwand, 1978. (ERIC Document Reproduction Service No. ED 153 327)

Leong-Hong, B., & Marron, B. *Database Administration: Concepts, Tools, Experiences, and Problems*. Washington, D.C.: National Bureau of Standards, 1978. (ERIC Document Reproduction Service No. ED 163 995)

Licklider, J. C. R. Social and economic impacts of information technology on education. In House of Representatives, Committee on Science and Technology, *Information Technology in Education* (96th Congress, Joint Hearings before the Subcommittee on Science, Research and Technology of the Committee on Science and Technology and the Subcommittee on Select Education of the Committee on Education and Labor, House of Representatives). Washington, D.C.: U.S. Government Printing Office, 1980, pp. 84–113.

Lund, C., & King D. T. Quickscore: A computerized test and survey analysis package. *Journal of Technological Horizons in Education*, 1978, *5*(3), 33–35, 39.

Maloney, R. K. DEIC: New Jersey's system for bringing data elements and items under control. In D. Green (Ed.), *Discovery: New Worlds of Educational Data Systems* (Association for Educational Data Systems Proceedings, Virginia Beach, Va., April 1975). (ERIC Document Reproduction Service No. ED 107 237)

Marcus, R. S., & Reitjes, J. F. *The Networking of Interactive Bibliographic Retrieval Systems*. Cambridge, Mass.: MIT, 1976. (ERIC Document Reproduction Service No. ED 125 533)

Massachusetts State Department of Education. *Field Test Results of the MISOE Management Information System for Occupational Education*. Boston: Massachusetts State Department of Education, 1974. (ERIC Document Reproduction Service No. ED 115 864)

McCorduck, P. *Machines Who Think*. San Francisco: Freeman, 1979.

Myers, E. M., & Topping, J. R. *Information Exchange Procedures Activity Structure* (Technical Report No. 63). Boulder, Colo.: Western Interstate Commission for Higher Education, 1974. (ERIC Document Reproduction Service No. ED 101 635)

Newman, W. N., & Sproull, R. F. *Principles of Interactive Computer Graphics* (2nd ed.). New York: McGraw-Hill, 1979.

Nonbibliographic databases on line. *On-Line Review*, June 1978, *2*(2), 125–126.

Noyce, R. N. Microelectronics. *Scientific American*, 1977, *237*(3), 62–69.

Paulhus, D. L. DSYSTM: A basic computer program for the casual analysis of contingency data. *Educational and Psychological Measurement*, 1977, *37*(3), 795–796.

Peterson, C. R., & Thain, J. W. A Monte Carlo program for simulating selection decisions from personnel tests. *Educational and Psychological Measurement*, 1976, *36*(1), 205–207.

Pierce, J. A. In C. Sippl, Jr., & R. J. Sippl, *Computer Dictionary and Handbook*. Indianapolis: Howard W. Sams & Co., 1980.

Powell, M. *Necessary Steps to Insure Availability of Data for Secondary Analysis*. Paper presented at the annual meeting of the American Educational Research Association, New York, April 1977. (ERIC Document Reproduction Service No. ED 137 384)

Rodgers, R., & Barefield, A. *LEXIS: Applications for Research in Communication and Law*. Paper presented at the meeting of the Eastern Communication Association, Philadelphia, May 1979. (ERIC Document Reproduction Service No. ED 169 603)

Schlattmann, H., & Wildgrube, W. A FORTRAN IV program for configural frequency analysis. *Educational and Psychological Measurement*, 1979, *39*(3), 673–675.

Sippl, C. J., Jr., & Sippl, R. J. *Computer Dictionary and Handbook*. Indianapolis: Howard W. Sams & Co., 1980.

Splittgerber, F. L. Computer-based instruction: A revolution in the making? *Educational Technology*, 1979, *19*(1), 20–26.

Steiger, J. H. MULTICORR: A computer program for fast, accurate, small-sample testing of correlational pattern hypotheses. *Educational and Psychological Measurement*, Fall 1979, *39*(3), 677–680.

Topping, L. S. Let's stop blaming MIS . . . and manage. *Cause/Effect*, September 1979, *2*, 34–38.

Tyzenhouse, J. Econometric and statistical bases for the noneconometrician. *Online*, 1978, *2*(2), 48–54.

U.S. House of Representatives Committee on Science and Technology. *Computers and the Learning Society* (Report prepared by the Subcommittee on Domestic and International Scientific Planning, Analysis, and Cooperation of the Committee on Science and Technology, U.S. House of Representatives, Ninety-fifth Congress). Washington, D.C.: U.S. Government Printing Office, 1978.

Vallee, J.; Johansen, R.; Lipinski, H.; Spangler, K.; Wilson, T.; & Hardy, A. *Group Communication through Computers: Social, Managerial, and Economic Issues* (Vol. 4). Menlo Park, Calif.: Institute for the Future, 1978.

Wisdom, J. C., & Houghton, B. *Non-bibliographic Data-bases: An Investigation into Their Uses within the Fields of Economics and Business Studies*. Liverpool, England: Liverpool Polytechnic, 1977. (ERIC Document Reproduction Service No. ED 190 086)

Wood, B. L. *Review of Scientific and Technical Numerical Database Activities*. Rockville, Md.: King Research, 1977. (ERIC Document Reproduction Service No. ED 162 904)

INNOVATION IN EDUCATION

See Change Processes; New Technologies in Education.

IN-SERVICE TEACHER EDUCATION

Recently, as defining in-service education has become a popular sport, several new labels have been introduced into the game: "staff development," "continuing teacher education," and "continuous education professional development." Probably an adjustment of Hass's short definition is as good as any: "Broadly conceived, in-service education includes all activities engaged in by the professional personnel during their service and designed to contribute to [professional] improvement" (1957, p. 13). Although this definition is very general, it does provide some useful constraints. It includes all teachers, but only those who are actively employed. Likewise, all types of in-service activity can be included, but only if they are intended to "contribute to [professional] improvement." The definition will serve as a guidepost in this article.

Context. In-service education is a massive, highly politicized, complex activity, affecting great numbers of people directly and many others indirectly. It is important to study the history and dimensions of in-service education, as well as the energizers that currently propel it and are likely to be important for the next decade.

Although the recent prominence of in-service education might suggest otherwise, it has a long history, and was not invented in the past ten years. From the beginning of public education, teacher competence has been the object of scrutiny, complaint, and regulation. In the beginning, trainers of in-service teachers were generally the town fathers. Upon appointment of the schoolmaster or schoolmistress, these public officials took pains to give advice and direction regarding the values to be inculcated in the town children. This training of teachers was primarily concerned with educational content rather than pedagogy, although affective areas such as discipline were also considered important. From this time until just recently, in-service education has emphasized either content or pedagogy, with little attention given to integrating the two.

A more formal type of in-service education began to appear about the mid-nineteenth century, in the form of "institutes" that "were designed to review and drill teachers in the elementary subjects" (Asher, 1967, p. 3). Such rudimentary programs were necessitated by a condition that Richey (1957, p. 36) refers to as "the tremendous but largely unfilled need for even modestly educated and professionally trained teachers."

Although these institutes were recognizable until about the middle of the twentieth century, other forms of teacher education began to appear about 1880. By that time, the period of high public concern about teacher incompetence seemed to diminish significantly. In addition, the institutes were not keeping up with the needs of teachers, and many teachers found them to be boring and repetitive. Consequently, newer approaches to in-service education were beginning to appear and become popular. Teachers' reading circles, and summer schools and extension courses sponsored by universities and normal schools (Asher, 1967; Tyler, 1971), began to fill some of the void left by the increasingly irrelevant institutes. Reading circles were aimed at motivating teachers to continue their own education through the reading and discussion of books of literary merit with colleagues. The more formal summer schools and extension courses provided the teacher with a more cosmopolitan view of education and with college credits. Even so, many teachers in the early part of the twentieth century did not possess a college degree or post–high school diploma (a situation found again in American education shortly after World War II).

From 1900 until approximately 1930, a major aim of in-service programs was "filling gaps in college degree requirements" (Tyler, 1971, p. 10). However, the 1930s brought a drastic change of focus in educational standards that paralleled a drastic change in the economic standard of most Americans. During the early 1930s economic conditions were so poor and job opportunities so limited that students stayed in school as long as possible. This necessitated the development of curricula with a new emphasis on vocational relevancy. Reform of education was a very serious economic necessity. In short, this reform led to new approaches to in-service teacher education, including the development of workshops and curriculum study and development activities.

During the past thirty years, in-service education has been revisited by past concerns and aims while at the same time developing in new ways. About 1950 the schools began to feel the strain of the postwar baby boom. Increases in the school population required emergency measures, particularly in the staffing of classrooms. Many teachers were hired who did not possess college degrees and had not fulfilled requirements for certification. Consequently, the primary activity of in-service education, at least until the early 1960s, was to provide for completion of degree and certification requirements.

While American schools were still feeling the effects of the drastic increase in population, the launching of *Sputnik* in 1957 threw them into another crisis. The Russian space activities brought heavy indictment from the public against the American education system. Science and mathematics programs, in particular, were widely criticized. The result was the initiation of national curriculum development projects in science and mathematics. These projects were typically centered at large universities across the nation and only minimally involved the classroom teacher. In-service programs during most of the 1960s, therefore, were designed to assist teachers in developing the skills necessary to implement these packaged programs. Toward the latter half of the decade, similar projects for English and social studies were also launched, but with considerably less enthusiasm and concentrated effort than was the case for science and mathematics. Nevertheless, during most of the 1960s the professional development of teachers reverted to a focus on molding teachers to fit the nationwide curricula—a focus that had dominated the field just thirty years earlier.

Although credentialing and standardization of curricula have been major thrusts of professional development programs since World War II, other ideas and emphases developed as well. During the 1970s some of these involved pressures for dramatic change in in-service teacher education. Probably the most controversial among these is the teacher center, reflective of the increased involvement of teachers and their organizations in the in-service effort.

Size. It is impossible to determine precisely how massive the enterprise of in-service education truly is. Recently it was reported (Yarger, Howey, & Joyce, 1980, p. B–4) that nearly half of all teachers in the United States presently hold a master's degree, and about 5 percent hold doctorates. Most in-service education is provided by colleges and school districts, and it is estimated that there are seventy to eighty thousand education professors, supervisors, and consultants presently engaged as full-time or part-time in-service instructors. That roughly provides a ratio of nearly one instructor for every twenty-five to thirty teachers presently employed. If one were to add those professionals who can be assumed to have some responsibility for in-service training of such administrators as principals and vice-principals, nonsupervisory instructional personnel, and others, one arrives at a figure of one in-service professional for approximately every ten teachers in the country. And these dramatic estimates do not include the teachers themselves—who may represent the single most important category of in-service instructors.

If each of the 2.1 million teachers in America were to take just one college course per year, and there were approximately twenty students per class, there would be more than one hundred thousand college classes devoted to in-service education. If all these classes were equally divided among the approximately fifteen hundred colleges and universities that prepare teachers, there would be approximately seventy in-service courses per year per institution. Truly, there are many more people engaged in in-service education than has generally been thought; the programs have a myriad of forms, and the enterprise operates on a major scale.

Importance. Although no one would deny that in-service education has been important for a long time, many factors seem to merge at this point in American educational history to underscore its importance today. First, the teachers who are in classrooms with children today will also be there tomorrow. In a recent survey of more than eight thousand teachers in three states (Yarger, Howey, & Joyce, 1980), the following demographic picture emerged. The "typical" teacher is a woman in her mid-

thirties. Chances are about even that she has a master's degree, and the odds are even greater that she has achieved permanent certification. This typical teacher has taught for about fourteen years. Inasmuch, then, as most teachers do not need additional credits in order to advance toward either master's degrees or certification, the historic reasons for in-service education have lost their potency.

Recently, however, the public media have begun to assail not only the educational competence of students in public schools but the competence of their teachers as well. The litany of complaints is all too familiar: students can't read, test scores are declining, student violence is on the upswing. In short, to say that there is heightened interest in the capabilities of American teachers would be euphemistic. Who can ignore, for example, *Time* magazine's effort ("Help! Teacher Can't Teach," 1980), which brought attention to inadequacies of classroom teachers? Although the *Time* article was not a direct assault on teacher education, it certainly raised the question of how allegedly illiterate teachers are getting into classrooms. Lyons (1980) has addressed this question very specifically and has placed the blame squarely on teacher education. These recent articles are cited only as examples of the current media interest in teacher competency—an interest that has led, quite naturally, to increased political interest in in-service teacher education. Notwithstanding the defensive reaction of the teaching profession, one would be hard-pressed not to acknowledge that the media blitz has created yet another reason to look closely at the field.

The current interest in in-service education and the recent phenomenon of a teacher surplus have unfortunately removed the focus of teacher education from the initial preparation programs for teachers. Preservice programs have clearly suffered from lack of attention. A 1977 study (Joyce, Yarger, & Howey) highlighted the inadequacies of preservice teacher education. For example, in many states it takes more hours of classroom instruction and supervised practice to become a hairdresser than an elementary teacher—and elementary teachers receive twice as much preparation as secondary teachers. To make matters even worse, the structure and content of preservice teacher education programs are heavily embedded in state regulations and certification requirements, and not amenable to rapid change. What emerges is yet another pressure to look seriously at in-service education and recognize its importance.

Finally, it is important to recognize the genuine interest that many practicing classroom teachers have in programs that will help them work with children more effectively. This point has been underscored by a study of thirty-seven federally funded teacher centers (Mertens & Yarger, 1981). One of the characteristics of these teacher centers has been voluntary participation by clients. In the typical project, there were 330 instances per month of voluntary participation in programs that reflected the interests of teachers. Thus, it is apparent that when teachers perceive the content of in-service education to be responsive to their needs, they participate in droves! Teacher interest in teacher centers is important for many reasons. It provides what may be the beginning for a truly professional culture, i.e., teachers willingly participating in their own professional improvement. Additionally, it should help mute some of the cynical views concerning classroom teachers held by the public. Finally, it has provided researchers with the opportunity to learn that when self-perceived needs are the crux for program development, short-term and classroom-focused in-service education is the result.

In short, although no one would deny the historical importance of in-service teacher education, many factors have recently converged to underscore its contemporary importance. These factors include not only the demographics of the teacher population but also public perceptions of the competency of both students and teachers, recognition of the shortcomings of preservice teacher education, and finally, and perhaps most importantly, the interest that teachers themselves have demonstrated in improving their professional skills.

Knowledge Base. Research is limited, existing knowledge is typically in the form of program descriptions and hortatory statements, and those who wish to implement in-service education must often rely on the conventional wisdom of practitioners. However, there is probably more knowledge available than can be tapped; the form of this knowledge is typically often not a part of the traditional methods of professional communication.

A program description typically provides a narrative account of the initiation, implementation, and/or evaluation of an in-service program or activity. Descriptions are abundant in the literature and provide in-service educators with an almost unlimited supply of ideas and information. Program descriptions, however, are not necessarily bound to data, and frequently serve the single purpose of advocacy. Good examples of program descriptions include Goodlad (1972) and Snow (1972). Pipes (1978) and Devaney (1979) provide examples of the growing number of monographs and books that include anthologies of program descriptions.

Case studies share many characteristics of program descriptions. However, they are typically written for the purpose of conveying accurate information about in-service programs. Case studies have a specified methodology; and some type of evidence (e.g., documents, interviews, or personal observations) is usually presented. Oja (1979) and McDonald (1980) are good examples of relevant case studies.

Surveys canvass large populations concerning important topics. True surveys take note of the issues of sampling, instrument design, return rates, response rates, social acceptability, and other important technicalities. Surveys often address topics that are fairly broad and abstract, but the data are usually accurate and generalizable. Studies by Ingersoll (1976), Byrd (1979), and Yarger, Howey, and Joyce (1980) are representative of the limited

number of true surveys available about in-service education.

Finally, experimental studies, although the highest order of research in in-service education, are almost impossible to conduct in a field setting. In an experimental study, not only are variables controlled but sampling is performed appropriately, subjects are assigned to treatment, and a true experimental manipulation of a variable is required. Although really scientific experimental studies are rare in the research on in-service education, quasi-experiments are more abundant. Good examples of the latter include the works of Carline (1970), Good and Brophy (1974), and McDonald and Davis (1978).

The important point to consider about the conditions of existing knowledge in in-service education is that there exists a tremendous problem of language precision; the literature is dominated by hortatory and advocative program descriptions; and studies that are generalizable and/or replicable are rare. Reliable research is simply insufficient to justify a claim of a body of research knowledge, although there is no lack of "paper." Those trying to learn about and understand in-service education must rely heavily on their critical reading skills, as well as on the experience and wisdom of in-service educators.

Program Content. As with so much of the field, it is necessary to make creative inferences in order to patch together an estimate of what constitutes the content of in-service education. With the exception of a single study (Mertens & Yarger, 1981), no reliable information regarding content could be uncovered. In this study of thirty-seven federally supported teacher center projects, the data are quite clear. When teachers are involved in program development, as they are in teacher centers, they put the focus on pedagogical skills—those that will make it possible for them to effectively work with children in classrooms. Additionally, teachers request and involve themselves in in-service programs related to basic skill areas, particularly reading and mathematics (although writing is also emphasized). Interestingly, woven through all areas selected by teachers is the priority put on materials development. It is clear that one of the richest prospective content areas, traditionally ignored by in-service education, is teacher-made instructional materials for children.

No systematic study of the content of college programs targeted at in-service teachers has ever been conducted. But if one looks at college catalogs focusing on graduate programs for teachers, two content areas emerge. First, one encounters the "general education" courses that are typically required for degrees: educational psychology, educational research, and others. Second, a large number of courses are related to career change: for example, educational administration, reading, guidance, and counseling. It is interesting to note that most graduate school catalogs (for the master's degree particularly) do not have a plethora of courses that would approximate the content interests expressed by teachers in the Mertens and Yarger study.

An inspection of certification requirements yields little more insight (Wollner, 1974, 1978). It is only recently that state departments of education have begun to place important restrictions on which courses may or may not count toward achieving permanent certification status. Historically, as long as teachers earned graduate credits these could be applied toward meeting certification requirements. More recently, however, state departments of education are requiring that teachers justify the content of courses related to certification, typically demanding that they be in the "tenure or professional" area. In most cases, the content of in-service teacher education one can infer from state certification requirements is not dissimilar to what is found in college catalogs. In fact, state certification requirements and college programs are often logically and practically related.

Although local school districts are noted for their lack of activity in in-service program development, there are so many school districts that one must look at the content of their programs in order to better understand the field. With notable exceptions (e.g., Los Angeles, California, and Lincoln, Nebraska) a typical school district may offer only two or three in-service programs per year. Often these programs are directly related to district goals: for example, a new K–12 writing program, districtwide discipline, or record keeping as prescribed by state law. Interestingly, school district programs seldom focus on direct aid to teachers in classrooms related to their ongoing task of instructing children.

Finally, one can look at federally sponsored in-service programs to obtain some sense of content. With the exception of the Teacher Centers Program, most federally sponsored in-service programs are categorical in nature; i.e., they emanate from a larger federal program designed to help a very specifically defined population. Thus, the bulk of the in-service programs sponsored with federal funds are directed toward helping teachers achieve such goals as understanding the instructional needs of the economically disadvantaged, the culturally different, the handicapped, and, more recently, the gifted and talented. Although few would deny the importance of developing in-service programs in these categorical areas, many critics point out that their narrow specificity of content tends to isolate and fragment them, and make their development very costly.

Obtaining valid information about the content of in-service education is relatively unsatisfactory at best. Often tied to college credit, certification, and/or degrees, much of the in-service education encountered by teachers focuses on either general degree requirements or career change programs. Less available are district programs focusing on specific district priorities and federal programs emerging from categorical legislation. Finally, when the needs of teachers as perceived by teachers are highlighted (as in teacher centers), pedagogical skills, curriculum areas, and instructional-materials development emerge as the important content areas.

Program Delivery. Discussions about delivery formats for in-service teacher education are particularly plagued by the problem of imprecise communication noted earlier. Thus any attempt to be highly specific in discussing in-service formats is precluded. But a general description of delivery formats includes five types: long-term programs of interrelated courses; long-term courses; short-term courses; individualized plans; and self-directed plans.

Long-term programs of interrelated courses. Long-term programs of interrelated courses in in-service format are almost exclusively related to the pursuit of advanced college degrees. Typically, programs of interrelated courses are designed to help teachers develop new skills, perhaps in quest of a career change. These efforts may be related to certification requirements and to salary increments. There is little reason to believe that such programs would exist if they were not either required or the source of real and tangible benefits for teachers. They are not the format of choice for teachers looking for support in their daily activities.

Long-term courses. Teachers frequently enroll in long-term courses (usually at a college or university) even though they are not enrolled in a specific degree program. Often, these courses are related either to certification requirements or to salary advancement. Sometimes they are part of a teacher developed program to learn new skills. Regardless, long-term courses are not usually designed to offer direct aid to teachers in classrooms, and are almost always attached to either a requirement or to an inducement.

Short-term courses. Short-term courses, usually meeting only two or three times, are less likely to be attached to any kind of requirement or incentive than are the long-term courses or interrelated programs. Data from the teacher center study suggest they are a format of choice. Teachers quite willingly become involved—particularly if a short-term course is designed to help them learn a specific skill that can be used in the classroom. Short-term courses emerge unevenly in the in-service domain, because they typically have no institutional base; that is, it is difficult to garner "line item" financial support for this type of program. Thus, they frequently emerge in alternative programs, in externally funded programs, and in those few school districts where extensive in-service programs have, in fact, been developed.

Individualized support. Probably the most startling finding of the teacher center study was that teachers were served more frequently through individualized help than through group activities such as courses. It is clearly a delivery format of teacher choice, and is typically exercised through provision of direct consultative services, facilitative services (matching teachers with resources, providing instructional materials), and materials and equipment for developing instructional materials. Unfortunately, individualized in-service education is labor-intensive and therefore costly. Also, like short-term courses, this type of format lacks an institutional base. It does ap-

FIGURE 1. *Levels of assessment of teacher competence in teacher education*

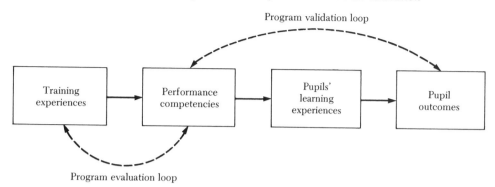

SOURCE: Medley, 1977.

pear, however, to be a high priority with practicing elementary and secondary teachers.

Self-directed learning. Finally, one cannot ignore the self-directed in-service education that characterizes any profession. Not only do teachers subscribe to magazines, purchase books, attend lectures, and think about their work; they also take educational trips, form informal study groups, and participate in a myriad of events that are self-directed and personal. It is impossible to estimate the pervasiveness of self-directed learning. Those involved with in-service education have been and are developing new and creative formats for serving their clients. Probably the most important point to remember, however, is that only programs of interrelated courses and courses taken separately are embedded in an institution and thus assured of support that guarantees survival over a long term.

Evaluation. Success of in-service education can be examined at three levels: judgments by the teachers themselves, researchers' measures of the effects on teachers' behavior and measures of how learned teacher behavior affects students. At the first level, there is a great deal of evidence; at the second, there is enough evidence to support some very clear positions; and at the third, productivity has been virtually nonexistent.

In a thorough investigation of evaluation results of in-service teacher education programs, Lawrence (1974) discovered several important characteristics. However, it is important to note that almost all of the nearly one hundred studies cited by Lawrence depend on participant perceptions. Although Lawrence's conclusions are probably valid, they are not confirmed either by demonstrated learning on the part of participating teachers or by improved learning on the part of children.

Lawrence's major conclusions were (1) that individualized in-service education tends to be better than single offerings for large groups; (2) that programs requiring active involvement tend to be better than those requiring passive-receptive involvement; (3) that demonstration of skills with supervised feedback tends to be better than provision of skills to be stored for future use; (4) that

teacher-help-teacher programs tend to be better than teacher-work-alone programs; (5) that in-service training integrated into a large program tends to be more effective than one-shot affairs; (6) that training that has an emerging design, with teacher input, tends to be better than totally preplanned training; and (7) that self-initiated training tends to be more effective than self-prescribed training.

Joyce and Showers (1980) looked specifically at the effects of training programs on the behavior of teachers. Although they reported dismay with the "spottiness" of the literature, they did review more than two hundred studies and were able to develop some interesting conclusions: for example, teachers can utilize feedback in training to develop both simple and complex teaching skills and strategies, and to implement curricula; teachers also have the ability to respond to autoinstructional methodologies quite rapidly. However, Joyce and Showers implicitly raise the question that McDonald and Davis (1978) raise explicitly: Is it possible for teachers to integrate the skills learned by in-service training into their repertoire of classroom behaviors so that they can use them over a long period of time? This is a difficult question to answer, and clearly demands more research in the future.

Finally, Medley (1977), in his summary of the teacher effectiveness literature, clearly demonstrates that some teacher behavior does affect student learning. He also wrestles with the problem of teacher education programs and their relationship to student learning. In his view (see Figure 1), one must separate the evaluation or research question into two distinct questions. First, as Joyce and Showers asked, can in-service programs produce demonstrable effects on teacher behavior? Second, can teachers who exhibit certain behaviors have a measurable effect on the learning of children? Medley cautions about attempting to jump from measures of teacher training to measures of student learning—the technical problems are grotesque. Rather, Medley's work suggests "linked" studies in which demonstrations of teacher learning are evident before the question is asked concerning student achievement. This domain of linked studies constitutes the null set in evaluations of the success of in-service teacher education. It is probably an area that will demand activity in the future, but at this point it simply does not exist.

Delving into the substance of in-service teacher education is an adventure. The state of existing knowledge is less than one would desire, leaving little choice but to speculate and make high inference judgments. Although in-service education does have content, is delivered in some format, and serves several purposes, the ability to learn about it and to communicate about it succinctly and with certainty is difficult in the early 1980s.

Governance and Support. Since the mid-nineteenth century, control and funding of education has been embedded in state and local governments, making education a major political activity in the United States. The term "political" is used in the best sense of the word. In fact, many view the political nature of American education to be crucial to the maintenance of a free and open society. Unfortunately, the political process that governs education is not only sometimes cumbersome but has come to connote evil and unpleasant things to many people. This entry does not deal with those aspects of "politics," but rather is grounded in the belief that the political nature of education is an asset rather than a liability.

Financing. Few would deny that allocation of resources to in-service teacher education is intimately linked to political activity. There are four distinct sources of financial support: federal, state, and school district funds and the personal resources of teachers themselves. If one is willing to be adventurous with the data that are available, some reasoned estimates of support can be made.

Feistritzer and Dobson (1980) suggest that approximately $270 million are invested at the federal level for the professional development of educators. Because professionals other than teachers are eligible for the use of these funds and because high administrative costs are associated with federal grants, it would seem safe to halve that figure. Thus, if $135 million are actually spent on in-service education for 2.1 million teachers, the federal government annually invests approximately $65 per teacher for in-service activity.

Data from states are more difficult to acquire. Since no one has yet taken on the arduous task of collating and equating these data across states, it makes sense to look at a single state that may be considered generous in support of in-service teacher education activities. For example, despite severe economic problems Michigan has committed "real" dollars to in-service education (Brictson, 1981). For the 1981 fiscal year, Michigan committed approximately $2.25 million, or about 0.2 percent of the total education budget. Therefore, for each of the approximately one-hundred fifty thousand teachers in Michigan, $15 of state money was devoted to in-service teacher education in 1981.

Developing an estimate of expenditures at the level of local school districts is also difficult. At least two studies (Yarger & Leonard, 1974; Van Ryn, 1977) are relevant.

Excluding administrative salaries that may be devoted to in-service teacher education, and accrued benefits to teachers based on salary increases as a result of credit, on the average, about 0.25 percent of local education budgets is set aside. Thus, local school districts typically allocate about $70 per teacher per year for in-service activities. Admittedly, these estimates are speculative. However, it would appear that combined input from federal, state, and local sources is somewhere in the vicinity of $150 per teacher per year.

Although it is virtually impossible to document the amount of money that teachers themselves expend on in-service activities, it is possible to make gross estimates. For example, if each teacher in America takes one course per year (obviously some take more and some take none), and if the average tuition for one course is assumed to be about $300, the investment of personal dollars in support of in-service activities doubles that provided by all public sources. Clearly, the largest single source of financial support for in-service education comes from teachers themselves.

The importance of this analysis is not the likelihood that teachers invest more in their own professional growth and development than do public sources. Rather, the important point is that the paucity of public money devoted to in-service education means that no institution (i.e., school district, university, or college) has accepted or has been vested with the responsibility for the in-service enterprise. School districts put little into in-service training, and universities and colleges and more likely to see it as a source of revenue than a source of expenditure. This lack of a "home base" for in-service education probably does more to inhibit the development and coordination of the enterprise than any other single fact. Until an institutional base is found, in-service education is probably destined to flounder, lacking both coordination and direction.

Control and direction. Given that policy is the result of a political process, then the question of policy development in in-service teacher education is important. Such policy development relates not only to the allocation of resources, but also to the important issue of who shall control those resources once allocated. Central is the question of "ownership." But, since policy does result from a political process, it is naive to think in terms of a single "owner." Rather, the question of ownership must revolve around the vested interest groups. What political strength can any single interest group bring to bear on the political process? There are many interest groups in in-service education, including, but not restricted to, teacher organizations, university and college groups, administrator groups, and school board associations. One must also take into account the bureaucracy designed to implement the initiatives of the political system. For example, collaborative decision making in in-service education, such as has been found in teacher centers, periodically in the Teacher Corps, and historically in the Urban-Rural School Development Program, is a bureaucratic contribution to the field.

The bureaucracy has contributed by facilitating the development of temporary systems within a permanent institution, and by giving new power and influence to specific constituent groups, such as community representatives in the Urban-Rural School Development Program and classroom teachers in the Teacher Centers Program.

Few in-service teacher education policies are developed by the federal government, which has a very limited role in educational policy; and with two exceptions (the Teacher Corps and the Teacher Centers Program) all in-service legislation is embedded in categorical programs that have other, primary purposes (e.g., bilingual education and education for the economically handicapped). Feistritzer and Dobson (1980) cite forty such programs. Thus, one probably should not look to the federal government for concise statements about control of in-service teacher education.

Pais (1977) could find no omnibus legislation at the state level in support of in-service education. Although legislation exists in such states as Michigan and Florida, and is imminent in New York, most state legislation for in-service education is, like federal legislation, linked to categorical programs with specifically defined purposes. Where omnibus state legislation has emerged, it is often linked to a teacher center–like structure, or closely tied to local initiative, as in New York.

In a real sense, state certification and licensure legislation are also linked to in-service teacher education. Historically, certification and licensure have been of the "program approval" type, that is, they have been tied to approved collegiate programs. Some states, such as Minnesota, are developing alternative approaches to certification and licensure, thus opening the door to different types of in-service programs for the future.

Predictions. Speculations about the future can be nothing more than reasoned guesses, and predictions are always risky. Yet, in a publication that appears once every decade, speculation seems to be appropriate. Thus, I risk offering, without comment, but on the basis of data presented in this article, the following predictions.

1. In the next generation, a great deal of in-service teacher education will be the result of educationally conservative mandates, and will be tied in one way or another to teacher competency. The public simply will not pay for in-service education formats that do not respond directly to what it considers to be needed initiatives.

2. Although colleges of education have been heavily criticized, their presence will not diminish, and probably will be slightly strengthened by their providing in-service training to increase basic teacher competency. There simply are no other qualified institutions around to do the job.

3. Even acknowledging that some states are beginning to invest small amounts of money in in-service education, the costs are so massive that teachers themselves will continue to pay the bulk.

4. Even though recent practices, particularly in teacher centers, have demonstrated a variety of new and individualized approaches to in-service education, the lack of an institutional base will make it difficult to anticipate widespread infusion of these practices into the enterprise.

5. As federal resources for in-service education diminish, and as those that remain flow more directly through the states, vested interest groups such as chief school officers and school board associations will gain in clout, as they will become more influential in decision making in state programs than they have been in federal programs.

6. Mandates, pleas, and cries for evaluation data to prove that students learn better will be intensified. But evidence to respond to these pleas will not significantly grow, because evaluation is costly and the technical problems are complex.

7. To the extent that state funds are directed to in-service education, it will become an item for collective bargaining.

These predictions are based on the assumption that we are entering a period of conservatism in education. In the years to come, in-service education may in fact become more important, and perhaps small amounts of public monies will continue to be invested. To the extent that this occurs, however, it is likely that the general dissatisfaction with education will exert a powerful pressure, and result in in-service teacher education resources being clearly targeted at improving teacher "competency." It is not likely that this trend will be overly popular with teachers.

Sam J. Yarger

See also Evaluation of Teachers; Faculty Development; Supervision of Teachers; Teacher Centers; Teacher Certification; Teacher Job Satisfaction; Teacher Selection and Retention.

REFERENCES

Asher, J. J. *Inservice Education: Psychological Perspectives.* San Francisco: Far West Regional Laboratory of Educational Research and Development, 1967 (ERIC Document Reproduction Service No. ED 015 891)

Brictson, P. Personal communication, March 10, 1981.

Byrd, D. M. *A Summary of Teachers', Administrators', and Professors' Perceptions of the Need for Teacher Inservice Education.* Unpublished doctoral dissertation, Syracuse University, 1979.

Carline, J. Inservice training—re-examined. *Journal of Research and Development in Education,* 1970, *4*(1), 103–115.

Devaney, K. (Ed.). *Building a Teachers' Center.* San Francisco: Far West Regional Laboratory for Educational Research and Development, 1979. (ERIC Document Reproduction Service No. ED 171 071)

Feistritzer, C. E., & Dobson, C. Federal funding for educational personnel development. In C. E. Feistritzer (Ed.), *The 1981 Report on Educational Personnel Development.* Washington, D.C.: Feistritzer Publications, 1980.

Good, T. L., & Brophy, J. E. Changing teacher and student behavior: An empirical investigation. *Journal of Educational Psychology,* 1974, *66*(3), 390–405.

Goodlad, J. I. Staff development: The league model. *Theory into Practice,* 1972, *11*(4), 207–214.

Hass, C. G. Inservice education today. In N. B. Henry (Ed.), *Inservice Education for Teachers, Supervisors, and Administrators: The Fifty-sixth Yearbook of the National Society for the Study of Education.* Chicago: National Society for the Study of Education, 1957.

Help! Teacher can't teach. *Time,* June 16, 1980, pp. 54–63.

Ingersoll, G. M. Assessing inservice needs through teacher responses. *Journal of Teacher Education,* 1976, *26*(2), 169–173. (ERIC Document Reproduction Service No. ED 104 820)

Joyce, B., & Showers, B. Improving inservice training: The message of research. *Education Leadership,* 1980, *37*(5), 379–385.

Joyce, B. R.; Yarger, S. J.; Howey, K. R.; Harbeck, K. M.; & Kluwin, T. N. *Preservice Teacher Education.* Palo Alto, Calif.: John Booksend Laboratories, 1977. (ERIC Document Reproduction Service No. ED 146 120)

Lawrence, G. *Patterns of Effective Inservice Education.* Tallahassee: Florida State Department of Education, 1974. (ERIC Document Reproduction Service No. ED 176 424)

Lyons, G. Why teachers can't teach. *Phi Delta Kappan,* October 1980, *62,* 108–112.

McDonald, F. J. *The New York City Teacher Center, Year One: Description, Research, and Evaluation.* Vol. 3 of *The Teacher Specialists: Their Training and Its Effects.* Princeton, N.J.: Educational Testing Service, 1980.

McDonald, F. J., & Davis, E. L. *The Effects of an Inservice Training Program on Teacher Performance and Pupil Learning.* Princeton, N.J.: Educational Testing Service, 1978.

Medley, D. M. *Teacher Competence and Teacher Effectiveness.* Washington, D.C.: American Association of Colleges for Teacher Education, 1977. (ERIC Document Reproduction Service No. ED 143 629)

Mertens, S. K., & Yarger, S. J. *Teacher Centers in Action.* Syracuse, N.Y.: Syracuse University, Syracuse Area Teacher Center, 1981.

Oja, S. N. Adapting research findings in psychological education: A case study. In *Adapting Educational Research: Staff Development Approaches.* Norman, Okla.: Teacher Corps Research Adaptation Cluster, 1979.

Paris, R. M. Inservice: Legislation and legal issues. In *Creative Authority and Collaboration* (ISTE Report 4). Syracuse, N.Y.: National Dissemination Center, 1977.

Pipes, L. *Collaboration for Inservice Teacher Education: Case Studies.* Washington, D.C.: ERIC Clearinghouse on Teacher Education, 1978. (ERIC Document Reproduction Service No. ED 151 327)

Richey, H. G. Growth of the modern conception of inservice education. In N. B. Henry (Ed.), *Inservice Education for Teachers, Supervisors, and Administrators: The Fifty-sixth Yearbook of the National Society for the Study of Education.* Chicago: National Society for the Study of Education, 1957.

Snow, R. E. *A Model Teacher Training System: An Overview* (Report No. RD-92). Palo Alto, Calif.: Stanford Center for Research and Development in Teaching, 1972. (ERIC Reproduction Service No. ED 066 437)

Teacher Centers (Commissioner's Report on the Education Professions 1975–1976, HEW Publication No. OE 77-12012). Washington, D.C.: U.S. Government Printing Office, 1977. (ERIC Document Reproduction Service No. ED 150 113)

Tyler, R. W. Inservice education of teachers: A look at the past and future. In L. Rubin (Ed.), *Improving Inservice Education: Proposals and Procedures for Change.* Boston: Allyn & Bacon, 1971. (ERIC Document Reproduction Service No. ED 052 154)

Van Ryn, M. Financing inservice education: Who should pay for what. *Educational Economics,* 1977, *2*(7), 9–10, 27.

Wollner, E. H. *Requirements for Certification for Elementary Schools, Secondary Schools, and Junior Colleges* (38th ed.). Chicago: University of Chicago Press, 1974.

Wollner, E. H. *Requirements for Certification for Elementary Schools, Secondary Schools, and Junior Colleges* (40th ed.). Chicago: University of Chicago Press, 1978.

Yarger, S. J.; Howey, K. R.; & Joyce, B. R. *Inservice Teacher Education.* Palo Alto, Calif.: Booksend Laboratory, 1980.

Yarger, S. J., & Leonard, A. J. *A Descriptive Study of the Teacher Center Movement in American Education.* Syracuse, N.Y.: Syracuse University, 1974. (ERIC Document Reproduction Service No. ED 098 159)

INSTRUCTION PROCESSES

"Instruction processes" is a broad term that may encompass most of the activities taking place in the classroom and the school as well as many activities taking place in the home. In addition, virtually any aspect of instruction—duration, source, group size, nature of the instructional activities, and specific teacher or student behaviors—is legitimately included in the construct "instruction processes." This article confines itself to a particular interpretation of the term "instruction processes" and devotes its attention to only one dimension of instruction, teaching strategy. Teaching strategy is defined as patterns of behavior, described in activity sequences.

In this article we discuss six teaching strategies: advance organizer, concept attainment, cognitive development, contingency management, self-management, and the basic practice strategy. These six strategies were selected because they are the most well-researched and/or most widely used in the classroom. There are exceptions to these criteria, however. Gaming and simulation is a well-known, moderately researched strategy, but it is discussed elsewhere. On the other hand, the basic practice strategy draws heavily on teacher-effectiveness literature, which is also discussed elsewhere. We chose to include it here because we believe the results of teacher-effectiveness research can be enhanced by building them into a teaching strategy, that is, a theoretically based sequence of activities.

Joyce and Weil (1980) organized the alternative models of teaching into four groups: information processing, personal, social interaction, and behavioral. Information processing models address the ways students can improve their ability to master information, including capacities to organize data, generate concepts, solve problems, and use verbal and nonverbal symbols. Information processing is concerned with intellectual functioning. The personal strategies address development of unique, individual realities, with attention to development of emotional life. Social interaction models emphasize the relationship of the individual to society or to other persons. These models seek to improve ability to relate to others and to engage in the democratic process. Finally, the behavioral strategies share a common theoretical base variously referred to as "learning theory," "social learning theory," and "behavior therapy." Behavioral models address a wide variety of goals, cognitive, affective, and social. The emphasis in this group is on changing behavior from less productive to more productive patterns.

Of the six strategies reviewed in this chapter, three belong to information processing and three come from the behavioral strategies. The distribution partly reflects the state of research. Information processing goals and behavioral methods are easier to study and measure than are social or affective strategies and goals. The distribution also reflects the recent emphasis by researchers and practitioners on intellectual development and, in the case of the behavioral models, on deportment as well. Role playing, not included in this review, is the only strategy in the social group, other than simulation, that has been researched to any extent. The results are promising in terms of promoting both interpersonal skills (Bohart, 1977; McClure, Chinsky, & Larcen, 1978) and intrapersonal development, as in the case of depression (Butler et al., 1980).

Despite the fact that space does not permit discussion of additional strategies in this article, the skewed distribution of teaching strategy research as it relates to the four group models offers an important message to researchers and practitioners alike. If schools are going to seriously address educational goals other than cognitive goals, more research and more application of programs and teaching strategies are necessary in the social and personal field.

Information Processing Strategies

In this section we present three teaching strategies that are based on theoretical approaches to information processing. Strategies designed to help learners develop and use more efficient ways of processing and organizing data come from a variety of sources (Joyce & Weil, 1980). The three strategies examined here all have a strong cognitive orientation; that is, they assume (1) the presence of some type of cognitive structure into which new information is organized and stored and (2) cognitive functioning, or thinking processes by which that information is moved into cognitive structure.

The advance organizer strategy is developed from Ausubel's theory of meaningful verbal learning. This strategy is built upon the idea that learning of new information can be facilitated through manipulation of the learner's cognitive structure. The second strategy, concept attainment, which is derived from the work of Bruner and his colleagues, is more concerned with cognitive functioning, or the actual thinking strategies used to process information. The third strategy, cognitive development, is based upon the work of Piaget and is concerned with the development of the thinking processes individuals use to interpret their environment. Underlying this work is the conviction that different thinking processes characterize the individual at different stages of cognitive development.

Advance Organizer Strategy. In addition to being based on a strong theoretical body of knowledge, the advance organizer strategy is of interest to educators for three reasons. First, it is clearly one of the most researched of all teaching strategies. More important, it is, as we will see, a strategy that research has indicated has great potential for instruction. Second, it is an elegant yet rather simple strategy to learn. Third, it has its greatest applicability for those teaching activities—lecturing and leading recitations—that are most common in the classroom.

Definitions and functions. According to Ausubel's theory of meaningful verbal learning, advance organizers (AO) are introduced in advance of new learning tasks and are formulated so that they take into account ideas and concepts already existing in the cognitive structure of the learner. They are presented at higher levels of abstractness, generality, and inclusiveness than the material to be learned, and they serve "to provide specifically relevant anchoring ideas for the more differentiated and detailed material that is subsequently presented" (Ausubel, 1977, pp. 167–168). Mayer (1979) maintains that advance organizers (AO) generally have five characteristics:

(1) Short set of verbal or visual information, (2) Presented prior to learning a larger body of to-be-learned information, (3) Containing no specific content from the to-be-learned information, (4) Providing a means of generating logical relationships among elements in the to-be-learned information, (5) Influencing the learner's encoding process. (p. 382)

Other than describing AO in general terms, Ausubel (1978) noted that one cannot provide more detailed information without specific knowledge of the characteristics of both the learner and the material to be learned.

Ausubel (1977), Barnes and Clawson (1975), Hartley and Davies (1976), and Mayer (1978) revealed that AO have secondary functions in addition to providing ideational scaffolding or a meaningful context for new learning material. According to those authors, an AO provides an overview of the more detailed information to follow and may influence the learning set by increasing student motivation and/or encouraging use of active encoding strategies on the part of the learner.

Ausubel labeled two types of advance organizers depending on the learner's degree of familiarity with the material. Expository organizers are used when the material to be learned is completely new, whereas comparative organizers are used when the material to be learned is "familiar or relatable to previously learned ideas" (1978, p. 252).

It is important to point out that AO are only part of Ausubel's theory of meaningful verbal learning. For Ausubel, cognitive structure is the most important variable influencing learning (Ausubel, 1980; Lawton & Wanska, 1979); therefore, learning can be facilitated by manipulating concepts and ideas within the learner's cognitive structure. Also for Ausubel, meaningful verbal learning is basically a subsumptive process whereby new and more highly differentiated learning material becomes assimilated into previously learned superordinate ideas/concepts. Within this framework, we can see that AO are designed to manipulate the overall cognitive structure of the learner by creating a new part of cognitive structure (Lawton & Wanska, 1977) that bridges the new learning material to the larger, already existing cognitive structure (assimilative context).

Research. The effectiveness of AO in promoting learning and retention has been a subject of debate and controversy. Basically, research on AO can be divided into three periods: (1) the early 1960s to the mid-1970s, when numerous studies were conducted; (2) the mid-1970s, when the results of these studies were brought together; and (3) the current period from the late 1970s to date, in which many of the methodological problems with earlier studies have been uncovered and corrected in newer studies, thus leading to more consistent and generalizable results (Lawton & Wanska, 1979; Mayer, 1978, 1979).

At least three major reviews of AO studies were conducted in the mid-1970s (Barnes & Clawson, 1975; Faw & Waller, 1976; Hartley & Davies, 1976). In the first two reviews the authors concluded, based on the investigations examined, that AO did not facilitate learning. The results from the third review were mixed. These reviews were instrumental in improving the quality of subsequent research by uncovering methodological flaws in the research studies analyzed. They also created a situation in which subsequent critiques of the reviews themselves helped define additional methodological flaws (Lawton & Wanska, 1977; Ausubel, 1978).

It is helpful to note some of the major research problems that allowed such contradictory conclusions to be drawn about the effectiveness of AO. The first seven problems (lack of control groups, lack of attention to aptitude-treatment interactions, lack of long-term studies, inequality of treatment time between experimental and control groups, lack of a clear definition of AO, novelty of treatment effects, and failure to have control groups use passages related to the material to be learned) were uncovered by the three reviews listed above. The last five were revealed in subsequent critiques of the three reviews:

- *Test-measure incompatibility* (Ausubel, 1978; Mayer, 1979). Most studies used tests that tended to measure verbatim retention of material and accumulation of detail, not meaningful verbal learning and long-term retention.
- *Failure to control for existing subsumers in cognitive structure* (Ausubel, 1978; Kozlow & White, 1980; Lawton & Wanska, 1977; Mayer, 1979). Without controlling for existing subsumers, it is impossible to judge whether AO are effective, for control group subjects may already have had sufficient knowledge to do equally well on the subsequent task. Mayer (1979) also pointed out that the mate-

rial to be learned may have a relevant subsumer embodied in it or may tend to elicit a relevant subsumer from the learner, a consideration that has been ignored by investigators.
- *Failure to assess the presence of appropriate bridge cognitive structures* (Ausubel, 1978; Kozlow & White, 1980; Mayer, 1979). Alexander, Frankiewicz, and Williams (1979) concluded that learners used in these experiments may lack the relevant ideational scaffolding to which potentially meaningful new knowledge could be related, making it impossible for them to utilize advance organizers.
- *Failure to show that the learners used the relevant subsumers* (Lawton & Wanska, 1977; Mayer, 1979).
- *Failure to analyze whether the main concept in the AO is an appropriate subsumer for the information in the learning material* (Kozlow & White, 1980). There is a need to analyze the conceptual "content of the passage to be learned to ascertain what kind of concepts are to be bridged to existing subsumers" (Ausubel, 1978, p. 254).

Investigations in the late 1970s were designed to overcome many of the methodological problems just outlined, and clearly indicated that AO facilitate learning, retention, and transfer (Alexander, Frankiewicz, & Williams, 1979; Kozlow & White, 1980; Lawton & Wanska, 1979; Luiten, 1980; Mayer, 1978, 1979). Mayer (1979) pointed out that a more important question than the overall effectiveness of AO is under what conditions AO are most conducive to learning. Although the results that follow are still somewhat tentative, they encompass the best available information about specific effectiveness of AO:

- Comparative organizers tend to be more facilitative than expository organizers (Kozlow & White, 1980).
- AO tend to aid lower ability learners more than higher-ability learners (Faw & Waller, 1976; Mayer, 1978).
- Subject areas where AO might be most helpful are science and mathematics (Mayer, 1979); it should be noted, however, that the degree of novelty and difficulty in a subject area is more important than the subject area per se.
- AO using both content and process concepts are more effective than AO using either content or process concepts; AO using process concepts have a greater facilitative effect than AO using content concepts (Lawton & Wanska, 1979).
- AO show greater facilitative effect when audiovisual aids are used (Kozlow & White, 1980).
- Written, visual, and oral-interactive AO have all been shown to facilitate learning and retention (Alexander, Frankiewicz, & Williams, 1979).
- Postorganizers may be as effective as AO (Alexander, Frankiewicz, & Williams, 1979; Hartley & Davies, 1976).
- AO are more likely to be effective when the material to be learned is difficult (Faw & Waller, 1976), technical or unfamiliar (Alexander, Frankiewicz, & Williams, 1979;

Mayer, 1979), or presented in a random and unorganized fashion (Mayer, 1978).

- AO are more likely to be effective with reception than with discovery learning (Hartley & Davies, 1976).
- AO are likely to have an inhibiting effect on affect and student thinking (Nugent, Tipton, & Brooks, 1980).
- AO have a greater effect on retention than on learning (Alexander, Frankiewicz, & Williams, 1979; Hartley & Davies, 1976), greater effects on measures of transfer than on retention, greater effects on measures of far transfer than on near transfer (Mayer, 1978, 1979), and greater effects on measures of conceptually related transfer (near-near) than on conceptually nonrelated transfer (near-far) (Lawton & Wanska, 1979).

It is important to emphasize that AO have implications for both curriculum and teaching (Joyce & Weil, 1980). In the curriculum, most textbooks are designed in such a fashion that a great deal of detailed, factual information must be learned before relevant subsumers are presented. Clearly, more work needs to be undertaken to provide relevant subsumers to learners before the presentation of factual information so new material can be meaningfully integrated into the learners' existing cognitive structure.

As we noted earlier, the AO strategy is described because it has great applicability to (1) common teaching activities (lecturing and leading recitations) and (2) common teaching objectives (imparting information and facts). Before any new material is presented to be learned, an AO can be used to help students retain the new information both by relating it to existing concepts in cognitive structure and by differentiating it from previously learned material. AO are especially effective for helping students learn the key concepts or principles of a subject area and the detailed facts and bits of information within those concept areas. The AO is a highly effective instructional strategy for all subject areas where the objective is meaningful assimilation of those concepts, principles, and facts.

An actual AO teaching strategy for institutional purposes would be designed to manipulate the cognitive structure of the learner in order to facilitate the assimilation of meaningful learning. In order to accomplish this, an AO teaching strategy would be designed to meet two formative objectives—to make the material potentially meaningful and to help the learner employ a meaningful learning set. Such a strategy would have the following phases: development of an appropriate AO, creations of a student learning set, presentation of the advance organizer, presentation of the new learning material, and the use of activities designed to reinforce the subsumptive learning process as new material is progressively differentiated beneath the AO subsumer.

Concept Attainment Strategy. The concept attainment (CA) strategy is concerned with two separate but related ideas: the nature of concepts themselves and the thinking processes used by individuals to learn concepts. The first two parts of this section are devoted to these

two ideas respectively. In the third part we examine applications of the CA strategy for classroom instruction.

Nature of concepts. Concepts are the key building blocks for the structure of knowledge of the various academic disciplines. They are the critical components of an individual's cognitive structure. According to Tennyson and Park (1980),

A concept is assumed to be a set of specific objects, symbols, or events which share common characteristics (critical attributes) and can be referenced by a particular name or symbol. Concept learning is thus regarded as the identification of concept attributes which can be generalized to newly encountered examples and discriminate examples from nonexamples. (p. 56)

Concepts can be thought of as information about objects, events, and processes that allows us to (1) differentiate various things or classes, (2) know relationships between objects, and (3) generalize about events, things, and processes (Klausmeier, 1977).

All concepts possess at least four components: attributes, examples, definition, and hierarchical relations. As we shall see later, it is by analyzing these components of a concept and preparing them for presentation in certain ways that a teacher facilitates CA.

The first component, "attributes," refers to the characteristics of a particular concept that help distinguish instances of the concept from noninstances. These characteristics, or attributes, may be relevant, irrelevant, or criterion-related. "Relevant" attributes are common to all examples of a concept whereas "irrelevant" attributes vary among examples of the concept, that is, are associated with certain examples of a concept but not with other examples of the same concept (Harris & Harris, 1973). "Attribute value" refers to the acceptable range for any given relevant attribute. "Criterion-related" attributes are those relevant attributes that distinguish the concept from other supraordinate or coordinate concepts (Joyce & Weil, 1980). An example will help make these distinctions clearer.

In Figure 1, the relevant attributes of the concept triangle are presented. These are closed geometric figure, three sides, and straight sides. Note that these relevant attributes may possess a range of values and still constitute a triangle; that is, the straight sides may be of various lengths as long as they are straight with three of them forming a closed figure. Irrelevant attributes include size, color, and position in space. The attribute three-sidedness is criterion-related because it distinguishes the concept triangle from the subordinate concept trapezoid and the superordinate concept polygon.

"Examples" of a concept possess all relevant attributes of the concept whereas "nonexamples" lack at least one relevant attribute. Both examples and nonexamples can vary in the irrelevant attributes they possess. A "rational set" is a set of examples and nonexamples in which "examples vary widely in irrelevant attributes, while the nonexamples differ from the examples in (if possible) only one

FIGURE 1. *Hierarchical relations of a concept*

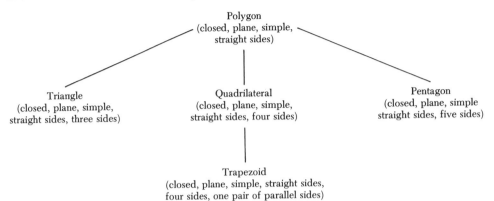

relevant attribute at a time" (Klausmeier & Feldman, 1975, p. 175). For instance, with our triangle example, a rational set would include examples that varied widely on such attributes as size and position in space, whereas nonexamples would always possess only two of the three relevant attributes.

"Concept definition" is the third component of a concept. To be most facilitative for concept attainment, concept definitions should contain references to both the relevant and criterion-related attributes of the concept (Harris & Harris, 1973; Klausmeier & Feldman, 1975).

The final component of concepts, "hierarchical relations," deals with relationships between concepts. For all concepts, hierarchical relations can be divided into three types—superordinate, subordinate, and coordinate—based upon relevant attributes (Tennyson, Tennyson, & Rothen, 1980). A concept is "subordinate" to another concept when it contains all the relevant attributes of the superordinate concept and at least one additional relevant attribute that further defines the concept. " 'Coordinate concepts' have the same number of relevant attributes but the values of one of the relevant attributes are varied to form different concepts, all of which are coordinate" (Harris & Harris, 1973, p. 14). In both these cases it is the criterion-related attribute that distinguishes concept types. In Figure 1, triangle, quadrilateral, and pentagon are all coordinate concepts that are subordinate to the superordinate concept polygon. Trapezoid in turn is subordinate to quadrilateral. The criterion-related attribute for the quadrilateral is four-sidedness. The same attribute for the trapezoid is at least one pair of parallel sides.

Much instruction that occurs in schools consists of the learning of concepts. The four components discussed in this section form the basis for concept learning and thus have important applications for the design and outcomes of instruction. Definitions that students are given may be inadequate because they do not articulate the relevant attributes. The examples that are provided may not clearly contrast the relevant and irrelevant attributes. Indeed, some instruction may not even include nonexamples, pro-

moting only a superficial understanding of a concept. Teachers who understand the nature of concepts are in a position to take it into account when they design instruction and when they check students' mastery of concepts.

Concept learning. Researchers disagree about how much understanding is necessary to claim that a concept has indeed been attained. Recent research leads us to conclude that it is more useful to discuss CA in terms of levels rather than in all-or-none terms. Harris and Harris (1973), for example, presented three levels of concept mastery: level one—(a) differentiating characteristics of correct instances and (b) discriminating examples from nonexamples; level two—(a) identifying relevant attributes, (b) defining the concept, and (c) understanding hierarchical concept relations; level three—(a) identifying irrelevant attributes and (b) understanding principles. Bruner, Goodnow, and Austin (1977) presented two levels of CA: behavioral and verbal, that is, ability to use a concept contrasted with ability to explain a concept.

Klausmeier and his associates also discussed CA in terms of levels. According to their model of conceptual learning and development, CA occurs in an invariant sequence of four levels: concrete, identity, classificatory, and formal (McMurray et al., 1977). In addition, CA can be analyzed within levels as either high or low (Klausmeier & Feldman, 1975). According to Klausmeier (1977), different cognitive strategies emerge as the learner matures. It is these emerging cognitive strategies that permit successively higher levels of CA; that is, they compose the prerequisites for CA at each level.

For Klausmeier, CA, at the concrete level, occurs when the learner recognizes an object previously encountered. The three essential cognitive operations for CA at this level are attending, discriminating, and remembering. CA at the identity level occurs when the learner recognizes a previously encountered object presented from a different spatiotemporal perspective or perceived with a different modality. The additional cognitive operation needed at this level is generalization of equivalence of forms. Classificatory CA takes place when the learner can classify instances as examples and nonexamples but cannot classify on the basis of relevant attributes or define the concept. Generalizing equivalence of instances is the new cognitive strategy needed at the classificatory level. A concept is attained at the formal level when the learner can define the concept by its relevant attributes, name relevant and criterion-related attributes, evaluate examples and nonexamples in terms of the presence or absence of relevant attributes, and name the concept. Generating and evaluating hypotheses about relevant and criterion-related attributes is the cognitive function needed for CA at the formal level.

Research. A good deal of research on CA is useful in helping one construct CA teaching strategies. We know that "focused instruction" in CA can facilitate learning and retention of concepts in a dramatic fashion (Klausmeier, 1977; McMurray et al., 1977). Specific procedures that have been shown to promote CA are presented under the following four headings:

- *Examples.* Selecting examples through an instance probability analysis (McMurray et al., 1977); using both examples and nonexamples (Tennyson & Park, 1980); providing rational sets (Klausmeier, 1977; Tennyson & Park, 1980); providing practice in identifying examples and nonexamples; presenting examples according to their coordinate concepts (Tennyson, 1980); simultaneously rather than successively presenting examples of coordinate concepts (Tennyson, Tennyson, & Rothen, 1980); presenting four examples at a time (Tennyson & Park, 1980); pairing examples and nonexamples (Klausmeier, 1977; McMurray et al., 1977); basing selection of the total number of examples primarily upon the learning characteristics of the students and secondarily upon the characteristics of the concept itself (Tennyson & Park, 1980); defining and emphasizing the relevant attributes of examples (McMurray et al., 1977).
- *Definition.* Using concept definition (Klausmeier & Feldman, 1975; Tennyson & Park, 1980); stating the definition in terms of the relevant attributes of the concept (Klausmeier & Feldman, 1975; Tennyson & Park, 1980); presenting the concept definitions before presenting the examples and nonexamples (Tennyson & Park, 1980); developing the definitions at the appropriate developmental level of the learner (Klausmeier & Feldman, 1975).
- *Definitions plus examples.* Using of combined sets of rational sets and a concept definition (Klausmeier & Feldman, 1975; Tennyson & Park, 1980).
- *Related teaching techniques.* Teaching students strategies for distinguishing between examples and nonexamples of a concept (Klausmeier, 1977; McMurray et al., 1977); teaching needed vocabulary at the beginning of the lesson (Klausmeier, 1977); actively involving students, and providing students feedback on a regular basis (Tennyson, 1980); creating a situation in which student and teacher control are balanced; and telling students

that they will be involved in concept attainment exercises (Bruner, Goodnow, & Austin, 1977).

Thinking strategies. The components of a concept, particularly its attributes and examples, play important roles in students' thought processes directed to concept attainment. Bruner, Goodnow, and Austin (1977) identified regularities in students' decision-making processes that they labeled "thinking strategies." Their research has implications for developing CA teaching strategies, for understanding students' responses during CA activities, and for facilitating the most optimal thinking strategies.

Strategy selection. In their work on CA, Bruner and his associates uncovered six distinct thinking strategies used to attain concepts and five sets of factors that affect selection of these strategies. The five factors that affect CA behavior follow:

- *Definition of task.* The prior set of the learner, that is, whether the learner is seeking to learn a concept or just a collection of isolated facts; the learner's expectancies about the concept; the subject's definition of what constitutes success in learning the concept; the learner's familiarity with and predilection for the relevant attributes of the concept; and the depth of understanding of the concept sought by the learner.
- *Nature of the instances encountered.* The number and kinds of attributes of examples and nonexamples; the order and frequency of presentation of examples and nonexamples, the amount of information needed to ensure CA, and the subject's ability to control the order of and timing of examples and nonexamples.
- *Nature of validation.* The sources, frequency, immediacy, ambiguity, and directness or indirectness of validation.
- *Anticipated consequences of categorizing.* The likelihood of anticipated consequences and the expected values of these consequences.
- *Nature of imposed restrictions.* The restrictions imposed on selection of strategies by the conditions under which the subject must work.

The six CA strategies are divided into selection and reception strategies based upon learning conditions. "Selection" strategies are used when the learner is free to choose concept instances (examples and nonexamples) in order to test hypotheses about concepts. With "reception" strategies the learner's "major area of freedom is in the hypotheses he chooses to adopt, not in the manner in which he can choose instances to test" (Bruner, Goodnow, & Austin, 1977, p. 126). In terms of instruction, this means that with selection strategies the teacher presents unlabeled examples of the concept and the students (1) inquire as to which of the presentations are examples and nonexamples and (2) attempt to construct positive examples on their own. With reception strategies the teacher presents examples of the concept that are labeled yes or no. Reception strategies are most often required for CA—both within the classroom and in everyday learning opportunities.

The four selection strategies can be divided into two groups: scanning strategies (successive and simultaneous) and focusing strategies (conservative and gambling). The major difference between groups is that when using scanning strategies the learner is testing hypotheses about concepts, whereas with focusing strategies the learner is concerned with concept attributes. "Successive scanning" consists of testing one hypothesis at a time," and "simultaneous scanning" requires the learner to hold more than one hypothesis at a time. Likewise, with focusing strategies, "conservative focusing" requires that only one attribute at a time be altered, whereas with "focus gambling" more than one attribute at a time is changed.

The two reception strategies are wholist and partist. The central rule for the wholist strategy is that the first example is used in toto as one's initial hypothesis. This original hypothesis is used to examine each successive example and is modified according to the information contained in those examples. The partist strategy "begins with the choice of an hypothesis about part of the initial exemplar encountered. When this hypothesis fails to be confirmed by some subsequent instance, the person seeks to change it by referring back to all instances previously met and making modifications accordingly" (Bruner, Goodnow, & Austin, 1977, p. 132).

According to Bruner and his colleagues, the wholist and focusing strategies are more advantageous than the partist or scanning strategies in terms of the four objectives noted earlier; that is, (1) instances encountered are more likely to contain the maximum information possible, (2) inference and memory are less strained, (3) risk is regulated to a greater degree, and (4) performance in CA is maximized. In terms of wholist and partist strategies, it was discovered that a learner has a marked tendency to use one or the other of these strategies consistently. It was also revealed that most people are wholist in their initial approach to CA problems.

Summary on CA. We would be remiss if we closed this section without providing some indication of the richness and importance of CA strategies for classroom instruction. Concepts are both the key building blocks of instructional materials, such as textbooks, and the main element of a learner's cognitive structure. Unfortunately, teaching of concepts often receives less emphasis than teaching of isolated facts and skills. If this situation is to be corrected, it is imperative that teachers possess the instructional tools to teach for CA.

A second problem of concept learning that occurs in schools is that concepts are presented in their entirety for consumption, that is, without reference to or analysis of the unique attributes that combine to form a specific concept. Again, the strategy discussed herein provides a mechanism to alleviate this problem. By dealing with both examples and nonexamples of concepts, by analyzing relevant and irrelevant attributes, by testing hypotheses, and by developing one's own examples, one learns concepts that are presented in a meaningful fashion so that they are understood, can be used to evaluate future instances, and can be related to other concepts.

Another reason why the CA teaching strategy is such a powerful tool is that it has widespread applicability. It can be used with all ages and grade levels and with all subject areas. It can also be used as both an instructional and an evaluation procedure. An actual CA teaching strategy would have the following four phases of activity: teacher presentation of the data in labeled examples of the concept in rational sets, student identification of concepts, student work to reinforce their understanding of the new concept, and activities designed to help students reinforce and broaden their thinking skills.

Cognitive Development Strategy. This section on the cognitive development (CD) strategy is divided into four parts. The first presents the Piagetian framework of cognitive development. Both the adaptation process and stages of development are described. The next section outlines the educational principles derived from Piaget's work and examines the role of the teacher in implementing a CD strategy. The third subsection is devoted to an examination of some of the applications of CD principles in classrooms.

The Piagetian framework. According to Piaget (1968, 1972), mental development is best explained as a process of equilibration: "the compensation resulting from the activities of the subject in response to external intrusion" (1968, p. 101). Equilibration in turn consists of two complementary aspects: functions and structures. Let us examine these two aspects in more detail.

The so-called constant functioning, which occurs at all stages or levels of development (Ginsburg & Opper, 1979; Rosen, 1977), is composed of the three activities of assimilation, accommodation, and adaptation. These three activities make up an ongoing process in which the individual interacts with the external environment and is in turn influenced by it. Thus, the individual assimilates the external world into already existing cognitive structures and in turn tends to change or alter these structures—to accommodate to the external world. Balancing of the processes, or equilibrium, between assimilation and accommodation is called "adaptation." The adaptation process itself will be different depending on the stage of cognitive development.

An example will help illustrate how intellectual adaptation follows incorporation and adjustment. A young child through previous bathing experiences has developed a schemata that objects float. When the child is presented with some new (nonfloating) toys, attempts are made to assimilate interactions with these new materials into the existing "objects float" schemata. After experiences with the new toys reveal to the child that these materials do not float, the existing schemata will be accommodated to fit the new experience; that is, in the process of assimilating the new toys, the child will accommodate the existing schemata (objects float) to meet the new reality of the environment (some objects float, some do not).

Function, as here discussed, is an invariant process that occurs at all stages of CD; what differs between stages is the nature of the structures used in adaptation, evolving from a perceptual and movement basis to higher mental operations (Piaget, 1968). These different structures, or methods, available to individuals to interpret and understand their environment are not innate, but evolve, becoming more complex and differentiated. These structures are the forms of mental activity Piaget used to classify the various stages of CD (Ginsburg & Opper, 1979). For example, the only structures available to the newborn infant are reflex activities. Through interactions with the environment (physical and social) and through maturation, young children develop progressively more advanced structures until they are able to act mentally upon environmental stimuli. It is important to point out that these stages of CD, with their characteristic structures or ways of viewing the world, occur in an invariant sequence. Each stage represents a "qualitatively different construction process" from other stages (Klausmeier, 1977, p. 183).

CD framework and instruction. The connection between Piaget's theory of CD and instruction can best be seen by examining the principles of learning inherent in and the role of the teacher suggested by this theory. Four principles of learning flow from Piaget's work on CD and are discussed in some detail by Ginsburg and Opper (1979) and McNally (1977). The first is that children should construct their own learning. The idea that children learn best when they construct their own meaning from experiences is not only the core of CD theory (Kuhn & Ho, 1980; Lavatelli, 1970) but is also the single most important and fundamental of Piaget's insights for educators (Ginsburg & Opper, 1979; McNally, 1977; Silberman, 1970).

For Piaget, to know is to act (Rosen, 1977). Children are the architects of their own knowledge and intelligence. Self-initiated learning and spontaneous work based on an individual's personal needs and interests are much more likely to lead to both optimal cognitive conflict and adaptation (McNally, 1977). The importance of the constructive role in learning means that students must be given extensive opportunities to manipulate and be active (Joyce & Weil, 1980); be free to choose what they will interact with (McNally, 1977); and act on the environment in a fashion consistent with developmental growth, that is, have experiences with concrete materials during learning before being expected to abstract (Richmond, 1970, Singer & Revenson, 1978).

The second related principle is that education should be child-centered. This principle follows logically from the constructionist principle and is based on Piaget's discovery that the key difference in the way children and adults approach reality, view the world, and use language is qualitative, not quantative as had previously been believed (Kohlberg & Gilligan, 1971; Osborn & Osborn, 1974). This

qualitative difference is in the nature of the structures used to interpret the world.

The third principle is that education should be individualized. Again, this follows directly from the constructionist principle. Given the wide diversity of existing schematas in the classroom and the importance of the role of students in selecting their own learning experiences, the teacher's goal in the CD strategy is to individualize instruction as much as possible: to create a learning environment in which each child can create his or her own learning experiences based on personal needs and interests (Ginsburg & Opper, 1979).

Development of this type of learning environment does not necessitate creation of an individual learning program for each child. This is true primarily because, within any given class, a large group of children will be functioning at a specific stage of development. Smaller groups of children will be functioning at stages of development either somewhat above or somewhat below this larger group. The teacher is interested in supplying a wide variety of environmental stimuli appropriate for the range of developmental levels in the class. These materials will then be used by different students at varying times to create learning experiences.

The fourth principle is that social interaction should play a significant role in the classroom. For Piaget, social interaction is valued for its effect on cognitive restructuring or adaptation (McNally, 1977). Such interaction forces students to present their own views logically and clearly, to clarify their thinking, and to defend and justify their opinions (Ginsburg & Opper, 1979). For Piaget, these social interaction experiences are as valuable in their own right for promoting cognitive development as are any physical/material experiences. The special role of social interaction in moral development is discussed later in this article.

The teacher working with the CD strategy performs in four separate but interrelated roles: (1) developer of the learning environment, (2) diagnostician of student development, (3) creator of cognitive conflict and facilitator in helping students achieve reequilibration after the introduction of such conflict, and (4) promoter of social interaction. All four roles are illustrated in the next subsection on CD applications. In terms of the CD strategies presented in this section, the roles of diagnostician and creator of cognitive conflict (disequilibrator) are the most significant. Therefore, we touch only briefly on the first and last functions.

In the role as constructor of the physical environment (for physical and logical types of knowledge), the teacher is primarily concerned with developing as rich and varied a material base as possible and organizing these materials into "centers" where students can work (Featherstone, 1971; Kohl, 1969; Stallings, 1977; Weikart et al., 1971). The idea is to create situations that encourage children to design their own stage-appropriate learning experiments (McNally, 1977). As facilitator for the social environment (for social knowledge), the teacher is primarily concerned with developing an environment characterized by warmth, respect, tolerance, and equality (Hersh, Paolitto, & Reimer, 1979; Jensen, 1977). The teacher fosters opportunities for students to collaborate during work periods and convenes the class on a regular basis for discussions about work done, work to be selected, group maintenance skills, etc. (Stallings, 1977; Weikart et al., 1971).

In the role as assessor of student thinking, the first responsibility of the teacher is to develop a kind of "intellectual empathy" with the learner (Gage & Berliner, 1979; Jensen, 1977; Rogers, 1969). The teacher must make a special effort to understand the experiences of a child and to see things from a child's point of view (Ginsburg & Opper, 1979).

Piaget provided the teacher with a special tool to use in diagnosing student thinking: the clinical method. Cowan (1978) outlined a six-step procedure for the clinical method. The most important step is the actual application of the method, or the clinical interview, a procedure designed to uncover students' thinking and reasoning abilities. The correctness or incorrectness of the answers presented by the student is important only insofar as it provides the interviewer with information about the quality of the student's thought processes (Case, 1975, 1978; Ginsburg & Opper, 1979; Wadsworth, 1978).

Wadsworth (1978) defined the clinical interview as an ongoing experimental process in which "the interviewer asks questions of a child, listens, observes, makes a hypothesis about the child's conceptual ability, and proceeds to ask more questions *based on the hypothesis* he has formed" (p. 225). The interviewer uses probing questions to get at underlying reasoning, provides conflict situations, makes countersuggestions, encourages the child to test predictions and verify answers, suggests helpful strategies, and shifts to related tasks to verify understanding (Cowan, 1978; Ginsburg & Opper, 1979). The interview is not a fixed set of questions but rather a set of skills to be used during a dynamic exchange between teacher and student. It is the key to understanding the world through the eyes of a child.

Two points about the use of the clinical interview in the classroom should be made. First, this procedure is used both formally and informally. In a formal setting the teacher structures an exchange or interview situation in order to ascertain information about a child's thinking processes and stage of development. This interview, based around a teacher-selected, predetermined assessment task, takes place in an area of relative isolation between the teacher and one student only. The primary goal is to help the teacher to function in other roles in relation to a particular child.

In the informal setting the teacher is still concerned with securing the same types of information, still uses that information to plan instruction, and generally follows the same dynamic exchange process as in the formal interview. The differences are (1) that the interview occurs as the teacher encounters the student already engaged in a self-selected task (e.g., dividing a box of blocks into two piles based upon some criterion, such as color) and (2) that the goal of helping the student move toward higher-level thinking processes (through the exchange) is more important than the goal of assessment for instructional planning. It is this type of informal assessment which the teacher can use on a regular basis in the classroom as one monitors student activity.

The second point to be made is that both formal and informal clinical interviews are based on the curriculum used in the classroom. That this is true with informal assessment is clear from our previous discussion of that role. It is important to point out that the formal, prestructured assessment tasks are designed to use the same types of curriculum materials and operations a child would normally use in the classroom. Osborn and Osborn (1974) presented twenty-eight assessment tasks and Wadsworth (1978) presented twenty-nine tasks that form the basis of the clinical interview. According to Wadsworth (1978), four criteria are used to determine if a student is at a particular level of reasoning: if the child can (1) make the "correct" judgment, (2) logically justify the response, (3) successfully resist a countersuggestion, and (4) produce a successful performance on a related behavioral task.

In their most important role, teachers are responsible for first creating disequilibrium or cognitive conflict and then facilitating cognitive restructuring (Cowan, 1978; Hersh, Paolitto, & Reimer, 1979). Treatments should be designed and materials organized for students with the understanding that they will act only if there is an imbalance between the environment and the individual, that is, if a state of disequilibrium or a cognitive conflict exists (Blatt & Kohlberg, 1973; Piaget, 1972). Thus treatments should be developed to promote ongoing assimilation, accommodation, and adaptation (Jensen & Chatterly, 1979; Richmond, 1970). According to CD theory, promoting cognitive conflict by influencing transformation in the internal or external environments leads to behavior that restabilizes equilibrium at a level that is more stable and progressive than the previous state of equilibrium. It is this constant readjustment process that constitutes mental development (Johnson & Johnson, 1979; Piaget, 1968).

Two further points need to be made. First, it is during this readjustment that teachers, using the same skills needed for the clinical interview, facilitate cognitive development. Whether working with one student or the entire class, teachers act as facilitators and guides. They ask questions, seek justifications, point out inconsistencies in thinking, etc.

Second, although in moral development the optimal degree of cognitive conflict can be achieved by using reasoning strategies one stage above the learner's current level of reasoning (Cooney, 1977; Enright, 1980; Kohlberg, 1971), no such clear statement can be made about the optimal level of conflict with cognitive development. Ginsburg and Opper (1979) and McNally (1977) suggested that new learning experiences be "moderately novel," that is, that they not be so incongruent that they are simply ignored or reworked to fit into current strategies, or so similar to what is already known that no restructuring is required.

Cognitive developmental applications. Four factors—maturation, adaptation, social interactions, and educational and cultural transmissions—interact to produce changes in developmental stages or acquisition of new structures (Dasen, 1977; Rosen, 1977; Singer & Revenson, 1978). The role of formal education in promotion of cognitive development has been the subject of much debate. The fact that Piaget emphasized invariant stage development and "spontaneous or incidental experience" (Ausubel, 1980, p. 227), that his work did not spell out the mechanisms of stage transition (Kuhn & Ho, 1980; Mussen, Conger, & Kagen, 1969), and that his work provided no "blueprints for instructional programs" (Enright, 1980, p. 27) has led some researchers to conclude that his work on CD theory offered little guidance or assistance for instructional designers. Others have argued and demonstrated that Piaget's work has great relevance for education (Case, 1978; Klausmeier, 1977; Vaidya & Chansky, 1980; Weikart et al., 1971; Zimmerman & Sassenrath, 1978). Our goal for the remainder of this subsection is to provide some indication of current CD applications and, where appropriate, review related research. We will look at schoolwide CD programs, subject area programs built upon CD principles, and an application of CD principles to moral development.

The broadest application of CD principles to the classroom has occurred in those situations in which the total organization of the class has been affected. The two clearest examples are the British primary schools (Featherstone, 1971; Silberman, 1970) and American "open education" schools (Holt, 1964, 1967, 1970; Kohl, 1969; Rogers, 1969). What these schools have in common is a philosophy about (1) the role of the teacher, (2) the way children learn, (3) the curriculum to be presented, and (4) the classroom organization (Featherstone, 1971). The teacher is not the transmitter of information but rather the facilitator of learning. The teacher's job is to provide as rich an environment as possible and to act as a type of stage manager, bringing children into contact with that environment. Learning in these schools is based upon the three principles that children learn by using procedures that make sense to them at any given time; that, to be meaningful, knowledge must be discovered; and that children must engage with concrete experiences to learn.

The curriculum to be learned is viewed as less important than the process used to learn. Episodic and incidental learning are considered more important than vertical progression through given academic subject areas. The curriculum tends to be more integrated than in traditional schools; that is, curricular areas tend to become fused rather than separated into discrete topics or areas. Organization of the classrooms and the school as a whole are

such that maximum individualization of learning and social interaction can occur. Open school classrooms are not characterized by desks and chairs but by interest centers, work stations, and open floor space where students can work and converse.

One of the best examples, in terms of both adherence to CD principles and experimental design, of the open school is the Ypsilanti Perry Preschool Project carried out by Weikart and his associates in Ypsilanti, Michigan (Weikart, 1974; Weikart et al., 1970, 1971). The Ypsilanti project was designed to assess the longitudinal effects of a CD-based preschool program (Cognitively Oriented Curriculum) on achievement of economically disadvantaged minority pupils. The program ran from October to May for twelve and a half hours per week for two years. There was also a ninety-minute home teaching session once a week for each student. Four waves of children received this two-year program; one group received a one-year program.

Each day was divided into six time blocks: planning time (twenty minutes), work time (forty minutes), cleanup time (fifteen minutes), juice and group time (thirty minutes), activity time (twenty minutes), and group evaluation meeting (ten minutes). All activities during the day, whether student-selected (work time) or teacher-directed (group evaluation time), were designed to facilitate student learning in the four content areas of classification, seriation or ordering, temporal relations, and spatial relations. In addition, the environment itself was structured to facilitate and reinforce learning objectives in these four areas; for example, materials in the room were put away differently during various times of the year depending on the goal being emphasized at any given time. The room itself was divided into five interest centers: large motor area (blocks), doll area, quiet corner, art corner, and group meeting and planning area. In addition to promoting cognitive development, the Cognitively Oriented Curriculum was designed, through the use of sociodramatic plays and group meetings, to facilitate socioemotional development as well.

Weikart et al. (1970) and Schweinhart and Weikart (1980) showed that exposure to the Cognitively Oriented Curriculum had a significant impact on students' cognitive abilities, achievement, and socioemotional development. Significant differences in achievement were maintained throughout the elementary years. The experimental group had test scores substantially higher than the control group's at the eighth-grade level. Up to age 15, the experimental group maintained a greater commitment to school, spent much less time receiving special educational services, and exhibited much less deviant behavior than did the control group.

There is at least one report of Weikart's Cognitively Oriented Curriculum being adopted to the primary grades (Stallings, 1977). In a comparison of the CD model with a programmed model of teaching, Stallings noted that the children in the CD model did better on a test of nonverbal problem solving but did not score as well on achievement tests in reading and math.

Global applications of Piagetian principles, although most often found at the early childhood level, have not been confined to that level of education. McNally (1977) discussed a comprehensive application of CD in the fifth and sixth-grades, and Rogers (1969) outlined a program for graduate school education.

In addition to these comprehensive applications of CD principles, the Piagetian framework has been used to guide development of programs within specific subject areas at all levels of education. Curricular programs based on CD theory are especially prevalent in mathematics (Nuffield Mathematics Program, Triad Laboratory, Dienes' Multi-Model Mathematics Program) and science (Science: A Process Approach, Science Curriculum Improvement Study, Elementary Science Study).

The Nuffield Mathematics Program is a good representative of these curricular programs. According to Cowan (1978), the Nuffield program is based on such Piagetian activities as ordering, classifying, and sorting. The activities in the Nuffield booklets follow the logical progress of development of mathematical reasoning in children. The program provides teachers with the basic conceptual principles from which to develop activities and experiences and concrete examples of these mathematical activities.

The program is based on self-directed activity and discovery within a structured environment. It uses a wide variety of materials, especially everyday materials in and around the school, in order to have children explore concepts from a variety of perspectives with concrete manipulatives. In one of the exercises, for example, students use various objects in the classroom (ropes, blocks) to gain some initial understanding of the concept of length. The Nuffield program also provides students with opportunities to record their observations, both concretely and abstractly, through such means as simple graphing exercises.

Research on the effectiveness of process approaches and discovery learning has provided mixed results. Two of the best studies on these topics (Bredderman, 1980; Worthen, 1968) allowed us to draw the following tentative conclusions:

- Process approaches in science appear to be more effective for disadvantaged than average groups of students and more effective for average than advantaged groups of students.
- Process approaches to science are not necessarily any more effective than laboratory and/or textbook approaches.
- Discovery learning in mathematics, although not more effective than expository learning in initial learning, is better for promoting retention and transfer and for helping students develop problem-solving approaches in new situations.

In addition McNally (1977) reported that both the Dienes' Multi-Model Mathematics program and the Method of En-

quiry approach to social studies resulted in children's developing a more favorable attitude to subject matter than did control groups of children.

Our final application of CD principles to education is in moral development. The important distinction here is not between comprehensive and subject-based programs but between social and physical knowledge. All the previous program applications were concerned primarily with physical and/or logical knowledge. Moral development is concerned with social knowledge. There are a number of CD-based applications of moral development (Nicholson, 1974). Here we will limit ourselves to an analysis of the work of Kohlberg and his associates at Harvard's Center for the Study of Moral Education (see Selman & Lieberman, 1974, for a description of a commercially developed moral development [MD] program based on Kohlberg's theories).

According to Kohlberg (1972) and Colby et al. (1977), three key assumptions are at the core of a CD theory of MD: (1) that a philosophical concept of moral development is required for intelligent thought about the education of social traits and values, (2) that there are invariant types of MD, and (3) that the stimulation of MD rests upon the stimulation of thinking and problem solving. Kohlberg (1970) identified six stages of MD. Each stage is defined by the values that enter into moral decisions (e.g., in stage 1, the value of life is based upon "the social status and physical attributes of its possessor"; in stage 4, life is valued because of "its place in a categorical moral or religious order of rights and duties" [Kohlberg, 1968, p. 498]) and the motivation used for moral action (Kohlberg, 1972).

MD, like CD, is not the result of direct instruction and teaching but rather the creation of understanding by the student (Kohlberg & Turiel, 1971). The aim of moral education is to stimulate the learner to progress to the next level of reasoning, not to teach fixed rules (Kohlberg, 1967, 1972; Kohlberg & Turiel, 1971; Selman & Lieberman, 1974). An excellent model of the role of the teacher in facilitating MD was developed by Hersh, Paolitto, and Reimer (1979). They listed seven general functions for the teacher and numerous specific tasks to use to stimulate MD.

In a moral development lesson the teacher in the role of creator of cognitive conflict attempts to facilitate MD by providing a conflict situation, exposing students to the next stage of moral reasoning, encouraging active participation in social interaction, and providing students with the opportunity to take on the roles of others (Kohlberg, 1971; Selman & Lieberman, 1974).

In the role of disequilibrator the teacher presents students with an open-ended moral dilemma (one in which there is uncertainty about what is right); uses diagnostic (clinical interview), questioning, and social organizing skills in an ongoing dialogue to make sure that students experience a conflict (are not able to assimilate the dilemma to current structures); and, using these same skills, facilitates MD through cognitive restructuring. Examples of teacher-student moral discussion dialogues can be found in Colby et al. (1977).

Using Kohlberg's "moral dilemma" approach to MD, researchers have been successful in raising moral reasoning skills, both between and within levels, for a wide variety of populations (Kohlberg, 1971). Colby et al. (1977) revealed that social studies teachers were effective in raising moral reasoning in high school–aged students; Kavanagh (1977) found that peer-directed groups were successful in raising moral reasoning; Blatt and Kohlberg (1973) found that adult-guided peer discussions of moral conflicts were successful in raising moral reasoning in junior and senior high school students of various races and socioeconomic levels; Kohlberg (1972) reported that the moral reasoning skills of prisoners had been increased using moral dilemmas; and Enright (1980) found that it was possible to increase by means of instruction the cognitive abilities (interpersonal conceptions, social problem solving, and moral judgment) of both first- and sixth-grade students.

From these CD applications, a two-step CD teaching strategy can be constructed. In the first phase of activity cognitive conflict or disequilibrium is established; that is, a learning experience is presented to the students that activates the adaptation function. In the second phase the teacher uses a series of patterned activities to ensure that new adaptation, in response to cognitive introduced in phase one, occurs at the most progressive level possible; that is, that there is maximum developmental movement.

The application of CD theory to the classroom is difficult for two reasons. First, the bridge from theory, especially that as complex and abstruse as Piaget's, to practice is always a difficult matter. We have attempted to create that bridge by establishing a middle ground between theory and application. That middle ground consists of CD principles of learning, CD teacher roles, and an analysis of the clinical method. Second, the CD principles of learning and CD teacher roles are, quite simply, ones that are contrary to those that have traditionally formed and are currently the core of practice in most schools. Significantly changes in both the value and goal structure of schools will be needed before CD applications can receive a fair hearing on a widespread basis.

Behavioral Strategies

"Behavioral strategies" refers to the array of approaches that are based upon psychological principles of learning aimed at changing human behavior. Variously referred to as "learning theory," "behavioral modification" (Bandura, 1969), "social learning theory" (Bandura & Walters, 1963), and "behavioral therapy" (Lazarus, 1971), behavioral strategies have become commonplace in school settings, especially in special education classes but increasingly among regular classrooms from preschool to secondary levels. Evidence of success for behavioral approaches abounds not only in clinical applications but also in educational programs (Rimm & Masters, 1979; Stallings & Kaskowitz, 1974; Thoresen, 1973). Until 1968 only one major journal was devoted to behavioral research; by 1981 there were over nine, not including school practitioner–oriented journals. Behavioral strategies have been successful in (1) promoting a wide range of academic behaviors from basic skills to creative writing; (2) creating desirable social behaviors, such as control of anger and aggression, as well as more assertive interpersonal communication; (3) eliminating self-defeating thought processes and establishing greater self-control over dysfunctional habits; and (4) altering phobic behavior and reducing anxiety.

Some behavioral strategies are more well-known than others. Most educators have heard of behavior modification. Less familiar are the self-management strategy, assertive training, relaxation and desensitization, and others. In this section we consider three of the most widely used and/or extensively researched strategies: contingency management, self-management, and the basic practice strategy. The last is a widely used though sometimes poorly implemented behavioral approach, better known as direct instruction.

Behavioral Theory. Behavioral theory originated with Pavlov's classical conditioning experiments (1927), Thorndike's experiments in reward learning (1898, 1911, 1913), and Watson's treatment of psychological disorders (1916, 1921). Only in the past twenty years, however, has behavioral theory been systematically applied in school and clinical settings. The work of Skinner (1953) and Wolpe (1958) greatly accelerated the use of behavioral strategies in nonlaboratory settings.

Behavioral theory is a collection of principles emanating from a common view of human behavior. Various behavioral strategies emphasize some principles more than others, or use different techniques, but they share a common set of assumptions about the development and alteration of human behavior (Joyce & Weil, 1980; Rimm & Masters, 1979).

Behaviorists believe that external forces in the environment cause people to respond in certain ways. These forces either elicit or depress particular responses; they increase or decrease the probability that behaviors will occur. The implications for teaching are enormous. If teachers are able to regulate the environmental forces that give rise to student behaviors, then they can shape those forces in such a way that learning and other important educational outcomes are enhanced.

Unlike in traditional psychodynamic thought, in behavioral theory the underlying causes of behavior are unimportant. What are critical are the observable behaviors that behaviorists believe can be altered by manipulating environmental forces. Even internal responses, such as anxiety or stress, can be altered with appropriate behavioral techniques. Behaviorists can describe virtually any problem area in terms of observable behaviors and of the environmental forces that serve to maintain or alter the problem behaviors. They have developed many ways of observing and measuring behaviors (Becker, 1973; Rimm & Masters, 1979). These powerful tools are available to the classroom teacher and along with them freedom from the viewpoint that students' progress is governed by internal processes that the teacher can neither observe nor change.

Behaviorists are optimists. They regard all behavior as a product of past learning and believe that through systematic application of learning principles even the most maladaptive behaviors can be changed. The role of the past in shaping a person's behavior is the determination of the environmental relationship currently operating to maintain the behavior. Once this relationship has been ascertained, procedures for altering the behavior can be determined. Remarkably, some very debilitating conditions, for example, phobias, self-mutilation, and stuttering, have been relieved in relatively short periods of time with behavioral strategies.

According to behaviorists, the same behavior may be the product of different stimuli; conversely, different behaviors may originate with a common stimulus. Therefore, the environmental manipulations for encouraging new behaviors are highly individualized and require setting specific, concrete objectives. Behavioral strategies may be conducted with groups, but the expectations for individual achievement must be differentiated. Variations in implementation (such as pacing or content) must be established to accommodate different individuals.

Behavioral strategies vary somewhat in the procedures they employ and the theoretical mechanisms that underlie those procedures. They all rest, however, on the view that a behavior is a response that is then reinforced by some action in the environment. Although it may not be clear what caused the person to make the response in the first place, behaviorists contend that the probability the individual will make the response again in the face of the same stimulus is increased because of the reinforcement that is received from the environment. In this way behavior gradually comes to be controlled by the particular stimulus, the discriminative stimulus. A "reinforcer" is any event that increases the probability of any behavior on which it is contingent.

Recent developments in behavioral research have modified the basic stimulus-response-reinforcement paradigm. With increased work on internal and covert responses, the revised paradigm, looks like this (Kanfer, 1973):

Stimulus → Biological   → Response → Reinforcing
             consequences   consequences

Thus, anxiety or negative thoughts (the biological state) elicited by a stimulus and mediating the response can be targets of behavioral control, as in the case of desensitization and cognitive restructuring strategies. The stimulus-response–reinforcing consequence paradigm is fundamental to behavioral theory. It is also referred to as the "contingency relationship"; that is, in the presence of a certain stimulus, a response is emitted that then receives reinforcement from the environment, further increasing the likelihood that in the presence of the same stimulus the response will be elicited.

Such contingency relationships occur regularly in classrooms and other instructional situations. For example, first-grade students learning to print are given a letter with instructions to copy it (the stimuli). With some effort they scrawl a reasonable approximation of the letter (the response). The teacher then enthusiastically praises the students for their product (the reinforcement). As the weeks move on the teacher will reinforce only very close representations of the letter. Students whose script is more primitive will be given corrective feedback and asked to try again. This example illustrates the contingency relationship as well as the principle of shaping. "Shaping" simply implies that the behavior that is ultimately desired does not always come forth in the first stages of instruction but is improved through successive approximation by changing the stimuli and/or the conditions of reinforcement. The correct formation of letters is a small unit of behavior out of which more complex patterns of responses are developed. In this way behavioral principles are applicable to simple behaviors as well as more complex ones. Unfortunately, the dynamics of the contingency relationship are not always harnessed effectively in the classroom. When everyone, including the teacher, laughs at the class clown, they are reinforcing inappropriate behavior, supporting rather than altering the contingency. Similarly, some teachers are not consistent in their reinforcement of appropriate behaviors or have not provided for careful shaping of desirable behaviors.

In the classroom, except in instances of programmed or computer-assisted instruction, the teacher readily assumes the role of reinforcer. Again, although this role may not always be carried out optimally according to behavioral theory, it is a commonly recognized activity of the teacher. Equally important, but perhaps less acknowledged, is the teacher's role in controlling the stimulus presentation. Often this function is abdicated to the publisher through the textbook and work sheet. Designers of programmed materials give careful thought to the sequential presentation of the stimulus material; however, the presentation of material in many textbooks does not follow behavioral principles. Yet much of what goes on in school is concerned with bringing students' behavior under the control of the subject matter stimulus. Gradually students are expected to discriminate among similar stimuli, responding differently according to their stimulus discriminations. At other times, as in the learning of classes of objects and events, students are expected to make the same response to different stimuli. Through the processes of stimulus discrimination and stimulus generalization, new skills and concepts are mastered. Serving in the role of instructional designer, the teacher can select and sequence material in such a way that these two processes are carefully controlled to maximize learning.

The instructional strategies that emanate from the basic behavioral paradigm and its processes rest on one or more of four learning models (Kanfer, 1973). "Classical conditioning" focuses on response substitution. Clients with phobias or students with test anxiety are taught to relax. Then the relaxation response is paired with the original fear-arousing stimulus, ultimately reducing the anxiety. In this instance relaxation is a response that is incompatible with anxiety. A more functional response is substituted for a less functional one.

"Operant conditioning," more widely used than the classical conditioning model, is based on carefully programming the consequences following a given response. Operant conditioning relies heavily on principles of reinforcement. Students' responses are altered by changing the consequences of the response or by using reinforcement to bring behavior under the control of new stimuli. Teachers can improve management in their classrooms simply by learning how to reinforce students for appropriate instead of inappropriate behavior (Becker, 1973).

"Observation learning" and/or "modeling" includes techniques of rehearsing new behaviors after observing them demonstrated by other persons. Observation can sometimes be effective without behavioral rehearsal (Kanfer, 1973). "Self-regulation" includes techniques from the first three learning models but is based on individuals' setting their own standards and being in charge of carrying out the behavioral strategies on their own.

Several behavioral strategies are described below. Of these contingency management relies primarily on operant conditioning principles, particularly reinforcement and to some extent stimulus control in the case of programmed instruction. Its complement, based on self-regulation, is the self-management strategy. The basic practice strategy, a popular instructional approach, incorporates stimulus control, reinforcement, and modeling. All three strategies have been successfully utilized in the classroom. The next section is a description of the strategies and their research results.

Contingency Management Strategy. Of all behavioral strategies contingency management, which emphasizes the use of rewarding and punishing consequences, is probably the most well-known among educators as well as the most widely used. The educational setting has provided the context for much of the behavioral research in the past ten years (Kazdin, 1981; Rimm & Masters, 1979).

This strategy has been applied to an enormous range of behaviors, including alteration of both prosocial and antisocial behaviors; modification of behaviors that require self-control, such as academic task completion or school attendance; and changes in cognitive or academic behaviors including a variety of skills in reading, mathematics, language arts, creative writing, and vocabulary development. Finally, contingency management has been credited with improvements in performance on standardized and intelligence tests (Hanley, 1970; Kazdin, 1981; Rimm & Masters, 1979; Staats, 1973).

Contingency management is multifaceted in its conceptual approaches and techniques. Within basic contingency management principles are several variations including the traditional behavior modification program, token systems, programmed instruction, and self-management. The first three represent externally controlled contingencies.

"Contingency management" refers to the systematic control of reinforcing stimuli such that reinforcement is presented at select times and only when the desired response appears. Based on the operant principle that behavior is influenced by the consequences that follow, people who implement a contingency management strategy must do a careful behavioral analysis of the problem situation (Kanfer, 1973). They must be aware of what stimulus and conditions activate the undesired response and what reinforcing stimulus maintains it; they must also know what constitutes both desirable and undesirable responses and what stimulus will be effective in reinforcing the desired behavior. Sometimes the solution for maladaptive behavior is simply to rearrange the environment so that the behavior is not elicited. Removing distractions can be enough to get some students back on task. Usually, however, it is necessary to set up a contingency management plan in which new behavior is identified, taught if necessary, and reinforced according to appropriate schedules of reinforcement.

Contingency management principles are so deceptively simple that many teachers claim to be implementing them already. It is unlikely, however, that large numbers of teachers are applying reinforcement procedures systematically, which is the only way this strategy can be effective. It is more likely that the principles are unsystematically and sporadically applied and/or that teachers are unknowingly reinforcing undesirable behaviors (Becker, 1973; Brophy, 1981; Hanley, 1970).

Reinforcement The contingency management strategy relies heavily upon systematic administration of reinforcement principles and, in some contingency management applications, such as programmed instruction, upon carefully planned stimulus presentation, or stimulus control. Reinforcers may be either positive or negative. "Positive reinforcers" are those events whose presence increases the response; money, affection, approval, and smiles are all examples of positive reinforcers. Another positive reinforcer is knowledge of results. During instruction, when students receive feedback that their answers are correct or their behavior is appropriate, they are positively reinforced. Programmed material is designed to give students immediate knowledge of results coupled with a high rate of successful (correct) responses. This may be why highly sequenced programmed materials seem to work well with students who have experienced little success in the past (Holland, 1960). At the same time, however, behavioral researchers believe that knowledge of results and even social reinforcement are not sufficient incentives for students who have had little learning success. "Token economy programs," which provide access to material reinforcers (candy, toys) or activity reinforcers (being read to, free time) are claimed to be especially appropriate for these students (Staats, 1973). "Feedback," or knowledge of results, has been effective in altering behavior; it has been even more effective when combined with praise or tokens (Kazdin, 1981).

"Negative reinforcement" strengthens desired responses either by removing something positive from the environment after an undesired response or by removing an aversive stimulus after a desired response (Becker, 1973; Rimm & Masters, 1979). Poor grades, disapproval, threats, and other forms of punishment control behavior because students generally want to avoid them. In general, the use of positive reinforcement is encouraged over negative reinforcement (Rimm & Masters, 1979). A negative reinforcer that is used in many classrooms with good results is "response cost" (Becker, 1973; Kazdin, 1972; Rimm & Masters, 1979). This technique involves taking away a reinforcer, such as tokens or points given as credits for reinforcers, or preferred activity, upon emission of an undesired response. In a given classroom students receive a certain amount of time each week for a free-choice activity. If undesirable behavior occurs during the week, the class or individual may lose a certain amount of the allocated free-choice time, this loss being the response cost. Other effective negative reinforcers are "time-out" (Becker, 1973; Rimm & Masters, 1979), and reprimands or "don't signals" provided they are delivered quietly (Becker, 1973). "Time-out" consists of removing a student from a situation, perhaps to a special corner of the room or to a quiet room for a period of time. It is important that the new environment be somewhat isolated and unstimulating.

Negative reinforcement is also, although inaccurately, known as "punishment"; however, "punishment" usually refers to negative reinforcement that consists of strong aversive stimuli, such as physical or verbal punishment and threats. In general, behaviorists agree that punishment should not be employed by teachers because students will soon learn to avoid the sources of punishment and may generate anger and fear reactions to people, places, or things associated with the punishment (Becker, 1971). Finally, as Bandura and Walters (1963) showed, punishment provides a model of aggression that children can then use in controlling others (Becker, 1973; Rimm & Masters, 1979).

Reinforcement appears to be a necessary part of successful behavior management and probably of instruction as well. Studies of the effect of rules, ignoring of disruptive behavior, and praise indicate that rules alone, and rules in conjunction with ignoring, were ineffective in altering behavior. Only the addition of praise reduced inappropriate behavior (Madsen, Becker, & Thomas, 1968). Comments intended to stop inappropriate behavior by telling students what not to do (e.g., "Tommy, stop touching him!") ultimately appear to increase the disruptive behav-

iors even though the behaviors may cease temporarily (Madsen et al., 1968).

Several types of reinforcers are available, including social (Stevenson, 1965), activity (Premack, 1965), material (Becker, 1971), token (Allyon & Azrin, 1968), and covert (Becker, 1973; Cautela, 1970; Rimm & Masters, 1979). Many of these reinforcers occur naturally in the environment, although not systematically and sometimes reinforcing undesirable behaviors, as when the teacher laughs at the student who is showing off.

The majority of reinforcers are "social," that is, those based on the behavior of people (Becker, 1973). Most individuals are responsive to other people and to some of the range of social reinforcement: smiles, verbal approval, attention, or physical contact (Lipe & Jung, 1971). Social reinforcers such as praise or touch are often used in school-based contingency management programs. They have the advantages of being easy to administer, naturally occurring, and more resistant to satiation than material reinforcers (Kazdin, 1981).

"Activity reinforcers" involve performing a preferred activity of any nature. Premack's principle states that you can get people to engage in one activity if you promise them the privilege of engaging in another more desirable behavior when they are finished (Premack, 1965). Giving students free time when they complete their work is an example of a commonly used and effective activity reinforcer. Others are academic games and entertaining reading material (Kazdin, 1981; Lovitt, Guppy, & Blattner, 1969).

"Material reinforcers" are consumables, such as candies, toys, and music. These work particularly well with young children, but people of all ages respond to valued consumables. Rimm and Masters (1979) pointed out that an added advantage of material reinforcers is that any individual who consistently delivers a material reinforcement acquires a positive valence.

"Token reinforcers" are objects with redeemable value; that is, they can be traded off for a reinforcer of another kind (social, material, or activity). Tokens may be made of anything (paper, metal, wood); usually they are chips of some sort. In the classroom the teacher identifies certain behaviors for which students may receive tokens at a particular rate of value. The earned tokens are then exchanged for reinforcers whose cost has been established. This type of contingency management program is known as a "token economy" and is usually, although not always, established for an entire class rather than one or two individuals. Token economies have been successfully implemented in school settings and have been found to produce greater behavior change than praise (Kazdin, 1977, 1981; Kazdin & Bootzin, 1972; O'Leary & Drabman, 1971).

The last type, "covert reinforcers," is relatively new to the behavioral literature. Only in the last few years have psychologists realized that the thoughts, images, and self-evaluations that individuals engage in contingent on their behavior have an important role in maintaining the behavior (Rimm & Masters, 1979). These covert responses can be altered in such a way that new behaviors can be established, particularly those involving self-control. This area, often referred to as "cognitive restructuring," is one of the newest behavioral fields and has proven to be important as behavioral principles have become increasingly applied to self-management (Lazarus, 1971; Rimm & Masters, 1979).

There are various means of assessing effectiveness of reinforcers for any student or group of students (Rimm & Masters, 1979). It is important to recognize that not all reinforcers are equally effective with each student and that the value of any one reinforcer to an individual changes with time and circumstance. Saturation is one obvious reason but personal preference is another. Some people are not as responsive to praise as others; other people are not reinforced by completing a task (Rimm & Masters). Forness (1973) postulated a seven-level reinforcement hierarchy ranging from edibles to competence (learning for learning's sake); variations of tokens, activity, and social approval (praise) rank in between (in ascending order). According to Forness, students should be rewarded at the highest possible level to which they can successfully respond.

Some effort has been made to look at the relative effectiveness of different reinforcers. The results are mixed. Benowitz and Brisse (1976) found material incentives to be more effective than social incentives in teaching spelling to fourth-grade students in lower-class communities. A previous study indicated material incentives were favorable to middle and lower socioeconomic groups (Benowitz & Rosenfield, 1973). Another study found no difference in effectiveness between token reinforcement and response cost in increasing students' attending behavior and improving accuracy on arithmetic problems (Hundert, 1976). In their review of studies, Rimm and Masters (1979) concluded that reinforcement and response-cost procedures appear to be equally effective. Some light may be shed on the question by a study looking at combinations of social and token reinforcement and cost contingency (Walker, Hops, & Feigenbaum, 1976). The results showed a 13 percent increase in the target behavior due to change in setting, an additional 12 percent improvement for social reinforcement, an additional 19 percent improvement for the addition of tokens, and another 17 percent increase when cost contingency was added. The combination of the three reinforcement types increased desirable behavior 96 percent. These findings indicate that combined application of several reinforcers may be more effective in reducing deviant behavior and increasing desirable behavior than any single reinforcer.

Research on reinforcers, indeed, on any instructional process, is hazardous because the instructional process can be either poorly or ably implemented. Effectiveness depends on accurate, relatively high-quality implementation. For example: There is some question about how cognizant students have to be about the contingency relationship before learning can occur (Rimm & Masters, 1979). Students may need to be clearly informed about the nature of the relationship if the reinforcer is to be effective. If this aspect of implementation does not occur or is not carried out well, then the contingency management program may be less effective than its potential. Similarly, teacher-effectiveness findings on praise are interesting to consider from a contingency management point of view. Although this literature generally concluded that praise is a desirable teacher behavior, particularly for students of low socioeconomic status (Kash & Borich, 1978; Medley, 1979), Brophy recently reevaluated the literature and his own thinking (Brophy, 1981). The data indicated that praise is used infrequently and without contingency, specificity, or credibility. It either is unrelated to appropriate behavior or is a poor substitute for accurate feedback. In terms of contingency management principles, the use of praise has been misinterpreted. Becker (1973) made the relevant point very nicely: "The frequency of use of positive social reinforcers (smiles, praise, etc.) per se is not related to improvement in behavior. *It matters when the teacher praises whom for what behavior*" (p. 102).

Several types of reinforcement schedules are practiced in behavioral strategies, including continuous reinforcement and intermittent reinforcement (Rimm & Masters, 1979). "Continuous reinforcement" (CRF) describes reinforcement that occurs after every appropriate response; "intermittent reinforcement" describes a reinforcement schedule that does not follow every response. The latter may occur on a fixed-ratio (FR) schedule, such as after every fifth response, or the ratio may change from time to time, a variable-ratio (VR) schedule.

Basically reinforcement should occur as soon as possible after a response is emitted and after every response (Skinner, 1953). Research showed that continuous-reinforcement schedules contribute to the most rapid acquisition of behavior; however, a variable-ratio schedule creates the most lasting response levels (Ferster & Skinner, 1957). Contingency management strategies often begin with continuous-reinforcement schedules and shift to variable-ratio schedules.

In early studies of contingency management, reinforcement was based on an individual's performance. More recently, the peer group has been incorporated into the contingency (Kazdin, 1981). One group contingency method provides reinforcement for the performance of the group as a whole. Another provides reinforcement for competing teams. Still another reinforces the individual but has the peer group share in the consequences. Finally, peers have also been successful as contingency managers (Nelson, Worell, & Polsgrove, 1973).

Group- and individually oriented contingencies are both effective, almost equally so (Kazdin, 1981; Litow, 1975; Rosenbaum, O'Leary, & Jacob, 1975). Generally teachers favor group contingencies because they are easier to administer and because the peer group participates in development of prosocial behavior (Kazdin, 1981).

Research. Until the recent past, "contingency management," perhaps more commonly called "behavior modification," was most often used in the service of classroom management to reduce disruptive behavior. In recent years it has gained more importance in the service of instruction to increase desirable academic behaviors: spelling, reading comprehension, composition and writing, study skills, academic output and accuracy, even creativity (Kazdin, 1981). It had always been assumed that increasing students' attentive behavior and decreasing disruptions would result in more time on-task. Logically and factually this is true, but recent behavioral research has found that increasing these task-related behaviors does not automatically result in increased levels of achievement of accuracy (Marholin & Steinman, 1977). On the other hand, reinforcing achievement and quality of work seems to improve the attentional behaviors necessary for work (Kazdin, 1980; Rimm & Masters, 1979). Rimm and Masters suggest that in general it may be more effective to establish contingency management programs that reinforce achievement and/or accuracy instead of task-related behavior, except for those populations in which students do not comprehend the task-related behaviors that are necessary to achieve; in this case, contingencies rewarding both task-related behavior and achievement might be most productive.

Programmed instruction processes rely heavily on (1) use of programs with which students can achieve a high degree of success, (2) careful presentation of material in small, sequential steps, and (3) immediate feedback as to correctness of the students' response to each step. Consequently, programmed instruction calls for continuous diagnosis, monitoring, and assessment.

Some models involve students working independently with programmed materials (Wang, 1976) or in a small group with an instructor who provides highly sequenced instructional material through questions and answers. The early childhood (K–3) behavioral analysis approach developed by Bushell at the University of Kansas provides students tokens if they respond correctly to a question (Stallings, 1977). The University of Oregon model developed by Engelman, Bereiter, and Becker places children in small groups with an instructor who delivers highly sequenced material in a scriptlike lesson presentation (Becker, 1977). The teacher directs rapidly paced questions to the whole group for choral response as a means of keeping all participants engaged and giving each student maximum practice. Occasionally the teacher addresses individuals but usually it is the entire group. In this model teachers initiate each stimulus (the question) and reinforce or modify the group response. Weekly testing uncovers any learning problems, for which students then receive the necessary instruction. The learning material and groupings are set up in such a way that students succeed about 90 percent of the time.

In these approaches students are expected to succeed academically and to persist at their learning task. It is assumed that a positive self-concept will develop through academic success and feelings of competence. Evaluation of the early education models developed as part of Project Follow Through confirms these assumptions (Becker, 1977; Dolan, 1981). Early childhood models based on the behavioral strategies of programmed instruction in general showed great gains in achievement and task persistence (despite a greater number of pupil absences) than less structured models (Stallings & Kaskowitz, 1974). The students also showed a sense of personal competence. When compared with the other models, the University of Oregon model produced more gains on cognitive and affective measures on all levels, kindergarten through third grade (Becker, 1977; Kazdin, 1981). The behavioral analysis program also produced highly favorable results. The gains in the Oregon program were evident in the fifth and sixth grades; the gains in the behavioral analysis program were also evident two years after the program terminated (Becker, 1977). Interestingly enough, less structured models appeared to be more successful than behavioral strategies on measures of problem solving skills, independence, cooperation, and question-asking (Stallings & Kaskowitz, 1974).

Although both were enormously successful, results of the Oregon direct instruction program slightly exceeded results of the Kansas behavioral analysis model. This finding may be due to the greater attention to stimulus control in the form of programmed learning materials in the Oregon program. Both programs placed emphasis on reinforcement, knowledge of results, and mastery; however, the particular techniques chosen differed as did other aspects of the instructional format.

Token systems have been successfully implemented from preschool to secondary levels with such diverse populations as low achievers, dropouts, and predelinquent and delinquent adolescents and with such a wide range of behaviors as attentive and disruptive behaviors, academic skills (in mathematics, reading, handwriting, spelling, and vocabulary), compositional skills, social behaviors, and speech problems (Drabman, 1976; Kazdin, 1977; Kazdin & Bootzin, 1972; O'Leary & Drabman, 1971). One of the major rationales for token systems is that for some children social reinforcers or knowledge of successful results may not be enough (Bijou et al., 1967; Kazdin, 1980; Staats, 1973). Evidence exists that the technique of token reinforcement adds something to the effects of contingency management programs based on social reinforcement (Kransner & Krasner, 1973).

The basic elements of a token system are the same as those for contingency management (systematic observation, designation of the desirable behaviors, selection of reinforcers, and formulation of the contingency), with the addition of the token as the medium of exchange and of the exchange rules. A token represents the backup reinforcer; for example, check marks (the token) may be exchanged for free time (the backup reinforcer). Krasner and Krasner (1973) pointed out that the tokens "are merely a gimmick" (p. 355) to help teachers and others in the classroom learn how (1) to observe behavior; (2) to act in a reinforcing manner, with contingent responses, and (3) to arrange the environment to maximize the timing of the reinforcement. Others have also pointed out the value of the token system in assisting the teacher to alter his or her behavior.

One of the first uses of token reinforcement systems in educational settings was the program established by O'Leary and Becker (1967) in a public school classroom. The program, designed to curb disruptive behaviors (e.g., talking, pushing), is a prototype of later token programs. Focusing on eight disruptive children, nearly one-half of the class, observers recorded students' behavior every thirty seconds for an hour and a half three days a week. When the token system was instituted the experimenter listed the desired behaviors (In Seat, Face Front, Raise Hand, Working, Pay Attention, Desk Clean) on the blackboard and explained that tokens would be given for these behaviors. The tokens could then be exchanged for such material reinforcers as candy and comics. Periodically the teacher then rated whether each child met the criteria.

Initially the tokens were exchanged at the end of each period; then they were accumulated for two days, three days, and finally four days. Gradually the backup reinforcers were faded out in favor of more traditional social reinforcers, such as teacher praise. Group points were awarded for the quietness of the group during the rating period. Other behavior management techniques, such as praise, time-out, and ignoring, were drawn upon as necessary. The token program successfully reduced deviant behavior during the token period.

Later programs, such as that of Wolf, Giles, and Hall (1968), designed to enhance academic behavior in low-achieving students, added variations: altering the rules for exchange in order to shape the amount and quality of work, to allow students to negotiate the amount of points to be awarded, to introduce long-range as well as short-range goals, and to reward events that occurred elsewhere, such as behavior in the remedial classroom and report card grades. Token systems differ in their effectiveness. Much of this difference may be due to subtle variations in the programs.

Most token systems are based on rewarding individuals; however, group contingencies have also been successfuly administered (Kazdin, 1977). Token systems have also been expanded to include many classrooms in a school as well as to bring parents into the program as contingency managers. Modifications that expand the contingency environments will help to generalize desired behaviors, generalization having been a problem with token systems (Krasner & Krasner, 1973; Rimm & Masters, 1979).

Without question, externally based contingency management procedures offer educators a well-documented approach to instruction and classroom management. The results from the Follow-Through evaluation and other individual studies are very promising. The increasing application of contingency management to academic skills and to more complex behaviors, such as composition writing, attests to its use for instructional purposes. In order for this to happen, more attention will need to be given to the curriculum, especially to task analysis and procedures of stimulus control.

Contingency management, however, is not a strategy that can be implemented casually. If it is to work, it must be implemented with a high degree of fidelity. Furthermore, generalization from one situation to another is not likely to occur unless teachers maintain the contingencies over time and unless some consistency across classrooms is developed. When this has occurred, as in the Follow-Through examples, behaviors have been sustained. Normally, however, behaviors are not maintained without special techniques to facilitate maintenance and transfer of training (Kazdin, 1981).

Self-management Strategy. The principles of stimulus control and reinforcement utilized in contingency management strategies are also the operating principles in the self-management strategy. In self-management, however, the emphasis is on teaching students ways of changing their own behavior, not on modifying their behavior through externally controlled contingencies and environmental alterations.

Self-management research is relatively recent, appearing within the last ten years. Despite its infancy, classroom applications of self-management have been reviewed several times (McLaughlin, 1976; O'Leary & Dubey, 1979; Rosenbaum & Drabman, 1979; Thomas, 1980). The findings are encouraging.

The rationale for self-management is both philosophical and practical (Kazdin, 1975; O'Leary & Dubey, 1979; Thomas, 1980). Philosophically, independent behavior is valued in our culture, and the intrinsic desire and continuing motivation to learn are espoused as important educational outcomes (Maehr, 1976). Thus, self-management techniques are seen as a means of freeing students from dependence on external reinforcement and as promoting a sense of personal control over learning (Thomas, 1980). Finally, critics of traditional behavior modification approaches believe that, for those students who do not succeed under externally determined goals and standards, behavior modification has a negative effect on self-regard, achievement, and commitment to learning.

On a more practical level, it is argued by some that teachers cannot easily implement external control techniques for a large group (O'Leary & Dubey, 1979). McLaughlin (1976) felt that contingency management techniques are expensive and logistically difficult, although this conclusion may be questioned. Others maintained that if students can control their own behavior, teachers can spend more time teaching and less time managing (Staats, 1973). Furthermore, if behavior is self-controlled it will be maintained when adults are not present; it is also more likely to generalize to new situations. Finally, many behaviors are not amenable to external contingency systems.

Behaviors that require self-control (such as studying, refraining from smoking, assertive social behaviors) have significant long-term rewards but minimal short-term payoffs. In addition, often the stimulus that maintains self-defeating behaviors is covert: what people say or think to themselves before engaging in the behavior. In these situations individuals must learn to instruct and reward themselves because the environment cannot control the necessary contingencies.

Component of self-management. Thomas defined self-management as "the transfer to students of responsibilities typically held by the teacher. This transfer may or may not involve systematic control procedures and can vary in complexity from training students to record instances of disruptive behavior to multiskill systems for teaching students to teach themselves" (1980, p. 218). Self-management techniques have been derived from a multistage model of self-regulation first proposed by Kanfer (1970). The three components of the multistage model are (1) self-monitoring, (2) self-evaluation, and (3) self-reinforcement. The self-regulation model includes the processes of deliberately giving attention to one's own behavior, comparing information gathered in that process to a given criterion, and administering reinforcement based on the degree to which the behavior matches or diverges from performance standards (Kanfer, 1975).

Self-management applications and research have utilized one or more components of self-control. A definition by Glynn, Thomas, and Shee (cited in McLaughlin, 1976) identified these components as

1. Self-assessment—the individual may examine his own behavior and decide whether or not he has performed a specific behavior or class of behaviors.
2. Self-recording—the individual may objectively record the frequency of his own performance of a given behavior or class of behaviors.
3. Self-determination of reinforcement—the individual may determine from all available reinforcers the nature and amount of reinforcement he should receive contingent upon his performance of a given behavior or class of behaviors.
4. Self-administration of reinforcement—the individual dispenses his own reinforcers (which may or may not be self-determined) contingent upon his performance of a given behavior or class of behaviors. (p. 632)

Studies of self-management often refer to self-assessment and self-recording as "self-monitoring" (Thomas, 1980). Other reviewers add the components of self-instruction or self-talk and self-determined criteria (O'Leary & Dubey, 1979; Rosenbaum & Drabman, 1979). Much of the research on self-management looks at the efficacy of these techniques in producing the desired behavior change. The next section discusses these results.

Research. Classroom research has generally focused on one or more components of self-management used as an intervention procedure either to create behavior change or to maintain behavior after experience with systematic external reinforcement. This section reviews the research first on individual components and then on more general findings and issues.

"Self-assessment" refers to several procedures by which students assess the quality and quantity of their own behavior (O'Leary & Dubey, 1979). In terms of the components discussed earlier, self-assessment includes Kanfer's components of self-monitoring and self-evaluation (Kanfer, 1970) and Glynn, Thomas, and Shee's components of self-recording and self-assessment (Glynn, Thomas, & Shee, 1973). In general, self-assessment alone does not appear to have an appreciable effect on changes in behavior (O'Leary & Dubey, 1979; Rosenbaum & Drabman, 1979). Self-assessment can make a significant contribution when added to an effective reward system and in that context can be as effective as external assessments (O'Leary & Dubey, 1979).

Studies have documented both the accuracy and inaccuracy of students' self-observation and recording (O'Leary & Dubey, 1979; Rosenbaum & Drabman, 1979). Training and other procedures seem to enhance the accuracy of students' self-recording (O'Leary & Dubey, 1979; Rosenbaum & Drabman, 1979); however, the self-recording does not have to be accurate to produce changes in behavior (O'Leary & Dubey, 1979).

O'Leary and Dubey (1979) identified three factors that might influence the effectiveness of self-assessment procedures: accuracy of assessments, difficulty of the task, and type of students. With respect to the latter the authors speculate that self-assessment might be useful with students who are clearly motivated to improve their behavior. This possibility is consistent with research demonstrating that self-assessment is successful in maintaining behavior that has been established with externally imposed token systems (O'Leary & Dubey, 1979).

Criterion setting alone (whether self- or externally imposed) does not improve behavior. If students who self-determine their criterion are subsequently rewarded for their achievement, they will outperform students who experience neither criteria nor contingent rewards (O'Leary & Dubey, 1979). Furthermore, self-determined contingencies can be as effective as externally imposed standards when both are combined with rewards (Bandura & Perloff, 1967; Felixbrod & O'Leary, 1973, 1974). The effectiveness of criterion setting, self or external, depends on a contingent reward.

Students may establish more lenient performance standards in contrast to externally imposed standards (O'Leary & Dubey, 1979; Rosenbaum & Drabman, 1979). This tendency can be altered by prompting the selection of more stringent standards (Rosenbaum & Drabman, 1979).

Self-reinforcement in combination with an explicit or implicit self-evaluation process is effective in modifying students' behavior (O'Leary & Dubey, 1979; Rosenbaum & Drabman, 1979). It can be as effective as or more effective than externally administered reinforcement. O'Leary and Dubey (1979) described self-reinforcement as "clearly one of the most powerful self-control procedures (p. 456).

Studies of self-administered reinforcement have dem-

onstrated a significant aptitude-treatment interaction between the motivation of the student and the effectiveness
of self-versus-external reward (Switzky & Haywood, 1974).
Students motivated by self-satisfaction responded better
to self-reinforcement; students who are externally oriented responded better to externally imposed reinforcement (O'Leary & Dubey, 1979).

"Self-instruction" is talking to oneself (Rosenbaum &
Drabman, 1979; Thomas, 1980). O'Leary and Dubey
(1979, p. 450) defined self-instruction as "verbal statements
to oneself which prompt, direct or maintain behavior."
They gave the example of an often repeated rule, such
as " 'i' before 'e' except after 'c'," as a commonly occurring
self-instruction. In clinical uses of self-management, clients
have been instructed to be aware of self-defeating
thoughts and to substitute more constructive ideation.
Typically, self-instruction with students involves teaching
them phrases to repeat that will remind them of behaviors
to stop and behaviors to engage in.

Self-instruction has been successfully used with children
as a sole intervention (O'Leary & Dubey, 1979). The technique appears to be effective provided students implement it and use it in areas in which they are skilled and
which are the focus of instruction (O'Leary & Dubey,
1979). Self-instruction procedures have also been effective
in treating such behavioral problems as anger and impulsivity (Snyder & White, 1979; Thomas, 1980).

Except for criterion setting, which requires the use of
rewards to be effective, research on self-management supports the techniques of self-assessment, self-determination
of criteria, and self-instruction when they are used alone.
Comprehensive self-control programs attempting to teach
students a wide range of techniques have met with some
success (O'Leary & Dubey, 1979) and have been especially
effective as maintenance strategies when externally imposed treatment programs are withdrawn. In general, self-
control procedures have been shown to be as effective
as similar externally controlled procedures. As more research is conducted, the conditions under which self-management is effective and for whom are gradually being
identified. Finally, self-management techniques appear to
produce behavioral changes that endure over time.

The activities of the self-management model based on
a formulation of Joyce and Weil (1980), are very similar
to an external contingency management program. The
major difference is that students are made aware of the
process and, as much as possible, are given responsibility
for decision making. The research on self-management
suggests that there should be a gradual phasing in of student responsibility. The major activities of self-management strategy are (1) providing the student with an introduction to behavior principles and skills; (2) establishing
baseline data about the target behavior—students may be
taught the procedures for self-assessment (O'Leary & Dubey, 1979; Rosenbaum & Drabman, 1979); (3) setting up
the contingency program, which may include self-administration of contingencies, self-determination of contingen-

cies, and self-instruction techniques (Rosenbaum & Drabman, 1979); (4) implementing and modifying the self-management program; and (5) withdrawal of contingencies
(Rosenbaum & Drabman, 1979). O'Leary and Dubey
(1979) make the point that self-management skills must
be taught, not just told. Teaching involves modeling,
prompting, reinforcement, and shaping.

Self-management and student motivation. Self-management strategy places the evaluation conditions in the
hands of students. Some educators have devoted considerable study to the relationship between motivation and
achievement (Alshuler, 1973; Covington & Berry, 1976;
McClelland, 1973) and to the development of continued
motivation (Maehr, 1976). For these researchers self-management and its logical extension, self-regulated learning
(Thomas, 1980), are crucial. Contrary to many researchers,
these individuals believe that low-achieving students who
experience an external locus of control can develop the
motivation to achieve and continue under self-managed
learning conditions (DeCharms, 1976; McClelland, 1978).
A study by Bugenthal, Whalen, and Henker (1977) showed
that self-control training was especially useful for hyperactive students who had an internal locus of control whereas
social reinforcement was more beneficial to students with
an external locus of control.

The dichotomy between contingency management and
self-management is an artificial one. The more important
question seems to be with whom and under what circumstances self-management will be productive. Many parameters are still to be uncovered, but self-management techniques appear to work optimally after students have
experienced controlled contingency management conditions. The literature also suggests that self-management
more readily matches the personality style of students having an internal locus of control; however, because they
may promote a sense of internal control, self-management
techniques are thought to be beneficial for students with
an external locus of control.

Basic Practice Strategy. The basic practice strategy
(BPS) also known as direct instruction, presented here is
an attempt to synthesize a large number of diverse research findings from the literature on teacher effectiveness
into a teaching strategy. In the sense of being empirically
derived as well as theoretically based, this strategy differs
from the other strategies.

The BPS is placed into the behavioral family because
we believe that its origins are in the theories of training
psychology and behavioral psychology (see Joyce & Weil,
1980, chap. 21). When considered in the context of these
two bodies of knowledge, the research findings take on
obvious and additional meaning. We also believe that synthesis of distinct teacher behaviors into functionally related activities (or patterns of behavior) will enhance the
effectiveness of the strategy and the power of teacher
training.

The discussion of the BPS includes a very brief description of the theoretical underpinnings and a relatively

lengthy review of the research findings from which the strategy is derived. A few words of caution are in order before we proceed to review the theory and research findings. First, we will be discussing research findings in the basic academic areas (especially reading and mathematics). The BPS may not be as suitable for objectives beyond skill acquisition and integration. Second, we will be examining what the research reveals about the association between teacher behavior and only two learning outcomes—cognitive achievement as defined by standardized achievement tests, and student attitudes. The BPS appears to be a highly effective strategy for promoting lower-level achievement (knowledge of facts and concepts). It may not be an appropriate model for obtaining other educational outcomes, such as critical thinking, problem solving, and creativity (Dunkin & Biddle, 1974; Madaus, Airasian, & Kellaghan, 1980; Peterson, 1979).

Training and behavioral psychology. "Training psychologists" have focused on training people to perform complex behaviors that involve a high degree of precision and often coordination with others as in being a crew member on a submarine. Their main contribution to the learning situation is in instructional design, particularly task definition and task analysis. Training psychology concentrates on conceptualizing performance goals, or tasks, breaking these tasks into smaller component tasks, developing training activities that ensure mastery of each subcomponent, and, finally, arranging the entire learning situation into sequences that ensure adequate transfer from one component to another and achievement of prerequisite learnings before more advanced ones.

Behavioral psychologists, like training psychologists, have focused on helping people acquire new behaviors, although generally less complex behaviors than those of concern to training psychologists. Whereas training psychologists have made important contributions to the preactive, or planning, aspects of instruction, behavioral psychologists speak to the interactive part of the learning situation, particularly the notions of modeling, reinforcement and feedback, and successive approximation. Behaviorists sometimes refer to their approach as "modeling with reinforced guided performance." As we review the diverse research findings on teacher effectiveness, it is relatively easy to perceive the relationship between the theoretical underpinnings of training and behavioral psychology and the empirical findings of basic-skills research.

Teaching-effectiveness research. In this section we review the research findings on which the BPS is based. We begin with a brief review of the learning environment variables under the control of the teacher, examine the role of the teacher as "manager of the learning task" (Soar & Soar, 1979) in more detail, and end with a brief discussion of the importance of two variables—time and success rate—as they relate to student achievement.

Researchers have uncovered at least five learning environment variables that are both subject to the influence

of the teacher and associated with student achievement in basic academic subjects:

- *Academic focus.* Teachers who emphasize an atmosphere of work in the classroom, who maintain a strong academic focus or task orientation, obtain more student engagement with learning tasks and, subsequently, greater achievement (Fisher et al., 1980; Madaus, Airasian, & Kellaghan, 1980; Rosenshine, 1970, 1979, 1980. "Academic focus" consists of emphasizing academic activity during lessons while strongly de-emphasizing the use of nonacademic materials (games, toys, puzzles) and non–academically oriented student-teacher interactions (questions about self, discussions of personal concerns) (Rosenshine, 1976, 1979).

- *Teacher direction and control.* Learning environments that are characterized as teacher-directed are associated with greater student involvement (Dunkin & Biddle, 1974; Rosenshine, 1979) and student achievement (Gage & Berliner, 1979; Soar & Soar, 1979). "Teacher direction and control" occurs when the teacher selects and directs learning tasks, determines grouping patterns, maintains a central role, keeps student choice and freedom at low levels, and minimizes the amount of nonacademic pupil talk.

- *Concern for academic progress—high teacher expectations for pupils.* Teachers who create learning environments in which more learning is expected of students tend to promote this effect (Madaus, Airasian, & Kellaghan, 1980; Rosenshine, 1976, 1979).

- *Student accountability and cooperation.* Students working in learning environments in which they are held accountable for their work and in which they work together, share supplies, and help each other tend to learn more than students in learning environments not characterized by cooperation and accountability (Fisher et al., 1980; Hertz-Lazarowitz, Sharan & Steinberg, 1980).

- *Nonnegative affect.* Although there is some disagreement about whether a learning environment characterized by positive affect (warm, positive, democratic atmosphere) does (Berliner, 1979; Medley, 1979) or does not (Dunkin & Biddle, 1974; Soar & Soar, 1979) promote achievement, there is ample evidence that negative affect inhibits student learning (Rosenshine, 1980; Soar & Soar, 1979).

The research on managing the learning task that is applicable to the BPS is discussed under the topics of structuring, teacher-student interaction, and supervisory activity. There are three basic types of structuring: (1) structuring moves made by the teacher at the beginning of a lesson, (2) internalized or "established" structure (Soar & Soar, 1979), and (3) structuring moves made during and after a lesson. Structuring activities made at the start of a lesson are designed to clarify for the learner the purposes, procedures, and actual content of the learning experience. Such clarification comes from providing students with a clear understanding of the lesson objective(s), the content to be covered, and the procedures (materials, instructional format, grouping patterns) to be used to learn the content.

There is substantial evidence that these initial structuring moves are associated with improved student engagement during the lesson and overall achievement (Block, 1980; Coker, Medley, & Soar, 1980; Fisher et al., 1980; Madaus, Airasian, & Kellaghan, 1980). All the following preinstructional structuring strategies have been shown to be positively correlated with student achievement: organizing learning materials in advance (Gage & Berliner, 1979); providing clear, explicit directions about work to be done (Coker, Medley, & Soar, 1980; Fisher et al., 1980; Medley, 1977); telling students about the materials they will use and the activities in which they will be engaged during the lesson (Berliner, 1979); using pretests (Hartley & Davies, 1976); revealing and/or discussing the objectives of the lesson (Faw & Waller, 1976; Hartley & Davies, 1976); and providing an overview of the lesson (Hartley & Davies, 1976).

The second type of structure is "established structure." This structure "represents internalization by pupils of limits of behavior, patterns of behavior that are carried out, and sequences of activities that have been established in the past" (Soar & Soar, 1979). The authors note that established structure (e.g., students knowing and practicing the rules about where to get supplies, how to use them correctly, how to clean up and return materials) reduces the need for interactions between teacher and student, about behavior that are negatively related to student achievement (Dunkin & Biddle, 1974; Rosenshine, 1979).

Structuring activities used during and after a lesson are a final type that have been correlated with pupil learning. Such teacher structuring moves as emphasizing concepts to be learned during the lesson, alerting students to important parts of a lesson, summing up sub-parts of a lesson, maintaining the flow between parts of the lesson by informing students of transitions and using adjoining relationship words ("now," "therefore," "because of"), and bringing the lesson together at the end with a summary have all been associated positively with student achievement (Dunkin & Biddle, 1974; Gage & Berliner, 1979).

Teacher-student interaction during lessons has received many labels, including "controlled practice," "substantive interaction," and "simple recitation." What all these terms have in common is a pattern of teacher explanation or presentation followed by a period of teacher-student interaction in which the teacher directs questions, students respond, and the teacher follows up with feedback and/or additional questions. The research evidence that this pattern of classroom construction is associated with student achievement is impressive (Fisher et al., 1980; Gall et al., 1978; Rosenshine, 1976; Soar & Soar, 1979). This pattern has been shown not only to promote learning of factual information, but also to be associated with (1) higher student engagement rates both during the interaction period and during later independent seatwork activities (Rosenshine, 1980), (2) "higher cognitive responsibilities," and

(3) more favorable student attitudes toward the subject area discussed during the interaction (Gall et al., 1978). For learning factual material, this interaction strategy may be the most effective method available (Dunkin & Biddle, 1974; Rosenshine, 1979).

A good deal of research has been undertaken to investigate the relationship between teacher behaviors during the interaction period and student achievement, that is, about teacher questions and teacher feedback. Some of the most important of the research findings in terms of the BPS are briefly outlined under the following headings:

- *Teacher questions.* There is support for the contention that teachers should be active and prolific questioners (Gage & Berliner, 1979); that teachers should use convergent questions with single answers and should minimize the use of open-ended and divergent questions (Rosenshine, 1976); that teachers should call on students by name before asking questions or ask questions in a patterned order (Gage & Berliner, 1979); that teachers should wait three seconds after asking questions before intervening (Soar & Soar, 1979); that it is better for teachers to ask questions students can answer correctly at least 75 percent of the time (Gage & Berliner, 1979; Rosenshine, 1976); that teachers should rely primarily upon direct academic questions and avoid nonacademic questions and responses (Rosenshine, 1979; Soar & Soar, 1979); that teachers should spend most of their time asking questions rather than responding to pupil-initiated questions (Fisher et al., 1980; Medley, 1977); and that teachers should use primarily lower-order cognitive questions (factual, knowledge recall) rather than higher-order cognitive questions (analysis, synthesis, evaluation) (Berliner, 1979; Gall et al., 1978; Medley, 1977; Soar & Soar, 1979).
- *Student responses.* There is some evidence that pupil responses to direct academic questions are associated with student achievement (Rosenshine, 1976); there is also evidence that the effectiveness of response patterns and subsequent teacher feedback may vary with the socioeconomic status of the pupils (Gage & Berliner, 1979).
- *Teacher responses and feedback.* Two common teaching practices during student-teacher interactions, redirecting unanswered questions to other students (Dunkin & Biddle, 1974; Gage & Berliner, 1979) and probing to get clarification or improved answers (Gage & Berliner, 1979), are correlated with student achievement in the basic-skills areas; waiting at least three seconds after a student response increases the quality of further student exploration (Soar & Soar, 1979); criticism providing information about the inappropriateness of student behaviors and a nonevaluative posture are both negatively associated with student learning (Fisher et al., 1980; Medley, 1977; Rosenshine, 1976); providing feedback that is academically oriented as opposed to behaviorally oriented is very strongly related to student achievement (Berliner, 1980; Fisher et al., 1980); although no consistent

pattern on the use of praise has been uncovered, it appears that praise that is targeted on specific responses and made dependent on the quality of those responses is correlated with achievement (Dunkin & Biddle, 1974; Gage & Berliner, 1979).

"Supervision" refers to teacher monitoring activities during periods of time when students are involved in seatwork, interacting with such materials as textbooks, workbooks, and work sheets. Since students spend between 55 and 70 percent of their time so engaged (Rosenshine, 1979), supervising activities associated with pupil learning can have a large impact on overall student achievement. Supervision of seatwork activities consists of the teacher making the rounds, questioning students, monitoring progress, keeping students "on-task," holding them accountable for their efforts, and providing feedback about the quality of their work. These procedures are very similar to those discussed under teacher-student interaction. The difference is that at this phase of the lesson the students are being directed primarily by the material with which they are engaged and only to a limited extent by the teacher.

Research is quite clear that pupil time spent in supervised seatwork activities is substantially more effective in promoting achievement than unsupervised practice time (Medley, 1977; Rosenshine, 1980). Students working either independently or in small groups without adult supervision spend considerably less time working with their materials than supervised groups: 68 to 73 percent versus 79 to 88 percent (Rosenshine, 1979). Thus, the often suggested pattern of having the teacher work with one or two students at a time appears to be dysfunctional for the class as a whole because of the lack of supervision for the remainder of the class (Rosenshine, 1976). A more effective pattern, and the one used in the BPS, limits instructional activities to groups and places the teacher in a supervisory role, as defined above, during seatwork activities.

Establishing the learning environment and managing the learning task are done so as to maximize student learning. It is important to point out, however, that all the teacher behaviors discussed so far do not lead directly to student achievement, but rather that they interact with two intervening variables—student time-on-task and student rate of success—that in turn are associated with student achievement. That is, all the teacher behaviors discussed so far and incorporated into the BPS are designed to create a structured, academically oriented learning environment in which students are (1) actively engaged (on-task) during recitation and seatwork activities and (2) experiencing a high rate of success (at least 75 percent). Time spent by pupils in which both these conditions are realized is referred to as "academic learning time" (ALT). Academic learning time is highly related to student achievement. Maximization of ALT is the goal of the BPS (see Peterson & Walberg, 1979, and Denham & Lieberman, 1980, for a fuller analysis of ALT).

In this section we reviewed the research about teacher behaviors and student achievement in the basic academic areas. Of all the models discussed in this paper none has greater applicability to the classroom. All the parts of the model (teacher presentation, recitation, seatwork, and other independent work) occur daily in almost every classroom in the country. What is unique about the BPS is that it (1) establishes a series of patterned teacher behaviors in a logical sequence based on these recurring activities and (2) establishes guidelines for teacher behaviors within the parts of the model based on the best available research findings to date. The BPS is a proven vehicle for those wishing to promote student achievement in the basic subject areas.

An actual BPS would contain the following five phases of activity: the structuring or orientation phase in which the teacher provides the learners with a clear understanding of the lesson objective, the procedures of the lesson, and the content of the lesson; in the second phase the teacher presents the new information to be learned; the third phase is a time of controlled practice during which the teacher leads a dialogue in which students receive structured practice in applying the newly introduced skill; phase four is a time for guided practice for students during individual seatwork; in phase five the student has an opportunity to practice the newly acquired skill in a situation (e.g., homework) independent of close teacher supervision.

Conclusions

Research results have demonstrated that instruction processes make a significant contribution to student outcomes. Furthermore, it appears that different instruction processes promote goals associated with a particular process. This conclusion contrasts with earlier reviews on teaching methods or strategies (Gage, 1969; Wallen & Travers, 1963).

We believe that one problem with previous research has been failure to conceptualize all the important dimensions of the instruction process as well as failure to describe them in specific patterns of behavior. As a result, it has been impossible to know whether an instruction process was well or poorly implemented. Research designs have not addressed this issue. A second problem has been the failure to recognize that instruction processes are designed to accomplish distinct objectives. It is misleading to compare instruction processes designed to promote different objectives, especially if the outcome represents only one of the processes. As teaching strategies have become more theoretically based and delineated into clearly describable patterns of behavior, the research findings have documented the contribution of teaching strategies to educational outcomes. Many of the isolated behaviors identified as part of the direct instruction repertoire of effective teachers can be more powerfully characterized, we believe, by describing them in terms of a teaching strategy.

Much of the entry was devoted to a review of research

and to behavioral descriptions of six teaching strategies drawn from information processing and behavioral models of teaching. The research highlighted the aspects of each strategy that contribute to its effectiveness. In general, all six strategies were demonstrated to be effective in promoting their desired educational outcomes. These strategies represent a repertoire of proven instruction processes for educational practitioners and behavioral maps for educational researchers. It should be noted that much less research has been devoted to those strategies designed to promote social and personal outcomes. If education is to seriously address these goals, more educational research and programs in these areas are needed.

Marsha L. Weil
Joseph Murphy

See also Classroom Organization; Homework; Independent Study; Individualized Systems of Instruction; Instructional Time and Learning; Media Use in Education; New Technologies in Education; Systems Design in Instruction.

REFERENCES

Alexander, L.; Frankiewicz, R. G.; & Williams, R. E. Facilitation of learning and retention of oral instruction using advance and post organizers. *Journal of Educational Psychology,* 1979, *71,* 701–707.

Allyon, T., & Azrin, N. *The Token Economy.* New York: Appleton-Century-Crofts, 1968.

Alschuler, A. S. *Developing Achievement Motivation in Adolescents.* Englewood Cliffs, N.J.: Educational Technology Publication, 1973.

Ausubel, D. The facilitation of meaningful verbal learning in the classroom. *Educational Psychologist,* 1977, *12,* 162–178.

Ausubel, D. In defense of advance organizers: A reply to the critics. *Review of Educational Research,* 1978, *48,* 251–257.

Ausubel, D. Enhancing the acquisition of knowledge. In M. Johnson (Ed.), *Toward Adolescence: The Middle School Years.* Chicago: University of Chicago Press, 1980.

Bandura, A. *Principles of Behavior Modification.* New York: Holt, Rinehart & Winston, 1969.

Bandura, A., & Perloff, B. Relative efficacy of self-monitored and externally imposed reinforcement systems. *Journal of Personality and Social Psychology,* 1967, *7,* 111–116.

Bandura, A., & Walters, R. H. *Social Learning and Personality Development.* New York: Holt, Rinehart & Winston, 1963.

Barnes, B. R., & Clawson, E. V. Do advance organizers facilitate learning? Recommendations for further research based on an analysis of thirty-two studies. *Review of Educational Research,* 1975, *45,* 637–659.

Becker, W. C. *Parents Are Teachers.* Champaign, Ill.: Research Press, 1971.

Becker, W. C. Applications of behavior principles in typical classrooms. In C. E. Thoresen (Ed.), *Behavior Modification in Education.* Chicago: National Society for the Study of Education, 1973.

Becker, W. C. Teaching reading and language to the disadvantaged: What we have learned from research. *Harvard Educational Review,* 1977, *47,* 418–543.

Benowitz, M. L., & Brisse, T. V. Effect of material incentives on classroom learning over a four-week period. *Journal of Educational Psychology,* 1976, *68,* 57–62.

Benowitz, M. L., & Rosenfield, J. G. Three types of incentives and the classroom learning of middle- and lower-class children. *Psychology in the Schools,* 1973, *10,* 79–83.

Berliner, D. Tempus educare. In P. Peterson & H. Walberg (Eds.), *Research on Teaching: Concepts, Findings, and Implications.* Berkeley, Calif.: McCutchan, 1979.

Bijou, S. W.; Birnbrauer, J. S.; Kidder, J. D.; & Tague, C. E. Programmed instruction as an approach to the teaching of reading, writing, and arithmetic to retarded children. In S. W. Bijou & D. M. Baer (Eds.), *Child Development: Readings in Experimental Analysis.* New York: Appleton-Century-Crofts, 1967.

Blatt, M., & Kohlberg, L. The effects of classroom moral discussion upon children's level of moral judgment. In L. Kohlberg & E. Turiel (Eds.), *Recent Research in Moral Development.* New York: Holt, Rinehart & Winston, 1973.

Block, J. H. Success rate. In C. Denham & A. Lieberman (Eds.), *Time to Learn.* Washington, D.C.: National Institute of Education, 1980.

Bohart, A. C. Role playing and interpersonal-conflict reduction. *Journal of Counseling Psychology,* 1977, *24,* 15–24.

Bredderman, T. Process curricula in elementary school service. *Evaluation in Education,* 1980, *4,* 43–44.

Brophy, J. Teacher praise: A functional analysis. *Review of Educational Research,* 1981, *51,* 5–32.

Bruner, J. S.; Goodnow, J. J.; & Austin, G. A. *A Study of Thinking.* Huntington, N.Y.: Robert E. Krieger, 1977.

Bugenthal, D. B.; Whalen, C. K.; & Henker, B. Causal attributions of hyperactive children and motivational assumptions of two behavior-change approaches: Evidence for an interactionist position. *Child Development,* 1977, *48,* 847–884.

Bulter, L.; Miezitis, S.; Friedman, R.; & Cole, E. The effects of two school-based intervention programs on depressive symptoms in preadolescents. *American Educational Research Journal,* 1980, *17,* 111–119.

Case, R. Gearing the demands of instruction to the developmental capacities of the learner. *Review of Educational Research,* 1975, *45,* 59–87.

Case, R. A developmentally based theory and technology of instruction. *Review of Educational Research,* 1978, *48,* 439–463.

Cautela, J. R. Covert reinforcement. *Behavior Therapy,* 1970, *1,* 33–50.

Coker, H.; Medley, D. M.; & Soar, R. S. How valid are expert opinions about effective teaching? *Phi Delta Kappan,* 1980, *62,* 131–134, 149.

Colby, A.; Kohlberg, L.; Fenton, E.; Speicher-Dubin, B.; & Lieberman, M. Secondary school moral discussion programmes led by social studies teachers. *Journal of Moral Education,* 1977, *6,* 90–111.

Cooney, E. W. Social-cognitive development: Applications to intervention and evaluation in the elementary grades. *Counseling Psychologist,* 1977, *6,* 6–9.

Covington, M. V., & Berry, R. G. *Self-worth and School Learning.* New York: Holt, Rinehart & Winston, 1976.

Cowan, P. A. *Piaget with Feeling: Cognitive, Social, and Emotional Dimensions.* New York: Holt, Rinehart & Winston, 1978.

Dasen, P. R. Introduction. In P. R. Dasen (Ed.), *Piagetian Psychology: Cross-cultural Contributions.* New York: Gardner Press, 1977.

DeCharms, R. *Enhancing Motivation in the Classroom.* New York: Irvington and Halsted-Wiley, 1976.

Denham, C., & Lieberman, A. *Time to Learn.* Washington, D.C.: National Institute of Education, 1980.

Dolan, L. Home, school, and pupil attitudes. *Evaluation in Education,* 1981, *4,* 265–358.

Drabman, R. S. Behavior modification in the classroom. In W. E. Craighead, A. E. Kazdin, & M. J. Mahoney (Eds.), *Behavior Modification: Principles, Issues, and Applications.* Boston: Houghton Mifflin, 1976.

Dunkin, M., & Biddle, B. *The Study of Teaching.* New York: Holt, Rinehart & Winston, 1974.

Enright, R. D. An integration of social cognitive developmental and cognitive processing: Educational applications. *American Educational Research Journal,* 1980, *17,* 21–41.

Faw, H. W., & Waller, T. G. Mathemagenic behaviours and efficiency in learning from prose materials: Review, critique, and recommendations. *Review of Educational Research,* 1976, *46,* 691–720.

Featherstone, J. *Schools Where Children Learn.* New York: Avon Books, 1971.

Felixbrod, J. J., & O'Leary, K. D. Effects of reinforcement on children's academic behavior as a function of self-determined and externally imposed contingencies. *Journal of Applied Behavioral Analysis,* 1973, *6,* 241–250.

Felixbrod, J. J., & O'Leary, K. D. Self-determination of academic standards by children: Toward freedom from external control. *Journal of Educational Psychology,* 1974, *66,* 845–850.

Ferster, C. B., & Skinner, B. F. *Schedules of Reinforcement.* New York: Appleton, 1957.

Fisher, C. W.; Berliner, D. C.; Filby, N. N.; Marliave, R.; Cahen, L. S.; & Dishaw, M. M. Teaching behaviors, academic learning time, and student achievement: An overview. In C. Denham & A. Lieberman (Eds.), *Time to Learn.* Washington, D.C.: National Institute of Education, 1980.

Forness, S. R. The reinforcement hierarchy. *Psychology in the Schools,* 1973, *10,* 168–177.

Gage, N. L., & Berliner, D. C. *Educational Psychology* (2nd ed.). Chicago: Rand McNally, 1979.

Gall, M. D.; Ward, B. A.; Berliner, D. C.; Cahen, L. S.; Winne, P. H.; Elashoff, J. D.; & Stanton, G. C. Effects of questioning techniques and recitation on student learning. *American Education Research Journal,* 1978, *15,* 175–199.

Ginsburg, H., & Opper, S. *Piaget's Theory of Intellectual Development* (2nd ed.). Englewood Cliffs, N.J.: Prentice-Hall, 1979.

Glynn, E. L.; Thomas, D. J.; & Shee, S. M. Behavioral self-control of on-task behavior in an elementary classroom. *Journal of Applied Behavioral Analysis,* 1973, *6,* 105–113.

Hanley, E. M. Review of research involving applied behavioral analysis in the classroom. *Review of Educational Research,* 1970, *40,* 597–625.

Harris, M. L., & Harris, C. W. *A Structure of Concept Attainment Abilities.* Madison: Wisconsin Research and Development Center for Cognitive Learning, 1973.

Hartley, J., & Davies, I. K. Preinstructional strategies: The role of pretests, behavioral objectives, overviews, and advance organizers. *Review of Educational Research,* 1976, *46,* 239–265.

Hersh, R. H.; Paolitto, D. P.; & Reimer, J. *Promoting Moral Growth: From Piaget to Kohlberg.* New York: Longman, 1979.

Hertz-Lazarowitz, R.; Sharan, S.; & Steinberg, R. Classroom learning style and cooperative behavior of elementary school children. *Journal of Educational Psychology,* 1980, *72,* 99–106.

Holland, J. R. Teaching machines: An application of principles from the laboratory. *Journal of Experimental Analysis of Behavior,* 1960, *3,* 275–287.

Holt, J. *How Children Fail.* New York: Dell, 1964.

Holt, J. *How Children Learn.* New York: Dell, 1967.

Holt, J. *What Do I Do Monday?* New York: Dell, 1970.

Hundert, J. The effectiveness of reinforcement, response cost, and mixed programs on classroom behaviors. *Journal of Applied Behavioral Analysis,* 1976, *9,* 107.

Jensen, L. C. *That's Not Fair: Helping Children Make Moral Decisions.* Provo, Utah: Brigham Young University Press, 1977.

Jensen, L., & Chatterley. Facilitating development of moral reasoning in children. *Journal of Moral Education,* 1979, *9,* 53–54.

Johnson, D. W., & Johnson, R. T. Conflict in the classroom: Controversy and learning. *Review of Educational Research,* 1979, *49,* 51–70.

Joyce, B. R., & Weil, M. *Models of Teaching* (2nd ed.). Englewood Cliffs, N.J.: Prentice-Hall, 1980.

Kanfer, F. H. Self-regulation: Research, issues, and speculations. In C. Neuringer & J. L. Michael (Eds.), *Behavior Modification in Clinical Psychology.* New York: Appleton-Century-Crofts, 1970.

Kanfer, F. H. Behavior modification: An overview. In C. E. Thoresen (Ed.), *Behavior Modification in Education.* Chicago: National Society for the Study of Education, 1973.

Kanfer, F. H. Self-management methods. In F. H. Kanfer & A. P. Goldstein (Eds.), *Helping People Change: A Textbook of Methods.* New York: Pergamon Press, 1975.

Kash, M. M., & Borich, G. D. *Teacher Behavior and Pupil Self-concept.* Reading, Mass.: Addison-Wesley, 1978.

Kavanagh, H. B. Moral education: Relevance, goals, and strategies. *Journal of Moral Education,* 1977, *6,* 121–130.

Kazdin, A. E. Response cost: The removal of conditioned reinforcers for therapeutic change. *Behavior Therapy,* 1972, *3,* 533–546.

Kazdin, A. E. *Behavior Modification in Applied Settings.* Homewood, Ill.: Dorsey Press, 1975.

Kazdin, A. E. *The Token Economy: A Review and Evaluation.* New York: Plenum, 1977.

Kazdin, A. E. *Behavior Modification in Applied Settings* (2nd ed.). Homewood, Ill.: Dorsey Press, 1980.

Kazdin, A. E. Behavior modification in education: Contributions and limitations. *Developmental Review,* 1981, *1,* 34–57.

Kazdin, A. E., & Bootzin, R. The token economy: An evaluative review. *Journal of Applied Behavior Analysis,* 1972, *5,* 343–372.

Klausmeier, H. J. Educational experience and cognitive development. *Educational Psychologist,* 1977, *12,* 179–196.

Klausmeier, H. J., & Feldman, K. V. Effects of a definition and a varying number of examples and nonexamples on concept attainment. *Journal of Educational Psychology,* 1975, *67,* 174–178.

Kohl, H. R. *The Open Classroom: A Practical Guide to a New Way of Teaching.* New York: Random House, Vintage Books, 1969.

Kohlberg, L. Moral and religious education and the public schools: A developmental view. In T. Sizer (Ed.), *Religion and Public Education.* Boston: Houghton Mifflin, 1967.

Kohlberg, L. Moral development. In D. L. Sills (Ed.), *International Encyclopedia of the Social Sciences.* New York: Macmillan and Free Press, 1968.

Kohlberg, L. Education for justice: A modern statement of the platonic view. In T. Sizer (Ed.), *Moral Education.* Cambridge, Mass.: Harvard University Press, 1970.

Kohlberg, L. Cognitive-developmental theory and the practice of collective moral education. In M. Wolins & M. Gottesman (Eds.), *Group Care: The Education Path of Youth Aliyah*. New York: Gordon & Breach, 1971.

Kohlberg, L. A cognitive-developmental approach to moral education. *Humanist*, November–December 1972, 13–16.

Kohlberg, L., & Gilligan, C. The adolescent as a philosopher: The discovery of the self in a postconventional world. *Daedalus*, 1971, *100*, 1051–1086.

Kohlberg, L., & Turiel, E. Moral development and moral education. In G. Lesser (Ed.), *Psychology and Educational Practice*. Glenview, Ill.: Scott, Foresman, 1971.

Kozlow, M. N., & White, A. L. Advance-organizer research. *Evaluation in Education*, 1980, *4*, 7–48.

Krasner, L., & Krasner, M. Token economies and other planned environments. In C. E. Thoresen (Ed.), *Behavior Modification in Education*. Chicago: National Society for the Study of Education, 1973.

Kuhn, D., & Ho, V. Self-directed activity and cognitive development. *Journal of Applied Developmental Psychology*, 1980, *1*, 119–133.

Lavatelli, C. S. *Piaget's Theory Applied to an Early Childhood Curriculum*. Boston: American Science and Engineering, 1970.

Lawton, J. T., & Wanska, S. K. Advance organizers as a teaching strategy: A reply to Barnes and Clawson. *Review of Educational Research*, 1977, *47*, 233–244.

Lawton, J. T., & Wanska, S. K. The effects of different types of advance organizers on classification learning. *American Educational Research Journal*, 1979, *16*, 223–239.

Lazarus, A. A. *Behavior Therapy and Beyond*. New York: McGraw-Hill, 1971.

Lipe, D., & Jung, S. M. Manipulating incentives to enhance school learning. *Review of Educational Research*, 1971, *41*, 249–280.

Litow, L. *Classroom Interdependent Group-oriented Contingencies: An Annotated Bibliography*. 1975. (ERIC Document Reproduction Service No. ED 134 886)

Lovitt, T. C.; Guppy, T. E.; & Blattner, J. E. The use of free-time contingency with fourth-graders to increase spelling accuracy. *Behavior Research and Therapy*, 1969, *7*, 151–156.

Luiten, J. W. Advance organizers in learning. *Evaluation in Education*, 1980, *4*, 49–50.

Madaus, G. F.; Airasian, P. W.; & Kellaghan, T. *School Effectiveness: A Reassessment of the Evidence*. New York: McGraw-Hill, 1980.

Madsen, C. H., Jr.; Becker, W. C., & Thomas, D. R. Rules, praise, and ignoring: Elements of elementary classroom control. *Journal of Applied Behavioral Analysis*, 1968, *1*, 139–150.

Madsen, C. H., Jr.; Becker, W. C.; Thomas, D. R.; Koser, L.; & Plager, E. An analysis of reinforcing functions of "sit down" commands. In R. K. Parker (Ed.), *Readings in Educational Psychology*. Boston: Allyn & Bacon, 1968.

Maehr, M. L. Continuing motivation: An analysis of a seldom-considered educational outcome. *Review of Educational Research*, 1976, *46*, 443–462.

Marholin, D., II, & Steinman, W. M. Stimulus control in the classroom as a function of the behavior reinforced. *Journal of Applied Behavioral Analysis*, 1977, *10*, 465–478.

Mayer, R. E. Advance organizers that compensate for the organization of text. *Journal of Educational Psychology*, 1978, *70*, 880–886.

Mayer, R. E. Can advance organizers influence meaningful learning? *Review of Educational Research*, 1979, *49*, 371–383.

McClelland, D. C. What is the effect of achievement motivation training in the school? In A. S. Alschuler (Ed.), *Developing Achievement Motivation in Adolescents*. Englewood Cliffs, N.J.: Educational Technology Publication, 1973.

McClelland, D. C. Managing motivation to expand human freedom. *American Psychologist*, 1978, *33*, 201–210.

McClure, L.; Chinsky, J. M.; & Larcen, S. W. Enhancing social problem-solving performance in an elementary school setting. *Journal of Educational Psychology*, 1978, *70*, 504–513.

McLaughlin, T. F. Self-control in the classroom. *Review of Educational Research*, 1976, *46*, 631–663.

McMurray, N. E.; Bernard, M. E.; Klausmeier, H. J.; Schilling, J. M.; & Vorwerk, K. Instructional design for accelerating children's concept learning. *Journal of Educational Psychology*, 1977, *69*, 660–667.

McNally, D. W. *Piaget, Education, and Teaching*. Hassocks, England: Harvester Press, 1977.

Medley, D. *Teacher Competence and Teacher Effectiveness: A Review of Process-Product Research*. Washington, D.C.: American Association of Colleges for Teacher Education, 1977. (ERIC Document Reproduction Service No. ED 143 629)

Medley, D. The effectiveness of teachers. In P. Peterson & H. Walberg (Eds.), *Research on Teaching: Concepts, Findings, and Implications*. Berkeley, Calif.: McCutchan, 1979.

Mussen, P. H.; Conger, J. J.; Kagan, J. *Child Development and Personality* (3rd ed.). New York: Harper & Row, 1969.

Nelson, C. M.; Worell, J.; & Polsgrove, L. Behaviorally disordered peers as contingency managers. *Behavior Therapy*, 1973, *4*, 270–276.

Nicholson, S. *Values, Feelings, and Morals: Part II. An Annotated Bibliography of Programs and Instructional Materials*. Washington, D.C.: American Association of Elementary-Kindergarten-Nursery Educators, 1974.

Nugent, G. C.; Tipton, T. J.; & Brooks, D. W. Use of introductory organizers in television instruction. *Journal of Educational Psychology*, 1980, *72*, 445–451.

O'Leary, D. K., & Drabman, R. Behavior modification of an adjustment class: A token reinforcement program. *Exceptional Children*, 1967, *37*, 637–642.

O'Leary, D. K., & Drabman, R. Token reinforcement programs in the classroom: A review. *Psychological Bulletin*, 1971, *75*, 379–398.

O'Leary, S. G., & Dubey, D. R. Applications of self-control procedures by children: A review. *Journal of Applied Behavior Analysis*, 1979, *12*, 449–465.

Osborn, J. D., & Osborn, D. K. *Cognitive Tasks: An Approach for Early Childhood Education*. Athens: University of Georgia, Early Childhood Education Learning Center, 1974.

Pavlov, I. P. *Conditioned Reflexes: An Investigation of Physiological Activity of the Cerebral Cortex* (G. V. Antrep, Trans.). New York: Oxford University Press, 1927.

Peterson, P. Direct instruction reconsidered. In P. Peterson & H. Walberg (Eds.), *Research on Teaching: Concepts, Findings, and Implications*. Berkeley, Calif.: McCutchan, 1979.

Peterson, P., & Walberg, H. *Research on Teaching: Concepts, Findings, and Implications*. Berkeley, Calif.: McCutchan, 1979.

Piaget, J. *Six Psychological Studies*. New York: Random House, Vintage Books, 1968.

Piaget, J. *Psychology of Intelligence*. Totowa, N.J.: Littlefield, Adams, 1972.

Premack, D. Reinforcement theory. In D. Levine (Ed.), *Nebraska Symposium on Motivation*. Lincoln: University of Nebraska Press, 1965.

Richmond, P. G. *An Introduction to Piaget.* New York: Basic Books, 1970.

Rimm, D. C., & Masters, J. C. *Behavior Therapy: Techniques and Empirical Findings* (2nd ed.). New York: Academic Press, 1979.

Rogers, C. R. *Freedom to Learn.* Columbus, Ohio: Merrill, 1969.

Rosen, H. *Pathway to Piaget: A Guide for Clinicians, Educators, and Developmentalists.* Cherry Hill, N.J.: Postgraduate International, 1977.

Rosenbaum, A. K.; O'Leary, D.; & Jacob, R. G. Behavioral intervention with hyperactive children: Group consequences as a supplement to individual contingencies. *Behavior Therapy,* 1975, *6,* 315–323.

Rosenbaum, M. S., & Drabman, R. S. Self-control training in the classroom: A review and critique. *Journal of Applied Behavioral Analysis,* 1979, *12,* 467–485.

Rosenshine, B. V. Classroom instruction. In N. L. Gage (Ed.), *The Psychology of Teaching Methods.* Chicago: University of Chicago Press, 1976.

Rosenshine, B. V. Content, time, and direct instruction. In P. Peterson & H. Walberg (Eds.), *Research on Teaching: Concepts, Findings, and Implications.* Berkeley, Calif.: McCutchan, 1979.

Rosenshine, B. V. Direct instruction. In C. Denham & A. Lieberman (Eds.), *Time to Learn.* Washington, D.C.: National Institute of Education, 1980.

Schweinhart, L. J., & Weikart, D. P. *Young Children Grow Up: The Effects of the Perry Preschool Program on Youths through age Fifteen.* Ypsilanti, Mich.: High Scope Educational Research Foundation, 1980.

Selman, R. L., & Lieberman, M. Primary-level curriculum: Cognitive developmental theory of moral reasoning. In D. D. Hearn (Ed.), *Values, Feelings, and Morals: Part I. Research and Perspectives.* Washington, D.C.: American Association of Elementary-Kindergarten-Nursery Educators, 1974. (ERIC Document Reproduction Service No. ED 095 472)

Silberman, C. E. *Crisis in the Classroom: The Remaking of American Education.* New York: Random House, Vintage Books, 1970.

Singer, D. G., & Revenson, T. A. *A Piaget Primer: How a Child Thinks.* New York: International Universities Press, 1978.

Skinner, B. F. *Science and Human Behavior.* New York: Macmillan, 1953.

Snyder, J. J., & White, M. J. The use of cognitive self-instruction in the treatment of behaviorally disturbed adolescents. *Behavior Therapy,* 1979, *10,* 227–235.

Soar, R. S., & Soar, R. M. Emotional climate and management. In P. Peterson & H. Walberg (Eds.), *Research on Teaching: Concepts, Findings, and Implications.* Berkeley, Calif.: McCutchan, 1979.

Staats, A. W. Behavior analysis and token reinforcement in educational behavior modification and curriculum research. In C. E. Thoresen (Ed.), *Behavior Modification in Education.* Chicago: National Society for the Study of Education, 1973.

Stallings, J. *Learning to Look.* Belmont, Calif.: Wadsworth, 1977.

Stallings, J., & Kaskowitz, D. H. *Follow-through Classroom Observation Evaluation: 1972–1973.* Menlo Park, Calif.: Stanford Research Institute, 1974.

Stevenson, H. W. Social reinforcement of children's behavior. In L. P. Lipsitt & C. C. Spiker (Eds.), *Advances in Child Development and Behavior* (2 vols.), New York: Academic Press, 1965.

Switzky, H. N., & Haywood, H. C. Motivational orientation and the relative efficacy of self-monitoring and externally imposed reinforcement systems in children. *Journal of Personality and Social Psychology,* 1974, *30,* 360–366.

Tennyson, C. L.; Tennyson, R. D.; & Rothen, W. Content structure and instructional control strategies as design variables in concept acquisition. *Journal of Educational Psychology,* 1980, *72,* 499–505.

Tennyson, R. D. Instructional control strategies and content structure as design variables in concept acquisition using computer-based instruction. *Journal of Educational Psychology,* 1980, *72,* 525–532.

Tennyson, R. D., & Park, O. Teaching of concepts: A review of instructional design research literature. *Review of Educational Research,* 1980, *50,* 55–70.

Thomas, J. W. Agency and achievement: Self-management and self-regard. *Review of Educational Research,* 1980, *50,* 213–240.

Thoresen, C. E. (Ed.). *Behavior Modification in Education.* Chicago: National Society for the Study of Education, 1973.

Thorndike, E. L. Animal intelligence: An experimental study of the associative process in animals. *Psychological Review,* 1898, *2*(8, Monograph Supplement).

Thorndike, E. L. *Animal Intelligence.* New York: Macmillan, 1911.

Thorndike, E. L. *The Psychology of Learning* (Educational Psychology, II). New York: Teachers College Press, 1913.

Vaidya, S., & Chansky, N. Cognitive development and cognitive style as factors in mathematics achievement. *Journal of Educational Psychology,* 1980, *72,* 326–330.

Wadsworth, B. J. *Piaget for the Classroom Teacher.* New York: Longman, 1978.

Walker, H. M.; Hops, H.; & Feigenbaum, E. Deviant classroom behavior as a function of combinations of social and token reinforcement and cost contingency. *Behavior Therapy,* 1976, *7,* 76–88.

Wallen, N. E., & Travers, R. M. W. Analysis and investigation of teaching methods. In N. L. Gage (Ed.), *Handbook of Research on Teaching.* Chicago: Rand McNally, 1963.

Wang, M. C. The self-schedule system: A brief description. In M. C. Wang (Ed.), *The Self-schedule System for Instructional-Learning Management in Adaptive School Learning Environments.* Pittsburgh, Pa.: University of Pittsburgh, Learning Research and Development Center, 1976.

Watson, J. B. The place of conditioned reflex in psychology. *Psychological Review,* 1916, *23,* 89–116.

Watson, J. B., & Rayner, P. Conditioned emotional reactions. *Journal of Experimental Psychology,* 1921, *3,* 1–14.

Weikart, D. Influencing children's values, feelings, and morals: Program development and problems. In D. D. Hearn (Ed.), *Values, Feelings, and Morals: Part I. Research and Perspectives.* Washington, D.C.: American Association of Elementary-Kindergarten-Nursery Educators, 1974.

Weikart, D.; Deloria, D.; Lawser, S.; & Wiegerink, R. *Longitudinal Results of the Ypsilanti Perry Preschool Project.* Ypsilanti, Mich.: High/Scope Educational Research Foundation, 1970.

Weikart, D.; Rogers, L.; Adcock, C.; & McClelland, D. *The Cognitively Oriented Curriculum: A Framework for Preschool Teachers.* Washington, D.C.: National Association for the Education of Young Children, 1971. (ERIC Document Reproduction Service No. ED 052 045)

Wolf, M. M.; Giles, D. K.; & Hall, R. V. Experiments with token reinforcement in a remedial classroom. *Behavior Research and Therapy,* 1968, *6,* 51–64.

Wolpe, J. *Psychotherapy by Reciprocal Inhibition.* Stanford, Calif.: Stanford University Press, 1958.

Worthen, B. R. Discovery and expository task presentation in elementary mathematics. *Journal of Educational Psychology* (Monograph Supplement), 1968, *59*, 1–13.

Zimmermann, M. J., & Sassenrath, J. M. Improvement in arithmetic and reading and discovery learning in mathematics (SEED). *Educational Research Quarterly*, 1978, *3*, 27–33.

INSTRUCTIONAL TIME AND LEARNING

Time, as a variable in research, has few trumpeters. It is, of course, recognized that instruction requires time and that motivation may cause a pupil to spend more time in study, but time, until recently, was considered a mere background variable. It seems invalid, however, if, in an experimental comparison, one treatment goes on longer than the other. Surely, the length of the school day or the school year is important to the amount learned. And many teachers recognize that one of their main goals is to manage the classroom so that pupils get the time, or put in the time, to learn.

Research on Instructional Time. The research on instructional time and learning shows a moderate and positive relationship. The more instructional time devoted to a course of study, the greater the achievement that generally results. Table 1 shows the correlations obtained in thirty-four studies of instructional time and learning measures (see Fredrick & Walberg, 1980, for a complete review of the studies). The typical correlation between amount of instruction and achievement is about .40 to .50, a correlation that leaves sufficient room for other effects, but that is comparatively strong and consistent.

The research can be grouped, as in Table 1, to reflect the category of time being examined: years of schooling, days of instruction, hours of class, and minutes of study. In each category of time under study, the relationship between quantity of instruction and achievement has been shown to be significant and moderate.

TABLE 1. *Correlations from studies of instructional time and achievement*

Time category	Number of studies		Range of correlations[1]	
	Total	Positive	Uncontrolled	Controlled
Years	6	6	.26 to .71	.20 to .60
Days	10	7	.32 to .69	.60*
Hours	7	7	.13 to .59	.09 to .47
Minutes	11	11	.15 to .53	.09 to .44

[1] The range of correlations is given for significant, positive studies. "Controlled correlations" are those in which another variable, such as ability or social class, has been partialed out.   * For the time category days, only one of the studies controlled for other variables.

Years of schooling. When time spent in a learning situation is measured over relatively long spans, the results show a modest but persistent association between the outcome measure and time. Various types of achievements— knowledge, intelligence, skills, language learning, cultural openness, and religious commitment—were each shown to be related to the amount of time spent in study. Correlations ranged between .26 and .71, although they were slightly lower when social class was controlled. There were indications in two of the studies that the logarithm of time was a better predictor than untransformed time, suggesting a diminishing return in achievement with ever larger amounts of time. Whether additional years of schooling cause an increase in achievement cannot be proven by the usual survey study. One can argue that those who achieve will tend to continue their schooling.

Days of instruction. The time variables in the range of days of instruction demonstrate a less consistent relationship to outcomes. Seven studies found a positive effect resulting from number of days of instruction, with correlations ranging from .32 to .69, although again, the correlation was lower in one study when poverty level was partialed out. Days of instruction are apparently more directly related to gains in achievement than to absolute achievement level. The relationship is also clarified if the outcome measure is specifically geared to the content covered. Some studies show the need for caution in combining various indicators into a composite measure, for not all time measures are valid predictors of outcomes.

Hours of classes. The studies in the range of hours of classes indicate a rather persistent connection between time spent on content and the achievement that results. Correlations ranged from .13 to .59. When relationships were analyzed by amount of variance explained, the proportion ranged from 3 percent to 22 percent, representing the amount explained after other variables had already been entered into the equations. Study time and other variables, such as satisfaction level, have a substantial amount of common variance when study time is controlled by the student. In some situations, added time may make up for a lack of achievement. Homework time may be as predictive as in-class time for producing achievement effects.

Minutes of study. The research studies that look at time use within the class period reported modest relationships between the variable and achievement. Reported correlations ranged from .15 to .53, but when other relevant variables (e.g., IQ, ability, readiness) were controlled, they ranged from .09 to .44. Refining the measure of time to reflect actual time devoted to the outcome being measured can be expected to increase the association. An interesting approach is to predict the time needed so that the ratio of time spent to time needed can be estimated (Carroll, 1963).

Current Research Strategies and Measures. The current research in the literature on instructional time seldom reports experimental comparisons with randomized assignment to treatments. The research strategy in the majority of studies seems to be one of two types, the types differing in the unit of analysis. Where long-term effects or gross numbers of variables are being entered in correlational analyses, the usual procedure has been to gather available indices of time and classroom process and then to summarize the relationships discovered by using the median school achievement or an even broader category as the unit under study. The other paradigm uses the student as the unit and explores individual time-on-task and other student or classroom variables as they relate to individual achievement.

The following list shows the variables that have been variously used as measures of instructional time:

Significant Variables

> Actual instruction time—composite
> Amount of cutting classes
> Attendance rate
> Hours of homework
> Industriousness
> Interruptions to the lesson
> Latenesses or tardiness
> Length of school year
> Logarithm of months of study
> Logarithm of practice time
> Logarithm of time allocated
> Minutes allocated to reading
> Minutes of silent reading
> Number of instructional days
> Number of late arrivals
> Number of students not involved
> Number of unexcused absences
> On- and off-task behaviors
> Opportunity to learn—composite
> Participation level
> Percentage of students attending to task
> Proportion of dropouts
> Proportion of time devoted to instruction
> Teacher-contact time
> Time allocated
> Time for homework
> Time in group instruction
> Time-on-task
> Time-on-task during instruction
> Time spent reading
> Time spent to learn: time needed to learn
> Wasted or dead time
> Willingness to devote study time
> Years of schooling

Nonsignificant variables

> Days that school is in session
> Frequency of homework
> Length of academic day
> Length of school year

Minutes allocated to reading
Number of late arrivals
Part-day attendance

Experimenters sometimes choose easy tallies of time that stand in for actual time spent in instruction. For example, in order to correlate years of schooling and achievement, variables such as dropout rate or proportion of graduates might replace a more exact calculation of how many years each member of the population under study had gone to school. Days of instruction have been studied by using attendance rate as the proxy. The easy tally may not be sufficiently exact, however. It appears that refining the validity of the measure of instructional time increases its correlation with learning. The time spent in class, for example, is not as closely related to achievement as is time-on-task.

Complexities in Relating Instructional Time to Achievement. Time often has a narrow range of variation. Causal studies are rarely conducted. If one varies instructional time, how does one provide filler for those who finish early? Time is not only a cause, but an effect of success in an activity. Use of time is related to socioeconomic variables. Out-of-class time is often unmeasured. Some pupils may study without being observed. Outcome measures are often too broadly constructed to measure the specific content taught during the time span under study. All of these issues complicate the study of time and learning.

Do people attend school longer because they learn more, or do they learn more because they attend school longer? Do school attendees review and update their previous learning more so than those who stop going to school? Does voluntary attendance exert sample selectivity that dilutes the clarity of results? These questions are incompletely resolved and are likely to occupy educational researchers and policy makers in the future.

In several studies, growth in achievement has reached a plateau or what is statistically seen as diminishing returns (Fredrick & Walberg, 1980). With such a plateau, additional time has only marginal impact on achievement, even though it had previously shown larger effect. The reasons for such diminishing returns may be the achievement measure itself (the test cannot detect the high-level gains), the mix of pupils (progressively more of them reach the ceiling of the skill and can improve no further), the instruction (the procedures may need change as students become skilled), or the nature of learning itself. Nonlinear terms (logarithm and the like) are frequently more precise than linear terms in explaining variances.

Another complexity revealed by research is that not all indices of instruction time are positively related to achievement. For example, a longer school year seems to coincide with a higher absence rate and has not been shown to predict achievement. Other indices may show significant correlations only by virtue of the fact that they, also, are related to socioeconomic level. Schools in high-poverty areas have lower attendance rates and higher dropout rates. Only by partialing out effects or doing experimental comparisons can one get close to a measure of the true relationship. The separate effects of instructional time and poverty are difficult to disentangle.

Time in itself is conceptually different from quantity of instruction as a variable, but usually the experimenter assumes that measuring time-on-task, for example, measures quantity of instruction. This is reasonable, but asking "How much time?" is not the same question as "How much instruction?" Some procedures may provide more instruction per unit of time than others.

There are several ways in which the true relationship between instructional time and achievement is hidden. The time variable may not measure the time devoted to study or to instruction very accurately. The sample of time measured may not be sufficient, or it may not be representative. The measure itself may be more unreliable than expected, or the measurement may itself alter the situation. Conversely, the achievement test or task may not fit the instruction that was timed. It may cover other areas or only partially measure the instructional content. Tests may also be insensitive to small gains in achievement when the length of time under study is short, and they may have ceiling effects when the instruction is very thorough. When the content is new to pupils and time and achievement are carefully measured, however, the correlation between the two is high.

A procedure that also raises the numerical relationship is the formation of composite measures of time usage. If, for example, one measures time lost by absences, tardiness, interruptions, transitions, and off-task activities, the deduction of each value weighted for the number of pupils affected will give a very useful indicator of the actual instructional minutes. If each separate entry is positively related to the outcome, even though only marginally strong, the composite weighted variable becomes quite firmly associated with achievement. The increase comes partly from additional sampling that the multiple measures provide.

Time is not always or only an independent variable. Instructional time may be increased as a response to poor achievement. Correlational forays that happen upon such situations may unwittingly uncover negative correlations.

Instructional time is usually more logically related to gains in achievement than to absolute achievement level, unless the period under study is very long. Gain scores are beset with a double-error term that can be discounted only by doubled attention to assuring the reliability of the gain. An interesting possibility is that measuring two variables, the time a student needs to learn certain content and the time spent on it, will bring researchers closer to understanding and affecting educational practice. These and other critical research issues are discussed in a long, critical review of the literature (Fredrick & Walberg, 1980).

Implications of Research Strategies for Practice. Just as there is densely packed language, there are instructional strategies that have high input. Can all pupils handle "packed" lessons? We need to learn how to distribute learning so that it has the maximum chance of being remembered and useful. How time-efficient is Socratic questioning or discovery learning? It takes five minutes to tell pupils something, an hour to have them experience it, and a week to have them discover it. Can we afford the luxury of discovery, or, on the other hand, the rate at which spoken discourse is forgotten? Will students like learning if teachers tell them something too many times?

Time spent is a necessary, but not a sufficient, condition for learning. For example, time spent on social interactions, classroom management, and other indirect or non-instructional tasks correlates negatively with gains in achievement (Stallings, 1980). Amount of whole-class instruction is often more positively related to outcome than is amount of individual seatwork (Evertson et al., 1980). Some types of instructional methods, including direct instruction, are apparently more effective in keeping pupils on task (Rutter et al., 1979).

There is a need to make the allocation of additional time possible in classrooms. Teachers do not purposely waste time, but perhaps a certain amount of lost time is inevitable in a school day. Keeping students on task requires insight or empathy that many teachers have not yet mastered. Learning depends on how the available time is spent. Learning by the less able pupil is especially hampered by larger amounts of dead time, when nothing instructional is happening.

There is evidence that large quantities of time are dissipated in the typical classroom. When interruptions to the lesson, in-movements and out-movements by pupils, time wasted, time missed by absent pupils, time lost to set up, clean-up, and starting late and finishing early are subtracted from the available time, as much as 25 percent is lost in classrooms showing good gains and 50 percent in those with poor achievement gains (Fredrick, 1977; Harnischfeger, 1980).

Stallings (1980) found that in-service meetings were efficient in helping teachers recognize these dissipations. Prescriptions for keeping on-task, for managing pupil work more effectively, and for increasing the more productive activities seemed to be followed readily when the prescription was based on an observational analysis of the teacher's behavior.

Noteworthy trends in research include analysis of which activities are actually occurring within the classroom and which of these are positively related to achievement. Interacting seems to increase achievement, but too much time spent on silent reading and class management actually decreases it. (Or is it that classes with decreased achievement seem to require too much time in management and in simply finding time to read?) The supportive action of reinforcing and giving positive feedback to lower-ability pupils is especially helpful (Stallings, 1980).

Pupils may be on-task, but their work may lose value if teacher is not teaching value (Rutter et al., 1979). Workshops with teachers seem to help them implement procedures for the more efficient and productive use of class time and interactions.

Models of School Process Variables Related to Outcomes. Models are helpful in organizing the array of variables that are potentially effective in explaining the variation in achievement outcomes. Often these models specify the direction of causality, the strength of relationship, and effects of output changes dependent on input variable changes. Most models have some affinity to work by Carroll (1963), who postulated that the degree of learning is related to the ratio of time spent to time required.

Leinhardt (1980) reviewed several production models in which time for instruction has a strong influence on the outcome measures. The models help guide the measurement of the instructional environment for purposes of evaluating effects. In the model prepared by Berliner (1979), the main construct used is academic learning time (ALT). It includes time allocated, time engaged, success rate of the pupils, and relevance of the task to the outcome. A model of achievement by Harnischfeger and Wiley (1977) considers teacher and pupil time to be a primary resource in education. Policy decisions, they say, should focus on optimizing the allocation of instruction time. The model that Bloom (1976) built over the years deals with variation among pupils in the time needed to achieve a specified level of performance. Such rate-of-learning differences are to be taken into account when designing curricula so that pupils are not left behind or left out. Centra and Potter (1980) review school and teacher effects in terms of modeling all the variables that affect school achievement. They note that time usage, while often treated as a between-school difference applied to groups of pupils, is actually more useful as a within-school effect that relates to individual pupil achievement.

A productivity model developed by Walberg (1981) demonstrates that several categories of independent variable need to be examined, in addition to instructional time, in order to investigate fully causal connections to achievement. The model draws on some economic principles to postulate that an increase in one variable can, to a limited extent, overcome the effect of weakness in another. It also shows that the effect of instructional time may best be explained by the curve known as an "ogive." Initially, the achievement resulting for an amount of study will be low, but as more bits of information or skill are brought together, the pace of gains in achievement picks up, and as an advanced level of achievement develops, the time required to add increments to that achievement level becomes ever larger.

Cooley and Leinhardt (1980) tested such a model of instructional dimensions. They included motivation levels, types of instructional events and interactions, the degree of structure and organization of the curriculum, and the opportunity to learn. The opportunity to learn was a measure of total time in instruction and of the overlap between the curriculum and the test. The opportunity variables were the most useful predictors of the achievement mea-

sures. Their correlation with achievement gains made during the year ranged from .11 to .40. Other variables ranged from −.25 to .26. Cooley and Leinhardt draw the following implications:

> We can see from the results that what goes on in a classroom has definite impact on what students learn during the course of an academic year. At least one-fourth of the variation in achievement gain is due to differences in classroom processes. . . . An elaborate innovative curriculum is unlikely to be effective if it requires sustained (as opposed to start-up) managerial time and effort on the part of a teacher, because such time is obtained at the expense of instruction. . . . opportunity is the strongest, most consistent predictor of achievement gains. Within opportunity, the variable that stands out is that which assesses the degree to which the children in the classroom have an opportunity to learn what was in the end-of-year achievement test. (pp. 22–23)

Directions for Future Research. Future research needs to test the models that have been developed so that the relative contribution of quantity and quality of instruction, entry-level skills, social and economic context, classroom environment, motivation and desire, and other variables may be analyzed not only by correlation-based designs, but by experimentally manipulated comparisons. There is definite need for causal connections to be made and to find out the extent to which instructional time can make up for low entry skills or low motivation.

In the foreseeable future, there will be indices attributed to each type of instructional activity (seatwork, film viewing, tutoring, group discussion, and the like). The indices will permit the estimation of the instructional impact that the activity has on achievement per unit of time. These indices will be adjusted for different age-groups or for pupils of particular entry characteristics. Sequences of such activities will have a code that indicates how well the particular sequence distributes the work required to learn. Farther ahead in the future, curricula made up of these sequenced and indexed activities will be built by teachers, school systems, and curriculum writers. These curricula will have known effects on achievement, and achievement areas themselves will eventually be similarly indexed as to the time and effort required to bring a group up to selected proficiency. At that point, schools will pick and choose what they have time and expertise to teach on the basis of projected outcomes and inputs.

Theories about the Time-Learning Relation. The first section of this article and the cited research and reviews make clear that the evidence for the positive relation of time and learning is voluminous and consistent. Aristotle made the point that experience teaches. The strength of the apparent relation, of course, depends on the subject matter, knowledge levels of the learner, design and measurements employed in the research, and other factors. Because of such consistent, lawlike relations, educational researchers see less need for more evidence, yet more need to deepen the relevance of research for educational policy and practice by developing theoretical and prescriptive models that take account of time, learning, and related variables. Student motivation and quality of instruction, for example, surely determine, in part, the efficiency of the use of time allocated for instruction and learning.

Although the mainstream of educational and psychological research on learning, both in laboratory and natural settings, has usually employed only a few variables, development in the microeconomics of productivity, advanced statistical method, and increased need to draw policy implications from inquiry are encouraging researchers to develop more explicit and comprehensive theoretical models that can be evaluated in practice as well as tested in large-scale empirical probes. Such models have the further advantage of calling attention to the pertinent empirical facts. As models, they should show the values of student, teacher, and parental time; the effect of forgoing opportunities in one area of learning for the sake of other achievement; and the fact of increasing or decreasing returns to time invested under the constraints of other factors. New research can also focus on the trade-offs in such choices as being a jack-of-all-trades or master of one.

Learning as a function of time. Two views of instructional time can be posited: "acceleration" and "enrichment" (Walberg, 1971, 1975). In both conceptions, learning is thought to be a function of ability and time, other things being equal. Enrichment, which is far more often used in conventional classrooms, holds time the same for all students, and the normal distribution of achievement scores is a function of the normal curve of initial ability. Acceleration, now often termed "mastery," chooses a fixed criterion level of achievement, which students are given varying time to achieve. Enrichment programs often assume that an achievement test samples the universe of content items that might be asked, and they often compare the scores of students with one another. Acceleration programs often assume that the test comprises the universe of content and equate student mastery of that universe by taking percentages correct on tests.

Both conceptions may be represented in the regression formula

$$\text{Learning} = a + b\,(\text{ability}) + c\,(\text{time}) + \text{error},$$

where a is a constant and b and c are regression weights that estimate the amount of increased learning linearly associated with a one-unit increment, respectively, in ability or time. This conventional formula used in research on time suggests that for a given criterion level of achievement or "mastery" in acceleration models of school learning, moderate-aptitude students require relatively moderate amounts of time; brighter students require correspondingly less; and duller students require correspondingly more. Extrapolating such linear reasoning to extremes, however, produces the absurd conclusions that geniuses learn instantaneously and that the feeble-minded require just a little more time than the subnormal. Walberg (1981) argues that aptitude and time multiplicatively substitute or compensate for one another, other things

being equal, at diminishing rates of marginal returns; ever larger amounts of time, approaching a poorly measured asymptote at infinity, are required to substitute for equal decrements of aptitude and vice versa. Thus, to attain the highest performance levels requires at least a small amount of time for a genius and an immense, possibly prohibitive, amount for the dull. Such relations can be tested by taking logarithms of the variables in the above equation.

Such log-log regressions are known as "Cobb-Douglas functions" in microeconomics, and Walberg (1981) argues that their properties of diminishing marginal returns and substitutability of production factors may be useful in studies of learning, especially when variables are measured over their full latent range. A useful property of such Cobb-Douglas regressions is the uniform and ready interpretability, because the metric raw regression weight is the estimated percentage increase in achievement associated with a 1 percent increase in time (or any other independent variable). Such interpretability may be important enough in its own right, even if the log transformation does not always make for better-fitting regressions. Actually, however, studies of physical training, computer-assisted instruction, language acquisition, and general school learning that have compared linear and logged equations instead of assuming linearity show the superior fit of the Cobb-Douglas form (Fredrick & Walberg, 1980).

Arthur (1977), for example, shows from swim-training data that at "1,000 yards a day one reaches 75% of the maximum training effort, and at 2,000 yards, 85%. In order to reach 95% of maximum, one needs to go 10,000 yards a day in training, and to get 99% to 100% one would need to go 16,000 yards a day," which would take as long as eight hours (p. 2). The variance accounted for by a logarithmic regression is .96, in contrast to .87 for the linear equation (Walberg, 1981). Although such things as chess, ballet, musical, scientific, and writing performance cannot be measured so precisely, they appear to show diminishing returns relative to time: good or even excellent performance by the usual standards may only require a half-hour to an hour a day of concentrated effort, but national rankings or one's best performance may require, among other things, three to ten hours of instruction and practice daily (pushing past some point, of course, may produce not only diminishing but negative returns).

Such immense amounts of time for truly outstanding performance, of course, require the sacrifice of large blocks of time, energy, and other resources that might have been spent on other worthy activities and goals. It may be difficult to see why such doubling and redoubling of effort should occur when the performance gains are minuscule, but it should be recalled that the value of first or second place in national or world rankings is great in competitive societies, even though the performance levels may vary only slightly in the upper range. The top twenty times for the one-mile run, for example, lie within a few seconds of one another.

Even if diminishing returns are pervasive in many

spheres of human activity and in nature, it should not be inferred that the principle always applies or can always be detected. It appears, on the contrary, that initial practice and learning may exhibit slow starting but gradually increasing returns relative to time. Novices in second language learning and sports, for example, often find that gains become easier and larger after initial hurdles are overcome and the base of experience enlarges. When other factors, such as instruction and environmental constraints, remain fixed, the gains can eventually be expected to stabilize and finally diminish as the limits of natural ability, environment, or measurement are approached. For beginners, the increase in distance run in a fixed time period or the number of words acquired in a foreign vocabulary can ordinarily be expected under a constant daily amount of practice, first, to increase; then, to stabilize; and finally, to diminish as the level of peak performance is approached. (Because of the accidents of mood, health, and circumstances, of course, actual learning curves exhibit zigs and zags rather than smooth, idealized curvature.) The limitations of the defined task or subject matter or the measurement of achievement may, in fact, set the levels where diminishing or zero returns take place. Memorization of the 144 multiplication facts through 12 times 12, for example, is likely to show acceleration when regularities such as the commutative law are recognized, but beyond, perhaps, the 135 easiest, facts of addition are likely to be memorized more slowly, and further memory progress after 144 on this universe of content is nearly impossible (unless perhaps speed of response, confidence, or other outcomes are credited).

Similarly, constraining a test to easy items, such as the multiplication facts through 6 times 6 for a given group, may result in 80 percent of the students getting at least 80 percent of items correct, but the latent achievement of some students may extend far beyond the arbitrary, low ceiling that the test is able to reveal. The magnitudes or ratios of performance of highest and lowest members of unselected (and particularly of uninstructed) groups may range beyond 10:1, as in the naming of national capitals, distances covered in sports, or vocabulary in foreign languages. The limited ratios of standardized test performance, typically, may reveal the manifest general attainment of standard mastery levels by conventional instruction or the limitations of the measurements, rather than the range of real or possible performance. Research progress in defining and measuring more comprehensively the vast range and variety of human activity and learning is likely to contribute much to the understanding and improvement of educational productivity. Computer-assisted adaptive testing is now capable, in principle, of overcoming some of the obstacles of conventional standardized tests.

Psychological theories of educational productivity. From extensive synthesis of thousands of empirical studies of school and college learning, Walberg and Uguroglu (1980) and colleagues (Walberg, Schiller, & Heartel, 1979)

assembled a great deal of evidence on the positive relations of learning not only to time (Fredrick & Walberg, 1980) but also to several other factors: student motivation and ability; quality of instruction; class, home, and peer-group social-psychological environments; and exposure to mass media such as television. The evidence is persuasive that all eight "productivity factors" should be taken into account. Each has consistent correlations and likely causal connections with learning. The causal directions among the factors, however, are by no means completely settled (Walberg & Uguroglu, 1980), since correlational studies leave open rival hypotheses. Students who have learned a great deal or who are encouraged by superior instruction or who are motivated by stimulating home environments, for example, may spend more time learning.

Correlational studies employing causal modeling, experiments that randomly assign students to educative conditions, and disciplined case studies in the remainder of this century should help sort out the causal directions more confidently for policy makers. Even now, however, it seems reasonable to conclude that the eight factors generally exert a positive influence on learning and can substitute for one another to some extent in the Cobb-Douglas equation. The production-function framework of eight factors serves to organize the past empirical research and also to call attention to factors not explicitly included in major instructional theories. The theories of Carroll (1963), Bloom (1976), and Harnishfeger and Wiley (1976), for example, may be interpreted as acceleration models within the production-function framework.

In Carroll's formulation,

$$\text{Degree of learning} = f\left(\frac{\text{Time actually spent}}{\text{Time needed}}\right),$$

the "numerator of this fraction will be equal to the smallest of the following three qualities: (1) opportunity—the time allowed for learning, (2) perseverance—the amount of time the learner is willing to engage actively in learning, and (3) ability—the amount of time needed to learn, increased by whatever amount necessary in view of the poor quality of instruction and lack of ability to understand less than optimal instruction. This last quality (time needed to learn after adjustment for quality of instruction and ability to understand instruction) is also the denominator of the fraction" (Carroll, 1963, p. 730). Recast in the production function, (1) opportunity becomes quantity of instruction, that is, time allowed including self-instructional time; (2) perseverance becomes motivation (an observer rating the percentage of engaged time being a reasonable proxy to measures of perseverance); (3) time needed becomes unadjusted ability; and (4) quality of instruction explicitly enters the equation rather than adjusting ability. Thus, rather than redefining all the independent variables in terms of time, the production function permits the assessment of the direct effect of each measured factor (including, because of their known connections with achievement, student age, the home environment, and the social environment of the class) in an explicit equation form.

Bloom's adaptation (1976) of the Carroll model may be written

$$\begin{pmatrix} \text{Level and type} \\ \text{of achievement} \\ \text{Affective outcomes} \\ \text{Rate of learning} \end{pmatrix} = f \begin{pmatrix} \text{Quality of instruction} \\ \text{Cognitive entry behaviors} \\ \text{Affective entry behaviors} \end{pmatrix}.$$

In the production function, affective outcomes would be considered a particular type of achievement, possibly involved in a feedback loop with motivation for subsequent achievement. Instead of measuring time to reach a criterion or gain in achievement divided by time to obtain a rate, time would directly enter the equation as an independent variable, quantity of instruction. The other variables have obvious correspondences in the production function. Thus, the sets of redefined variables in the Carroll and Bloom models may be hypothesized to show substitutability and diminishing returns of the function.

The usual problems of operational definition, measurement error, and lack of factor variation may account for the occasional lack of significant fit of learning to time, but the production function suggests that misspecification may also be a problem. Bringing more of the production factors into the equation, finding data in which time varies over a greater range, and taking logarithms may help considerably. More specifically, the form of the production function suggests nonlinear relations among time and the other factors that seem more conceptually defensible than the linear assumptions that pervade the research.

The Harnischfeger and Wiley model (1977) distinguishes different types of classroom events and hence argues for specificity in measuring time that is instructionally used as opposed to that which fulfills other purposes. In the model, the teacher's on-task time and the students' on-task time both enter the production function. Out-of-class time is also included in the model, a need demonstrated by the entry of hours of homework as a predictor of achievement in several studies reviewed here. As Kifer (1975) argues, "Addition of time-related variables in the home should increase the explanatory power of 'time' models and provide a means to explore further the effects of academic achievement on the personality characteristics of the learner" (p. 208). Accordingly, Harnischfeger and Wiley (1977) rightly call not only for more specific measures of classroom time components but also of study time outside of school.

Limitations of Achievement Tests. Despite the powerful ways that microeconomic production functions serve to consolidate research and policy, especially with respect to time allocation, they also serve to caution attempts to maximize only one output. Despite the numerous ability and achievement tests available, they tend to measure only one major factor, verbal-educational accomplishment—surely an important aspect of human quality, but by no means the only one. Performance on such tests predicts subsequent grades and performance on similar tests. For samples of adults who have attained the same amount of education, however, neither test scores nor grades predict indicators of success in later life, such as income, participation in community activities, self-concept, supervisor-related and peer-related effectiveness, and number of prizes, written works, patents, and other accomplishments. Rather, engagement in independent, self-sustained ventures and extracurricular activities during the high school and college years forecasts adult success (Walberg, 1981).

How much effort should be given to the production of test achievement? The "law of increasing relative costs" in economics states that to produce equal additional amounts of one good, other things being equal, larger and larger amounts of other goods must be sacrificed (Samuelson, 1980, p. 26). Thus, in setting achievement goals on the usual tests and the earliest or most effective, cost-efficient, and rapid means of attaining them, educators, parents, and students should consider the extent to which other goals, opportunities, and experiences, valuable for the present or future, must be sacrificed. The causal mechanisms and the costs and benefits of other goals and their trade-offs with test achievement cannot always be accurately estimated, but research in the last decade, as well as the prospects for the next decade, seem likely to continue advancing not only the scientific understanding of human learning, but also educational policies and practices.

Conclusions.   Learning is produced in schools in a context of many variables. One variable operating is time—time spent in homework, on a lesson, during a school year, or in a lifetime of schooling. The other variables may have their effects, other things being equal, to the extent that they are given time to work.

Time devoted to school learning appears to be a modest predictor of achievement. For some types of new material, when other variables are experimentally or statistically controlled, time may be the best predictor. When material is familiar, often taught, or imprecisely measured, then time may appear a weak and insignificant predictor. To the extent that additional time is used to make up partially for ineffective instruction or inability, it may even be negatively correlated with achievement. It is apparent that, in schools, time can be easily lost, and time use in one classroom can radically differ from that in another, even though the same content is ostensibly being taught.

A recent survey of high school administrators, asked to rank discipline problems, indicated that the top three problems—skipping class, truancy, and lateness—involved the loss of instructional time (Duke, 1978). The survey showed the practical importance of time in the minds of school administrators. Quantity of instruction should be a candidate for inclusion in many educational research studies, either as a potentially manipulable policy variable under the partial and joint control of educators, parents, and students, or as a control variable to estimate more precisely the effects of other educational variables on student achievement.

Recent work on productivity models has served to organize the large body of research on school and classroom variables, which include instructional time. These models will also help guide future research as it focuses on sorting out the causes and effects that operate among the many variables existent in the teaching situation.

Herbert J. Walberg
Wayne C. Fredrick

See also Achievement Testing; Attendance Policy; Comparative School Achievement; Instruction Processes; Learning.

REFERENCES

Arthur, R. J. Masters' swimming program stimulates physical fitness. *Swim-Master*, 1977, *6*, 1–2.

Berliner, D. C. Tempus educare. In P. L. Peterson & H. J. Walberg (Eds.), *Research on Teaching: Concepts, Findings, and Implications*. Berkeley, Calif.: McCutchan, 1979.

Bloom, B. S. *Human Characteristics and School Learning*. New York: McGraw-Hill, 1976.

Carroll, J. B. A model of school learning. *Teachers College Record*, 1963, *64*, 723–733.

Centra, J. S., & Potter, D. A. School and teacher effects: An interrelational model. *Review of Educational Research*, 1980, *50*, 273–291.

Cooley, W. W., & Leinhardt, G. The instructional dimensions study. *Educational Evaluation and Policy Analysis*, 1980, *2*, 7–25.

Duke, D. L. How administrators view the crisis in school discipline. *Phi Delta Kappan*, 1978, *59*, 325–330.

Evertson, C. M.; Anderson, C. W.; Anderson, L. M.; & Brophy, J. E. Relationships between classroom behaviors and student outcomes in junior high mathematics and English classes. *American Educational Research Journal*, 1980, *17*, 43–60.

Fredrick, W. C. The use of classroom time in high schools above or below the median reading score. *Urban Education*, 1977, *11*, 459–464.

Fredrick, W. C., & Walberg, H. J. Learning as a function of time. *Journal of Educational Research*, 1980, *73*, 183–194.

Harnischfeger, A. Curricular control and learning time: District policy, teacher strategy, and pupil choice. *Educational Evaluation and Policy Analysis*, 1980, *2*, 19–30.

Harnischfeger, A., & Wiley, D. E. The teaching-learning process in elementary schools: A synoptic view. *Curriculum Inquiry*, 1976, *6*, 5–43.

Harnischfeger, A., & Wiley, D. E. Conceptual issues in models of school learning. *Studies of Educative Processes* (Report No. 10). Chicago: Cemrel, Inc., 1977.

Kifer, E. Relationships between academic achievement and personality characteristics: A quasi-longitudinal study. *American Educational Research Journal*, 1975, *12*, 191–210.

Leinhardt, G. Modeling and measuring educational treatment in evaluation. *Review of Educational Research*, 1980, *50*, 393–420.

Rutter, M.; Maughan, B.; Mortimore, P.; Ouston, J.; & Smith, A. *Fifteen Thousand Hours*. Cambridge, Mass.: Harvard University Press, 1979.

Samuelson, P. *Economics*. New York: McGraw-Hill, 1980.

Stallings, J. Allocated academic learning time revisited, or beyond time-on-task. *Educational Researcher*, 1980, *9*, 11–16.

Walberg, H. J. Models for optimizing and individualizing school learning. *Interchange*, 1971, *2*, 15–27.

Walberg, H. J. Psychological theories of educational individualization. In H. Talmadge (Ed.), *Systems of Individualized Education*. Berkeley, Calif.: McCutchan, 1975.

Walberg, H. J. Psychological theory of educational productivity. In F. H. Farley & N. Gordon (Eds.), *Psychology and Education: The State of the Union*. Chicago: National Society for the Study of Education, 1981.

Walberg, H. J.; Schiller, D.; & Heartel, G. D. The quiet revolution in educational research. *Phi Delta Kappan*, 1979, *61*, 179–183.

Walberg, H. J., & Uguroglu, M. Motivation and educational productivity: Theories, results and implications. In J. Fyans, Jr. (Ed.), *Achievement Motivation: Theory and Research*. New York: Plenum, 1980.

INTELLIGENCE

Intelligence has been a heavily researched psychological construct during the present century. Most of the research on intelligence has been devoted to the construction and testing of "explicit" theories of intelligence, whereas a less sizable research effort has been devoted to the discovery of "implicit" theories of intelligence. Explicit theories are constructed by "experts" (i.e., psychologists or other scientists) and are based or at least tested on data that are the result of people performing tasks presumed to measure intelligent behavior. The present paper is concerned, for the most part, with progress in the field of research on explicit theories of intelligence.

Implicit Theories. Implicit theories, however, are of interest as well. These are theories that reside in the minds of the people (psychologists or laypersons) who construct them. Since these theories already exist, it is the psychologist's goal to discover rather than create them. The data for research on implicit theories are people's communications regarding their notions as to the nature of intelligence.

One important issue in research on implicit theories concerns deciding which group of people should be studied. The group studied typically has been "experts" on intelligence. The most well-known example is a symposium that appeared in the *Journal of Educational Psychology* in 1921. Fourteen experts replied to the question of what they "conceive 'intelligence' to be, and by what means it can best be measured by group tests" ("Intelligence and Its Measurement," 1921, p. 123). Among the definitions given were: (1) the power of good responses from the point of view of truth or fact (E. L. Thorndike); (2) the ability to carry on abstract thinking (L. M. Terman); (3) having learned or ability to learn to adjust oneself to the environment (S. S. Colvin); (4) ability to adapt oneself adequately to relatively new situations in life (R. Pintner); (5) the capacity for knowledge and knowledge possessed (V. A. C. Henmon); (6) a biological mechanism by which the effects of a complexity of stimuli are brought together and given a somewhat unified effect in behavior (J. Peterson); (7) the capacity to inhibit an instinctive adjustment, the capacity to redefine the inhibited instinctive adjustment in the light of imaginally experienced trial and error, and the volitional capacity to realize the modified instinctive adjustment as overt behavior to the advantage of the individual as a social animal (L. L. Thurstone); (8) the capacity to acquire capacity (H. Woodrow); (9) the capacity to learn or to profit by experience (W. F. Dearborn).

Although it seems as if there were nearly as many definitions as experts, a broad view indicates two themes running through these definitions: the capacity to learn from experience and adaptation to one's environment. More recently, Ferguson (1954) has viewed intelligence primarily in terms of the ability to transfer training, and Piaget (1972) has defined intelligence largely in terms of one's adaptation to the environment.

A more sophisticated approach to studying implicit theories has been suggested by Neisser (1979). In his view, intelligence is organized around an ideal case, or "prototype." One's intelligence is defined by the degree of resemblance to this prototype. Whereas a consensually validated concept of intelligence would emerge if there were a single prototype, it appears that there exist multiple prototypes (Sternberg et al., 1981). The definitional approach is a useful way to discover what people mean by "intelligence," but not to discover what "intelligence" means. Neisser (1979) has studied informally Cornell undergraduates' conceptions of intelligence; Cantor (1973) and Bruner, Shapiro, and Tagiuri (1958) have studied other groups of adults more formally. Siegler and Richards (in press) studied adults' conceptions of children's intelligence, whereas Yussen and Kane (in press) studied children's conceptions of their own intelligence.

Explicit Theories. Explicit theories of human intelligence have differed primarily in terms of the basic unit of analysis hypothesized to account for individual differences in intelligent behavior. Not only have different basic units of ability been proposed, but there have been different conceptions of how these basic units are represented in the mind and how they are organized with respect to one another. We can conveniently organize a review of research on intelligence according to the alternative basic units that have been proposed and then differentiate within these categories in terms of different theories proposed to explain how each of these units accounts for intelligent behavior.

The three basic units to be discussed are the stimulus-response (S-R) bond, the factor, and the elementary information process (or component). These units derive from the three major kinds of theories of intelligence: learning theories, factor theories, and cognitive (or information-processing) theories. Although these are not meant to be mutually exclusive categories, they do serve to discriminate classes of theories in terms of the paradigms generating the theories.

Stimulus-response theories. Since stimulus-response (S-R) theorizing has had limited influence upon theory and research in intelligence, we will treat it briefly. The role of the S-R bond concept in theorizing about intelligence can be traced back to Thorndike (1911; Thorndike et al., 1928), who, like subsequent S-R theorists, viewed intelligence primarily in terms of the ability to learn. In early S-R theorizing, intelligence was understood in terms of the buildup of simple S-R bonds. A more sophisticated and variegated view has been proposed by Gagné (1970), who suggested that there are eight kinds of learning, which differ among themselves in both the quantity and quality of S-R bonds involved. From simplest to most complex, these are signal learning (Pavlovian conditioning), stimulus-response learning (operant conditioning), chaining (complex operant conditioning), verbal association, discrimination learning, concept learning, rule learning, and problem solving.

Factor theories. In most traditional investigations of intelligence, the basic unit of analysis has been the factor. The paradigm in which this unit has been defined and used is referred to as the "differential," "psychometric," of "factorial" paradigm. Factors are obtained by "factor analyzing" a matrix of intercorrelations (or covariances) between scores on tests of mental abilities. Factor analysis tends to group into single factors observable sources of individual difference variation that are highly correlated with each other, and to group into different factors observable sources of variation that are only modestly correlated or not at all correlated with each other. These new groupings are each proposed to represent unitary, latent sources of individual differences at some level of analysis. Theorists generally agree that other levels of analysis, in which factors would either be further subdivided or further combined, would be possible as well.

The earliest factorial theory of the nature of intelligence was formulated by the inventor of factor analysis, Charles Spearman. Spearman's analysis (1927) of relations among the kinds of mental tests he and other psychologists had been administering led him to propose a "two-factor" theory of intelligence. According to this theory, intelligence comprises two kinds of factors, a general factor and specific factors. General ability, or *g*, as measured by the general factor, is required for performance on mental tests of all kinds. Each specific ability, as measured by each specific factor, is required for performance on just one kind of mental test. Thus, there are as many specific factors as there are tests, but only a single general factor. Spearman suggested that the ability underlying the general factor could best be understood as a kind of "mental energy."

Godfrey Thomson's reassessment (1939) of Spearman's individual differences data led him to accept Spearman's hypothesis of a general factor running through the range of mental ability tests; it led him to reject Spearman's interpretation of this factor, however. Thomson disputed Spearman's claim that the general factor represented a single underlying source of individual differences. Instead, he proposed that the appearance of a general factor was due to the workings of a multitude of mental "bonds," including reflexes, learned associations between stimuli, and the like. Performance of any particular task activates large numbers of these bonds. Some bonds will be required for the performance of virtually any task requiring mental effort, and these bonds in combination will give rise to the appearance of a general factor.

Thurstone (1938), like Thomson (1939), accepted Spearman's hypothesis of a general factor. But he disputed the importance of this factor. He argued that it is a "second-order" factor or phenomenon, one which arises only because the primary or "first-order" factors are related to each other. What are these primary factors, or as Thurstone called them, "primary mental abilities"? Thurstone suggested that they include verbal comprehension (measured by tests such as knowledge of vocabulary), word fluency (measured by tests requiring rapid word production, for example, a listing of as many words as a person can think of that have *c* as their third letter), number (measured by tests of arithmetic reasoning and computation), spatial visualization (measured by tests requiring mental manipulation of geometric forms), perceptual speed (measured by tests requiring rapid visual scanning, for example, proofreading), memory (measured by tests of recall and recognition of previously presented information), and reasoning (measured by tests such as number series, which require people to say which of several numbers should come next in a given series of numbers).

Guilford (1967) has parted company from the majority of factorial theorists by refusing to acknowledge the existence of any general factor at all in human intelligence. Instead, Guilford has proposed that intelligence comprises 120 elementary abilities, each of which involves the action of some operation upon some content to produce some product.

Probably the most widely accepted factorial description of intelligence is a hierarchical one. The concept of a hierarchical theory can be traced back at least to Burt (1940), and more sophisticated hierarchical factor theories have been proposed by Jensen (1970), who reviews a variety of hierarchical theories, and by Vernon (1971). In Jensen's theory, intelligence is viewed as comprising two levels: associative learning ability (called Level I); and conceptual learning and problem solving (called Level II and corresponding to Spearman's *g*). Vernon has proposed that intelligence can be described as comprising abilities at varying levels of generality. At the highest or most general level is a general factor, encompassing all tasks. This is followed in turn by (1) major group factors, including a verbal-educational factor and a practical-mechanical factor; (2) minor group factors; and (3) specific factors. Humphreys (1962) has proposed a sophisticated hierarchical theory that combines aspects of the Burt-Vernon tradition of hierarchical factor analysis with aspects of Guttman's facet analysis (1954), in which intelligence is subdivided in terms of logical dimensions. Cattell (1971) and Horn (1968) have pro-

posed a theory according to which the general factor noted by Spearman (1927) is alleged to comprise two subfactors: crystallized ability, measured by tests such as vocabulary and general information; and fluid ability, measured by tests such as abstract analogies and abstract series completions. The direction of such hierarchical conceptualizations of intelligence is best shown in the recent work of Hakstian and Cattell (1974, 1978). They have tested Cattell's triadic theory of ability structure (1971) and have found evidence for three strata of abilities, reflected in different levels of factor intercorrelations. Currently, they argue for the higher-stratum capacities of visualization capacity, general perceptual speed, memory, and general retrieval capacity in addition to crystallized and fluid intelligence. These are derived from approximately twenty primary abilities (agencies). Three third-stratum factors have emerged in support of triadic theory: (1) original fluid intelligence; (2) the capacity to concentrate; and (3) school culture, which represents the effects of acculturation, especially formal schooling.

Cognitive Approaches. "Cognitive" theories of mental processing have shown increasing influence in research on intelligence. Although there is no single universally accepted cognitive theory of intelligence, a common element in most of these theories is a unit of analysis that can be described as an elementary information process, or component. This is a unit or process that operates upon internal representations of objects or symbols (Newell & Simon, 1972; Sternberg, 1977, 1980). The component may translate a sensory input into a conceptual representation, transform one conceptual representation into another, or translate a conceptual representation into a motor output. What is considered elementary enough to be labeled a component depends upon the desired level of theorizing.

A number of theories have been proposed during the past decade that might be labeled, at least loosely, as componential. We will organize our review of these componential or, at least, cognitive approaches to individual differences and intelligence into four major categories of theory and research: (1) cognitive correlates; (2) cognitive components; (3) cognitive training; and (4) cognitive contents.

Cognitive correlates. A first major approach has been labeled the "cognitive correlates" approach. Research conducted under this very general rubric has been concerned with specification of the information-processing abilities that are able to discriminate subjects of high and low aptitude, generally in the domain of verbal intelligence. The typical methodology involves separating groups of subjects into high and low aptitude on the basis of a standard psychometric ability test and then administering a series of standard information-processing tasks. Response latency to simple stimuli is typically measured as the dependent variable. Hunt (1976, 1978; Hunt, Frost, & Lunneborg, 1973; Hunt & Lansman, 1975; Hunt, Lunneborg, & Lewis, 1975) has proposed that individual differences in the efficacy of execution of information-processing components such as those found in simple tasks studied in the cognitive psychologist's laboratory are a significant source of individual differences in higher-order verbal ability as measured by standard tests of intelligence. For the most part, a general model of memory has depicted the transfer of information from sensory memory to short-term, intermediate-term, and long-term storage as under executive control (see Atkinson & Shiffrin, 1968). This model has motivated the search for correlations between information processing measures and psychometric abilities. The results of these studies include the findings that high verbal scorers (1) are faster when access to long-term memory is required; (2) are better in a serial recall task; and (3) have faster access to letter name codes as shown in the smaller difference between name matches and physical identity matches in the Posner and Mitchell (1967) letter-matching paradigm. This last difference is often reflected in a correlation of about −.30 between a score on a verbal college entrance test and the difference between name match (*Aa* match in name but not physical appearance) and physical match (*AA* match in physical appearance and name) latencies. However, there are several methodological problems with these findings, and replication studies by other investigators have revealed additional problems that need to be ironed out. Chiang and Atkinson (1976) were able to replicate this finding of a relationship between short-term processing speed and verbal aptitude only when their data were analyzed separately by sex. Males with higher processing rates, but females with lower processing rates, were high verbal. Keating and Bobbitt (1978) demonstrated that these relationships may be a function of developmental level, and others have argued that task-specific factors may delimit the proposed relationship (Bisanz & Resnick, 1978; Hogaboam & Pellegrino, 1978). It is conceivable that differences in processing of verbal versus nonverbal material may be related to verbal and nonverbal intellectual factors. Cognitive strategies may also mediate the relationship. Hunt has demonstrated (see Hunt, 1978; Hunt, Lunneborg, & Lewis, 1975; MacLeod, Hunt, & Mathews, 1978) that in tasks in which solution strategies may be either verbal or visuo-spatial, such as the Clark and Chase (1972) sentence-picture verification task, the effect of task complexity on processing speed may be a function of the type of strategy employed. Pellegrino and Glaser (1979) use this work as a prime example of why the "cognitive correlates" approach is problematic. Whereas most "cognitive correlates" research to date has attempted to differentiate high and low verbal subjects on the dimension of processing speed, many cognitive dimensions will likely prove relevant to variation in aptitude. Therefore, we will no doubt be accumulating a wealth of data on process differences that are correlated with aptitude differences, and we will have to understand these process differences in terms of the measures used initially to identify the aptitude groups (Pellegrino & Glaser, 1979). A more direct analysis of psychometric task components would perhaps serve our goals better.

Cognitive components. Such an analysis is characteristic of the "cognitive components" approach. "Cognitive components" researchers attempt to analyze directly the processes involved in intellectual behavior rather than trying to find behavioral correlates of such behavior. Among the cognitive psychologist's tools are computer simulation, protocol analysis, and mathematical modeling. All of these, alone or in combination, have proven useful in identifying the components of simple and complex human information processing in laboratory and psychometric intellectual tasks.

Carroll (1976, 1981) has attempted to analyze existing information processing and psychometric tasks in terms of component processes. In the earlier study, he used the French, Ekstrom, and Price (1963) kit of reference tests for cognitive factors, which includes seventy-four tests and twenty-four factors. Using a model similar to that used by Hunt and his colleagues, Carroll (1976) devised a classification scheme that would help to account for individual differences in task performance in terms of elementary cognitive processes. More recently, Carroll (1981) has completed a meta-analysis of experimental cognitive work in order to refine this classification system. The notion of the Elementary Cognitive Task (ECT) has been developed to classify paradigms and processes in cognitive psychology. Using what he terms a Dual Time Representation (DTR) chart, Carroll logically analyzes both the experimenter and subject operations in published reports of cognitive experiments (e.g., Jensen, 1980; Keating & Bobbitt, 1978) and then simulates the processes in the ECTs with the aid of computer programs. With the ultimate goal of predicting outcomes of cognitive experiments, Carroll has specified eight tentative paradigms and ten types or classes of processes. The paradigms are (1) perceptual apprehension; (2) reaction time and movement; (3) evaluation–decision; (4) stimulus matching–comparison; (5) naming–reading–association; (6) episodic memory readout; (7) analogical reasoning; and (8) algorithmic manipulation. The processes include (1) the monitor, or executive control; (2) attention; (3) apprehension; (4) perceptual integration; (5) encoding; (6) comparison; (7) corepresentation–formation; (8) corepresentation–retrieval; (9) transformation; and (10) response execution.

In addition to delineating these sources of individual differences in cognitive tasks, Carroll (1981) has set the goal of determining the factorial structure of such individual differences and the nature of the relationship between these factors and the traditional psychometrically assessed mental abilities. For example, Carroll reanalyzed Jensen's data (1979, 1980) from thirteen tests of reaction time, movement time, and psychometric ability. Jensen (1979; Jensen & Munro, 1979) has found that simple reaction time and movement time in a choice reaction-time paradigm are moderately correlated with scores on the Raven (1965) Progressive Matrices. Carroll found three uncorrelated factors and no evidence for a Spearman *g* factor. With the exception of the Raven Progressive Matrices score (the Raven is a test of nonverbal, intellectual skill), reaction time, movement time, and psychometric variables loaded on separate factors. There are numerous difficulties with this sort of meta-analytic approach, as Carroll notes. Many of the studies analyzed have small numbers of subjects, and it is risky to infer common underlying processes from loadings on the same factor. Carroll prefers to depend upon loadings on separate factors to conclude tentatively that tests are either measuring different psychological processes or at least are subject to the control of different task and stimulus characteristics. Despite these cautions, Carroll has found, from about twenty-five different correlation matrices, that factors sort themselves roughly according to the types of paradigms and processes in his classification system as well as according to the type of dependent measure—reaction time or accuracy.

Sternberg (1979, 1980) proposes that many kinds of tasks are hierarchically interrelated by means of information-processing components. In his theory, components are described that are perhaps able to account at one level for an interesting portion of what we call "intelligent behavior." Components have three properties in Sternberg's system: duration, difficulty, and probability of execution. The various kinds of components are classified by their function and level of generality.

There are at least six kinds of functions in Sternberg's componential theory of intelligence. Metacomponents, which are higher-order control processes used for problem solving, planning, and decision making, include (1) decision as to what the problem is that needs solution; (2) selection of lower-order components; (3) selection of a strategy for combining lower-order components; (4) selection of a representation for information; (5) decision regarding the tradeoff of speed and accuracy; and (6) solution monitoring. Performance components are actual problem solving processes, and include, among others (1) encoding of the problem's terms; (2) inference, or the detection of one or more relations between two objects; (3) mapping, or relating aspects of previous situations to the present one; (4) application, which is the use of relations inferred between past elements of the situation and decisions made about them in the past to help make current decisions; (5) justification, or the verification of the better or best of available options; and (6) response, which is the communication of the problem solution. Acquisition, retention, and transfer components are skills involved in learning new information, retrieving previously acquired information, and generalizing retained information from one situational context to another.

There are three levels of generality of components: (1) general components are required to perform all tasks of a given type; (2) class components are required to perform a subset of at least two tasks of a given type; and (3) specific components are required for the performance of a single task.

Earlier research by Sternberg and colleagues (see Stern-

berg, 1980, for a review) has concentrated on the identification of performance components, whereas more recent research is concentrating on metacomponents and acquisition, retention, and transfer components.

Cognitive training. The cognitive training approach to understanding mental abilities can be used in conjunction with either of the two previous approaches as well as with some other approach. The crux of the approach is described by Campione, Brown, and Ferrara (in press). Detailed cognitive task analysis is used to construct programs (instructional or computer) that can be used to teach a human subject or computer to perform better on that task. Failure of the program to result in successful task performance is used to analyze further the theory's weaknesses. Belmont and Butterfield (1977), Borkowski and Wanschura (1974), and Campione and Brown (1978) have used the training approach in the domains of learning and memory; Feuerstein (1979a), Holzman, Glaser, and Pellegrino (1976), and Linn (1973) have used it in the domains of reasoning and problem solving. An interesting and theoretically important outcome of many of these studies is that successful training, in terms of durability and generalizability, is contingent upon training of components at the executive level (e.g., Sternberg's metacomponents) and the lower-order process level (e.g., performance components) (e.g., Belmont, Butterfield, & Ferretti, in press; Feuerstein, 1979a, 1979b).

At a practical level, the cognitive-training approach can be helpful in telling us what aspects of cognitive functioning are and are not trainable with reasonable amounts of effort, and in actually effecting improvement in individuals' cognitive functioning. Successful training may suggest processes or strategies that subjects are capable of performing although it may not suggest that subjects will or are likely to use those strategies spontaneously. Failure to train, on the other hand, could mean several different things: (1) the component may not be trainable because it is not in the realm of natural cognitive or intellectual functioning; (2) the component to be trained was not accessible to conscious strategies (e.g., the component has been automatized and is difficult to alter); (3) the wrong methods were used to train a component that is an aspect of intelligence and is trainable; or (4) the component is an aspect of intelligence and is trainable, but not in the population being investigated.

Cognitive contents. A fourth approach has not as yet been applied directly to the study of intellectual abilities, but it appears to be promising for such a purpose. The "cognitive contents" approach seeks to compare the performances of experts and novices in complex tasks, such as the solution of physics problems (Chi, Feltovich, & Glaser, 1981; Larkin et al., 1980); the selection of moves and strategies in chess and other games (Chase & Simon, 1972; deGroot, 1966; Reitman, 1976; and the acquisition of domain-related information by groups of people at different levels of expertise (Chiesi, Spilich, & Voss, 1979;

Spilich et al., 1979). Research on expert-novice differences in a variety of task domains suggests that the way information is stored in and retrieved from long-term memory can account in large part for substantial differences in performance between experts and novices. This view would suggest that a possible locus of differences between more and less mentally able people is in their abilities to organize information in long-term memory in a way that makes it readily accessible for a variety of purposes (see Egan & Greeno, 1973). Presumably, information stored in such a flexible way is maximally available for transfer from old to new problem situations.

Comparison of cognitive approaches. Whereas we have outlined four different types of cognitive approaches to research on intelligence, it is important to note that these approaches are compatible. In particular, the distinction between the "cognitive correlates" and "cognitive components" approaches is weak. Both have the goal of understanding the relationships between psychometrically assessed mental abilities and theoretically derived conceptions of cognitive processing. Whereas the emphasis in the "correlates" approach is on discovering which elements of information processing are related to measures of intelligence, the emphasis in the "components" approach is on directly analyzing intelligent behavior, as assessed by standard tests, in terms of information-processing components. In the past, the "correlates" investigators have relied on relatively simple information-processing tasks and the "components" researchers on more complex problem solving tasks. Neither emphasis upon simple nor complex tasks is sufficient; future progress in this area will likely result from intensive analysis of tasks designed to tap the complete constellations of human information-processing skills. These two approaches may be combined in a productive manner, as has already been demonstrated in a related research domain by Frederiksen (1980), who has used analysis of covariance structures to study reading skills. This approach allows direct tests of theoretical relationships between information-processing components and psychometric abilities when these relationships have been derived via logical or empirical analysis of cognitive processing.

Interrelationships among theories. The alternative units discussed above are not mutually exclusive; on the contrary, they are complementary. Stimulus-response theorizing concentrates upon the external or environmental contingencies that lead to various kinds of responses, whereas factorial and componential theorizing concentrate upon the internal effects of these contingencies. Factorial models tend to be structural ones, although they often contain clear implications for understanding information processing; componential models tend to be process ones, although they often contain clear implications for understanding how information is structured. Sternberg (1980), along with Carroll (1976) and others, proposes that factors can be understood in terms of components.

But components should not be viewed as superseding factors, since for at least some educational purposes (such as predicting performance), factors are probably still the preferred unit of analysis. For other educational purposes (such as training performance), components are probably the preferred unit of analysis (Sternberg, 1981b).

The early differential psychologists, such as Galton, Binet, Spearman, and Thurstone, were also early cognitive psychologists. Although we have suggested that the factorial and cognitive approaches to the study of intelligence are different in some important ways, there is nothing in either kind of theory that prohibits merging of perspectives. The work of Hunt, Carroll, Sternberg, and Frederiksen suggests fruitful lines of research in this regard. Such integration of theories and methodologies has been called for repeatedly since Cronbach's paper (1957) on the two disciplines of scientific psychology, and the message was clear in many of the papers in a recent volume on intelligence (Resnick, 1976). Certain of the theories noted earlier help place interrelations among alternative units of analysis into sharper perspective. Spearman's general factor (1927), for example, has often been understood in terms of individual differences in people's abilities to implement Spearman's three principles of cognition (1923)—apprehension of experience (encoding stimuli), education of relations (inferring rules), and education of correlates (applying rules). Guilford's theory (1967) has clear process implications, in that one of the three facets in Guilford's structure-of-intellect cube isolates processes as factors. And in Jensen's theory (1970), Level I intelligence can be understood in terms of the relatively simple kinds of associative learning studied by early S-R theorists, whereas Level II intelligence can be understood in terms of the more complex kinds of conceptual learning studied only by later S-R theorists (such as Gagné, 1970). In sum, then, the various units are compatible, not contradictory. They highlight different aspects of the global and ill-defined concept of intelligence.

Directions for Future Research. There has been a growing concern in research on intellectual functioning for a reexamination of definitions of intelligent behavior. Investigators have asked, for example, whether we have focused too much on laboratory-type tasks that may not be reflective of everyday behavior and on definitions of intelligent behavior that may be quite different from one culture to another. This last suggestion has received some support (Berry, 1974; Cole et al., 1971; Cole & Scribner, 1974; Goodnow, 1976; Wober, 1974; see also Neisser, 1976, 1979). Sternberg (1980), however, interpreted the available evidence as providing no support for the notion that the components of human intelligence or the ways in which these components are organized differ across cultures; but the evidence does provide considerable support for the notion that the relative importance of the various components differs across cultures, as does the importance of components as distinguished from other aspects of adaptive functioning. Berry (1980), however, claims there is a need for further exploration of the possibility that intelligence or cognition has different structures in different populations. Only more empirical work will shed light on this debate.

There is some work in progress relevant to research on intelligent behavior in non–laboratory-type tasks. Cole and his colleagues (see Laboratory for Comparative Human Cognition, forthcoming) are beginning to examine the issue of whether one can measure the intelligence of individuals participating in group problem-solving situations. Sternberg (1981a) is currently investigating practical intelligence, and others are studying what might be described as social intelligence (Archer, 1980; Rosenthal et al., 1979).

Whereas we have suggested rather strongly in this review that research on cognitive processes, particularly from the human information processing perspective, has and will continue to be at the forefront of research on intelligence, it is also the case that advances in cognitive theories of intelligence have lagged behind advances in cognitive theory, in general. Perhaps this is an adaptive check against pursuing fads in experimental psychology, but there are at least two general issues in cognitive psychology that have been heavily researched recently and are likely to continue to receive serious attention, particularly from researchers on intelligence. These are the distinctions between automatic and controlled (conscious) information processes and the strategies of allocation of attentional resources in complex information-processing tasks. Both of these issues involve the role of attention in intellectual functioning.

The notion of attentional control in cognition has received a great deal of consideration since the memory work of Atkinson and Shiffrin (1968). We have referred to this notion in several of the cognitive theories of intelligence, and many other investigators in cognitive psychology and developmental psychology have stressed the importance of conscious, strategic control of performance in most cognitive tasks. The concepts of metamemory (Kreutzer, Leonard, & Flavell, 1974), metacognition (Brown, 1978), and metacomponents (Sternberg, 1980) are common terms in the cognitive psychological vocabulary, and their role in theory is in general to account for the coordination of the numerous psychological processes that must be utilized in successful problem solving of all kinds. Emphasis on the conscious strategizing involved in cognitive tasks has, however, overshadowed until recently the role of automatic processes that are not under strategic control but may affect task performance just as strongly. Automatic processing proceeds without the allocation of conscious attention to stimuli or stimulus attributes but can result in a response to a stimulus nevertheless (LaBerge & Samuels, 1974; Logan, 1980, Posner & Snyder, 1975; Schneider & Shiffrin, 1977).

Hunt (1978), in his "cognitive correlates" work on verbal ability and short-term memory efficiency, refers to the information-free mechanistic processes (automatic and controlled) as one of the three sources of individual differences in cognitive processing; the other two sources are knowledge and general strategies, such as rehearsal strategies and metacognitive strategies. Hunt is not alone in conceptualizing automatic processes to result from extensive practice with control processes; therefore, he views control processes to be variable or transient and thus not reliable long-term predictors of performance, and automatic processes to be more stable traits. If controlled strategies are transient predictors of performance and automatic processes are invariant traits, then it may be that neither can account for individual differences in complex task performance and that higher-level executive strategies will provide a better account (see Pellegrino & Glaser, 1979). On the other hand, we cannot ignore the evidence that processes continue to develop in efficiency of execution once automaticity has been achieved. It is possible that the way in which automatic and controlled processing are coordinated within a single task may explain more of the variance in cognitive task performance than will measurement of performance components considered in isolation or executive strategies that consider only conscious allocation of attention (Kaye et al., 1981; Logan, 1980).

There has been a recent increase in the number of investigators of cognition concerned with the allocation of attention during complex problem solving. In particular, there has been much research dealing with the changes in information processing when subjects are required to perform two or more tasks simultaneously. It is hypothesized that the allocation of processing resources in dual task or multiple-task environments will successfully explain a greater proportion of variance in intelligence than have performance components considered either in isolation or in simple information-processing tasks (Hawkins, Rodriguez, & Reicher, 1979; Lansman & Hunt, 1980). By studying people's ability to perform multiple tasks presented simultaneously, it is hoped that we will learn a great deal about how people function in their everyday lives when confronted with complex tasks.

In closing, it is clear that the future of research on intelligence will proceed along a plurality of lines. Many conceptions of intelligence have been proposed in the past, but not all have received experimental attention. It is likely that we will continue to learn about intelligence in laboratory task environments as well as in the "real world" as psychologists in both the cognitive and psychometric traditions expand their research to include a greater variety of tasks studied from a multiplicity of perspectives.

Robert J. Sternberg
Daniel B. Kaye

See also Cognitive Development; Creativity; Gifted Persons; Individual Differences; Intelligence Measurement; Mental Retardation; Neurosciences; Psychology.

REFERENCES

Archer, D. *How to Expand Your Social Intelligence Quotient.* New York: M. Evans, 1980.

Atkinson, R. C., & Shiffrin, R. M. Human memory: A proposed system and its control processes. In K. W. Spence & J. T. Spence (Eds.), *The Psychology of Learning and Motivation* (Vol. 2). New York: Academic Press, 1968.

Belmont, J. M., & Butterfield, E. C. The instructional approach to developmental cognitive research. In R. V. Kail, Jr. & J. Hagen (Eds.), *Perspectives on the Development of Memory and Cognition.* Hillsdale, N. J.: Lawrence Erlbaum Associates, 1977.

Belmont, J. M.; Butterfield, E. C.; & Ferretti, R. To secure transfer of training, instruct self-management skills. In D. K. Detterman & R. J. Sternberg (Eds.), *How Much Can Intelligence Be Increased?* Norwood, N.J.: Ablex, forthcoming.

Berry, J. W. Radical cultural relativism and the concept of intelligence. In J. W. Berry & P. R. Dasen (Eds.), *Culture and Cognition, Readings in Cross-cultural Psychology.* London: Methuen, 1974.

Berry, J. W. Cultural universality of any theory of human intelligence remains an open question. *Behavioral and Brain Sciences,* 1980, *3,* 584–585.

Bisanz, J. H., & Resnick, L. B. Changes with age in two components of visual search speed. *Journal of Experimental Child Psychology,* 1978, *25,* 129–142.

Borkowski, J. G., & Wanschura, P. B. Mediational processes in the retarded. In N. R. Ellis (Ed.), *International Review of Research in Mental Retardation* (Vol. 7). New York: Academic Press, 1974.

Brown, A. L. Knowing when, where, and how to remember: A problem of metacognition. In R. Glaser (Ed.), *Advances in Instructional Psychology* (Vol. 1). Hillsdale, N.J.: Lawrence Erlbaum Associates, 1978.

Bruner, J. S.; Shapiro, D.; & Tagiuri, R. The meaning of traits in isolation and in combination. In R. Tagiuri & L. Petrollo (Eds.), *Person Perception and Interpersonal Behavior.* Stanford, Calif.: Stanford University Press, 1958.

Burt, C. *The Factors of the Mind.* London: University of London Press, 1940.

Campione, J. C., & Brown, A. L. Toward a theory of intelligence: Contributions from research with retarded children. *Intelligence,* 1978, *2,* 279–304.

Campione, J. C.; Brown, A. L.; & Ferrara, F. Research with slow-learning children: Implications for the concept of intelligence. In R. J. Sternberg (Ed.), *Handbook of Human Intelligence.* New York: Cambridge University Press, forthcoming.

Cantor, N. *Prototypicality and Personality Judgments.* Unpublished doctoral dissertation, Stanford University, 1973.

Carroll, J. B. Psychometric tests as cognitive tasks: A new "structure of intellect." In L. B. Resnick (Ed.), *The Nature of Intelligence.* Hillsdale, N.J.: Lawrence Erlbaum Associates, 1976.

Carroll, J. B. Ability and task difficulty in cognitive psychology. *Educational Researcher,* 1981, *10,* 11–21.

Cattell, R. B. *Abilities: Their Structure, Growth, and Action.* Boston: Houghton Mifflin, 1971.

Chase, W. G., & Simon, H. A. The mind's eye in chess. In W. G. Chase (Ed.), *Visual Information Processing.* New York: Academic Press, 1972.

Chi, M. T. H.; Feltovich, P. J.; & Glaser, R. Categorization and representation of physics knowledge by experts and novices. *Cognitive Science,* 1981, *5,* 121–152.

Chiang, A., & Atkinson, R. C. Individual differences and interrela-

tionships among a select set of cognitive skills. *Memory and Cognition,* 1976, *4,* 661–672.

Chiesi, H. L.; Spilich, G. J.; & Voss, J. F. Acquisition of domain-related information in relation to high and low domain knowledge. *Journal of Verbal Learning and Verbal Behavior,* 1979, *18,* 257–273.

Clark, H. H., & Chase, W. G. On the process of comparing sentences against pictures. *Cognitive Psychology,* 1972, *3,* 472–517.

Cole, M.; Gay, J.; Glick, J. A.; & Sharp, D. W. *The Cultural Context of Learning and Thinking.* New York: Basic Books, 1971.

Cole, M., & Scribner, S. *Culture and Thought: A Psychological Introduction.* New York: Wiley, 1974.

Cronbach, L. J. The two disciplines of scientific psychology. *American Psychologist,* 1957, *12,* 671–684.

deGroot, A. D. Perception and memory versus thought: Some old ideas and recent findings. In B. Kleinmuntz (Ed.), *Problem Solving: Research Method and Theory.* New York: Wiley, 1966.

Egan, D. E., & Greeno, J. G. Acquiring cognitive structure by discovery and rule learning. *Journal of Educational Psychology,* 1973, *64,* 85–97.

Ferguson, G. A. On learning and human ability. *Canadian Journal of Psychology,* 1954, *8,* 95–112.

Feuerstein, R. *The Dynamic Assessment of Retarded Performers: The Learning Potential Assessment Device, Theory, Instruments, and Techniques.* Baltimore: University Park Press, 1979. (a)

Feuerstein, R. *Instrumental Enrichment: An Intervention Program for Cognitive Modifiability.* Baltimore: University Park Press, 1979. (b)

Frederiksen, J. R. Component skills in reading: Measurement of individual differences through chronometric analysis. In R. E. Snow, P. A. Federico, & W. E. Montague (Eds.), *Aptitude, Learning, and Instruction* (Vol. 1). Hillsdale, N.J.: Lawrence Erlbaum Associates, 1980.

French, J. W., Ekstrom, R. B., & Price, L. A. *A Kit of Reference Tests for Cognitive Factors.* Princeton, N.J.: Educational Testing Service, 1963.

Gagné, R. M. *The Conditions of Learning* (2nd ed). New York: Holt, Rinehart & Winston, 1970.

Goodnow, J. J. The nature of intelligent behavior: Questions raised by cross-cultural studies. In L. B. Resnick (Ed.), *The Nature of Human Intelligence.* Hillsdale, N.J.: Lawrence Erlbaum Associates, 1976.

Guilford, J. P. *The Nature of Human Intelligence.* New York: McGraw-Hill, 1967.

Guttman, L. A new approach to factor analysis: The radex. In P. E. Lazarsfeld (Ed.), *Mathematical Thinking in the Social Sciences.* Glencoe, Ill.: Free Press, 1954.

Hakstian, A. R., & Cattell, R. B. The checking of primary ability structure on a broader basis of performances. *British Journal of Educational Psychology,* 1974, *44,* 140–154.

Hakstian, A. R., & Cattell, R. B. Higher-stratum ability structures on a basis of twenty primary abilities. *Journal of Educational Psychology,* 1978, *70,* 657–669.

Hawkins, H. L.; Rodriguez, E.; & Reicher, G. M. *Is Time-sharing a General Ability?* (NR150–407 ONR Technical Report No. 3). Eugene: University of Oregon, Department of Psychology, 1979.

Hogaboam, T. W., & Pellegrino, J. W. Hunting for individual differences in cognitive processes: Verbal ability and semantic processing of pictures and words. *Memory and Cognition,* 1978, *6,* 189–193.

Holzman, T. G.; Glaser, R.; & Pellegrino, J. W. Process training derived from a computer simulation theory. *Memory and Cognition*, 1976, *4*, 349–356.

Horn, J. L. Organization of abilities and the development of intelligence. *Psychological Review*, 1968, *75*, 242–259.

Humphreys, L. G. The organization of human abilities. *American Psychologist*, 1962, *17*, 475–483.

Hunt, E. B. Varieties of cognitive power. In L. B. Resnick (Ed.), *The Nature of Intelligence*. Hillsdale, N.J.: Lawrence Erlbaum Associates, 1976.

Hunt, E. B. Mechanics of verbal ability. *Psychological Review*, 1978, *85*, 109–130.

Hunt, E. B.; Frost, N.; & Lunneborg, C. Individual differences in cognition: A new approach to intelligence. In G. H. Bower (Ed.), *The Psychology of Learning and Motivation* (Vol. 7). New York: Academic Press, 1973.

Hunt, E. B., & Lansman, M. Cognitive theory applied to individual differences. In W. K. Estes (Ed.), *Handbook of Learning and Cognitive Processes: Introduction to Concepts and Issues* (Vol. 1). Hillsdale, N.J.: Lawrence Erlbaum Associates, 1975.

Hunt, E. B.; Lunneborg, C.; & Lewis, J. What does it mean to be high verbal? *Cognitive Psychology*, 1975, *7*, 194–227.

Intelligence and its measurement. *Journal of Educational Psychology*, 1921, *12*, 123–147, 195–216, 271–275.

Jensen, A. R. Hierarchical theories of mental ability. In W. B. Dockrell (Ed.), *On Intelligence*. Toronto: Ontario Institute for Studies in Education, 1970.

Jensen, A. R. *g*: Outmoded theory or unconquered frontier? *Creative Science and Technology*, 1979, *2*, 16–29.

Jensen, A. R. *Bias in Mental Testing*. New York: Free Press, 1980.

Jensen, A. R., & Munro, E. Reaction time, movement time, and intelligence. *Intelligence*, 1979, *3*, 121–126.

Kaye, D. B.; Brown, S. W.; Post, T. A.; & Plude, D. J. The development of letter-processing efficiency. *Memory and Cognition*, 1981, *9*, 378–388.

Keating, D. P., & Bobbitt, B. L. Individual and developmental differences in cognitive processing components of mental ability. *Child Development*, 1978, *49*, 155–167.

Kreutzer, M. A.; Leonard, C.; & Flavell, J. H. An interview study of children's knowledge about memory. *Monographs of the Society for Research in Child Development*, 1974, *40*(1).

LaBerge, D., & Samuels, S. J. Toward a theory of automatic information processing in reading. *Cognitive Psychology*, 1974, *6*, 293–323.

Laboratory for Comparative Human Cognition. Culture and intelligence. In R. J. Sternberg (Ed.), *Handbook of Human Intelligence*. New York: Cambridge University Press, forthcoming.

Lansman, M., & Hunt, E. B. *Individual Differences in Secondary Task Performance*. University of Washington, Department of Psychology, 1980.

Larkin, J. H.; McDermott, J.; Simon, D. P.; & Simon, H. A. Models of competence in solving physics problems. *Cognitive Science*, 1980, *4*, 317–345.

Linn, M. C. The role of intelligence in children's responses to instruction. *Psychology in the Schools*, 1973, *10*, 67–75.

Logan, G. D. Attention and automaticity in Stroop and priming tasks: Theory and data. *Cognitive Psychology*, 1980, *12*, 523–553.

MacLeod, C. M.; Hunt, E. B.; & Mathews, N. N. Individual differences in the verification of sentence-picture relationships. *Journal of Verbal Learning and Verbal Behavior*, 1978, *17*, 493–507.

Neisser, U. General, academic, and artificial intelligence. In L. B. Resnick (Ed.), *The Nature of Intelligence*. Hillsdale, N.J.: Lawrence Erlbaum Associates, 1976.

Neisser, U. The concept of intelligence. In R. J. Sternberg & D. K. Detterman (Eds.), *Human Intelligence: Perspectives on Its Theory and Measurement*. Norwood, N.J.: Ablex, 1979.

Newell, A., & Simon, H. *Human Problem Solving*. Englewood Cliffs, N.J.: Prentice-Hall, 1972.

Pellegrino, J. W., & Glaser, R. Cognitive correlates and components in the analysis of individual differences. In R. J. Sternberg & D. K. Detterman (Eds.), *Human Intelligence: Perspectives on Its Theory and Measurement*. Norwood, N.J.: Ablex, 1979.

Piaget, J. *The Psychology of Intelligence*. Totowa, N.J.: Littlefield, Adams, 1972.

Posner, M. I., & Mitchell, R. Chronometric analysis of classification. *Psychological Review*, 1967, *74*, 392–409.

Posner, M. I., & Snyder, C. R. R. Facilitation and inhibition in the processing of signals. In P. M. Rabbitt & S. Dornic (Eds.), *Attention and Performance* 5. New York: Academic Press, 1975.

Raven, J. C. *Advanced Progressive Matrices: Sets I and II*. London: Lewis, 1965.

Reitman, J. S. Skilled perception in Go: Deducing memory structures from inter-response times. *Cognitive Psychology*, 1976, *8*, 336–356.

Resnick, L. B. (Ed.), *The Nature of Intelligence*. Hillsdale, N.J.: Lawrence Erlbaum Associates, 1976.

Rosenthal, R.; Hall, J.; DiMatteo, M. R.; Rogers, P. L.; & Archer, D. *Sensitivity to Nonverbal Communication: The PONS Test*. Baltimore: Johns Hopkins Press, 1979.

Schneider, W., & Shiffrin, R. Controlled and automated human information processing: I. Detection, search, and attention. *Psychological Review*, 1977, *84*, 1–66.

Siegler, R. S., & Richards, D. D. The development of intelligence. In R. J. Sternberg (Ed.), *Handbook of Human Intelligence*. New York: Cambridge University Press, forthcoming.

Spearman, C. *The Nature of "Intelligence" and the Principles of Cognition*. London: Macmillan, 1923.

Spearman, C. *The Ability of Man*. New York: Macmillan, 1927.

Spilich, G. J.; Vesonder, G. T.; Chiesi, H. L.; & Voss, J. F. Text processing of domain-related information for individuals with high and low domain knowledge. *Journal of Verbal Learning and Verbal Behavior*, 1979, *18*, 275–290.

Sternberg, R. J. *Intelligence, Information Processing, and Analogical Reasoning: The Componential Analysis of Human Abilities*. Hillsdale, N.J.: Lawrence Erlbaum Associates, 1977.

Sternberg, R. J. The nature of mental abilities. *American Psychologist*, 1979, *34*, 214–230.

Sternberg, R. J. Sketch of a componential subtheory of human intelligence. *Behavioral and Brain Sciences*, 1980, *3*, 573–614.

Sternberg, R. J. The nature of intelligence. *New York University Education Quarterly*, 1981, *12*, 3, 10–17. (a)

Sternberg, R. J. Cognitive-behavioral approaches to the training of intelligence in the retarded. *Journal of Special Education*, 1981, *15*, 165–183. (b)

Sternberg, R. J.; Conway, B. E.; Ketron, J. L.; & Bernstein, M. People's conceptions of intelligence. *Journal of Personality and Social Psychology*, 1981, *41*, 37–55.

Thomson, G. H. *The Factorial Analysis of Human Ability*. London: University of London Press, 1939.

Thorndike, E. L. *Animal Intelligence: Experimental Studies*. New York: Macmillan, 1911.

Thorndike, E. L.; Bregman, E. O.; Cobb, M. V.; & Woodyard,

E. I. *The Measurement of Intelligence.* New York: Teachers College, 1928.

Thurstone, L. L. *Primary Mental Abilities.* Chicago: University of Chicago Press, 1938.

Vernon, P. E. *The Structure of Human Abilities.* London: Methuen, 1971.

Wober, M. Towards an understanding of the Kiganda concept of intelligence. In J. W. Berry & P. R. Dasen (Eds.), *Culture and Cognition: Readings in Cross-cultural Psychology.* London: Methuen, 1974.

Yussen, S. R., & Kane, P. Children's concept of intelligence. In S. R. Yussen (Ed.), *The Growth of Insight in Children.* New York: Academic Press, forthcoming.

INTELLIGENCE MEASUREMENT

Intelligence measurement has been embroiled in controversy ever since psychologists and educators first concerned themselves with it seventy-five years ago. It continues to be controversial to the present day because mental test scores have often been used to open or close doors to educational or vocational opportunity. The difficulty stems not so much from the tests themselves as from widely held misunderstandings as to their legitimate uses and limitations, and confusion about the nature of intelligence itself (Brody & Brody, 1976; Tuddenham, 1962, 1969).

What to Measure: Conceptions of Intelligence

Intelligence-in-General. In 1904 Alfred Binet was asked by the Paris public school authorities to develop a means for identifying pupils unable to profit by instruction in ordinary classrooms, so that they might be given special education better suited to their needs. After some false starts, Binet hit upon a solution known to history as the 1905 Binet scale (Binet & Simon, 1905). It consisted of a series of brief, varied cognitive tasks arranged in order of difficulty—defining words, repeating strings of digits or words after one hearing, reasoning problems, repeating the thought of a passage, reproducing designs from memory, etc. From this small beginning have come virtually all modern intelligence tests. Yet Binet was not concerned with the definition or theory of intelligence as an abstract variable. His objective was pragmatic. He tested a child on a variety of cognitive activities similar to those encountered in daily life, and struck an average to serve as an index of all-round adaptive adequacy, and a basis for predicting success in school. What he measured can reasonably be called "intelligence-in-general."

General Intelligence. In 1904 Charles Spearman in England published an epochal paper setting forth a theory of mental organization based upon a mathematical analysis of the intercorrelations among children's grades and measures of their sensory acuity. Observing that all his measures were positively intercorrelated, Spearman concluded that to a degree they were measuring the same thing. He assumed this to be an underlying mental trait, and labeled it *g*. It soon became clear that tests composed of numerous items of varied kinds, such as Binet's, were particularly good measures of *g*. In contrast to Binet's interest, however, Spearman's was theoretical. He believed he had demonstrated the existence of an underlying mental dimension, which soon came to be known as "general intelligence."

Goddard's Hereditarian Views. Binet testing was introduced to the United States in 1911 by Henry Goddard, director of the Vineland Training School in New Jersey, an institution for children who had suffered since birth from severe mental and physical disabilities. Although we would now regard some of these as congenital, Goddard attributed them all to defective heredity. He seized upon Spearman's theory of general intelligence to explain variations in mental ability, and grafted on to it his own belief that such variations were largely determined by the genes and essentially unmodifiable (Goddard, 1920). Espousing at the same time Binet's test, Spearman's theory, and his own hereditarian views, Goddard was largely responsible for three widely adopted but highly dubious propositions: that there is such a thing as general intelligence; that it is determined by the quality of one's heredity; and that the Binet test is the measure of this cognitive dimension.

Implications. Much of today's public controversy over tests and testing has followed from mistaking scores on Binet's pragmatic instrument for measurements of Spearman's theoretical variable. Yet there is a sharp difference between the views of Binet and Spearman. General intelligence is analogous to height, with the important proviso that stature is visible and can be measured directly, whereas intelligence is underlying, inferential, and can only be estimated. Intelligence-in-general is analogous to health, which has many aspects, even though people can be ordered on a quantitative rating scale of health overall. Perhaps the most fundamental difference between the two perspectives is in philosophical position. Spearman believed that general intelligence really exists, as a trait in the mind. This view is the premise that lies behind queries as to whether intelligence tests are good measures of intelligence.

The alternative view, sometimes called nominalism, is that intelligence is merely a label for a broad array of complex cognitive functions. A behavior sequence can be evaluated in different ways. If we choose to evaluate it with respect to its adaptive adequacy, we can judge how intelligent—that is, how adaptive—it is. We can judge persons, also, to be intelligent or unintelligent on the basis of their typical behavior, without endowing them with an inner faculty of intelligence. From this perspective, the question is not whether intelligence tests are good measures of intelligence, but rather to what degree and in what circumstances intelligence tests permit useful prediction of concrete variables such as success in school or on the job.

Factor Theories of Intelligence

In the years since Spearman and Binet psychologists have wrestled with two central questions of intelligence measurement: what to measure, and how to measure it. The first question is basically theoretical; the second is pragmatic. Developments on these two levels have been surprisingly independent of one another. Consider first the factor theories of intelligence offered by Spearman and his successors.

Spearman's Theory of Two Factors. On inspecting his table of intercorrelations, Spearman observed that if the test variables were listed by row and by column in the order of their average intercorrelations, a pattern was obtained in which the highest values were at the upper left, and decreased regularly in both the horizontal and vertical directions. With artificial data the pattern is easy to see (Table 1). Spearman, borrowing an idea from physics, thought that departures from this ideal in real data were attributable to the ubiquitous presence of "errors of measurement," and he invented statistical formulas to evaluate and correct for such errors. Spearman, as mentioned, interpreted the fact that all correlations were positive to mean that all his variables were measuring the same underlying faculty or dimension, g, and that the tests with the largest average correlations were the best measures of g (Spearman, 1904). Spearman's theory could not be proved, but it was compatible with the observed data, provided the numerical value of all possible tetrads (i.e., sets of four correlations differing in the sequence of their subscripts) vanished, that is, were numerically equal to zero within limits of measurement error. (As an example, one such tetrad is marked by arrows on Table 1.)

$$(r_{AE} \times r_{BF}) - (r_{AF} \times r_{BE}) = 0;$$

or numerically,

$$(.45 \times .32) - (.36 \times .40) = 0.$$

Another formula enabled one to determine the degree to which each test was determined by the common, underlying dimension (i.e., to determine the correlation between the test and g).

$$\sqrt{\frac{r_{AE} \times r_{AF}}{r_{EF}}} = r_{Ag};$$

or numerically,

$$\sqrt{\frac{.45 \times .36}{.20}} = .90.$$

Because g determined only a portion of individual differences in scores on any real test, Spearman, by the same logic, inferred that each test measured not only g but a second underlying dimension, s, that was different from test to test. Because each s was found only in one test, it was useless for predicting any other variable and could be ignored. Spearman called his interpretation—that tests all measured g plus a specific s unique to each test—the "theory of two factors" (more accurately, $1 + n$ factors, as there were as many s's as tests), or simply the "Theory of factors."

Thomson's Sampling Theory. Both Binet and Terman, author of the Stanford-Binet, were critical of Spearman's theory (Tuddenham, 1962). The most cogent opposition, however, came from G. L. Thomson at Edinburgh, who proposed instead what has been called the sampling theory of intelligence, an interpretation clearly more compatible with Binet's views. According to Thomson (1920, 1951) the correlation between two tests arises not because both are measuring the same underlying factor, but simply because they make overlapping cognitive demands. Tests differ in the variety and complexity of the knowledge and skills they call upon. The more complex a test is, the more likely it is to overlap other tests, whereas a test that makes narrow demands will be less likely to overlap. Thus it is the breadth or narrowness of the tests, and not the existence of one or a few common factors in the mind, that accounts for the pattern of intercorrelations in a group of tests.

Perhaps because Thomson's theory offered only an al-

TABLE 1. *Intercorrelations among six tests (artificial data)*

Test	A	B	C	D	E	F
A	—	.72	.63	.54	.45	.36
B	.72	—	.56	.48	.40	.32
C	.63	.56	—	.42	.35	.28
D	.54	.48	.42	—	.30	.24
E	.45	.40	.35	.30	—	.20
F	.36	.32	.28	.24	.20	—
Correlation with g[1]	.90	.80	.70	.60	.50	.40

[1] The correlation between any two tests is equal to the product of their respective correlations with g.

ternative to Spearman's, not a refutation, and because Spearman's general intelligence construct seemed like the dimensions of physics—force, gravity, etc.—most psychologists adhered to Spearman's view. Its overthrow, when it came, was on empirical grounds. In many correlation tables not all the tetrad differences were close enough to zero! At first Spearman argued that "undue similarity" between two or three tests in the battery was to blame but, as Thomson pointed out, the experimenter was likely to detect undue similarity only after the fact, and find it necessary to alter the battery of tests in order to protect the theory.

Later Spearman allowed, in such cases, not only g and each test's own s, but also minor factors involved in only two or three tests and thus intermediate in generality between g and s. The admission of such factors fundamentally damaged the elegance and simplicity of Spearman's theory. Moreover, accumulating evidence suggested that g might actually consist of two components: v:ed, found in tests that required verbal skill and depended upon education; and k:m, found in tests involving practical–spatial–mechanical ability.

Multiple-factor Theories. L. L. Thurstone (1938) resolved the issue by inverting the factor problem. Instead of trying to demonstrate the adequacy of Spearman's single common factor g, he invented statistical means to analyze a correlation table into as many common factors as were required to account for the empirical correlation coefficients. From Thurstone's investigation of the intercorrelations of some fifty-six intelligence tests, there emerged at least seven factors, which he called "primary abilities." These factors were V, verbal; W, word fluency; N, number; M, associative memory; S, spatial; P, perceptual speed; and R, reasoning—a set of constructs uncomfortably reminiscent of the "faculties" into which speculative philosophers had divided the mind a century earlier. Nor was Thurstone's the ultimate factorial resolution. With the advent of large computers, investigators were able to use much larger and more varied batteries of tests, and these in turn led to the identification of more and more factors. Perhaps the apogee of this trend is J. P. Guilford's ambitious Structure-of-the-Intellect model (Guilford, 1967). It allows for at least 120 factors of intelligence, of which eighty-seven have been "discovered."

Many complications and controversies in the field of factor analysis are tangential to the present topic. It is clear, however, that g has been replaced by a horde of common factors less general than g. Factor analysis, invented by Spearman to buttress his theory of general intelligence, no longer provides a definite answer to the fundamental question "How many types or traits of intelligence are there?" Indeed, one can generate as many mental factors as one chooses, depending upon how trivial one is willing to let them be. But this takes one back to the nominalist position that the question is meaningless, as there are as many types of intelligence as there are people. Each person is unique in genetic endowment and experi-

ential history, and cognitive functions are sampled differently from test to test because no two tests use exactly the same content. From this point of view, factors offer a classification of test content rather than a mapping of the mind.

Nevertheless, and despite the circularity of its logic, the factor analytic paradigm, by defining intelligence as a finite set of trait dimensions, has provided one answer to the question of what to measure. Several well-known multiscore batteries have been derived from factorial research, for example, Thurstone's Tests of Primary Mental Abilities (PMA), the U.S. Employment Service's General Aptitude Test Battery (GATB) (U.S. Employment Service, 1970), and the Meeker (1969) tests for some of the variables of Guilford's structure of the intellect. Multiscore tests give more information and are presumably more useful than the single-score IQ test for counseling or job assignment. The single-score test predicts reasonably well, however, a much broader array of criteria than do the narrower factor scales. Except for the relationship between numerical reasoning score and mathematics and science grades, it has proved difficult to improve predictions of course grades much beyond the level obtainable with the best single-score instruments.

Recent Theories of Intelligence. The conflict among the various factor descriptions of intelligence has led some investigators to propose variables of a somewhat different kind. An example is the crystallized intelligence–fluid intelligence distinction of Horn and Cattell (1966), the former referring to learned, that is, "cultural" strategies and information used in cognitive tasks, and the latter to a more biological capacity for resourcefulness and innovation in problem solving. Yet Horn himself characterizes the crystallized component as a swollen verbal factor and the fluid component as a swollen reasoning factor, thus reducing the variables to something close to the much older division of g into v:ed and k:m (Horn, 1976).

Jensen (1969) has distinguished level I intelligence (simple associative learning) from level II intelligence (conceptual ability). Level I is best measured by memory span and rote learning. Level II involves cognitive transformations of the input, and is close to IQ. He offers evidence that different ethnic groups have similar score distributions on level I measures, whereas black and lower-class children on the average show a significant disadvantage on tests of level II.

In all these attempts to specify the components of intelligence, the implicit goal has been to predict intellectual achievement of different kinds in order to select individuals for particular instructional programs. Intelligence tests to date have given teachers an alibi to excuse failure, but very little guidance as to how to help the child with learning difficulties. Recently there has arisen a radically different formulation of the problem of what to measure. The new goal is to discover individual difference variables that will suggest how to teach different kinds of people. Clearly there is room for both approaches. Tests will continue to be needed as a basis for selecting the most promising individuals to train for professions in which only a relatively few candidates are required. To improve the effectiveness of instruction in the basics that everyone must learn, we need tests that classify children according to their preferred ways of learning. The first efforts in this direction were to discover aptitude–treatment interactions, a topic ably summarized by Cronbach and Snow (1977). Aptitude in this sense covers many kinds of variables, but the results thus far have been on the whole inconsistent, unstable, and disappointing.

At a 1921 symposium fourteen prominent psychologists contributed as many different definitions of intelligence. Their collective wisdom had almost no impact upon test constructors faced with deciding what content to include or exclude. The only definition still widely quoted was by Boring (1923); he said that intelligence was that which intelligence tests tested. In 1974 another such symposium was held at which a new generation of psychologists addressed the old question "What is intelligence?" (Resnick, 1976). Their approach was very different from that of the 1921 group. Most of them were experimental psychologists interested in discovering variables of cognitive behavior analogous to the successive stages of problem solving by computer, from encoding the input to checking the output.

A popular article by Simon (1981) illustrates how computer simulation can be used to elucidate human cognitive processes, and perhaps define variables with more direct implications for teaching than factors have proved to have. The work of Sternberg (1977), Carroll (1976), and others may provide such variables. Psychochronometry, the measurement of the temporal duration of intervening processes in information processing (Jensen, 1980b), may also prove useful.

Two cautions are in order, however. First, most information-processing research has been done by experimental psychologists more interested in man as a species than in individual men. It remains to be seen whether or not individual differences in the variables of information-processing theory will aid us in adapting teaching to the strengths and weaknesses of the individual.

Second, computers are basically logic machines. They are enormously powerful at manipulating numbers or other symbols, provided the problems can be precisely formulated and solved by rule, as in algebra. Human beings do not always think in this way. For example, Rosch has pointed out that human categorizing in real life goes on in the absence of decisively defining features (see Neisser, 1979). It seems improbable that the most uniquely "human" aspects of intelligence—creativity, social intuition, humor, even detecting absurdities as on the Stanford-Binet—can be encompassed by variables derived from the logic of computers.

Without really settling the issue of *what* to measure, let us turn to problems in deciding *how* to measure intelligence.

How to Measure: Problems in Intelligence Measurement

The discussion thus far has been concerned with the conceptualization of intelligence, but it has ignored the pragmatic problems that have arisen in creating a measuring instrument.

Measurement in the strict sense requires a scale whose units are equal and start from a true zero point. Stature, weight, and reaction time all can be measured. In contrast, intelligence must be gotten at indirectly. It has traditionally been "measured" on a mental test made up of a multiplicity of separate items (words to be defined, number series to be repeated, etc.), each of which can be scored pass or fail. If the items are closely spaced in average difficulty, different subjects near the top of their range will pass somewhat different items. In principle, each such pattern of success and failure constitutes a type of intelligence. Because it is not feasible to deal with a large number of patterns test constructors from Binet's day to the present have disregarded individual differences in which items were passed, and simply counted their number. Persons taking the test can then be located serially from best to worst along a single, ordinal dimension. Such was Binet's first, 1905 scale.

Age Scales. The number of items a child passes will depend very heavily upon the child's age. To score the number of items passed is meaningless unless there are data for comparison—on how many items other children pass. The major innovation in Binet's 1908 and 1911 scales was to group the items by level according to the age at which from 50 to 90 percent of normal children passed them. Although the allocation of tests to age levels was rather crude, it permitted the examiner to express the developmental level, that is, the "mental age" of a given child, as the highest age level at which the child could pass all the items, plus additional age credit for each item passed above this level. This is the essential pattern of the age scale adopted for the Stanford-Binet and many other intelligence tests in the United States and elsewhere.

Such a scale has serious statistical limitations. A subject's failure to pass any item would not mean zero intelligence in the sense of zero inches or zero pounds, because one might invent an easier item that the subject could pass. Nor can it be assumed that the "distance" from one age level to the next is the same at all levels of the scale. If there were no yardsticks, we could measure height, using Binet's approach, by cutting a stick equal in length to the height of the average child in each age group. A given child's stature would then be expressed as a "height age," that is, the age of the average child whose stick most closely matched the height of the child in question. Visual inspection would soon reveal, however, that the increments between successive sticks were not equal but grew smaller (except during the adolescent growth spurt), and vanished altogether in the postadolescent years when everyone stops growing. The same phenomenon may characterize the growth of intelligence, but our scales conceal it. Nevertheless, mental age scales have the undoubted merit of providing an easily understood way to describe differences between children in general level of ability.

The IQ. Lewis M. Terman's thorough revision and American restandardization, the Stanford-Binet Intelligence Scale of 1916, provided a longer, more carefully calibrated scale than Binet's, with much more precise instructions for administration and scoring, but Terman's major innovation was the introduction of the IQ. A mental age (MA) does not indicate how bright a child is unless one takes into simultaneous account his chronological age (CA). A German psychologist, W. Stern (1912), suggested that dividing MA by CA would yield an absolute index of brightness. Terman adopted the suggestion, although his allocation of test items to age levels was primarily by MA. The use of a quotient is legitimate if the scale has a zero point and equal intervals. Its fundamental inappropriateness for an ordinal scale was not recognized at the time, although Simon, Binet's collaborator, called the IQ a betrayal of Binet's work (Wolf, 1973).

In practice, the IQ concept worked well enough during the elementary years when the increments in performance from year to year were large enough to camouflage the fundamental problems. For children of high school age, and especially for adults, the problems were inescapable. Terman was forced to resort to two unsatisfactory expedients to preserve the meaning of IQs. An example will clarify the problem and Terman's solution.

Assume that a very bright child aged exactly 4 years passes all the tests allocated to age level V (the basal level), plus enough additional items to earn a total mental age of 6 years. The child's IQ is 6/4, or dropping decimals, 150. To maintain this level the test should permit the child to earn an MA of 15 when he reaches the age of 10, and of 30 years at 20. When we recall the "stick method" of measuring stature, the difficulty becomes apparent. After adolescence there is very little annual gain in ability, and no items that 29-year-olds fail but 30-year-olds pass. Terman's solution was simply to add at the top of the scale very difficult items whose mental-age value was arbitrary in the sense that it corresponded to no actual age cohort, but was required to provide the "top" needed to preserve the IQs of the gifted. This device suffices for children of average ability during the school years. However, a bright child would be penalized as he grew older. The one in the example would start to decline in IQ after he attained a CA of 12 years 8 months even if he passed every item and earned an MA of 19 years, the maximum possible. Similarly, an average person with an IQ of 100 (i.e., MA = CA) during childhood would start to decline after age 19, and obtain an IQ of only 50 at age 38, an absurd state of affairs. To avoid this outcome, Terman adopted the second expedient: basing the IQs of youths and adults not only on artificial MAs, but also, regardless of their real ages, on artificial CAs corresponding to the point at which annual increments in intelligence cease. Which CA to use

was another problem. In 1916 Terman decided upon 16 years for persons 16 years of age or older. Thus the maximum possible IQ for an adult was 19/16 or 119. Apparently he set the level too high, as Binet testing of U.S. Army recruits in World War I, a less able group than Terman's standardization sample, yielded an average MA of only 13 (Yerkes, 1921).

In 1937 an improved Stanford-Binet was published (Terman & Merrill, 1937; McNemar, 1942). Two closely parallel alternate forms were provided, the test was extended at both the lower and upper levels, and the fixed CA for calculating adult IQ was set at 15. The fundamental statistical difficulty was palliated but not cured by these improvements. A 1960 revision and 1972 restandardization, while retaining the age scale arrangement of items, provided tables for obtaining IQs that were essentially standard scores by age (Terman & Merrill, 1973).

Point Scales. In 1939 David Wechsler produced the first carefully constructed test intended explicitly for adults, the Wechsler-Bellevue Intelligence Scale (Wechsler, 1939; Matarazzo, 1972). Observing that adults actually did worse on mental tests as they grew older, Wechsler believed that the fixed CA denominator for adults used on the Stanford-Binet misrepresented adult changes in ability. His solution was to abandon altogether the concept of MA and the age scale format, used since Binet, in favor of a point scale format. Instead of items allocated to age level by difficulty without regard for content, Wechsler fixed on ten basic content types. Five were verbal tests: information, similarities, arithmetic, comprehension, and digit span (plus vocabulary). Five were performance tests: picture completion, picture arrangement, block design, object assembly, and coding. He then assembled items ranging from easy to difficult within each content type.

Each item of a given type earned points toward the score on that subtest. Since raw scores in the different content types were incommensurable, all were transformed into standard scores on the basis of data from the younger adults in the standardization sample. These standard scores were added to provide a sum of standard scores on the verbal subtests, a sum on the nonverbal subtests, and a grand sum on the full scale. Using the empirical mean and standard deviation of each age cohort of adults, these sums of standard scores were again transformed into standard scores with a mean of 100 and a standard deviation of fifteen points, separately for verbal tests, for performance tests, and for the full scale. These standard scores Wechsler called IQs, although no MA or ratio is involved. The fundamental scale is still an ordinal one, but the level of an individual is assessed by comparison not with older or younger people, but with people of the same age. The group average is taken as the zero point, and the standard deviation of the distribution is used as a unit to assess a person's relative rarity above or below the average of that person's age group.

The point scale format is superior to the age scale from a statistical point of view, and tests on this pattern are quicker and easier to construct. Although the details differ, the same scheme was used in Wechsler's later individual mental tests—the 1949 Wechsler Intelligence Scale for Children (WISC), revised in 1974; the 1955 Wechsler Adult Intelligence Scale (WAIS), revised in 1981; and the 1963 Wechsler Preschool and Primary Scale (WPPSI).

Point scale format has typically been used also in group tests intended for adults, in the army as well as in schools. The famous Army Alpha, a group test used for mental classification of soldiers during World War I, was a point scale, as were its nonverbal analog, Army Beta, and the comparable test used for much of World War II, the Army General Classification Test (AGCT-1). Such tests resembled the individual tests in content, but were adapted as necessary for group administration. They were often standardized on large samples and had good reliability, but their claims to validity usually rested upon their correlation with one of the better individual tests, usually the Stanford-Binet.

Later group tests, especially those intended for use in counseling in high schools and colleges, were constructed on the basis of factor analytic studies to yield not one but several scores. The Differential Aptitude Tests (DAT) and the Scholastic Aptitude Test (SAT) also yield more than a single score. However, they are based not on factor analysis, but on analysis of the complex skills involved in educational curricula and the world of work. [See Buros (1975) for reviews and data on all current tests. Standard texts on testing—for example, Anastasi (1982)—provide background.]

Test Validity

Discussions of test validity usually distinguish among content validity, construct validity, and predictive validity (see *Standards*, 1974). How valid are intelligence tests from these perspectives?

Content Validity. Content validity is most easily assessed in an achievement test of a well-defined subject such as high school mathematics. An evaluator can easily check the test items for coverage of all the topics taught, and for the appropriateness of the balance among them. To evaluate a test of Binet's intelligence-in-general in the same fashion, we would need careful inventories of all the cognitive activities in which children of each age level engage in the course of an ordinary week, so that a test really could be built on sampling principles. The crucial consideration would be that the content be varied, and we would need to take care that the content was representative of the "average expectable environment" of all those for whom the test was intended. No such inventory exists. If we had one, we might find that the test strongly resembled the ones we have now. A surprisingly limited number of item types meet the criteria of brevity, simplicity, ease of scoring, etc. In the course of this century psychologists already have developed most of them.

Construct Validity. The correspondence between a tangible test and an intangible psychological construct is hard to demonstrate. It is inferred from the fit between theoretical predictions and empirical findings, but empirical findings are usually subject to more than one interpretation. Factorial validity, a special case of construct validity (since factors are constructs), is an exception. It is measured by the correlation between test and factor, and can be calculated, as we have seen. For Spearman the most valid tests of g were obtained by combining a broad variety of items, regardless of content, to permit the numerous specifics to cancel out and the average to approximate a measure of the pure g. This argument implies Binet's actual procedure. Not surprisingly, intelligence tests as a group are very good measures of g.

The factorial validity of multiscore, factor-based tests also can be calculated, but the set of factors selected from among an infinity of mathematically equivalent sets is chosen to maximize correlations between factors and tests. Since the nature of the factor is then deduced from its pattern of test correlations, it is hard to decide which is the independent variable and which is the dependent one. Those who wish to establish the "construct validity" of intelligence test batteries by means of multiple factor analysis find that the technique accommodates too many models of intelligence to provide a clear demonstration.

One is thrown back upon Boring's operational view that intelligence is what the tests test. Indeed for many years, roughly from 1916 to 1940, the Stanford-Binet constituted both the definition and the measure of intelligence. The "validity" of a host of tests was established if the correlation between the new instrument and the Stanford-Binet was sufficiently high. Even today, for those who prefer a single-dimension model, the Stanford-Binet, together with WISC-R and WAIS-R, constitute the standard of excellence.

Predictive Validity. A more manageable question concerns the predictive validity of intelligence tests, that is, what other important variables can be predicted from them.

IQ constancy. An initial question concerns "IQ constancy"—the degree to which an IQ measurement at one age is predictive of IQ at a later age. Psychologists for many years (and the laity even today) have been inclined to accept the notion that because the IQ is an index independent of age, an individual's IQ will be always the same, apart from minor errors of measurement, unless there is a catastrophic accident to the nervous system. This belief had two sources: the notion, popularized by Goddard but not validated by research even to this day, that intelligence differences are founded almost entirely upon hereditary differences; and, the fact that the mean IQ was roughly 100 and the standard deviation roughly fifteen or sixteen points at all age levels. It was not realized that although well-standardized tests have this property, it is only a statistical consequence of proper scaling. Individuals may show

IQ fluctuations through time that are not evident in the data for group averages. Empirical findings on the same individuals tested repeatedly (e.g., Honzik, Macfarlane, & Allen, 1948; McCall, Appelbaum, & Hogarty, 1973) have demolished belief in IQ constancy. Although testings close together in time are similar, the correlations are lower the younger the individuals concerned and the longer the interval between tests. Indeed, the correlations between scores in infancy and adulthood are virtually zero, which should not be too surprising. A person who takes the same intelligence test twice will be tested the second time, if the interval is appreciable, on items that differ in content, and probably in function measured, despite the common label of the scale itself. Mental tests necessarily sample functions with respect to which people show individual differences. In infancy these are largely matters of sensory and motor maturation. Verbal functions enter when children learn to talk, and become increasingly important at the higher age levels when abstract thinking ability, which largely involves words and their relationships, is involved.

Prediction of other variables. Although correlations between different intelligence tests are usually positive, the size of the relationships depends upon the similarity in the content of the two tests. Intercorrelations between individual subtests of WISC-R range from as low as .14 (Coding versus Similarities, age $6\frac{1}{2}$) to as high as .75 (Vocabulary versus Information, age $16\frac{1}{2}$). Verbal IQ correlates with performance IQ in the range of .65 to .75 at different ages. Correlations between WISC-R verbal IQ and Stanford-Binet are nearly as high as their respective reliabilities permit. Correlations of Stanford-Binet with WISC-R performance IQ are lower. Guilford (1967) reports zero correlations among measures of a few of the factors in his Structure-of-the-Intellect model. Differences in overlap of functions sampled and in degree of heterogeneity of the people tested can yield a variety of results.

For some, the validity of intelligence tests rests upon their correlation with such variables as teachers' ratings or school grades, but such correlations are not without ambiguity. Quite apart from errors in comparing one child with another, teachers tend to distribute their grades or ratings across the whole scale, and to make insufficient allowance for differences in level from classroom to classroom. Moreover, as Binet noted long ago, teachers' judgments of intelligence are inevitably confounded with personal attraction, judgments of effort, etc. Also, the correlations tend to decline when the children reach adolescence and begin to leave school, because the range of ability shrinks. In short, the existence of positive correlations between teachers' judgments and test scores is evidence of a degree of overlap between the test and the teachers' observations, but limitations and problems with the ratings preclude obtaining very high correlations regardless of the merit of the test.

Intelligence, achievement, and aptitude. Correlations of intelligence tests with achievement tests are appreciably higher than with school marks, because the same test-taking skills and attitudes enter into both variables, and because the tests often overlap in content. The inclusion of items requiring reading in the Stanford-Binet and of arithmetic problems in WISC-R guarantees correlation with school achievement tests regardless of differences in the labels attached to the tests.

Those who consider intelligence tests direct measures of hereditary potential often characterize children whose MAs are higher than their achievement scores as "underachievers," that is, as failing to learn as much as they can. Although they receive less attention, overachievers are equally numerous, and, by the same logic, are learning more than they can! In fact, both types of tests measure what has been learned, both "content" (word meanings, number facts, etc.) and strategies for problem solving. The achievement test measures mostly what has been learned in the classroom; the intelligence test draws upon broader contexts. The difficulty with treating intelligence as a linear, unitary trait would seem to indicate that intelligence tests are best thought of as "general achievement" tests, on which scores depend largely, though by no means entirely, upon material learned outside the classroom.

Intelligence tests can also be considered "general aptitude" tests, as the difference between an aptitude test and an achievement test is largely a matter of the tester's purpose (for other views, see Green, 1974). Potential cannot be measured, but must be inferred. The only basis for predicting future learning is a measurement of past learning. Test items of the same type may occur on an achievement test to assess mastery of college chemistry and on a medical aptitude test, because chemistry achievement is a valid predictor of success in the preclinical curriculum of medical school. Of course, if students have had no opportunity to study chemistry, their test performances would provide no basis for predicting their potential if circumstances were to permit them to study it. All children want to master the things that are important to them, even though they may have little interest in school-imposed tasks. It is for this reason that the intelligence test, which draws upon a much broader sampling of the child's cognitive resources than the achievement test, is better able to predict scholastic performance in improved circumstances, for example, better teaching, new role models, or reduction of family stress. If circumstances do not change, the achievement test will prove the better predictor of later academic achievement. Clearly, however, children whose extrascholastic backgrounds are culturally different or intellectually impoverished may give little evidence of their true potential, even on the intelligence test.

Bias in Intelligence Measurement. The original impetus to mental testing arose because school people observed that some children were much more competent than others at learning material prescribed by the school. Tests were intended to discriminate between those who *could* not learn and those who did not learn in school, but whose accomplishment in non–school learning measured by the IQ test demonstrated that they were capable of learning what suited them. Intelligence tests were useful not only for identifying the slow learners needing special educational attention, but also those whose poor classroom performance, for whatever reason, masked superior abilities. With the recent pressure to remove inequalities in our treatment of ethnic minorities, some have professed to see evidence of bias in the tests themselves, if the test score distributions of different ethnic groups differ in their averages or variabilities.

Much of the objection to use of mental tests with minority groups comes from those who consciously or unconsciously accept the Spearman-Goddard reification of intelligence as an underlying trait determined almost entirely by heredity, and accept intelligence tests as measuring this trait. The problem lies with the Spearman-Goddard premise, not with the tests. Tests measure individual differences, but are neutral as to the origin of these differences, and cannot be taken as measures of native ability without many qualifications. Certainly it is impossible to impute score differences on mental tests to innate ability differences unless one can justifiably assume that the content the tests draw upon is equally available to all, and that all children are equally familiar with, and comfortable in, the testing situation. Test content tends to be drawn from the ordinary experiential and language background of subjects who are white and middle class. To the degree that the experiences and language of individuals differ from this average expectable background, the tests will be biased as measures of native endowment. They may be quite sensitive measures, however, of relative acculturation. It is hard to see what genuine social ends are served by banning tests that identify children who need special help, just because the tests do not support egalitarian beliefs.

In the United States repeated studies have ranked Asians (Chinese and Japanese) as high as, or slightly higher than, whites, followed by Chicanos, with blacks lowest. Blacks typically test on the average about one standard deviation lower than whites. Variability is roughly equal (Tyler, 1965; Loehlin, Lindzey, & Spuhler, 1975). The distributions overlap, with roughly 16 percent of blacks above the white mean. Groups differ not only in average level, but in specific areas. Blacks tend to do relatively better on verbal measures. Chicanos tend to do poorly, on the average, on verbal measures in English, but on nonverbal scales that emphasize numerical or spatial reasoning their performance approaches that of whites. Working-class children typically test lower than middle class, and rural groups lower than urban ones. Sex differences are negligible, because items favoring one sex over the other have been eliminated by test constructors.

The difficulty is that the facts can be interpreted from either a biological or a sociological perspective. A huge research literature has been generated in trying to disentangle the relative contributions of nature and nurture to mental test performance. In a thorough review Vernon (1979) concluded that none of the research to date has really settled the question. Readers of this literature must be careful to keep in mind that heritability does not mean unmodifiability, and that specific percentages assigned to hereditary causes and other percentages to environmental ones refer to sources of variability in a group, not causes in an individual. Both a full complement of genes and a viable physical and social environment are essential. Attempts to assess their separate contributions in an individual are meaningless. Moreover, the total group variance must always add up to 100 percent. Several studies have assigned roughly 80 percent of variance to genetic sources, but the subjects were usually white and middle class. Within this group IQ resemblances among family members of different degrees of relationship fit well the predictions made from the genetic hypothesis (Bouchard & McGue, 1981). The genetic variance in most studies is large because intragroup differences in social and educational background tend to be small. The conclusions cannot be extrapolated to intergroup comparisons. Conversely, intrapair differences among identical twins are wholly owing to environmental differences (some of which are prenatal), because the two individuals come from a single fertilized egg and have identical genes. Paradoxically, the more we succeed in equalizing environmental advantage for all people, the larger will be the proportion of total test score variance associated with genetic differences (Herrnstein, 1973).

Culture fair tests. Some have argued that intelligence tests should be abandoned in favor of "culture fair" tests such as Progressive Matrices (Raven, 1951) or the Culture Fair Test (Cattell, 1940) in order to place all children on the same footing. Such tests typically eschew the use of language or mathematical symbols, and rely upon measuring observation of differences in pictorial details or spatial arrangements as a basis for scoring (Lambert, 1964). Tyler (1972), in a review of the research, concluded, however, that certain minorities may be more handicapped on pictorial than on verbal items. The former typically have somewhat lower correlations with achievement test scores and school grades than do conventional tests, precisely because skill in manipulating verbal and quantitative content important to the criterion variables has been eliminated. Nevertheless, they may play a useful part in assessing those who do not speak English or who come from radically different cultural backgrounds. Even if the content were equally novel to all (a condition difficult to guarantee when typical culture fair test content also occurs in commercial games and puzzles), members of different classes or ethnic groups would still differ in such intangibles as willingness to keep striving in the face of defeat, willingness to hurry, or willingness to work for goals set by strange adults. These attitudes are enshrined in the white-middle-class value system, but not necessarily in those of different cultures. Yet differences in these variables contribute to the validity of intelligence tests as predictors of achievement in the middle-class school.

Criteria of bias. Some writers accept the existence of ethnic or class differences as *prima facie* evidence of bias. Such an inference rests not on empirical results of any kind but rather on the sociopolitical dogma of equality, and forecloses discussion at the outset. Jensen (1980a), who has reviewed the problem, offers two criteria of bias that are susceptible to empirical investigation. First, a test is biased if the order of difficulty of the constituent items differs for different groups. Evidence is incomplete, but two recent studies of WISC and WISC-R items (Miele, 1979; Sandoval, 1979) showed the same ordering for blacks and whites. Although there was a significant race-by-item interaction for a few items at certain age levels, the interaction accounted for only 1 or 2 percent of the total variance.

Second, a test is biased if its validity for predicting school or job performance differs in different ethnic groups. A preponderance of evidence indicates that there is little difference in the regression lines predicting academic achievement of blacks and of whites (Weiss & Davison, 1981). One study (Lunemann, 1972) found that intelligence tests tended to overpredict black performance and underpredict that of whites. The data appear not to support the notion that tests discriminate against all but middle-class whites. Kamin (1974) arrives at the opposite conclusion. Rejoinders have been offered by Hebb (1978) and Herrnstein (1981). Reactions by various specialists to Jensen's work on bias are appended to a summary (Jensen, 1980c) of his book. Given the present political climate, the work in this area remains intensely controversial.

Mercer (1973, 1979) has offered a complex set of procedures, the System of Multicultural Pluralistic Assessment (SOMPA), which is designed to "correct" IQs of minority children by making due allowance for cultural disadvantage. Implicit in such approaches is the Spearman–Goddard view that intelligence tests measure a genetically determined *g* in middle-class whites, but require adjustment to be applied to children of other groups. Goodman (1977), on the other hand, has been severely critical of Mercer's "diagnosticism." If intelligence tests are regarded simply as measures of the adequacy of children's behavioral repertories for dealing with school demands rather than an evaluation of their genes, then the question is not how bright they are in some absolute sense, but simply which educational experiences among the available alternatives will help each child the most. Even if a test is regarded as mostly a measure of relative acculturation, it can provide useful information in making such educational decisions. None of these considerations are likely to have much influence if procrustean courts reject them and detect "unfairness" in the fact that test score distributions of different groups are not all alike. The case of *Larry P.*, which resulted in the banning of intelligence tests in California when making certain educational decisions, is a pertinent example (Lambert, 1981).

And what of the future? A recent American Educational Research Association symposium (1979) posed the question "Intelligence tests in the year 2000: What forms will they take and what purposes will they serve?" The seven contributors offered a variety of prophecies, including testing by computer, measuring variables derived from developmental theories such as Vigotsky's, and measuring information-processing components of intelligence. Several suggested, however, a continuing use for tests that are not much different from those we have now. It is noteworthy that experts in the field still recognize the enduring social utility of Binet's reform of seventy-five years ago, even though the pendulum seems for the present to have swung the other way.

Read D. Tuddenham

See also Aptitude Measurement; Individual Differences; Intelligence; Measurement in Education; Norms and Scales; Psychology.

REFERENCES

American Educational Research Association Symposium. Intelligence tests in the year 2000: What forms will they take and what purposes will they serve? *Intelligence*, 1979, *3*, 215–306.
Anastasi, A. *Psychological Testing* (5th ed.). New York: Macmillan, 1982.
Binet, A., & Simon, T. Méthodes nouvelles pour le diagnostic du niveau intellectuel des anormaux. *Année Psychologique*, 1905, *11*, 191–244.
Boring, E. G. Intelligence as the tests test it. *New Republic*, 1923, *35*, 35–37.
Bouchard, T. J., Jr., & McGue, N. Familial studies of intelligence: A review. *Science*, 1981, *212*, 1055–1059.
Brody, E. B., & Brody, N. *Intelligence: Nature, Determinants, and Consequences*. New York: Academic Press, 1976.
Buros, O. K. (Ed.). *Intelligence Tests and Reviews*. Highland Park, N.J.: Gryphon, 1975.
Carroll, J. B. Psychometric tests as cognitive tasks: A new "structure of intellect." In L. B. Resnick (Ed.), *The Nature of Intelligence*. Hillsdale, N.J.: Lawrence Erlbaum Associates, 1976.
Cattell, R. B. A culture-free intelligence test. *Journal of Educational Psychology*, 1940, *31*, 161–179.
Cronbach, L. J., & Snow, R. E. *Aptitudes and Instructional Methods: A Handbook for Research on Interactions*. New York: Irvington, 1977.
Goddard, H. H. *Human Efficiency and Levels of Intelligence*. Princeton, N.J.: Princeton University Press, 1920.
Goodman, J. F. The diagnostic fallacy: A critique of Jane Mercer's concept of mental retardation. *Journal of School Psychology*, 1977, *15*, 197–206.
Green, D. R. (Ed.). *The Aptitude-Achievement Distinction*. Monterey, Calif.: CTB/McGraw-Hill, 1974.
Guilford, J. P. *The Nature of Human Intelligence*. New York: McGraw-Hill, 1967.
Hebb, D. O. Open letter to a friend who thinks the IQ is a social evil. *American Psychologist*, 1978, *33*, 1143–1144.
Herrnstein, R. J. *IQ in the Meritocracy*. Boston: Little, Brown, 1973.
Herrnstein, R. J. Try again, Dr. Albee. *American Psychologist*, 1981, *36*, 424.

Honzik, M. P.; Macfarlane, J. W.; & Allen, L. The stability of mental test performance between two and eighteen years. *Journal of Experimental Education*, 1948, *17*, 309–324.

Horn, J. L. Human abilities: A review of research and theory in the early 1970's. *Annual Review of Psychology*, 1976, *27*, 437–485.

Horn, J. L., & Cattell, R. B. Refinement and test of the theory of fluid and crystallized ability intelligences. *Journal of Educational Psychology*, 1966, *57*, 253–276.

Jensen, A. R. Jensen's theory of intelligence: A reply. *Journal of Educational Psychology*, 1969, *60*, 427–431.

Jensen, A. R. *Bias in Mental Testing*. New York: Free Press, 1980. (a)

Jensen, A. R. Chronometric analysis of intelligence. *Journal of Social and Biological Structures*, 1980, *3*, 103–122. (b)

Jensen, A. R. Précis of *Bias in Mental Testing*. *Behavioral and Brain Sciences*, 1980, *3*, 325–371. (c)

Kamin, L. J. *The Science and Politics of IQ*. Hillsdale, N.J.: Lawrence Erlbaum Associates, 1974.

Lambert, N. M. The present status of the culture-fair testing movement. *Psychology in the Schools*, 1964, *1*, 318–330.

Lambert, N. M. Psychological evidence in *Larry P.* v. *Wilson Riles:* An evaluation by a witness for the defense. *American Psychologist*, 1981, *36*, 937–952.

Loehlin, J. C.; Lindzey, G.; & Spuhler, J. N. *Race Differences in Intelligence*. San Francisco: Freeman, 1975.

Lunemann, A. *The Predictive Validity of IQ Tests for Different Ethnic Groups in a Desegregated Elementary School Setting*. Unpublished doctoral dissertation, University of California, Berkeley, 1972.

Matarazzo, J. D. *Wechsler's Measurement and Appraisal of Adult Intelligence*. Baltimore: Williams & Wilkins, 1972.

McCall, R. B.; Appelbaum, M. L.; & Hogarty, P. S. Developmental changes in mental performance. *Monographs of the Society for Research in Child Development*, 1973, *38*(3, Serial No. 150).

McNemar, Q. *The Revision of the Stanford-Binet Scale: An Analysis of the Standardization Data*. Boston: Houghton Mifflin, 1942.

Meeker, M. N. *The Structure of Intellect: Its Interpretation and Uses*. Columbus, Ohio: Merrill, 1969.

Mercer, J. R. *Labeling the Mentally Retarded*. Berkeley: University of California Press, 1973.

Mercer, J. R., & Lewis, J. F. *System of Multicultural Pluralistic Assessment: Conceptual and Technical Manual*. New York: Psychological Corporation, 1979.

Miele, F. Cultural bias in the WISC. *Intelligence*, 1979, *3*, 149–164.

Neisser, U. The concept of intelligence. *Intelligence*, 1979, *3*, 217–227.

Raven, J. C. *Guide to Using Progressive Matrices*. London: H. K. Lewis, 1951.

Resnick, L. B. (Ed.). *The Nature of Intelligence*. Hillsdale, N.J.: Lawrence Erlbaum Associates, 1976.

Sandoval, J. The WISC-R and internal evidence of test bias with minority groups. *Journal of Consulting and Clinical Psychology*, 1979, *47*, 919–927.

Simon, H. A. Studying human intelligence by creating artificial intelligence. *American Scientist*, 1981, *69*, 300–309.

Spearman, C. General intelligence objectively determined and measured. *American Journal of Psychology*, 1904, *15*, 201–293.

Standards for Educational and Psychological Tests. Washington, D.C.: American Psychological Association, 1974.

Stern, W. *Die psychologische Methoden der Intelligenzprüfung*. Leipzig: Barth, 1912.

Sternberg, R. J. *Intelligence, Information Processing, and Analogical Reasoning: The Componential Analysis of Human Abilities*. Hillsdale, N.J.: Lawrence Erlbaum Associates, 1977.

Terman, L. M. *The Measurement of Intelligence*. Boston: Houghton Mifflin, 1916.

Terman, L. M., & Merrill, M. A. *Measuring Intelligence*. Boston: Houghton Mifflin, 1937.

Terman, L. M., & Merrill, M. A. *Stanford-Binet Intelligence Scale*. Boston: Houghton Mifflin, 1973.

Thomson, G. H. The general factor fallacy in psychology. *British Journal of Psychology*, 1920, *10*, 319–326.

Thomson, G. H. *The Factorial Analysis of Human Ability* (5th ed.). London: University of London Press, 1951.

Thurstone, L. L. *Primary Mental Abilities*. Chicago: University of Chicago Press, 1938.

Tuddenham, R. D. The nature and measurement of intelligence. In L. Postman (Ed.), *Psychology in the Making: Histories of Selected Research Problems*. New York: Knopf, 1962.

Tuddenham, R. D. Intelligence. In R. L. Ebel (Ed.), *Encyclopedia of Educational Research* (4th ed.). New York: Macmillan, 1969.

Tyler, L. E. *The Psychology of Human Differences* (3rd ed.). New York: Appleton-Century-Crofts, 1965.

Tyler, L. E. Human abilities. *Annual Review of Psychology*, 1972, *23*, 177–206.

United States Employment Service. *Manual for the USES General Aptitude Test Battery*. Washington, D.C.: U.S. Employment Service, 1970.

Vernon, P. E. *Intelligence: Heredity and Environment*. San Francisco: Freeman, 1979.

Wechsler, D. *The Measurement of Adult Intelligence*. Baltimore: Williams & Wilkins, 1939.

Wechsler, D. *Wechsler Preschool and Primary Scale of Intelligence*. New York: Psychological Corporation, 1963.

Wechsler, D. *Wechsler Intelligence Scale for Children, Revised*. New York: Psychological Corporation, 1974.

Wechsler, D. *Wechsler Adult Intelligence Scale, Revised*. New York: Psychological Corporation, 1981.

Weiss, D. J., & Davison, M. L. Test theory and methods. *Annual Review of Psychology*, 1981, *32*, 629–658.

Wolf, T. H. *Alfred Binet*. Chicago: University of Chicago Press, 1973.

Yerkes R. M. (Ed.). Psychological examining in the United States Army. *Memoirs of the National Academy of Sciences*, 1921, *15*.

INTERESTS MEASUREMENT

The measurement of educational and vocational interests has been one of the most widely addressed topics in vocational psychology, one that has a history reaching back to the early years of this century. Although the evolution of career interest inventories has been based on the conceptualizations underlying just a few instruments, and primarily one of them, and although fewer than a dozen instruments predominate in use today, scores of them have been developed. *The Eighth Mental Measurements Year-*

book (Buros, 1978) lists approximately fifty career and interest measures, and other literature includes reports of many more. (For some recent examples, see Alley, Berberich, & Wilbourn, 1977; Begin, 1977; Cunningham, Slonaker, & Riegel, 1975; Droege & Hawk, 1977; and Hanson, 1974.) The more widely used instruments have been the focus of a great deal of research to establish predictive, concurrent, and, more recently, construct validity, and to document use and add to the growing sets of occupational norms. The proliferation of instruments and research studies could not, however, have taken place without a receptive audience for them. The use of career interest inventories has become firmly established in career and educational counseling. One recent estimate puts at about 3.5 million the number of interest inventories that are scored annually by the three major test-scoring services or self-scored by users of the Self-directed Search (Tittle & Zytowski, 1978).

Constructing Inventories. The earliest approaches to measuring career interests consisted of directly asking individuals which of a number of occupations they were interested in. Responses to questions of this kind were generally superficial and unrealistic, probably reflecting the fact that young people are relatively naive about most occupations and have a tendency to focus only on those characteristics or aspects of an occupation that are particularly salient to them (Fryer, 1931). A less direct method, introduced by E. K. Strong, Jr., in 1927, made use of the Strong Vocational Interest Blank (SVIB). The empirical keying method he used was based on the notion that people in one occupation could be distinguished from people in others on the basis of their common interests in occupational things and also in matters such as interpersonal relationships and leisure-time activities. The SVIB used hundreds of items consisting of a wide variety of specific activities, kinds of people, or kinds of materials. In selecting the items, Strong attempted to list those things likely to be within the experiences of adolescents rather than those that could acquire meaning only after one engaged in an occupation. Most items in the Strong tests require respondents to indicate whether they like, dislike, or are indifferent to the content of the item. Scoring patterns were established solely on the basis of comparing the responses of men and, later, women in a specific occupation to the responses of all other men or women answering the items. Test takers are given scores on all specific occupational scales for which there are adequate norm data. This method of test construction relies entirely on acquired test data to describe the interests of members of specific occupations. Strong's development of the procedures has stood as the model for subsequent construction of other instruments, both career interest inventories and personality inventories.

The Kuder instruments, starting with the Kuder Preference Record (KPR) in 1940, used a completely different approach to test development. The items, forced-choice triads, each consisted of three different activities to which

students responded by indicating which was the most liked and which was the least liked. Kuder used factor analyses to identify clusters of interests and then organized items into descriptive scales. The intended result was to indicate a person's relative interest in a small number of occupational areas rather than in many specific occupations. The Kuder instruments provide scores on ten interest scales: Outdoor, Mechanical, Computational, Scientific, Persuasive, Artistic, Literary, Musical, Social Service, and Clerical. Early use of the Kuder instruments was based more on the logical relationships and content validity of the tests than on empirical data. The term "rational keying" was used to describe this method of inventory construction.

Since their introduction, both the Strong and Kuder inventories have been revised several times, and a series of forms has evolved for each (Campbell, 1971; Campbell et al., 1974; Kuder, 1966a, 1966b). Perhaps the most significant changes in the Strong instruments took place in 1974 with the publication of the Strong-Campbell Interest Inventory (SCII). These changes addressed issues involving charges of sex bias and the need to link operational definitions of interests with theoretical constructs. Although all interest inventories had been using separate norms for males and females, the Strong instruments had also been using separate forms. The problem of a lack of theoretical framework for interest inventories had been noted previously by several researchers, and is cogently described by Crites (1969). The 1974 SCII merged the women's and men's forms, dropped a masculinity–femininity scale, and simultaneously introduced scoring on six general occupational themes: Realistic, Artistic, Social, Enterprising, Investigative, and Conventional. These themes were based on Holland's classification of interests (1973), which had received support from a number of studies. They bear a close resemblance to the interest scales of the Kuder inventories. Since previous research on the Strong forms had resulted in the development of basic interest scales (also similar to Kuder's), individual scores on the SCII could be generated for 124 occupational scales as well as 23 basic interest scales embedded within the six occupational themes. The SCII also included a number of administrative indices for detecting response sets and for predicting the likelihood of a person's continuing education through high school, college, and graduate school (Campbell, 1974; Campbell et al., 1974). A previous version of the SVIB had contained the latter kind of index, but at least one study, which accumulated data over a five-year period, concluded that it did not differentiate between college students who graduated and those who did not (Wright, 1976).

Another milestone in test construction methodology was the introduction of the Kuder Occupational Interest Survey (KOIS). In developing the KOIS, an empirical keying similar to that used for the Strong inventories was employed. However, the KOIS method did not employ the men or women in general reference groups. It was scored by comparing an individual's response pattern directly with the patterns of occupational criterion groups through point-biserial correlation procedures. Scales on this test were developed for both occupational and college-major groups, as well as for a number of semiskilled occupations (Kuder, 1966a).

Although the initial approaches to the development of these inventories were almost diametrically opposed, recent developments demonstrate a growing number of similarities between them. Modifications of the Strong instruments hold the promise of more sophisticated interpretation of scores in counseling situations. In addition, they contain the potential for linking the instruments into a network of constructs that may ultimately permit the generation of additional knowledge about career interests within the larger picture of the individual's development and personality. The evolution of the Kuder instruments toward more empirically based procedures promises to improve the usefulness of the inventory, particularly in its applicability across occupational strata.

With growing sophistication in test development and scoring methods for interest inventories, computer scoring has become commonplace, and mandatory for some instruments. Partly as a reaction to this and partly arising from his theory of interests, Holland (1970, 1971) introduced the Self-directed Search. This instrument requires users to summarize their occupational daydreams, their favorite activities, their competencies, their knowledge of various occupations, and their self-estimates and relate them to appropriate occupations. This development has met with mixed success (see reviews in Buros, 1978).

Research on Inventories. Interest inventories, particularly the Strong and Kuder, and more recently the ACT Interest Inventory, have been the object of some of the most extensive research in psychological literature. Early studies grouped around several problem areas. A great deal of data were and still are gathered to establish occupational and general interest scale norms. There are numerous reports of test use in specific contexts and of the use of modified inventories with specific occupational or cultural samples. The stability of measured interests is a critical characteristic of tests that are used in counseling to assist students in making career and educational decisions. It has been the object of a number of longitudinal studies covering periods ranging from one to twenty years. The validity of various scales for predicting job entry, occupational success, and academic majors has been addressed frequently. For general reviews, examples of these kinds of studies, and discussions of persistent problems, see Anastasi (1976), Campbell (1971), Canfield (1941), Crites (1969), Crosby and Windsor (1941), Darley and Hagenah (1955), Hanson (1974), Hanson (1978), Kuder (1970), Strong (1955), and Super and Crites (1962). It is undoubtedly because of the extent of these research studies that interest inventories have come to be highly regarded in the field. Cronbach (1960), in evaluating the SVIB, said that it was "the most highly developed and best understood of the

inventories; indeed, it ranks very near the top among psychological tests of all types" (p. 434).

The use of interest inventories with minorities and women has received increasing attention in recent years in both the research and policy domains. Lamb's work (1978) comparing criterion-related validity and interest structures on the ACT Interest Inventory for white, black, native American, oriental American, and Spanish-surnamed college student samples indicates that use of the inventory is equally appropriate for any of these groups. This finding may be generalizable to other inventories resembling ACT but is probably not applicable to students of a younger age. It is consistent with similar studies done by others, but few of them have been done. Because of the evidence (or lack of it) collected to date, potential cultural bias of the inventories and their use has not been considered a pressing enough problem to generate a large amount of research interest.

The problem of using career interest inventories with women is considerably more complex and persistent, and it has received more attention. Interest inventory test construction procedures were originally based on the pervasive sociocultural assumption of differential occupational appropriateness for women and men. The result was that separate forms, separate interest and occupational scales, and separate norms were developed for men and women. These instrument characteristics were entrenched within a counseling and guidance context that perpetuated the view of the world of work as consisting of "men's work" and "women's work," and therefore restricted career and educational options for both sexes, but particularly for women. With the passage of Title IX of the Educational Amendments of 1972 (Public Law 92-318) and the amendments of 1976, sex-biased counseling and guidance practices were prohibited. Professional organizations (particularly the Association for Measurement and Guidance in Education), the National Institute of Education, and the publishers of career interest inventories themselves have all been instrumental in addressing the problems of sex bias in interest measurement. Within the last ten years, the social, legal, and many of the technical issues have been defined; research on several aspects of sex bias has been conducted; the characteristics of various interest inventories have been scrutinized; new norming and scoring procedures have been devised; and new guidelines and interpretive materials have been developed for the use of the measures (Diamond, 1975; Tittle & Zytowski, 1978).

In short, important changes have taken place in career interest measurement since its inception many years ago. These changes have been due to a continuing scrutiny of the inventories and how they work, the constant need to update and revise norms, the development of technical innovations, the need for grounding interest measurement within a theoretical framework, and the imperatives of addressing changing social policies and consciousness. Changes continue to be made. Research that addresses all fronts continues to be called for. One of the most important areas for future research is to discover how different kinds of inventories work differently for members of different sexes, cultures, occupations, and socioeconomic groups. Such studies may add not only to improved use of the instruments in educational contexts, but also to continued development of the theory that permits understanding and prediction of related phenomena.

Patricia M. Kay

See also Attitude Measurement; Career Guidance; Counseling; Individual Differences; Measurement in Education; Personality Assessment.

REFERENCES

Alley, W. E.; Berberich, G. L.; & Wilbourn, J. M. *Development of Factor-referenced Subscales for the Vocational Interest-Career Examination*. Brooks Air Force Base, Texas: Air Force Human Resources Laboratory, 1977. (ERIC Document Reproduction Service No. ED 156 721)

Anastasi, A. *Psychological Testing* (4th ed.). New York: Macmillan, 1976.

Begin, L. The Canadian Occupational Interest Inventory. *School Guidance Worker*, 1977, *32*, 38–41.

Buros, O. K. *The Eighth Mental Measurements Yearbook*. Highland Park, N.J.: Gryphon Press, 1978.

Campbell, D. P. *Handbook for the Strong Vocational Interest Blank*. Stanford, Calif.: Stanford University Press, 1971.

Campbell, D. P. *Manual for the Strong-Campbell Interest Inventory*. Stanford, Calif.: Stanford University Press, 1974.

Campbell, D. P.; Crichton, L.; Hansen, J. I.; & Webber, P. A new edition of the SVIB: The Strong-Campbell Interest Inventory. *Measurement and Evaluation in Guidance*, 1974, *7*.

Canfield, A. A. Administering Form BB of the Kuder Preference Record, half length. *Journal of Applied Psychology*, 1941, *32*, 481–494.

Crites, J. O. Interests. In R. L. Ebel (Ed.), *Encyclopedia of Educational Research* (4th ed.). New York: Macmillan, 1969. (ERIC Document Reproduction Service No. ED 040 587)

Cronbach, L. J. *Essentials of Psychological Testing* (2nd ed.). New York: Harper & Brothers, 1960.

Crosby, R. C., & Windsor, A. L. The validity of students' estimates of their own interests. *Journal of Applied Psychology*, 1941, *25*, 408–414.

Cunningham, J. W.; Slonaker, E.; & Riegel, N. B. *The Development of Activity Preference Scales Based on Systematically Derived Work Dimensions: An Ergometric Approach to Interest Measurement*. Washington, D.C.: National Institute of Education, 1975.

Darley, J. G., & Hagenah, T. *Vocational Interest Measurement: Theory and Practice*. Minneapolis: University of Minnesota Press, 1955.

Diamond, E. E. (Ed.). *Issues of Sex Bias and Sex Fairness in Career Interest Measurement*. Washington, D.C.: U.S. Government Printing Office, 1975. (ERIC Document Reproduction Service No. ED 113 609)

Droege, R. C., & Hawk, J. Development of a U.S. Employment Service Interest Inventory. *Journal of Employment Counseling*, 1977, *14*, 65–71.

Fryer, D. H. *The Measurement of Interests*. New York: Holt, 1931.

Hanson, G. R. *Assessing the Career Interests of College Youth:*

Summary of Research and Applications. Iowa City, Iowa: American College Testing Program, 1974. (ERIC Document Reproduction Service No. ED 109 525)

Hanson, J. C. Age differences and empirical scale construction. *Measurement and Evaluation in Guidance*, 1978, *11*, 78–87.

Holland, J. *The Self-directed Search*. Palo Alto, Calif.: Consulting Psychologists Press, 1970.

Holland, J. A theory-ridden, computerless, impersonal vocational guidance system. *Journal of Vocational Behavior*, 1971, pp. 167–176. (ERIC Document Reproduction Service No. ED 043 892)

Holland, J. *Making Vocational Choices: A Theory of Careers*. Englewood Cliffs, N.J.: Prentice-Hall, 1973.

Kuder, G. F. *Kuder Occupational Interest Survey: General Manual*. Chicago: Science Research Associates, 1966. (a)

Kuder, G. F. The occupational interest survey. *Personnel and Guidance Journal*, 1966, *45*, 72–77. (b)

Kuder, G. F. Some principles of interest measurement. *Educational and Psychological Measurement*, 1970, *30*, 205–226.

Lamb, R. R. Validity of the ACT Interest Inventory for minority group members. In C. Tittle & D. G. Zytowski (Eds.), *Sex-fair Interest Measurement: Research and Implications*. Washington, D.C.: National Institute of Education, 1978.

Strong, E. K., Jr. *Vocational Interests Eighteen Years after College*. Minneapolis: University of Minnesota Press, 1955.

Super, D. E., & Crites, J. O. *Appraising Vocational Fitness by Means of Psychological Tests* (Rev. ed.). New York: Harper & Brothers, 1962.

Tittle, C. K., & Zytowski, D. G. (Eds.). *Sex-fair Interest Measurement: Research and Implications*. Washington, D.C.: National Institute of Education, 1978. (ERIC Document Reproduction Service No. ED 166 416)

Wright, J. C. Research in brief: The SVIB academic achievement score and college attrition. *Measurement and Evaluation in Guidance*, 1976, *8*, 258–259.

INTERNATIONAL EDUCATION

The term "international education" was used increasingly during the sixties and seventies as an umbrella term describing a variety of activities and programs designed to encourage the flow of ideas and people across cultural and geographic boundaries. Such activities have included student and faculty exchanges; technical cooperation to help other countries build their educational institutions and programs; international, multicultural, multiethnic, and language studies in U.S. schools and institutions; programs to prepare professionals for international service; public affairs programs to inform and involve the American public in the discussion of world events and foreign policy issues; and information exchange activities, designed to benefit both foreign and U.S. scholars, businessmen, government officials, and citizens.

Implicit or explicit in most definitions of international education (Fraser, 1965; Griffin & Spence, 1970; Marklund, 1980; President's Commission on Foreign Language and International Studies, 1979a; Shane, 1969; Spaulding &

Singleton, 1968; Sutton, 1974; Task Force on International Education, 1966) are notions that such activities and programs are essential if we are to prepare a citizenry capable of dealing with the challenges of the modern world, its shrinking resources, and its increasingly interdependent social, political, and economic elements. Implicit, also, is the notion that we must work cooperatively with other nations of the world, both rich and poor, to help assure progress in meeting the basic needs of all people.

The concern for international education is not unique to the United States. Public and private organizations throughout the world are involved in research, training, technical assistance activities, and publications on all aspects of international education. Some of these organizations are the Institute of Education of the European Cultural Foundation in Paris; the International Movement Toward Educational Change (IMTEC) in Oslo; the Organization for Economic Cooperation and Development (OECD) in Paris; l'Association des Universités Partiellement ou Entièrement de Langue Française (AUPELF) in Montreal; the United Nations University in Tokyo; and the Institute of International Education in Stockholm. The Ford Foundation sponsored a series of studies in the mid-seventies which showed that needs for international studies in European and American institutions have similar dimensions (*International Studies in Six European Countries,* 1976). The United Nations Children's Fund (UNICEF) has described international and global education programs in elementary schools throughout the world (Miller, 1977). O'Connor (1980) examines world studies in the European classroom. European foundations, such as the Netherlands Universities Foundation for International Cooperation (NUFFIC), perform functions similar to those of funding groups in the U.S. in stimulating international activities in education (*NUFFIC Annual Report,* 1978).

These examples of foreign interest in international education illustrate the global context within which international education interests in the U.S. should be viewed. This article, however, because of space limitations, concentrates on trends within the United States. The first section deals with historical and legislative underpinnings of international education interests in the United States. The second section surveys trends within the convergent strands usually associated with the term "international education." Significant terminology within the field of international education includes "technical assistance," "comparative and development education," "educational and cultural exchange," "foreign language and area studies," "global issues," "multicultural and multiethnic education," "education for international understanding," "global education" and "outreach programs in international education." A third, brief section speculates on trends in the 1980s.

Historical Underpinnings. International education, loosely defined as the purposeful movement of ideas and scholars across cultural and geographic boundaries, has roots lost in history. Comparative educators such as Brick-man (cited in Fraser, 1965) trace the first technical assistance activities to biblical times when, in the tenth century B.C., King Solomon made a request of King Hiram of Tyre for skills and materials to construct the Holy Temple in Jerusalem. In subsequent centuries, virtually every great civilization is replete with examples of cultures adapting ideas from one another and of scholars and students from many countries mingling in various institutionalized forms of education.

Prior to World War II, there were relatively few "international studies" specialists in U.S. universities and schools. Returned missionaries, journalists, and foreign service officers and their offspring provided a type of network of international studies specialists (McCaughey, 1980). The advent of World War II found the United States woefully inadequate not only in terms of military preparedness but also in terms of specialists who understood the languages and cultures of the world where combat and occupation troops were expected to operate. As a result, the government hastily funded the establishment of language and area studies courses at some sixty-five universities (Task Force on International Education, 1966). These courses, which were established primarily for military training purposes, can be considered the seeds of post–World War II language and area studies programs in higher education.

Post–World War II era. The end of World War II generated an explosion of interest in all facets of international education. The United States led the movement to establish the United Nations and its specialized agencies, most notably the United Nations Educational, Scientific, and Cultural Organization (UNESCO); the Food and Agriculture Organization (FAO); the World Health Organization (WHO); the World Bank; and a variety of smaller agencies.

The establishment of the United Nations marked the threshold of a new era of foreign relations for the United States. This new era spawned a host of new federal agencies and programs—among them, the International Cooperation Administration (established in 1955 to replace the Economic Cooperation Administration and other programs and in 1961, to become, the Agency for International Development); the Central Intelligence Agency; the United States Information Agency (to become the International Communication Agency in the late seventies); the Bureau of Educational and Cultural Affairs of the Department of State (to be merged with the International Communication Agency in the late seventies); and the Bureau of International Organizations of the Department of State.

These new agencies and programs were established in response to the international challenges of the postwar period. Early legislation, such as the Marshall Plan, was designed to assist in European reconstruction but was later broadened to include technical and financial assistance and cooperation in the developing world. The Fulbright Act of 1946 authorized the use of surplus local currencies owned by the U.S. government abroad for programs of educational exchange. The legislation was broadened by the Smith-Mundt Act of 1948 to authorize dollar appropriations and further broadened by the Fulbright-Hays Act of 1961, which provided support for strengthening language and area competence in the United States through special programs abroad.

In the late fifties, other events affected the direction of international education. Following the launching of *Sputnik* in 1957, the National Defense Education Act of 1958 was passed. Title VI provided support for language and area studies in American universities and for language institutes to improve language teaching in the public schools. Concurrently, various foundations, especially the Ford Foundation, offered "institution-building" grants to colleges and universities to stimulate the internationalization of the curriculum and to encourage various kinds of international activities on campus. Finally, the Peace Corps, established in 1961, provided an opportunity for Americans of all ages to learn about the quotidian lives of others through international service.

The late 1960s and the 1970s. Such was the context of the mid-sixties when former President Lyndon B. Johnson proposed the passage of the International Education Act of 1966, proclaiming in his message to Congress that "ideas, not armaments, will shape our lasting prospects for peace. The conduct of our foreign policy will advance no faster than the curriculum of our classrooms" (Task Force, 1966, p. 17). Congressman Adam Clayton Powell, then Chairman of the House Committee on Education and Labor, suggested that the act was to support "international education—education to function effectively in a multicultural universe" through federal programs to "enable our schools and universities to carry forward the essential training and research in international studies" (Task Force, 1966, p. xii).

The International Education Act of 1966 was never funded. Although Title VI of the National Defense Education Act continued to receive modest funding through the seventies, the mood of Congress, during the Vietnam War and its aftermath, appeared to be unfavorable to increased funding of the broad goals of the International Education Act.

The seventies also encountered a diminishing interest of the major foundations in international studies. The Ford Foundation institutional grants of the sixties, designed to assist higher education institutions in developing international programs, ceased. Numerous private consulting firms were created and began to compete with universities for technical assistance contracts under the gradually diminishing foreign aid programs of the Agency for International Development (AID). The Peace Corps turned from its earlier goals of encouraging young people to engage in dialogue with peoples of other cultures to a more focused goal of providing technical assistance, but enthusiasm among many young people for such work declined.

In the early seventies, new social, economic, and political problems emerged from new global realities. The oil crisis is perhaps the best example. The changing political climate also figured among the new realities. The United States was no longer in the unchallenged position of political and economic leadership of the post–World War II years. At the same time, domestic concerns relating to ethnic and cultural groups within the United States began to overshadow the concern for international relationships of earlier years.

Social and political activism on the part of ethnic and racial minorities as well as shifts on the part of educators with respect to theoretical, ideological, and conceptual views of cultural diversity gave rise to multicultural and multiethnic education (Flint, 1980). Title VII of the Emergency School Aid Act of 1972, for example, addresses the need for curriculum materials and instructional strategies that focus on the language and culture of American minority groups.

It was in this context of international and domestic ferment and change that the Carter administration assumed power in 1977. With its emphasis on human rights and international dialogue, the administration felt that the time was ripe for a fresh look at the state of international education in the United States. In 1978, based upon the recommendations of legislators such as Representative Paul Simon and educational interest groups such as the American Council on Education (1975), Carter appointed a President's Commission on Foreign Language and International Studies, consisting of twenty-five distinguished educators, businessmen, journalists, and legislators. The report of the commission portrays a dramatic picture of the decline in both funding of and institutional commitment to foreign languages and international studies in the seventies (President's Commission on Foreign Language and International Studies 1979a, 1979b). A ringing introduction links foreign language and international studies to national interests in security and business and suggests that the "situation cries out for a better comprehension of our place and our potential in a world that, though it expects much from America, no longer takes American supremacy for granted" (President's Commission, 1979b, p. 2). The president's commission quotes extensively from an Educational Testing Service study of children in grades 4, 8, and 12, in twenty states, which presents dramatic evidence of the extent of student illiteracy in world affairs (Pike et al., 1979).

The commission recommends a broad program of federal support for foreign language and international studies in schools, colleges, and universities; support for college and university training and research programs; increased funding of international educational exchange programs and for citizens' education programs in international affairs; cooperative programs with business and industry; the strengthening of coordination and administration within the federal government for such programs, plus a continuing private National Commission on Foreign Language and International Studies to monitor and report on progress in the area.

Even though professional response to the report has

been favorable (Lambert, 1980; "President's Commission on Foreign Language and International Studies," 1980), immediate prospects for substantial federal funding of the programs suggested by the commission appear bleak. The Reagan administration has proposed sizable budget cuts in all legislation affecting international education. Nevertheless, the commission's report has provided yet another rallying point for the various interested groups in pursuing more consistent and integrated policies of international education.

Institutional support among colleges, universities, and state departments of education for international education activities may be on the upswing. As examples of such support, a recent internal study at Michigan State University (International Studies Programs Review and Planning Committee, 1980) recommends the strengthening of all aspects of international programming on campus; and a statement by the International Affairs Committee of the National Association of State Universities and Land Grant Colleges (1981) suggests a renewal of U.S. resolve to assist developing countries and posits that such commitments can be strengthened under the leadership of the Board for International Food and Agriculture Development (BIFAD), created by Congress under Title XII of the Foreign Assistance Act. The American Association of Colleges for Teacher Education and the International Council for the Education of Teachers continue to promote collaborative activity with teacher education groups in other countries. Community and junior colleges are expanding their commitment to international education (American Association of Community and Junior Colleges, 1978; Harrington & Clarkson, 1979; Schultz & Terrell, 1979. The Council for Interinstitutional Leadership at the University of Alabama urges international education consortia programs (Emplaincourt & Bush, 1979); an Illinois Task Force on Foreign Language and International Studies recommends a comprehensive statewide program (Illinois State Board of Education, 1979).

In a study on international programs in higher education, Burn (1980) points out that "when international activities and programs are centrally coordinated they reinforce each other and become more central to the institution in terms of both structure and priority" (p. 143). Many institutions share this notion as evidenced by the increased efforts during the seventies to set up international programs offices. One example is the University Center for International Studies at the University of Pittsburgh, an administrative unit that coordinates all international education activities at that institution. The level of administrative direction ranges from Vice-President for International Studies at Texas A & M University to Dean of International Studies and Programs at Michigan State University to Director of the Center for International Studies at the University of Pittsburgh. Comprehensive international studies centers frequently have responsibility for coordinating area studies programs, international exchanges, foreign students, technical assistance projects

abroad, faculty research in international studies, outreach programs, and transnational interinstitutional relationships. Funds to support partially many of these activities may come from a broad range of federal agencies, as noted in an eighty-four-page American Council on Education compendium of federal agency programs that support international education (Owens, 1977). A more recent, yet unexhaustive inventory, compiled by the Federal Interagency Committee on Education, lists some 181 international education programs of at least 28 federal agencies (Wiprud, 1980).

Major Trends. International education is not a clearly defined professional or disciplinary term. Rather, it is a useful term to label a wide range of activities and research interests. In this section we examine trends in several definable areas within international education. If one thinks of the various areas as strands of interest, it is clear that the various strands intersect in many ways. For instance, technical assistance activities of the federal government and of international agencies have drawn on universities and their faculties to implement the field programs; and this has stimulated campus interest in international, comparative, and development education. Similarly, the technical assistance programs have stimulated educational and cultural exchange activities that, in turn, have been supportive in many ways of foreign language and area studies on college and university campuses. Finally, the various concerns for multicultural and multiethnic studies in domestic U.S. education have drawn on models similar to those prevalent in the international area studies programs and on earlier interests in education for international understanding.

Technical assistance activities. One might hypothesize that it was the major development of technical assistance activities in the decades following World War II that triggered interest within the United States in all aspects of international education. The leadership in scholarly international studies exercised by returned foreign correspondents, missionaries, and foreign-service officers and their children was rapidly challenged by faculty members who returned to campus after service in a technical assistance project. Institutions that undertook such projects often used them as devices for strengthening faculty interest and commitment to international studies. Many of them established international programs offices designed to involve faculty members in overseas assistance activities and to create area and/or international studies programs on campus.

The sixties were a period of great ferment in higher education institutions, which were considering ways of using technical cooperation programs to strengthen academic and scholarly interests at home (Morrill, 1960). Some scholars wrote compellingly of the significance of such programs for universities (Gardner, 1963; Humphrey, 1967; Sutton, 1979). Coombs and Bigelow (1965) examined the significance of such programs for the field of education; Harbison and Meyers (1964) legitimized investment in education throughout the world as a major contribution to economic development; and Education and World Affairs (1966), the predecessor of the International Council for Educational Development, did case studies of six American universities that represented different models of institutionalizing for effective higher education involvement in international education. Interest in international education was not limited to area studies. It also permeated the various professional schools, ranging from business and public administration to agriculture, engineering, law, medicine, public health, and education (Sanders, 1968). A number of universities established consortia (e.g., the Midwest Consortium for International Activities) with the idea that many technical assistance activities would require the resources of more than one university. Others formed councils (e.g., the Pennsylvania Council for International Education) designed to encourage a broad range of cooperation among higher education institutions with international interests.

During the seventies, attention was increasingly turned to broader interests in global education, education for interdependence, and multicultural and ethnic education. This attention has been accompanied by a decline in U.S. legislative funding of technical assistance activities. When the Marshall Plan was instituted at the end of World War II, U.S. official development assistance amounted to 2.49 percent of the gross national product (GNP). Although the foreign aid budgets of most Western nations have been increasing since then, U.S. assistance has declined steadily, and in 1979, only 0.19 percent of the GNP was so allocated (McNamara, 1980). The Reagan administration is proposing further cuts in economic assistance abroad; and it appears that the U.S. will further withdraw from collaborative economic and social development activities around the world.

Given that much of the leadership in international education during the sixties and seventies came from scholars and professionals who had been drawn into technical assistance activities early in their careers, one could posit that the dramatic decline in U.S. support for such activity will have an impact on international education leadership in the future.

Comparative and development education. The increasing involvement of U.S. educational institutions in overseas educational development activities during the fifties and sixties and the concurrent movement of U.S. faculty abroad to help other countries in the development of their educational systems led to considerable ferment in the comparative education field. Whereas traditional comparative education tended to deal with the statics of education in various countries (i.e., the structure and organization of education, the curriculum, or the enrollment at various levels), the sixties and seventies witnessed an emphasis on the study of the dynamics of education in individual countries around the world (i.e., the effect of different kinds of intervention in educational systems and the interaction of education, society, and the economy).

Some scholars defined this new interest as "development education" (Spaulding & Singleton, 1968; "The States of the Art," 1977).

A 1977 issue of the *Comparative Education Review*, devoted to the "state of the art," is noteworthy in including little on the statics of education. Most of the issue deals with conflict and equilibrium paradigms as applied to questions of education and social change; economic models for assessing the cost and benefit of educational investment at different levels and in differing contexts; the effect of education on social equity; and equity (or the lack of it) in access to and success in education around the world.

Comparative and development education are synthetic fields that draw upon the various disciplines and professions relevant to the study of educational phenomena. In fact, literature of interest in the field is often found in social science and professional journals rather than in education journals. Similarly, the various programs and centers in comparative, international, and development education at major universities (e.g., University of Pittsburgh; Stanford; Harvard; Teachers College, Columbia; University of Massachusetts) tend to have interdisciplinary faculty and to draw students from undergraduate fields other than education.

Significant research trends in comparative and development education affect to some degree international and bilateral policies in educational development around the world, and assistance policies, in turn, affect research trends. For instance, although U.S. aid policy included projects in the field of education as far back as the fifties, it was not until economists, such as Schultz (1963) and Harbison and Meyers (1964), espoused education as investment rather than consumption that the assistance community began to place high priority on educational development in other countries.

The turning point may have come in 1962 when Eugene R. Black, then president of the World Bank, announced that the International Development Association, a World Bank affiliate, would grant loans for education. The bank's first education credits were granted to Tunisia in the amount of $5 million for secondary school construction. Bank interest in education accelerated through the sixties and seventies, and by June 1979, it had supported 192 education projects in 81 countries, mostly through a cooperative program with the United Nations Educational, Scientific and Cultural Organization (UNESCO) begun in 1964 (World Bank, 1980a).

Although the World Bank concentrates on capital assistance, UNESCO, in cooperation with the United Nations Development Program (UNDP), assists developing countries by providing teams of experts to help establish rational educational plans and to assist in training counterparts to manage educational institutions, curriculum development centers, and other specialized programs in national education systems. The United Nations Children's Fund (UNICEF) collaborates with both UNESCO and the World Bank in providing school equipment and other services useful in primary education and primary teacher training.

In the early seventies, the various multilateral and bilateral aid groups, including several foundations, sponsored a series of conferences at Bellagio, Italy, that set the stage for increased collaboration in educational development activities. An early report of the Bellagio meetings suggests a strong economic bias in the support of education for development (Ward, 1974). Although earlier policies had stressed assistance at the secondary, vocational, and higher levels in order to provide specialized personnel for economic development, subsequent policy statements by the World Bank (1980a, 1980b) and the Agency for International Development (1980) suggest increased support at the primary or basic education level in order to assist countries in achieving social equity. It was the rapid expansion of upper-level education and the increasing problem in many countries of underemployed high-level personnel that led economists to recommend increased support at the base of the pyramid—the basic education level.

The effects of various aid policies on educational development in recipient countries needs more systematic study (Spaulding, 1981). A 1976 study charts the complexities of European and American involvement in educational aid (Parkinson, 1976); another study prescribes various guidelines building on the earlier Bellagio conferences (Phillips, 1976). For a microperspective of what happens in the field when a bilateral or multilateral educational assistance project is undertaken, few studies equal that of Havelock and Huberman (1978), which examines a number of cases in various countries and builds theory concerning the elements influencing the success or failure of projects. Similarly, Spaulding and Gillette undertook case studies of UNESCO's functional literacy projects and suggested sources of impediments to the full attainment of planned goals and objectives (United Nations Development Program, 1976).

A 1968 report of the Agency for International Development (AID) assessed a broad range of projects undertaken abroad by land grant universities in the fifties and sixties and suggested ways of improving and expanding the programs. Adiseshiah (1979) and MacKinnon (1979) reviewed the history of international interventions in the field of education and suggested that we have moved from aid to cooperation. Sutton (1979) examined the problems of maintaining effective worldwide relationships between universities, and Dawson (1978) examined problems of rural development in less developed countries and ways of organizing a foreign aid program.

There are many actors involved in policy setting and in field implementation of aid programs, but the interaction dynamics among the actors is complex and poorly understood. The picture is further complicated by what might be called "filtering organizations." Dozens, if not hundreds, of private organizations, both profit and non-profit, undertake various kinds of educational assistance activities throughout the world. Many of these, especially

church-related groups, have small amounts of their own funding. Most depend, however, on contracts and grants from governments and foundations. Typical groups are the Academy for Educational Development; World Education, Incorporated; the American Institutes for Research; and the New Transcentury Foundation. These organizations tend to follow the funds available and to develop institutional policies that are infused into the projects they manage.

AID, in turn, recognizes that it is dependent upon institutional resources in the United States to implement its aid policies. Accordingly, foreign aid legislation in the sixties and seventies provided for AID funding of centers in the United States that can provide research and personnel pools necessary for effective implementation of aid policy. Accordingly, Michigan State University's Center for Nonformal Education has been funded over a period of more than a decade to pursue research, to provide information services, and to provide personnel in nonformal education—an AID priority. World Education, Incorporated (a private, nonprofit group, Stanford University's Center for Communication Research, and the Academy for Educational Development in Washington, D.C. have also received such funding. To some degree, these contractual programs are beneficial in building up U.S. institutional capability to understand educational assistance needs and in facilitating more effective international educational collaboration.

In a less direct way, the World Bank has collaborated with U.S. and foreign institutions by borrowing faculty for policy study and project planning and evaluation activities. The bank also operates an Economic Development Institute in Washington, D.C., which trains small numbers of government officials from abroad in educational as well as other types of planning (World Bank, 1975). Similarly, there are various training efforts, especially in language, run by organizations such as the Defense Language Institute, the Foreign Service Institute, the Missionary Training School (run by the Mormons), and the Summer Institute of Linguistics. Many of the people trained in these programs embark upon some kind of work related to development education when they complete their training.

Educational and cultural exchange. The movement of people beyond their own borders for structured educational and cultural experiences has continued to accelerate since World War II. The network of institutions and organizations involved in such activities is vast. It includes intergovernmental agencies, U.S. government agencies, academic and scholarly organizations, private voluntary organizations, professional exchange organizations, and international wings of various professional organizations in specialized fields. The range of such programs is outlined in a publication of the U.S. Department of State (1975).

Although the flow of personnel is both to and from the United States, the trend most often noted is that of increasing numbers of foreign students coming to the United States. In 1954, there were 19,124 undergraduate and

12,110 graduate students from abroad in the United States. This figure increased to 149,024 undergraduates and 114,916 graduate students in 1978, and projections suggest that there will be about 408,000 undergraduates and 266,000 graduate students by 1990 (National Center for Educational Statistics, 1980; Winkler & Agarwal, 1980).

Foreign student enrollment has significant implications for U.S. foreign policy since many of these students return to their home country to become leaders (Angell, 1979; Coombs, 1964; Elder, 1961; Frankel, 1965; Jacobson, 1979; Spaulding & Coelho, 1980; Thomson & Laves, 1963). Kenneth Thompson of the Rockefeller Foundation, for instance, is quoted by Arnove (1980) as claiming that "66 percent of all East African faculty have been Rockefeller Foundation scholars or holders of Special Lectureships established with Rockefeller Foundation funding" (p. 56). There are also implications for the curriculum and programs of American colleges and universities for the communities that host foreign students (Burn, 1978; Jenkins, 1978; National Liaison Committee on Foreign Student Admissions, 1971; President's Commission on Foreign Language and International Studies, 1979a, 1979b; Sanders, 1963; Spitzberg, 1980). Furthermore, literally hundreds of studies have explored what happens to foreign students while they are abroad, from the point of view of both academic achievement and adaptation and coping (Coelho & Ahmed, 1980; Cormack, 1962; Cussler, 1962; Eide, 1970; Klineberg, 1976; Klineberg & Hull, 1979; Walton, 1967). A review of over 450 studies on foreign students in the United States illustrates the diversity of such research (Spaulding and Flack, 1976). Although numerous studies with a psychological, sociological, anthropological, or educational management bias have been done on academic and adjustment problems, few attempt to integrate knowledge stemming from these disparate disciplinary biases. There is limited theory in the field, and what little exists does not tend to attract a longitudinal research following.

Policy and administrative recommendations generated by such studies seem to be ignored. Few colleges and universities attempt to adjust curriculum to the needs of foreign students, many of whom are from developing countries with manpower and technological problems substantially different from those of the United States. Although many colleges and universities have well-developed foreign-student offices, these typically deal with financial and housing problems rather than academic issues. Academic departments, in turn, tend to take the position that the foreign student is on campus to study what is considered important in the United States.

Few follow-up studies have been done on foreign students after they return home. Larger numbers of studies have been pursued on the migration of high-level talent—the so-called brain-drain—that is, those students who do not return home (Adams, 1968; Bhavati, 1975; Bhavati Partington, 1976; Glaser, 1974; Glaser & Habers, 1973, 1978; Myers, 1972). In this area, however, the research literature is contradictory, with a number of studies suggesting that, even from an economic viewpoint, such migration is good for the sending country because such migrants would probably be underemployed at home and they contribute to the home economy in terms of funds repatriated from abroad. Other studies, especially in the medical field, suggest that there should be—and indeed there have been—increasing attempts to encourage medical students to return and remain home to provide needed services there.

Governmental interest in attracting students from abroad has declined steadily over the years, perhaps, in part, because foreign-student arrivals continue to increase despite diminishing U.S. government support. The number of foreign students aided under the Fulbright-Hays Act has declined from 1,853 in 1966 to 1,166 in 1978. Financial aid for foreign students under AID programs has declined from 6,827 grants in 1964 to 902 in 1979. With over 250,000 foreign students in the United States each year in the late seventies, it is obvious, then, that the majority are either self-supporting or are supported by scholarships from their own governments or from international organizations such as the United Nations specialized agencies.

The economic impact of these students on local communities and on universities has rarely been studied. If one estimates that each student spends at least $10,000 a year on tuition and living expenses in the United States (and those who bring families spend much more), these students bring some $2.5 billion a year into the U.S. economy. Only in the early eighties are studies of these economic issues being planned (e.g., by Donald R. Winkler of the School of Public Administration of the University of Southern California). Such studies must include not only a concern for the effect on university budgets, but also an examination of the impact of total funds imported into the local community by the foreign students.

There has been little study of the magnitude or effect of organized programs of foreign study and cultural exchange experiences for U.S. scholars, students, and citizens. Notwithstanding the call for greater awareness by all Americans of the interdependencies in today's world, there has been little policy support at the governmental level for increased foreign experiences on the part of Americans. Most efforts are privately organized either by voluntary organizations or by scholarly and professional organizations. Some exceptions are the Peace Corps, which is no longer promoted as a cultural exchange activity but as a technical assistance function of the U.S. government, and modest programs of educational and cultural exchange under the International Communication Agency and the Fulbright program.

Study abroad on the part of U.S. students has not followed the pattern of foreign students in the United States. Minuscule numbers of U.S. students pursue degrees in foreign universities. Most programs of study abroad are organized by U.S. institutions that borrow facilities and occasional faculty from foreign institutions for special programs geared to the curriculum the students are following in the United States. A few American colleges exist abroad (e.g., the American College in Paris), but these are not encouraged by U.S. education policy. Such institutions are considered foreign institutions under federal higher education legislation and are not eligible for student or institutional aid under federal programs. The State Department, in turn, which subsidizes American overseas schools, considers such institutions American institutions and therefore ineligible for programs available to foreign institutions. American colleges abroad are a mistakenly neglected element in American higher education policy in an age when interrelationships with other countries are becoming more critical to every aspect of our social, economic, and political life.

Foreign language and area studies. Literature related to international studies and foreign language education tends to be interrelated at the policy and organizational level but distinct at the substantive level. Thus, legislation often covers both simultaneously. Structures such as area studies centers at universities also cover both, and there is some degree of overlap of professional interests in organizations such as the International Studies Association. However, foreign language specialists tend to have their own professional organizations (the Modern Language Association and the various associations of teachers of specific languages), often intersecting with professional associations of linguists. Essentially, then, those interested in international area studies and in foreign languages represent an interdisciplinary group of people, primarily from the various social science disciplines and from foreign language fields.

The term "area studies" refers to the study of foreign peoples and cultures from the perspectives of different disciplines. Area studies programs usually require students to study the history, social, political, and cultural dimensions; literature and art; and one or more of the languages of a country or region (Lambert, 1973). In most cases, the study of an area is not the student's major, but rather complements a major in a given discipline (Tonkin & Edwards, 1981). Many institutions offer certificates attesting to the student's area specialization, thus making the area specialization similar to a minor (Bonham, 1981).

International relations is a subfield of political science that deals with the international system and the interactions among actors in that system. Actors consist of nation states, governmental organizations, nongovernmental organizations, multinational corporations, and other groups or individuals who interact across national boundaries. The field has a well-defined body of literature, research paradigms and methodologies, and professional publications and organizations.

Foreign language training is only one component of the international dimension in education (Cadoux, 1977; Luce, 1978; Renshaw, 1972; Strasheim, 1979). Language is the key that unlocks the door to other cultures and is,

in fact, a direct reflection of culture. Logically, it seems that the only valid way to study another culture is through its mode of thought. A mastery of idiom enables the learner to gain access to the culture and to establish an intimate relationship with it, thereby experiencing what its members feel, think, see, and understand (Rettig, 1968). Ideally, such an experience in human understanding instills in the student a high level of tolerance for those who are different from members of his own cultural group. As a result, the foreign language speaker will contribute his share, minute as it may be, to world understanding and to an enrichment of human relationships. There is much to be said about the intrinsic and extrinsic values of foreign language competence in this globally interdependent era (Lantolf, 1977; President's Commission on Foreign Language and International Studies, 1979a; Simon, 1977; Turner, 1974).

Global issues. Many scholars, professionals, and businessmen are interested in the global dimensions of such issues as hunger, population, energy, arms control, law of the sea, foreign trade, transnational business relationships, and the like. Many faculty on university campuses interested in such issues do not identify with the various area study centers or with language programs on campus (Tonkin & Edwards, 1981). They see themselves, perhaps, as "transnational" specialists (President's Commission on Foreign Language and International Studies, 1979a), not particularly interested in any one foreign society or culture or foreign nation, but rather in the worldwide dynamics of a particular problem. These specialists increasingly identify with professional organizations that are interdisciplinary in nature and with a number of groups that can be loosely grouped under the term "futurology." The focus upon global issues is a critical conceptual and organizational problem for the future in international studies. Perhaps the most provocative presentation of this point of view is a study commissioned by the Club of Rome (Botkin, Elmandjra, & Malitza, 1979).

Multicultural education. To further confound the international studies picture, the past two decades have seen an attempt to conceptualize areas of study generally called "ethnic or multicultural studies." These interests are rooted not in a response to a need to understand and interact more intelligently with other countries and peoples, but rather in a concern for creating an informed citizenry who can deal with a multicultural and multiethnic domestic scene.

The American Association of Colleges for Teacher Education (AACTE) presented one of the best statements on multicultural education: "Multicultural education is education which values cultural pluralism. Multicultural education affirms that schools should be oriented toward the cultural enrichment of all children and youth through programs rooted to the preservation and extension of cultural diversity as a fact of life in American society.... Multicultural education reaches beyond awareness and understanding of cultural differences. More important than the acceptance and support of these differences is the recognition of the right of these different cultures to exist" (AACTE, 1973, pp. 264–265).

Interestingly, strands in this domestic interest seem to be comparable to the comparative and development education interests in the international arena. There are those who see multicultural and ethnic studies as the teaching of the history and culture of different ethnic groups in the United States (similar to comparative education until recent years); but others see such studies as an effort to get various segments of society to understand the dynamics of development and change within different ethnic groups so as to help the various groups work together more effectively toward satisfactory economic, social, and political relationships in the future (comparable to "development education" in the international sphere). Nonetheless, a search of ERIC files shows that the two areas, international studies and multicultural-multiethnic studies, are distinct entities in the minds of those at work in each field.

Education for international understanding. In its 1972 report, the International Commission on the Development of Education (Faure et al., 1972) asserted that "one mission of education is to help men see foreigners not as abstractions but as concrete beings, with their own reasons, sufferings, and joys, and to discern a common humanity among the various nations" (p. 153). A UNESCO recommendation, adopted in 1974, outlined the guiding principles of education for international understanding. This type of education promotes understanding, tolerance, and friendship among all nations, racial, or ethnic groups and furthers the activities of the United Nations toward the maintenance of peace (UNESCO, 1974). Instilling positive attitudes towards peace, justice, and human rights in young people is organized around the existing curricula by the incorporation of a global perspective in the regular course offerings rather than through new courses in global studies. Education for international understanding should begin as early as possible. The development of political knowledge, beliefs, and values is a lifelong process that begins in infancy (Remy et al., 1975). Since the period from 6 to 14 years of age, however, seems to be most crucial in the development of attitudes toward peoples of other cultures and nations, the primary and middle schools have a vital role to play in fostering a greater awareness, understanding, and appreciation of other cultures.

Because of young children's tendency to see themselves as the center of the universe (Piaget & Weil, 1951), primary education should first focus on the development of attitudes and skills that help pupils recognize and respect their own individuality. Then, to enable children to deal with the increasingly complex concepts of family, community, ethnic and cultural groups, state, nation, and the family of mankind, teachers should adopt a spiral approach, moving from the familiar to the unknown (Piaget & Weil, 1951; UNESCO, 1976). At the secondary level, students are better able to deal both cognitively and affectively

with the difficult concepts and generalizations involved in education for peace and understanding of others. Simulations in which students can play a participatory role are often quite effective tools in teaching world problems (Whipp, 1980). Throughout the educational process, however, the focus must always be on the unity of mankind and the respect for diversity and differences (Lamden, 1979; Leestma, 1978; UNESCO, 1976).

Perhaps the best example of this type of education is the UNESCO Associated Schools Project for Education in International Cooperation and Peace. The goal of this project, which was launched in 1953, is to promote international cooperation and peace through formal schooling. Any existing school may apply to participate in this experimental project. Although individual schools design and implement their own curricular activities, they need to concentrate on four basic topics: world problems and the role of the United Nations system in solving them; human rights; other countries and cultures; and man and his environment. Today, approximately thirteen hundred primary, secondary, and teacher-training institutions in seventy-four countries are participating in this project (UNESCO, no date; Sato, 1979; Struwe, 1979).

Global education. A trend exists in the seventies and early eighties for a new, synthetic area to emerge, usually under the titles of "global education," "education for global awareness," "education for interdependence," or "education for global interdependence." Those using the above terminology are attempting to cut across traditional disciplinary and professional interests embedded in earlier terminology. Viewing the world as a single system, they suggest educational approaches that prepare citizens to cope with an increasingly complex domestic and international community of interests (Anderson, 1979; Becker, 1979; Posvar, 1980). At least one state, Pennsylvania, has appointed a statewide global education task force and has articulated global education goals for the future of the education system in the state. Various citizens' associations, such as the United Nations Association, issue publications and study documents dealing with interdependence and global issues, and the new terminology is even beginning to appear in publications issued by some of the more traditional international studies groups.

Anderson (1979) has perhaps thus far done the most thorough study of the meaning and significance of global education. He defines global education as "efforts to bring about changes in the content, in the methods, and in the social context of education in order to better prepare students for citizenship in a global age" (p. 15). Anderson's definition implies that students who are currently enrolled in the nation's schools are becoming citizens within the context of a global era in human history; that citizens in a global age must develop competencies that have not been traditionally emphasized by schools; and that certain changes must take place in the educational process if schools are to become more effective agents of citizen education in a global age.

The impetus for global education came from a major study on goals, needs, and priorities in international education at the elementary and secondary level, funded in 1966 by the U.S. Office of Education. The report of the study team called for a new definition of international education and emphasized the need to prepare children and youth to live in an interdependent global society (Becker, 1969).

In 1978, Leestma, then Associate Commissioner for Institutional Development and International Education, U.S. Office of Education, outlined the five underlying concerns of the global perspective approach to education: unity and diversity of mankind; international human rights; global interdependence; intergenerational responsibility; and international cooperation. These five major themes should permeate all global curricula.

The educational system is obviously the best channel for fostering global awareness. Yet, despite the importance of reaching children before they form prejudices and stereotypes, few primary school teachers engage children in activities with a global component (American Council on Education, 1975). A 1979 nationwide survey of college students to determine their understanding of the world and world issues suggests that change may not come about very rapidly: education majors (the teachers of the future) scored lowest on the knowledge test (Barrows, Klein, & Clark, 1981). A number of public and private internationally oriented organizations as well as professional education associations have developed curriculum models, guidelines, and materials to assist classroom teachers in adopting a global approach. Simonson (1977) has developed one such curriculum model for world study based on three levels of awareness: global consciousness (grades K–4); global specialization (grades 3–9); and global understanding (grades 6–12). Remy et al. (1975) offer useful guidelines for designing world studies programs based on a variety of orientations. Mehlinger et al. (1979) provide their readers with sample lessons from a global studies project for middle schools sponsored by the Indiana University Social Studies Development Center. The Center for Global Perspectives of the New York Friends Group, Inc. issues a quarterly publication, *Intercom*, which provides a myriad of classroom tools, resources, and ideas for teachers.

Since the Becker report (1969) there has been a growing feeling, especially among the professional associations of social studies teachers, that students need to know and understand more about other peoples and cultures and about the challenges humankind faces in an increasingly interdependent world. Attempts have been made to introduce new forms of international and global education in high schools throughout the country (Starr, 1979). One example is the High School for International Service, started by the Center for International Service (headed by Harold Taylor) of the College of Staten Island, in collaboration with a 2,000-pupil school near the college. There are also cases of schools deliberately created with a global education perspective, for example, the Friends World College, the Monterey Institute of International Studies, the Thunderbird schools, and the School for International Training of the Experiment for International Living. Although a number of state departments of education have been promoting global education as a concept, there is little indication that many school systems are adopting strong programs of global and international education on a systemwide basis.

Outreach programs. In an effort to link the expertise of university faculty in international studies with the needs of the local community and schools, area studies centers developed outreach programs (e.g., Egerton, 1980). The impetus for outreach activities came largely from the requirement that National Defense Education Act Title VI centers devote the equivalent of at least 15 percent of the funds awarded to them to such university-community linkage activities. Outreach activities include in-service education programs for teachers, public lecture series, colloquia, conferences, summer institutes, media productions, studies of curriculum development, and film series, with a view toward increasing citizen involvement in foreign policy making (Alger, 1978). As Mehlinger and Ehman (1974) argue, such programs not only enrich the specific target audience (such as high school teachers) but also enhance undergraduate education.

Trends in the 1980s. International education is a cluster of concepts represented by a variety of institutional patterns. Each is shaped by federal legislation, which itself has changed in its emphases over time. Historically, the field has consisted of, perhaps, two major strands of interest: the idealistic, which has stressed education and exchange experiences for the purpose of encouraging international understanding and peace, and the pragmatic, which has stressed the need for this nation to prepare internationally sophisticated manpower who can more effectively serve the political, economic, and social needs of the country and the world.

The early eighties find little federal legislative support for the idealistic strand of international education. Programs such as the Peace Corps have been slashed to about fifty-five hundred volunteers in 1981 compared to over fifteen thousand in 1968. Economic and social aid under the Reagan administration will be earmarked for use primarily in cases where the recipient country is clearly significant from a strategic viewpoint.

The pragmatic strand of international education, however, may receive increased support in the early and mideighties. While there appears to be less federal government interest in international understanding, there is an increased awareness of the need for greater sophistication in dealing with international and transnational problems and issues. This fact suggests probable rethinking on the allocation of federal funds. Language and area studies funds will no longer be given exclusively to area centers and language programs simply because the existence of more regional and language specialists is assumed to be good. Funds increasingly will be earmarked for programs that deal with transnational economic, social, and political issues, as well as problems that transcend national and even regional interests. Funds for global education at the elementary through undergraduate-university levels will probably give priority to in-school and outreach programs that do more than teach young people and citizens about the cultures and customs of other countries. Priority will be given to those programs that attempt to educate a citizenry in the social, economic, and political interdependencies among nations and among cultural groups in the United States.

Research funds will be scarce for conclusion-oriented and theory-oriented research but will be more plentiful if social scientists and professionals can team up to demonstrate the usefulness of research in solving problems. Policy makers who control resource allocation will be less interested in studies that describe current problems and their history. They are increasingly interested in ways to predict, with some degree of accuracy, the future effect of alternative interventions. Interests in cross-cultural research will gradually merge with those in economic development and social engineering.

Higher education institutional structures will continue to lag behind conceptual frameworks. Language and area studies centers will resist the trend toward broader-based structures that stress problem-oriented and issue-oriented research with a transnational and interregional focus. The resistance will be exacerbated by departmental and disciplinary boundaries that will remain strong, especially as budgetary constraints in the eighties strengthen the competition for scarce resources. Private foundations and industries may increase support for conclusion-oriented and theory-oriented research, thus taking up some of the slack of diminished federal support. Nevertheless, such research will receive relatively less support both from the federal government and from private sources than it has received in the past.

Similar problems will plague international, global, multicultural, and multiethnic education at the elementary and secondary levels. Substantial changes in established curriculum areas that should be affected by the new trends will come about slowly. Although state departments of education and local school systems will be eager to benefit from federal funds available for these areas, there will be continued competition among those who identify with the various strands, and there will only be nominal cooperation among the various projects and programs labeled international, global, or multicultural and multiethnic.

Urgently needed is a coherent network of interest groups to lobby on a national basis for international education support. This suggests both a disbanding of interests, so that the value of each group can be made concrete and clear to legislators and policy makers, and a coordinated lobbying effort among all the groups. Until recently, social science and language groups have supported traditional notions of language and areas studies. There has been a reasonable coordination among these groups

through organizations such as the Social Science Research Council, the American Council of Learned Societies, and the various national organizations with language and area affiliations. Professional schools at the university level and private voluntary organizations primarily concerned with international and global issues have much less effective coordinating bodies at the national level. Each professional association, nevertheless, often has an international special-interest group or organization (e.g., in the field of education, the American Educational Research Association, the Association for Educational Communications and Technology, the International Reading Association, the Association for Supervision and Curriculum Development, the American Association of Colleges for Teacher Education, the Comparative and International Education Society; and in the field of development studies, the Society for International Development). One hopes that the International Studies Association (ISA) is able to pull together the various social science and issues-oriented professional groups; but even the ISA is heavily dominated by social scientists and gets only token participation on the part of professional groups.

An encouraging sign is the establishment of a privately supported National Council on Foreign Language and Area Studies, an outgrowth of the 1979 President's Commission of Foreign Language and Area Studies. The council, under its first executive director, Allen Kassof, and his successor, Rose Lee Hayden, has been able to continue the impetus of the president's commission. It has established a number of task forces to circumstantiate the need for federal support of international education in the eighties, including one to identify the need for foreign area specialists in the United States, another to identify issues and problem-oriented studies necessary to the national interest (e.g., in business, education, government), and a third to examine needs in kindergarten through undergraduate education. The council's work will generate recommendations for a national support system for international education that will probably include a rationale for national institutes to focus on critical areas of needed research and training, federal subsidies for university centers in international education, and various regional-support and state-support infrastructures.

On the positive side, it may be that the educational imperatives of an interdependent world are becoming so clear to all in the educational enterprise that traditional programs and their component disciplines are becoming truly internationalized. It may also be that the trend toward infusing this state of mind in all aspects of our educational systems has progressed past the takeoff point. If so, the future will see increasing innovation in education for global interdependence and in all of the related convergent strands.

As with any interdisciplinary field, it takes some time to establish coherent theories, conceptual frameworks, and a body of research literature that is more than episodic in nature. Most of the existing literature in international education is in the form of position papers, evaluative reports, and other attempts to legitimize a point of view. We hope that in the future there will be more systematic research on the various strands in international education. In addition, more interdisciplinary and interprofessional research is needed to clarify the relationships among the topics of interest generally identified with international education. The promise and the challenge today is that international education will increasingly be viewed by all in the educational enterprise as a core concept for making contemporary education more relevant to a highly interdependent world.

Seth Spaulding
Judith Colucci
Jonathan Flint

See also Comparative Education; National Development and Education.

REFERENCES

Adams, W. (Ed.). *The Brain Drain.* New York: Macmillan, 1968.

Adiseshiah, M. S. From international aid to international cooperation: Some thoughts in retrospect. (I) *International Review of Education,* 1979, *25,* 213–230.

Agency for International Development. *Building Institutions to Serve Agriculture: A Summary Report of the Committee on Institutional Cooperation–Agency for International Development Rural Development Research Project.* Washington, D.C.: U.S. Department of State, 1968. (Eric Document Reproduction Service No. ED 043 737)

Agency for International Development. *Education and Human Resources: Policy Statement for the Agency for International Development.* Washington, D.C.: AID, March 1980. (Mimeo)

Alger, C. F. Extending responsible public participation in international affairs. *International Educational and Cultural Exchange,* 1978, *14,* 17–21.

American Association of Colleges for Teacher Education Commission on Multicultural Education. No one model American. *Journal of Teacher Education,* 1973, *24,* 264–265.

American Association of Community and Junior Colleges. *Internationalizing Community Colleges.* Washington, D.C.: The Association, 1978.

American Council on Education, International Education Project. *Education for Global Interdependence.* Washington, D.C.: The Council, 1975.

Anderson, L. *Schooling and Citizenship in a Global Age: An Exploration of the Meaning and Significance of Global Education.* Bloomington: Indiana University, Social Studies Development Center, 1979.

Angell, R. C. *The Quest for World Order.* Ann Arbor: University of Michigan Press, 1979.

Arnove, R. S. Comparative education and world systems analysis. *Comparative Education Review,* 1980, *24,* 48–62.

Barrows, T. S.; Klein, F.; & Clark, J. L. D. *What College Students Know and Believe about Their World.* New Rochelle, N.Y.: Change Magazine Press, 1981.

Becker, J. M. *An Examination of Objectives, Needs, and Priorities in International Education in U.S. Secondary and Elementary Schools.* Washington, D.C.: U.S. Office of Education, 1969. (ERIC Document Reproduction Service No. ED 031 612)

Becker, J. M. (Ed.). *Schooling for a Global Age.* New York: McGraw-Hill, 1979.

Bhavati, Y. N. *The Brain Drain and Taxation.* Amsterdam: North Holland Publishing, 1975.

Bhavati, Y. N., & Partington, M. (Eds.). *Taxing the Brain Drain: A Proposal.* Amsterdam: North Holland Publishing, 1976.

Bonham, G. (Ed.). *Education and the World View.* New Rochelle, N.Y.: Change Magazine Press, 1981.

Botkin, J. W.; Elmandjra, H.; & Malitza, M. *No Limits to Learning: Bridging the Human Gap.* Elmsford, N.Y.: Pergamon Press, 1979.

Burn, B. B. (Ed.). *Higher Education Reform: Implications for Foreign Students.* New York: Institute of International Education, 1978.

Burn, B. B. *Expanding the International Dimension of Higher Education.* San Francisco: Jossey-Bass, 1980.

Cadoux, R. Trends in language and cultural studies. In S. K. Bailey (Ed.), *Higher Education in the World Community.* Washington, D.C.: American Council on Education, 1977.

Coelho, G. V., & Ahmed, P. I. *Uprooting and Development: Dilemmas of Coping with Modernization.* New York: Plenum, 1980.

Coombs, P. H. *The Fourth Dimension of Foreign Policy: Educational and Cultural Affairs.* New York: Harper & Row, 1964.

Coombs, P. H., & Bigelow, K. *Education and Foreign Aid.* Cambridge, Mass.: Harvard University Press, 1965.

Cormack, M. L. *An Evaluation of Research on Educational Exchange.* Washington, D.C.: U.S. Department of State, Bureau of Educational and Cultural Affairs, 1962.

Cussler, M. T. *Review of Selected Studies Affecting International Educational and Cultural Affairs.* Washington, D.C.: U.S. Advisory Commission on International and Cultural Affairs, 1962.

Dawson, A. Suggestions for an approach to rural development by foreign aid programmes. *International Labour Review,* 1978, *117,* 391–404.

Education and World Affairs. *The University Looks Abroad: Approaches to World Affairs at Six American Universities.* New York: Walker & Co. and Education and World Affairs, 1966.

Egerton, J. International outreach from Kentucky. *Change,* 1980, *12,* 51–53.

Eide, I. (Ed.). *Students and Links between Cultures.* Oslo: Universitetsforlaget, 1970.

Elder, R. W. *The Foreign Leader Program.* Washington, D.C.: Brookings Institution, 1961.

Emplaincourt, M., & Bush, W. (Eds.). International education. *Acquainter Special Issue,* 1979. University, Ala.: Council for Interinstitutional Leadership. (ERIC Document Reproduction Service No. ED 180 347)

Faure, E.; Herrera, F.; Kaddoura, A. R.; Lopes, H.; Petrovsky, A. V.; Rahnema, M.; & Ward, F. C. *Learning to Be: The World of Education Today and Tomorrow.* Paris: UNESCO, 1972.

Flint, J. K. *Present and Future Directions in Multicultural Teacher Education.* Paper presented at the National Conference of the National Council of States on Inservice Education, San Diego, December 1980. (Available from the author at the University of Pittsburgh, Pittsburgh, Pa. 15260)

Frankel, C. *The Neglected Aspect of Foreign Affairs: American Educational and Cultural Policy Abroad.* Washington, D.C.: Brookings Institution, 1965.

Fraser, S. *Governmental Policy in International Education.* New York: Wiley, 1965.

Gardner, J. A. *A Beacon of Hope: The Exchange of Persons Program.* Washington, D.C.: U.S. Government Printing Office, 1963.

Glaser, W. A. *Brain Drain and Study Abroad.* New York: Columbia University, Bureau of Applied Social Science Research, 1974.

Glaser, W. A., & Habers, C. *The Migration and Return of Professionals.* New York: Columbia University Press, 1973.

Glaser, W. A., & Habers, C. *The Brain Drain: Emigration and Return.* Elmsford, N.Y.: Pergamon Press, 1978.

Griffin, W. H., & Spence, R. B. *Cooperative International Education.* Washington, D.C.: Association for Supervision and Curriculum Development, 1970. (ERIC Document Reproduction Service No. ED 039 203)

Harbison, F. A., & Meyers, C. A. *Education, Manpower, and Economic Growth: Strategies of Human Resource Development.* New York: McGraw-Hill, 1964.

Harrington, F. H., & Clarkson, S. International linkages: The community college role. *New Directions for Community Colleges,* 1979, *7,* 101–107.

Havelock, R. G., & Huberman, A. M. *Solving Educational Problems.* New York: Praeger, 1978.

Humphrey, R. (Ed.). *Universities and Development Assistance Abroad.* Washington, D.C.: American Council on Education, 1967.

Illinois State Board of Education, Task Force on Foreign Language and International Studies. Report of the Illinois Task Force on Foreign Language and International Studies. *Bulletin of the Illinois Foreign Language Teachers Association,* 1979, *11,* 9–42.

International Studies in Six European Countries: United Kingdom, France, Federal Republic of Germany, Sweden, Netherlands, Italy (Reports to the Ford Foundation). New York: Ford Foundation, 1976. (ERIC Document Reproduction Service No. ED 175 734)

International Studies Programs Review and Planning Committee. *International Education at Michigan State University in an Interdependent World.* East Lansing: University of Michigan, Office of International Programs, 1980.

Jacobson, H. K. *Networks of Interdependence.* New York: Knopf, 1979.

Jenkins, H. M. International education and NAFSA, 1948–1978. *International Education and Cultural Exchange,* 1978, *14,* 13–16.

Klineberg, O. *International Educational Exchange.* The Hague: Mouton, 1976.

Klineberg, O., & Hull, W. F. *At a Foreign University: An International Study of Adaptation and Coping.* New York: Praeger, 1979.

Lambert, R. D. Language and area studies review. *American Academy of Political and Social Science* (Monograph 17). Philadelphia: American Academy of Political and Social Science, 1973. (ERIC Document Reproduction Service No. ED 197 101)

Lambert, R. D. (Ed.). New directions in international education. *Annals of the American Academy of Political and Social Science,* 1980, *449.*

Lamden, J. Differences. *Comment: A Research/Action Report on Wo/Men. 12,* Washington, D.C.: American Council on Education, Office of Women in Higher Education, 1979.

Lantolf, J. P. Aspects of change in foreign language study. *Modern Language Journal,* 1977, *61,* 242–251.

Leestma, R. Global education. *American Education,* 1978, *14,* 1–8.

Luce, L. F. The new mediators: Foreign language departments in a post-modern era. *Association of Departments of Foreign Languages Bulletin,* 1978, *10,* 25–30.

MacKinnon, A. R. From international aid to international cooperation: Some thoughts in retrospect. (II) *International Review of Education,* 1979, *25,* 231–247.

Marklund, S. *Internationalization of Education: Some Concepts and Questions.* Stockholm: University of Stockholm, Institute for International Education, 1980.

McCaughey, R. A. In the land of the blind: American international studies in the 1930's. *Annals of the American Academy of Political and Social Science,* 1980, *449,* 1–16.

McNamara, R. S. *Address to the Board of Governors.* Washington, D.C.: World Bank, September 30, 1980.

Mehlinger, H. D., & Ehman, L. *Toward Effective Instruction in Secondary Social Studies.* Boston: Houghton Mifflin, 1974.

Mehlinger, H. D.; Hutson, H.; Smith, V.; & Wright, B. *Global Studies for American Schools.* Washington, D.C.: National Education Association, 1979. (ERIC Document Reproduction Service No. ED 183 456)

Miller, M. (Ed.). Education for a changing world. *UNICEF News,* 1977, *93.*

Morrill, J. L. *The University and World Affairs.* New York: Ford Foundation, 1960.

Myers, R. G. *Education and Emigration.* New York: McKay, 1972.

National Association of State Universities and Land Grant Colleges, International Affairs Committee. *Statement on U.S. Assistance to Developing Countries.* Washington, D.C.: The Association, 1981.

National Center for Educational Statistics. *Full-time Equivalent Enrollment in All Institutions of Higher Education by Enrollment Level and Type of Institution, 1970–1988.* Washington, D.C.: U.S. Government Printing Office, 1980.

National Liaison Committee on Foreign Student Admissions. *The Foreign Graduate Student: Priorities for Research and Action.* New York: College Entrance Examination Board, 1971. (ERIC Document Reproduction Service No. ED 047 604)

Netherlands Universities Foundation for International Cooperation Annual Report, 1977. The Hague: NUFFIC, 1978.

O'Connor, E. *World Studies in the European Classroom: Education and Culture.* Strasbourg, France: Council for Cultural Cooperation, 1980. (Available from Manhattan Publishing Company, 80 Brook Street, P.O. Box 650, Croton, N.Y. 10520).

Owens, B. *International Education: A Compendium of Federal Agency Programs.* Washington, D.C.: American Council on Education, International Education Project, 1977. (ERIC Document Reproduction Service No. ED 159 941)

Parkinson, N. *Educational Aid and National Development.* London: Macmillan, 1976. (U.S. distribution by Holmes & Meier, New York).

Phillips, H. M. *Educational Cooperation between Developed and Developing Countries.* New York: Praeger, 1976.

Piaget, J., & Weil, A. M. The development in children of the idea of the homeland and of relations with other countries. *International Social Science Journal,* 1951, *3,* 561–578.

Pike, L. W.; Barrows, T. S.; Mahoney, M. H.; & Jungeblut, A. *Other Nations, Other People: A Survey of Student Interests, Knowledge, Attitudes, and Perceptions.* Washington, D.C.: U.S. Government Printing Office, 1979. (ERIC Document Reproduction Service No. ED 189 190)

Posvar, W. W. Toward an academic response: Expanding international dimensions. *Change,* 1980, *12,* 23–28.

President's Commission on Foreign Language and International Studies. *Background Papers and Studies.* Washington, D.C.: U.S. Government Printing Office, 1979. (a)

President's Commission on Foreign Language and International Studies. *Strength through Wisdom: A Critique of U.S. Capability.* Washington, D.C.: U.S. Government Printing Office, 1979. (b) (ERIC Document Reproduction Service No. ED 176 599)

President's Commission on Foreign Language and International Studies. *Modern Language Journal,* 1980, *64.*

Remy, R. C.; Nathan, J. A.; Becker, J. M.; & Torney, J. V. *International Learning and International Education in a Global Age.* Washington, D.C.: National Council for the Social Studies, 1975. (ERIC Document Reproduction Service No. ED 107 566)

Renshaw, J. P. Foreign language and intercultural studies in present-day college curricula. *Journal of Higher Education,* 1972, *48,* 295–302.

Rettig, J. W. Foreign language study: A proposal. *Liberal Education,* 1968, *54,* 429–434.

Sanders, I. T. *The Professional Education of Students from Other Lands.* New York: Council on Social Work Education, 1963.

Sanders, I. T. *The Professional School and World Affairs.* Albuquerque: University of New Mexico Press, 1968.

Sato, T. Education for international understanding in Japanese schools. *Prospects: Quarterly Review of Education,* 1979, *9,* 216–222.

Schultz, R. E., & Terrell, R. International education: A vehicle for staff revitalization. *New Directions for Community Colleges,* 1979, *7,* 37–47.

Schultz, T. W. *The Economic Value of Education.* New York: Columbia University Press, 1963.

Shane, H. G. (Ed.). *The United States and International Education.* Chicago: University of Chicago Press and National Society for the Study of Education, 1969.

Simon, P. Battling language chauvinism. *Change,* 1977, *9,* 10.

Simonson, R. Global awareness: A curriculum plan for world study. *National Association of Secondary School Principals Bulletin,* 1977, *61,* 75–79.

Spaulding, S. The impact of international assistance organizations on the development of education. *Comparative Education,* 1981, *17,* 207–213.

Spaulding, S., & Coelho, G. V. Research on students from abroad: The neglected policy implications. In G. V. Coelho & P. I. Ahmed, *Uprooting and Development: Dilemmas of Coping with Modernization.* New York: Plenum, 1980.

Spaulding, S., & Flack, M. *The World's Students in the United States: A Review and Evaluation of Research on Foreign Students.* New York: Praeger, 1976.

Spaulding, S., & Singleton, J. (Eds.). International and development education (Special issue). *Review of Educational Research,* 1968, *38.*

Spitzberg, I. J., Jr. (Ed.). *Universities and the International Distribution of Knowledge.* New York: Praeger, 1980.

Starr, S. F. International high schools: Their time has come. *Phi Delta Kappan,* 1979, *60,* 743–744.

The State of the Art (Special issue). *Comparative Education Review,* 1977, *21.*

Strasheim, L. A. An issue on the horizon: The role of foreign languages in global education. *Foreign Language Annals,* 1979, *12,* 29–33.

Struwe, K. The Danish UNESCO schools project. *Prospects: Quarterly Review of Education,* 1979, *9,* 203–209.

Sutton, F. X. The international liaison of universities: History, hazards, and opportunities. *Educational Record,* 1979, *60,* 318–325.

Sutton, F. X.; Ward, F. C.; Perkins, J. A.; & Östergren, B. *Internationalizing Higher Education: A United States Approach* (Occasional paper 13). New York: International Council for Educational Development, 1974. (ERIC Document Reproduction Service No. ED 098 890)

Task Force on International Education. *International Education: Past, Present, Problems, and Prospects.* Washington, D.C.: Committee on Education and Labor; House of Representatives; and U.S. Government Printing Office, 1966. (ERIC Document Reproduction Service No. ED 087 643)

Thomson, C. A., & Laves, W. *Cultural Relations and U.S. Foreign Policy.* Bloomington: Indiana University Press, 1963.

Tonkin, H., & Edwards, J. *The World in the Curriculum: Curricular Strategies for the Twenty-first Century.* New Rochelle, N.Y.: Change Magazine Press, 1981.

Turner, P. R. Why Johnny doesn't want to learn a foreign language. *Modern Language Journal,* 1974, *58,* 191–196.

United Nations Development Program and United Nations Educational, Scientific, and Cultural Organization. *The Experimental World Literacy Program: A Critical Assessment.* New York: UNDP and UNESCO, 1976.

United Nations Educational, Scientific, and Cultural Organization. *UNESCO Associated Schools Project* (Information packet). Paris: UNESCO, n.d.

United Nations Educational, Scientific, and Cultural Organization. *Recommendation Concerning Education for International Understanding, Cooperation, and Peace and Education Relating to Human Rights and Fundamental Freedoms* (Adopted by the General Conference at its eighteenth session). Paris: UNESCO, 1974.

United Nations Educational, Scientific, and Cultural Organization. *International Meeting of Experts on the Role of Social Studies in Education for Peace and Respect for Human Rights* (Report Ed-76, CONF. 631, COL. 5). Paris: UNESCO, 1976.

U.S. Department of State, Bureau of Educational and Cultural Affairs. *Directory of Contacts for International Education: Cultural and Scientific Programs.* Washington, D.C.: U.S. Government Printing Office, 1975. (ERIC Document Reproduction Service No. ED 101 651)

Walton, B. J. *Foreign Student Exchange in Perspective.* Washington, D.C.: U.S. Department of State, Office of External Research, 1967.

Ward, F. C. (Ed.) *Education and Development Reconsidered.* New York: Praeger, 1974.

Whipp, L. T. Simulating world crises. *Change,* 1980, *12,* 56–58.

Winkler, D. R., & Agarwal, V. B. *The Migration of Foreign Students to the United States.* Unpublished manuscript prepared for the National Institute of Health, December 1980. (Available from author at the School of Public Administration, University of Southern California, Los Angeles, Calif. 90007)

Wiprud, H. R. *International Education Programs of the U.S. Government: An Inventory.* Washington, D.C.: U.S. Government Printing Office, 1980.

World Bank. *Training for Development.* Washington, D.C.: World Bank, 1975.

World Bank. *Education Sector Policy Paper.* Washington, D.C.: World Bank, 1980. (a)

World Bank. *World Development Report, 1980.* Washington, D.C.: World Bank, 1980. (b)

ITEM ANALYSIS

The creation of an educational measuring instrument is a complex process that involves many steps and many different techniques. An important component of the overall test development process is the writing of items to the specifications of the test plan. This is a difficult task for which the item writer must not only have a complete mastery of the content area, but also a thorough understanding of the population of examinees for whom the test is intended.

The classical source on the techniques of item writing is *Achievement Testing* by Hawkes, Lindquist, and Mann, (1936) and much of this material is replicated in Wesman (1971). But even when these techniques are employed by a skilled item writer, the resulting items are an enigma. It is not possible to evaluate an item as "good" or "bad" by inspection alone. The content covered may be appropriate, the distractors plausible, and the vocabulary at the level of the target population of examinees, yet the item may be "bad" in some sense. Within this context item analysis techniques have been developed to provide information about test items that can be used in their evaluation.

Two basic technical properties (parameters) of an item have been defined: (1) item difficulty, a measure of whether the item is easy or hard for the examinees; and (2) item discrimination, the degree to which an item can distinguish between examinees having different criterion variable scores. Thus, an item can be described as easy (of low difficulty) or hard (of high difficulty) and as one that has a particular degree of discriminating power. In the test development process the test is administered to a random sample from the target population and the item response data analyzed to yield estimators of these parameters for each item in the test. It should be noted that the numerical values of the summary statistics estimating these two properties do not intrinsically define a good or bad item. Rather they represent two technical pieces of information that must be evaluated within the overall context (content, vocabulary level, intended population, role within the whole test) of the item.

There are two different measurement theories upon which to base the definition of the item parameters: classical test theory and latent trait/item response theory. Because each of these theories leads to a unique definition of the item parameters and their interpretation, separate but parallel discussions of item analysis and its uses under the two theories are presented here.

Classical Test Theory. The basic item analysis model under classical test theory is a correlational one in which an item variable is correlated with a criterion variable. The item variable is a hypothetical variable that is conceptualized as a wrong to right continuum. The criterion variable is the trait being measured by the test. In practice, however, the criterion variable is usually the total test score, and in some applications it can be a variable external to the test such as grade-point average. Assuming there is a bivariate normal relationship between the item and criterion variable, the two item parameters are defined as follows: (1) item difficulty, the proportion of the population of examinees who answer the item correctly; and (2) item discrimination, the product-moment correlation between the item and criterion variables for the population of examinees responding to the item. In actual practice these parameters are estimated by sample statistics and an estimate of item difficulty is simply the proportion of the group of examinees who answered the item correctly. A value of .10 corresponds to a difficult item whereas a value of .90 would be associated with an easy item. Thus the index is more properly a measure of item easiness, than of item difficulty. However, tradition dictates that the latter terminology be used.

Because the item discrimination index involves the hypothetical item variable that cannot be measured directly, correlations other than the product moment are used. The most popular, biserial r is a function of the assumption made as to how the observed dichotomous item response is related to the hypothetical item variable.

With biserial r, the assumption made is that the hypothetical item variable is normally distributed but dichotomized by a value, γ, that delimits an area equal to the item difficulty. In reality the only data available are on whether or not an item was answered correctly. Thus the correlation is between the criterion variable and a dichotomous $(1, 0)$ variable. Two alternative formulas are available for the biserial correlation coefficient (Walker & Lev, 1953):

$$r_{\text{bis}} = \frac{M_R - M_W}{S_T}\left(\frac{PQ}{h}\right)$$

or

$$r_{\text{bis}} = \frac{M_R - M_T}{S_T}\left(\frac{P}{h}\right),$$

where M_R = mean test score of examinees answering the item correctly;

M_W = mean test score of examinees answering the item incorrectly;

M_T = mean test score of the total group of examinees;

S_T = standard deviation of the test scores of the total group;

P = item difficulty;

$Q = 1 - P$; and

h = height of the normal density at the deviate that delimits an area equal to the item difficulty.

The numerical values of biserial r range from -1 to $+1$, but if underlying assumptions are violated, values greater than unity are possible. Such deviate values are often encountered when a few examinees who have extreme test scores are the only ones to answer the item correctly. On the basis of McNamara and Dunlap's formula for the asymptotic variance of biserial r (McNamara & Dunlap, 1934), the standard error is

$$\sigma_{r_{\text{bis}}} = \frac{\sqrt{\dfrac{PQ}{h}} - r_{\text{bis}}^2}{\sqrt{N}},$$

where N is the sample size. A formula for the small sample variance of biserial r is not known, but the asymptotic formula yields reasonable values for samples as small as 30.

The user of item analysis techniques must keep in mind that the obtained item statistics are estimators of the actual parameter values. As such they will have sampling distributions and thus a given value may not be replicated in subsequent testing. Baker (1965) has studied the sampling distribution of several item discrimination indices and has shown that they have considerable variability when small samples ($N < 60$) are used, and thus values obtained on the bases of these small samples should be interpreted with caution.

During the 1920s and 1930s it was common practice to develop *ad hoc* item discrimination indices. These indices were usually based on the product-moment correlation coefficient and involved algebraic or other manipulations to reduce the computations involved. However, in their now classical study of the validation of test items, Long and Sandiford (1935) showed that the items with the highest value on one index are often the ones with the lowest values on another index. They concluded that the best item discrimination indices are those with a solid mathematical basis, such as biserial r.

Computational procedures. One of the nice features of using classical item analysis is that the underlying data processing is relatively simple. The answer key is used to score the tests and the mean M_T, and variance, S_T^2, of the test scores are calculated. Then, for each item, the number of examinees giving correct answers and the sum of their test scores are computed. On the basis of this information the item difficulty, P, and M_R can be calculated, and the formula for biserial r evaluated. Although the process can be performed manually or by using a pocket calculator, to do so is laborious when the test has more than a few items. In our modern world of electronics technology, the bulk of item analysis is carried out by computers and the answer sheets scanned by optical mark readers. (See Baker, 1971, for an extended presentation.) The result is a very complete analysis of the data. Because the underlying computations are simple, they can be implemented easily on a small "personal" computer.

Test construction and analysis. An important part of the test construction process is the establishment of a pool of items for which item statistics are available. Such a pool of "precalibrated" items enables the user to select items from the pool to meet the specifications in the underlying test plan. The statistics of the items selected are used to obtain a desired test score distribution, assuming the population of examinees is similar to that used to precalibrate the items. For example, the distribution of the values of the item difficulties has a direct impact on the test score distribution. Ebel (1965) has shown that clustering the item difficulties around a value of .5 yields a symmetric test score distribution with a moderate amount of spread. When the item difficulties are uniformly distributed over the range .10 to .90, the test score distribution has a smaller variance than in the previous case. The use of only extreme values of item difficulty (.10 and .90) results in a test score distribution that is very peaked near its mean and has a smaller variance than either of the previous two examples. From these results it is clear that the wider the distribution of the item difficulty values in a test, the smaller the variance of the test scores and the lower the value of the reliability coefficient (Ebel, 1965).

The spread in value of the item discrimination indices is not so important as their average level. The higher the level, the greater the discrimination among examinees. Since internal consistency reliability depends upon the separability of examinees, the higher the average value of the discrimination indices in a test, the higher the internal consistency reliability coefficient and the larger the test score variance.

When precalibrated items are available, the test constructor has considerable flexibility in selecting items to achieve desired test characteristics. However, the test statistics computed from the item statistics are simply preliminary indicators. Only when the test has been administered and analyzed can one obtain the actual test statistics. But when proper test development procedures are employed the predicted and obtained test statistics should show reasonable agreement. In an iterative test development sequence one can fine-tune the test statistics by selecting items with particular statistical characteristics.

For discussion purposes, a somewhat arbitrary distinction is made here between test construction and test analysis. In the latter case it is assumed that a test already exists and that the purpose of item analysis is to aid in the interpretation of test data resulting from an administration of the test. When the item responses of the examinees are analyzed, either by hand or by computer, the mean and variance of the test scores and an internal consistency reliability coefficient are obtained, as are the item difficulty and item discrimination indices for each item. In a test analysis situation the task is to utilize this information to ascertain the characteristics of the test and its items for the group of examinees involved. The item analysis data also are extremely valuable in curriculum evaluation. For example, an item that is too difficult may indicate that a concept was not grasped. A distractor with a high positive value of its discrimination index may indicate that students learned the wrong thing.

The basic idea is to use the technical characteristics of the item (P, r_{bis}) to identify items that warrant attention. However, there is a danger of overreliance on the item statistics to the point where only the index values are interpreted. In many situations the content of an item, and its relation to the overall plan of the test and other substantive matters outweigh the numerical values of its item statistics. The converse is also true; often perfectly awful items will yield highly desirable values of the item statistics. Henryssen (1971) has presented a rather complete description of the role of item statistics within test construction and analysis under classical test theory.

Latent Trait/Item Response Theory. Since the publication of the fourth edition of the *Encyclopedia of Educational Research* (1969), a modern theory of measurement called latent trait or item response theory (LTT/IRT) has come into wide use. Actually this theory has been evolving since the turn of the century, but its recent emergence as a significant element in measurement practice can be attributed primarily to two factors: (1) its conceptual superiority over the classical approach, and (2) the availability of computer programs that implement the parameter estimation procedures. Since classical test theory is a theory of test scores, item analysis is a set of techniques that is rather disjoint from the basic theory. In sharp contrast LTT/IRT is based on the parameters of the items that make up the test. As a result the item analysis techniques are inextricably intertwined with the theory itself, and so it is necessary to have a basic understanding of the theory in order to use these techniques. The basic concepts of the theory underlying the use of item analysis are described in the following, as a basis for subsequent discussion; the reader is referred to Allen and Yen (1979) and Lord (1980) for more comprehensive presentations.

The Item Characteristic Curve. The basic building block of LTT/IRT is an item, and the technical characteristics of an item are couched in terms of the parameters of an item characteristic curve (ICC). This curve is the functional relation between the probability of correct response to an item and a hypothetical latent trait. The latter, denoted by θ and referred to generically as "ability," is a construct such as intelligence, scholastic ability, or arithmetic ability that the item is attempting to measure. The functional relationship is best depicted graphically as in Figure 1. The horizontal axis is the ability scale. It has a midpoint of zero, a unit of measurement equal to one, and a theoretical range from $-\infty$ to $+\infty$. The vertical axis is the probability of correct response to the item, $P_i(\theta_j)$ where i indexes the item and j the ability level. The curved line relating the two variables is the item characteristic curve.

The basic ICC model is the normal ogive given by

$$P_i(\theta_j) = \frac{1}{\sqrt{2\pi}\,\sigma}\int_{-z}^{\infty} \exp[-t^2/2]\,dt,$$

where $Z = \dfrac{(\theta_j - \mu_i)}{\sigma_i} = \alpha_i(\theta_j - \beta_i);$

$\beta_i = \mu_i;$ and

$\alpha_i = 1/\sigma_i.$

FIGURE 1. *Item characteristic curve, $\beta = .5$, $\alpha = 1.0$*

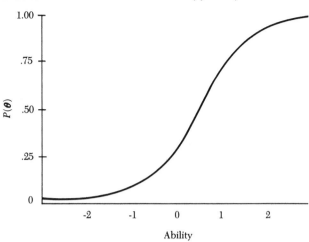

Specifically, β_i is the point on the ability scale where the probability of correct response is one-half for examinees of that ability. In the literature β_i is referred to as the item difficulty parameter because a hard item will have a value of $\beta_i > 0$ and an easy item a value of $\beta_i < 0$. This difficulty parameter has theoretical limits of $-\infty$ to $+\infty$ but obtained values usually fall between -4 and $+4$. The item discrimination index α_i is defined as the reciprocal of the standard deviation of the normal ogive. A rather flat ogive has an underlying σ that is numerically large and a steep ogive has a small σ associated with it, thus an item that discriminates sharply among ability levels will yield a large numerical value of α_i. Although the theoretical range of α_i is from $-\infty$ to $+\infty$, the value is usually in the range $0 \leq \alpha_i \leq 2.5$ and negative values of α_i are undesirable for the correct response to an item. For interpretation purposes α_i can be thought of as the slope of the ICC at the point β_i. Given an ICC model and these two parameters, the relationship between ability level and probability of correct response to an item can be completely specified. Despite the use of a common terminology the item difficulty parameter of LTT/IRT has a completely different meaning from that of classical test theory. It is not a measure of the proportion of examinees getting the item correct.

Models for the ICC other than the normal ogive are also employed in practice. The logistic ogive is very widely used and is defined by

$$P_i(\theta_j) = \frac{1}{1 + \exp[-\alpha_1(\theta_j - \beta_i)]},$$

where α_i, β_i are as given previously. The logistic model has the advantage over the normal ogive of not involving an integral and hence can be evaluated easily using a pocket calculator. If the value of the logistic discrimination parameter α_i is multiplied by 1.702, the logistic ogive specified will match the normal ogive having the same value of α_i to within .01 over the full ability scale (Haley, 1952). As a result the logistic model is often substituted for the normal ogive to reduce the computational burden of item analysis. A second ICC model based upon the logistic ogive is the Rasch model (Rasch, 1960, 1966a, 1966b), given by

$$P_i(\theta_j) = \frac{1}{1 + \exp[-(\theta_i - \beta_i)]}$$

It is simply the two-parameter logistic with the item discrimination parameter set to an a priori value of unity. Another extension of the logistic model is the Birnbaum (1968) three-parameter (logistic) model. Under this model

$$P_i(\theta_j) = c_i + (1 - c_i) \frac{1}{1 + \exp[-\alpha_i(\theta_j - \beta_i)]} .$$

This model takes into account the fact that low-ability examinees get an item correct more often than is expected under the two-parameter logistic model. In the literature the parameter c_i is often referred to as a guessing parameter (see Hambelton & Cook, 1977). However, Lord (1974) indicates that c_i should not be interpreted in this way. To be a guessing parameter c_i should be a function of ability, but in the Birnbaum model it is independent of ability. As a result c_i as the lower asymptote of the ICC is the correct concept. One of the major problems with using Birnbaum's three-parameter model is that c_i is very difficult to estimate from item response data (Lord, 1975; Wood, Wingersky, & Lord, 1976).

The ICC model to be used in an item analysis is selected by the person analyzing or constructing a test. The choice of models can determine which of the available computer programs will be used and the approach one takes to interpreting the results of the item analysis.

The information function.   One can conceptualize a conditional distribution of ability estimates, $\hat{\theta}$, yielded by examinees who share a common underlying ability level θ. This conditional distribution will have a mean θ and variance $\sigma_{\hat{\theta}}^2$. The amount of information is a concept due to Sir R. A. Fisher and in our context is defined as $I(\theta) = 1/\sigma_{\hat{\theta}}^2$. Thus the larger the variance of the $\hat{\theta}$ at a given θ level, the less information one has about an examinee's unknown ability level. Under LTT/IRT the amount of information can be obtained for a test and for the individual items in a test at each ability level. Birnbaum (Chaps. 17, 20) has defined the test information function based upon a normal ogive ICC model as:

$$I(\theta_j) = \sum_{i=1}^{n} \alpha_i^2 \frac{[h_i(\theta_j)]^2}{P_i(\theta_j) Q_i(\theta_j)} ,$$

where $P_i(\theta_j)$ is obtained by evaluating the item characteristic curve model at θ_j;

$h_i(\theta_j)$ = normal ordinate delineating $P_i(\theta_j)$; and

n = number of items in the test.

The amount of information contributed by an individual item is given by

$$I_i(\theta_j) = \alpha_i^2 \frac{[h_i(\theta_j)]^2}{P_i(\theta_j) Q_i(\theta_j)}$$

and then

$$I(\theta_j) = \sum_{i=1}^{n} I_i(\theta_j).$$

Under a logistic ICC model we have

$$I(\theta_j) = \sum_{i=1}^{n} \alpha_i^2 P_i(\theta_j) Q_i(\theta_j).$$

The test information function plays a role in LTT/IRT that is related to that of the reliability coefficient in classical test theory. The usual reliability coefficient is defined as the product-moment correlation between test scores on two parallel tests. As such it depends not only on the test but also on the group of subjects taking the test (Samejima, 1977). Under LTT/IRT the situation is radically different in that the test information function is intrinsic to the test, depending only upon the ability scale and the ICCs of the items in the test. Since the test information function is evaluated at each ability level, the amount of information will be unique to each level. Thus under LTT/IRT one uses the test information function to examine how well the test is estimating ability over the range of interest. Consequently the information function is a much more powerful concept than reliability, both theoretically and in practice.

Estimation procedures.   Under LTT/IRT two sets of parameters must be estimated from the item response data. Assuming a two-parameter model such as the normal or logistic for the ICC, there will be two n-item parameters to be estimated for a test having n items. Since classical test theory was a theory of test scores, the only information desired about an examinee was his raw test score. However, under LTT/IRT the raw test score has little intrinsic value as the goal is to estimate an examinee's ability directly. Thus the second set of parameters to be estimated are the ability levels of the N examinees who respond to the test items, and so a total of two $n + N$ parameters are to be estimated.

The estimation of the necessary parameters is a computationally complex process that can only be accomplished effectively with digital computers. As a result a number of different computer programs are available for the estimation process. The two most accessible are LOGIST (Wood, Wingersky, & Lord, 1976) and BICAL (Wright and Mead, 1976). The former is based on the Birnbaum three-parameter model but will also handle a one-parameter or two-parameter model. The latter is specialized to the Rasch model, which has a single item parameter.

Test construction.   All of the key elements for the application of LTT/IRT on the basis of dichotomously scored items are now in place. The data yielded by an administration of a test can be analyzed and interpreted, new tests that meet a priori specifications can be constructed from pools of precalibrated items, and new and unique testing procedures can be developed to take advantage of the constructs of the theory. With LTT/IRT the test norming process is known as test calibration (a term attributed to Wright, 1968). To calibrate a test a population of subjects is used as the calibration group. The item response data obtained by administering the test to the calibration group are analyzed via the estimation procedure. The results are the estimated values of the item parameters α_i, β_i for each of the n items and the estimated ability levels $\hat{\theta}_j$ for the N examinees expressed in a metric that has a midpoint of zero and a unit of measurement of one for that group. Since the basis of these estimates is a calibration group, they are treated as if they are the parameters. In the terminology of LTT/IRT the items have been precalibrated, that is, their parameters are known.

One of the most powerful features of LTT/IRT is the conceptual framework it provides for the test construction process. When an item pool containing precalibrated items is available, LTT/IRT furnishes the test constructor with a versatile repertoire of techniques based on the ICC parameters α_i, β_i and the test information function. These two facets of the theory allow the test constructor to devise tests for very specialized as well as very broad purposes. As representative of the many different tests that this spectrum encompasses, examples of both types are described in the following.

For example, if one specifies that a given ability level, θ_c, has a particular interpretation, it is possible to screen examinees on the basis of their estimated ability. Persons with $\hat{\theta}$ scores above this level would be eligible for specialized treatment, such as a scholarship, entrance into a particular program, or special recognition. Persons with $\hat{\theta}$ scores below θ_c would be ineligible. The basic task is to construct a test that will separate such persons as sharply as possible at the critical ability level. To accomplish this items should be selected that have $\beta_i = \theta_c$ and the maximum possible value of α_i. Choosing only items with $\beta_i = \theta_c$ results in two things. First, it focuses the resources of the test at the point on the ability scale of interest. Second, it capitalizes on the discriminating power of the item since the maximum slope of the ICC occurs at θ_c. Thus the item will make its sharpest discrimination at this point. The test information function plays an important role here as it indicates how well the ability level is being estimated. For a screening test the maximum of $I(\theta)$ should occur at θ_c. When it does, the standard error of $\hat{\theta}$ is at its minimum. Consequently the simplest screening test is one with k equivalent items having $\beta_i = \theta_c$ and a large common value of α_i. Under these conditions the test information function would have a maximum at θ_c. To illustrate this case a test was constructed of thirty equivalent items having $\beta_i = 2.0$ and $\alpha_i = .80$. Table 1 contains the test information function under a normal ICC model for this screening test, denoted by ST 1. Although equivalent items were used, the moderate α_i values resulted in a test information function with a gradual peaking rather than a sharp peak, but the maximum occurred at $\theta = 2.0$.

This case is rather unrealistic, however, as it would be very difficult to build an item pool containing equivalent items for all possible values of θ_c of interest. In a very large pool, items in the neighborhood of a given θ_c would be available, but the associated α_i could vary considerably. The test construction task then becomes one of doing one's best with the available items. Again the strategy would be to pick a sufficient number of items whose β_i was approximately θ_c and the largest value of α_i available. This strategy would maximize the test information function in the neighborhood of θ_c. Table 1 also contains the test information function for a thirty-item screening test with $\theta_c = 2.0$, denoted as ST 2, constructed in this manner. Compared with the equivalent items test, the test information function reaches a lower maximum, has a somewhat broader peak, and does not tail off as rapidly. One would conclude that the equivalent items test is the better screening test.

The typical educational or psychological instrument is intended to be used to measure across a range of the ability continuum, and thus a unique set of issues arises in the conceptualization of the test construction process. As was the case with screening tests, the two basic test construction tools are the ICC and the information function. The test constructor uses these to design a test that will measure all ability levels within the range of interest in some optimal fashion. A fundamental decision is whether to allocate items via their difficulty parameters along the ability continuum or to cluster them at the mean. When the goal is to measure over a broad range, the optimal test information function is a horizontal line having the maximum possible value of $I(\theta)$. This would indicate that each ability level is estimated with the same degree of precision. However, obtaining such a test information function is very difficult. The underlying problem is that $I(\theta) = \Sigma I_i(\theta)$ and the individual item information curves are bell-shaped and symmetric about β_i, and their maximum height is a function of α_i^2. The problem is to obtain a horizontal line from a composite of such curves. Let us explore this test construction problem via the use of several different ICC mixtures. As usual a large precalibrated item pool will be assumed.

A logical choice for the items of a broad-range test would be to space the items evenly along the ability scale according to their difficulty parameters. Let us assume that the ability range of interest is -2.5 to $+2.5$ and that a sixty-item test is to be constructed. In this case an item would be located every $.10\sigma$ along the ability continuum. Since the maximum height of the item information function depends upon α_i^2, its value must be selected. If a large value of α_i is used, the item information function will peak rapidly in the region of β_i and $I_i(\theta)$ will be reasonably large at this point. When a low value of α_i is used, the item information function will have a rather smooth hump and the maximum amount of information obtained at β_i will be less than the previous case. Although its level is low, some discrimination does occur over a wider range

TABLE 1. *Test information function for various tests*

	$I(\theta)$										
Test	−2.5	−2.0	−1.5	−1.0	−.5	0	.5	1.0	1.5	2.0	2.5
ST 1			.47	1.18	2.52	4.56	7.11	9.65	11.53	12.22	11.53
ST 2			.68	1.12	1.92	3.32	5.52	8.11	10.12	10.63	9.47
A	25.01	36.16	39.54	36.90	33.94	32.91	32.49	32.22	31.54	26.65	16.61
B	4.25	4.67	5.01	5.25	5.37	5.37	5.25	5.01	4.67	4.26	3.79
C	12.15	21.72	33.52	45.73	54.26	55.68	49.37	37.26	23.47	12.83	6.85
D	4.26	4.75	5.17	5.47	5.64	5.67	5.55	5.30	4.93	4.46	3.93
E	6.73	10.69	15.34	20.20	24.40	26.66	26.02	22.45	16.97	11.25	6.72

of ability. Thus the design trade-off is good discrimination in a small range versus lower discrimination over a wider range of ability.

To illustrate the former, two tests are constructed from precalibrated items under a logistic model. All sixty items in test A have $\alpha_i = 1.7$ but the values of β_i are uniformly distributed over the ability continuum as specified previously. The test information function of test A is shown in Table 1 and bears no resemblance to that for a typical item. Over the relatively flat section the test information has a value of roughly 30 and the standard error of $\hat{\theta}$ would be about .18, which is quite small.

Test B differs from test A only in that the common value of α_i is .40. Table 1 also presents the test information function for test B. It is rather flat over the ability continuum from −2.0 to +2.0. However, its average height is about 5.0, which corresponds to a standard error of $\hat{\theta}$ equal to .45. Although the test information function for test B is reasonably uniform over a broad range, its low level suggests that the test does a rather poor job of estimating ability over that range. In this example A is clearly a better broad-range test. Even in the regions where the test information curve of test A is decreasing rapidly, the amount of information is many times greater than that of test B in the same region. Since the β_i of the items has a similar distribution in both tests, the sharp difference in the amounts of information is attributable to the differences in levels of the item discrimination parameters.

The second strategy for a broad-range test is to use items whose difficulty parameters are clustered around the mean of the ability continuum. Again our interest is in the form of the test information function. As was the case in the first strategy, the role of high and low item discrimination indices is also of interest. Three different hypothetical tests are used to explore the present strategy. Test C employs sixty items having normally distributed β_i ($\mu_\beta = 0$, $\sigma_\beta = 1$) and a common $\alpha_i = 1.7$. Test D is the same as test C except that the common value of α_i is .40. Test E is the same as test C except that the α_i is normally distributed ($\mu_\alpha = 1.0$, $\sigma_\alpha = .2$). This final test, in a crude sense, corresponds to the situation where one does not have the luxury of a large item pool and must use available items.

The test information function for test C is shown in Table 1. The curve is decidedly bell-shaped with a maximum near $\theta = -.25$ and is reasonably symmetrical. A rather large amount of information ($I(\theta) = 56$) was obtained near the middle (−.5 to +.5) of the ability scale, reflecting the high common level of α_i. However, the high value of $I(\theta)$ was not retained and as $|\theta + .25|$ increased $I(\theta)$ decreased rapidly, reaching 22 at $\theta = -2.0$ and 13 at $\theta = +2.0$. Clustering the β_i around $\bar{\theta}$ appears to be the cause of the bell shape of the information function for this test.

The test information function for test D is also given in Table 1. Because of the common but low value of α_i, the function has a very small average value of roughly $I(\theta) = 5.0$. Although β_i was distributed in the same fashion as in test C, only a modest peaking of the test information function can be observed.

The values of α_i for test E varied around an average of 1.0 and the level of its test information function was intermediate to that of tests C and D. The maximum amount of information was 26.7, which occurred at $\theta = 0.0$. The function was bell-shaped but well rounded rather than sharply peaked. The amount of information at the extremes ($\theta = \pm2.5$) was about one-fourth (6.8) of the maximum (26.7). The impact of using a variable α_i appears to a reduction of the kurtosis of the test information function.

Given these two strategies for constructing a broad-range test and their variations, the test constructor must now use that information to make a choice. The absolute level of the test information function is important and is heavily dependent on the average value of the α_i. The larger the values of α_i, the larger the amount of information and the greater the precision of the ability estimate. The test constructor must also decide whether the precision is to be the same at all ability levels. As can be seen from the various test information functions, the usual price one pays for uniform precision is lower overall levels of precision. The tests with β_i clustered near μ_θ yielded larger amounts of information near the middle of the ability scale than did the tests with uniformly distributed β_i.

The ICCs and item information and test information functions provide considerable insight into the properties of tests constructed under LTT/IRT. However, the test constructor must base the ultimate choice of items on such factors as the test plan, the intended use of the test, and the target population.

Although the test construction procedures described involved a two-parameter ICC model, they are also applicable to other models. In the case of the Rasch model only the item difficulty parameter β_i can be used to adjust the test information function as the item discrimination parameter has an a priori value of unity. The book *Best Test Design* (Wright & Stone, 1979) contains a comprehensive presentation of test construction procedures using the Rasch model. The Birnbaum three-parameter model has an additional item parameter, c_i, that influences the item information function and hence the test information function. Since guessing behavior decreases the precision with which an examinee's ability is estimated, achieving a desired level of the test information function may require additional manipulation of the items used in the test in order to take the c_i parameter into account. The reader is referred to Lord (1980) for a detailed account of the test construction process using the Birnbaum three-parameter model.

A unique application of precalibrated items under LTT/IRT is what is known as tailored or adaptive testing. Here the items administered to each individual should be appropriate to the ability level of that individual. Given a set of precalibrated items, a subset of n items can be administered sequentially under control of a branching rule. The response to an item determines the difficulty of the next item to be administered. In other words, if the item were answered correctly, the next item would be more difficult, and conversely. The process is continued until a stopping criterion is met. This paradigm has served as the basic concept underlying a variety of tailored testing techniques. Lord (1968, p. 1005) has recognized that LTT/IRT provides a much better basis for tailored testing than does classical test theory. The advantage arises from the item invariance principle whereby an examinee's ability can be estimated by an arbitrary set of items selected from a pool of precalibrated items. Also, the estimated ability of each individual will be in the metric of the calibration group. Given this, tailored testing reduces to finding the best scheme for selecting the set of items from the item pool to be administered to each individual. The theoretically optimal approach is to use only those items whose difficulty parameter, β_i, matches the examinee's ability. Unfortunately an examinee's ability is not known in advance, and hence the sequential scheme must be used to "zero in" on the unknown ability. To accomplish this, a particular tailored testing procedure is based on three components: the branching rule, the scoring procedure, and the stopping criteria. Many schemes and variations are possible within each of these components and the overall result is a very large set of potential tailored testing procedures. Weiss (1974) has presented an excellent review of the most important approaches. Research based on both actual testing and simulation studies shows clearly

that tailored testing requires fewer items than conventional tests and yields ability estimates with good precision over a wide range. In addition, the basic tailored testing procedures are simple enough to implement on a "personal" microcomputer.

Test analysis. When an existing test is being analyzed the role of item analysis is similar for the two measurement theories. However, the item parameters under LTT/IRT do a better job of conveying the characteristics of the item. Specifically, the difficulty parameter, β_i, locates an item on the ability scale. Thus items can be compared in terms of where they function, which is not possible with classical indices. An item with $\beta = +1.5$ can be described as functioning among high-ability students. An item with $\beta = -.2.0$ is one that functions with low-ability students. Given this information, the item content and other features of these items can be studied to ascertain why each item functions where it does. This is a different concept from that of classical item difficulty, which simply says that over all examinees the item was easy or hard. A large value of the item discrimination parameter would indicate that the item functions within a narrow range of ability centered on the value of β_i. Such items would be rather specific with respect to which examinees are impacted by the item. Conversely, an item with a low value of α_i would function over a broader range of ability. Again, comparisons of the content, structure, etc., of such items should reveal why the items discriminate differentially.

The item and test information functions can also be part of the test analysis. As shown in the foregoing, these functions indicate how well the ability levels are being estimated. Thus if a particular level has a small amount of information, one should interpret the ability estimate with caution, especially in a decision-making context. Again, LTT/IRT is a very rich theory in terms of the technical information it provides to those interpreting the results of a test analysis.

Recent advances. Up to this point it was assumed that an item was dichotomously scored, a choice that is somewhat arbitrary. There are many testing situations in which one could properly use a "graded" response. In such cases the hypothetical item response variable is divided into three or more ordered categories and an examinee's response is assigned to a response category. For example, one could categorize the possible responses with regard to their level of understanding of a concept. Because the response categories are mutually exclusive and exhaustive, the response category probabilities at any point on the ability scale must sum to unity. In addition, the requirement that the response categories be ordered means that the item difficulty parameters β_{ik} (where k, $1 \leq k \leq m$ denotes a response category) must also be ordered. Samejima (1969, 1972, 1973) has published extensively on the theoretical aspects of the graded response and has used both normal and logistic models for the item characteristic curves.

The availability of item parameter estimation techniques for the graded response case makes item analysis of rating scales possible. Since most scales involve a single underlying variable, the examinees can be located on a latent trait continuum and the item response categories can also be located along the same continuum. If the item functions properly, the difficulty parameters of the item response categories should be neatly ordered along that continuum. Unevenly spaced or improperly sequenced values of β_{ik} would identify less than optimal items.

A logical extension of the graded response is to remove the restriction that the response categories be ordered. In this situation a subject's response is simply identified by the response category to which it belongs. Bock (1972) has labled this situation a nominal response case inasmuch as the response categories form a nominal scale. Logically, the situation can be considered an extension of dichotomous scoring to polychotomous scoring. Because the item response is measured on a nominal scale, a total test score cannot be obtained but an ability estimate can be found for each examinee. Bock has employed the multivariate generalization of the logistic response function as the model for the set of ICCs involved.

Although few item writers employ nominal response items, the approach provides a solution to the problem of simultaneous estimation of the parameters of all response categories for a multiple-choice item. This has long been an unsolved problem in item analysis. Bock (1972) has shown that the correct response and distractors of a multiple-choice item can be treated as a nominal response item, and so, by using the estimation procedures for the nominal response case, estimates of α_{ik}, β_{ik} can be found for all the item response categories. The LOGOG computer program (Kolakowski & Bock, 1973) implements these procedures for an n-item test and also yields ability estimates for the examinees.

A group of European psychometricians has been developing an extension of the Rasch model known as the linear logistic test model (LLTM) (see Fischer, 1977; Spada, 1977). The starting point for this model is the usual one-parameter logistic model. Each item in a test is considered to entail a common set of cognitive operations. For example, the difficulty of elementary school arithmetic problems may be a function of the student's recognition of the type of problem, the magnitude of the numbers involved, the complexity of the procedure, etc. Each of these factors is considered a cognitive operation and has a parameter associated with it. Given this logic, the Rasch item difficulty parameter is defined as a linear function of the cognitive operation parameter and

$$\beta_i = \sum_{i=1}^{m} Q_{ik} \psi_k + c,$$

where ψ_k = a basic parameter corresponding to cognitive operation k;

Q_{ik} = weight of operation k in item i; and

c = an unknown constant.

In practice the Q_{ik} play the role of the elements in a design matrix and the ψ_k are estimated using maximum likelihood estimation procedures. Fischer (1977) applied LLTM to the problem of measuring change over time when the examinees were subjected to a number of different educational treatments but were administered a common achievement examination. The goal was to measure the effect of the particular treatments and to separate this effect from natural changes in achievement over time. Whitely (1981a,1981b) has extended the work on linear logistic test models to include components of ability that are allocated to the cognitive operations.

These new multicomponent models provide a means of relating achievement test results to underlying cognitive operations, curricular procedures, teaching methods, and the like. The interesting feature is that they yield a definition of the usual item difficulty parameter in terms of yet a more detailed set of parameters. It is too early to predict the impact of this development on item analysis practice. However, it is currently a very active research area.

Summary.   The item analysis techniques of classical test theory have been used for more than half a century. These procedures are well known and simplified explanations abound in elementary measurement textbooks; for example, see Stanley and Hopkins (1972) or Hills (1981). The most serious defect of the classical item parameters is that they are group dependent (Weiss & Davidson, 1981). Thus the indices can be interpreted only within the context of a given group of examinees. Despite this limitation, the experienced measurement person develops a clinical skill in interpreting the values of the item statistics in many different contexts.

As a relative newcomer to the measurement scene, the basic precepts of the latent trait theory/item response theory is not widely known nor its applications widespread among practioneers. Nonetheless, LTT/IRT is the state of the art in measurement theory. Because it is based on the parameters of the test item, item analysis plays a prominant role. The item parameters, β_i, α_i, have simple yet powerful interpretations that greatly facilitate the understanding of test results. In addition, the item parameters can be invariant with respect to the group taking the test. LTT/IRT is also capable of extensions such as to graded and nominal response models as well as to multicomponent models. As a result of this richness, LTT/IRT should be the standard basis for item analysis.

Frank B. Baker

See also Measurement in Education; Norms and Scales; Reliability of Measurement; Validity of Tests.

REFERENCES

Allen, M. J., & Yen, W. M. *Introduction to Measurement Theory.* Monterey, Calif.: Brooks/Cole, 1979.

Baker, F. B. An investigation of the sampling distributions of item discrimination indices. *Psychometrika*, 1965, *30*, 165–178.

Baker, F. B. Automation of test scoring, reporting, and analysis.

In R. L. Thorndike (Ed.), *Educational Measurement*. Washington, D.C.: American Council on Education, 1971.

Birnbaum, A. Some latent trait models and their use in inferring an examinee's ability. In F. M. Lord & M. R. Novick, *Statistical Theories of Mental Test Scores*. Reading, Mass.: Addison-Wesley, 1968.

Bock, R. D. Estimating item parameters and latent ability when responses are scored in two or more nominal categories. *Psychometrika*, 1972, *37*, 29–51.

Ebel, R. L. *Measuring Educational Achievement*. Englewood Cliffs, N.J.: Prentice-Hall, 1965.

Fischer, G. H. Linear logistic test models: Theory and application. In H. Spada & W. F. Kempf (Eds.), *Structural Models of Thinking and Learning*. Vienna: Huber, 1977.

Haley, D. C. *Estimation of the Dosage Mortality Relationship When the Dose Is Subject to Error*. (Technical Report No. 15). Stanford, Calif.: Stanford University, Applied Mathematics and Statistics Laboratory, 1952.

Hambleton, R. K., & Cook, L. L. Latent trait models and their use in the analysis of educational test data. *Journal of Educational Measurement*, 1977, *14*, 75–96.

Hawkes, H. E.; Lindquist, E. F.; & Mann, C. R. *The Construction and Use of Achievement Examinations*. Boston: Houghton Mifflin, 1936.

Henryssen, S. Gathering, analyzing, and using data on test items. In R. L. Thorndike (Ed.), *Educational Measurement*. Washington, D.C.: American Council on Education, 1971.

Hills, J. R. *Measurement and Evaluation in the Classroom*. Columbus, Ohio: Merrill, 1981.

Kolakowski, D., & Bock, R. D. *LOGOG, Maximum Likelihood Item Analysis and Test Scoring: Logistic Model for Multiple Item Response*. Ann Arbor, Mich.: National Educational Resources, 1973.

Lippey, G. (Ed.). *Computer-assisted Test Construction*. Englewood Cliffs, N.J.: Educational Technology Publications, 1974. (ERIC Document Reproduction Service No. ED 096 948)

Long, J. A., & Sandiford, P. *The Validation of Test Items* (Bulletin No. 3). Toronto: University of Toronto Press, Department of Educational Research, 1935.

Lord, F. M. An analysis of the verbal Scholastic Aptitude Test using Birnbaum's three-parameter logistic model. *Educational and Psychological Measurement*, 1968, *28*, 989–1020.

Lord, F. M. Individualized testing and item characteristic curve theory. In D. H. Krantz et al. (Eds.), *Contemporary Development in Mathematical Psychology*. San Francisco: Freeman, 1974. (ERIC Document Reproduction Service No. ED 069 783)

Lord, F. M. *Evaluation with Artificial Data of a Procedure for Estimating Ability and Item Characteristic Curve Parameters* (Research Bulletin 75-33). Princeton, N.J.: Educational Testing Service, 1975.

Lord, F. M. *Applications of Item Response Theory to Practical Testing Problems*. Hillsdale, N.J.: Lawrence Erlbaum Associates, 1980.

Lord, F. M., & Novick, M. R. *Statistical Theories of Mental Test Scores*. Reading, Mass.: Addison-Wesley, 1968.

McNamara, W. J., & Dunlap, J. W. A graphical method of computing the standard error of biserial *r*. *Journal of Experimental Education*, 1934, *2*, 274–277.

Rasch, G. *Probabilistic models for some intelligence and attainment tests*. Copenhagen: Danish Institute for Educational Research, 1960.

Rasch, G. An individualistic approach to item analysis. In P. Lazarsfeld & N. V. Henry, *Readings in Mathematical Social Science*. Chicago: Science Research Associates, 1966. (a)

Rasch, G. An item analysis which takes individual differences into account. *British Journal of Mathematical and Statistical Psychology*, 1966, *19*, 49–57. (b)

Samejima, F. Estimation of latent ability using a response pattern of graded scores (Monograph 17). *Psychometrika*, 1969, *34*, (2), 1–97.

Samejima, F. A general model for free response data (Monograph 18). *Psychometrika*, 1972, *37* (2), 1–68.

Samejima, F. Hogomeneous case of the continuous response model. *Psychometrika*, 1973, *38*, 203–219.

Samejima, F. A use of the information function in tailored testing. *Applied Psychological Measurement*, 1977, *1*, 233–247.

Spada, H. Logistic models of learning and thought. In H. Spada, & W. F. Kempf (Eds.), *Structural Models of Thinking and Learning*. Vienna: Huber, 1977.

Stanley, J. C., & Hopkins, K. D. *Educational and Psychological Measurement and Evaluation*. Englewood Cliffs, N.J.: Prentice-Hall, 1972.

Walker, H., & Lev, J. *Statistical Inference*. New York: Holt, 1953.

Weiss, D. J. *Strategies of Adaptive Ability Measurement* (Research Report 74-5). Minneapolis: University of Minnesota, Department of Psychology, Psychometric Methods Program, 1974. (ERIC Document Reproduction Service No. ED 104 930)

Weiss, D. J., & Davidson, M. L. Review of test theory and methods. *Annual Review of Psychology*, 1981, *32*, 629–658.

Wesman, A. G. Writing and test items. In R. L. Thorndike (Ed.), *Educational Measurement*. Washington, D.C.: American Council on Education, 1971.

Whitely, S. W. Multicomponent latent trait models for ability tests. *Psychometrika*, 1981a, *45*, 479–494.

Whitely, S. W. Measuring aptitude processes with multicomponent latent trait models. *Journal of Education Measurement* 1981b, *18*(2), 67–84.

Wood, R. L.; Wingersky, M. S.; & Lord, F. M. *LOGIST: A Computer Program for Estimating Ability and Item Characteristic Curve Parameters* (Research Memorandum 76-6). Princeton, N.J.: Educational Testing Service, 1976.

Wright, B. D. Sample-free test calibration and person measurement. *Proceedings of the 1967 Invitational Conference on Testing Problems*. Princeton, N.J.: Educational Testing Service, 1968. (ERIC Document Reproduction Service No. ED 017 810)

Wright, B. D., & Mead, R. S. *BICAL: Calibrating Rating Scales with the Rasch Model* (Research Memorandum 23A). Chicago: University of Chicago, Department of Education, Statistical Laboratory, 1976.

Wright, B. D., & Stone, M. H. *Best Test Design*. Chicago: MESA Press, 1979.

JK

JEWISH EDUCATION

Jewish education in the United States is voluntary, religious, heterogenous, and autonomous. It is neither centrally controlled nor funded by government. Jewish education in America is divided into several religious ideologies, which, in turn, are further divided into different subgroups. Detailed descriptions of the major religious ideologies (i.e., Orthodox, Conservative, and Reform) and their various subgroupings do not fall within the purview of this article; only their educational programs are discussed. Jewish schools are financed by tuition and philanthropy. Local and national religious and educational agencies provide financial assistance, guidance, and services, but actual operation and control of education is retained by each individual school.

Historical Background. The biblical injunction "and thou shalt teach them diligently to thy children" was faithfully observed by Jews throughout the millenia. Originally there were no schools. Fathers taught their sons biblical texts and the oral tradition, and mothers trained their daughters. During postbiblical times, family-centered instruction began giving way to a new community-based system of education. Whereas, heretofore, masters taught only select, small groups of gifted individuals, the Men of the Great Assembly (ca. 500 B.C.E.) founded large academies for higher learning, enrolling substantial numbers of students. Secondary schools were established by the sage Shimon ben Shatakh (ca. first century C.E.), and elementary schools were organized by the high priest Joshua ben Gamla at about the same time (Drazin, 1940). The latter's educational contribution was singled out by the Talmud for special commendation. Thus evolved a universal, noncompulsory system of education (Morris, 1934). In Europe, the elementary school was known as "Heder" and "Talmud Torah." (In its broadest sense, the term "Torah" means "teaching" or "instruction"; specifically, the term refers to the sacred texts that form the core of Jewish

learning and, generally, to the whole body of doctrines and laws derived from these texts.)

These talmudic schools were exclusively male schools. Traditional Jews perpetuated this total educational differentiation between the sexes until the early part of the twentieth century. Education was not confined to schools; learning was a lifelong process. Adults, mostly men, attended daily classes after work. On the Sabbath and holidays, everyone came to public lectures.

Throughout history, Jews have had a thirst for knowledge and an insatiable passion for scholarship. The lifelong pursuit of learning represents an unusual blend of doing one's duty and enjoying it. Education, in its broadest sense, has always been a priority on the agenda of the Jewish people. Indeed, the history of Jewish education is the history of the Jewish people.

Theological Foundations. Without the religious imperative, Jewish education could never have become a primary force in the shaping of the character of the Jewish people. Were it not for the fact that Torah was endowed by tradition with an aura of cosmological mysticism and perceived as the sacred, infinite repository of heavenly wisdom, the children of Israel could not have produced lawgivers, prophets, sages, and masters. A comprehension of a few of the basic tenets of Judaism which underlie educational theory and practice is indispensable to the understanding of Jewish education.

God, Torah, and Israel. Judaism's faith is pure monotheism. The Creator is noncorporeal and infinite. His being and essence are beyond the range of human comprehension. Yet, his existence is known to us by his creation, the universe, and everything therein.

The Almighty communicates with humankind through Torah, prophets, and Torah-true scholars. He entered into a covenant with the children of Israel and elected them to be the recipients and guardians of Torah, to serve as his "witnesses," and to be a "light unto the nations" by conveying his teachings to the human race. People communicate with God through Torah study, a Torah-true life-style, prayer, and worship. This relationship between God and Israel by no means excludes other people. Although Jews do not proselytize, they accept converts from every race and creed. Closeness to God may be attained by all righteous persons, even without the faith of Israel.

The educational goals and practices based on these beliefs are the teaching of Torah, faith, prayer, worship, and uniqueness of Israel. Children are taught to cherish their identity and to live proudly as Jews; and, although they should respect other people and religions and be law-abiding citizens, they must know what makes a Jew different.

God, the Creator, the source of life and all existence, is the Eternal One. Everything else in the universe, from the microcosmic to the macrocosmic, is temporal and was created by him. Such theories as evolution do not really stand in total contradiction to faith. Talmudic opinion has it that there were other creations preceding the present one. The age of the earth and the universe may run into billions of years. Tradition will not accept that the universe came into being without creation. There are some scientists who indeed accept the theory of spontaneous creation. Believers in the biblical account of creation no longer face a unanimous scientific community hostile to the belief in creation (Jastrow, 1978). Opposite the Darwinian theory of the evolution of humankind stands the elevating and dignifying belief that humans were created in the image of God. To tell a child that God has endowed all humans with intelligence and an immortal soul is more inspiring and challenging than to describe a descent from animal life. Judaism and objective science can coexist without any undue friction. What Judaism does reject is subjective and *a priori* atheistic scientism. Jewish educational institutions from elementary through graduate schools follow the same curriculum as their public counterparts. Science is taught objectively, without doctrinal strictures.

The moral dimension. Morality is an integral part of Judaism and permeates virtually all of its teachings and practices. Each person is a free agent, obligated to abide by high ethical standards. For example, the end does not justify the means in the pursuit of justice. Thus, the biblical commandment "justice, justice shall thou pursue" has been interpreted to mean that justice must be pursued with justice only, not by illegal or unethical means. The Torah enjoins everyone to walk in the ways of the Almighty. This requirement to emulate God is viewed by the rabbis of the Talmud as an ethical imperative: "Even as He is merciful so should you be merciful." Expanded a prominent moralist: "Even as He is a creator, so should you be a creator. A person must create his own self" (Levovitz, 1972). Not only are we free and accountable for our deeds, but we are also responsible for shaping our personalities. People cannot absolve themselves of guilt by claiming that their hot temper or bad environment led them to criminal or sinful acts. The freedom to act and create is vouchsafed with limitations encompassing all human experience. There is an ethic, not only of action but also of

feeling. A hungry person has to forego nonkosher food; a merchant gives up lucrative profits on Saturdays; disruptive, compulsive emotions must be controlled; and, a husband must abstain from conjugal relations with his wife during her menstrual cycle until her immersion in a ritual bath (Soloveitchik, 1978).

One's intellectual development, if it is not complemented by ongoing emotional and moral growth, does not constitute a full and complete education. Hence, education must be confluent and comprehensive. Students have to be taught the time-honored virtues of modesty, thrift, respect, hard work, politeness, charity, reverence, and discipline.

Way of life. Centuries before John Dewey, Jews were learning by doing. The greatness of the study of Torah is predicated on its being translated into action, says the Talmud, the massive compendium of Jewish wisdom, lore, and law. The practice of Judaism is not a mere set of rituals and worship, but a total way of life. Starting with circumcision and ending with burial rites, Judaism demands full adherence to complex and strict sets of laws, defined by *halakhah,* a divine system of norms regulating all human conduct.

Food has to be kosher, as prescribed by law, and duly certified by religious authorities. Sex is sanctified by nuptial rites; marriage and divorce are regulated by religious law and entrusted to rabbis only. Work is strictly forbidden on Saturdays and religious holidays; commerce, labor, and interpersonal relations must be conducted in consonance with high standards of honesty and integrity. Charity must be generously given. Governments and laws of the land must be respected. These are only some of the areas of life governed by *halakhah.*

Daily life is based on an affirmation of the inherent dignity and sanctity of physical life because there is "beautiful spirituality in this world" (ibn Paquda, 1970). But above all life and existence on earth towers human life. The transcendental soul within all human beings renders human life sacred and inviolate.

Educational implications. In order to initiate children into the Jewish way of life, teachers do not rely upon books alone, no matter how sacred the text. Intellectual learning must be accompanied by religious experiences at school, at home, and in the community so that students' self-esteem, self-realization, and fulfillment may be fostered. As they experience their religion, students are taught that doing a *mitzvah* (religious commandment or good deed) must be pleasant, aesthetic, and joyful. Finally, teachers must never be mere dispensers of knowledge, but models of forthright and respectable behavior.

Administrative and Educational Data. In 1959, Jewish schools in America, elementary and secondary, reported a total of 553,600 students (Dushkin & Engelman, 1959). Enrollment has been declining since the 1960s, largely because of a lower birthrate. In 1979, enrollment dropped to 357,107. Schools under Reform auspices, mostly Sunday schools, represented about 35 percent of the total enrollment; Conservative schools represented 30 percent; Orthodox schools represented 25 percent; and communal, independent, and Yiddish schools represented 10 percent. The Yiddish schools, still viable in Canada and South America, have ceased to be a significant factor in Jewish education in the United States. The day schools show steady growth, constituting now 26.3 percent of the total school population. About one-half of the students in Jewish schools still attend afternoon supplementary schools; about one-fourth are in day schools; and a similar number are in Sunday schools (American Association for Jewish Education, 1979c).

In 1980, there were 84,300 students in Orthodox day schools, of which 17,000 were secondary and 67,300 were elementary (Torah Umesorah, National Society for Hebrew Day Schools, 1980). Approximately one-half of the graduates of elementary day schools do not continue in secondary schools. Although the 1980 rate of growth has leveled off in the Orthodox community, enrollment in Conservative and Reform day schools has been on the increase and totals approximately 12,000 pupils (American Association for Jewish Education, 1979c). It was reported in 1959 that approximately 40–45 percent of the Jewish child population, ages 5–14, received some Jewish schooling (Dushkin & Engelman, 1959). A recent study in Los Angeles, the second largest Jewish community in America, reports similar findings (Phillips, 1980).

Financial data. In 1959, it was estimated that an aggregate annual total of $60 million was spent on Jewish elementary and secondary schools. About one-half of the income was derived from tuition, 7 percent from federation allocations, and the rest from contributions (Dushkin & Engelman, 1959). The 1979 overall educational budget of Jewish schools in America was about $280 million (Ackerman, 1980). In 1979, the annual average cost per pupil in elementary day schools ranged from $1,600 to $2,000. This sum includes operating costs, not capital expenses. Secondary day schools spent about $4,300 per student. In public schools, the cost was $1,782 per pupil in 1977 (American Association for Jewish Education, 1979a). Tuition fees in day schools have been rising steadily, averaging $2,000 in 1979, with many children receiving full or partial scholarships (Ackerman, 1980). On the average, tuition covers no more than 50 percent of the day-school budget. Allocations by federations have risen, averaging 13 percent of the school's budget. The rest of the income comes from fund-raising activities. By contrast, tuition fees in afternoon schools average about $105 (American Association for Jewish Education, 1979b).

Whereas a generation ago most of the Jewish teachers were foreign-born, the number of American-born teachers has been rising. Salary scales are generally lower than those in public schools. In Los Angeles, the Bureau of Jewish Education has equalized the salaries of Jewish teachers with those of their public school counterparts. Salaries of principals and consultants are more equitable. There exists a shortage of personnel at all levels (Ackerman, 1980).

School systems and their curricula. A number of school systems exist for the education of Jewish youth.

1. *Early childhood schools.* These include nursery and kindergarten classes. The curriculum includes Bible stories, Hebrew language studies, and religious experiences and activities.

2. *Sunday schools.* These schools are mostly under Reform auspices. Children study religion and history and engage in such activities as drama, dance, arts and crafts, and projects.

3. *Afternoon Hebrew schools.* Students meet twice weekly after public school hours and on Sunday morning, for a total of six hours per week. These schools are sponsored by all ideologies, but are the mainstay of Conservative education. Generally, these are congregational schools operated by synagogues. The Orthodox afternoon school is called "Talmud Torah." The Hebrew school curriculum consists of Hebrew language studies, prayer book studies, religious observances, history, and activities. Very little Bible is taught, if any.

4. *Afternoon high schools.* These generally follow the six-hour-a-week pattern. Hebrew, Bible, and literature are added to the subjects taught in elementary Hebrew schools.

5. *Day schools.* One-half of the school day is given to studies of Hebrew language, Bible, prayer, Jewish law, social studies, Talmud, and to extracurricular activities. The other half of the day is spent in general studies patterned after local public school curricula. Day schools have been almost exclusively under Orthodox auspices, but in recent years, the Conservative and Reform groups have entered this field. There are also a small number of community or nondenominational schools. Day schools, unlike the afternoon Hebrew schools, are generally communal schools, not attached to any one synagogue.

6. *Secondary day schools.* The curricula include Hebrew language and literature studies, talmudic studies, and religious thought, in addition to subjects taught in the elementary day school.

7. *Yeshivah.* Whereas the term "day school" may denote either an Orthodox, Conservative, Reform, secular, or communal school, yeshivah is an exclusively Orthodox institution. There are Hasidic yeshivoth where the language of instruction is Yiddish and the curriculum primarily consists of Pentateuch, talmudic, and rabbinic subjects. There are yeshivoth where the language of instruction is English and the curriculum is quite similar to that of Hasidic yeshivoth. In yeshivoth where the language of instruction is Hebrew, the curriculum includes subjects similar to those in Hasidic yeshivoth, plus more Bible, Hebrew literature, and social studies. Whereas day-school hours of instruction range from twelve to twenty per week, yeshivoth offer about thirty to thirty-five hours per week of Jewish instruction. This increase is accomplished by a long school day, Sunday sessions, and a longer school year.

8. *The metivta or yeshivah high school.* This secondary school is run along curricular lines parallel to the elementary yeshivah. These schools offer intensive programs and long hours of instruction. Hours of Jewish instruction may range from thirty to forty per week. Day schools may be coeducational, but not yeshivoth, and especially not metivtoth, where separate schools for boys and girls are maintained.

9. *Yeshivah gedolah.* A few such schools for college-age men have existed in the United States for some time. After World War II, scores of such yeshivoth opened throughout the country. Talmudic and rabbinic studies, plus Jewish thought and ethics, constitute the curriculum. The language of instruction is either Yiddish or English. Enrollment in these higher yeshivoth is estimated to range from 7,000 to 9,000. In Israel, there are about 18,000 such students. In some yeshivoth, the students attend colleges or universities concurrently. In others, the students are engaged in Torah studies exclusively. In New York, Yeshiva University and Touro College offer both sacred and general university studies.

10. *Yeshivah for baalei teshuvah.* Traditionally, a yeshivah *gedolah* was a school for college-age men graduates of a yeshivah high school, who had to pass an entrance examination in order to be admitted. It would have been unthinkable for a yeshivah to accept total beginners. In recent years, special yeshivoth for *baalei teshuvah* were opened in Israel and elsewhere for students ignorant of their Jewish heritage.

Some of the students are former drug addicts, or members of cults, whereas others are successful professionals, all sharing a yearning for spirituality. The religious rehabilitation work done by these yeshivoth extends now to women, too. There are now several thousand such students in the United States and in Israel.

11. *Kolel.* These schools were originally established as postgraduate schools for talmudic and rabbinic research in nineteenth-century Lithuania by Rabbi Israel Salanter, but remained virtually unknown. After the decimation of European learning centers during the holocaust of World War II, the kolel setting for young married scholars reemerged as the best medium for the advancement of postgraduate Torah-true learning. There are probably close to 1,000 young men enrolled in kolelim in the United States. In Israel, their number is much larger. These young scholars are idealists, subsisting on meager stipends; they spend the best years of their lives studying, researching, and publishing works. Future scholars, authors, rabbis, and educators will emerge from these talmudic schools.

Women in Jewish education. Historically, formal Jewish education was male-oriented. Young boys attended schools, and adults either studied in a yeshivah or continued their Torah studies informally. There were no schools for girls and women. Whatever formal instruction certain women received—and there were some notable women scholars—was done in the privacy of their homes. Within the family and in the community, life was male-dominated. Women had to be sheltered and protected against promiscuity and lewdness. The family was always the woman's

domain. The cultivation of children's ethical concepts and behavior (the very development of their personalities) was in the hands of women. Husbands were instructed to "love their wives as themselves, honor them more than themselves, guide their sons and daughters in the ways of the upright, and marry off their daughters at an early age."

In keeping with the religious concepts of modesty and sexual purity, women were prohibited by *halakhah* to mingle with men, to serve in positions of community leadership, and to take part in other functions that would take them out of the family circle. Surely, Jewish law does place restrictions on women. Traditional homes are male-directed, the father being considered the head of the household. Yet, if the father is "head" of the family, the mother is its "heart." In terms of children's respect, the mother and father are equal, and the husband must give priority to his wife's needs.

Although male superiority seems well established, secular Jews, Reform Jews, and many Conservative Jews do not accept this tradition, and they have initiated such changes as eliminating the segregation of the sexes in temples and synagogues, ordaining women rabbis, engaging female cantors, and so forth. Challenged by the feminists, these Jews consider it their duty to wipe out all inequities between the sexes.

Orthodox Jews generally differentiate economic, social, cultural, and legal barriers from religious barriers between the sexes. All nonreligious discrimination against women ought to be eliminated, but laws of modesty, sanctity, and family life are not subject to change. Orthodox Jews point to the frequent breakup of the modern family, teenage pregnancies, drug addiction, lack of parental controls, and disregard for law and authority as a vindication of their position. These serious problems, which plague modern societies, usually do not exist in traditional families and communities. Having other moral priorities, Orthodox men and women willingly forego the equality offered by feminists.

The Orthodox position, however, has some flexibility. The emergence of Bais Yaakov schools for girls early in this century, sanctioned by the leading Torah authorities of the time, represents prudence and judicious selectivity. The law itself is not subject to change, but methods of implementation do change because of new sets of conditions within society. Thus, when newspapers, magazines, paperbacks, and radios began penetrating the home, and when compulsory secular education and changing social conditions began affecting the minds and attitudes of young girls, a new set of threatening circumstances arose. Realizing that without meaningful formal religious schooling the girls were simply not equipped to handle the challenges posed by a changing world, the rabbis decided to endorse and support the Bais Yaakov schools. The very fact that a creative and inspiring woman, Sara Schenirer, conceived the idea of a Bais Yaakov movement and stood at its helm, was in itself a change and a prediction of things to come. The Bais Yaakov school system ranges from early childhood through college-level seminaries. The seminaries train teachers and have probably close to 1,000 students, but many of the graduates do not become teachers.

Teacher-training institutions. There are some thirty Jewish teacher-training institutions in the United States and Canada. Of these, 35 percent are under Orthodox auspices, either as seminaries, teacher colleges, or pedagogic institutes attached to yeshivoth. The pedagogic institutes are coordinated by Torah Umesorah, the National Society for Hebrew Day Schools. About 16 percent are under Conservative-traditional auspices, 13 percent are operated as Hebraic-national schools; 7 percent are Reform schools; and about 29 percent are classified as interdenominational-communal and secular Yiddishist schools (Dushkin, 1970). In 1970, a total of 2,968 students were enrolled in these schools, and only about 37 percent intended to become teachers. Despite the shortage of personnel, teachers are generally underpaid, and this insufficient pay is perhaps the single most important factor compelling teachers to seek other pursuits (Dushkin, 1970).

The Hebrew teacher colleges have been declining in stature and enrollment. Although some innovative programs are attempted, these schools can only supply a small portion of the teachers needed. It seems that in the future the yeshivoth *gedoloth,* with their pedagogic institutes, and the Bais Yaakov and similar women's seminaries, will provide most of the teachers for the Orthodox school system. It is probable that other movements will also have to utilize these resources as some already do.

Curricular goals and objectives. Each ideology perpetuates its interpretation of Judaism through school curricula. The various subjects included in these curricula and the educational goals of each group are consonant with their respective theologies. Detailed pronouncements are spelled out in official curricula (Baum, 1979; Ruffman, 1959; Syme, 1975).

Numerous informal educational programs exist in the Jewish community. These programs are offered by the various ideologies, Zionist and congregational youth groups, Jewish centers, Chabad-Lubavitch Hasidim, and others. Programs consist of camping, retreats, study groups in Israel, social and cultural events, national contests, and much more. Various courses in Jewish studies are offered at colleges and universities. Synagogues and other groups conduct adult education programs.

Although the entire educational enterprise is noncentralized, many schools tend to affiliate with local or national agencies. On the local level, almost all sizable Jewish communities have boards or bureaus of Jewish education. These central agencies, sponsored or supported by local federations, provide various pedagogic and consultative services to affiliated schools and distribute federation-allocated subventions. These local agencies are affiliated with the American Association for Jewish Education, a national umbrella organization. Many schools affiliate or associate with national bodies representing their respective ideological movements. These national agencies provide services in the form of publications, curricular guides, codes of practice, placement of personnel, arbitration, and consultation.

Summary. Jewish education in the United States does not reach substantial numbers of Jewish children. There are an estimated 5,860,900 Jews in this country (Chenkin & Miran, 1980). Approximately 360,000 students are enrolled in elementary and secondary Jewish schools, which is less than one-half of the school-age population. The problem is further compounded by the fact that a majority of these 360,000 students receive either a Sunday school or a Hebrew school education, which, at best, is shallow and short-lived, leaving little impact on adult life. Students who attend day schools and meshivoth, especially yeshivah high schools, do receive a solid Jewish education and remain committed to Jewish ideals and traditions.

Yet, one must not be overly harsh when judging Jewish education in America. The American Jewish community is a relatively young community. It took time for immigrants who fled from various European lands to establish themselves economically in the United States. At first, they organized charitable and social services, many of which have benefited Jews and non-Jews alike. Hospitals, orphanages, homes for the aged, cemeteries, organizations, synagogues, and schools had to be developed *de novo.* In addition to local needs, Jews in America did not forget their international obligations. Whether to help the families they left behind, to assist Jews in settling Palestine, to rescue persecuted Jews from pogroms (or from behind the Iron Curtain), or to rehabilitate and save the remnants of the holocaust, it was the American Jew who held out a helping brotherly hand.

All these great welfare, relief, and rescue operations consumed money, time, and energy. Thus, even as American Jews were busy saving other Jews, they often overlooked their own children, who grew up ignorant of their Jewish cultural heritage. Moreover, in their strong desire to "Americanize," the immigrant generation considered public school and college education for their children as top priority. Some of them erroneously assumed that shedding past religious practices and ethnic mores would pave the way for acculturation and acceptance by the larger American society. Thus, Jewish education was inadvertently relegated to a supplementary appendixlike status. The American melting pot was hard at work.

In recent years, some solid gains have been scored in Jewish education, especially by day schools and yeshivoth. The cataclysmic events of the holocaust, the awe-inspiring saga of the establishment and existence of the state of Israel after 2,000 years of Jewish exile, plus a coming-of-age at home, have converged and placed Jewish consciousness, identity, ethnicity, and religious education high on the agenda of the American Jewish community. One may expect this new awareness to spur further expansion of the day school and yeshivah movements, large-scale adult education programs, more returnees *(baalei teshuvah),* and community-wide efforts to raise the levels of knowledge and religiosity (Kaminetsky, 1976).

It seems that the same factors that have motivated Jews throughout history to preserve their way of life are functioning in America, too. These factors range from nostalgic, historic sentimentalism to an abiding commitment to the Covenant. The driving force behind the Jewish educational enterprise in America, and elsewhere, is the mystique of Israel's eternal spirit: a spirit seeking transcendental horizons beyond materialism and hedonism. Nowadays, there is a renewed quest for genuine religious learning and experience. There seems to be a brighter future in store for Jewish education in America. Truly, the words of the prophet are beginning to come true: "Behold, days are coming, said the Lord God, when I will send a famine in the land, not a famine for bread, nor a thirst for water, but to hear the words of the Lord" (Amos 8:11).

Zalman F. Ury

See also Private Schools; Religion and Education.

REFERENCES

Ackerman, W. I. Jewish education today. In *American Jewish Yearbook, 1980.* New York and Philadelphia: American Jewish Committee, Jewish Publication Society of America, 1980.
American Association for Jewish Education. *Information Bulletin No. 41: Budgeting and Financing in Jewish Day Schools.* New York: The Association, 1979. (a)
American Association for Jewish Education. *Information Bulletin No. 43: Tuition Fee Scales and Policies in Jewish Schools, 1978–1979.* New York: The Association, 1979. (b)
American Association for Jewish Education. *Information Bulletin No. 44: Jewish School Census, 1978–1979.* New York: The Association, 1979. (c)
Baum, E. (Ed). *Curriculum Guide for Afternoon Religious Schools.* New York: National Commission on Torah Education, Yeshiva University, 1979.
Chenkin, A., & Miran, M. Jewish population in the United States. In *American Jewish Yearbook, 1980.* New York and Philadelphia: American Jewish Committee, Jewish Publication Society of America, 1980.
Drazin, N. *History of Jewish Education from 515 B.C.E. to 200 C.E.* Baltimore: Johns Hopkins Press, 1940.
Dushkin, A. M. *Comparative Study of the Jewish Teacher Training Schools in the Diaspora.* Jerusalem: Institute of Contemporary Jewry, Hebrew University, 1970.
Dushkin, A. M., & Engelman, U. Z. *Jewish Education in the United States.* New York: American Association for Jewish Education, 1959.
ibn Paquda, B. *Duties of the Heart* (2nd Treatise, M. Hyamson, Trans.). Jerusalem and New York: Feldheim, 1970.
Jastrow, R. Have astronomers found God? *New York Times Magazine,* June 25, 1978, pp. 18–24.
Kaminetsky, J. A program for the day school movement in the seventies and beyond. *Tradition,* 1976, *16*(1), 124.
Levovitz, Y. *Daat Hokhmah U-Musar* (Vol. 3). Tel Aviv: Greenberg, 1972.
Morris, N. *The Jewish School.* New York: Jewish Education Committee Press, 1934.
Phillips, B. *Los Angeles Jewish Community Survey.* Los Angeles: Jewish Federation Council of Greater Los Angeles, 1980.
Ruffman, L. L. *Curriculum Outline for the Congregational School* (Rev. ed.). New York: United Synagogue Commission on Jewish Education, 1959.
Soloveitchik, J. B. Catharsis. *Tradition,* 1978, *17*(2), 45–47.
Syme, D. *Goals of Reform Jewish Education.* New York: Union of American Hebrew Congregations, Department of Education, 1975.
Torah Umesorah, National Society for Hebrew Day Schools. *Tempo* (Report No. 11). New York: The Society, 1980.

JUDICIAL DECISIONS

Before 1954, constitutional adjudication affecting education was an important but infrequent occurrence. The largest proportion of the suits involved disputes over the scope of the basic legal authority delegated by state legislatures to local school boards. For example, historically important struggles were fought over the meaning of statutes delegating authority to the school boards to control the admission and attendance of pupils, the school instructional program, student and teacher conduct, the disposition of school funds, the purchasing and selling of school property, the construction of school buildings, the raising of taxes, and the operation of the transportation system. Litigation also touched upon the interpretation of legislation on school board elections, the holding of school board meetings, and the alteration of school district boundaries. In addition, suits were brought over contract disputes between school boards and their teachers, the teachers' union, and other suppliers of services and products. Finally, courts were asked to determine if school districts were liable as a result of the commission of allegedly tortious actions (Peterson, Rossmiller, & Volz, 1978).

Since 1954 constitutional litigation, while not supplanting the types of litigation listed above, has increased dramatically, with important implications for all levels of education, whether public or private. Accompanying the rise in constitutional litigation has been the promulgation of new federal statutes both supplying new financial aid to public schools and threatening the cutoff of that aid if certain discriminatory practices are not halted. This body of legislation has itself been a second new source of litigation.

These two new areas of litigation have involved the judiciary in disputes that differ from the earlier litigation both in degree and kind. The most radical and noticeable difference is that today the courts are frequently asked to decide cases affecting the well-being of whole social classes and racial minorities; cases that reshape complex bureaucracies; and cases that use social scientific, and psychological and medical, evidence. Courts today must choose among differing philosophies of education, conflicting views of the role of educational institutions in a democracy, and alternative visions of society. This broadening of the issues has in turn meant a change in the form, structure, and processes of litigation. Plaintiffs, defendants, and the judge all now take on new roles and must exercise new skills in carrying forward these cases to resolution (Chayes, 1976; Fiss, 1979). The result has been the evolution of a new body of constitutional doctrine; a changed relationship among judiciary, legislatures, and school districts; and a potential for the expansion of judicial influence on education.

Recent constitutional developments affecting education fall into six areas: the scope of federal power; limits on governmental socialization; establishment of procedural requirements; limits on the use of coercive rules; equal protection; and rights of political participation (Tribe, 1978; Yudof et al., 1981).

Federal Legislative Power. One of the more important constitutional developments of the twentieth century has been the expansive interpretation the federal judiciary has given to article 1 §8 of the Constitution, which grants Congress the power to collect taxes for the general welfare. By interpreting this clause as conferring not just a power to tax but also a power to spend money on such areas as education that are not expressly mentioned as within the province of Congress, the Supreme Court has made possible a dramatic change in the federal system governing education (*United States* v. *Butler*, 297 U.S. 1 (1936); van Geel, 1976). Subsequent decisions have expanded federal power by making clear that the power to spend includes a significant power to control by means of regulations attached to the use of the federally supplied money. *Fullilove* v. *Klutznick*, 448 U.S. 448 (1980); *Lau* v. *Nichols*, 414 U.S. 563 (1974); *Helvering* v. *Davis*, 301 U.S. 619 (1937). To the extent that there are limits on the exercise of Article I power, they are in provisions outside that article such as the Bill of Rights or the Constitution's implicit protections of state sovereignty. For example, in *National League of Cities* v. *Usery*, 426 U.S. 833 (1976), the Court invalidated a law that extended federal minimum wage and maximum hour provisions to local government on the grounds that these were matters that should remain in the control of state and local government since they were essential to their separate and independent existence. This decision throws into doubt the constitutionality of proposed federal legislation to regulate collective bargaining in public elementary and secondary educational institutions. But it is important to note that federal legislative power also exists pursuant to grants of authority in the Thirteenth, Fourteenth, and Fifteenth amendments to enforce those amendments. An important civil rights statute passed by Congress pursuant to its authority in the Thirteenth Amendment has been held to be applicable to private schools, thereby, in effect, prohibiting racially restricted private schools. 42 U.S.C. §1981 *Runyon* v. *McCrary*, 427 U.S. 160 (1976).

Although the states are endowed with power pursuant to the Tenth Amendment to support and operate public school systems, they (and their agents, school boards and their employees) are nevertheless subject to the external check of the Bill of Rights made applicable to the states through the Fourteenth Amendment, as well as being subject to the Fourteenth, Thirteenth, and Fifteenth amendments themselves. Of the many values enshrined in these provisions, among the most important are those protected by the First Amendment, in particular the rights of free speech and religion and the associated right of freedom of belief. Relying on these clauses as well as the guarantees of liberty in the clauses of the Fifth and Fourteenth amendments, the courts have moved toward defining a "sphere of intellect and spirit" which is to be free of governmental control: "[I]n a free society one's beliefs should be shaped by his mind and his conscience rather than coerced by the State." *Abood* v. *Detroit Board of Education*, 431 U.S. 209, 235 (1977). At the same time the Supreme Court has explicitly recognized as legitimate the interest of the government in instructing the young in the value of patriotism and those other social, political, and moral values that, once learned, permit a student to take his or her place in the community. *Ambach* v. *Norwick*, 441 U.S. 68 (1979). Although this governmental interest has been deemed to be strong enough to warrant compulsory education laws and curricular requirements for public and private schools, given the recognition of a student's interest in autonomy, the question is inevitably one of balance. How far may government go to foster a sense of shared values and viewpoints before it exceeds the limitations imposed upon it by a decent respect for the child's autonomy?

The Supreme Court addressed this question in three cases decided in the 1920s, cases that laid the foundation for the dual public and private school system now in place in the United States. In those cases the Court protected the right of private schools to continue to exist, protected the right of parents to send their children to private school, and established that only reasonable regulations of private schooling would be tolerated, thereby assuring that private schools could continue to offer a type of education which was not by reason of state law forced to be an exact copy of the public school program. See *Pierce* v. *Society of Sisters*, 268 U.S. 510 (1925); *Meyer* v. *Nebraska*, 262 U.S. 390 (1923); *Farrington* v. *Tokushige*, 273 U.S. 284 (1926). A premise running through those decisions, sometimes only implicitly supportive, was that government would not be permitted wholly to take over the education of children with a view to graduating students all of whom share the same values, beliefs, and attitudes.

But despite the strong protection given by the Supreme Court to a right to send one's child to private schools, the Court has at the same time made it clear that there is no right to receive governmental financial support to make the exercise of that right financially easier. *Committee for Public Education and Religious Liberty* v. *Nyquist*, 413 U.S. 756 (1973); *Norwood* v. *Harrison*, 413 U.S. 455 (1973); *Brusca* v. *State of Missouri ex rel. State Board of*

Education, 332 F. Supp. 275 (E.D. mo. 1971), *aff'd,* 405 U.S. 1050 (1972) *(per curiam).* Even when states voluntarily have attempted to provide financial support to private schools, the result has been a spate of often successful challenges based on the establishment clause of the First Amendment. Thus today transportation to private schools may be paid for by government; books may be loaned by the state to private school students, but audiovisual and other equipment may not be loaned to the school itself; under special restrictions certain forms of services may be provided by the state to private school pupils, and the state may reimburse private schools, subject to other conditions, for the costs of administering state-mandated standardized tests. *Committee for Public Education and Religious Liberty* v. *Regan,* 444 U.S. 646 (1980); *Wolman* v. *Walter,* 433 U.S. 229 (1977); *Meek* v. *Pittenger,* 421 U.S. 349 (1975); *Lemon* v. *Kurtzman,* 403 U.S. 602 (1971); *Board of Education* v. *Allen,* 392 U.S. 236 (1968); *Everson* v. *Board of Education,* 330 U.S. 1 (1947).

Aid to private religious schools is constitutionally sensitive because it places the government positively in support of particular religious orthodoxies, an issue that may also arise in the context of the public school itself. At the most general level the basic questions are whether the Constitution should be interpreted to impose upon school districts a duty not to reject books and materials, or not to refuse to hire or fire teachers, for religious or ideological reasons; whether the Constitution should be read to impose upon school districts a duty not to impose a single identifiable perspective, religion, ideology, or other viewpoint; and whether the Constitution should be read to require school boards to assure that the curriculum is neutral, or balanced, and representative of the diversity of views in the community. These are difficult questions, and the cases to date provide only partial answers (Stern, 1979; Yudof, 1979).

As for religion, the Supreme Court has taken an unequivocal position against the holding, by school officials during the regular school day, of religious ceremonies, and the posting of a religious text like the Ten Commandments on classroom walls. But although the Court has prohibited these explicitly religious activities in the public schools (see *Stone* v. *Graham,* 66 L.Ed.2d 199 (1981); *Abington School District* v. *Schempp,* 374 U.S. 203 (1963)), lower courts have permitted the celebration in school of such holidays as Christmas by means of music, art, literature, and drama having religious themes (if presented in a prudent and objective manner and as a traditional part of the cultural and religious heritage of the particular holiday) and by means of religious symbols (when used as a teaching aid or resource and provided such symbols are displayed as an example of the cultural and religious heritage of the holiday and are of a temporary nature). *Florey* v. *Sioux Falls School District,* 619 F.2d 1311 (7th Cir. 1980) *(en banc).* An invocation and benediction have also been permitted at a public high school graduation ceremony if attendance is voluntary. *Wiest* v. *Mt. Lebanon School*

District, 457 Pa. 166, 320 A.2d 362 (1974), *cert. denied,* 419 U.S. 967 (1974).

Turning to the avowedly secular portion of the school program, as noted above, the Supreme Court has acknowledged as legitimate the state's interest in inculcating in students certain civic and patriotic virtues, but at the same time the Court has moved to impose limits on the pursuit of that purpose. The most important decision remains that in *West Virginia State Board of Education* v. *Barnette,* 319 U.S. 624 (1943), in which the Court, while permitting school districts to continue to have a daily flag salute ceremony, prohibited schools from requiring students to participate. Although the underlying principle of the case has not been identified with certainty, one plausible interpretation of the case is that the flag salute involved a coerced confession of belief that the Court arguably deemed to be an affront to dignity, an improper means of state communication and socialization.

Relying on the decision in *Barnette,* and other important decisions protective of freedom of speech and academic freedom, the most recent challenges have been to school officials' decisions refusing to purchase recommended books for use in the classroom or ordering the removal of specified books from the library. To date, only lower courts have ruled in these cases and the results have been mixed, with plaintiffs winning in some suits but losing in others. See *Zykan* v. *Warsaw Community School Corp.,* 631 F.2d. 1300 (7th Cir. 1980); *Pico* v. *Board of Education, Island Trees Union Free School District,* 638 F.2d 404 (2d Cir. 1980), *cert. granted,* 50.U.S.L.W. 3083 (6/1/81); *Bicknell* v. *Vergenees Union High School,* 638 F.2d 438 (2d. Cir. 1980); *Cary* v. *Board of Education,* 598 F.2d 535 (10th Cir. 1979); and *Minarcini* v. *Strongsville City School District,* 541 F.2d 577 (6th Cir. 1976). There is no agreement as to the limits, if any, on the discretion of school boards to control the selection of text and library books.

The legal situation is somewhat clearer when school boards attempt to purge their schools of students or teachers with whom they are in disagreement. Today the free speech rights of students and teachers are given judicial protection as long as the exercise of those rights neither materially disrupts the operation of the school nor frustrates the interest of the state and school board in getting their message across. By protecting these individual rights the courts have assured that at least to a limited extent, the public schools will be marketplaces of ideas, forums in which something additional may be said and heard beyond that which has received official approval. See *Healy* v. *James,* 408 U.S. 169 (1972); *Tinker* v. *Des Moines Independent School District,* 393 U.S. 503 (1969); *James* v. *Board of Education,* 461 F.2d 566 (2d Cir.), *cert. denied,* 409 U.S. 1042 (1972); *Parducci* v. *Rutland,* 316 F. Supp. 352 (M.D. Ala. 1970). To further assure that a "pall of orthodoxy" is not thrown over the classroom, the Supreme Court has opposed attempts to keep Communists out of the classroom who had no specific intent to further the unlawful goals of the Communist party and were not active members of the party. *Keyishian* v. *Board of Regents*, 385 U.S. 589 (1967). However, in 1979 the Court upheld a law that prohibited aliens who were eligible to seek U.S. citizenship, but had not, from holding teaching posts on the ground that the state's prohibition was rationally related to the promotion of the governmental interest in having students educated in certain civic virtues and duties, a task which, in the state's view, aliens could not accomplish. *Ambach* v. *Norwick*, 441 U.S. 68 (1979).

Procedural Requirements. It is only a short step from protection of the autonomy of the individual mind to protection of dignity and, arguably, the due process clause of the Fourteenth Amendment ("nor shall any State deprive any person of life, liberty, or property, without due process of law") has embedded in it the ideals that governmental actions should approach the individual as a person who is to be consulted about what is done with him or her, and that governmental decisions should not involve unfair or mistaken deprivations of liberty or other entitlements. Pursuant to these values the Supreme Court has required that decisions by school officials which deprive a student or teacher of an interest protected by the Constitution (e.g., continued access to a publicly provided education or continuation in a job to which the individual has an entitlement founded in state law) must be preceded by a hearing that may vary in formality depending in part on the severity of the likely deprivation. *Board of Regents* v. *Roth*, 408 U.S. 564 (1972); *Perry* v. *Sindermann*, 408 U.S. 593 (1972); *Goss* v. *Lopez*, 419 U.S. 565 (1975). More recent cases indicate that there are important limitations as to when the Constitution does require such a hearing: proving the existence of a state-created legal entitlement is now more difficult. *Bishop* v. *Wood*, 426 U.S. 341 (1976). Also, the Court has said that even a brief informal hearing is not required before a school official may administer corporal punishment (*Ingraham* v. *Wright*, 430 U.S. 651 (1977)) or dismiss a student for academic reasons from graduate school (*Board of Curators* v. *Horowitz*, 435 U.S. 78 (1978)).

Coercive Rules. Although the value of personal dignity has been used by the Supreme Court as a basis for imposing at least some modicum of restraint on the school's power over children, the effort to get the courts to recognize a value in autonomy and self-defined identity has met with considerable judicial resistance when it comes to the efforts of school officials to control the hair and dress styles of students and teachers. To be sure, some courts have recognized the existence of a protectable interest within the vague contours of the due process clause of the Fourteenth Amendment, but others have stoutly maintained that whatever interest a student or teacher may have in controlling their outward appearance is too trivial to warrant the expenditure of judicial effort to regulate the regulators of hair and dress styles. See, for example, *Zeller* v. *Donegel School District*, 517 F.2d 600 (3d Cir. 1975); *Miller* v. *School District No. 167*, 495 F.2d 658 (7th Cir. 1974); *Richards* v. *Thurston*, 424 F.2d 1281 (1st Cir. 1970).

Neither have the privacy interests of students gained strong judicial protection. Today most lower courts have said that evidence of criminal or school rule violations seized by school administrators in contravention of the limitations against unreasonable searches and seizures embodied in the Fourth Amendment may be used against the student in school disciplinary hearings. The current trend in judicial decisions, however, is one that excludes the use of such evidence in criminal proceedings. *People* v. *Scott D.*, 34 N.Y. 2d 483, 315 N.E. 2d 466, 358 N.Y.S. 2d 403 (1974); and see *Morale* v. *Grigel*, 422 F. Supp. 988 (D.N.H. 1976); but see *Caldwell* v. *Cannady*, 340 F. Supp. 835 (N.D. Tex. 1972). Finally, the Court has said that even severe beatings by public school officials in the name of administering corporal punishment do not constitute cruel and unusual punishment within the meaning of that constitutional phrase. *Ingraham* v. *Wright*, 430 U.S. 651 (1977).

Equal Protection. Judicial concern for the values of dignity and respect has shaped not only the interpretations of the First Amendment and to a more limited extent the due process clause of the Fourteenth Amendment, but also the elaboration by the judiciary of the generalities of the equal protection clause of the Fourteenth Amendment. Most notably, the Supreme Court's school desegregation opinions may be understood as resting on the principle that when government acts it should treat all people as if they were endowed with equal dignity, or as if they deserved equal respect (Karst, 1977). Significantly, such a principle does not preclude affirmative action to assist minorities when the appropriate institution, e.g., a legislature or court, formally recognizes that there has been a historical wrong which warrants correction, for in that circumstance the expectations of nonminorities that may be frustrated are not due the same relative degree of respect. See *Fullilove* v. *Klutznick*, 448 U.S. 448 (1980); *Regents of the University of California* v. *Bakke*, 438 U.S. 265 (1978); *Brown* v. *Board of Education*, 347 U.S. 483 (1954).

From this principle the Supreme Court has deduced that the purposeful segregation of the races in schools is impermissible, but that to prove an intent to segregate, something more must be shown than that the effects of a board's policies were to produce racially imbalanced schools (van Geel, 1980). The Court also has said that school boards which in 1954, at the time of the *Brown* decision, were maintaining dual school systems have been, since that time, automatically under a continuous constitutional obligation to disestablish their dual systems. Such districts must prove that after 1954 their policies affirmatively were directed toward ending segregation and did not even have the unintended effect of perpetuating it. See *Columbus Board of Education* v. *Penick*, 443 U.S. 449 (1979); *Dayton Board of Education* v. *Brinkman*, 443 U.S. 526 (1979); *Arlington Heights* v. *Metropolitan Housing Corp.*, 429 U.S. 252 (1977); *Washington* v. *Davis*, 426 U.S. 229 (1976); *Keyes* v. *School District No. 1., Denver*, 413 U.S. 189 (1973).

School districts that have been found purposefully to have promoted segregation are exposed to the equitable powers of the courts to fashion remedies to rid the system of the improperly caused segregation—remedies that may include extensive intradistrict busing, remedial education programs, and perhaps even interdistrict busing in special circumstances. See *Evans* v. *Buchanan*, 582 F.2d. 750 (3d Cir. 1978), *cert. denied*, 446 U.S. 923 (1980); *Millikan* v. *Bradley*, 433 U.S. 267 (1977); *Millikan* v. *Bradley*, 418 U.S. 717 (1974); *Swann* v. *Charlotte-Mecklenburg Board of Education*, 402 U.S. 1 (1971). In the Supreme Court's most recent decisions it has moved to limit the instances in which district-wide remedies may be imposed by the lower courts; for example, a finding of a small number of specific violations, says the Court, does not provide a promise for a system-wide remedy—it only means that the quantum of segregation purposefully caused in the specific schools involved has to be corrected. *Dayton Board of Education* v. *Brinkman*, 433 U.S. 406 (1976), and see *Dayton Board of Education* v. *Brinkman*, 443 U.S. 526 (1979).

Except for the race cases, the Supreme Court itself has not been active in dealing with discrimination in the public schools—on the basis of gender, limited English-speaking ability, or handicap; since these topics have been addressed by Congress, discussion is reserved for later sections. The Supreme Court itself, however, was asked to deal with discrimination on the basis of wealth in *San Antonio Independent School District* v. *Rodriguez*, 411 U.S. 1 (1973). There the Court rejected the claim that Texas's system of finance, which produced great differences among the districts of the state in the amount of money spent per pupil, was a violation of the equal protection clause simply because the differences coincided with and arguably were caused by inequalities in the amount of property wealth per pupil in those districts. Since that Supreme Court decision, however, litigation attacking inequalities in expenditures per pupil among districts has gone forward with considerable success in state courts, based on a variety of interpretations of what the respective state constitutions require of the state legislatures (Yudof et al., 1981).

Rights of Political Participation. In a variety of ways, and with the use of the First Amendment and the equal protection clause, the Court has laid out a number of principles designed to assure that the political process for controlling public education is not restricted or closed to certain people and groups. Impermissible are laws excluding those from voting in school elections who neither own nor lease property in the district, nor are parents of children enrolled in the schools. *Kramer* v. *Union Free School District No. 15*, 395 U.S. 621 (1969). Also unconstitutional are electoral arrangements, such as the at-large election system, when established with the purpose of preventing black or other minority representation on the school board. *Mobile* v. *Bolden*, 446 U.S. 55 (1980); *White* v. *Regester*, 412 U.S. 755 (1973). And teachers have been afforded protection so that they may without undue fear for their jobs attempt to shape the policies of their school boards. First, publicly criticizing school board policies may not, unless there are special circumstances present in the case, be a basis for dismissal. *Pickering* v. *Board of Education*, 391 U.S. 563 (1968); also see *Givhan* v. *Western Line Consolidated School District*, 439 U.S. 410 (1979). Second, several lower courts have assured teachers of the constitutional right to join a union and to engage aggressively in union activities. *Hickman* v. *Valley Local School District Board of Education*, 619 F.2d 606 (6th Cir. 1980); *McLaughlin* v. *Tilendis*, 398 F.2d 287 (7th Cir. 1968). Finally, the Supreme Court has invalidated a state employment commission's order requiring a school board to prohibit teachers who are not union representatives from speaking at open meetings of the school board at which public participation is permitted even if the speech is addressed to the subject of pending collective bargaining negotiations. *City of Madison* v. *Wisconsin Employment Relations Commission*, 429 U.S. 167 (1976).

The Normative Perspective on Judicial Review. Ever since the Supreme Court seized and simultaneously was ceded the power of judicial review, the central question has been how the judiciary shall exercise this power. *Marbury* v. *Madison*, 1 Cranch 137 (1803). An important segment of the advocates of judicial restraint argue that the Court may not discover or invent new fundamental values which are to be afforded protection by the Constitution, but may only act when the Constitution clearly specified the value to be preferred. Judges must stick close to the text, its history, and their fair implications, and must show deference and respect to the independent judgment of the other branches of government, which are more nearly representative of the majority viewpoint (Bork, 1971). In contrast, there are others who argue that the courts may and must give voice to, develop, and shape the widely shared ideals and values of society, not all of which could be embodied expressly in the language of the Constitution. Advocates of this ethical theory of review believe that doing right, achieving justice, is more important than limiting the role of the Court to the one of keeping the majoritarian process as unfettered as possible (Perry, 1979, 1978). A third theory of the role of the Court rejects the ethical theory as inviting judges to impose their own subjective values. It stresses that the Court's function should be only to ensure an open political process, protecting politically powerless minorities by ensuring their participation in the processes and distributions of government (Ely, 1980).

Each of these perspectives has its own quarrel with the decisions the courts have reached. First of all, for example, advocates of restraint say the result in *Pierce* v. *Society of Sisters* (the case that upheld the right of parents to send their children to private school) cannot be sustained by the Court's reasoning and are doubtful it can be sustained by any rationale; they argue that the courts have too cavalierly accepted proof of racial discrimination, leading to excessive judicial involvement in the schools; but they congratulate the courts on giving government leeway to socialize students as the government sees fit. Second, adherents of the view that the Courts should serve an ethical function praise the desegregation decisions but argue that the courts have not gone far enough in dealing with racially harmful practices; they are critical of courts that have let school districts regulate hair and dress styles and other matters of personal autonomy and privacy. Third, advocates of the judiciary promoting an open and fair political process disagree with the positions of the two other kinds of theorists in some respects but agree with them in certain respects. For example, they praise the racial integration cases, and those cases protecting free speech and rights of political participation, at the same time rejecting as inappropriate any judicial effort to protect students and teachers from hair and dress codes; but they approve of *Pierce* v. *Society of Sisters* for its prevention of government capturing control of all education, which might in turn damage the possibility of freely formed public opinion that is so crucial to an open political process.

Interpreting Statutes. Judicial power includes not only the power of judicial review but also the power to interpret statutes in the face of a conflict over their meaning. Beginning in the middle of the 1970s, the truly active exercise of judicial review began to wane while the exercise of the interpretative powers of the courts increased and was used to expand the meaning of federal legislation intended to end discrimination on the basis of race, gender, and handicap. The relative waning of judicial review can be accounted for by the fact that the Supreme Court increasingly came to view the exercise of judicial review as inconsistent with both the principle of federalism and that of majority rule, whereas the power even liberally to interpret the statutes of Congress was fully legitimate since the Court could claim, with some plausibility, that when it extended the meaning of a statute it was only executing the will of the majority as embodied in a preexisting law. From a political perspective, using this tactic, the Court shielded itself from the full brunt of critics of social reform, pressing forward in the name of what Congress intended instead of declaring the law as a seeming *ipse dixit*.

There are numerous examples of the judiciary's willingness to give expansive interpretations of the acts of Congress. Shortly after the Civil Rights Act of 1964 (42 U.S.C. §2000c) was passed—the law prohibits discrimination on the basis of race, color, or national origin in programs receiving federal funds on pain of loss of those funds—the courts approved as consistent with the intent of Congress strong regulations and guidelines designed to promote integration in all public school districts receiving federal funds. *United States* v. *Jefferson County Board of Education*, 372 F.2d 836 (5th Cir. 1966), *aff'd*, 380 F.2d 385 (5th Cir. 1967) *(en banc)*. Some years later the Supreme Court agreed that Title IV might be read to render illegal actions that simply has the effect of discriminating, even though no purposeful design was present. *Lau* v. *Nichols*, 414 U.S. 563 (1974). (More recently a majority of the Court

seemed to be moving away from that position. *Regents of the University of California* v. *Bakke*, 438 U.S. 265 (1978).) In *Lau* the Court also upheld an interpretation of Title VI which said that illegal discrimination exists when a school does not offer assistance in learning English to a student who can't take advantage of the program offered because of limited ability to speak and understand English. Title VII of the Civil Rights Act of 1964, which is concerned with discrimination in employment, has been interpreted to mean that a discriminatory purpose need not be proved, only a discriminatory effect need be established. *International Brotherhood of Teamsters* v. *United States*, 431 U.S. 324 (1977). A similar interpretation was placed on the Emergency School Aid Act, 20 U.S.C. §1601(a). *Board of Education* v. *Harris*, 100 S. Ct. 363 (1979). In *Cannon* v. *University of Chicago*, 441 U.S. 677 (1979), despite the absence of any express authorization for it in the statute, the Court concluded that Title IX of the Educational Amendments of 1972, an act designed to prohibit discrimination on the basis of gender in programs receiving federal funds, authorized private enforcement suits in addition to explicitly authorized official implementation efforts. Section 1983 (42 U.S.C. §1983) was interpreted to extend to public school officials, thereby providing a means for students and teachers whose constitutional rights were violated by school officials to sue for monetary damages. *Wood* v. *Strikland*, 420 U.S. 308 (1975). Section 1981 (42 U.S.C. §1981) was extended to private schools, thereby prohibiting racially discriminatory admissions policies by private schools. *Runyon* v. *McCrary*, 427 U.S. 160 (1976). And the lower courts especially have been active in giving liberal interpretations of P.L. 94-142, thereby forcing school districts to, for example, provide deaf students with "signers" who would accompany them to class and provide simultaneous translations of oral English proceedings. *Camenisch* v. *University of Texas*, 616 F.2d. 127 (5th Cir. 1980); *Rowley* v. *Board of Education of Hendrick Hudson*, 632 F.2d 945 (2d Cir. 1980); also see *Southeastern Community College* v. *Davis*, 442 U.S. 397 (1979). Finally, the courts have even been pressing the federal government for more vigorous enforcement of the legislation it has been charged with enforcing. *Alexander* v. *Holmes City Board of Education*, 396 U.S. 19 (1969); *Adams* v. *Richardson*, 480 F.2d 1159 (D.C. Cir. 1973); *Adams* v. *Califano*, 430 F. Supp. 118 (D.D.C. 1977); *Brown* v. *Weinberger*, 417 F. Supp. 1215 (D.D.C. 1976); *Adams* v. *Weinberger*, 391 F. Supp. 269 (D.D.C. 1975).

At the same time that the courts have been enforcing civil rights legislation, they have also had to deal with legislation designed to limit courts' use of busing as a remedy to end segregation. See the Equal Educational Opportunity Act of 1974, 20 U.S.C. §§1701 et seq.; 90 Stat. 1434 (1976). Now, instead of liberally expanding upon the intent of Congress, courts have taken a crabbed view of the legislation, narrowing its scope, thereby leaving courts the same degree of discretion to order busing that they enjoyed prior to the passage of these laws. *Morgan* v. *Kerri-*

gan, 530 F.2d 401, 412 (1st Cir. 1976), *cert. denied,* 426 U.S. 935 (1976). See also *Brinkman* v. *Gilligan,* 518 F.2d 853, 856 (6th Cir. 1975), *cert. denied,* 423 U.S. 1000 (1975); *Evans* v. *Buchanan,* 416 F. Supp. 328, 362 (D. Del. 1976).

Interaction of Three Branches. The three branches of government can be, and have been simultaneously, institutions that serve as checks and as supports. The courts have the authority both to frustrate the wills of legislators and administrators and to legitimize and expand upon what they have undertaken. For their part the legislatures can pass, and have passed, laws that affirm the rules, principles, and policies advanced by the judiciary while also resolving political conflicts among values and interests that the judiciary may have left unresolved. But legislatures may also actively seek to undo the courts' work by passing legislation that seeks to exploit ambiguities in the decrees, or directly overrules the decrees, or directly attacks judicial power. The federal administration working through Congress can, of course, attempt to check or expand the courts' work. In addition, the administration is also in the position, as a law enforcement agency, vigorously or not so vigorously to enforce the "law of the land," or, using its access to the media, to rally support or opposition to courts' rulings.

The interaction of judiciary, Congress, and the federal administration can be illustrated by a brief recounting of the recent history of federal policy toward racial segregation (Wilkinson, 1979). The Supreme Court, after decisively taking the lead in seeking to end legally enforced racial segregation in 1954, withdrew from the field of action, delegating primary responsibility to the federal district courts and refusing for many years thereafter to entertain most of the desegregation suits brought to it for review. But little significant change occurred despite, or because of, the requirement for "all deliberate speed." The disinterested-to-hostile attitude of the Eisenhower administration toward the *Brown* decision failed to encourage desegregation and may have contributed to the rise of what was sometimes trumpeted as "massive resistance." However, the Reverend Martin Luther King, Jr., and his organization marched in the early 1960s and in so doing raised the moral conscience of the nation, an effort that ultimately led to the declaration by Congress in Title VI of the Civil Rights Act of 1964 that any program receiving funds would lose its funds if it discriminated on the basis of race. The Johnson administration, which had ushered the law through Congress in the name of an assassinated president, John F. Kennedy, took the law seriously, and the then Department of Health, Education, and Welfare (HEW) promulgated guidelines that defined in a more specific way than had heretofore been stated by court or agency what constituted racial discrimination. Now the shoe was on the other foot, for it was the courts that embraced these guidelines as to what the Constitution itself required. The Supreme Court, lower federal courts, and the administration, in concert for the first time, pushed forward together on ending the southern dual school system.

But in 1968 Richard Nixon won the presidency, partly on a platform that opposed "massive desegregation." The result was first a request by the administration to the Fifth Circuit Court of Appeals to delay the implementation of a desegregation plan for certain Mississippi school districts—a delay that the Fifth Circuit granted and the Supreme Court unanimously overturned. More importantly for the long term, the administration took the responsibility for enforcement of Title VI out of HEW and placed it in the hands of the Justice Department, which was to work solely through the courts, not by means of administrative action that could lead to a cutoff of federal funds. Since that time, despite a court order requiring HEW to begin fund-cutoff proceedings against over a hundred southern districts, little change came from actions by HEW or the new Department of Education. (HEW, starting with the Carter administration in 1976, turned most of its energies toward defining and ending discrimination against students of limited English-speaking ability, women, and the handicapped.) As for the Justice Department, it has continued to develop and bring desegregation suits at the number of three or four a year. Meanwhile, the courts continued to expand the notion of *de jure* segregation and the remedial obligation that a school board incurred because of having segregated purposefully. These developments led to a congressional revolt, directed specifically against busing, but not expressly against the underlying principles that form the ultimate premise of the judiciary's busing orders. The resulting antibusing legislation, as noted above, has been interpreted by the courts in such a way as to avoid placing themselves under a legal obligation to stop doing what they had been doing before. Nevertheless, the Supreme Court in recent decisions has moved to restrict the occasions on which the district courts may issue district-wide desegregation orders, which inevitably entail busing.

The history of federal policy toward racial segregation, when viewed in conjunction with the history of other reform efforts that have drawn inspiration and doctrinal guidance from the original civil rights effort (e.g., the efforts to end discrimination on the basis of gender, deficiency in English, and handicap), can be seen as having a certain pattern. First comes judicial action gingerly sketching out a somewhat inchoate notion of a constitutional right. Second, the political activism that led to the bringing of the suit in the first place continues in the form of efforts to assure implementation of the court's decree, in the form of additional suits seeking similar or even expanded versions of the right announced in the first suit, and in the form of legislative lobbying. Difficulties and uncertainties, conflicts of values, and even conflicts of rights may now become evident as people explore through action and in print the implications of the judicial decrees. Third, legislative action insures affirmation in a statute of the principles announced by the court but at the same time, perhaps, attempts some reconciliation of the conflicts in values and rights that have now surfaced. For example, legislation reforming school finance and federal legislation directed toward ending discrimination on the basis of gender both represent attempts to write into a statute the principles of court decisions, but also to take into account other important values such as the values of local control and privacy, respectively. Fourth, there may then follow a vigorous administrative enforcement effort, as occurred under the Carter administration on behalf of women (especially in higher education settings), the handicapped, and students with deficiencies in English. Fifth, there may then follow a political reaction resulting in a reduction of the federal enforcement effort and a return by reformers to the courts to maintain the reform movement. For a time, the courts may press forward as before, but the political reaction may at least serve to check further expansion of their doctrines, which now have been clearly shown to not only harm vested interests but also to vitiate other important rights of which the courts themselves are protective.

Impact of the Courts. Sorting out the unique contribution of judicial decrees to educational policy decisions and practices of other branches of government, let alone estimating the impact of judicial decrees on the achievement of students or the degree of student unrest or violence in the schools, is no easy matter (Wasby, 1970; Dahl, 1957; Casper, 1976). Yet claims have been made, including (1) statements that the courts are now running the schools; (2) statements that judicial decrees protective of student rights are importantly responsible for disruption and violence in the schools; and (3) assertions that the *Brown* decision itself may be responsible for making overt and undisguised racism a rarely espoused position today. These and other similar claims are virtually impossible to disprove or prove, but some evidence does exist that helps to place the impact of the courts in perspective. First, even in the most extreme circumstances when the judiciary has ordered the implementation of remedial programs to correct for past racially discriminatory policies, these orders are often not the result of judicial fiat, but the product of a complex bargaining process among school officials, interested community groups, and a special master appointed by the court. These remedies are political solutions as much as they are solutions logically deduced from legal principle and imposed by a court (Buckholz, et al., 1978; Berger, 1978). Next, most judicially created rules and required remedies are stated in general language capable of a number of interpretations, thereby leaving state legislatures and school boards with considerable leeway within the meaning of the rule itself. See, for example, *Tinker* v. *Des Moines Independent School District*, 393 U.S. 503 (1969); *Robinson* v. *Cahill*, 62 N.J. 473, 303 A.2d 273 (1973). Hence the basic effect of much litigation may not be to impose a specific policy, but to raise higher on the political agenda of the other branches of government an issue that otherwise would have probably been taken

up at a later date (Lehne, 1978). Furthermore, there is evidence that judicial decrees, e.g., the prohibition against prayers in schools, are regularly ignored in many districts (Way, 1968; Birkby, 1969; Dolbeare & Hammond, 1971). In any event, litigation occasionally produces no change or may produce change that hurts the very people the litigation was intended to help (Horowitz, 1977). Nevertheless, the common wisdom holds that the courts have been an important factor in promoting public acceptance of the values of equality, dignity, and respect—a point that, although difficult to establish with unambiguous empirical evidence, appears to be a plausible hypothesis that should stand until contrary evidence is brought forward to refute it.

Tyll van Geel

See also Equity Issues in Education; Federal Influence on Education; Financing Schools; Governance of Schools; Legislation; State Influences on Education.

REFERENCES

Berger, C. J. Away from the court house and into the field: The odyssey of a special master. *Columbia Law Review*, 1978, *78*, 707–738.

Birkby, R. H. The Supreme Court and the Bible Belt: Tennessee reaction to the *Schempp* decision. *Midwestern Journal of Political Science*, 1969, *10*, 304–319.

Bork, R. H. Neutral principles and some First Amendment problems. *Indiana Law Journal*, 1971, *47*, 1–35.

Buckholz, R. E., Jr.; Copper, D. J.; Gettner, A.; Guggenheimer, J.; Rosenthal, E. S.; & Rotenberg, M. B. Special project: The remedial process in institutional reform litigation. *Columbia Law Review*, 1978, *78*, 784–929.

Casper, J. D. The Supreme Court and national policy making. *American Political Science Review*, 1976, *70*, 50–63.

Chayes, A. The role of the judge in public law litigation. *Harvard Law Review*, 1976, *89*, 1281–1316.

Dahl, R. Decision making in a democracy: The Supreme Court as a national policy maker. *Journal of Public Law*, 1957, *6*, 279–295.

Dolbeare, K. M., & Hammond, P. E. *The School Prayer Decisions*. Chicago: University of Chicago Press, 1971.

Ely, J. H. *Democracy and Distrust*. Cambridge, Mass.: Harvard University Press, 1980.

Fiss, O. M. Foreword: The forms of justice. *Harvard Law Review*, 1979, *93*, 1–58.

Horowitz, D. *The Courts and Social Policy*. Washington, D.C.: Brookings Institution, 1977.

Karst, K. L. Foreword: Equal citizenship under the Fourteenth Amendment. *Harvard Law Review*, 1977, *91*, 1–68.

Kirp, D. L. Law, politics, and equal educational opportunity. *Harvard Educational Review*, 1977, *47*, 117–137.

Lehne, R. *The Quest for Justice*. New York: Longman, 1978.

Perry, M. J. The abortion funding cases: A comment on the Supreme Court's role in American government. *Georgetown Law Journal*, 1978, *66*, 1191–1245.

Perry, M. J. Modern equal protection: A conceptualization and appraisal. *Columbia Law Review*, 1979, *79*, 1023–1084.

Peterson, L. J.; Rossmiller, R. A.; & Volz, M. *The Law and Public School Operation* (2d ed.). New York: Harper & Row, 1978.

Stern, N., Challenging the ideological exclusions of curriculum materials: Rights of students and parents. *Harvard Civil Rights–Civil Liberties Law Review*, 1979, *14*, 485–528.

Tribe, L. *American Constitutional Law*. Mineola, N.Y.: Foundation Press, Inc., 1978.

van Geel, T. Does the Constitution establish a right to an education? *School Review*, 1974, *82*, 293–326.

van Geel, T. *Authority to Control the School Program*. Lexington, Mass.: Heath, 1976.

van Geel, T. Racial discrimination from Little Rock to Harvard. *Cincinnati Law Review*, 1980, *49*, 49–98.

Wasby, S. L. *The Impact of the United States Supreme Court*. Dorsey Press, 1970.

Way, H. F., Jr., Survey research on judicial decisions: The prayer and Bible reading cases. *Western Political Quarterly*, 1968, *21*, 189–205.

Wilkinson, J. H., III. *From Brown to Bakke: The Supreme Court and School Integration, 1954–1978*. Oxford, England: Oxford University Press, 1979.

Yudof, M. G., When governments speak: Toward a theory of government expression and the First Amendment. *Texas Law Review*, 1979, *57*, 863–918.

Yudof, M.; Kirp, D. L.; van Geel, T.; & Levin B. *Educational Policy and the Law*. Berkeley, Calif.: McCutchan, 1981.

JUNIOR AND COMMUNITY COLLEGE EDUCATION

American higher education is noteworthy in the educational history of the world because of the continued expansion of opportunity and availability of education through the postsecondary levels. In many ways this expansion is best characterized by the creation and development of the American community college. This expansion is indicative of a philosophical commitment to postsecondary education, which has grown continuously throughout the nation's history. It began with institutions that provided opportunity for a limited few (elitism, education of socioeconomic and political elites); it continued to expand through institutions in which opportunity for an increased number of people became the objective (meritocracy, education for those who have demonstrated that they can personally benefit from continued educational opportunity); and it achieved a high level in institutions committed to a philosophy of higher education for all (mass higher education, educational opportunity made available in some form at the postsecondary level to everyone). In the 1970s, new emphasis was placed upon a commitment to lifelong education for each person. Although other countries have developed similar commitments to continued education for their citizens, many of the world's educational systems have taken the American community college as a model.

The terms "junior college" and "community college" are not used in this article with any particular philosophical connotation. Although some writers describe junior colleges as institutions with more limited programs and more restrictive commitments than community colleges, there are many junior colleges that do not fit this description. "Community college" is a more recent descriptive term; community colleges are generally more vitally involved in the community than was true of the older junior colleges; and the "junior college" designation tends to emphasize associate degree work. Nevertheless, the two terms will be used on an interchangeable basis in this article, with no attempt to attach special meanings to either term. This discussion will focus on locally oriented postsecondary institutions that provide two-year degrees (Associate in Arts or Associate in Science) for those who wish to transfer to a baccalaureate program, that offer a variety of occupational programs of varying length, and that make a diversity of opportunities for lifelong education accessible to all in the communities they serve.

The junior college and community college are largely creations of the twentieth century. The first public institution so recognized was Joliet Junior College, established in 1901 in Illinois. Growth was slow but steady during the 1910s and 1920s. The Depression years, with low income and high unemployment levels, gave impetus to education as an alternative to inactivity and as preparation for jobs requiring specialized training. During this period, junior colleges grew in both number and size.

Many colleges temporarily ceased to operate during World War II, but these years were not important in terms of overall development. After 1945, the growth was rapid and almost universal. During the 1950s, several states created statewide plans for community college expansion and began implementing those plans. By the early 1970s, authorities in most states had established community or junior colleges in all regions of their respective states. This development has continued, with strong emphasis upon the creation of multilocation institutions, with both permanent and temporary centers, particularly in urban areas.

At an early stage, before 1940, there were a number of independent or privately supported junior colleges, particularly in New England, New York, and the South. These were small, often church-related, and usually limited-purpose colleges. However, as the number of new public institutions rapidly increased, making the community college the dominant type, the privately supported junior colleges became less important and less representative of two-year institutions. By 1980, fewer than 200 community and junior colleges (approximately 15 percent of the total) were classified as independent. They accounted for less than 4 percent of the total enrollment in two-year colleges. The public community college, even though still sometimes called junior college, has become the typical and dominant example of this extension of public education into the postsecondary level.

Another type of institution that was developed in the 1940s but saw its greatest growth after 1960 is the technical institution or technical college. This institution is similar to the community college in that it is public in governance and support, postsecondary in level of curriculum emphasis, community-oriented in program focus, and designed to serve a defined clientele in completing a program short of the baccalaureate degree. Usually technical colleges or institutions offer few if any liberal arts or general education courses or degrees. Most of them are public; few are independent (although some are proprietary). Accounting for less than 10 percent of all two-year postsecondary institutions, these technical colleges enroll a very small percentage of total enrollment at this level.

Two-year branch campuses of universities are also found in a few states. These offer educational programs similar to those of community colleges, but are usually neither community-oriented nor locally controlled. The central campus of the university carries full responsibility for their operation and program control. Faculty are selected by the university departments and operational policy is made at the central university campus.

Community colleges have been philosophically committed to universal access, open-door admission, no or low tuition, local (community) orientation, program diversity, and lifelong educational opportunity. Quality is assumed to be measured by the degree of improvement a person achieves as well as his or her attainment of competence in defined areas. Quality is not accomplished through stringent admission requirements that eliminate certain portions of the population. Since service to the local community is a major focus for these institutions, they are committed to providing educational opportunities to people who may not be accepted in other institutions. Emphasis is placed upon people having an opportunity to meet their own needs and to achieve their own improvement.

The community college curriculum is often classified into seven specific categories: (1) courses, most often organized into a two-year format, that prepare people for specific employment in a defined job or job cluster; (2) courses, most often organized into an Associate in Arts format, that prepare people for transfer to the junior level of a baccalaureate degree program at a four-year college or university; (3) courses, usually organized into a defined associate degree program format, that are best described as a general education program and that may also be used as a basis for transferring to a four-year college or university; (4) single courses or small clusters of courses that are used to upgrade individual skills, create new areas of competence, or otherwise provide improvement of a personal and individual nature; (5) courses, increasingly required but often self-prescribed, that provide remedial, corrective, and improvement education for those who have not previously mastered the basic skills in literacy, mathematics, or other subjects; (6) courses, workshops, or conferences, usually noncredit, that provide a variety of lifelong educational opportunities to local citizens; and (7) courses or programs that are designed to meet the specific needs of people with special problems or learning impairments.

Not all community colleges offer a complete program in the seven areas listed above. Some institutions may se-lect one or more for concentration and thus limit their offerings. In multilocation institutions, concentrations in one or more areas may be limited to a specific location and are therefore not available at all locations.

Research into the history and philosophy of the community junior college movement originated with McDowell (1919) and Koos (1925). More recently, Henry (1956), Medsker (1960), Fields (1962), Blocker (1965), Thornton (1972), Monroe (1972), and Gleazer (1980) have described in perspective the history, mission, philosophical commitments, and development of these institutions. Koos originally described these colleges as democratizing influences having a socializing effect upon the general populace. He also predicted their impact upon the reorganization of the structure of higher education. Subsequently, authors have for the most part substantiated this analysis and documented it in more detail. Gleazer sees the community college as an influential agent for community as well as individual improvement.

Community college students are demographically different from typical college students. Recent figures indicate an older student; 29 years is the median age, although the age range may extend from 14 to 90 years in a single institution. There are more women than men (52 percent as compared with 48 percent), and the imbalance is increasing. There are more part-time than full-time enrollees and more noncredit than credit students. Community college students work in full-time and part-time jobs, are members of households in their communities, and participate broadly in all phases of the life of their communities. Being a student is not necessarily the major concern in their lives. Their motivations for attending college are varied and unpredictable.

Research studies have repeatedly confirmed these characteristics and have demonstrated how the student body has changed over the years. Earlier studies by Clark (1960), Medsker (1960), Wattenbarger (1963), Knoell and Medsker (1964), Tillery (1964), Cross (1968), and Koos (1970) demonstrated the differences between the typical college student who attends a four-year college or university and the community college student. Subsequent studies have shown how these differences were even greater in the 1970s and are projected into the 1980s (Knoell, 1976; Knoell & McIntyre, 1974). Reports of the American Association of Community and Junior Colleges (AACJC) pointed out that between 1970 and 1977 the proportion of learners between 14 and 19 years of age fell from 36 percent to 32 percent. However, almost half the nation's undergraduates aged 25 to 32 were enrolled in two-year colleges in 1977. Forty-five percent of the community college enrollment was over 22 years old, and over 20 percent of those enrolling for the first time came from families with incomes of less than $12,500 for 1977. Also, almost 39 percent of the nation's minority students was enrolled in two-year colleges. These colleges also enrolled a larger percentage of physically handicapped students than did other segments of higher education (Astin, 1978).

Factors Influencing Change. The philosophical commitments as well as the generally accepted values of community college leadership have resulted in the student body described above. These same values and commitments are also the origin of the problems that affect the continued development of the community colleges. Rapid expansion during the 1950s and 1960s resulted in a growth pattern of increasing service and responsibility. The number of students served in community colleges increased from 196,710 in 1938/39 to 4,487,872 in fall 1979. The number of institutions changed from 258 public colleges and 317 private colleges in 1938/39 to 1,044 public colleges and 186 private colleges in 1979 (Gilbert, 1980). This public-sector growth, however, has been much slower since 1975. Several factors, most of them common to all postsecondary education, have influenced the change.

First, the number of high school graduates in this country has been decreasing each year since the early 1970s. This is largely a result of a decreasing birthrate. Since fewer students are graduating from high school each year, fewer are enrolling in college during the subsequent year. The pool from which these students come is shrinking, and competition for those coming from that pool is increasing. Four-year colleges and universities are affected by the size of the pool and have placed increased emphasis upon marketing techniques and recruitment procedures. Students who are identified in high school as merit scholars are subjected to strong recruitment pressures by baccalaureate-degree–awarding institutions. The increasing emphasis on recruitment or marketing has caused community colleges to study their situations with care, to collect and analyze the available data, to evaluate their programs and their staff, to seek adequate financial support, to plan with more knowledge of and concern for the total market, and to develop programs, courses, and activities to meet locally defined needs.

Second, the need for education beyond high school has been questioned in the literature and in the general press. However, employers expect the people they hire to come with defined skills and competencies that are often not taught in high school. The increased emphasis upon occupational education has placed the community colleges in competition with area vocational-technical schools, technical colleges, adult education programs in public school districts, and certain proprietary schools. This rivalry has limited the full development of occupational programs in the community colleges to a greater or lesser extent.

Third, the dual influences of inflation and low financial support have severely inhibited community college budgets and financial planning. Since many colleges in a number of states began operation as locally supported colleges with low or no tuition, the shift to increased state support and higher student fees has been accepted with some reluctance and no little fear. However, heavy demands on local property taxes for supporting grades K–12, for providing local police and fire protection, and for funding other local public services have made *ad valorem* real estate taxation a less desirable source of support income than was the case in the past. According to the theories of public finance pointed out by Wattenbarger (1966), the benefits of community college education spread beyond the locality served by a particular college. These benefits are based upon studies in the field of economics that (1) describe more specifically the economic benefits of education; (2) illustrate the interdependent market economy and the geographically mobile population that may be associated with the global nature of the results of education; (3) stress that education has a function in promoting social mobility and in providing for equity in economic opportunity; (4) assert that the social benefits of education are not associated with family ability to pay and social position; (5) prove that there is an indivisible character in the benefits of education and that even nonstudents will receive sizable benefits from educational expenditures; (6) propose that education can be used consciously as a governmental policy to break the cycle of poverty as well as to overcome the lack of motivation among certain low-income groups; (7) recommend that taxation of people be based upon broad general principles rather than the exact determination of benefits received from educational services; and (8) conclude that the optimum in expenditures for education should be a political decision rather than a decision made upon measured market value. The result of these and other factors, often limited to a particular state, is that financial support has shifted more and more to the state level, with some increase in student tuition fees. This shift, however, has caused several problems that affect the program development of the institutions. The typical pattern of state support for higher education is formula-driven, based upon "full-time equivalents" (FTE), most often limited to credit enrollment, occasionally limited to daytime students, and provided on a single-cost basis. Several of the factors in the FTE formula do not take into account the philosophical commitments of the community college as distinct from the commitments of the four-year institution. The more expensive occupational programs are not often considered in FTE formulas; services needed by part-time students are inadequately provided; the round-the-clock schedule of course offerings in a community college are not typical of a dormitory college; non-credit programs, although a minor activity in a typical college, constitute a major part of the program in a community college. State support solves a number of problems, but creates others.

State Support. Three factors (decreasing numbers of young people, disenchantment with higher education, and lower effective financial support) have convinced many political as well as educational leaders that statewide planning for all of higher education is a necessity. The trend toward state support has also caused a serious consideration of state control and state operation. State-level planning has become a generally accepted state responsibility since the 1950s.

Several states led the way in the development of statewide plans for community colleges (Florida, 1957; Virginia, 1967; Mississippi, 1969; West Virginia, 1971; Maryland, 1973). Other states developed statewide plans for all of higher education (New York, 1960; Illinois, 1964; Maine, 1968; New Jersey, 1970; Oklahoma, 1970). A few states also developed similar plans for technical education at the postsecondary level (Florida, 1964; Indiana, 1966; Washington, 1970). Not all of these plans were implemented, but large enough groups of studies were used as blueprints for growth and development to illustrate their value. The federal government's support of planning has been demonstrated through planning agencies ("1202 Commissions") found in all but one state.

The authorities who developed statewide plans were concerned with mission statements and role clarification for various types of institutions, articulation between levels of education, assignment of responsibility, resource allocation, and provisions for growth and expansion of institutions, programs, and opportunities.

The statewide plans also provide a basis within a state for discussing various institutional missions and for clarifying the roles of each level of postsecondary education. The tendency to convert community colleges into four-year institutions was stopped by these statewide plans in some states. In a number of instances, the location and establishment of new institutions were based on a rational framework provided by the statewide plans; the procedures for curriculum and program development were clarified; and the processes for quality controls were established.

Problems of Articulation. As community colleges became a major entry point for students into baccalaureate degree programs, the concern for articulation between community colleges and universities or four-year colleges became more pressing. During the 1960s, a number of conferences were held; in the 1970s, the American Council on Education as well as the Southern Regional Education Board provided continued attention. Several states developed policy statements and full-faith and credit agreements that attempted to establish procedures and to promote basic agreements, although other states continued to leave the problem up to individual institutions. A core program was adopted by Georgia and Texas to facilitate smooth transfer from one level to another. After being in use for more than ten years as a state board of education regulation (1969), the Florida articulation policies were enacted into law by the state legislature in 1979. New Jersey developed a full-faith and credit policy in 1973. Other states have also made specific progress.

Continued interest and concern for articulation between community colleges and universities caused the American Council on Education, the Southern Regional Education Board, and similar organizations to sponsor conferences and to foster discussions. In spite of these efforts, however, the problems appear to persist. The conclusions of a series of doctoral dissertations pointed out persistent

problems. Wattenbarger (1976) summarized some of these studies:

1. There is a need to establish sound and well-conceived articulation policies to guide the various institutions in developing their own procedures.
2. The continuous attention of responsible leaders to active communication between institutions is of primary importance.
3. The development of an articulation counseling office in each university is necessary; a similar liaison responsibility exists for each community college and warrants the appointment of responsible parties to that office.
4. Improved academic counseling at both the community colleges and the universities is needed.
5. Improved on-campus communication with transfer students is needed as soon as they arrive.
6. University recruitment appears to be generally ineffective in influencing student decisions about attending an institution. These energies and resources could be used more effectively in acquainting the public with the programs and available curriculum as the major recruitment thrust.
7. Privately supported colleges need to inform the community colleges more completely and accurately concerning their junior-level admission policies and procedures. Demonstration of a positive posture is very much needed.
8. Constant and continued attention to these problems and their solutions is required. There are no permanent solutions.

On the other hand, little attention has been given to problems of articulation between high schools and community colleges. The need for career counseling and realistic approaches to continued education seems obvious but is seldom met. A few studies relating to vocational and technical education have been conducted (Bender, 1973). Articulation will continue to be a major concern at all levels.

Financing. The financing of community colleges has been pointed out as a major problem in the continuing development of these institutions. Each of the fifty states has developed unique financial procedures. Those may, however, be classified into four general types: (1) states in which institutions negotiate with the legislature for appropriations (negotiated budget funding); (2) states using an FTE formula based on a set amount per unit (unit-rate formula funding); (3) states attempting to equalize by providing a combination of state and local funding (minimum foundation funding); and (4) states basing allocations at least in part upon the cost differentials of various programs (cost-based program funding). In an analysis of these various procedures, the last type, although currently used by only fourteen or fifteen states, is considered to be the best for carrying out the community college program commitments (Martorana & Wattenbarger, 1978). The major development in recent years has been an increasing dependence upon state sources, with a concurrent decrease in income from local tax sources.

Studies by Breneman of the Brookings Institution and Hyde of the Educational Commission of the States will seek to identify the future trends that may develop relative to financing these institutions. Studies by Wattenbarger, Cage, and Arney (1970) at the Institution of Higher Education, University of Florida, analyze state support patterns. These research activities point toward five major problem areas relative to finance: (1) maintaining the traditional community college tuition-free or low-tuition policy; (2) balancing state support with decreases in local support; (3) relating resource apportionment formulas to community college philosophical commitments; (4) providing for the objectives of equity, efficiency, and variable program costs, as well as student access in the improved financial support programs; and (5) supporting programs for part-time learners, older learners, learners who have educational disabilities, and learners who take noncredit courses.

The commitment to access was implemented to some extent by a low-tuition or tuition-free policy. Although California has been the only state to maintain a tuition-free policy, most community colleges have kept fees as low as possible. A recent trend, however, appears to be in the direction of increasing these fees. Several states attempt to place a limit on the portion of the total cost paid by students. This may be placed at 25 percent of total cost as computed or 33 percent of the total student expenditure (various states have varied requirements). As a result of increased costs, however, this limit has been continuously raised during recent years.

In simple terms, those authorities that fund community colleges have not provided the means for these colleges to implement their philosophical goal, the creation of full-service institutions with unlimited capacity. Instead, they have sought ways to limit that goal. Limitations placed upon increased enrollment, upon numbers of FTEs to be served, upon types of programs to be supported, upon available financial aid for students, and upon funds available for new facilities have been typical. These limitations prevent the college from being accessible to all who wish to attend. The extent to which these limitations inhibit enrollment will vary from place to place and from time to time. State-level monitoring has been used to maintain the legislative expression of policy and has, thereby, increased state controls at the expense of local decision making.

Faculty. Community college faculty have been generally supportive of the philosophical mission of the college. Studies by Montgomery (1962), Mills (1968), and Benoit (1978) indicated that the overwhelming majority of community college faculty in Florida were supportive of the philosophy commonly expressed. Similar studies of faculty in other states come to the same conclusions. Studies in the 1950s and 1960s indicated that a large proportion of the faculty came from secondary schools and senior colleges to teach in the community colleges. However, a number of university programs as well as in-service education programs have now prepared a cadre of people specially prepared for teaching at this level. O'Banion (1972), in describing the staff needs of community colleges, stresses the need for affective as well as cognitive education in preservice preparation of community college faculty.

Studies by Cohen (1973), Gaff (1975), Richardson (1975), and Smith (1976, 1980) emphasize that in-service and staff development programs have assumed a large role in faculty improvement and preparation for working with the type of students usually found in community colleges. Much of the faculty support for the mission of these colleges may be attributed to faculty development programs.

Competencies required of community college faculty are uniquely different from those required of high school or traditional college faculty. Seven types of community college faculty are needed (Wattenbarger, 1971):

1. Faculty who teach courses directly related to an occupation. These are usually persons who have some experience in that occupation as well as knowledge of how to teach the requisite competencies.
2. Faculty who are prepared to teach general education courses and who can organize such courses into a viable and relevant experience. People who do this well are in short supply, and progress in this area has been limited and often entirely centered upon the liberal arts rather than general education.
3. Faculty who are expected to teach courses comparable to those taken during the freshman and sophomore years of a four-year degree. These persons need preparation and competence similar to those expected of university faculty without the latter's emphasis upon research.
4. Faculty who are specially competent in learning resources and course organization. These are persons who prepare teaching materials, who are familiar with multimedia techniques, and who serve as complementary teachers to the classroom faculty.
5. Faculty who serve in leadership roles in helping faculty to evaluate their work, to develop innovative approaches, and to achieve personal improvement. Because of the diverse student body, the multiple objectives of the community colleges, and the variety of community needs, the community colleges need this type of person to a far greater extent than other institutions with more limited roles and more specific focuses.
6. Faculty who are specially prepared to work with older students. Since the learning styles and educational needs of the majority of community college students do not fit the patterns of the youthful college student, there is need for a part of the faculty to have the special competency needed to work with lifelong learners.
7. Faculty who are prepared for counseling and the variety of other student development services that are essential in dealing with the persons who attend community colleges.

The rapid growth in the number and scope of community colleges during the 1950s and 1960s brought many persons into community college employment who were not prepared in most of these areas. However, the more stable growth of the 1970s and the more generally available preservice preparation, as well as the greater emphasis upon in-service improvement, have resulted in faculty who are recognized as special community college faculty. Staff development programs emphasize their special competencies.

Community college faculty have also been concerned about their personal as well as professional status. The *Chronicle of Higher Education* reported that, as of 23 September 1981, 470 two-year campuses had selected a collective bargaining agent to represent their faculties. Collective bargaining has become an important consideration on many campuses. Poole (1975) analyzed the influence of collective bargaining upon written policies of governance and concluded that the greatest concern in negotiation of contracts centered around grievance procedures, followed by participation in the process of selecting administrators. Concern for salaries, although important, did not appear to be the most important area of conflict. Ross and Flakus-Mosqueda (1980) reported that twelve states had passed special laws covering collective bargaining for community colleges, although these institutions were often already covered by laws affecting elementary and secondary schools or colleges and universities, depending upon the state structure. Thirty-one states have some kind of law providing coverage for collective bargaining in elementary and secondary schools; only a few more (eight) do not also include colleges and universities as a part of the same provisions or similar ones. The community colleges tend to follow the direction of the elementary and secondary school systems in most states.

A major concern of community college authorities has always been student development services. Early discussions by Koos (1925) emphasized the guidance and counseling responsibilities assumed by community colleges. The McConnell (1965) report to the Carnegie Corporation described national trends and evaluated the status of student services at that time. Student personnel services were judged to be inadequate. O'Banion and Thurston (1972) reevaluated the situation and projected future directions. Matson (1972) provided a status survey of progress countrywide and concluded that student personnel functions were well established and were, in general, minimally supported. She further stressed that a movement toward a closer working relationship with the instructional program had not developed great momentum in very many community colleges. Collins (1967) outlined the services that are needed in a community college: precollege information, registration and records, appraisal, counseling, orientation, remediation, co-curricular activities, health services, financial assistance, placement services, housing, food services, research and evaluation, and community services. These items were still the basis for evaluating

student development services in 1980. The special needs of particular types of students were summarized by Cross (1971), Purdy and Bloom (1974), and Cacciola (1979). These studies conclude that the need to provide programs for students who have not been continuing their education in the past is paramount. These students include minority students, women, older adults, disabled students, culturally deprived students, and those from low-income families. The unique needs of these groups require student development services that have not ordinarily been available in community colleges. Greater attention to career counseling for all students, as well as to placement services, becomes increasingly important. Computer-assisted counseling is a technique now used in many institutions. Financial aid, encouraged in part by the increased availability of funds from federal sources, has placed a high priority on this service in many community colleges. Remediation services, emphasizing student development, have become a major concern in almost all community colleges and are often independent of other student services.

Roueche and Snow (1979) described a model for developmental education with emphasis upon the teacher as the key element. In this model, vital supportive services included counselors, peer helpers, and a well-equipped learning center. Active organizational support included specific efforts toward recruitment; simplified registration; organized orientation activities; competent staff services enhanced through a well-supported staff development program; clear objectives outlined and understood by students; integrative experiences organized for cognitive, affective, and psychomotor skills, with systematic evaluation procedures; and active communication procedures including the total faculty. Roueche and Mink (1980) called for a reeducation of the faculty in order to improve the literacy of the students.

Gollattscheck and co-workers (1976) projected a community college with influence in community development. Gleazer (1980) discussed a community college with emphasis upon lifelong educational opportunity. He described six qualities that characterize superior community colleges:

1. *Adaptability:* the capability of responding to new conditions, new demands, new circumstances. The ease and speed with which change occurs is a clear differentiation from the typical college or university's reluctance to change.
2. *Awareness:* continuing sensitivity to community needs and community directions. The formal and informal methods used to achieve this knowledge are primary objectives.
3. *Continuation of relationships:* emphasis upon the continuing existence of the institution. Each individual in the community should be encouraged to look to the college throughout his or her learning lifetime.
4. *Extension of opportunity:* emphasis upon the college's responsibility to seek learners who may not otherwise

be in touch with it. Marketing techniques used by the college include identification and active recruitment of unserved students in the community, as well as provision of particular services.

5. *Accommodation of diversity:* emphasis upon the open-door philosophy, which means willingness and commitment to provide educational opportunity to everyone, including many who have not been considered "college material" in the past. The diverse educational needs of the postsecondary community, throughout a lifetime but short of the baccalaureate, are the focus of the community college.

6. *Provision of a nexus:* exercise by the college of a connective function, since it cannot itself provide all services to every student all the time. Ability to identify outside sources of help for learners and to aid them in getting in touch with that help is a part of the college's lifelong educational commitment.

Future Prospects. As the community colleges move into the last twenty years of the twentieth century, there still exists a gap between stated philosophical commitments and level of achievement. A major difficulty arises because of financial support patterns. Most if not all community colleges are not provided funds that will enable them to carry out the total services envisioned above. Financial support is based upon a traditional FTE student enrolled in college-credit courses. There is usually little or no direct support for many desirable services. Indirect support may come from a number of sources, including fees, grants, budget transfers, temporary special funding, and community gifts. None of these provides a sound basis for continuing planned program support.

The future seems to include (1) continued growth of part-time enrollments, since the community college clientele need to work as they learn; (2) continued increase in the number of older adult learners who will use the community college for retraining, personal improvement, and recreation; (3) continued emphasis upon educational development centers that diagnose and prescribe educational improvement activities on an individual basis; (4) continued growth in occupational programs designed to prepare learners for specific occupations, especially those with local job opportunities; (5) continued improvement of general education programs designed to prepare effective and knowledgeable citizens to take an active role in local, state, and national community life; (6) continued development of community-centered educational and cultural activities, not necessarily connected to either credit or noncredit courses; (7) continued pressures to increase tuition fees and other user fees, and, simultaneously, continued emphasis upon financial aid for learners; (8) increased attention to placement services, especially for those who have completed programs, but also for those currently enrolled; (9) increased centralization at regional (within states) and state levels, especially in relationship to program development and student services; (10) increased emphasis upon individualized courses in which

students progress at their own pace; (11) increased emphasis upon competency-based education in which desired student competencies are clearly defined by faculty; (12) increased use of computer services in record keeping, analyzing information, counseling learners, and managing institutions; (13) increased concern over need for faculty improvement through evaluation and development plans; (14) a need for increased concern regarding relevant general education programs; (15) continued emphasis upon sound marketing techniques, with special attention to market segments; and (16) focus upon service in international education as it relates to local community life.

If those who are responsible for community college development and operation are not alert, sensitive, competent, and informed, the colleges will suffer from (1) a loss of students who aim for a baccalaureate degree (many of them will attend four-year institutions as a result of active recruitment on the part of these institutions); (2) inadequate financial support for noncredit courses, with an increased emphasis upon user fees that will deteriorate these programs; (3) faculty complacency, which will result in poor teaching and negative results (students will not participate); (4) insufficient information, which will result in poor management practices and the diversion of funds to meet crises; and (5) increasing state control, which will be detrimental to the quality of programs and procedures.

James L. Wattenbarger

See also Adult Education; Financing Colleges and Universities; Higher Education; History and Philosophy of Higher Education; Organization and Administration of Higher Education; State Influences on Education; Undergraduate Instruction; Vocational Education.

REFERENCES

Astin, A. W. *The American Freshman: National Norms for Fall, 1977.* Los Angeles: University of California, 1978. (ERIC Document Reproduction Service No. ED 136 660)

Bender, L. W. *Articulation of Secondary and Post-secondary Occupational Education Programs* (Information Series No. 76, VT020727). Columbus: Ohio State University, 1973. (ERIC Document Reproduction Service No. ED 090 392)

Benoit, R. J. *Characteristics and Attitudes of Florida Community College Faculty.* Unpublished doctoral dissertation, University of Florida, 1978.

Blocker, C. E.; Plummer, R. H.; & Richardson, R. C., Jr. *The Two-year College: A Social Synthesis.* Englewood Cliffs, N.J.: Prentice-Hall, 1965.

Cacciola, R. M. Sources and information: Special programs for special populations. *Serving New Populations.* P. Walsh (Ed.). *New Directions for Community Colleges.* Monograph No. 27 (1979): 91–100. (ERIC Document Reproduction Service No. ED 175 520)

Clark, B. R. *The Open Door College.* New York: McGraw-Hill, 1960.

Cohen, A. M. (Ed.). *Toward a Professional Faculty.* San Francisco: Jossey-Bass, 1973.

Collins, C. C. *Junior College Student Personnel Programs: What They Are and What They Should Be.* Washington D.C.: American Association of Junior Colleges, 1967.

Cross, K. P. *The Junior College Students: A Research Description.* Princeton N.J.: Educational Testing Service, 1968.

Cross, K. P. *Beyond the Open Door.* San Francisco: Jossey-Bass, 1971.

Fields, R. R. *The Community College Movement.* New York: McGraw-Hill, 1962.

Gaff, J. G. *Toward Faculty Renewal.* San Francisco: Jossey-Bass, 1975.

Gilbert, F. (Ed.). *1980 Community, Junior, and Technical College Director.* Washington, D.C.: American Association of Community and Junior Colleges, 1980.

Gleazer, E., Jr. *The Community College: Values, Vision, and Vitality.* Washington, D.C.: American Association of Community and Junior Colleges, 1980. (ERIC Document Reproduction Service No. ED 129 386)

Gollattscheck, J. F.; Harlacher, E. L.; Roberts, E.; & Wygal, B. R. *College Leadership for Community Renewal.* San Francisco: Jossey-Bass, 1976.

Henry, N. B. (Ed.). *The Public Junior College: The Fifty-fifth Yearbook of the National Society for the Study of Education* (Part 1). Chicago: University of Chicago Press, 1956.

Knoell, D. *Through the Open Door* (Commission Report No. 76-1). Sacramento, Calif.: Postsecondary Education Commission, 1976.

Knoell, D., & McIntyre, C. *Planning Colleges for the Community.* San Francisco: Jossey-Bass, 1974.

Knoell, D., & Medsker, L. *Factors Affecting Performance of Transfer Students from Two- and Four-year Colleges: With Implications for Coordination and Articulation.* (Cooperative Research Project No. 1133). Berkeley, Calif.: Center for Study of Higher Education, 1964. (ERIC Document Reproduction Service No. ED 003 047)

Koos, L. V. *The Junior College Movement.* Boston: Ginn & Co., 1925.

Koos, L. V. *The Community College Student.* Gainesville: University of Florida Press, 1970.

Martorana, S. V., & Wattenbarger, J. L. *Principles, Practices, and Alternatives in State Methods of Financing Community Colleges and an Approach to Their Evaluation, with Pennsylvania a Case State Center for Study of Higher Education* (Report No. 32). University Park: Pennsylvania State University, 1978.

Matson, J. Perspectives on student personnel services. *Junior College Journal,* March 1972, *42,* 48–52.

McConnell, T. R. *Junior College Personnel Programs—Appraisal and Development: A Report to the Carnegie Corporation.* 1965. (ERIC Document Reproduction Service No. ED 013 065)

McDowell, F. M. *The Junior College.* (U.S. Bureau of Education Bulletin, 1919, *35*). Washington, D.C.: U.S. Government Printing Office.

Medsker, L. L. *The Junior College: Progress and Prospect.* New York: McGraw-Hill, 1960.

Mills, E. *Analysis of Degree of Faculty Satisfactions in Florida Community Junior Colleges.* Unpublished doctoral dissertation, University of Florida, 1968.

Monroe, C. R. *Profile of the Community College.* San Francisco: Jossey-Bass, 1972.

Montgomery, D. M. *An Analysis of Faculty Acceptance of and Commitment to the State Mission of the Florida Community Junior College.* Unpublished doctoral dissertation, Florida State University, 1962.

O'Banion, T. *Teachers for Tomorrow.* Tucson: University of Arizona Press, 1972.

O'Banion, T., & Thurston, A. (Eds.). *Student Development Programs in the Community Junior College.* Englewood Cliffs, N.J.: Prentice-Hall, 1972.

Poole, L. H. *The Confluence of Collective Bargaining upon Written Policies of Governance in Selected Community/Junior Colleges.* Unpublished doctoral dissertation, University of Florida, 1975.

Purdy, L., & Bloom, J. Humanizing student services: Sources and information. *Humanizing Student Services.* C. E. Blocker (Ed). *New Directions for Community Colleges,* Winter 1974, *8,* 101–110.

Richardson, R. C. Staff development: A conceptual framework. *Journal of Higher Education,* May-June 1975, *46,* 303–312.

Ross, D., & Flakus-Mosqueda, P. *Case Book 11: State Education Collective Bargaining Laws* (Report No. F80-5). Denver: Education Commission of the States, 1980.

Roueche, J. E., & Mink, O. G. *Holistic Literacy in College Teaching.* New York: Media Systems Corporation, 1980.

Roueche, J. E., & Snow, J. J. *Overcoming Learning Problems.* San Francisco: Jossey-Bass, 1979.

Smith, A. B. *Faculty Development and Evaluation in Higher Education* (ERIC/HE Research Report No. 8). Washington, D.C.: American Association of Higher Education, 1976. (ERIC Document Reproduction Service No. ED 132 891)

Smith, A. B. *National Research Project on the Status of Staff, Program, and Organizational Development in Community Colleges.* Lexington, Ky.: American Association of Community and Junior Colleges National Council for Staff, Program, and Organizational Development, 1980.

Thornton, J. *The Community Junior College.* New York: Wiley, 1972.

Tillery, H. D. *Differential Characteristics of Entering Freshmen at the University of California and Their Peers at California Junior Colleges.* Unpublished doctoral dissertation, University of California at Berkeley, 1964.

Wattenbarger, J. L. *Five Years of Progress.* Tallahassee: Florida State Department of Education, 1963.

Wattenbarger, J. L. Implications of new developments in economics and public finance for community college administrators. In *Conference Proceedings on Administering the Community College in a Changing World.* (Buffalo Studies, Vol. 11, No. 1, June 1966). Buffalo: State University of New York.

Wattenbarger, J. L. Staffing the community colleges: Who, where, why, and how? *Junior College Staffing 1975–1980.* Normal: Illinois State University, 1971.

Wattenbarger, J. L. College transfer students: New focus, old problems. *College Board Review.* Summer 1976, *100.*

Wattenbarger, J. L.; Cage, B. N.; & Arney, L. H. *The Community Junior College: Target Population, Program Costs, and Cost Differentials.* Gainsville, Fla.: National Educational Finance Project, 1970. (ERIC Document Reproduction Service No. ED 045 068)

JUNIOR HIGH AND MIDDLE SCHOOL EDUCATION

The nature and purpose of junior high and middle school education continues to need clarification. The confusion concerns a school unit that is separate from both elementary school and high school, but in need of relationship to them. This long-term problem besetting junior high and middle school education is now almost a century old. The United States was the first of the modern, Western nations to recognize a need to establish a separate, specialized school program interposed between elementary school and high school. The establishment of the junior high school movement closely followed upon a major reorganization of American public elementary and secondary education.

Until the final decade of the nineteenth century, American public schools embodied a structure of eight years of elementary school and four years of high school. In 1888, Charles Eliot, then president of Harvard University, initiated a national movement seeking to lower the age of entering college freshmen. This necessitated reorganizing and shortening the scope of the public school years. The National Education Association (1894) endorsed Eliot's recommendation, resulting in the rapid shift to a symmetrical balance of six years each in elementary and secondary schools. The new organization was designed to allow talented, college-bound students to complete secondary school in as few as four years. The emergence, shortly after, of the junior high school movement saw the six years of secondary education divide into combinations of grades 7–8 and 9–12, and of grades 7–9 and of 10–12.

Lounsbury (1954) and Toepfer (1962a, 1962b) suggest that the uncertainty surrounding the origin of the junior high school stemmed from its emergence almost immediately as a subdivision of the newly constituted six-year high school. Eichhorn (1980) and Toepfer (1962 a & b) report that school systems in Richmond, Indiana; Lawrence, Kansas; and New York City had established separate middle-grades school units as early as 1887. The rationale for such innovations was based upon locally identified concerns that learners require separate program emphasis in grade 7, grade 8, or grades 7–9. Prior to the junior high school movement initiated by the reorganization of secondary schools in Berkeley, California, and Columbus, Ohio, in 1909, these early efforts sought to make local school programs more responsive to the educational needs of the junior high school age-group.

Early historians of the junior high school movement (Bennett, 1919; Briggs, 1920; Koos, 1927) assumed that the primary purpose of the early junior high movement was to respond to the educational needs of young adolescents. This is only partially true. Examination of local reports in those pioneer settings (Bunker, 1909; Stoddard, 1909) as well as school board minutes (*Berkeley, California, Board of Education Minutes,* 1909; *Columbus, Ohio, Board of Education Minutes,* 1909) reveal such primary causes as overcrowding and shortage of classroom space in the middle grades but not in the high schools. At that time, the majority of students left school to work after completing grade 9. School board minutes reveal a strong need to provide more specialized classrooms for the middle-grades age-group. Although some pedagogical rationale was part of these and other early moves toward a

junior high school unit, a true educational and curricular rationale (Gruhn & Douglass, 1947; Noar, 1953; VanTil, Vars, & Lounsbury, 1961) concerning the junior high school did not develop until the 1920s. Thus the instructional rationale for the initial junior high movement was at least as much logistical as pedagogical.

The Junior High School Movement. The term "junior high school" was first used in Columbus, Ohio, in 1909, to describe the program at Indianola Junior High School. Aside from its crowded conditions, local reporting ("Indianola Junior High," 1909) saw the school as providing a "fairly liberal" and special educational program for pupils unable to continue beyond grade 9 (it also provided a certificate to the junior high school graduate). While Berkeley called its intermediate program an "introductory high school" (Bunker, 1909), the programs in both districts aimed to provide a miniature high school education. Although early writers (Bunker, 1909; Fullerton, 1910) alluded to special needs of learners in grades 7–9, virtually nothing in the content or organization of the early junior high school differed substantially from the senior high school program. The option for study in "manual training and domestic arts" (industrial arts, cooking, and sewing) was the only difference in curriculum exposure. However, later authors (Alexander, 1964; Curtis, 1966; Vars, 1965a) foresaw problems in the fact that the junior high school was too often a "junior edition of the senior high," as did a number of early writers. Davis (1918) and Glass (1924) saw a growing problem of the early junior high to be its failure to develop a program that was especially responsive to the educational needs of the young adolescent. Floyd (1932) was perhaps the first to recommend that teacher preparation for junior high teachers differ from that of both elementary and high school teachers. In concept, then (Powers, 1928), the early junior high school was largely an administrative reorganization of the secondary school, dividing it into two units of either grades 7–9 and 10–12 or of grades 7–8 and 9–12. Although some movement to a specifically different program was attempted in various localities, early reviews of program change in the junior high school (Landsittel, 1928; Rogers, 1921; Tryon, Smith, & Rood, 1927) found little general departure other than extending typical secondary school approaches down into grades 7–9.

This failure to sharply define a specific educational rationale contributed greatly to the general lack of understanding of the junior high school by professional educators and lay people alike. Yet the movement expanded. Efforts to compare the effectiveness of the junior high school with other patterns of schooling were limited and inconclusive (Carpenter, 1928; Clem & Roberts, 1930; Glass, 1930; Gruhn, 1940; Mills, 1931; Smith, 1935). Kirby (1927) noted that, despite a general lack of conclusive evidence concerning its educational effectiveness, over two-thirds of the nation's cities of 100,000 population or more, as well as increasing numbers of rural communities, had adopted the junior high school or were moving in that direction.

Northby (1941) reported a continued growth of junior and junior-senior high schools (combinations both of grades 7–8 and 9–12, and of grades 7–9 and 10–12), substantiating the acceptance of the junior high format in the majority of American school districts.

The difference between the grade 7–8 and grade 7–9 patterns developed from a number of factors. Local needs for classroom space, size of districts, and secondary school teacher certification demands all contributed to the lack of any single format for the junior high, even concerning the specified grades included. The Carnegie unit requirement for secondary schools was probably the greatest deterrent to the development of a grade 7–9, grade 10–12 pattern in junior and senior high schools. These requirements demanded that academic courses meet for set minimum minutes weekly for a set number of classes weekly. This standardization worked against flexibility in schedule and discriminated against nonacademic areas of study. Studies of its impact (Toepfer, 1962a; Tompkins & Gaumlitz, 1954) show that the extension of Carnegie unit requirements beginning in 1910, established both time and unit requirements for grades 9–12. Glass (1924), reported that Carnegie requirements had so standardized the ninth-grade program throughout the nation that the junior high program was limited. In those communities where the local junior high program attempted to respond to the learning needs of seventh-graders and eighth-graders, the Carnegie unit requirements terminated all such concerns in the ninth-grade program. Thus, whether or not a district had a grade 7–8 or grade 7–9 junior high, its program emphasis could only extend through grade 8 if that program differed at all from Carnegie unit requirements in the ninth-grade.

Achievements. Although no concentric educational pattern or program dominated in the junior high era, programs did become more responsive to the needs of learners. The development of adolescent psychology began to define and sharpen differences between young adolescents and more mature adolescents. The impact of studies on adolescent psychology (Ausubel, 1954; Blos, 1941; Jersild & Tasch, 1949; Strang, 1957; Wattenberg, 1957) resulted in a range of efforts to have the junior high school develop a more responsive curriculum. This was translated into a range of interesting program alternatives and a wide range of applications.

The concerns for general education in the junior high led to the development of the term "core curriculum" (Glass, 1923b). The growing awareness of the transitional aspect of the junior high and the consequent need to facilitate the elementary school–high school continuum led to a focus upon common learnings to be provided by the junior high. Initially this development translated into subjects such as English, social studies, science, mathematics and health as curriculum constants for each year of junior high. These subject areas were separated from considerations of exploratory, tryout courses that also included a guidance function. Tryon, Smith, and Rood (1927) found

that although not a common strand in the majority of junior high programs, an increasing effort was made to differentiate between "core" and exploratory concerns in junior high schools.

The translation of the common learning found in "core" subject areas into the concept of a "core curriculum" was an important achievement of the junior high school. According to this concept, general education and common learning transcend the boundaries of single subject matter areas. The correlation of subject areas under the supervision of a single teacher permits various levels of correlation, fusion, and planning of subject matter. A rich literature developed around this concept and its techniques (Alberty, 1944; Faunce & Bossing, 1951; Vars, 1969a; Wright, 1958), which caused some initiation of this practice within the high school (Alberty & Lurry, 1957). The strategies and tactics of this approach involved "block time" and other scheduling departures, as well as the principle of synthesized learning as opposed to the fragmented learning facilitated by departmentalized instruction. While still operational in a limited number of junior high and middle schools today, lack of definitive preservice and in-service experiences for teachers curtailed the expansion of the core curriculum approach. Related to core curriculum strategies, however, was the growth of pupil-teacher planning in the junior high school. Writers offered means to involve junior high learners in planning with their teachers with interesting results (Burton, 1944; Giles, 1942; Krug, 1957; Parrish & Waskin, 1958). Again, however, the development of such capacities was not adequately facilitated by teacher preparation programs.

Exploration was an initial objective of the junior high school, and attempts to offer nonacademic tryout experiences (Briggs, 1920; Gruhn & Douglass, 1947; Koos, 1927; Noar, 1953; Smith, 1925; VanTil, Vars, & Lounsbury, 1961) were among the most successful accomplishments of the junior high. The purpose of such activities was to try out and explore, by means of intrinsically worthwhile material, the interests, aptitudes, and capacities of students. Limitations occurred in local settings where emphasis was placed on evaluating and grading successful as opposed to unsuccessful exploratory learning.

An early achievement of the junior high school, later utilized by the high school, was the concept of the "homeroom." The homeroom was originated by Hieronimus (1917) on the premise that young adolescents require daily time for interaction with a teacher in a noninstructional setting. His coining of the term "teacher-adviser in the junior high" was the source for contemporary attempts to develop adviser-advisee programs in the middle school.

Guidance in the junior high was initially a downward extension of high school practices. The first text on the junior high school by Douglass (1916) and the text on guidance by Edgerton and Herr (1924) do not mention any kind of junior high school guidance program. As guidance and counseling developed into more responsive programs in the high school, concerns emerged to provide vocational counseling for the majority of students who entered the world of work upon completing junior high (Edgerton & Herr, 1924; Glass, 1923b). This led to the specification of junior high guidance approaches (Koos & Kefauver, 1932) concerning vocational, academic, and personal counseling needs. The Depression of 1929 meant that virtually all junior high students continued into high school because of the lack of opportunity to enter the world of work.

Extracurricular activities were an innovation in the junior high school, later adapted and extended by the high school. The socialization function recommended for early junior high programs (Bennett, 1919; Briggs, 1920) was implemented through early efforts in the "extra-curriculum" (Counts, 1926; Kitson, 1926). These efforts were designed to capture the spontaneous interests of young adolescents (Terry, 1926), and extracurricular activities were seen as a means to that end. Briggs (1922) reported a range of practices and guidelines for developing such effective extracurricular programs.

Thus, although it developed no single approach, the institution of the junior high school did develop a number of responsive departures from the conventional academic program. Whereas a lack of strategic focus hindered development and understanding of the junior high school pattern, a range of effective tactical responses to the needs of the junior high age-group did evolve. However, the uniqueness of effective programs and the failure of the junior high to synthesize concentric program models continued to plague its growth.

Continuing problems. Despite successes, junior high schools had difficulty in developing a curricular rationale specifically responsive to the total range of needs of its learner population (Faunce & Clute, 1961). The problem of the Carnegie unit, considered earlier, continued to hinder the development of a junior high unit free from high school regulations. In addition, teacher preparation did not respond to the particular instructional demands of the junior high school (Dixon, 1965; Toepfer, 1965; Vars, 1965b). A political problem in some states concerned teacher certification (Ackerman, 1962; Conant, 1960; Erickson, 1964; Hoots, 1963; Johnson, 1962; MacNaughton, 1961; Pabst, 1962; Spencer, 1960; Wiley, 1962), especially as related to the lack of specific preparation for teachers at the junior high level. This was tied to the problem of certification requirements for elementary and secondary certification and involved that segment of state bureaucracy administering junior high requirements. In this respect, the overwhelming number of states administered the junior high program under the authority of the department of secondary education, thereby appearing to support the idea of junior high education as "early secondary education." It certainly contributed (Lounsbury, 1960) to efforts to adapt procedures that were effective in the high school to the junior high, where they were often poorly suited. Furthermore the junior high age-group was characterized by a variety of casually utilized descriptors; terms such as "preadolescent," "young adolescent," "early ado-

lescent," "emerging adolescent," and "junior high school learner" had a range of meanings. This descriptive vagueness was symptomatic of a greater problem: the continuing failure of the junior high school to examine its program in light of the research on the nature of the learner that began to multiply in the 1950s and early 1960s.

A variety of specific works (Bayer & Bayley, 1959; Bayley, 1956; Gesell, Ilg, & Ames, 1956; Inhelder & Piaget, 1958; Mussen & Jones, 1957) gave reason to suspect that the junior high needed to make a massive effort to respond to the unique physical, intellectual, and social realities in youngsters between 10 and 14 years of age. The question did not pertain to the validity of the aims of the junior high. Howell (1948) and Koos (1955) had identified the original aims of the junior high to be as valid as ever. The problem appeared to be a growing discrepancy between the responsiveness of the junior high to its constituents and the changing realities of the age-group confirmed by growing research. Few junior high schools had been attentive to the implications of the developmental tasks of early adolescence (Havighurst, 1952) or the attempts to specify these tasks for the junior high (Lilienthal & Tryon, (1950a,b), Faunce & Clute, 1961). The junior high literature increasingly pointed to needs for school programs to be more responsive to the junior high learner (Cooper & Peterson, 1949; Segal, 1951; Shipp, 1951). As such concerns were unheeded in junior high practice, an even more imperative issue arose: the degree to which the junior high could viably respond to the changing dimension of educational needs in the 10-year-old to 14-year-old population. By the early 1960s, the questions of Buell (1962) and Skogberg and Johnson (1963) set the stage for comparing the junior high to a newer organizational pattern, that of the middle school. The question of examining alternatives to the junior high school was now possible.

The Middle School. The middle school entered the scene amid confrontation and debate. Almost immediately, an adversarial relationship developed between proponents of the junior high and the middle school. Howard (1959) raised a series of objective questions about the degree to which a reorganized junior high or an alternative organization could better respond to the unmet educational needs of young adolescents. Separate grade organizations of many sorts other than the traditional junior high arrangement had existed throughout the nation for years. However, there was still not a thought of organized alternatives to set against the junior high. The idea of a grade 6–8 school was not totally new, by any means. For instance, because of separate grade K–8 elementary school and grade 9–12 high school districts in Illinois, many junior high schools had been grade 6–8 for decades. However, with the growth of grade 5–8 and grade 6–8 program alternatives to the junior high format in the early 1960s, the term "middle school" was popularized. Debate and confrontation between advocates of the middle school and the junior high format added little to efforts to identify advantages or the relative effectiveness of one form over the other. The literature reflected the need to seriously question any such differences (Douglass, 1966; Gruhn, 1967; Hull, 1965; Johnson, 1962), much as Kirby (1927) asked of the new junior high school in 1927. Gastworth (1966) identified the problems inherent in moving to an alternative pattern based only upon superficial criticism of the junior high. However, the early growth of the middle school may simply have reflected the growing impatience among those who had long but unsuccessfully attempted to move the junior high toward a more responsive educational program. This investment of hope in the new middle school format, rather than in the junior high format, was captured in much of the literature of the time. Nickerson (1966), Regan (1967), Rice (1964), and Rowe (1967) each spoke out strongly in terms of specific junior high practices that seemed impervious to efforts to improve them. As middle schools began to spread, Alexander (1964, 1966) emerged as an objective source for those interested in seeking a more effective program for intermediate schools. His writings took an unbiased look at the capacities of the junior high and called for serious planning of an improved organizational pattern (1966) before making a poorly conceptualized decision to move to the middle school format. The instances of improved middle grades programs he found in the growing data on the middle school were effectively stated in his highly definitive text (Alexander et al., 1969). Although individual, effective junior high programs continued, it was clear that the institution of the junior high school would be seriously challenged by the middle school movement. This challenge was confirmed in early surveys of middle-grades programs. Cuff (1967) found 499 middle schools in 1965; Alexander (1968b) found 1,101; Compton (1976) found 3,723 in 1976; and Brooks (1978) found 4,060 middle schools. It is obvious that middle schools continue to be the fastest growing format of school organization in the nation (*Middle-level Schools,* 1981).

Objectives. The original objectives of the junior high have not been drastically revised by the middle school movement. Howell (1948) and Koos (1955) both identified the problem of the junior high as one of more effectively meeting these objectives, rather than of changing them. Curtis (1968) sought to define and separate different middle-grades patterns. He defined the junior high as a grade 7–8 or grade 7–9 pattern, emphasizing early secondary education. The middle school was defined as a grade 6–8 pattern, seeking to achieve the initial junior high objectives outside the limits of early secondary education. He saw the middle school as an evolutionary attempt to meet the educational needs of the age 10 to age 14 population, without imposing secondary school limitations. He used the term "intermediate school" to describe the grade 5–8 pattern, viewing it essentially as a revolutionary attempt to reorganize both elementary and secondary education according to a virtual 4–4–4 grade pattern. He recommended that local districts examine the maturational profiles of youngsters carefully before accepting any specific pattern of reorganization.

Transescence. The concept of the operational middle school program was initially best described by Eichhorn (1966). He described the middle school as an educational program that is more effectively responsive to learner needs than the existing junior high format. Eichhorn's work established a continuing effort to examine the research in areas of physical, social, emotional, and intellectual development of youngsters of middle school age as a basis for developing a more responsive educational program in the middle school. Early efforts of the middle school focused upon specifying the developmental needs of the specified age-group. Since social tasks and emotional needs are determined by physical growth and expectations derived from a youngster's stage of physical development, early studies sought to establish contemporary standards of physical growth. The problem faced by the junior high in lacking a single, communicative descriptor for the middle-grades population was inherited by the middle school movement. For example, previous terms did not define the developmental stage of human growth found in the middle-grades years. However, Eichhorn (1966) coined such a descriptor by defining that stage in life as "transescence" and the learner in that stage as a "transescent": "Transescence: the stage of development which begins prior to the onset of puberty and extends through the early stages of adolescence. Since puberty does not begin for all at precisely the same chronological age in human development, the transescent designation is based upon the many physical, social, emotional and intellectual changes that appear prior to the puberty cycle to the time in which the body gains a practical degree of stabilization over these complex pubescent changes" (p. 3).

Using this descriptor for the specified age-group, proponents of the middle school sought to base organizational changes in the middle school upon the realities of physical growth during transescence. Tanner's works (1961, 1962) had identified the reality of earlier onset of pubescence, and Forbes (1968) focused upon the nature of the physical-medical data of earlier pubescent arrival. The early middle school validated its shift to a grade 6–8 format on the grounds that earlier onset of pubescence and earlier maturation at approximately age 14 raised serious questions about a grade 7–9 organizational structure. This rationale contended that most sixth-graders and some fifth-graders had the physical growth and capabilities found in seventh-graders a decade previously and that most eighth-graders could perform in the manner of ninth-graders of ten years past. Likewise, most contemporary ninth-graders were viewed as having far more in common as learners, as well as in physical maturation, with high school students rather than younger students. The physical growth and body changes typically viewed as initiating adolescent tasks were now supported by medical and physiological findings, which suggested an altered grade organization for the middle grades. Dorothy Eichorn (1968) synthesized the existing data on variation in growth rate during transcence. The research of Jones (1957, 1963) and Mussen and Jones (1957) studied the longitudinal difference between boys and girls in terms of the late or early onset of pubescence. This research suggested the areas in which a reorganized middle-grades unit might expect to be more responsive to human needs.

In concept, then, the initial junior high school and initial middle school were quite different. The junior high was seen to be largely an administrative reorganization of secondary education that gradually developed a curricular rationale in response to its pedagogic objectives. The middle school approach was primarily a curriculum-planning response to the educational needs of transescents. At the same time, the junior high had increasing difficulty in meeting learner needs within its organizational limitations. In basing its reorganization on medical research about changing physical growth patterns, the early middle school was far less of an administrative reorganization than its predecessor. Alexander (1973) found the middle school to be more educationally responsive and able to escape the dominance of "early secondary" education inherent in many junior high settings. Earlier, Howard (1956) saw that a grade 6–8 organization could eliminate the Carnegie unit high school requirements as a major limiting factor in transescent educational programs, something not possible in the grade 7–9 junior high format. The removal of Carnegie unit limitations in the middle grades finally realized Glass's concern (1924): "There can be only one college-preparatory unit in the public school system. This has been the senior high school and this school must continue to be the sole agency responsible for accrediting pupils to the higher institutions" (p. 15).

Continuing medical investigations and research into physical growth during transescence has extended the basis for new educational responses in the middle school. Among a growing range of medical studies, several are particularly helpful in formulating educational tasks for programs during transescence. Daniel and Brown (1979), Drash (1976), Frisch, (1974), Marshall and Tanner (1969, 1970a,b), and Tanner (1971) provide a range of data confirming the need to identify physical changes that the school must consider in planning programs, facilities, and schedules, among other educational concerns. Sequencing of growth, capacities to sit, need for physical movement, and capacities for attention and concentration need to be considered in terms of these data. Compton (1978) examined the relationship of growth and development to nutritional needs of transescents in school settings. Bromberg, Commins, and Friedman (1980) synthesized the existing physical and mental health data concerning the stage of transescence.

Programs and strategies. In attempting to respond to the changing physical growth needs of transescents, the middle school concept sought to correlate physical growth and social, emotional, and intellectual demands. Eichhorn (1966) had designed a curriculum model that

was refined after careful planning with medical researchers at Pittsburgh Childrens Hospital. The Boyce Medical Study (Eichhorn, 1973) utilized the results of medical investigations of the total population of a middle school both to specify age characteristics of transescents and to develop a more responsive curriculum model. Age characteristics were established, based upon the correlation of physical growth profiles with social and emotional maturational tasks. Combined with ability and achievement profiles, this model is a highly responsive means of organizing and grouping students for instruction. This designation of developmental age, rather than chronological age, broke through a long-standing problem that graded organization could not overcome in both junior high and middle school settings. Eichhorn (1973) found that in any middle school population, the variance in relationship of chronological age to physical development means that a traditional, graded structure based on chronological age cannot be sufficiently responsive. In the greatest extremes, there are some 11-year-olds who are fully pubescent, and some 14-year-olds who are completely prepubescent. The concept of developmental age, along with multiaged grouping, was organized as a more responsive replacement for a grade structure totally dependent upon chronological age. Continuing study (Eichhorn, 1975, 1979; Lawrence, 1980) views this departure to be more responsive to individual growth and developmental patterns as well as to improved learning and achievement in the middle school. Lipsitz (1977, 1980) specified a social-psychological framework for viewing transescent needs that both school and society must address.

Responsiveness to developmental patterns and the capacity to provide an organizational setting more appropriate to the earlier onset of growth and maturity may well differentiate the middle school from the junior high school most clearly. As junior high schools today develop a more responsive curricular rationale and program, they are still limited by the capacities of youngsters to function in grade 7–8 and grade 7–9 settings. However, the middle school and new intermediate grade patterns surpass the limits of the grade 7–8 junior high in another dimension. Alexander (1968a) has described the advantage of organizing at least three years in a middle-grades unit. The first year usually involves a great adjustment to a new environment and regimen. Study shows that in the second year, students begin to become comfortable in the new setting. The inclusion of only two grades in the middle unit means that another trauma in adjustment comes with the move to a new organizational unit in the third year.

It is difficult to differentiate sharply between strategies, structures, and programs in the contemporary junior high school and those in the middle school. Almost any innovative middle-grades procedure is certain to be utilized in both junior high and middle schools. Team teaching, departmentalization, flexible and modular scheduling, house plans, school-within-a-school, minicourses, intramural and extramural programs, adviser-advisee, and home-base guidance programs all have been utilized in junior high schools and middle schools as well as in secondary schools. Thornburg (1970) pointed out the degree to which middle-grades learning depends upon individual and group maturation. The degree to which schools for transescents utilize as wide a range of alternatives as possible may determine their effectiveness. The wide range of variation in everything from physical, social, and emotional maturity to learning styles in any single middle-grades population spells the need to provide the widest possible range of strategies and departures (Eichhorn, 1977; Toepfer, 1977). To that end, the program emphases of both the middle school movement and continuing junior high efforts interface in their attempts to offer learners a more effectively responsive educational program. The growing combined efforts of both middle schools and junior high schools appear to be resulting in a philosophically united middle-grades movement.

Middle-grades Education. The growing emergence of a nonadversarial middle-grades movement is seen as a means to provide the true three-stage public educational system that has been long awaited by proponents of the junior high concept. The articulation of the three units—early childhood schools, transescent schools, and adolescent schools—appears to be at hand. The growing convergence of junior high and middle school curricular objectives appears to be overcoming the concerns of Stewart (1975) and moving toward a program for effective middle-grades education recommended by Dilg and Gatewood (1975). Progress in this direction has been most clearly seen in the definition of a curricular rationale and philosophy unique to transescent educational needs as separate from those of early childhood and mature adolescence. Thornburg (1980) believes that the holistic educational needs of transescents cannot be fulfilled by any single organizational pattern. Instead, alternative patterns are more appropriate to the philosophical concerns of middle grades than any one rigid sequence of program elements. This has been an improvement over earlier efforts to set specific program arrangements against others in a search for some ideal, master plan for all middle-grades settings. Two reports provide the opportunity to view this progress in middle-grades education. In a national shadow study of junior high learners, Lounsbury and Marani (1964) observed the need to base middle-grades strategies upon the needs of middle-grades learners. Lounsbury, Marani, and Compton (1980) in a similar study on the middle school, suggest that specific middle-grades program components be selected only if they respond to transescent educational needs. The wider acceptance of the findings of the second study at the present time seems to confirm a growth in educational perspective. Educators now seem to be seeking more responsive middle-grades programs, rather than a rigid set of program elements, as was the case in the 1960s.

Contemporary problems and strategies. Arth (1979) has considered the reasons why the necessary elements of learning cannot always be provided through a single middle-grades program. Alexander and George (1981) present a range of contemporary middle-grades programs operational in districts throughout the nation. They provide educators with extensive examples for both planning and adapting programs to transescent needs at the local school district level.

Whereas no specific pattern defines an effective middle-grades program, the following synthesis of elements is found in a growing number of them. A range of organizational arrangements for instruction as opposed to a single instructional mode is generally preferred. Cooperative staff plans seek to minimize the isolation of the individual teacher in planning middle-grades instruction. The age characteristics of transescents serve as the basis for middle-grades curricula and methodologies. Similarly, evaluation of growth and learning is based upon local definition of transescent age characteristics and capacities. An understanding of the developmental patterns of middle-grades learners is a priority for ongoing staff development. Specific program components vary throughout the nation, but these central concerns predominate in increasing numbers of middle-grades school programs.

Furthermore, middle-grades learning strategies differ from elementary and high school models. The implications of the work of Inhelder and Piaget (1958) and Piaget (1969) for learning during transescence have resulted in the considerable influence of so-called Piagetian concerns. Arlin (1975) postulates a fifth Piagetian stage as possible between age 12 and age 14. Furth and Wachs (1974) suggest further implications from Piagetian work for the middle grades. Sund (1976) and Sund and Carin (1977) present specific teaching and learning strategies for transescents based upon application of Piaget's theories of learning to that age-group. Shayer, Kuchemann, and Wylam (1976) and Shayer and Wylam (1978) find that even the brightest transescents may not learn as well as tradition has assumed.

Most recently, the implications of brain growth periodization for the period between ages 10 and 14 suggest new possibilities for improving the responsiveness of middle-grades curricula. Epstein (1977, 1978, 1980) presents new consideration of the expectations for intellectual growth during transescence, related to the alternating periods of brain growth and brain-growth plateau found in most youngsters during the age spans of 10 to 12 years and 12 to 14 years.

The implications of these data have been examined increasingly in terms of the general educational concerns of transescence, rather than any specific pattern of school organization. Although specific concerns such as grades and program components may be more appropriate for certain schools and communities, there appears to be a growing positive trend to reject arbitrary designation of any one organizational pattern as exclusively superior to all others.

Teacher education. The number of states moving toward separating the preparation and certification of middle-grades teachers from those of teachers at elementary and high school levels remains small. However, the growth of middle-grades programs in individual states, as well as the differentiation of middle-grades teacher preparation, contrasts markedly with the complete lack of such efforts in the junior high school movement. Whereas Compton (1973) described unique teacher needs in transescent school settings, George, Malinka, and Pumerantz (1975) found teacher certification to reflect few of these concerns in their national survey. Malinka (1971) elaborated the needed specialization of teacher education in the middle grades initially recommended by Shearron (1970). Curtis (1972) specified the shortcomings of "add-on" middle-grades certification in the light of efforts to formulate separate middle-grades teacher certification and preparation. Florida's efforts to develop teacher education modules in a middle school certification program (George, 1975) and the development of separate state certification in Georgia established precedents for future moves in that direction by other states. The University of Georgia (1977) program, combining state requirements and university preparation programs, serves as a national model for such certification. The increasing number of states moving toward special certification and preparation of middle-grades teachers now includes Alabama, Illinois, Indiana, Kansas, Michigan, Ohio, Pennsylvania, Virginia, and West Virginia. The concerns identified by George and McEwin (1976) and McEwin (1977) are finding a response in the spreading efforts of states to prepare a uniquely educated teacher for the middle grades. The needs identified as critical by Vars (1969b) are being served, and the increasing supply of separately educated middle-grades teachers gives cause for optimism.

Klingele (1979) has identified the impact of improved middle-grades instructional strategies upon teacher preparation needs. Progress in refining middle school educational patterns means that "cosmetic" packages added on to predominantly elementary or high school teacher education programs will not provide the kind of training necessary for successful teachers of transescent learners. Anderson and Snyder (1979) considered the equally crucial roles of staff development and in-service education in preparing current faculty for effective teaching in middle-grades school settings. Johnston and Markle (1979b) synthesized the instructional behaviors of middle-grades teachers in a data base for the design of both preservice and inservice middle-grades teacher education activities. Tyrrell and Natko (1979) focused upon the specific interpersonal skills required for middle-grades teaching as opposed to other levels of teaching. The admonitions of Applegate (1977) and Johnston et al. (1977) have been considered in the contemporary development of teacher education and certification programs for the middle grades. Bearden and Gillan (1980) and Walter and Fanslow (1980) find in their investigations that the gap between transescent educational needs and teacher preparation is narrowing in those states that have organized separate programs for middle-grades teacher education.

Research. The junior high era suffered from a lack of broad, as well as specific, research needed to validate its effectiveness over other patterns of middle-grade education. Critical topics lacking data include the comparative effectiveness of alternative junior high patterns and the relation of teacher preparation to successful performance. Whereas the middle school movement initially shared this lack, the past decade has seen the development of increased efforts to provide necessary data for the entire middle-grades movement.

The investigations of Gatewood (1973) and Wiles and Thomason (1975) describe beginning efforts to research middle-grades practices and to identify their effectiveness. Johnston and Markle (1978, 1979a) and Johnston (1985) have collected and reported contemporary middle-grades research in a series of annual research reports. Toepfer and Marani (1980) have described specific school-based and naturalistic studies carried out with transescents in both school and social settings. McCann (1980) provides a perspective for present and emerging research needs in middle-grades education.

The literature in the latter stage of the junior high school movement identified increasing limits in the junior high school's capacity to respond to changing needs in its learner population. Although initially adversarial in its relation to the junior high, the middle school movement has become a catalyst in uniting the middle-grades movement. This middle-grades movement has the apparent potential to develop an articulated, three-stage, educational program of early childhood, transescent, and adolescent education. The history of program and curriculum development, as well as the data base growing available on transescent learners and their unique educational needs, is enabling junior high and middle school education to earn the credibility and respect it has long sought.

Conrad F. Toepfer, Jr.

See also Curriculum Development and Organization; Preadolescent Development; Secondary Education.

REFERENCES

Ackerman, R. E. The preparation of junior high school teachers. *Journal of Teacher Education*, March 1962, *13*, 69–71.

Alberty, A. *Reorganizing the High School Curriculum.* New York: Macmillan, 1944.

Alberty, E., & Lurry, L. *Developing a High School Core Program.* New York: Macmillan, 1957.

Alexander, W. M. The junior high school: A changing view. *Bulletin of the National Association of Secondary School Principals,* March 1964, *48*, 15–24.

Alexander, W. M. What educational plan for the in-between-ager? *National Education Association Journal*, March 1966, *55*, 30–32.

Alexander, W. M. New organizational patterns for the middle

school years. In A. Frazier (Ed.), *The New Elementary School.* Washington, D.C.: Association for Supervision and Curriculum Development, 1968. (a)

Alexander, W. M. *A Survey of Organizational Patterns of Reorganized Middle Schools* (Final Report No. 7-D-026). Gainesville: University of Florida Press, 1968. (b) (ERIC Document Reproduction Service No. ED 024 121)

Alexander, W. M. What has the middle school achieved to date? *Transescence: The Journal on Emerging Adolescent Education,* Spring 1973, *1,* 13–18.

Alexander, W. M., & George, P. *The Exemplary Middle School.* New York: Holt, Rinehart & Winston, 1981.

Alexander, W. M., Williams, E. L.; Compton, M.; Himes, V. A.; Prescott, D.; & Kealy, R. *The Emergent Middle School* (2nd enlarged ed.). New York: Holt, Rinehart & Winston, 1969.

Anderson, R. H., & Snyder, K. J. Preparation of staff for middle school implementation. *Middle School Journal,* August 1979, *10,* 5, 27, 29–30.

Applegate, J. The rhetoric of middle-grade teacher preparation: A look at the last ten years. *Middle School Journal,* August 1977, *8,* 5, 22–23.

Arlin, P. Cognitive development in adulthood: A fifth stage? *Developmental Psychology,* 1975, *2,* 602–606.

Arth, A. Supporting the crucial decision to more closely match teacher presentation style with young adolescent preferred learning style in middle school. *Transescence: The Journal on Emerging Adolescent Education,* 1979, *8,* 9–12.

Ausubel, D. P. *Theory and Problems of Adolescent Development.* New York: Grune & Stratton, 1954.

Bayer, S. M., & Bayley, N. *Growth Diagnosis.* Chicago: University of Chicago Press, 1959.

Bayley, N. Individual patterns of development. March 1956, *27,* 45–74.

Bearden, I. R., & Gillan, R. Middle school teacher: Rate yourself. *Middle School Journal,* August 1980, *11,* 16–17.

Bennett, G. V. *The Junior High School.* Baltimore: Warwick & York, 1919.

Berkeley, California, Board of Education Minutes. November 30, 1909, p. 293.

Blos, P. *The Adolescent Personality.* New York: Appleton-Century-Crofts, 1941.

Briggs, T. H. *The Junior High School.* Boston: Houghton Mifflin, 1920.

Briggs, T. H. Extra-curricular activities in the junior high school. *Educational Administration and Supervision,* January 1922, *8,* 1–9.

Bromberg, D.; Commins, C.; & Friedman, S. B. Protecting physical and mental health. In M. Johnson, Jr. (Ed.), *Toward Adolescence: The Middle School Years: Seventy-ninth Yearbook of the National Society for the Study of Education* (Part 1). Chicago: University of Chicago Press, 1980.

Brooks, K. The middle school: A national survey. *Middle School Journal,* February 1978, *9,* 6–7.

Buell, C. E. What grades in the junior high school? *Bulletin of the National Association of Secondary School Principals,* February 1962, *46,* 14–22.

Bunker, F. A plan for the reorganization of the intermediate grades. *Sierra Educational News and Review,* December 1909, *5,* 13–19.

Burton, W. H. *The Guidance of Learning Activities.* New York: Appleton-Century-Crofts, 1944.

Carpenter, L. H. *A Study of the Effects of the Junior High School Organization of Wabash, Indiana.* Unpublished master's thesis, University of Chicago, 1928.

Clem, O. M., & Roberts, H. M. The tenth-year progress of junior high school and elementary school pupils. *Journal of Educational Research,* March 1930, *21,* 288–296.

Columbus, Ohio, Board of Education Minutes. June 7, 1909, p. 47.

Compton, M. F. How do you prepare to teach transescents? *Educational Leadership,* December 1973, *31,* 215–216.

Compton, M. F. The middle school: A status report. *Middle School Journal,* June 1976, *6,* 3–5.

Compton, M. F. The physiological enigma of early adolescence. In M. F. Compton (Ed.), *A Source Book for the Middle School.* Athens, Ga.: Educational Associates, 1978.

Conant, J. B. *Education in the Junior High Years.* Princeton, N.J.: Educational Testing Service, 1960.

Cooper, D. H., & Peterson, O. E. *Schools for Young Adolescents: The Upper-Elementary and Lower-Secondary Grades.* Chicago: Superintendents' Study Club, 1949.

Counts, G. S. Procedures in evaluating extra-curricular activities. *School Review,* June 1926, *34,* 419–421.

Cuff, W. A. Middle schools on the march. *Bulletin of the National Association of Secondary School Principals,* February 1967, *51,* 82–86.

Curtis, T. E. Crucial times for the junior high school. *New York State Education,* February 1966, *48,* 30–35.

Curtis, T. E. Rationale for the middle school. *Impact on Instructional Improvement,* Winter 1968, *8,* 6–10.

Curtis, T. E. Preparing teachers for middle and junior high schools. *Bulletin of National Association of Secondary School Principals,* May 1972, *56,* 61–70.

Daniel, W. A., Jr., & Brown, R. T. Adolescent physical maturation. *Journal of Current Adolescent Medicine,* 1979, *1,* 27–30.

Davis, C. O. Junior high schools in the North Central Association territory, 1917–1918. *School Review,* April 1918, *26,* 324–326.

Dilg, C. A., & Gatewood, T. E. *The Middle School We Need.* Washington, D.C.: Association for Supervision and Curriculum Development, 1975. (ERIC Document Reproduction Service No. ED 113 821)

Dixon, N. R. The search for jhs teacher. *Clearing House,* October 1965, *40,* 82–85.

Douglass, A. A. (Ed.) *The Junior High School: Fifteenth Yearbook of the National Society for the Study of Education* (Part 3). Bloomington, Ind.: Public School Publishing, 1916.

Douglass, H. R. What type of organization of schools? *Journal of Secondary Education,* December 1966, *41,* 358–364.

Drash, A. Variations in pubertal development and the school system. *Transescence: The Journal on Emerging Adolescent Education,* 1976, *4,* 14–26.

Edgerton, A. H., & Herr, L. A. Present status of guidance activities in the public schools. In A. Edgerton (Ed.), *Vocational Guidance and Vocational Education for the Industries: Twenty-third Yearbook of the National Society for the Study of Education* (Part 2). Bloomington, Ind.: Public School Publishing, 1924.

Eichhorn, D. H. *The Middle School.* New York: Center for Applied Research in Education, 1966. (ERIC Document Reproduction Service No. ED 032 623)

Eichhorn, D. H. The Boyce Medical Study. In N. Atkins & P. Pumerantz (Eds.), *Educational Dimensions of the Emerging Adolescent Learner.* Springfield, Mass.: Educational Leadership Institute, 1973.

Eichhorn, D. H. Middle school developmental age-grouping: A promising change. *Transescence: The Journal on Emerging Adolescent Education*, 1975, *3*, 18–22.

Eichhorn, D. H. Middle school learner characteristics: The key to alternative programs. In P. George (Ed.), *The Middle School: A Look Ahead*. Fairborn, Ohio: National Middle School Association, 1977.

Eichhorn, D. H. Middle school developmental age-grouping: A needed consideration. *Colorado Journal of Educational Research*, Fall 1979, *19*, 19–21.

Eichhorn, D. H. The school. In M. Johnson, Jr. (Ed.), *Toward Adolescence: The Middle School Years: Seventy-ninth Yearbook of the National Society for the Study of Education* (Part 1). Chicago: University of Chicago Press, 1980.

Eichorn, Dorothy H. Variations in growth rate. *Childhood Education*, January 1968, *44*, 286–291.

Epstein, H. T. A neuroscience framework for restructuring middle school curricula. *Transescence: The Journal on Emerging Adolescent Education*, 1977, *5*, 6–11.

Epstein, H. T. Growth spurts during brain development: Implications for educational policy. In J. Chall & A. Mirsky (Eds.), *Education and the Brain: Seventy-seventh Yearbook of the National Society for the Study of Education* (Part 2). Chicago: University of Chicago Press, 1978.

Epstein, H. T. Brain growth and cognitive functioning. In D. Steer (Ed.), *The Emerging Adolescent: Characteristics and Implications*. Fairborn, Ohio: National Middle School Association, 1980.

Erickson, J. H. Specialized training for junior high school teachers. *Teachers College Journal*, March 1964, *35*, 172–174.

Faunce, R. C., & Bossing, N. L. *Developing the Core Curriculum*. Englewood Cliffs, N.J.: Prentice-Hall, 1951.

Faunce, R. C., & Clute, M. J. *Teaching and Learning in the Junior High School*. Belmont, Calif.: Wadsworth, 1961.

Floyd, O. R. *The Preparation of Junior High School Teachers* (U.S. Office of Education Bulletin, No. 20). Washington, D.C.: U.S. Government Printing Office, 1932.

Forbes, G. Physical aspects of early adolescence. In T. Curtis (Ed.), *The Middle School*. Albany: State University of New York at Albany, 1968. (ERIC Document Reproduction Service No. ED 032 623)

Frisch, R. E. Crucial weight at menarche, initiation of the adolescent growth spurt, and the control of puberty. In C. Grumbach, I. Grove, & R. Moyer (Eds.), *The Control of the Onset of Puberty*. New York: Wiley, 1974.

Fullerton, C. H. Report of the principal of Indianola School. In *Annual Report of the Board of Education of the City of Columbus, Ohio for the Year Ending August 10, 1910*. Columbus, Ohio: Board of Education, 1910.

Furth, H., & Wachs, H. *Thinking Goes to School: Piaget's Theory into Practice*. New York: Oxford University Press, 1974.

Gastworth, P. Questions facing the middle school. *High Points*, June 1966, *48*, 40–47.

Gatewood, T. E. What research says about the middle school. *Educational Leadership*, December 1973, *31*, 221–224.

George, P. *Middle School Teacher Certification*. Gainesville: University of Florida, 1975.

George, P.; Malinka, R.; & Pumerantz, P. Middle school teacher certification: A national survey. *Educational Leadership*, December 1975, *32*, 213–216.

George, P., & McEwin, K. *Middle School Teacher Education: A Progress Report*. Unpublished manuscript, University of Florida at Gainesville, 1976.

Gesell, A.; Ilg, F. L.; & Ames, L. B. *Youth: The Years from Ten to Sixteen*. New York: Harper & Brothers, 1956.

Giles, H. H. *Teacher-Pupil Planning*. New York: Harper & Brothers, 1942.

Glass, J. M. The junior high school. *The New Republic*, November 7, 1923, *36*, 19–22. (a)

Glass, J. M. The reorganization of the seventh, eighth, and ninth grades: Program of studies. *School Review*, September 1923, *31*, 519–520. (b)

Glass, J. M. *Curriculum Practices in the Junior High and Grades Five and Six* (Supplementary Education Monographs No. 25). Chicago: University of Chicago Press, 1924.

Glass, L. *The Relative Achievement in Senior High School of Graduates and Non-graduates of Junior High School*. Unpublished master's thesis, University of Pennsylvania, 1930.

Gruhn, W. T. *An Investigation of the Relative Frequency of Curriculum and Related Practices Contributing to the Realization of the Basic Functions of the Junior High School*. Unpublished doctoral dissertation, University of North Carolina, 1940.

Gruhn, W. T. What do principals believe about grade organization? *Journal of Secondary Education*, April 1967, *42*, 169–174.

Gruhn, W. T., & Douglass, H. R. *The Modern Junior High School*. New York: Ronald Press, 1947.

Havighurst, R. J. *Developmental Tasks and Education*. New York: Longmans, Green, 1952.

Hieronimus, N. C. The teacher-advisor in the junior high school. *Educational Administration and Supervision*, February 1917, *3*, 91–95.

Hoots, W. R. Junior high teacher certification. *Bulletin of the National Association of Secondary School Principals*, October 1963, *47*, 44–48.

Howard, A. W. The Carnegie Unit. *Clearing House*, November 1956, *39*, 135–139.

Howard, A. W. Which years in junior high? *Clearing House*, March 1959, *33*, 227–230.

Howell, C. E. Junior high: How valid are its original aims? *Clearing House*, October 1948, *23*, 75–88.

Hull, J. H. Are junior high schools the answer? *Educational Leadership*, December 1965, *23*, 213–216.

Indianola Junior High. *Columbus Evening Dispatch*, August 31, 1909, p. 10.

Inhelder, B., & Piaget, J. *Growth of Logical Thinking from Childhood to Adolescence*. New York: Basic Books, 1958.

Jersild, A. T., & Tasch, R. J. *Children's Interests and What They Suggest to Education*. New York: Columbia University, Teachers College, Bureau of Publications, 1949.

Johnson, M., Jr. School in the middle-junior high: Education's problem child. *Saturday Review*, July 1962, *45*, 40–42.

Johnston, J. H. (Ed.) *Middle School Research Studies*. Fairborn, Ohio: National Middle School Association, 1980.

Johnston, J. H., & Markle, G. C. (Eds.) *Middle School Research Annual*. Laramie: University of Wyoming, Center for Research and Publications, 1978.

Johnston, J. H., & Markle, G. C. (Eds.) *Middle School Research Annual*. Laramie: University of Wyoming, Center for Research and Publications, 1979. (a)

Johnston, J. H., & Markle, G. C. What research says to the practitioner about teacher behavior. *Middle School Journal*, May 1979, *10*, 14–15. (b)

Johnston, J. H.; Markle, G.; Hogan, J.; & Smith, D. Students' perception of the ideal middle school teacher. *Middle School Journal*, August 1977, *8*, 6–7.

Jones, M. C. The late careers of boys who were early- or late-maturing boys. *Child Development,* March 1957, *28,* 113–128.

Jones, M. C. Self-conceptions, motivations, and interpersonal attitudes of early- and late-maturing girls. In R. Grinde (Ed.), *Studies in Adolescence.* New York: Macmillan, 1963.

Kirby, T. E. Preface. In R. A. Fritz, *An Evaluation of Two Special Purposes of the Junior High School: Economy of Time and Bridging the Gap* (University of Iowa Studies in Education IV, No. 5). Iowa City: University of Iowa Press, 1927.

Kitson, H. D. Extra-curricular activities as a means of guidance. *Vocational Guidance Magazine,* May 1926, *4,* 356–361.

Klingele, W. E. *Teaching in Middle Schools.* Boston: Allyn & Bacon, 1979.

Koos, L. V. *The Junior High School.* Boston: Ginn, 1927.

Koos, L. V. *Junior High School Trends.* New York: Harper & Brothers, 1955.

Koos, L. V., & Kefauver, G. N. *Guidance in Secondary Schools.* New York: Macmillan, 1932.

Krug, E. *Curriculum Planning* (2nd ed.). New York: Harper & Brothers, 1957.

Landsittel, F. C. Scholastic accomplishment in the junior high school. *Journal of Educational Research,* 1928, *18,* 127–135.

Lawrence, G. Do programs reflect research about physical development? *Middle School Journal,* May 1980, *11,* 12–14.

Lilienthal, J. W., & Tryon, C. Developmental tasks, 1: The concept and its importance. In *Fostering Mental Health in Our Schools: 1950 Yearbook of the Association for Supervision and Curriculum Development.* Washington, D.C.: National Education Association, 1950. (a)

Lilienthal, J. W., & Tryon, C. Developmental tasks, 2: Discussion of specific tasks and implications. In *Fostering Mental Health in Our Schools: 1950 Yearbook of the Association for Supervision and Curriculum Development.* Washington, D.C.: National Education Association, 1950. (b)

Lipsitz, J. *Growing Up Forgotten: A Review of Research and Programs concerning Early Adolescence (Report to the Ford Foundation).* Lexington, Mass.: Heath, Lexington Books, 1977.

Lipsitz, J. The age group. In M. Johnson, Jr. (Ed.), *Toward Adolescence—The Middle-School Years: Seventy-ninth Yearbook of the National Society for the Study of Education* (Part 1). Chicago: University of Chicago Press, 1980.

Lounsbury, J. H. *The Role and Status of the Junior High School.* Unpublished doctoral dissertation, George Peabody College, 1954.

Lounsbury, J. H. How the junior high school came to be. *Educational Leadership,* December 1960, *18,* 145–147.

Lounsbury, J. H., & Marani, J. V. *The Junior High School We Saw: One Day in the Eighth Grade.* Washington, D.C.: Association for Supervision and Curriculum Development, 1964.

Lounsbury, J. H.; Marani, J. V.; & Compton, M. F. *The Middle School in Profile: A Day in the Seventh Grade.* Fairborn, Ohio: National Middle School Association, 1980.

MacNaughton, R. A. Junior high school teaching deserves its own training. *Ohio Schools,* January 1961, *39,* 18–22.

Malinka, R. M. *Teaching in the Middle School: Implications for Certification and Fundamentals* (U.S. Office of Education Booklet). Washington, D.C.: U.S. Government Printing Office, 1971. (ERIC Document Reproduction Service No. ED 083 251)

Marshall, W. A., & Tanner, J. M. Variations in the pattern of pubertal changes in boys. *Archives of Diseases in Childhood,* 1970, *45,* 10. (a)

Marshall, W. A., & Tanner, J. M. Variations in the pattern of pubertal changes in girls. *Archives of Diseases in Childhood,* 1970, *44,* 291. (b)

McCann, C. K. (Ed.). *Perspectives on Middle School Research.* Cincinnati: University of Cincinnati, College of Education, 1980. (ERIC Document Reproduction Service No. ED 188 325)

McEwin, C. K. The middle school: An institution in search of teachers. In P. George (Ed.), *The Middle School: A Look Ahead.* Fairborn, Ohio: National Middle School Association, 1977.

Middle-level Schools in the United States: A Study of the Demography of Schools for Early Adolescents (Report of the National Institute of Education). Washington, D.C.: U.S. Government Printing Office, 1981.

Mills, H. C. *The Comparative Efficiency of the 8-4 and 6-3-3 Systems of Schools.* Unpublished doctoral dissertation, Harvard University, 1931.

Mussen, P. H., & Jones, N. C. Self-conceptions, motivations, and interpersonal attitudes of late- and early-maturing boys. *Child Development,* 1957, *28,* 243–248.

National Education Association. *Report of the Committee of Ten on Secondary Studies.* New York: American Book, 1894.

Nickerson, N. C. *Junior High Schools Are on the Way Out.* Dansville, Ill.: Interstate Printers & Publishers, 1966.

Noar, G. *The Junior High School Today and Tomorrow.* Englewood Cliffs, N.J.: Prentice-Hall, 1953.

Northby, A. S. Secondary education: Organization. In W. Monroe (Ed.), *Encyclopedia of Educational Research.* New York: Macmillan, 1941.

Pabst, R. L. The junior high school teacher's certificate: Something new in teacher education. *Junior High Newsletter,* December 1962, *1,* 2–3.

Parrish, L., & Waskin, Y. *Teacher-Pupil Planning for Better Classroom Learning.* New York: Harper & Brothers, 1958.

Piaget, J. *Psychology of Intelligence* (M. Pierce & D. E. Berlyne, Trans.). Totowa, N.J.: Littlefield, Adams, 1969.

Powers, J. O. Is the junior high realizing its declared objectives? *School Life,* 1928, *14,* 76–79.

Regan, E. E. The junior high is dead. *Clearing House,* November 1967, *41,* 150–151.

Rice, A. H. What's wrong with junior highs? Nearly everything. *Nation's Schools,* November 1964, *74,* 30–32.

Rogers, J. H. Junior high school curricula and programs. *School Review,* 1921, *29,* 196–198.

Rowe, R. N. Why we abandoned our traditional junior high. *Nation's Schools,* January 1967, *77,* 80–82.

Segal, D. *Frustration in Adolescent Youth: Its Development and Implications for School Programs* (U.S. Office of Education Bulletin, No. 1). Washington, D.C.: U.S. Government Printing Office, 1951.

Shayer, M.; Kuchemann, D.; & Wylam, H. The distribution of Piagetian stages of thinking in British middle and secondary school children. *British Journal of Educational Psychology,* February 1976, *46,* 164–173.

Shayer, M., & Wylam, H. The distribution of Piagetian stages of thinking in British middle and secondary school children: Fourteen- to sixteen-year-olds and sex differences. *British Journal of Educational Psychology,* 1978, *68,* 62–70.

Shearron, G. *A Proposed Program for the Preparation of Middle School Teachers* (Report available from the College of Education, Division of Elementary Education). Athens: University of Georgia, 1970.

Shipp, F. T. 4-4-4-3: New plan for school organization. *School Executive,* September 1951, *71,* 62.

Skogberg, A. H., & Johnson, M., Jr. The magic numbers of 7,8,9:

Is this structure really best for junior high schools? *National Education Association Journal*, March 1963, *52*, 50–51.

Smith, H. P. The relative efficiency of the junior high versus the conventional eight-grade type of school. *Journal of Educational Research*, 1935, *29*, 276–280.

Smith, W. A. *The Junior High School*. New York: Macmillan, 1925.

Spencer, H. B. Preparing teachers for the junior high school. *Bulletin of the National Association of Secondary School Principals*, April 1960, *44*, 85–87.

Stewart, W. J. What causes a middle school to be ineffective: Student-centered teaching approach. *Clearing House*, September 1975, *49*, 23–25.

Stoddard, J. J. Report of the president of the board. *Annual Report of the Board of Education of the City of Columbus for the Year Ending August 31, 1909*. Columbus, Ohio: Board of Education, 1909.

Strang, R. *The Adolescent Views Himself: A Psychology of Adolescence*. New York: McGraw-Hill, 1957.

Sund, R. B. *Piaget for Educators*. Columbus, Ohio: Merrill, 1976.

Sund, R. B., & Carin, A. *Creative Questioning and Sensitive Listening Techniques* (2nd ed.). Columbus, Ohio: Merrill, 1977.

Tanner, J. M. *Education and Physical Growth*. London: University of London Press, 1961.

Tanner, J. M. *Growth at Adolescence* (2nd ed.). Oxford: Blackwell Scientific Publications, 1962.

Tanner, J. M. Sequence, tempo, and individual growth and development of boys and girls aged twelve to sixteen. In J. Kagan & R. Coles (Eds.), *Twelve to Sixteen: Early Adolescence*. New York: Norton, 1971.

Terry, P. W. General survey of practices: Junior high schools. In L. Koos (Ed.), *Extra-curricular Activities: Twenty-fifth Yearbook of the National Society for the Study of Education* (Part 2). Bloomington, Ind.: Public School Publishing Company, 1926.

Thornburg, H. D. Learning and maturation in middle-school-age youth. *Clearing House*, November 1970, *44*, 150–155.

Thornburg, H. D. The total early adolescent. *Transescence: The Journal on Emerging Adolescent Education*, 1980, *8*(2), 22–26.

Toepfer, C. F., Jr. *Evolving Curricular Patterns in Junior High Schools: An Historical Study*. Unpublished doctoral dissertation, University of Buffalo, 1962. (a)

Toepfer, C. F., Jr. The historical development of patterns of junior high school organization in America. *Bulletin of the National Association of Secondary School Principals*, February 1962, *46*, 181–184. (b)

Toepfer, C. F., Jr. Who should teach in junior high? *Clearing House*, October 1965, *40*, 74–76.

Toepfer, C. F., Jr. The middle school as a multiple school: A means for survival. In P. George (Ed.), *The Middle School: A Look Ahead*. Fairborn, Ohio: National Middle School Association, 1977.

Toepfer, C. F., Jr., & Marani, J. V. School-based research. In M. Johnson, Jr. (Ed.), *Toward Adolescence—The Middle School Years: Seventy-ninth Yearbook of the National Society for the Study of Education* (Part 1). Chicago: University of Chicago Press, 1980.

Tompkins, E., & Gaumlitz, W. H. *The Carnegie Unit: Its Origin, Status, and Trends* (U.S. Department of Health, Education, and Welfare Bulletin 1954, No. 7). Washington, D.C.: U.S. Government Printing Office, 1954.

Tryon, R. M.; Smith, H. L.; & Rood, A. F. The program of studies in seventy-eight junior high school centers. *School Review*, January 1927, *35*, 96–107.

Tyrrell, R., & Natko, J. Person-centered teachers for emerging adolescents. *Middle School Journal*, May 1979, *10*, 18–19, 26–27.

University of Georgia. *A Program for the Preparation of Middle School Teachers* (Report available from the College of Education, Division of Elementary Education). Athens: University of Georgia, 1977.

VanTil, W.; Vars, G. F.; & Lounsbury, J. H. *Modern Education for the Junior-School Years*. New York: Bobbs-Merrill, 1961.

Vars, G. F. Change and the junior high school. *Educational Leadership*, December 1965, *23*, 187–189. (a)

Vars, G. F. Preparing junior-high teachers. *Clearing House*, October 1965, *40*, 77–81. (b)

Vars, G. F. *Common Learning: Core and Interdisciplinary Team Approaches*. Scranton, Pa.: International Textbook, 1969. (a)

Vars, G. F. Teacher preparation for the middle school. *High School Journal*, December 1969, *53*, 172–177. (b)

Walter, J. M., & Fanslow, A. M. Professional competencies of middle school teachers. *Middle School Journal*, August 1980, *11*, 23–24, 29.

Wattenburg, W. W. Preadolescents in the junior high. *Educational Leadership*, May 1957, *17*, 473–477.

Wiles, J., & Thomason, J. Middle school research, 1968–1974: A Review of substantial studies. *Educational Leadership*, March 1975, *33*, 421–423.

Wiley, W. D. Teaching success of junior high school teachers as it relates to type of credential held. *Bulletin of National Association of Secondary School Principals*, February 1962, *46*, 382–384.

Wright, G. S. *Block-time and the Core Program in the Junior High School* (U.S. Department of Health, Education, and Welfare Bulletin, No. 6). Washington, D.C.: U.S. Government Printing Office, 1958.

JUVENILE DELINQUENCY

See Behavior Problems; Behavioral Treatment Methods; Correctional Education; Discipline; Psychological Services; Truants and Dropouts.

KINDERGARTEN EDUCATION

See Early Childhood Development; Early Childhood Education; Home-School Relationships; Parent Education; Readiness.

L

LABOR AND EDUCATION

This article on labor and education examines the role of organized labor and higher education in the development of nonvocational educational programs for trade union officers, activists, and, more recently, workers in general. Labor studies, which this movement has come to be called, is unlike other areas of study with longer traditions in academe currently engaged in gaining legitimization on the campus. A brief examination of the historical development of this movement will set the stage for a delineation of the important educational questions facing labor studies today.

Because labor studies is emerging on the campus from an extension division base and at a time of budgetary constraints, questions of academic acceptance are overemphasized in the literature. Therefore, questions of curricular redundancy with other academic departments, questions of the utilization of scarce resources between noncredit extension and credit-bearing degree offerings, questions regarding the locus of power, and more recently questions of curricular design predominate in the literature. After examining the historical bases of the movement, this article will highlight the literature delineating many of the key educational issues that confront labor studies professionals.

Education has long been an important concern of organized labor in the United States. As early as 1829, the Working Men's Party, believing that "liberty rested on a wide diffusion of knowledge" (Taft, 1964, p. 16), demanded the abolition of the pauper's oath as a prerequisite for free elementary education and the establishment of a free, equal, universal, and republican system of education. Between 1830 and 1880, labor unions were organized in this country in response to specific problems confronting workers. As a result of worsening economic conditions and counterattacks by employers and government, many of these unions were forced out of existence, but most of these fledgling unions viewed education as a vehicle for social change. The Knights of Labor, organized during this period, listed education as one of its three major planks because it believed education could abolish the wage system and replace it with a cooperative commonwealth. When the American Federation of Labor (AFL) became the dominant labor federation, it no longer viewed education as a vehicle for promoting a new social order. Instead, this federation supported free public education because it could ensure that working people would "get the best there is in life, regardless of the system under which (they) live" (Perkins, 1927, p. 34). Consistent with this position, the AFL continues to support free public education. Today, the education department of the American Federation of Labor/Congress of Industrial Organizations (AFL-CIO), in cooperation with one of its affiliates, the American Federation of Teachers (AFT), closely monitors and testifies on all educational legislation proposed in Congress. It is obvious why unions that represent educators, the producers of the educational product, such as the AFT, the National Education Association (NEA), and the American Association of University Professors (AAUP), monitor and lobby educational legislation, but the AFL-CIO's education department also invests considerable energy monitoring public education legislation to ensure that its members, who are also educational consumers, are represented. In addition, many national and international unions, especially those representing skilled workers, are actively interested in public vocational education and apprenticeship training. Each year, thousands of union workers, mainly in the construction, maritime, and printing trades, attend educational programs for skill improvement in their chosen trades.

Although organized labor is involved in these diverse public educational programs, the scope of this article is limited to examining labor's involvement in the nonvocational education of its members. Labor's interest in the education of its members has waxed and waned throughout the twentieth century. Although a continuous thread of educational activity for adult workers has developed through this century and, in chronological sequence, has been named workers' education, labor education, and, more recently, labor studies, labor's interest has not always been consistently high. For the last two decades, however, organized labor has displayed renewed interest in this type of education. For instance, the AFL-CIO established the George Meany Labor Studies Center in Silver Springs, Maryland, and the United Automobile Workers (UAW) established the Walter and May Reuther Family Education Center in Black Lake, Michigan. Other labor organizations have developed close relationships with nearby colleges and provide educational opportunities for their members, many times at the union headquarters.

Workers' Education. Workers' education was imported into the United States from Great Britain, where the term is still used to identify the movement for the education of workers. In 1901, Walter Vrooman, an American and one of the founders of Ruskin College in Great Britain, the oldest, continuously existing labor college in the world, approached the executive council of the AFL asking for its endorsement for a labor college in the United States. Although his request was refused, nevertheless, Vrooman launched Ruskin College; first in Missouri, later in Illinois, and finally in Ruskin, Florida, where it closed in 1917.

Before unions became actively involved in workers' education in the post–World War I period, three distinguishable organizations provided educational opportunities for working people: (1) such organizations as the Workmen's Circle, founded by Jewish migrants in New York City's Lower East Side, used education to socialize immigrant workers to the United States; (2) political organizations such as the Socialist party, which advocated education as a prerequisite for a workers' cooperative and commonwealth; and (3) organizations, such as the Women's Trade Union League (WTUL) and the Industrial Department of the Young Women's Christian Association (YWCA), which developed educational activities for working women (Peters & McCarrick, 1976).

Direct trade-union involvement began in cooperation with these endeavors. For instance: (1) the Work People's College, founded in Duluth, Minnesota (1908), to acculturate Finnish immigrants, became closely associated with the Industrial Workers of the World; (2) the Rand School of the Social Sciences, founded in New York City (1906) by the Socialist party, provided educational services for the International Ladies' Garment Workers' Union (ILGWU) and the Amalgamated Clothing Workers of America (ACWA), until these unions established their own educational departments in 1916 and 1917, respectively; and (3) the WTUL established a school for women union organizers in Chicago in 1914.

The post–World War I era was a boom for union-sponsored workers' education. During the 1920s, City Central Labor bodies affiliated with the AFL established more than 300 labor colleges throughout the United States, those in Seattle, Milwaukee, and Boston being the most successful. In 1921, the University of California, in close cooperation with the California Federation of Labor, expanded its extension program to include a program specifically geared for workers. In that same year, Brookwood Labor College initiated its two-year resident program at Katonah, New York. In April, the Workers Educational Bureau (WEB) was formed in New York City to coordinate workers' education services conducted under trade union auspices.

Another important workers' education endeavor, not conducted under trade union auspices, also began in 1921: The Bryn Mawr Summer School for Women Workers in Industry. A number of other schools were initially organized to educate women workers in industry and were, for the most part, conducted on college campuses during the summer months. Because these schools were not conducted under official trade union auspices, they could not join the WEB, and therefore they formed their own coordinating organization, known as the Affiliated Summer Schools for Women Workers in Industry (Dwyer, 1977a).

These educational programs were organized by "progressives" both within and without the AFL. These "progressives" believed that the basic aim of workers' education was to encourage a change in the social order. To this end, James Maurer, a socialist, contended that "the basic purpose of workers' education is the role of an intelligent guide to a new social order . . . and the ultimate liberation of the working masses" (Report, 1927, p. 12). Likewise, Hulet M. Wells stated, "Education in our universities and colleges is essentially capitalistic in that it glorifies competition. . . . Education that may properly be called labor education is essentially socialistic, in that it glorifies cooperation and seeks to produce an efficient social and industrial order" (Shafer, 1921, p. 790).

The various groups that sponsored worker education programs in the 1920s filled the ideological spectrum from radical political parties to the much more conservative state universities. For this reason alone, it is evident that, although the basic objective of the vast majority of workers' education programs was a change in the social order, each program defined the objectives and methods of achieving the new social order according to its own ideology (Dwyer, 1977b).

As long as progressives controlled the workers' education programs and conservatives controlled the leadership positions within the AFL, conflict was inevitable. The battleground for this conflict became the WEB, with the final struggle taking place at the 1929 convention, where the conservative AFL forces consolidated their power in the WEB and expelled many of the progressives, including Brookwood Labor College, labeling them communistic, pro-Soviet, antireligious, and a threat to the labor movement (Morris, 1958). James Maurer announced that he was forced to resign the presidency of the WEB because of certain distressing trends in the American workers' education movement. Tendencies he feared included the denial of the purpose of workers' education as an intelligent guide to a new social order; the encouragement of conducting workers' education programs in cooperation with state universities, rather than in independent educational organizations like Brookwood; and a proposed change in the WEB constitution that would deny the right of representation on the executive board of the WEB to all groups except the AFL and its affiliated international unions.

Coupled with the AFL's failure to support workers' education programs it could not control, economic and social changes in the early 1930s also hastened the decline of workers' education. The AFL, which never made a serious financial commitment to workers' education, ignored it completely in the face of the Depression. With its membership severely reduced, organized labor's thoughts were on survival not education. As a result, all 300 city labor colleges closed their doors by 1935. Even the independent workers' education programs suffered financial problems in this period. Most, including Brookwood, Barnard, Vineyard Shore, and other programs, were forced to close.

The WEB, responding to the wishes of the AFL and attempting to salvage workers' education, turned to the state universities to provide activities (Dwyer, 1976). These joint union-university education programs generally lasted one week during the summer, and then labor's presence faded from the campus until the next year. Most cases, involving universities in workers' education were not very successful. Thus, the first few years of the 1930s saw the fortunes of workers' education in deep decline.

Labor Education. The changing social, political, and economic conditions of the New Deal affected the very nature of workers' education, modifying its goals to such an extent that it was eventually renamed "labor education." The New Deal brought with it a rash of labor legislation, including the National Labor Relations Act, the Fair Labor Standards Act, and the Davis–Bacon Act, which helped to legitimatize the American labor movement. Combined with this legitimization, the social and economic climate of the country enhanced the rise of the Congress of Industrial Organizations (CIO) in 1935 and added to the upsurge of union membership, which swelled the ranks of CIO unions to 3.7 million members by 1937.

As a result of the meteoric growth of the labor movement and the impact of friendly labor laws, the educational needs of organized labor shifted. Education for social change was no longer the central concern in labor education as it had been in workers' education. Between 1935 and 1937, it seemed that new local unions were being formed daily. Contracts had to be negotiated, grievances processed, and local union meetings conducted. There simply were not enough union members who had the required leadership skills. It became necessary to train local union leaders in public speaking, parliamentary procedure, grievance handling, shop-steward skills, and other practical union subjects. Educationally, what this new era ushered in was known as labor education, and its goal was to educate for organizational imperatives of the union movement.

As this new wave of labor education developed in the latter part of the 1930s, the actual organizations responsible for the education shifted from city labor colleges and independent workers' education programs to individual unions. As mass production industries organized, labor education became an integral part of local unions. Education departments were established in new unions representing automobile, rubber, steel, and textile workers. In addition, older unions, such as the mineworkers and the machinists, began to offer labor education (Ware, 1946).

Even the federal government's entry into labor education during the depression sought practical education that could assist the labor movement. The Works Progress Administration (WPA) hired unemployed teachers and instructed them in the techniques of teaching adult workers. During the life of this project (1933–1943), the program conducted courses for one million workers in thirty-six states.

During World War II, labor education, like almost everything else, was subordinated to the war effort. However, with the cessation of hostilities and the return to civilian life of thousands of workers, labor-management relations became inflamed. During the war, wages had been kept down, but prices had managed to spiral upward. In contract negotiations of 1946, unions expected to make up lost ground. More American workers went on strike in 1946 than in any previous year. Every major industry in the United States suffered at least one strike. Federal legislators responded to this conflict swiftly and decisively, enacting the Taft–Hartley Labor Act, which attempted to curtail union power. In the highly industrialized states, legislation took more positive forms, laws creating institutes of labor-management relations at state universities "to promote harmony and cooperation between management and labor" (Public Laws, 1947).

Although the University of Wisconsin had been involved in both workers' education and labor education at least once a year since 1925, and Rutgers University had had a similar involvement since 1931, not until the period after World War II did several state universities in the industrial Northeast and Midwest begin year-round labor education programs in their extension divisions. These university programs, like their union counterparts, stressed utilitarian training to strengthen the union organization. In 1950, a study of university labor education programs concluded that "demand is growing throughout the labor movement for instruction in utilitarian 'tool' subjects like collective bargaining, public speaking, parliamentary procedure, and time study" (Kerrison, 1951).

With the influx of universities into labor education, however, it was only a matter of time before they began experimenting with liberalizing the curriculum and attempting to provide course progression. The first national effort to expand the curriculum occurred when eight university labor education programs received a grant from the Fund for Adult Education and established the Inter-University Labor Education Committee (IULEC) in 1951. In 1956, after the IULEC grant expired, the former executive secretary reported that "within the last few years, . . . there has been a noticeable broadening of the scope of programs, particularly with a view to including programs on international affairs, community participation and health programs" (Mire, 1956, p. 793). After the expiration of the IULEC grant in 1956, another central agency, the National Institute of Labor Education (NILE) was established for the effective promotion and development of cooperative labor education projects between unions and universities. Although the suggestions for broader curriculum content and the development of a systematic progression of curriculum developed out of the IULEC, it was NILE that began extensive experimentation in these new areas by subsidizing long-term labor education programs at several universities.

Labor Studies. As these long-term, liberal-arts-based programs for union members developed around the United States, offering credit-bearing degree programs for union people was the logical next step. Once again, changing social, economic, and political forces triggered the expansion from noncredit labor education to credit-bearing labor studies. The 1960s found American society wracked by a higher degree of internal turmoil than at any time since the Depression. Every institution within the society, including education, came under scrutiny. Among the goals of student demonstrators were the liberalization of admission policies and the establishment of more relevant curricula in such areas as urban, black, and Hispanic studies. Coupled with this threat from student activists, many in organized labor, alert to opportunities to increase labor's share of educational resources that higher education had disproportionately allocated to business, banking, industry, and agriculture, applied pressure for degree programs in labor studies. Parallel pressure to create degree programs came from university labor educators who found traditional, short-term, episodic "tool" courses, such as labor union administration and collective bargaining, insufficient to prepare union members and officials for the increasingly far-reaching and complex problems faced in the 1960s (Levine, 1966). Parenthetically, after World War II, union workers in the United States were better educated. By the early 1970s, the average member of the civilian work force had a high school diploma, and many had some college study. Given this increase in educational attainment, significant numbers of working people possessed the necessary credentials to enter institutions of higher education. In response to the general pressure in American society for credentialization, union workers have urged their union organization to concern itself with higher educational opportunities as a fringe benefit to enhance occupational mobility.

Labor-studies degree programs started in the latter half of the 1960s. In 1972, there were only seven such degree programs in the United States; in 1973, the number

jumped to twenty; and in 1975, it increased to forty-nine. There were between seventy-five and one hundred labor-studies degree programs in 1980, according to one estimate, and one author has tagged labor studies as a growth sector in higher education (Gray, 1976).

Not only higher education has been concerned with the development of labor studies, but the organized labor movement has also been involved. The UAW education department has urged community and junior colleges in areas of concentrated union membership to establish labor studies degree programs. The union has published a guide and curriculum design for colleges to use in implementing an associate degree program in labor studies. The AFL-CIO, in concert with Antioch College, is offering a labor studies degree program at its George Meany Labor Studies Center. Meanwhile, AFL-CIO affiliates, like the New York City Central Labor Council, have been instrumental in establishing and maintaining labor studies degree programs in local colleges (Stack & Hutton, 1980).

As with most new area studies, labor studies is not universally accepted as a viable academic pursuit. Many in academe do not understand what the area of labor studies really is, and labor studies faculty cannot yet agree on its philosophical underpinnings and curriculum parameters. At the same time that these faculty are striving for a common identity, higher education budgets are being severely restricted, causing program retrenchment, which forces academic administrators to scrutinize educational programs and eliminate academic duplication. Today, some academics believe that labor studies is in fact just one aspect of an older area study that also focuses on the study of labor-industrial relations. To illustrate the differences and similarities between labor studies and industrial relations, the next section examines briefly their intellectual heritage.

Key Issues in Labor Studies. Many key issues confront the labor education and labor studies professional in higher education today. Chiefly, they center on labor studies' search for identity, and they involve such questions as (1) Is labor studies a viable area of study, or is it one aspect of industrial relations? (2) Does labor studies fill a void in labor education, or is it simply an attempt to gain academic respectability? (3) Should labor studies provide a general liberal arts education or is career-oriented, applied social science research more appropriate? (4) Who will control the academic program—the labor movement or the community of labor education scholars?

Industrial relations versus labor studies. Given the conditions of university budgets, the question of the integrity of the subject matter of labor studies vis-à-vis industrial relations is crucial. Though not every faculty member in labor studies can agree on a definition of labor studies, all agree that the subject is distinct from industrial relations. Golatz (1977) contends that the study of labor transcends collective bargaining and spills over into the psychological, sociological, and political dynamics of worldwide phenomena. "Thus labor is no longer perceived as one aspect of industrial relations; instead industrial relations is viewed as one of the several areas on which the labor presence impinges" (p. 17).

Dwyer, Galvin, and Larson (1977) define labor studies as an interdisciplinary liberal arts area of study based in the social sciences with its parameters defined by the nature of work, the individual's relationship to work, the organizations workers form to protect and enhance their interests, and those institutions and nonwork phenomena that are affected by and, in turn, affect the work process and the workers.

Boyle (1977) agrees that labor studies is not industrial and labor relations because, like Golatz, he believes labor studies constitutes a discipline in its own right. "It deals with workers, their unions, their organizational policies, practices, structures, and activities. It encompasses the study of a world-wide social, economic, political, psychological and ideological mass movement which affects every aspect of national life in both the civilized world and developing areas of the world," (p. 142). No scholar in industrial relations has felt threatened enough by the nascent labor studies, or this analysis of their differences, to respond in writing, but some have orally rejected this argument. They believe that industrial relations provides unbiased, objective scholarship in labor-management relations, and that it is labor studies that is biased toward labor, not industrial relations toward management. In short, labor studies, to these industrial relations scholars, is nothing more than an ideological intrusion (i.e., university study with a working-class bias masquerading as objective scholarship).

Labor education versus labor studies. Not only is the value of labor studies being questioned by those academics in other subject matter areas that impinge on the study of labor, it is also being questioned from its very roots. Although labor studies traces its higher education lineage directly to the noncredit labor education extension programs developed after World War II, many university and college labor-education extension specialists believe that labor studies degree programs are detrimental to the educational needs of the labor movement. Labor education proponents fear that labor studies degree programs will siphon off the extension programs' vitally needed resources. Lieberthal (1977) contends that more and more priority will go to the credit and degree programs. "More and more faculty efforts will go to the imitation of on-campus activities including the writing for journals" (p. 243).

Lieberthal (1980a) further hypothesizes that labor studies degree programs will educate the best working-class students out of the labor movement and into middle-class professional occupations. This will occur, he contends, because credit courses, degree programs, tests, and grades have nothing to do with education, but are merely unnecessary trappings that promote the vocational ends of higher education, middle-class professional occupations.

Finally, the supporters of labor education extension programs fear that the subject matter they teach is not as interesting to reach as the courses in the labor-studies degree programs. Lieberthal (1980b) blames conventional university wisdom "that treats steward training, contract bargaining, and union administration as if they are simple intellectually unchallenging subjects" (p. 70). Against this conventional wisdom, he argues that the noncredit instructor, like the credit instructor, (1) must thoroughly know the subject matter to be taught; (2) must utilize analytical ability in the development of stimulating ideas and discussion material; and (3) must possess teaching ability to present and prepare classroom material (Lieberthal, 1980a).

Many labor studies professionals place greater reliance on labor studies than on labor education, but Nash has been most critical of traditional labor education. Nash (1978b) views university labor education as a marginal occupation, not respected in the academy or in the labor movement. The labor educator is a facilitator of "communication and transaction between organized labor and higher education, two institutions that for most of their pasts have been suspicious of, if not hostile to each other. Ironically, despite—or perhaps because of—this mediating function and the background of most as union activists, labor educators have a marginal relationship to both institutions" (p. 40). Nash (1978b) believes that labor educators are discriminated against in academia because they are perceived as partisan supporters of union objectives both inside and outside institutions of higher learning, and as such they need to be watched closely. This discrimination is further compounded by the fact that most labor education programs are administratively housed in the extension division of the institution; a division treated at best as a stepchild of the college or university. So prevalent is the feeling that extension education has been discriminated against by the higher education community, that the authors of a major study of university labor education did not believe it necessary to document that claim (Rogin & Rachlin, 1968).

Not only are labor educators treated as second-class citizens in the academy, they also "lack the authority and professional stature to persuade union leaders to accept labor education as an effective support for achieving the aims of unions" (Nash, 1978b, p. 51). As the role of the labor leaders grows exceedingly complex, they turn not to the labor educator for knowledge, but to actuaries, lawyers, economists, and other professionals. The traditional professional-client model does not apply to labor educators and union leaders. Nash suggests four reasons why this relationship never developed.

First, the very nature of union leadership and the political nature of the union stress the transfer of customs, insights, information, and beliefs orally. In contrast, "the formal training and educational methods of universities are not welcome in this social arrangement (Nash, 1978b). Therefore, rather than stimulating critical thinking or pioneering investigation, union leaders want education to promote and gain support for their policies (Linton, 1965).

Second, union leaders often sit on the boards of directors

of universities, as well as on the advisory boards of the labor extension programs; and, in these capacities, they approve appointments of directors of labor programs, and influence, review, and evaluate the types of educational programs offered ("Joint Statement," 1977). Such activities negate labor's role as a client.

Third, some labor educators believe that their close association with union leaders "makes labor education too conformist to union official attitudes and prevents them from exploring social problems that are not of prime concern to the union or from treating controversial subjects like civil rights" (Rogin & Rachlin, 1968, p. 193).

Fourth, the labor educator is concerned with losing the union leader's support if that leader believes that the education program is producing too many dissidents, some of whom might run against him at the next election. Nash (1978a), therefore, concludes that the relationship more closely resembles a customer requesting the services he or she desires than a client seeking advice of the professional.

The controversy then is between labor educators who believe that they are doing a worthwhile job and want to maintain the status quo, and others, like Nash, who believe that labor education is at best a marginal occupation adding little to the academy or to the labor movement. Labor education critics believe that a shift to labor studies can enhance the labor faculty's position within both the institution of higher learning and the labor movement. Nash (1978a) contends that university labor education does not have the integrated sequence of courses, the activities, or the stable student body that are an integral part of the social structure of the typical college, and that a distinct body of codified knowledge about unions and the world of work has not been defined. As a consequence, there is no structure for creating, ordering, and transmitting knowledge of labor and work to persuade its union clients that labor education can solve their problems (Nash, 1978a). To remedy this situation, labor educators must concentrate on those areas that will legitimize them in the academy while enhancing their status with the union clientele. Nash, therefore, supports the move toward labor studies degree programs, believing this change may solve these weaknesses in labor education.

Generalist versus applied social scientist. Taking Nash's arguments to their logical conclusion means that labor faculties, as they conform to the academy, will need to become subject matter specialists. Lieberthal (1977), on the other hand, lauds the generalist perspective of labor educators. "While a generalist cannot penetrate the mysteries of a discipline as profoundly as a specialist, the generalist can frequently meet the needs of union people with greater effectiveness" (p. 240). Nash (1978a) counters that one of the problems with labor educators is the cursory or superficial knowledge that they bring to a given subject area.

This debate between the generalist and the specialist is not confined to those who disagree about the efficacy of labor studies degree programs; even among those who support degree programs there is controversy. Three distinct schools of thought are prevalent. The first includes those who believe that Lieberthal's notion of a generalist should be transferred to academic credit education. The faculty member should be a "renaissance scholar," fluent in any subject that might be of interest to the student. A second group (its members call themselves generalists) believes that labor studies as a social science study can make workers effective union activists once they are made aware of "their history, the nature of work in this and other cultures, and theories of work and social organizations" (Goode, 1980, p. 69). A third group, consisting of specialists, believes that labor studies will gain importance only if its teaching is based on thorough applied social science research in areas that can aid unions in solving their problems. Applied research, geared to labor's concerns, in such social science disciplines as economics, political science, psychology, and sociology is of utmost importance to the specialist (Craypo, 1979). This debate is between the generalist, who believes that once working people understand the nature of their predicament, they will be prepared to remedy their situation, and the specialist, who believes the nature of society is so complex that working people need to be prepared with new tools (i.e., applied social science research) to remedy their plight.

The question of control. Maybe the most important question for university labor programs is who controls the program—the community of labor education professionals or the client group, the labor movement. This is not a new concern. The struggles within the WEB of the 1920s centered on who would control the educational program—the progressive educators or the conservative leadership of the AFL. Today, as higher education faces the threat of declining enrollment, labor studies stand poised, ready to introduce a previously underrepresented clientele to higher education, the adult union worker (Gray, 1976). Many colleges and universities today employ the tenets of unions—higher education cooperation to recruit adult union workers into college degree programs (Stack & Hutton, 1980). Although this alliance between unions and the academy is new and may prove to be of mutual benefit to those involved, the question of control may become the central concern in this relationship.

Even though many, if not most, union and university labor educators oppose the shift to labor studies degree programs, these programs continue to develop among colleges and universities. The various degree programs fall into four basic administrative categories. First, and most prevalent, is the labor studies department within traditional colleges. Examples are Rutgers University and Pennsylvania State University where the academic departments grew out of noncredit labor education extension programs. Many colleges and universities that have labor studies departments, but did not have a labor education extension tradition, received assistance in establishing their degree programs from nearby state universities with ongoing labor education extension programs.

The second model was initially developed by District Council 37, American Federation of State, County, and Municipal Employees (AFSCME) in New York City. The union invited the College of New Rochelle to establish a degree program for union members at union headquarters. More recently, District 65, UAW has developed a similar program with Hofstra University, and Local 237 of the International Brotherhood of Teamsters has begun a program with the City College of New York. Though labor studies is an option, these programs generally tend to be broad-based, liberal arts degree offerings, specifically adapted for union workers (Taaffee & Litwak, 1980).

The third model was pioneered at Wayne State University through its University Studies and Weekend College Program. Working closely with the UAW, the college developed a creative delivery system and an innovative curriculum, designed to provide traditionally denied working adults access to higher education. Currently, the Wayne State faculty, utilizing a grant from the Fund for the Improvement of Post-Secondary Education, has established a program called "To Educate the People Consortium," which is assisting other colleges to implement the curriculum and delivery system in an attempt to educate working people (Stack & Pascal, 1980). This program, too, contains a labor studies component, though much of the education is general, liberal arts degree courses.

The final model and the least prevalent is the "Labor College." In this model, the entire undergraduate degree program is developed with a "labor studies focus" (Dwyer & Torgoff, 1980).

Summary. Throughout the twentieth century, educational programs for union workers have continued unabated. At various times, organized labor actively supported these endeavors, and at other times the unions' interest in this education waned. Three distinct historical phases—workers' education, labor education, and most recently labor studies—have been delineated. Labor studies' impact has been chiefly in institutions of higher learning, where many unions have focused their efforts to expand educational opportunities for union members and their families.

With the development of labor studies degree programs, many key issues confront labor education, and labor studies professionals. Among these key issues are the debate between labor studies and industrial relations; labor education and general education for union workers; and also the question of the scope of the labor studies curriculum, and the locus of control between the academy and the labor movement.

Because of labor studies' recent advent on the campus, and the preoccupation to legitimatize its role in academe, many important educational questions have not been addressed. For instance, there is little or no empirical information on the student body, especially on the comparative achievement of students in labor studies programs. In addi-

tion, the profession has yet to debate, let alone agree on, the core competencies necessary for a labor studies graduate.

Generally, the issues found in the literature evolve from labor studies' search for identity. Only when the profession feels sufficiently secure will it move to explore educational issues that signal the maturation process of an accepted area of study.

Richard E. Dwyer

See also Adult Education; Industrial Training.

REFERENCES

Boyle, G. Functions of university labor education programs. *Labor Studies Journal*, 1977, *2*, 139–144.

Craypo, C. Introduction, special issue on the impact of changing corporate structure and technology. *Labor Studies Journal*, 1979, *3*, 195–200.

Dwyer, R. Union-university cooperation: The education of organized labor at the university. *Journal of General Education*, 1976, *28*, 145–160.

Dwyer, R. Evolution of the Affiliated Schools in workers' education from coordination to educational service. *Labor Studies Journal*, 1977, *3*, 37–49. (a)

Dwyer, R. Workers' education, labor education, labor studies: A historical delineation. *Review of Educational Research*, 1977, *47*, 179–207. (b)

Dwyer, R.; Galvin, M.; & Larson, S. Labor studies: In quest of industrial justice. *Labor Studies Journal*, 1977, *2*, 95–131.

Dwyer, R., & Torgoff, C. A labor college. In H. Stack & C. Hutton (Eds.), *Building New Alliances: Labor Unions and Higher Education*. San Francisco: Jossey-Bass, 1980.

Golatz, H. Labor studies: New kid on campus. *Labor Studies Journal*, 1977, *2*, 15–22.

Goode, B. Liberal education for labor. *Labor Studies Journal*, 1980, *5*, 62–69.

Gray, L. Labor studies credit and degree programs: A growth sector of higher education. *Labor Studies Journal*, 1976, *1*, 34–51.

Joint statement on effective cooperation between organized labor and higher education. *Labor Studies Journal*, 1977, *1*, 291–295.

Kerrison, I. *Workers' Education at the University Level*. New Brunswick, N.J.: Rutgers University Press, 1951.

Levine, H. Will labor educators meet today's challenges? *Industrial Relations*, 1966, *5*, 97–106.

Lieberthal, M. On the academization of labor education. *Labor Studies Journal*, 1977, *1*, 235–245.

Lieberthal, M. Osmotic process in labor education and labor studies. *Labor Studies Journal*, 1980, *5*, 115–123. (a)

Lieberthal, M. Tool subjects as disciplines. *Labor Studies Journal*, 1980, *5*, 70–71. (b)

Linton, T. *A Historical Examination of the Purposes and Practices of the United Automobile Workers of America, 1936–1959*. Ann Arbor: University of Michigan School of Education, 1965.

Mire, J. Developments in university labor education programs. *Monthly Labor Review*, 1956, *79*, 793–795.

Morris, J. *Conflict within the AFL*. Ithaca, N.Y.: Cornell University Press, 1958.

Nash, A. Labor education, labor studies, and the knowledge factor. *Labor Studies Journal*, 1978, *3*, 5–18. (a)

Nash, A. The university labor educator: A marginal occupation. *Industrial and Labor Relations Review*, 1978, *32*, 40–55. (b)

Perkins, G. Address. In *Proceedings of the Fifth National Convention of the Workers' Education Bureau, 1927*. New York: Workers' Education Bureau, 1927.

Peters, R., & McCarrick, J. Roots of public support for labor education, 1900–1945. *Labor Studies Journal*, 1976, *1*, 109–129.

Public Law 307. *Statutes of the State of New Jersey*, 1947.

Report of the Executive Committee Workers' Education Bureau of America to the Fifth Annual Convention in New York City, April 22–24, 1927. New York: Workers' Education Bureau, 1927.

Rogin, L., & Rachlin, M. *Labor Education in the United States*. Washington, D.C.: National Institute of Labor Education, 1968.

Shafer, R. Working People's Education. *North American Review*, 1921, *214*, 786–794.

Stack, H., & Hutton, C. (Eds.). *Building New Alliances: Labor Unions and Education*. San Francisco: Jossey-Bass, 1980.

Stack, H., & Pascal, O. The University Studies and Weekend College Program: Beyond access. In H. Stack & C. Hutton (Eds.), *Building New Alliances: Labor Unions and Higher Education*. San Francisco: Jossey-Bass, 1980.

Taaffee, T., & Litwak, E. A union campus. In H. Stack & C. Hutton (Eds.), *Building New Alliances: Labor Unions and Higher Education*. San Francisco: Jossey-Bass, 1980.

Taft, P. *Organized Labor in American History*. New York: Harper & Row, 1964.

Ware, C. *Labor Education in Universities: A Study of University Programs*. New York: American Labor Education Service, 1946.

LABORATORY EXPERIENCES IN TEACHER EDUCATION

Most teacher-educators subscribe to the position that good teacher-preparation curricula should contain more than college courses and student teaching experiences. They agree that teacher trainees should be provided with a set of experiences that fall somewhere between "learning about" teaching and "doing it" in the field, that serve to bridge the gap between principles and practices (e.g., Conant, 1964; Cruickshank, 1971). These experiences should actively involve trainees in laboratory and/or clinical exercises intended to broaden their practical understanding of teaching and learning in schools, to facilitate acquisition of selected teaching skills appropriate for use in classrooms, to increase attitudes of self-confidence in themselves and understanding of youngsters, and to encourage transfer of knowledge of teaching and learning from university or college courses to field settings.

Indeed, the position favoring such pre-student-teaching laboratory experiences has been provided the status of a convention in teacher education by the adoption of National Council for the Accreditation of Teacher Education (NCATE) standards for basic teacher education programs. These standards mandate a professional-studies compo-

nent that includes laboratory and clinical experiences (Standards for Accreditation, 1979). Data from recent surveys of teacher-education practice suggest that inclusion of such laboratory experiences as simulation, microteaching, protocol materials, and computer-assisted instruction is the rule rather than the exception in American preservice teacher preparation (Johnson, 1968; Joyce et al., 1977; Kuuskraa, Morra, & Brashear, 1977; Sherwin, 1974).

Despite apparent agreement concerning the desirability of pre-student-teaching laboratory experiences, at present we do not understand which experiences should be included, how they should be organized, and, most important, what they supply to a teacher-education program. This article will attempt to offer answers to such questions, to the extent they exist, and will suggest avenues of pursuit when such answers are not currently available.

The variety of pre-student-teaching laboratory experiences offered by American teacher-education institutions is large and varied. Yet they lack consistency and order. Most are not based on well-understood, tested, and refined models or principles, but at best they grow from a variety of assumptions about what good teaching is and how it can be trained. Often, these experiences reflect nothing more than the feelings and intuitions of independent teacher educators concerning what constitutes worthwhile or appropriate activities.

Through the literature on teacher education are scattered hundreds of reports of individual efforts to provide experiences that link university or college course work with the practice of student teaching. Most of these reports amount to statements of "We-did-this-and-we-think-it-works." Because they are not soundly based in any principles of learning or teaching or because they do not offer verification of such principles or test aspects of models applied to teacher education, these efforts are of limited value. The success they report can only be understood in terms of the idiosyncratic characteristics of the individuals engaged in the activity. They do not illuminate or inform additional efforts in other settings.

Occasionally, through this literature, exceptions stand out. For the past fifteen years a number of efforts have been advanced to design and test pre-student-teaching laboratory experiences that proceed from supportable principles of teaching, learning, and professional growth and that yield information useful both for improving the effects of those activities on their participants and for replicating their results in other settings. The variety, even within this narrower body of literature, is still great. The types of activities reported are diverse. The permutations within each type are more numerous still. Because of this diversity, it will be impossible to consider in these pages all or even most of these activities. Instead, attention is focused here on the three types of pre-student-teaching laboratory experiences that appear to dominate the field: microteaching, protocol materials, and simulations, including those assisted by computer.

An examination of these types of pre-student-teaching

laboratory experiences reveals that they appear to aim at a limited number of instructional outcomes, including acquisition of concepts, principles, skills, and attitudes. We have therefore examined each type of laboratory experience by asking, "What does this experience have as its instructional goal? How well is that goal accomplished? Why does the experience seem to succeed or fail in achieving that goal? What needs to be done to increase success?"

Microteaching. In the early 1960s some educator-researchers at Stanford University recognized the significance of newly developed videotape technology for providing teacher trainees with immediate "knowledge of results" about their teaching performance. Coupling this capability with an emphasis on mastery of tightly defined teaching skills and with learning experiences based on exemplary models of teaching behavior, the Stanford group developed the concept of microteaching (Allen, 1966).

In the following years other researchers and teacher educators attempted to look more closely at microteaching and the possibilities it offers for improving teacher education. The process was taken apart and its components examined and weighed. Its principles have been adapted to in-service as well as preservice training programs. Finally, its effects on teaching performance have been assessed.

First, a definition of the term "microteaching." Examination of the original Stanford work and subsequent reports from other sources concerning microteaching suggests that, in its most complete form, microteaching is distinguished by seven characteristics. First, the trainee is taught the characteristics of a particular teaching skill, for example "verbal redirection." This instruction generally involves both an explanation of the skill and an exhibition of a model of the skill in use. Second, the subject trainee teaches a lesson to a small number of pupils, generally four to six. During this lesson the trainee's aim is to utilize the target skill whenever appropriate. Third, the lesson is of short duration, 6 to 10 minutes. Fourth, the lesson is recorded. Fifth, within a few minutes after completing the lesson the trainee receives feedback by viewing a replay of the lesson. Sixth, within a short time after viewing the replay the trainee replans and reteaches the lesson to a new group of pupils. Seventh, this teach-review-reteach cycle continues until both the training coordinator and the trainee are satisfied.

More than any other form of pre-student-teaching laboratory experience, microteaching has been the subject of research aimed at understanding the effects of variation in its basic components. One component receiving considerable attention is the model used to acquaint trainees with the target skill. Results of research in this area strongly suggest that use of a model during initial instruction benefits skill acquisition. However, the form that the model should take, written or filmed, is still in question. A general rule of thumb may be that the form of the model depends on the nature of the skill—for example, a nonverbal skill requires a visual model (see Allen et al.,

1967; Gall, Dinning, & Banks, 1972; Koran, Snow, & McDonald, 1971).

A second component is the nature of the pupils taught by the trainee during the teaching phase of the program. Conclusions here must be quite tentative. With respect to initial performance of the skill, it appears that use of peers as "pupils" may help trainees, perhaps because they feel more comfortable with or can elicit empathy from their fellows. However, with respect to the tendency to complete the transfer from training to the classroom, the use of youngsters as pupils may be more advantageous (see Johnson & Pancrazio, 1970; Steinbach & Butts, 1969).

A third component of microteaching that has received attention of researchers is the type of feedback provided to trainees. Though the initial design of microteaching utilized videotape as feedback source, no researchers have been able to establish the superiority of videotape over much less expensive audiotape, at least when the target skills involve verbal teacher behavior (Acheson, Tucker, & Zigler, 1974; Gall, 1972; Hiscox & Van Mondfrans, 1972).

A fourth component is the supervision offered trainees during feedback. First, though providing one-on-one supervision is expensive in terms of personnel time, there seems to be general agreement that the presence of a supervisor enhances training effects (McIntyre, 1972; Pisano, 1974). Second, it appears that to be most effective in bringing about change between teach-reteach cycles, the supervisor should adopt a directive as opposed to a nondirective posture (Kise, 1971).

Considerable research effort has been aimed at verifying the effects of microteaching in trainees. The specific instructional outcomes of microteaching that have attracted the most attention are technical teaching skills and trainee attitudes. In the last fifteen years, a prominent movement in teacher education has been the inclusion of the "technical skills of teaching" as objectives of credential programs (for a summary of this development, see McKnight, 1978). Various authors have suggested that the task of teaching may be seen to include the employment of a variety of specific technical skills, technical to teaching because they may be used independently of the content being taught and skills because they are purposeful teacher behaviors, the successful exhibition of which can be refined with practice (Allen & Ryan, 1969; Berliner, 1969; Gage, 1972; Smith, Cohen, & Pearl, 1969). A wide variety of technical skills have been proposed, including set induction, closure, probing and higher-order questioning, reinforcement, planned repetition, cue attendance, responsiveness, and inference generation. While the experimental work needed to verify the place of these skills in the teaching act has proceeded slowly (for some examples of work in this area see Berliner, 1976; Gage, 1976; Peterson, Marx, & Clark, 1978), the inclusion of technical skills as content in teacher education programs has been common in recent years. As an example, most competency-based teacher-education programs propose to develop technical skills of teaching in their graduates. More important for our consideration here, pre-student-teaching laboratory experiences have been seen as especially appropriate places for providing training in such skills.

Most teacher educators include microteaching in their programs for the purpose of offering training in the technical skills of teaching. Such inclusion is based on two assumptions: the first that skill training via microteaching will cause trainees initially to acquire the targeted technical skill rapidly and with a high degree of efficiency, and the second that microteaching will ensure that the targeted skills thus acquired will be used in the classroom subsequent to training. When searching for support for these assumptions in the literature, one must distinguish between two basic measurement approaches used by researchers. Some researchers have measured performance by utilizing what Rosenshine (1970) has called "high-inference" measurement instruments. These instruments require an observer to record impressions and/or estimations of characteristics of the teaching/learning encounter that cannot be observed directly but can only be inferred. Such characteristics might include teachers' "effectiveness," "enthusiasm," or "organization" or students' "interest" or "involvement." Other researchers have utilized "low-inference" instruments that require the observer to identify and record the occurrence of specific overt behaviors such as questions asked by teachers or time within a lesson devoted to student talk. To reach conclusions concerning the effects of microteaching on skill acquisition, it is necessary to focus, in the following pages, on those research projects that attempted to measure skill utilization with low-inference instrumentation.

Following this strategy, a search of the literature reveals a preponderance of evidence in support of the first assumption on which use of microteaching should be based—that is, that microteaching training increases initial acquisition of target skills (for examples of such research see Borg, 1972; Kissock, 1971; Perrott, 1976; Reed, Van Mondfrans, & Smith, 1970; Saunders et al., 1975; Shea, 1974). If initial acquisition of technical skills were the only criteria for including microteaching as a pre-student-teaching laboratory experience, teacher educators would be well advised by these results to make such an inclusion.

The weight of evidence supporting the second assumption—that microteaching increases the range of technical skills actually employed by the trainee in the classroom subsequent to training—is, however, much less substantial. While Borg et al. (1969) and Raymond (1973) reported that microteaching trainees demonstrated a significant increase in the use of target skills, other investigators have not succeeded in obtaining similar results (Copeland, 1975; Copeland & Doyle, 1973; Katz, 1976; Kissock, 1971; Peterson, 1973).

Though the results at first seem disappointing, further examination of these reports reveals an interesting tendency. Other researchers have performed similar studies using as subjects experienced teachers who are enrolled in in-service training. These studies with in-service sub-

jects report that microteaching has considerable effect on classroom performance (Borg, 1972; Borg et al., 1969; Perrott et al., 1975; Stowitschek & Hofmeister, 1974). Interestingly, in the 1969 study, which yielded positive results for microteaching with preservice subjects, Borg and his colleagues used the same materials (the Far West Laboratory's Minicourse Program) that had produced good results with in-service teachers. In this study, while Borg and his colleagues noted significant results with the preservice subjects, they also noted that the gains for their experimental group were not nearly so great as were gains exhibited by in-service teachers who had taken the same program.

Such tendencies as these require further speculation. Why do beginning teachers not benefit from microteaching experiences as well as experienced teachers do? Examination of the raw data in these studies, wherever such data are available, opens interesting possibilities regarding this disparity. First, it will be remembered that there exists considerable support for the proposition that when measured in the laboratory at the close of training, subjects demonstrate that they have acquired the targeted skills. If lack of use of the targeted skills in the field following training is to be attributed to the subjects' simply forgetting the skills, then one would expect to find a high rank-order correlation between subjects' scores on the laboratory test and those on the field test, but in an examination of laboratory and field-test scores, no correlation was detected. Subjects who scored highest on the laboratory test were just as likely to score below their fellow subjects on the field test as they were to score above them. This tendency suggests that simple lack of retention—forgetting—cannot explain declining scores on field tests. It suggests that, instead, other relatively powerful variables are affecting the tendency of beginning teacher trainees to utilize the target skills in their student teaching classrooms.

In an effort to identify variables influencing trainees' use of target skills in classrooms subsequent to training, Copeland (1977, 1978) conducted a series of studies, the results of which suggest that the cooperating teachers with whom the trainees work in classrooms after completing microteaching training influence the trainees' use of the targeted skills in at least two ways. In the first, labeled "direct influence," cooperating teachers who have been trained in techniques of instructional supervision (Boyan & Copeland, 1978) appear to offer sufficient support and encouragement to assure student teachers' use of target skills in the classroom after training. The second, and in many ways the more intriguing way in which cooperating teachers influence student teacher classroom behavior, was labeled by Copeland "indirect influence." His results suggest that student teachers who taught with cooperating teachers who consistently used the targeted skills were significantly more likely to use the skills themselves. This tendency did not appear, however, to be the result of a straightforward modeling effect, as was initially hypothesized. Instead, it appeared to relate to the effect of the pupils who had been taught first by the cooperating teacher and subsequently by the student teacher.

Here Doyle and Ponder's (1975) conception of a classroom ecological system appears to aid understanding. It may be that the cooperating teacher's tendency to use or not use a particular teaching skill became, over time, an accepted part of the ecological system of the classroom. That is, the skill's use was an accustomed part of the ongoing behavior patterns in those rooms where the cooperating teacher used the skill. When entering such classrooms to teach, the student teacher's observation of the cooperating teacher was not necessary. If the student teacher simply attempted to use the skill previously acquired via microteaching, its use would be accepted as normal for that classroom's ecological system and the other components of the system, in this case the pupils, would respond appropriately. The student teacher would thus experience success and become more likely to use the skill. Conversely, if a student teacher had as part of his or her tentative teaching repertoire a skill acquired previously in a microteaching program, and attempted to use it in a classroom in which the skill was not a part of the current ecological system, the other components of the system would be less likely to respond to the skill's use. Lack of such response would result in a decreased likelihood that the student teacher would use the skill in the future.

Consider again the results, cited above, which showed consistent positive transfer from microteaching to the classroom when experienced teachers were the subjects of the research. A characteristic of microteaching training when applied to experienced teachers (via such packages as the Far West Laboratory's Minicourses) is that the subjects use their *own* pupils when they teach the microlessons. As they continue the teach-review-reteach cycle, not only may experienced teachers be training themselves, they may be training their pupils as well. Experienced teachers' participation in microteaching training may initiate changes in the ecological system of their classrooms. Pupils learn to respond to the skills. Thus, the likelihood of future use of the skills is increased. On the other hand, student teachers who typically experience microteaching training in laboratories separate from their student teaching assignments have no opportunity to shape the system into which they will move to engage in student teaching. The likelihood of their future use of the target skills is not enhanced by unintentional pupil training.

These findings suggest that if trainees are to acquire specific technical skills of teaching, microteaching is an appropriate beginning. They also suggest, however, that microteaching alone is not sufficient. If student teachers are to continue use of skills acquired via microteaching during pre-student-teaching laboratory experiences, steps must be taken to ensure that the student teaching environments they enter subsequent to microteaching are supportive of their newly acquired skills. Either the cooperating teachers should be trained to give direct supervisory support that will reinforce the student teachers' use of the target skills, or the cooperating teachers must use the target skills in their own teaching so that use of the skills is an accepted part of their classroom ecological systems.

In addition to aiding in the acquisition of technical skills of teaching, microteaching may also have as an appropriate goal the modification of credential students' attitudes. Attitudes of teachers toward pupils, toward the subject matter they teach, toward the teaching act, and even toward themselves as teachers have long been subjects of interest in teacher education. As an example, teachers' attitudes toward themselves as persons, their self-concept, have been studied by a number of researchers. Positive self-esteem and a sense of personal adequacy held by teachers have been related to generalized success in teaching (Garvey, 1970; Hatfield, 1961). More specifically, pupils of teachers whose self-concept is higher demonstrate higher academic achievement than do pupils of teachers with lower self-concept (Sears & Hilgard, 1964; Hamacheck, 1971).

It is not surprising, then, that student teacher self-confidence has been a dependent variable of interest in microteaching research. Huber and Ward (1969) reported that participants in microteaching evidenced increased confidence in themselves and in their teaching abilities. Stanton (1978) found significant differences in scores that favored subjects who participated in microteaching on the Tennessee Self-concept Scale. These higher scores were interpreted to mean an increase in overall level of self-esteem, which is characteristic of persons who, like themselves, feel they have worth and value, have confidence in themselves, and act accordingly. The above findings are supported by those by Belt (1967) and Randall (1972).

Several researchers have reported shifts in other attitudes attributable to microteaching. For example, Jaus (1977) and Sparks and McCallon (1974) found that subjects acquired positive attitudes toward the content of their practice lessons—for example, a process approach to science, as a result of microteaching involvement. Similar findings are reported by Stanley (1970).

In summary, there appears to be a considerable research base supporting the inclusion of microteaching as a pre-student-teaching laboratory experience in teacher education. Participation in microteaching appears to assure initial acquisition of selected technical skills of teaching and to be associated with shifts in participants' attitudes. Further, skills acquired by doing microteaching may be used in student teaching classrooms subsequent to training *if* the nature of those classrooms supports such use.

Microteaching is, however, a relatively expensive training technique, because one-on-one supervision is normally required to provide adequate feedback. Access to different pupils for each teach-reteach lesson is difficult. As with all training techniques, the benefits and costs must be weighed by the user.

Protocol Materials. With considerable support from the U.S. Office of Education in the early 1970s, a number of projects across the United States were undertaken to develop a new technique for teacher education: protocol materials. The original concept of protocol materials was records—filmed, videotaped, audio-recorded or written—of events of educational significance that illustrate concepts. Though the concepts may originate from fields such as psychology, sociology, anthropology, or philosophy, they must have particular relevance for categorizing and understanding teaching and learning behaviors in classrooms. By presenting a set of protocol materials that contain a series of events depicting a particular concept, teacher educators hope that their students will acquire the concept, be able to recognize its occurrence in classrooms, and thus be able to respond more intelligently and purposefully to classroom events.

Approximately 140 separate protocol materials products have been developed as a result of this effort, and most are currently available from the individual developers or from the National Resource Dissemination Center at the University of South Florida.

Cooper (1975) has pointed out that the greatest proportion of funds and energies in the protocol projects was directed at development of the materials rather than their evaluation. As a result, efforts to evaluate the effects of protocol materials on student teachers have been less than were hoped for. Researchers who have studied the effects of protocol materials have focused on three types of educational outcomes hypothesized to result from their use: acquisition of concepts, of technical teaching skills, and of attitudes. Each of these outcomes is considered below.

Classrooms are very complicated places. Large numbers of people, with a variety of purposes, interact in diverse ways in a small area. Much that takes place in classrooms is peculiar, if not unique, to the classroom environment. One of the primary tasks of new teachers is to develop ways of making conceptual order out of the apparent diversity of the classrooms into which they enter. They must be able to see the myriad persons, things, processes, and interactions they encounter not as unique items unlike any other but as examples of a much smaller number of understood classes of things and events.

Perceiving such order in classrooms depends upon the possession of concepts. Bruner wrote of the utility of concepts when he observed that "in order to cope with the environment we categorize: we render discriminately different things equivalent . . . we respond to them in terms of their class membership rather than their uniqueness" (Bruner, Goodnow, & Austin, 1956, p. 1). While a beginning teacher may perceive different students as they move hither and yon about the classroom, each with apparently different direction, speed and style, an experienced teacher will categorize each instance of pupil movement as being appropriately necessary for the learning task (e.g., returning a book to a shelf, beginning work in a learning center) or inappropriate movement (e.g., moving closer to a friend for conversation, beginning a dispute over possession of a booklet). The experienced teacher's ability to recognize individual pupil movement as examples of these

two classes of pupil movement—appropriate and inappropriate—allows that teacher to deal intelligently with the classroom environment, to make decisions, and to act on them.

Acquisition of a conceptual scheme that lends order and meaning to the diversity of classrooms is a crucial goal in the education of beginning teachers. Though it is a process that begins very early in a trainee's education and continues well beyond obtaining a credential, it is possible that much of the process can be intensely pursued during pre-student-teaching laboratory experiences.

In their book *Teachers for the Real World* (1969), Smith, Cohen, and Pearl observe: "Teachers fail because they have not been trained calmly to analyze new situations against a firm background of relevant theory. Typically, they base their interpretations of behavior on intuition and common sense. . . . If the teacher is incapable of understanding classroom situations, the actions he takes will often increase his difficulties" (pp. 28–29). Recognizing that concepts provide the basic elements of relevant theory, Smith and colleagues proposed the development of protocol materials for training prospective teachers to acquire the concepts necessary to effective teaching.

The most common question addressed by evaluators of protocol materials is "Can trainees perform better on tests of concept acquisition as a result of instruction using protocol materials?" This question, which focuses on immediate posttraining behavior, is usually addressed by displaying filmed vignettes of classroom behavior and asking trainees to identify instances of the target concepts as they occur. The evidence supporting a positive answer to this question appears to be solid. A number of evaluation efforts have reported significant effects of protocol materials on trainees' abilities to identify target concepts in such settings (Borg, 1973; Gliessman & Pugh, 1976; Pugh & Gliessman, 1976; Berliner et al., 1973; Kleucker, 1974). These findings are certainly encouraging. Because immediate posttreatment effects have been found so consistently, it is certainly possible that protocol materials have utility in concept training. Before such confidence can be realistically justified, however, the answers to a second research question must be examined.

In addition to verifying trainees' acquisition of concepts with immediate posttreatment measures, it is important to ask, "Are trainees able to use the concepts that were the targets of protocol-materials training to inform their subsequent understanding of classrooms?" This question asks whether the concepts, once acquired, in fact serve as organizing tools to aid the trainees' understanding of teaching and learning behaviors, especially subsequent to training when trainees acquire the full responsibility for the classroom. Though such a question could be answered by using research techniques such as interviews and ethnographic observations, no attempts to do so have been reported. The lack of attention to this question is both puzzling and unfortunate. Until it is addressed, the utility of protocol materials as a technique for increasing concept acquisition useful in teaching must remain in question.

There are two other areas of caution in the protocol-materials movement. For teachers, the utility of concepts derives from their ability to aid in the understanding of classrooms. Doyle (1977) has suggested that one of the most difficult tasks in learning to teach is "learning the texture of the classroom" (p. 2). Protocol materials seem eminently appropriate for teaching student teachers this texture, but in most cases they have not been used to do so. The large majority of the protocol materials currently available have as their content concepts related to teachers and their behavior, not pupils and learning behavior. Though the notion of protocol materials originally put forth by Smith and his colleagues clearly focused on learning, teaching, and their interaction, and though the concepts defined by Hudgins (1974) to guide protocol-materials developers clearly emphasized pupils as well as their teachers, the tendency of most developers has been to produce materials focused on teaching behavior: questioning, reinforcement, and presentation techniques. (There are exceptions, including materials developed at Southern Illinois University, which focused on features of black speech, and those developed at the Far West Laboratory for Educational Research and Development, which focused on pupils engaged in group processes.) Materials that teach only concepts of teacher behavior are not sufficient to improve understanding of the texture of classrooms.

The tendency to focus on teacher behavior may derive from a second area of caution in the protocol-materials movement. Though protocol materials were originally intended to teach concepts, as development proceeded through the early 1970s many developers grew to see their products' primary purpose as skill instruction. The emphasis turned from acquiring concepts that aid in understanding classrooms to acquiring skills that should be used when teaching. This evolution of purpose may be one reason why so many protocol materials focus on teacher behavior. It may also suggest that the protocol materials movement pulled up short of its true potential as envisioned by Smith and his colleagues. (See Cruickshank, 1974, for a discussion of this and other variations in the protocol materials movement.) Others would, however, maintain that regardless of the original purpose for developing protocol materials, the acquisition of teaching skills is a perfectly legitimate instructional goal. In fact, as much research effort has been devoted to verifying the ability of protocol materials to deliver skill facility as has been devoted to inquiry concerning concept acquisition.

The use of protocol materials for teaching skills in a program of pre-student-teaching laboratory experiences is based on the same two assumptions suggested above for supporting microteaching. The first assumption is that skill training via protocol materials will increase the probability that initial acquisition of the target skills will be both rapid and efficient. The second assumption is that use of protocol materials will extend the range of technical skills employed by the trainee in the classroom subsequent to training. A number of researchers have tested the first of these assumptions. Kleucker (1974) reported that learning to identify instances of a teaching skill depicted as a protocol of teaching behavior had a significant effect on the trainees' frequency of skill use when measured immediately after training in a simulated teaching situation. These findings are supported by those of Wagner (1973) and Santiesteban and Koran (1977). In each of these studies skill usage was seen to increase without overt practice but only as a result of observing protocols of the target skill. Koran, Snow, and McDonald (1971) found that supplementing practice with protocols depicting the target skill was necessary to produce significant change in the use of that skill. Gliessman, Pugh, and Bielat (1978) report similar results and also report a significant relationship between the level of concept acquisition and the level of skill utilization exhibited immediately after training in a laboratory setting.

The above evidence concerning the first assumption is quite encouraging and may even suggest that the elaborate practice characteristic of microteaching may not be necessary for acquisition of some teaching skills. Unfortunately, the second assumption—that the use of protocol materials extends the range of skills used subsequent to training in classrooms—has not been the subject of any disciplined inquiry that might give it support. No reports have been published of efforts to follow subjects from protocol training experiences into actual teaching situations and to verify increased use of the target skills after some passage of time. The issue of the transfer and persistence of skills after initial acquisition deserves examination. Confidence in the ability of protocol materials to deliver durable improvement in skill usage must await the results of such work.

Simulation. A third educational technique appropriate for pre-student-teaching laboratory experiences is simulation. Though they vary widely in both form and content, most simulation training experiences attempt to recreate, in a limited form, some aspect of the real world of teaching and then to engage the learner in an interaction with that recreation.

Gagné (1962) has suggested that training-oriented simulations should have at least three characteristics. First is representation. A simulation must reliably represent what it intends to simulate. It must portray those important situational characteristics in a way that maximizes fidelity to the portion of the real world that is the setting of the training. Transfer from training to work settings has been presumed by many to depend on such fidelity of representation. Gagné's second characteristic is control. Simulations must allow for control over critical situational characteristics so that planned variation can be employed. Trainees do not proceed willy-nilly through simulated training experiences, their movement governed by whim and chance. Their experiences must be contrived and controlled so as to maximize learning outcomes. When chance is part of a simulated experience, it is introduced systematically. Gagné's third characteristic of simulated training is omission. It is necessary that simulations be designed to omit certain situational characteristics. If all characteristics of the real world were contained in the activity, that activity would not be a simulation but a slice of reality. Situational characteristics may be omitted because they are considered unimportant and the expense of including them is not justified, or because their inclusion would pose danger to the trainee or lend an excess of unpredictability to the activity. One central task faced by simulation developers is, therefore, to decide which situational characteristics require inclusion to ensure sufficient fidelity to what is being simulated and which may be excluded in the interest of economy, safety, or control.

Strictly speaking, both pre-student-teaching laboratory experiences previously discussed here—protocol materials and microteaching—are simulations. They both attempt to represent aspects of the real world of teaching, limited by omitting unimportant characteristics, in a controlled manner that allows for purposeful training to occur. Megarry (1981) has proposed an array of simulation techniques for teacher education, organized by the amount of structure present. Techniques in this array range from open-ended activities with little structure, such as discussion of critical incidents and case studies, to very structured activities including simulation games, action mazes, and computer-based exercises. Protocol materials and microteaching fall in the middle of her array. The simulation activities we consider in this and the following sections— role playing, simulation games, and computer-based exercises—are distinguished by a somewhat higher degree of organization and structure.

In a relatively optimistic preview of simulation in teacher training, Cruickshank (1971) lists a number of advantages for including simulations in teacher education. They include (1) simulations establish a setting wherein the trainee is able to bring together theory and practice, (2) they require trainees to act instead of just thinking and to bear the consequences of their activities, (3) they offer an arena for action that is both physically and psychologically safe, (4) personal involvement in decisions and action create a high motivational quality, (5) they offer much more control over the training experience than the relatively haphazard experience of student teaching, (6) they broaden the training horizon by allowing trainees to engage in simulated situations not otherwise conveniently available (e.g., inner-city and rural schools, varieties of grade levels, team-teaching situations), and (7) personal and anecdotal experience suggests that they work, that they do have demonstrable training effects on participants.

While all Cruickshank's alleged advantages of simulation would seem quite beneficial, the last is most in need of evidence. Is participation in simulated teaching activities related to change in participants behavior? At the time that Cruickshank proposed these advantages, evidence for the benefits of simuation was sketchy. Unfortunately, the intervening years have not added appreciably to this evidence. The question of training effects is still uncertain, not because of conflicts in research findings but because of a lack of them. Gordon (1972) has observed that the open-ended nature of most simulation activities, their emphasis on processes, and a lack of appropriate instruments have combined to contribute to this lack of research findings.

One of the earliest and most elaborate attempts at teacher training via simulation, "Mr. Land's Sixth Grade" (Kersh, 1963), required a trainee, standing in a mockup of the front of a classroom, to watch a large rear-projection screen onto which were displayed filmed examples of pupil classroom behavior containing potential problems. The trainee was encouraged to decide upon and then to act out a response to the pupil behavior. The trainer would then select one of four filmed sequences for projection as a consequence of the trainee's intervention. The selected film clip might show the problem getting worse, persisting, or subsiding, depending on the judged adequacy of the trainee's response. "Mr. Land's Sixth Grade" was thus hypothesized to utilize an operant conditioning model to teach principles of behavior management. In addition to acquisition of such principles, participation in the simulation was also hypothesized to offer training in problem-solving skills—especially problem recognition and solution generation—and to shape the trainee's attitudes toward teaching and toward self. Evidence supporting these hypotheses is mixed. While some studies produced positive results (Kersh, 1965; Vlcek, 1966), others found none (Beals, 1970).

Other investigators followed Kersh's lead in developing simulated training materials (examples include "The Teaching Problems Laboratory," Cruickshank, Broadbent, & Bubb, 1967; "The Inner City Simulation Laboratory," Cruickshank, 1969; "Inner City Teaching," Diehl, 1979; "Project Insite," Marten, Denfee, & Buffie, 1970). In most of these projects, validation of training effects appears to have taken a back seat to the initial development effort. A few exceptions have reported data supporting the assumptions that simulation training delivers skill acquisition (Cruickshank & Broadbent, 1969; Gaffga, 1967; Marsh, 1979), though these skills tend to be of a type that is broader—problem solving, application of principles, decision making—than the technical skills that are the typical targets of other training such as microteaching. There is also evidence that participation in simulations may produce attitudinal shifts (Marsh, 1979; Smith, 1975).

What is the place of simulation in pre-student-teaching laboratory experiences today? Much of the development and research work in simulation for teacher education was done between 1965 and 1975. Though more recent efforts are much less numerous, one such project is that of Cruikshank et al. (undated), "Reflective Teaching," a technique that uses peers as "pupils" in simulated teaching situations, requires trainees to teach short lessons with specific learning outcomes, and encourages deliberate postteaching reflection and examination of the experience. Preliminary evaluation results offer strong support for the claim that reflective teaching promotes student's abilities to think in a more complex manner when considering the acts of teaching and learning. Reflective teaching also appears to reduce anxiety about teaching.

Cruickshank, Clingan, & Peters (1979) recently reviewed surveys of teacher-training methods and found evidence suggesting a decline in use of simulations by teacher educators in recent years (though he points out that the nature of the data reviewed does not allow this conclusion to be held with any confidence). He further speculates that if there has been a decline in simulation for teacher education in recent years, it may be due to a combination of factors, including the high cost in resources and time for producing and using simulation materials and the training required to use such an approach.

While the basic intent of simulation in teacher education may be appropriate, Marsh (1979) suggests that some of the assumptions implicit in the simulation programs developed thus far should be questioned. Is it necessary, she asks, for simulation experiences to be characterized by such a wide and costly range of detail—photos, film, and background materials on pupils, school, and community and so on? (Some evidence reported by Kersh, 1965, suggests true fidelity to the reality of the classroom may not be necessary.) Is there an overemphasis on problems between teacher and student, possibly establishing an undesirable state of tension? Isn't teaching more than a collection of techniques for dealing with specific classroom problems? Isn't the development of integrated teaching/ curriculum models important? Is a limited time lag between practicing simulated decision making and undertaking similar experiences in actual classrooms important? With questions such as these, Marsh may be opening avenues for some of the badly needed research in simulation for teacher education.

Computer-assisted simulation. Although current interest in simulation for teacher education, at least as measured by research activity in the field, may not be as high as was anticipated ten years ago, one promising extension of this technique that does appear to command substantial current interest is the application of computer technology to teacher education. A central requisite for success in any learning experience is provision of feedback to learners by which they can determine the adequacy of their performance. Most simulations useful as pre-student-teaching laboratory experiences attempt to provide learners with feedback of some sort that will enable them to shape future responses as they work through the simulation. Providing feedback that is specific and immediate proves to be the major occupation of the trainer in many

simulation activities, a factor responsible for the typical high involvement time of staff in conducting simulations. Application of computer technology to simulations offers the promise of freeing the activities from constant attention by trained staff, thereby making use of such activities more practical.

Most applications of computer technology to teacher education have been simulations, similar to those discussed above, that confront trainees with problem situations and require solutions to be generated. Perhaps the best example of this type of activity is the University of Iowa's "Interactive Incidents from Classroom, School and Community" computerized simulation (Lunetta & Zalewski, 1974). Containing twenty-two simulated problem incidents, this program requires the learner to select a response to the problem and then immediately offers the consequences of application of the selected response. The learner continues selecting responses and observing consequences until the problem is solved or dissolves into chaos. Typical simulated situations include "Klepto" (materials are stolen from the classroom), "Note" (a note is being passed around the class), "No Work" (a student appears to be idle).

While use of such computerized simulations is quite intriguing, as yet there is little evidence that supports assumptions of trainee change as a result of such use. Aside from the author's claims (Lunetta, 1977) of trainee satisfaction, the only attempt at studying learning outcomes from this computer-simulated instruction was undertaken by Reynolds and Simpson (1980). They found no differences in affective responses of subjects toward computer-simulated instruction when compared to small-group discussion or role playing. They suggest that these findings, when coupled with the economy of instructor time offered by the Lunetta system, argues in favor of computer simulation. Sampling considerations, instrumentation, and the focus exclusively on affective outcomes serve to make these findings even more tentative.

Similar work done with other computer-simulated packages (Flake, 1975; Ascroft, 1979) offer no further basis for confidence. At this point, the possible effects of such training techniques on students' acquisition of concepts, principles, teaching skills, or attitudes are simply unknown. The field awaits inquiry.

A quite different application of computers in pre-student-teaching laboratory experiences is represented by "Computer Assisted Teacher Training System" (CATTS) (Semmel, 1975). The applications of computers discussed above involve trainees in problem situations and require selection of alternate responses. CATTS is a system for providing feedback to trainees as they proceed through teaching activities in real time. It has four components— teaching station, observation station, computerized data processing, and feedback medium—and requires an observer to record data concerning trainee behavior during the act of teaching and to encode the data using a touch-tone system. The data are processed by a computer and, within microseconds, displayed to the teacher in an easily understandable form, generally on a cathode-ray tube mounted in the rear of the classroom. The trainee is thus offered data reflecting current behavior, which can be compared against intentions as the trainee continues teaching.

Evidence concerning the effects of CATTS on learner performance is both more plentiful and more encouraging than that concerning the effects of other systems for applying computers to pre-student-teaching laboratory training discussed above. Sitko and Semmel (1976) describe substantial evidence supporting the assumption that the CATTS system brings about changes in trainees' use of specific skills related to question-response interaction. An intriguing study of the application of CATTS (Semmel, 1976), though not in a preservice training setting, went as far as looking at the effects of the training intervention on pupil outcomes. In this study immediate feedback to teachers concerning their interaction patterns with pupils was offered via the CATTS system. Changes in teacher behavior that resulted from this feedback were statistically related to changes in the interaction patterns and social status of rejected pupils in the classroom.

Summary. As the above review suggests, research and development efforts in pre-student-teaching laboratory experiences have characteristically emphasized development. Attempts to verify instructional outcomes of such experiences are few and have produced tentative but in many cases encouraging results. Attempts to conceptualize models of such experiences and to examine components of these models systematically have been even fewer, with the possible exception of microteaching. Yet such examination would seem to be a necessary prerequisite for application of these models to teacher-education settings that vary so widely in terms of intended outcomes, trainee and trainer characteristics, available resources, and settings for training.

In addition to the specific types reviewed above, a number of developers have, over the past ten years, proposed other pre-student-teaching laboratory experiences that offer imaginative variation both in intended instructional outcomes and in strategies for attaining these outcomes. Examples of such experiences include empathy training (Kelly, Reavis, & Latham, 1977), enthusiasm training (Collins, 1978), and interpersonal-skills training (Thurman, 1971). Teacher educators would like to believe that these experiences, like their cousins reviewed in detail here, hold sufficient promise for providing the needed bridge between academic training and performance in the field. Whether such promises can be fulfilled can only be answered with time and hard work.

Willis D. Copeland

See also Competency-Based Teacher Education; Field Experiences in Teacher Education; Games and Simulations; Laboratory Schools; Student Teaching.

REFERENCES

Acheson, K. A.; Tucker, P. E.; & Zigler, C. J. *The Effects of Two Microteaching Variations: Written versus Videotape Modeling and Audiotape versus Videotape Feedback.* Paper presented at the annual meeting of the American Educational Research Association, 1974. (ERIC Document Reproduction Service No. ED 088 835)

Allen, D. W. *Microteaching: A Description.* Stanford, Calif.: Stanford University School of Education, 1966. (ERIC Document Reproduction Service No. ED 019 224)

Allen, D. W.; Berliner, D. L.; McDonald, F. J.; & Sobol, F. T. *A Comparison of Different Modeling Procedures in the Acquisition of a Teaching Skill.* Paper presented at the annual meeting of the American Educational Research Association, 1967. (ERIC Document Reproduction Service No. ED 011 261)

Allen, D. W., & Ryan, K. A. *Microteaching.* Reading, Mass.: Addison-Wesley, 1969.

Ascroft, R. A. M. SLATE: An instructional planning simulation. *McGill Journal of Education,* 1979, *14*(2), 231–237.

Beals, P. E. *Classroom Simulation as a Substitute for Live Prestudent Teaching Laboratory Experiences.* Paper presented at the annual meeting of the American Educational Research Association, 1970. (ERIC Document Reproduction Service No. ED 037 401)

Belt, W. D. *Microteaching Observed and Critiqued by a Group of Trainees.* Paper presented at the annual meeting of the American Research Association, 1967. (ERIC Document Reproduction Service No. ED 011 890)

Berliner, D. C. *Microteaching and the Technical Skills Approach to Teacher Training.* (Technical Report No. 8). Palo Alto, Calif.: Stanford Center for Research and Development in Teaching, 1969. (ERIC Document Reproduction Service No. ED 034 707)

Berliner, D. C.; Golden, G.; Bierly, M.; Codori, C.; Hunter, L.; Loeding, D.; & Porteus, K., *Protocols on Group Process.* San Francisco: Far West Laboratory for Educational Research and Development, 1973.

Berliner, D. C. Impediments to the study of teacher effectiveness. *Journal of Teacher Education,* 1976, *27*(1), 5–14.

Borg, W. R. The minicourse as a vehicle for changing teacher behavior: A three-year follow-up. *Journal of Educational Psychology,* 1972, *63,* 572–579.

Borg, W. R. Protocols: Competency-based teacher education modules. *Educational Technology,* 1973, *13,* 17–20.

Borg, W. R.; Kallenbach, W.; Morris, M.; & Friebel, A. Videotape feedback and microteaching in a teacher training model. *Journal of Experimental Education,* 1969, *37,* 9–16.

Boyan, N. J., & Copeland, W. D. *The Instructional Supervision Training Program.* Columbus, Ohio: Merrill, 1978.

Bruner, J. S.; Goodnow, J. J.; & Austin, G. A. *A Study of Thinking.* New York: Wiley, 1956.

Collins, M. L. Effects of enthusiasm training on preservice elementary teachers. *Journal of Teacher Education,* 1978, *29*(1), 53–57.

Conant, J. B. *The Education of American Teachers.* New York: McGraw-Hill, 1964.

Cooper, J. E. A survey of protocol materials evaluation. *Journal of Teacher Education,* 1975, *26*(1), 69–77.

Copeland, W. D. The relationship between microteaching and student teacher classroom performance. *Journal of Educational Research,* 1975, *68,* 289–293.

Copeland, W. D. Some factors related to student teacher classroom performance following microteaching training. *American Educational Research Journal*, 1977, *14*(2), 147–157.

Copeland, W. D. Processes mediating the relationship between cooperating-teacher behavior and student teacher classroom performance. *Journal of Educational Psychology.* 1978, *70*(1), 95–100.

Copeland, W. D., & Doyle, W. Laboratory skill training and student teacher classroom performance. *Journal of Experimental Education*, 1973, *42*, 16–21.

Cruickshank, D. R. *Inner City Simulation Laboratory.* Chicago: Science Research Associates, 1969.

Cruickshank, D. R. Teacher education looks at simulation: A review of selected uses and research results. In P. J. Tansey (Ed.), *Educational Aspects of Simulation.* New York: McGraw-Hill, 1971, pp. 185–203.

Cruickshank, D. R. The protocol materials movement: An exemplar of efforts to wed theory and practice in teacher education. *Journal of Teacher Education*, 1974, *25*(4), 300–311.

Cruickshank, D. R., & Broadbent, F. W. *An Investigation to Determine Effects of Simulation Training on Student Teaching.* Paper presented at the annual meeting of the American Educational Research Association, 1969.

Cruickshank, D. R.; Broadbent, F. W.; & Bubb, R. L. *Teaching Problems Laboratory.* Chicago: Science Research Associates, 1967.

Cruickshank, D. R.; Clingan, M. L.; & Peters, J. The state of the art of simulation in teacher education. *Simulation/Games in Learning*, 1979, *9*(2), 72–82.

Cruickshank, D. R.; Kennedy, J. J.; Holton, J.; Nott, D. E.; & Williams, E. J. *A Summative Evaluation of the Outcomes of Reflective Teaching.* Columbus: Ohio State University, n.d. (Mimeo)

Diehl, B. Current simulation gaming in Australia. *Simulation and Games*, 1979, *10*(3), 265–274.

Doyle, W. *Learning the Classroom Environment: An Ecological Analysis of Induction into Teaching.* Paper presented at the annual meeting of the American Educational Research Association, 1977. (ERIC Document Reproduction Service No. ED 135 782)

Doyle, W., & Ponder, G. A. Classroom ecology: Some concerns about a neglected dimension of research on teaching. *Contemporary Education*, 1975, *46*(3), 182–188.

Flake, J. L. Interactive computer simulations for teacher education. *Educational Technology*, 1975, *15*, 54–57.

Gaffga, R. M. *Simulation: A Model for Observing Student Teaching Behavior.* Unpublished doctoral dissertation, University of Tennessee, 1967.

Gage, N. L. *Teacher Effectiveness and Teacher Education: The Search for a Scientific Basis.* Palo Alto, Calif.: People Books, 1972.

Gage, N. L. A factorially designed experiment on teacher structuring, soliciting, and reading. *Journal of Teacher Education*, 1976, *27*(1), 35–39.

Gagné, R. M. Simulators. In R. Glaser (Ed.), *Training Research and Education.* Pittsburgh, Pa.: University of Pittsburgh Press, 1962, 223–246.

Gall, M.; Dinning, B.; & Banks, H. *Comparison of Instructional Media in a Minicourse on Higher Cognitive Questioning.* Paper presented at the annual meeting of the American Educational Research Association, 1972. (ERIC Document Reproduction Service No. ED 064 326)

Garvey, R. Self-concept and success in student teaching. *Journal of Teacher Education*, 1970, *23*, 356–361.

Gliessman, D., & Pugh, R. C. The development and evaluation of protocol films of teacher behavior. *A V Communications Review*, 1976, *24*, 21–48.

Gliessman, D.; Pugh, R. C.; & Bielat, B. *Acquiring Teaching Skills through Concept-based Training.* Paper presented at the annual meeting of the American Association of Colleges of Teaching Education, February 1978.

Gordon, A. K. *Games for Growth.* Chicago: Science Research Associates, 1972.

Hamacheck, E. E. *Encounters with the Self.* New York: Holt, Rinehart & Winston, 1971.

Hatfield, A. B. An experimental study of the self-concept of student teachers. *Journal of Educational Research*, 1961, *55*, 87–89.

Hiscox, S. B., & Van Mondfrans, A. P. *Feedback Conditions and Type of Teaching Skill in Microteaching.* Paper presented at the annual meeting of the American Educational Research Association, 1972. (ERIC Document Reproduction Service No. ED 064 249)

Huber, J., & Ward, B. E. Pre-service confidence through microteaching. *Supervisors Quarterly*, 1969, *5*(2), 22–28.

Hudgins, B. B. *Performance Education: A Catalogue of Concepts in the Pedagogical Domain of Teacher Education.* Albany: Multi-state Consortium on Performance-based Education, 1974.

Jaus, H. H. Using microteaching to change elementary teachers' attitudes toward science instruction. *School Science and Mathematics*, 1977, *77*, 402–406.

Johnson, J. A. *A National Survey of Student Teaching Programs.* (No. 6-8182, Grant No. OEG 3-7-068182-2635). Washington, D.C.: U.S. Office of Education, 1968. (ERIC Document Reproduction Service No. ED 023 643)

Johnson, W. D., & Pancrazio, S. R. *The Effectiveness of the Microteaching Environments in Preparing Undergraduates for Student Teaching.* Paper presented at the annual meeting of the American Educational Research Association, 1970.

Joyce B.; Yarger, S.; Howey, K.; Harbeck, K.; & Kluwin, T. *Preservice Teacher Education.* Palo Alto, Calif.: Center for Educational Research and Development, 1977.

Katz, G. Use of minicourse instruction with student teachers of educable mentally retarded children. *Journal of Educational Research*, 1976, *69*, 355–359.

Kelly, E.; Reavis, C.; & Latham, W. A study of two empathy-training models in elementary education. *Journal of Instructional Psychology*, 1977, *4*(4), 40–46.

Kersh, B. Y. *Classroom Simulation: A New Dimension in Teacher Education.* Monmouth: Oregon State System of Higher Education, Teaching Research Division, 1963. (ERIC Document Reproduction Service No. ED 003 613)

Kersh, B. Y. *Classroom Simulation: Further Studies on Dimensions of Realism* (Final Report). Monmouth: Oregon State System of Higher Education, Teaching Research Division, 1965. (ERIC Document Reproduction Service No. ED 010 176)

Kise, J. E. *Microteaching: A Study in Specific and General Behavior of Supervisors.* Unpublished doctoral dissertation, University of Akron, 1971.

Kissock, C. *A Study to Test the Value of Microteaching in a Program of Video Modelling Instruction in the Development of Higher Order Question-asking on the Part of Pre-service Teachers.* Unpublished doctoral dissertation, University of Minnesota, 1971.

Kleucker, J. C. Effects of protocol and training materials. In *Ac-

quiring Teaching Competencies: Reports and Studies (No. 6). Bloomington: Indiana University, National Center for the Development of Training Materials in Teacher Education, 1974.

Koran, M. L., Snow, R. E.; & McDonald, F. J. Teacher aptitude and observational learning of a teaching skill. *Journal of Educational Psychology,* 1971, *62,* 219–228.

Kuuskraa, V. A.; Morra, F.; & Brashear, J. P. *Condition of Teacher Education, 1977.* Washington, D.C.: Lewin & Associates, 1977. (ERIC Document Reproduction Service No. ED 143 644)

Lunetta, V. N. Human transactions and classroom management: A computer-based unit in teacher education. *Educational Technology,* 1977, *17,* 35–37.

Lunetta, V. N., & Zalewski, L. J. *Interactive Incidents from Classroom, School, and Community.* Washington, D.C.: National Science Teachers Association, 1974. (ERIC Document Reproduction Service No. ED 095 031)

Marsh, C. J. Teacher education simulations: The "Challenge of Change" example. *British Journal of Teacher Education,* 1979, *5*(1) 63–71.

Marten, M.; Denfee, M.; & Buffie, E. Simulation-focus on decision-making. *Bulletin of the School of Education, Indiana University,* 1970, *46,* 3–48.

McIntyre, D. I. *Microteaching Practice, Collaboration with Peers, and Supervisory Feedback as Determinants of the Effects of Microteaching.* Stirling, Scotland: University of Stirling, Department of Education, 1972. (Mimeo)

McKnight, P. C. *Development of the Technical Skills of Teaching.* Paper presented at the annual meeting of the American Educational Research Association, 1978. (ERIC Document Reproduction Service No. ED 171 699)

Megarry, J. Simulations, games, and the professional education of teachers. *Journal of Education for Teaching,* January 1981, *7*(1), 25–39.

Perrott, E. Changes in teaching behavior after participating in a self-instructional microteaching course. *Educational Media International,* 1976, *1,* 16–25.

Perrott, E.; Appletree, A.; Heap, B.; & Watson, E. Changes in teaching behavior after completing a self-instructional microteaching course. *Programmed Learning and Educational Technology,* 1975, *12*(6), 348–362.

Peterson, P. L.; Marx, R. W.; & Clark, C. M. Teacher planning, teacher behavior, and student achievement. *American Educational Research Journal,* 1978, *15*(3), 417–432.

Peterson, T. L. Microteaching and pre-service education of teachers. *Journal of Educational Research,* 1973, *67,* 34–36.

Pisano, D. P. *The Effects of Supervisory Feedback on Behavior and Attitudes in the Microteaching of Elementary School Science.* Unpublished doctoral dissertation, Temple University, 1974.

Pugh, R. C., & Gliessman, D. *Measuring the Effects of a Protocol Film Series: Instrument Development and Use.* Bloomington: Indiana University Center for Development in Teacher Education, 1976. (ERIC Document Reproduction Service No. ED 123 254)

Randall, R. W. *The Effects of Videotaped Microteaching on the Self-concepts of Social Studies Student Teachers.* Unpublished doctoral dissertation, University of Kentucky, 1972.

Raymond, A. The acquisition of non-verbal behaviors by preservice science teachers and their application during student teaching. *Journal of Research in Science Teaching,* 1973, *10*(1), 13–24.

Reed, C. L.; Van Mondfrans, A. P.; & Smith, T. M. *The Effect of Microteaching, Directive and Non-directive Lectures on*

Achievement and Attitudes in a Basic Educational Psychology Course. Paper presented at the annual meeting of the American Educational Research Association, 1970. (ERIC Document Reproduction Service No. ED 037 390)

Reynolds, D. S., & Simpson, R. D. Pilot study using computer-based simulations on human transactions and classroom management. *Science Education,* 1980, *64*(1), 35–41.

Rosenshine, B. Evaluation of classroom instruction. *Review of Educational Research,* 1970, *40,* 279–300.

Santiesteban, A. J., & Koran, J. J. Acquisition of science teaching skills through psychological modeling and concomitant student learning. *Journal of Research in Science Teaching,* 1977, *14*(3), 199–207.

Saunders, W.; Gull, M. D.; Nielson, E.; & Smith, G. The effects of variations in microteaching on prospective teachers' acquisition of questioning skills. *Journal of Educational Research,* 1975, *69,* 3–8.

Sears, P. L., & Hilgard, E. The effects of classroom conditions on the strength of achievement motive and work output in elementary school children. In E. Hilgard (Ed.), *Theories of Learning and Instruction: NSSE Yearbook.* Chicago: University of Chicago Press, 1964, pp. 182–209.

Semmel, M. I. Application of systematic classroom observation to the study and modification of pupil-teacher interactions in special education. In R. A. Weinberg & F. H. Hood (Eds.), *Observation of Pupils and Teachers in Mainstream and Special Education Settings: Alternative Strategies.* University of Minnesota, Leadership Training Institute/Special Education, 1975, pp. 231–264. (ERIC Document Reproduction Service No. ED 108 423)

Semmel, M. I. *The Improvement of Social Status among Rejected Pupils through the Modification of Teacher Behavior Using the Computer-assisted Teacher Training System (CATTS): An Inservice Training Application of CATTS.* Bloomington: Indiana University, Center for Innovation in Teaching the Handicapped, 1976. (ERIC Document Reproduction Service No. ED 162 469)

Shea, J. *The Relative Effectiveness of Student Teaching versus a Combination of Student Teaching and Microteaching.* Paper presented at the annual meeting of the American Educational Research Association, 1974. (ERIC Document Reproduction Service No. ED 087 782)

Sherwin, S. *Teacher Education: A Status Report.* Princeton, N.J.: Educational Testing Service, 1974. (ERIC Document Reproduction Service No. ED 096 287)

Sitko, M., & Semmel, M. I. *The Effectiveness of a Computer-assisted Teacher Training System (CATTS) in the Development of Reading and Listening Comprehension Instructional Strategies of Preservice Special Education Trainees in a Tutorial Classroom Setting.* Bloomington: Indiana University, Center for Innovation in Teaching the Handicapped, 1976. (ERIC Document Reproduction Service No. ED 162 467)

Smith, B. O.; Cohen, S. B.; & Pearl, A. *Teachers for the Real World.* Washington, D.C.: American Association of Colleges for Teacher Education, 1969. (ERIC Document Reproduction Service No. ED 027 267)

Smith, C. L. Personality and attitudinal shift under a simulated teaching experience. *Improving College and University Teaching,* 1975, *23,* 229–231.

Sparks, R. L., & McCallon, E. L. Microteaching: Its effect on student attitudes in an elementary science methods course. *Science Education,* 1974, *58*(4), 483–487.

Standards for Accreditation of Teacher Education. Washington,

LABORATORY SCHOOLS

1019

D.C.: National Council for Accreditation of Teacher Education, 1979.

Stanley, F. A. *A Comparison Study of the Effects of Pre-service Teachers Presenting One or Two Microteaching Lessons to Different-sized Groups of Peers on Selected Teaching Behaviors and Attitudes in an Elementary Science Methods Course.* Unpublished doctoral dissertation, Michigan State University, 1970.

Stanton, H. E. Self-concept change through the microteaching experience. *British Journal of Teacher Education*, 1978, *4*(2), 119–123.

Steinbach, A., & Butts, D. P. A comparative study of the effects of practice with elementary children or with peers in the science methods course. *Journal of Research in Science Teaching*, 1969, *6*, 316–321.

Stowitschek, J. J., & Hofmeister, A. M. Effects of minicourse instruction on teachers and pupils. *Exceptional Children*, 1974, *40*, 490–495.

Thurman, J. H. Relative effectiveness of four methods of training prospective teachers in interpersonal skills. *Journal of Educational Research*, 1971, *65*(1), 19–22.

Vlcek, C. Classroom simulation in teacher education. *Audiovisual Instructor*, 1966, *11*(2), 86–90.

Wagner, A. C. Changing teacher behavior: A comparison of microteaching and cognitive discrimination training. *Journal of Educational Psychology*, 1973, *64*, 299–305.

LABORATORY SCHOOLS

Van Til (1969) refers to the ideal laboratory school as an educational mecca: "a center of enlightenment [to attract] educators from near and far to observe the best in education" (p. 1). In an address to fellow laboratory-school directors, Goodlad (1971) employs a quite different metaphor: "It's nice to be with my friends on death row" (p. 31). These images reflect both the influential past and uncertain future of laboratory schools in the United States (McGeogh, 1972).

Historians disagree over the origin of the laboratory school. Barnard (1851) claims that the first was in Potsdam, Germany, in 1825. Monroe (1912) points to Johann Friedrick Herbart's practice school at the University of Königsberg as the forerunner. Cordasco (1963) cites E. C. Trappe's university practice school at the University of Halle in 1779. There is agreement that laboratory schools were organized for one primary purpose: the provision of a controlled environment in which future teachers could observe master teachers, begin to teach, and develop their pedagogical skills.

Laboratory schools in the United States evolved in response to the same need. In 1830, Samuel Read Hall incorporated a teacher-training course and practice teaching into the curriculum of his academy in Andover, Massachusetts (McCarrel, 1933). The first college-associated laboratory school apparently was attached to the normal school in Albany, New York, in 1845. The Albany "model school"

not only served as a training site for teachers but also began the practice of charging tuition that would become characteristic of so many laboratory schools (Johnson, 1968).

From 1850 to 1890, most teachers were trained in normal schools (Mattingly, 1975). The first concern of these institutions was to provide lessons in practical pedagogy (Stone, 1968), or what Silberman (1970) calls "some knowledge of subject matter, along with a bag of tricks—the so-called art of teaching" (p. 419). The second approach was the continuation of the moralistic tradition from the early 1800s, when teachers were hired more for their moral character than for their pedagogical skill. The close association between the practical and moral approaches to teacher training implied that the strength of a school was based on the character of the individual teachers (Mattingly, 1975). Most laboratory schools of the latter nineteenth century reflected this view. The schools were model schools in which future teachers could observe model teaching by the master teacher, model discipline, and the newest equipment (Bixby & Mitzel, 1965).

Increasingly, attention was given to the emerging science of education. In the laboratory school attached to the Oswego Normal School, Edward Sheldon instructed future teachers in Pestalozzian techniques; from 1860 to 1880, students were taught to employ the famous object lessons and to practice educating the head, heart, and hand of pupils. The laboratory school at Illinois State University took the Herbartian approach as teachers in training acquired the five formal steps of pedagogy. Looking back at this period, Hutton (1965) wrote, "It would be gratifying to add that under the intellectual stimulus of Herbartianism normal schools and their model schools gave vigorous leadership in developing a science of education whose hallmarks were research and experimentation. No such claim can be made" (p. 17).

By the end of the nineteenth century, scholars such as Cyrus Pierce, Nicholas Murray Butler, and John Dewey had become dismayed by the shoddy preparation of teachers. In 1890, Butler built Teachers College at Columbia University, which integrated more rigorous academic study and teacher training (Cremin, Shannon, & Townsend, 1954). In 1896, Dewey established the Laboratory School at the University of Chicago. He believed that teacher training required the fusion of theory and practice: "Pedagogical instruction is effective in proportion as the theory of the classroom is accompanied by actual school work" (Dewey, 1896, pp. 332–333). However, Dewey's school was not founded to train teachers. In theory and practice it was much more, and as such, it reflected the second major tradition of the laboratory school—the possibility of a center for research and experimentation.

The Laboratory School was designed specifically to test Dewey's radical theories (Dewey, 1899, 1916, 1965) about the education of children and youth (Cremin, 1961; Kelly, 1970). Two of its first teachers, Mayhew and Edwards (1965), wrote a detailed history of the Dewey school in the 1896–1904 period, describing its curriculum, pedagogical methods, personnel, organization, and evaluation techniques and reporting that it was quite specifically a laboratory for the Departments of Psychology and Pedagogy of the University of Chicago. Dewey (1902) wrote of the school: "Only the scientific aim, the conduct of a laboratory comparable to other scientific laboratories can furnish a reason for the maintenance by the university of an elementary school . . . It is not a normal school or a department for the training of teachers" (pp. 96–97). Whereas some schools needed to train the rank and file of teachers, others (including the Laboratory School) existed to educate leaders, including professors, teacher trainers, and administrators. Dewey (1896) believed that "our educational systems were in need of some kind of direction and systemization from expert sources" (p. 354). If government was not to take the lead, as in Europe, then it must be the universities.

Under his leadership, the Laboratory School was not only a place where teachers taught and children learned, but a "place where children, teachers, parents and the principal learned and grew" (Sarason, 1971, p. 197). Inquiry was the cornerstone of the school. Edwards (1965) observed that the most significant product of the school was the development of the student's learning processes. Faculty members from the University of Chicago indeed became involved closely with the life of the school. Teacher training was not a course, but rather an on-going activity. Sarason (1971) points out that Dewey was not as concerned as most principals are today with running his school smoothly; instead, he was interested in how and where problems arose and how they were solved.

This new prototype of a laboratory school did not collapse when Dewey left in 1904, but it did change. De Pencier (1967) indicates that the commitment to research and experimentation continued under the leadership of Charles Hubbard Judd (1909–1919) and Henry Morrison (1919–1928). Morrison (1926) added the terms "unit" and "mastery" to the educational lexicon, and teachers in the school continued to produce textbooks, articles, curriculum materials, monographs, and book reviews of high quality and in large numbers (Parker, 1931). However, in the 1930s, the intellectual ties between the school and the university began to weaken, and by the 1960s, the Laboratory School had become a college preparatory school that was occasionally, but not primarily, experimental. Although the Laboratory School had a profound impact on the organization of the American classroom and its curriculum, Sarason (1971, 1972) suggests that few public schools came to regard teachers, administrators, and parents with the intrinsic respect found in Dewey's school. The roots of contemporary teacher boredom and dissatisfaction can be traced in certain measure to this failure.

Difficulties Faced by Laboratory Schools. Some laboratory schools that retained their scholarly orientation from the early 1900s to the middle of the century, were forced to close their doors or reduce programs because of financial concerns, selective admissions policies, or academic reasons (Bixby & Mitzel, 1965). Most of the schools that persisted held to the traditional purposes of teacher training, demonstration, and observation (Eubank, 1931). Kelly (1965) surveyed 178 laboratory schools and found that 62 rated student teaching as their primary function, whereas only 27 rated research as a first commitment, even past mid-century.

As much as laboratory schools appeared to be stable centers for teacher training and related activities, they encountered serious difficulties in the period after the Second World War. Lathrop and Beal (1965) found that between 1955 and 1965, twenty schools closed, and many more survived only with program reductions. Howd and Browne (1970) reported that in the 1964–1969 period, forty schools closed, five were to be closed in the immediate future, and twenty had experienced various grade-level reductions (Cardinell, 1978). Quick's examination (1972) of laboratory-school closings in Michigan indicated that the "most influential factor related to the demise of the campus laboratory school was the rapid growth of the state colleges during the 1950's and 1960's and their transformation into multi-purpose universities" (p. 23).

As the demands for teachers increased rapidly in the United States, laboratory schools were ill prepared to handle student-teaching demands. A policy of scheduling student-teaching programs in public school settings emerged and solidified. Forced into a subordinate role in the expanding university, the laboratory school was unable to compete successfully with other units in the annual budget process. State legislators and university trustees began to diminish or eliminate financial support (Howd & Browne, 1970).

Van Til (1969) found other basic difficulties. In order to be a feasible research center, the laboratory schools needed a representative student population, yet their students typically were wealthier, more intellectual, and more burdened with special problems. Increasingly, parents did not want their children to be used as guinea pigs (Friedman, Brinlee, & Hayes, 1980). Teachers could not devote much time to research because of their teaching responsibilities and their second-class status within the university milieu. Van Til added that most professors avoided the schools, while others used them as a means of testing pet but unimportant theories. In trying to be everything to everyone, the laboratory schools were floundering, and many were closing (Goodlad, 1971).

A governmental policy change in the funding of research and experimentation had a devastating impact. "Increasingly, the innovation in education comes from massive projects financed by the federal government or by foundations. Decreasingly do significant innovations come from the laboratory school" (Van Til, 1969, p. 13). These research efforts were centered most often in public schools and school systems. As a result, laboratory schools came into direct competition with public schools (as well as new federally supported regional laboratories and research development centers) on the two issues that had provided their bedrock purposes: teacher training and research (Abrams, 1971). Although few of the research and development programs (such as Title III of Public Law 89-10) led to permanent changes, such fund sources continued to be available through the 1970s. Universities, too, began to take a new approach to research. Braddock (1968) argues that some "made the ghetto school, rather than the college campus, their laboratory" (p. 3). Laboratory schools had taken pride in the excellence of their uniqueness, but these policy changes permitted the public schools to take the lead in research and development.

Self-Reevaluation. Once again, laboratory schools began to determine a future related more closely to the research function than to the teacher-training function (Wiles, 1958; Cornthwaite, 1972). The Howd and Browne survey (1970) of 208 laboratory schools documented a rising trend: "Whereas provision of student teaching experiences was a primary objective of the schools in 1964, the principal aim of many schools in 1969 was to serve as a center for observation and pre-student teaching participation of college students with children in the classroom and increased emphasis upon research, experimentation, and in-service education" (p. 9). In addition, those schools that were creating new buildings or enlarging old ones gave the need for a facility for research and experimentation as a primary reason for the new construction. Some laboratory schools changed their names to "centers" to emphasize their resemblance to teacher centers (Quigley & Chaves, 1974), as the relationship between laboratory schools and in-service teacher education began to grow (Ball, 1971; Driscoll & Wheeler, 1980).

New Directions. Only a few laboratory schools appear to have national visibility and influence at this time. The laboratory school at UCLA was the lone survivor of California state budget cuts in the 1960s. It would thrive in the 1970s, because it eliminated student teaching and devoted itself to experimentation and innovative program development (Goodlad, 1971; Devaney, 1971). Its successful nongraded academic programs have drawn nationwide attention. The principal of this laboratory school has described seven specific research areas for such institutions (Hunter, 1971).

An even more influential prototype may be developing in Hawaii (Krause, 1978). The campus laboratory school at the University of Hawaii began to collaborate with the Curriculum Research and Development Group of the university in 1966. This coalition has produced many changes, the most important of which involved, instead of teacher training, a new commitment to research, experimentation, and development of new curriculum materials. Several programs initiated by the group or state programs tested successfully in the laboratory school have been disseminated to the public schools of the state, which uniquely comprise a single school district.

As the laboratory schools enter a new decade, they face formidable problems. First, financial constraints will continue to limit research and experimentation efforts. Second, adherence to the tradition of serving too many functions and roles will be a handicap. Competition with government- and grant-sponsored research in public settings will constitute a third issue. The great volume of recent research has centered on culturally deprived, handicapped, and learning-disabled students, few of whom are represented in the population of the typical laboratory school.

Such problems will be towering, yet they are not necessarily insurmountable. School financing in the 1980s will be challenging for public and private institutions as well as laboratory schools. Where purpose is clear, money should be available. Van Til (1969) argues that laboratory-school advocates must "realistically adapt the function and purpose of each individual laboratory school to contemporary reality" (p. 13). The UCLA and University of Hawaii schools give evidence of such redefinition, using core activities of research, development, and dissemination as the basis for responding to field needs. Strong laboratory schools in the 1980s will tend to focus on important, yet limited, areas of inquiry and service. Competition with the public schools could prove fatal to many laboratory schools. Goodlad (1971) claims that "you justify a laboratory school by providing what the rest of American education is not providing" (p. 40). Thus, the coming task of laboratory schools may not be one of competition, but one of finding important new problems for consideration.

Conclusions. Initially, laboratory schools spread as the need to train teachers accelerated. Some changed direction as the educational climate of the early 1900s dictated a need for experimentation, curriculum revision, and innovation. The strain between training and experimentation has persisted into the current period (Young, 1967). As yet, no third rallying point for laboratory schools has emerged clearly. Laboratory schools that will thrive must meet the educational needs of individual students, parents, teachers, and communities. An emerging policy issue in the decade ahead has to do with the impact of laboratory schools on a relatively local level. There may be mainland counterpoints to the Hawaii plan: laboratory schools that serve a particular locality. Such schools could capitalize on their ties with a university and direct contact with a school setting in ways that have been difficult for regional laboratories to attain.

Howd and Browne (1970) wrote, "There is mounting evidence to show that a serious reexamination of purposes for campus laboratory schools is underway in an effort to define a unique role for such schools" (p. 9). The situation in the early 1980s is much the same. Laboratory schools probably will not have a great national impact in the coming decade. They may, however, have important local or regional impact as they define roles in research, experimentation, and dissemination that are congruent with local needs and problems (Florida, Department of Education, 1976). The laboratory school enjoys a long tradition of service, but it will continue to exist only if it can provide responses of high quality to a local community.

R. Bruce McPherson
Glenn W. McGee

See also Field Experiences in Teacher Education; Laboratory Experiences in Teacher Education; Student Teaching; Teacher Education Programs.

REFERENCES

Abrams, P. Crisis in the lab school. *National Association of Laboratory Schools Newsletter*, 1971, *13*, 50–63.

Ball, E. E. *Northern Kentucky In-service Innovation Center.* 1971. (ERIC Document Reproduction Service No. ED 080 489)

Barnard, H. *On Normal Schools.* Hartford: Case, Tiffany, 1851.

Bixby, P. W., & Mitzel, H. E. (Eds.). *Campus School to a Research and Dissemination Center.* University Park: Pennsylvania State University, 1965.

Braddock, C. What's going on in the lab schools? *Southern Education Report*, 1968, *3*, 3–7.

Cardinell, C. F. *New Paths for America's Laboratory Schools.* Paper presented at the School of Education, Indiana State University, May 3, 1978.

Cordasco, F. *A Brief History of Education.* Paterson, N.J.: Littlefield, Adams, 1963.

Cornthwaite, D. L. *Defining the Role and Functions of Campus Laboratory Schools for the Decade of the Seventies through an Investigation of Studies Completed between 1965 and 1970.* Unpublished doctoral dissertation, George Washington University, 1972.

Cremin, L. A. *The Transformation of the School.* New York: Knopf, 1961.

Cremin, L. A.; Shannon, D. A.; & Townsend, M. E. *A History of Teachers College, Columbia University.* New York: Columbia University Press, 1954.

De Pencier, I. *The History of the Laboratory Schools.* Chicago: Quadrangle, 1967.

Devaney, K. *U.C. and the Public Schools.* Berkeley: University of California, 1971.

Dewey, J. Pedagogy as a university discipline. *University of Chicago Record*, 1896, *1*, 353–355.

Dewey, J. *The School and Society.* Chicago: University of Chicago Press, 1899.

Dewey, J. *The Child and the Curriculum.* Chicago: University of Chicago Press, 1902.

Dewey, J. *Democracy and Education.* New York: Macmillan, 1916.

Dewey, J. The theory of the Chicago experiment. In K. C. Mayhew & A. C. Edwards, *The Dewey School.* New York: Atheling, 1965.

Driscoll, R. L., & Wheeler, D. *Teacher Education Center: A Displaced Campus School?* 1980. (ERIC Document Reproduction Service No. ED 182 298)

Edwards, A. C. The evolution of Mr. Dewey's principles of education. In K. C. Mayhew & A. C. Edwards, *The Dewey School.* New York: Atheling, 1965.

Eubank, L. A. The organization and administration of laboratory schools in state teachers colleges. *Northeast Missouri State Teachers College Bulletin*, 1931, *31.*

Florida, Department of Education. *Study of State Coordination of Research and Development Efforts for Education.* Tallahassee: Florida State Department of Education, 1976.

Friedman, M. A.; Brinlee, P. S.; & Hayes, P. *Improving Teacher Education: Resources and Recommendations.* New York: Longman, 1980.

Goodlad, J. The role of laboratory schools in innovation and experimentation. *National Association of Laboratory Schools Newsletter*, 1971, *13*, 31–49.

Howd, M. C., & Browne, K. A. *National Survey of Campus Laboratory Schools, 1969.* Washington, D.C.: American Association of Colleges for Teacher Education, 1970.

Hunter, M. Expanding roles of laboratory schools. *Phi Delta Kappan*, 1971, *52*, 14–19.

Hutton, H. Historical background of the campus school in America. In P. W. Bixby & H. E. Mitzel (Eds.), *Campus School to a Research and Dissemination Center.* University Park: Pennsylvania State University, 1965.

Johnson, J. *A Brief History of Student Teaching.* Dekalb, Ill.: Creative Educational Publishing Company, 1968.

Kelly, E. H. *College-controlled Laboratory Schools in the United States, 1964.* Washington, D.C.: American Association of Colleges for Teacher Education, 1965.

Kelly, E. H. The historical development of the campus laboratory school. In R. C. Blockman (Ed.), *Laboratory School, U.S.A.: Studies and Readings.* Lafayette: University of Southwestern Louisiana, 1970.

Krause, L. *From a Campus Laboratory School to a Research and Development Center.* Honolulu: University of Hawaii, 1978.

Lathrop, R. L., & Beal, D. K. Current status of selected college-related schools. In P. W. Bixby & H. E. Mitzel (Eds.), *Campus School to a Research and Dissemination Center.* University Park: Pennsylvania State University, 1965.

Mattingly, P. H. *The Classless Profession.* New York: New York University Press, 1975.

Mayhew, K. C., & Edwards, A. C. *The Dewey School.* New York: Atheling, 1965.

McCarrel, F. *The Development of the Training School.* Nashville, Tenn.: George Peabody College for Teachers, 1933.

McGeogh, D. M. Phoenix or dodo bird? The evolution of the campus laboratory school. *National Association of Laboratory Schools Newsletter*, 1972, *13*, 8–21.

Monroe, P. *History of Education.* New York: Macmillan, 1912.

Morrison, H. C. *The Practice of Teaching in the Secondary School.* Chicago: University of Chicago Press, 1926.

Parker, B. G. *An Introductory Course in Science in the Intermediate Grades.* Chicago: University of Chicago Press, 1931.

Quick, D. M. Campus laboratory schools: Why are they being eliminated? *National Association of Laboratory Schools Newsletter*, 1972, *13*, 22–30.

Quigley, L. A., & Chaves, A. (Eds.). *Report of the Task Force on Teacher Education and Laboratory Schools.* Boston: Massachusetts State College System, 1974.

Sarason, S. B. *The Culture of the School and the Problem of Change.* Boston: Allyn & Bacon, 1971.

Sarason, S. B. *The Creation of Settings and the Future Societies.* San Francisco: Jossey-Bass, 1972.

Silberman, C. *Crisis in the Classroom.* New York: Random House, 1970.

Stone, J. C. *Breakthrough in Teacher Education.* San Francisco: Jossey-Bass, 1968.

Van Til, W. *The Laboratory School: Its Rise and Fall?* Address to the national meeting of the Laboratory Schools Administrators Association, Chicago, February 1969.

Wiles, K. The role of the laboratory school in educational research. In *The Role of the Laboratory School in Teacher Education.*

Report of a conference at the P. K. Yonge Laboratory School, College of Education, University of Florida, November 23–25, 1958.

Young, B. J. *Roles and Functions of Laboratory Schools.* Madison: Wisconsin State University System, 1967.

LAND GRANT COLLEGES

See Federal Influence on Education; History and Philosophy of Higher Education.

LANGUAGE DEVELOPMENT

Child language development has been a target of scientific inquiry for at least 200 years. Perhaps the earliest attempt to collect normative data on language acquisition was by the German philosopher Tiedemann, who published his observations in 1787, followed by physiologists in the mid-nineteenth century. The first systematic and detailed chronicle of language development was published by Preyer in 1882 (Bar-Adon & Leopold, 1971). The subject also merited serious consideration from Darwin (1971 [1877]) and other scientists concerned with the development of the human species, since understanding the nature of language development in children was seen as a key to understanding the phylogeny of mankind itself. The process of language acquisition has since been studied within a wide range of disciplines, including philosophy, psychology, anthropology, education, and linguistics, and from as wide a range of perspectives. Language development has thus been of interest as a biological, spiritual, and social phenomenon defining human existence, integrally related with cognitive development and all other aspects of each individual and with the culture that it helps to transmit from generation to generation in each society.

Observational and experimental reports in the vast literature that has accumulated reflect changing foci of interest within each of the disciplines represented, as well as shifting theoretical concepts of the nature of language, appropriate sources of data and data collection procedures, and interpretive frames. The study of language acquisition in the past few decades has focused in turn primarily on vocabulary, phonology, syntax, semantics, pragmatics, and discourse, corresponding to the changes of focus and paradigm shifts in the study of language more generally. Aspects of language that are not of central concern during any specific period still continue to receive at least peripheral consideration by researchers who are not primarily "theorists."

Theoretical Base. Because the theoretical perspective of the researcher has influenced the nature of the questions that have been asked, data collection and organization procedures, and the interpretation of results, some under-standing of recent theoretical bases will aid in understanding the nature of current knowledge about language development and will help to explain some of the apparently conflicting findings and conclusions.

Structuralist-experimentalist. The structuralist model for linguistic description, which was dominant in the forties and fifties, fostered an empiricist approach to the study of language acquisition: language was thought to be determined entirely by the environment, and the child was striving "to learn the language exactly as his environment speaks it" (Leopold, 1948, p. 14). The importance of simple imitation in the acquisition process was brought into question, however, and generally augmented by concepts of selective reinforcement borrowed from behaviorist psychology (see Bloomfield, 1933; Skinner, 1957). With respect to phonology, this perspective was summarized by McCarthy (1950) in the revised edition of the *Encyclopedia of Educational Research:* "Most writers are agreed . . . that the child does not learn to make new sounds by imitation, but that his attention is called to those sounds in his own vocal repertoire which are close approximations to real words and thus they are repeated more often" (p. 166).

The primary approach to research on child language shifted from the earlier detailed observations of individual children in naturalistic contexts to more carefully controlled experimental study of (usually elicited) language data from large numbers of subjects. This shift resulted in the discounting of much of the earlier observational data and in the limitation of most research during this period to children's recognition and production of discrete language forms, largely to the exclusion of attention to developing communication abilities. The change in research perspective was articulated by Carroll (1960) in the third edition of the *Encyclopedia of Educational Research:* "One of the basic drawbacks in the available research literature is that it is based mainly on observations in naturalistic settings. Theories of language-learning cannot ultimately be tested unless an experimental approach is adopted" (p. 745).

A major goal of the structuralists-experimentalists was to discover general patterns, and quantitative studies in this paradigm included research on frequencies of different speech sounds produced at various age levels, amounts of language produced in particular units of time, numbers of words understood, ratio of different words to total words produced ("type-token ratio"), length of sentences, and percentage of words produced in different grammatical categories (summarized in McCarthy, 1950, 1954). Individual variation was not considered interesting or significant, although a number of studies documented systematic differences in language development according to sex (McCarthy, 1953), socioeconomic status (Young, 1941), and intelligence (Smith, 1957; Spiker & Irwin, 1949).

One of the major contributions of this theoretical model was the consideration of child language as a system to be discovered in its own right and not just as an imperfect realization of adult speech. This perspective led to the categorization of words in early child language as Class I, II, and III ("operators") or A, B, C, and D ("nonoperators") by Miller and Ervin (1964), and to Braine's (1963) positing of a "pivot grammar" at the stage when children begin producing two words in sequence, with words seen as belonging to "pivot" and "open" classes, roughly comparable with function and content words in traditional analyses (e.g., in the utterance *more sing, more* is a "pivot" word, and *sing* belongs to the "open" class). Although Braine adopted the use of generative rules in his descriptive model, his approach basically reflected the structuralist philosophy, and was soon displaced by other models.

Generative-transformational. The generative-transformational approach to grammatical description was launched with the publication of Noam Chomsky's *Syntactic Structures* (1957). Chomsky (see also 1959, 1965) stimulated new directions in research on child language development with his claim that knowing a language does not mean knowing a finite set of sentences (no matter how large), but rather an internalized set of rules (the grammar), which allows the creation and interpretation of an infinite number of possible sentences, including many that have perhaps never before been uttered. The key question for the study of language acquisition from this "rationalist" perspective is how, from the limited sample of speech to which any child is exposed, he or she inductively arrives at this set of rules. Chomsky and his followers have claimed that this accomplishment would not be possible unless the child were guided by some innate notions about the nature of language in general—universal structural principles to (in some way) guide the organization of input data and hypothesis formation. The existence of an innate language acquisition device (LAD) was hypothesized, and evidence was sought to account for its nature and content (see McNeill, 1966, 1970, 1971).

The basic assumption of this "nativist" model is that children are thought to be "biologically equipped with certain clues about the nature of language" (Cook-Gumperz, 1981, p. 28), and they set about "actively searching [the] speech environment for structures that correspond to those clues. In this model although a rich or impoverished environment can affect the rate of development, the crucial aspects of language are not derived from speech input but imposed on it" (Bates, 1976b, p. 1).

Most of the early research of this era was concerned with demonstrating that child language development is indeed a process of rule formation (e.g., Brown & Fraser, 1963) and with discovering what features might be universal (see Slobin, 1970). The focus of studies within this model was the acquisition of syntax, and relatively little attention was paid to phonology or semantics (see review in van der Geest, 1974).

Bloom's (1970) work represented a pioneering effort that formed a transition to certain current directions. She showed the inadequacy of Braine's model (as did Menyuk, 1971) to deal with ambiguous sentences containing two

"open-class" words such as *Mommy sock,* which could be accounted for only by recognizing differences in grammatical relations, as subject-object in the interpretation 'Mommy put on [Kathryn's] sock' and possessor–object possessed in the interpretation 'Mommy's sock'. At the same time, Bloom was the first in recent years to make explicit use of contextual information in the study of child language, arguing that the ambiguity in a sentence such as the foregoing example was determinable only by attention to the context of utterance.

Case grammar. Beginning in the late sixties, the basic distinction that Chomsky made between syntax and semantics was challenged by other linguists (e.g., Fillmore, 1968; McCawley, 1968), who considered the two systems essentially integrated, and semantics (meaning) as the more basic component of language. One theoretical model that has had a major impact on research into language acquisition is that of Fillmore (1968), who characterizes the primary underlying structure of language as involving a small set of semantic case relationships existing between verbs (propositional predicates) of sentences and one or more noun phrases (called "arguments" in propositional logic), such as agent, object, dative (goal), and locative. In English, cases are marked primarily by prepositions, while other languages such as Latin or Turkish might use suffixes, postpositions, or other devices. The English genitive (possessive) case, for example, is marked two ways: by *of* and by -*s*.

Additionally, Fillmore's early formulation of "case grammar" considered a sentence as containing a modality component, which was interpreted in language acquisition research to include the meaningful intonational contours of preverbal infancy (Ingram, 1971; Kernan, 1970).

The applicability of Fillmore's case grammar model (and derivations thereof) to the description of child language has been recognized by Slobin (1970), Brown (1973), and Bowerman (1973), among others. It has been found particularly suitable for describing one-word speech, because a semantic case or role such as "object" or "agent" could be assigned to a single word without having to make reference to syntactic structures that were not yet overtly produced. Additionally, some of the problems encountered in applying earlier models disappear with case grammar, because "a semantic approach which derives grammar from relations among perceived aspects of the real world opens the way to a theoretical treatment of one word as structurally continuous with later grammatical development" (Greenfield & Smith, 1976, p. 15). For example, Kernan (1970) argued that the shift from the two-word to the three-word stage could be seen in a case grammar framework as simply involving the addition of a second case to the verbal proposition. Fillmore's model also facilitated comparison between typologically quite different languages and thus contributed to the search for universals in language acquisition.

Speech-act theory. Theoretical interest in "speech acts" (Austin, 1962; Searle, 1969) has focused on speakers' intent in making an utterance, such as reporting, commanding, and inquiring. An important concept is that some utterances (called "performatives") accomplish certain functions just by being said—for example, the act of promising, of requesting, or of making a declaration like *You're fired* or *I resign*. These are distinguished from referential use of language, which has propositional content. This linguistic theory is based on the work of such pragmatic philosophers as Austin (1962), Grice (1975), and Searle (1969), though its ethnocentricity has been criticized by Silverstein (1977).

Researchers in child language acquisition have applied this model to the study of children's communicative intent and how it relates to lexical development (see Bates, 1976a; Clark & Clark, 1977; Greenfield & Smith, 1976). Hypotheses developed from this perspective have been particularly enlightening with respect to the growth of communication in infancy, and to a concept of continuous communicative development from "proto speech acts" (Bruner, 1975; Dore, 1975) to complex verbalization, rather than an abrupt beginning of "grammar" only when two words are first used in sequence (the structuralist and generative-transformational views). Eisenberg (1978), however, finds speech-act theory to be too confining to be useful.

With the growth of interest within linguistic theory during the seventies toward pragmatics and the recognition of meaning as central to language, attention in language acquisition research shifted to such topics as the functions that language serves for children and the relationship of form and meaning. From this perspective, these topics are seen to comprise the essential tasks of early language development: (1) learning to use language to achieve particular goals, and (2) determining the relation between regularly occurring linguistic patterns and regularly occurring contexts and experiences, which provide meaning. This latter task is essentially a "mapping" problem for the child—one of mapping the relation of what he or she hears to the surrounding world (Clark, 1977).

Sociolinguistics. As recently as the late sixties, theories of language acquisition were focusing primarily on the biological or innate factors in the process and were relegating the social context of language learning to an amorphous sociolinguistic milieu from which children somehow constructed their language.

Within the past decade, however—with rapid developments taking place within linguistic theory, moving toward a concern for discourse processes and conversational interaction—research on language development has placed emphasis on discovering what communicative strategies children use, on how these are developed, and on how input is structured in the process of social interaction.

The shift of focus has also entailed a shift away from experimental research procedures toward ethnographic modes of investigation. From this perspective, it is considered possible to understand how language is learned only if the process is observed and analyzed within its natural social and cultural setting and in the context of conscious or unconscious socialization or enculturation.

Much of the recent research on language development has been influenced by work in sociolinguistics and by its emphasis on the social and interactional nature of language and language use. Research from this perspective does not focus so much on development of the referential functions of language as on the interactional ones, and although the development of speech is still of central interest, a broader scope of communicative behaviors is being investigated (e.g., Carter, 1975; Gleason & Weintraub, 1978; Halliday, 1975).

Seen from the sociolinguistic viewpoint, the task of children learning language is much greater in scope and complexity than just acquiring "linguistic competence" (Chomsky, 1965), which includes only the ability to understand and produce grammatically correct utterances. They must acquire "communicative competence" (Hymes, 1964), which includes not only phonological, syntactic, and semantic systems but rules for their appropriate use and interpretation in different social contexts.

The essential assumption of the interactional model is that the acquisition of communicative competence is the result of interaction processes within a sociocultural context, and not merely the automatic unfolding of innate, preprogrammed behavior. Descriptive data from a wide variety of speech communities clearly support this perspective (reviewed in Saville-Troike, 1982).

Language Development, Cognition, and Culture. The relationship between language and cognitive development has long been of interest (e.g., Luria, 1959; Piaget, 1926; Piaget & Inhelder, 1969; Vygotsky, 1964 [1934]), with Piaget's model emphasizing the priority of cognition in relation to language structures, and Luria's the progressive "internalization of speech" as cognitive abilities develop.

The most common current position is that cognitive development occurs before and quite independently of language development, and indeed that language acquisition is heavily dependent on prior conceptualization; that is, meaning precedes verbalization (Bloom, 1973; Nelson, 1974a), or "new forms first express old functions" (Slobin, 1973, p. 184). When new meanings (or functions) require expression, children make use of whatever "old forms" are available. Bowerman (1981) adds a note of caution regarding attempts to explain language development by reference to "cognition first," however. "Cognition first" cannot account for cross-cultural phenomena; for example, children acquiring Navajo need the concepts "distributive" and "aggregate plural," alienable and inalienable possession, and certain complicated distinctions of aspect and gender, which are not required for children learning English.

An alternative perspective is provided by Halliday, who claims that children use language in part to construct their conceptual framework, that "a child constructs a reality for himself largely through language" (1975, p. 120). Bowerman (1976, 1980) also presents data that indicate children may use a word they do not yet have a meaning for, and then attempt to construct meaning from the context and usage they have observed, and further support comes from studies, discussed below, that focus on language development through interaction.

According to Halliday, his perspective "is complementary to the cognitive one, not contradictory to it . . . locating [the higher level of semiotic organization] not in the cognitive system but in the social system" (1975, p. 139), but there is disagreement on this point. For example, Greenfield & Smith (1976) consider it an "untenable position" in relation to their view that language is based on a preexisting conceptual framework.

Another aspect of the relationship between language and cognitive development that appears somewhat contradictory is that very young children produce metaphorical utterances (Bloom, 1973; Carlson & Anisfeld, 1969), and yet experimental research suggests this ability is acquired much later, after basic language skills (Gardner, 1974; Jakobson, 1960). Other research indicates children know more about metaphor than the experimental tasks allow them to display; they are limited by content knowledge, knowledge of when metaphoric interpretation is appropriate, and knowledge of conventionalized interpretations (Gentner, 1977, 1978). Apparently contradictory data may also be due to a shift from inventive language use in early childhood, to a stage of literalism, and back to creativity (Gardner et al., 1978).

One aspect of children's cognitive development that may have been underestimated because of the linguistic requirements is the ability to make inferences from verbal messages. Piaget (1926) asserted that the logical structure of children before the formal operations stage could deal with objects and their properties but not with reasoning about propositions (Falmagne, 1975). However, many recent studies have demonstrated that children are capable of all kinds of inferencing as soon as they have the requisite linguistic and memorial competence (e.g., Bryant & Trabasso, 1971; Neimark & Chapman, 1975; Trabasso, 1980).

Beyond the early years of childhood and fairly simple issues (e.g., the gradual unfolding of distinctions in color terminology), the interrelation of linguistic and cognitive development has been little examined. In a book-length treatment of cognitive development, for instance, Flavell (1977) devotes only ten pages to communication and language, and those ten pages deal primarily with the growth of children's ability to modify the content of discourse in relation to the information needs of listeners (e.g., blindfolded versus seeing). He reports that while some experiments seemed to show that this ability was not acquired until the age of 8, others employing a gamelike approach elicited such behavior from 3-year-olds.

There are a number of dimensions along which the study of language and cognitive development could be examined. These include such matters as the ability to recognize hierarchical relationships among vocabulary items (e.g., bird-robin; vegetable-lettuce; metal-iron), to comprehend various types of humor (e.g., puns, situational jokes), to formulate rules for sequences of behavior (e.g., games, school routines), to stage analogies, to organize events in narrative accounts, to compose poetry or comparable forms, to construct generalizations, and to recognize contradictories. Additional data of a cross-cultural nature are especially needed, to avoid the dangers of prematurely positing universals on the basis of behavior in one language and one culture (see reviews of existing cross-cultural data in Bowerman, 1981; Cole & Scribner, 1974).

A very significant direction of research that is certain to have a growing impact on the study of discourse (text) construction and interpretation during the coming decade is the application of schema theory, as it has been adapted from the field of artificial intelligence. Cognitive schemata, or "scripts," which are developed through experience, enable individuals to interpret linguistic and behavioral text in personal interaction settings as well as in the process of reading. Reading itself is seen as a constructive interaction between the text and the reader, with the reader constructing an interpretation as he or she proceeds. Schemata that are brought to bear in interpretation include knowledge of discourse structures and appropriate rules of interaction (e.g., story grammars, "logical" or rhetorical structure of argumentation, organization of conversations versus public speeches, mutual responsibilities of participants, etc.), as well as knowledge of facts, events, values, attitudes, and relationships in the "real world" or some particular subcultural component thereof.

Most text is spoken or written with the presupposition that the reader will bring to it schemata that are congruent with those of the speaker or writer. To the extent that these schemata are shared, or the hearer-reader possesses metacognitive strategies to detect gaps and inadequacies and to seek to repair them, communication will be more or less successful. To use a simple example, a text beginning "Once upon a time" will identify for hearers or readers familiar with the genre that this is likely to be a folk tale, and they will be able to predict that it is likely to be about royal figures and magical events. In short, the identification can trigger a schema for this type of story that will aid a hearer or reader in the comprehension of the text through matching of intake with internally generated expectations.

It is coming to be increasingly realized that proficient hearers or readers of language do not in fact attend to every word that they hear or read, but probably sample the received text only to the extent necessary to create a satisfactory internal representation and seek clarification (repetition, expansion, rereading, etc.) only when a coherent interpretation fails. A major task of formal education is to assist students to internalize the schemata and strategies, both linguistic and extralinguistic, to enable them to comprehend (i.e., construct adequate interpretations of) complex textual language, especially that dealing with abstract conceptual structures. (For research data and programmatic discussion, see Johnson-Laird & Wason, 1977; Schlesinger, 1977; Spiro, Bruce, & Brewer, 1980; Steffensen, Jogdeo, & Anderson, 1979; van Dijk, 1980.)

In most industrialized nations, formal education is to a large extent linguistically mediated, so the relation of language and cognitive development is obviously an issue of the greatest educational import. The Finnish researchers Skutnabb-Kangas and Toukomaa (1976) have, on the basis of Finnish immigrants in Sweden, argued that native language education, at least through the age of 10, is important for the attainment of successful academic achievement in a second language where those involved are members of a socially subordinated group. That the effects do not hold for majority-group students from middle-class backgrounds and supportive homes (e.g., English-speaking Canadian students in French immersion programs; see Swain, 1978) suggests that the factors inhibiting academic achievement among linguistic minorities may be as much cultural and attitudinal (on the part of the majority) as linguistic, but language clearly plays a role (see review in Troike, 1978).

Evidence from a variety of sources suggests that sociolinguistic factors may have a powerful effect on the types of cognitive development that school curricula are designed to foster and reward. It must be remembered that the school is a fairly late cultural invention, and the forms of thinking inculcated therein, as well as the forms of language used as a medium of instruction, are very specific to this cultural context. The failure of many students, both of the majority culture and different subcultures, to achieve in school may be in some measure the result of a failure to acquire the complex linguistic structures and forms of discourse used to mediate the teaching and learning of cognitive skills.

Cummins (1979) has argued that the acquisition of "academic language" forms and uses is a prerequisite to academic achievement (which may be regarded as a surrogate measure of cognitive development, at least of a particularly defined band on a cognitive spectrum). He has emphasized, as have others, that much academic discourse is "context-reduced" language, as opposed to the "context-embedded" language with which students are familiar in interpersonal interactional settings. Context-reduced language requires the hearer (or reader) to construct mental contexts largely from the language text itself, since the situational context cannot be utilized, to interpret the linguistic message, or to seek clarification from an interlocutor. The ability to process and learn from information presented and constructed in context-reduced texts is at the heart of the educational enterprise.

As Michaels and Cook-Gumperz (1979) have shown, students from nonmajority backgrounds may be accustomed to other patterns of rhetorical and discourse organization, and may for this reason have difficulty in processing academic prose. Although much effort has been expended on reading problems as a source of low achievement in school, research has shown that the same difficulties show up when a text is heard as when it is read (Daneman & Carpenter, 1980), indicating that many of the problems basically arise from failure to acquire the necessary metacognitive strategies for processing context-reduced prose. The fact that these problems tend to be more frequent among lower socioeconomic status students undoubtedly reflects in part the greater congruity between the language used in the home background of the middle-class students and that used in the school (which is a middle-class institution).

Personality-related factors, which are also partly social and cultural in origin, may also have an effect. Students who are found to be "field-independent" on the basis of Embedded Figures tests appear to be able to handle context-reduced prose better than "field-sensitive" (dependent) students, who are likely to perform better at interpreting information communicated in interpersonal interaction (Cazden & Leggett, 1976; Ramirez, Herold, & Castañeda, 1975; Witkin & Goodenough, 1976).

Whatever the origins of differences in ability to process context-reduced language, Oller (1980a) has claimed that there is a general factor of language proficiency that exhausts most of the reliable variance on various subtasks of listening, speaking, reading, and writing. He further (1980b) equates this with Spearman's g, and proposes that putative measures of intelligence are essentially equivalent to measures of language proficiency. Put another way, "intelligence" (as defined by scores on tests) is simply a reflection of an underlying general language ability (presumably, again, relative to a particular spectrum of context-reduced language used in school and in testing situations). An anthropologically oriented perspective, however, might see school achievement and language proficiency test performance as primarily measures of acculturation to middle-class knowledge and language use (Troike, 1981).

Although language acquisition is generally considered to be primarily a cognitive process, it is clearly a social process as well, and one that must take place within the context of social interaction. Just as some innate language development capabilities must be posited to explain the rate and sequence of children's acquisition of their native language code, we must also assume that all human infants are born with the capacity to develop patterned rules for appropriate language use from whatever input is provided within their speech community.

All components of a communicative event are potential input to children in their construction of meaning from language (e.g., setting, people participating in or listening to the interaction), with the social identity of the participants evidently the most salient (Slobin, 1967). This is particularly evident for children in a bilingual (or even multilingual) setting, who learn to use two (or more) languages at the same time, distinguishing them by interlocutors (McClure, 1977; Weir, 1962). Halliday's (1975) functional-interactional approach is consonant with this view, claiming that children learn the meaning of language because of the systematic relation between what they hear and what is going on around them. Children's intent to communicate arises naturally out of the system of shared assumptions and understandings that result from the regularities and rituals of their early socialization (Cook-Gumperz, 1977). Children begin to use language within this framework of presupposed knowledge, where verbalizations are only part of the message communicated by them or by adults. Halliday's treatment of acquisition considers such factors as the language that the child is reacting to and its meaning potential, the situational environment of interaction (including the roles and status of participants), the variety of language used in any specific communicative event, the linguistic system itself (both its potential and how it is constructed by the child), and the social structure within which the interaction is taking place.

Early studies on the effects of expansions and modeling by adults on child language development yielded no significant results (Brown, Cazden, & Bellugi, 1968; Cazden, 1965), but Blount (1975) suggests this may be because the range of language forms and processes they tested for was too broad. He further notes that the systematic deletion of imitations or expansions of child speech in Brown's (1973) calculation of the frequency of morpheme use by adults and its effect on order of acquisition may have led to false conclusions. Blount suggests (and more recent research confirms) that parental speech has at least as great an influence on child language development in interactions that are initiated by the child as in those that are initiated by the parent. Lieven (1978) reports that a child is an initiator as much as a responder in many situations and thus controls his or her own opportunities for language learning. Wells (1981) describes the strategies that children use to engage adults in conversation and prolong the interaction.

Children's role in their own language learning appears to be far more active than models that focused on either conditioning or innate capacity led us to believe. Children are essentially participant-observers of communication, like small ethnographers, learning and inductively developing language rules through processes of observation and interaction.

The common practice of focusing observation and description exclusively on "verbal" features may also have obscured important data for understanding the development of communication ability. Von Raffler-Engel and Rea (1978) report that much of the interaction between adults and children is nonverbal, or paralinguistic, with children often confirming understanding or triggering repetitions or paraphrases with grunts, facial expressions, or head nods. The scope of at least some recent research has expanded to include interactional phenomena traditionally considered "nonverbal" aspects of communication (e.g., Carter, 1975; Wiener, Shilkret, & Devoe, 1980; Wood, 1976), but many more data are needed.

There has been significant disagreement about the age

and extent to which children use language to interact with others. The disagreement reflects at least in part differences in social and cultural influences on communicative behavior that would result in differential answers to these questions. Piaget (1926) claimed that children's speech is primarily egocentric, with early conversation essentially collective monologue, and that such interactional linguistic forms as commands and requests are a later development. He reported that even at 6½ years, more than one-half of children's utterances are egocentric: repetition, monologue, and collective monologue. The social factors involved are illustrated by Keenan's (1974) challenge to Piaget's conclusions in reporting that her twins exhibited such interactional strategies as turn taking before the age of 3, but also by Garvey's (1977) lack of success in replicating Keenan's results with young children who were not acquainted.

One of the most important contributions of a cross-cultural perspective on language development is the awareness it creates of the great diversity in the social context in which development takes place. Different cultures contain tremendous differences in child-rearing practices and beliefs about appropriate behaviors with children—and yet language acquisition is to a remarkable extent a similar process around the world. Thus, while language development takes place in the process of social interaction (and would be impossible in a social vacuum), full understanding of the process will require research from cognitive perspectives as well.

Development of Forms and Functions. For analytic purposes, it is useful to consider language as a complex of component systems that are organized hierarchically. The smallest units of speech are sounds (the phonological system), which are used to represent morphemes and words (the lexical system). These are in turn combined into units of phrases, clauses, and sentences (the syntactic system), which may occur in sequences or interact with the utterances of others (the discourse system). Cross-cutting all levels must be consideration of meaning (semantics), the functions of language use (pragmatics), and appropriateness for social and cultural contexts. Many linguists see language organized in levels, with meaning forming the deepest level, which is linked by means of the grammar (syntax) to the words and morphemes that form the surface level and are represented by speech (or, alternatively, by writing or manual signs).

Phonology. Recent research on the acquisition of phonology has been influenced primarily by two theoretical perspectives: focus on language universals versus focus on variability. Adequate description and understanding of the process must incorporate both views. (For a review of these and other theoretical perspectives on phonological development, see Ferguson & Garnica, 1975.)

The universal perspective sees the development of the phonological system of any language as essentially the unfolding of an increasing set of meaningful distinctions children interpret and produce. Jakobson (1941) accounts for these progressive distinctions in terms of a hierarchy of distinctive features. The distinctions between vocalic and nonvocalic (like /a/ and /p/) are the first to be made; distinctions between continuant and noncontinuant (like /m/ and /b/ or /f/ and /t/) are developed a little later; distinctions between voiced and voiceless consonants (like /b/ and /p/ or /d/ and /t/) are developed later still.

The set of possible distinctive features in all human languages is relatively small (Chomsky & Halle, 1968; Jakobson, Fant, & Halle, 1963), but each unique language makes use of some of these distinctions and not others, or the features pattern in different ways into meaningful units of sound (phonemes). Jakobson claims that the order in which features are distinguished by children is the same for all languages, although the nature and pattern of the developing phonological system depends on which sounds are phonemic in the language each child is hearing and learning to speak.

Research on child language development has not supported Jakobson's theory in its strongest form, since order of acquisition has proved to be variable (even for the same language). At least part of the variation that has been found in the order of phonological development may be attributed to the different lexical items being produced by individual children (Ferguson & Farwell, 1975). Linguistic environment has also been considered as a potential factor in variability, especially in studies of identical versus fraternal twins, raised together and apart (see Leonard, Newhoff, & Mesalam, 1980, for a review of these studies). Leonard, Newhoff, and Mesalam (1980) report that female identical twins exhibit almost as much difference in order and rate of phonological development as ten unrelated children of the same age that they studied, however, indicating that linguistic environment is not sufficient to explain the variation. Other factors contributing to variation include individual strategies in the acquisition of phonology, more general differences in learning styles, and accidents of language input (Ferguson, 1979).

The fact that some sounds are produced in early words and then seemingly "unlearned" is also problematic for a strong interpretation of Jakobson's theory. This is possibly because sounds are produced first as part of a phonological idiom, imitating adult speech, and later modified to fit into the regularized system that is developing (see Leonard, Newhoff, & Mesalam, 1980; Moskowitz, 1970). This would be congruent with evidence that the early contrastive units acquired by children are words, not sounds (Ferguson & Farwell, 1975; Macken, 1977; Menn, 1976; Vihman, 1976). These words are not yet distinguished by phonemic principles, and a child's pronunciation of the same word may be variable.

Early phonological development may be summarized in the context of four broad stages in infant communication (Kaplan & Kaplan, 1971; reviewed in Dale, 1976).

1. *Crying (beginning at birth).* Many infants seem to have variants of their cry, and parents often infer different "meanings," such as pain, hunger, frustration, or boredom.

Such interpretation is probably heavily dependent on context; when removed from context (e.g., not knowing when the infant last ate), Müller, Hollien, and Murray (1974) found that parents could not infer the reason for crying.

2. *Other vocalizations (beginning about 1 month) and cooing (about 2 months).* Vocalization becomes much more varied, and articulatory organs are used (e.g., tongue and lips). Cooing usually involves production of the back vowel /u/ with rounded lips.

3. *Babbling (begins by 5–6 months).* Vocalizations are much more like speech, with frequent consonantlike sounds and syllables of consonant plus vowel (CV). Intonation patterns begin to resemble those of adults. Although speechlike, the sounds produced at this stage seem to be very similar for all infants, no matter what language is spoken in their environment (Atkinson, MacWhinney, & Stoel, 1970). Infants who hear either English or Arabic will both produce pharyngeal fricatives, for instance, but because the sound does not occur in English, it will be lost in the process of phonological development; it will be retained by children acquiring Arabic because it is part of the phonological system of the adult language.

4. *Patterned speech (begins about 11–12 months).* The transition from babbling to patterned speech may be gradual or abrupt and sometimes is marked by a period of complete silence. Syllabic structure diversifies from the V and CV already acquired to include also VCV, VC, and CVCV (reduplication), and single meaningful words are produced.

Perceptive competence generally precedes productive distinctions (e.g., Menyuk & Anderson, 1969; see Edwards, 1975, for counterevidence in a few instances). This order is illustrated by accounts of children responding negatively to adults' attempts to imitate their pronunciation; for example, "a child asked if he could come along on a trip to the 'mewwy-go-wound.' . . . 'No,' said David firmly, 'you don't say it wight' " (Maccoby & Bee, 1965, p. 67). Although the general principle seems to hold, the anecdotal and experimental sources of data are brought into question by Priestly (1980).

Virtually all children have mastered the phonological system of their native language by 7 or 8 years, or more precisely, the variety of that language spoken in their region and by members of their social group. They have also developed systematic variation appropriate in different social contexts (see reviews by Keller-Cohen, 1978; Roeper & McNeill, 1973). For example, Labov (1966) and Wolfram (1969) report that black children use more final consonant clusters in the presence of whites than in the presence of blacks, and one 6-year-old child I knew developed a lisp when a best friend lost his front teeth (Saville-Troike, 1982). Young children are also developing evaluative attitudes toward variable pronunciation of their language, related to concepts of self and others' identity.

Variability in child language is currently of great interest to researchers in this field, and better understanding of its nature and functions should be forthcoming.

Words and their meanings. The first words spoken by children cannot be considered "parts of speech" comparable to categories of words in adult grammar, because they are complete utterances in themselves. In their review of early studies on one-word speech, Greenfield and Smith (1976) note that this property in words designating and commenting on objects has long been recognized. In 1893, Stevenson wrote: In the infant's speech, these words are not nouns, but equivalent to whole sentences. When a very young child says "water," he is not using the word merely as the name of an object so designated by us, but with the value of an assertion, something like "I want water," or "there is water" (cited in Greenfield & Smith, 1976, p. 18).

There is evidence that children's nonverbal actions and perceptions are structured in terms of such semantic functions (cases) as agent, object, or location, and that the first words are used in reference to these semantic relations (Greenfield & Smith, 1976). Linguists are now in fairly general agreement that these one-word utterances cannot be characterized in terms of grammatical structure, since young children exhibit no knowledge of syntax in the traditional sense (see Bloom, 1973) but rather in terms of semantic or functional intent (see Dore, 1975)—that is, as "speech acts."

Halliday (1975) is one who claims that the earliest meaning in child language is functional, or pragmatic, in origin, and depends on the interactional context of communication as much as on emerging linguistic structures. The order in which the functions were acquired by his son was instrumental, regulatory, interactional, and personal (all about 9 months); heuristic and imaginative (15 months); and informative (21 months).

Greenfield and Smith (1976) also report their data in terms of a time sequence for the acquisition of linguistic functions. These include

1. Performatives (10–11 months). Utterances are an integral part of action—for example, *hi, bye-bye, mm.*
2. Names of people (about 12 months). First used when the person can be heard but is not in sight.
3. Vocatives (about 15 months). Used to get attention for a subsequent utterance.
4. Object of a demand (16–18 months). For example, *spoon* if they want one.
5. Object of a direct action (19 months). For example, *spoon* if mother removes it.
6. Instrument of an action (21 months). For example, *spoon* if someone is eating with one.

The sequential use of a single lexical item like *spoon* to express different semantic relations illustrates the developmental nature of this process.

The age when a child first utters single words is variable, as is the length of time this stage lasts before he or she begins to put words together. Onset is usually early in the second year, and production of some children is limited to single-word utterances for 8–10 months or even longer (Bloom & Lahey, 1978). During this period, children are not merely learning new words but developing their phonological system, learning the meanings of different kinds of words, and learning to use words in relation to a variety of contexts and activities.

What children pay attention to is reflected in early vocabulary development; for instance, their attention to actions is reflected in early choice of "words that refer to agents, movers, and doers" (Keller-Cohen, 1978, p. 463; cf. Clark, 1978; Nelson, 1973, 1974a). In the acquisition of antonymous adjectives, children generally acquire the positive adjectives first: *big* before *small, tall* before *short,* and *wide* before *narrow* (Donaldson & Wales, 1970; Klatzky, Clark, & Macken, 1973). Keller-Cohen (1978) reports suggestions that "the positive member is learned first because it refers to the end of the dimension with the greatest extent, and that great extent is particularly salient for the young child" (p. 464). She also cites evidence that suggests children's preference for containment and contact may partially account for the acquisition of *in* before *under* (Clark, 1973a) and *come* before *go* (Clark & Garnica, 1974).

Another view is presented by Greenfield and Smith (1976), who argue that "the child first expresses what is relatively uncertain or informative. . . . Applied to polar opposite states, uncertainty would be change" (p. 218). The first term to be used in a pair that expresses opposite meaning will be the one that indicates change; for example, a child in their study used *on* when he wanted something turned on that was usually off, and used *out* before *in* because he wanted to get pennies out of a bank (contrary to the containment preference principle suggested above but congruent with attention to movement and action). Which term in such pairs would refer to a change in natural state depends at least to some extent on the salient objects in the child's environment and on the situations in which the terms are used.

Nelson (1973) distinguishes between the words in early vocabularies that are "referential" and those that are "expressive" (i.e., that do and do not make reference to objects, respectively). In studies of the first fifty words acquired by a large number of subjects, she and others report different children use proportionately more of one type or the other. First-born children use more referential words, and later-born children more social routine words, such as *hi* and *bye-bye,* and this difference is also reflective of the different social contexts of language acquisition.

Vocabulary development (and by implication, knowledge of the domains to which the vocabulary pertains) may also reflect to a significant degree the ordering of priorities within a culture or subculture and serves as an index of socialization or enculturation. For example, the typical school curriculum does not introduce the terms and concepts for cardinal directions until about the fourth- or fifth-grade level, but Navajo children already master them even before starting school, because of the importance of directions in the religious beliefs and practices of the community (Saville-Troike, 1982).

Sherk's (1973) comparison of the spontaneous speaking

vocabulary of lower-class children who were 4, 5, and 6 years old (mostly black) and from Missouri (LC) and middle-class (mostly white) children from New England (MC) showed the following differences in frequencies of lexical occurrences:

	LC	MC
apron	1	743
vegetables	6	165
trash	52	0
whip	23	3
party	9	800

Sherk drew the invalid inference that the differences reflected differing topics of interest; a more valid conclusion is that the terms simply mirror differences in experience. Further, the occurrence only among the lower-class group of terms such as *chitlins, skillet, lingo, shoats*, 'poor people,' *pokey, okra, greens*, and *fetch* must be attributed to regional and ethnic differences in experience rather than social class differences, as inferred in this study. Indeed, all situated meaning in language depends on the dictates of cultural experience (cf. Cook-Gumperz, 1977).

It is hard to say with assurance when a child has "learned" a word. "Knowing" a word fully means at least knowing its pronunciation; its primary referential meaning (its denotation); its range of application; its differentiation from related words in the same domain (e.g., *running* versus *jogging*); its associational significance (its connotation); its metaphoric uses; its categorical memberships (features it shares with other groups of words, such as animate noun, stative verb); its grammatical and semantic collocational or co-occurrence relationships with other words or word classes (e.g., transitive verbs require objects; rocks don't drink milk); its metalinguistic existence (e.g., how it is spelled, how to refer to it, its paradigmatic memberships); and its sociolinguistic or pragmatic properties (e.g., whether it is a taboo word, whether it is a "hard word," whether it is appropriate for intimate use). To some extent we continue throughout life renewing and revising our knowledge of words, as we hear them pronounced differently, encounter them in novel contexts, or find them used in new ways. Thus language development truly never stops.

It cannot be assumed, therefore, that children "know" a word just because they use it in a specific context. The development of meaning requires experience with the referent in a variety of contexts, understanding it in relation to many others, and forming a network of semantic categories and subcategories. Research on this aspect of language acquisition has focused on different ways children know words at various stages in their development, which accounts for many discrepancies in reports of the rate of vocabulary acquisition.

The first meaning assigned to a word is restricted to the specific context in which the word is learned (underex-

tension), such as *dog* referring only to the neighbor's pet (Anglin, 1975; Bloom, 1973). The child then learns that *dog* refers to other creatures, makes a generalization about the semantic domain to which the word might apply, and typically uses *dog* to refer to all four-legged animals (overextension). This hypothesis formation, testing, and revision continues through childhood (Bloom, 1973; Brown, 1965; Greenfield, 1973). The perceptual criteria that foster such overextension include shape, size, texture, and movement but evidently not color (Clark, 1973b); e.g., children may extend *dog* to all fuzzy, four-legged animals with tails, but not to other brown objects.

Overextension of the use of *dog* does not necessarily mean that the child recognizes the differences among dogs, cats, sheep, and horses. Clark (1973a) believes overextension is evidence that the child has fewer semantic components than are required for adult meaning, or it may indicate that the child recognizes similarities and has identified a larger semantic domain but does not yet have the productive vocabulary to refer to the other animals (Bloom & Lahey, 1978). A counter hypothesis is suggested by Bridges, Sinha, and Walkerdine (1981). Rather than assume a direct link between perception and language (or action), they propose a "functional core hypothesis, which assumes that the relationship between language—specifically, word meanings—and perception is mediated by a separate, functionally based conceptual system" (p. 142). The primary difference is the level of abstraction at which concepts or categories are thought to exist (see also Rosch, 1977).

According to Nelson and Nelson (1978), changes in linguistic and cognitive systems follow the following stages:

1. Idiosyncratic first steps
2. General-rule state (few generally broad rules)
3. Many-rule state (rapid change, additions, revisions)
4. Integration and consolidation (stable, coordinated rules)
5. Flexible extension (adaptive, conscious rule use)

Overall linguistic and cognitive development does not take place at an even rate. Nelson and Nelson attribute this unevenness to "pendulum" swings, which include (1) shifts from rapid acquisition of new skills and rules to limited growth while old skills and rules are repeatedly applied; and (2) shifts from one quality to its opposite, as from broad to narrow, from stable to unstable, and from loosely related components to a highly integrated and complex level (p. 226).

Stage 4 (integration and consolidation) in the development of the semantic system is reached when the child has a basic working vocabulary of about 500 words, when the system becomes "rigidified." This corresponds to Piaget's (1965) and Vygotsky's (1934) stage of word realism. The sequence of development may be repeated beyond early childhood as new semantic domains are differentiated. This process has been studied by deVos (1977) in relation to differentiated usage of *cup, glass, bowl*, and *vase* by children 3 to 10 years old (an adaptation of research with adults by Labov, 1973), by Neimark (1974) in relation to clothing, and by Nelson (1974b) and Rosner and Hayes (1976) in relation to furniture. (These studies are described in Nelson & Nelson, 1978.)

MacGinitie (1969) reported in his review of the literature for the fourth edition of the *Encyclopedia of Educational Research* that "vocabulary is somewhat outside current trends of study but in many practical respects remains an index of development outweighing all others" (p. 693). The same may be said over a decade later. While the acquisition of vocabulary has been a key component in research on the development of phonological, semantic, and pragmatic aspects of language, it has received little recent attention from linguists and psychologists as a developing system in its own right. This neglect may be justified by the imperatives of linguistic theory, and by the self-contained nature of the linguistic subsystems that have received attention, but the importance of vocabulary development to learning to read and other aspects of formal schooling suggests that greater research focus on vocabulary *per se* would be useful for education. In the meantime, there is abundant research from earlier periods, which continues to be used as a basis for curriculum development (for an extensive bibliography, see Dale & Razik, 1963), and educators continue to compile word lists and frequencies. In general, however, educational research in this area does not incorporate recent findings from other areas of language study (e.g., linguistics and psychology) or recent perspectives from these fields on methods for data collection and analysis.

Morphology. Slobin (1973, p. 205) posits the following sequence as the universal pattern for the acquisition of grammatical inflections on words (illustrated here with past tense forms in English):

1. No marking (e.g., *break, drop*)
2. Appropriate marking in limited cases (e.g., *broke, drop*)
3. Overgeneralization of marking (e.g., *breaked, dropped*)
4. Full adult system (e.g., *broke, dropped*)

Similarly, the pattern for the acquisition of plurals is generally (1) *foot, cat;* (2) *feet, cat;* (3) *foots, cats;* (4) *feet, cats.* The third stage represents a level where the regular rule for forming past tense and plural (adding *-ed* and *-s,* respectively) has been acquired and is overgeneralized. The irregular forms *(broke, feet)* used in the second stage were probably learned as separate lexical items and are probably relearned in stage 4 as exceptions to the general rule. Cazden (1968) illustrates this process in one child's use of *went* and *goed* from ages 27 to 50 months:

went:	27	32	. . .	47	48	49	50
goed:				47		49	

This child used *went* correctly as early as 27 months, but *goed* at 47 and 49 months. The age at which this overgeneralization occurs is variable; for example, another child in

Cazden's study used *comed* three times between 25 and 27 months after she had used *came* correctly 11 times between 20 and 22 months.

The regular plural inflection in English requires further development to distinguish three allomorphs (phonologically different forms of the same morpheme): -/ɨz/ after words that end with /s,z,š,ž,č,j/, as in *glasses* and *watches;* -/z/ after other voiced consonants and all vowels, as in *dogs* and *toes;* and -/s/ after other voiceless consonants, as in *cats.* Acquisition of this distinction was tested by Berko (1958) using a now classic procedure with nonsense names and cartoon pictures—for example, saying, "This is a wug; these are two _____," expecting *wugs* in response. With children 4 to 7 years, she found 67 percent errors with names requiring -/ɨz/, and only 25 percent with names requiring -/z/. (The relative infrequency of -/ɨz/ in the language a child hears may account for this order of development.) At least the regular forms of the past tense and plural are acquired by the time a child enters school. Derivational morphology (generally used to derive one part of speech from another—e.g., noun + *-ical* → adjective; adjective + *-ly* → adverb) continues to develop throughout the school years and has an important bearing on students' ability to comprehend and produce complex abstract prose. Although most persons by adulthood have acquired full control of the inflectional system of the language, there are great individual differences in the control of the derivational system (particularly with regard to morphemes of Latinate and Romance origins).

Morphological development has not been a major focus for recent research on the acquisition of English as a native language, but there is increasing interest in comparative studies across languages and language families (see especially Ferguson & Slobin, 1973; and Blount, 1975, and Bowerman, 1981, for reviews of the literature). Summaries of research based primarily on development of English may be found in Brown (1973) and Dale (1976).

Syntax. Children begin to string two or more words together at about 18 months, but there are pauses between each, and they are given equal stress, giving the impression of a sequence of one-word utterances (Schlesinger, 1975). Soon after, however, they come to be combined in a single intonation contour (question, statement, or emphatic).

As at the one-word stage, two-word utterances are structured in terms of their semantic relations. The same basic set is found for all children at this stage, no matter what language they are learning, and is generally related to universals in the development of sensorimotor intelligence (Piaget & Inhelder, 1969; for discussion see Sinclair, 1971; McCune-Nicolich, 1981). The following list is from Brown (1973, p. 173), with examples compiled by Wells (1981, p. 84):

1. Agent and action *(Adam go)*
2. Action and object *(Kick ball)*
3. Agent and object *(Mummy sock)*
4. Action and locative *(Sit chair)*

5. Entity and locative *(Lady home)*
6. Possessor and possession *(Daddy chair)*
7. Entity and attributive *(Yellow block)*
8. Demonstrative and entity *(That dog)*

Early multiple-word utterances are often called "telegraphic" because, as in telegrams, "function words" (elements of primarily grammatical function) are typically missing—for example, prepositions, articles, copulas *(be)*, and auxiliary verbs (Brown & Bellugi, 1964; Brown & Fraser, 1963). Function words and inflections are gradually added in the development process, and sentences become longer and hierarchically organized (e.g., a noun phrase is used in place of a single noun; sentences are embedded within sentences).

Mean length of utterance (MLU) is sometimes used as a measure of syntactic development. MLU is calculated by counting the number of morphemes (e.g., *cat* = 1, *cats* = 2, *cats'* = 3) used in a sample of speech by a child, and dividing by the number of "utterances" (essentially, sentences) in the speech sample. Although in general, length of utterance increases with age, Shipley, Smith, and Gleitman (1969) found no significant correlation between age and median length of utterance from 18 to 33 months of age. While MLU is a heuristically convenient measure, it is simplistic in nature, because it fails to distinguish different types of syntactic complexity and may be affected by interview variables such as setting, topic, or interviewer (cf. Labov's 1969 study refuting the claim that black children were nonverbal).

"Minimal terminable units" (T-units) appear to form a more linguistically relevant measure. Developed by Hunt (1965) and used most extensively in studies of growth in writing complexity, T-units consist of any predication that could stand alone together with any other material (including subordinate clauses) connected with it. The T-unit has the advantage over the MLU and other measures that it does not give extra weight even to very long sentences that are formed only by conjoining clauses with *and.*

In Hunt's study of writing at grades 4, 8, and 12, compared with the writing of "superior adults" in *Harper's* and the *Atlantic,* he found a consistent pattern of growth. O'Donnell, Griffin, and Norris (1967) conducted a similar study following Hunt's model (and adding spoken samples beginning in kindergarten), with closely similar results. A major finding was that the complexity of written language quickly outpaced that of speech, which did not change greatly in syntactic complexity from kindergarten through seventh grade.

The development of syntax is related to both cognitive development and grammatical complexity. Children begin to use conjunctions by about 4 years (Johansson & Sjölin, 1975; Miller, 1973), but consistently appropriate use for logical coordination requires further cognitive development and continues developing throughout the elementary school years (Inhelder & Piaget, 1964; Neimark & Slotnik, 1970). The order of acquisition is also related to semantic complexity; for example, *and* appears before *but* because it is semantically less complex (Halliday and Hasan, 1976, analyze *but* as incorporating both the logical meaning of *and* and the meaning "adversative"), and *because* precedes *even though* for the same reason (McClure & Steffensen, 1980).

When children begin to use complex sentences (i.e., sentences containing embedded or subordinated sentential constructions), the order in which events happen is usually the order in which they are mentioned (Clark, 1971; French & Brown, 1977; Hatch, 1971; Johnson, 1975), but grammatical structure is also involved. Since main clauses are also ordered first (Amidon & Carey, 1972; Coker, 1978), *before* appears before *after* in children's language. Regardless of the conjunction used, however, 5-year-olds have difficulty remembering information mentioned in a subordinate clause, and even older children remember information from a main clause more readily (Amidon, 1976). Studies of the understanding and production of relative clauses have generally shown that those that follow the main clause are easier for children than those that are center-embedded; for example, *The boy kicked the dog that bit him* is easier than *The dog that bit the boy ran away* (see de Villiers et al., 1979, for a review).

An important concept that has been developed in recent research is that the process of increasing length and complexity of syntax (and, for English, derivational morphology) goes along with the decontextualization of utterances. All meaning before the onset of language is contained within the nonverbal context; the meaning of early words is created within meaningful nonverbal contexts, and these verbalizations themselves increasingly serve to create meaning apart from the immediate experiences being shared by speaker and hearer (cf. Bruner, 1975; Carter, 1975).

Decontextualization begins when children use language to refer to objects, people, or actions not present in the immediate environment and continues until even emotions can be expressed entirely through the medium of the language code. For instance, aggression is often expressed physically by young children (at least among English speakers), but this behavior comes to be supplemented with verbal taunts and chants by the age of 5, and may develop into one of the complex verbal dueling forms of later childhood and adolescence.

The ability to decontextualize (or better, to symbolize and construct context linguistically) is essential in developing skills to communicate with others who do not share the same social and personal experiences, and eventually in learning to read and to write, where the text itself must carry the message and other interactional clues are not available (see the earlier discussion of "reduced-context" prose and academic achievement). Bernstein's (1971) distinction between "restricted" and "elaborated" codes related to social class and modes of socialization has not been supported by recent research (see Edwards, 1976, and

Robinson, 1978, for reviews). The systematically different linguistic styles described probably do represent different degrees of contextualization in language use, however, and the development of facility in a highly decontextualized variety as part of the linguistic repertoire is probably related to sociocultural differences in literary tradition and experiences (Wells, 1981).

Many aspects of syntactic development are still not well understood. Although it is clear that children use a regular principle for ordering words as soon as they begin putting two together, for instance, there is some disagreement about whether this is a semantic principle (e.g., actor first, then action; see Braine, 1976) or a focusing principle (e.g., more important information first, then less important; see MacWhinney, 1975).

Another unanswered question is how children develop metalinguistic awareness of syntactic classes independently of the semantics involved. A plausible hypothesis proposed by Bowerman (1973) and de Villiers and de Villiers (1978) is that learners first take advantage of the correlation between syntactic and semantic categories: for instance, most verbs are actions, and most subjects are agents. At some point, and in an unknown way, the semantic categories are reorganized into syntactic ones.

Evidence for the interaction of syntax and semantics can be found in studies of 4-to-5-year-olds' comprehension of English active and passive sentences (Maratsos, Kuczaj, & Fox, 1977). When verbs are actional (e.g., *hold, hit*), the subject is semantically in an agentive role, and when verbs are "nonactional" (e.g., *see, remember*), the subject semantically is in an experiencer role (see Fillmore, 1968). The children in the study by Maratsos et al. had evidently not acquired a general passive rule that operated on both types of verbs because they did much better with the first type (with semantically agentive subjects) than with the latter. It is quite possible there is a hierarchy in the concept development of "subject" that says agents are more subject like than words in other semantic categories, comparable to the hierarchy that has been posited to account for purely linguistic phenomena.

The nature and effect of adult language input on language development has in general constituted one of the major foci for research in the last decade and one of its most important contributions to cumulative knowledge in the field (see especially Snow & Ferguson, 1977; Wells, 1981). Adult-initiated dialogue with children may contribute to syntactic development by serving as a stimulus and by providing part of the content, which they can use in their own response (Greenfield & Smith, 1976). The value of such input depends on how it relates to the children's production and on their stage in language development (e.g., see Newport, Gleitman, & Gleitman, 1977).

Discourse. Once children begin using multiple-word utterances, they need to develop strategies for cohesion and interaction, as they do for the sequencing and integration of sentences into longer units of language, such as narratives and conversations (Tierney & Mosenthal, 1981).

As part of developing appropriate use of pronouns and articles, for instance, children must learn to judge what is known, or not known, to the hearer. A distinction between *known* and *new information* is made by 2-year-olds learning a variety of languages (Bates, 1976a; MacWhinney, 1975). Children acquiring a language with relatively free word order use the ordering of words to indicate new information, while children acquiring a language with relatively fixed word order (like English) tend to use contrastive stress. The use of anaphoric pronouns to make this distinction is relatively late in appearing (Keenan, 1977), as is correct selection of indefinite (first-mention) versus definite (subsequent-mention) articles (Maratsos, 1976). Children do not consistently use the definite article for referents known to the hearer but not in the immediate linguistic context until they are about 9 years old (Warden, 1976).

Unlike adults, young English-speaking children frequently achieve cohesion and topic relevance in peer dialogue by repeating all or part of the preceding utterance, and they "use repetition with varying prosodic/intonational markers in place of a variety of adult speech acts and semantic forms to add information that is not coded lexically" (Cook-Gumperz, 1981, p. 34). In sequences of more than one sentence, Applebee (1980) finds evidence of such cohesive devices as word repetition and pronominal reference as early as 3 years. Keenan (1974) reports her twin sons at age 2 years, 9 months could already develop and sustain a cooperative dialogue over several turns. These were constructed by "focusing on a sequence of sound (sound play) or a constituent within an antecedent turn and reproducing it (with or without modification) in the next turn" (p. 163).

Turn taking is among the earliest conversational rules to be acquired (Bloom, Rocissano, & Hood, 1976). Getting someone's attention is a basic initial component of early interactions (Atkinson, 1978; Scollon, 1976). Keenan, Schieffelin, and Platt (1976) report that children's early strategies include self-repetition, vocatives, increased volume, and gestures. Other interaction skills include acknowledging another speaker (e.g., by producing a similar utterance) and sustaining an interaction. Developing conversational competence includes learning to follow such conversational maxims as those outlined by Grice (1975), including "be informative" (provide for the informational needs of the listener) and "be relevant" (keep comments relevant to the topic at hand). Research on the acquisition of these and other conversational principles is reviewed by Keller-Cohen (1978).

The development of oral discourse strategies to a certain level is probably essential for interpreting them in decontextualized written language, and research on the relation of this aspect of oral language development to reading is of great potential significance for schooling. Many have clearly not been developed by the time children enter first grade (e.g., C. Chomsky, 1969, reports problems in oral comprehension of forward pronominalization even for 10-year-olds), and this may create difficulties in the interpretation of written texts.

Children's use of nonlinguistic clues for functional interpretation is documented by Ervin-Tripp (1981): even very young children responded to the intent of the speaker in her experiments, based on their understanding of the particular situation being portrayed, and when they were as young as 3 years were as likely to respond appropriately to indirect requests as to direct ones, at least as long as the desired object was mentioned.

By 4 years of age, children's request forms vary depending on whether they believe the addressee is willing to do what is requested. Garvey (1977) reports the use of tag questions when a child is in doubt that the other will comply, and Bates (1976a) found that Italian children modify request forms by such strategies as using diminutives and compliments, or shifting from imperatives to interrogatives. The age of the addressee is also a factor, as is relative size if the addressee is another child (Owens, 1979).

The early development of pragmatic competence is also evidenced in Cook-Gumperz's (1981) analysis of verbal persuasion strategies used by 3- and 4-year-olds with one another. Although still very limited in linguistic resources, they combine all at their command in the creative (and often successful) endeavor.

Eisenberg (1978), in a study of over 200 videotaped "adversative episodes" (interactional situations involving contradiction, denial, refusal, and conflicting claims) between pairs of acquainted and unacquainted children aged 2 years, 10 months to 5 years, 7 months, found an extensive array of linguistic means used to seek, accomplish, or reject cooperative play activity and sharing or exchanging of toys. Noncompliance with requests or demands included five types of verbal response strategies: (1) explicit negation, (2) explanation, (3) countering, (4) temporizing, or (5) evasion, in addition to (6) no response. Multiple alternative strategies were often tried in turn to achieve and resist compliance. Particularly interesting was the fact that children were able to recognize an utterance of the form *I'm playing with it now* as an implicit negative response to a request or demand *I want to play with the car/Give me the car.*

Children use language to create and maintain a social hierarchy in their peer group, often with routines, known to all in the group, that have predetermined responses and are thus controlled by the initiator. Weininger (1978) described "knock-knock" routines started by socially subordinate children in a Texas kindergarten, which then forced higher-ranking children to respond and interact with them. Directives are often used by children to establish a power position, with compliance by others interpreted as their accepting lesser status. English-speaking children use fewer imperative forms between equals than do adults, but they direct more to subordinates (Mitchell-Kernan & Kernan, 1977). Thus this does not appear to represent a developmental stage in acquiring adult communicative competence but rather a difference in linguistic strategies.

Language Development and Schooling. It is usually only in school that children's language development takes place at a technical level (i.e., explicitly formulated and conscious), as children find out about the grammar they have already acquired informally. Rules are explained by adults (usually based on the concept of a formal "standard," which does not always realistically reflect actual usage), and deviations are corrected. Written language skills are most likely to be taught in a technical mode, and more advanced oral rhetorical skills may also be developed at this level.

During this decade, there has been a strong growth of interest in research on the ethnography of schooling, which has included attention to patterns of language behavior used in the classroom (Green & Wallat, 1981; Mehan, 1979). One of the things that this research has shown is that teachers often differentially reinforce the language skills of high and low achievers and of students from different social and ethnic backgrounds.

Some speech events are unique to, or first encountered in, the context of school. One of the first performance routines learned by kindergarten students is "show and tell," or "sharing time," which is usually considered a major step toward more complex public speaking and is designed to teach rules for appropriate speaking that are learned either from observing others or through explicit correction of errors. Other classroom-specific communicative phenomena are rigid turn taking, with a raised hand to request a turn; the effects of spatial and seating arrangements on interaction; and peer interaction that is initiated and controlled by an adult. Students often informally acquire skills in manipulating such situations to their own advantage, including techniques for feigning involvement or disfluency (see Cazden, John, & Hymes, 1972).

In educational programs where the language of instruction is essentially the same code that the children have learned at home, the oral language development that takes place through formal education is primarily new vocabulary, new rules for speaking, practice in interpretation and use of a more formal style, and skills for public performance. Most emphasis is placed on acquiring a new channel of communication (writing) and on the skills and conventions involved in its interpretation (reading) and use. As is increasingly becoming realized, the written language is not just "talk written down" but is often quite different in syntactic complexity and organizational structure from interpersonal speech. At more advanced levels, students are introduced to various genres of literary form and may be encouraged to practice producing them.

The study of discourse and pragmatics constitutes the most productive area of both oral and written language development research of the late seventies and early eighties (e.g., see also Bates, 1976a; Boggs, 1978; Dickson, 1981; Ochs & Schefflein, 1979), and will probably continue as such in the near future. Research on developmental and subcultural differences is potentially of great significance for instructional materials and procedures in reading and language arts, particularly as they relate to the education of children from linguistically and culturally diverse environments.

Muriel Saville-Troike

See also Bilingual Education; Cognitive Development; English Language Education; Intelligence; Learning; Reading; Speech Communication.

REFERENCES

Amidon, A. Children's understanding of sentences with contigent relations: Why are temporal and conditional connectives so difficult? *Journal of Experimental Child Psychology,* 1976, *22,* 423–437.

Amidon, A., & Carey, P. Why five-year-olds cannot understand "before" and "after." *Journal of Verbal Learning and Verbal Behavior,* 1972, *11,* 417–473.

Anglin, J. *The Extensions of the Child's First Terms of Reference.* Paper presented at the Society for Research in Child Development, 1975.

Applebee, A. N. Children's narratives: New directions. *Reading Teacher,* 1980, *34,* 137–142.

Atkinson, M. Prerequisites for reference. In E. O. Keenan (Ed.), *Studies in Developmental Pragmatics.* New York: Academic Press, 1978.

Atkinson, K.; MacWhinney, B.; & Stoel, C. An experiment on the recognition of babbling. *Papers and Reports on Child Language Development,* 1970, *1.*

Austin, J. L. *How to Do Things with Words.* London: Oxford University Press, 1962.

Bar-Adon, A., & Leopold, W. F. (Eds.). *Child Language: A Book of Readings.* Englewood Cliffs, N.J.: Prentice-Hall, 1971.

Bates, E. *Language and Context: The Acquisition of Pragmatics.* New York: Academic Press, 1976. (a)

Bates, E. Pragmatics and sociolinguistics in child language. In D. M. Morehead & A. E. Morehead (Eds.), *Directions in Normal and Deficient Child Language.* Baltimore: University Park Press, 1976. (b)

Berko, J. The child's learning of English morphology. *Word,* 1958, *14,* 150–177.

Bernstein, B. *Class, Codes, and Control.* Boston: Routledge & Kegan Paul, 1971.

Bloom, L. M. *Language Development: Form and Function in Emerging Grammars.* Cambridge, Mass.: MIT Press, 1970.

Bloom, L. M. *One Word at a Time: The Use of Single-word Utterances before Syntax.* The Hague: Mouton, 1973.

Bloom, L. M., & Lahey, M. *Language Development and Language Disorders.* New York: Wiley, 1978.

Bloom, L. M.; Rocissano, L.; & Hood, L. Adult-child discourse: Developmental interaction between information processing and linguistic knowledge. *Cognitive Psychology,* 1976, *8,* 521–552.

Bloomfield, L. *Language.* New York: Henry Holt, 1933.

Blount, B. G. Studies in child language: An anthropological view (Review article). *American Anthropologist,* 1975, *77,* 580–600.

Boggs, S. T. The development of verbal disputing in part-Hawaiian children. *Language in Society,* 1978, *7,* 325–344.

Bowerman, M. *Early Syntactic Development: A Cross-Linguistic Study with Special Reference to Finnish.* Cambridge, England: Cambridge University Press, 1973.

Bowerman, M. Semantic factors in the acquisition of rules for word use and sentence construction. In D. M. Morehead & A. E. Morehead (Eds.), *Directions in Normal and Deficient Child Language.* Baltimore: University Park Press, 1976.

Bowerman, M. The structure and origin of semantic categories in the language learning child. In M. L. Foster & S. Brandes (Eds.), *Symbol as Sense.* New York: Academic Press, 1980.

Bowerman, M. Language development. In H. C. Triandis & A. Heron (Eds.), *Developmental Psychology.* Vol. 4 of *Handbook of Cross-cultural Psychology.* Boston: Allyn & Bacon, 1981.

Braine, M. D. S. The ontogeny of English phrase structure: The first phase. *Language,* 1963, *39,* 1–13.

Braine, M. D. S. Children's first word combinations. *Monographs of the Society for Research in Child Development,* 1976, *41*(1, Serial No. 164).

Bridges, A.; Sinha, C.; & Walkerdine, V. The development of comprehension. In G. Wells (Ed.), *Learning through Interaction: The Study of Language Development.* Cambridge, England: Cambridge University Press, 1981.

Brown, R. *Social Psychology.* New York: Free Press, 1965.

Brown, R. *A First Language: The Early Stages.* Cambridge, Mass.: Harvard University Press, 1973.

Brown, R., & Bellugi, U. Three processes in the child's acquisition of syntax. *Harvard Educational Review,* 1964, *34,* 133–151.

Brown, R.; Cazden, C.; & Bellugi, U. The child's grammar from I to III. In J. P. Hill (Ed.), *Minnesota Conference on Child Psychology.* Minneapolis: University of Minnesota Press, 1968.

Brown, R., & Fraser, C. The acquisition of syntax. In U. Bellugi & R. Brown (Eds.), The acquisition of language. *Monographs of the Society for Research in Child Development,* 1963, *29,* 43–79.

Bruner, J. S. The ontogenesis of speech acts. *Journal of Child Language,* 1975, *2,* 1–20.

Bryant, P., & Trabasso, T. Transitive inferences and memory in young children. *Nature,* 1971, *232,* 456–458.

Carlson, P., & Anisfeld, M. Some observations on the linguistic competence of a two-year-old child. *Child Development,* 1969, *40,* 565–575.

Carroll, J. B. Language development. In C. W. Harris (Ed.), *Encyclopedia of Educational Research* (3rd ed.). New York: Macmillan, 1960.

Carter, A. L. The transformation of sensorimotor morphemes into words. *Papers and Reports on Child Language Development,* 1975, *10,* 31–47.

Cazden, C. B. *Environmental Assistance to the Child's Acquisition of Grammar.* Unpublished doctoral dissertation, Harvard University, 1965.

Cazden, C. B. The acquisition of noun and verb inflections. *Child Development,* 1968, *39,* 433–438.

Cazden, C.; John, V.; & Hymes, D. (Eds.). *Functions of Language in the Classroom.* New York: Teachers College Press, 1972.

Cazden, C. B., & Leggett, E. L. Culturally responsible education. In *Proceedings of the Conference on Research and Policy Implications of the Task Force Report of the U.S. Office of Civil Rights.* Austin: Southwest Educational Development Laboratory, 1976.

Chomsky, C. *The Acquisition of Syntax in Children from Five to Ten.* Cambridge, Mass.: MIT Press, 1969.

Chomsky, N. A. *Syntactic Structures.* The Hague: Mouton, 1957.

Chomsky, N. A. Review of *Verbal Behavior* by B. F. Skinner. *Language,* 1959, *35,* 26–58.

Chomsky, N. A. *Aspects of the Theory of Syntax.* Cambridge, Mass.: MIT Press, 1965.

Chomsky, N. A., & Halle, M. *The Sound Pattern of English.* New York: Harper, 1968.

Clark, E. V. On the acquisition of the meaning of "before" and "after." *Journal of Verbal Learning and Verbal Behavior,* 1971, *10,* 266–275.

Clark, E. V. Non-linguistic strategies and the acquisition of word meanings. *Cognition,* 1973, *2,* 161–182. (a)

Clark, E. V. What's in a word? On the child's acquisition of semantics in his first language. In T. E. Moore (Ed.), *Cognitive Development and the Acquisition of Language.* New York: Academic Press, 1973b.

Clark, E. V. Strategies and the mapping problem in first language acquisition. In J. Macnamara (Ed.), *Language Learning and Thought.* New York: Academic Press, 1977.

Clark, E. V. Building a vocabulary: Words for objects, actions, and relations. In P. Fletcher & M. A. Garman (Eds.), *Studies in Language Acquisition.* Cambridge, England: Cambridge University Press, 1978.

Clark, E. V., & Garnica, O. Is he coming or going? On the acquisition of deictic verbs. *Journal of Verbal Learning and Verbal Behavior,* 1974, *13,* 559–572.

Clark, H. H., & Clark, E. V. *Language and Psychology.* New York: Harcourt Brace Jovanovich, 1977.

Coker, P. L. Syntactic and semantic factors in the acquisition of "before" and "after." *Journal of Child Language,* 1978, *5,* 261–278.

Cole, M., & Scribner, S. *Culture and Thought.* New York: Wiley, 1974.

Cook-Gumperz, J. Situated instructions: Language socialization of school-age children. In S. Ervin-Tripp & C. Mitchell-Kernan (Eds.), *Child Discourse.* New York: Academic Press, 1977.

Cook-Gumperz, J. Persuasive talk: The social organization of children's talk. In J. Green & C. Wallat (Eds.), *Ethnography and Language in Educational Settings.* Norwood, N.J.: Ablex, 1981.

Cummins, J. Linguistic independence and the educational development of bilingual children. *Review of Educational Research,* 1979, *49,* 222–251.

Cummins, J. *The Role of Primary Language Development in Promoting Educational Success for Language Minority Students.* Paper prepared for the California State Department of Education Compendium on Bilingual-Bicultural Education, 1981.

Dale, E., & Razik, T. *Bibliography of Vocabulary Studies* (2nd rev. ed.). Ohio State University, Bureau of Education Research Services, 1963.

Dale, P. *Language Development: Structure and Function* (2nd ed.). New York: Holt, Rinehart & Winston, 1976.

Daneman, M., & Carpenter, P. Individual differences in working memory and reading. *Journal of Verbal Learning and Verbal Behavior,* 1980, *19,* 450–466.

Darwin, C. A biographical sketch of an infant. *Mind,* 1877, *2,* 285–294. (Reprinted in A. Bar-Adon & W. F. Leopold (Eds.), *Child Language: A Book of Readings.* Englewood Cliffs, N.J.: Prentice-Hall, 1971.)

de Villiers, J. G., & de Villiers, P. A. Semantics and syntax in the first two years: The output of form and function and the form and function of the input. In F. D. Minifie & L. L. Lloyd (Eds.), *Communicative and Cognitive Abilities: Early Behavioral Assessment.* Baltimore: University Park Press, 1978.

de Villiers, J. G.; Tager Flushberg, H. B.; Hakuta, K.; & Cohen, M. Children's comprehension of relative clauses. *Journal of Psycholinguistic Research,* 1979, *8,* 499–518.

DeVos, L. F. *The Role of Form and Function in the Development of Natural Language Concepts.* Unpublished manuscript, Yale University, 1977. (Cited in Nelson & Nelson, 1978.)

Dickson, W. P. (Ed.). *Children's Oral Communication Skills.* New York: Academic Press, 1981.

Donaldson, M., & Wales, R. J. On the acquisition of some relational terms. In J. R. Hayes (Ed.), *Cognition and the Development of Language.* New York: Wiley, 1970.

Dore, J. Holophrases, speech acts, and language universals. *Journal of Child Language,* 1975, *2,* 21–40.

Edwards, A. D. *Language in Culture and Class.* London: Heinemann Education, 1976.

Edwards, M. L. Perception and production in child phonology: The testing of four hypotheses. *Journal of Child Language,* 1975, *1,* 205–219.

Eisenberg, A. R. *An Analysis of the Preschooler's Use of Language in the Resolution of an Adversative Episode.* Unpublished masters' thesis, Johns Hopkins University, 1978.

Ervin-Tripp, S. Data presented in a lecture at the Center for the Study of Reading, University of Illinois, April 1981.

Falmagne, R. J. *Reasoning: Representation and Process.* Hillsdale, N.J.: Lawrence Erlbaum Associates, 1975.

Ferguson, C. A. Phonology as an individual access system: Some data from language acquisition. In C. J. Fillmore, D. Kempler, & W. S.-Y. Wang (Eds.), *Individual Differences in Language Ability and Language Behavior.* New York: Academic Press, 1979.

Ferguson, C. A., & Farwell, C. Words and sounds in early language acquisition. *Language,* 1975, *51,* 419–439.

Ferguson, C. A., & Garnica, O. K. Theories of phonological development. In E. H. Lenneberg & E. Lenneberg (Eds.), *Foundations of Language Development: A Multidisciplinary Approach* (Vol. 1). New York: Academic Press, 1975.

Ferguson, C. A., & Slobin, D. I. (Eds.). *Studies of Child Language Development.* New York: Holt, Rinehart & Winston, 1973.

Fillmore, C. J. The case for case. In E. Bach & R. T. Harms (Eds.), *Universals in Linguistic Theory.* New York: Holt, Rinehart & Winston, 1968.

Flavell, J. H. *Cognitive Development.* Englewood Cliffs, N.J.: Prentice-Hall, 1977.

French, L. A., & Brown, A. L. Comprehension of "before" and "after" in logical and arbitrary sequences. *Journal of Child Language,* 1977, *4,* 247–256.

Gardner, H. Metaphors and modalities: How children project polar adjectives onto diverse domains. *Child Development,* 1974, *45,* 84–91.

Gardner, H.; Winner, E.; Bechhofer, R.; & Wolf, D. The development of figurative language. In K. E. Nelson (Ed.), *Children's Language* (Vol. 1). New York: Gardner Press, 1977.

Garvey, C. Play with language and speech. In S. Ervin-Tripp & C. Mitchell-Kernan (Eds.), *Child Discourse.* New York: Academic Press, 1977.

Gentner, D. Playing with words (review of *Speech Play* by B. Kirshenblatt-Gimblett, Ed.). *Contemporary Psychology,* 1977, *22,* 762–763.

Gentner, D. On relationship meaning: The acquisition of verb meaning. *Child Development,* 1978, *47,* 988–998.

Gleason, J. B., & Weintraub, S. Input language and the acquisition of communicative competence. In K. E. Nelson (Ed.), *Children's Language* (Vol. 1). New York: Gardner Press, 1978.

Green, J. L., & Wallat, C. (Eds.). *Ethnography and Language in Educational Settings.* Norwood, N.J.: Ablex, 1981.

Greenfield, P. Who is "dada?" Some aspects of the semantic and phonological development of a child's first words. *Language and Speech*, 1973, *16*, 34–43.

Greenfield, P., & Smith, J. *The Structure of Communication in Early Language Development*. New York: Academic Press, 1976.

Grice, H. P. Logic and conversation. In P. Cole & J. L. Morgan (Eds.), *Syntax and Semantics: Speech Acts* (Vol. 3). New York: Academic Press, 1975.

Halliday, M. A. K. *Learning How to Mean: Explorations in the Development of Language*. London: Edward Arnold, 1975.

Halliday, M. A. K., & Hasan, R. *Cohesion in English*. London: Longmans, 1976.

Hatch, E. The young child's comprehension of the time connectives. *Child Development*, 1971, *42*, 2111–2113.

Hunt, K. W. *Grammatical Structures Written at Three Grade Levels*. Champaign, Ill.: National Council of Teachers of English, 1965.

Hymes, D. Introduction: Toward Ethnographies of communication. In J. Gumperz & Hymes (Eds.), The ethnography of communication. *American Anthropologist*, 1964, *55*(5, Part 2), 1–34.

Ingram, D. Transitivity in child language. *Language*, 1971, *47*, 888–910.

Inhelder, B., & Piaget, J. *The Early Growth of Logic in the Child*. New York: Norton, 1964.

Jakobson, R. *Kindersprache, Aphasie, and Allgemeine Lautgesetze*. Uppsala, Sweden: 1941. [*Child Language, Aphasia, and Phonological Universals*. The Hague: Mouton, 1968.]

Jakobson, R. Linguistics and poetics. In T. Sebeok (Ed.), *Style in Language*. Cambridge, Mass.: MIT Press, 1960.

Jakobson, R.; Fant, C. G. M.; & Halle, M. *Preliminaries to Speech Analysis*. Cambridge, Mass.: MIT Press, 1963.

Johansson, B. S., & Sjölin, B. Preschool children's understanding of the coordinators "and" and "or." *Journal of Experimental Child Psychology*, 1975, *19*, 233–240.

Johnson, H. J. The meaning of "before" and "after" for preschool children. *Journal of Experimental Child Psychology*, 1975, *19*, 88–99.

Johnson-Laird, P. N., & Wason, P. C. (Eds.). *Thinking: Readings in Cognitive Science*. Cambridge: Cambridge University Press, 1977.

Kaplan, E., & Kaplan, G. The prelinguistic child. In J. Elliot (Ed.), *Human Development and Cognitive Processes*. New York: Holt, Rinehart & Winston, 1971.

Keenan, E. O. Conversational competence in children. *Journal of Child Language*, 1974, *1*, 163–183.

Keenan, E. O. Making it last. In S. Ervin-Tripp & C. Mitchell-Kernan (Eds.), *Child Discourse*. New York: Academic Press, 1977.

Keenan, E. O.; Schieffelin, B. B.; & Platt, M. L. Propositions across speakers and utterances. *Papers and Reports on Child Language Development*, 1976, *12*, 127–143.

Keller-Cohen, D. Context in child language. *Annual Review of Anthropology*, 1978, *7*, 453–482.

Kernan, K. T. Semantic relationships and the child's acquisition of language. *Anthropological Linguistics*, 1970, *12*, 171–187.

Klatzky, R. L.; Clark, E. V.; & Macken, M. Asymmetries in the acquisition of polar adjectives: Linguistic or conceptual? *Journal of Experimental Child Psychology*, 1973, *16*, 32–46.

Labov, W. *The Social Stratification of English in New York City*. Washington, D.C.: Center for Applied Linguistics, 1966.

Labov, W. The logic of nonstandard English. In J. Alatis (Ed.), *Monograph Series on Languages and Linguistics* (No. 22). Washington, D.C.: Georgetown University Press, 1969.

Labov, W. The boundaries of words and their meanings. In C.-J. N. Bailey & R. W. Shuy (Eds.), *New Ways of Analyzing Variation in English*. Washington, D.C.: Georgetown University Press, 1973.

Leonard, L. B.; Newhoff, M.; & Mesalam, L. Individual differences in early child phonology. *Applied Psycholinguistics*, 1980, *1*, 7–30.

Leopold, W. F. The study of child language and infant bilingualism. *Word*, 1948, *4*, 1–17.

Lieven, E. Conversations between mothers and young children: Individual differences and their implications for the study of language learning. In N. Waterson & C. Snow (Eds.), *The Development of Communication: Social and Pragmatic Factors in Language Acquisition*. New York: Wiley, 1978.

Luria, A. R. The direct function of speech in development and dissolution. *Word*, 1959, *15*, 341–352.

Maccoby, E. E., & Bee, H. L. Some speculations concerning the lag between perceiving and performing. *Child Development*, 1965, *36*, 367–377.

MacGinitie, W. M. Language development. In R. L. Ebel (Ed.), *Encyclopedia of Educational Research* (4th ed.). New York: Macmillan, 1969.

Macken, M. Developmental reorganization of phonology: A hierarchy of basic units of acquisition. *Papers and Reports on Child Language Development*, 1977, *14*, 1–36.

MacWhinney, B. Pragmatic patterns in child syntax. *Papers and Reports on Child Language Development*, 1975, *10*, 153–165.

Maratsos, M. P. *The Use of Definite and Indefinite Reference in Young Children*. Cambridge, England: Cambridge University Press, 1976.

Maratsos, M.; Kuczaj, S. A.; & Fox, D. E. *Some Empirical Studies in the Acquisition of Transformational Relations: Passives, Negatives, and the Past Tense*. Paper presented at the Minnesota Symposium of Child Psychology, Minneapolis, 1977.

McCarthy, D. Language development. In W. S. Monroe (Ed.), *Encyclopedia of Educational Research* (2nd ed.). New York: Macmillan, 1950.

McCarthy, D. Some possible explanations of sex differences in language development and disorders. *Journal of Psychology*, 1953, *35*, 115–160.

McCarthy, D. Language development in children. In L. Carmichael (Ed.), *A Manual of Child Psychology* (2nd ed.). New York: Wiley, 1954.

McCawley, J. D. The role of semantics in a grammar. In E. Bach & R. T. Harmes (Eds.), *Universals in Linguistic Theory*. New York: Holt, Rinehart & Winston, 1968.

McClure, E. Aspects of code-switching in the discourse of bilingual Mexican-American children. In M. Saville-Troike (Ed.), *Linguistics and Anthropology*. Washington, D.C.: Georgetown University Press, 1977.

McClure, E., & Steffensen, M. S. *A Study of the Use of Conjunctions across Grades and Ethnic Groups* (Technical Report No. 158). Urbana: University of Illinois, Center for the Study of Reading, 1980.

McCune-Nicolich, L. The cognitive bases of relational words in the single-word period. *Journal of Child Language*, 1981, *8*, 15–34.

McNeill, D. Developmental psycholinguistics. In F. Smith & G. A. Miller (Eds.), *The Genesis of Language*. Cambridge, Mass.: MIT Press, 1966.

McNeill, D. *The Acquisition of Language: The Study of Developmental Psycholinguistics*. New York: Harper, 1970.

McNeill, D. Explaining linguistic universals. In J. Morton (Ed.), *Biological and Social Factors in Psycholinguistics*. London: Logos Press, 1971.

Mehan, H. *Learning Lessons*. Cambridge, Mass.: Harvard University Press, 1979.

Menn, L. Evidence for an interactionist-discovery theory of child phonology. *Papers and Reports on Child Language Development*, 1976, *12*, 169–177.

Menyuk, P. *The Acquisition and Development of Language*. Englewood Cliffs, N.J.: Prentice-Hall, 1971.

Menyuk, P., & Anderson, S. Children's identification and reproduction of /w/, /r/, and /l/. *Journal of Speech and Hearing Research*, 1969, *5*, 39–52.

Michaels, S., & Cook-Gumperz, J. A study of sharing time with first-grade students: Discourse narratives in the classroom. In *Proceedings of the Fifth Annual Meeting of the Berkeley Linguistics Society*. Berkeley, Calif.: Berkeley Linguistics Society, 1979.

Miller, W. The acquisition of grammatical rules by children. In C. A. Ferguson & D. I. Slobin (Eds.), *Studies of Child Language Development*. New York: Holt, Rinehart & Winston, 1973.

Miller, W., & Ervin, S. The development of grammar in child language. In U. Bellugi & R. Brown (Eds.), The acquisition of language. *Monographs of the Society for Research in Child Development*, 1964, *29*, 9–33.

Mitchell-Kernan, C., & Kernan, K. T. Pragmatics of directive choice among children. In S. Ervin-Tripp & C. Mitchell-Kernan (Eds.), *Child Discourse*. New York: Academic Press, 1977.

Moskowitz, A. *Acquisition of Phonology* (Working Paper No. 34). Berkeley: University of California, Language Behavior Research Laboratory, 1970.

Müller, E.; Hollien, H.; & Murry, T. Perceptual responses to infant crying: Identification of cry types. *Journal of Child Language*, 1974, *1*, 89–95.

Neimark, E. Natural language concepts: A failure to replicate. *Child Development*, 1974, *45*, 508–511.

Neimark, E., & Chapman, R. Development of the comprehension of logical quantifiers. In R. J. Falmagne (Ed.), *Reasoning: Representation and Process*. Hillsdale, N.J.: Lawrence Erlbaum Associates, 1975.

Neimark, E., & Slotnick, N. Development of the understanding of logical connectives. *Journal of Educational Psychology*, 1970, *61*, 451–460.

Nelson, K. Structure and strategy in learning to talk. *Monographs of the Society for Research in Child Development*, 1973, *38*(1–2, Serial No. 149).

Nelson, K. Concept, word, and sentence: Interrelations in acquisition and development. *Psychological Review*, 1974, *81*, 267–285. (a)

Nelson, K. Variations in children's concepts by age and category. *Child Development*, 1974, *45*, 577–584. (b)

Nelson, K. E., & Nelson, K. Cognitive pendulums and their linguistic realization. In K. E. Nelson (Ed.), *Children's Language* (Vol. 1). New York: Gardner Press, 1978.

Newport, E. L.; Gleitman, H.; & Gleitman, L. R. Mother, I'd rather do it myself: Some effects and non-effects of maternal speech style. In C. A. Ferguson & C. E. Snow (Eds.), *Talking to Children: Language Input and Acquisition*. Cambridge, England: Cambridge University Press, 1977.

Ochs, E., & Schefflein, B. B. (Eds.). *Developmental Pragmatics*. New York: Academic Press, 1979.

O'Donnell, R. C.; Griffin, W. J.; & Norris, R. C. *Syntax of Kindergarten and Elementary School Children: A Transformational Analysis*. Champaign, Ill.: National Council of Teachers of English, 1967.

Oller, J. W. A comment on specific variance versus global variance in certain EFL tests. *Teachers of English to Speakers of Other Languages Quarterly*, 1980, *14*, 527–530. (a)

Oller, J. W. A language factor deeper than speech: More data and theory for bilingual assessment. In J. Alatis (Ed.), *Current Issues in Bilingual Education*. Washington, D.C.: Georgetown University Press, 1980. (b)

Owens, M. *Solicitation Techniques among English-speaking Children in the U.S.: The Use of Direct and Indirect Request Forms*. Unpublished doctoral dissertation, Georgetown University, 1979.

Piaget, J. *The Language and Thought of the Child*. New York: Harcourt, Brace & World, 1926.

Piaget, J. *The Child's Conception of the World*. Newark, N.J.: Littlefield Adams & Co., 1965.

Piaget, J., & Inhelder, B. *The Psychology of the Child*. New York: Basic Books, 1969.

Priestly, T. M. S. Homonymy in child language. *Journal of Child Language*, 1980, *7*, 413–427.

Ramirez, M.; Herold, P. L.; & Castañeda, A. Field sensitivity and field independence in children. In *New Approaches to Bilingual, Bicultural Education* (Rev. ed.). Austin, Tex.: Dissemination and Assessment Center for Bilingual Education, 1975.

Robinson, W. P. *Language Mangement in Education: The Australian Context*. Sydney: George Allen & Unwin, 1978.

Roeper, T., & McNeill, D. Review of child language. *Annual Review of Anthropology*, 1973, *2*, 127–137.

Rosch, E. Classification of real-word objects: Origins and representation in cognition. In P. Johnson-Laird & P. Wason (Eds.), *Thinking*. Cambridge, England: Cambridge University Press, 1977.

Rosner, S. R., & Hayes, D. S. *A Developmental Study of Category Item Production*. Unpublished manuscript, University of Iowa, 1976. (Cited in Nelson & Nelson, 1978.)

Saville-Troike, M. *The Ethnography of Communication: An Introduction*. Oxford, England: Basil Blackwell & Mott, 1982.

Schlesinger, I. M. Grammatical development: The first steps. In E. H. Lenneberg & E. Lenneberg (Eds.), *Foundations of Language Development: A Multidisciplinary Approach* (Vol. 1). New York: Academic Press, 1975.

Schlesinger, I. M. *Production and Comprehension of Utterances*. Hillsdale, N.J.: Lawrence Erlbaum Associates, 1977.

Scollon, R. *Conversations with a One-year-old: A Case Study of the Developmental Foundation of Syntax*. Honolulu: University of Hawaii Press, 1976.

Searle, J. *Speech Acts*. London: Cambridge University Press, 1969.

Sherk, J. K. *A Word-count of Spoken English of Culturally Disadvantaged Preschool and Elementary Pupils*. Kansas City: University of Missouri, 1973.

Shipley, E. F.; Smith, C. S.; & Gleitman, L. R. A study in the acquisition of language: Free responses to commands. *Language*, 1969, *45*, 322–343.

Silverstein, M. Cultural prerequisites to grammatical analysis. In M. Saville-Troike (Ed.), *Linguistics and Anthropology*. Washington, D.C.: Georgetown University Press, 1977.

Sinclair, H. Sensorimotor action patterns as a condition for the acquisition of syntax. In R. Huxley & E. Ingram (Eds.), *Language Acquisition: Models and Methods*. New York: Academic Press, 1971.

Skinner, B. F. *Verbal Behavior.* New York: Appleton-Century-Crofts, 1957.

Skutnabb-Kangas, T., & Toukomaa, P. *Teaching Migrant Children's Mother Tongue and Learning the Language of the Host Country in the Context of the Socio-cultural Situation of the Migrant Family.* Helsinki: Finnish National Commission for UNESCO, 1976.

Slobin, D. E. Universals of grammatical development in children. In W. Levelt & G. B. F. d'Arcais (Eds.), *Advances in Psycholinguistic Research.* Amsterdam: North Holland, 1970.

Slobin, D. I. (Ed.). *A Field Manual for Cross-cultural Study of the Acquisition of Communicative Competence.* Berkeley: University of California, 1967.

Slobin, D. I. Cognitive prerequisites for the development of grammar. In C. A. Ferguson & D. I. Slobin (Eds.), *Studies of Child Language Development.* New York: Holt, Rinehart & Winston, 1973.

Smith, M. E. Relation between word variety and mean letter-length of words with chronological and mental ages. *Journal of Genetic Psychology,* 1957, *56,* 27–43.

Snow, C. E., & Ferguson, C. A. (Eds.). *Talking to Children: Language Input and Acquisition.* Cambridge, England: Cambridge University Press, 1977.

Spiker, C. C., & Irwin, O. C. The relationship between IQ and indices of infant speech sound development. *Journal of Speech and Hearing Disorders,* 1949, *14,* 335–343.

Spiro, R. F.; Bruce, B. C.; & Brewer, W. F. (Eds.). *Theoretical Issues in Reading Comprehension.* Hillsdale, N.J.: Lawrence Erlbaum Associates, 1980.

Steffensen, M. S.; Jogdeo, C.; & Anderson, R. C. A cross-cultural perspective on reading comprehension. *Reading Research Quarterly,* 1979, *15,* 10–29.

Swain, M. French immersion: Early, late, or partial? *Canadian Modern Language Review,* 1978, *34,* 577–586.

Tiedemann, D. [Über die Entwicklung der Seelenfähigkeiten bei Kindern.] Observations on the development of the mental faculties of children. In A. Bar-Adon & W. F. Leopold (Eds.), *Child Language: A Book of Readings.* Englewood Cliffs, N.J.: Prentice-Hall, 1971. (Originally published, 1787)

Tierney, R. J., & Mosenthal, J. Discourse comprehension as a production: Analyzing text structure and cohesion. In J. Langer & M. Smith-Burkey (Eds.), *Reader Meets Author/Bridging the Gap: A Psycholinguistic and Sociolinguistic Perspective.* International Reading Association, 1981.

Trabasso, T. On making and assessment of inferences during reading. In J. T. Guthrie (Ed.), *Reading Comprehension and Education.* Newark, Del.: International Reading Association, 1980.

Troike, R. C. Research evidence for the effectiveness of bilingual education. *Journal of the National Association for Bilingual Education,* 1978, *3,* 13–24.

Troike, R. C. *SCALP: Social and Cultural Aspects of Language Proficiency.* Paper presented at the Language Proficiency Assessment Symposium, Warrenton, Va., March 1981.

van der Geest, T. *Evaluation of Theories on Child Grammars.* The Hague: Mouton, 1974.

van Dijk, T. A. Story comprehension: An introduction. *Poetics,* 1980, *9,* 1–21.

Vihman, M. From pre-speech to speech: On early phonology. *Papers and Reports on Child Language Development,* 1976, *12,* 230–244.

von Raffler-Engel, W., & Rea, C. *The Influence of the Child's Communicative Style on the Conversational Behavior of the Adult.* Paper presented at the First International Congress for the Study of Child Language, Tokyo, August 1978.

Vygotsky, L. S. *Thought and Language.* Cambridge, Mass.: MIT Press, 1962. (Originally published, 1934.)

Warden, D. The influence of context on children's use of identifying expressions and references. *British Journal of Psychology,* 1976, *61,* 101–112.

Weininger, J. C. G. Communicative strategy among children in a bilingual school environment (K–3). In J. E. Redden (Ed.), *Proceedings of the Second International Conference on Frontiers in Language Proficiency and Dominance Testing.* Carbondale: Southern Illinois University, 1978.

Weir, R. *Language in the Crib.* The Hague: Mouton, 1962.

Wells, G. *Learning through Interaction: The Study of Language Development.* Cambridge, England: Cambridge University Press, 1981.

Wiener, M.; Shilkret, R.; & Devoe, S. "Acquisition" of communicative competence: Is language enough? In M. R. Key (Ed.), *The Relationship of Verbal and Nonverbal Communication.* The Hague: Mouton, 1980.

Witkin, H. A., & Goodenough, D. R. Field independence and interpersonal behavior. In *Psychological Bulletin.* Princeton, N.J.: Educational Testing Service, 1976.

Wolfram, W. *Detroit Negro Speech.* Washington, D.C.: Center for Applied Linguistics, 1969.

Wood, B. S. *Children and Communication: Verbal and Nonverbal Language Development.* Englewood Cliffs, N.J.: Prentice-Hall, 1976.

Young, F. M. An analysis of certain variables in a developmental study of language. *Genetic Psychology Monographs,* 1941, *23,* 3–141.

LEARNING

"Learning" is the relatively permanent change in a person's knowledge or behavior due to experience. This definition has three components: (1) the duration of the change is long-term rather than short-term; (2) the locus of the change is the content and structure of knowledge in memory or the behavior of the learner; (3) the cause of the change is the learner's experience in the environment rather than fatigue, motivation, drugs, physical condition, or physiological intervention.

Behaviorist theories of learning focus primarily on changes in behavior, that is, changes in what the learner *does;* cognitive theories focus primarily on changes in the content or structure of knowledge in memory, that is, changes in what the learner *knows* (Bower & Hilgard, 1981). Research on learning has traditionally involved both animal and human research. Before the late 1950s, behaviorist theories dominated the field, and animal research was emphasized. More recently, cognitive theories have appeared, and human research in "real world settings" is emphasized (Neisser, 1976).

"Learning" refers to the acquisition of knowledge or behavior; "performance" refers to the actual behavior that a learner exhibits on a given occasion. A distinction must be made between learning and performance, since people's performance may not always give a direct indication of what they have learned. For example, performance on a test of learned material may be affected by the place where the test is administered, the stress experienced by the learner, the format of the test, cues provided by the test, and so on. This distinction between learning and performance has serious practical and theoretical implications. Since learning cannot be directly observed and measured (unless physiological measures are used), one can only indirectly infer that learning has occurred through observing changes in performance.

This article summarizes basic information concerning four major kinds of learning tasks: (1) response learning—in which the learner acquires a new response; (2) concept learning—in which the learner acquires a new rule based on experience with instances; (3) verbal learning—in which the learner acquires the ability to produce a list of verbal responses; and (4) prose learning—in which the learner acquires new factual knowledge from connected discourse. Each task represents a kind of learning that may take place in educational settings. For each task, a description and a summary of basic research findings are provided.

Response Learning

In response learning, the outcome of learning is a change in a single aspect of the learner's behavior. Examples of response learning include learning to say "four" when presented with a flash card that says "2 + 2," learning to pull a handle at a water fountain in order to get a drink, and learning to keep quiet while the teacher is lecturing. In particular, this section describes two types of response learning: classical conditioning and instrumental conditioning.

In "classical conditioning," the learner already possesses a strong stimulus-response bond, such that whenever the stimulus is presented (called the "unconditioned stimulus," or US), the learner produces the associated response (called the unconditioned response, or UR). Classical conditioning involves presenting an originally neutral stimulus (called the "conditioned stimulus," or CS) close in time with the (US). The typical time sequence for classical conditioning trials is CS followed by US followed by UR. After many such trials in which the CS and US are paired in time, the CS presented alone will elicit a response similar to the US. This response is called the "conditioned response" (or CR). Thus, in classical conditioning the learner has no control over what stimuli are presented.

An early experiment by Pavlov (1927) demonstrates the classical conditioning situation. First, Pavlov noticed that as soon as he presented meat powder (the US) to a dog, the dog produced saliva (the UR). He also noticed that if he presented the sound of a metronome (the CS), no saliva was produced. In order to produce conditioning, Pavlov presented the tone; then a few seconds later he presented the food, and then the dog salivated. After several such conditioning trials, Pavlov presented the tone alone without any food. The tone elicited some saliva from the dog (the CR). Apparently, the dog had come to associate the sound of the metronome with meat powder and thus learned to give the same kind of response to both stimuli.

Pavlov suggested that since the tone occurred close in time with the food, the tone became a signal that acquired the same meaning as the meat powder itself. Thus, according to this stimulus substitution theory, the CS tends to become the US. However, in contrast to Pavlov, several researchers have found that the CS and US may produce quite different responses in animals (Bindra & Palfai, 1967, Blanchard & Blanchard, 1969). A more recent *information theory* proposed by Rescorla (1967) is that the CS serves to provide information to the learner concerning what is about to follow.

In "operant conditioning," a reinforcement (called an "unconditioned stimulus," or US) is contingent upon the learner's response (called conditioned response, or CR). A "discriminative stimulus" (S+ or S−) refers to any aspect of the learning situation that serves to elicit (S+) or to inhibit (S−) the response; thus, S+ or S− is similar to the CS in classical conditioning. The experimenter must wait for the learner to make the conditioned response; as soon as the CR is produced, the US is administered. The typical sequence for a conditioning trial is S+ followed by CR followed by US. Thus, in "instrumental conditioning," the learner's behavior is instrumental in obtaining the US.

An early experiment by Thorndike (1898) demonstrates the instrumental conditioning task. Thorndike placed a hungry cat into a cage that he called a "puzzle box." There were many objects inside the puzzle box, including a latch that could open the door and let the cat out to eat. The first time the cat was put into the puzzle box, it performed many useless behaviors, such as scratching at the walls or pouncing on objects, until eventually it pulled the latch. As soon as the cat did this, the door opened, and it was free to eat some food that was nearby. On succeeding trials, the cat executed fewer useless behaviors and was faster in pulling the latch. After much practice, the cat quickly pulled the latch upon being placed in the puzzle box. In this example, the discrimination stimulus (S+) is some aspect of the puzzle box, the conditioned response (CR) is pulling the latch, and the reinforcement or unconditioned stimulus (US) is the opening of the door for food.

Thorndike (1898, 1932) concluded that the cat learned by "trial and error and accidental success." The cat executed many behaviors until one "worked." Based on this line of research, Thorndike proposed several basic laws of learning, including the law of effect and the law of exercise. The "law of effect" states that responses in a given situation that result in a satisfying state of affairs are more likely to be performed in that situation in the future, whereas responses to a given situation that do not result in a satisfying state of affairs are less likely to be performed in that situation in the future. Skinner (1938) and Ferster and Skinner (1957) later reformulated the law of effect in terms of the role of reinforcement in learning. The "law of exercise" states that responses that have been previously practiced many times in a given situation are more likely to be performed when that situation occurs again. In other words, practice with reinforcement increases the tendency to execute a response correctly.

Thorndike is notable because he easily moved between the experimental laboratory and the school classroom, between psychological theory and educational practice. For example, his work on mathematics instruction (Thorndike, 1922) emphasized rewarding correct responses to computational problems and the extensive use of drill and practice. Unfortunately, Thorndike's mixture of psychology and education was not emulated by psychologists during the mid-1900s, and there was very little communication between learning theorists working on artificial tasks and educational psychologists working on everyday teaching problems. However, Skinner (1938, 1957, 1958) represents a modern attempt, in the Thorndike tradition, to cross the bridge between psychological theory and practical classroom instruction.

There are several important differences between instrumental and classical conditioning. (1) The critical time sequence in classical conditioning is the CS–US interval; the critical time sequence in instrumental conditioning is the CR–US interval. (2) The learner has no control over presentation of the US in classical conditioning; the learner does control presentation of the US in instrumental conditioning. (3) The CR is elicited by the classical conditioning situation; the CR must be discovered by the learner in the instrumental learning situation. (4) The CR and UR are similar in classical conditioning; the CR need not have any similarity to the UR in instrumental conditioning. (5) The CS is obvious in classical conditioning, but it may not be obvious in instrumental conditioning.

Factors Influencing Classical Conditioning. Classical conditioning may be most relevant for learning emotional responses, such as the fear of certain classroom situations or materials (Bolles, 1979). Research on classical conditioning with animals reveals the following general results. (1) The production of CRs is generally larger for stronger USs; for example, more saliva is produced as a CR when larger amounts of food are used as the US (Wagner et al., 1964; Smith, 1968; Ost & Lauer, 1965; Sheafor & Gormezano, 1972). (2) The production of CRs is generally larger for stronger CSs; for example, more saliva is produced for a louder tone (Gray, 1965; Grice, 1968; Tarpy & Mayer, 1978). (3) The optimal interval between onset of the CS and onset of the US varies from about a half-second to several seconds, depending on the type of CR and the nature of the learner (Tarpy & Mayer, 1978; Ross & Ross, 1971; Fitzgerald & Martin, 1971; Deane, 1965). (4) The production of CRs is generally stronger if the US is never omitted during training; the more times the US fails to follow the CS during training, the weaker the CR

(Ross & Hartman, 1965; Fitzgerald, 1963; Wagner et al., 1964; Thomas & Wagner, 1964).

In addition, four procedures have been suggested for the sequencing of the CS and US in classical conditioning.

1. *Simultaneous conditioning* involves starting and stopping the presentations of the CS and US at the same time, such as presenting the tone at the same time the food is placed in a dog's mouth.
2. *Delayed conditioning* involves presenting the CS before the US, and continuing to present the CS at least until the US is presented (or until it is terminated).
3. *Trace conditioning* involves presenting and stopping the CS, waiting some amount of time, and then presenting the US.
4. *Backward conditioning* involves presenting the CS after the US has been presented and stopped.

In general, for many kinds of responses, backward and simultaneous conditioning result in very slight or no learning; in addition, delayed conditioning tends to result in easier learning than trace conditioning, especially if longer retention intervals are used in trace conditioning (Black, Carlson, & Solomon, 1962; Schneiderman, 1966; Manning, Schneiderman, & Lordahl, 1969; Pavlov, 1927; Gormezano & Moore, 1969; Tarpy & Mayer, 1978).

Factors Influencing Instrumental Conditioning. Instrumental conditioning allows for four different types of procedures (Tarpy & Mayer, 1978).

1. *Reward training* involves producing a positive stimulus (i.e., a stimulus that is satisfying to the learner) following the CR. In this case, the US is a positive reinforcement that serves to increase the frequency or strength of the CR.
2. *Escape training* involves terminating a negative stimulus (i.e., a stimulus that is aversive for the learner) following the CR; *avoidance training* involves preventing a negative stimulus from occurring if the CR is produced. In both cases, the US is a negative reinforcement that serves to increase the frequency or strength of the CR.
3. *Punishment training* refers to presenting a negative stimulus following the CR. Punishment has the effect of suppressing performance.
4. *Omission training* refers to presenting a positive stimulus as long as the learner does not produce the CR, but terminating the positive stimulus when the CR is produced. This procedure is the opposite to reward training and serves to decrease the frequency and strength of the CR.

Conditioning. This section focuses on reward training because it is the most common type of instrumental conditioning used with humans, including applications in programmed instruction systems and in behavior modification programs. Research with animals has produced the following general findings. (1) Speed and resilience of learning are positively related to the size and satisfaction value of the reinforcer (Kintsch, 1962; Meltzer & Brahlek, 1968;

Roberts, 1969; Kraeling, 1961). (2) Speed and resilience of learning are positively related to the motivation level of the learner, such as how long the learner has been deprived of food (Weinstock, 1972; Pavlik & Reynolds, 1963; Zaretsky, 1965; Capaldi, 1971). (3) Speed and resilience of learning are negatively related to the delay of reinforcement following the CR (Tarpy & Sawabini, 1974; Renner, 1964).

In addition, the speed and resilience of learning are related to the schedule of reinforcement. Five basic schedules are

1. *Continuous* or *100 Percent Schedule.* Reinforcement is presented after every CR.
2. *Fixed Interval Schedule.* The learning situation is broken into several equal-time segments, and the first CR produced during each interval is reinforced.
3. *Fixed Ratio Schedule.* Reinforcement is given following some fixed number of CRs, such as one reinforcer after each five CRs.
4. *Variable Interval Schedule.* Reinforcement is administered after some CRs, such that on the average there is one reinforcement per time interval.
5. *Variable Ratio Schedule.* Reinforcement is given following some CRs, such that on the average there is one reinforcement per certain number of CRs.

A review of research on animal learning reveals that continuous reinforcement produces a higher rate of responding during training but also a faster drop in responding during extinction; in addition, the rate of responding is generally higher for ratio than for interval schedules, but the transition is easier from continuous to interval schedules than from continuous to ratio schedules (Tarpy & Mayer, 1978).

Extinction. Like conditioning, extinction depends on a procedure. Following instrumental conditioning, extinction involves no longer presenting the US when the learner produces a CR. In extinction, the reward (US) is omitted, resulting in a drop in the level of responding. When the level of producing the CR falls to its preconditioning baseline, the CR is said to be extinguished.

Extinction of instrumentally conditioned responses in animals generally takes the following forms. (1) Extinction is more rapid if the size of the reinforcement has been larger during conditioning (Roberts, 1969; Wagner, 1961; Campbell, Batsche, & Batsche, 1972). (2) Extinction may be less rapid if reinforcement has been delayed during conditioning (Tarpy & Sawabini, 1974). (3) Extinction may be more rapid if conditioning has involved continuous rather than intermittent schedules of reinforcement (Ratliff & Ratliff, 1971; Tarpy & Mayer, 1978). (4) Extinction may be more rapid if many conditioning trials have been given with strong reinforcements and continuous schedules; however, extinction may be slower if many conditioning trials have been given using weak reinforcements and intermittent schedules (Ison, 1962; Ison & Cook, 1964). Thus, techniques that slow down the rate of learning tend to have the effect of making learned behavior (CR) more resistant to extinction.

Generalization and discrimination. During conditioning a learner may learn to produce a certain CR (such as pressing a bar) in the presence of a certain CS (such as a green light). "Stimulus generalization" refers to the tendency of the learner to make the CR also in the presence of stimuli that are similar to the CS (such as less bright green lights); the strength of the CR depends on the similarity between the presented stimulus and the previous CS (Kalish, 1969; Prokasy & Hall, 1963; Tarpy & Mayer, 1978). "Response generalization" refers to the tendency of the learner to produce CRs that are similar to the behavior that led to reinforcement.

"Stimulus discrimination" refers to the tendency to produce different responses to different stimuli. For example, a different response is required to a door marked "IN" and to a door marked "OUT," or to a green traffic light and to a red traffic light. "Response discrimination" refers to the tendency to distinguish aspects of one's CR that are critical in obtaining the US from those that are not. Although a review of generalization and discrimination is beyond the scope of this article, the interested reader is referred to Bolles (1979).

Feedback. One extension of research on animal instrumental conditioning has involved the role of feedback in human learning. "Feedback" refers to information that informs learners about the success or accuracy of their actions. Thus, feedback involves providing the learner with "knowledge of results." In human learning of simple instrumental responses, feedback appears to be a crucial factor. In a typical study (Trowbridge & Carson, 1932), blindfolded subjects were asked to draw lines that were exactly three inches long, and were given practice totaling one hundred trials. Subjects who were given no feedback after each response showed no improvement over the hundred trials. Subjects who were given qualitative feedback—told whether or not they were close to three inches—showed strong improvement. Subjects who were given quantitative feedback—told the extent to which their lines were too long or too short—showed the strongest improvement. More recently, researchers have shown that feedback is most important early in learning a new response, but may not be crucial after a student has acquired his or her own "internal reference mechanism" (Bilodeau, Bilodeau, & Schumsky, 1959; Newell, 1974; Adams, 1976). The implication of this work is that practice on new material should allow for external feedback, especially early in learning.

Learning Hierarchies. Gagné and his associates (Gagné et al., 1962; Gagné & Briggs, 1974; Gagné, 1968) have extended the work on animal instrumental conditioning by focusing on the transfer of training of simple responses in humans. Gagné (1968) has argued that many skills may be analyzed into a hierarchy of behaviors, using a learning hierarchy. A "learning hierarchy" is generated by stating the to-be-learned skill as a specific behavior. For example, the skill might be to "subtract whole numbers of any size." The next step is to ask "What would you have to know how to do in order to perform this task, after being given only instructions?" (Gagné, et al., 1962). For example, to subtract whole numbers, one subordinate skill is to "subtract in successive columns without borrowing."

In a typical study, Gagné et al. (1962) developed a learning hierarchy for a simple arithmetic skill. In teaching the component skills, the researchers claimed that one should start at the lowest level in the hierarchy that the student cannot perform, and work up. Results indicated that subjects rarely learned a higher skill without already knowing the lower skill. More recently, Resnick and her colleagues (Resnick, Wang, & Kaplan, 1973; Resnick & Ford, 1981) have found that learning hierarchies are useful in prescribing and assessing sequences of instruction when the to-be-learned material can be specified as behaviors. However, recent studies have suggested that teaching from the bottom to the top of a learning hierarchy, as prescribed by Gagné (1968), may inhibit more able learners (Resnick & Ford, 1981; Caruso & Resnick, 1972; Resnick, Siegel, & Kersh, 1971).

Additional information concerning instrumental and classical conditioning may be obtained from the following sources: Bolles (1979), Bower and Hilgard (1981), Skinner (1974), Tarpy (1975), Houston (1976), Rachlin (1976), and Keller (1969).

Concept Learning

In a typical concept learning task, an item, such as a word, a picture, or an object, is presented. The learner tries to determine which of two (or more) categories it should be placed into. Then the learner is told which category the item belongs in, and the next item is presented. This procedure is continued until the learner is able to predict correctly the category for a long string of presented items. Concept learning tasks correspond to some classroom activities, such as learning to name pictures of animals in a picture book or learning to recognize printed letters of the alphabet. In addition, the learning of language involves concept learning.

Early work by Bruner, Goodnow, and Austin (1956) provides an example of the concept learning situation. They used eighty-one stimulus cards, which consisted of four dimensions with three values for each: shapes of objects were squares, circles, or crosses; number of objects on a card was one, two, or three; color of objects was red, green, or black; number of borders on a card was one, two, or three. In a typical experiment, using the "reception method," subjects were shown a chart consisting of all eighty-one cards and were allowed to indicate which card they wanted as an instance. Then the experimenter told whether or not the card was in the target category, and the subject could ask for another card, and so on. Results indicated that subjects followed several different kinds of strategies, such as focusing on one dimension at a time

or trying to remember all features of positive instances. Thus, a major contribution of this study is that subjects use a variety of active learning strategies during concept learning rather than being passively "reinforced" by the situation. More recently, Laughlin (1973) has proposed more precise descriptions of these strategies.

Hypothesis Testing. Learners may be able to perform on concept learning tasks either by forming and testing hypotheses about the correct rule (noncontinuity theory) or by learning by reinforcement (continuity theory). Noncontinuity learning involves all-or-none learning, in which a person generates a hypothesis concerning the correct rule; this hypothesis is maintained if it predicts category membership of stimuli but is replaced if it does not. Continuity learning involves building associations between each feature of a presented stimulus and its category name; thus, each time a stimulus is assigned to a category, the associations are strengthened. Levine (1975) provides a historical review of the two theories of concept learning.

The Kendlers (Kendler & D'Amato, 1955; Kendler & Kendler, 1959; Kendler & Kendler, 1962, 1975) provided evidence that there is a developmental change from reinforcement learning in preverbal children to hypothesis testing in older children and adults. In a typical experiment, a student is presented with pairs of stimuli that vary in color and size. First the student may learn to choose the large object. Then a shift takes place. For a reversal shift, the new rule is to choose the smaller object rather than the larger. For a nonreversal shift, the new rule may be to choose the black object rather than the white object. According to a reinforcement theory, four associations must be broken for a reversal shift (small-black is no; small-white is no; large-black is yes; large-white is yes), whereas only two must be broken for a nonreversal shift (small-black is no; large-white is yes); therefore, reinforcement theory predicts that a reversal shift is more difficult to learn than a nonreversal shift. According to a mediational theory, similar to a hypothesis-formation theory, the opposite prediction is generated. The results suggest that humans have both systems available during learning, but younger children are more likely to rely on reinforcement learning. Similar results have been obtained using a better-controlled "optional shift" procedure (Kendler & Kendler, 1975).

Another test of the continuity versus noncontinuity issue was performed by Bower and Trabasso (1963, 1964; Trabasso & Bower, 1968). For example, students were given a concept learning task for many trials. Before they actually learned to respond at a consistently correct level, the rule was reversed for some learners. According to continuity theory, assuming students are learning by reinforcement, the reversal should greatly hinder learning. According to noncontinuity theory, assuming students are forming hypotheses, the reversal should not affect learning since they have not yet found the right hypothesis. Results with adults indicated that hypothesis testing best described learning, whereas analogous studies with animals favored reinforcement learning.

Based on a careful review of these and other studies, Levine (1975) concluded that hypothesis-testing strategies are often used by adults and some older children. Thus, reinforcement theories that were developed to account for animal learning do not seem to be adequate to describe complex human learning.

Cue Salience. Learners may pay attention to some features of a stimulus more readily than others; that is, some cues are more salient for a learner than others. For example, Heidbreder (1946, 1947) performed a concept-learning experiment in which the stimuli were pictures representing concrete objects (such as "tree"), geometric forms (such as "circle"), and numbers (such as "five"). Heidbreder found evidence for a "dominance hierarchy" of cues in which concrete objects were easiest to learn and abstract numbers most difficult. More recently, Trabasso (1963; Trabasso & Bower, 1968) used flower designs that varied in number of leaves, shape of leaves, angle of branches, color of flower, and so on. Students learned very quickly when the concepts were based on color but learned very slowly when the concepts were based on angle. Apparently students tend to pay attention to certain cues (such as color or shape) more readily than other cues. In addition, Trabasso and Bower (1968) and Trabasso (1963) found that weightings of cue salience are cumulative; for example, if color and angle are redundant, then learning is faster than if just one cue is relevant.

The task may be able to focus a learner's attention on relevant dimensions of a stimulus. For example, in an early study, Hull (1920) used Chinese characters as stimuli. When the critical features of the stimuli were printed in red ink, learning was greatly enhanced. Similarly, Zeaman and House (1963) found that mentally retarded students tend to have more trouble in determining the cues to which they should attend than in forming rules. For example, when the relevant dimension is pointed out to them, the pattern of learning is similar to that for normal learners.

Task Variables. The difficulty of learning a concept, as measured by the number of trials needed to learn, depends on several features of the task. First, the type of rule influences learning (Bourne, 1966; Haygood & Stevenson, 1967; Bourne, Ekstrand, & Dominowski, 1971; Bourne, 1970). For example, a single value rule (such as "Choose the red object") is easier to learn than a rule involving two values (such as color and shape). In addition, a conjunctive rule (such as "Choose red squares") is easier to learn than a disjunctive rule (such as "Choose the red or the square or the red square"); a conditional rule (such as "If it's red, then it must be square") is easier to learn than a biconditional (such as "If it's red, then it must be square, and if it's square, it must be red"). Bourne (1974) suggests that the learner starts with a simple assumption about the rule—most consistent with a conjunctive concept—and then must learn to alter the assumption for more complex rules. Similarly, Hunt, Marin, and Stone (1966) and Trabasso, Rollins, and Shaughnessy (1971) have shown that more complex rules require a longer set of decisions.

Second, increasing the number of relevant dimensions decreases solution time since a subject can pay attention to any dimension to solve the problem; increasing the number of irrelevant dimensions or values on a dimension makes learning more difficult presumably because the subject is more likely to choose an irrelevant hypothesis (Bourne, 1966; Bourne, Ekstrand, & Dominowski, 1971; Bourne & Haygood, 1959).

Finally, subjects seem to learn faster from positive instances than negative instances (Bourne, Ekstrand, & Dominowski, 1971; Friebergs & Tulving, 1961). However, some subjects are able to learn to make use of negative instances if they are given practice (Friebergs & Tulving, 1961).

Prototypes versus Distinctive Features. When the stimuli are complex visual patterns or objects, learners may be able to perform on concept learning tasks either by forming an internal prototype or by focusing on a distinctive feature of the stimulus. Forming a prototype involves averaging all the instances of a category into a schematic representation. Focusing on distinctive features involves the opposite process; instead of averaging, the learner focuses on just those few features that characterize the stimulus.

Several researchers (Posner & Keele, 1968, 1970; Posner, 1969; Franks & Bransford, 1971) have shown that learners form prototypes for complex visual patterns. For example, subjects were shown a series of distortions of a basic dot pattern, in which several dots were moved in different ways in each distortion. On a recognition test, subjects were most confident about seeing the basic dot pattern, although it had never been presented (Posner, 1969). In addition, subjects were just as likely to recognize distortions of the pattern that had been presented as distortions that had not (Posner & Keele, 1968, 1970). Apparently, subjects abstracted a prototypical basic pattern of dots rather than focusing on the features of each separate instance.

More recently, Reed (1972) and Hyman and Frost (1974) found that subjects use both strategies in concept learning for faces. Some subjects tend to rely on prototype abstraction, and others rely on distinctive features. In addition, Neumann (1977) has shown that when the stimuli are extremely complex, subjects tend to use a distinctive features strategy, but when the stimuli are simpler or more familiar (such as faces), there is a higher tendency to use prototype abstraction strategies. Apparently, there are both individual differences and situational differences in the learner's tendency to use one or the other strategy.

Structure of Categories. Rosch (1975a, 1975b) found that the learning of "natural categories" in the real world may be different from learning artificial categories such as those used by Bruner, Goodnow, & Austin (1956). For example, Rosch (1975a) suggests that most natural categories, such as "student," are "fuzzy" in the sense that the boundary lines are not firm. She found that subjects were able to rate the "goodness of fit" of instances to a category: "chair" was rated as good example of "furniture"; "lamp" was a poorer example; and "pillow" was an even poorer example. In addition, students were faster in answering questions about typical examples (such as "Is a chair a piece of furniture?") than less typical examples (such as "Is a lamp a piece of furniture?").

Rosch and Mervis (1975) have suggested that all members of a natural category have a "family resemblance"—that is, there is a basic core of features for the category such that each instance contains some but not all of the features. For example, not all birds have the characteristics of "flying" and "smallness" and "singing," but these features are found in many birds. In a typical experiment, Rosch and Mervis (1975) asked students to list the features of several instances of pieces of furniture. Results indicated that most instances shared some of the basic furniture features, but not all instances possessed all of the basic features.

Finally, Rosch and her colleagues (Rosch et al., 1976; Rosch & Lloyd, 1978) have found that people are better able to use "basic level" categories (such as "table") than "superordinate level" categories (such as "furniture") or "subordinate level" categories (such as "kitchen table"). Further, they argue that children begin to learn to classify objects at the basic level (Rosch et al., 1976). Newport and Bellugi (1978) have shown that restricted languages such as American Sign Language (ASL) focus mainly on the basic level for their signs.

Additional information concerning concept learning may be obtained from the following sources: Neimark and Santa (1975); Mervis and Rosch (1981); Bourne, Ekstrand, and Dominowski (1971); and Levine (1975).

Verbal Learning

In verbal learning tasks, a list of items (such as words or pictures) or pairs of items is presented. The items may be presented in visual form (such as printed on a sheet of paper) or in auditory form (such as spoken words), and the list may be repeated any number of times. Then a test is given to determine how much is remembered. The test may involve any of the following. (1) Recall tests ask the learner to recite or write down all the items that can be remembered, similar to essay tests on school exams. (2) Recognition tests ask the learner to determine whether a given item was or was not on the presented list, similar to multiple-choice tests on school exams. (3) Relearning tests ask the learner to learn the material again, similar to restudying old material.

Verbal learning tasks correspond to many types of rote learning that take place in schools, such as learning to recite the alphabet or to count numbers or the months of the year. Three major paradigms are used in verbal learning tasks, each corresponding to a particular type of rote school learning. (1) In "serial learning," a student is given a list of items to be memorized in order. An example of a serial learning task is learning to recite the names of the U.S. presidents in chronological order. (2) In "paired-associate learning," a student is given a list of pairs of items. For each pair, the student must learn to recite the second item (the response term) whenever the first item (the stimulus term) is presented. An example of a paired-associate learning task is learning to recite the capital of a state whenever the teacher gives the name of the state. (3) In "free-recall list learning," a student is given a list of items to be recalled in any order. An example of a free recall list learning task is to recite the names of all the countries in Europe.

The first major study of rote verbal learning was conducted by the German psychologist Herman Ebbinghaus in 1885. Ebbinghaus's study serves as an example of a verbal learning task. In a typical study (1964 [1885]), he read a list of nonsense syllables to himself at a constant rate. Each nonsense syllable consisted of a consonant-vowel-consonant triplet that was not a word. He read the list over many times, always in the same order. Eventually, after many repetitions, he was able to recite the entire list in order. Later, after a certain length of time, Ebbinghaus tried to relearn the list in the same way. Savings in relearning occurred when it took fewer repetitions to relearn the list than it took to learn it originally.

Two important results emerged from the Ebbinghaus study that are still well-established facts today. (1) Learning curve—there is a direct relationship between how much Ebbinghaus practiced a list, and how much he learned from the list. Each additional amount of practice seemed to add a constant amount to how much Ebbinghaus learned; however, once he had practiced a great deal on a list, additional practice did not seem to add as much. (2) Forgetting curve—there is a direct relationship between how much time he waited between original learning and the subsequent test, and how much he remembered from the list. The largest drop occurred within the first twenty minutes or the first hour, and very little additional forgetting occurred after a day. Apparently, when many lists of rote material are learned, a great deal of the material is forgotten after a very short time.

Based on these studies, Ebbinghaus viewed learning as the building of associations in memory, and he viewed forgetting as due to the interference of new competing associations. As can be seen from this summary, Ebbinghaus concentrated on isolating variables that influenced "how much is learned." Among the most persistent variables are rate of presentation, amount of practice, and amount of time since learning. Ebbinghaus's method involved well-controlled laboratory studies that used artificial materials.

The remainder of this section presents some of the best-established facts concerning rote verbal learning tasks. These include meaningfulness effects, serial position effects, practice effects, transfer effects, interference effects, organization effects, levels-of-processing effects, state-dependent effects, and mnemonic effects.

Meaningfulness Effects. One of the best-established facts concerning rote learning tasks is that high-meaningful words are easier to learn and remember than low-meaningful words. This result is obtained when meaningfulness is measured by the number of associations a person has for the word (Archer, 1960; Glaze, 1928; Palermo & Jenkins, 1964; Noble, 1952, 1963; Cofer, 1971; Underwood & Schultz, 1960; Cieutat, Stockwell, & Noble, 1958), by the frequency of the word in ordinary printed and spoken language (French, Carter, & Koenig, 1930; Howes, 1966; Jones & Wepman, 1966; West, 1953; Thorndike & Lorge, 1944; Kucera & Francis, 1967; Miller, Newman, & Friedman, 1958; Mann, 1944; Hall, 1954; Deese, 1959; Cofer, 1971), by the sequential order of the letters (Underwood & Schultz, 1960), or by the tendency of the word to elicit clear images (Paivio, 1971; Paivio, Smythe, & Yuille, 1968; Paivio, Yuille, & Madigan, 1968). Paivio (1971) argues that the imagery value of a word—the tendency of a word to elicit a vivid image—is highly correlated with word frequency and association value; however, in a series of controlled studies, imagery value was found to be the most important factor determining the meaningfulness of a word. More recently, Wittrock, Marks, and Doctrow (1975) have found large improvements in retention of prose passages when familiar, concrete words are substituted for unfamiliar, abstract words.

Serial Position Effects. A second major fact concerning the learning of lists is that the position of a word on a list influences how well it is learned. In general, words at the beginning and end of the list are better remembered than words in the middle of the list, and any distinctive word is remembered better regardless of its position (Murdock, 1974). Thus, there are three major effects. (1) The "primary effect" refers to the fact that the first few words are remembered better than words in the middle of the list. (2) The "recency effect" refers to the fact that the last few words on the list are remembered better than words in the middle of the list. (3) The "distinctiveness effect" (or von Restorff effect) refers to the fact that a word that is different, such as a word printed in red rather than black ink or a boy's name in a list of girls' names, is remembered better than other words regardless of its serial position.

Several researchers have argued that the beginning and end of a list, as well as distinctive words in the list, serve as cognitive landmarks that provide anchors to which words may be attached in memory (Ebenholtz, 1972; Jensen, 1962; Glanzer & Dolinsky, 1965; Goulet, Bone, & Barker, 1967; McLaughlin, 1966; Coppage & Harcum, 1967). A complementary explanation for the recency effect is that learners hold the last few words of the list in a temporary short-term memory store and thus are able to produce these words first on a recall test; the explanation for the primacy effect is that the first few words enter an empty short-term memory store and thus have more time to be transferred to long-term memory (Postman & Phillips, 1965; Glanzer & Cunitz, 1966; Tulving & Arbuckle, 1963; Craik, 1970). This theory correctly predicts that when the recall test is delayed, the last few words of the list in short-term memory are lost and the recency effect is eliminated (Craik, 1970; Postman & Phillips, 1965; Glanzer & Cunitz, 1966). An implication of this work is that students are more likely to remember the beginning of a lesson than any other part; for example, Kieras (1978) has found that students remember topic sentences of paragraphs better than other sentences.

Practice Effects. Since Ebbinghaus's early work in 1885 (Ebbinghaus, 1964), it has been well established that the repetition of a list tends to increase the amount learned. In addition, Ebbinghaus found that studying a list once a day for six days resulted in more learning than studying an equivalent list six times all in one day. This work suggested that distributed practice (or spaced practice) is more effective than massed practice for rote learning. Support for this idea has been obtained, especially for long lists, fast presentation rates, or unfamiliar stimulus material (Underwood, 1961; Underwood, Kapelak, & Malmi, 1976).

One explanation for the superiority of distributed practice is that it takes time for a memory trace to be consolidated into a structural change in nerve cells. Thus, when learning is massed, only one consolidation may take place; however, when learning is distributed, many different consolidations may take place (Hebb, 1949, 1958). Another explanation is that learners have more opportunities to rehearse information mentally when it is distributed (Rundus, 1971). Finally, another explanation is that learners may associate a word with only one context for massed practice, but they are able to associate it with many different contexts when distributed practice is used. Thus, the word is stored in more different contexts in memory when distributed practice is used (Martin, 1968, 1972; Melton, 1970; Glenberg, 1976). Although all three explanations are compatible, Glenberg (1976) has provided evidence that most strongly supports the context theory.

Transfer Effects. "Transfer" refers to the effects of prior learning on the learning of new material. Positive transfer occurs when previous learning makes new learning easier; negative transfer occurs when previous learning makes new learning more difficult. In general, the more two tasks have in common, the more likely it is that learning of one will result in positive transfer to the other (Osgood, 1949).

Specific transfer is transfer between two learning tasks when the tasks share some components. For example, learning three-column addition has some components in common with learning one-column addition, such as knowing number facts for all pairs of digits or recognizing written numerals. General transfer is transfer that cannot be attributed to any shared components among tasks. For example, general study skills learned in one course may transfer to another course even though none of the content is the same. Thune (1951) has distinguished between two aspects of general transfer: warm-up and learning-to-learn. "Warm-up" refers to an increase in performance on learning word lists during a session; "learning-to-learn" refers to a general increase in performance on learning word lists over the course of several days.

Interference Effects. Interference effects occur when memory for newly learned material is hurt by previous or subsequent learning. Proactive interference occurs when something that was previously learned influences one's ability to remember some newly learned material. For example, if one learns the names of parts of the body in French, recall of the French names may be more difficult if the person has previously learned the names in German. Retroactive interference occurs when something that is subsequently learned influences one's ability to remember learned material. For example, if one learns the names of parts of the body in French, recall of the French names may be more difficult if the person subsequently learns the names in German.

In a summary of research on proactive interference, Underwood (1957) found that the recall of word lists depended on how many previous lists had been learned and recalled. With no prior lists, recall was about 75 percent on the average, but this fell to about 25 percent with five to ten prior lists. More recently, Wickens (1970, 1972) demonstrated a technique that allows for "release from proactive interference." If a student learns four lists of words, with all words from the same general category, recall tended to fall from about 90 percent on list 1 to below 40 percent on list 4; however, if the words in the fourth list are from a completely different category, recall jumps back to very high levels, as if the learner were "released from proactive interference." The implication is that there will be less interference (hence more learning) if one changes the context from time to time during learning.

Organization Effects. Another major fact concerning the learning of word lists is that subjects tend to organize the words mentally into categories rather than retain the exact order of presentation (Bousfield, 1953; Bousfield & Cohen, 1953; Bousfield, Cohen, & Whitmarsh, 1958; Tulving, 1962; Bower, 1970). For example, Bousfield (1953) read a list of sixty nouns to subjects and asked them to recall the words. The list contained fifteen words from each of four categories such as animals, vegetables, jobs, and names. The words were presented in random order, no two consecutive words coming from the same category, but in recalling the words, subjects tended to "cluster" them by category. Even when the list had no obvious categories, subjects tended to impose their own "subjective organization" on recall (Tulving, 1962). In another study, Bower et al. (1969) presented a word list organized in a logical way or a random way. Recall was higher when the logical categories were made clear during learning.

In addition, there is evidence that subjects learn about the category of the words as well as the specific letters

of the word. For example, Underwood (1965) found than many of the errors subjects make in learning long word lists involve remembering words that have the same meaning as actual words in the list (such as remembering "happy" instead of "glad") rather than remembering words that have the same sound or similar letters. Apparently, even rote learning of word lists involves active categorization processes by the learner.

Levels-of-Processing Effects. "Levels of processing" refers to the idea that the more deeply a word list is processed, the better it will be remembered. According to Craik and Lockhart (1972), words may be processed at several levels ranging from low-level sensory analysis of the physical characteristics of the letters to high-level semantic analysis of word meaning. Orienting tasks that require semantic processing, such as telling whether each word belongs in a certain category, result in better recall than orienting tasks that require sensory processing, such as circling every vowel (Tresselt & Mayzner, 1960; Jenkins, 1974; Hyde & Jenkins, 1969, 1973; Till & Jenkins, 1973; Walsh & Jenkins, 1973).

Similar results have been obtained using prose passages. For example, outlining a passage or even being told to read carefully resulted in better recall performance than circling every letter *e* (Arkes, Schumacher, & Gardner, 1976). Rothkopf (1970) has suggested that adjunct questions in text encourage "mathemagenic activity"—that is, learners must actively process the text. For example, when text passages are accompanied by principle-based questions, posttest performance is qualitatively different than when the text is accompanied by rote questions (Watts & Anderson, 1971; Mayer, 1975a).

More recently, Bransford and his colleagues (Bransford, 1979; Morris, Bransford & Franks, 1977) have introduced the concept of "transfer appropriate processing," the idea that different types of processing are required for different types of tests. For example, semantic processing tends to result in better performance on recall tests but poorer performance on tests of the specific physical characteristics of the words; physical processing tends to result in better performance on tests of physical details but poorer performance on recall tests (Morris, Bransford, & Franks, 1977; Stein, 1978). Tversky (1973) has provided evidence that learners can adjust their processing strategies based on what kind of test they expect. For example, of subjects given a series of pictures, some were told to expect a recall test and some to expect a recognition test. Subjects who expected a recall test performed better on a recall test than subjects who expected a recognition test, and subjects who expected a recognition test performed better on recognition than subjects who expected a recall test. Apparently, different kinds of processing are appropriate for different kinds of tests, and subjects adjust their processing to correspond to the expected type of test.

State-dependent Effects. Another reliable finding about rote learning is that lists are more easily remembered as the similarity of the test situation to the learning situation increases. For example, Baddeley (1976) has reviewed a series of studies in which word lists learned under water were recalled better under water, or word lists learned while under the influence of alcohol were recalled best under the same state (Godden & Baddeley, 1975; Goodwin et al., 1969). One hypothesis concerning such state-dependent memory effects is that when the test state and learning state match, there are more contextual cues available to aid in retrieving the information. Thus, state-dependent effects may be stronger for tests that require retrieval (such as recall) than for recognition tests (Baddeley, 1976).

Tulving and his associates (Tulving & Thomson, 1971, 1973; Tulving & Watkins, 1975; Watkins & Tulving, 1975) have introduced a similar idea called "encoding specificity." The idea is that remembering will be enhanced if the same cues are available during the test as during learning. For example, if the word "light" was associated with "head" during learning, it will be easier to remember "light" if a test gives a cue such as "head" than if it gives a cue such as "dark" (Tulving & Thomson, 1973). Apparently, it is useful to try to re-create the original context of learning, including similar stimulus cues and locations.

Mnemonic Effects. Finally, there is some evidence that general techniques for enhancing rote learning can be taught. For example, Brown and DeLoache (1978) reviewed research on teaching mnemonic strategies to children. In general, recognition performance was enhanced when students were taught to use rehearsal and taxonomic categorization in rote list learning (Flavell, 1970; Flavell & Wellman, 1977; Wellman, 1977). In addition, there is evidence that older children use these strategies spontaneously (Brown & DeLoache, 1978).

In paired-associate learning, the keyword method has been used to enhance the learning of foreign language vocabulary. For example, to learn that *carta* means "letter," one can find a keyword of "cart" from *carta* and then build an association between "cart" and "letter" such as visualizing a letter in a cart. The keyword method has been effective in a number of studies (Pressley, 1977; Pressley & Levin, 1977; Pressley & Dennis-Rounds, 1980; Atkinson & Raugh, 1975; Raugh & Atkinson, 1975). In addition, Bower (1972) and Rowher (1973; Rowher & Bean, 1973) have found great improvement in paired-associate learning when subjects were asked to form visual images or sentences containing the two words in each paired associate.

There are several other techniques that have received both practical and research support. The method of loci involves relating each item on a list to a particular series of locations such as places around a room (Yates, 1966; Higbee, 1977; Lorayne & Lucas, 1974). The pegword method involves memorizing a list such as "one is a bun, two is a shoe," etc., and then associating each word on a new list to its "peg" on the peglist (Paivio, 1971; Higbee, 1977; Lorayne & Lucas, 1974). The elaboration method involves putting the list into one's own words. For exam-

ple, Bower & Clark (1969) asked subjects to make up a running story involving words from a list that were presented one at a time. Recall was dramatically higher for subjects who produced a running story involving the listed words than for subjects who tried to memorize in their normal way.

Additional information concerning verbal memory may be obtained from the following sources: Postman (1975), Peterson (1977), Wickelgren (1981), Klatzky, (1980), Wingfield (1979), Kausler (1974).

Prose Learning

In prose learning tasks, a passage such as a story or a lesson is presented, usually in visual form, as in a book or on a computer terminal screen, or auditory form, as on a tape recording. Then a test is given to determine what is remembered. The test may involve recall, recognition, or answering questions.

The first major research on prose learning, conducted by Bartlett in 1932, provides a good example of prose learning tasks. In a typical study, Bartlett used the "method of serial production," a procedure similar to the children's game of "telephone." The first subject was presented with an unfamiliar folk story, "The War of the Ghosts," and asked to reproduce the story from memory. The reproduced version was presented to the next subject, who then was asked to reproduce the story from memory. This reproduced version was passed on to the next subject, and so on. The passage changed in a systematic way as it was passed from subject to the next, the resulting stories showing evidence of (1) flattening—details were dropped out; (2) sharpening—a few details were retained and elaborated upon; (3) rationalization—the story became more coherent, with all mystical aspects recast into a more conventional plot.

Based on these studies, Bartlett rejected the view that learning involves passively recording experience or that remembering involves finding a particular idea in memory. Instead, Bartlett concluded as follows. (1) Learning is a schematic process. Learners engage in an active "effort after meaning" in which they try to "assimilate" new material to existing feelings or knowledge. Details are not always learned, because learners focus on the main theme or "schema" for the passage. (2) Remembering is a reconstructive process. When asked to remember the passage, a subject may use general impressions along with a few remembered details to generate a version that seems like the original.

As can be seen, research on prose learning focuses on questions such as how the learner processes new information, how the learner organizes and structures new information in memory, and how the learner retrieves information. Although Bartlett performed early studies on prose learning that addressed these questions, intensive research in this area has occurred mainly within the past ten years (Cofer, 1976).

This section describes several of the best-established findings concerning prose learning: abstraction effects, levels effects, schema effects, prior knowledge effects, inference effects, text organization effects, and mathemagenic effects.

Abstraction Effects. "Abstraction" is the tendency of learners to pay attention to and remember the gist of a passage rather than the specific wording of the sentences. For example, Sachs (1967) asked students to listen to a passage about the invention of the telescope. On a subsequent delayed test, a sentence was presented and subjects were asked to judge whether this sentence in verbatim form had been in the passage. Students were proficient at noticing a sentence that was factually different from the passage; however, they were unable to distinguish a verbatim sentence from one that was a factually correct reworded version. Similarly, Bransford and Franks (1971) read a list of sentences to subjects and then gave a verbatim recognition test. Subjects were able to notice sentences that were factually inconsistent with the presented information, but they could not distinguish verbatim sentences from similar sentences that were factually correct. In addition, subjects were most confident about seeing longer sentences that joined several of the shorter ones, even though these longer sentences had never been presented. Apparently, subjects abstract the general meaning of the sentences but lose the specific verbatim wordings of the sentences (Jarvella, 1971; Sachs, 1967; Bransford & Franks, 1971, 1972; Franks & Bransford, 1972, 1974).

These results do not mean that people are unable to remember specific details, but rather that in many learning situations people assume that the goal is general understanding rather than verbatim memory. Verbatim recognition is increased, for example, when stimuli are presented visually (Katz & Gruenewald, 1974), when forced-choice tests are used (Anderson & Bower, 1973; Griggs & Keen, 1977), when sentences are embedded in a confusing list (Moeser, 1976), or when instructions call for verbatim learning (Barclay, 1973; Bransford, 1979).

Levels Effects. The "levels effect" refers to the idea that learning and remembering a particular piece of information from a passage depends on where it fits into the overall organization of the passsage. Passages may be analyzed into a hierarchy of parts, like an outline. Information that is important for the theme of the passage, as indicated by a high level in the text structure, is generally learned and remembered better than information from lower levels.

In an early study, Johnson (1970) asked students to rate the importance of idea units in passages based on how closely the idea units related to the theme. Then other subjects read and recalled the passage. Subjects tended to recall the most important idea units best, the second highest level next best, and so on, with poorest recall for idea units rated as least important. This levels effect suggests that learners make an active effort to learn informa-

tion that is most related to the general theme rather than information about details.

Kintsch has developed a technique for converting a passage into a text base—a hierarchy of propositions from the passage. In general, propositions that are high in the text base are recalled better than those at lower levels in the text base (Kintsch, 1974, 1976). Meyer developed a different technique for representing the organization of idea units in a passage, in which the passage may be represented as a sort of outline. As in Kintsch's studies, information that was essential in the outline was remembered better than information from more detailed levels (Meyer & McConkie, 1973; Meyer, 1975, 1977). Similar results have been obtained with young readers (Brown & Smiley, 1977) and using various systems for determining level of importance (Chiesi, Spilich, & Voss, 1979; Spilich et al., 1979; Mayer & Cook, 1981).

Schema Effects. More recently, Rumelhart (1975) and Thorndyke (1977) have devised a system for describing the organization of the parts of a story. A story grammar is a list of rules that specify the hierarchical relationships among events or states in a story. For example, four main "slots" to be filled in a story are the setting, the theme, the plot, and the resolution. The setting may consist of several parts, such as characters, location, and time. The theme consists of an event or goal. The plot consists of series of episodes, each consisting of goals, attempts, and outcomes. The resolution consists of an event or state. According to Thorndyke, older subjects have already learned to fill in these slots as they read a story, beginning with the four main parts and working down.

Thorndyke (1977) tested the story grammar idea by asking subjects to listen to a story and then try to recall it. Subjects tended to recall information from the top of the story grammar hierarchy (such as setting, theme, resolution) better than information lower down in the hierarchy. In addition, if the sentence corresponding to the theme was left out of the story, recall was much poorer. Apparently, subjects try to build a framework for a story and fill in the slots; however, if the theme is unclear, subjects may not be able to generate the right framework for the story. More recently, Voss and Bisanz (1982) have found that younger children tend to focus on actions rather than motives in a story line.

Schank and Abelson (1976) have suggested that people possess a large set of scripts for many common episodes. A script is a generalized set of expectations concerning a class of events. For example, the "restaurant script" may consist of slots such as "entering," "ordering," and so on. People may use their scripts for comprehending new information, and many failures to understand new information may occur when teacher and student are using different underlying scripts. Story grammars and scripts may be seen as more specific descriptions of Bartlett's "schema."

Prior Knowledge Effects. The prior knowledge that a learner brings to a learning situation can influence how the learner interprets new information. Prior knowledge can thus be used to establish a context or schema, into which new information is assimilated (Bransford, 1979). For example, Anderson et al. (1977) asked students to listen to an ambiguous passage that could be interpreted as either a story about a card game or a story about a music jam session. Music majors were more likely to remember things that were consistent with the jam session interpretation, while other students were more likely to remember things that were consistent with the card game interpretation. Similar results have been reported by other researchers (Schallert, 1976; Bransford, 1979; Anderson, 1977).

There is also evidence that learners have some control over the perspective they use for interpreting new information. For example, Pichert and Anderson (1977) presented a passage describing two boys playing in a house. Some subjects were asked to read the passage from the perspective of a home buyer; other subjects were asked to read it from the perspective of a burglar. On a recall test, subjects taking the home buyer perspective were more likely to recall things such as the fact that there was a leak in the roof, whereas subjects taking the burglar perspective were more likely to recall things such as the fact that there was a color TV. Similar results were obtained in other studies (Bransford, 1979). For example, Spilich et al. (1979) found that when people who are experts in a particular domain listen to a passage concerning this domain, they recall qualitatively different kinds of information than those who are novices.

It is also possible to manipulate a learner's perspective or schema on a passage by providing the learner with a topic or title for a passage. For example, Bransford and Johnson (1972) presented a vague passage to subjects, giving them a title (e.g., "Washing Clothes") either before they read, after they read, or not at all. Subjects rated the passage low in comprehensibility and recalled very little information when they had no title or were given the title after reading; however, subjects given the title before reading rated the passage much higher in comprehensibility and recalled more than twice as much information. Similar results were obtained by Dooling and Lachman (1971) and by Dooling and Mullet (1973) in which presenting a title before an ambiguous passage aided recall but presenting the title after the passage did not. Apparently the title provides a context for the subjects so that they can relate the new information to appropriate previous experience.

Inference Effects. Another major fact concerning prose learning is that people tend to make inferences during learning. Three kinds of inferences are case grammar presuppositions, conceptual dependency inferences, and logical deductions.

"Case grammar" (Fillmore, 1968, 1971) refers to the idea that each predicate (or verb) implies certain role relations. For example, "hit" suggests that there should be an agent (such as a "batter"), an object (such as a "ball"),

and an instrument (such as a "bat"). Thus, a learner comes to the learning situation with a storehouse of "presuppositions"—such as that the idea "hitting" requires an instrument. Even when a sentence excludes one of these role relations, subjects are likely to "remember" the sentence with all appropriate role relations (Kintsch, 1974; Meyer, 1975; Grimes, 1972; Perfetti, 1972; Wanner, 1974).

"Conceptual dependency" (Schank, 1972) refers to the idea that learners must make inferences concerning the relations among ideas in a passage, such as "cause-effect." For example, Kintsch (1976) reported a study in which students read a story containing the sentences "A burning cigarette was carelessly discarded. The fire destroyed many acres of virgin forest." Performance on a delayed test revealed that learners were just as fast in verifying that a cigarette started the fire as were subjects who had actually read that verbatim information. Recently, Mayer and Cook (1981) asked students to listen to a passage about radar. Students who were asked to repeat each phrase of the passage verbatim during learning showed considerably fewer inferences on a recall test than students who were asked to listen only. Apparently, mature learners use their prior knowledge in order to make appropriate inferences.

In a linear reasoning task, subjects are given premises such as "A is taller than B," "B is taller than C," "C is taller than D." In a series of studies, Potts (1972, 1974) found that students who read the premises were more accurate and faster in answering questions that involved inferences (such as "Is A taller than D?") than in answering questions about the premises (such as "Is B taller than C?"). Such results suggest that learners were able to build an integrated representation that included all inferences at the time of encoding. More recently, Mayer (1978) showed that the tendency of learners to make inferences at the time of encoding could be manipulated by varying the learning situation. Similarly, Frederiksen (1975) asked students to read a passage that contained many premises that could be combined. Subjects who were told to be prepared for a written test recalled many of the facts but made few inferences when asked to recall; subjects who were asked to try to solve the problem presented in the passage also recalled many of the facts but tended to make many inferences when asked to recall.

Text Organization Effects. What is learned from a lesson may depend on how the lesson is organized. For example, Bromage and Mayer (1981) found that organizing a technical passage around general principles resulted in better problem-solving transfer performance than organizing the passage by topic. Similarly, organizing a mathematics lesson so that it moves from familiar prerequisite concepts to formal definitions and algorithms resulted in better problem-solving transfer performance than using a lesson that moved from the formal to the familiar (Mayer, 1975b).

Advance organizers may serve to increase the meaningfulness of technical text. An advance organizer is a short verbal or pictorial introduction that provides a context for organizing the subsequent passage. Early research by Ausubel and his colleagues (Ausubel, 1968, 1977; see also Mayer, 1979a) found small but significant improvements in the retention of text material when advance organizers were used. For example, in a typical study (Ausubel & Youssef, 1963), students read a passage about Buddhism after reading either an advance organizer that pointed to the general relation between Christianity and Buddhism or a nonorganizing historical introduction. Performance on a retention test was higher for the advance organizer group, presumably because the organizer provided "ideational scaffolding" into which text material could be "anchored."

More recently, Mayer (1979b) and Royer and Cable (1975) have found that concrete models may serve as effective advance organizers for technical and scientific passages. For example, Mayer used a concrete model as an advance organizer for a computer programming manual; the model showed a picture of a computer with memory as an erasable scoreboard, input as a ticket window, output as a message pad, and executive control as a shopping list. The results of a long series of experiments revealed that concrete models served to enhance the recall of conceptual information (rather than technical information) and to enhance problem-solving performance on transfer tests (rather than retention tests). In addition, these effects seemed to be strongest for learners who lacked prerequisite knowledge in the domain, and for materials that were presented in a poorly organized way. Although some studies fail to demonstrate advance organizer effects (Barnes & Clawson, 1975), many failures are due to inadequate measurement of learning outcomes or inadequate experimental design (Mayer, 1979b; Ausubel, 1978; Lawton & Wanska, 1977). Apparently, advance organizers and concrete models provide an assimilative context that can be used during learning (Mayer, 1979a, 1979b).

Mathemagenic Effects. Mathemagenic activities (Rothkopf, 1970) are learner behaviors that enhance learning. Under appropriate conditions, mathemagenic activities, such as answering adjunct questions or taking notes, have measurable effects on improving learning.

Adjunct questions are questions that occur within prose passages, such as review questions in a textbook. In general, performance on a final retention test is enhanced when adjunct questions are incorporated into the text (Anderson & Biddle, 1975; Rothkopf & Bisbicos, 1967; DuBois, Alverson, & Staley, 1979). In particular, posttest performance is enhanced on information that was tested in adjunct questions—that is, intentional learning—but performance may be unaffected or hindered on information that was not tested in adjunct questions—that is, incidental learning (Rothkopf & Bisbicos, 1967; Anderson & Biddle, 1975).

One explanation of these results is that adjunct questions serve to direct the learner's attention. For example,

placing questions before each section of a passage may serve to limit the focus of the learner and thus result in poorer overall posttest performance than placing questions after each section of a passage (Anderson & Biddle, 1975; DuBois, Alverson, & Staley, 1979). Similarly, using just one type of question tends to limit the learner's reading strategy and posttest performance (Watts & Anderson, 1971; Mayer, 1975a; McConkie, Rayner, & Wilson, 1973).

Note taking is another mathemagenic technique that may aid learning. In a recent review, Faw and Waller (1976) noted, as Peters (1972) had earlier, that note taking has the strongest effect when the presentation rate is slow and when subjects can review their notes. Several researchers have found note taking to aid retention, but others have not (DiVesta & Gray, 1972, 1973; Peters, 1972; Peper & Mayer, 1978). Peper and Mayer (1978) have shown that note taking seems to have its strongest effects on tests of transfer rather than on retention, and on recall of main concepts rather than details. Wittrock (1974) has suggested that "learning is a generative process" in which the learner must actively build the to-be-learned material in memory. For example, Wittrock reported a study in which students recalled much more from a passage when they were asked to summarize paragraphs as they read. Similarly, Rickards and August (1975) have found student-generated underlining to enhance certain kinds of learning. Thus, note taking and underlining may serve as ways of encouraging learners to actively integrate new information with existing knowledge. This idea is supported by the finding that note taking has its strongest effects for low-knowledge learners (Peper & Mayer, 1978).

Additional information concerning prose learning may be obtained from the following sources: Bransford (1979), Cofer (1976), Meyer (1975), Graesser (1981), Kintsch (1974), Reder (1980).

Richard E. Mayer

See also Cognition and Memory; Cognitive Development; Language Development; Mathematical Behavior of Children; Motivation; Psychology; Readiness; Transfer of Learning.

REFERENCES

Adams, J. A. *Learning and Memory: An Introduction.* Homewood, Ill.: Dorsey, 1976.

Anderson, J. R., & Bower, G. H. *Human Associative Memory.* New York: Wiley, 1973.

Anderson, R. C. The notion of schemata and the educational enterprise. In R. C. Anderson, R. J. Spiro, & W. E. Montague (Eds.), *Schooling and the Acquisition of Knowledge.* Hillsdale, N.J.: Lawrence Erlbaum Associates, 1977.

Anderson, R. C., & Biddle, W. B. On asking people questions about what they are reading. In G. Bower (Ed.), *Psychology of Learning and Motivation* (Vol. 9). New York: Academic Press, 1975.

Anderson, R. C.; Reynolds, R. E.; Schallert, D. L.; & Goetz, E. T. Frameworks for comprehending discourse. *American Educational Research Association*, 1977, *14*, 367–381.

Archer, E. J. A re-evaluation of the meaningfulness of all possible CVC trigrams. *Psychological Monographs,* 1960, *74* (Whole No. 497).

Arkes, H. R.; Schumacher, G. M.; & Gardner, E. T. Effects of orienting tasks on the retention of prose material. *Journal of Educational Psychology,* 1976, *68,* 536–545.

Atkinson, R. C., & Raugh, M. R. An application of the mnemonic keyword method to the acquisition of Russian vocabulary. *Journal of Experimental Psychology: Human Learning and Memory,* 1975, *104,* 126–133.

Ausubel, D. P. *Educational Psychology: A Cognitive View.* New York: Holt, Rinehart & Winston, 1968.

Ausubel, D. P. The facilitation of meaningful verbal learning in the classroom. *Educational Psychologist,* 1977, *12,* 162–178.

Ausubel, D. P. In defense of advance organizers: A reply to the critics. *Review of Educational Research,* 1978, *48,* 251–257.

Ausubel, D. P., & Youssef, M. Role of discriminability in meaningful parallel learning. *Journal of Educational Psychology,* 1963, *54,* 331–336.

Baddeley, A. D. *The Psychology of Memory.* New York: Basic Books, 1976.

Barclay, J. R. The role of comprehension in remembering sentences. *Cognitive Psychology,* 1973, *4,* 229–254.

Barnes, B. R., & Clawson, E. U. Do advance organizers facilitate learning? Recommendations for further research based on an analysis of thirty-two studies. *Review of Educational Research,* 1975, *45,* 637–659.

Bartlett, F. C. *Remembering: A Study in Experimental and Social Psychology.* London: Cambridge University Press, 1932.

Bilodeau, E. A.; Bilodeau, I. M.; & Schumsky, D. A. Some effects of introducing and withdrawing knowledge of results early and late in practice. *Journal of Experimental Psychology,* 1959, *58,* 142–144.

Bindra, I., & Palfai, T. Nature of positive and negative incentive motivational effects on general activity. *Journal of Comparative and Physiological Psychology,* 1967, *63,* 288–297.

Black, A. H.; Carlson, N. J.; & Solomon, R. L. Exploratory studies of the conditioning of autonomic responses in curarized dogs. *Psychological Monographs,* 1962, *76* (Whole No. 548).

Blanchard, R. J., & Blanchard, D. C. Crouching as an index of fear. *Journal of Comparative and Physiological Psychology,* 1969, *67,* 370–375.

Bolles, R. C. *Learning Theory* (2nd ed.). New York: Holt, Rinehart & Winston, 1979.

Bourne, L. E., Jr. *Human Conceptual Behavior.* Boston: Allyn & Bacon, 1966.

Bourne, L. E., Jr. Knowing and using concepts. *Psychological Review,* 1970, *77,* 546–556.

Bourne, L. E., Jr. An inference model for conceptual rule-learning. In R. L. Solso (Ed.), *Theories in Cognitive Psychology: The Loyola Symposium.* Hillsdale, N.J.: Lawrence Erlbaum Associates, 1974.

Bourne, L. E., Jr.; Ekstrand, B. R.; & Dominowski, R. L. *The Psychology of Thinking.* Englewood Cliffs, N.J.: Prentice-Hall, 1971.

Bourne, L. E., & Haygood, R. C. The role of stimulus redundancy in concept identification. *Journal of Experimental Psychology,* 1959, *58,* 232–238.

Bousfield, W. A. The occurrence of clustering in the recall of randomly arranged associates. *Journal of General Psychology,* 1953, *49,* 229–240.

Bousfield, W. A., & Cohen, B. H. The effects of reinforcement on the occurrence of clustering in the recall of randomly arranged associates. *Journal of Psychology,* 1953, *36,* 67–81.

Bousfield, W. A.; Cohen, B. H.; & Whitmarsh, G. A. Associative clustering in the recall of words of different toxonomic frequencies of occurrence. *Psychological Reports,* 1958, *4,* 39–44.

Bower, G. H. Organizational factors in memory. *Cognitive Psychology,* 1970, *1,* 18–46.

Bower, G. H. Mental imagery in associative learning. In L. W. Gregg (Ed.), *Cognition in Learning and Memory.* New York: Wiley, 1972.

Bower, G. H., & Clark, M. C. Narrative stories as mediators for serial learning. *Psychonomic Science,* 1969, *14,* 181–182.

Bower, G. H.; Clark, M. C.; Lesgold, A. M.; & Winzenz, D. Hierarchical retrieval schemes in recall of categorized word lists. *Journal of Verbal Learning and Verbal Behavior,* 1969, *8,* 323–343.

Bower, G. H., & Hilgard, E. R. *Theories of Learning* (5th ed.). Englewood Cliffs, N.J.: Prentice-Hall, 1981.

Bower, G. H., & Trabasso, T. R. Reversals prior to solution in concept identification. *Journal of Experimental Psychology,* 1963, *66,* 409–418.

Bower, G. H., & Trabasso, T. R. Concept identification. In R. C. Atkinson (Ed.), *Studies in Mathematical Psychology,* Stanford, Calif.: Stanford University Press, 1964, pp. 32–94.

Bransford, J. D. *Human Cognition: Learning, Understanding, and Remembering.* Belmont, Calif.: Wadsworth, 1979.

Bransford, J. D., & Franks, J. J. The abstraction of linguistic ideas. *Cognitive Psychology,* 1971, *2,* 331–350.

Bransford, J. D., & Franks, J. J. The abstraction of linguistic ideas: A review. *Cognition,* 1972, *2,* 211–249.

Bransford, J. D., & Johnson, M. K. Contextual prerequisites for understanding: Some investigations of comprehension and recall. *Journal of Verbal Learning and Verbal Behavior,* 1972, *11,* 717–726.

Bromage, B. K., & Mayer, R. E. Relationship between what is remembered and creative problem-solving performance in science learning. *Journal of Educational Psychology,* 1981, *73,* in press.

Brown, A. L., & DeLoache, J. S. Skills, plans, and self-regulation. In R. S. Siegler (Ed.), *Children's Thinking: What Developments?* Hillsdale, N.J.: Lawrence Erlbaum Associates, 1978.

Brown, A. L., & Smiley, S. S. Rating the importance of structural units of prose passages: A problem of metacognitive development. *Child Development,* 1977, *48,* 1–8.

Bruner, J. S.; Goodnow, J. J.; & Austin, G. A. *A Study of Thinking.* New York: Wiley, 1956.

Campbell, P. E.; Batsche, C. J.; & Batsche, G. M. Spaced-trials reward magnitude effects in the rat: Single versus multiple food pellets. *Journal of Comparative Physiological Psychology,* 1972, *81,* 360–364.

Capaldi, E. D. Simultaneous shifts in reward magnitude and level of food deprivation. *Psychonomic Science,* 1971, *23,* 357–359.

Caruso, J. L., & Resnick, L. B. Task structure and transfer in children's learning of double classification skills. *Child Development,* 1972, *43,* 1297–1308.

Chiesi, H. L.; Spilich, G. J.; & Voss, J. F. Acquisition of domain-related information in relation to high and low domain-related knowledge. *Journal of Verbal Learning and Verbal Behavior,* 1979, *18,* 257–273.

Cieutat, V. J.; Stockwell, F. E.; & Noble, C. E. The interaction of ability and amount of practice with stimulus meaningfulness (m, m') in paired-associate learning. *Journal of Experimental Psychology,* 1958, *56,* 193–202.

Cofer, C. N. Properties of verbal materials and verbal learning. In J. W. Kling & L. A. Riggs (Eds.), *Woodworth and Schlosberg's Experimental Psychology.* New York: Holt, Rinehart & Winston, 1971.

Cofer, C. N. (Ed.), *The Structure of Human Memory.* San Francisco: Freeman, 1976.

Coppage, E. W., & Harcum, E. R. Temporal versus structural determinants of primacy in strategies of serial learning. *Journal of Verbal Learning and Verbal Behavior,* 1967, *6,* 487–490.

Craik, F. I. M. The fate of primary items in free recall. *Journal of Verbal Learning and Verbal Behavior,* 1970, *9,* 143–148.

Craik, F. I. M., & Lockhart, R. S. Levels of processing: A framework for memory research. *Journal of Verbal Learning and Verbal Behavior,* 1972, *11,* 671–684.

Deane, G. E. Cardiac conditioning in the albino rabbit using three CS-UCS intervals. *Psychonomic Science,* 1965, *3,* 119–120.

Deese, J. Influence of inter-item associative strength upon immediate free recall. *Psychological Reports,* 1959, *5,* 305–312.

DiVesta, F. J., & Gray, G. S. Listening and note-taking. *Journal of Educational Psychology,* 1972, *63,* 8–14.

DiVesta, F. J., & Gray, G. S. Listening and note-taking: Immediate and delayed recall as functions of variations in thematic continuity, note taking, and length of listening-review intervals. *Journal of Educational Psychology,* 1973, *64,* 278–287.

Dooling, D. J., & Lachman, R. Effects of comprehension on retention of prose. *Journal of Experimental Psychology,* 1971, *88,* 216–222.

Dooling, D. J., & Mullet, R. L. Locus of thematic effects on retention of prose. *Journal of Experimental Psychology,* 1973, *97,* 404–406.

DuBois, N. F.; Alverson, G. F.; & Staley, R. K. *Educational Psychology and Instructional Decisions.* Homewood, Ill.: Dorsey, 1979.

Ebbinghaus, H. *Memory* (H. A. Ruger & C. E. Bussenius, Trans.). New York: Dover, 1964. (Originally published as *Über das Gedachtnis.* Leipzig: Duncker & Humbolt, 1885).

Ebenholtz, S. M. Serial learning and dimensional organization. In G. N. Bower (Ed.), *The Psychology of Learning and Motivation: Advances in Research and Theory* (Vol. 5). New York: Academic Press, 1972, pp. 267–314.

Faw, H. W., & Waller, T. G. Mathemagenic behaviors and efficiency in learning from prose. *Review of Educational Research,* 1976, *46,* 691–720.

Ferster, C. B., & Skinner, B. F. *Schedules of Reinforcement.* New York: Appleton-Century-Crofts, 1957.

Fillmore, C. J. The case for case. In E. Bach & R. T. Harms (Eds.), *Universals of Linguistic Theory.* New York: Holt, Rinehart & Winston, 1968, pp. 1–90.

Fillmore, C. J. Some problems for case grammar. In R. J. O'Brien (Ed.), *Linguistics Developments of the Sixties—Viewpoints for the Seventies: Monograph Series on Languages and Linguistics,* 1971, *24,* 35–56.

Fitzgerald, R. D. Effects of partial reinforcement with acid on the classically conditioned salivary response in dogs. *Journal of Comparative and Physiological Psychology,* 1963, *56,* 1056–1060.

Fitzgerald, R. D., & Martin, G. K. Heart-rate conditioning in rats as a function of interstimulus interval. *Psychological Reports,* 1971, *29,* 1103–1110.

Flavell, J. H. Developmental studies of mediated memory. In H. W. Reese & L. P. Lipsitt (Eds.), *Advances in Child Development and Behavior* (Vol. 5). New York: Academic Press, 1970.

Flavell, J. H., & Wellman, H. M. Metamemory. In R. V. Kail & J. W. Hagen (Eds.), *Perspectives on the Development of Memory and Cognition.* Hillsdale, N.J.: Lawrence Erlbaum Associates, 1977.

Franks, J. J., & Bransford, J. D. Abstraction of visual patterns. *Journal of Experimental Psychology,* 1971, *90,* 65–74.

Franks, J. J., & Bransford, J. D. The acquisition of abstract ideas. *Journal of Verbal Learning and Verbal Behavior,* 1972, *11,* 311–315.

Franks, J. J., & Bransford, J. D. Memory for syntactic form as a function of semantic context. *Journal of Experimental Psychology,* 1974, *103,* 1037–1039.

Frederiksen, C. H. Effects of context-induced processing operations on semantic information acquired from discourse. *Cognitive Psychology,* 1975, *7,* 139–166.

French, N. R.; Carter, C. W.; & Koenig, W. The words and sounds of telephone conversations. *Bell System Technical Journal,* 1930, *9,* 290–324.

Friebergs, V., & Tulving, E. The effect of practice on utilization of information from positive and negative instances in concept identification. *Canadian Journal of Psychology,* 1961, *15,* 101–106.

Gagné, R. M. Learning hierarchies. *Educational Psychologist,* 1968, *6,* 1–9.

Gagné, R. M., & Briggs, L. J. *Principles of Instructional Design.* New York: Holt, Rinehart & Winston, 1974.

Gagné, R. M.; Mayor, J. R.; Garstens, H. L.; & Paradise, N. E. Factors in acquiring knowledge of a mathematical skill. *Psychological Monographs: General and Applied,* 1962, *76* (Whole No. 526).

Glanzer, M., & Cunitz, A. R. Two storage mechanisms in free recall. *Journal of Verbal Learning and Verbal Behavior,* 1966, *5,* 351–360.

Glanzer, M., & Dolinsky, R. The anchor for the serial position curve. *Journal of Verbal Learning and Verbal Behavior,* 1965, *4,* 267–273.

Glaze, J. A. The association value of nonsense syllables. *Journal of Genetic Psychology,* 1928, *35,* 255–266.

Glenberg, A. M. Monotonic and nonmonotonic lag effects in paired-associate and recognition memory paradigms. *Journal of Verbal Learning and Verbal Behavior,* 1976, *15,* 1–16.

Godden, D. R., & Baddeley, A. D. Context-dependent memory in two natural environments: On land and under water. *British Journal of Psychology,* 1975, *66,* 325–332.

Goodwin, D. W.; Powell, B.; Bremer, D.; Hoine, H.; & Stern, J. Alcohol and recall: State dependent effects in man. *Science,* 1969, *163,* 1358.

Gormezano, I., & Moore, J. W. Classical conditioning. In M. H. Marx (Ed.), *Learning: Processes.* New York: Macmillan, 1969.

Goulet, L. R.; Bone, R. N.; & Barker, D. D. Serial position, primacy, and the von Restorff isolation effect. *Psychonomic Science,* 1967, *9,* 529–530.

Graesser, A. C. *Prose Comprehension beyond the Word.* New York: Springer-Verlag, 1981.

Gray, J. A. Stimulus intensity dynamism. *Psychological Bulletin,* 1965, *63,* 180–196.

Grice, G. R. Stimulus intensity and response evocation. *Psychological Review.* 1968, *75,* 359–373.

Griggs, R. A., & Keen, D. M. The role of test procedure in linguistic integration studies. *Memory and Cognition,* 1977, *5,* 685–689.

Grimes, J. E. *The Thread of Discourse.* Ithaca, N.Y.: Cornell University Press, 1972.

Hall, J. F. Learning as a function of word frequency. *American Journal of Psychology*, 1954, *67*, 138–140.

Haygood, R. C., & Stevenson, M. Effects of number of irrelevant dimensions in nonconjunctive concept learning. *Journal of Experimental Psychology*, 1967, *74*, 302–304.

Hebb, D. O. *Organization of Behavior*. New York: Wiley, 1949.

Hebb, D. O. *A Textbook of Psychology*. Philadelphia: Saunders, 1958.

Heidbreder, E. The attainment of concepts, Part 1: Terminology and methodology. *Journal of Psychology*, 1946, *35*, 173–189.

Heidbreder, E. The attainment of concepts, Part 3: The process. *Journal of Psychology*, 1947, *24*, 93–108.

Higbee, K. L. *Your Memory: How it Works and How to Improve It*. Englewood Cliffs, N.J.: Prentice-Hall, 1977.

Houston, J. P. *Fundamentals of Learning*. New York: Academic Press, 1976.

Howes, D. A word count of spoken English. *Journal of Verbal Learning and Verbal Behavior*, 1966, *5*, 572–604.

Hull, C. L. Quantitative aspects of the evolution of concepts. *Psychological Monographs*, 1920, *28* (No. 123).

Hunt, E. B.; Marin, J.; & Stone, P. I. *Experiments in Induction*. New York: Academic Press, 1966.

Hyde, T. S., & Jenkins, J. J. Differential effects of incidental tasks on the organization of recall of a list of highly associated words. *Journal of Experimental Psychology*, 1969, *82*, 472–481.

Hyde, T. S., & Jenkins, J. J. Recall of words as a function of semantic, graphic, and syntactic orienting tasks. *Journal of Verbal Learning and Verbal Behavior*, 1973, *12*, 471–480.

Hyman, R., & Frost, N. Gradients and schema in pattern recognition. In P.M.A. Rabbitt (Ed.), *Attention and Performance* (Vol. 5). New York: Academic Press, 1974.

Ison, J. R. Experimental extinction as a function of number of reinforcements. *Journal of Experimental Psychology*, 1962, *64*, 314–317.

Ison, J. R., & Cook, P. E. Extinction performance as a function of incentive magnitude and number of acquisition trials. *Psychonomic Science*, 1964, *1*, 245–246.

Jarvella, R. J. Syntactic processing of connected speech. *Journal of Verbal Learning and Verbal Behavior*, 1971, *10*, 409–416.

Jenkins, J. J. Remember that old theory of memory? Well, forget it! *American Psychologist*, 1974, *29*, 785–795.

Jensen, A. R. An empirical theory of the serial-position effect. *Journal of Psychology*, 1962, *53*, 127–142.

Johnson, R. E. Recall of prose as a function of the structural importance of linguistic units. *Journal of Verbal Learning and Verbal Behavior*, 1970, *9*, 12–20.

Jones, L. V., & Wepman, J. M. *A Spoken Word Count*. Chicago: Language Research Associates, 1966.

Kalish, H. I. Stimulus generalization. In M. H. Marx (Ed.), *Learning: Processes*. New York: Macmillan, 1969.

Katz, S., & Gruenewald, P. The abstraction of linguistic ideas in "meaningful" sentences. *Memory and Cognition*, 1974, *2*, 737–741.

Kausler, D. H. *Psychology of Verbal Learning and Memory*. New York: Academic Press, 1974.

Keller, F. S. *Learning: Reinforcement Theory*. New York: Random House, 1969.

Kendler, H. H.; & D'Amato, M. F. A comparison of reversal and nonreversal shifts in human concept formation. *Journal of Experimental Psychology*, 1955, *49*, 165–174.

Kendler, H. H., & Kendler, T. S. Vertical and horizontal processes in problem-solving. *Psychological Review*, 1962, *69*, 1–16.

Kendler, H. H., & Kendler, T. S. From discrimination learning to cognitive development: A neobehaviorist odyssey. In W. K. Estes (Ed.), *Handbook of Learning and Cognitive Processes* (Vol. 1). Hillsdale, N.J.: Lawrence Erlbaum Associates, 1975.

Kendler, T. S., & Kendler, H. H. Reversal and nonreversal shifts in kindergarten children. *Journal of Experimental Psychology*, 1959, *58*, 56–60.

Kieras, D. E. Good and bad structure in simple paragraphs: Effects of apparent theme, reading time, and recall. *Journal of Verbal Learning and Verbal Behavior*, 1978, *17*, 13–28.

Kintsch, W. Runway performance as a function of drive strength and magnitude of reinforcement. *Journal of Comparative and Physiological Psychology*, 1962, *55*, 882–887.

Kintsch, W. *The Representation of Meaning in Memory*. Hillsdale, N.J.: Lawrence Erlbaum Associates, 1974.

Kintsch, W. Memory for prose. In C. N. Cofer (Ed.), *The Structure of Human Memory*. San Francisco: Freeman, 1976, pp. 90–113.

Klatzky, R. L. *Human Memory* (2nd ed.). San Francisco: Freeman, 1980.

Kraeling, D. Analysis of amount of reward as a variable in learning. *Journal of Comparative and Physiological Psychology*, 1961, *54*, 560–565.

Kucera, H., & Francis, W. N. *Computational Analysis of Present-day American English*. Providence: Brown University Press, 1967.

Laughlin, P. R. Selection strategies in concept attainment. In R. L. Solso (Ed.), *Contemporary Issues in Cognitive Psychology: The Loyola Symposium*. New York: Halsted Press, 1973.

Lawton, J. T., & Wanska, S. K. Advance organizers as a teaching strategy: A reply to Barnes and Clawson. *Review of Educational Research*, 1977, *47*, 233–244.

Levine, M. *A Cognitive Theory of Learning: Research on Hypothesis Testing*. Hillsdale, N.J.: Lawrence Erlbaum Associates, 1975.

Lorayne, H., & Lucas, J. *The Memory Book*. New York: Ballantine, 1974.

Mann, M. B. Studies in language behavior: The quantitative differentiation of samples of written language. *Psychological Monograph*, 1944, *56* (Whole No. 255), 41–74.

Manning, A. A.; Schneiderman, N.; & Lordahl, D. S. Delay versus trace heart rate classical discrimination conditioning in rabbits as a function of ISI. *Journal of Experimental Psychology*, 1969, *80*, 225–230.

Martin, E. Stimulus meaningfulness and paired-associate transfer: An encoding variability hypothesis. *Psychological Review*, 1968, *75*, 421–441.

Martin, E. Stimulus encoding in learning and transfer. In A. W. Melton & E. Martin (Eds.), *Coding Processes in Human Memory*. New York: Halsted Press, 1972, pp. 59–84.

Mayer, R. E. Forward transfer of different reading strategies evoked by test-like events in mathematics text. *Journal of Educational Psychology*, 1975, *67*, 165–169. (a)

Mayer, R. E. Information processing variables in learning to solve problems. *Review of Educational Research*, 1975, *45*, 525–541. (b)

Mayer, R. E. Qualitatively different storage and processing strategies used for linear reasoning tasks due to meaningfulness of premises. *Journal of Experimental Psychology: Human Learning and Memory*, 1978, *4*, 5–18.

Mayer, R. E. Twenty years of research on advance organizers: Assimilation theory is still the best predictor of results. *Instructional Science*, 1979, *8*, 133–167. (a)

Mayer, R. E. Can advance organizers influence meaningful learning? *Review of Educational Research*, 1979, *49*, 371–383. (b)

Mayer, R. E., & Cook, L. K. Effects of shadowing on prose comprehension and problem-solving. *Memory and Cognition*, 1981, *9*, 101–109.

McConkie, G. W.; Rayner, K.; & Wilson, S. J. Experimental manipulation of reading strategies. *Journal of Educational Psychology*, 1973, *65*, 1–8.

McLaughlin, J. P. The von Restorff effect in serial learning: Serial position of the isolate and length of list. *Journal of Experimental Psychology*, 1966, *72*, 603–609.

Melton, A. W. The situation with respect to the spacing and repetitions and memory. *Journal of Verbal Learning and Verbal Behavior*, 1970, *9*, 596–606.

Meltzer, D., & Brahlek, J. A. Quantity of reinforcement and fixed-interval performance. *Psychonomic Science*, 1968, *12*, 207–208.

Mervis, C. B., & Rosch, E. Categorization of natural objects. In M. R. Rosenzweig & L. W. Porter (Eds.), *Annual Review of Psychology*, 1981, *32*, 89–116.

Meyer, B. J. F. *The Organization of Prose and Its Effects on Memory.* Amsterdam: North Holland, 1975.

Meyer, B. J. F. The structure of prose: Effects on learning and memory and implications for educational practice. In R. C. Anderson, R. J. Spiro, & W. E. Montague (Eds.), *Schooling and the Acquisition of Knowledge.* Hillsdale, N.J.: Lawrence Erlbaum Associates, 1977.

Meyer, B. J. F., & McConkie, G. W. What is recalled after hearing a passage? *Journal of Educational Psychology*, 1973, *65*, 109–117.

Miller, G. A.; Newman, E. B.; & Friedman, E. A. Length-frequency statistics for written English. *Information and Control*, 1958, *1*, 370–389.

Moeser, S. D. Inferential reasoning in episodic memory. *Journal of Verbal Learning and Verbal Behavior*, 1976, *15*, 193–212.

Morris, C. D.; Bransford, J. D.; & Franks, J. J. Levels of processing versus transfer appropriate processing. *Journal of Verbal Learning and Verbal Behavior*, 1977, *16*, 519–533.

Murdock, B. B., Jr. *Human Memory: Theory and Data.* Hillsdale, N.J.: Lawrence Erlbaum Associates, 1974.

Neimark, E. D., & Santa, J. L. Thinking and concept attainment. In *Annual Review of Psychology* (Vol. 26). Palo Alto, Calif.: Annual Review, 1975, pp. 173–205.

Neisser, U. *Cognition and Reality.* San Francisco: Freeman, 1976.

Neumann, P. G. Visual prototype formation with discontinuous representation of dimensions of variability. *Memory and Cognition*, 1977, *5*, 187–197.

Newell, K. M. Knowledge of results and motor learning. *Journal of Motor Behavior*, 1974, *6*, 235–244.

Newport, E. L., & Bellugi, U. Linguistic expression of category levels in a visual gesturing language. In E. Rosch & B. B. Lloyd (Eds.), *Cognition and Categorization.* Hillsdale, N.J.: Lawrence Erlbaum Associates, 1978.

Noble, C. E. An analysis of meaning. *Psychological Review*, 1952, *59*, 421–430.

Noble, C. E. Meaningfulness and familiarity. In C. N. Cofer & B. S. Musgrave (Eds.), *Verbal Behavior and Learning: Problems and Processes.* New York: McGraw-Hill, 1963.

Osgood, C. E. The similarity paradox in human learning: A resolution. *Psychological Review*, 1949, *56*, 132–143.

Ost, J. W. P., & Lauer, D. W. Some investigations of classical salivary conditioning in the dog. In W. F. Prokasy (Ed.), *Classical Conditioning: A Symposium.* New York: Appleton-Century-Crofts, 1965.

Paivio, A. *Imagery and Verbal Processes.* New York: Holt, Rinehart & Winston, 1971.

Paivio, A.; Smythe, P. C.; & Yuille, J. C. Imagery versus meaningfulness of nouns in paired-associate learning. *Canadian Journal of Psychology*, 1982, *22*, 427–441.

Paivio, A.; Yuille, J. C.; & Madigan, S. Concreteness, imagery, and meaningfulness values for 925 nouns. *Journal of Experimental Psychology Monograph Supplement*, 1968, *76*(1, Part 2).

Palermo, D. S., & Jenkins, J. J. *Word Association Norms: Grade School through College.* Minneapolis: University of Minnesota Press, 1964.

Pavlik, W. B., & Reynolds, W. F. Effects of deprivation schedule and reward magnitude on acquisition and extinction performance. *Journal of Comparative and Physiological Psychology*, 1963, *56*, 452–455.

Pavlov, I. P. *Conditional Reflexes.* London: Oxford University Press, 1927.

Peper, R. J., & Mayer, R. E. Note-taking as a generative activity. *Journal of Educational Psychology*, 1978, *70*, 514–522.

Perfetti, C. A. Psychosemantics: Some cognitive aspects of structural meaning. *Psychological Bulletin*, 1972, *78*, 241–259.

Peters, D. L. Effects of note-taking and rate of presentation on short-term objective test performance. *Journal of Educational Psychology*, 1972, *63*, 276–280.

Peterson, L. R. Verbal learning and memory. In M. R. Rosenzweig & L. W. Porter (Eds.), *Annual Review of Psychology*, 1977, *28*, 393–416.

Pichert, J. W., & Anderson, R. C. Taking different perspectives on a story. *Journal of Educational Psychology*, 1977, *69*, 309–315.

Posner, M. I. Abstraction and the process of recognition. In G. H. Bower & J. T. Spence (Eds.), *The Psychology of Learning and Motivation* (Vol. 3), New York: Academic Press, 1969, pp. 44–96.

Posner, M. I., & Keele, S. W. On the genesis of abstract ideas. *Journal of Experimental Psychology*, 1968, *77*, 353–363.

Posner, M. I., & Keele, S. W. Retention of abstract ideas. *Journal of Experimental Psychology*, 1970, *83*, 304–308.

Postman, L. Verbal learning and memory. In M. R. Rosenzweig & L. W. Porter (Eds.), *Annual Review of Psychology*, 1975, *26*, 291–336.

Postman, L., & Phillips, L. W. Short-term temporal changes in free recall. *Quarterly Journal of Experimental Psychology*, 1965, *17*, 132–138.

Potts, G. R. Information-processing strategies used in the encoding of linear orderings. *Journal of Verbal Learning and Verbal Behavior*, 1972, *11*, 727–740.

Potts, G. R. Storing and retrieving information about ordered relationships. *Journal of Experimental Psychology*, 1974, *103*, 431–439.

Pressley, M. Imagery and children's learning: Putting the picture in developmental perspective. *Review of Educational Research*, 1977, *47*, 585–622.

Pressley, M., & Dennis-Rounds, J. Transfer of a mnemonic keyword strategy at two age levels. *Journal of Educational Psychology*, 1980, *72*, 575–582.

Pressley, M., & Levin, J. R. Developmental differences in subjects' associative learning strategies and performance: Assessing a hypothesis. *Journal of Experimental Child Psychology*, 1977, *24*, 431–439.

Prokasy, W. F., & Hall, J. F. Primary stimulus generalization. *Psychological Review,* 1963, *70,* 310–322.

Rachlin, H. *Behavior and Learning.* San Francisco: Freeman, 1976.

Ratliff, R. G., & Ratliff, A. R. Runway acquisition and extinction as a joint function of magnitude of reward and percentage of rewarded acquisition trials. *Learning and Motivation,* 1971, *2,* 289–295.

Raugh, M. R., & Atkinson, R. C. A mnemonic method for learning a second-language vocabulary. *Journal of Educational Psychology,* 1975, *67,* 1–16.

Reder, L. M. The role of elaboration in the comprehension and retention of prose: A critical review. *Review of Educational Research,* 1980, *50,* 5–54.

Reed, S. K. Pattern recognition and categorization. *Cognitive Psychology,* 1972, *3,* 382–407.

Renner, K. E. Delay of reinforcement: An historical review. *Psychological Bulletin,* 1964, *61,* 341–361.

Rescorla, R. A. Pavlovian conditioning and its proper control procedures. *Psychological Review,* 1967, *74,* 71–80.

Resnick, L. B., & Ford, W. W. *The Psychology of Mathematics for Instruction.* Hillsdale, N.J.: Lawrence Erlbaum Associates, 1981.

Resnick, L. B.; Siegel, A. W.; & Kersh, E. Transfer and sequence in learning double classification skills. *Journal of Experimental Child Psychology,* 1971, *11,* 139–149.

Resnick, L. B.; Wang, M. C.; & Kaplan, J. Task analysis in curriculum design: A hierarchically sequenced introductory mathematics curriculum. *Journal of Applied Behavior Analysis,* 1973, *6,* 679–710.

Rickards, J. P., & August, G. J. Generative underlining strategies in prose recall. *Journal of Educational Psychology,* 1975, *67,* 860–865.

Roberts, W. A. Resistance to extinction following partial and consistent reinforcement with varying magnitudes of reward. *Journal of Comparative and Physiological Psychology,* 1969, *67,* 395–400.

Rosch, E. Cognitive representations of semantic categories. *Journal of Experimental Psychology: General,* 1975, *104,* 192–223. (a)

Rosch, E. On the internal structure of semantic categories. In T. E. Moore (Ed.), *Cognitive Development and the Acquisition of Language.* New York: Academic Press, 1975. (b)

Rosch, E., & Lloyd, B. B. *Cognitive and Categorization.* Hillsdale, N. J.: Lawrence Erlbaum Associates, 1978.

Rosch, E., & Mervis, C. B. Family resemblances: Studies in the internal structure of categories. *Cognitive Psychology,* 1975, *7,* 573–605.

Rosch, E.; Mervis, C. B.; Gray, W.; Johnson, D.; & Boyes-Braem, P. Basic objects in natural categories. *Cognitive Psychology,* 1976, *8,* 382–439.

Ross, L. E., & Hartman, T. F. Human-eyelid conditioning: The recent experimental literature. *Genetic Psychology Monographs,* 1965, *71,* 177–220.

Ross, S. M., & Ross, L. E. Comparison of trace and delay classical eyelid conditioning as a function of interstimulus interval. *Journal of Experimental Psychology,* 1971, *91,* 165–167.

Rothkopf, E. Z. The concept of mathemagenic activities. *Review of Educational Research,* 1970, *40,* 325–336.

Rothkopf, E. Z., & Bisbicos, E. Selective facilitative effects of interspersed questions on learning from written material. *Journal of Educational Psychology,* 1967, *58,* 56–61.

Rowher, W. D., Jr. Elaboration and learning in childhood and adolescence. In H. W. Reese (Ed.), *Advances in Child Development and Behavior* (Vol. 18). New York: Academic Press, 1973.

Rowher, W. D., Jr., & Bean, J. P. Sentence effects and noun-pair learning: A developmental interaction during adolescence. *Journal of Experimental Child Psychology,* 1973, *15,* 521–533.

Royer, J. M., & Cable, G. W. Facilitated learning in connected discourse. *Journal of Educational Psychology,* 1975, *67,* 116–123.

Rumelhart, D. E. Notes on a schema for stories. In D. G. Bobrow & A. Collins (Eds.), *Representation and Understanding.* New York: Academic Press, 1975, pp. 211–236.

Rundus, D. Analysis of rehearsal processes in free recall. *Journal of Experimental Psychology,* 1971, *89,* 63–77.

Sachs, J. D. S. Recognition memory for syntactic and semantic aspects of connected discourse. *Perception and Psychophysics,* 1967, *1,* 437–442.

Schallert, D. L. Improving memory for prose: The relationship between depth of processing and context. *Journal of Verbal Learning and Verbal Behavior,* 1976, *15,* 621–632.

Schank, R. C. Conceptual dependency: A theory of natural language understanding. *Cognitive Psychology,* 1972, *3,* 552–631.

Schank, R. C., & Abelson, R. P. *Scripts, Plans, Goals, and Understanding: An Inquiry into Human Knowledge Structures.* Hillsdale, N.J.: Lawrence Erlbaum Associates, 1976.

Schneiderman, N. Interstimulus interval function of the nicitating membrane response of the rabbit under delay versus trace conditioning. *Journal of Comparative and Physiological Psychology,* 1966, *62,* 397–402.

Sheafor, P. J., & Gormezano, I. Conditioning the rabbit's (oryctolagus cuniculus) jaw-movement response: US magnitude effects on URs, CRs, and pseudo-CRs. *Journal of Comparative and Physiological Psychology,* 1972, *81,* 449–456.

Skinner, B. F. *The Behavior of Organisms.* Engelwood Cliffs, N.J.: Prentice-Hall, 1938.

Skinner, B. F. *Verbal Behavior.* New York: Prentice-Hall, Appleton-Century-Crofts, 1957.

Skinner, B. F. Teaching machines. *Science,* 1958, *128,* 969–977.

Skinner, B. F. *About Behaviorism.* New York: Knopf, 1974.

Smith, M. C. CS-US interval and US intensity in classical conditioning of the rabbit's nicitating membrane responses. *Journal of Comparative and Physiological Psychology,* 1968, *66,* 679–687.

Spilich, G. J.; Vesonder, G. T.; Chiesi, H. L.; & Voss, J. F. Text processing of domain-related information for individuals with high- and low-domain knowledge. *Journal of Verbal Learning and Verbal Behavior,* 1979, *18,* 275–290.

Stein, B. S. Depth of processing re-examined: The effects of precision of encoding and test appropriateness. *Journal of Verbal Learning and Verbal Behavior,* 1978, *17,* 165–174.

Tarpy, R. M. *Basic Principles of Learning.* Glenview, Ill.: Scott, Foresman, 1975.

Tarpy, R. M., & Mayer, R. E. *Foundations of Learning and Memory.* Glenview, Ill.: Scott, Foresman, 1978.

Tarpy, R. M., & Sawabini, F. L. Reinforcement delay: A selective review of the last decade. *Psychological Bulletin,* 1974, *81,* 984–997.

Thomas, E., & Wagner, A. R. Partial reinforcement of the classically conditioned eyelid response in the rabbit. *Journal of Comparative and Physiological Psychology,* 1964, *58,* 157–158.

Thorndike, E. L. Animal intelligence. An experimental study of the associative process in animals. *Psychological Monographs,* 1898, *2*(Whole No. 8).

Thorndike, E. L. *The Psychology of Arithmetic.* New York: Macmillan, 1922.

Thorndike, E. L. *The Fundamentals of Learning*. New York: Teachers College, 1932.

Thorndike, E. L., & Lorge, I. *The Teacher's Word Book of 30,000 Words*. New York: Columbia University Press, 1944.

Thorndyke, P. W. Cognitive structures in comprehension and memory of narrative discourse. *Cognitive Psychology*, 1977, *9*, 77–110.

Thune, L. E. Warm-up effects as a function of level of practice in verbal learning. *Journal of Experimental Psychology*, 1951, *42*, 250–256.

Till, R. E., & Jenkins, J. J. The effects of cued orienting tasks on the free recall of words. *Journal of Verbal Learning and Verbal Behavior*, 1973, *12*, 489–498.

Trabasso, T. R. Stimulus emphasis and all-or-none learning in concept identification. *Journal of Experimental Psychology*, 1963, *65*, 398–406.

Trabasso, T. R., & Bower, G. H. *Attention in Learning*. New York: Wiley, 1968.

Trabasso, T. R.; Rollins, H.; & Shaughnessy, E. Storage and verification stages in processing concepts. *Cognitive Psychology*, 1971, *2*, 239–289.

Tresselt, M. E., & Mayzner, M. S. A study of incidental learning. *Journal of Psychology*, 1960, *50*, 338–347.

Trowbridge, M. H., & Carson, H. An experimental study of Thorndike's theory of learning. *Journal of General Psychology*, 1932, *7*, 245–258.

Tulving, E. Subjective organization in free recall of "unrelated" words. *Psychological Review*, 1962, *69*, 344–354.

Tulving, E., & Arbuckle, T. Y. Sources of intratrial interference in immediate recall of paired associates. *Journal of Verbal Learning and Verbal Behavior*, 1963, *1*, 321–334.

Tulving, E., & Thomson, D. M. Retrieval processes in recognition memory: Effect of associative context. *Journal of Experimental Psychology*, 1971, *87*, 116–124.

Tulving, E., & Thomson, D. M. Encoding specificity and retrieval processes in episodic memory. *Psychological Review*, 1973, *80*, 352–373.

Tulving, E., & Watkins, M. J. Structure of memory traces. *Psychological Review*, 1975, *84*, 261–275.

Tversky, B. Encoding processes in recognition and recall. *Cognitive Psychology*, 1973, *5*, 275–287.

Underwood, B. J. Interference and forgetting. *Psychological Review*, 1957, *64*, 49–60.

Underwood, B. J. Ten years of massed practice on distributed practice. *Psychological Review*, 1961, *68*, 229–247.

Underwood, B. J. False recognition produced by implicit verbal responses. *Journal of Experimental Psychology*, 1965, *70*, 122–129.

Underwood, B. J.; Kapelak, S. M.: & Malmi, R. A. The spacing effect: Additions to the theoretical and empirical puzzles. *Memory and Cognition*, 1976, *4*, 391–400.

Underwood, B. J., & Schultz, R. W. *Meaningfulness and Verbal Learning*. Philadelphia: Lippincott, 1960.

Voss, J. F., & Bisanz, G. L. Models and methods used in the study of prose comprehension and learning. In S. Black & B. K. Britton (Eds.), *Expository Text*. Hillsdale, N.J.: Lawrence Erlbaum Associates, 1982.

Wagner, A. R. Effects of amount and percentage of reinforcement and number of acquisition trials on conditioning and extinction. *Journal of Experimental Psychology*, 1961, *62*, 234–242.

Wagner, A. R.; Siegel, S.; Thomas, E.; & Ellison, G. D. Reinforcement history and the extinction of a conditioned salivary response. *Journal of Comparative and Physiological Psychology*, 1964, *58*, 354–358.

Walsh, D. A., & Jenkins, J. J. Effects of orienting tasks on free recall in incidental learning: "Difficulty," "effort," and "process" explanations. *Journal of Verbal Learning and Verbal Behavior*, 1973, *12*, 481–488.

Wanner, E. *On Remembering, Forgetting, and Understanding Sentences*. The Hague: Mouton, 1974.

Watkins, M. J., & Tulving, E. Episodic memory: When recognition fails. *Journal of Experimental Psychology: General*, 1975, *104*, 5–29.

Watts, G. H., & Anderson, R. C. Effects of three types of inserted questions on learning from prose. *Journal of Educational Psychology*, 1971, *62*, 387–394.

Weinstock, R. B. Maintenance schedules and hunger drive: An examination of the rat literature. *Psychological Bulletin*, 1972, *78*, 311–320.

Wellman, H. M. The early development of intentional memory behavior. *Human Development*, 1977, *20*, 86–101.

West, M. *A General-Service List of English Words, with Semantic Frequencies and a Supplementary Word List for the Writing of Popular Science and Technology*. New York: Longmans, Green, 1953.

Wickelgren, W. A. Human learning and memory. In M. R. Rosenweig & L. W. Porter (Eds.), *Annual Review of Psychology*, 1981, *32*, 21–52.

Wickens, D. D. Encoding categories of words: An empirical approach to meaning. *Psychological Review*, 1970, *77*, 1–15.

Wickens, D. D. Characteristics of word encoding. In A. W. Melton & E. Martin (Eds.), *Coding Processes in Human Memory*. New York: Halsted Press, 1972, 191–215.

Wingfield, A. *Human Learning and Memory: An Introduction*. New York: Harper & Row, 1979.

Wittrock, M. C. Learning as a generative process. *Educational Psychologist*, 1974, *11*, 87–95.

Wittrock, M. C.; Marks, C. B.: & Doctorow, M. J. Reading as a generative process. *Journal of Educational Psychology*, 1975, *67*, 484–489.

Yates, F. A. *The Art of Memory*. Chicago: University of Chicago Press, 1966.

Zaretsky, H. H. Runway performing during extinction as a function of drive and incentive. *Journal of Comparative and Physiological Psychology*, 1965, *60*, 463–464.

Zeaman, D., & House, B. J. The role of attention in retardate discrimination learning. In N. R. Ellis (Eds.), *Handbook of Mental Deficiency: Psychological Theory and Research*. New York: McGraw-Hill, 1963.

LEARNING CENTERS

See Computer-Based Education; Media Use in Education; Study Skills.